COLLINS
POCKET
DICTIONARY
AND
THESAURUS

HarperCollins*Publishers*

First Edition 1993

New Edition 1998
Reprinted 1998 (twice)
Latest reprint 1999

©HarperCollins Publishers 1993, 1998

The HarperCollins website address is
www.**fire**and**water**.com

ISBN 0 00 472119-5

A catalogue record for this book
is available from the British Library.

Typeset by Morton Word Processing Ltd.
Scarborough, England

Printed and bound in Great Britain by
Caledonian International Book Manufacturing Ltd,
Glasgow, G64

CONTENTS

EDITORIAL STAFF

FEATURES OF THE DICTIONARY AND THESAURUS

Short, clear definitions

will not last long **perishing** *adj Inf* very cold

perjure *v* be guilty of perjury **perjury** *n* crime of false testimony on oath

perk *n* incidental benefit from employment

perky *adj* lively, cheerful

perm *n* long-lasting curly hairstyle ~*v* give a perm

permanent *adj* continuing in same state; lasting **permanence** *n*

permeate *v* pervade; pass through pores of **permeable** *adj*

Spelling help with changes in form of entry word

permit *v* -mitting, -mitted allow; give leave to ~*n* warrant or licence to do something **permissible** *adj* **permission** *n* **permissive** *adj* (too) tolerant, esp. sexually

permutation *n Maths* arrangement of a number of quantities in every possible order

pernicious *adj* wicked; harmful

pernickety *adj Inf* fussy

——————————— THESA

Headwords in **colour** for ease of use

per, publication, serial

perish be killed, die, expire, lose one's life, pass away; decay, decompose, rot, waste

perjury false statement, forswearing, oath breaking

permanent abiding, constant, durable, enduring, eternal, everlasting, fixed, immutable, invariable, lasting, perpetual, persistent, stable, unchanging

permeate fill, impregnate, penetrate, pervade, saturate

permissible acceptable, allowable, all right, authorized, lawful, legal, legitimate, O.K. *or* okay *Inf*, permitted

Restrictive labels show context of use

permission assent, authorization, consent, freedom, go-ahead *Inf*, green light, leave, licence, permit, sanction

permissive free, lax, liberal, tolerant

permit *v* agree, allow, authorize, consent, give leave *or* permission, let, li-

FEATURES OF THE DICTIONARY AND THESAURUS

peroxide *n short for* HYDROGEN PEROXIDE

perpendicular *adj/n* (line) at right angles to another; (something) exactly upright — **Parts of speech**

perpetrate *v* perform or be responsible for (something bad)

perpetual *adj* continuous; lasting forever **perpetuate** *v* make perpetual; not to allow to be forgotten **perpetuity** *n*

perplex *v* puzzle; bewilder **perplexity** *n*

persecute *v* oppress because of race, religion etc. **persecution** *n*

persevere *v* persist, maintain effort **perseverance** *n*

persist *v* continue in spite of obstacles or objections **persistence** *n* **persistent** *adj*

person *n* individual (human) being; body of human being; *Grammar* classification of pronouns and verb forms according to the person speaking, — **Restrictive labels**

U R U S ─────────────

cense, sanction ~*n* licence, pass, passport, warrant

perpetrate carry out, commit, do, execute, perform

perpetual abiding, endless, enduring, eternal, everlasting, immortal, lasting, perennial, permanent — Generous choice of **synonyms**

perpetuate maintain, preserve, sustain

perplex baffle, bewilder, confound, confuse, mystify, puzzle, stump

persecute harass, ill-treat, maltreat, oppress, torment, victimize

perseverance dedication, determination, doggedness, persistence, resolution, tenacity

persevere carry on, continue, go on, keep going, maintain, persist — Headwords in **colour** for ease of use

persist continue, persevere; carry on, continue, keep up, last, remain

persistence doggedness, endurance, perseverance, tenacity

persistent determined, dogged, per-

ABBREVIATIONS USED IN THE TEXT

abbrev	abbreviation		Lit	Literary
adj	adjective			
adv	adverb		masc	masculine
Afr	African		Maths	Mathematics
Amer	American		Med	Medicine
Anat	Anatomy		Mil	Military
Arch	Archaic		Mus	Music
Aust	Australian		Myth	Mythology
Bot	Botany		n	noun
Brit	Britain, British		N	North(ern)
			Naut	Nautical
Canad	Canadian		NZ	New Zealand
cap.	capital			
Chem	Chemistry		Obs	Obsolete
comb.	combining		Offens	Offensive
conj	conjunction		oft.	often
Dial	Dialect		orig.	originally
E	East(ern)		Pathol	Pathology
Eng	England, English		pert.	pertaining
e.g.	for example		Photog	Photography
esp.	especially		pl	plural
etc.	et cetera		Poet	Poetic
			prep	preposition
fem	feminine		pron	pronoun
Fig	Figurative			
Fr	French		S	South(ern)
			Scot	Scottish
Geog	Geography		sing.	singular
			Sl	Slang
Hist	History			
			US(A)	United States
Inf	Informal			(of America)
interj	interjection		usu.	usually
kg	kilogram(s)		v	verb
km	kilometre(s)		Vulg	Vulgar
Lat	Latin		W	West(ern)
lb(s)	pound(s)			

A a

a, an *adj* the indefinite article meaning one; *an* is used before vowels

AA Alcoholics Anonymous; Automobile Association

aardvark *n* S Afr. anteater

aback *adv* **taken aback** startled

abacus *n* counting device of beads on wire frame

abandon *v* desert; give up ~*n* freedom from inhibitions etc. **abandoned** *adj* deserted; uninhibited; wicked

abase *v* humiliate, degrade

abashed *adj* ashamed

abate *v* make or become less

abattoir *n* slaughterhouse

abbey *n* community of monks or nuns; abbey church **abbot** *n* head of monastery

abbreviate *v* shorten **abbreviation** *n*

shortened word or phrase

abdicate *v* give up (throne etc.)

abdomen *n* belly **abdominal** *adj*

abduct *v* carry off, kidnap

aberration *n* deviation from normal; lapse

abet *v* **abetting, abetted** help, esp. in doing wrong

abeyance *n* **in abeyance** not in use

abhor *v* **abhorring, abhorred** loathe **abhorrence** *n* **abhorrent** *adj*

abide *v* **abiding, abode** *or* **abided** endure; *Obs* reside **abide by** obey

ability *n* competence, power

abject *adj* wretched; servile

ablaze *adj* burning

able *adj* capable, competent, or talented **ably** *adv*

abnormal *adj* not usual or typical;

THESAURUS

---

abandon *v* desert, forsake, jilt, leave, leave behind ~*n* dash, wantonness, wildness

abbey cloister, convent, friary, monastery, nunnery, priory

abbreviate abridge, abstract, compress, condense, contract, curtail, cut, reduce, shorten, summarize, trim, truncate

abbreviation abridgment, abstract, compendium, compression, condensation, contraction, curtailment, digest, epitome, précis, reduction, résumé, shortening, summary, synopsis, trimming, truncation

abdicate abandon, abjure, abnegate, cede, forgo, give up, quit, relinquish, renounce, resign, retire, step down *Inf*, surrender, vacate, waive, yield

abduct carry off, kidnap, run off with, seize, snatch *Sl*

abeyance in abeyance hanging fire, pending, shelved, suspended

abhor abominate, detest, hate, loathe,

shrink from, shudder at

abhorrent abominable, detestable, disgusting, distasteful, hated, horrible, horrid, loathsome, odious, offensive, repulsive

abide accept, bear, brook, endure, put up with, stand, submit to, suffer, tolerate

abide by agree to, conform to, follow, obey, observe, submit to

ability aptitude, capability, capacity, competence, competency, expertise, facility, faculty, flair, force, gift, knack, power, proficiency, skill, talent

abject base, cringing, despicable, dishonourable, fawning, grovelling, ignominious, low, mean, servile, slavish, submissive, vile, worthless

able accomplished, adept, adequate, capable, clever, competent, effective, efficient, experienced, expert, fit, gifted, proficient, qualified, skilful, skilled, talented

odd **abnormally** *adv* **abnormality** *n*
aboard *adv* on, onto ship, train, or aircraft
abode *n* home; dwelling
abolish *v* do away with **abolition** *n*
abominate *v* detest **abominable** *adj* **abomination** *n* loathing; the object loathed
Aborigine *n* original inhabitant of Australia
abort *v* terminate (a pregnancy) prematurely; end prematurely and unsuccessfully **abortion** *n* **abortive** *adj* unsuccessful
abound *v* be plentiful
about *adv* on all sides; nearly; astir ~*prep* round; near; concerning **about-turn** *n* turn to the opposite

direction
above *adv* higher up ~*prep* over; higher than, more than; beyond
abrasion *n* place scraped (e.g. on skin); a wearing down **abrasive** *n* substance for grinding, polishing etc. ~*adj* causing abrasion; grating
abreast *adv* side by side
abridge *v* shorten
abroad *adv* to or in a foreign country; at large
abrupt *adj* sudden; blunt; steep **abruptly** *adv*
abscess *n* gathering of pus
abscond *v* leave secretly
absent *adj* away; missing ~*v* keep away **absence** *n* **absentee** *n* one who stays away **absently** *adv*

———————————— THESAURUS ————————————

abnormal atypical, curious, deviant, eccentric, exceptional, extraordinary, irregular, odd, oddball *Inf,* peculiar, queer, singular, strange, uncommon, unusual, weird
abnormality deformity, deviation, eccentricity, exception, flaw, irregularity, oddity, peculiarity, strangeness, weirdness
abolish annul, axe *Inf,* blot out, cancel, destroy, do away with, eliminate, end, eradicate, extinguish, invalidate, nullify, obliterate, overthrow, overturn, put an end to, quash, rescind, revoke, suppress, terminate, void, wipe out
abolition cancellation, destruction, elimination, end, ending, eradication, extermination, extinction, obliteration, overthrow, overturning, revocation, suppression, termination, wiping out
abominable base, contemptible, despicable, detestable, disgusting, execrable, foul, horrible, horrid, loathsome, obnoxious, odious, repellent, repugnant, repulsive, revolting, terrible, vile

abomination antipathy, aversion, detestation, disgust, distaste, hate, hatred, repugnance, revulsion
abound be plentiful, crowd, flourish, increase, luxuriate, overflow, proliferate, swarm, swell, teem, thrive
about *prep* as regards, concerned with, concerning, dealing with, on, re, referring to, regarding, relative to; adjacent, beside, circa *used with dates,* close to, near, nearby; around, encircling, on all sides, round, surrounding ~*adv* almost, approaching, approximately, around, close to, more or less, nearing, nearly, roughly
above *prep* beyond, exceeding, higher than, on top of, over, upon
abroad in foreign lands, out of the country, overseas
abrupt blunt, brisk, brusque, curt, direct, gruff, impolite, rough, rude, short, terse
absence absenteeism, truancy; default, defect, deficiency, lack, need, omission, privation, want
absent away, elsewhere, gone, lacking, missing, not present, out, truant, unavailable, wanting

absolute *adj* complete; unrestricted; pure **absolutely** *adv* completely ~*interj* certainly

absolve *v* free from, pardon

absorb *v* suck up; engross; take in **absorption** *n* **absorbent** *adj*

abstain *v* refrain **abstention** *n* **abstinence** *n*

abstemious *adj* sparing in eating and drinking

abstract *adj* existing only in the mind; not concrete ~*n* summary ~*v* remove; summarize **abstracted** *adj* preoccupied **abstraction** *n*

abstruse *adj* hard to understand

absurd *adj* ridiculous **absurdity** *n*

abundant *adj* plentiful **abundantly**
adv **abundance** *n* great amount

abuse *v* misuse; address rudely ~*n* wrong treatment; insulting comments **abusive** *adj* **abusively** *adv*

abut *v* abutting, abutted adjoin

abysmal *adj* immeasurable, very great; *Inf* extremely bad **abysmally** *adv*

abyss *n* very deep gulf or pit

AC alternating current

acacia *n* gum-yielding tree or shrub

academy *n* society to advance arts or sciences; institution for specialized training; *Scot* secondary school **academic** *adj* of a place of learning; theoretical ~*n* member of college or university

———————————————— THESAURUS ————————————————

absolute complete, downright, entire, out-and-out, outright, perfect, pure, sheer, thorough, total, unqualified, utter; autocratic, despotic, dictatorial, full, sovereign, supreme, unbounded, unconditional, unlimited, unrestricted

absorb consume, devour, digest, drink in, exhaust, imbibe, receive, soak up, suck up, take in; captivate, engage, engross, fascinate, fill, fill up, fix, hold, immerse, occupy, preoccupy, rivet

abstain avoid, cease, desist, forbear, forgo, give up, keep from, refrain, refuse, renounce, shun, stop, withhold

abstention abstaining, abstinence, avoidance, forbearance, refraining, refusal, self-control, self-denial

abstinence forbearance, moderation, self-denial, self-restraint, soberness, sobriety, temperance

abstract *adj* abstruse, complex, conceptual, deep, general, occult, philosophical, profound, separate, subtle, theoretical ~*n* digest, epitome, essence, outline, précis, résumé, summary, synopsis ~*v* detach, extract, isolate, remove, separate, steal, take

away, withdraw

absurd crazy, farcical, foolish, idiotic, illogical, irrational, laughable, ludicrous, nonsensical, preposterous, ridiculous, senseless, silly, stupid

abundant ample, bountiful, copious, exuberant, filled, full, lavish, luxuriant, overflowing, plenteous, plentiful, profuse, rich, teeming

abuse *v* damage, exploit, harm, hurt, ill-treat, injure, maltreat, mar, misapply, misuse, oppress, spoil, wrong; curse, defame, disparage, insult, libel, malign, revile, scold, slander, smear, swear at, vilify ~*n* damage, exploitation, harm, hurt, ill-treatment, imposition, maltreatment, misapplication, misuse, oppression, spoiling, wrong; blame, castigation, censure, cursing, defamation, disparagement, insults, invective, libel, reproach, revilement, scolding, slander, swearing, tirade, vilification

academic *adj* bookish, erudite, highbrow, learned, lettered, literary, scholarly, scholastic, school, studious; conjectural, notional, speculative, theoretical ~*n* don, fellow, lecturer, master, professor, tutor

accede v agree; attain (office etc.)

accelerate v (cause to) increase speed **acceleration** n **accelerator** n mechanism to increase speed

accent n stress or pitch in speaking; mark to show this; style of pronunciation ~v emphasize

accentuate v stress, emphasize

accept v take, receive; admit, believe; agree to **acceptable** adj **acceptance** n

access n right or means of entry ~v Computers obtain (data) **accessible** adj easy to approach **accessibility** n

accession n attaining of office, right etc.; addition

accessory n supplementary part of car, woman's dress etc.; person assisting crime

accident n event happening by chance; mishap, esp. causing injury **accidental** adj **accidentally** adv

acclaim v applaud, praise ~n applause **acclamation** n

acclimatize v accustom to new climate or environment

accolade n public approval; honour;

accede accept, acquiesce, admit, agree, assent, comply, concede, concur, consent, endorse, grant, yield; assume, attain, come to, enter upon, inherit, succeed, succeed to as heir

accelerate expedite, forward, further, hasten, hurry, quicken, speed, speed up, spur

acceleration expedition, hastening, hurrying, quickening, speeding up, spurring, stimulation

accent n beat, emphasis, force, rhythm, stress; inflection, intonation, modulation, pronunciation, tone ~v accentuate, stress, underline, underscore

accept obtain, receive, secure, take; accede, acknowledge, acquiesce, admit, adopt, affirm, agree to, approve, believe, buy Sl, consent to, recognize, swallow Inf; acknowledge, admit, assume, take on, undertake

acceptable agreeable, gratifying, pleasant, pleasing, welcome; adequate, admissible, all right, fair, moderate, passable, satisfactory, so-so Inf, tolerable

acceptance obtaining, receipt, securing, taking; accession, acknowledgment, acquiescence, admission, adoption, affirmation, agreement, approbation, approval, assent, belief, compliance, concession, concur-

rence, consent, cooperation, O.K. or okay Inf, permission, recognition, seal of approval; deference, standing, submission; acknowledgment, admission, assumption, undertaking

access admission, admittance, course, door, entrance, entrée, entry, key, path, road

accessible achievable, at hand, attainable, available, handy, near, nearby, obtainable, on hand, possible, reachable, ready

accessory addition, adornment, attachment, component, decoration, extra, frill, trim, trimming

accident calamity, casualty, chance, collision, crash, disaster, misadventure, mischance, misfortune, mishap, pile-up; chance, fate, fortune, hazard, luck

accidental casual, chance, fortuitous, haphazard, incidental, random, uncertain, unexpected, unforeseen, unintended, unintentional, unplanned

acclaim v applaud, approve, celebrate, cheer, clap, commend, exalt, extol, hail, honour, laud, praise, salute, welcome ~n acclamation, applause, approbation, approval, celebration, commendation, exaltation, honour, plaudits, praise, welcome

acclimatize accommodate, accustom, adapt, adjust, become seasoned

token of knighthood

accommodate *v* supply, esp. with lodging; oblige; adapt **accommodating** *adj* obliging **accommodation** *n* lodgings

accompany *v* -nying, -nied go with; supplement; occur with; play music to support a soloist **accompaniment** *n*

accomplice *n* one assisting another in crime

accomplish *v* carry out; finish **accomplished** *adj* complete; proficient

accord *n* (esp. in accord with) agreement, harmony ~*v* (cause to) be in accord with; grant **according to** as stated by; in conformity with **accordingly** *adv* as the circumstances suggest; therefore

accordion *n* musical instrument with bellows and reeds

accost *v* approach and speak to

account *n* report; importance; statement of moneys received, paid, or owed; person's money held in bank ~*v* regard as; give reason, answer (for) **accountable** *adj* responsible **accountancy** *n* keeping, preparation of business accounts **accountant** *n* accounting *n*

accoutrements *pl n* equipment, esp. military; trappings

accredited *adj* authorized, officially recognized

accrue *v* be added; result

accumulate *v* gather; collect **accumulation** *n*

accurate *adj* exact, correct **accurately**

——————— THESAURUS ———————

to, get used to, inure, naturalize

accommodate billet, board, cater for, harbour, house, lodge, put up, quarter, shelter; aid, assist, furnish, help, oblige, provide, serve, supply

accommodating complaisant, considerate, cooperative, friendly, helpful, hospitable, kind, obliging, polite, unselfish, willing

accommodation board, digs *Brit inf*, harbouring, house, housing, lodging(s), quartering, quarters, shelter, sheltering

accompany attend, conduct, convoy, escort, go with, usher

accomplice accessory, ally, assistant, associate, collaborator, colleague, confederate, helper, henchman, partner

accomplish achieve, attain, bring off *Inf*, carry out, complete, conclude, do, effect, execute, finish, fulfil, manage, perform, produce, realize

accomplished adept, cultivated, expert, gifted, masterly, polished, practised, proficient, skilful, skilled, talented

accordingly as a result, consequently, ergo, hence, in consequence, so, therefore, thus

according to as believed by, as maintained by, as stated by, in the light of; after, after the manner of, in accordance with, in keeping with, in line with, in step with, in the manner of

account *n* chronicle, description, history, narration, narrative, recital, record, relation, report, statement, story, tale, version; *Commerce* balance, bill, book, books, charge, inventory, invoice, ledger, reckoning, register, score, statement, tally ~*v* assess, believe, calculate, consider, count, deem, esteem, estimate, hold, judge, rate, reckon, regard, think, value

accountable amenable, answerable, charged with, liable, obliged, responsible

accredited appointed, certified, commissioned, endorsed, guaranteed, licensed, official, recognized, sanctioned, vouched for

accumulate accrue, amass, build up, collect, gather, grow, hoard, increase,

adv **accuracy** *n*

accursed *adj* under a curse; detestable

accuse *v* charge with wrongdoing; blame **accusation** *n*

accustom *v* make used to, familiarize **accustomed** *adj* usual; used (to); in the habit (of)

ace *n* one at dice, cards, dominoes; *Tennis* winning serve; *Inf* expert

acetylene *n* colourless, flammable gas

ache *n* continuous pain ~*v* to be in pain **aching** *adj*

achieve *v* accomplish, gain **achievement** *n*

acid *adj* sharp, sour ~*n* *Chem* compound which combines with bases to form salts **acidic** *adj* **acidity** *n*

acknowledge *v* admit, recognize; say one has received **acknowledgment** *n*

acme *n* highest point

acne *n* pimply skin disease

acorn *n* fruit of the oak tree

acoustic *adj* of sound and hearing **acoustics** *pl* *n* science of sounds; features of room or building as regards sounds heard in it

acquaint *v* make familiar, inform **acquaintance** *n* person known; personal knowledge

acquiesce *v* agree, consent **acquiescence** *n*

——————— T H E S A U R U S ———————

pile up, stockpile, store

accumulation aggregation, build-up, collection, gathering, heap, hoard, increase, mass, pile, stack, stock, stockpile, store

accuracy carefulness, correctness, exactitude, precision, strictness, truth, truthfulness, veracity

accurate close, correct, exact, faithful, faultless, just, meticulous, precise, proper, regular, right, scrupulous, spot-on *Brit inf*, strict, true, truthful, unerring

accusation allegation, attribution, charge, complaint, imputation, incrimination, indictment, recrimination

accuse blame, censure, charge, impute, incriminate, indict, recriminate, tax

accustom acclimatize, adapt, familiarize, habituate, inure, season, train

accustomed acclimatized, adapted, familiar, given to, habituated, in the habit of, inured, seasoned, trained, used; common, conventional, customary, established, everyday, expected, habitual, normal, ordinary, regular, routine, set

ache *v* hurt, pain, smart, suffer, throb, twinge

achieve accomplish, attain, bring about, carry out, complete, do, earn, effect, execute, finish, fulfil, gain, get, obtain, perform, procure, reach, win

achievement accomplishment, attainment, completion, execution, fulfilment, performance, production, realization

acid acrid, biting, pungent, sharp, sour, tart

acidity acridity, bitterness, pungency, sharpness, sourness, tartness

acknowledge accept, acquiesce, admit, allow, concede, confess, declare, grant, own, profess, recognize, yield; answer, notice, react to, recognize, reply to, respond to, return

acquaint announce, apprise, disclose, divulge, enlighten, inform, let (someone) know, notify, reveal, tell

acquaintance associate, colleague, contact

acquiesce accept, agree, assent, bow to, comply, concur, conform, consent, give in, submit, yield

acquiescence acceptance, agreement, assent, compliance, concur-

acquire *v* gain, get **acquisition** *n* act of getting; material gain

acquit *v* -quitting, -quitted declare innocent; settle (a debt); behave (oneself) **acquittal** *n*

acre *n* measure of land, 4840 square yards

acrid *adj* pungent, sharp

acrimony *n* bitter feeling or language **acrimonious** *adj*

acrobat *n* one skilled in gymnastic feats, esp. in circus etc. **acrobatic** *adj* **acrobatics** *pl n*

acronym *n* word formed from initial letters of other words

across *adv/prep* crosswise; from side to side; on or to the other side

acrylic *n* synthetic fibre

act *n* thing done, deed; doing; law or decree; section of a play ~*v* perform, as in a play; exert force, work, as mechanism; behave **acting** *n* ~*adj* temporary **action** *n* operation; deed; gesture; expenditure of energy; battle; lawsuit **active** *adj* in operation; busy, occupied; brisk, energetic **activate** *v* **actively** *adv* **activity** *n* **actor, actress** *n* one who acts in a play, film etc.

actual *adj* existing in the present; real

———————————— THESAURUS ————————————

rence, conformity, consent, giving in, submission, yielding

acquire amass, attain, buy, collect, earn, gain, gather, get, obtain, pick up, procure, realize, receive, score *Sl*, secure, win

acquisition buy, gain, possession, prize, property, purchase

acquit absolve, clear, deliver, discharge, exculpate, exonerate, free, fulfil, liberate, release, relieve, vindicate

acquittal absolution, clearance, discharge, exculpation, exoneration, liberation, release, relief, vindication

acrimonious astringent, bitter, caustic, censorious, cutting, irascible, mordant, petulant, pungent, rancorous, sarcastic, severe, sharp, spiteful, tart, testy, trenchant, vitriolic

act *n* action, blow, deed, doing, execution, exertion, exploit, feat, operation, performance, step, stroke, undertaking; bill, decree, edict, enactment, law, measure, ordinance, resolution, statute; performance, routine, show, sketch, turn ~*v* acquit, bear, behave, carry, carry out, comport, conduct, do, enact, execute, exert, function, go about, make, move, operate, perform, react, serve, strike,

take effect, undertake, work; act out, characterize, enact, impersonate, mime, mimic, perform, personate, personify, play, play *or* take the part of, portray, represent

acting *adj* interim, provisional, substitute, surrogate, temporary ~*n* dramatics, impersonation, performance, performing, portrayal, portraying

action accomplishment, achievement, act, deed, feat, move, operation, performance, step, stroke, undertaking; battle, combat, conflict, fighting, warfare; case, cause, lawsuit, litigation, proceeding, prosecution, suit

activate actuate, animate, arouse, energize, galvanize, get going, impel, initiate, kick-start, mobilize, motivate, move, prod, prompt, propel, rouse, set going, set in motion, set off, start, stimulate, stir, switch on, trigger (off), turn on

active acting, astir, at work, doing, functioning, in action, in force, in operation, live, moving, operative, running, working; bustling, busy, engaged, full, involved, occupied, on the go *Inf*, on the move; alert, animated, diligent, energetic, industrious, lively, nimble, on the go *Inf*, quick, spirited, sprightly, spry, vi-

actuality *n* **actually** *adv* really, indeed

actuary *n* expert in insurance statistics

actuate *v* activate

acumen *n* keen discernment

acupuncture *n* medical treatment by insertion of needles into the body

acute *adj* shrewd; sharp; severe *~n* accent (´) over letter **acutely** *adv*

AD anno Domini

ad *n* abbrev. of ADVERTISEMENT

adage *n* proverb

adagio *adj/n Mus* slow (passage)

adamant *adj* unyielding

Adam's apple projecting part at front of throat

adapt *v* alter for new use; modify;

change **adaptable** *adj* **adaptation** *n*

adaptor, -er *n* device for connecting two electrical appliances to a single socket

add *v* join; increase by; say further **addition** *n* **additional** *adj* **additionally** *adv* **additive** *n* something added, esp. to foodstuffs

addendum *n* (*pl* **-da**) thing to be added

adder *n* small poisonous snake

addict *n* one who has become dependent on something **addicted** *adj* **addiction** *n*

addle *v* make or become rotten, muddled

address *n* direction on letter; place

————— THESAURUS —————

brant, vigorous, vital, vivacious

activity action, animation, bustle, exertion, hurly-burly, hustle, labour, life, liveliness, motion, movement, stir, work

actual absolute, categorical, certain, definite, factual, indisputable, indubitable, physical, positive, real, substantial, tangible, undeniable, unquestionable; current, existent, extant, live, living, present, present-day, prevailing

actually as a matter of fact, de facto, essentially, indeed, in fact, in reality, in truth, literally, really, truly

acute clever, discerning, discriminating, incisive, intuitive, keen, observant, perceptive, perspicacious, sharp, smart, subtle; pointed, sharp, sharpened

adamant determined, firm, fixed, immovable, inexorable, inflexible, insistent, intransigent, obdurate, relentless, resolute, rigid, set, stiff, stubborn, unbending, uncompromising, unrelenting, unyielding

adapt accommodate, adjust, alter, apply, change, comply, conform, convert, fit, habituate, make, match,

modify, prepare, qualify, remodel, shape, suit, tailor

adaptable adjustable, compliant, easy-going, flexible, malleable, modifiable, plastic, pliant, resilient, versatile

adaptation adjustment, alteration, change, conversion, modification, refitting, shift, transformation, variation, version

add amplify, append, attach, augment, enlarge by, include, increase by, supplement; add up, compute, count up, reckon, sum up, total, tot up

addict dope-fiend *Sl*, freak *Inf*, junkie *Inf*, user *Inf*

addicted dedicated, dependent, devoted, hooked *Sl*, obsessed, prone

addiction craving, dependence, habit, obsession

addition adding, adjoining, affixing, amplification, attachment, augmentation, enlargement, extension, inclusion; addendum, adjunct, appendage, appendix, extension, extra, gain, increase, increment, supplement

additional added, add-on, extra, fresh, further, more, new, other,

where one lives; speech ~*v* mark destination; speak to; direct

adenoids *pl n* tissue at back of nose

adept *adj* skilled ~*n* expert

adequate *adj* sufficient, suitable; not outstanding **adequacy** *n* **adequately** *adv*

adhere *v* stick to; be firm in opinion etc. **adherence** *n* **adherent** *n* **adhesion** *n* **adhesive** *adj/n*

ad hoc *adj/adv* for a particular occasion only

adieu *interj* farewell

adjacent *adj* lying near, next (to)

adjective *n* word which qualifies a noun

adjoin *v* be next to; join

adjourn *v* close (meeting etc.) temporarily; *Inf* move elsewhere **adjourn-**

ment *n*

adjudge *v* declare; decide

adjudicate *v* judge; sit in judgment **adjudication** *n* **adjudicator** *n*

adjunct *n* person or thing added or subordinate

adjure *v* earnestly entreat

adjust *v* adapt; alter slightly, regulate **adjustable** *adj* **adjustment** *n*

adjutant *n* military officer who assists superiors

ad-lib *v* improvise ~*n* improvised remark

administer *v* manage; dispense, as justice etc.

administrate *v* manage (an organization) **administration** *n* management, supervision; governing body **administrative** *adj* **administrator** *n*

——————— THESAURUS ———————

spare, supplementary

address *n* abode, domicile, dwelling, home, house, location, lodging, pad *Sl*, place, residence; discourse, dissertation, lecture, oration, sermon, speech, talk ~*v* discourse, give a speech, give a talk, harangue, lecture, orate, sermonize, speak, talk

adept able, accomplished, adroit, dexterous, expert, practised, proficient, skilful, skilled, versed

adequacy competence, fairness, sufficiency, tolerability

adequate capable, competent, enough, fair, passable, satisfactory, sufficient, suitable, tolerable

adhere attach, cement, cling, fasten, fix, glue, glue on, hold fast, paste, stick, stick fast

adhesive *adj* clinging, gummy, holding, sticking, sticky, tacky, tenacious ~*n* glue, gum, paste

adjacent adjoining, alongside, beside, bordering, close, near, neighbouring, next door, touching

adjourn defer, delay, discontinue, interrupt, postpone, prorogue, put off,

put on the back burner *Inf*, recess, stay, suspend

adjournment deferment, delay, discontinuation, interruption, recess, stay, suspension

adjudicate adjudge, arbitrate, decide, determine, judge, referee, settle, umpire

adjudication arbitration, decision, determination, finding, judgment, pronouncement, ruling, settlement, verdict

adjust adapt, alter, arrange, compose, convert, dispose, fit, fix, harmonize, make conform, measure, modify, order, reconcile, redress, regulate, remodel, set, settle, suit

adjustable flexible, malleable, modifiable, movable, tractable

adjustment adaptation, alteration, arrangement, arranging, fitting, fixing, modification, ordering, rectification, redress, regulation, remodelling, setting, tuning

administer conduct, control, direct, govern, handle, manage, oversee, run, superintend, supervise

admiral *n* naval officer of highest rank

admire *v* regard with approval, respect, or wonder **admirable** *adj* **admirably** *adv* **admiration** *n* **admirer** *n* **admiring** *adj*

admit *v* **-mitting, -mitted** confess; accept as true; allow; let in **admissible** *adj* **admission** *n* permission to enter; entrance fee; confession **admittance** *n* permission to enter **admittedly** *adv*

admonish *v* reprove; exhort **admonition** *n*

ad nauseam *Lat* to a boring or disgusting extent

ado *n* fuss

adolescence *n* period of life just before maturity **adolescent** *n/adj* young (person)

adopt *v* take as one's child; take up, as principle, resolution **adoption** *n*

adore *v* love intensely; worship **adorable** *adj* **adoration** *n* **adoring** *adj*

adorn *v* decorate

adrenal *adj* near the kidney **adrenalin** *n* hormone secreted by adrenal glands

adrift *adj/adv* drifting; *Inf* detached; *Inf* off course

———————————— THESAURUS ————————————

administration conduct, control, direction, execution, government, management, overseeing, performance, provision, running, superintendence, supervision; executive, governing body, government, management, ministry, term of office

admirable commendable, estimable, excellent, exquisite, fine, laudable, meritorious, praiseworthy, rare, superior, valuable, wonderful, worthy

admiration adoration, affection, amazement, appreciation, approval, astonishment, delight, esteem, pleasure, praise, regard, respect, surprise, wonder

admire adore, appreciate, approve, esteem, idolize, look up to, praise, prize, respect, think highly of, value, worship

admirer beau, boyfriend, lover, suitor, sweetheart, wooer; devotee, disciple, enthusiast, fan, follower, partisan, supporter, worshipper

admissible acceptable, allowable, allowed, passable, permissible, permitted, tolerable, tolerated

admission access, entrance, entrée, entry, initiation, introduction; acknowledgment, allowance, avowal, concession, confession, declaration, disclosure, divulgence, profession, revelation

admit allow, allow to enter, give access, initiate, introduce, let in, receive, take in; acknowledge, affirm, avow, concede, confess, declare, disclose, divulge, own, profess, reveal; agree, allow, grant, let, permit, recognize

adolescence boyhood, girlhood, minority, teens, youth

adolescent *adj* boyish, girlish, growing, immature, juvenile, puerile, teenage, young, youthful ~*n* juvenile, minor, teenager, youngster, youth

adopt accept, appropriate, approve, assume, choose, embrace, endorse, espouse, follow, maintain, ratify, select, support, take on, take over, take up; foster, take in

adoption acceptance, approbation, appropriation, approval, assumption, choice, embracing, endorsement, espousal, ratification, support, taking on, taking over, taking up; adopting, fosterage, fostering, taking in

adore admire, cherish, dote on, esteem, exalt, glorify, honour, idolize, love, revere, reverence, venerate, worship

adorn array, bedeck, beautify, deck, decorate, embellish, enhance, enrich, festoon, garnish, gild the lily, grace,

adroit *adj* skilful; clever **adroitly** *adv*

adulation *n* flattery

adult *adj* grown-up; mature ~*n* mature person, animal or plant

adulterate *v* make impure by addition **adulteration** *n*

adultery *n* sexual unfaithfulness of a husband or wife **adulterer** *n* **adulterous** *adj*

advance *v* bring forward; suggest; lend (money); go forward; improve in position or value ~*n* progress; movement forward; improvement; a loan ~*adj* ahead in time or position **advanced** *adj* at a late stage; not elementary; ahead of the times **advancement** *n*

advantage *n* more favourable position or state **advantageous** *adj*

advent *n* arrival, coming; (*with cap.*) the four weeks before Christmas

adventure *n* exciting undertaking or happening **adventurous** *adj*

adverb *n* word added to verb etc. to modify meaning

adverse *adj* hostile; unfavourable **adversary** *n* enemy **adversely** *adv* **adversity** *n* distress, misfortune

advert *n* *Inf* advertisement

advertise *v* publicize; give notice of, esp. in newspapers etc.; make public request (for) **advertisement** *n* **advertising** *adj/n*

advice *n* counsel; notification

————————— THESAURUS —————————

ornament, trim

adulation blandishment, fawning, fulsome praise, servile flattery, sycophancy, worship

adult *adj* full grown, fully developed, fully grown, grown-up, mature, of age, ripe ~*n* grown-up

advance *v* accelerate, bring forward, bring up, come forward, elevate, go ahead, go forward, go on, hasten, move onward, move up, press on, proceed, progress, promote, send forward, send up, speed, upgrade; adduce, allege, cite, offer, present, proffer, put forward, submit, suggest; *Inf,* pay beforehand, raise *price,* supply on credit ~*n* advancement, amelioration, betterment, breakthrough, furtherance, gain, growth, improvement, progress, promotion, step; appreciation, credit, deposit, down payment, increase *in price,* loan, prepayment, retainer, rise *in price* ~*adj* beforehand, early, foremost, forward, in front, leading, prior

advanced avant-garde, extreme, forward, higher, late, leading, precocious, progressive

advantage aid, ascendancy, asset, assistance, avail, benefit, blessing, boon, convenience, edge, gain, good, help, interest, lead, profit, service, start, superiority, sway, upper hand, use, utility, welfare

advantageous dominant, favourable, superior

adventure chance, contingency, enterprise, escapade, experience, exploit, hazard, incident, occurrence, risk, speculation, undertaking, venture

adventurous adventuresome, audacious, bold, dangerous, daredevil, daring, enterprising, foolhardy, have-a-go *Inf,* hazardous, headstrong, intrepid, rash, reckless, risky

adverse conflicting, contrary, detrimental, disadvantageous, hostile, inexpedient, inopportune, negative, opposing, opposite, reluctant, repugnant, unfavourable, unfortunate, unfriendly, unlucky, unwilling

adversity affliction, bad luck, calamity, disaster, distress, hardship, hard times, ill-fortune, ill-luck, misery, misfortune, mishap, reverse, sorrow, suffering, trial, trouble, woe

advertise advise, announce, declare,

advise v offer advice; give notice (of) **advisable** adj expedient **advisedly** adv deliberately **adviser, -or** n **advisory** adj

advocate n one who pleads the cause of another, esp. in court of law; Scot barrister ~v recommend **advocacy** n

aeon n long period of time

aerate v charge liquid with gas; expose to air

aerial adj operating in the air; pertaining to aircraft ~n part of radio etc. receiving or sending radio waves

aerobatics pl n stunt flying

aerobics pl n (with sing v) exercise system designed to increase oxygen in the blood **aerobic** adj

aerodrome n airfield

aerodynamics pl n (with sing v) study of air flow, esp. round moving solid bodies **aerodynamic** adj

aeronautics pl n (with sing v) science of air navigation and flying in general

aeronautical adj

aeroplane n heavier-than-air flying machine

aerosol n (substance dispensed from) pressurized can

aerospace n earth's atmosphere and space beyond

aesthetic adj relating to principles of beauty **aesthetics** pl n study of beauty **aesthetically** adv **aesthete** n

afar adv from, at, or to, a great distance

affable adj polite and friendly

affair n thing done or attended to; business; happening; sexual liaison; pl personal or business interests; matters of public interest

affect v act on; move feelings; make show of **affectation** n show, pretence **affected** adj making a pretence; moved; acted upon **affection** n fondness, love **affectionate** adj **affectionately** adv

display, inform, make known, notify, praise, proclaim, promote, promulgate, publicize, publish, puff, tout

advertisement ad Inf, advert Brit inf, announcement, bill, blurb, circular, commercial, display, notice, placard, poster, promotion, publicity, puff

advice admonition, caution, counsel, guidance, help, injunction, opinion, recommendation, suggestion, view

advisable apt, desirable, expedient, fit, fitting, judicious, politic, profitable, proper, prudent, seemly, sensible, sound, suitable, wise

advise admonish, caution, commend, counsel, enjoin, recommend, suggest, urge

advocate v advise, argue for, campaign for, champion, defend, encourage, espouse, favour, plead for, press for, promote, propose, recommend, speak for, support, uphold, urge ~n

backer, campaigner, champion, counsellor, defender, promoter, proposer, speaker, spokesman, supporter, upholder

affable amiable, benevolent, benign, civil, congenial, cordial, courteous, friendly, genial, good-humoured, good-natured, kindly, mild, obliging, pleasant, sociable, urbane

affair activity, business, circumstance, concern, episode, event, happening, incident, interest, matter, occurrence, proceeding, project, question, subject, transaction, undertaking; amour, intrigue, liaison, relationship, romance

affect act on, alter, bear upon, change, concern, influence, interest, involve, modify, regard, relate to, sway, transform; assume, contrive, feign, imitate, pretend, sham, simulate

affectation appearance, artificiality,

affidavit *n* written statement on oath

affiliate *v/n* (join as an) associate **affiliation** *n*

affinity *n* natural liking; resemblance; chemical attraction

affirm *v* assert positively; make solemn declaration **affirmation** *n* **affirmative** *adj/n* positive (statement)

affix *v* fasten (to)

afflict *v* cause to suffer **affliction** *n*

affluent *adj* wealthy **affluence** *n*

afford *v* to be able to (buy, do); provide **affordable** *adj*

affront *v/n* insult

afield *adv* **far afield** far away

aflame *adv/adj* burning

afloat *adv* floating; at sea

afoot *adv* astir; on foot

aforesaid *adj* previously mentioned

afraid *adj* frightened; regretful

afresh *adv* again, anew

African *adj* of Africa **African violet** house plant with pink or purple flowers

aft *adv* towards stern of ship

after *adv* later; behind ~*prep* behind; later than; on the model of; pursuing ~*conj* later than **afters** *pl n* dessert

afterbirth *n* membrane expelled after a birth

aftermath *n* result, consequence

afternoon *n* time from noon to evening

aftershave *n* lotion applied to face after shaving

afterwards, afterward *adv* later

again *adv* once more; in addition

against *prep* in opposition to; in contact with; opposite

agape *adj/adv* open-mouthed

——————— THESAURUS ———————

façade, false display, insincerity, mannerism, pose, pretence, pretentiousness, sham, show, simulation

affected artificial, assumed, conceited, contrived, counterfeit, feigned, insincere, mannered, precious, pretended, pretentious, put-on, sham, simulated, stiff, studied, unnatural

affection attachment, care, desire, feeling, fondness, friendliness, good will, inclination, kindness, liking, love, tenderness, warmth

affectionate attached, caring, devoted, doting, fond, friendly, kind, loving, tender, warm, warm-hearted

affinity analogy, closeness, compatibility, connection, correspondence, kinship, likeness, relation, relationship, resemblance, similarity

affirm assert, attest, aver, avouch, avow, certify, confirm, declare, maintain, state, swear, testify

affirmation assertion, averment, avouchment, avowal, confirmation, declaration, oath, pronouncement, ratification, statement, testimony

affirmative agreeing, approving, assenting, concurring, confirming, consenting, positive

afflict burden, distress, grieve, harass, hurt, oppress, pain, plague, trouble, try, wound

affluence abundance, fortune, opulence, plenty, profusion, prosperity, riches, wealth

affluent moneyed, opulent, prosperous, rich, wealthy, well-off, well-to-do

afford bear, spare, stand, sustain

afraid alarmed, anxious, apprehensive, cowardly, faint-hearted, fearful, frightened, intimidated, nervous, scared, timid, timorous

after afterwards, behind, below, following, later, subsequently, succeeding, thereafter

again afresh, anew, another time, once more; also, besides, furthermore, in addition, moreover, on the contrary, on the other hand

against anti *Inf*, contra *Inf*, counter, hostile to, in contrast to, in defiance

agate *n* semiprecious quartz

age *n* length of time person or thing has existed; time of life; period of history; long time; maturity, old age *~v* make or grow old **aged** *adj* old *~pl n* old people **ageing** *n/adj*

agenda *pl n (with sing v)* list of things to be attended to

agent *n* one authorized to act for another; person or thing producing effect **agency** *n* organization providing service; business, premises of agent

aggrandize *v* make greater in size, power, or rank

aggravate *v* make worse or more severe; *Inf* annoy **aggravation** *n*

aggregate *v* gather into mass *~adj*

gathered thus *~n* mass, sum total; gravel etc. for concrete

aggression *n* unprovoked attack; hostile activity **aggressive** *adj* **aggressively** *adv*

aggrieved *adj* upset, angry

aghast *adj* appalled

agile *adj* nimble; quick **agility** *n*

agitate *v* stir, shake up; trouble; stir up public opinion (for or against) **agitation** *n* **agitator** *n*

aglow *adj* glowing

AGM Annual General Meeting

agnostic *n* one who believes that we cannot know whether God exists

ago *adv* in the past

agog *adj/adv* eager, astir

——————— THESAURUS ———————

of, in opposition to, in the face of, opposed to, opposing, resisting, versus; abutting, close up to, facing, fronting, in contact with, on, opposite to, touching, upon

age *n* date, day(s), duration, epoch, era, generation, lifetime, period, span, time; advancing years, decline *of life,* majority, maturity, old age, senescence, senility, seniority *~v* decline, deteriorate, grow old, mature, mellow, ripen

aged age-old, ancient, antique, elderly, getting on, grey, hoary, old, superannuated

agency bureau, business, department, office, organization

agenda calendar, diary, list, plan, programme, schedule, timetable

agent advocate, deputy, emissary, envoy, factor, go-between, negotiator, rep *Inf,* representative, substitute, surrogate; agency, cause, force, instrument, means, power, vehicle

aggravate exacerbate, exaggerate, heighten, increase, inflame, intensify, magnify, make worse, worsen; *Inf* annoy, exasperate, gall, get on one's nerves *Inf,* hassle *Inf,* irk, irritate,

nark *Brit, Aust, & NZ sl,* needle *Inf,* nettle, pester, provoke, tease, vex

aggression assault, attack, encroachment, injury, invasion, offence, offensive, onslaught, raid

aggressive belligerent, destructive, hostile, offensive, pugnacious, quarrelsome

agile active, acute, alert, brisk, clever, lithe, lively, nimble, quick, sharp, sprightly, spry, supple, swift

agitate beat, convulse, disturb, rock, rouse, shake, stir, toss; alarm, arouse, confuse, disquiet, distract, disturb, excite, faze, ferment, fluster, incite, inflame, perturb, rouse, trouble, unnerve, upset, work up, worry

agitation convulsion, disturbance, rocking, shake, shaking, stir, stirring, tossing, turbulence, upheaval; alarm, arousal, clamour, commotion, confusion, discomposure, disquiet, distraction, disturbance, excitement, ferment, flurry, fluster, incitement, outcry, stimulation, trouble, tumult, turmoil, upheaval, upset, worry

agitator demagogue, firebrand, inciter, rabble-rouser, revolutionary, stirrer *Inf,* troublemaker

agony *n* extreme suffering **agonize** *v* suffer agony; worry greatly **agonizing** *adj*

agoraphobia *n* fear of open spaces **agoraphobic** *adj/n*

agree *v* **agreeing, agreed** be of same opinion; consent; harmonize; approve **agreeable** *adj* willing; pleasant **agreeably** *adv* **agreement** *n*

agriculture *n* (science of) farming **agricultural** *adj*

aground *adv* (of boat) touching bottom

ahead *adv* in front; onwards

ahoy *interj* ship's hailing cry

aid *v/n* help, support

aide *n* assistant

AIDS *n* disease that destroys the body's immune system

ail *v* trouble; be ill **ailing** *adj* **ailment** *n* illness

aim *v* direct (weapon etc.); intend ~*n* aiming; intention **aimless** *n* without purpose **aimlessly** *adv*

ain't *Nonstandard* am not; is not; are not; has not; have not

air *n* (gases of) earth's atmosphere; breeze; tune; manner; *pl* affected manners ~*v* expose to air; communicate, make known **airless** *adj* stuffy **airy** *adj* well-ventilated; jaunty, nonchalant **air bed** inflatable mattress **air conditioning** control of temperature and humidity in building **aircraft** *n* flying machines generally; aeroplane **airfield** *n* landing and taking-off area

——————— THESAURUS ———————

agony affliction, anguish, distress, misery, pain, pangs, suffering, throes, torment, torture, woe

agree accede, acquiesce, admit, allow, assent, be of the same mind, comply, concede, concur, consent, engage, grant, permit, see eye to eye, settle; accord, answer, chime, coincide, conform, correspond, fit, get on (together), harmonize, match, square, suit, tally

agreeable acceptable, congenial, delightful, enjoyable, gratifying, pleasant, pleasing, pleasurable, satisfying, to one's liking, to one's taste; acquiescent, amenable, approving, complying, concurring, consenting, in accord, responsive, sympathetic, well-disposed, willing

agreement accord, accordance, compatibility, compliance, concert, concord, concurrence, conformity, congruity, consistency, correspondence, harmony, similarity, union, unison; arrangement, bargain, compact, contract, covenant, deal *Inf*, pact, settlement, treaty, understanding

agriculture culture, farming, husbandry, tillage

aground ashore, beached, foundered, grounded, high and dry, on the rocks, stranded, stuck

ahead along, at an advantage, at the head, before, forwards, in advance, in front, in the foreground, in the lead, leading, on, onwards, winning

aid *v* abet, assist, befriend, encourage, favour, help, promote, relieve, second, serve, subsidize, succour, support, sustain ~*n* assistance, benefit, encouragement, favour, help, promotion, relief, service, succour, support

aim *v* aspire, attempt, design, direct, endeavour, intend, level, mean, plan, point, propose, purpose, resolve, seek, set one's sights on, sight, strive, take aim (at), train, try, want, wish ~*n* ambition, aspiration, course, design, desire, direction, end, goal, intent, intention, mark, object, objective, plan, purpose, scheme, target, wish

aimless chance, erratic, haphazard, pointless, purposeless, random, stray, undirected, unguided, unpredictable,

for aircraft **air force** armed force using aircraft **air gun** discharged by compressed air **airline** *n* company operating aircraft **airliner** *n* large passenger aircraft **air mail** mail sent by aircraft **airman** *n* member of air force **airplay** *n* performances of a record on radio **airport** *n* station for civilian aircraft **air raid** attack by aircraft **airship** *n* lighter-than-air flying machine with means of propulsion **airstrip** *n* strip of ground where aircraft can take off and land **airtight** *adj* not allowing passage of air **airworthy** *adj* fit to fly

aisle *n* passage between rows of seats

ajar *adv* partly open

akimbo *adv* with hands on hips

akin *n* related by blood; alike

alabaster *n* white, decorative stone

à la carte *Fr* selected freely from the menu

alacrity *n* eager willingness

à la mode *Fr* fashionable

alarm *n* fright; apprehension; danger signal ~*v* frighten; alert **alarming** *adj*

alas *interj* cry of grief

albatross *n* large sea bird

albino *n* (*pl* **-nos**) individual lacking pigmentation

album *n* book for photographs, stamps etc.; collection of items in book or record form

alchemy *n* medieval form of chemistry **alchemist** *n*

alcohol *n* intoxicating fermented liquor; class of organic chemical substances **alcoholic** *adj* of alcohol ~*n* person addicted to alcoholic drink **alcoholism** *n*

alcove *n* recess

alder *n* tree related to the birch

alderman *n* formerly, senior local councillor

ale *n* kind of beer

alert *adj* watchful; brisk ~*n* warning ~*v* warn; draw attention to **alertness** *n*

alfresco *adv/adj* in the open air

wayward

air *n* atmosphere, heavens, sky; blast, breath, breeze, draught, puff, waft, whiff, wind, zephyr; ambience, appearance, atmosphere, aura, bearing, character, demeanour, effect, feeling, flavour, impression, look, manner, mood, quality, style, tone, vibes *Sl* ~*v* aerate, expose, freshen, ventilate; circulate, communicate, declare, disclose, display, disseminate, divulge, exhibit, expose, express, give vent to, make known, make public, proclaim, publicize, reveal, tell, utter, voice

airless breathless, close, heavy, muggy, oppressive, stale, stifling, stuffy, suffocating, sultry, unventilated

airy blowy, breezy, draughty, fresh, gusty, light, lofty, open, spacious, uncluttered, well-ventilated, windy; animated, blithe, buoyant, cheerful, cheery, chirpy *Inf,* debonair, gay,

happy, high-spirited, jaunty, light, light-hearted, lively, merry, nonchalant

alarm *v* distress, frighten, panic, scare, startle, terrify, unnerve; alert, arouse, signal, warn ~*n* anxiety, dismay, distress, fear, fright, panic, scare, terror, unease; alarm-bell, alert, bell, danger signal, distress signal, siren, warning

alarming dismaying, distressing, disturbing, frightening, scaring, shocking, startling, terrifying

alcoholic *n* boozer *Inf,* dipsomaniac, drunk, drunkard, hard drinker, inebriate, soak *Sl,* sot, sponge *Inf,* toper, wino *Inf*

alert *adj* agile, attentive, brisk, careful, heedful, lively, nimble, observant, on guard, on the ball *Inf,* perceptive, quick, ready, spirited, sprightly, vigilant, wary, watchful, wide-awake ~*n*

algae *pl n* (*sing* **alga**) various water plants

algebra *n* method of calculating, using symbols to represent quantities

alias *adv* otherwise ~*n* (*pl* **aliases**) assumed name

alibi *n* plea of being elsewhere at time of crime

alien *adj* foreign; different in nature; repugnant (to) ~*n* foreigner **alienate** *v* estrange; transfer **alienation** *n*

alight[1] *v* get down; land

alight[2] *adj* burning; lit up

align *v* bring into line or agreement; ally, side (with) **alignment** *n*

alike *adj/adv* similar(ly)

alimentary canal food passage in body

alimony *n* allowance paid to separated or divorced spouse

alive *adj* living; active; aware; swarming

alkali *n* (*pl* **-lis**) substance which combines with acid and neutralizes it, forming a salt **alkaline** *adj*

all *adj* the whole of, every one of ~*adv* entirely ~*n* the whole; everything, everyone **all right** *adj* adequate, satisfactory; unharmed ~*interj* expression of approval

allay *v* relieve, soothe

allege *v* state without proof **allegation** *n* **allegedly** *adv*

allegiance *n* loyalty, esp. to one's country

allegory *n* symbolic story, poem **allegorical** *adj*

allegro *adv/adj/n* Mus fast (passage)

allergy *n* abnormal sensitivity to a specific substance **allergic** *adj*

alleviate *v* ease, lessen

alley *n* narrow street; enclosure for skittles

alliance *n* union, e.g. by treaty, agree-

———————— THESAURUS ————————

alarm, signal, siren, warning ~*v* alarm, forewarn, inform, notify, signal, warn

alias *adv* also called, also known as, otherwise, otherwise known as ~*n* assumed name, *nom de guerre, nom de plume*, pen name, pseudonym, stage name

alibi defence, explanation, plea

alien *adj* adverse, exotic, foreign, inappropriate, incompatible, not native, opposed, outlandish, remote, repugnant, separated, strange, unfamiliar ~*n* foreigner, outsider, stranger

alight[1] *v* come down, descend, disembark, dismount, get down, get off, land, light, perch, settle, touch down

alight[2] *adj* ablaze, aflame, blazing, burning, fiery, flaming, flaring, lighted, lit, on fire

alike analogous, corresponding, equal, equivalent, even, identical, parallel, similar, the same, uniform

alive animate, breathing, having life, living, subsisting; active, existent, existing, extant, functioning, in existence, in force, operative; active, alert, animated, awake, brisk, cheerful, chirpy Inf, eager, energetic, full of life, lively, quick, spirited, sprightly, spry, vigorous, vital, vivacious

all *adj* every bit of, the complete, the entire, the sum of, the total of, the whole of; each, each and every, every, every one of, every single ~*n* aggregate, entirety, everything, sum, sum total, total, total amount, totality, whole ~*adv* altogether, completely, entirely, fully, totally, utterly, wholly

allege advance, affirm, assert, aver, avow, charge, claim, declare, maintain, plead, profess, put forward, state

allergic affected by, sensitive, susceptible

allergy antipathy, hypersensitivity, sensitivity, susceptibility

ment, or marriage

alligator *n* animal of crocodile family found in America

alliteration *n* beginning of successive words with same sound

allocate *v* assign as a share **allocation** *n*

allot *v* **-lotting, -lotted** allocate **allotment** *n* distribution; portion of land rented for cultivation; portion allotted

allow *v* permit; set aside; acknowledge **allowable** *adj* **allowance** *n*

alloy *n* metallic mixture

allude *v* refer (to) **allusion** *n*

allure *v* entice ~*n* attractiveness **alluring** *adj*

ally *v* **-lying, -lied** join by treaty, friendship etc. ~*n* friend **allied** *adj*

almanac *n* calendar of tides, events etc.

almighty *adj* all-powerful; *Inf* very great

almond *n* tree of peach family; its edible seed

almost *adv* very nearly

alms *pl n* gifts to the poor

aloft *adv* on high; overhead

alone *adj/adv* by oneself, by itself; without equal, unique

along *adv* lengthwise; together (with); forward ~*prep* over the length of

alongside *adv/prep* beside

aloof *adj* indifferent; at a distance

aloud *adv* loudly; audibly

alphabet *n* set of letters used in writing a language

already *adv* previously; sooner than

———————————— T H E S A U R U S ————————————

alley alleyway, backstreet, lane, passage, passageway, pathway, walk

alliance affinity, agreement, association, coalition, combination, confederation, federation, league, marriage, pact, treaty, union

allied affiliated, associated, bound, combined, confederate, connected, in league, joined, kindred, married, related, unified, united, wed

allot allocate, apportion, assign, budget, designate, earmark, set aside, share out

allotment allocation, grant, lot, measure, portion, quota, ration, share, stint; kitchen garden, patch, plot, tract

allow approve, authorize, endure, let, permit, sanction, stand, suffer, tolerate; allocate, allot, assign, deduct, give, grant, provide, set aside, spare; acknowledge, acquiesce, admit, concede, confess, grant, own

allowable acceptable, admissible, all right, appropriate, approved, permissible, suitable, tolerable

allowance admission, concession,

sanction, sufferance, toleration; allocation, amount, grant, lot, measure, pension, portion, quota, ration, share, stint, stipend, subsidy; concession, deduction, discount, rebate, reduction

all right *adj* acceptable, adequate, fair, O.K. *or* okay *Inf*, passable, satisfactory

allusion glance, hint, indirect reference, innuendo, intimation, mention, suggestion

ally accessory, accomplice, associate, collaborator, colleague, confederate, friend, helper, partner

almighty absolute, all-powerful, omnipotent, supreme

almost about, all but, approximately, as good as, close to, just about, nearly, not quite, practically, virtually

alone abandoned, apart, deserted, desolate, detached, forsaken, isolated, lonely, lonesome, only, separate, single, sole, solitary, unaccompanied, unaided, unassisted, unattended, unescorted

aloud audibly, clearly, distinctly, in-

expected

Alsatian *n* large wolflike dog

also *adv* besides, moreover **also-ran** *n* loser in a contest

altar *n* Communion table; sacrificial table

alter *v* change, make or become different **alterable** *adj* **alteration** *n*

altercation *n* quarrel

alternate *v* (cause to) occur by turns ~*adj* in turn; every second **alternately** *adv* **alternative** *n* one of two choices ~*adj* replacing **alternatively** *adv*

although *conj* despite the fact that

altitude *n* height, elevation

alto *n* (*pl* **-tos**) *Mus* male singing voice or instrument above tenor; contralto

altogether *adv* entirely; in total

altruism *n* unselfish concern for others

aluminium *n* light nonrusting silvery metal

always *adv* at all times; for ever

am *first person sing. of* BE

a.m. before noon

amalgamate *v* mix, (cause to) combine **amalgamation** *n*

amass *v* collect in quantity

amateur *n* one who does something for interest not money; unskilled practitioner **amateurish** *adj*

amaze *v* surprise greatly, astound **amazing** *adj* **amazement** *n*

ambassador *n* senior diplomatic representative overseas

amber *n* yellow fossil resin

—————————— THESAURUS ——————————

telligibly, out loud, plainly

already as of now, at present, before now, by now, by that time, by then, by this time, even now, previously

also additionally, along with, and, as well, as well as, besides, further, furthermore, in addition, including, into the bargain, moreover, on top of that, plus, to boot, too

alter adapt, adjust, amend, change, convert, modify, recast, reform, remodel, reshape, revise, shift, transform, turn, vary

alteration amendment, change, difference, diversification, metamorphosis, modification, revision, shift, transformation, variance, variation

alternate *v* act reciprocally, fluctuate, follow in turn, interchange, intersperse, oscillate, rotate, substitute, take turns, vary ~*adj* alternating, every other, every second

alternative *n* choice, option, other *of two,* preference, recourse, selection, substitute

although albeit, despite the fact that, even if, even supposing, even though, notwithstanding, tho' *US or poet,*

though, while

altogether absolutely, completely, fully, perfectly, quite, thoroughly, totally, utterly, wholly; all in all, all things considered, as a whole, collectively, generally, in general, *in toto,* on the whole

always consistently, continually, ever, evermore, every time, forever, *in perpetuum,* invariably, perpetually, repeatedly, unceasingly, without exception

amass accumulate, aggregate, assemble, collect, compile, garner, gather, heap up, hoard, pile up, rake up, scrape together

amateur dabbler, dilettante, layman, nonprofessional

amaze alarm, astonish, astound, bewilder, bowl over *Inf,* daze, shock, stagger, startle, stun, stupefy, surprise

amazement astonishment, bewilderment, confusion, marvel, perplexity, shock, surprise, wonder

ambassador agent, attaché, consul, deputy, diplomat, emissary, envoy, legate, minister, plenipotentiary,

ambidextrous *adj* able to use both hands with equal ease

ambience *n* atmosphere of a place

ambiguous *adj* having more than one meaning; obscure **ambiguity** *n*

ambition *n* desire for success; goal, aim **ambitious** *adj*

ambivalence *n* simultaneous existence of conflicting emotions

amble *v/n* (move at an) easy pace

ambulance *n* conveyance for sick or injured people

ambush *v/n* attack from hiding

ameliorate *v* improve

amen *interj* so be it

amenable *adj* easily controlled; answerable

amend *v* correct; alter **amendment** *n*

amenity *n* (*oft. pl*) useful or pleasant facility or service

amiable *adj* friendly, kindly

amicable *adj* friendly **amicably** *adv*

amid, amidst *prep* among

amiss *adj* wrong ~*adv* faultily

ammonia *n* pungent alkaline gas

ammunition *n* projectiles that can be discharged from weapon; facts that can be used in argument

amnesia *n* loss of memory

amnesty *n* general pardon

amoeba *n* (*pl* -bas, -bae) microscopic single-celled animal

amok *adv* **run amok** run about in a violent frenzy

among, amongst *prep* in the midst of; of the number of; between; with one another

amoral *adj* having no moral standards

amorous *adj* inclined to love

amorphous *adj* without distinct shape

amount *v* come, be equal (to) ~*n*

——————————— THESAURUS ———————————

representative

ambiguous doubtful, dubious, equivocal, inconclusive, indefinite, indeterminate, obscure, puzzling, uncertain, unclear, vague

ambition aspiration, desire, drive, eagerness, enterprise, longing, striving, yearning, zeal; aim, aspiration, desire, dream, end, goal, hope, intent, objective, purpose, wish

ambitious aspiring, avid, desirous, driving, eager, enterprising, hopeful, intent, purposeful, striving, zealous

ambush *n* cover, hiding, hiding place, lying in wait, retreat, shelter, trap

amenable acquiescent, agreeable, open, persuadable, responsive, susceptible, tractable

amend alter, ameliorate, better, change, correct, enhance, fix, improve, mend, modify, rectify, reform, remedy, repair, revise

amendment alteration, amelioration, change, correction, emenda-

tion, improvement, modification, reform, remedy, repair, revision; addendum, addition, adjunct, alteration, attachment, clarification

amenity advantage, comfort, convenience, facility, service

amiable affable, agreeable, benign, charming, cheerful, engaging, friendly, genial, kind, kindly, lovable, obliging, pleasant, pleasing, sociable, winsome

ammunition armaments, explosives, munitions, powder, rounds, shot and shell

amnesty absolution, dispensation, forgiveness, general pardon, immunity, oblivion, remission *of penalty*, reprieve

among, amongst amid, amidst, in association with, in the middle of, in the midst of, midst, with; between, to each of; in the company of, in the group of, in the number of, out of; by all of, by the joint action of, by the whole of, mutually, with one another

quantity; sum total

amp *n* ampere; *Inf* amplifier

ampere *n* unit of electric current

ampersand *n* sign (&) meaning *and*

amphetamine *n* synthetic medicinal stimulant

amphibian *n* animal that lives first in water then on land; vehicle, plane adapted to land and water **amphibious** *adj*

amphitheatre *n* arena surrounded by rising tiers of seats

ample *adj* big enough; large, spacious **amply** *adv*

amplify *v* **-fying, -fied** increase; make bigger, louder etc. **amplification** *n* **amplifier** *n*

amplitude *n* spaciousness, width

amputate *v* cut off (limb etc.) **amputation** *n*

amulet *n* thing worn as a charm against evil

amuse *v* entertain; cause to laugh or smile **amusing** *adj* **amusement** *n*

an *see* A

anachronism *n* something put in wrong historical period

anaconda *n* large snake which kills by constriction

anaemia *n* deficiency of red blood cells **anaemic** *adj* pale, sickly

anaesthetic *n/adj* (drug) causing loss of sensation **anaesthetist** *n* **anaesthetize** *v*

anagram *n* word(s) whose letters can be rearranged to make new word(s)

anal *see* ANUS

analgesic *adj/n* (drug) relieving pain

analogy *n* likeness in certain respects **analogous** *adj* similar

analysis *n* (*pl* **-ses**) separation into elements or components; evaluation, study **analyse** *v* examine critically; determine constituent parts **analyst** *n* **analytical** *adj*

anarchy *n* absence of government and law; disorder **anarchic** *adj* **anarchist** *n* one who opposes all forms of government

anathema *n* anything detested; curse of excommunication or denunciation

anatomy *n* (study of) bodily structure; detailed analysis **anatomical** *adj* **anatomist** *n*

ancestor *n* person from whom another is descended; forerunner **ancestral** *adj* **ancestry** *n*

anchor *n* heavy implement dropped

——————— THESAURUS ———————

amount expanse, extent, magnitude, mass, measure, number, quantity, supply, volume; addition, aggregate, extent, sum total, total, whole

ample abounding, abundant, big, bountiful, broad, capacious, commodious, copious, expansive, extensive, full, generous, great, large, lavish, liberal, plenteous, plentiful, plenty, profuse, rich, roomy, spacious, substantial, wide

amuse beguile, charm, cheer, divert, enliven, entertain, occupy, please, recreate, regale

amusement cheer, delight, diversion, enjoyment, entertainment, fun, gratification, interest, laughter, mer-

riment, mirth, pleasure, recreation, sport; distraction, diversion, entertainment, game, hobby, joke, lark, pastime, prank, recreation, sport

amusing charming, cheerful, comical, delightful, diverting, droll, enjoyable, entertaining, funny, humorous, interesting, jocular, laughable, lively, merry, pleasant, pleasing, witty

analyse estimate, evaluate, examine, investigate, judge, test; break down, consider, dissect, dissolve, divide, resolve, separate, study

analysis breakdown, dissection, dissolution, division, enquiry, examination, investigation, scrutiny, separation, sifting, test; estimation, evalu-

to stop vessel drifting; any similar device ~*v* secure with anchor **anchorage** *n* act, place of anchoring

anchovy *n* small savoury fish of herring family

ancient *adj* belonging to former age;
very old

ancillary *adj* subordinate, auxiliary

and *conj* word used to join words and
sentences, introduce a consequence
etc.

andante *adv/adj/n Mus* moderately
slow (passage)

androgynous *adj* having male and
female characteristics

android *n* robot resembling a human

anecdote *n* short account of a single
incident **anecdotal** *adj*

anemone *n* flower related to buttercup

anew *adv* afresh, again

angel *n* divine messenger; guardian
spirit; very kind person **angelic** *adj*

anger *n* extreme annoyance; wrath ~*v*

make angry **angry** *adj* **angrily** *adv*

angina *n* severe pain accompanying
heart disease

angle *n* meeting of two lines or surfaces; point of view ~*v* bend at an angle; fish **angler** *n* one who fishes for
sport **angling** *n*

Anglican *adj/n* (member) of the
Church of England

Anglo- *comb. form* English or British,
as in **Anglo-Scottish, Anglo-Ital-
ian**

angora *n* goat with long white silky
hair; cloth or wool of this

anguish *n* great mental or bodily pain
anguished *adj*

angular *adj* (of people) bony; having
angles; measured by an angle

animal *n* living creature that can
move at will; beast ~*adj* of animals;
sensual

animate *v* give life to; enliven; inspire; actuate; make cartoon film of
animated *adj* **animation** *n* **animator** *n*

———— THESAURUS ————

ation, opinion, study

ancestor forebear, forefather, precursor, progenitor

ancient aged, antediluvian, antiquated, antique, archaic, early, hoary,
old, olden, old-fashioned, out-of-
date, superannuated, timeworn

and along with, also, as well as,
furthermore, in addition to, including, moreover, plus, together with

anecdote reminiscence, short story,
sketch, story, tale, yarn

angel archangel, cherub, divine messenger, guardian spirit, seraph

anger *n* annoyance, displeasure, exasperation, fury, ill humour, ill temper,
indignation, ire, irritability, irritation,
outrage, passion, pique, rage, resentment, spleen, temper, vexation,
wrath ~*v* affront, annoy, displease,
enrage, exasperate, excite, gall, incense, infuriate, irritate, madden,

nettle, offend, outrage, pique, provoke, rile, vex

angle *n* bend, corner, crook, crotch,
cusp, edge, elbow, intersection, knee,
nook, point; approach, aspect, outlook, perspective, point of view, position, side, slant, standpoint, viewpoint ~*v* cast, fish

angler fisher, fisherman

angry annoyed, choleric, displeased,
enraged, exasperated, furious, heated, hot, ill-tempered, incensed, indignant, infuriated, irascible, irate,
ireful, irritable, irritated, nettled, out-
raged, passionate, piqued, provoked,
raging, resentful, wrathful

animal *n* beast, brute, creature ~*adj*
bestial, bodily, brutish, carnal, fleshly, gross, physical, sensual

animate activate, embolden, encourage, enliven, excite, fire, impel, incite, inspire, invigorate, kindle,

animosity *n* hostility, enmity

animus *n* hatred; animosity

aniseed *n* liquorice-flavoured seed of plant

ankle *n* joint between foot and leg

annals *pl n* yearly records

annex *v* append, attach; take possession of **annexation** *n*

annexe *n* extension to a building; nearby building used as an extension

annihilate *v* reduce to nothing, destroy utterly **annihilation** *n*

anniversary *n* yearly return of a date; celebration of this

anno Domini *Lat* in the year of our Lord

annotate *v* make notes upon **annotation** *n*

announce *v* make known, proclaim **announcement** *n* **announcer** *n*

annoy *v* vex; irritate **annoyance** *n*

annual *adj* yearly ~*n* plant which completes its life cycle in a year; book published each year **annually** *adv*

annul *v* -nulling, -nulled make void, cancel **annulment** *n*

anodyne *n* thing that relieves pain or distress ~*adj* relieving pain or distress

anoint *v* smear with oil or ointment; consecrate with oil

anomaly *n* irregular or abnormal thing **anomalous** *adj*

anon. anonymous

anonymous *adj* without (author's) name **anonymously** *adv* **anonymity** *n*

anorak *n* waterproof hooded jacket

anorexia *n* loss of appetite **anorexic** *adj/n*

another *pron/adj* one other; a different one; one more

———————————————— THESAURUS ————————————————

move, quicken, revive, rouse, spark, spur, stimulate, stir, urge

animated active, airy, ardent, brisk, buoyant, dynamic, ebullient, elated, energetic, enthusiastic, excited, fervent, lively, passionate, quick, sparky, spirited, sprightly, vibrant, vigorous, vital, vivacious, vivid, zealous, zestful

animation action, activity, airiness, ardour, briskness, buoyancy, dynamism, ebullience, elation, energy, enthusiasm, excitement, exhilaration, fervour, gaiety, high spirits, life, liveliness, passion, pep, sparkle, spirit, sprightliness, verve, vibrancy, vigour, vitality, vivacity, zeal, zest

animosity animus, antagonism, antipathy, bad blood, bitterness, enmity, hate, hatred, hostility, ill will, malice, rancour, resentment

annihilate abolish, destroy, eradicate, exterminate, extinguish, obliterate, wipe out

announce advertise, broadcast, declare, disclose, give out, intimate,

make known, proclaim, promulgate, publish, report, reveal, tell

announcement advertisement, broadcast, bulletin, communiqué, declaration, disclosure, intimation, proclamation, publication, report, statement

annoy aggravate *Inf,* anger, bedevil, bore, bother, displease, disturb, exasperate, get on one's nerves *Inf,* harass, harry, hassle *Inf,* irk, irritate, madden, molest, nark *Brit, Aust, & NZ sl,* needle *Inf,* nettle, pester, plague, provoke, rile, ruffle, tease, trouble, vex

annoyance anger, bother, displeasure, disturbance, exasperation, hassle *Inf,* irritation, nuisance, provocation, trouble, vexation

anomaly abnormality, departure, eccentricity, exception, incongruity, inconsistency, irregularity, oddity, peculiarity, rarity

anonymous incognito, nameless, unacknowledged, unidentified, unknown, unnamed, unsigned

answer v reply (to); be accountable (for, to); match; suit ~n reply; solution **answerable** adj

ant n small social insect **anteater** n animal which feeds on ants

antagonist n opponent **antagonism** n **antagonistic** adj **antagonize** v arouse hostility in

Antarctic adj/n (of) south polar regions

ante- comb. form before, as in **antechamber**

antecedent adj/n (thing) going before

antelope n deerlike animal

antenatal adj of care etc. during pregnancy

antenna n (pl **-nae**) insect's feeler; aerial

anterior adj to the front; before

anthem n song of loyalty; sacred choral piece

anther n pollen sac of flower

anthology n collection of poems

anthracite n slow-burning coal

anthrax n infectious disease of cattle and sheep

anthropoid adj/n manlike (ape)

anthropology n study of origins, development of human race

anti- comb. form against, as in **anti-aircraft**

antibiotic n/adj (of) substance used against bacterial infection

antibody n substance which counteracts bacteria

anticipate v expect; look forward to; foresee **anticipation** n

anticlimax n sudden descent to the trivial or ludicrous

anticlockwise adv/adj in the opposite direction to the rotation of the hands of a clock

antics pl n absurd behaviour

anticyclone n high-pressure area and associated winds

antidote n counteracting remedy

antifreeze n liquid added to water to prevent freezing

antihistamine n drug used esp. to treat allergies

antimony n brittle, bluish-white metal

antipathy n dislike, aversion

antiperspirant n substance used to reduce sweating

antipodes pl n regions on opposite side of the globe **antipodean** adj

antique n object valued because of its age ~adj ancient; old-fashioned **antiquarian** n collector of antiques **antiquated** adj out-of-date **antiquity** n

—————— THESAURUS ——————

answer n acknowledgment, defence, explanation, reaction, refutation, rejoinder, reply, report, response, retort, return, riposte ~v acknowledge, explain, react, rejoin, reply, resolve, respond, retort, return, solve

answerable accountable, chargeable, liable, responsible, subject, to blame

antagonism antipathy, conflict, contention, discord, dissension, friction, hostility, rivalry

antagonize aggravate Inf, alienate, anger, annoy, disaffect, estrange, gall, insult, irritate, nark Brit, Aust, &

NZ sl, offend, repel, rub (someone) up the wrong way Inf

anthem canticle, chant, chorale, hymn, psalm

anticipate await, count upon, expect, forecast, foresee, foretell, hope for, look for, predict

anticipation awaiting, expectancy, expectation, foresight, foretaste, forethought, hope, premonition

anticlimax bathos, disappointment, letdown

antipathy antagonism, aversion, bad blood, disgust, dislike, distaste, enmity, hatred, hostility, ill will, loath-

great age; former times

antiseptic *n/adj* (substance) preventing infection ~*adj* free from infection

antisocial *adj* avoiding company; (of behaviour) harmful to society

antithesis *n* (*pl* -**ses**) direct opposite; contrast

antler *n* branching horn of certain deer

antonym *n* word of opposite meaning to another

anus *n* open end of rectum **anal** *adj*

anvil *n* heavy iron block on which a smith hammers metal

anxious *adj* uneasy; concerned **anxiety** *n* **anxiously** *adv*

any *adj/pron* one indefinitely; some; every **anybody** *n* **anyhow** *adv* **anyone** *n* **anything** *n* **anyway** *adv* **anywhere** *adv*

aorta *n* main artery carrying blood from the heart

apace *adv* swiftly

apart *adv* separately, aside; in pieces

apartheid *n* (esp. formerly in S Africa) official policy of segregation

apartment *n* room; flat

apathy *n* indifference; lack of emotion **apathetic** *adj*

ape *n* tailless monkey; imitator ~*v* imitate

aperitif *n* alcoholic appetizer

aperture *n* opening, hole

apex *n* (*pl* **apexes**, **apices**) top, peak; vertex

aphid *n* small insect which sucks the sap from plants

aphorism *n* maxim, clever saying

aphrodisiac *adj/n* (substance) exciting sexual desire

apiece *adv* for each

aplomb *n* assurance

apocalypse *n* prophetic revelation, esp. of the end of the world **apocalyptic** *adj*

apocryphal *adj* of questionable authenticity

apology *n* expression of regret for a

——————————— T H E S A U R U S ———————————

ing, rancour, repugnance

antique *adj* aged, ancient, elderly, old; archaic, obsolete, old-fashioned, outdated ~*n* bygone, heirloom, relic

antiquity age, elderliness, old age, oldness; ancient times, distant past, olden days

antiseptic *adj* aseptic, clean, hygienic, pure, sanitary, sterile, unpolluted ~*n* bactericide, disinfectant, germicide, purifier

antisocial alienated, misanthropic, reserved, retiring, unfriendly, unsociable, withdrawn

anxiety apprehension, care, concern, disquiet, distress, misgiving, nervousness, restlessness, solicitude, suspense, tension, unease, uneasiness, worry

anxious apprehensive, careful, concerned, distressed, disturbed, fearful, fretful, in suspense, nervous, restless,

solicitous, tense, troubled, uneasy, watchful, worried

apart afar, alone, aside, away, cut off, distant, distinct, divorced, excluded, independent, isolated, separate, singly, to itself, to oneself, to one side; asunder, in bits, in pieces, into parts, to bits, to pieces

apartment accommodation, compartment, quarters, room, rooms, suite

apathetic cool, emotionless, impassive, insensible, passive, stoic, stoical, torpid, unconcerned, unemotional, unfeeling, uninterested, unmoved, unresponsive

apathy coolness, impassivity, indifference, listlessness, passivity, stoicism, torpor, unconcern, unresponsiveness

apocryphal doubtful, dubious, equivocal, fictitious, legendary, mythical, questionable, spurious, un-

fault; poor substitute (for) **apologetic** *adj* **apologetically** *adv* **apologize** *v*

apoplexy *n* paralysis caused by broken or blocked blood vessel in the brain **apoplectic** *adj* of apoplexy; *Inf* furious

Apostle *n* one of the first disciples of Jesus; (*without cap.*) enthusiastic supporter of a cause

apostrophe *n* mark (') showing omission of letter(s)

appal *v* **-palling, -palled** dismay, terrify **appalling** *adj Inf* terrible

apparatus *n* equipment for performing experiment, operation etc.

apparel *n* clothing

apparent *adj* seeming; obvious; acknowledged **apparently** *adv*

apparition *n* ghost

appeal *v* (*with* **to**) make earnest request; be attractive; apply to higher court *~n* request; attractiveness **appealing** *adj*

appear *v* become visible or present; seem, be plain; be seen in public; perform **appearance** *n* an appearing; aspect; pretence

appease *v* pacify, satisfy **appeasement** *n*

append *v* join on, add

appendicitis *n* inflammation of the appendix

appendix *n* (*pl* **-dixes, -dices**) supplement; *Anat* small worm-shaped part of the intestine

appertain *v* belong, relate to

———————————— THESAURUS ————————————

substantiated, unverified

apologetic contrite, penitent, sorry

apologize ask forgiveness, beg pardon, express regret, say sorry

apology confession, defence, excuse, extenuation, vindication

appal alarm, astound, daunt, dismay, harrow, horrify, outrage, petrify, scare, shock, terrify, unnerve

appalling alarming, astounding, awful, daunting, dire, dreadful, fearful, frightful, ghastly, godawful *Sl*, grim, harrowing, hellacious *US sl*, hideous, horrible, horrid, horrifying, intimidating, petrifying, scaring, shocking, terrible, terrifying

apparatus appliance, device, equipment, gear, implements, machine, machinery, materials, means, mechanism, outfit, tackle, tools, utensils

apparent blatant, clear, conspicuous, discernible, distinct, evident, indubitable, manifest, marked, obvious, open, overt, patent, plain, understandable, unmistakable, visible

apparently it appears that, it seems that, on the face of it, ostensibly, outwardly, seemingly, superficially

appeal *n* entreaty, invocation, petition, plea, prayer, request, suit, supplication; allure, attraction, beauty, charm, fascination *~v* adjure, apply, ask, beg, beseech, call, call upon, entreat, implore, petition, plead, pray, refer, request, solicit, sue, supplicate; allure, attract, charm, engage, entice, fascinate, interest, invite, please, tempt

appear arise, arrive, attend, be present, come forth, come into sight, come out, come to light, develop, emerge, issue, loom, materialize, occur, surface, turn out, turn up; (like *or* as if), occur, seem, strike one as; be apparent, be clear, be evident, be obvious, be plain; act, enter, perform, play, play a part, take part

appearance advent, arrival, debut, emergence, introduction, presence; air, aspect, bearing, demeanour, expression, face, figure, form, image, look, looks, manner; front, guise, image, impression, outward show, pretence

appendix addition, adjunct, postscript, supplement

appetite *n* desire, inclination, esp. for food **appetizer** *n* something stimulating appetite **appetizing** *adj*

applaud *v* praise by clapping; praise loudly **applause** *n*

apple *n* round, firm fleshy fruit; tree bearing it

appliance *n* piece of equipment, esp. electrical

apply *v* -plying, -plied utilize; lay or place on; devote; have reference (to); make request (to) **applicable** *adj* relevant **applicant** *n* **application** *n* request for a job etc.; diligence; use;

function **applied** *adj* put to practical use

appoint *v* assign to a job or position; fix, equip **appointment** *n* engagement to meet; (selection for a) job

apportion *v* divide out in shares

apposite *adj* appropriate

appraise *v* estimate value of **appraisal** *n*

appreciate *v* value at true worth; be grateful for; understand; rise in value **appreciable** *adj* noticeable **appreciably** *adv* **appreciation** *n* **appreciative** *adj*

——————————————— THESAURUS ———————————————

appetite craving, demand, desire, hunger, liking, longing, passion, relish, stomach, taste, zeal, zest

appetizing delicious, inviting, mouthwatering, palatable, savoury

applaud approve, cheer, clap, commend, eulogize, extol, laud, praise

applause acclamation, approval, cheering, cheers, hand-clapping, laudation, ovation, plaudit, praise

appliance apparatus, device, gadget, implement, instrument, machine, mechanism, tool

applicable apposite, appropriate, apt, fit, fitting, germane, pertinent, relevant, suitable, useful

applicant candidate, inquirer, petitioner, suitor, suppliant

application function, pertinence, practice, purpose, relevance, use, value; appeal, claim, inquiry, petition, request, requisition, suit; assiduity, attentiveness, commitment, dedication, diligence, effort, hard work, industry, perseverance, study

apply bring into play, bring to bear, carry out, employ, engage, execute, exercise, exert, practise, put to use, use, utilize; appertain, be applicable, be appropriate, bear upon, be fitting, be relevant, fit, pertain, refer, relate, suit; anoint, bring into contact with,

cover with, lay on, paint, place, put on, smear, spread on, touch to; claim, inquire, make application, petition, put in, request, requisition, solicit, sue; be diligent, be industrious, commit, concentrate, dedicate, devote, direct, give, pay attention, persevere, study, try, work hard

appoint assign, choose, commission, delegate, elect, install, name, nominate, select

appointment arrangement, assignation, consultation, date, engagement, interview, meeting, rendezvous, session; assignment, job, office, place, position, post, situation

apportion allocate, allot, assign, deal, dispense, distribute, divide, dole out, measure out, mete out, share

appreciate be appreciative, be grateful for, be indebted, be obliged, be thankful for, give thanks for; acknowledge, be alive to, know, perceive, realize, recognize, take account of, understand; esteem, like, prize, rate highly, regard, relish, respect, savour, treasure, value; gain, grow, improve, increase, inflate, rise

appreciation acknowledgment, gratitude, indebtedness, obligation, thanks; admiration, assessment, awareness, cognizance, enjoyment,

apprehend *v* arrest; understand; dread **apprehension** *n* anxiety **apprehensive** *adj*

apprentice *n* person learning a trade; novice

apprise *v* inform

approach *v* draw near (to); set about; address request to; approximate to ~*n* a drawing near; means of reaching

or doing; approximation **approachable** *adj*

approbation *n* approval

appropriate *adj* suitable, fitting ~*v* take for oneself; allocate **appropriately** *adv*

approve *v* think well of, commend; authorize **approval** *n*

approx. approximate(ly)

——————————— T H E S A U R U S ———————————

esteem, knowledge, liking, perception, realization, recognition, regard, relish, respect, sensitivity, sympathy, valuation; gain, growth, improvement, increase, rise

appreciative beholden, grateful, indebted, obliged, thankful; admiring, aware, cognizant, conscious, enthusiastic, mindful, perceptive, pleased, respectful, responsive, sensitive, sympathetic, understanding

apprehend arrest, capture, catch, lift *Sl*, pinch *Inf*, run in *Sl*, seize, take, take prisoner; appreciate, comprehend, conceive, grasp, know, perceive, realize, recognize, think, understand

apprehension alarm, anxiety, concern, disquiet, doubt, dread, fear, foreboding, misgiving, mistrust, trepidation, unease, uneasiness, worry

apprehensive afraid, alarmed, anxious, concerned, fearful, foreboding, mistrustful, uneasy, worried

apprentice beginner, learner, novice, pupil, student

approach *v* advance, catch up, come close, come near, come to, draw near, gain on, meet, move towards, near, push forward, reach; appeal to, apply to, make advances to, make a proposal to, make overtures to, sound out; approximate, be comparable to, be like, come close to, come near to, compare with, resemble ~*n* access, advance, advent, arrival, av-

enue, coming, drawing near, entrance, nearing, passage, road, way; approximation, likeness, semblance; attitude, course, manner, means, method, mode, procedure, style, technique, way

appropriate *adj* apposite, apropos, apt, becoming, befitting, belonging, congruous, correct, felicitous, fit, fitting, opportune, pertinent, proper, relevant, right, seemly, suitable, to the point, to the purpose, well-suited, well-timed ~*v* annex, arrogate, assume, commandeer, confiscate, expropriate, impound, seize, take, take over, take possession of, usurp

approval acquiescence, agreement, assent, authorization, blessing, compliance, confirmation, consent, countenance, endorsement, leave, licence, mandate, O.K. *or* okay *Inf*, permission, sanction, the go-ahead *Inf*, the green light *Inf*; acclaim, admiration, applause, appreciation, approbation, commendation, esteem, favour, good opinion, liking, praise, regard, respect

approve acclaim, admire, applaud, appreciate, be pleased with, commend, esteem, favour, have a good opinion of, like, praise, regard highly, respect, think highly of; accede to, accept, advocate, agree to, allow, assent to, authorize, bless, concur in, confirm, consent to, countenance, endorse, give the go-ahead *Inf*, give the green light *Inf*, go along with,

approximate *adj* nearly correct; inexact ~*v* come or bring close; be almost the same as **approximately** *adv* **approximation** *n*

Apr. April

après-ski *n* social activities after skiing

apricot *n* orange-coloured fruit related to plum

April *n* fourth month

apron *n* covering worn in front to protect clothes; in theatre, strip of stage before curtain; on airfield, tarmac area where aircraft stand, are loaded etc.

apropos *adv* with reference to ~*adj* appropriate

apt *adj* suitable; likely; quick-witted **aptitude** *n* **aptly** *adv*

aqualung *n* breathing apparatus used in underwater swimming

aquamarine *n* precious stone ~*adj* greenish-blue

aquarium *n* (*pl* **aquariums, aquaria**) tank for water animals or plants

aquatic *adj* living, growing, done in or on water

aqueduct *n* artificial channel for water, esp. one like a bridge

aquiline *adj* like an eagle

arable *adj* suitable for growing crops

arbiter *n* judge, umpire **arbitrary** *adj* despotic; random **arbitrate** *v* settle (dispute) impartially **arbitration** *n* **arbitrator** *n*

arboreal *adj* of or living in trees

arc *n* part of circumference of circle or similar curve

arcade *n* row of arches on pillars; covered walk or avenue

arcane *adj* secret

arch[1] *n* curved structure spanning an opening; a curved shape; curved part of the sole of the foot ~*v* form, make into, an arch

arch[2] *adj* knowingly playful

———————— THESAURUS ————————

mandate, O.K. *or* okay *Inf,* pass, permit, ratify, recommend, uphold

approximate *adj* close, near; estimated, inexact, loose, rough ~*v* approach, border on, come close, come near, resemble, touch, verge on

approximately about, almost, around, circa *used with dates,* close to, generally, just about, loosely, more or less, nearly, not far off, relatively, roughly

approximation conjecture, estimate, estimation, guess, guesswork, rough calculation, rough idea

apt applicable, apposite, appropriate, befitting, correct, fit, fitting, germane, pertinent, proper, relevant, seemly, suitable, to the point, to the purpose; disposed, given, inclined, liable, likely, of a mind, prone, ready, astute, bright, clever, expert, gifted, ingenious, intelligent, prompt, quick, sharp, skilful, smart, talented,

teachable

aptitude bent, disposition, inclination, leaning, predilection, proclivity, proneness, propensity, tendency; ability, aptness, capability, capacity, cleverness, faculty, flair, gift, giftedness, intelligence, knack, proficiency, quickness, talent; applicability, appositeness, appropriateness, fitness, relevance, suitability, suitableness

arbitrary capricious, erratic, fanciful, inconsistent, optional, personal, random, subjective, unreasonable, whimsical, wilful

arbitrate adjudge, adjudicate, decide, determine, judge, mediate, referee, settle, umpire

arbitration adjudication, decision, judgment, settlement

arc arch, bend, bow, crescent, curve, half-moon

arch[1] archway, curve, dome, span, vault

arch- *comb. form* chief, as in **archangel, archenemy**

archaeology *n* study of ancient times from remains **archaeologist** *n*

archaic *adj* old, primitive **archaism** *n* word no longer in use

archbishop *n* chief bishop

archery *n* skill, sport of shooting with bow and arrow **archer** *n*

archetype *n* prototype; perfect specimen **archetypal** *adj*

archipelago *n* (*pl* **-go(e)s**) group of islands

architect *n* person qualified to design buildings; contriver **architecture** *n*

archives *pl n* collection of records, documents etc.

Arctic *adj* of north polar region; (*without cap.*) very cold **~n** north polar region

ardent *adj* intensely enthusiastic; passionate **ardently** *adv*

ardour *n* enthusiasm; zeal

arduous *adj* hard to accomplish

are *pres. tense of* BE (*used with you, we and they*)

area *n* surface extent; two-dimensional expanse enclosed by boundary; region; part; field of activity

arena *n* space in middle of amphitheatre or stadium; sphere, territory

argon *n* gas found in the air

argue *v* quarrel, offer reasons (for); debate **arguable** *adj* **arguably** *adv* **argument** *n* **argumentative** *adj*

aria *n* song in opera etc.

arid *adj* dry; dull

———————— THESAURUS ————————

arch² artful, frolicsome, knowing, mischievous, pert, playful, roguish, saucy, sly, waggish, wily

architect designer, master builder, planner

architecture building, construction, design, planning

archives annals, chronicles, documents, papers, records, registers, rolls

ardent avid, eager, enthusiastic, fervent, fiery, hot, impassioned, intense, keen, passionate, spirited, vehement, warm, zealous

ardour avidity, eagerness, enthusiasm, feeling, fervour, fire, heat, intensity, keenness, passion, spirit, vehemence, warmth, zeal

arduous burdensome, difficult, exhausting, fatiguing, hard, harsh, heavy, onerous, painful, punishing, rigorous, severe, steep, strenuous, taxing, tiring, tough, troublesome

area district, locality, neighbourhood, patch, plot, realm, region, sector, sphere, stretch, territory, tract, turf *US sl*, zone; part, portion, section, sector

arena amphitheatre, field, ground, park *US & Canad.*, ring, stadium, stage; battleground, domain, field, lists, province, realm, scene, scope, sphere, territory, theatre

argue altercate, bandy words, bicker, disagree, dispute, fall out *Inf*, feud, fight, have an argument, quarrel, squabble, wrangle; assert, claim, contend, controvert, debate, discuss, dispute, expostulate, hold, maintain, plead, question, reason, remonstrate; demonstrate, evince, exhibit, imply, indicate, point to, show, suggest

argument altercation, barney *Inf*, clash, controversy, difference of opinion, disagreement, dispute, feud, fight, quarrel, row, squabble, wrangle; assertion, claim, contention, debate, discussion, dispute, plea, pleading, remonstrance, remonstration; case, defence, dialectic, ground(s), logic, polemic, reason, reasoning

argumentative belligerent, combative, contrary, opinionated, quarrelsome

arise *v* arising, arose, arisen get up; rise (up); come about

aristocracy *n* upper classes **aristocrat** *n* **aristocratic** *adj*

arithmetic *n* science of numbers

ark *n* Noah's vessel

arm¹ *n* upper limb from shoulder to wrist; anything similar, as branch of sea, supporting rail of chair etc.; sleeve **armful** *n* **armhole** *n* **armpit** *n* hollow under arm at shoulder

arm² *v* supply with weapons; take up arms ~*pl n* weapons; war; heraldic emblem

armada *n* large fleet

armadillo *n* (*pl* -los) S Amer. animal protected by bony plates

armistice *n* truce

armour *n* defensive covering; plating of tanks, warships etc.; armoured fighting vehicles **armoury** *n*

army *n* military land force; great number

aroma *n* sweet smell **aromatic** *adj*

around *prep/adv* on all sides (of); somewhere in or near; approximately; in a circle; here and there

arouse *v* awaken, stimulate

arraign *v* accuse, indict

arrange *v* set in proper order; make agreement; plan; adapt music **arrangement** *n*

——————————— THESAURUS ———————————

arid barren, desert, dried up, dry, parched, sterile, torrid, waterless

arise appear, begin, come to light, commence, crop up *Inf,* emanate, emerge, ensue, follow, happen, issue, occur, originate, proceed, result, set in, spring, start, stem; ascend, climb, lift, mount, move upward, rise, soar, tower

aristocracy elite, gentry, *haut monde,* nobility, noblesse *Lit,* patricians, peerage, upper class

aristocrat aristo *Inf,* grandee, lady, lord, noble, nobleman, patrician, peer

aristocratic blue-blooded, elite, gentlemanly, highborn, lordly, noble, patrician, titled, upper-class, well-born

arm¹ *n* appendage, limb, upper limb; bough, branch, department, division, extension, offshoot, section, sector

arm² *v esp. with weapons* array, deck out, equip, furnish, issue with, outfit, provide, rig, supply; mobilize, muster forces, prepare for war, take up arms

armour armour plate, covering, protection, sheathing, shield

army armed force, land forces, legions, military, soldiers, soldiery, troops; array, horde, host, multitude, pack, swarm, throng, vast number

aroma bouquet, fragrance, odour, perfume, redolence, savour, scent, smell

aromatic balmy, fragrant, perfumed, pungent, redolent, savoury, spicy

around *prep* about, encircling, enclosing, on all sides of, surrounding; about, approximately, circa *used with dates,* roughly ~*adv* about, all over, everywhere, here and there, in all directions, on all sides, throughout, to and fro; at hand, close, close at hand, close by, near, nearby, nigh *Arch or dial*

arouse agitate, awaken, call forth, enliven, excite, foster, goad, incite, inflame, instigate, kindle, move, provoke, quicken, rouse, sharpen, spark, spur, stimulate, stir up, summon up, waken, wake up, warm, whet, whip up

arrange array, class, dispose, file, form, group, line up, marshal, order, organize, position, range, rank, set out, sort; adjust, agree to, come to terms, compromise, construct, contrive, determine, devise, plan, prepare, schedule, settle; adapt, instru-

array *n* order, esp. military; dress; imposing show ~*v* set out; dress richly

arrears *pl n* money owed

arrest *v* detain by legal authority; stop; catch attention ~*n* seizure by warrant **arresting** *adj* striking

arrive *v* reach destination; (*with* at) reach, attain; *Inf* succeed **arrival** *n*

arrogance *n* conceit **arrogant** *adj* **arrogantly** *adv*

arrow *n* shaft shot from bow

arsenal *n* stores for guns etc.

arsenic *n* soft, grey, very poisonous metallic element

arson *n* crime of intentionally setting property on fire

art *n* human skill as opposed to nature; creative skill in painting, poetry, music etc.; any of the works produced thus; craft; knack; *pl* branches of learning other than science; wiles

artful *adj* wily **artfully** *adv* **artist** *n* one who practises fine art, esp. painting **artiste** *n* professional entertainer **artistic** *adj* **artistry** *n* **artless** *adj* natural, frank **arty** *adj* ostentatiously artistic

artefact, artifact *n* something made by man

artery *n* tube carrying blood from heart; any main channel of communications

arthritis *n* painful inflammation of joint(s) **arthritic** *adj/n*

artichoke *n* thistle-like plant with edible flower

article *n* item, object; short written piece; *Grammar* words the, a, an; clause in a contract **articled** *adj* bound as an apprentice

articulate *adj* fluent; clear, distinct ~*v* utter distinctly **articulated** *adj* jointed

———————— THESAURUS ————————

ment, orchestrate, score

arrangement array, classification, design, display, disposition, form, line-up, order, organization, rank, setup *Inf*, structure, system; adaptation, instrumentation, interpretation, orchestration, score, version

array arrangement, collection, display, disposition, exhibition, formation, line-up, marshalling, muster, order, parade, show, supply

arrest *v* apprehend, capture, catch, detain, lay hold of, lift *Sl*, run in *Sl*, seize, take, take into custody, take prisoner ~*n* apprehension, capture, cop *Sl*, detention, seizure

arrival advent, appearance, entrance, occurrence, taking place

arrive appear, befall, come, enter, get to, happen, occur, reach, show up *Inf*, take place, turn up

arrogance bluster, conceit, hauteur, insolence, loftiness, lordliness, pomposity, pompousness, presumption, pretentiousness, pride, scornfulness,

superciliousness, swagger

arrogant assuming, blustering, conceited, contemptuous, disdainful, haughty, high-handed, imperious, insolent, lordly, overbearing, pompous, presumptuous, pretentious, proud, scornful, supercilious

arsenal ammunition dump, armoury, arms depot, magazine, ordnance depot, stock, stockpile, store, storehouse, supply

art adroitness, aptitude, artistry, craft, craftsmanship, dexterity, expertise, facility, ingenuity, knack, knowledge, mastery, method, profession, skill, trade, virtuosity

artful crafty, cunning, deceitful, designing, intriguing, sharp, shrewd, sly, tricky, wily

article commodity, item, object, piece, substance, thing, unit; composition, discourse, essay, feature, item, paper, piece, story, treatise

articulate *adj* clear, coherent, comprehensible, eloquent, expressive,

artifice *n* contrivance, trick **artificial** *adj* synthetic; insincere **artificially** *adv*

artillery *n* large guns on wheels; troops who use them

artisan *n* craftsman

artiste *see* ART

as *adv/conj* denoting: comparison; similarity; equality; identity; concurrence; reason

asbestos *n* fibrous mineral which does not burn

ascend *v* go, come up; climb **ascendancy** *n* dominance **ascent** *n*

ascertain *v* find out

ascetic *n/adj* (person) practising severe self-denial

ascribe *v* attribute, assign

asexual *adj* without sex

ash[1] *n* remains of anything burnt **ashen** *adj* pale

ash[2] *n* deciduous timber tree; its wood

ashamed *adj* feeling shame

ashore *adv* on shore

aside *adv* to, on one side; privately ~*n* words spoken so as not to be heard by all

asinine *adj* stupid, silly

ask *v* make request or inquiry; invite; require

askance *adv* with mistrust

askew *adv* awry

asleep *adj/adv* sleeping

asp *n* small poisonous snake

asparagus *n* plant with edible young shoots

aspect *n* appearance; outlook; side

———————— THESAURUS ————————

fluent, intelligible, lucid, meaningful, vocal ~*v* enunciate, express, pronounce, say, speak, state, talk, utter, voice

artificial man-made, manufactured, plastic, synthetic; bogus, counterfeit, ersatz, fake, imitation, mock, sham, simulated, specious, spurious

artistic aesthetic, beautiful, creative, cultivated, cultured, decorative, elegant, exquisite, graceful, imaginative, refined, sensitive, stylish

as *conj* at the time that, during the time that, just as, when, while; in the manner that, in the way that, like; because, considering that, seeing that, since; in the same manner with, in the same way that, like; for instance, like, such as ~*prep* being, in the character of, in the role of, under the name of

ascend climb, float up, fly up, go up, lift off, mount, move up, rise, scale, slope upwards, soar, take off, tower

ascent climb, climbing, mounting, rise, rising, scaling, upward movement; gradient, incline, ramp, rise, upward slope

ascetic *n* abstainer, hermit, monk, nun, recluse ~*adj* abstemious, abstinent, austere, celibate, frugal, harsh, plain, puritanical, rigorous, self-denying, self-disciplined, severe, Spartan, stern

ascribe assign, attribute, charge, credit, impute, put down, refer, set down

ashamed bashful, blushing, crestfallen, discomfited, distressed, embarrassed, guilty, humiliated, mortified, prudish, reluctant, remorseful, shamefaced, sheepish, shy, sorry

aside alone, alongside, apart, away, beside, in reserve, on one side, out of mind, privately, separately, to one side, to the side

ask inquire, interrogate, query, question, quiz; appeal, apply, beg, beseech, claim, crave, demand, entreat, implore, petition, plead, pray, request, seek, solicit, sue, supplicate; bid, invite, summon

asleep dead to the world *Inf,* dormant, dozing, sleeping, slumbering

aspect air, appearance, attitude, bearing, condition, countenance, de-

aspen *n* type of poplar tree

aspersion *n* (*usu. pl*) malicious remark

asphalt *n* covering for road surfaces etc.

asphyxiate *v* suffocate **asphyxiation** *n*

aspic *n* jelly used to coat meat, eggs, fish etc.

aspidistra *n* plant with long tapered leaves

aspire *v* have great ambition **aspiration** *n* **aspiring** *adj*

aspirin *n* (tablet of) drug used to relieve pain and fever

ass *n* donkey; fool

assail *v* attack, assault; criticize **assailable** *adj* **assailant** *n*

assassin *n* one who kills for money or political reasons **assassinate** *v* **assassination** *n*

assault *n/v* attack

assemble *v* meet, bring together; put together **assembly** *n*

assent *v* agree ~*n* agreement

assert *v* declare strongly, insist upon **assertion** *n* **assertive** *adj* **assertively** *adv*

assess *v* fix value or amount of; evaluate **assessment** *n* **assessor** *n*

asset *n* valuable or useful person, thing; *pl* things that can be used to

———————— THESAURUS ————————

meanour, expression, look, manner; angle, facet, feature, side

aspire aim, crave, desire, dream, hanker, hope, long, pursue, seek, wish

aspiring *adj* ambitious, eager, hopeful, wishful, would-be

assassin executioner, hatchet man *Sl*, hit man *Sl*, killer, murderer

assassinate blow away *Sl, chiefly US*, eliminate *Sl*, hit *Sl*, kill, liquidate, murder, slay

assault *n* aggression, attack, charge, invasion, offensive, storm, storming, strike ~*v* attack, charge, invade, lay into *Inf*, set about, set upon, storm

assemble accumulate, amass, bring together, call together, collect, come together, congregate, convene, convoke, flock, forgather, gather, marshal, meet, muster, rally, summon; connect, construct, erect, fabricate, fit together, join, make, piece together, set up

assembly accumulation, aggregation, body, collection, company, conference, congregation, council, crowd, diet, flock, gathering, group, house, mass, meeting, rally, throng; construction, erection, fabrication,

manufacture

assent *v* accede, accept, acquiesce, agree, allow, approve, comply, concur, consent, grant, permit ~*n* acceptance, accord, acquiescence, agreement, approval, consent, permission, sanction

assert affirm, allege, avow, contend, declare, maintain, profess, state, swear

assertion affirmation, allegation, attestation, avowal, contention, declaration, profession, pronouncement, statement; defence, insistence, maintenance, stressing, vindication

assertive aggressive, confident, decided, decisive, demanding, dogmatic, domineering, emphatic, firm, forceful, forward, insistent, overbearing, positive, self-assured, strongwilled

assess compute, determine, estimate, evaluate, fix, gauge, judge, rate, value, weigh; fix, impose, levy, rate, tax, value

assessment determination, estimate, judgment, rating, valuation; charge, demand, duty, evaluation, impost, levy, rate, rating, tax, taxation, toll

raise money

assiduous *adj* persevering **assiduously** *adv*

assign *v* appoint; allot; transfer **assignation** *n* secret meeting **assignment** *n*

assimilate *v* take in; incorporate; (cause to) become similar **assimilation** *n*

assist *v* give help to **assistance** *n* **assistant** *n*

associate *v* link, connect; join; keep company; combine, unite ~*n* partner; friend; subordinate member ~*adj* affiliated **association** *n*

assonance *n* rhyming of vowel sounds but not consonants

assorted *adj* mixed **assortment** *n* mixture

assume *v* take for granted; pretend; take on assumption *n*

assure *v* tell positively, promise; make sure; insure against loss, esp. of life **assurance** *n* **assured** *adj* sure; confident, self-possessed

aster *n* plant with starlike flowers

asterisk *n* star (*) used in printing

astern *adv* in, behind the stern; backwards

———— THESAURUS ————

asset advantage, aid, benefit, blessing, boon, help, resource, service; *pl* capital, estate, funds, goods, holdings, means, money, possessions, property, reserves, resources, valuables, wealth

assign appoint, choose, name, nominate, select; allocate, allot, consign, give, grant

assignment appointment, charge, commission, duty, job, mission, position, post, responsibility, task

assist aid, back, boost, collaborate, cooperate, expedite, facilitate, further, help, reinforce, second, serve, succour, support, sustain, work for, work with

assistance aid, backing, boost, collaboration, cooperation, furtherance, help, helping hand, reinforcement, relief, service, succour, support

assistant accessory, accomplice, aide, ally, associate, auxiliary, backer, collaborator, colleague, helper, helpmate, henchman, partner

associate *v* affiliate, ally, combine, connect, couple, join, league, link, mix, pair, relate, unite, yoke ~*n* ally, colleague, companion, comrade, co-worker, follower, friend, mate, partner

association alliance, band, clique,

club, company, confederacy, confederation, cooperative, corporation, federation, fraternity, group, league, order, partnership, society, syndicate, union; blend, bond, combination, concomitance, connection, correlation, identification, mixture, pairing, relation, tie, union

assorted different, diverse, diversified, heterogeneous, mixed, motley, sundry, varied, various

assortment array, choice, collection, diversity, hotchpotch, jumble, medley, *mélange,* miscellany, mishmash, mixture, selection, variety

assume accept, believe, expect, fancy, imagine, presuppose, suppose, surmise, suspect, take for granted, think; affect, feign, imitate, impersonate, mimic, put on, sham, simulate; accept, enter upon, put on, set about, shoulder, take on, take over, take responsibility for, take up, undertake

assumption belief, conjecture, inference, premise, premiss, presumption, surmise

assurance affirmation, declaration, guarantee, oath, pledge, promise, vow, word, word of honour

assure guarantee, pledge, promise, swear, vow; make certain, make sure,

asteroid *n* small planet

asthma *n* illness in which one has difficulty breathing **asthmatic** *adj/n*

astigmatism *n* inability of lens (esp. of eye) to focus properly

astir *adv* on the move

astonish *v* amaze, surprise, stun **astonishment** *n*

astound *v* astonish greatly **astounding** *adj*

astral *adj* of the stars

astray *adv/adj* off the right path; into error or sin

astride *adv* with legs apart

astringent *adj* sharp; stopping bleeding ~*n* astringent substance

astrology *n* foretelling of events by stars **astrologer** *n* **astrological** *adj*

astronaut *n* one trained for travel in space

astronomy *n* scientific study of heavenly bodies **astronomer** *n* **astronomical** *adj* very large; of astronomy **astronomically** *adv*

astute *adj* perceptive, shrewd **astutely** *adv*

asunder *adv* apart; in pieces

asylum *n* refuge, place of safety; *Obs* mental hospital

asymmetry *n* lack of symmetry **asymmetrical** *adj*

at *prep/adv* denoting: location in space or time; rate; condition or state; amount; direction; cause

atheism *n* belief that there is no God **atheist** *n*

athletics *pl n* sports such as running, jumping, throwing etc. **athlete** *n* athletic *adj* **athleticism** *n*

atlas *n* book of maps

atmosphere *n* gases surrounding earth etc.; prevailing mood **atmospheric** *adj* **atmospherics** *pl n* radio interference

atoll *n* ring-shaped coral island enclosing lagoon

atom *n* smallest unit of matter which can enter into chemical combination; any very small particle **atomic** *adj* **atomizer** *n* instrument for discharging liquids in a fine spray **atomic bomb** bomb with immense power derived

——————— T H E S A U R U S ———————

seal, secure

astonish amaze, astound, bewilder, confound, daze, stagger, stupefy, surprise

astonishment amazement, awe, bewilderment, stupefaction, surprise, wonder

astounding amazing, astonishing, bewildering, breathtaking, impressive, staggering, striking, stunning, stupefying, surprising

astray *adj/adv* adrift, afield, amiss, lost, off, off course, off the mark, off the right track, off the subject; into error, into sin, to the bad, wrong

astute adroit, artful, bright, calculating, canny, clever, crafty, cunning, intelligent, keen, knowing, perceptive, sagacious, sharp, shrewd, sly, subtle, wily

asylum harbour, haven, refuge, retreat, safety, sanctuary, shelter; *Old-fashioned* funny farm *Facetious*, hospital, institution, loony bin *Sl*, madhouse *Inf*, mental hospital, nuthouse *Sl*, psychiatric hospital

atheism godlessness, paganism, scepticism

atheist pagan, sceptic, unbeliever

athlete competitor, contender, contestant, runner, sportsman

athletic *adj* able-bodied, active, energetic, fit, muscular, powerful, robust, strapping, strong, sturdy, vigorous ~*pl n* contests, exercises, gymnastics, races, sports

atmosphere air, heavens, sky; air, aura, character, climate, feel, feeling, flavour, mood, quality, spirit, surroundings, tone, vibes *Sl*

from nuclear fission or fusion **atomic energy** nuclear energy

atonal *adj* (of music) not in an established key

atone *v* make amends (for) **atonement** *n*

atop *prep* on top of

atrocious *adj* extremely cruel; horrifying; *Inf* very bad **atrociously** *adv* **atrocity** *n*

atrophy *n* wasting away ~*v* **-phying, -phied** waste away

attach *v* join, fasten; attribute **attached** *adj* (*with* **to**) fond of **attachment** *n*

attaché *n* specialist attached to diplomatic mission **attaché case** flat rectangular briefcase

attack *v* take action against; criticize; set about with vigour; affect adversely ~*n* attacking action; bout **attacker** *n*

attain *v* arrive at; achieve **attainable** *adj* **attainment** *n*

attempt *v/n* try

attend *v* be present at; accompany; (*with* **to**) take care of; pay attention to **attendance** *n* an attending; persons attending **attendant** *n/adj* **attention** *n* notice; heed; care; courtesy **attentive** *adj* giving attention; considerately helpful

————————— THESAURUS —————————

atom fragment, grain, iota, jot, mite, molecule, particle, scrap, shred, speck, spot, tittle, trace, whit

atone (*with* **for**) answer for, compensate, do penance for, make amends for, make redress, make reparation for, make up for, pay for, recompense, redress

atrocious barbaric, brutal, cruel, fiendish, infamous, infernal, inhuman, monstrous, ruthless, savage, vicious, wicked

atrocity abomination, barbarity, brutality, crime, cruelty, enormity, evil, horror, outrage, villainy

attach add, adhere, bind, connect, couple, fasten, fix, join, link, secure, stick, tie, unite

attached affectionate towards, devoted, fond of, possessive

attachment bond, clamp, connection, connector, coupling, fastening, joint, junction, link, tie

attack *n* assault, charge, foray, incursion, inroad, invasion, offensive, onset, onslaught, raid, rush, strike; access, bout, convulsion, fit, paroxysm, seizure, spasm, spell, stroke ~*v* assault, charge, fall upon, invade, raid, rush, set about, set upon, storm; abuse, blame, blast, censure, criticize, impugn, malign, put down, revile, vilify

attacker aggressor, assailant, assaulter, intruder, invader, raider

attain accomplish, achieve, arrive at, bring off, complete, earn, fulfil, gain, get, grasp, reach, realize, secure, win

attainment act, accomplishment, achievement, acquirement, acquisition, arrival at, completion, feat, fulfilment, gaining, getting, obtaining, procurement, reaching, realization, reaping, winning; ability, accomplishment, achievement, art, capability, competence, gift, mastery, proficiency, skill, talent

attempt *n* attack, bid, crack *Inf*, endeavour, go *Inf*, shot *Inf*, stab *Inf*, try, undertaking, venture ~*v* endeavour, essay, experiment, have a crack *Inf*, have a go *Inf*, have a shot *Inf*, have a stab *Inf*, seek, strive, tackle, take on, try, undertake, venture

attend appear, be at, be here, be present, be there, frequent, go to, haunt, show oneself, show up *Inf*, turn up, visit; hear, heed, listen, look on, mark, mind, note, notice, observe, pay attention, pay heed, regard,

attest v bear witness to

attic n space within roof

attire v/n dress, array

attitude n mental view, opinion; posture, pose; disposition, behaviour

attorney n person legally appointed to act for another, esp. a lawyer

attract v draw (attention etc.); arouse interest of; cause to come closer (as magnet etc.) **attraction** n **attractive** adj

attribute v regard as belonging to or produced by ~n quality or characteristic **attributable** adj **attribution** n

attrition n wearing away

attune v tune; adjust

atypical adj not typical

aubergine n purple fruit eaten as vegetable

auburn adj/n reddish brown

auction n public sale in which goods are sold to the highest bidder ~v sell by auction **auctioneer** n

audacious adj bold; impudent **audaciously** adv **audacity** n

audible adj able to be heard **audibly** adv

audience n people assembled to listen or watch; formal interview

audio- comb. form relating to sound or hearing **audio** adj of, for sound or hearing

audiovisual adj involving both sight and hearing

audit n official examination of accounts ~v examine accounts

——————— THESAURUS ———————

watch (with **to**) apply oneself to, concentrate on, devote oneself to, look after, see to, take care of

attendance audience, crowd, gate, house, number present, turnout

attendant aide, assistant, auxiliary, companion, escort, flunky, follower, guard, guide, helper, servant, steward, usher, waiter

attention concentration, consideration, heed, mind, scrutiny, thinking, thought, thoughtfulness; consideration, notice, recognition, regard; care, concern, looking after, ministration, treatment

attentive alert, careful, concentrating, heedful, mindful, observant, regardful, studious, watchful

attic garret, loft

attitude approach, frame of mind, mood, opinion, outlook, position, posture, stance, standing, view; air, aspect, bearing, carriage, condition, demeanour, manner, pose, position, posture, stance

attract allure, charm, decoy, draw, enchant, endear, engage, entice, incline, interest, invite, lure, tempt

attraction allure, charm, draw, enticement, fascination, interest, lure, magnetism

attractive agreeable, appealing, beautiful, captivating, charming, engaging, fair, fetching, good-looking, gorgeous, handsome, interesting, inviting, lovely, magnetic, pleasing, pretty, seductive, tempting

attribute v apply, assign, blame, charge, lay at the door of, refer ~n aspect, characteristic, facet, feature, indication, mark, note, point, property, quality, quirk, sign, symbol, trait, virtue

audacious adventurous, bold, brave, courageous, daredevil, daring, fearless, intrepid, rash, reckless, risky

audacity adventurousness, boldness, bravery, courage, daring, nerve, rashness, recklessness; cheek, chutzpah US & Canad inf, defiance, effrontery, impertinence, impudence, insolence, nerve

audible clear, discernible, distinct

audience congregation, crowd, gathering, house, listeners, viewers; consultation, hearing, interview,

auditor *n*

audition *n* test of prospective performer ~*v* set, perform such a test
auditorium *n* (*pl* **-toriums, -toria**) place where audience sits

Aug. August

augment *v* increase, enlarge

augur *v* foretell

August *n* eighth month

auk *n* northern sea bird

aunt *n* father's or mother's sister; uncle's wife **auntie** *n Inf* aunt

au pair *n* young foreigner who receives board and lodging in return for housework etc.

aura *n* atmosphere considered distinctive of person or thing

aural *adj* of, by ear

auricle *n* outside ear; an upper cavity of heart

aurora *n* (*pl* **-ras, -rae**) lights in the sky radiating from polar regions; dawn

auspices *pl n* patronage **auspicious** *adj* giving hope of future success

auspiciously *adv*

austere *adj* severe; without luxury **austerity** *n*

authentic *adj* genuine **authentically** *adv* **authenticate** *v* make valid **authenticity** *n*

author *n* (*fem* **authoress**) writer; originator

authority *n* legal power or right; delegated power; influence; permission; expert; board in control **authoritarian** *n/adj* (person) insisting on strict obedience **authoritative** *adj* **authorize** *v* empower; permit **authorization** *n*

autism *n* disorder causing children to become withdrawn and divorced from reality **autistic** *adj*

auto- *comb. form* self, as in **autosuggestion**

autobiography *n* life of person written by himself **autobiographical** *adj*

autocrat *n* absolute ruler; despotic person **autocratic** *adj* **autocracy** *n*

Autocue *n Trademark* electronic tele-

——————— THESAURUS ———————

reception

auspicious bright, encouraging, favourable, fortunate, happy, hopeful, lucky, propitious, rosy

austere cold, forbidding, grave, grim, hard, serious, severe, solemn, stern, stiff; abstemious, abstinent, puritanical, sober, solemn, Spartan

austerity coldness, harshness, inflexibility, rigour, solemnity, sternness; economy, rigidity, self-denial

authentic actual, authoritative, faithful, genuine, real, reliable, true, valid

authenticity actuality, genuineness, truth, truthfulness, validity

author composer, creator, father, founder, inventor, maker, mover, originator, parent, planner, producer, writer

authoritarian autocratic, despotic, dictatorial, disciplinarian, doctri-

naire, domineering, harsh, imperious, rigid, severe, strict, tyrannical

authority charge, command, control, domination, dominion, force, government, influence, might, power, prerogative, right, rule, strength, supremacy, sway, weight; authorization, licence, permission, permit, sanction, warrant; arbiter, expert, master, professional, scholar, specialist, textbook

authorize empower, enable, entitle, give authority; allow, approve, confirm, countenance, give leave, license, permit, ratify, sanction, warrant

autocracy absolutism, despotism, dictatorship, tyranny

autocratic absolute, all-powerful, despotic, dictatorial, domineering, imperious, tyrannical, tyrannous,

vision device displaying speaker's script unseen by audience

autogiro, autogyro *n* (*pl* **-ros**) self-propelled aircraft with unpowered rotor

autograph *n* signature ~*v* sign

automatic *adj* operated or controlled mechanically; done without conscious thought ~*adj/n* self-loading (weapon) **automatically** *adv* **automation** *n* introduction of automatic devices in industry **automaton** *n* robot; person who acts mechanically

automobile *n* motorcar

autonomy *n* freedom; right of self-government **autonomous** *adj*

autopsy *n* postmortem

autumn *n* season after summer **autumnal** *adj*

auxiliary *adj/n* (person) helping, subsidiary

avail *v* be of use, advantage ~*n* benefit **available** *adj* obtainable; accessible **availability** *n*

avalanche *n* mass of snow, ice, sliding down mountain; any great quantity

avant-garde *adj* innovative and progressive

avarice *n* greed for wealth **avaricious** *adj*

avenge *v* take vengeance for

avenue *n* wide street; approach; double row of trees

aver *v* **averring, averred** affirm, assert

average *n* middle or usual value ~*adj* ordinary ~*v* calculate an average; form an average

averse *adj* disinclined **aversion** *n* (object of) dislike

avert *v* turn away; ward off

aviary *n* enclosure for birds

aviation *n* art of flying aircraft **aviator** *n*

avid *adj* keen; greedy (for) **avidly** *adv*

avocado *n* (*pl* **-dos**) tropical pear-shaped fruit

avoid *v* keep away from; refrain from;

unlimited

automatic mechanical, push-button, robot, self-activating, self-propelling, self-regulating; habitual, mechanical, perfunctory, routine, unconscious

autonomous free, independent, self-governing, sovereign

autonomy freedom, home rule, independence, self-determination, self-government, self-rule, sovereignty

auxiliary accessory, aiding, ancillary, assisting, helping, reserve, secondary, subsidiary, substitute, supplementary

available accessible, applicable, at hand, free, handy, obtainable, on hand, on tap, ready, to hand, vacant

avalanche landslide, landslip, snowslide, snow-slip; barrage, deluge, flood, inundation, torrent

avant-garde *adj* experimental, ground-breaking, innovative, innovatory, pioneering, progressive, unconventional, way-out *Inf*

avaricious close-fisted, covetous, grasping, greedy, mean, miserly, parsimonious, penurious, stingy

avenge hit back, punish, repay, requite, retaliate, revenge, take satisfaction for, take vengeance

avenue access, approach, boulevard, channel, course, drive, entrance, entry, pass, path, road, route, street, way

average *n* mean, medium, midpoint, norm, normal, par, rule, run, standard ~*adj* fair, general, indifferent, mediocre, middling, moderate, normal, not bad, ordinary, regular, so-so *Inf*, standard, tolerable, typical

averse disinclined, hostile, ill-disposed, loath, opposed, reluctant, unfavourable, unwilling

avid ardent, devoted, eager, enthusiastic, fanatical, fervent, intense, keen,

not allow to happen **avoidable** *adj* **avoidance** *n*

avow *v* declare; admit **avowal** *n* **avowed** *adj*

await *v* wait or stay for; be in store for

awake *v* awaking, **awoke, awoken** emerge or rouse from sleep; (cause to) become alert ~*adj* not sleeping; alert **awaken** *v* awake **awakening** *n*

award *v* give formally ~*n* thing awarded

aware *adj* informed, conscious **awareness** *n*

awash *adv* covered by water

away *adv* absent, apart, at a distance, out of the way ~*adj* not present

awe *n* dread mingled with reverence ~*v* astonish, frighten **awesome** *adj*

awful *adj* dreadful; *Inf* very great **awfully** *adv* in an unpleasant way; *Inf* very much

awhile *adv* for a time

awkward *adj* clumsy; difficult; inconvenient; embarrassed **awkwardly** *adv* **awkwardness** *n*

awl *n* tool for boring wood etc.

———————————— THESAURUS ————————————

passionate, zealous

avoid avert, bypass, circumvent, dodge, elude, escape, evade, keep away from, prevent, shirk, shun, sidestep, steer clear of

await anticipate, expect, look for, stay for, wait for; attend, be in readiness for, be in store for, be ready for, wait for

awake alert, alive, aroused, attentive, aware, conscious, not sleeping, observant, on guard, on the alert, on the lookout, vigilant, wakeful, waking, watchful, wide-awake

awaken activate, alert, arouse, awake, call forth, excite, incite, kindle, provoke, revive, rouse, stimulate, stir up, wake

awakening *n* activation, arousal, awaking, revival, rousing, stimulation, stirring up, waking, waking up

award *v* accord, allot, apportion, assign, bestow, confer, decree, endow, gift, give, grant, hand out, render ~*n* decoration, gift, grant, prize, trophy, verdict

aware alive to, apprised, attentive, cognizant, conscious, conversant, familiar, knowing, mindful, sensible, wise *Inf*

awareness appreciation, attention, consciousness, familiarity, knowledge, mindfulness, perception, reali-

zation, recognition, understanding

away *adv* abroad, elsewhere, from here, from home, hence, off; apart, at a distance, far, remote; aside, out of the way, to one side ~*adj* abroad, elsewhere, gone, not here, not present, not there, out

awe *n* admiration, amazement, astonishment, dread, fear, horror, respect, reverence, terror, veneration, wonder ~*v* amaze, astonish, cow, daunt, frighten, horrify, impress, intimidate, stun, terrify

awesome alarming, amazing, astonishing, awe-inspiring, awful, breathtaking, daunting, dreadful, fearful, fearsome, formidable, frightening, horrible, horrifying, imposing, impressive, intimidating, magnificent, majestic, overwhelming, redoubtable, shocking, solemn, stunning, stupefying, terrible, terrifying, wonderful

awful alarming, appalling, deplorable, dire, distressing, dreadful, fearful, frightful, ghastly, gruesome, hideous, horrible, nasty, shocking, terrible, ugly, unpleasant

awfully badly, disgracefully, disreputably, dreadfully, unforgivably, unpleasantly, wickedly, woefully, wretchedly

awkward artless, blundering, bun-

awning *n* (canvas) roof to protect from weather

AWOL *adj Mil* absent without leave

awry *adv* crookedly; amiss ~*adj* crooked; wrong

axe *n* tool for chopping; *Inf* dismissal from employment ~*v Inf* dismiss from employment

axiom *n* generally accepted principle

axiomatic *adj*

axis *n* (*pl* **axes**) (imaginary) line round which body spins

axle *n* shaft on which wheels turn

aye *interj* yes ~*n* affirmative answer or vote

azalea *n* genus of shrubby flowering plants

azure *adj* sky-blue

———————— THESAURUS ————————

gling, clownish, clumsy, coarse, gauche, gawky, graceless, ham-fisted, inelegant, inept, inexpert, lumbering, maladroit, oafish, rude, stiff, uncoordinated, uncouth, ungainly, ungraceful, unpolished, unrefined, unskilful, unskilled; cumbersome, difficult, inconvenient, troublesome, unhandy, unmanageable, unwieldy; annoying, difficult, disobliging, exasperating, intractable, irritable, perverse, prickly, stubborn, touchy, troublesome, trying, unhelpful

awkwardness clumsiness, coarseness, gaucheness, gaucherie, gawkiness, gracelessness, inelegance, ineptness, inexpertness, maladroitness, oafishness, rudeness, stiffness, uncoordination, uncouthness, ungainliness; delicacy, embarrassment, inconvenience; difficulty, stubbornness, touchiness, unhelpfulness

axe *n* chopper, hatchet **the axe** *Inf* cancellation, cutback, discharge, dismissal, termination, the boot *Sl*, the chop *Sl*, the order of the boot *Sl*, the sack *Inf*, wind-up ~*v* chop, cut down, fell, hew

axiom adage, aphorism, dictum, fundamental, maxim, postulate, precept, principle, truism

axiomatic accepted, assumed, fundamental, given, granted, manifest, self-evident, understood, unquestioned

axis axle, centre line, pivot, shaft, spindle

axle axis, pin, pivot, rod, shaft, spindle

B b

BA Bachelor of Arts

babble *v/n* (make) foolish, incoherent speech

babe *n* baby

baboon *n* large monkey

baby *n* infant **baby-sitter** *n* one who cares for children when parents are out **baby-sit** *v*

bachelor *n* unmarried man

bacillus *n* (*pl* **bacilli**) minute organism sometimes causing disease

back *n* hind part of anything, e.g. human body; part opposite front; part further away or less used; (position of) player in ball games ~*adj* situated behind; earlier ~*adv* at, to the back; in, into the past; in return ~*v* move backwards; support; put wager on; provide with back; provide with musical accompaniment **backer** *n* backward *adj* behind in education **backwardness** *n* **backwards** *adv* to rear,

past, worse state **backbite** *v* slander absent person **backbone** *n* spinal column; strength of character **backcloth, backdrop** *n* painted cloth at back of stage **backdate** *v* make effective from earlier date **backfire** *v* (of plan, scheme, etc.) fail to work; ignite wrongly **backgammon** *n* game played with draughtsmen and dice **background** *n* space behind chief figures of picture etc.; past history of person **backhand** *n* stroke made with hand turned backwards **backlash** *n* sudden adverse reaction **backside** *n* rump

bacon *n* cured pig's flesh

bacteria *pl n* (*sing* **bacterium**) microscopic organisms **bacterial** *adj* **bacteriology** *n*

bad *adj* **worse, worst** faulty; harmful; evil; severe; rotten; *Sl* very good **badly** *adv*

badge *n* distinguishing emblem

--- THESAURUS ---

baby babe, bairn *Scot*, child, infant, newborn child

back *n* backside, end, far end, hind part, hindquarters, posterior, rear, reverse, stern, tail end ~*adj* end, hind, hindmost, posterior, rear, tail ~*v* backtrack, go back, regress, retire, retreat, reverse, turn tail, withdraw; abet, advocate, assist, champion, countenance, encourage, endorse, favour, finance, sanction, second, side with, sponsor, subsidize, support, sustain, underwrite

backer advocate, benefactor, patron, promoter, second, sponsor, subscriber, supporter, underwriter, well-wisher

backfire boomerang, disappoint, fail, flop *Inf*, miscarry, rebound, recoil

background breeding, circumstances, credentials, culture, educa-

tion, environment, experience, history, qualifications, tradition, upbringing

backlash backfire, reaction, recoil, repercussion, resentment, response, retaliation

backward behind, behindhand, dense, dull, retarded, slow, stupid, subnormal, undeveloped

bad defective, deficient, faulty, imperfect, inadequate, incorrect, inferior, poor, substandard, unsatisfactory; damaging, dangerous, detrimental, harmful, hurtful, injurious, ruinous, unhealthy; base, corrupt, criminal, delinquent, evil, immoral, mean, sinful, vile, villainous, wicked, wrong; decayed, mouldy, off, putrid, rancid, rotten, sour, spoiled

badge brand, device, emblem, mark, sign, token

badger *n* burrowing night animal ~*v* pester, worry

badminton *n* game played with rackets and shuttlecocks

baffle *v* check, frustrate, bewilder ~*n* device to regulate flow of liquid etc.

bag *n* sack; measure of quantity; woman's handbag ~*v* **bagging, bagged** bulge; sag; put in bag; kill as game, etc. **baggy** *adj* loose

bagatelle *n* trifle; game like pinball

baggage *n* suitcases, luggage

bagpipes *pl n* musical wind instrument

bail[1] *n Law* security given for person's reappearance in court ~*v* (obtain) release on security

bail[2] *n Cricket* crosspiece on wicket

bail[3] *also* **bale** *v* empty water from boat **bail out** parachute

bailiff *n* land steward, agent

bait *n* food to entice fish; any lure ~*v* lure; persecute

baize *n* smooth woollen cloth

bake *v* cook or harden by dry heat ~*v* make bread, cakes etc. **baker** *n* **bakery** *n* **baking powder** raising agent used in cooking

balalaika *n* Russian musical instrument, like guitar

balance *n* pair of scales; equilibrium; surplus; sum due on an account; difference between two sums ~*v* weigh; bring to equilibrium

balcony *n* platform outside window; upper seats in theatre

bald *adj* hairless; plain; bare **balding** *adj*

bale *n/v* bundle or package

baleful *adj* menacing

balk *v* swerve, pull up; thwart; shirk ~*n* hindrance

ball[1] *n* anything round; globe, sphere, esp. as used in games ~*v* gather into a mass **ball bearings** steel balls used to lessen friction

ball[2] *n* assembly for dancing **ballroom** *n*

ballad *n* narrative poem; simple song

ballast *n* heavy material put in ship to steady it

ballet *n* theatrical presentation of dancing and miming **ballerina** *n*

ballistics *pl n* (*with sing v*) scientific study of motion of projectiles

balloon *n* large bag filled with air or

———————————————— THESAURUS ————————————————

badly carelessly, defectively, faultily, imperfectly, inadequately, incorrectly, ineptly, poorly, shoddily, wrong, wrongly

bag *v* acquire, capture, catch, gain, get, kill, land, shoot, take, trap

baggage bags, belongings, equipment, gear, luggage, suitcases

baggy billowing, bulging, droopy, floppy, ill-fitting, loose, oversize, roomy, sagging, seated, slack

bail[1] *n* bond, guarantee, guaranty, pledge, security, surety, warranty

bail[2], **bale** *v* dip, drain off, ladle, scoop

bait *n* allurement, attraction, bribe, decoy, enticement, inducement, lure, snare, temptation ~*v* entice, lure, se-

duce, tempt; irritate, needle *Inf,* persecute, provoke, tease, torment

balance *n* correspondence, equilibrium, equipoise, equity, equivalence, evenness, parity, symmetry; difference, remainder, residue, rest, surplus ~*v* adjust, compensate for, counteract, counterbalance, equalize, equate, make up for, neutralize, offset

bald baldheaded, depilated, hairless; uncovered

balk demur, evade, flinch, hesitate, jib, recoil, refuse, resist, shirk; baffle, bar, check, defeat, hinder, obstruct, prevent, thwart

ball globe, orb, pellet, sphere

ballast balance, equilibrium, sand-

gas ~*v* puff out

ballot *n* voting, usually by paper ~*v* vote

balm *n* healing or soothing (ointment)

balmy *adj* (of weather) mild and pleasant

balsa *n* Amer. tree with light but strong wood

balsam *n* resinous aromatic substance

bamboo *n* large tropical treelike reed

bamboozle *v* mystify, hoax

ban *v* **banning, banned** prohibit, forbid, outlaw ~*n* prohibition; proclamation

banal *adj* commonplace, trite **banality** *n*

banana *n* tropical treelike plant; its fruit

band¹ *n* strip used to bind; range of frequencies **bandage** *n/v* (apply) strip of cloth for binding wound

band² *n* company; company of musi-

cians ~*v* bind together

bandanna *n* handkerchief

bandit *n* outlaw; robber

bandwagon *n* **jump on the bandwagon** join something that seems assured of success

bandy *v* **bandying, bandied** toss from one to another **bandy-legged** *adj* curving outwards

bane *n* person or thing causing misery or distress **baneful** *adj*

bang *n* sudden loud noise; heavy blow ~*v* make loud noise; beat; slam

banger *n* *Sl* sausage; *Inf* old car; loud firework

bangle *n* ring worn on arm or leg

banish *v* exile; drive away

banisters *pl n* railing on staircase

banjo *n* (*pl* **-jos**) musical instrument like guitar

bank¹ *n* mound of earth; edge of river etc. ~*v* enclose with ridge; pile up

bank² *n* establishment for keeping,

———————— THESAURUS ————————

bag, stabilizer, weight

ballot election, poll, polling, vote, voting

balm balsam, cream, lotion, ointment, salve

balmy clement, mild, pleasant, summery, temperate

ban *v* banish, debar, disallow, exclude, forbid, outlaw, prohibit, proscribe, restrict, suppress ~*n* boycott, censorship, embargo, prohibition, proscription, restriction, suppression, taboo

banal clichéd, commonplace, everyday, hackneyed, humdrum, old hat, ordinary, pedestrian, platitudinous, stale, stereotyped, stock, threadbare, tired, trite, vapid

band¹ bandage, belt, bond, chain, cord, fetter, ribbon, shackle, strap, strip, tie

band² assembly, association, body, clique, club, company, coterie, crew

Inf, gang, horde, party, society, troop; ensemble, group, orchestra

bandage compress, dressing, gauze, plaster

bandit brigand, crook, desperado, freebooter, gangster, gunman, hijacker, marauder, outlaw, pirate, robber, thief

bane affliction, *bête noire,* blight, burden, calamity, curse, despair, destruction, disaster, downfall, plague, ruin, scourge, torment, trial, trouble

bang *n* boom, burst, clang, clap, clash, detonation, explosion, peal, pop, shot, slam, thud, thump; blow, box, bump, cuff, hit, knock, punch, smack, stroke, wallop *Inf,* whack ~*v* bash *Inf,* beat, bump, clatter, crash, hammer, knock, pound, rap, slam, strike, thump

banish deport, drive away, eject, evict, exclude, exile, expel, ostracize, outlaw

lending, exchanging etc. money ~*v* put in bank; keep with bank **banker** *n* **banking** *n* **banknote** *n* written promise of payment **bank on** rely on

bankrupt *n* one who fails in business, insolvent debtor ~*adj* financially ruined ~*v* make bankrupt **bankruptcy** *n*

banner *n* placard; flag

banns *pl n* public declaration of intended marriage

banquet *n/v* feast

banshee *n* spirit whose wailing warns of death

bantam *n* small chicken; very light boxing weight

banter *v* make fun of ~*n* light, teasing language

baptize *v* immerse in, sprinkle with water ceremoniously; christen **baptism** *n*

bar *n* rod or block of any substance; obstacle; rail in law court; body of lawyers; counter where drinks are served; unit of music ~*v* **barring, barred** fasten; obstruct; exclude ~*prep* except **barman** *n* (*fem* **barmaid**)

barb *n* sharp point curving backwards; cutting remark **barbed** *adj*

barbarous *adj* savage, brutal, uncivilized **barbarian** *n* **barbaric** *adj* **barbarism** *n* **barbarity** *n*

barbecue *n* meal cooked outdoors over open fire ~*v* cook thus

barber *n* person who shaves beards and cuts hair

barbiturate *n* derivative of barbituric acid used as drug

bare *adj* uncovered; naked; plain; scanty ~*v* make bare **barely** *adv* only just **barefaced** *adj* shameless

bargain *n* something bought at fa-

bank[1] *n* embankment, heap, mass, mound, pile, ridge; brink, edge, margin, shore, side ~*v* amass, heap, mass, mound, pile, stack

bank[2] *n* depository, fund, hoard, repository, reserve, savings, store, storehouse ~*v* deal with, deposit, keep, save

bankrupt broke *Inf*, destitute, exhausted, failed, impoverished, insolvent, lacking, ruined, spent

banner colours, ensign, flag, pennant, standard, streamer

banquet dinner, feast, meal, repast, revel, treat

banter *v* chaff, deride, jeer, jest, joke, kid *Inf*, make fun of, rib *Inf*, ridicule, taunt, tease ~*n* badinage, derision, jeering, jesting, joking, kidding *Inf*, mockery, repartee, ribbing *Inf*, ridicule

baptism christening; beginning, debut, dedication, initiation, introduction

bar *n* batten, crosspiece, paling, pole, rail, rod, shaft, stake, stick; deterrent, hindrance, impediment, obstacle, rail, railing, stop; bench, court, courtroom, dock, law court; *Law* barristers, counsel, court, tribunal; canteen, counter, inn, lounge, pub *Inf*, public house, saloon, tavern ~*v* barricade, bolt, fasten, latch, lock, secure; ban, exclude, forbid, hinder, keep out, obstruct, prevent, prohibit, restrain

barb bristle, point, prickle, prong, quill, spike, spur, thorn; cut, dig, gibe, insult, sarcasm, scoff, sneer

barbarian *n* hooligan, lout, ruffian, savage, vandal

barbaric primitive, rude, uncivilized, wild

barbarism coarseness, crudity, savagery

bare denuded, exposed, naked, nude, peeled, shorn, stripped, unclothed, undressed; barren, blank, empty,

vourable price; agreement ~*v* haggle, negotiate

barge *n* flat-bottomed freight boat ~*v* *Inf* bump (into), push

baritone *n* (singer with) second lowest adult male voice ~*adj* of, for this voice

barium *n* white metallic element

bark[1] *n/v* (utter) sharp loud cry of dog etc.

bark[2] *n* outer layer of tree

barley *n* grain used for food and making malt

barmy *adj Sl* insane

barn *n* building to store grain, hay etc. **barnyard** *n*

barnacle *n* shellfish which sticks to rocks and ships

barometer *n* instrument to measure pressure of atmosphere **barometric** *adj*

baron *n* (*fem* **baroness**) member of lowest rank of peerage; powerful businessman **baronial** *adj*

baronet *n* lowest British hereditary title

baroque *adj* extravagantly ornamented

barque *n* sailing ship

barracks *pl n* building for lodging soldiers

barrage *n* heavy artillery fire; continuous heavy delivery of questions etc.; dam across river

barrel *n* round wooden vessel; tube of gun etc.

barren *adj* sterile; unprofitable

barricade *n* improvised barrier ~*v* block

barrier *n* fence, obstruction

barrister *n* advocate in the higher law courts

barrow *n* small wheeled handcart; wheelbarrow

barter *v/n* (trade by) exchange of goods

base[1] *n* bottom, foundation; starting point; centre of operations ~*v* found, establish **baseless** *adj* **basement** *n* lowest storey of building

base[2] low, mean; despicable

baseball *n* game played with bat and

lacking, mean, open, poor, scanty, scarce, unfurnished, vacant, void, wanting

bargain *n* (cheap) purchase, discount, giveaway, good buy, good deal, good value, reduction, snip *Inf*; agreement, business, compact, contract, negotiation, pact, pledge, promise, stipulation, transaction, treaty, understanding ~*v* barter, buy, deal, haggle, sell, trade, traffic

bark[1] *n/v* bay, growl, howl, snarl, woof, yap, yelp

bark[2] *n* casing, cortex *Anat & Bot*, covering, crust, husk, rind, skin

barrage battery, bombardment, gunfire, salvo, shelling, volley

barren childless, infertile, sterile; arid, desert, desolate, dry, empty, unfruitful, unproductive, unprofitable,

waste

barricade *n* barrier, blockade, bulwark, fence, obstruction, palisade, rampart, stockade ~*v* bar, block, blockade, defend, fortify, obstruct, protect, shut in

barrier bar, barricade, blockade, boundary, ditch, fence, obstacle, obstruction, railing, rampart, stop, wall; difficulty, drawback, hindrance, impediment, limitation, obstacle, restriction, stumbling block

barter bargain, exchange, haggle, sell, swap, trade, traffic

base[1] *n* bed, bottom, foot, foundation, groundwork, pedestal, rest, stand, support; basis, core, essence, essential, fundamental, heart, key, origin, principle, root, source; camp, centre, headquarters, home, post,

ball; ball used in this game

bash *Inf v* strike violently *~n* blow; attempt

bashful *adj* shy, modest

basic *adj* relating to, serving as base; fundamental; necessary **basically** *adv*

basics *pl n* fundamental principles, facts etc.

basil *n* aromatic herb

basin *n* deep circular dish; harbour; land drained by river

basis *n* (*pl* -ses) foundation; principal constituent

bask *v* lie in warmth and sunshine

basket *n* vessel made of woven cane, straw etc. **basketball** *n* ball game played by two teams

bass¹ *n* lowest part in music; bass singer or voice *~adj* of bass

bass² *n* sea fish

basset *n* type of smooth-haired dog

bassoon *n* woodwind instrument of low tone

bastard *n* child born of unmarried parents; *Inf* unpleasant person *~adj* illegitimate; spurious

bastion *n* projecting part of fortification; defence

bat¹ *n* club used to hit ball in cricket etc. *~v* **batting, batted** strike with bat

bat² *n* nocturnal mouselike flying animal

batch *n* group or set of similar objects

bated *adj* **with bated breath** anxiously

bath *n* vessel or place to bathe in; water for bathing; act of bathing *~v* wash **bathroom** *n*

bathe *v* **bathing, bathed** swim; apply liquid; wash; immerse in water *~n* swim; wash **bather** *n*

baton *n* stick, esp. of policeman, conductor, marshal

battalion *n* military unit of three companies

———————— T H E S A U R U S ————————

settlement, starting point, station *~v* build, construct, depend, derive, establish, found, ground, hinge, locate, station

base² contemptible, corrupt, depraved, despicable, dishonourable, disreputable, evil, ignoble, immoral, infamous, scandalous, shameful, sordid, vile, villainous, wicked

baseless groundless, unfounded, unjustified, unsubstantiated

bash *v* belt *Inf,* biff *Sl,* break, crash, crush, deck *Sl,* hit, punch, slosh *Brit sl,* smash, sock *Sl,* strike, wallop *Inf*

bashful blushing, coy, diffident, nervous, reserved, retiring, self-conscious, sheepish, shrinking, shy, timid, timorous

basic central, essential, fundamental, indispensable, intrinsic, key, necessary, primary, underlying, vital

basics brass tacks *Inf,* core, essentials, facts, hard facts, nitty-gritty *Inf,* practicalities, principles, rudiments

basis base, bottom, footing, foundation, ground, groundwork, support

bask laze, lie in, loll, lounge, relax, sunbathe

bastard *n* illegitimate (child), love child *~adj* counterfeit, false, illegitimate, imperfect, impure, irregular, misbegotten, sham, spurious

bastion bulwark, citadel, defence, fortress, prop, rock, stronghold, support

bat bang, hit, rap, smack, strike, swat, thump, wallop *Inf,* whack

batch accumulation, amount, collection, crowd, group, lot, pack, set

bath *n* ablution, douche, shower, soak, tub, wash *~v* bathe, clean, scrub down, soak, soap, sponge, tub, wash

bathe *v* cleanse, immerse, moisten, rinse, soak, steep, wash, wet *~n* dip, swim

baton club, mace, rod, staff, stick, truncheon, wand

batten *n* strip of wood ~*v* (*esp. with down*) fasten

batter *v* strike continuously ~*n* mixture of flour, eggs, milk, used in cooking

battery *n* connected group of electrical cells; accumulator; number of similar things occurring together; *Law* assault by beating; number of guns

battle *n* fight between armies ~*v* fight **battle-axe** *n* large heavy axe; *Inf* domineering woman

battlement *n* wall with openings for shooting

battleship *n* heavily armed and armoured fighting ship

batty *adj Inf* crazy, silly

bauble *n* showy trinket

bawdy *adj* obscene, lewd

bawl *v/n* cry; shout

bay¹ *n* wide inlet of sea

bay² *n* space between two columns; recess

bay³ *n/v* bark **at bay** cornered; at a distance

bayonet *n* stabbing weapon fixed to rifle ~*v* **bayonetting, bayonetted** stab

with this

bazaar *n* market (esp. in the East); sale for charity

bazooka *n* powerful rocket launcher

B & B bed and breakfast

BBC British Broadcasting Corporation

BC before Christ

be *v* (*present tense I* **am**, *he, she is, we, you, they* **are**; *present participle* **being**; *past tense I, he, she* **was**, *we, you, they* **were**; *past participle* **been**) live; exist; have a state or quality

beach *n* shore of sea ~*v* run boat on shore

beacon *n* fire used to give signal; lighthouse, buoy

bead *n* little ball pierced for threading; drop of liquid **beaded** *adj* **beady** *adj* small and glittering

beagle *n* small hound

beak *n* projecting horny jaws of bird; anything similar; *Sl* magistrate

beaker *n* large drinking cup; glass vessel used by chemists

beam *n* long thick piece of wood; ray of light etc. ~*v* aim light, radio waves etc. (to); shine; smile broadly

bean *n* edible seed of various legumi-

batten board up, clamp down, cover up, fasten down, fix, nail down, secure

batter assault, bash *Inf*, beat, belabour, break, buffet, clobber *Sl*, lash, pelt, pound, pummel, smash, smite, thrash

battery assault, attack, beating, mayhem, onslaught, physical violence, thumping

battle action, attack, combat, encounter, engagement, fight, fray, hostilities, skirmish, war, warfare

bawl bellow, call, clamour, howl, roar, shout, yell

bay¹ cove, gulf, inlet, sound

bay² alcove, niche, nook, opening, recess

bay³ bark, bell, clamour, cry, growl, howl, yelp

bazaar exchange, market, marketplace, mart; bring-and-buy, fair, fête

be be alive, breathe, exist, inhabit, live

beach coast, sands, seashore, seaside, shingle, shore, strand

beacon beam, bonfire, flare, lighthouse, sign, signal, watchtower

bead blob, bubble, dot, drop, droplet, globule, pill

beak bill, neb *Arch or dial,* nib

beam *n* girder, joist, plank, rafter, spar, support, timber; gleam, glimmer, glint, glow, radiation, ray, shaft, streak, stream ~*v* glare, gleam, glitter, glow, radiate, shine, transmit; grin, laugh, smile

nous plants

bear[1] *v* **bearing, bore, born** *or* **borne** carry; support; produce; endure; press (upon) **bearer** *n*

bear[2] *n* heavy carnivorous animal

beard *n* hair on chin ~*v* oppose boldly

bearing *n* support for mechanical part; relevance; behaviour; direction; relative position

beast *n* four-footed animal; brutal man **beastly** *adj*

beat *v* **beating, beat, beaten** strike repeatedly; overcome; surpass; stir vigorously; flap (wings); make, wear (path); throb ~*n* stroke; pulsation; appointed course; basic rhythmic unit of music ~*adj Sl* exhausted **beater** *n*

beau *n* (*pl* **beaux**) suitor

beauty *n* loveliness, grace; beautiful

person or thing **beautiful** *adj* beautifully *adv* **beautician** *n* person who gives beauty treatments

beaver *n* amphibious rodent; its fur ~*v* work industriously

becalmed *adj* (of ship) motionless through lack of wind

because *adv/conj* by reason of, since

beckon *v* summon by signal

become *v* **becoming, became, become** come to be; suit **becoming** *adj* suitable

bed *n* piece of furniture for sleeping on; garden plot; bottom of river; layer, stratum ~*v* **bedding, bedded** lay in a bed; plant **bedding** *n* **bedpan** *n* container used as lavatory by bedridden people **bedridden** *adj* confined to bed **bedroom** *n* **bedsit** *n* one-roomed flat **bedstead** *n*

bear bring, carry, convey, move, take, tote, transport; beget, breed, bring forth, generate, give birth to, produce, yield; allow, endure, permit, put up with *Inf*, stomach, suffer, tolerate, undergo

bearing air, aspect, attitude, behaviour, carriage, demeanour, deportment, manner, mien, posture; connection, import, pertinence, relation, relevance; *Naut* course, direction, point of compass

beast animal, brute, creature; barbarian, brute, fiend, monster, ogre, sadist, savage, swine

beastly barbarous, bestial, brutal, brutish, coarse, cruel, depraved, inhuman, monstrous, sadistic, savage; awful, foul, mean, nasty, unpleasant

beat *v* bang, batter, break, buffet, cane, clobber *Sl*, cudgel, drub, flog, hit, knock, lambast(e), lash, maul, pound, punch, strike, thrash, whip; conquer, defeat, excel, master, outdo, outrun, overcome, subdue, surpass, vanquish ~*n* blow, hit, lash,

punch, slap, strike, stroke, swing, thump; flutter, palpitation, pulsation, pulse, throb; circuit, course, path, rounds, route, way; accent, cadence, measure, metre, rhythm, stress, time

beautiful appealing, attractive, charming, comely, delightful, exquisite, fair, fine, good-looking, gorgeous, graceful, handsome, lovely, pleasing, radiant, stunning *Inf*

beauty attractiveness, bloom, charm, elegance, fairness, glamour, grace; belle, charmer, cracker *Sl*, goodlooker, stunner *Inf*, Venus

because as, by reason of, in that, on account of, owing to, since, thanks to

beckon bid, gesticulate, gesture, motion, nod, signal, summon, wave at

become alter to, be transformed into, change into, evolve into, grow into, mature into, ripen into; embellish, enhance, fit, flatter, grace, harmonize, ornament, set off, suit

becoming attractive, comely, flattering, graceful, neat, pretty, tasteful

bed bedstead, berth, bunk, cot,

bedevil v -illing, -illed harass or torment

bedlam n noisy confused scene

bedraggled adj messy and wet

bee n insect that makes honey

beech n European tree with smooth greyish bark and small nuts

beef n flesh of cattle for eating; Inf complaint ~v Inf complain **beefy** adj muscular **beefburger** n flat grilled or fried cake of minced beef

beer n fermented alcoholic drink made from hops and malt **beer parlour** Canad licensed place where beer is sold to the public

beet n any of various plants with root used for food **beetroot** n type of beet plant with a dark red root

beetle n class of insect with hard upper-wing cases

befall v befalling, befell, befallen happen (to)

befit v befitting, befitted be suitable

for or appropriate to

before prep in front of; in presence of; in preference to; earlier than ~adv earlier; in front ~conj sooner than

beforehand adv previously

befriend v become a friend to

beg v begging, begged ask earnestly; ask for money or food **beggar** n

begin v -ginning, -gan, -gun (cause to) start **beginner** n **beginning** n

begonia n tropical plant

begrudge v grudge, envy anyone the possession of

beguile v charm, fascinate; amuse; deceive

behalf n on behalf of in the interest of

behave v act in particular way; act properly **behaviour** n conduct

behead v cut off the head of

behest n charge, command

behind prep further back or earlier than ~adv in the rear

behold v beheld, behold or beholden

———— THESAURUS ————

couch, divan, pallet; area, border, garden, patch, plot, row, strip

bedlam chaos, clamour, commotion, confusion, furore, hubbub, noise, pandemonium, tumult, turmoil, uproar

bedridden confined, incapacitated, laid up Inf

beef Inf brawn, flesh, muscle, physique, robustness, sinew, strength

before prep earlier than, in advance of, in front of, in the presence of, prior to ~adv ahead, earlier, formerly, in advance, in front, previously, sooner

beforehand before now, earlier, in advance, previously, sooner

befriend advise, aid, assist, back, benefit, favour, help, patronize, side with, stand by, succour, support, sustain, uphold, welcome

beg beseech, crave, desire, entreat, implore, importune, petition, plead, pray, request, solicit, supplicate;

cadge, call for alms, sponge on

beggar cadger, mendicant, scrounger Inf, sponger Inf, supplicant, tramp, vagrant

begin commence, embark on, initiate, instigate, institute, prepare, set about, set on foot, start

beginner amateur, apprentice, fledgling, freshman, greenhorn Inf, initiate, learner, neophyte, novice, recruit, starter, student, trainee, tyro

beginning birth, commencement, inauguration, inception, initiation, onset, opening, origin, outset, preface, prelude, rise, rudiments, source, start

begrudge be jealous, envy, grudge, resent

behave act, function, operate, perform, run, work; conduct oneself properly, mind one's manners

behaviour actions, bearing, carriage, conduct, demeanour, deportment, manner, manners, ways

watch, see

beholden *adj* bound in gratitude

beige *n* undyed woollen cloth; its colour

being *n* existence; that which exists; creature; *present participle of* BE

belated *adj* late; too late

belch *v* expel wind by mouth; eject violently ~*n* this act

beleaguered *adj* besieged; surrounded or beset

belfry *n* bell tower

belie *v* show to be untrue

believe *v* regard as true or real; have faith **belief** *n* **believable** *adj* **believer** *n*

belittle *v* regard, speak of, as having little worth

bell *n* hollow metal instrument giving ringing sound when struck; electrical device emitting ring

belle *n* beautiful woman

bellicose *adj* warlike

belligerent *adj* hostile, aggressive; making war **belligerence** *n*

bellow *v/n* roar; shout

bellows *pl n* instrument for creating stream of air

belly *n* stomach ~*v* **bellying, bellied** swell out

belong *v* be property of; be member of; have an allotted place; pertain to **belongings** *pl n* personal possessions

beloved *adj* much loved ~*n* dear one

below *adv* beneath ~*prep* lower than

belt *n* band; girdle; zone ~*v Inf* thrash

bemoan *v* grieve over

bemuse *v* confuse, bewilder

bench *n* long seat; seat or body of judges etc.

bend *v* **bending, bent** (cause to) form a curve

beneath *prep* under, lower than ~*adv*

——————— THESAURUS ———————

behind *prep* after, at the back of, at the rear of, following, later than ~*adv* after, afterwards, following, in the wake (of), next, subsequently

behold consider, contemplate, discern, eye, look at, observe, regard, scan, view, watch, witness

being actuality, existence, life, living, reality; entity, essence, nature, soul, spirit, substance; animal, beast, body, creature, human being, individual, living thing, mortal, thing

belated delayed, late, overdue, tardy

belief admission, assurance, confidence, conviction, credit, feeling, impression, judgment, notion, opinion, persuasion, reliance, theory, trust, view; credence, credo, creed, doctrine, dogma, faith, ideology, principles, tenet

believable acceptable, credible, creditable, imaginable, likely, plausible, possible, reliable, trustworthy

believe accept, be certain of, be convinced of, buy *Sl*, count on, credit,

depend on, have faith in, hold, swallow *Inf*, swear by, trust

believer adherent, convert, devotee, disciple, follower, proselyte, supporter

belong be at the disposal of, be held by, be owned by; be allied to; be a member of, be associated with, be included in

belongings effects, gear, goods, personal property, possessions, stuff, things

beloved adored, cherished, darling, dear, dearest, loved, precious, sweet

below *adv* beneath, down, lower, under, underneath ~*prep* inferior, lesser, lesser than, subject, subordinate

belt band, girdle, girth, sash, waistband

bench form, pew, seat, settle; court, courtroom, judge, judges, judiciary, magistrate, magistrates

bend *v* bow, buckle, contort, curve, diverge, flex, incline, lean, stoop, swerve, turn, twist, veer, warp ~*n* an-

below

benefit n advantage, profit; money paid to unemployed etc. ~v **-fiting, -fited** do good to; receive good **benefactor** n (fem **benefactress**) one who helps or does good to others; patron **beneficial** adj

benevolent adj kindly, charitable **benevolence** n

benign adj kindly, favourable

bent adj curved; resolved (on); Inf corrupt; Inf deviant ~n inclination

benzene n one of group of flammable liquids used as solvents etc.

bequeath v leave property etc. by will **bequest** n bequeathing; legacy

berate v scold harshly

bereave v **-reaved** or **-reft** deprive of, esp. by death **bereavement** n

beret n round, close-fitting hat

beriberi n tropical disease caused by

vitamin B deficiency

berry n small juicy stoneless fruit

berserk adj frenzied

berth n ship's mooring place; place to sleep in ship ~v moor

beryl n variety of crystalline mineral, e.g. aquamarine, emerald

beseech v **beseeching, besought** entreat, implore

beset v **besetting, beset** surround with danger, problems

beside prep by the side of, near; distinct from **besides** adv/prep in addition (to)

besiege v surround

besotted adj drunk; foolish; infatuated

best adj/adv superlative of GOOD and WELL ~v defeat **best man** groom's attendant at wedding **bestseller** n book sold in great numbers

———————— T H E S A U R U S ————————

gle, arc, bow, corner, crook, curve, hook, loop, turn, twist

beneath prep below, inferior to, less than, lower than, unbefitting, underneath, unworthy of ~adv below, in a lower place, underneath

beneficial advantageous, favourable, healthful, helpful, useful, valuable, wholesome

benefit n advantage, aid, asset, blessing, boon, favour, gain, good, help, interest, profit, use ~v advance, aid, assist, avail, better, enhance, further, improve, profit, promote, serve

bent adj angled, arched, bowed, crooked, curved, hunched, twisted; (with **on**) determined, inclined, insistent, resolved, set ~n ability, aptitude, flair, forte, inclination, knack, penchant, proclivity, propensity, talent

bequeath bestow, commit, endow, entrust, give, grant, hand down, leave to by will, pass on, will

bereavement death, deprivation,

loss

berserk crazy, frenzied, insane, mad, manic, rabid, raging, violent, wild

berth n anchorage, dock, harbour, haven, pier, port, quay, wharf; bed, billet, bunk

beside abreast of, adjacent to, alongside, at the side of, close to, near, nearby, neighbouring, next door to, next to, overlooking

besides adv also, as well, further, furthermore, in addition, moreover, otherwise, too, what's more

besiege beleaguer, beset, blockade, encircle, encompass, hedge in, hem in, lay siege to, shut in, surround

best adj chief, finest, first, first-class, foremost, highest, leading, outstanding, perfect, pre-eminent, superlative, supreme; apt, correct, most desirable, most fitting, right; greatest, largest, most ~adv advantageously, excellently, most fortunately; extremely, greatly, most deeply, most fully, most highly

bestial *adj* like a beast, brutish

bestir *v* **bestirring, bestirred** rouse to activity

bestow *v* give, confer

bet *v* **betting, bet** *or* **betted** agree to pay money if wrong in guessing result of contest ~*n* money so risked

bête noire *n* (*pl* *bêtes noires*) particular dislike

betray *v* be disloyal to; reveal, divulge; show signs of **betrayal** *n*

better *adj/adv comparative of* GOOD *and* WELL ~*v* improve

between *prep/adv* in the intermediate part, in space or time; indicating reciprocal relation or comparison

bevel *n* angled surface ~*v* **-elling, -elled** slope, slant

beverage *n* drink

bevy *n* flock or group

bewail *v* lament

beware *v* be on one's guard

bewilder *v* puzzle, confuse

bewitch *v* charm, fascinate

beyond *adv* farther away ~*prep* on the farther side of; out of reach of

bias *n* (*pl* **biases**) slant; inclination ~*v* **-asing, -ased** influence, affect **biased** *adj* prejudiced

bib *n* cloth put under child's chin when eating; top of apron

Bible *n* sacred writings of the Christian religion **biblical** *adj*

bibliography *n* list of books on a subject

bicentenary *n* 200th anniversary

biceps *n* two-headed muscle, esp. of upper arm

——————— THESAURUS ———————

bestial animal, beastly, brutal, brutish, carnal, depraved, gross, inhuman, low, savage, sensual, sordid, vile

bestow accord, allot, award, commit, confer, donate, entrust, give, grant, impart, lavish, present

bet *v* chance, gamble, hazard, pledge, risk, speculate, stake, venture, wager ~*n* ante, gamble, hazard, pledge, risk, speculation, stake, venture, wager

betray be disloyal, break with, double-cross *Inf*, inform on, sell out *Inf*; disclose, divulge, evince, expose, give away, lay bare, let slip, reveal, show, tell, tell on, uncover, unmask

betrayal disloyalty, double-cross *Inf*, double-dealing, duplicity, falseness, perfidy, sell-out *Inf*, treachery, treason, trickery; disclosure, revelation, telling

better *adj* bigger, excelling, finer, fitter, greater, higher quality, larger, preferable, superior, surpassing, worthier; cured, fitter, healthier, improving, more healthy, on the mend *Inf*, progressing, recovering, stronger, well; bigger, greater, larger, longer ~*adv* in a more excellent manner, in a superior way, to a greater degree

between amidst, among, halfway, in the middle of, mid

beverage draught, drink, liquid, liquor, refreshment

beware avoid, be careful, be cautious, be wary, guard against, heed, look out, mind, shun, steer clear of, take heed, watch out

bewilder bemuse, confound, confuse, daze, flummox, mix up, mystify, perplex, puzzle

bewitch allure, beguile, charm, enchant, entrance, fascinate, spellbind

beyond above, apart from, at a distance, away from, before, farther, out of range, out of reach, over, past, remote

bias favouritism, inclination, leaning, narrow-mindedness, one-sidedness, partiality, prejudice, proneness, propensity, tendency, turn, unfairness

biased distorted, one-sided, partial, prejudiced, slanted, swayed, twisted, warped, weighted

bicker v/n quarrel over petty things

bicycle n vehicle with two wheels **bicyclist** n

bid v **bidding, bid** or **bade, bid** or **bidden** offer; say; command; invite ~n offer, esp. of price; try; Card games call **bidder** n **bidding** n command

bide v remain; dwell; await

bier n frame for coffin

bifocal adj having two focal lengths **bifocals** pl n spectacles having bifocal lenses

big adj **bigger, biggest** of great size, height, number, power etc. **bighead** n Inf conceited person **big-headed** adj

bigamy n crime of marrying a person while one is still legally married to someone else **bigamist** n

bigot n person intolerant of ideas of others **bigoted** adj **bigotry** n

bike n short for BICYCLE or MOTORBIKE

bikini n (pl **-nis**) woman's two-piece swimming costume

bilberry n small moorland plant with edible blue berries

bile n fluid secreted by the liver; ill temper **bilious** adj nauseous, nauseating

bilge n bottom of ship's hull; dirty water collecting there; Inf nonsense

bilingual adj speaking, or written in, two languages

bill[1] n written account of charges; draft of Act of Parliament; poster; commercial document ~v present account of charges; announce by advertisement

bill[2] n bird's beak

billet n/v (provide) civilian quarters for troops

billiards n game played on table with balls and cues

billion n thousand million, 10^9; Obs million million, 10^{12}

billow n swelling wave ~v swell

bin n receptacle for corn, refuse etc.

binary adj composed of, character-

——————— T H E S A U R U S ———————

bicker argue, disagree, dispute, fight, quarrel, squabble

bid v offer, proffer, propose, submit, tender; call, greet, say, tell, wish; ask, call, charge, command, desire, direct, enjoin, instruct, invite, require, solicit, summon, tell ~n offer, price, proposal, proposition, sum, tender; attempt, effort, try, venture

bidding behest, call, charge, command, demand, invitation, order, request, summons

big bulky, burly, colossal, enormous, extensive, gigantic, great, huge, hulking, immense, large, mammoth, massive, prodigious, sizable, spacious, substantial, vast, voluminous; eminent, important, leading, main, powerful, principal, prominent, serious, significant, valuable, weighty; generous, gracious, heroic, magnanimous, noble, princely

bigoted biased, dogmatic, illiberal, intolerant, narrow-minded, opinionated, prejudiced, sectarian

bigotry bias, discrimination, dogmatism, fanaticism, intolerance, narrow-mindedness, prejudice, racialism, racism, sectarianism

bill[1] n account, charges, invoice, reckoning, score, statement, tally; measure, projected law, proposal; advertisement, broadsheet, circular, handbill, handout, leaflet, notice, placard, playbill, poster ~v charge, debit, figure, invoice

bill[2] beak, mandible, neb Arch or dial, nib

billet n accommodation, barracks, lodging, quarters ~v accommodate, berth, quarter, station

billow n breaker, surge, swell, tide, wave ~v balloon, puff up, rise up, roll, surge, swell

ized by, two; dual

bind v **binding, bound** tie fast; tie round; oblige; seal; constrain; bandage; cohere; put (book) into cover **binder** n **binding** n cover of book; tape for hem etc.

binge n Inf spree

bingo n game of chance in which numbers drawn are matched with those on a card

binoculars pl n telescope made for both eyes

bio- comb. form life, living, as in **biochemistry**

biodegradable adj capable of decomposition by natural means

biography n story of one person's life **biographer** n **biographical** adj

biology n study of living organisms **biological** adj **biologist** n

bionic adj having physical functions aided by electronic equipment

biopsy n examination of tissue from a living body

biped n two-footed animal

birch n tree with silvery bark; rod for punishment ~v flog

bird n feathered animal

birdie n Golf score of one stroke under par

Biro n Trademark ballpoint pen

birth n bearing, or the being born, of offspring; parentage, origin **birthday** n **birthmark** n blemish on the skin

biscuit n dry, small, thin variety of cake

bisect v divide into two equal parts

bisexual adj sexually attracted to both men and women

bishop n clergyman governing diocese; chess piece

bison n large wild ox; Amer. buffalo

bistro n small restaurant

bit¹ n fragment, piece

bit² n biting, cutting part of tool; mouthpiece of horse's bridle

bit³ n Computers smallest unit of information

bitch n female dog, fox, or wolf; Offens sl spiteful woman **bitchy** adj

bite v **biting, bit, bit** or **bitten** cut into, esp. with teeth; grip; rise to the bait; corrode ~n act of biting; wound so made; mouthful **biting** adj piercing or keen; sarcastic

bitter adj sour tasting; (of person) re-

———————— T H E S A U R U S ————————

bind v attach, fasten, glue, hitch, lash, paste, rope, secure, stick, strap, tie, tie up; compel, constrain, force, necessitate, oblige

binding adj compulsory, indissoluble, irrevocable, mandatory, obligatory, unalterable

biography account, curriculum vitae, CV, life, life story, memoirs, profile, record

birth childbirth, delivery, nativity, parturition; ancestry, background, blood, breeding, descent, genealogy, line, lineage, nobility, pedigree, race, stock, strain; beginning, emergence, genesis, origin, rise, source

bisect cut in half, cut in two, divide in two, halve

bit¹ chip, crumb, fragment, grain, iota, jot, mite, morsel, part, piece, scrap, slice, speck, tittle, whit

bit² brake, check, curb, restraint, snaffle

bitchy catty Inf, malicious, mean, nasty, rancorous, snide, spiteful, venomous, vicious, vindictive

bite v chew, clamp, crunch, crush, cut, gnaw, grip, hold, nibble, nip, pierce, pinch, rend, seize, snap, tear, wound ~n itch, nip, pinch, prick, sting, tooth marks, wound; food, light meal, morsel, mouthful, piece, snack

biting bitter, cold, cutting, freezing, harsh, penetrating, piercing, sharp; caustic, cutting, incisive, mordant,

sentful; sarcastic **bitterly** *adv* **bitterness** *n*

bittern *n* wading bird

bitumen *n* viscous substance occurring in asphalt, tar etc.

bivouac *n* temporary encampment of soldiers, hikers etc. ~*v* **bivouacking, bivouacked** camp

bizarre *adj* unusual, weird

blab *v* **blabbing, blabbed** reveal secrets; chatter idly

black *adj* of the darkest colour; without light; dark; evil ~*n* darkest colour; black dye, clothing etc.; (*with cap.*) person of dark-skinned race ~*v* boycott in industrial dispute **blacken** *v* make black; defame **blackball** *v* vote against, exclude **blackberry** *n* plant with dark juicy berries, bramble **blackbird** *n* common European songbird **blackboard** *n* dark surface for writing on with chalk **black box** *Inf.* name for FLIGHT RECORDER **blackhead** *n*

small dark spot on skin **blackleg** *n* strikebreaker **blacklist** *n* list of people considered suspicious ~*v* put on such a list **black market** illegal buying and selling of goods **black spot** dangerous place, esp. on a road

blackguard *n* scoundrel

blackmail *v* extort money by threats ~*n* extortion **blackmailer** *n*

blackout *n* complete failure of electricity supply; state of temporary unconsciousness; obscuring of lights as precaution against night air attack

blacksmith *n* person who works in iron

bladder *n* membranous bag to contain liquid

blade *n* edge, cutting part of knife or tool; leaf of grass etc.; sword

blame *n* censure; culpability ~*v* find fault with; censure **blameless** *adj* **blameworthy** *adj*

blanch *v* whiten, bleach; turn pale

——————— THESAURUS ———————

sarcastic, scathing, sharp, stinging, vitriolic, withering

bitter acid, acrid, astringent, sharp, sour, tart, unsweetened, vinegary; hostile, morose, rancorous, resentful, sore, sour, sullen

bitterness acerbity, acidity, sharpness, sourness, tartness; grudge, hostility, pique, rancour, resentment

bizarre curious, eccentric, extraordinary, fantastic, freakish, grotesque, ludicrous, odd, off-beat, outlandish, outré, peculiar, queer, strange, unusual, weird

black *adj* dark, dusky, ebony, inky, jet, murky, sable, starless, swarthy; bad, evil, iniquitous, nefarious, villainous, wicked

blacken befoul, cloud, darken, make black, smudge, soil; decry, defame, defile, denigrate, dishonour, malign, slander, smear, smirch, stain, sully, taint, tarnish, vilify

blacklist *v* ban, bar, boycott, debar, exclude, expel, ostracize, preclude, proscribe, reject, snub, vote against

blackmail *n* bribe, exaction, extortion, hush money *Sl*, intimidation, protection *Inf*, ransom

blackout *n* power cut, power failure; coma, faint, oblivion, swoon, unconsciousness

blame *n* accusation, censure, charge, complaint, condemnation, criticism, recrimination, reproach, reproof; culpability, fault, guilt, incrimination, liability, onus, responsibility ~*v* accuse, admonish, censure, charge, chide, condemn, criticize, disapprove, find fault with, hold responsible, reprehend, reproach, reprove, tax, upbraid

blameless above suspicion, clean, faultless, guiltless, innocent, in the clear, irreproachable, perfect, stainless, unblemished, upright, virtuous

blancmange *n* jellylike pudding made from milk

bland *adj* devoid of distinctive characteristics; smooth in manner **blandly** *adv*

blank *adj* without marks or writing; empty; vacant, confused ~*n* empty space; cartridge containing no bullet **blankly** *adv*

blanket *n* thick bed cover; concealing cover ~*v* cover, stifle

blare *v* sound loudly and harshly ~*n* such sound

blarney *n* flattering talk

blasé *adj* indifferent through familiarity; bored

blaspheme *v* show contempt for God, esp. in speech **blasphemous** *adj* **blasphemy** *n*

blast *n* explosion; shock wave; gust of wind; loud sound ~*v* blow up; blight

blatant *adj* obvious **blatantly** *adv*

blaze[1] *n* strong fire or flame; brightness; outburst ~*v* burn strongly; be very angry

blaze[2] *v* establish trail ~*n* white mark on horse's face

blazer *n* type of jacket worn esp. for sports

bleach *v* make or become white ~*n* bleaching substance

bleak *adj* cold, exposed; dismal **bleakness** *n*

bleary *adj* with eyes dimmed, as with tears, sleep

bleat *v* cry, as sheep; say plaintively ~*n* sheep's cry

bleed *v* **bleeding, bled** lose blood; draw blood from

bleep *n* short high-pitched sound

blameworthy discreditable, indefensible, inexcusable, iniquitous, reprehensible, reproachable, shameful

bland boring, dull, flat, humdrum, insipid, tasteless, tedious, vapid, weak

blank *adj* bare, clean, clear, empty, plain, spotless, unfilled, unmarked, void, white; at a loss, bewildered, confounded, confused, nonplussed, uncomprehending ~*n* emptiness, empty space, gap, nothingness, space, vacancy, vacuum, void

blanket *n* cover, coverlet, rug; carpet, cloak, coat, coating, covering, envelope, film, layer, mantle, sheet, wrapper, wrapping ~*v* cloak, cloud, coat, conceal, cover, hide, mask, obscure

blare blast, boom, clang, honk, hoot, peal, resound, roar, trumpet

blaspheme curse, damn, desecrate, execrate, profane, swear

blasphemous godless, impious, profane, sacrilegious, ungodly

blasphemy cursing, desecration, execration, impiety, impiousness, profanity, sacrilege, swearing

blast *n* bang, blow-up, burst, crash, explosion, outburst, salvo, volley; blow, clang, honk, peal, scream, toot, wail ~*v* blow up, break up, burst, demolish, destroy, explode, ruin, shatter

blatant brazen, conspicuous, flagrant, glaring, naked, obvious, ostentatious, outright, overt, prominent, sheer

blaze *n* bonfire, conflagration, fire, flame, flames; beam, brightness, flare, flash, glare, gleam, glitter, glow, light, radiance ~*v* beam, burn, fire, flame, flare, flash, glare, gleam, glow, shine

bleach blanch, fade, grow pale, lighten, peroxide, wash out, whiten

bleak bare, barren, chilly, cold, desolate, exposed, gaunt, open, raw, windswept, windy; cheerless, depressing, dismal, dreary, gloomy, grim, hopeless, joyless, sombre, unpromising

bleed exude, flow, gush, lose blood, ooze, run, seep, shed blood, spurt,

bleeper *n*

blemish *n* defect ~*v* make defective **blemished** *adj*

blend *v* mix ~*n* mixture **blender** *n* electrical appliance for mixing food

bless *v* **blessing, blessed** *or* **blest** consecrate; ask God's favour for; make happy **blessed** *adj* **blessing** *n*

blether *v* speak at length, esp. foolishly ~*n* foolish or babbling talk

blight *n* plant disease; harmful influence ~*v* injure

blighter *n* *Inf* irritating person

blind *adj* unable to see; heedless; closed at one end ~*v* deprive of sight ~*n* window screen; pretext **blindly**

adv **blindness** *n* **blindfold** *v/n* (cloth used to) cover the eyes

blink *v* wink; twinkle ~*n* gleam **blink** at ignore **on the blink** *Inf* not working

blip *n* repetitive sound or visible pulse, e.g. on radar screen

bliss *n* perfect happiness **blissful** *adj* **blissfully** *adv*

blister *n* bubble on skin; surface swelling ~*v* form blisters (on) **blistering** *adj* very hot; extremely harsh

blithe *adj* happy **blithely** *adv*

blitz *n* concentrated attack

blizzard *n* blinding storm of wind and snow

bloated *adj* swollen **bloater** *n* smoked

——————— THESAURUS ———————

trickle, weep; drain, draw *or* take blood, exhaust, extort, extract, fleece, milk, reduce, sap

blemish *n* blot, blotch, blur, defect, disfigurement, disgrace, dishonour, fault, flaw, imperfection, mark, smudge, speck, spot, stain, taint

blend *v* coalesce, combine, compound, fuse, intermix, merge, mingle, mix, unite ~*n* alloy, amalgam, composite, compound, concoction, fusion, mix, mixture, synthesis, union

bless consecrate, dedicate, exalt, extol, glorify, hallow, magnify, ordain, praise, sanctify, thank

blessed adored, beatified, divine, hallowed, holy, revered, sacred, sanctified; endowed, favoured, fortunate, lucky

blessing benediction, benison, consecration, dedication, grace, invocation, thanksgiving; advantage, benefit, boon, bounty, favour, gain, gift, godsend, good fortune, help, kindness, profit, service, windfall

blight *n* canker, decay, disease, fungus, infestation, mildew, pest, rot ~*v* blast, destroy, injure, nip in the bud, ruin, shrivel, wither

blind *adj* eyeless, sightless, unseeing, unsighted, visionless; careless, heedless, ignorant, inattentive, inconsiderate, indifferent, insensitive, neglectful, oblivious, prejudiced, thoughtless, unaware of, unconscious of, uncritical, undiscerning, unmindful of, unobservant, unreasoning ~*n* camouflage, cloak, cover, façade, feint, front, mask, screen, smoke screen

blindly aimlessly, at random, confusedly, frantically, indiscriminately, instinctively, madly, purposelessly, wildly

bliss beatitude, blessedness, ecstasy, euphoria, happiness, heaven, joy, paradise, rapture

blissful delighted, ecstatic, elated, enchanted, euphoric, happy, joyful, rapt, rapturous

blister abscess, boil, canker, carbuncle, cyst, pimple, sore, swelling, ulcer

blithe buoyant, carefree, cheerful, cheery, debonair, happy, jaunty, light-hearted, merry, sprightly, vivacious

blitz assault, attack, blitzkrieg, bombardment, offensive, onslaught, raid, strike

herring

blob *n* soft mass or drop

block *n* solid (rectangular) piece of wood, stone etc.; obstacle; pulley with frame; large building of offices, flats etc. ~*v* obstruct, stop up; shape **blockage** *n* **blockhead** *n* stupid person **block letter** plain capital letter

blockade *n* physical prevention of access, esp. to port ~*v* prevent access

bloke *n Inf* fellow, chap

blond *adj* (*fem* **blonde**) (of hair) light-coloured ~*n* person with light-coloured hair

blood *n* red fluid in veins; kindred ~*v* initiate (into hunting, war etc.) **bloodless** *adj* **bloody** *adj* covered in blood; savage; extreme ~*adv Sl* extremely ~*v* make bloody **blood bath** massacre **bloodhound** *n* large dog used for tracking **bloodshed** *n* slaughter **bloodshot** *adj* (of eyes) inflamed **bloodthirsty** *adj* cruel **bloody-minded** *adj* deliberately unhelpful

bloom *n* flower; prime; glow ~*v* be in flower; flourish

bloomer *n Inf* mistake

bloomers *pl n* wide, baggy knickers

blossom *n* flower ~*v* flower; flourish

blot *n* spot, stain ~*v* **blotting, blotted** spot, stain; obliterate; soak up ink **blotter** *n*

blotch *n* dark spot ~*v* make spotted

blouse *n* light, loose upper garment

blow¹ *v* **blowing, blew, blown** make a current of air; pant; drive air upon or into; drive by current of air; make sound; *Sl* squander ~*n* blast; gale **blower** *n* **blowfly** *n* fly which infects food etc. **blowlamp** *n* small burner with very hot flame **blowout** *n* sudden puncture in tyre; uncontrolled escape of oil, gas, from well; *Sl* large meal **blow up** explode; fill with air; *Inf* enlarge photograph; *Inf* lose one's temper

blow² *n* stroke, knock; sudden misfortune

blowzy *adj* slovenly, sluttish

———————— T H E S A U R U S ————————

blizzard blast, gale, snowstorm, squall, storm, tempest

blob ball, bead, bubble, drop, droplet, globule, lump, mass, pearl

block *n* bar, brick, cake, chunk, cube, hunk, ingot, lump, mass, piece, square; bar, barrier, blockage, hindrance, impediment, jam, obstacle, obstruction, stoppage ~*v* choke, clog, close, obstruct, plug, stop up

blockade barricade, barrier, closure, hindrance, impediment, obstacle, obstruction, restriction, siege, stoppage

blond, blonde fair, fair-haired, flaxen, golden-haired, light

blood gore, lifeblood, vital fluid; ancestry, birth, descent, extraction, family, kindred, kinship, lineage, relations

bloodshed blood bath, butchery, carnage, gore, killing, massacre, murder, slaughter

bloodthirsty brutal, cruel, ferocious, inhuman, ruthless, savage, vicious, warlike

bloody bleeding, blood-soaked, bloodstained, raw; cruel, ferocious, fierce, savage

bloom *n* blossom, blossoming, bud, flower; beauty, flush, freshness, glow, health, heyday, lustre, perfection, prime, radiance, rosiness ~*v* blossom, blow, bud, burgeon, open, sprout

blossom *n* bloom, bud, flower, flowers ~*v* bloom, burgeon, flower; bloom, develop, flourish, grow, mature, progress, prosper, thrive

blot *n* mark, patch, smear, smudge, speck, splodge, spot; blemish, blur, defect, disgrace, fault, flaw, spot, stain, taint ~*v* mark, smudge, spot,

blubber *v* weep ~*n* whale fat
bludgeon *n* short thick club ~*v* strike with one; coerce
blue *adj* of the colour of sky; depressed; indecent ~*n* colour of sky; dye or pigment ~*pl Inf* depression; form of jazz music ~*v* **blueing, blued** make blue **bluish** *adj* **bluebell** *n* wild spring flower **bluebottle** *n* blowfly
blueprint *n* copy of drawing; original plan
bluff¹ *n* cliff, steep bank; *Canad* clump of trees ~*adj* hearty; blunt
bluff² *v/n* (deceive by) pretence
blunder *n/v* (make) clumsy mistake
blunt *adj* not sharp; (of speech) abrupt ~*v* make blunt **bluntly** *adv*
blur *v* **blurring, blurred** make, become less distinct ~*n* something indistinct

blurb *n* statement recommending book etc.
blurt *v* utter suddenly
blush *v* become red in face; be ashamed ~*n* this effect **blusher** *n* cosmetic to give rosy colour to face
bluster *v/n* (indulge in) noisy, aggressive behaviour **blustery** *adj* (of wind) gusty
BO *Inf* body odour
boa *n* large, nonpoisonous snake; long scarf of fur or feathers
boar *n* male pig; wild pig
board *n* broad, flat piece of wood, card etc.; table; meals; group of people who administer company ~*v* cover with planks; supply food daily; enter ship etc.; take daily meals **boarder** *n* **boardroom** *n*

———————— THESAURUS ————————

stain, taint
blow ¹ *v* blast, breathe, exhale, fan, pant, puff, waft; flow, rush, stream, whirl; bear, buffet, drive, fling, flutter, sweep, waft; pipe, play, sound, trumpet, vibrate ~*n* blast, draught, flurry, gale, gust, puff, strong breeze, tempest, wind
blow² *n* bang, bash *Inf*, buffet, knock, punch, rap, smack, stroke, thump, wallop *Inf*, whack; bombshell, calamity, catastrophe, disappointment, disaster, jolt, misfortune, reverse, setback, shock, upset
blow up blast, bomb, burst, detonate, explode, go off, rupture, shatter; distend, enlarge, expand, fill, inflate, swell; blow up, enlarge, magnify
blue azure, cobalt, navy, sapphire, ultramarine; dejected, depressed, despondent, dismal, downcast, downhearted, down in the mouth, fed up, gloomy, glum, low, melancholy, sad, unhappy
blueprint design, draft, layout, outline, pattern, pilot scheme, plan, pro-

ject, prototype, scheme, sketch
bluff *v* deceive, delude, fake, feign, humbug, lie, mislead, pretend, sham ~*n* bluster, boast, deceit, deception, fake, feint, fraud, humbug, idle boast, lie, mere show, pretence, sham, show, subterfuge
blunder *n* error, fault, mistake, oversight, slip ~*v* botch, bungle, err
blunt dull, rounded, unsharpened; bluff, brusque, forthright, frank, impolite, outspoken, plain-spoken, rude, tactless, trenchant
blur *v* cloud, darken, dim, fog, mask, obscure, soften ~*n* blear, confusion, dimness, fog, haze, indistinctness, obscurity
blush colour, crimson, flush, redden, turn red
bluster *v* boast, brag, bulldoze, bully, domineer, hector, rant, roar, storm, swagger, swell, vaunt ~*n* bombast, bragging, bravado, crowing, swagger
board *n* panel, plank, slat, timber; daily meals, food, meals, provisions; committee, conclave, council, directorate, directors, panel, trustees ~*v*

boast v speak too much in praise of oneself; brag of; have to show ~n thing boasted (of) **boastful** adj

boat n small open vessel; ship ~v sail about in boat **boater** n flat straw hat **boatswain** n ship's officer in charge of equipment

bob v **bobbing, bobbed** move up and down; move jerkily; cut (women's) hair short ~n jerking motion; short hairstyle; weight on pendulum etc.

bobbin n reel for thread

bobble n small, tufted ball

bobby n Inf police officer

bobsleigh n sledge for racing ~v ride on this

bode v be an omen of

bodice n upper part of woman's dress

bodkin n large blunt needle

body n whole frame of man or animal; corpse; main part; substance; group regarded as single entity **bodily** adj/ adv **bodyguard** n escort to protect

important person **bodywork** n outer shell of motor vehicle

boffin n Inf scientist

bog n wet, soft ground **boggy** adj **bog down** stick as in a bog

bogey n thing that causes fear; Golf score of one stroke over par

boggle v stare, be surprised

bogus adj sham, false

bohemian n/adj (person) leading unconventional life

boil[1] v (cause to) change from liquid to gas, esp. by heating; cook or become cooked by boiling; Inf be hot; Inf be angry ~n boiling state **boiler** n equipment providing hot water

boil[2] n inflamed swelling on skin

boisterous adj wild; noisy

bold adj daring, presumptuous; prominent **boldly** adv **boldness** n

bole n tree trunk

bolero n (pl **-ros**) Spanish dance; short loose jacket

——————— T H E S A U R U S ———————

accommodate, feed, house, lodge, put up, quarter, room; embark, embus, enplane, enter, entrain, mount

boast v be proud of, exhibit, flatter oneself, possess, show off; bluster, brag, crow, exaggerate, puff, strut, swagger, talk big Sl, vaunt ~n avowal, brag, swank Inf, vaunt

boastful cocky, conceited, crowing, egotistical, puffed-up, swaggering

bodily adj carnal, corporeal, material, physical, tangible ~adv altogether, collectively, completely, en masse, entirely, fully, totally, wholly

body build, figure, form, frame, physique, shape, torso, trunk; cadaver, carcass, corpse, dead body, remains; bulk, essence, main part, mass, material, matter, substance; association, band, collection, company, congress, corporation, society

bog fen, marsh, mire, morass, peat bog, quagmire, slough, swamp

bogey apparition, bogeyman, goblin, hobgoblin, imp, spectre, spirit, spook Inf, sprite

bogus artificial, counterfeit, dummy, fake, false, forged, fraudulent, imitation, phoney or phony Inf, sham, spurious

bohemian avant-garde, eccentric, exotic, left bank, nonconformist, offbeat, unconventional, unorthodox

boil v agitate, bubble, churn, effervesce, fizz, foam, froth, seethe

boisterous bouncy, clamorous, impetuous, loud, noisy, riotous, rollicking, rowdy, rumbustious, unrestrained, unruly, uproarious, vociferous, wild

bold adventurous, audacious, brave, courageous, daring, dauntless, enterprising, fearless, gallant, heroic, intrepid, valiant; bright, colourful, conspicuous, eye-catching, flashy, lively, loud, prominent, spirited, striking,

bollard *n* post to secure mooring lines; post in road as barrier

bolster *v* support, uphold ~*n* long pillow; pad, support

bolt *n* bar or pin (esp. with thread for nut); rush; lightning; roll of cloth ~*v* fasten; swallow hastily; rush away

bomb *n* explosive projectile; any explosive device ~*v* attack with bombs **bomber** *n* aircraft that drops bombs; person who throws or plants a bomb **bombard** *v* shell; attack (verbally) **bombshell** *n* shocking surprise

bombastic *adj* pompous

bona fide *Lat* genuine

bonanza *n* sudden wealth

bond *n* thing which binds; link; written promise ~*v* bind

bondage *n* slavery

bone *n* hard substance forming skeleton; piece of this ~*v* take out bone **bony** *adj* **bone-idle** *adj* extremely lazy

bonfire *n* large outdoor fire

bongo *n* (*pl* **-gos, -goes**) small drum played with fingers

bonk *v Inf* hit; have sexual intercourse (with)

bonnet *n* hat with strings; cap; cover of motor vehicle engine

bonny *adj* beautiful, handsome

bonsai *n* (art of growing) dwarf trees, shrubs

bonus *n* (*pl* **bonuses**) extra (unexpected) payment or gift

boo *interj* expression of disapproval; exclamation to surprise esp. child ~*v* make this sound

boob *n Sl* foolish mistake; female breast

booby trap harmless-looking object which explodes when disturbed

boogie *v Inf* dance quickly to pop music

book *n* sheets of paper bound together; literary work ~*v* reserve room, ticket etc.; charge with legal offence; enter name in book **booklet** *n* **bookkeeping** *n* systematic recording of business transactions **bookmaker** *n* one who takes bets **bookworm** *n* person devoted to reading

boom[1] *n* sudden commercial activity; prosperity ~*v* prosper

boom[2] *v/n* (make) deep sound

boom[3] *n* long spar for bottom of sail

boomerang *n* curved wooden missile

———— THESAURUS ————

strong, vivid

bolt *n* bar, catch, latch, lock; peg, pin, rivet, rod; spring, sprint ~*v* bar, fasten, latch, lock, secure; cram, devour, gobble, gorge, gulp, guzzle, stuff, wolf; abscond, bound, dash, escape, flee, fly, hurtle, jump, leap, run, rush, spring, sprint

bomb *n* bombshell, charge, device, explosive, grenade, mine, missile, projectile, rocket, shell, torpedo ~*v* attack, blow up, bombard, destroy, shell, strafe, torpedo

bombard assault, blast, blitz, bomb, fire upon, open fire, shell, strafe; assail, attack, barrage, beset, besiege, harass, hound

bond *n* band, binding, chain, cord, fastening, fetter, link, shackle, tie; affinity, attachment, connection, link, relation, tie, union; compact, contract, covenant, guarantee, obligation, pledge, promise, word ~*v* bind, connect, fasten, fix together, fuse, glue, gum, paste

bonus benefit, bounty, commission, dividend, extra, gift, gratuity, handout, prize, reward

book *n* album, diary, jotter, notebook, pad; manual, publication, roll, textbook, tome, tract, volume, work ~*v* arrange for, bill, charter, engage, line up, make reservations, organize, reserve, schedule

boom[1] *n* advance, development, expansion, gain, growth, improvement,

of Aust. Aborigines, which returns to the thrower

boon n something helpful, favour

boor n rude person **boorish** adj

boost n encouragement; upward push; increase ~v encourage; push **booster** n

boot n covering for the foot and ankle; luggage space in car; Inf kick ~v Inf kick

booth n stall; cubicle

bootleg v make, carry, sell illicit goods, esp. alcohol ~adj produced, sold illicitly **bootlegger** n

booty n plunder, spoil

booze n/v Inf (consume) alcoholic drink

border n margin; frontier; limit; strip of garden ~v provide with border; adjoin

bore¹ v pierce hole ~n hole; calibre of

gun

bore² v make weary by repetition ~n tiresome person or thing **boredom** n **boring** adj

boron n chemical element used in hardening steel etc.

borough n town

borrow v obtain on loan; copy, steal **borrower** n

borstal n formerly prison for young criminals

borzoi n tall dog with long, silky coat

bosom n human breast

boss n person in charge of or employing others ~v be in charge of; be domineering over **bossy** adj overbearing

botany n study of plants **botanical** adj **botanist** n

botch v spoil by clumsiness ~n blunder

———— THESAURUS ————

increase, spurt, upsurge ~v develop, expand, flourish, gain, grow, increase, intensify, prosper, spurt, succeed, swell, thrive

boom² v bang, blast, crash, explode, resound, reverberate, roar, roll, rumble, thunder ~n bang, blast, burst, clap, crash, explosion, roar, rumble, thunder

boon advantage, benefaction, benefit, blessing, favour, gift, grant, present, windfall

boost n encouragement, help, praise, promotion; addition, expansion, improvement, increase, increment, jump, rise ~v advance, advertise, assist, encourage, foster, further, improve, inspire, plug Inf, praise, promote, support, sustain; elevate, heave, hoist, lift, push, raise, shove, thrust

border bound, boundary, bounds, brim, brink, confine, confines, edge, hem, limit, limits, lip, margin, rim, skirt, verge; borderline, boundary,

frontier, line, march

bore¹ v drill, mine, penetrate, pierce, sink, tunnel ~n borehole, calibre, drill hole, shaft, tunnel

bore² v be tedious, bother, exhaust, fatigue, pall on, tire, trouble, vex, wear out, weary, worry ~n bother, drag Inf, nuisance, pain Inf, pest

boredom apathy, dullness, ennui, flatness, monotony, sameness, tediousness, tedium, weariness

boring dead, dull, flat, humdrum, insipid, monotonous, routine, stale, tedious, tiresome, tiring, unexciting, uninteresting, unvaried, wearisome

borrow take on loan, use temporarily; acquire, adopt, appropriate, copy, imitate, obtain, pilfer, pirate, simulate, steal, take, use, usurp

bosom breast, bust, chest

boss chief, director, employer, executive, foreman, gaffer Inf, chiefly Brit, governor Inf, head, leader, manager, master, overseer, owner, supervisor

botch v blunder, bungle, cobble, fum-

both *adj/pron* the two

bother *v* pester; perplex; trouble ~*n* fuss, trouble

bottle *n* vessel for holding liquid; its contents ~*v* put into bottle; restrain **bottleneck** *n* narrow outlet which impedes smooth flow

bottom *n* lowest part; bed of sea etc.; buttocks ~*adj* lowest ~*v* put bottom to; base (upon); get to bottom of **bottomless** *adj*

bough *n* branch of tree

boulder *n* large rock

boulevard *n* broad street or promenade

bounce *v* (cause to) rebound on impact ~*n* rebounding; quality causing this; *Inf* vitality **bouncer** *n* person who removes unwanted people from nightclub etc. **bouncing** *adj* vigorous

bound¹ *n* (*usu. pl*) limit ~*v* restrict **boundary** *n* **boundless** *adj*

bound² *v/n* spring, leap

bound³ *adj* on a specified course

bound⁴ *adj* committed; certain; tied

bounty *n* liberality; gift; premium **bounteous, bountiful** *adj*

bouquet *n* bunch of flowers; aroma; compliment

bourbon *n* US whisky made from maize

bourgeois *n/adj* middle class

bout *n* period of time spent doing something; contest, fight

boutique *n* small shop, esp. one selling clothes

bow¹ *n* weapon for shooting arrows; implement for playing violin etc.; ornamental knot; bend ~*v* bend

bow² *v* bend body in respect, assent etc.; submit; bend downwards; crush ~*n* bowing

bow³ *n* fore end of ship

bowel *n* (*oft. pl*) part of intestine; in-

———————— THESAURUS ————————

ble, mar, mend, mess, muff, patch, screw up *Inf,* spoil

bother *v* alarm, annoy, concern, dismay, distress, disturb, harass, hassle *Inf,* inconvenience, irritate, molest, nag, pester, plague, put out, trouble, upset, vex, worry ~*n* annoyance, bustle, difficulty, flurry, fuss, hassle *Inf,* inconvenience, irritation, nuisance, pest, problem, strain, trouble, vexation, worry

bottom *n* base, basis, bed, deepest part, depths, floor, foot, foundation, groundwork, lowest part, pedestal, support ~*adj* base, basement, basic, fundamental, ground, last, lowest

bounce *v* bound, bump, jump, leap, rebound, recoil, ricochet, spring, thump ~*n* bound, elasticity, give, rebound, recoil, resilience, spring, springiness; animation, dynamism, energy, go *Inf,* life, liveliness, pep, vigour, vitality, vivacity, zip *Inf*

bound¹ *n* (*usu. pl*) border, boundary,

confine, edge, extremity, fringe, limit, line, march, margin, rim, verge

bound² *v/n* bounce, caper, frisk, gambol, hurdle, jump, leap, pounce, prance, skip, spring, vault

bound³ *adj* committed, compelled, forced, obligated, obliged, pledged, required; certain, destined, doomed, fated, sure; cased, fastened, fixed, secured, tied, tied up

boundary barrier, border, borderline, bounds, brink, confines, edge, extremity, fringe, frontier, limits, margin, precinct

boundless endless, immense, incalculable, inexhaustible, infinite, measureless, unbounded, unending, unlimited, untold, vast

bouquet bunch of flowers, buttonhole, garland, nosegay, posy, wreath; aroma, fragrance, perfume, redolence, savour, scent

bout competition, contest, encounter, engagement, fight, match, set-to

side of anything

bowl¹ round vessel, deep basin; drinking cup; hollow

bowl² wooden ball; *pl* game played with such balls ~*v* roll or throw ball in various ways **bowler** *n* **bowling** *n*

bowler *n* man's low-crowned stiff felt hat

box¹ *n* (wooden) container, usu. rectangular; its contents; any boxlike cubicle or receptacle ~*v* put in box; confine **box office** place where tickets are sold

box² *v* fight with fists, esp. with padded gloves on; strike ~*n* blow **boxer** *n* one who boxes; large dog resembling bulldog **boxing** *n*

box³ *n* evergreen shrub used for hedges

boy *n* male child; young man **boyish** *adj* **boyfriend** *n* woman's male companion

boycott *v* refuse to deal with or participate in ~*n* such refusal

bra *n* woman's undergarment, supporting breasts

brace *n* tool for boring; clamp; pair; support; *pl* straps to hold up trousers ~*v* steady (oneself) as before a blow;

support **bracelet** *n* ornament for the arm **bracing** *adj* invigorating

bracken *n* large fern

bracket *n* support for shelf etc.; group; *pl* marks, () used to enclose words etc. ~*v* enclose in brackets; connect

brackish *adj* (of water) slightly salty

brag *v* **bragging, bragged** boast ~*n* boastful talk **braggart** *n*

braid *v* interweave; trim with braid ~*n* anything plaited; ornamental tape

Braille *n* system of printing for blind, with raised dots

brain *n* mass of nerve tissue in head; intellect ~*v* kill by hitting on head **brainy** *adj* **brainchild** *n* creative idea of a person **brainwash** *v* force someone to change beliefs **brainwave** *n* sudden, clever idea

braise *v* stew in covered pan

brake *n* instrument for slowing motion of wheel on vehicle ~*v* apply brake to

bramble *n* prickly shrub

bran *n* sifted husks of corn

branch *n* limb of tree; local office ~*v* bear branches; diverge; spread

brand *n* trademark; class of goods;

——————— THESAURUS ———————

bow *v* bend, droop, genuflect, incline, make obeisance, nod, stoop; accept, comply, concede, defer, give in, relent, submit, surrender, yield ~*n* bending, bob, genuflexion, nod

box¹ carton, case, chest, container, pack, package, trunk

box² *v* exchange blows, fight, spar; buffet, clout *Inf*, cuff, hit, punch, slap, strike, wallop *Inf*, whack ~*n* blow, buffet, cuff, punch, slap, stroke, wallop *Inf*

boxer fighter, prizefighter, pugilist

boy fellow, junior, lad, schoolboy, stripling, youngster, youth

boycott ban, bar, black, blackball, blacklist, exclude, outlaw, prohibit,

proscribe, refuse, reject, spurn

boyfriend admirer, date, follower, lover, man, suitor

bracing brisk, cool, crisp, exhilarating, fresh, invigorating, lively, refreshing, stimulating, tonic, vigorous

brainy bright, brilliant, clever, intelligent, smart

brake *n* check, constraint, control, curb, rein, restraint ~*v* check, decelerate, halt, moderate, reduce speed, slacken, slow, stop

branch arm, bough, limb, offshoot, prong, ramification, shoot, spray, sprig; chapter, department, division, local office, office, part, section, subdivision, subsection, subsidiary, wing

particular kind; mark made by hot iron; burning piece of wood ~*v* burn with iron; mark; stigmatize **brand-new** *adj* absolutely new

brandish *v* flourish, wave

brandy *n* spirit distilled from wine

brash *adj* bold, impudent

brass *n* alloy of copper and zinc; group of brass wind instruments; *Inf* money; *Inf* (army) officers ~*adj* made of brass

brassiere *n* bra

brat *n* unruly child

bravado *n* showy display of boldness

brave *adj* courageous; splendid ~*n* warrior ~*v* defy, meet boldly **bravery** *n*

bravo *interj* well done!

brawl *v/n* (take part in) noisy fight

brawn *n* muscle; strength; pickled pork **brawny** *adj*

bray *n/v* (make) donkey's cry

brazen *adj* of, like brass; shameless ~*v* (*usu.* with **out**) face, carry through with impudence

brazier *n* pan for burning coals

breach *n* opening; breaking of rule etc. ~*v* make a gap in

bread *n* food make of flour baked; food; *Sl* money **breadwinner** *n* main earner in family

breadth *n* extent across, width; largeness of view, mind

break *v* **breaking, broke, broken** part by force; shatter; burst; destroy; become broken; fail to observe; disclose; interrupt; surpass; weaken; accustom (horse) to being ridden; decipher (code); open, appear; come suddenly ~*n* fracture; gap; opening; separation; interruption; respite; interval; *Inf* opportunity **breakable** *adj* **breakage** *n* one that breaks; wave beating on shore **breakdown** *n* collapse; failure to function; analysis **breakfast** *n* first meal of the day **break-in** *n* illegal entering of building **breakneck** *adj* fast and dangerous **breakthrough** *n* important advance **breakwater** *n* barrier to break force of waves

bream *n* broad, thin fish

——————— THESAURUS ———————

brand *n* hallmark, label, mark, sign, stamp, symbol, trademark; cast, class, grade, kind, make, quality, sort, species, type, variety ~*v* burn, burn in, label, mark, scar, stamp; denounce, disgrace, expose, mark, stigmatize

brandish display, exhibit, flourish, raise, shake, swing, wield

bravado bluster, boastfulness, bombast, brag, swagger

brave bold, courageous, daring, fearless, gallant, heroic, intrepid, plucky, resolute, valiant

bravery boldness, courage, daring, fortitude, gallantry, grit, guts *Inf*, hardiness, heroism, intrepidity, mettle, pluck, spirit, valour

brawl *v* battle, dispute, fight, quarrel, row *Inf*, scrap *Inf*, scuffle, wrangle,

wrestle ~*n* argument, battle, broil, clash, disorder, dispute, fight, fracas, fray, free-for-all *Inf*, quarrel, row *Inf*, rumpus, scrap *Inf*, uproar, wrangle

brawny athletic, beefy *Inf*, burly, hardy, lusty, muscular, powerful, robust, strapping, strong, sturdy, thickset, well-built

breach break, chasm, cleft, crack, fissure, gap, hole, opening, rent, rift, rupture, split; infringement, offence, transgression, trespass, violation

bread diet, fare, food, nourishment, nutriment, provisions, subsistence, sustenance

breadth latitude, span, spread, wideness, width; freedom, latitude, liberality, openness, permissiveness

break *v* batter, burst, crack, crash, demolish, destroy, divide, fracture,

breast *n* human chest; milk-secreting gland on woman's chest; seat of the affections *~v* face, oppose; reach summit of **breaststroke** *n* stroke in swimming

breath *n* air used by lungs; life; respiration; slight breeze **breathe** *v* inhale and exhale (air); live; rest; whisper **breather** *n* short rest **breathing** *n* **breathless** *adj* **breathtaking** *adj* causing awe or excitement

Breathalyser *n* *Trademark* device that estimates amount of alcohol in breath **breathalyse** *v*

breech *n* buttocks; hind part of anything **breeches** *pl n* trousers

breed *v* **breeding, bred** generate; rear; be produced; be with young *~n* offspring produced; race, kind **breeder** *n* **breeding** *n* result of good upbringing

breeze *n* gentle wind **breezy** *adj* windy; lively

brethren *pl n* brothers

brevity *n* conciseness of expression; short duration

brew *v* prepare liquor, as beer; make drink, as tea; plot; be in preparation;

———————— THESAURUS ————————

fragment, part, rend, separate, shatter, shiver, smash, snap, splinter, split, tear; breach, disobey, disregard, infringe, transgress, violate; demoralize, dispirit, enfeeble, impair, incapacitate, subdue, tame, undermine, weaken; *of a record, etc.* beat, better, cap *Inf,* exceed, excel, go beyond, outdo, outstrip, surpass, top; appear, burst out, emerge, erupt, happen, occur *~n* breach, cleft, crack, division, fissure, fracture, gap, gash, hole, opening, rent, rift, rupture, split, tear; alienation, breach, disaffection, estrangement, rift, rupture, separation, split; breather *Inf,* halt, interlude, intermission, interruption, interval, let-up *Inf,* lull, pause, recess, respite, rest, suspension

breakdown collapse, disintegration, disruption, failure, stoppage; analysis, detailed list, diagnosis, dissection, itemization

breakthrough advance, development, discovery, find, gain, improvement, invention, leap, progress

breath air, exhalation, gasp, gulp, inhalation, pant, respiration, wheeze; faint breeze, flutter, gust, puff, sigh, waft, zephyr

breathe draw in, gasp, gulp, inhale and exhale, pant, puff, respire,

wheeze; articulate, express, murmur, say, sigh, utter, voice, whisper

breathless exhausted, gasping, gulping, out of breath, panting, spent, wheezing, winded

breathtaking amazing, astonishing, awe-inspiring, awesome, exciting, impressive, magnificent, moving, overwhelming, stunning *Inf,* thrilling

breed *v* bear, beget, bring forth, engender, generate, hatch, multiply, originate, procreate, produce, propagate, reproduce; bring up, cultivate, develop, foster, instruct, nourish, nurture, raise, rear *~n* brand, class, extraction, family, ilk, kind, line, lineage, pedigree, progeny, race, sort, species, stock, strain, type, variety

breeding civility, conduct, courtesy, cultivation, culture, gentility, manners, polish, refinement, urbanity

breeze air, draught, flurry, gust, waft, whiff, zephyr

breezy airy, blowy, blustery, fresh, gusty, squally, windy; airy, animated, blithe, carefree, casual, cheerful, chirpy *Inf,* debonair, easy-going, free and easy, jaunty, light, light-hearted, lively, spirited, sunny, upbeat *Inf,* vivacious

brevity conciseness, economy, pithiness, succinctness, terseness; imper-

n beverage produced by brewing **brewer** *n* **brewery** *n*

briar, brier *n* prickly shrub

bribe *n* anything offered or given to gain favour ~*v* influence by bribe **bribery** *n*

bric-a-brac *n* small ornamental objects

brick *n* oblong mass of hardened clay used in building ~*v* build, block etc. with bricks **bricklayer** *n*

bride *n* (*masc* **bridegroom**) woman about to be, or just, married **bridal** *adj* **bridesmaid** *n*

bridge¹ structure for crossing river etc.; something joining or supporting other parts; raised narrow platform on ship; upper part of nose ~*v* make bridge over, span

bridge² *n* card game

bridle *n* headgear of horse; curb ~*v* put on bridle; restrain; show resentment

brief *adj* short in duration; concise; scanty ~*n* document containing facts of legal case; summary; *pl* underpants; panties ~*v* give instructions **briefly** *adv* **briefcase** *n* flat case for carrying papers, books etc.

brier *see* BRIAR

brigade *n* subdivision of army; organized band **brigadier** *n* high-ranking army officer

brigand *n* bandit

bright *adj* shining; full of light; cheerful; clever **brighten** *v* **brightly** *adv* **brightness** *n*

brilliant *adj* shining; sparkling; splen-

———————————— THESAURUS ————————————

manence, transience

brew *v* boil, ferment, infuse *tea,* make *beer,* seethe, soak, steep, stew; breed, concoct, contrive, develop, devise, excite, foment, form, gather, hatch, plan, plot, project, scheme, start, stir up

bribe *n* allurement, enticement, graft *Inf,* hush money *Sl,* incentive, inducement, kickback *US,* pay-off *Inf* ~*v* buy off, corrupt, get at, grease the palm *or* hand of *Sl,* lure, pay off *Inf,* reward, square, suborn

bribery *n* buying off, corruption, graft, inducement, payola *Inf*

bridge *n* arch, flyover, overpass, span, viaduct; band, bond, connection, link, tie ~*v* arch over, attach, bind, connect, couple, cross, cross over, extend across, go over, join, link, reach across, span, traverse, unite

bridle *v* check, constrain, control, curb, govern, master, moderate, repress, restrain, subdue; bristle, get angry, raise one's hackles, rear up

brief *adj* fast, fleeting, little, momentary, quick, short, short-lived, swift,

transitory; compressed, concise, crisp, curt, laconic, pithy, short, succinct, terse, to the point ~*n* case, contention, data, defence; abstract, digest, epitome, outline, précis, sketch, summary, synopsis ~*v* advise, explain, fill in *Inf,* instruct, prepare, prime

briefly concisely, cursorily, curtly, hastily, hurriedly, in brief, in outline, in passing, momentarily, precisely, quickly, shortly

bright beaming, blazing, brilliant, effulgent, flashing, gleaming, glistening, glittering, glowing, illuminated, intense, luminous, radiant, resplendent, shining, sparkling, twinkling, vivid; clear, clement, cloudless, fair, lucid, pleasant, sunny, unclouded; cheerful, chirpy *Inf,* gay, genial, glad, happy, jolly, joyful, joyous, lively, merry, vivacious; acute, astute, aware, brilliant, clever, ingenious, intelligent, inventive, keen, quick, quick-witted, sharp, smart

brighten clear up, enliven, gleam, glow, illuminate, lighten, light up,

did; very clever; distinguished **brilliance, brilliancy** n

brim n margin, edge, esp. of river, cup, hat **brimful** adj

brine n salt water; pickle

bring v **bringing, brought** fetch; carry with one; cause to happen

brink n edge of steep place

brisk adj active, vigorous **briskly** adv

brisket n meat from breast

bristle n short stiff hair ~v stand erect; show temper **bristly** adj

Brit. Britain; British

brittle adj easily broken; curt

broach v introduce (subject); open

broad adj wide, spacious, open; obvious; coarse; general **broaden** v **broadly** adv **broadcast** v transmit by radio or television; make widely known ~n

radio or television programme **broadcaster** n **broadcasting** n **broad-minded** adj tolerant **broadside** n discharge of guns; strong (verbal) attack

brocade n rich woven fabric with raised design

broccoli n type of cabbage

brochure n pamphlet

brogue n stout shoe; dialect, esp. Irish accent

broil v US grill

broke adj Inf having no money

broker n one employed to buy and sell for others

bromide n chemical compound used in medicine and photography

bromine n liquid element used in production of chemicals

bronchial adj of branches in the

shine; become cheerful, gladden, hearten, perk up

brilliant ablaze, bright, dazzling, glittering, glossy, intense, luminous, radiant, refulgent, scintillating, shining, sparkling, vivid; accomplished, acute, astute, brainy, clever, discerning, expert, gifted, intellectual, intelligent, penetrating, profound, quick, talented; celebrated, distinguished, eminent, exceptional, famous, glorious, magnificent, outstanding, splendid, superb

brim border, brink, circumference, edge, lip, margin, rim, skirt, verge

bring accompany, bear, carry, conduct, convey, deliver, escort, fetch, gather, guide, import, lead, take, transfer, transport, usher; cause, contribute to, create, effect, engender, inflict, occasion, produce, result in, wreak

brink border, brim, edge, fringe, frontier, limit, margin, point, rim, skirt

brisk active, agile, alert, bustling, busy, energetic, lively, nimble, quick, speedy, spry, vigorous, vivacious

bristle n barb, hair, prickle, spine, stubble, thorn, whisker ~v be angry, bridle, flare up, rage, see red, seethe

brittle breakable, crisp, crumbly, delicate, fragile, frail, shivery

broad ample, extensive, large, roomy, spacious, vast, voluminous, wide, widespread; comprehensive, far-reaching, general, inclusive, sweeping, universal, unlimited, wide, wide-ranging

broadcast v air, beam, radio, relay, show, televise, transmit; advertise, announce, circulate, disseminate, make public, proclaim, promulgate, publish, report, spread ~n programme, show, transmission

broaden develop, enlarge, expand, extend, increase, open up, spread, stretch, swell, widen

broad-minded catholic, flexible, indulgent, liberal, open-minded, permissive, responsive, tolerant, unbiased, unprejudiced

brochure booklet, circular, folder, handbill, leaflet, pamphlet

broker agent, dealer, factor, go-

windpipe **bronchitis** *n* inflammation of bronchial tubes

bronco *n* (*pl* -**cos**) *US* wild pony

brontosaurus *n* large plant-eating dinosaur

bronze *n* alloy of copper and tin ~*adj* made of, or coloured like, bronze ~*v* give appearance of bronze to

brooch *n* ornamental pin

brood *n* family of young, esp. of birds ~*v* sit, as hen on eggs; fret over **broody** *adj*

brook[1] *n* small stream

brook[2] *v* put up with

broom *n* brush for sweeping; yellow-flowered shrub **broomstick** *n* handle of broom

bros. brothers

broth *n* thick soup

brothel *n* house of prostitution

brother *n* son of same parents; one closely united with another **brotherly** *adj* **brotherhood** *n* fellowship; association **brother-in-law** *n* brother of husband or wife; husband of sister

brow *n* ridge over eyes; forehead; eyebrow; edge of hill **browbeat** *v* frighten with threats

brown *adj* of dark colour inclining to red or yellow ~*n* the colour ~*v* make, become brown

Brownie *n* junior Girl Guide

browse *v* look through (book etc.) in a casual manner; feed on shoots and leaves

bruise *v* injure without breaking skin ~*n* contusion, discoloration caused by blow **bruiser** *n* tough person

brunch *n* breakfast and lunch combined

brunette *n* woman of dark complexion and hair ~*adj* dark brown

brunt *n* chief shock of attack

brush[1] *n* device with bristles, hairs etc. used for cleaning, painting etc.; act of brushing; brief contact; skirmish; bushy tail ~*v* apply, remove, clean, with brush; touch lightly

brush[2] *n* thick shrubbery

brusque *adj* curt

between, intermediary, middleman

bronze brownish, chestnut, copper, reddish-brown, rust, tan

brood *n* breed, chicks, children, clutch, family, hatch, infants, issue, litter, offspring, progeny, young ~*v* agonize, dwell upon, fret, meditate, mope, muse, repine, ruminate, think upon

brook burn, stream, watercourse

brother kin, kinsman, relation, relative, sibling; associate, colleague, companion, comrade, fellow member, mate, partner

brotherhood camaraderie, companionship, comradeship, fellowship, friendliness, kinship; alliance, association, clan, clique, community, coterie, fraternity, guild, league, society, union

brotherly affectionate, amicable, be-

nevolent, cordial, fraternal, friendly, kind, neighbourly, sympathetic

brown auburn, bronze, brunette, chestnut, chocolate, coffee, dark, dun, dusky, hazel, rust, sunburnt, tan, tanned, tawny

browse dip into, leaf through, look through, peruse, scan, skim, survey; crop, eat, feed, graze, nibble, pasture

bruise *v* blacken, blemish, contuse, crush, damage, deface, discolour, injure, mar, mark ~*n* blemish, contusion, discoloration, injury, mark, swelling

brush[1] *n* besom, broom, sweeper; clash, conflict, fight, fracas, scrap *Inf*, set-to *Inf*, skirmish, tussle ~*v* buff, clean, paint, polish, sweep, wash; contact, flick, glance, graze, kiss, scrape, stroke, sweep, touch

brush[2] *n* bushes, copse, scrub,

Brussels sprout vegetable like a tiny cabbage

brute *n* any animal except man; crude, vicious person ~*adj* animal; sensual; stupid; physical **brutal** *adj* **brutality** *n* **brutally** *adv*

BSc Bachelor of Science

BST British Summer Time

bubble *n* hollow globe of liquid, blown out with air; something insubstantial ~*v* rise in bubbles **bubbly** *adj*

bubonic plague acute infectious disease characterized by swellings

buccaneer *n* pirate

buck *n* male deer, or other male animal; act of bucking; *US & Aust sl* dollar ~*v* (of horse) attempt to throw rider **buckshot** *n* lead shot in shotgun shell

bucket *n* vessel, round with arched handle, for water etc. **bucketful** *n*

buckle *n* metal clasp for fastening belt, strap etc. ~*v* fasten with buckle; warp, bend

bud *n* shoot containing unopened leaf, flower etc. ~*v* **budding, budded** begin to grow

budge *v* move, stir

budgerigar *also* **budgie** *n* small Aust. parakeet

budget *n* annual financial statement; plan of systematic spending ~*v* make financial plan

buff¹ *n* leather from buffalo hide; light yellow colour; polishing pad ~*v* polish

buff² *n* expert

buffalo *n* type of cattle

buffer *n* device to lessen impact

buffet¹ *n* blow, slap ~*v* strike with blows; contend against

buffet² *n* refreshment bar; meal at which guests serve themselves; sideboard

buffoon *n* clown; fool

bug *n* any small insect; *Inf* disease, infection; concealed listening device ~*v* annoy; listen secretly

bugbear *n* object of needless terror; nuisance

bugger *n Sl* unpleasant person or thing

bugle *n* instrument like trumpet

build *v* **building, built** construct by putting together parts; develop ~*n* make, form **builder** *n* **building** *n*

———————— T H E S A U R U S ————————

shrubs, thicket, undergrowth

brutal bloodthirsty, cruel, ferocious, heartless, inhuman, merciless, pitiless, remorseless, ruthless, savage, uncivilized, vicious

brute animal, beast, creature, wild animal; barbarian, beast, devil, fiend, monster, ogre, sadist, savage, swine

bubble *n* bead, blister, drop, droplet, globule ~*v* boil, effervesce, fizz, foam, froth, seethe, sparkle

buckle *n* catch, clasp, clip, fastener ~*v* catch, clasp, close, fasten, hook, secure; bend, bulge, cave in, collapse, crumple, fold, twist, warp

bud *n* germ, shoot, sprout ~*v* burgeon, develop, grow, shoot, sprout

budge dislodge, give way, inch,

move, propel, push, remove, roll, shift, slide, stir

budget *n* allowance, cost, finances, funds, means, resources ~*v* apportion, cost, cost out, estimate, plan, ration

buffer bumper, cushion, fender, intermediary, safeguard, screen, shield

buffet¹ *n* bang, blow, bump, cuff, jolt, knock, push, rap, shove, slap, smack ~*v* bang, batter, beat, box, bump, knock, pound, push, rap, shove, slap, strike, thump

buffet² *n* café, cafeteria, cold table, counter, cupboard, snack bar

bug *Inf n* disease, germ, microorganism, virus ~*v* eavesdrop, listen in, spy, tap, wiretap

building society organization where money can be borrowed or invested

bulb *n* modified leaf bud emitting roots from base, e.g. onion; globe surrounding filament of electric light **bulbous** *adj*

bulge *n* swelling; temporary increase ~*v* swell

bulk *n* size; volume; greater part; cargo ~*v* be of weight or importance **bulky** *adj*

bull *n* male of cattle; male of various other animals **bulldog** *n* thickset breed of dog **bulldozer** *n* powerful tractor for excavating etc. **bullfight** *n* public show in which bull is killed **bullock** *n* castrated bull **bull's-eye** *n* centre of target

bullet *n* projectile discharged from rifle, pistol etc.

bulletin *n* official report

bullion *n* gold or silver in mass

bully *n* one who hurts or intimidates weaker people ~*v* **bullying, bullied**

bulrush *n* tall reedlike marsh plant

bulwark *n* rampart; any defence

bum *n Sl* buttocks, anus

bumble *v* perform clumsily

bumblebee *n* large hairy bee

bumf *also* **bumph** *n Inf* official papers

bump *n* knock; thud; swelling ~*v* strike or push against **bumper** *n* horizontal bar on motor vehicle to protect against damage ~*adj* abundant

bumpkin *n* simple country person

bumptious *adj* self-assertive

bun *n* small, round cake; round knot of hair

bunch *n* number of things tied or growing together; group, party ~*v* gather together

bundle *n* package; number of things tied together ~*v* tie in bundle; send (off) without ceremony

———————————— T H E S A U R U S ————————————

build *v* assemble, construct, erect, fabricate, form, make, put up, raise; base, begin, constitute, establish, inaugurate, originate, set up, start ~*n* body, figure, form, frame, physique, shape

building dwelling, edifice, fabric, house, pile, structure

bulge *n* bump, lump, protuberance, swelling; boost, increase, rise, surge ~*v* dilate, distend, enlarge, expand, project, protrude, sag, stand out, stick out, swell

bulk immensity, largeness, magnitude, massiveness, size, substance, volume, weight; body, greater part, lion's share, main part, majority, major part, mass, most

bullet missile, pellet, projectile, shot, slug

bulletin announcement, communiqué, dispatch, message, news flash, notification, report, statement

bully *v* browbeat, bulldoze *Inf,* coerce,

cow, domineer, hector, intimidate, oppress, persecute, push around *Sl,* terrorize, tyrannize

bulwark bastion, buttress, defence, fortification, rampart, redoubt

bump *n* bang, blow, crash, hit, impact, jar, jolt, knock, rap, shock, smash, thud, thump; bulge, contusion, knob, knot, lump, protuberance, swelling ~*v* bang, crash, hit, knock, slam, smash into, strike

bumptious arrogant, boastful, brash, cocky, conceited, egotistic, forward, full of oneself, impudent, overbearing, presumptuous, pushy *Inf*

bunch *n* batch, bouquet, bundle, clump, cluster, collection, heap, lot, mass, parcel, pile, quantity, sheaf, spray, stack, tuft ~*v* assemble, bundle, cluster, collect, crowd, flock, group, herd, mass, pack

bundle *n* bag, bale, box, carton, crate, pack, package, packet, pallet, parcel, roll; assortment, batch, bunch, col-

bung n stopper for cask ~v stop up; Sl sling

bungalow n one-storeyed house

bungle v/n botch

bunion n inflamed swelling on foot or toe

bunk n narrow shelflike bed

bunker n large storage container for coal etc.; sandy hollow on golf course; underground defensive position

bunny n Inf rabbit

bunting n material for flags

buoy n floating marker anchored in sea ~v prevent from sinking **buoyancy** n **buoyant** adj

burden n load; weight, cargo; anything difficult to bear ~v load, encumber **burdensome** adj

bureau n (pl -reaus) writing desk; office; government department **bureaucracy** n government by officials; body

of officials **bureaucrat** n

burgeon v bud; flourish

burglar n one who enters building to commit crime esp. theft **burglary** n **burgle** v

burgundy n name of various wines, white and red

burlesque n/v caricature

burly adj sturdy, stout, robust

burn v burning, burned or burnt destroy or injure by fire; be on fire; be consumed by fire ~n injury, mark caused by fire **burning** adj intense; urgent

burnish v/n polish

burp v/n Inf belch

burrow n hole dug by rabbit etc. ~v dig

bursar n official managing finances of college etc. **bursary** n scholarship

burst v break into pieces; break suddenly into some expression of feeling;

——————— T H E S A U R U S ———————

lection, group, heap, mass, pile, quantity ~v bale, bind, fasten, pack, tie, tie up, truss, wrap

bungle blunder, botch, butcher, make a mess of, mar, mess up, miscalculate, mismanage, muff, ruin, screw up Inf, spoil

buoy beacon, float, guide, marker, signal

buoyant afloat , floating, light

burden n affliction, anxiety, care, clog, load, onus, sorrow, strain, stress, trial, trouble, weight, worry ~v bother, encumber, load, oppress, overload, saddle with, strain, tax, weigh down, worry

bureau desk, writing desk; agency, branch, department, division, office, service

bureaucracy administration, civil service, government, ministry, officialdom

bureaucrat civil servant, mandarin, minister, officer, official, public

servant

burglar housebreaker, pilferer, robber, sneak thief, thief

burial entombment, exequies, funeral, interment, obsequies

burlesque n caricature, mock, mockery, parody, satire, send-up Brit inf, spoof Inf, takeoff Inf ~v ape, caricature, exaggerate, imitate, lampoon, make fun of, mock, parody, ridicule, satirize, send up Brit inf, take off Inf

burly beefy, big, bulky, hefty, muscular, powerful, stocky, stout, strapping, strong, sturdy, well-built

burn be ablaze, be on fire, blaze, flame, flare, flash, flicker, glow, smoke; char, ignite, incinerate, kindle, light, parch, scorch, set on fire, shrivel, singe, toast, wither

burning ardent, eager, earnest, fervent, frantic, intense, passionate, vehement, zealous

burrow n den, hole, lair, retreat, shelter, tunnel ~v delve, dig, excavate,

shatter, break violently *~n* bursting; explosion; outbreak; spurt

bury *v* **burying, buried** put underground; inter; conceal **burial** *n/adj*

bus *n* large motor vehicle for passengers

bush *n* shrub; uncleared country **bushy** *adj* shaggy **bushbaby** *n* treeliving, nocturnal Afr. animal

bushel *n* dry measure of eight gallons

business *n* occupation; commercial or industrial establishment; trade; responsibility; work **businesslike** *adj* **businessman** *n* **businesswoman** *n*

busker *n* street entertainer **busk** *v*

bust[1] *n* sculpture of head and shoulders; woman's breasts

bust[2] *Inf v* burst; make, become bankrupt; raid; arrest *~adj* broken; bankrupt

bustle *v* be noisily busy *~n* fuss, commotion

busy *adj* actively employed; full of activity *~v* **busying, busied** occupy **busily** *adv* **busybody** *n* nosy person

but *conj* without; except; yet; still; besides; *adv* only

butane *n* gas used for fuel

butch *adj* *Inf* aggressively masculine

butcher *n* one who kills animals for food, or sells meat; savage man *~v* slaughter **butchery** *n*

butler *n* chief male servant

butt[1] *n* thick end; unused end

——————————— T H E S A U R U S ———————————

hollow out, scoop out, tunnel

burst *v* blow up, break, crack, explode, fly open, fragment, puncture, rupture, shatter, shiver, split, tear apart *~n* bang, blast, blowout, blowup, breach, break, crack, discharge, explosion, rupture, split

bury embed, engulf, implant, sink, submerge; entomb, inearth, inhume, inter, lay to rest; conceal, cover, cover up, hide, secrete, stow away

bush hedge, plant, shrub, shrubbery, thicket; brush, scrub, the wild

busily actively, briskly, carefully, diligently, earnestly, energetically, industriously, intently, speedily, strenuously

business calling, career, craft, employment, function, job, line, métier, occupation, profession, pursuit, trade, vocation, work; company, concern, enterprise, firm, organization, venture; commerce, dealings, industry, manufacturing, selling, trade, trading, transaction

businesslike correct, efficient, methodical, orderly, organized, practical, professional, regular, systematic, thorough, well-ordered

businessman, businesswoman capitalist, employer, entrepreneur, executive, financier, industrialist, merchant, tradesman, tycoon

bust bosom, breast, chest, torso

bustle *v* bestir, dash, fuss, hasten, hurry, rush, scamper, scramble, scurry, stir *~n* activity, ado, agitation, commotion, excitement, flurry, fuss, haste, hurry, stir, to-do, tumult

busy active, assiduous, brisk, diligent, employed, engaged, engrossed, hard at work, industrious, occupied, on duty, slaving, working; active, energetic, full, hectic, hustling, lively, restless, tireless, tiring

but *conj* further, however, moreover, nevertheless, on the contrary, on the other hand, still, yet; bar, barring, except, excepting, excluding, notwithstanding, save, with the exception of *~adv* just, merely, only, simply, singly, solely

butcher *n* destroyer, killer, murderer, slaughterer, slayer *~v* carve, clean, cut, cut up, dress, joint, prepare, slaughter; assassinate, cut down, destroy, exterminate, kill, massacre, slaughter, slay

butt² *n* target; object of ridicule

butt³ *v* strike with head; interrupt ~*n* blow made with head

butter *n* fatty substance got from cream by churning ~*v* spread with butter; flatter

buttercup *n* plant with glossy, yellow flowers

butterfly *n* insect with large wings

butterscotch *n* kind of hard, brittle toffee

buttock *n* (*usu. pl*) rump, protruding hind part

button *n* knob, stud for fastening dress; knob that operates doorbell, machine etc. ~*v* fasten with buttons **buttonhole** *n* slit in garment to pass button through; flower worn on lapel etc. ~*v* detain (unwilling) person in conversation

buttress *n* structure to support wall; prop ~*v* support

buxom *adj* full of health, plump

buy *v* buying, bought get by payment, purchase; bribe ~*n* thing purchased **buyer** *n*

buzz *v/n* (make) humming sound **buzzer** *n* **buzzword** *n* fashionable

word

buzzard *n* bird of prey

by *prep* near; along; past; during; not later than; through use or agency of; in units of ~*adv* near; aside; past **by and by** soon **by and large** on the whole

by- *comb. form* subsidiary, near, as in **byproduct, bystander**

bye *n Sport* situation where player or team wins by default of opponent

bye-bye *interj Inf* goodbye

by-election *n* election to fill vacant seat

bygone *adj* past, former ~*n* (*oft. pl*) past occurrence; small antique

bylaw *n* law, regulation made by local authority

bypass *n* road for diversion of traffic from overcrowded centres ~*v* make detour round

byre *n* cowshed

byte *n Computers* sequence of bits processed as single unit of information

byway *n* secondary or side road

byword *n* well-known name or saying

————— THESAURUS —————

butt¹ handle, hilt, shaft, shank, stock

butt² Aunt Sally, dupe, mark, object, point, subject, target, victim

butt³ *v/n* With or of the head or horns buck, buffet, bump, jab, knock, poke, prod, punch, push, ram, shove, thrust

buy *v* get, invest in, obtain, pay for, procure, purchase, shop for ~*n* acquisition, bargain, deal, purchase

by *prep* along, beside, by way of, close to, near, next to, over, past, via; through, through the agency of, under the aegis of ~*adv* aside, at hand, away, beyond, close, handy, in reach, near, past, to one side

bypass avoid, circumvent, depart from, detour round, deviate from, get round, go round, pass round

C c

C *Chem* carbon; Celsius; Centigrade
c. circa
cab *n* taxi; driver's compartment on lorry etc.
cabal *n* small group of intriguers; secret plot
cabaret *n* floor show at a nightclub
cabbage *n* green vegetable
cabin *n* hut, shed; small room, esp. in ship
cabinet *n* piece of furniture with drawers or shelves; outer case of television, radio etc.; committee of politicians
cable *n* strong rope; wires conveying electric power, television signals etc.; telegraph ~*v* telegraph by cable **cable car** vehicle pulled up slope on cable
cache *n* secret hiding place; store of food etc.
cackle *v/n* (make) chattering noise, as of hen
cacophony *n* disagreeable sound; discord of sounds
cactus *n* (*pl* **cactuses, cacti**) spiny succulent plant
cad *n* unchivalrous person
cadaver *n* corpse **cadaverous** *adj*
caddie, caddy *n* golfer's attendant
caddy *n* small box for tea
cadence *n* fall or modulation of voice in music or verse
cadenza *n Mus* elaborate solo passage
cadet *n* youth in training, esp. for armed forces
cadge *v* get (food, money etc.) by begging
cadmium *n* metallic element
caecum *n* (*pl* -**ca**) part of large intestine
Caesarean section surgical operation to deliver a baby
caesium *n* metallic element
café *n* small restaurant serving light refreshments **cafeteria** *n* self-service restaurant
caffeine *n* stimulating chemical found in tea and coffee
caftan *n see* KAFTAN
cage *n* enclosure, box with bars or wires, esp. for keeping animals or birds ~*v* put in cage, confine **cagey** *adj* wary
cagoule *n* lightweight anorak
cairn *n* heap of stones, esp. as monument or landmark
cajole *v* persuade by flattery, wheedle
cake *n* baked, sweet, bread-like food; compact mass ~*v* harden (as of mud)
calamine *n* soothing ointment
calamity *n* disaster **calamitous** *adj*
calcium *n* metallic element, the basis of lime
calculate *v* estimate; compute; make reckonings **calculable** *adj* **calculating** *adj* shrewd; scheming **calculation** *n* **calculator** *n* electronic device for making calculations

---

THESAURUS

---

cab minicab, taxi, taxicab
cabin berth, chalet, cot, cottage, crib, hovel, hut, lodge, shack, shanty, shed; berth, compartment, deckhouse, quarters, room
cabinet case, closet, commode, cupboard, dresser, locker; administration, assembly, council, counsellors, ministry
cage *v* confine, coop up, fence in, impound, imprison, lock up, mew, pound, restrain, shut up
cajole beguile, coax, decoy, entice, flatter, inveigle, lure, mislead, seduce, tempt, wheedle
cake bar, block, cube, loaf, lump, mass, slab
calculate adjust, compute, consider,

calendar *n* table of months and days in the year; list of events

calf[1] *n* (*pl* **calves**) young of cow and other animals; leather of calf's skin

calf[2] *n* (*pl* **calves**) fleshy back of leg below knee

calibre *n* size of bore of gun; capacity, character **calibrate** *v*

calico *n* (*pl* **-coes, -cos**) cotton cloth

call *v* speak loudly to attract attention; summon; telephone; name; shout; pay visit ~*n* shout; animal's cry; visit; inner urge; demand **caller** *n* **calling** *n* vocation, profession **call up** summon to serve in army; imagine

calligraphy *n* handwriting

callipers *pl n* instrument for measuring diameters

callous *adj* hardened, unfeeling

callow *adj* inexperienced

callus *n* area of hardened skin

calm *adj/v* (make, become) still, tranquil; (make) composed ~*n* absence of wind **calmly** *adv* **calmness** *n*

calorie *n* unit of heat; unit of energy from foods

calypso *n* (*pl* **-sos**) (West Indies) improvised song

cam *n* device to change rotary to reciprocating motion

camaraderie *n* spirit of comradeship, trust

camber *n* curve on road surface

cambric *n* fine white linen or cotton cloth

camcorder *n* portable video camera and recorder

camel *n* animal of Asia and Africa, with humped back

camellia *n* ornamental shrub

cameo *n* (*pl* **cameos**) medallion, brooch etc. with design in relief; small part in film etc.

camera *n* apparatus used to make photographs **cameraman** *n*

camisole *n* underbodice

camouflage *n* disguise, means of avoiding enemy observation ~*v* disguise

camp[1] *n* (place for) tents of hikers,

count, determine, enumerate, estimate, figure, gauge, judge, rate, reckon, value, weigh, work out

calculation answer, computation, estimate, judgment, reckoning, result

calibre bore, diameter, gauge, measure; ability, capacity, endowment, faculty, force, gifts, merit, parts, quality, scope, stature, talent, worth

call *v* announce, arouse, awaken, cry, cry out, hail, proclaim, rouse, shout, waken, yell; assemble, bid, collect, contact, convene, convoke, gather, invite, muster, phone, rally, ring up *Inf, chiefly Brit*, summon, telephone; christen, describe as, designate, dub, entitle, label, name, style, term ~*n* cry, hail, shout, signal, whoop, yell

calling employment, life's work, line, métier, mission, occupation, profession, province, pursuit, trade, vocation, work

callous cold, hard-bitten, hardened, hardhearted, harsh, heartless, indifferent, insensitive, obdurate, soulless, thick-skinned, uncaring, unfeeling, unresponsive, unsympathetic

calm *adj* balmy, mild, pacific, peaceful, placid, quiet, restful, serene, smooth, still, tranquil, windless; collected, composed, cool, equable, impassive, imperturbable, relaxed, sedate, self-possessed, unemotional, unexcited, unfazed *Inf*, unmoved, unruffled ~*v* hush, mollify, placate, quieten, relax, soothe

calmness calm, composure, equability, hush, peace, peacefulness, placidity, quiet, repose, serenity, smoothness, stillness, tranquillity; composure, coolness, dispassion, equanimity, impassivity, self-possession

army etc.; group supporting political party etc. ~v form or lodge in camp

camp² *adj Inf* homosexual; consciously artificial

campaign *n/v* (organize) series of co-ordinated activities for some purpose, e.g. political, military

camphor *n* solid essential oil with aromatic taste and smell

campus *n* grounds of university

can¹ *v* (*past tense* **could**) be able; have the power; be allowed

can² *n* container, usu. metal, for liquids, foods ~v **canning, canned** put in can **canned** *adj* preserved in can; (of music) previously recorded

canal *n* artificial watercourse; duct in body

canary *n* yellow singing bird

canasta *n* card game played with two packs

cancan *n* high-kicking dance

cancel *v* **-celling, -celled** cross out; annul; call off **cancellation** *n*

cancer *n* malignant growth or tumour **cancerous** *adj*

candid *adj* frank, impartial **candour** *n*

candidate *n* one who seeks office etc.; person taking examination **candidacy, candidature** *n*

candle *n* stick of wax with wick; light **candelabrum** *n* (*pl* **-bra**) large, branched candle holder **candlestick** *n*

candy *n* crystallized sugar; *US* confectionery in general ~v **candying, candied** preserve with sugar **candyfloss** *n* fluffy mass of spun sugar

cane *n* stem of small palm or large grass; walking stick ~v beat with cane

canine *adj* like, pert. to, dog ~n sharp pointed tooth

canister *n* container, usu. of metal, for storing dry food

canker *n* eating sore; thing that destroys, corrupts

cannabis *n* hemp plant; drug derived from this

cannelloni *pl n* tubular pieces of pasta filled with meat etc.

cannibal *n* one who eats human flesh **cannibalism** *n*

cannon¹ *n* (*pl* **-ons** or **-on**) large gun **cannonball** *n* heavy metal ball

cannon² *n* billiard stroke ~v make this stroke; rebound, collide

cannot *negative form of* CAN¹

canny *adj* shrewd; cautious

canoe *n* (*pl* **-oes**) very light boat pro-

—————————— THESAURUS ——————————

camouflage *n* blind, cloak, concealment, cover, deceptive markings, disguise, front, guise, mask, masquerade, mimicry, screen, subterfuge ~v cloak, conceal, cover, disguise, hide, mask, obscure, screen, veil

camp¹ bivouac, camp site

camp² affected, artificial, effeminate, mannered, ostentatious, posturing

campaign attack, crusade, drive, expedition, offensive, push

cancel abolish, annul, blot out, call off, cross out, delete, efface, eliminate, erase, expunge, obliterate, obviate, quash, repeal, repudiate, rescind, revoke

cancer blight, canker, carcinoma

Pathol, corruption, evil, growth, malignancy, pestilence, rot, tumour

candid blunt, downright, fair, frank, free, impartial, just, open, outspoken, plain, straightforward, truthful, unprejudiced, upfront *Inf*

candidate applicant, aspirant, competitor, contender, contestant, entrant, nominee, runner

candour forthrightness, frankness, honesty, openness, outspokenness, truthfulness

cannon big gun *Inf,* field gun, gun, mortar

canny acute, artful, astute, careful, cautious, circumspect, clever, judicious, knowing, prudent, sagacious,

pelled with paddle ~v travel by canoe

canon n law or rule, esp. of church; standard; list of saints **canonize** v enrol in list of saints

canopy n covering over throne, bed etc. ~v **-opying, -opied** cover with canopy

cant n hypocritical speech; technical jargon; slang, esp. of thieves ~v use cant

cantankerous adj quarrelsome

cantata n choral work

canteen n place in factory, school etc. where meals are provided

canter n/v (move at) easy gallop

cantilever n beam, girder etc. fixed at one end only

canvas n coarse cloth used for sails, painting on etc.

canvass v solicit votes, contributions etc.; discuss

canyon n deep gorge

cap n covering for head; lid, top ~v **capping, capped** put a cap on; outdo

capable adj able; competent; having the power **capability** n

capacity n power of holding; room; volume; function, role; ability

cape[1] n covering for shoulders

cape[2] n headland

caper n skip; frolic; escapade ~v skip, dance

capillary n small blood vessel

capital n chief town; money; large-sized letter ~adj involving or punishable by death; chief; excellent **capitalism** n economic system based on private ownership of industry **capitalist** n/adj **capitalize** v convert into capital; (with on) turn to advantage

capitulate v surrender

capon n castrated cock fowl fattened for eating

cappuccino n (pl **-nos**) coffee with steamed milk

caprice n whim, freak **capricious** adj

capsize v (of boat) overturn accidentally

——————— THESAURUS ———————

sharp, shrewd, subtle, wise

canopy awning, covering, shade, sunshade

cant n humbug, hypocrisy, insincerity, lip service, pretence

cantankerous bad-tempered, captious, contrary, crabby, crotchety Inf, crusty, difficult, disagreeable, grumpy, irascible, irritable, peevish, perverse, quarrelsome, testy, tetchy

canter n/v amble, jog, lope

canvass analyse, campaign, electioneer, examine, inspect, investigate, poll, scan, sift, solicit, study

cap v beat, better, cover, crown, exceed, excel, finish, outdo, outstrip, overtop, run rings around Inf, surpass, top, transcend

capable able, accomplished, adapted, adept, apt, clever, competent, efficient, fitted, gifted, masterly, proficient, skilful, suited, talented

capacity amplitude, compass, extent, range, room, scope, size, space, volume; function, office, position, post, province, role, service, sphere; ability, brains, cleverness, competence, competency, facility, faculty, forte, genius, gift, intelligence, power, readiness, strength

cape head, headland, point, promontory

caper v bounce, bound, cavort, dance, frisk, frolic, gambol, hop, jump, leap, romp, skip, spring

capital n assets, cash, finances, funds, investment(s), means, money, principal, property, resources, stock, wealth, wherewithal ~adj cardinal, central, chief, foremost, important, leading, main, major, paramount, pre-eminent, prime, principal, vital

capitalism free enterprise, free market, laissez faire, private enterprise,

capstan *n* machine to wind cable

capsule *n* case for dose of medicine

Capt. Captain

captain *n* commander of vessel or company of soldiers; leader ~*v* be captain of **captaincy** *n*

caption *n* heading, title of article, picture etc.

captive *n* prisoner ~*adj* taken, imprisoned **captivate** *v* fascinate **captivity** *n*

capture *v* seize, make prisoner ~*n* seizure, taking **captor** *n*

car *n* road vehicle; passenger compartment

carafe *n* glass water bottle for the table, decanter

caramel *n* burnt sugar for cooking; chewy sweet

carat *n* weight used for gold, diamonds etc.; measure used to state fineness of gold

caravan *n* large vehicle for living in, pulled by car etc.; company of merchants travelling together

caraway *n* plant with spicy seeds used in cakes etc.

carbohydrate *n* any compound containing carbon, hydrogen and oxygen, esp. sugars and starches

carbon *n* nonmetallic element, substance of pure charcoal, found in all organic matter **carbonate** *n* salt of carbonic acid **carbon copy** copy made with carbon paper; very similar person or thing **carbon dioxide** colourless gas exhaled in respiration

carbuncle *n* inflamed ulcer, boil or tumour

carburettor *n* device for mixing petrol with air in engine

carcass, carcase *n* dead animal body

card *n* thick, stiff paper; piece of this giving identification etc.; illustrated card sending greetings etc.; playing card; *pl* any card game **cardboard** *n* thin, stiff board made of paper pulp **cardsharp** *n* cheating card player

cardiac *adj* pert. to the heart **cardiograph** *n* instrument which records movements of the heart **cardiology** *n* study of heart diseases

cardigan *n* knitted jacket

cardinal *adj* chief, principal ~*n* rank next to the Pope in R.C. church **cardinal numbers** 1,2,3 etc.

care *v* be anxious; have regard or liking (for); look after; be disposed to ~*n* attention; protection; anxiety; caution **careful** *adj* **careless** *adj* **carefree** *adj* **caretaker** *n* person in charge of premises

——————— THESAURUS ———————

private ownership

capsize keel over, overturn, tip over, turn over, turn turtle, upset

capsule lozenge, pill, tablet

captain boss, chief, commander, head, leader, master, officer, skipper

captivate allure, attract, beguile, bewitch, charm, dazzle, enchant, enslave, enthral, entrance, fascinate, infatuate, lure, mesmerize, seduce, win

captive *n* convict, detainee, hostage, internee, prisoner, slave ~*adj* caged, confined, ensnared, imprisoned, incarcerated, locked up, restricted, subjugated

captivity confinement, custody, detention, imprisonment, incarceration, internment, servitude, slavery

capture *v* arrest, catch, nail *Inf*, secure, seize, take, take prisoner ~*n* arrest, imprisonment, seizure

car automobile, machine, motor, motorcar, vehicle

carcass body, cadaver *Med*, corpse, dead body, hulk, remains, shell, skeleton

cardinal capital, central, chief, essential, first, foremost, greatest, highest, important, leading, main, preeminent, primary, prime, principal

career *n* course through life; profession; rapid motion ~*v* run or move at full speed

caress *v* fondle, embrace, treat with affection ~*n* affectionate embrace or touch

caret *n* mark (Λ) showing where to insert word etc.

cargo *n* (*pl* **-goes**) load, freight, carried by ship, plane etc.

caribou *n* reindeer

caricature *n* likeness exaggerated to appear ridiculous ~*v* portray in this way

carnage *n* slaughter

carnal *adj* fleshly, sensual

carnation *n* cultivated flower

carnival *n* festive occasion; travelling fair

carnivorous *adj* flesh-eating **carnivore** *n*

carol *n/v* **-olling, -olled** (sing) song or hymn of joy

carouse *v* have merry drinking spree **carousal** *n*

carousel *n* US merry-go-round; rotating device for holding slides

carp[1] *n* freshwater fish

carp[2] *v* find fault; nag

carpenter *n* worker in timber **carpentry** *n*

carpet *n* heavy fabric for covering floor

carriage *n* railway coach; bearing; horse-drawn vehicle **carriageway** *n* part of road along which traffic passes in a single line

carrion *n* rotting dead flesh

carrot *n* plant with orange-red edible root; inducement

carry *v* **carrying, carried** convey, transport; capture, win; effect; be-

———————— T H E S A U R U S ————————

care attention, caution, consideration, direction, forethought, heed, management, pains, prudence, regard, vigilance, watchfulness; charge, control, custody, keeping, management, protection, supervision, ward; anxiety, burden, concern, disquiet, interest, pressure, responsibility, solicitude, stress, trouble, vexation, woe, worry

career *n* calling, employment, life work, livelihood, occupation, pursuit, vocation

careful accurate, attentive, cautious, chary, circumspect, conscientious, discreet, fastidious, heedful, painstaking, precise, prudent, scrupulous, thoughtful, thrifty; alert, concerned, judicious, mindful, particular, protective, solicitous, vigilant, wary, watchful

careless absent-minded, forgetful, hasty, heedless, incautious, indiscreet, negligent, perfunctory, remiss, thoughtless, unconcerned, unguard-

ed, unmindful, unthinking; inaccurate, irresponsible, lackadaisical, neglectful, offhand, slapdash, slipshod, sloppy *Inf*

caress *v* cuddle, embrace, fondle, hug, kiss, pet, stroke ~*n* cuddle, embrace, hug, kiss, pat, stroke

caretaker concierge, curator, custodian, janitor, keeper, porter, warden, watchman

cargo baggage, consignment, contents, freight, goods, lading, load, merchandise, shipment, tonnage, ware

caricature *n* burlesque, cartoon, farce, lampoon, parody, satire, takeoff *Inf*, travesty ~*v* burlesque, distort, lampoon, mimic, mock, parody, ridicule, satirize, send up *Brit inf*, take off *Inf*

carnival celebration, fair, festival, fête, fiesta, gala, holiday, revelry

carriage; cab, coach, vehicle; air, bearing, behaviour, conduct, demeanour, gait, manner, mien, pos-

have; (of projectile, sound) reach **car-rier** n

cart n open (two-wheeled) vehicle ~v carry in cart; carry with effort **cart-horse** n heavily built horse **cartwheel** n sideways somersault

carte blanche Fr complete authority

cartel n industrial alliance for fixing prices etc.

cartilage n firm elastic tissue in the body; gristle

cartography n map making

carton n cardboard or plastic container

cartoon n drawing, esp. humorous or satirical; sequence of drawings telling story **cartoonist** n

cartridge n case containing charge for gun; container for film etc.

carve v cut; hew; sculpture; engrave; cut (meat) in pieces or slices **carving** n

cascade n waterfall

case[1] n instance; circumstance; question at issue; arguments supporting particular action etc.; Med patient; lawsuit **in case** so as to allow for eventualities

case[2] n box, sheath, covering; receptacle; box and contents ~v put in a case

cash n money, banknotes and coins ~v turn into or exchange for money **cashier** n one in charge of receiving and paying of money

cashier v dismiss from office

cashmere n fine soft fabric made from goat's wool

casino n (pl **-nos**) building, institution for gambling

cask n barrel

casket n small case for jewels etc.

casserole n fireproof cooking dish; stew

cassette n plastic container for film, magnetic tape etc.

cassock n clergyman's long tunic

cast v throw or fling; shed; deposit (a vote); allot, as parts in play; mould ~n throw; squint; mould; that which is shed or ejected; set of actors; type or quality **castaway** n shipwrecked person **cast-iron** adj made of hard, brittle type of iron; rigid or unchallengeable **cast-off** adj/n discarded (garment)

————— THESAURUS —————

ture, presence

carry bear, bring, conduct, convey, fetch, haul, hump Brit sl, lift, lug, move, relay, take, transfer, transmit, transport

carton box, case, pack, package

cartoon animated film, animation, comic strip, lampoon, parody, satire, sketch, takeoff

cartridge charge, round, shell

carve chip, chisel, cut, divide, engrave, etch, form, hack, hew, inscribe, mould, sculpt, sculpture, slash, slice, whittle

cascade n cataract, deluge, falls, flood, fountain, outpouring, shower, torrent, waterfall

case[1] example, illustration, instance,

occasion, occurrence, specimen; circumstance(s), condition, context, dilemma, event, plight, position, predicament, situation, state Law action, cause, dispute, lawsuit, proceedings, process, suit, trial

case[2] box, cabinet, capsule, carton, cartridge, casket, chest, compact, container, crate, holder, receptacle, shell, suitcase, tray, trunk

cash bullion, charge, coin, coinage, currency, dosh Brit & Aust sl, dough Sl, funds, money, notes, payment, ready money, resources, wherewithal

cashier n bank clerk, banker, bursar, clerk, teller

cast v chuck Inf, drive, drop, fling, hurl, impel, launch, lob, pitch, proj-

castanets *pl n* two small curved pieces of wood clicked together in hand

caste *n* section of society in India; social rank

caster sugar *also* **castor sugar** *n* finely powdered sugar

castigate *v* rebuke severely

castle *n* fortress

castor *n* bottle with perforated top; small swivelled wheel on table leg etc.

castor oil *n* vegetable medicinal oil

castrate *v* remove testicles **castration** *n*

casual *adj* accidental; unforeseen; occasional; unconcerned; informal **casually** *adv* **casualty** *n* person killed or injured in accident, war etc.

cat *n* any of various feline animals, esp. small domesticated furred animal **catty** *adj* spiteful **catcall** *n* derisive cry **catkin** *n* drooping flower spike **catnap** *v/n* doze **Catseye** *n Trademark* glass reflector set in road to indicate traffic lanes **catwalk** *n* narrow platform

cataclysm *n* (disastrous) upheaval; deluge

catacomb *n* underground chamber for burial

catalogue *n* descriptive list ~*v* make such list of

catalyst *n* substance causing or assisting a chemical reaction without taking part in it

catamaran *n* type of sailing boat with twin hulls

catapult *n* small forked stick with sling for throwing stones; launching device ~*v* launch with force

cataract *n* waterfall; downpour; disease of eye

catarrh *n* inflammation of mucous membrane

catastrophe *n* great disaster **catastrophic** *adj*

catch *v* **catching, caught** take hold of; hear; contract disease; be in time for; detect; be contagious; get entangled; begin to burn ~*n* seizure; thing that holds, stops etc.; what is caught; *Inf* snag, disadvantage **catcher** *n* **catching** *adj* **catchy** *adj* (of tune) easily remembered

catechism *n* instruction by questions and answers

category *n* class, order **categorize** *v*

ect, shed, shy, sling, throw, thrust, toss ~*n* fling, lob, throw, thrust, toss; actors, characters, company, players

castle chateau, citadel, fortress, keep, mansion, stronghold, tower

casual accidental, chance, contingent, fortuitous, irregular, occasional, random, unexpected, unforeseen, unpremeditated; blasé, indifferent, informal, nonchalant, offhand, perfunctory, relaxed, unconcerned

casualty loss, sufferer, victim

catalogue directory, index, inventory, list, record, register, roll, roster, schedule

catastrophe adversity, affliction, blow, calamity, cataclysm, devasta-

tion, disaster, failure, fiasco, ill, mischance, misfortune, mishap, reverse, tragedy, trial, trouble

catch *v* apprehend, arrest, capture, clutch, ensnare, entrap, grab, grasp, grip, lay hold of, lift *Sl*, nail *Inf*, seize, snare, snatch, take; detect, discover, expose, find out, surprise, unmask ~*n* bolt, clasp, clip, fastener, hasp, hook, hook and eye, latch; disadvantage, drawback, fly in the ointment, hitch, snag, stumbling block, trap, trick

catching contagious, infectious, infective, transferable, transmittable

categorical absolute, direct, downright, emphatic, explicit, express,

categorical *adj* positive

cater *v* provide, esp. food **caterer** *n*

caterpillar *n* hairy grub of moth or butterfly

catharsis *n* relief of strong suppressed emotions **cathartic** *adj*

cathedral *n* principal church of diocese

Catherine wheel *n* rotating firework producing sparks

catholic *adj* universal; including whole body of Christians; (*with cap.*) relating to R.C. church ~*n* (*with cap.*) adherent of R.C. church **Catholicism** *n*

cattle *pl n* pasture animals, esp. oxen, cows **cattleman** *n*

cauldron *n* large pot used for boiling

cauliflower *n* variety of cabbage with edible white flowering head

cause *n* that which produces an effect; reason; motive; charity, movement; lawsuit ~*v* bring about, make happen

causeway *n* raised path over marsh etc.

caustic *adj* burning; bitter ~*n* corrosive substance

cauterize *v* burn with caustic or hot iron

caution *n* heedfulness, care; warning ~*v* warn **cautionary** *adj* **cautious** *adj*

cavalcade *n* procession

cavalier *adj* careless, disdainful ~*n* courtly gentleman; *Obs* horseman; (*with cap.*) supporter of Charles I

cavalry *n* mounted troops

cave *n* hollow place in the earth; den

cavern *n* deep cave **cavernous** *adj*

cavity *n* hollow **caveman** *n* prehistoric cave dweller

caviar, caviare *n* salted sturgeon roe

cavil *v* **-illing, -illed** make trifling objections

cavort *v* prance, frisk

CB Citizens' Band

CBE Commander of the British Empire

cc cubic centimetre

CD compact disc **CD-ROM** compact disc storing written information, displayed on VDU

cease *v* bring or come to an end **ceaseless** *adj* **ceasefire** *n* temporary truce

cedar *n* large evergreen tree

———————— T H E S A U R U S ————————

positive, unequivocal, unqualified

category class, department, division, grade, head, heading, list, order, rank, section, sort, type

cater furnish, outfit, provide, provision, purvey, supply, victual

cattle beasts, cows, livestock, stock

cause *n* agent, beginning, creator, genesis, maker, origin, prime mover, producer, root, source, spring; account, agency, aim, basis, consideration, end, grounds, incentive, inducement, motivation, motive, object, purpose, reason ~*v* begin, bring about, compel, create, effect, engender, generate, give rise to, incite, induce, lead to, motivate, occasion, precipitate, produce, provoke,

result in

caustic acrid, astringent, biting, burning, corroding, corrosive, keen, mordant

caution *n* care, carefulness, circumspection, discretion, forethought, heed, prudence, vigilance, watchfulness; admonition, advice, counsel, injunction, warning ~*v* admonish, advise, tip off, urge, warn

cautious alert, cagey *Inf*, careful, chary, circumspect, discreet, guarded, heedful, judicious, prudent, tentative, vigilant, wary, watchful

cave cavern, den, grotto, hollow

cavern cave, hollow, pothole

cavity crater, hole, hollow, pit

cease come to an end, conclude, de-

cede *v* yield, give up, transfer

cedilla *n* accent (‚) below letter

ceilidh *n* informal social gathering for dancing

ceiling *n* inner, upper surface of a room

celebrate *v* have festivities to mark (happy day, event etc.); observe (birthday etc.); perform (religious ceremony etc.); praise publicly **celebrated** *adj* famous **celebration** *n* **celebrity** *n* famous person; fame

celery *n* vegetable with long juicy edible stalks

celestial *adj* heavenly, divine

celibacy *n* unmarried state **celibate** *adj/n*

cell *n* small room in prison; small cavity; minute, basic unit of living matter; device converting chemical into electrical energy **cellular** *adj*

cellar *n* underground room for storage; stock of wine

cello *n* (*pl* -**los**) stringed instrument of violin family

Cellophane *n Trademark* transparent wrapping

cellulose *n* fibrous carbohydrate

Celsius *adj/n* (of) scale of temperature from 0° to 100°

cement *n* fine mortar; glue ~*v* unite as with cement

cemetery *n* burial ground

cenotaph *n* monument to one buried elsewhere

censor *n* one authorized to examine films, books etc. and suppress parts considered unacceptable ~*v* suppress **censorious** *adj* fault-finding **censorship** *n*

censure *n*/*v* blame

census *n* official counting of people, things etc.

cent *n* hundredth part of dollar etc.

centaur *n* mythical creature, half man, half horse

centenary *n* 100 years; celebration of hundredth anniversary ~*adj* pert. to a hundred

centigrade *adj/n* another name for CELSIUS

centimetre *n* hundredth part of metre

centipede *n* small segmented animal with many legs

centre *n* midpoint; pivot; place for

———————— THESAURUS ————————

sist, die away, end, fail, finish, halt, leave off, refrain, stay, stop, terminate

ceaseless constant, continuous, endless, eternal, everlasting, incessant, never-ending, nonstop, perpetual, unending, untiring

celebrate commend, drink to, eulogize, exalt, extol, glorify, honour, keep, laud, observe, praise, proclaim, rejoice, reverence, toast

celebrated distinguished, eminent, famed, famous, glorious, illustrious, notable, popular, prominent, renowned, well-known

celebration carousal, festival, festivity, gala, jubilee, revelry

celebrity big name, dignitary, luminary, megastar *Inf*, name, personage, personality, star, superstar, V.I.P.

cell cavity, chamber, compartment, cubicle, dungeon, stall

cement *v* attach, bind, bond, glue, gum, join, plaster, seal, solder, stick together, unite, weld

cemetery burial ground, churchyard, graveyard

censor blue-pencil, bowdlerize, cut, expurgate

censure *n* blame, castigation, condemnation, criticism, disapproval, rebuke, remonstrance, reprimand, reproach, reproof, stricture ~*v* abuse, blame, castigate, condemn, criticize, denounce, lambast(e), rebuke, reprimand, reproach, reprove, scold, tear

specific organization or activity **central** *adj* **centralize** *v* **centrally** *adv*

centurion *n* Roman commander of 100 men

century *n* 100 years; any set of 100

ceramics *pl n* (*with sing v*) art, techniques of making clay, porcelain objects **ceramic** *adj*

cereal *n* any edible grain; (breakfast) food

cerebral *adj* pert. to brain

ceremony *n* formal observance; sacred rite; courteous act **ceremonial** *adj/n*

certain *adj* sure; inevitable; some, one; moderate (in quantity, degree etc.) **certainly** *adv* **certainty** *n*

certify *v* -fying, -fied declare formally; guarantee **certificate** *n* written declaration

cervix *n* (*pl* -vixes, -vices) neck, esp. of womb **cervical** *adj*

cessation *n* stop, pause

cesspool, cesspit *n* covered pit for sewage

cf. compare

chafe *v* make sore or worn by rubbing; warm; vex

chaff *n* husks of corn; worthless matter ~*v* tease

chaffinch *n* small songbird

chagrin *n* vexation, disappointment ~*v* embarrass

chain *n* series of connected rings; thing that binds; connected series of things or events; surveyor's measure ~*v* fasten with a chain; restrain

chair *n* movable seat, with back, for one person; seat of authority ~*v* preside over; carry in triumph **chairman** *n* one who presides over meeting **chairperson** *n* **chairwoman** *n*

chalet *n* Swiss wooden house

chalice *n* *Poet* cup

chalk *n* white substance, carbonate of lime; crayon ~*v* mark with chalk **chalky** *adj*

challenge *v* call to fight or account; dispute; stimulate ~*n* challenging **challenger** *n*

chamber *n* (room for) assembly; compartment; cavity; *pl* office or

——————— THESAURUS ———————

into *Inf*, upbraid

central chief, essential, fundamental, inner, interior, main, mean, median, mid, middle, principal

centralize amalgamate, concentrate, condense, converge, incorporate, unify

centre core, crux, focus, heart, hub, mid, middle, pivot

ceremonial *adj* formal, ritual, solemn, stately ~*n* ceremony, formality, rite, ritual, solemnity

ceremony commemoration, function, observance, parade, rite, ritual, service, show

certain actual, ascertained, assured, constant, convinced, dependable, established, fixed, incontrovertible, indubitable, plain, positive, reliable, settled, true, undeniable, unmistak-

able, valid

certainty assurance, confidence, conviction, faith, inevitability, positiveness, sureness, trust, validity

certificate credential(s), diploma, document, licence, testimonial

certify assure, attest, authenticate, aver, avow, confirm, declare, endorse, guarantee, show, testify, validate, verify, witness

chain *n* coupling, fetter, link, manacle, shackle, union; progression, sequence, series, set, string, succession, train ~*v* bind, enslave, fetter, handcuff, manacle, restrain, shackle, tether

challenge *v* brave, claim, dare, defy, demand, dispute, investigate, object to, provoke, question, require, stimulate, summon, tax, try

apartment of barrister **chambermaid** *n* woman who cleans bedrooms

chameleon *n* lizard with power of changing colour

chamois *n* goatlike mountain antelope; soft pliable leather

champ *n* munch noisily; be impatient

champagne *n* light, sparkling white wine

champion *n* one that excels all others; defender of a cause ~*v* fight for **championship** *n*

chance *n* unpredictable course of events; luck; opportunity; possibility; risk; probability ~*v* risk; happen ~*adj* casual, unexpected **chancy** *adj*

chancel *n* part of a church where altar is

chancellor *n* high officer of state; head of university

chandelier *n* hanging frame with branches for lights

change *v* alter, make or become different; put on (different clothes, fresh coverings); put or give for another; exchange ~*n* alteration; variety; coins; balance received on payment **changeable** *adj*

channel *n* bed of stream; strait; deeper part of strait; groove; means of conveying; band of radio frequencies; television broadcasting station ~*v* groove; guide

chant *n* simple song or melody; rhythmic slogan ~*v* utter chant; speak monotonously

chaos *n* disorder, confusion **chaotic** *adj*

chap[1] *v* **chapping, chapped** (of skin) become raw and cracked

chap[2] *n Inf* fellow, man

chapati *n* thin unleavened bread used in Indian cookery

chapel *n* place of worship; division of church with its own altar

chaperon, chaperone *n* one who

chamber bedroom, compartment, cubicle, enclosure, hall, hollow, room

champion conqueror, defender, guardian, hero, patron, protector, title holder, upholder, victor, warrior, winner

chance *n* accident, casualty, coincidence, destiny, fate, fortune, luck, misfortune, peril, providence; likelihood, occasion, odds, opening, opportunity, possibility, probability, prospect, scope, time, window; gamble, hazard, risk, speculation, uncertainty ~*v* endanger, gamble, hazard, risk, stake, try, venture, wager; befall, betide, come about, come to pass, fall out, happen, occur

change *v* alter, convert, diversify, fluctuate, metamorphose, moderate, modify, mutate, reform, remodel, reorganize, restyle, shift, transform, vary, veer; barter, convert, displace, exchange, interchange, remove, re-

place, substitute, swap *Inf*, trade, transmit ~*n* alteration, difference, innovation, metamorphosis, modification, mutation, permutation, revolution, transformation, transition

changeable capricious, erratic, fickle, fitful, fluid, inconstant, irregular, mercurial, mobile, protean, shifting, temperamental, uncertain, uneven, unpredictable, unreliable, unsettled, unstable, unsteady, vacillating, variable, versatile, volatile, wavering

channel *n* canal, duct, furrow, groove, gutter, main, passage, route, strait ~*v* conduct, convey, direct, guide, transmit

chant *n* carol, chorus, melody, psalm, song ~*v* intone, recite, sing, warble

chaos anarchy, bedlam, confusion, disorder, pandemonium, tumult

chaotic anarchic, confused, deranged, disordered, disorganized, lawless, purposeless, riotous, topsy-

attends young unmarried lady in public ~*v* attend in this way

chaplain *n* clergyman attached to prison, college etc.

chapter *n* division of book; assembly of clergy; organized branch of society

char *v* **charring, charred** scorch

character *n* nature; qualities making up individuality; moral qualities; eccentric person; fictional person **characteristic** *adj* typical ~*n* distinguishing feature **characterize** *v* mark out; describe

charade *n* absurd act; *pl* word-guessing game

charcoal *n* charred wood

charge *v* ask as price; bring accusation against; lay task on; attack; fill (with electricity); make onrush, attack ~*n* price; accusation; attack; command; accumulation of electricity **chargeable** *adj* **charger** *n* that which charges, esp. electrically; war-horse

chargé d'affaires head of small diplomatic mission

chariot *n* two-wheeled vehicle used in ancient fighting; state carriage **charioteer** *n*

charisma *n* special power of individual to inspire fascination, loyalty etc. **charismatic** *adj*

charity *n* giving of help, money to needy; organization for this; love, kindness **charitable** *adj*

charlatan *n* impostor

charm *n* attractiveness; anything that fascinates; amulet; magic spell ~*v* bewitch; delight **charmer** *n* **charming** *adj*

chart *n* map of sea; tabulated statement ~*v* map

charter *n* document granting privileges etc. ~*v* let or hire; establish by charter **chartered** *adj* officially qualified

turvy, tumultuous, uncontrolled

chapter clause, division, episode, part, period, phase, section, stage, topic

character calibre, cast, complexion, constitution, disposition, make-up, nature, personality, quality, reputation, temper, temperament, type; honour, integrity, rectitude, strength, uprightness; card *Inf*, eccentric, nut *Sl*, oddball *Inf*, oddity, original, queer fish *Brit inf*; part, persona, portrayal, role

characteristic *adj* distinctive, distinguishing, individual, peculiar, representative, singular, special, specific, symbolic, typical ~*n* attribute, faculty, feature, mark, peculiarity, property, quality, trait

charge *v* accuse, arraign, blame, impeach, indict, involve; bid, command, enjoin, exhort, instruct, order, require ~*n* amount, cost, expendi-

ture, expense, outlay, payment, price, rate; accusation, allegation, imputation, indictment; assault, attack, onset, rush, sortie

charitable benevolent, bountiful, generous, kind, lavish, liberal, philanthropic

charity alms-giving, assistance, benefaction, donations, fund, gift, hand-out, largess *or* largesse, philanthropy, relief

charm *n* allure, appeal, attraction, desirability, enchantment, fascination, magic, magnetism, sorcery, spell ~*v* allure, attract, beguile, bewitch, cajole, captivate, delight, enchant, entrance, fascinate, mesmerize, please

charming appealing, attractive, bewitching, captivating, delightful, engaging, lovely, pleasant, pleasing, seductive, winning, winsome

chart *n* blueprint, diagram, graph, map, plan, table ~*v* graph, map out,

charwoman n woman paid to clean office, house etc.

chary adj cautious, sparing

chase v hunt, pursue; drive from, away, into etc. ~n pursuit, hunting

chasm n deep cleft

chassis n (pl **chassis**) framework of motor vehicle

chaste adj virginal; pure; modest; virtuous **chastity** n

chasten v correct by punishment; subdue **chastise** v inflict punishment on

chat v **chatting, chatted** talk idly or familiarly ~n such talk **chatty** adj

chateau n (pl **-teaux** or **-teaus**) (esp. in France) castle, country house

chattel n any movable property

chatter v talk idly or rapidly; rattle teeth ~n idle talk **chatterbox** n person who chatters incessantly

chauffeur n (fem **chauffeuse**) paid driver of motorcar

chauvinism n irrational feeling of superiority **chauvinist** n/adj

cheap adj low in price; of little value; inferior **cheaply** adv **cheapen** v **cheapskate** n Inf miserly person

cheat v deceive; practise deceit to gain advantage ~n fraud

check v stop; control; examine ~n stoppage; restraint; brief examination; pattern of squares; threat to king at chess **checkmate** n/v (make) final winning move **checkout** n counter in supermarket where customers pay **check-up** n examination (esp. medical) to see if all is in order

Cheddar n smooth hard cheese

cheek n side of face below eye; Inf impudence **cheeky** adj

cheep v/n (utter) high-pitched cry, as of young bird

cheer v comfort; gladden; encourage by shouts; shout applause ~n shout of approval; happiness; mood **cheer-**

————— THESAURUS —————

outline, plot, shape, sketch

charter n contract, deed, document, franchise, indenture, privilege, right

chase course, drive, drive away, expel, follow, hound, hunt, pursue, put to flight, run after, track

chaste austere, decent, elegant, immaculate, incorrupt, innocent, modest, moral, neat, pure, quiet, refined, restrained, simple, unaffected, undefiled, virtuous, wholesome

chat v chatter, gossip ~n chatter, gossip, talk, tête-à-tête

chatter v/n babble, blather, chat, gossip, natter, prattle

cheap bargain, cut-price, economical, inexpensive, keen, low-priced, reduced, sale; common, dime-a-dozen Inf, inferior, paltry, poor, secondrate, shoddy, tatty, tawdry, worthless

cheat v beguile, con Inf, deceive, defraud, double-cross Inf, dupe, fleece, fool, hoax, hoodwink, mislead, rip off

Sl, swindle, thwart, trick, victimize; baffle, check, defeat, deprive, foil, frustrate, prevent, thwart ~n charlatan, cheater, con man Inf, deceiver, dodger, double-crosser Inf, impostor, knave, rogue, shark, sharper, swindler, trickster

check v bar, bridle, control, curb, delay, halt, hinder, impede, inhibit, limit, obstruct, pause, repress, restrain, retard, stop, thwart; compare, confirm, enquire into, examine, inspect, investigate, look at, look over, make sure, monitor, note, probe, scrutinize, study, test, tick, verify ~n constraint, control, curb, damper, hindrance, impediment, limitation, obstruction, rein, restraint, stoppage; examination, inspection, investigation, research, scrutiny, test

cheek audacity, brazenness, disrespect, effrontery, gall Inf, impertinence, impudence, insolence, nerve,

ful *adj* **cheerless** *adj* **cheery** *adj*

cheerio *interj Inf* goodbye

cheese *n* food made from solidified curd of milk **cheesy** *adj* **cheesecake** *n* dessert made from biscuits and cream cheese

cheetah *n* large, swift, spotted feline animal

chef *n* head cook

chemistry *n* science concerned with properties of substances and their combinations and reactions **chemical** *n/adj* **chemically** *adv* **chemist** *n* dispenser of medicines; shop that sells medicines etc.; one trained in chemistry

chemotherapy *n* treatment of disease by chemicals

chenille *n* soft cord, fabric of silk or worsted

cheque *n* written order to banker to pay money from one's account; printed slip of paper used for this **chequebook** *n* **cheque card** banker's card

chequer *n* marking as on chessboard; marble, peg etc. used in games ~*v* mark in squares; variegate **chequered** *adj*

cherish *v* treat tenderly

cherry *n* small red fruit with stone; tree bearing it

cherub *n* (*pl* **cherubim, cherubs**) winged creature with human face; angel **cherubic** *adj*

chess *n* game played on chequered board **chessman** *n* piece used in chess

chest *n* upper part of trunk of body; large, strong box **chest of drawers** piece of furniture containing drawers

chestnut *n* tree bearing large nut in prickly husk; *Inf* old joke ~*adj* reddish-brown

chevron *n Mil* V-shaped braid designating rank

chew *v* grind with teeth ~*n* chewing **chewy** *adj* **chewing gum** flavoured gum

chianti *n* red Italian wine

chic *adj* stylish ~*n* stylishness

chicane *n* obstacle on racing circuit **chicanery** *n* trickery

chick *n* young of birds, esp. of hen; *Sl* girl, young woman **chickpea** *n* edible pealike seed

chicken *n* domestic fowl; *Sl* coward ~*adj* cowardly **chickenpox** *n* infectious disease

chicory *n* salad plant whose root is used instead of coffee

chide *v* **chiding, chid, chid** *or* **chidden** scold

chief *n* head or principal person ~*adj* principal, foremost **chiefly** *adv* **chieftain** *n* leader of tribe

——————— THESAURUS ———————

temerity

cheer *v* brighten, buoy up, cheer up, comfort, console, elate, elevate, encourage, enliven, exhilarate, gladden, hearten, incite, inspirit, solace, uplift, warm; acclaim, applaud, clap, hail, hurrah ~*n* cheerfulness, comfort, gaiety, gladness, glee, hopefulness, joy, liveliness, merriment, merry-making, mirth, optimism, solace

cheerful blithe, bright, buoyant, cheery, chirpy *Inf,* contented, enthusiastic, gay, glad, happy, hearty, jaun-

ty, jolly, joyful, light-hearted, merry, optimistic, pleasant, sparkling, sprightly, sunny, upbeat *Inf*

cherish care for, cling to, comfort, encourage, entertain, foster, harbour, hold dear, nourish, nurse, prize, shelter, support, sustain, treasure

chest box, case, casket, crate, trunk

chew bite, champ, crunch, gnaw, grind, masticate, munch

chief *n* boss *Inf,* captain, commander, director, governor, head, leader, lord, manager, master, principal, ruler,

chiffon *n* gauzy material

chihuahua *n* breed of tiny dog

chilblain *n* inflamed sore on hands, legs etc. due to cold

child *n* (*pl* **children**) young human being; offspring **childish** *adj* silly **childlike** *adj* of or like a child; innocent **childhood** *n*

chill *n* coldness; cold with shivering; anything that discourages ~*v* make, become cold **chilly** *adj* cold; unfriendly

chilli *n* small red hot-tasting seed pod

chime *n* sound of bell ~*v* ring harmoniously; agree; strike (bells)

chimney *n* (*pl* **-neys**) vertical passage for smoke

chimpanzee *n* ape of Africa

chin *n* part of face below mouth **chinwag** *n Inf* chat

china *n* fine earthenware, porcelain; cups, saucers etc.

chinchilla *n* S Amer. rodent with soft, grey fur

chink *n* cleft, crack

chintz *n* cotton cloth printed in coloured designs

chip *n* splinter; place where piece has

been broken off; thin strip of potato, fried; tiny wafer of silicon forming integrated circuit ~*v* **chipping, chipped** chop into small pieces; break small pieces from; break off **chip in** interrupt; contribute

chipmunk *n* small, striped N Amer. squirrel

chiropodist *n* one who treats disorders of feet **chiropody** *n*

chirp, chirrup *n/v* (make) short, sharp cry **chirpy** *adj Inf* happy

chisel *n* cutting tool ~*v* **-elling, -elled** cut with chisel; *Sl* cheat

chit *n* informal note

chitchat *n* gossip

chivalry *n* bravery and courtesy; medieval system of knighthood **chivalrous** *adj*

chive *n* herb with onion flavour

chlorine *n* nonmetallic element, yellowish-green poison gas **chloride** *n* bleaching agent **chlorinate** *v* disinfect

chloroform *n* volatile liquid formerly used as anaesthetic

chlorophyll *n* green colouring matter in plants

chock *n* block or wedge

────────────── T H E S A U R U S ──────────────

superintendent ~*adj* capital, cardinal, central, especial, essential, foremost, grand, highest, key, leading, main, most important, outstanding, predominant, pre-eminent, premier, prevailing, principal, superior, supreme, uppermost, vital

chiefly especially, essentially, in general, in the main, largely, mainly, mostly, on the whole, principally, usually

child baby, brat, descendant, infant, issue, juvenile, kid *Inf*, little one, minor, offspring, progeny, sprog *Sl*, toddler, tot, youngster *Inf*

childhood boyhood, girlhood, immaturity, infancy, minority, schooldays, youth

childlike artless, credulous, guileless, ingenuous, innocent, naive, simple, trustful, trusting, unfeigned

chill *v* congeal, cool, freeze, refrigerate ~*adj* bleak, chilly, cold, freezing, raw, sharp, wintry

chilly breezy, brisk, cold, crisp, draughty, fresh, nippy, sharp; hostile, unfriendly, unsympathetic, unwelcoming

chip *n* dent, flake, flaw, fragment, nick, notch, paring, scrap, scratch, shaving, wafer

chivalrous bold, brave, courteous, courtly, gallant, gentlemanly, heroic, high-minded, honourable, knightly, true, valiant

chivalry courage, courtesy, courtli-

chocolate *n* confectionery, drink made from ground cacao seeds

choice *n* act or power of choosing; alternative; thing or person chosen ~*adj* select, fine

choir *n* band of singers

choke *v* hinder, stop the breathing of; smother, stifle; obstruct; suffer choking ~*n* act, noise of choking; device to increase richness of petrol-air mixture **choker** *n* tight-fitting necklace

cholera *n* deadly infectious disease

choleric *adj* bad-tempered

cholesterol *n* substance found in animal tissue and fat

choose *v* **choosing, chose, chosen** pick out, select; take by preference; decide, think fit **choosy** *adj*

chop *v* **chopping, chopped** cut with blow; hack ~*n* cutting blow; cut of meat with bone **chopper** *n* short axe; *Inf* helicopter **choppy** *adj* (of sea) having short, broken waves

chopsticks *pl n* implements used by Chinese for eating food

choral *adj* of, for a choir

chorale *n* slow, stately hymn tune

chord *n* simultaneous sounding of musical notes

chore *n* (unpleasant) task

choreography *n* art of arranging dances, esp. ballet **choreographer** *n*

chorister *n* singer in choir

chortle *v/n* (make) happy chuckling sound

chorus *n* (music for) band of singers; refrain ~*v* sing or say together

chow[1] *n Inf* food

chow[2] *n* thick-coated dog with curled tail, orig. from China

Christ *n* Jesus of Nazareth

Christian *n/adj* (person) following, believing in Christ **christen** *v* baptize; give name to **christening** *n* **Christianity** *n*

Christmas *n* festival of birth of Christ

chrome, chromium *n* metal used in alloys and for plating

chromosome *n* microscopic gene-carrying body in the tissue of a cell

chronic *adj* lasting a long time; habitual; *Inf* serious; *Inf* of bad quality

chronicle *n/v* (write) record of historical events

chronological *adj* arranged in order of time

chrysalis *n* (*pl* **chrysalises**) resting state of insect; case enclosing it

chrysanthemum *n* garden flower of various colours

chub *n* freshwater fish

chubby *adj* plump

chuck *v Inf* throw; pat affectionately (under chin); give up

chuckle *v/n* (make) soft laugh

chuffed *adj Inf* pleased, delighted

——————— THESAURUS ———————

ness, gallantry, politeness

choice *n* alternative, election, option, pick, preference, say, selection, variety ~*adj* best, dainty, elect, elite, excellent, exclusive, exquisite, hand-picked, nice, precious, prize, rare, select, special, uncommon, valuable

choke bar, block, bung, clog, close, congest, constrict, dam, gag, obstruct, occlude, overpower, smother, stifle, stop, strangle, suffocate, suppress, throttle

choose adopt, designate, elect, fix on,

opt for, pick, prefer, see fit, select, settle upon, single out, take, wish

chore burden, duty, job, task

chortle cackle, chuckle, crow, guffaw

chorus choir, choristers, ensemble, singers, vocalists

chronicle *n* account, annals, diary, history, journal, narrative, record, story ~*v* enter, narrate, record, recount, register, relate, report, set down, tell

chuck cast, discard, fling, heave, hurl, pitch, shy, sling, throw, toss

chum *n Inf* close friend **chummy** *adj*

chunk *n* thick, solid piece **chunky** *adj*

church *n* building for Christian worship; (*with cap.*) whole body or sect of Christians; clergy

churlish *adj* rude or surly

churn *n* large container for milk; vessel for making butter ~*v* shake up, stir; (*with* **out**) produce rapidly

chute *n* slide for sending down parcels, coal etc.

chutney *n* pickle of fruit, spices etc.

CIA *US* Central Intelligence Agency

CID Criminal Investigation Department

cider *n* fermented drink made from apples

cigar *n* roll of tobacco leaves for smoking **cigarette** *n* finely-cut tobacco rolled in paper for smoking

cinch *n Inf* easy task

cinder *n* remains of burned coal

cinema *n* building used for showing of films; films generally

cinnamon *n* spice from bark of Asian tree

cipher, cypher *n* secret writing; arithmetical symbol; person of no importance

circa *Lat* about, approximately

circle *n* perfectly round figure; ring; *Theatre* section of seats above main level of auditorium; group, society with common interest ~*v* surround; move round **circular** *adj* round ~*n* letter sent to several persons **circulate** *v* move round; pass round; send round **circulation** *n* flow of blood; act of moving round; extent of sale of newspaper etc.

circuit *n* complete round or course; area; path of electric current; round of visitation **circuitous** *adj* indirect

circumcise *v* cut off foreskin of **circumcision** *n*

circumference *n* boundary line, esp. of circle

circumflex *n* accent (^) over a letter

circumnavigate *v* sail right round

circumscribe *v* confine, bound, limit

circumspect *adj* cautious

circumstance *n* detail; event; *pl* state of affairs; condition in life, esp. financial; surroundings or things accompanying an action **circumstantial** *adj*

circumvent *v* outwit, evade, get round

circus *n* (*pl* **-cuses**) (performance of)

——————————— T H E S A U R U S ———————————

chunk block, hunk, lump, mass, piece, portion, slab, wad

churlish boorish, crabbed, harsh, ill-tempered, impolite, morose, oafish, rude, sullen, surly, uncivil, uncouth, unmannerly, vulgar

cinema big screen *Inf*, films, flicks *Sl*, movies, pictures

circle *n* band, circumference, coil, cordon, cycle, disc, globe, lap, loop, orb, perimeter, revolution, ring, round, sphere, turn; assembly, clique, club, company, coterie, crowd, fellowship, fraternity, group, set, society ~*v* circumnavigate, coil, compass, curve, encircle, enclose, encompass, envelop, gird, hem in, re-

volve, ring, rotate, surround, tour

circuit area, compass, course, journey, lap, orbit, revolution, round, route, tour, track

circulate broadcast, diffuse, distribute, issue, make known, promulgate, propagate, publicize, publish, spread

circulation circling, flow, motion, rotation; currency, distribution, spread

circumference border, boundary, bounds, circuit, edge, extremity, fringe, limits, outline, perimeter, rim, verge

circumstance accident, condition, contingency, detail, element, event, fact, factor, happening, incident, item, occurrence, particular, posi-

acrobats, clowns, performing animals etc.

cirrhosis *n* disease of liver

cirrus *n* (*pl* **-ri**) high wispy cloud

cistern *n* water tank

citadel *n* city fortress

cite *v* quote; bring forward as proof **citation** *n* quoting; commendation for bravery etc.

citizen *n* member of state, nation etc.; inhabitant of city **citizenship** *n*

citrus fruit lemons, oranges etc.

city *n* large town

civic *adj* pert. to city or citizen

civil *adj* relating to citizens; not military; refined, polite; *Law* not criminal **civilian** *n* nonmilitary person **civility** *n*

civilize *v* bring out of barbarism; refine **civilization** *n* refinement; cultured society **civilized** *adj*

claim *v* demand as right; assert; call for ~*n* demand for thing supposed due; right; thing claimed **claimant** *n*

clairvoyance *n* power of seeing things not present to senses **clairvoyant** *n/adj*

clam *n* edible mollusc

clamber *v* to climb awkwardly

clammy *adj* moist and sticky

clamour *n/v* (make) loud outcry **clamorous** *adj*

clamp *n* tool for holding ~*v* fasten with or as with clamp; (*with* **down**) become stricter

clan *n* collection of families of common ancestry; group

clandestine *adj* secret; sly

clang *v* (cause to) make loud ringing sound ~*n* this sound

clap *v* **clapping, clapped** (cause to) strike with noise; strike (hands) together; applaud; pat; place or put quickly ~*n* hard, explosive sound; slap

claret *n* dry red wine

clarify *v* **-fying, -fied** make or become clear **clarification** *n* **clarity** *n*

clarinet *n* woodwind instrument

clash *n* loud noise; conflict, collision ~*v* make clash; come into conflict; strike together

clasp *n* hook or fastening; embrace ~*v*

———————— THESAURUS ————————

tion, respect, situation

cite adduce, advance, allude to, enumerate, evidence, extract, mention, name, quote, specify; *Law* call, subpoena, summon

citizen burgher, dweller, freeman, inhabitant, ratepayer, resident

city conurbation, megalopolis, metropolis, municipality

civic community, municipal, public

civil civic, domestic, home, interior, municipal, political; affable, civilized, courteous, courtly, obliging, polished, polite, refined, urbane, wellbred, well-mannered

civilization culture, development, education, enlightenment, progress, refinement, sophistication; community, nation, people, polity, society

civilize cultivate, educate, enlighten,

improve, polish, refine, tame

civilized cultured, educated, enlightened, humane, polite, tolerant

claim *v* allege, ask, assert, call for, collect, demand, exact, hold, insist, maintain, need, pick up, profess, require, take, uphold ~*n* application, assertion, call, demand, petition, privilege, protestation, request, requirement, right, title

clan band, brotherhood, clique, faction, family, fraternity, group, race, sect, sept, set, society, tribe

clap acclaim, applaud, cheer

clarify clear up, elucidate, explain, make plain, resolve, shed light on, simplify

clarity definition, explicitness, intelligibility, lucidity, precision, simplicity, transparency

fasten; embrace, grasp

class *n* any division, order, kind, sort; rank; group of school pupils; division by merit; quality ~*v* assign to proper division **classy** *adj Inf* stylish, elegant

classify *v* **-fying, -fied** arrange methodically in classes **classification** *n*

classic *adj* of highest rank, esp. of art; typical; famous ~*n* (literary) work of recognized excellence; *pl* ancient Greek and Latin literature **classical** *adj* refined, elegant; of ancient Greek and Latin culture

clatter *n* rattling noise ~*v* (cause to) make clatter

clause *n* part of sentence; article in formal document

claustrophobia *n* abnormal fear of confined spaces **claustrophobic** *adj*

clavicle *n* collarbone

claw *n* sharp hooked nail of animal ~*v* tear with claws

clay *n* fine-grained earth, plastic when wet, hardening when baked; earth **clayey** *adj*

clean *adj* free from dirt; pure; guiltless; trim ~*adv* so as to leave no dirt; entirely ~*v* free from dirt **cleaner** *n* **cleanliness** *n* **cleanly** *adv* **cleanse** *v* make clean

clear *adj* pure, bright; free from cloud; transparent; plain, distinct; without defect; unimpeded ~*adv* brightly; wholly, quite ~*v* make clear; acquit; pass over; make as profit; free from obstruction, difficulty; become clear, bright, free, transparent **clearly** *adv* **clearance** *n* **clearing** *n* land cleared of trees

cleave¹ *v* **cleaving, clove** *or* **cleft, clo-**

─────────── THESAURUS ───────────

clash *n* brush, collision, conflict, confrontation, difference of opinion, disagreement, fight ~*v* conflict, cross swords, feud, grapple, quarrel, war, wrangle

clasp *n* brooch, buckle, catch, clip, grip, hasp, hook, pin, snap ~*v* clutch, connect, embrace, enfold, fasten, grapple, grasp, grip, hold, hug, press, seize, squeeze

class caste, category, collection, department, division, genus, grade, group, grouping, kind, league, order, rank, set, sort, species, sphere, status, type, value

classic *adj* best, finest, first-rate, masterly; archetypal, definitive, exemplary, ideal, master, model, standard, typical ~*n* exemplar, masterpiece, model, standard

classical chaste, elegant, pure, refined, restrained, symmetrical, well-proportioned; Attic, Augustan, Grecian, Greek, Hellenic, Latin, Roman

classification analysis, arrangement, categorization, codification, grading,

sorting, taxonomy

classify arrange, catalogue, codify, dispose, distribute, file, grade, rank, sort

clause article, chapter, condition, paragraph, part, passage, section; heading, item, point, rider, stipulation

claw nail, nipper, pincer, talon, tentacle

clean *adj* faultless, fresh, hygienic, immaculate, pure, sanitary, spotless, squeaky-clean, unsoiled, unstained, unsullied, washed; chaste, decent, exemplary, good, honourable, impeccable, innocent, moral, pure, respectable, undefiled, upright, virtuous ~*v* bath, cleanse, disinfect, do up, dust, launder, mop, purge, purify, rinse, scour, scrub, sponge, swab, sweep, wash, wipe

clear *adj* bright, cloudless, fair, fine, light, luminous, shining, sunny, unclouded, undimmed; apparent, audible, blatant, coherent, definite, distinct, evident, explicit, express, lu-

ven *or* **cleft** (cause to) split **cleavage** *n* **cleaver** *n* short chopper

cleave² *v* **cleaving, cleaved** stick, adhere; be loyal

clef *n* Mus mark to show pitch

cleft *n* crack, fissure, chasm

clematis *n* climbing plant

clement *adj* merciful; gentle; mild **clemency** *n*

clench *v* set firmly together; grasp, close (fist)

clergy *n* body of ministers of Christian church **clergyman** *n*

clerical *adj* of clergy; of office work **cleric** *n* clergyman

clerk *n* subordinate who keeps files etc.; officer in charge of records, correspondence etc.

clever *adj* intelligent; able, skilful, adroit **cleverly** *adv*

cliché *n* (*pl* -s) stereotyped hackneyed phrase

click *n/v* (make) short, sharp sound

client *n* customer **clientele** *n* clients

cliff *n* steep rock face **cliffhanger** *n*

thing which is exciting and full of suspense

climate *n* condition of country with regard to weather **climatic** *adj*

climax *n* highest point, culmination **climactic** *adj*

climb *v* go up or ascend **climber** *n*

clinch *v* conclude (agreement)

cling *v* **clinging, clung** adhere; be firmly attached to **clingfilm** *n* thin polythene wrapping material

clinic *n* place for medical examination, advice or treatment **clinical** *adj*

clink *n* sharp metallic sound ~*v* (cause to) make this sound

clip¹ *v* **clipping, clipped** cut with scissors; cut short ~*n* Inf sharp blow **clipping** *n* thing cut out, esp. newspaper article

clip² *n/v* **clipping, clipped** (attach with) gripping device

clipper *n* fast sailing ship

clique *n* small exclusive set; faction, group of people

clitoris *n* part of female genitals

——————— THESAURUS ———————

cid, manifest, obvious, palpable, patent, plain, pronounced, recognizable, unambiguous, unequivocal; empty, free, open, smooth, unhampered, unhindered, unimpeded, unlimited, unobstructed ~*v* clean, erase, purify, refine, sweep away, tidy (up), wipe; absolve, acquit, excuse, exonerate, justify, vindicate; jump, leap, miss, pass over, vault; break up, brighten, clarify, lighten

clearly beyond doubt, distinctly, evidently, obviously, openly, overtly, seemingly, undeniably, undoubtedly

clever able, adroit, apt, astute, brainy Inf, bright, canny, capable, cunning, deep, discerning, expert, gifted, ingenious, intelligent, inventive, keen, knowing, quick, rational, sagacious, sensible, shrewd, skilful, smart, talented, witty

client applicant, buyer, consumer, customer, dependant, habitué, patient, protégé, shopper

clientele clients, customers, following, market, regulars, trade

cliff bluff, crag, escarpment, face, overhang, precipice, rock face, scar, scarp

climate region, temperature, weather

climax acme, apogee, culmination, head, height, highlight, high spot Inf, peak, summit, top, zenith

climb ascend, clamber, mount, rise, scale, shin up, soar, top

cling adhere, be true to, clasp, cleave to, clutch, embrace, fasten, grasp, grip, hug, stick, twine round

clip¹ crop, curtail, cut, cut short, dock, pare, prune, shear, shorten, snip, trim

clip² *v* attach, fasten, fix, hold, pin,

clitoral *adj*

cloak *n/v* (cover with) loose outer garment; disguise **cloakroom** *n*

clobber *v Inf* beat, batter

clock *n* instrument for measuring time **clockwise** *adv/adj* in the direction that the hands of a clock rotate **clockwork** *n* wind-up mechanism for clocks, toys etc.

clod *n* lump of earth

clog *v* **clogging**, **clogged** hamper, impede, choke up ~*n* wooden-soled shoe

cloister *n* covered pillared arcade; monastery or convent **cloistered** *adj* secluded

clone *n* cells of same genetic constitution as another, derived by asexual reproduction; *Inf* lookalike ~*v* replicate

close¹ *adj* near; compact; crowded; intimate; almost equal; careful, searching; confined; secret; unventilated; niggardly; restricted ~*adv* nearly; tightly **closely** *adv* **close-up** *n* close view

close² *v* shut; stop up; prevent access to; finish; come together; grapple ~*n* end; shut-in place; precinct of cathedral **closure** *n*

closet *n* small private room; *US* cupboard ~*adj* secret ~*v* **closeting**, **closeted** shut away in private

clot *n* mass or lump (of blood); *Inf* fool ~*v* **clotting**, **clotted** (cause to) form into lumps

cloth *n* woven fabric **clothe** *v* **clothing**, **clothed** *or* **clad** put clothes on **clothes** *pl n* dress; bed coverings **clothing** *n*

cloud *n* vapour floating in air; state of gloom ~*v* darken; become cloudy **cloudy** *adj*

clout *n Inf* blow; influence, power ~*v* strike

———— THESAURUS ————

staple

cloak *n* blind, cape, coat, cover, front, mantle, mask, pretext, shield, wrap ~*v* camouflage, conceal, cover, disguise, hide, mask, obscure, screen, veil

clog block, bung, burden, congest, dam up, hamper, hinder, impede, jam, obstruct, occlude, shackle, stop up

close¹ adjacent, adjoining, approaching, at hand, handy, hard by, imminent, impending, near, nearby, neighbouring, nigh, upcoming; compact, congested, cramped, cropped, crowded, dense, impenetrable, jampacked, packed, short, solid, thick, tight; attached, confidential, dear, devoted, familiar, inseparable, intimate, loving; airless, heavy, humid, muggy, oppressive, stale, stifling, stuffy, suffocating, sweltering, thick

close² *v* bar, block, choke, clog, confine, cork, fill, lock, obstruct, plug, seal, secure, shut, shut up, stop up; axe *Inf*, cease, complete, conclude, discontinue, end, finish, shut down, terminate, wind up ~*n* cessation, completion, conclusion, culmination, denouement, end, ending, finale, finish, termination

cloth dry goods, fabric, material, stuff, textiles

clothe attire, dress, fit out, outfit, rig, robe

clothes, clothing attire, costume, dress, ensemble, garb, garments, gear *Inf*, get-up *Inf*, habits, outfit, togs *Inf*, wardrobe, wear

cloud *n* billow, darkness, fog, gloom, haze, mist, murk, obscurity, vapour ~*v* darken, dim, eclipse, obscure, overcast, overshadow, shade, shadow, veil

cloudy blurred, confused, dark, dim, dismal, dull, dusky, gloomy, hazy, leaden, muddy, murky, overcast, sombre, sullen, sunless

clove *n* pungent spice

clover *n* forage plant

clown *n* circus comic

club *n* thick stick; bat; association; suit at cards ~*v* **clubbing, clubbed** strike; join

cluck *v/n* (make) noise of hen

clue *n* indication, esp. of solution of mystery or puzzle **clueless** *adj* stupid

clump[1] *n* cluster of plants

clump[2] *v/n* (move with) heavy tread

clumsy *adj* awkward **clumsily** *adv* **clumsiness** *n*

cluster *n/v* group, bunch

clutch *v* grasp eagerly; snatch (at) ~*n* grasp, tight grip; device enabling two revolving shafts to be (dis)connected at will

clutter *v* cause obstruction, disorder ~*n* disordered mass

cm centimetre

Co. Company; County

co- *comb. form* together, jointly, as in

coproduction

c/o care of; carried over

coach *n* long-distance bus; large four-wheeled carriage; railway carriage; tutor, instructor ~*v* instruct

coagulate *v* curdle, clot

coal *n* mineral used as fuel; glowing ember

coalesce *v* unite

coalition *n* alliance

coarse *adj* rough; unrefined; indecent **coarsely** *adv* **coarseness** *n*

coast *n* sea shore ~*v* move under momentum **coastal** *adj* **coaster** *n* small ship; small mat

coat *n* sleeved outer garment; animal's fur; covering layer ~*v* cover **coating** *n* covering layer

coax *v* persuade

cob *n* short-legged stout horse; male swan; head of corn

cobalt *n* metallic element; blue pigment from it

———————————— THESAURUS ————————————

clown *n* buffoon, comedian, dolt, fool, harlequin, jester, joker, pierrot, prankster

club bat, bludgeon, cosh *Brit*, cudgel, stick, truncheon; association, circle, clique, company, fraternity, group, guild, lodge, order, set, society, union

clue evidence, hint, indication, inkling, intimation, lead, pointer, sign, suggestion, suspicion, tip, tip-off, trace

clumsy awkward, blundering, bumbling, bungling, gauche, gawky, heavy, ill-shaped, inept, klutzy *US & Canad sl*, lumbering, maladroit, ponderous, uncoordinated

cluster *n* batch, bunch, clump, collection, gathering, group, knot ~*v* assemble, bunch, collect, flock, gather

clutch catch, clasp, cling to, embrace, grab, grapple, grasp, grip, seize

coach *n* bus, car, carriage, vehicle; instructor, teacher, trainer, tutor ~*v* cram, drill, instruct, prepare, train, tutor

coalition alliance, amalgamation, association, bloc, combination, compact, confederacy, confederation, integration, league, merger, union

coarse boorish, brutish, foulmouthed, gruff, loutish, rough, rude, uncivil

coarseness bawdiness, crudity, indelicacy, poor taste, ribaldry, roughness, smut, uncouthness, unevenness

coast *n* beach, border, coastline, seaside, shore, strand ~*v* cruise, drift, freewheel, get by, glide, sail, taxi

coat *n* fleece, fur, hair, hide, pelt, skin, wool; coating, covering, layer, overlay ~*v* apply, cover, plaster, smear, spread

coax allure, beguile, cajole, decoy, entice, flatter, persuade, prevail upon, soothe, talk into, wheedle

cobble v patch roughly; mend shoes ~n round stone **cobbler** n

cobra n poisonous, hooded snake

cobweb n spider's web

cocaine n addictive narcotic drug used medicinally

cochineal n scarlet dye

cock n male bird, esp. of domestic fowl; tap; hammer of gun ~v draw back to firing position; raise, turn **cockerel** n young cock

cockatoo n crested parrot

cockle n shellfish

cockpit n pilot's seat, compartment in small aircraft

cockroach n insect pest

cocktail n mixed drink of spirits; appetizer

cocky adj conceited, pert

cocoa n powdered seed of cacao tree; drink made from this

coconut n large, hard nut

cocoon n sheath of insect in chrysalis stage

COD cash on delivery

cod n large sea fish

coda n Mus final part of musical composition

code n system of letters, symbols to transmit messages secretly; scheme of conduct; collection of laws **codify** v -**fying**, -**fied**

codeine n pain-killing drug

coerce v compel, force **coercion** n

coexist v exist together **coexistence** n

C of E Church of England

coffee n seeds of tropical shrub; drink made from these

coffer n chest for valuables

coffin n box for corpse

cog n one of series of teeth on rim of wheel **cogwheel** n

cogent adj convincing

cogitate v think, reflect, ponder **cogitation** n

cognac n French brandy

cognizance n knowledge **cognizant** adj

cohabit v live together as husband and wife

cohere v stick together, be consistent **coherent** adj capable of logical speech, thought; connected, making sense **cohesion** n tendency to unite **cohesive** adj

cohort n troop; associate

coiffure n hairstyle

coil v twist into winding shape ~n series of rings; anything coiled

coin n piece of money; money ~v stamp; invent **coinage** n

coincide v happen together **coincidence** n chance happening **coincidental** adj

coke[1] n residue left from distillation of coal, used as fuel

coke[2] n Coca-Cola; Sl cocaine

Col. Colonel

cola n flavoured soft drink

colander n strainer for food

cold adj lacking heat; indifferent, unmoved; unfriendly ~n lack of heat; illness, marked by runny nose etc. **coldly** adv **cold-blooded** adj lacking pity

coleslaw n cabbage salad

——————— T H E S A U R U S ———————

cocky arrogant, brash, cocksure, conceited, lordly, swaggering, vain

code cipher; canon, convention, custom, ethics, etiquette, manners, maxim, rules, system

coil curl, entwine, loop, snake, spiral, twine, twist, wind, wreathe

coincide be concurrent, coexist, synchronize

coincidence accident, chance, eventuality, fluke, luck, stroke of luck

cold adj arctic, biting, bitter, bleak, chill, chilly, cool, freezing, frigid, frosty, frozen, harsh, icy, parky Brit inf, raw, wintry; aloof, distant, frigid, indifferent, reserved, standoffish, un-

colic *n* severe pains in the intestines

collaborate *v* work with another **collaboration** *n* **collaborator** *n*

collage *n* (artistic) composition of bits and pieces stuck together on background

collapse *v* fall; fail ~*n* act of collapsing; breakdown **collapsible** *adj*

collar *n* band, part of garment, worn round neck ~*v* seize **collarbone** *n* bone joining shoulder blade to breast bone

collate *v* compare carefully

collateral *n* security pledged for loan

colleague *n* fellow worker

collect *v* gather, bring, come together **collected** *adj* calm **collection** *n* **collective** *n* factory, farm etc. owned by its workers ~*adj* shared **collectively** *adv* **collector** *n*

college *n* place of higher education **collegiate** *adj*

collide *v* crash together **collision** *n*

collie *n* breed of sheepdog

colliery *n* coal mine

colloquial *adj* pert. to, or used in, informal conversation **colloquialism** *n*

collusion *n* secret agreement for a fraudulent purpose **collude** *v*

cologne *n* perfumed liquid

colon[1] *n* mark (:) indicating break in a sentence

colon[2] *n* part of large intestine

colonel *n* commander of regiment or battalion

colonnade *n* row of columns

colony *n* body of people who settle in new country; country so settled **colonial** *adj* **colonist** *n* **colonize** *v* **colonization** *n*

colossal *adj* huge, gigantic

colour *n* hue, tint; complexion; paint; pigment; *Fig* semblance, pretext; timbre, quality; *pl* flag; *Sport* distinguishing badge, symbol ~*v* stain, paint; disguise; influence or distort; blush **colourful** *adj* bright; interesting **colourless** *adj* **colour-blind** *adj* unable to distinguish between certain colours

colt *n* young male horse

——————— THESAURUS ———————

feeling, unmoved ~*n* chill, chilliness, coldness, frigidity, frostiness, iciness, inclemency

collaborate cooperate, join forces, participate, team up, work together

collaborator associate, colleague, confederate, co-worker, partner, team-mate

collapse *v* break down, cave in, come to nothing, crumple, fail, faint, fall, fold, founder, give way, subside ~*n* breakdown, cave-in, disintegration, downfall, exhaustion, failure, faint

colleague ally, assistant, associate, auxiliary, collaborator, companion, comrade, fellow worker, helper, partner, team-mate, workmate

collect accumulate, amass, assemble, gather, heap, hoard, save, stockpile; assemble, congregate, convene, converge, rally

collected calm, composed, cool, placid, poised, self-possessed, serene, unfazed *Inf*, unruffled

collection accumulation, anthology, compilation, heap, hoard, mass, pile, set, stockpile, store; assembly, assortment, cluster, company, crowd, gathering, group

collide clash, conflict, crash, meet head-on

collision accident, bump, crash, impact, pile-up *Inf*, smash

colony community, outpost, province, settlement, territory

colour *n* complexion, dye, hue, paint, pigment, shade, tincture, tinge, tint ~*v* dye, paint, stain, tinge, tint; disguise, distort, embroider, falsify, garble, gloss over, misrepresent, pervert, prejudice, slant, taint; blush, burn, crimson, flush, go crimson, redden

columbine *n* garden flower

column *n* long vertical pillar; division of page; body of troops **columnist** *n* journalist writing regular feature

coma *n* unconsciousness **comatose** *adj*

comb *n* toothed instrument for tidying hair; cock's crest; mass of honey cells ~*v* use comb on; search

combat *v/n* fight, contest **combatant** *n* **combative** *adj*

combine *v* join together ~*n* syndicate, esp. of businesses **combination** *n* **combine harvester** machine to harvest and thresh grain

combustion *n* process of burning **combustible** *adj*

come *v* **coming, came, come** approach, arrive, move towards; reach; occur; originate (from); become **comeback** *n Inf* return to active life; retort **comedown** *n* decline in status; disappointment **comeuppance** *n Inf* deserved punishment

comedy *n* light, amusing play; humour **comedian** *n* (*fem* **comedienne**) entertainer who tells jokes

comely *adj* good-looking

comet *n* luminous heavenly body

comfort *n* ease; (means of) consolation ~*v* soothe; console **comfortable** *adj* giving comfort; well-off **comfortably** *adv* **comforter** *n*

comic *adj* relating to comedy; funny

————————— THESAURUS —————————

colourful bright, brilliant, intense, motley, multicoloured, rich, variegated, vivid; characterful, distinctive, graphic, interesting, lively, picturesque, rich, stimulating, unusual, vivid

colourless characterless, dreary, insipid, lacklustre, tame, uninteresting, vapid

column; pillar, post, shaft, support, upright; cavalcade, file, line, list, procession, queue, rank, row, string, train

coma insensibility, oblivion, somnolence, stupor, trance, unconsciousness

comb *v* dress, groom, untangle; hunt, rake, ransack, rummage, scour, screen, search, sift, sweep

combat action, battle, conflict, contest, encounter, engagement, fight, skirmish, struggle, war, warfare

combination amalgam, blend, coalescence, composite, meld, mix, mixture

combine amalgamate, bind, blend, bond, compound, connect, cooperate, fuse, incorporate, integrate, join (together), link, marry, meld, merge, mix, pool, unify, unite

come advance, appear, approach, arrive, become, draw near, enter, happen, materialize, move, move towards, near, occur, originate, turn out, turn up *Inf*; appear, arrive, attain, enter, materialize, reach, show up *Inf*, turn up *Inf*; fall, happen, occur, take place; arise, emanate, emerge, end up, flow, issue, originate, result, turn out

comeback rally, rebound, recovery, resurgence, return, revival, triumph

comedown anticlimax, blow, decline, demotion, disappointment, humiliation, reverse

comedy chaffing, drollery, facetiousness, farce, fun, hilarity, humour, jesting, joking, slapstick, witticisms

comfort *n* cosiness, creature comforts, ease, luxury, wellbeing; aid, alleviation, cheer, consolation, ease, encouragement, help, relief, succour, support ~*v* cheer, commiserate with, console, encourage, gladden, hearten, reassure, relieve, solace, soothe

comfortable agreeable, ample, commodious, convenient, cosy, delightful, easy, enjoyable, homely, loose,

~*n* comedian; magazine of strip cartoons **comical** *adj*

comma *n* punctuation mark (,)

command *v* order; rule; compel; have in one's power ~*n* order; power of controlling; mastery; post of one commanding; jurisdiction **commandant** *n* **commandeer** *v* seize for military use **commander** *n* **commandment** *n*

commando *n* (*pl* **-dos**) (member of) special military unit

commemorate *v* keep in memory by ceremony **commemoration** *n* **commemorative** *adj*

commence *v* begin

commend *v* praise; entrust **commendable** *adj* **commendation** *n*

commensurate *adj* equal; in proportion

comment *n/v* remark; gossip; note **commentary** *n* explanatory notes; spoken accompaniment to film etc. **commentate** *v* **commentator** *n*

commerce *n* trade **commercial** *adj* of business, trade etc. ~*n* advertisement, esp. on radio or television

commiserate *v* sympathize with **commiseration** *n*

commission *n* authority; (body entrusted with) some special duty; agent's payment by percentage; document appointing to officer's rank; committing ~*v* charge with duty; *Mil* confer a rank; give order for **commissioner** *n*

commissionaire *n* uniformed doorman

———————— THESAURUS ————————

pleasant, relaxing, restful, roomy, snug; affluent, prosperous, well-off, well-to-do

comic *adj* amusing, comical, droll, facetious, farcical, funny, humorous, joking, light, witty

command *v* bid, charge, compel, demand, direct, enjoin, order, require; administer, control, dominate, govern, handle, head, lead, manage, reign over, rule, supervise, sway ~*n* behest, bidding, decree, direction, directive, edict, fiat, injunction, instruction, mandate, order, precept, requirement

commander boss, captain, chief, C in C, C.O., commanding officer, director, head, leader, officer, ruler

commemorate celebrate, honour, immortalize, keep, observe, pay tribute to, remember, salute

commemoration ceremony, honouring, memorial service, observance, remembrance, tribute

commence begin, embark on, enter upon, initiate, open, originate, start

commend acclaim, applaud, approve, compliment, eulogize, extol, praise, recommend

comment *n* observation, remark, statement; commentary, criticism, elucidation, explanation, exposition, note ~*v* mention, note, observe, opine, point out, remark, say, utter

commentary analysis, critique, description, exegesis, explanation, narration, notes, review, treatise, voiceover

commentator reporter, sportscaster; annotator, critic, expositor, interpreter, scholiast

commerce business, dealing, exchange, trade, traffic

commercial business, mercantile, sales, trade, trading

commission *n* appointment, authority, charge, duty, employment, errand, function, mandate, mission, task, trust, warrant; board, committee, delegation, deputation, representative; allowance, cut, fee, percentage, royalties ~*v* appoint, authorize, contract, delegate, depute, empower, engage, nominate, order, se-

commit v -mitting, -mitted give in charge; be guilty of; pledge; send for trial **commitment** n **committal** n

committee n body appointed, elected for special business

commode n chest of drawers; stool containing chamber pot

commodity n article of trade

commodore n senior naval or air officer; president of yacht club

common adj shared by all; public; ordinary; inferior ~n land belonging to community; pl ordinary people; (with cap.) House of Commons **commoner** n one not of the nobility **commonly** adv **commonplace** adj ordinary ~n trite remark **commonwealth** n republic; (with cap.) federation of self-governing states

commotion n stir, disturbance

commune[1] v converse intimately **communion** n sharing of thoughts, feelings etc.; (with cap.) (participa-

tion in) sacrament of the Lord's Supper

commune[2] n group living together and sharing property, responsibility etc. **communal** adj for common use

communicate v impart, convey; reveal ~v give or exchange information; have connecting door **communicable** adj **communication** n giving information; message; (usu. pl) means of exchanging messages **communicative** adj willing to talk

communiqué n official announcement

communism n doctrine that all means of production etc. should be property of community **communist** n/adj

community n body of people living in one district; the public; joint ownership; similarity

commute v travel daily some distance to work; exchange; reduce

lect, send

commit carry out, do, enact, execute, perform, perpetrate

commitment duty, engagement, liability, obligation, responsibility, tie; assurance, guarantee, pledge, promise, undertaking, vow, word

common accepted, general, popular, prevailing, universal, widespread; average, conventional, customary, daily, everyday, familiar, frequent, general, humdrum, obscure, ordinary, plain, regular, routine, run-of-the-mill, simple, standard, stock, usual, workaday; coarse, hackneyed, inferior, low, pedestrian, plebeian, stale, trite, undistinguished, vulgar

commotion ado, agitation, bustle, disorder, disturbance, excitement, ferment, furore, fuss, hubbub, racket, riot, rumpus, to-do, tumult, turmoil, upheaval, uproar

communal collective, community,

general, joint, public, shared

commune n collective, community, cooperative, kibbutz

communicate acquaint, announce, be in contact, be in touch, connect, convey, correspond, declare, disclose, divulge, impart, inform, make known, pass on, phone, proclaim, publish, report, reveal, ring up Inf, chiefly Brit, signify, spread, transmit, unfold

communication connection, contact, conversation, correspondence, link, transmission; disclosure, dispatch, information, intelligence, message, news, report, statement, word

communism Bolshevism, collectivism, Marxism, socialism, state socialism

community association, body politic, brotherhood, commonwealth, company, district, general public, locality, people, populace, population,

(punishment) **commuter** n

compact[1] adj closely packed; solid; terse ~v make, become compact **compact disc** small audio disc played by laser

compact[2] n small case to hold face powder etc.

compact[3] n agreement

companion n comrade

company n gathering of persons; companionship; guests; business firm; division of regiment

compare v notice likenesses and differences; liken; be like; compete with **comparability** n **comparable** adj **comparative** adj relative; *Grammar* denoting form of adjective, adverb meaning *more* **comparison** n act of comparing

compartment n part divided off

compass n instrument for showing north; (*usu. pl*) instrument for drawing circles; scope ~v surround; comprehend; attain

compassion n pity, sympathy **compassionate** adj

compatible adj agreeing with **compatibility** n

compatriot n fellow countryman

compel v **-pelling, -pelled** force

compendium n (*pl* **-diums, -dia**) collection of different games; summary **compendious** adj brief but inclusive

compensate v make up for; recompense **compensation** n

compere n one who introduces cabaret, television shows etc. ~v act as compere

———————— T H E S A U R U S ————————

public, residents, society, state

compact close, compressed, condensed, dense, firm, impenetrable, impermeable, pressed together, solid, thick; brief, concise, epigrammatic, laconic, pithy, pointed, succinct, terse, to the point

companion accomplice, ally, associate, colleague, comrade, confederate, consort, crony, friend, partner

company assemblage, assembly, band, body, circle, collection, convention, coterie, crew, crowd, ensemble, gathering, group, league, party, set, throng, troop, troupe, turnout; association, business, concern, corporation, establishment, firm, house, partnership, syndicate

comparable a match for, as good as, commensurate, equal, equivalent, in a class with, on a par, proportionate, tantamount; akin, alike, corresponding, related, similar

compare (*with* **with**) balance, collate, contrast, juxtapose, set against, weigh

comparison contrast, distinction,

juxtaposition

compartment alcove, bay, berth, booth, carriage, cell, chamber, cubicle, locker, niche, pigeonhole, section

compassion commiseration, condolence, fellow feeling, heart, humanity, kindness, mercy, pity, softheartedness, sorrow, sympathy, tenderness

compatible accordant, adaptable, agreeable, congenial, congruent, congruous, consistent, consonant, harmonious, in harmony, in keeping, like-minded, reconcilable, suitable

compel coerce, constrain, dragoon, drive, enforce, exact, force, impel, make, oblige, railroad *Inf,* restrain, squeeze, urge

compensate balance, cancel (out), counteract, make up for, offset, redress; atone, indemnify, make good, make restitution, recompense, refund, reimburse, remunerate, repay, requite, reward, satisfy

compensation amends, atonement, damages, indemnity, payment, remuneration, reparation, restitution, re-

compete v (oft. with **with**) strive in rivalry, contend for **competition** n rivalry; contest **competitive** adj **competitor** n

competent adj able; properly qualified; sufficient **competence** n

compile v make up from various sources **compilation** n

complacent adj self-satisfied **complacency** n

complain v grumble; make known a grievance; (with **of**) make known that one is suffering from **complaint** n grievance; illness

complement n something making up a whole; complete amount ~v add to, make complete **complementary** adj

complete adj perfect; ended; entire; thorough ~v make whole; finish **completely** adv **completion** n

complex adj intricate, compound, involved ~n group of related buildings; obsession **complexity** n

complexion n look, colour of skin, esp. of face; aspect, character

complicate v make involved, difficult **complication** n

———————— THESAURUS ————————

ward, satisfaction

compete be in the running, challenge, contend, contest, emulate, fight, pit oneself against, rival, strive, struggle, vie

competent able, adapted, appropriate, capable, clever, equal, fit, proficient, qualified, sufficient, suitable

competition contention, contest, emulation, opposition, rivalry, strife, struggle; championship, contest, event, head-to-head, puzzle, quiz, tournament

competitive aggressive, ambitious, antagonistic, at odds, combative, cutthroat, dog-eat-dog, opposing, rival, vying

competitor adversary, antagonist, challenger, competition, contestant, opponent, opposition, rival

compile amass, collect, cull, garner, gather, organize, put together

complacent contented, gratified, pleased, satisfied, self-assured, selfrighteous, self-satisfied, serene, smug, unconcerned

complain bemoan, bewail, bleat, carp, contend, deplore, find fault, fuss, grieve, groan, grouch Inf, grouse, growl, grumble, lament, moan, whine, whinge Inf

complaint accusation, annoyance,

charge, criticism, dissatisfaction, fault-finding, grievance, grouch Inf, grouse, grumble, lament, moan, plaint, protest, remonstrance, trouble, wail; affliction, ailment, disease, disorder, illness, malady, sickness

complete adj accomplished, concluded, ended, finished; all, entire, full, intact, integral, unabridged, unbroken, undivided, whole; consummate, deep-dyed usu. derog, perfect, thorough, total, utter ~v accomplish, achieve, cap, close, conclude, crown, discharge, do, end, execute, fill in, finalize, finish, fulfil, perfect, perform, realize, round off, settle, terminate, wrap up Inf

completely absolutely, altogether, en masse, entirely, from beginning to end, fully, heart and soul, in full, in toto, perfectly, quite, solidly, thoroughly, totally, utterly, wholly

complex circuitous, complicated, intricate, involved, knotty, labyrinthine, mingled, mixed, tangled, tortuous

complexion colour, colouring, hue, pigmentation, skin, skin tone

complicate confuse, entangle, interweave, involve, make intricate, muddle, snarl up

complication complexity, confusion,

complicity *n* partnership in wrong-doing

compliment *n/v* praise **complimentary** *adj* expressing praise; free of charge

comply *v* **complying, complied** do as asked **compliance** *n* **compliant** *adj*

component *n* part, constituent of whole

compose *v* put in order; write, invent; make up; calm **composer** *n* one who composes, esp. music **composite** *adj* made up of distinct parts **composition** *n* **composure** *n* calmness

compos mentis *Lat* sane

compost *n* decayed vegetable matter for fertilizing soil

compound¹ *n* substance, word, made up of parts ~*adj* not simple; composite ~*v* mix, make up; make worse; compromise

compound² *n* enclosure containing houses etc.

comprehend *v* understand; include **comprehensible** *adj* **comprehension** *n* **comprehensive** *adj* taking in much; pert. to education of children of all abilities

compress *v* squeeze together; make smaller ~*n* pad of lint applied to wound, inflamed part etc. **compressible** *adj* **compression** *n* **compressor** *n*

comprise *v* include, contain

———————— T H E S A U R U S ————————

entanglement, intricacy, mixture, web

compliment *n* admiration, bouquet, commendation, congratulations, courtesy, eulogy, favour, flattery, honour, praise, tribute ~*v* commend, congratulate, extol, felicitate, flatter, laud, pay tribute to, praise, salute

complimentary appreciative, approving, commendatory, congratulatory, eulogistic, flattering, panegyrical; courtesy, free, free of charge, giveaway, gratis, gratuitous

comply accede, accord, acquiesce, adhere to, agree to, conform to, consent to, discharge, follow, fulfil, obey, observe, perform, respect, satisfy

component constituent, element, ingredient, item, part, piece, unit

compose build, compound, comprise, constitute, construct, fashion, form, make, make up, put together

composition arrangement, configuration, constitution, design, form, formation, layout, make-up, structure; creation, essay, exercise, literary work, opus, piece, study, treatise, work, writing

composure aplomb, calm, calmness,

collectedness, coolness, dignity, ease, equanimity, placidity, poise, sedateness, self-assurance, self-possession, serenity, tranquillity

compound *n* alloy, amalgam, blend, combination, composite, composition, conglomerate, fusion, medley, meld, mixture, synthesis ~*adj* complex, composite, conglomerate, intricate, multiple, not simple ~*v* amalgamate, blend, coalesce, combine, concoct, fuse, intermingle, meld, mingle, mix, synthesize, unite

comprehend assimilate, conceive, discern, fathom, grasp, know, make out, perceive, see, take in, understand

comprehension discernment, grasp, intelligence, judgment, knowledge, perception, realization, sense, understanding

comprehensive all-embracing, all-inclusive, blanket, broad, catholic, complete, encyclopedic, exhaustive, extensive, full, inclusive, sweeping, thorough, umbrella, wide

compress compact, concentrate, condense, constrict, cram, crowd, crush, press, shorten, summarize

compromise *n* coming to terms by giving up part of claim ~*v* settle by making concessions; expose to suspicion

compulsion *n* act of compelling; urge **compulsive** *adj* **compulsory** *adj* not optional

compunction *n* regret

compute *v* calculate **computation** *n*

computer *n* electronic machine for processing information **computerize** *v*

comrade *n* friend

con[1] *v* **conning, conned** *Inf* swindle

con[2] *n* vote against

concave *adj* rounded inwards

conceal *v* hide **concealment** *n*

concede *v* admit truth of; give up

conceit *n* vanity **conceited** *adj*

conceive *v* believe; become pregnant; devise **conceivable** *adj*

concentrate *v* focus (one's efforts etc.); increase in strength; devote all attention ~*n* concentrated substance **concentration** *n*

concentric *adj* having the same centre

concept *n* abstract idea **conceptual** *adj*

conception *n* idea, notion; act of conceiving

concern *v* relate to; worry; (*with* **in** or **with**) involve (oneself) ~*n* affair; worry; business, enterprise **concerned** *adj* worried; involved **concerning** *prep* about

——— THESAURUS ———

comprise be composed of, consist of, contain, embrace, encompass, include, take in

compromise *n* accommodation, accord, adjustment, agreement, concession, give-and-take, settlement, trade-off ~*v* adjust, agree, concede, give and take, go fifty-fifty *Inf*, meet halfway, settle, strike a balance

compulsive compelling, driving, irresistible, obsessive, uncontrollable, urgent

compulsory binding, forced, imperative, mandatory, required, requisite

comrade ally, associate, colleague, companion, confederate, crony, fellow, friend, partner

concave cupped, depressed, excavated, hollowed, indented, sunken

conceal bury, cover, disguise, dissemble, hide, keep dark, keep secret, mask, obscure, screen, secrete, shelter, stash *Inf*

concede acknowledge, admit, allow, confess, grant, own; cede, give up, hand over, surrender, yield

conceit arrogance, complacency, egotism, narcissism, pride, swagger, vainglory, vanity

conceited arrogant, cocky, egotistical, immodest, overweening, puffed up, self-important, swollen-headed, vain

conceivable believable, credible, imaginable, possible, thinkable

conceive apprehend, believe, comprehend, envisage, fancy, grasp, imagine, realize, suppose, understand; create, design, devise, form, formulate, produce, project, purpose, think up

concentrate consider closely, focus attention on, put one's mind to, rack one's brains

concept hypothesis, idea, image, impression, notion, theory, view

concern *v* affect, apply to, bear on, be relevant to, interest, involve, pertain to, regard, touch; bother, disquiet, distress, disturb, make anxious, make uneasy, perturb, trouble, worry ~*n* affair, business, charge, field, interest, involvement, job, matter, mission, responsibility, task; anxiety, attention, burden, care, consideration, disquiet, distress, heed, responsibil-

concert *n* musical entertainment; agreement **concerted** *adj* mutually planned **concertina** *n* musical instrument with bellows **concerto** *n* (*pl* -tos, -ti) composition for solo instrument and orchestra

concession *n* act of conceding; thing conceded

conch *n* seashell

conciliate *v* win over from hostility **conciliation** *n* **conciliatory** *adj*

concise *adj* brief, terse

conclave *n* private meeting

conclude *v* finish; deduce; settle; decide **conclusion** *n* **conclusive** *adj* decisive

concoct *v* make mixture; contrive **concoction** *n*

concord *n* agreement; harmony

concourse *n* crowd; large, open place in public area

concrete *n* mixture of sand, cement etc. ~*adj* specific; actual; solid

concubine *n* woman cohabiting with man; secondary wife

concur *v* -curring, -curred agree; happen together **concurrent** *adj* **concurrently** *adv*

concussion *n* brain injury

condemn *v* blame; find guilty; doom; declare unfit **condemnation** *n*

condense *v* concentrate; turn from gas to liquid **condensation** *n*

condescend *v* treat graciously one regarded as inferior; stoop **condescension** *n*

———— THESAURUS ————

ity, solicitude, worry; business, company, enterprise, establishment, firm, house, organization

concerned anxious, bothered, distressed, disturbed, exercised, troubled, uneasy, upset, worried; active, implicated, interested, involved, mixed up, privy to

concerning about, apropos of, as regards, as to, in the matter of, on the subject of, re, regarding, relating to, respecting, touching, with reference to

conciliate appease, disarm, mediate, mollify, pacify, placate, propitiate, reconcile, restore harmony, soothe, win over

concise brief, compact, compressed, condensed, laconic, pithy, short, succinct, summary, terse, to the point

conclude cease, close, come to an end, complete, end, finish, round off, terminate; assume, decide, deduce, gather, infer, judge, suppose, surmise

conclusion close, completion, end, finale, finish, result; agreement, conviction, decision, deduction, inference, judgment, opinion, resolution,

settlement, verdict

conclusive clinching, convincing, decisive, definite, definitive, final, irrefutable, ultimate, unanswerable

concoction blend, brew, compound, creation, mixture, preparation

concrete *adj* actual, definite, explicit, factual, material, real, sensible, specific, substantial, tangible

concur accord, acquiesce, agree, approve, assent, coincide, combine, consent, cooperate, harmonize, join

condemn blame, censure, damn, denounce, disapprove, reproach, reprove, upbraid; convict, damn, doom, proscribe, sentence

condemnation blame, censure, denouncement, denunciation, disapproval, reproach, reprobation, reproof, stricture; conviction, damnation, doom, judgment, proscription, sentence

condense abridge, compact, compress, concentrate, contract, curtail, epitomize, précis, shorten, summarize

condescend patronize, talk down to; bend, deign, lower oneself, see fit,

condiment *n* seasoning for food

condition *n* state or circumstances; thing on which something else depends; prerequisite; physical fitness ~*v* accustom; regulate; make fit **conditional** *adj* dependent on events **conditioner** *n* liquid to make hair or clothes feel softer

condolence *n* sympathy

condom *n* sheathlike rubber contraceptive worn by man

condone *v* overlook, forgive

conducive *adj* leading (to)

conduct *n* behaviour; management ~*v* guide; direct; manage; transmit (heat etc.) **conduction** *n* **conductor** *n* person in charge of bus etc.; director of orchestra; substance capable of transmitting heat etc.

conduit *n* channel or pipe for water, cables etc.

cone *n* tapering figure with circular base; fruit of pine, fir etc. **conical** *adj*

confectionery *n* sweets, cakes etc. **confectioner** *n*

confederate *n* ally; accomplice ~*v* unite **confederation** *n* alliance of political units

confer *v* -ferring, -ferred grant; talk with **conference** *n* meeting for consultation

confess *v* admit; declare one's sins orally to priest **confession** *n* **confessional** *n* confessor's box **confessor** *n* priest who hears confessions

confetti *pl n* bits of coloured paper thrown at weddings

confide *v* (*with*) tell secrets; entrust **confidence** *n* trust; assurance; intimacy; secret **confident** *adj* certain; self-assured **confidential** *adj* private; secret

——————— THESAURUS ———————

stoop, submit, unbend *Inf*

condition *n* case, circumstances, plight, position, predicament, shape, situation, state, state of affairs, *status quo*; arrangement, article, demand, limitation, modification, prerequisite, provision, proviso, qualification, requirement, requisite, restriction, rider, rule, stipulation, terms; fettle, fitness, health, kilter, order, shape, state of health, trim ~*v* accustom, adapt, educate, equip, habituate, inure, make ready, prepare, ready, tone up, train, work out

conditional contingent, dependent, limited, provisional, qualified, subject to, with reservations

conduct *n* attitude, bearing, behaviour, carriage, comportment, demeanour, deportment, manners, mien *Lit,* ways; administration, control, direction, guidance, leadership, management, organization, running, supervision ~*v* administer, carry on, control, direct, govern, handle, lead,

manage, organize, preside over, regulate, run, supervise

confer consult, converse, deliberate, discourse, parley, talk

conference congress, consultation, convention, convocation, discussion, forum, meeting, seminar, symposium, teach-in

confess acknowledge, admit, allow, concede, confide, disclose, divulge, grant, own, own up, recognize; reveal

confession acknowledgment, admission, avowal, disclosure, revelation

confide admit, breathe, confess, disclose, divulge, impart, reveal, whisper

confidence belief, credence, dependence, faith, reliance, trust; aplomb, assurance, boldness, courage, firmness, nerve, self-possession, self-reliance

confident certain, convinced, counting on, positive, satisfied, secure, sure; assured, bold, dauntless, fearless, self-assured, self-reliant

configuration n shape

confine v keep within bounds; shut up **confines** pl n limits **confinement** n being confined; childbirth

confirm v make sure; strengthen; make valid; admit as member of church **confirmation** n **confirmed** adj long-established

confiscate v seize by authority **confiscation** n

conflict n struggle; disagreement ~v be at odds with; clash

conform v comply with accepted standards etc.; adapt to rule, pattern, custom etc. **conformist** n **conformity** n

confound v perplex; confuse **confounded** adj Inf damned

confront v face; bring face to face with **confrontation** n

confuse v bewilder; jumble; make unclear; mistake **confusion** n

conga n dance by people in single file; large drum

congeal v solidify

congenial adj pleasant

congenital adj existing at birth; dating from birth

conger n sea eel

congest v overcrowd or clog **congestion** n

conglomerate n substance com-

──────── T H E S A U R U S ────────

confidential classified, intimate, off the record, private, privy, secret

confine bind, bound, cage, enclose, hem in, hold back, imprison, incarcerate, intern, keep, limit, repress, restrain, restrict, shut up, straiten

confirm assure, buttress, clinch, establish, fix, fortify, reinforce, settle, strengthen; approve, authenticate, bear out, corroborate, endorse, ratify, sanction, substantiate, validate, verify

confirmation evidence, proof, substantiation, testimony, verification; acceptance, agreement, approval, assent, endorsement, ratification, sanction

confirmed chronic, habitual, hardened, ingrained, inured, inveterate, long-established, rooted, seasoned

conflict n battle, clash, combat, contention, contest, encounter, engagement, fight, head-to-head, strife, struggle, war, warfare; antagonism, bad blood, difference, disagreement, discord, dissension, friction, hostility, interference, opposition, strife, variance ~v be at variance, clash, collide, combat, contend, contest, differ, disagree, fight, interfere, strive, struggle

conform adapt, adjust, comply, fall in

with, follow, follow the crowd, obey, run with the pack, yield

conformity allegiance, compliance, observance, orthodoxy

confound amaze, astonish, astound, baffle, bewilder, confuse, dumbfound, flummox, mix up, mystify, nonplus, perplex, startle, surprise

confrontation conflict, contest, crisis, encounter, head-to-head, set-to Inf, showdown Inf

confuse baffle, bemuse, bewilder, flummox, mystify, nonplus, obscure, perplex, puzzle

confusion bemusement, bewilderment, mystification, perplexity, puzzlement; bustle, chaos, clutter, commotion, disarrangement, disorder, disorganization, hodgepodge US, hotchpotch, jumble, mess, muddle, pig's breakfast Inf, shambles, tangle, turmoil, untidiness, upheaval

congenial adapted, affable, agreeable, compatible, favourable, fit, friendly, genial, kindly, kindred, like-minded, pleasant, pleasing, suitable, sympathetic, well-suited

congestion bottleneck, clogging, crowding, jam, mass, overcrowding, surfeit

posed of smaller elements; business organization comprising many companies **conglomeration** *n*

congratulate *v* express pleasure at good fortune, success etc. **congratulations** *pl n*

congregate *v* assemble; flock together **congregation** *n* assembly, esp. for worship

congress *n* formal assembly; legislative body

conifer *n* cone-bearing tree **coniferous** *adj*

conjecture *n/v* guess **conjectural** *adj*

conjugal *adj* of marriage

conjugate *v Grammar* inflect verb in its various forms **conjugation** *n*

conjunction *n* union; simultaneous happening; part of speech joining words, phrases etc. **conjunctive** *adj*

conjunctivitis *n* inflammation of membrane of eye

conjure *v* produce magic effects; perform tricks **conjuror, -er** *n*

conker *n Inf* horse chestnut

connect *v* join together, unite; associate in the mind **connection, connexion** *n* association; connecting thing; relation

connive *v* conspire

connoisseur *n* expert in fine arts

connote *v* imply, mean in addition **connotation** *n*

conquer *v* overcome; defeat; be victorious **conqueror** *n* **conquest** *n*

conscience *n* sense of right or wrong **conscientious** *adj*

conscious *adj* aware; awake; intentional **consciousness** *n*

conscript *n* one compulsorily enlisted for military service ~*v* enlist thus **conscription** *n*

consecrate *v* make sacred **consecration** *n*

———— THESAURUS ————

congratulate compliment, felicitate

congratulations best wishes, compliments, felicitations, good wishes, greetings

congregate assemble, collect, come together, convene, converge, convoke, flock, forgather, gather, mass, meet, muster, rally, rendezvous, throng

congregation assembly, brethren, crowd, fellowship, flock, host, laity, multitude, parish, parishioners, throng

congress assembly, conclave, conference, convention, convocation, council, delegates, diet, house, legislature, meeting, parliament, representatives

connect affix, ally, cohere, combine, couple, fasten, join, link, relate, unite

connoisseur aficionado, arbiter, authority, buff *Inf*, devotee, expert, judge, savant, specialist

conquer beat, crush, defeat, get the

better of, humble, master, overcome, overpower, overthrow, quell, rout, subdue, triumph, vanquish

conqueror champion, hero, lord, master, vanquisher, victor, winner

conquest annexation, appropriation, coup, invasion, occupation, subjection, takeover; defeat, discomfiture, mastery, overthrow, rout, triumph, victory

conscience moral sense, principles, scruples, still small voice

conscientious careful, diligent, exact, faithful, meticulous, painstaking, particular, punctilious, thorough

conscious alert, alive to, awake, aware, clued-up *Inf*, cognizant, percipient, responsive, sensible, sentient, wise to *Sl*; calculated, deliberate, intentional, knowing, premeditated, studied, wilful

consciousness apprehension, attention, awareness, knowledge, realization, recognition, sensibility

consecutive *adj* in unbroken succession **consecutively** *adv*

consensus *n* widespread agreement

consent *v* agree to ~*n* permission; agreement

consequence *n* result, outcome; importance **consequent** *adj* **consequential** *adj* important **consequently** *adv* therefore

conserve *v* keep from change etc.; preserve ~*n* jam **conservation** *n* protection of environment **conservationist** *n* **conservative** *adj/n* (person) tending to avoid change; moderate (person) **conservatory** *n* greenhouse

consider *v* think over; examine; make allowance for; be of opinion that con-

siderable *adj* important; large **considerably** *adv* **considerate** *adj* thoughtful towards others **consideration** *n* act of considering; recompense **considering** *prep* taking into account

consign *v* hand over; entrust **consignment** *n* goods consigned **consignor** *n*

consist *v* be composed of **consistency** *n* agreement; degree of firmness **consistent** *adj* **consistently** *adv*

console[1] *v* comfort, cheer in distress **consolation** *n*

console[2] *n* bracket; keyboard etc. of organ; cabinet for television, radio etc.

consolidate *v* combine; make firm **consolidation** *n*

———————— T H E S A U R U S ————————

consecrate dedicate, devote, exalt, hallow, ordain, sanctify, set apart

consecutive following, in sequence, in turn, running, sequential, successive, uninterrupted

consent *v* accede, acquiesce, agree, allow, approve, assent, comply, concede, concur, permit, yield ~*n* agreement, approval, assent, compliance, go-ahead *Inf,* O.K. *or* okay *Inf,* permission, sanction

consequent ensuing, following, resultant, resulting, subsequent, successive

conservation custody, economy, maintenance, preservation, protection, safeguarding, safekeeping, saving, upkeep

conservative cautious, conventional, hidebound, reactionary, right-wing, sober, traditional

conserve hoard, husband, keep, nurse, preserve, protect, save, store up, take care of

consider chew over, cogitate, consult, contemplate, deliberate, discuss, meditate, ponder, reflect, revolve, ruminate, study, weigh

considerable important, influential,

noteworthy, renowned, significant; abundant, ample, appreciable, goodly, great, large, lavish, marked, much, plentiful, reasonable, substantial, tidy, tolerable

considerate concerned, discreet, kind, kindly, mindful, obliging, patient, tactful, thoughtful, unselfish

consideration attention, contemplation, deliberation, discussion, examination, perusal, reflection, regard, review, scrutiny, study, thought

considering all in all, in the light of, in view of

consignment batch, delivery, goods, shipment

consist (*with* **of**) amount to, be composed of, be made up of, comprise, contain, embody, include, incorporate, involve

consistent constant, dependable, regular, steady, true to type, unchanging, undeviating

consolation cheer, comfort, ease, encouragement, help, relief, solace, succour, support

console cheer, comfort, encourage, relieve, solace, soothe

consolidate fortify, reinforce, secure,

consommé *n* clear meat soup

consonant *n* sound, letter other than a vowel ~*adj* agreeing with, in accord **consonance** *n*

consort *v* associate ~*n* husband, wife, esp. of ruler **consortium** *n* (*pl* -tia) association of banks, companies etc.

conspicuous *adj* noticeable

conspire *v* plot together **conspiracy** *n* **conspirator** *n*

constable *n* policeman **constabulary** *n* police force

constant *adj* unchanging; steadfast; continual ~*n* quantity that does not vary **constancy** *n* loyalty **constantly** *adv*

constellation *n* group of stars

consternation *n* alarm, dismay

constipation *n* difficulty in emptying bowels **constipated** *adj*

constituent *adj* making up whole ~*n* component part; elector **constituency** *n* body of electors; parliamentary division

constitute *v* form; found **constitution** *n* composition; health; principles on which state is governed **constitutional** *adj* inborn; statutory ~*n* walk for good of health

constrain *v* force **constraint** *n* compulsion; restriction

constriction *n* squeezing together **constrict** *v* **constrictor** *n* snake that squeezes its prey

construct *v* build; put together **construction** *n* **constructive** *adj* positive

construe *v* interpret

consul *n* government representative in a foreign country **consulate** *n* consul's office

———— THESAURUS ————

stabilize, strengthen

conspicuous clear, discernible, easily seen, evident, manifest, noticeable, obvious, patent, perceptible, visible

conspiracy collusion, confederacy, frame-up *Sl*, intrigue, machination, plot, scheme, treason

conspirator intriguer, plotter, schemer, traitor

conspire contrive, devise, hatch treason, intrigue, machinate, manoeuvre, plot, scheme

constant even, firm, fixed, habitual, immutable, invariable, permanent, perpetual, regular, stable, steadfast, steady, unbroken, unvarying; ceaseless, continual, endless, eternal, everlasting, incessant, interminable, nonstop, perpetual, persistent, relentless, sustained, unrelenting

consternation alarm, anxiety, awe, bewilderment, confusion, dismay, distress, dread, fear, fright, horror, panic, shock, terror

constituent *adj* basic, component, elemental, essential, integral ~*n* component, element, essential, factor, ingredient, part, principle, unit

constitute comprise, create, enact, establish, fix, form, found, make, make up, set up

constitution establishment, formation, organization

constitutional *adj* congenital, inborn, inherent, intrinsic, organic; chartered, statutory, vested

constrain bind, compel, drive, force, impel, oblige, pressure, urge

constraint compulsion, force, necessity, pressure, restraint; check, curb, damper, deterrent, hindrance, limitation, rein, restriction

construct assemble, build, compose, create, design, erect, establish, fabricate, fashion, form, formulate, found, frame, make, manufacture, organize, put up, raise, set up, shape

construction assembly, building, composition, creation, edifice, erection, fabric, fabrication, figure, form, shape, structure

constructive helpful, positive, prac-

consult *v* seek advice, information from **consultancy** *n* **consultant** *n* specialist, expert **consultation** *n* **consultative** *adj*

consume *v* eat or drink; engross; use up; destroy **consumer** *n* **consumption** *n*

consummate *v/adj* perfect; complete **consummation** *n*

cont. continued

contact *n* touching; being in touch; useful acquaintance ~*v* get in touch with **contact lens** lens fitting over the eyeball

contagious *adj* communicable by contact, catching

contain *v* hold; have room for; comprise; restrain **container** *n*

contaminate *v* pollute; make radio-active **contamination** *n*

contemplate *v* meditate on; gaze upon; intend **contemplation** *n*

contemporary *adj* existing at same time; modern ~*n* one of same age **contemporaneous** *adj*

contempt *n* scorn, disgrace; wilful disrespect of authority **contemptible** *adj* **contemptuous** *adj* showing contempt

contend *v* strive, dispute; maintain (that) **contender** *n* competitor **contention** *n* **contentious** *adj*

content¹ *adj* satisfied; willing (to) ~*v* satisfy ~*n* satisfaction **contented** *adj* **contentment** *n*

content² *n* thing contained; *pl* index of topics

contest *n* competition ~*v* dispute;

tical, productive, useful, valuable

consult ask, compare notes, confer, consider, debate, deliberate, interrogate, question, refer to, take counsel, turn to

consultant adviser, authority, specialist

consultation appointment, conference, council, deliberation, dialogue, discussion, examination, hearing, interview, meeting, session

consume absorb, deplete, drain, eat up, employ, exhaust, expend, finish up, lavish, lessen, spend, use, use up, utilize, vanish, waste, wear out

consumer buyer, customer, purchaser, shopper, user

contact *n* approximation, contiguity, junction, juxtaposition, touch, union; acquaintance, connection ~*v* approach, call, communicate with, get hold of, get *or* be in touch with, reach, ring (up) *Inf, chiefly Brit*, speak to, write to

contagious catching, epidemic, infectious, spreading

contain accommodate, enclose, have

capacity for, hold, incorporate, seat

container holder, receptacle, vessel

contemplate brood over, consider, deliberate, meditate, observe, ponder, reflect upon study; consider, design, envisage, expect, foresee, intend, mean, plan, propose, think of

contemporary *adj* coexistent, synchronous; à la mode, current, happening *Inf*, in fashion, latest, modern, newfangled, present, present-day, recent, up-to-date ~*n* compeer, fellow, peer

contempt derision, disdain, disrespect, mockery, neglect, scorn

contemptible abject, base, despicable, ignominious, low, mean, shameful, vile

contemptuous arrogant, condescending, derisive, disdainful, haughty, scornful

contend clash, compete, contest, cope, emulate, grapple, jostle, litigate, skirmish, strive, struggle, vie; affirm, allege, argue, assert, aver, avow, debate, dispute, hold, maintain

compete for **contestant** *n*

context *n* words coming before and after a word or passage

continent¹ *n* large continuous mass of land **continental** *adj*

continent² *adj* in control of bodily functions

contingent *adj* depending (on) ~*n* group part of larger group **contingency** *n*

continue *v* remain; carry on; resume; prolong **continual** *adj* **continually** *adv* **continuation** *n* **continuity** *n* logical sequence **continuous** *adj*

contort *v* twist out of normal shape

contortion *n* **contortionist** *n*

contour *n* outline, shape, esp. mountains, coast etc.

contra- *comb. form* against

contraband *n/adj* smuggled (goods)

contraception *n* prevention of conception **contraceptive** *adj/n*

contract *v* make or become smaller; enter into agreement; incur ~*n* agreement **contraction** *n* **contractor** *n* one making contract, esp. builder **contractual** *adj*

contradict *v* deny; be inconsistent with **contradiction** *n* **contradictory** *adj*

————————— T H E S A U R U S —————————

content¹ *adj* agreeable, at ease, comfortable, contented, fulfilled, satisfied, willing to accept ~*v* appease, delight, gladden, gratify, humour, indulge, mollify, placate, please, reconcile, satisfy, suffice ~*n* comfort, ease, gratification, peace, peace of mind, pleasure, satisfaction

content² burden, essence, gist, ideas, matter, meaning, significance, substance, text, thoughts

contented at ease, at peace, cheerful, comfortable, glad, gratified, happy, pleased, satisfied, serene, thankful

contentment comfort, ease, equanimity, fulfilment, gladness, gratification, happiness, peace, pleasure, repletion, satisfaction, serenity

contest *n* competition, game, head-to-head, match, tournament, trial ~*v* argue, challenge, debate, dispute, doubt, oppose, question, compete, contend, fight, fight over, strive, vie

contestant aspirant, candidate, competitor, contender, player

context background, connection, frame of reference, framework, relation

contingency accident, chance, eventuality, happening, incident, possibility, uncertainty

continual constant, endless, eternal, everlasting, frequent, incessant, interminable, perpetual, recurrent, regular, unceasing

continually all the time, always, constantly, endlessly, eternally, incessantly, interminably, repeatedly

continuation extension, furtherance, sequel, supplement

continue abide, carry on, endure, last, live on, persist, remain, rest, stay, stay on, survive

continuity cohesion, connection, flow, progression, sequence, succession

continuous connected, constant, extended, prolonged, unbroken, unceasing, undivided, uninterrupted

contract *v* abridge, compress, condense, curtail, dwindle, lessen, narrow, reduce, shrink, shrivel, tighten; agree, arrange, bargain, clinch, close, come to terms, covenant, engage, enter into, negotiate, pledge, stipulate ~*n* agreement, arrangement, bargain, bond, compact, convention, covenant, deal *Inf*, engagement, pact, settlement, treaty, understanding

contradict be at variance with, belie, challenge, contravene, counter, counteract, deny, dispute, negate,

contraflow *n* flow of traffic in opposite direction

contralto *n* (*pl* **-tos**) lowest female voice

contraption *n* gadget; device

contrary *adj* opposed; perverse ~*n* the exact opposite ~*adv* in opposition

contrast *v* bring out, show difference ~*n* striking difference

contravene *v* infringe

contribute *v* give, pay to common fund; help to occur; write for the press **contribution** *n* **contributor** *n*

contrite *adj* remorseful **contrition** *n*

contrive *v* arrange; devise, invent **contrivance** *n*

control *v* **-trolling, -trolled** command; regulate; direct, check ~*n* power to direct or determine; curb, check; *pl*

instruments to control car, aircraft etc. **controller** *n*

controversy *n* debate **controversial** *adj*

contusion *n* bruise

conundrum *n* riddle

conurbation *n* large built-up area

convalesce *v* recover health after illness, operation etc. **convalescence** *n* **convalescent** *adj/n*

convection *n* transmission of heat by currents

convene *v* call together, assemble **convenor, -er** *n* **convention** *n* assembly; treaty; accepted usage **conventional** *adj* (slavishly) observing customs of society; customary; (of weapons, war etc.) not nuclear

convenient *adj* handy; favourable to

———————— THESAURUS ————————

oppose

contradiction conflict, contravention, denial, inconsistency, opposite

contradictory antagonistic, antithetical, conflicting, contrary, incompatible, inconsistent, opposite, paradoxical

contrary *adj* adverse, anti, clashing, contradictory, counter, discordant, hostile, inimical, opposed, opposite

contrast *v* compare, differ, differentiate, distinguish, oppose, set in opposition, set off ~*n* comparison, difference, disparity, dissimilarity, distinction, divergence, foil, opposition

contribute add, afford, bestow, chip in, donate, furnish, give, provide, subscribe, supply

contribution addition, bestowal, donation, gift, grant, subscription

contributor freelance, journalist, journo *Sl*, reporter

contrite humble, penitent, regretful, remorseful, repentant, sorrowful, sorry

contrive concoct, construct, create, design, devise, engineer, fabricate,

frame, improvise, invent, manufacture; arrange, bring about

control *v* command, conduct, direct, dominate, govern, handle, have charge of, lead, manage, manipulate, oversee, pilot, reign over, rule, steer, superintend, supervise; bridle, check, constrain, contain, curb, hold back, limit, master, rein in, repress, restrain, subdue ~*n* authority, charge, command, direction, discipline, government, guidance, jurisdiction, management, mastery, oversight, rule, supervision, supremacy; brake, check, curb, limitation, regulation, restraint

controversial at issue, contentious, debatable, disputable, disputed, open to question, under discussion

controversy argument, contention, debate, discussion, dispute, dissension, polemic, quarrel, row, squabble, strife, wrangle

convalescence improvement, recovery, recuperation, rehabilitation, return to health

convalescent *adj* on the mend, re-

needs, comfort **convenience** *n* ease, comfort, suitability; public toilet *~adj* (of food) quick to prepare **conveniently** *adv*

convent *n* religious community, esp. of nuns

convention *see* CONVENE

converge *v* tend to meet

conversant *adj* familiar (with), versed in

converse[1] *v* talk (with) *~n* talk **conversation** *n* **conversational** *adj*

converse[2] *adj* opposite, reversed *~n* the opposite **conversely** *adv*

convert *v* apply to another purpose; change; transform; cause to adopt (another) religion, opinion *~n* converted person **conversion** *n* **convertible** *n* car with folding roof *~adj* capable of being converted

convex *adj* curved outwards

convey *v* transport; impart; *Law* transfer **conveyance** *n* **conveyancer** *n* one skilled in legal forms of transferring property **conveyancing** *n* **conveyor belt** continuous moving belt

convict *v* prove or declare guilty *~n* criminal serving prison sentence **conviction** *n* verdict of guilty; being convinced, firm belief

convince *v* persuade by evidence or argument **convincing** *adj*

convivial *adj* sociable

convoluted *adj* involved; coiled **convolution** *n*

convoy *n* party (of ships etc.) travelling together for protection *~v* escort

convulse *v* shake violently; affect with spasms **convulsion** *n*

coo *n/v* cooing, cooed (make) cry of

———— T H E S A U R U S ————

covering, recuperating

convene assemble, bring together, call, come together, congregate, gather, meet, muster, rally

convenience accessibility, appropriateness, availability, fitness, handiness, opportuneness, serviceability, suitability, usefulness, utility

convenient accessible, at hand, available, close at hand, handy; appropriate, beneficial, commodious, fitted, helpful, labour-saving, opportune, seasonable, suitable, suited, timely, useful, well-timed

convention assembly, conference, congress, convocation, council, delegates, meeting; code, custom, etiquette, formality, practice, propriety, protocol, tradition, usage

converge combine, come together, focus, gather, join, meet, merge, mingle

conversation chat, colloquy, communion, conference, converse, dialogue, discourse, discussion, exchange, gossip, talk, tête-à-tête

converse *n* antithesis, contrary, obverse, opposite, reverse

conversion adaptation, alteration, modification, reconstruction, reorganization; change, transformation, transmutation; change of heart, rebirth, reformation, regeneration

convert *v* adapt, apply, modify, remodel, reorganize, restyle, revise; alter, change, transform, transmute, transpose, turn

convey bear, bring, carry, conduct, fetch, forward, grant, guide, move, send, support, transmit, transport

convict *v* condemn, find guilty, imprison, sentence *~n* criminal, culprit, felon, lag *Sl*, malefactor, prisoner

conviction assurance, certainty, confidence, firmness, reliance

convince assure, bring round, persuade, satisfy, sway, win over

convincing believable, cogent, conclusive, credible, impressive, incontrovertible, likely, persuasive, plausible, powerful, probable, telling

convoy *n* armed guard, attendance,

doves

cook v prepare food, esp. by heat; undergo cooking ~n one who prepares food **cooker** n apparatus for cooking **cookery** n **cookie** n US biscuit

cool adj moderately cold; calm; lacking friendliness ~v make, become cool **coolly** adv

coop[1] n/v (shut up in) cage

coop[2], **co-op** n cooperative society or shop run by one

cooperate v work together **cooperation** n **cooperative** adj willing to cooperate; (of an enterprise) owned collectively ~n collectively owned enterprise

co-opt v add to group

coordinate v bring into order, harmony ~adj equal in degree, status etc. **coordination** n **coordinator** n

coot n small black water bird

cop n Sl policeman

cope v deal successfully (with); tolerate or endure

coping n sloping top course of wall

copious adj abundant

copper[1] n reddish-brown metal; coin

copper[2] n Inf policeman

coppice, copse n small wood

copulate v unite sexually **copulation** n

copy n imitation; single specimen of book ~v copying, copied make copy of, imitate **copyright** n legal exclusive right to print and publish book, work of art etc. ~v protect by copyright

coquette n flirt

coracle n small round boat

coral n hard substance made by sea polyps

cord n thin rope or thick string; ribbed fabric

cordial adj sincere, warm ~n fruit-flavoured drink

cordon n chain of troops or police ~v form barrier round

cordon bleu (of cookery) of the very

———————— THESAURUS ————————

attendant, escort, guard, protection

cool adj chilled, chilly, nippy; calm, collected, composed, deliberate, imperturbable, level-headed, placid, quiet, relaxed, self-possessed, serene, unemotional, unexcited, unfazed Inf, unruffled; aloof, distant, frigid, indifferent, lukewarm, offhand, reserved, unfriendly ~v chill, cool off, freeze, lose heat, refrigerate

cooperate aid, assist, collaborate, combine, concur, conspire, contribute, help, join forces, pitch in, pull together, work together

cooperation assistance, collaboration, give-and-take, helpfulness, participation, responsiveness, teamwork, unity

cooperative accommodating, helpful, obliging, responsive, supportive

coordinate correlate, harmonize, integrate, match, mesh, organize, relate

cope cope with deal, encounter, handle, struggle, tangle, tussle, weather, wrestle; carry on, manage, struggle through, survive

copious abundant, ample, bountiful, extensive, exuberant, full, generous, lavish, liberal, luxuriant, overflowing, plenteous, plentiful, profuse, rich

copy n counterfeit, duplicate, facsimile, forgery, image, imitation, likeness, model, pattern, photocopy, print, replica, replication, representation, reproduction ~v counterfeit, duplicate, photocopy, reproduce, transcribe; ape, echo, emulate, follow, imitate, mimic, mirror, repeat, simulate

cord line, rope, string, twine

cordial affable, affectionate, agreeable, cheerful, congenial, friendly, genial, hearty, sociable, warm, warm-hearted, welcoming, whole-

highest standard

corduroy *n* cotton fabric with velvety, ribbed surface

core *n* seed case of apple; innermost part ~*v* take out core

corgi *n* small Welsh dog

coriander *n* herb

cork *n* bark of an evergreen Mediterranean oak tree; stopper for bottle etc. ~*v* stop up with cork **corkscrew** *n* tool for pulling out corks

corm *n* underground stem like a bulb

cormorant *n* large voracious sea bird

corn[1] *n* grain, fruit of cereals **corny** *adj Inf* trite, oversentimental **corned beef** beef preserved in salt **cornflakes** *pl n* breakfast cereal **cornflour** *n* finely ground maize **cornflower** *n* blue flower growing in cornfields

corn[2] *n* horny growth on foot

cornea *n* transparent membrane covering front of eye

corner *n* part where two sides meet; remote or humble place; *Business* monopoly ~*v* drive into position of no escape; establish monopoly; move round corner **cornerstone** *n* indispensable part

cornet *n* trumpet with valves; cone-shaped ice cream wafer

cornice *n* moulding below ceiling

cornucopia *n* horn overflowing with fruit and flowers

corollary *n* inference from a preceding statement; deduction

coronary *adj* of blood vessels surrounding heart ~*n* coronary thrombosis **coronary thrombosis** disease of the heart

coronation *n* ceremony of crowning a sovereign

coroner *n* officer who holds inquests on unnatural deaths

coronet *n* small crown

corporal[1] *adj* of the body

corporal[2] *n* noncommissioned officer below sergeant

corporation *n* body of persons legally authorized to act as an individual **corporate** *adj*

corps *n* (*pl* **corps**) military force; any organized body of persons

corpse *n* dead body

corpulent *adj* fat **corpulence** *n*

corpus *n* (*pl* **corpora**) main part or body of something

corpuscle *n* minute particle, esp. of blood

corral *n US* enclosure for cattle

correct *v* set right; indicate errors in; punish ~*adj* right, accurate **correctly** *adv* **correction** *n* **corrective** *n/adj*

——————— THESAURUS ———————

hearted

core centre, crux, essence, gist, heart, kernel, nub, nucleus, pith

corner *n* angle, bend, crook, joint; cavity, cranny, hideaway, hide-out, hole, niche, nook, recess, retreat ~*v* bring to bay, run to earth, trap

corny banal, commonplace, dull, feeble, hackneyed, maudlin, mawkish, sentimental, stale, trite

corporation association, corporate body, society

corps band, body, company, crew, detachment, division, regiment, squadron, troop, unit

corpse body, cadaver, carcass

correct *v* adjust, amend, cure, improve, rectify, redress, reform, remedy, right; admonish, chastise, chide, discipline, punish, reprimand, reprove ~*adj* accurate, exact, faultless, flawless, just, precise, regular, right, strict, true

correction adjustment, alteration, amendment, improvement, modification; admonition, castigation, chastisement, discipline, punishment, reproof

correctly accurately, perfectly, precisely, properly, rightly

correlate *v* bring into reciprocal relation **correlation** *n*

correspond *v* be similar (to); exchange letters **correspondence** *n* **correspondent** *n* writer of letters; one employed by newspaper etc. to report on particular topic

corridor *n* passage

corroborate *v* confirm

corrode *v* eat into **corrosion** *n* **corrosive** *adj*

corrugated *adj* ridged

corrupt *adj* lacking integrity; involving bribery; wicked ~*v* make evil; bribe; make rotten **corruption** *n*

corsage *n* (flower worn on) bodice of woman's dress

corset *n* close-fitting undergarment to support the body

cortege *n* formal (funeral) procession

cortex *n* (*pl* **-tices**) outer layer of brain etc.

cortisone *n* synthetic hormone used medically

cosh *n* blunt weapon ~*v* strike with one

cosine *n* in a right-angled triangle, ratio of adjacent side to hypotenuse

cosmetic *n/adj* (preparation) to improve appearance only

cosmic *adj* relating to the universe; vast

cosmopolitan *adj/n* (person) familiar with many countries

cosmos *n* the universe considered as an ordered system

cosset *v* pamper, pet

cost *n* price; expenditure of time, labour etc.; damage ~*v* have as price; entail payment, or loss of **costly** *adj* valuable; expensive

costume *n* style of dress of particular

———————————————— THESAURUS ————————————————

correspond accord, agree, be consistent, coincide, conform, dovetail, fit, harmonize, match, square, tally; communicate, exchange letters

correspondence agreement, analogy, coincidence, comparison, conformity, congruity, correlation, fitness, harmony, match, relation, similarity; communication, letters, mail, post, writing

correspondent *n* letter writer, pen friend *or* pal; contributor, journalist, journo *Sl*, reporter

corridor aisle, hallway, passage, passageway

corrode canker, consume, corrupt, eat away, erode, rust, waste, wear away

corrosive acrid, caustic, erosive, virulent, wasting, wearing

corrupt *adj* dishonest, fraudulent, rotten, shady *Inf*, unprincipled, unscrupulous, venal; decadent, degenerate, depraved, evil, immoral, perverted, sinful, wicked ~*v* bribe, debauch, demoralize, deprave, entice, fix *Inf*, lure, pervert, subvert

corruption breach of trust, bribery, bribing, demoralization, dishonesty, extortion, fraud, graft *Inf*, jobbery, profiteering, shadiness, venality; decadence, degeneration, depravity, evil, immorality, impurity, iniquity, perversion, sinfulness, vice, viciousness, wickedness

corset belt, bodice, girdle

cosmetic *adj* beautifying, superficial, surface

cosmopolitan sophisticated, universal, urbane, well-travelled, worldly, worldly-wise

cost *n* amount, charge, expenditure, expense, figure, outlay, payment, price, rate, worth; damage, detriment, expense, harm, hurt, injury, loss, penalty, sacrifice, suffering ~*v* come to, sell at

costly dear, excessive, expensive, extortionate, highly-priced, steep *Inf*, valuable

place or time

cosy *adj* snug, comfortable

cot *n* child's bed

cote *n* shelter for animals or birds

coterie *n* social clique

cottage *n* small house **cottage cheese** mild, soft cheese **cottage pie** dish of minced meat and potato

cotton *n* plant with white downy fibres; cloth of this

couch *n* piece of furniture for reclining on ~*v* put into (words)

cougar *n* puma

cough *v* expel air from lungs with sudden effort and noise ~*n* act of coughing

could *past tense of* CAN[1]

coulomb *n* unit of electric charge

council *n* deliberative or administrative body; local governing authority of town etc. **councillor** *n*

counsel *n* -selling, -selled advice; barrister(s) ~*v* advise, recommend **counsellor** *n*

count[1] *v* reckon, number; consider to be; be reckoned in; depend (on); be

of importance ~*n* reckoning; total number; act of counting **countless** *adj* too many to be counted **countdown** *n* counting of the seconds before an event

count[2] *n* nobleman **countess** *n* noblewoman

countenance *n* face, its expression ~*v* support, approve

counter[1] *n* horizontal surface in bank, shop etc., on which business is transacted

counter[2] *adv* in opposite direction ~*v* oppose

counter- *comb. form* reversed, opposite, rival, retaliatory, as in **counterclaim, counterproductive**

counteract *v* neutralize

counterattack *v/n* attack in response to attack

counterbalance *n* weight balancing another ~*v* act as balance

counterfeit *adj* sham, forged ~*n* imitation, forgery ~*v* imitate with intent to deceive; forge

counterfoil *n* part of cheque, receipt

costume attire, clothing, dress, ensemble, garb, get-up *Inf*, livery, outfit, uniform

cosy comfortable, homely, intimate, secure, sheltered, snug, warm

cottage cabin, chalet, hut, lodge, shack

cough *v* bark, clear one's throat, hack, hawk ~*n* bark, hack

council assembly, board, cabinet, chamber, conference, congress, convention, diet, house, parliament, synod

counsel *n* admonition, advice, caution, consideration, direction, forethought, guidance, information, recommendation, suggestion, warning; advocate, attorney, barrister, lawyer, legal adviser, solicitor ~*v* admonish, advise, advocate, caution, exhort, in-

struct, recommend, urge, warn

count add (up), calculate, cast up, check, compute, enumerate, estimate, number, reckon, score, tally, tot up; carry weight, matter, rate, signify, tell, weigh

counter *adv* against, contrarily, conversely, in defiance of, versus ~*v* answer, hit back, meet, offset, parry, resist, respond, retaliate, return, ward off

counterbalance balance, compensate, make up for, offset, set off

counterfeit *adj* bogus, copied, faked, false, feigned, forged, fraudulent, imitation, phoney *or* phony *Inf*, pseudo *Inf*, sham, simulated, spurious ~*n* copy, fake, forgery, fraud, imitation, reproduction, sham ~*v* copy, fabricate, fake, feign, forge, imitate, im-

etc. kept as record

countermand v cancel (previous order)

counterpane n bed covering

counterpart n something complementary to another

counterpoint n melody added as accompaniment to given melody

countersign v sign document already signed by another

countersink v enlarge top of hole to take head of screw, bolt etc. below surface

countertenor n male alto

country n region; nation; people of nation; land of birth; rural districts **countryman** n (fem **countrywoman**) **countryside** n

county n division of country

coup n successful stroke; (short for **coup d'état**) sudden, violent seizure of government

coup de grace Fr decisive action

coupé n sporty style of motorcar

couple n two, pair; husband and wife ~v connect, fasten together; join, associate **couplet** n two lines of verse **coupling** n connecting device

coupon n ticket entitling holder to discount, gift etc.

courage n bravery, boldness **courageous** adj **courageously** adv

courgette n type of small vegetable marrow

courier n messenger; person who guides travellers

course n movement in space or time; direction; sequence; line of action; series of lectures etc.; any of successive parts of meal; area where golf is played; racetrack ~v hunt; run swiftly; (of blood) circulate

court n space enclosed by buildings, yard; area for playing various games; royal household; body with judicial powers, place where it meets, one of

———— **THESAURUS** ————

personate, pretend, sham, simulate

counterpart complement, copy, duplicate, equal, fellow, match, mate, supplement, tally, twin

countless endless, incalculable, infinite, legion, limitless, measureless, myriad, uncounted, untold

country; land, part, region, terrain, territory; commonwealth, kingdom, nation, people, realm, sovereign state, state; citizens, community, electors, inhabitants, nation, people, populace, public, society, voters; fatherland, homeland, motherland, nationality, native land; backwoods, farmland, green belt, outdoors, provinces, rural areas, wide open spaces *Inf*

county province, shire

coup action, deed, exploit, feat, manoeuvre, stratagem, stroke, stunt, *tour de force*

couple n brace, duo, pair, twosome

~v buckle, clasp, conjoin, connect, hitch, join, link, marry, pair, unite, wed, yoke

courage balls *Taboo sl*, boldness, bottle *Brit sl*, bravery, daring, fearlessness, fortitude, gallantry, guts *Inf*, mettle, nerve, pluck, valour

courageous audacious, bold, brave, daring, fearless, gallant, hardy, heroic, indomitable, intrepid, plucky, valiant

course advance, continuity, development, flow, march, movement, order, progress, sequence, succession; channel, direction, line, orbit, passage, path, road, route, tack, track, trail, trajectory, way; lapse, passage, passing, sweep, term, time; conduct, manner, method, mode, plan, policy, procedure, programme; classes, course of study, curriculum, lectures, programme, schedule, studies; circuit, lap, race, racecourse

its sittings ~v woo; seek, invite **courti-er** n one who frequents royal court **courtly** adj ceremoniously polite; characteristic of a court **court card** king, queen or jack at cards **court martial** court for trying naval or military offences **courtship** n wooing **courtyard** n enclosed paved area

courtesy n politeness **courteous** adj

cousin n son or daughter of uncle or aunt

cove n small inlet of coast

coven n gathering of witches

covenant n agreement; compact ~v agree to a covenant

cover v place over; extend; spread; bring upon (oneself); protect; travel over; include; be sufficient; report ~n covering thing; shelter; insurance **coverage** n **coverlet** n top covering of bed

covert adj secret, sly

covet v long to possess, esp. what belongs to another **covetous** adj

cow[1] n (pl **cows**) female of bovine and other animals **cowboy** n ranch worker who herds cattle; Inf irresponsible worker

cow[2] v frighten, overawe

coward n one who lacks courage **cowardice** n **cowardly** adj

cower v crouch in fear

cowl n monk's hooded cloak; hooded top for chimney

———————————————— THESAURUS ————————————————

court n cloister, courtyard, piazza, plaza, quadrangle, square, yard; hall, manor, palace; attendants, royal household, suite, train; bar, bench, court of justice, lawcourt, tribunal ~v chase, date, go (out) with, serenade, take out, walk out with, woo; cultivate, curry favour with, fawn upon, flatter, pander to, solicit

courteous affable, attentive, civil, courtly, elegant, gallant, gracious, mannerly, polished, polite, refined, respectful, urbane, well-bred, well-mannered

courtesy affability, civility, elegance, gallantry, good breeding, good manners, graciousness, polish, politeness, urbanity

courtier attendant, follower, squire, train-bearer

courtyard area, enclosure, playground, quad, quadrangle, yard

covenant bargain, commitment, compact, concordat, contract, convention, pact, promise, stipulation, treaty, trust

cover v cloak, conceal, cover up, curtain, disguise, eclipse, hide, hood, house, mask, obscure, screen, se-crete, shade, shroud, veil; defend, guard, protect, reinforce, shelter, shield; describe, detail, investigate, narrate, recount, relate, report, tell of, write up ~n cloak, cover-up, disguise, façade, front, mask, pretence, screen, smoke screen, veil; concealment, defence, guard, hiding place, protection, refuge, sanctuary, shelter, shield; compensation, indemnity, insurance, payment, protection

covet begrudge, crave, desire, envy, fancy Inf, hanker after, long for, lust after, thirst for, yearn for

covetous avaricious, envious, grasping, greedy, jealous, mercenary, yearning

coward chicken Sl, craven, faint-heart, poltroon, renegade, sneak, wimp Inf

cowardly base, craven, faint-hearted, fearful, lily-livered, scared, shrinking, soft, spineless, weak, yellow Inf

cowboy cattleman, cowhand, drover, gaucho S Amer, herder, herdsman, rancher, stockman

cower cringe, crouch, draw back, fawn, flinch, grovel, quail, shrink, skulk, sneak, tremble

cowslip *n* wild primrose

coxswain, cox *n* steersman of boat

coy *adj* (pretending to be) shy, modest **coyly** *adv*

coyote *n* prairie wolf

coypu *n* aquatic rodent

crab *n* edible crustacean **crabbed** *adj* (of handwriting) hard to read **crabby** *adj* bad-tempered

crab apple wild sour apple

crack *v* split partially; break with sharp noise; break down, yield; *Inf* tell (joke); solve, decipher; make sharp noise ~*n* sharp explosive noise; split; flaw; *Inf* joke; chat; *Sl* highly addictive form of cocaine; *adj Inf* very skilful **cracker** *n* decorated paper tube, pulled apart with a bang, containing toy etc.; explosive firework; thin dry biscuit **crackers** *adj Sl* crazy **cracking** *adj* very good **crackle** *n/v* (make) sound of repeated small cracks **crackpot** *n Inf* eccentric person

cradle *n* infant's bed ~*v* hold or rock as in a cradle; cherish

craft[1] *n* skilled trade; skill, ability; cunning **crafty** *adj* cunning, shrewd **craftsman** *n* (*fem* **craftswoman**) **craftsmanship** *n*

craft[2] *n* vessel; ship

crag *n* steep rugged rock

cram *v* **cramming, crammed** stuff; prepare quickly for examination

cramp[1] *v* hinder

cramp[2] *n* painful muscular contraction

cranberry *n* edible red berry

crane *n* wading bird with long legs; machine for moving heavy weights ~*v* stretch neck **crane fly** long-legged insect

cranium *n* (*pl* **-niums, -nia**) skull **cranial** *adj*

crank *n* arm at right angles to axis, for turning main shaft; *Inf* eccentric person ~*v* start (engine) by turning crank **cranky** *adj* eccentric

———————— THESAURUS ————————

coy arch, backward, bashful, demure, evasive, modest, prudish, reserved, retiring, self-effacing, shrinking, shy, skittish, timid

crack *v* break, burst, chip, chop, fracture, snap, splinter, split; break down, collapse, give way, go to pieces, lose control, succumb, yield ~*n* burst, clap, crash, explosion, pop, report, snap; breach, break, chink, chip, cleft, cranny, crevice, fissure, fracture, gap, rift, split; *Sl* dig, gag *Inf*, insult, jibe, joke, quip, witticism; *adj Sl* ace, choice, elite, excellent, first-class, first-rate, hand-picked, superior, world-class

cradle *n* cot, crib, Moses basket ~*v* hold, lull, nestle, nurse, rock, support

craft[1] business, calling, line, occupation, trade, vocation, work; ability, aptitude, art, artistry, cleverness, dexterity, expertise, ingenuity, skill,

technique, workmanship

craft[2] aircraft, barque, boat, plane, ship, spacecraft, vessel

craftsman artificer, artisan, maker, master, skilled worker, smith, technician, wright

craftsmanship artistry, expertise, mastery, technique, workmanship

crafty artful, astute, calculating, canny, cunning, deceitful, devious, foxy, scheming, sharp, shrewd, sly, subtle, tricky, wily

cram compact, compress, crowd, crush, force, jam, overcrowd, overfill, pack, pack in, press, ram, shove, squeeze, stuff

cramp[1] *v* check, clog, confine, encumber, hamper, handicap, hinder, impede, inhibit, obstruct, restrict, shackle

cramp[2] *n* ache, crick, pain, pang, shooting pain, spasm, stiffness,

cranny *n* small opening

crash *v* (cause to) make loud noise; (cause to) fall with crash; smash; collapse; cause (aircraft) to hit land or water; collide with; move noisily ~*n* loud, violent fall or impact; collision; uncontrolled descent of aircraft; sudden collapse; bankruptcy **crash helmet** protective helmet

crass *adj* grossly stupid

crate *n* large (usu. wooden) container for packing goods

crater *n* mouth of volcano; bowl-shaped cavity

cravat *n* man's neckcloth

crave *v* have very strong desire for; beg **craving** *n*

craven *adj* cowardly

crawl *v* move on hands and knees; move very slowly; ingratiate oneself; swim with crawl stroke; be overrun (with) ~*n* crawling motion; racing stroke at swimming

crayfish *n* edible freshwater crustacean

crayon *n* stick or pencil of coloured wax etc.

craze *n* short-lived fashion; strong desire; madness **crazed** *adj* **crazy** *adj* insane; very foolish; madly eager (for)

creak *n/v* (make) grating noise

cream *n* fatty part of milk; food like this; cosmetic like this; yellowish-white colour; best part ~*v* take cream from; take best part from; beat to creamy consistency **creamy** *adj*

crease *n* line made by folding; wrinkle ~*v* make, develop creases

———————————— **THESAURUS** ————————————

twinge

cranny breach, chink, cleft, crack, crevice, fissure, gap, hole, interstice, nook, opening, rift

crash *v* come a cropper *Inf,* dash, fall, give way, hurtle, lurch, overbalance, pitch, plunge, topple; bang, bump (into), collide, crash-land *an aircraft,* drive into, have an accident, hit, plough into, wreck ~*n* bang, boom, clang, clash, racket, smash; accident, bump, collision, jar, jolt, pile-up *Inf,* smash, thud, thump, wreck; bankruptcy, collapse, debacle, depression, downfall, failure, ruin, smash

crass asinine, boorish, bovine, coarse, dense, doltish, gross, insensitive, obtuse, stupid, unrefined

crate *n* box, case, container, packing case, tea chest

crater depression, dip, hollow, shell hole

crave cry out for *Inf,* desire, fancy *Inf,* hanker after, hope for, hunger after, long for, lust after, need, pine for, thirst for, want, yearn for; ask, beg, beseech, entreat, implore, petition,

plead for, pray for, seek, solicit, supplicate

crawl advance slowly, creep, drag, go on all fours, inch, pull *or* drag oneself along, slither, wriggle, writhe; cringe, fawn, grovel, humble oneself, ingratiate oneself, toady

craze enthusiasm, fad, fashion, infatuation, mania, mode, novelty, passion, rage, thing, trend, vogue

crazy barking mad *Sl,* berserk, cuckoo *Inf,* delirious, demented, deranged, idiotic, insane, loopy *Inf,* mad, mental *Sl,* nuts *Sl,* off one's head *Sl,* of unsound mind, potty *Inf,* round the bend *Sl,* unbalanced, unhinged; bizarre, eccentric, fantastic, odd, oddball *Inf,* outrageous, peculiar, ridiculous, silly, strange, wacko *Sl,* weird

creak *v* grate, grind, groan, rasp, scrape, scratch, screech, squeak, squeal

cream cosmetic, liniment, lotion, ointment, salve; best, *crème de la crème,* elite, flower, pick, prime

crease *n* bulge, fold, groove, line, overlap, pucker, ridge, ruck, tuck,

create *v* bring into being; make; *Inf* make a fuss **creation** *n* **creative** *adj* imaginative, inventive **creativity** *n* **creator** *n*

creature *n* living being

crèche *n* day nursery for very young children

credentials *pl n* testimonials; letters of introduction

credible *adj* worthy of belief **credibility** *n*

credit *n* commendation; source of honour; trust; good name; system of allowing customers to pay later; money at one's disposal in bank etc. ~*v* attribute, believe; put on credit side of account **creditable** *adj* bringing honour **creditor** *n* one to whom debt is due

credulous *adj* too easy of belief, gullible **credulity** *n*

creed *n* statement of belief

creek *n* narrow inlet on coast

creep *v* **creeping, crept** move slowly, stealthily; crawl; act in servile way; (of flesh) feel shrinking sensation ~*n* creeping; *Sl* repulsive person; *pl* feeling of fear or repugnance **creeper** *n* creeping or climbing plant **creepy** *adj*

cremation *n* burning of corpses **cremate** *v* **crematorium** *n* building where corpses are cremated

creole *n* language developed from mixture of languages

creosote *n* oily liquid used for preserving wood

———— THESAURUS ————

wrinkle ~*v* crinkle, crumple, double up, fold, pucker, ridge, ruck up, rumple, screw up, wrinkle

create beget, bring into being, coin, compose, concoct, design, develop, devise, form, formulate, generate, hatch, initiate, invent, make, originate, produce, spawn

creation establishment, formation, foundation, inception, institution, laying down, origination, production, setting up; formation, generation, genesis, making, procreation, siring

creative artistic, clever, fertile, gifted, imaginative, ingenious, inspired, inventive, original, productive, stimulating, visionary

creator architect, author, begetter, designer, father, God, inventor, maker, originator, prime mover

creature animal, beast, being, brute, dumb animal, living thing, lower animal, quadruped

credentials authorization, card, certificate, deed, diploma, docket, licence, missive, passport, recommendation, reference(s), testimonial, title, voucher, warrant

credibility believability, integrity, plausibility, reliability, tenability, trustworthiness

credible believable, conceivable, imaginable, likely, plausible, possible, probable, reasonable, tenable, thinkable

credit *n* acclaim, acknowledgment, approval, commendation, fame, glory, honour, kudos, merit, praise, recognition, thanks, tribute *v* (*with* **with**) accredit, ascribe to, assign to, attribute to, impute to, refer to; accept, bank on, believe, depend on, have faith in, rely on, trust

creditable admirable, commendable, deserving, estimable, exemplary, honourable, laudable, meritorious, praiseworthy, reputable, respectable, worthy

credulity blind faith, gullibility, naiveté, silliness, simplicity

creed articles of faith, belief, canon, catechism, confession, credo, doctrine, dogma, principles

creek bay, bight, cove, inlet

creep skulk, slink, sneak, steal, tiptoe; crawl, glide, insinuate, slither,

crepe *n* fabric with crimped surface

crescendo *n* (*pl* **-dos**) *Mus* gradual increase of loudness

crescent *n* (shape of) moon seen in first or last quarter

cress *n* various plants with edible pungent leaves

crest *n* tuft on bird's or animal's head; top of mountain, wave etc.; badge above shield of coat of arms **crestfallen** *adj* disheartened

cretin *n* person afflicted by retardation; *Inf* stupid person **cretinous** *adj*

crevasse *n* deep open chasm

crevice *n* cleft, fissure

crew *n* ship's, aircraft's company; *Inf* gang

crib *n* child's cot; rack for fodder; plagiarism ~*v* copy dishonestly

cribbage *n* card game

crick *n* cramp esp. in neck

cricket[1] *n* chirping insect

cricket[2] *n* game played with bats, ball and wickets **cricketer** *n*

crime *n* violation of law; wicked act **criminal** *adj/n*

crimson *adj/n* (of) rich deep red

cringe *v* shrink, cower; behave obsequiously

crinkle *v/n* wrinkle

crinoline *n* hooped petticoat or skirt

cripple *n* disabled person ~*v* disable

crisis *n* (*pl* **crises**) turning point; time of acute danger

crisp *adj* brittle; brisk; clear-cut; fresh ~*n* very thin, fried slice of potato **crispy** *adj* **crispbread** *n* thin dry biscuit

crisscross *v* go in crosswise pattern ~*adj* crossing in different directions

criterion *n* (*pl* **-ria**) standard of judgment

critical *adj* fault-finding; discerning; skilled in judging; crucial, decisive **critically** *adv* **critic** *n* one who passes judgment; writer expert in judging works of literature, art etc. **criticism** *n* **criticize** *v*

———————— THESAURUS ————————

squirm, worm, wriggle, writhe

crescent half-moon, new moon, old moon, sickle

crest apex, crown, head, peak, pinnacle, ridge, summit, top

crestfallen dejected, depressed, despondent, disappointed, disconsolate, downcast, downhearted

crevice chink, cleft, crack, cranny, fissure, fracture, gap, hole, rent, rift, slit, split

crew hands, (ship's) company, (ship's) complement; company, corps, gang, party, posse, squad, team, working party

crib *v Inf* cheat, pilfer, pirate, plagiarize, purloin, steal

crime fault, felony, misdeed, misdemeanour, offence, outrage, transgression, trespass, unlawful act, violation, wrong

criminal *adj* bent *Sl*, corrupt, crooked

Inf, culpable, felonious, illegal, illicit, immoral, indictable, lawless, nefarious, unlawful, unrighteous, vicious, villainous, wicked, wrong ~*n* convict, crook *Inf*, culprit, delinquent, evildoer, felon, lag *Sl*, lawbreaker, malefactor, offender, villain

cripple *v* disable, enfeeble, incapacitate, lame, maim, paralyse, weaken

crisis climax, crunch *Inf*, crux, height, turning point; catastrophe, dilemma, dire straits, disaster, emergency, exigency, mess, plight, predicament, quandary, strait, trouble

crisp brittle, crispy, crumbly, crunchy, firm, fresh, unwilted

criterion canon, gauge, measure, norm, principle, rule, standard, test, yardstick

critic analyst, authority, commentator, connoisseur, expert, judge, pundit, reviewer

croak *v/n* (utter) deep hoarse cry

crochet *n/v* (do) handicraft like knitting

crock *n* earthenware pot **crockery** *n* earthenware dishes etc.

crocodile *n* large amphibious reptile

crocus *n* small bulbous plant

croft *n* small farm

croissant *n* crescent-shaped bread roll

crone *n* witchlike old woman

crony *n* intimate friend

crook *n* hooked staff; *Inf* swindler, criminal **crooked** *adj* twisted; deformed; dishonest

croon *v* sing in soft tone

crop *n* produce of cultivated plants; harvest; pouch in bird's gullet; whip; short haircut ~*v* **cropping, cropped** cut short; produce crop; (of animals) bite, eat down **cropper** *n Inf* heavy fall; disastrous failure **crop up** *Inf* happen unexpectedly

croquet *n* lawn game played with balls and hoops

croquette *n* fried ball of minced meat, fish etc.

cross *n* structure or symbol of two intersecting lines or pieces; such a structure as means of execution; symbol of Christian faith; any thing in shape of cross; affliction; hybrid ~*v* move or go across (something); intersect; meet and pass; mark with lines across; (*with* **out**) delete; place in form of cross; make sign of cross; breed by intermixture; thwart ~*adj* angry; transverse; contrary **crossing** *n* intersection of roads, rails etc.; part of street where pedestrians are expected to cross **cross-country** *adj/adv* by way of open fields **cross-examine** *v* examine witness already examined by other side **cross-examination** *n* **cross-eyed** *adj* having eyes turning inward **cross-ply** *adj* (of tyre) having fabric cords in outer casing running diagonally **cross-reference** *n* reference within text to another part of text **crossroads** *n* **crossword puzzle** puzzle built up of intersecting words, indicated by clues **The Cross** cross on which Jesus Christ was executed

crotch *n* angle between legs

——————— THESAURUS ———————

critical carping, censorious, derogatory, disapproving, disparaging, fault-finding, scathing; accurate, analytical, diagnostic, discerning, discriminating, fastidious, judicious, penetrating, perceptive, precise; crucial, dangerous, deciding, decisive, grave, momentous, perilous, precarious, risky, serious, urgent, vital

criticism bad press, censure, character assassination, disapproval, disparagement, fault-finding, stick *Sl*, stricture; analysis, appraisal, appreciation, assessment, comment, commentary, critique, evaluation, judgment, notice, review

criticize censure, condemn, disapprove of, disparage, lambast(e), slate *Inf*, tear into *Inf*

croak *v* caw, gasp, grunt, squawk

crook cheat, criminal, racketeer, robber, shark, swindler, thief, villain

crooked bent, bowed, crippled, curved, deformed, disfigured, distorted, hooked, irregular, misshapen, tortuous, twisted, twisting, warped, winding, zigzag; *Inf* bent *Sl*, corrupt, criminal, deceitful, dishonest, dishonourable, dubious, fraudulent, illegal, questionable, shady *Inf*, shifty, underhand, under-the-table, unlawful, unscrupulous

crop *n* fruits, gathering, harvest, produce, reaping, vintage, yield

crop up appear, arise, emerge, happen, occur, spring up, turn up

cross *n* crucifix, rood; crossing, crossroads, intersection, junction; blend,

crotchet *n* musical note

crotchety *adj Inf* bad-tempered

crouch *v* bend low; huddle down close to ground; stoop

croupier *n* person dealing cards, collecting money etc. at gambling table

crouton *n* piece of toasted bread served in soup

crow[1] *n* large black carrion-eating bird

crow[2] *v* utter cock's cry; boast ~*n* cock's cry

crowbar *n* iron bar

crowd *n* throng, mass ~*v* flock together; cram, pack; fill with people

crown *n* monarch's headdress; royal power; various coins; top of head; summit, top; perfection of thing ~*v* put crown on; occur as culmination; *Inf* hit on head

crucial *adj* decisive, critical; *Inf* very important **crucially** *adv*

crucible *n* small melting pot

crucifix *n* (*pl* -es) cross; image of (Christ on the) Cross **crucifixion** *n* **crucify** *v*

crude *adj* vulgar; in natural or raw state; rough **crudely** *adv* **crudity** *n*

cruel *adj* causing pain or suffering **cruelly** *adv* **cruelty** *n*

cruet *n* small container for salt, pepper etc.

cruise *v* travel about in a ship ~*n* voyage **cruiser** *n* ship that cruises; warship

crumb *n* fragment of bread

———————— THESAURUS ————————

combination, crossbreed, cur, hybrid, mixture, mongrel ~*v* bridge, cut across, extend over, ford, meet, pass over, ply, span, traverse, zigzag; crisscross, intersect, intertwine, lace; blend, crossbreed, hybridize, interbreed, mix ~*adj* angry, annoyed, churlish, disagreeable, fractious, ill-humoured, ill-tempered, impatient, irascible, irritable, peevish, petulant, querulous, ratty *Brit & NZ inf*, short, snappy, sullen, surly, tetchy; crosswise, intersecting, oblique, transverse

cross-examine catechize, grill *Inf*, interrogate, pump, question, quiz

crouch bend down, bow, duck, hunch, kneel, squat, stoop

crow boast, brag, exult, gloat, glory in, strut, swagger, triumph, vaunt

crowd *n* army, assembly, bevy, company, flock, herd, horde, host, mass, mob, multitude, pack, press, rabble, swarm, throng ~*v* cluster, congregate, flock, gather, huddle, mass, muster, surge, swarm, throng

crown *n* circlet, coronet, tiara; emperor, empress, king, monarch, monarchy, queen, royalty, ruler, sovereign, sovereignty ~*v* adorn, dignify, festoon, honour, invest, reward; cap, complete, consummate, finish, fulfil, perfect, round off, surmount, terminate, top

crucial central, critical, decisive, pivotal, searching, testing, trying

crude boorish, coarse, crass, dirty, gross, indecent, lewd, obscene, smutty, tactless, tasteless, uncouth, vulgar; natural, raw, unprocessed, unrefined; clumsy, makeshift, primitive, rough, rough-hewn, rude, rudimentary, sketchy, undeveloped, unfinished, unpolished

crudity coarseness, crudeness, impropriety, indelicacy, lewdness, obscenity, vulgarity

cruel barbarous, brutal, callous, cold-blooded, ferocious, fierce, hard, hard-hearted, harsh, heartless, inhuman, inhumane, malevolent, painful, remorseless, sadistic, savage, severe, spiteful, unfeeling, unkind, vengeful, vicious

cruelty bestiality, brutality, callousness, depravity, ferocity, harshness, inhumanity, sadism, savagery, sever-

crumble *v* break into small fragments; collapse **crumbly** *adj*

crumpet *n* flat, soft cake eaten with butter; *Sl* sexually desirable woman or women

crumple *v* (cause to) collapse; make or become creased

crunch *n* sound made by chewing crisp food, treading on gravel etc.; *Inf* critical situation ~*v* make crunching sound **crunchy** *adj*

crusade *n* medieval Christian war; concerted action to further a cause ~*v* take part in crusade **crusader** *n*

crush *v* compress so as to break; break to small pieces; defeat utterly ~*n* act of crushing; crowd of people etc.

crust *n* hard outer part of bread; similar casing **crusty** *adj* having crust; bad-tempered

crustacean *n* hard-shelled animal, e.g. crab, lobster

crutch *n* staff with crosspiece to go under armpit of lame person; support; crotch

crux *n* (*pl* **cruxes, cruces**) that on which a decision turns

cry *v* **crying, cried** weep; utter call; shout; beg (for); proclaim ~*n* loud utterance; call of animal; fit of weeping

crypt *n* vault, esp. under church **cryptic** *adj* secret, mysterious

crystal *n* transparent mineral; very clear glass; cut-glass ware; form with symmetrically arranged plane surfaces **crystalline** *adj* **crystallize** *v* form into crystals; become definite

cu. cubic

cub *n* young of fox and other animals; (*with cap.*) junior Scout

cubbyhole *n* small enclosed space

cube *n* solid figure with six equal square sides; cube-shaped block; product obtained by multiplying number by itself twice ~*v* multiply thus **cubic** *adj*

cubicle *n* enclosed section of room

cuckoo *n* (*pl* **-oos**) migratory bird; its call

cucumber *n* long fleshy green fruit used in salad

cud *n* food which ruminant animal brings back into mouth to chew again

cuddle *v* hug; lie close and snug, nestle ~*n* hug **cuddly** *adj*

———————— THESAURUS ————————

ity, spite, spitefulness, venom

cruise *v* coast, sail, voyage ~*n* boat trip, sail, sea trip, voyage

crumb atom, bit, grain, mite, morsel, particle, scrap, shred, sliver, snippet, *soupçon*, speck

crumble bruise, crumb, crush, fragment, granulate, grind, pound, powder; break up, collapse, come to dust, decay, decompose, degenerate, deteriorate, disintegrate, fall apart, go to pieces *Inf*, moulder, perish

crumple break down, cave in, collapse, fall, give way, go to pieces; crease, crush, pucker, rumple, screw up, wrinkle

crusade campaign, cause, drive, holy war, movement

crush break, bruise, compress, crease, crumble, crumple, crunch, mash, pound, pulverize, smash, squeeze, wrinkle; conquer, overcome, overpower, overwhelm, put down, quell, stamp out, subdue, vanquish

crust coat, coating, covering, layer, outside, shell, skin, surface

crusty brittle, crisp, crispy, friable, hard, short, well-baked, well-done

cry *v* bawl, bewail, blubber, lament, shed tears, snivel, sob, wail, weep, whimper, whine, whinge *Inf*; bawl, bellow, call, call out, exclaim, howl, roar, scream, screech, shout, shriek, whoop, yell ~*n* howl, lament, lamentation, snivel, snivelling, sob, sobbing, wailing, weep, weeping

cudgel *n* short thick stick ~*v* **-elling, -elled** beat with cudgel

cue[1] *n* signal to act or speak; hint

cue[2] *n* long tapering rod used in billiards

cuff[1] *n* ending of sleeve

cuff[2] *v* strike with open hand ~*n* blow with hand

cuisine *n* style of cooking; food cooked

cul-de-sac *n* (*pl* **culs-de-sac**) street open only at one end

culinary *adj* of, for, suitable for, cooking or kitchen

cull *v* select; take out animals from herd

culminate *v* reach highest point; come to a head **culmination** *n*

culottes *pl n* women's trousers flared like skirt

culpable *adj* blameworthy

culprit *n* one guilty of offence

cult *n* system of worship; devotion to some person, thing

cultivate *v* till and prepare (ground); develop, improve; devote attention to **cultivated** *adj* cultured **cultivation** *n*

culture *n* state of manners, taste and intellectual development; cultivating **cultural** *adj* cultured *adj*

culvert *n* drain under road

cumbersome *adj* unwieldy

cummerbund *n* sash worn round waist

cumulative *adj* becoming greater by successive additions

cumulus *n* (*pl* **-li**) round billowing cloud

cunning *adj* crafty, sly ~*n* skill in deceit or evasion

———————— THESAURUS ————————

cub offspring, whelp, young

cue hint, key, nod, prompting, reminder, sign, signal, suggestion

cul-de-sac blind alley, dead end

culminate climax, close, conclude, end, end up, finish, terminate

culmination acme, apex, apogee, climax, completion, conclusion, consummation, crown, finale, height, peak, perfection, pinnacle, summit, top, zenith

culpable answerable, at fault, blameworthy, guilty, in the wrong, liable, reprehensible, sinful, to blame, wrong

culprit criminal, delinquent, felon, guilty party, miscreant, offender, sinner, villain, wrongdoer

cult body, church faction, clique, denomination, faith, following, party, religion, school, sect; admiration, craze, devotion, reverence, veneration, worship

cultivate farm, harvest, plant, plough, prepare, tend, till, work; better, bring on, cherish, civilize, devel-op, foster, improve, promote, refine, train

cultivation advancement, advocacy, development, encouragement, enhancement, fostering, furtherance, help, nurture, patronage, promotion, support

cultural artistic, broadening, civilizing, edifying, educational, educative, elevating, enriching, humane, humanizing, liberal

culture civilization, customs, life style, mores, society, the arts, way of life; accomplishment, breeding, education, elevation, enlightenment, erudition, good taste, improvement, refinement, sophistication, urbanity

cultured accomplished, advanced, educated, enlightened, erudite, genteel, knowledgeable, polished, refined, scholarly, urbane, versed, well-bred, well-informed, well-read

cumbersome awkward, bulky, clumsy, heavy, unmanageable, unwieldy, weighty

cunning *adj* artful, astute, canny,

cup *n* small drinking vessel with handle; various cup-shaped formations; cup-shaped trophy as prize ~*v* **cupping, cupped** shape as cup (hands etc.) **cupful** *n* **cupboard** *n* piece of furniture with door, for storage

cur *n* dog of mixed breed; contemptible person

curate *n* parish priest's appointed assistant

curator *n* custodian, esp. of museum

curb *n* check, restraint ~*v* restrain; apply curb to

curd *n* coagulated milk **curdle** *v* turn into curd, coagulate

cure *v* heal, restore to health; remedy; preserve (fish, skins etc.) ~*n* remedy; course of medical treatment; restoration to health **curable** *adj*

curfew *n* official regulation prohibiting movement of people, esp. at night; deadline for this

curio *n* (*pl* **curios**) rare or curious thing sought for collections

curious *adj* eager to know, inquisitive; puzzling, odd **curiosity** *n* curiously *adv*

curl *v* take, bend into spiral or curved shape ~*n* spiral lock of hair; spiral **curly** *adj*

curlew *n* large long-billed wading bird

curmudgeon *n* bad-tempered person

currant *n* dried type of grape; fruit of various plants allied to gooseberry

current *adj* of immediate present; in general use ~*n* body of water or air in motion; transmission of electricity **currently** *adv* **currency** *n* money in use; state of being in use

curriculum *n* (*pl* **-lums, -la**) specified course of study **curriculum vitae** outline of career

curry *n* highly-flavoured, pungent condiment; dish flavoured with it ~*v* **currying, curried** prepare, flavour dish with curry

curse *n* profane or obscene expression of anger etc.; magic spell; affliction ~*v* utter curse, swear (at); afflict

———— THESAURUS ————

crafty, devious, guileful, knowing, Machiavellian, sharp, shifty, shrewd, subtle, tricky, wily ~*n* artfulness, astuteness, craftiness, deceitfulness, deviousness, guile, shrewdness, slyness, trickery

cup beaker, chalice, draught, drink, goblet, teacup

curb *n* brake, bridle, check, control, deterrent, limitation, restraint ~*v* bite back, bridle, check, constrain, contain, control, hinder, impede, inhibit, moderate, muzzle, repress, restrain, restrict, subdue, suppress

cure *v* alleviate, ease, heal, help, make better, mend, rehabilitate, relieve, remedy; dry, kipper, pickle, preserve, salt, smoke ~*n* antidote, healing, medicine, panacea, remedy, restorative, treatment

curiosity interest, prying; freak, marvel, novelty, oddity, phenomenon, rarity, sight, spectacle, wonder

curious inquiring, inquisitive, interested, puzzled, questioning, searching; bizarre, exotic, extraordinary, mysterious, novel, odd, peculiar, puzzling, quaint, queer, rare, singular, strange, unconventional, unique, unorthodox, unusual

curl *v* bend, coil, corkscrew, crimp, crinkle, crisp, curve, entwine, loop, meander, ripple, spiral, turn, twine, twirl, twist, wind, wreathe, writhe

currency bills, coinage, coins, money, notes

current *adj* accepted, circulating, common, customary, general, in the news, ongoing, popular, present, prevailing, prevalent, rife, widespread ~*n* course, draught, flow, jet, river, stream, tide

cursor *n* movable point showing position on computer screen

cursory *adj* hasty, superficial

curt *adj* rudely brief, abrupt

curtail *v* cut short

curtain *n* hanging drapery at window etc. ~*v* provide, cover with curtain

curtsy, curtsey *n/v* (perform) woman's bow

curve *n* line of which no part is straight ~*v* bend into curve

cushion *n* bag filled with soft stuffing or air, to support or ease body ~*v* provide, protect with cushion; lessen effects of

cushy *adj Inf* easy

custard *n* dish made of eggs and milk; sweet sauce of milk and cornflour

custody *n* guardianship, imprisonment **custodian** *n* keeper, curator

custom *n* habit; practice; usage; business patronage; *pl* taxes levied on imports **customary** *adj* usual, habitual

customer *n* one who enters shop to buy, esp. regularly; purchaser

cut *v* **cutting, cut** sever, wound, divide; pare, detach, trim; intersect; reduce, decrease; abridge; *Inf* ignore (person) ~*n* act of cutting; stroke; blow, wound; reduction; fashion, shape; *Inf* share **cutter** *n* **cutting** *n* piece cut from plant; article from newspaper; passage for railway ~*adj* keen, piercing; hurtful **cutthroat** *n* killer ~*adj* murderous; fiercely competitive

cute *adj* appealing, pretty

cuticle *n* dead skin, esp. at base of fingernail

cutlass *n* curved sword

cutlery *n* knives, forks etc.

cutlet *n* small piece of meat

cuttlefish *n* sea mollusc like squid

———— THESAURUS ————

curse *n* blasphemy, expletive, oath, obscenity, swearword; evil eye, execration, hoodoo *Inf,* jinx; affliction, bane, burden, calamity, disaster, evil, hardship, misfortune, ordeal, plague, scourge, torment, tribulation, trouble, vexation ~*v* blaspheme, swear, use bad language

curt abrupt, blunt, brief, brusque, gruff, offhand, rude, sharp, short, snappish, tart, terse

curtail abbreviate, abridge, contract, cut, cut back, decrease, dock, lessen, lop, pare down, reduce, shorten, trim, truncate

curtain *n* drape *chiefly US,* hanging ~*v* conceal, drape, hide, screen, shroud, shut off, shutter, veil

curve *n* arc, bend, camber, loop, turn ~*v* arc, arch, bend, bow, coil, hook, inflect, turn, twist, wind

cushion *n* beanbag, hassock, headrest, pad, pillow ~*v* bolster, buttress, cradle, dampen, deaden, muffle, soften, stifle, support

custody arrest, confinement, detention, imprisonment, incarceration

custom habit, manner, routine, way, wont

customary accepted, accustomed, acknowledged, common, confirmed, conventional, everyday, familiar, fashionable, general, normal, ordinary, popular, regular, routine, traditional, usual

customer buyer, client, consumer, patron, regular *Inf,* shopper

cut *v* chop, cleave, divide, gash, incise, lacerate, nick, notch, pierce, score, sever, slash, slice, slit, wound; contract, cut back, decrease, lower, rationalize, reduce, slash, slim (down); abbreviate, abridge, condense, curtail, delete, edit out, excise, shorten ~*n* gash, graze, groove, incision, laceration, nick, rip, slash, slit, stroke, wound; cutback, decrease, economy, fall, lowering, reduction, saving

CV curriculum vitae

cwt. hundredweight

cyanide *n* extremely poisonous chemical compound

cybernetics *pl n* (*with sing v*) comparative study of control mechanisms of electronic and biological systems

cyclamen *n* plant with flowers having turned-back petals

cycle *n* recurrent, complete series or period; bicycle ~*v* ride bicycle **cyclical** *adj* **cyclist** *n* bicycle rider

cyclone *n* circular storm

cygnet *n* young swan

cylinder *n* roller-shaped body, of uniform diameter **cylindrical** *adj*

cymbal *n* one of two brass plates struck together to produce clashing sound

cynic *n* one who believes the worst about people or outcome of events **cynical** *adj* **cynicism** *n* being cynical

cypress *n* coniferous tree with very dark foliage

cyst *n* sac containing liquid secretion or pus **cystitis** *n* inflammation of bladder

Czar, Tsar *n* emperor, esp. of Russia 1547-1917

———————— THESAURUS ————————

cutthroat *n* assassin, butcher, executioner, hit man *Sl*, killer, murderer, thug ~*adj* barbarous, bloodthirsty, bloody, cruel, ferocious, homicidal, murderous, savage, thuggish, violent; competitive, dog-eat-dog, fierce, relentless, ruthless, unprincipled

cutting *adj* biting, bitter, chill, keen, numbing, penetrating, piercing, raw, sharp, stinging

cycle age, circle, era, period, phase, revolution, rotation

cynic doubter, pessimist, sceptic, scoffer

cynical derisive, ironic, misanthropical, mocking, pessimistic, sarcastic, sardonic, sceptical, scornful, sneering

cynicism disbelief, doubt, misanthropy, pessimism, sarcasm, scepticism

D d

dab *v* **dabbing, dabbed** apply with momentary pressure ~*n* small mass

dabble *v* splash about; be amateur (in)

dachshund *n* short-legged long-bodied dog

dad, daddy *n Inf* father **daddy-longlegs** *n Inf* fly with long thin legs

daffodil *n* yellow spring flower

daft *adj* foolish, crazy

dagger *n* short stabbing weapon

dahlia *n* garden plant of various colours

daily *adj/adv* (done) every day ~*n* daily newspaper; charwoman

dainty *adj* delicate; choice; fastidious ~*n* delicacy **daintiness** *n*

dairy *n* place for processing milk and its products

dais *n* raised platform

daisy *n* flower with yellow centre and white petals

dale *n* valley

dally *v* **-lying, -lied** trifle; loiter

Dalmatian *n* white dog with black spots

dam *n/v* **damming, dammed** (barrier to) hold back flow of waters

damage *n* injury, harm; *pl* compensation for injury ~*v* harm

damask *n* patterned woven material; velvety red

dame *n Obs* lady; (*with cap.*) title of lady in Order of the British Empire; *Sl* woman

damn *v* **damning, damned** condemn; curse ~*interj* expression of annoyance etc. **damnable** *adj* **damnation** *n*

damp *adj* moist ~*n* moisture ~*v* make damp; deaden **dampen** *v* damp **damper** *n* anything that discourages; plate in flue

damson *n* small dark-purple plum

dance *v* move with rhythmic steps, to music; bob up and down; perform (dance) ~*n* rhythmical movement; social gathering **dancer** *n*

dandelion *n* yellow-flowered wild

THESAURUS

dabble dally, dip into, play at, potter, tinker, trifle (with)

dagger bayonet, dirk, poniard, skean

daily *adj* diurnal, everyday, quotidian; common, commonplace, day-to-day, everyday, ordinary, regular, routine ~*adv* day after day, every day, often, once a day, regularly

dainty charming, delicate, elegant, fine, graceful, neat, petite, pretty

dam *n* barrage, barrier, hindrance, obstruction, wall ~*v* barricade, block, check, choke, confine, hold back, hold in, obstruct, restrict

damage *n* destruction, devastation, harm, hurt, injury, loss, suffering; *pl* fine, indemnity, reimbursement, reparation, satisfaction ~*v* deface, harm, hurt, impair, injure, mar, mu-

tilate, ruin, spoil, tamper with, wreck

damn *v* blast, castigate, censure, condemn, criticize, denounce, denunciate, lambast(e), pan *Inf*, slam *Sl*, slate *Inf*; abuse, curse, execrate, imprecate, revile, swear; condemn, doom, sentence

damp *adj* clammy, dank, dewy, dripping, drizzly, humid, misty, moist, muggy, sodden, soggy, sopping, wet ~*n* dampness, darkness, dew, drizzle, fog, humidity, mist, moisture, vapour ~*v* dampen, moisten, wet; allay, check, chill, cool, curb, dash, deaden, deject, diminish, discourage, dull, inhibit, moderate, restrain, stifle

dance *v* caper, frolic, gambol, hop, jig, prance, rock, skip, spin, sway, swing, trip ~*n* ball, dancing party,

plant

dandruff *n* dead skin in small scales among the hair

dandy *n* man excessively concerned with smartness of dress *~adj Inf* excellent

danger *n* exposure to harm; peril **dangerous** *adj* **dangerously** *adv*

dangle *v* hang loosely

dank *adj* damp and chilly

dapper *adj* neat, spruce

dappled *adj* marked with spots

dare *v* have courage (to); challenge *~n* challenge **daring** *adj/n* **daredevil** *adj/n* reckless (person)

dark *adj* without light; gloomy; deep in tint; unenlightened *~n* absence of light **darken** *v* **darkly** *adv* **darkness** *n* **dark horse** person, thing about whom little is known

darling *adj/n* beloved (person)

darn *v* mend (hole) by sewing

dart *n* small pointed missile; darting motion; small seam *pl* indoor game played with numbered target *~v* throw, go rapidly

dash *v* move hastily; throw, strike violently; frustrate *~n* rush; small amount; smartness; punctuation mark (-) showing change of subject **dashing** *adj* lively, stylish **dashboard** *n* instrument panel

dastardly *adj* mean

data *pl n* (*oft. with sing v*) series of facts; information **database** *n* store of information

date[1] *n* day of the month; time of occurrence; appointment *~v* mark with date; reveal age of; exist (from); become old-fashioned **dated** *adj*

——————— THESAURUS ———————

knees-up *Brit inf,* social

danger hazard, insecurity, jeopardy, menace, peril, risk, threat, venture, vulnerability

dangerous alarming, exposed, hazardous, insecure, menacing, nasty, perilous, risky, threatening, treacherous, ugly, unsafe

dangle depend, flap, hang, hang down, sway, swing, trail

dare *v* brave, gamble, hazard, make bold, presume, risk, stake, venture; challenge, defy, goad, provoke, taunt *~n* challenge, defiance, provocation, taunt

daring *adj* adventurous, bold, brave, fearless, game *Inf,* impulsive, intrepid, plucky, rash, reckless, valiant, venturesome *~n* balls *Taboo sl,* boldness, bottle *Brit sl,* bravery, courage, fearlessness, grit, guts *Inf,* nerve *Inf,* pluck, spirit, temerity

dark *adj* black, dusky, ebony, sable, swarthy; cloudy, dim, dingy, gloomy, indistinct, murky, overcast, pitch-black, pitchy, shadowy, shady, sun-

less, unlit *~n* darkness, dimness, dusk, gloom, murk

darkness dark, dimness, dusk, gloom, murk, nightfall, obscurity, shade, shadiness, shadows

darling *adj* adored, beloved, cherished, dear, precious, treasured *~n* beloved, dear, dearest, love, sweetheart

darn mend, patch, repair, sew up, stitch

dart bound, dash, flash, flit, fly, race, run, rush, shoot, spring, sprint, tear, whiz

dash *v* bolt, bound, dart, fly, haste, hasten, hurry, race, run, rush, speed, spring, sprint, tear; break, crash, destroy, shatter, shiver, smash; confound, dampen, disappoint, discourage, frustrate, thwart

dashing bold, daring, debonair, exuberant, gallant, plucky, spirited, swashbuckling

data details, documents, facts, figures, information, input, materials, statistics

date² *n* fruit of palm

daub *v* paint roughly

daughter *n* one's female child
daughter-in-law *n* son's wife

daunt *v* frighten into giving up purpose **daunting** *adj*

dawdle *v* idle, loiter

dawn *n* daybreak; beginning ~*v* begin to grow light; (begin to) be understood

day *n* period of 24 hours; time when sun is above horizon; time period **daybreak** *n* dawn **daydream** *n* idle fancy ~*v* have such fancies **daydreamer** *n* **daylight** *n* natural light; dawn

daze *v* stun, bewilder ~*n* bewildered state **dazed** *adj*

dazzle *v* blind, confuse with brightness; impress greatly **dazzling** *adj*

DC direct current

de- *comb. form* removal of, from, reversal of, as in **delouse, desegregate**

deacon *n* (*fem* **deaconess**) one who assists in a church

dead *adj* no longer alive; obsolete; numb; lacking vigour; complete ~*n* (*oft. pl* **the dead**) dead person(s) ~*adv* utterly **deaden** *v* **deadly** *adj* fatal; deathlike ~*adv* as if dead; extremely **deadline** *n* limit of time allowed **deadlock** *n* standstill **deadpan** *adj* expressionless

deaf *adj* without hearing; unwilling to listen **deafen** *v* make deaf **deafness** *n*

deal¹ *v* dealing, dealt distribute; act; treat; do business (with, in) ~*n* agreement; treatment; share **dealer** *n*

──────── THESAURUS ────────

date age, epoch, era, period, stage, time; appointment, assignation, engagement, meeting, rendezvous, tryst

dated antiquated, archaic, obsolete, old-fashioned, old hat, out, outdated, out of date, passé, unfashionable

daub *v* coat, cover, paint, plaster, slap on *Inf,* smear

daunt alarm, appal, cow, dismay, frighten, intimidate, overawe, scare, subdue, terrify

dawdle dally, delay, hang about, idle, lag, loaf, loiter, potter, waste time

dawn *n* daybreak, daylight, morning, sunrise ~*v* break, brighten, gleam, glimmer, lighten

day daylight, daytime, twenty-four hours, working day; date, particular day, point in time, set time, time

daybreak break of day, cockcrow, crack of dawn, dawn, first light, morning, sunrise, sunup

daydream *n* dream, fancy, fantasy, pipe dream, wish ~*v* dream, fancy, fantasize, imagine, muse

daylight sunlight, sunshine

dazed baffled, bemused, bewildered, confused, dizzy, fuddled, light-headed, muddled, numbed, perplexed, shocked, staggered, stunned, stupefied

dazzle bedazzle, blind, blur, confuse, daze; amaze, astonish, awe, bowl over *Inf,* impress, overawe, overpower, overwhelm, strike dumb, stupefy

dead deceased, defunct, departed, extinct, gone, inanimate, late, lifeless, passed away, perished; callous, cold, dull, frigid, glassy, glazed, indifferent, spiritless, torpid, unresponsive, wooden; boring, dull, flat, ho-hum *Inf,* insipid, stale, tasteless, uninteresting, vapid

deadlock dead heat, draw, full stop, halt, impasse, stalemate, tie

deadly baleful, baneful, dangerous, deathly, destructive, fatal, lethal, malignant, mortal, noxious, pernicious, poisonous, venomous

deaf hard of hearing, stone deaf; oblivious, unconcerned, unhearing, unmoved

deafen din, drown out, make deaf, split the eardrums

deal[2] *n* (plank of) pine wood

dean *n* university official; head of cathedral chapter

dear *adj* beloved; precious; expensive ~*n* beloved one **dearly** *adv*

dearth *n* scarcity

death *n* dying; end of life; end **deathly** *adj/adv*

debacle *n* utter collapse, rout, disaster

debase *v* lower in value

debate *v* argue, esp. formally ~*n* formal discussion **debatable** *adj* **debater** *n*

debauched *adj* leading life of depraved self-indulgence **debauchery** *n*

debilitate *v* weaken

debit *Accounting n* entry in account of sum owed ~*v* enter as due

debonair *adj* suave, genial

debrief *v* report result of mission

debris *n* rubbish

debt *n* what is owed; state of owing **debtor** *n*

debunk *v* expose falseness of, esp. by ridicule

debut *n* first appearance in public **debutante** *n* girl making society debut

Dec. December

deca- *comb. form* ten, as in **decalitre**

decade *n* period of ten years

decadent *adj* deteriorating; morally corrupt **decadence** *n*

decaffeinated *adj* (of tea, coffee) with caffeine removed

decant *v* pour off (wine) **decanter** *n* stoppered bottle

decapitate *v* behead

decathlon *n* athletic contest for men

——————— THESAURUS ———————

deal *v* bargain, buy and sell, do business, negotiate, sell, stock, trade, traffic; allot, apportion, assign, bestow, dispense, distribute, divide, dole out, give, reward, share ~*n* agreement, arrangement, bargain, contract, pact, transaction, understanding

dealer merchant, purveyor, supplier, trader, tradesman, wholesaler

dear *adj* beloved, cherished, close, darling, esteemed, familiar, favourite, intimate, precious, prized, respected, treasured; costly, expensive, high-priced ~*n* angel, beloved, darling, loved one, precious, treasure

dearly extremely, greatly, profoundly, very much

death bereavement, decease, demise, departure, dying, end, exit, expiration, loss, passing, release; destruction, downfall, end, extinction, finish, grave, ruin, undoing

deathly gaunt, ghastly, grim, haggard, pale, pallid, wan; deadly, extreme, fatal, intense, mortal, terrible

debase cheapen, degrade, demean, devalue, disgrace, dishonour, drag down, humble, lower, reduce, shame

debatable arguable, borderline, controversial, disputable, doubtful, dubious, in dispute, moot, open to question, questionable, uncertain, unsettled

debate *v* argue, contend, contest, discuss, dispute, question, wrangle ~*n* argument, contention, controversy, discussion, disputation, dispute

debris bits, dross, fragments, litter, pieces, remains, rubbish, rubble, ruins, waste, wreck, wreckage

debt arrears, bill, commitment, debit, due, duty, liability, obligation, score

debtor borrower, defaulter, insolvent

debunk cut down to size, deflate, disparage, expose, lampoon, mock, puncture, ridicule, show up

debut beginning, bow, coming out, entrance, inauguration, initiation, introduction, launching

decadent corrupt, debased, decaying, declining, degenerate, degraded,

with ten events

decay v rot; decline ~n rotting

decease n death ~v die **deceased** adj/n dead (person)

deceive v mislead, delude **deceit** n fraud; duplicity **deceitful** adj

decelerate v slow down

December n twelfth month

decent adj respectable; fitting; adequate; Inf kind **decency** n

deception n deceiving; trick **deceptive** adj misleading

decibel n unit for measuring intensity of sound

decide v settle; give judgement; come to a decision **decided** adj unmistakable; resolute **decidedly** adv **decision**

n **decisive** adj final; able to make (quick) decisions **decisiveness** n

deciduous adj (of trees) losing leaves annually

decimal adj relating to tenths ~n decimal fraction **decimalization** n **decimal point** dot between unit and fraction

decimate v destroy or kill a tenth of, large proportion of

decipher v make out meaning of; decode

deck n floor, esp. one covering ship's hull; turntable of record player ~v decorate **deck chair** folding canvas chair

declaim v speak rhetorically

———— THESAURUS ————

depraved, dissolute, immoral

decay v crumble, decline, degenerate, deteriorate, disintegrate, dissolve, dwindle, moulder, shrivel, sink, spoil, wane, wither; decompose, mortify, perish, putrefy, rot

deceased adj dead, defunct, departed, expired, finished, former, gone, late

deceit artifice, cheating, cunning, dissimulation, double-dealing, duplicity, fraud, hypocrisy, pretence, slyness, treachery, trickery

deceitful crafty, designing, dishonest, disingenuous, double-dealing, duplicitous, fallacious, false, fraudulent, hypocritical, illusory, insincere, treacherous, two-faced, underhand, untrustworthy

deceive betray, cheat, con Inf, delude, double-cross Inf, dupe, ensnare, entrap, fool, hoax, hoodwink, mislead, outwit, swindle, take in Inf, trick

decency correctness, courtesy, decorum, etiquette, good form, good manners, modesty, propriety, seemliness

decent becoming, chaste, comely,

decorous, delicate, fit, modest, nice, polite, presentable, proper, pure, respectable, seemly, suitable

deception cunning, deceit, duplicity, fraud, fraudulence, guile, hypocrisy, imposition, insincerity, treachery, trickery

deceptive deceitful, delusive, dishonest, fake, false, fraudulent, illusory, misleading, mock, specious, spurious, unreliable

decide adjudicate, choose, commit oneself, conclude, decree, determine, elect, end, purpose, resolve, settle

decipher construe, crack, decode, explain, interpret, make out, read, reveal, solve, understand, unfold, unravel

decision conclusion, finding, judgment, outcome, resolution, result, ruling, sentence, settlement, verdict

decisive absolute, conclusive, critical, crucial, definite, definitive, fateful, final, influential, significant; determined, firm, forceful, incisive, resolute, strong-minded

deck v adorn, array, attire, beautify, bedeck, bedight, clothe, decorate, dress, embellish, festoon, grace,

declare *v* announce formally; state emphatically **declaration** *n*

decline *v* refuse; slope downwards; deteriorate; diminish ~*n* deterioration; diminution; downward slope

decode *v* convert from code into ordinary language **decoder** *n*

decompose *v* rot

decongestant *adj/n* (drug) relieving (esp. nasal) congestion

decontaminate *v* render harmless

decor *n* decorative scheme

decorate *v* beautify; paint room etc.; invest (with medal etc.) **decoration** *n* **decorative** *adj* **decorator** *n*

decorum *n* propriety, decency **deco-**

rous *adj*

decoy *n* bait, lure ~*v* lure, be lured as with decoy

decrease *v* diminish, lessen ~*n* diminishing

decree *n/v* **-creeing, -creed** (give) order having the force of law

decrepit *adj* old; worn out

decry *v* **-crying, -cried** disparage

dedicate *v* commit wholly to special purpose; inscribe or address; devote **dedicated** *adj* **dedication** *n*

deduce *v* draw as conclusion

deduct *v* subtract **deductible** *adj* **deduction** *n* deducting; amount subtracted; conclusion

———————— T H E S A U R U S ————————

ornament

declaim harangue, hold forth, lecture, proclaim, rant, recite, speak

declaration announcement, edict, manifesto, notification, promulgation, pronouncement; affirmation, assertion, disclosure, revelation, statement, testimony

declare affirm, announce, assert, attest, aver, avow, claim, confirm, maintain, proclaim, profess, pronounce, state, swear, testify

decline *v* abstain, avoid, deny, forgo, refuse, reject, say 'no', turn down; decrease, diminish, drop, dwindle, ebb, fade, fail, fall, fall off, flag, lessen, shrink, sink, wane ~*n* deterioration, downturn, dwindling, falling off, lessening, recession, slump

decorate adorn, beautify, deck, embellish, enrich, festoon, grace, ornament, trim; colour, furbish, paint, paper, renovate; cite, honour

decoration adornment, embellishment, enrichment, ornamentation, trimming; award, badge, colours, emblem, garter, medal, order, ribbon, star

decorum behaviour, breeding, decency, dignity, etiquette, gentility,

good grace, good manners, gravity, politeness, propriety, protocol, respectability, seemliness

decoy *n* attraction, bait, enticement, inducement, lure, pretence, trap ~*v* allure, bait, deceive, ensnare, entice, entrap, inveigle, lure, seduce, tempt

decrease *v* abate, contract, curtail, cut down, decline, diminish, drop, dwindle, ease, fall off, lessen, lower, reduce, shrink, wane ~*n* cutback, decline, ebb, falling off, loss, reduction, shrinkage

decree *n* act, canon, command, edict, enactment, law, mandate, order, precept, proclamation, regulation, ruling, statute ~*v* command, decide, determine, dictate, enact, lay down, ordain, order, prescribe, proclaim

decrepit aged, crippled, debilitated, feeble, frail, incapacitated, infirm, weak

dedicate commit, devote, give over to, pledge, surrender

dedicated committed, devoted, enthusiastic, purposeful, single-minded, wholehearted, zealous

deduce conclude, derive, draw, gather, glean, infer, reason, understand

deduct decrease by, reduce by, re-

deed *n* action; exploit; legal document

deem *v* judge, consider, regard

deep *adj* extending far down; at, of given depth; profound; hard to fathom; (of colour) dark; (of sound) low *~n* deep place; the sea *~adv* far down etc. **deeply** *adv* **deepen** *v*

deer *n* (*pl* **deer**) ruminant animal typically with antlers in male

deface *v* spoil or mar surface

defame *v* speak ill of **defamation** *n* **defamatory** *adj*

default *n* failure to act, appear or pay *~v* fail (to pay)

defeat *v* vanquish; thwart *~n* overthrow

defecate *v* empty the bowels

defect *n* lack, blemish *~v* desert **defection** *n* **defective** *adj* **defector** *n*

defend *v* protect, ward off attack; support by argument **defence** *n* protection; justification; statement by accused person in court **defenceless** *adj* **defendant** *n* person accused in court **defender** *n* **defensible** *adj* **defensive** *adj* serving for defence *~n* attitude of defence

defer[1] *v* -ferring, -ferred postpone

defer[2] *v* -ferring, -ferred submit to opinion or judgement of another **deference** *n* obedience; respect **deferential** *adj*

deficient *adj* lacking in something **de-**

move, subtract, take away, take from, withdraw

deduction decrease, diminution, discount, reduction, subtraction; conclusion, consequence, finding, inference, reasoning, result

deed act, action, exploit, fact, feat, reality

deep *adj* bottomless, broad, far, profound, wide, yawning; extreme, grave, great, intense, profound; *of a sound* bass, booming, full-toned, low, low-pitched, resonant, sonorous

default *n* absence, defect, failure, lack, lapse, neglect, nonpayment, omission, want *~v* defraud, dodge, evade, fail, neglect

defeat *v* beat, conquer, crush, master, overpower, overthrow, overwhelm, quell, repulse, rout, subdue, subjugate, vanquish *~n* conquest, debacle, overthrow, repulse, rout

defect *n* blemish, blotch, error, failing, fault, flaw, imperfection, mistake, spot, taint, want *~v* change sides, desert, go over, rebel, revolt

defective broken, faulty, flawed, imperfect, inadequate, incomplete, insufficient, not working, out of order

defence armament, cover, deterrence, guard, immunity, protection, resistance, safeguard, security, shelter; apologia, argument, excuse, exoneration, explanation, justification, plea, vindication; *Law* alibi, case, denial, plea, rebuttal, testimony

defend cover, fortify, guard, keep safe, preserve, protect, screen, secure, shelter, shield; assert, champion, endorse, espouse, justify, maintain, plead, stand by, stand up for, support, sustain, uphold, vindicate

defender bodyguard, escort, guard, protector; advocate, champion, patron, sponsor, supporter, vindicator

defer[1] adjourn, delay, hold over, postpone, protract, put off, set aside, shelve, suspend, table

defer[2] accede, bow, capitulate, comply, give in, give way to, respect, submit, yield

defiance challenge, contempt, disobedience, disregard, insolence, insubordination, opposition, rebelliousness, spite

deficiency defect, demerit, failing, fault, flaw, frailty, shortcoming, weakness

ficiency *n* **deficit** *n* amount by which sum of money is too small

defile *v* soil; sully

define *v* state meaning of; mark out **definite** *adj* exact; clear; certain **definitely** *adv* **definition** *n* **definitive** *adj* conclusive

deflate *v* (cause to) collapse by release of gas from **deflation** *n Economics* reduction of economic and industrial activity

deflect *v* (cause to) turn from straight course **deflection** *n*

deform *v* spoil shape of; disfigure **deformity** *n*

defraud *v* cheat, swindle

defrost *v* make, become free of frost, ice; thaw

deft *adj* skilful, adroit

defunct *adj* dead, obsolete

defuse *v* remove fuse of bomb etc.; remove tension

defy *v* **-fying, -fied** challenge, resist successfully **defiance** *n* resistance **defiant** *adj* openly and aggressively hostile

degenerate *v* deteriorate to lower level ~*adj* fallen away in quality ~*n* degenerate person **degeneration** *n* **degenerative** *adj*

degrade *v* dishonour; debase; reduce; decompose chemically **degradable** *adj* **degradation** *n*

degree *n* step, stage in process; university rank; unit of measurement

dehydrate *v* remove moisture from

deify *v* **-fying, -fied** make a god of **deity** *n* god

deign *v* condescend

déjà vu Fr feeling of having experienced something before

dejected *adj* miserable **dejection** *n*

delay *v* **delaying, delayed** postpone; linger ~*n* delaying

——————— THESAURUS ———————

deficit arrears, default, deficiency, loss, shortage, shortfall

define describe, designate, detail, determine, explain, expound, interpret, specify, spell out

definite clear, clear-cut, determined, exact, explicit, express, fixed, marked, obvious, particular, precise, specific

definitely absolutely, categorically, certainly, clearly, easily, finally, indubitably, obviously, plainly, positively, surely, undeniably, unequivocally, unmistakably, unquestionably, without doubt

definition clarification, description, elucidation, explanation, exposition

deflate collapse, contract, exhaust, flatten, puncture, shrink, void

deflect bend, diverge, glance off, shy, sidetrack, swerve, turn, twist, veer, wind

defraud cheat, delude, dupe, embezzle, fleece, outwit, swindle, trick

deft able, adept, adroit, agile, clever, dexterous, expert, handy, neat, nimble, proficient, skilful

defy beard, brave, challenge, confront, dare, despise, disregard, face, flout, provoke, scorn, slight, spurn

degenerate *v* decay, decline, deteriorate, fall off, lapse, regress, rot, sink, slip, worsen ~*adj* base, corrupt, debased, debauched, decadent, degraded, depraved, dissolute, fallen, immoral, low, mean

degrade cheapen, corrupt, debase, demean, discredit, disgrace, dishonour, humble, humiliate, impair, pervert, shame

degree class, grade, level, order, position, rank, standing, station, status

dejected cast down, crestfallen, depressed, despondent, disconsolate, disheartened, down, downcast, gloomy, glum, low, melancholy, miserable, morose, sad, wretched

delay *v* defer, hold over, postpone,

delectable *adj* delightful

delegate *n* representative ~*v* send as deputy; entrust **delegation** *n*

delete *v* remove, erase **deletion** *n*

deliberate *adj* intentional; well-considered; slow ~*v* consider **deliberately** *adv* **deliberation** *n*

delicate *adj* exquisite; fragile; requiring tact **delicacy** *n* elegance; delicious food

delicatessen *n* shop selling esp. imported or unusual foods

delicious *adj* delightful, pleasing to taste

delight *v* please greatly; take great pleasure (in) ~*n* great pleasure **de-**lightful *adj* charming

delinquent *n/adj* (one) guilty of delinquency **delinquency** *n* (minor) offence or misdeed

delirium *n* disorder of mind, esp. in feverish illness; violent excitement **delirious** *adj*

deliver *v* carry to destination; hand over; release; give birth or assist in birth (of); utter **deliverance** *n* rescue **delivery** *n*

dell *n* wooded hollow

delta *n* alluvial tract at river mouth

delude *v* deceive; mislead **delusion** *n*

deluge *n* flood, downpour ~*v* flood, overwhelm

─────────── THESAURUS ───────────

procrastinate, prolong, protract, put off, shelve, stall, suspend ~*n* check, deferment, hindrance, hold-up, postponement, procrastination, stay, stoppage, suspension, wait

delegate *n* agent, ambassador, commissioner, deputy, envoy, legate, representative, vicar

delegation commission, contingent, deputation, embassy, envoys, legation, mission

delete blot out, cancel, cross out, cut out, dele, edit, efface, erase, expunge, obliterate, remove, rub out

deliberate *adj* calculated, conscious, considered, designed, intentional, planned, premeditated, purposeful, studied, thoughtful, wilful ~*v* cogitate, consider, consult, debate, discuss, meditate, mull over, ponder, reflect, think, weigh

deliberation care, carefulness, caution, circumspection, consideration, coolness, forethought, meditation, prudence, purpose, reflection, speculation, study, thought, wariness

delicacy elegance, exquisiteness, fineness, lightness, nicety, precision, subtlety; dainty, luxury, relish, savoury, titbit, treat

delicate accurate, deft, detailed, exquisite, minute, precise, skilled; ailing, debilitated, flimsy, fragile, frail, sickly, slender, slight, tender, weak; considerate, diplomatic, discreet, sensitive, tactful

delicious appetizing, choice, dainty, luscious, mouthwatering, savoury, tasty, toothsome

delight *v* amuse, charm, cheer, divert, enchant, gratify, please, ravish, rejoice, satisfy, thrill ~*n* ecstasy, enjoyment, gladness, gratification, happiness, joy, pleasure, rapture, transport

delightful agreeable, amusing, captivating, charming, delectable, engaging, enjoyable, entertaining, heavenly, pleasant, pleasurable, thrilling

deliver bear, bring, carry, cart, convey, distribute, transport; cede, commit, give up, grant, hand over, make over, relinquish, resign, surrender, transfer, turn over, yield

delivery consignment, conveyance, dispatch, distribution, handing over, surrender, transfer, transmission, transmittal

delude beguile, cheat, con *Inf,* deceive, dupe, fool, hoax, hoodwink, kid *Inf,* misguide, mislead, take in

de luxe rich, sumptuous; superior in quality

delve v (*with* into) search intensively; dig

demagogue n mob leader or agitator

demand v ask as giving an order; call for as due, necessary ~n urgent request; call for **demanding** adj requiring effort

demean v degrade, lower

demeanour n conduct, bearing

demented adj mad, crazy **dementia** n mental deterioration

demerit n undesirable quality

demi- comb. form half, as in **demigod**

demijohn n large bottle

demilitarize v prohibit military presence

demise n death; conveyance by will or lease

demobilize v disband (troops); discharge (soldier)

democracy n government by the people or their elected representatives; state so governed **democrat** n advocate of democracy **democratic** adj

demolish v knock to pieces; destroy utterly **demolition** n

demon n devil, evil spirit

demonstrate v show by reasoning, prove; describe, explain; make exhibition of support, protest etc. **demonstrable** adj **demonstration** n **demonstrative** adj expressing feelings; pointing out; conclusive **demonstrator** n one who takes part in a public demonstration; assistant in laboratory etc.

demoralize v deprive of courage; undermine morally

demote v reduce in rank **demotion** n

——————— THESAURUS ———————

Inf, trick

deluge cataclysm, downpour, flood, overflowing, spate, torrent

de luxe choice, costly, elegant, exclusive, expensive, grand, opulent, palatial, rich, select, special, splendid, splendiferous *Facetious,* sumptuous, superior

demand v ask, challenge, inquire, interrogate, question, request; call for, cry out for, entail, involve, necessitate, need, require, take, want ~n bidding, charge, inquiry, interrogation, order, question, request, requisition

demanding challenging, difficult, exacting, exhausting, hard, taxing, tough, trying

demeanour air, bearing, behaviour, carriage, conduct, deportment, manner, mien

democracy commonwealth, government by the people, representative government, republic

democratic autonomous, egalitarian, popular, populist, representative, republican, self-governing

demolish bulldoze, destroy, dismantle, flatten, knock down, level, overthrow, pulverize, raze, ruin, tear down, trash *Sl;* annihilate, defeat, destroy, overthrow, overturn, undo, wreck

demonstrable attestable, certain, evident, evincible, incontrovertible, indubitable, irrefutable, obvious, positive, self-evident, undeniable, unmistakable, verifiable

demonstrate display, establish, evidence, exhibit, indicate, prove, show, testify to; describe, explain, illustrate, make clear, show how, teach; march, parade, picket, protest, rally

demonstration confirmation, display, evidence, exhibition, expression, illustration, manifestation, proof, testimony, validation; explanation, exposition, presentation, test, trial; march, mass lobby, parade, picket, protest, rally, sit-in

demur v -murring, -murred make difficulties, object ~n demurring

demure adj reserved

den n hole of wild beast; small room, esp. study

denigrate v belittle

denim n strong cotton fabric

denizen n inhabitant

denomination n particular sect or church; name, esp. of class or group **denominator** n divisor in fraction

denote v stand for; show

denouement n unravelling of plot

denounce v speak violently against; accuse **denunciation** n

dense adj thick, compact; stupid **density** n

dent n/v (make) hollow or mark by blow or pressure

dental adj of teeth or dentistry **dentist** n surgeon who attends to teeth **dentistry** n art of dentist **denture** n (usu. pl) set of false teeth

denude v strip, make bare

deny v -nying, -nied declare untrue; contradict; reject; refuse to give **denial** n

deodorant n substance to mask odour

depart v go away; start out; vary; die **departure** n

department n division; branch **departmental** adj

depend v (usu. with on) rely entirely; live; be contingent **dependable** adj reliable **dependant** n one who relies on another **dependent** adj depending on **dependence, dependency** n

———————— THESAURUS ————————

demoralize cripple, daunt, deject, depress, disconcert, discourage, dishearten, dispirit, undermine, unnerve, weaken

demure decorous, diffident, grave, modest, reserved, reticent, retiring, sedate, shy, sober, staid, unassuming

den cave, cavern, haunt, hide-out, hole, lair, shelter

denial contradiction, disavowal, disclaimer, dismissal, dissent, negation, prohibition, rebuff, refusal, renunciation, repudiation, repulse, retraction, veto

denigrate belittle, besmirch, blacken, calumniate, decry, defame, disparage, impugn, knock Inf, malign, revile, rubbish Inf, run down, slag (off) Sl, slander, vilify

denote betoken, designate, express, imply, import, indicate, mark, mean, show, signify, typify

denounce accuse, attack, castigate, censure, condemn, decry, impugn, proscribe, revile, stigmatize, vilify

dense close, compact, compressed, condensed, heavy, impenetrable,

opaque, solid, substantial, thick, thickset

dent n chip, crater, depression, dimple, dip, hollow, impression, indentation, pit ~v depress, dint, hollow, imprint, press in, push in

deny contradict, disagree with, disprove, oppose, rebuff, refute; abjure, disavow, discard, disclaim, disown, recant, reject, renege, renounce, repudiate, retract, revoke

depart decamp, disappear, escape, exit, go, go away, leave, migrate, quit, remove, retire, retreat, set forth, start out, vanish, withdraw

department district, division, province, region, sector; branch, bureau, division, office, section, station, subdivision, unit

departure exit, exodus, going, leave-taking, leaving, removal, retirement, withdrawal; branching out, change, difference, innovation, novelty, shift, variation

depend bank on, build upon, calculate on, confide in, count on, lean on, reckon on, rely upon, trust in, turn

depict *v* give picture of; describe **depiction** *n*

deplete *v* empty; reduce **depletion** *n*

deplore *v* lament, regret; denounce **deplorable** *adj*

deploy *v* organize (troops) in battle formation **deployment** *n*

depopulate *v* (cause to) be reduced in population **depopulation** *n*

deport *v* expel, banish **deportation** *n*

deportment *n* behaviour

depose *v* remove from office; make statement on oath

deposit *v* set down; give into safe keeping; let fall ~*n* thing deposited; money given in part payment; sediment **deposition** *n* statement written and attested; act of deposing or depositing **depositor** *n* **depository** *n*

depot *n* storehouse

deprave *v* make bad, corrupt **depravity** *n*

deprecate *v* express disapproval of

depreciate *v* (cause to) fall in value, price; belittle **depreciation** *n*

depress *v* affect with low spirits; lower **depression** *n* hollow; low spirits; low state of trade

deprive *v* dispossess **deprivation** *n* **deprived** *adj* lacking adequate food, care, amenities etc.

dept. department

THESAURUS

to; be based on, be contingent on, be determined by, be subject to, hinge on, rest on

dependent counting on, defenceless, helpless, immature, reliant, relying on, vulnerable, weak; conditional, contingent, depending, determined by, liable to, relative, subject to

deplete consume, decrease, drain, empty, evacuate, exhaust, expend, impoverish, lessen, milk, reduce, use up

deplorable calamitous, dire, disastrous, distressing, grievous, lamentable, melancholy, miserable, pitiable, regrettable, sad, unfortunate, wretched; disgraceful, disreputable, execrable, opprobrious, reprehensible, scandalous, shameful

deplore bemoan, bewail, grieve for, lament, mourn, regret, rue, sorrow over; abhor, censure, condemn, denounce, deprecate, disapprove of, object to

depose break, cashier, degrade, demote, dethrone, dismiss, displace, downgrade, remove from office

deposit *v* drop, lay, locate, place, precipitate, put, settle, sit down ~*n* down payment, instalment, money (*in bank*), part payment, pledge, retainer, security, stake, warranty

depot repository, storehouse, warehouse

deprave corrupt, debase, debauch, degrade, demoralize, pervert, seduce, vitiate

depreciate decrease, deflate, devalue, lessen, lose value, lower, reduce

depreciation depression, devaluation, drop, fall, slump; belittlement, derogation, detraction, disparagement

depress cast down, chill, damp, deject, desolate, discourage, dishearten, dispirit, oppress, sadden, weigh down

depression dejection, despair, despondency, dolefulness, downheartedness, gloominess, hopelessness, low spirits, melancholy, sadness; *Commerce* downturn, economic decline, hard *or* bad times, inactivity, lowness, recession, slump, stagnation

deprive bereave, despoil, dispossess, divest, expropriate, rob, strip, wrest

deprived bereft, denuded, destitute, disadvantaged, forlorn, in need, in want, lacking, needy, poor

depth *n* (degree of) deepness; deep place; intensity

deputy *n* assistant; delegate **deputation** *n* **deputize** *v* act as deputy

derange *v* put out of place, order; make insane

deregulate *v* remove regulations or controls from

derelict *adj* abandoned; falling into ruins **dereliction** *n* neglect of duty; abandonment

deride *v* treat with contempt, ridicule **derision** *n* **derisive** *adj* **derisory** *adj*

derive *v* get, come from **derivation** *n* **derivative** *adj*

dermatitis *n* inflammation of skin

derogatory *adj* belittling

derv *n* diesel oil for road vehicles

descant *n Mus* decorative variation to basic melody

descend *v* come or go down; spring from; be transmitted; attack **descendant** *n* person descended from an ancestor **descent** *n*

describe *v* give detailed account of **description** *n* **descriptive** *adj*

desecrate *v* violate sanctity of; profane

desert[1] *n* uninhabited and barren region

desert[2] *v* abandon, leave; run away from service **deserter** *n* **desertion** *n*

desert[3] *n* (*usu. pl*) what is due as reward or punishment

deserve *v* show oneself worthy of

design *v* sketch; plan; intend ~*n* sketch; plan; decorative pattern; project **designer** *n/adj*

———————— THESAURUS ————————

depth abyss, deepness, drop, extent, measure, profundity

deputation commission, delegates, delegation, embassy, envoys, legation

deputize act for, stand in for, understudy

deputy agent, ambassador, commissioner, legate, lieutenant, proxy, representative, substitute, surrogate

derelict abandoned, deserted, discarded, forsaken, neglected, ruined

derisory contemptible, insulting, laughable, ludicrous, outrageous, preposterous, ridiculous

derivation ancestry, basis, beginning, descent, etymology, foundation, genealogy, origin, root, source

derive collect, deduce, draw, elicit, extract, follow, gain, gather, get, glean, infer, obtain, procure, receive, trace

descend alight, dismount, drop, fall, go down, move down, plunge, sink, subside, tumble; be handed down, be passed down, derive, issue, originate, proceed, spring

descent coming down, drop, fall, plunge, swoop; ancestry, extraction, family tree, genealogy, heredity, lineage, origin, parentage

describe characterize, define, depict, detail, explain, express, illustrate, narrate, portray, recount, relate, report, specify, tell

description account, characterization, detail, explanation, narrative, portrayal, report, representation, sketch

desert[1] solitude, waste, wasteland, wilderness, wilds

desert[2] *v* abandon, abscond, betray, decamp, defect, forsake, give up, jilt, leave, leave stranded, maroon, quit, rat (on), relinquish, renounce, resign, throw over, vacate, walk out on *Inf*

deserter absconder, defector, escapee, fugitive, runaway, traitor, truant

deserve be entitled to, be worthy of, earn, gain, justify, merit, procure, rate, warrant, win

design *v* describe, draft, draw, outline, plan, sketch, trace; aim, conceive, contrive, create, devise, intend,

designate *v* name, appoint ~*adj* appointed but not yet installed

desire *v* wish, long for; ask for ~*n* longing; expressed wish; sexual appetite **desirable** *n* worth having; attractive **desirability** *n* **desirous** *adj*

desist *v* cease, stop

desk *n* writing table

desolate *adj* uninhabited; neglected; solitary; forlorn ~*v* lay waste; overwhelm with grief **desolation** *n*

despair *v* lose hope ~*n* loss of all hope; cause of this

desperate *adj* reckless from despair; hopelessly bad **desperately** *adv* desperation *n* **desperado** *n* (*pl* -does) reckless, lawless person

despise *v* look down on as inferior **despicable** *adj* base, contemptible, vile

despite *prep* in spite of

despoil *v* plunder, rob

despondent *adj* dejected, depressed

despot *n* tyrant, oppressor **despotic** *adj* **despotism** *n*

dessert *n* sweet course, or fruit, served at end of meal

destination *n* place one is bound for

——————— THESAURUS ———————

make, originate, plan, project, propose, purpose, scheme, think up ~*n* blueprint, draft, drawing, model, outline, plan, scheme, sketch

designer artificer, creator, deviser, inventor, originator, stylist

desirable advisable, agreeable, beneficial, eligible, enviable, good, pleasing, preferable, profitable, worthwhile; alluring, attractive, fascinating, fetching, seductive

desire *v* aspire to, covet, crave, fancy, hanker after, hope for, long for, thirst for, want, wish for, yearn for; ask, entreat, importune, petition, request, solicit ~*n* appetite, craving, hankering, longing, need, thirst, want, wish; appetite, concupiscence, lasciviousness, lechery, libido, lust, lustfulness, passion

desist abstain, break off, cease, discontinue, end, forbear, give up, kick *Inf*, leave off, pause, refrain from, stop, suspend

desolate bare, barren, bleak, desert, dreary, godforsaken, ruined, solitary, uninhabited, waste, wild; abandoned, bereft, comfortless, dejected, depressing, despondent, dismal, downcast, forlorn, forsaken, gloomy, lonely, melancholy, miserable, wretched

desolation destruction, devastation, havoc, ravages, ruin, ruination

despair *v* despond, give up, lose heart, lose hope ~*n* anguish, depression, desperation, gloom, hopelessness, melancholy, misery, wretchedness

desperate dangerous, daring, determined, foolhardy, frantic, furious, hasty, headstrong, impetuous, madcap, rash, reckless, risky, violent, wild; despairing, forlorn, hopeless, irrecoverable, irretrievable, wretched

desperately badly, dangerously, gravely, perilously, seriously, severely

despise abhor, deride, detest, disdain, disregard, flout, loathe, look down on, neglect, revile, scorn, slight

despite *prep* against, even with, in spite of, in the face of, notwithstanding, regardless of

despondent blue, dejected, depressed, despairing, disconsolate, discouraged, disheartened, dismal, doleful, down, downcast, gloomy, glum, hopeless, in despair, low, melancholy, miserable, morose, sad, sorrowful, wretched

despotic absolute, arbitrary, arrogant, authoritarian, autocratic, dictatorial, domineering, imperious, oppressive, tyrannical, unconstitutional

destine v ordain beforehand; set apart from fate

destitute adj in absolute want

destroy v ruin; put an end to; demolish **destroyer** n small, swift warship **destructible** adj **destruction** n ruin **destructive** adj

desultory adj aimless; unmethodical

detach v unfasten, separate **detachable** adj **detached** adj standing apart; disinterested **detachment** n aloofness; detaching; body of troops on special duty

detail n particular; small or unimportant part; treatment of anything item

by item; soldier assigned for duty ~v relate in full; appoint

detain v keep under restraint; keep waiting **detention** n

detect v find out or discover **detection** n **detective** n policeman detecting crime **detector** n

détente n lessening of international tension

deter v -terring, -terred discourage; prevent **deterrent** adj/n

detergent n/adj cleaning (substance)

deteriorate v become or make worse **deterioration** n

determine v decide; fix; be deciding

———————— THESAURUS ————————

destination harbour, haven, journey's end, landing-place, resting-place, station, stop, terminus

destine allot, appoint, assign, consecrate, decree, design, devote, doom, earmark, fate, intend, mark out, ordain, predetermine, purpose, reserve

destiny doom, fate, fortune, lot, portion

destitute distressed, down and out, flat broke *Inf*, impoverished, indigent, insolvent, moneyless, needy, penniless, poor

destroy annihilate, blow to bits, crush, demolish, desolate, devastate, dismantle, eradicate, kill, ravage, raze, ruin, shatter, slay, smash, trash *Sl*, wipe out, wreck

destruction demolition, devastation, downfall, end, extermination, havoc, liquidation, massacre, ruin, ruination, slaughter, wreckage, wrecking

destructive baleful, baneful, calamitous, cataclysmic, catastrophic, damaging, deadly, deleterious, detrimental, devastating, fatal, harmful, hurtful, injurious, lethal, pernicious, ruinous

detach cut off, disconnect, disengage, disentangle, disjoin, disunite, divide, free, isolate, loosen, remove, separate, sever, tear off, uncouple, unfasten

detachment aloofness, coolness, indifference, remoteness; detail, patrol squad, unit

detail n aspect, component, count, element, fact, factor, feature, item, particular, point, respect, specific, technicality ~v allocate, appoint, assign, charge, commission, delegate, detach, send

detain check, delay, hinder, hold up, impede, keep, keep back, retard, slow up (or down), stay, stop; arrest, confine, hold, intern, restrain

detect catch, descry, distinguish, identify, note, notice, observe, recognize, scent, spot

detective C.I.D. man, constable, investigator, private eye, sleuth *Inf*

detention confinement, custody, delay, hindrance, holding back, imprisonment, restraint

deter caution, check, damp, daunt, debar, discourage, dissuade, frighten, hinder, inhibit from, intimidate, prevent, prohibit, put off, restrain, stop, talk out of

detergent n cleaner, cleanser ~adj cleaning, cleansing, purifying

deteriorate decline, degenerate, de-

factor in; come to an end; come to a decision **determination** *n* determining; resolute conduct; resolve **determined** *adj* resolute

detest *v* hate, loathe **detestable** *adj*

dethrone *v* remove from position of authority

detonate *v* (cause to) explode **detonation** *n* **detonator** *n*

detour *n* roundabout way

detract *v* take away (a part) from, diminish **detractor** *n*

detriment *n* harm done, loss, damage **detrimental** *adj*

deuce *n* card with two spots; *Tennis* forty all; in exclamatory phrases, the devil

devalue, devaluate *v* reduce in value **devaluation** *n*

devastate *v* lay waste; ravage **devastated** *adj* extremely shocked **devastation** *n*

develop *v* **developing, developed** bring to maturity; elaborate; evolve; treat photographic film to bring out image; improve or change use of (land); grow to maturer state **developer** *n* **development** *n*

deviate *v* diverge **deviant** *n/adj* (person) deviating from normal, esp. in sexual practices **deviation** *n* **devious** *adj* deceitful; roundabout **deviousness** *n*

device *n* contrivance; scheme

——————————— THESAURUS ———————————

grade, deprave, depreciate, go downhill *Inf*, lower, spoil, worsen

determination backbone, constancy, conviction, dedication, doggedness, drive, firmness, fortitude, perseverance, persistence, resolution, resolve, single-mindedness, steadfastness, tenacity, willpower

determine arbitrate, conclude, decide, end, finish, fix upon, ordain, regulate, settle

determined bent on, constant, dogged, firm, fixed, intent, persistent, purposeful, resolute, set on, single-minded, steadfast, tenacious, unflinching, unwavering

deterrent check, curb, discouragement, disincentive, hindrance, impediment, obstacle, restraint

detest abominate, despise, execrate, hate, loathe

detour bypass, byway, diversion

detract diminish, lessen, lower, reduce, take away from

detriment damage, disservice, harm, hurt, injury, loss, mischief, prejudice

detrimental adverse, baleful, deleterious, destructive, harmful, inimical, injurious, pernicious, prejudicial,

unfavourable

devastate demolish, desolate, despoil, destroy, lay waste, level, pillage, plunder, ravage, raze, ruin, sack, spoil, total *Sl*, trash *Sl*, waste, wreck

devastation demolition, depredation, desolation, destruction, havoc, pillage, plunder, ravages, ruin, ruination

develop advance, cultivate, evolve, foster, grow, mature, progress, promote, prosper, ripen; amplify, augment, broaden, dilate upon, elaborate, enlarge, expand, unfold, work out

development advance, advancement, evolution, expansion, growth, improvement, increase, maturity, progress, progression, spread, unfolding; change, circumstance, event, happening, incident, issue, occurrence, outcome, result, situation, upshot

deviate avert, bend, deflect, depart, differ, digress, diverge, drift, err, part, stray, swerve, turn, turn aside, vary, veer, wander

deviation alteration, change, deflec-

devil *n* personified spirit of evil; person of great wickedness, cruelty etc.; *Inf* fellow; *Inf* something difficult or annoying **devilish** *adj* **devilment** *n* **devilry** *n* **devil-may-care** *adj* happy-go-lucky

devise *v* plan

devoid *adj* (*usu. with* of) empty

devolve *v* (cause to) pass on to another **devolution** *n* devolving

devote *v* give up exclusively (to person, purpose etc.) **devoted** *adj* loving **devotee** *n* ardent enthusiast **devotion** *n* deep affection; dedication; *pl* prayers

devour *v* eat greedily

devout *adj* deeply religious

dew *n* moisture from air deposited as small drops at night

dexterity *n* manual skill **dexterous** *adj*

diabetes *n* various disorders characterized by excretion of abnormal amount of urine **diabetic** *n/adj*

diabolic *adj* devilish **diabolical** *adj Inf* extremely bad

diadem *n* crown

diagnosis *n* (*pl* -ses) identification of disease from symptoms **diagnose** *v*

diagonal *adj/n* (line) from corner to corner

diagram *n* drawing, figure, to illustrate something

dial *n* face of clock etc.; plate marked with graduations on which pointer moves; numbered disc on front of

———— THESAURUS ————

tion, departure, digression, discrepancy, disparity, divergence, inconsistency, irregularity, shift, variance, variation

device apparatus, appliance, contraption, contrivance, gadget, gimmick, gismo *or* gizmo *Sl*, implement, instrument, invention, tool, utensil; artifice, design, dodge, expedient, gambit, manoeuvre, plan, ploy, project, purpose, ruse, scheme, shift, stratagem, stunt, trick

devil demon, fiend, Satan; beast, brute, demon, monster, ogre, rogue, savage, terror, villain

devious calculating, deceitful, dishonest, evasive, indirect, insidious, insincere, scheming, sly, surreptitious, treacherous, tricky, underhand, wily

devise arrange, conceive, concoct, construct, contrive, design, dream up, form, formulate, frame, imagine, invent, plan, plot, prepare, project, scheme, think up

devoid barren, bereft, deficient, denuded, destitute, empty, free from, lacking, unprovided with, vacant,

void, wanting, without

devote allot, apply, appropriate, assign, commit, concern oneself, dedicate, enshrine, give, pledge, reserve

devoted ardent, caring, committed, concerned, constant, dedicated, devout, faithful, fond, loving, loyal, staunch, steadfast, true

devour bolt, consume, cram, eat, gobble, gorge, gulp, guzzle, pig out on *Sl*, stuff, swallow, wolf

devout godly, holy, orthodox, pious, prayerful, pure, religious, reverent, saintly

dexterity adroitness, artistry, deftness, expertise, facility, finesse, handiness, knack, mastery, neatness, nimbleness, proficiency, skill, smoothness, touch

diagnose analyse, determine, distinguish, identify, interpret, pinpoint, pronounce, recognize

diagnosis analysis, examination

diagonal *adj* angled, cross, crossways, crosswise, oblique, slanting

diagram chart, drawing, figure, layout, outline, plan, representation, sketch

telephone ~v **dialling, dialled** operate telephone

dialect n characteristic speech of district

dialogue n conversation

dialysis n (pl **dialyses**) Med filtering of blood through membrane to remove waste products

diameter n (length of) straight line through centre of circle **diametrically** adv completely

diamond n very hard and brilliant precious stone; rhomboid figure; suit at cards

diaphragm n muscle between abdomen and chest

diarrhoea n excessive looseness of the bowels

diary n daily record of events; book for this

diatribe n violently bitter verbal attack, denunication

dice pl n (sing **dice, die**) cubes each with six sides marked one to six for games of chance ~v gamble with dice; Cookery cut vegetables into small cubes

dichotomy n division into two parts

dictate v say or read for another to transcribe; prescribe; impose ~n bidding **dictation** n **dictator** n absolute ruler **dictatorial** adj **dictatorship** n

diction n choice and use of words; enunciation

dictionary n book listing, alphabetically, words with meanings etc.

did past tense of DO

die[1] v **dying, died** cease to live; end; Inf look forward (to) **die-hard** n/adj (person) resisting change

die[2] n shaped block to form metal in forge, press etc.

diesel adj pert. to internal-combustion engine using oil as fuel ~n this engine; the fuel

diet n restricted or regulated course of feeding; kind of food lived on ~v follow a diet, as to lose weight **dietary** adj

differ v be unlike; disagree **difference** n unlikeness; point of unlikeness; disagreement; remainder left after subtraction **different** adj **differently** adv

differential adj varying with circum-

———————— **THESAURUS** ————————

dialect accent, idiom, jargon, language, patois, pronunciation, provincialism, speech, tongue, vernacular

dialogue communication, conference, conversation, converse, discourse, discussion, interlocution

diary appointment book, chronicle, daily record, day-to-day account, engagement journal

dictate read out, say, speak, transmit, utter; command, decree, direct, enjoin, impose, lay down, ordain, order, prescribe

dictator absolute ruler, autocrat, despot, oppressor, tyrant

diction language, phraseology, phrasing, style, usage; articulation, delivery, elocution, enunciation, inflection, intonation, pronunciation,

speech

dictionary concordance, encyclopedia, glossary, lexicon, vocabulary, wordbook

die croak Sl, decease, depart, expire, finish, kick the bucket Sl, pass away, perish; decay, decline, disappear, dwindle, ebb, end, fade, lapse, pass, sink, vanish, wane, wilt, wither

die-hard n fanatic, old fogy, reactionary, zealot ~adj dyed-in-the-wool, immovable, inflexible, intransigent, reactionary

diet n abstinence, dietary, fast, regime, regimen; commons, fare, food, nourishment, provisions, rations, sustenance ~v fast, lose weight, reduce, slim

differ be dissimilar, be distinct,

stances ~*n* mechanism in car etc. allowing back wheels to revolve at different speeds; difference between two rates of pay **differentiate** *v* serve to distinguish between, make different; discriminate

difficult *adj* requiring effort, skill etc.; not easy; obscure **difficulty** *n* difficult task, problem; embarrassment; hindrance; trouble

diffident *adj* lacking confidence

diffuse *v* spread slowly ~*adj* widely spread; loose, wordy **diffusion** *n*

dig *v* digging, dug work with spade; turn up with spade; excavate; thrust into ~*n* piece of digging; thrust; jibe;

pl Inf lodgings

digest *v* prepare (food) in stomach etc. for assimilation; bring into handy form by summarizing ~*n* methodical summary **digestible** *adj* **digestion** *n* **digestive** *adj*

digit *n* finger or toe; numeral **digital** *adj*

dignity *n* stateliness; gravity; worthiness **dignify** *v* -fying, -fied give dignity to **dignitary** *n* holder of high office

digress *v* deviate from subject **digression** *n*

dike *n see* DYKE

dilapidated *adj* in ruins

dilate *v* widen, expand **dilation** *n*

———— THESAURUS ————

contradict, contrast, depart from, diverge, run counter to, stand apart, vary

difference alteration, change, contrast, deviation, differentiation, discrepancy, disparity, dissimilarity, distinction, divergence, diversity, variation, variety; distinction, exception, idiosyncrasy, peculiarity, singularity; argument, clash, conflict, contention, contretemps, controversy, debate, disagreement, discordance, dispute, quarrel, row, strife, tiff, wrangle

different altered, at variance, changed, clashing, contrasting, deviating, disparate, dissimilar, divergent, diverse, inconsistent, opposed, unlike; assorted, diverse, manifold, many, miscellaneous, multifarious, numerous, several, some, sundry, varied, various

differentiate contrast, discern, discriminate, distinguish, mark off, separate, tell apart

difficult arduous, demanding, formidable, hard, laborious, onerous, painful, strenuous, toilsome, uphill, wearisome

difficulty awkwardness, hardship, labour, pain, painfulness, strain, tribulation; deep water, dilemma, distress, fix *Inf,* hot water *Inf,* jam *Inf,* mess, pickle *Inf,* plight, predicament, quandary, spot *Inf,* tight spot, trial, trouble

diffident backward, bashful, doubtful, hesitant, insecure, meek, modest, reluctant, reserved, self-conscious, sheepish, shrinking, shy, timid, unsure, withdrawn

dig *v* break up, burrow, delve, excavate, grub, hoe, hollow out, mine, penetrate, pierce, quarry, scoop, till, tunnel, turn over ~*n* jab, poke, prod, punch, thrust; barb, cutting remark, gibe, insult, jeer, quip, taunt, wisecrack *Inf*

digest absorb, assimilate, concoct, dissolve, incorporate; absorb, assimilate, consider, contemplate, grasp, master, meditate, ponder, study, take in, understand

dignitary notability, notable, personage, public figure, V.I.P., worthy

dignity decorum, grandeur, gravity, majesty, nobility, propriety, solemnity, stateliness

digress depart, deviate, diverge, drift, expatiate, ramble, stray, turn aside, wander

dilemma *n* position offering choice only between unwelcome alternatives

dilettante *n* (*pl* **dilettanti, -tes**) person who enjoys fine arts as pastime; dabbler

diligent *adj* hard-working **diligently** *adv* **diligence** *n*

dill *n* herb with medicinal seeds

dilute *v* reduce (liquid) in strength, esp. by adding water **dilution** *n*

dim *adj* **dimmer, dimmest** faint, not bright; mentally dull; unfavourable ~*v* **dimming, dimmed** make, grow dim **dimly** *adv*

dime *n US* 10-cent piece

dimension *n* measurement, size

diminish *v* lessen **diminutive** *adj* very small

diminuendo *adj/adv Mus* (of sound) dying away

dimple *n* small hollow in surface of skin, esp. of cheek

din *n* continuous roar of confused noises ~*v* **dinning, dinned** ram (fact,

opinion etc.) into

dine *v* eat dinner **diner** *n*

dinghy *n* small open boat; collapsible rubber boat

dingo *n* (*pl* **-goes**) Aust. wild dog

dingy *adj* dirty-looking, dull

dinner *n* chief meal of the day; official banquet

dinosaur *n* extinct reptile, often of gigantic size

dint *n* **by dint of** by means of

diocese *n* district, jurisdiction of bishop

diode *n Electronics* device for converting alternating current to direct current

dip *v* **dipping, dipped** plunge or be plunged partly or for a moment into liquid; take up in ladle, bucket etc.; direct headlights of vehicle downwards; go down; slope downwards ~*n* act of dipping; bathe; downward slope; hollow

diphtheria *n* infectious disease caus-

———————— THESAURUS ————————

dilapidated battered, broken-down, crumbling, decayed, decaying, decrepit, falling apart, in ruins, neglected, ramshackle, rickety, ruined, run-down, shabby, shaky, tumble-down, worn-out

dilemma difficulty, embarrassment, mess, perplexity, plight, predicament, problem, puzzle, quandary, spot *Inf*, strait

diligence activity, application, assiduity, attention, attentiveness, care, constancy, industry, perseverance

diligent active, assiduous, attentive, busy, careful, conscientious, constant, earnest, hard-working, indefatigable, industrious, laborious, persevering, persistent, studious, tireless

dilute *v* adulterate, cut, thin (out), water down, weaken

dim *adj* cloudy, dark, darkish, dusky, grey, overcast, poorly lit, shadowy;

dense, doltish, dozy *Brit inf*, dull, obtuse, slow, stupid, thick ~*v* blur, cloud, darken, dull, fade, lower, obscure, tarnish, turn down

diminish abate, contract, curtail, cut, decrease, lessen, lower, reduce, retrench, shrink, weaken

diminutive little, midget, miniature, minute, petite, pygmy *or* pigmy, small, teensy-weensy, tiny, wee

din babel, clamour, clangour, clash, clatter, commotion, crash, hullabaloo, noise, outcry, pandemonium, racket, row, shout, uproar

dingy colourless, dark, dim, dirty, discoloured, drab, dreary, dull, dusky, faded, gloomy, grimy, murky, obscure, seedy, shabby, soiled, sombre

dinner banquet, collation, feast, meal, refection, repast, spread *Inf*

dip *v* bathe, douse, duck, dunk, immerse, plunge, rinse, souse; ladle,

ing breathing difficulties

diphthong *n* union of two vowel sounds

diploma *n* document vouching for person's proficiency

diplomacy *n* management of international relations; tactful dealing **diplomat** *n* **diplomatic** *adj*

dipper *n* ladle, scoop; bird (water ouzel)

dipsomania *n* uncontrollable craving for alcohol **dipsomaniac** *n/adj*

dire *adj* terrible; urgent

direct *v* control, manage, order; point out the way; aim *~adj* frank; straight; immediate; lineal **direction** *n* direct-

ing; aim; instruction **directive** *adj/n* **directly** *adj* **directness** *n* **director** *n* one who directs, esp. a film; member of board managing company **directorial** *adj* **directorship** *n* **directory** *n* book of names, addresses, streets etc.

dirge *n* song of mourning

dirk *n* short dagger

dirt *n* filth; soil; obscene material **dirty** *adj* unclean; obscene; unfair; dishonest

dis- *comb. form* negation, opposition, deprivation; in many verbs indicates undoing of the action of simple verb

disable *v* make unable; cripple, maim **disabled** *adj* **disability** *n*

———— T H E S A U R U S ————

scoop, spoon *~n* douche, drenching, ducking, immersion, plunge, soaking; bathe, dive, plunge, swim; basin, concavity, depression, hole, hollow, incline, slope; decline, drop, fall, lowering, sag, slip, slump

diplomacy statecraft, statesmanship; craft, delicacy, discretion, finesse, savoir-faire, skill, subtlety, tact

diplomat go-between, mediator, moderator, negotiator, politician

diplomatic adept, discreet, polite, politic, prudent, sensitive, subtle, tactful

dire alarming, awful, calamitous, cataclysmic, catastrophic, cruel, disastrous, horrible, ruinous, terrible, woeful; dismal, dreadful, fearful, gloomy, grim, ominous, portentous

direct *v* administer, advise, conduct, control, govern, guide, lead, manage, oversee, preside over, regulate, rule, run, superintend, supervise; guide, indicate, lead, show *~adj* candid, frank, honest, open, outspoken, sincere, straight, upfront *Inf*

direction administration, charge, command, control, government, guidance, leadership, management, order, oversight, supervision; aim,

bearing, course, line, path, road, route, track, way

directly exactly, precisely, straight, unswervingly; candidly, face-to-face, honestly, in person, openly, personally, plainly, point-blank, straightforwardly, truthfully, unequivocally

director administrator, chairman, chief, controller, executive, governor, head, leader, manager, organizer, principal, producer

dirt dust, filth, grime, impurity, mire, muck, mud, slime, smudge, stain, tarnish; clay, earth, loam, soil

dirty filthy, foul, grimy, grotty *Sl*, grubby, messy, mucky, muddy, nasty, polluted, soiled, sullied, unclean; corrupt, crooked, dishonest, fraudulent, illegal, treacherous, unfair, unscrupulous, unsporting

disability affliction, ailment, defect, disorder, handicap, impairment, infirmity, malady

disable cripple, damage, handicap, immobilize, impair, incapacitate, paralyse, prostrate, unfit, unman, weaken

disabled bedridden, crippled, handicapped, incapacitated, infirm, lame, mangled, mutilated, paralysed, weak

disabuse v undeceive, disillusion; free from error

disadvantage n drawback; hindrance ~v handicap **disadvantaged** adj deprived, discriminated against **disadvantageous** adj

disaffected adj ill-disposed **disaffection** n

disagree v -greeing, -greed be at variance; conflict; (of food etc.) have bad effect on **disagreeable** adj **disagreement** n

disallow v reject as invalid

disappear v cease to be visible; cease to exist **disappearance** n

disappoint v fail to fulfil (hope) **disappointment** n

disarm v deprive of weapons; win over **disarming** adj removing hostility, suspicion **disarmament** n

disarray v throw into disorder ~n disorderliness

disaster n sudden or great misfortune **disastrous** adj

disband v (cause to) cease to function as a group

disbelieve v reject as false

disburse v pay out money

disc n thin, flat, circular object; record **disc jockey** announcer playing records

discard v reject; cast off

discern v make out; distinguish **discernible** adj **discerning** adj discriminating

discharge v release; dismiss; emit; perform (duties), fulfil (obligations); fire off; unload; pay ~n discharging; being discharged

disciple n follower of a teacher

—————— THESAURUS ——————

disadvantage damage, detriment, disservice, harm, hurt, injury, loss, prejudice

disagree be discordant, be dissimilar, conflict, contradict, counter, depart, deviate, differ, diverge, vary

disagreeable bad-tempered, churlish, cross, difficult, disobliging, ill-natured, irritable, peevish, rude, surly, unfriendly, unlikable, unpleasant

disagreement difference, discrepancy, disparity, divergence, incompatibility, incongruity, variance; argument, clash, conflict, debate, difference, discord, dispute, dissent, division, falling out, quarrel, row, squabble, wrangle

disappear abscond, depart, drop out of sight, ebb, escape, fade away, flee, fly, go, pass, recede, retire, wane, withdraw; cease, die out, dissolve, end, evaporate, expire, fade, pass away, perish, vanish

disappearance departure, desertion, eclipse, evanescence, evaporation,

fading, flight, loss, passing, vanishing

disappoint dash, deceive, disenchant, dishearten, disillusion, dismay, dissatisfy, fail, let down, sadden, vex

disappointment discontent, disenchantment, disillusionment, distress, failure, frustration, regret

disarray confusion, dismay, disorder, disunity, indiscipline, unruliness, upset

disaster accident, adversity, blow, calamity, catastrophe, misadventure, mischance, misfortune, mishap, reverse, ruin, stroke, tragedy, trouble

disastrous adverse, catastrophic, destructive, detrimental, devastating, dire, dreadful, fatal, hapless, harmful, ill-fated, ill-starred, ruinous, terrible, tragic, unfortunate, unlucky, untoward

discard abandon, cast aside, dispense with, dispose of, ditch Sl, drop, get rid of, jettison, reject, scrap, shed

discharge v absolve, acquit, allow to go, clear, free, liberate, pardon, re-

discipline *n* training that produces orderliness, obedience, self-control; system of rules etc.; punishment ~*v* train; punish **disciplinarian** *n* person practising strict discipline **disciplinary** *adj*

disclaim *v* deny, renounce **disclaimer** *n*

disclose *v* make known **disclosure** *n*

disco *n* club etc. for dancing to recorded music

discolour *v* stain

discomfit *v* embarrass

discomfort *n* inconvenience

disconcert *v* ruffle, upset

disconnect *v* break connection; stop supply of electricity, gas etc.

disconsolate *adj* very unhappy

discontent *n* lack of contentment

discontinue *v* bring to an end

discord *n* strife; disagreement of sounds **discordant** *adj*

discount *v* reject as unsuitable; deduct from usual price ~*n* amount deducted from cost

discourage *v* reduce confidence of; deter; show disapproval of **discouragement** *n*

lease, set free; discard, dismiss, expel, oust; accomplish, carry out, do, execute, fulfil, observe, perform; detonate, explode, fire, let off, let off, shoot ~*n* blast, burst, discharging, explosion, firing, report, salvo, shot, volley; acquittal, clearance, liberation, pardon, release, remittance

disciple apostle, believer, convert, devotee, follower, learner, partisan, proselyte, pupil, student, supporter

disciplinarian despot, martinet, stickler, taskmaster, tyrant

discipline *n* drill, exercise, method, practice, regulation; conduct, control, orderliness, regulation, restraint, strictness; chastisement, correction, punishment ~*v* break in, bring up, check, control, drill, educate, exercise, form, govern, instruct, prepare, regulate, restrain, train

disclose broadcast, communicate, confess, divulge, impart, leak, let slip, make known, make public, publish, relate, reveal, tell, unveil, utter

discolour fade, mar, mark, rust, soil, stain, streak, tarnish, tinge

discomfit ache, annoyance, disquiet, distress, hardship, hurt, irritation, nuisance, pain, soreness, trouble, uneasiness, vexation

disconcert abash, agitate, disturb,

fluster, nonplus, perplex, perturb, rattle *Inf,* ruffle, take aback, trouble, unnerve, unsettle, upset, worry

disconnect cut off, detach, divide, part, separate, sever, take apart, uncouple

disconsolate dejected, desolate, despairing, dismal, forlorn, gloomy, heartbroken, hopeless, inconsolable, melancholy, miserable, sad, unhappy, wretched

discontinue abandon, axe *Inf,* break off, cease, drop, end, finish, give up, halt, interrupt, pause, put an end to, quit, refrain from, stop, suspend, terminate

discord clashing, conflict, contention, difference, dispute, dissension, disunity, division, friction, opposition, row, rupture, strife, variance, wrangling; cacophony, din, dissonance, harshness, jangle, jarring

discount *v* disbelieve, disregard, ignore, overlook, pass over; lower, mark down, rebate, reduce, take off ~*n* allowance, concession, cut, cut price, deduction, rebate, reduction

discourage abash, awe, cast down, damp, dampen, dash, daunt, deject, demoralize, depress, dishearten, dismay, frighten, intimidate, overawe, psych out *Inf,* scare, unnerve

discourse *n* conversation; speech ~*v* speak, converse

discourteous *adj* showing bad manners

discover *v* (be the first to) find; learn about for first time **discovery** *n*

discredit *v* damage reputation of; cast doubt on; reject as untrue ~*n* disgrace; doubt

discreet *adj* prudent, circumspect

discrepancy *n* variation, as between figures

discrete *adj* separate, distinct

discretion *n* quality of being discreet; freedom to act as one chooses **discretionary** *adj*

discriminate *v* show prejudice; distinguish between **discriminating** *adj* showing good taste **discrimination** *n*

discursive *adj* rambling

discus *n* disc-shaped object thrown in athletic competition

discuss *v* exchange opinions about; debate **discussion** *n*

———— T H E S A U R U S ————

discouragement dejection, depression, despair, despondency, disappointment, dismay, hopelessness, low spirits, pessimism

discourse *n* chat, communication, conversation, converse, dialogue, discussion, speech, talk ~*v* confer, converse, debate, declaim, discuss, speak, talk

discourteous abrupt, abusive, bad-mannered, brusque, curt, ill-mannered, impolite, insolent, off-hand, rude, uncivil, ungentlemanly, ungracious, unmannerly

discover come across, come upon, dig up, find, light upon, locate, turn up, uncover, unearth; ascertain, descry, detect, determine, discern, disclose, espy, find out, learn, notice, perceive, realize, recognize, reveal, see, spot, suss (out) *Sl,* uncover

discovery ascertainment, detection, disclosure, exploration, finding, introduction, location, origination, revelation; breakthrough, coup, find, findings, innovation, invention, secret

discredit *v* blame, bring into disrepute, censure, defame, degrade, detract from, disgrace, dishonour, disparage, reproach, slander, slur, smear, vilify; challenge, deny, disbelieve, discount, dispute, distrust, doubt, mistrust, question ~*n* asper-

sion, censure, disgrace, dishonour, disrepute, ignominy, ill-repute, odium, reproach, scandal, shame, slur, smear, stigma; distrust, doubt, mistrust, question, scepticism, suspicion

discreet careful, cautious, circumspect, considerate, diplomatic, discerning, guarded, judicious, politic, prudent, reserved, tactful, wary

discrepancy conflict, difference, disagreement, disparity, dissimilarity, dissonance, divergence, incongruity, inconsistency, variance, variation

discretion acumen, care, carefulness, caution, consideration, diplomacy, discernment, good sense, judgment, maturity, prudence, sagacity, tact, wariness

discriminate favour, show bias, show prejudice, single out, treat differently, victimize; assess, differentiate, discern, distinguish, evaluate, separate, sift

discriminating acute, astute, critical, cultivated, discerning, fastidious, keen, particular, refined, selective, sensitive, tasteful

discrimination bias, bigotry, favouritism, inequity, intolerance, prejudice, unfairness

discuss argue, confer, consider, converse, debate, deliberate, examine, go into, review, sift, thrash out, ventilate

disdain *n/v* scorn **disdainful** *adj*
disease *n* illness
disembark *v* land from ship etc.
disembodied *adj* (of spirit) released from bodily form
disembowel *v* **-elling, -elled** remove the entrails of
disenchanted *adj* disillusioned **disenchantment** *n*
disengage *v* release
disfavour *n* disapproval
disfigure *v* mar appearance of
disgrace *n* shame, dishonour ~*v* bring shame upon **disgraceful** *adj*

disgracefully *adv*
disgruntled *adj* vexed; put out
disguise *v* change appearance of, make unrecognizable; conceal ~*n* device to conceal identity
disgust *n/v* (affect with) violent distaste, loathing
dish *n* shallow vessel for food; portion or variety of food ~*v* serve (up)
dishearten *v* weaken hope, enthusiasm etc.
dishevelled *adj* untidy
dishonest *adj* not honest or fair **dishonesty** *n*

———— THESAURUS ————

discussion analysis, argument, colloquy, conference, consideration, consultation, conversation, debate, deliberation, dialogue, discourse, examination, exchange, review, scrutiny, symposium
disdain *n* arrogance, contempt, derision, dislike, hauteur, indifference, scorn, sneering
disease *n* affliction, ailment, complaint, condition, disorder, ill health, illness, indisposition, infection, infirmity, malady, sickness, upset
disembark alight, arrive, get off, go ashore, land
disfavour disapprobation, disapproval, dislike, displeasure
disfigure blemish, damage, deface, deform, distort, injure, maim, mutilate, scar
disgrace *n* baseness, degradation, dishonour, disrepute, ignominy, infamy, odium, opprobrium, shame ~*v* abase, bring shame upon, defame, degrade, discredit, disfavour, dishonour, disparage, humiliate, reproach, shame, slur, stain, stigmatize, sully, taint
disgraceful contemptible, degrading, detestable, discreditable, dishonourable, disreputable, ignominious, infamous, low, mean, scandalous,

shameful, shocking, unworthy
disgruntled annoyed, discontented, displeased, dissatisfied, grumpy, irritated, malcontent, peeved, peevish, petulant, put out, sulky, sullen
disguise *v* deceive, dissemble, dissimulate, fake, falsify, fudge, gloss over, misrepresent; cloak, conceal, cover, hide, mask, screen, secrete, shroud, veil ~*n* cloak, costume, cover, mask, screen, veil
disgust *n* abhorrence, abomination, antipathy, aversion, detestation, dislike, distaste, hatred, loathing, nausea, repugnance, repulsion, revulsion ~*v* nauseate, offend, outrage, put off, repel, revolt, sicken
dish bowl, plate, platter, salver; fare, food, recipe
dishearten cast down, crush, damp, dampen, dash, daunt, deject, depress, deter, discourage, dismay, dispirit
dishonest corrupt, crafty, deceitful, deceiving, designing, disreputable, double-dealing, false, fraudulent, lying, mendacious, perfidious, treacherous, unfair, unprincipled, unscrupulous, untrustworthy
dishonesty corruption, deceit, duplicity, falsehood, fraud, fraudulence, graft *Inf*, mendacity, sharp practice,

dishonour v treat with disrespect ~n lack of respect; shame, disgrace **dishonourable** adj

disillusion v destroy ideals of ~n disenchantment

disinfectant n substance that prevents or removes infection **disinfect** v

disinformation n false information intended to mislead

disingenuous adj not sincere

disinherit v deprive of inheritance

disintegrate v fall to pieces

disinterested adj free from bias or partiality

disjoint v put out of joint; break the natural order of **disjointed** adj (of language) incoherent; disconnected

disk n computer storage device

dislike v consider unpleasant or disagreeable ~n feeling of not liking

dislocate v put out of joint **dislocation** n

dislodge v drive out from previous position

disloyal adj deserting one's allegiance **disloyalty** n

dismal adj depressing

dismantle v take apart

dismay v dishearten, daunt ~n consternation

dismember v tear limb from limb

dismiss v discharge from employment; send away; reject **dismissal** n **dismissive** adj scornful

dismount v get off horse, bicycle

disobey v refuse or fail to obey **dis-**

——————— T H E S A U R U S ———————

treachery

dishonour v abase, blacken, corrupt, debase, debauch, defame, degrade, discredit, disgrace, shame, sully ~n discredit, disfavour, disgrace, disrepute, ignominy, infamy, obloquy, odium, opprobrium, reproach, scandal, shame

dishonourable base, despicable, discreditable, disgraceful, ignoble, infamous, scandalous, shameful

disinfect clean, cleanse, decontaminate, fumigate, purify, sterilize

disinfectant antiseptic, germicide, sterilizer

disinherit cut off, disown, dispossess, oust, repudiate

disintegrate break up, crumble, disunite, fall apart, fall to pieces, separate, shatter, splinter

disinterested detached, equitable, even-handed, impartial, impersonal, neutral, unbiased

dislike v abhor, abominate, be averse to, despise, detest, disapprove, disfavour, hate, loathe, object to, scorn, shun ~n animosity, animus, antagonism, antipathy, aversion, detesta-

tion, disapproval, disgust, distaste, enmity, hatred, hostility, loathing, repugnance

disloyal disaffected, faithless, false, perfidious, seditious, subversive, traitorous, treacherous, two-faced, unfaithful, unpatriotic, untrustworthy

disloyalty deceitfulness, double-dealing, falseness, falsity, inconstancy, infidelity, perfidy, treachery, treason

dismal bleak, cheerless, dark, depressing, despondent, discouraging, dreary, forlorn, gloomy, lugubrious, melancholy, sad, sombre, sorrowful

dismay v affright, alarm, appal, distress, frighten, horrify, paralyse, scare, terrify, unnerve ~n agitation, alarm, anxiety, apprehension, distress, dread, fear, fright, horror, panic, terror

dismiss cashier, discharge, lay off, oust, remove; disband, disperse, dissolve, free, let go, release, send away

dismissal discharge, expulsion, notice, removal, the (old) heave-ho Inf, the sack Inf; adjournment, end, release

obedience *n* disobedient *adj*

disorder *n* confusion; ailment disorderly *adj* disorganized; unruly

disorganized *adj* lacking order, arrangement

disorientate *v* cause (someone) to lose his bearings, confuse disorientation *n*

disown *v* refuse to acknowledge

disparage *v* belittle

disparity *n* inequality; incongruity disparate *adj* utterly different

dispassionate *adj* impartial

dispatch, despatch *v* send off promptly; finish off ~*n* speed; official message

dispel *v* -pelling, -pelled drive away

dispense *v* deal out; make up (medicine); administer (justice) dispensable *adj* dispensary *n* place where medicine is made up dispensation *n* dispense with do away with; manage without

disperse *v* scatter dispersal *n*

dispirited *adj* dejected

displace *v* move from its place; take place of displacement *n*

display *v/n* show

displease *v* offend; annoy displeasure *n*

————— THESAURUS —————

disobedience insubordination, mutiny, noncompliance, recalcitrance, revolt, unruliness, waywardness

disobedient contrary, defiant, disorderly, insubordinate, intractable, mischievous, naughty, obstreperous, refractory, undisciplined, unruly, wilful

disobey defy, disregard, flout, ignore, infringe, overstep, rebel, resist, transgress, violate

disorderly chaotic, confused, disorganized, indiscriminate, irregular, jumbled, messy, untidy; disruptive, lawless, obstreperous, rebellious, riotous, rowdy, ungovernable, unlawful, unmanageable, unruly

disown cast off, deny, disallow, disavow, disclaim, reject, renounce, repudiate

dispassionate calm, collected, composed, cool, imperturbable, moderate, quiet, serene, sober, temperate, unemotional, unexcitable, unfazed *Inf*, unmoved

dispatch, despatch *v* conclude, discharge, dispose of, expedite, finish, perform, settle ~*n* account, bulletin, communication, communiqué, document, instruction, item, letter, message, missive, news, piece, report, story

dispense allocate, allot, apportion, assign, deal out, disburse, distribute, dole out, mete out, share; administer, apply, carry out, direct, discharge, enforce, execute, implement, operate, undertake

disperse broadcast, circulate, diffuse, disseminate, dissipate, distribute, scatter, spread, strew

dispirited crestfallen, dejected, depressed, despondent, discouraged, disheartened, down, downcast, gloomy, glum, in the doldrums, low, morose, sad

displace derange, disarrange, disturb, misplace, move, shift, transpose; crowd out, oust, replace, succeed, supersede, supplant, take the place of

display *v* betray, demonstrate, disclose, evidence, evince, exhibit, expose, manifest, open, present, reveal, show, unveil; expand, extend, model, open out, spread out, unfold, unfurl ~*n* array, demonstration, exhibition, exposition, exposure, manifestation, presentation, revelation, show; pageant, parade, pomp, show, spectacle

displease anger, annoy, disgust, dissatisfy, exasperate, incense, irk, irritate, offend, pique, provoke, put out,

dispose *v* arrange; distribute; deal with **disposable** *adj* designed to be thrown away after use **disposal** *n* disposition *n* temperament; arrangement **dispose of** sell; get rid of

disprove *v* show to be incorrect

dispute *v* debate, discuss; call into question; contest ~*n* disagreement **disputable** *adj*

disqualify *v* make ineligible **disqualification** *n*

disquiet *n* anxiety, uneasiness

disregard *v* ignore ~*n* lack of attention, respect

disrepair *n* state of bad repair, neglect

disrepute *n* bad reputation **disreputable** *adj*

disrespect *n* lack of respect **disrespectful** *adj*

disrupt *v* throw into disorder **disruption** *n* **disruptive** *adj*

———— THESAURUS ————

rile, upset, vex

displeasure anger, annoyance, disapproval, dislike, dissatisfaction, distaste, indignation, irritation, offence, pique, resentment, vexation, wrath

disposal clearance, discarding, ejection, relinquishment, removal, riddance, scrapping, throwing away

dispose adjust, arrange, array, determine, distribute, fix, group, marshal, order, place, put, range, rank, regulate, set, settle, stand

dispose of; bestow, give, make over, part with, sell, transfer; bin *Inf,* chuck *Inf,* destroy, discard, dump *Inf,* get rid of, jettison, junk *Inf,* scrap, unload

disposition character, constitution, make-up, nature, spirit, temper, temperament

disprove confute, controvert, discredit, expose, invalidate, negate, prove false, rebut, refute

dispute *v* argue, brawl, clash, contend, debate, discuss, quarrel, row, squabble, wrangle; challenge, contest, contradict, controvert, deny, doubt, impugn, question ~*n* argument, brawl, conflict, disagreement, discord, disturbance, feud, friction, quarrel, strife, wrangle

disqualification disenablement, disentitlement, elimination, exclusion, incompetence, ineligibility, rejection

disqualify debar, declare ineligible, disentitle, preclude, prohibit, rule out

disquiet alarm, anxiety, concern, disquietude, distress, fear, foreboding, fretfulness, restlessness, trepidation, trouble, uneasiness, unrest, worry

disregard discount, disobey, ignore, laugh off, make light of, neglect, overlook, pass over

disreputable base, contemptible, derogatory, discreditable, disgraceful, dishonourable, disorderly, ignominious, infamous, low, mean, notorious, scandalous, shameful, shocking, unprincipled, vicious, vile

disrepute disesteem, disfavour, disgrace, dishonour, ignominy, infamy, shame, unpopularity

disrespect contempt, discourtesy, dishonour, disregard, impertinence, impoliteness, impudence, insolence, irreverence, rudeness

disrespectful bad-mannered, contemptuous, discourteous, ill-bred, impertinent, impolite, impudent, insolent, insulting, irreverent, misbehaved, rude, uncivil

disrupt agitate, confuse, disorder, disorganize, disturb, spoil, throw into disorder, upset

dissatisfaction annoyance, disappointment, discontent, dismay, displeasure, distress, exasperation, frustration, irritation, regret, unhappiness

dissatisfied *adj* not pleased, disappointed **dissatisfaction** *n*

dissect *v* cut up (body) for detailed examination

dissemble *v* pretend, disguise

disseminate *v* spread abroad

dissent *v* differ in opinion ~*n* such difference **dissension** *n*

dissertation *n* written thesis

disservice *n* ill turn, wrong

dissident *n/adj* (one) not in agreement, esp. with government

dissimilar *adj* not alike, different

dissipate *v* scatter; waste, squander

dissipated *adj* **dissipation** *n*

dissociate *v* separate, sever

dissolute *adj* lax in morals

dissolution *n* break up; termination

dissolve *v* absorb or melt in fluid; annul; disappear; scatter **dissolvable, dissoluble** *adj*

dissuade *v* advise to refrain, persuade not to

distance *n* amount of space between two things; remoteness; aloofness **distant** *adj*

distaste *n* dislike **distasteful** *adj*

distemper *n* disease of dogs; paint

———— THESAURUS ————

dissatisfied disappointed, discontented, disgruntled, displeased, fed up, frustrated, unfulfilled, unhappy

dissect anatomize, cut up *or* apart, dismember, lay open

disseminate broadcast, circulate, diffuse, disperse, distribute, propagate, publish, scatter, sow, spread

dissension conflict, contention, difference, disagreement, discord, dispute, dissent, quarrel, strife

dissent *v* decline, differ, disagree, object, protest, refuse, withhold approval ~*n* difference, disagreement, discord, nonconformity, objection, opposition, refusal, resistance

dissertation discourse, essay, exposition, thesis, treatise

disservice bad turn, disfavour, harm, ill turn, injury, injustice, wrong

dissident *n* agitator, dissenter, rebel, recusant ~*adj* discordant, heterodox, nonconformist, schismatic

dissimilar different, disparate, divergent, diverse

dissipate burn up, deplete, expend, fritter away, lavish, misspend, run through, spend, squander, waste

dissociate detach, disconnect, distance, divorce, isolate, segregate, separate, set apart

dissolute abandoned, corrupt, debauched, degenerate, depraved, immoral, lax, lewd, libertine, licentious, loose, profligate, vicious, wanton, wild

dissolution breaking up, disintegration, division, divorce, parting, resolution, separation

dissolve flux, fuse, melt, soften, thaw; crumble, decompose, diffuse, disappear, disintegrate, disperse, dissipate, dwindle, evaporate, fade, melt away, perish, vanish, waste away

dissuade deter, discourage, disincline, divert, expostulate, put off, remonstrate, urge not to, warn

distance absence, extent, gap, interval, lapse, length, range, reach, remoteness, remove, separation, space, span, stretch, width

distant abroad, afar, far, faraway, far-flung, far-off, outlying, out-of-the-way, remote, removed; aloof, cold, cool, formal, haughty, reserved, restrained, standoffish, stiff, unapproachable, unfriendly

distaste abhorrence, antipathy, aversion, disfavour, disgust, dislike, displeasure, horror, loathing, repugnance, revulsion

distasteful abhorrent, disagreeable, displeasing, obnoxious, offensive, repugnant, repulsive, undesirable, un-

distend v swell out **distension** n

distil v -tilling, -tilled vaporize and recondense a liquid; purify **distillation** n **distiller** n maker of alcoholic drinks **distillery** n

distinct adj easily seen; definite; separate **distinctly** adv **distinction** n point of difference; act of distinguishing; repute, high honour **distinctive** adj characteristic

distinguish v make difference in; recognize; honour; (usu. with **between** or **among**) draw distinction, grasp difference **distinguishable** adj **distinguished** adj

distort v put out of shape; misrepresent **distortion** n

distract v draw attention away; divert; perplex, drive mad **distraction** n agitation; amusement

distraught adj frantic, distracted

distress n trouble, pain ~v afflict

distribute v deal out; spread **distribution** n **distributor** n

district n region, locality; portion of territory

distrust v regard as untrustworthy ~n suspicion, doubt

disturb v intrude on; trouble, agitate, unsettle **disturbance** n

——————— THESAURUS ———————

inviting, unpalatable, unpleasant, unsavoury

distil condense, evaporate, express, purify, rectify, refine, vaporize

distinct apparent, clear, clear-cut, decided, definite, evident, lucid, manifest, marked, noticeable, obvious, patent, plain, recognizable, sharp, well-defined; different, dissimilar, individual, separate, unconnected

distinction contrast, difference, differential, division, separation; discernment, discrimination, penetration, perception, separation; credit, eminence, honour, importance, merit, name, note, prominence, quality, rank, renown, reputation, repute, worth

distinguish decide, determine, differentiate, discriminate, judge, tell apart; discern, know, make out, perceive, pick out, recognize, see, tell

distinguished celebrated, eminent, famed, famous, illustrious, notable, noted, well-known

distort bend, buckle, contort, deform, disfigure, misshape, twist, warp, wrench, wrest; bias, colour, falsify, garble, misrepresent, pervert, slant, twist

distract divert, draw away, sidetrack,

turn aside; agitate, bewilder, confound, confuse, disturb, harass, madden, perplex, puzzle, torment, trouble

distraction agitation, bewilderment, commotion, confusion, discord, disorder, disturbance; amusement, beguilement, diversion, entertainment, pastime, recreation

distress n affliction, agony, anguish, anxiety, desolation, discomfort, grief, heartache, misery, pain, sadness, sorrow, torment, torture, woe, worry ~v afflict, agonize, bother, disturb, grieve, harass, harrow, pain, sadden, torment, trouble, upset, worry, wound

distribute administer, allocate, allot, assign, deal, dispense, dispose, divide, dole out, give, measure out, mete, share, spread

distribution allocation, allotment, division, dole, partition, sharing

district area, community, locality, neighbourhood, parish, quarter, region, sector, vicinity, ward

distrust v be sceptical of, be suspicious of, disbelieve, discredit, doubt, misbelieve, question, suspect ~n disbelief, doubt, misgiving, mistrust, qualm, question, scepticism, suspi-

disuse n state of being no longer used **disused** adj

ditch n long narrow hollow dug in ground for drainage etc. ~v Inf abandon

dither v be uncertain or indecisive ~n this state

ditto n (pl -tos) the same

ditty n simple song

divan n bed, couch without back or head

dive v plunge under surface of water; descend suddenly; go deep down into ~n act of diving; Sl disreputable bar or club **diver** n

diverge v get farther apart; separate

diverse adj different, varied **diversify** v -**fying, -fied** make varied **diversity** n

divert v turn aside; amuse **diversion** n

divide v make into parts, split up; distribute, share; become separated ~n watershed **dividend** n share of profits

divine adj of, pert. to God; sacred ~v guess; predict **divinity** n being divine; study of theology

division n act of dividing; part of whole; barrier; section; difference in opinion etc.; Maths method of finding how many times one number is contained in another; army unit **divisible** adj **divisive** adj causing disagreement

────────── THESAURUS ──────────

cion, wariness

disturb bother, disrupt, interfere with, interrupt, intrude on, pester, rouse, startle; agitate, alarm, annoy, distract, distress, excite, fluster, harass, hassle Inf, perturb, ruffle, shake, trouble, unnerve, unsettle, upset, worry

disturbance agitation, bother, confusion, disorder, distraction, hindrance, interruption, intrusion, perturbation, upset

disuse decay, discontinuance, idleness, neglect

ditch n channel, drain, dyke, furrow, gully, moat, trench, watercourse ~v chuck Inf, discard, dispose of, drop, get rid of, jettison, junk Inf, scrap

dither falter, haver, hesitate, oscillate, waver

dive v dip, disappear, drop, duck, fall, jump, leap, pitch, plummet, plunge, submerge, swoop ~n dash, jump, leap, lunge, plunge, spring

diverge branch, divide, fork, part, radiate, separate, split, spread

diverse different, dissimilar, distinct, separate, unlike, varying; assorted, miscellaneous, several, sundry, varied, various

diversion change, deflection, detour, deviation, digression, variation; amusement, delight, distraction, enjoyment, entertainment, game, pastime, play, pleasure, recreation, relaxation, sport

diversity assortment, difference, heterogeneity, medley, multiplicity, range, variance, variegation, variety

divert deflect, redirect, switch, turn aside

divide cut (up), detach, disconnect, part, partition, segregate, separate, sever, shear, split, subdivide; allocate, allot, apportion, deal out, dispense, distribute, dole out, measure out, portion, share

dividend bonus, extra, gain, plus, portion, share, surplus

divine adj celestial, godlike, heavenly, holy, spiritual, superhuman, supernatural ~v conjecture, deduce, discern, foretell, guess, infer, intuit, perceive, suppose, surmise, suspect, understand

divinity deity, divine nature, godliness, holiness, sanctity; religion, religious studies, theology

divisible fractional, separable, splittable

divorce *n/v* (make) legal dissolution of marriage; split **divorcé** *n* (*fem* **divorcée**) divorced person

divulge *v* reveal

DIY do-it-yourself

dizzy *adj* feeling dazed, unsteady **dizziness** *n*

DJ disc jockey

DNA *n abbrev. for* deoxyribonucleic acid, main constituent of the chromosomes of all organisms

do *v* **doing, did, done** perform, effect, finish; work at; solve; suit; provide; *Sl* cheat; act; fare; suffice; makes negative and interrogative sentences and expresses emphasis ~*n Inf* celebration **do away with** destroy **do up** fasten; renovate

Doberman pinscher large black-and-tan dog

docile *adj* willing to obey, submissive

docility *n*

dock[1] *n* artificial enclosure for loading or repairing ships ~*v* put or go into dock **docker** *n* **dockyard** *n*

dock[2] *n* solid part of tail; stump ~*v* cut short; deduct (an amount) from

dock[3] *n* enclosure in criminal court for prisoner

dock[4] *n* coarse weed

docket *n* piece of paper sent with package etc.

doctor *n* medical practitioner; one holding university's highest degree ~*v* treat medically; repair; falsify (accounts etc.)

doctrine *n* what is taught; belief, dogma **doctrinaire** *adj* stubbornly insistent about applying theories

document *n* piece of paper etc. providing information ~*v* furnish with proofs

————————————— T H E S A U R U S —————————————

division cutting up, detaching, dividing, partition, separation; branch, category, class, compartment, department, group, head, part, portion, section, sector, segment

divorce *n* breach, break, decree nisi, dissolution, disunion, rupture, separation, severance, split-up ~*v* annul, disconnect, dissociate, disunite, divide, part, separate, sever, split up

divulge betray, confess, declare, disclose, exhibit, expose, impart, leak, let slip, make known, proclaim, publish, reveal, tell, uncover

dizzy faint, giddy, reeling, shaky, staggering, swimming, wobbly

do *v* accomplish, achieve, act, carry out, complete, conclude, discharge, end, execute, finish, perform, produce, work; bring about, cause, create, effect, produce; *Inf* cheat, con *Inf,* deceive, defraud, dupe, fleece, hoax, swindle, trick; act, behave, carry oneself, conduct oneself; fare, get along, get on, make out, manage, proceed

~*n Inf* affair, event, function, gathering, occasion, party

do away with destroy, exterminate, kill, liquidate, murder, slay

docile biddable, compliant, manageable, obedient, pliant, submissive, tractable

docility compliance, meekness, obedience, pliancy, submissiveness

dock *n* harbour, pier, quay, waterfront, wharf ~*v* anchor, berth, drop anchor, land, moor, put in, tie up

doctor *n* general practitioner, G.P., medical practitioner, physician ~*v* treat; botch, cobble, fix, mend, patch up, repair; alter, change, disguise, falsify, fudge, pervert, tamper with

doctrine article, belief, canon, concept, conviction, creed, dogma, opinion, precept, principle, teaching, tenet

document *n* certificate, legal form, paper, record, report ~*v* authenticate, back up, certify, cite, corroborate, detail, instance, substantiate,

documentary *adj/n* (of) type of film dealing with real life

dodder *v* totter, as with age

dodge *v* (attempt to) avoid by moving quickly; evade *~n* trick, act of dodging **dodgy** *adj Inf* untrustworthy

Dodgem *n Trademark* car used for bumping other cars in rink at funfair

dodo *n* (*pl* **dodos, dodoes**) large extinct bird

doe *n* female of deer, hare, rabbit

does *third person sing. of* DO

doff *v* take off

dog *n* domesticated carnivorous four-legged mammal; male of wolf, fox and other animals; person (in contempt, abuse or playfully) *~v* **dogging, dogged** follow closely **dogged** *adj* persistent, tenacious **dog-ear** *n* turned-down corner of page in book **dog-end** *n Inf* cigarette end; rejected piece of anything **dogfight** *n* close combat between fighter aircraft; rough fight **dogleg** *n* sharp bend **dogsbody** *n Inf* one carrying out menial tasks

doggerel *n* trivial verse

dogma *n* article of belief **dogmatic**

adj asserting opinions with arrogance

doily *n* small lacy mat to place under cake, dish etc.

doldrums *pl n* state of depression; region of light winds and calms near the equator

dole *n Inf* payment made to unemployed *~v* (*usu. with* **out**) distribute

doleful *adj* dreary, mournful

doll *n* child's toy image of human being

dollar *n* standard monetary unit of many countries, esp. USA

dollop *n Inf* semisolid lump

dolly *n* doll; wheeled support for film, TV camera

dolphin *n* sea mammal with beaklike snout

domain *n* lands held or ruled over; sphere of influence

dome *n* rounded roof; something of this shape

domestic *adj* of, in the home; home-loving; (of animals) tamed; of, in one's own country *~n* house servant **domesticate** *v* tame

domicile *n* person's regular place of abode

support, validate, verify

dodge *v* dart, duck, shift, sidestep, swerve, turn aside; avoid, deceive, elude, fend off, get out of, shirk, shuffle, trick *~n* device, feint, ploy, ruse, scheme, stratagem, subterfuge, trick, wile

dog *n* bitch, canine, cur, hound, man's best friend, mongrel, pup, puppy *~v* follow, haunt, hound, plague, pursue, shadow, track, trail, trouble

dogged determined, firm, immovable, persevering, persistent, resolute, staunch, steadfast, steady, tenacious, unflagging, unshakable

dogma article, belief, creed, doctrine, precept, principle, tenet

dogmatic arbitrary, arrogant, assertive, categorical, dictatorial, downright, emphatic, imperious, obdurate, overbearing, peremptory

doldrums blues, boredom, depression, dullness, ennui, gloom, inertia, listlessness, malaise, stagnation, tedium

dole *n* allowance, alms, benefit, gift, grant, parcel, pittance, portion, quota, share *v* (*with* **out**) administer, allocate, allot, assign, deal, dispense, distribute, divide, give, hand out, share

domestic family, home, household, private; house, house-trained, pet, tame, trained; indigenous, internal, native, not foreign

dominate v rule, control; (of heights) overlook; be most influential **dominance** n **dominant** adj **domination** n **domineering** adj imperious

dominion n sovereignty; rule; territory of government

dominoes pl n game played with 28 oblong flat pieces marked with spots

don¹ v **donning, donned** put on (clothes)

don² n fellow or tutor of college; Spanish title, Sir

donate v give **donation** n **donor** n

done past participle of DO

donkey n (pl **-eys**) ass

doodle v/n scribble

doom n fate; ruin; judicial sentence ~v condemn; destine **doomsday** n day of Last Judgment; dreaded day

door n hinged barrier to close entrance **doorway** n

dope n narcotic drug; Inf stupid person ~v drug **dopey, dopy** adj

dormant adj not active; sleeping

dormitory n sleeping room with many beds

dormouse n small hibernating mouselike rodent

dorsal adj of, on back

dose n amount (of drug etc.) ~v give doses to **dosage** n

dossier n set of papers on particular subject

dot n small spot, mark ~v **dotting, dotted** mark with dots; sprinkle

dote v (with **on** or **upon**) be passionately fond of **dotage** n senility

double adj of two parts, layers etc.; twice as much or many; designed for two users ~adv twice; to twice the amount or extent; in a pair ~n person or thing exactly like another; quantity twice as much as another; sharp turn; running pace ~v make, become double; increase twofold; fold in two; turn sharply **doubly** adv **double bass** lowest member of violin family **double-cross** v betray

———— THESAURUS ————

dominant ascendant, assertive, commanding, controlling, governing, leading, presiding, ruling, superior, supreme

dominate control, direct, govern, lead, master, monopolize, overbear, rule, tyrannize; bestride, loom over, overlook, stand over, survey, tower above

domination authority, command, control, influence, mastery, power, rule, superiority, supremacy, sway

dominion ascendancy, authority, command, control, government, mastery, power, rule, sovereignty, supremacy, sway

don dress in, get into, pull on, put on, slip on or in to

donate bestow, gift, give, present, subscribe

donation alms, benefaction, boon, contribution, gift, grant, gratuity, lar-

gess or largesse, offering, present, subscription

donor almsgiver, benefactor, contributor, donator, giver

doom n catastrophe, death, destiny, destruction, downfall, fate, fortune, lot, portion, ruin ~v condemn, consign, damn, decree, destine, judge, sentence

door egress, entrance, entry, exit, ingress, opening

dope drugs, narcotic, opiate

dormant asleep, inactive, inert, latent, quiescent, sleeping, sluggish, slumbering, suspended

dose draught, drench, measure, portion, potion, prescription, quantity

dot n atom, circle, dab, fleck, full stop, iota, jot, mark, mite, mote, point, speck, speckle, spot

dotage feebleness, imbecility, old age, second childhood, senility,

doubt v suspect; hesitate to believe; call in question ~n (state of) uncertainty **doubtful** adj **doubtless** adv certainly; presumably

dough n flour or meal kneaded with water; Sl money **doughnut** n sweetened and fried piece of dough

doughty adj hardy, resolute

dour adj grim, severe

douse v thrust into water; extinguish (light)

dove n bird of pigeon family **dovetail** v fit closely, neatly together

dowager n widow with title or property from husband

dowdy adj shabbily dressed

dowel n wooden, metal peg

down[1] adv to, in, or towards, lower position; (of payment) on the spot ~prep from higher to lower part of; along ~adj depressed ~v knock, pull, push down; Inf drink **downward** adj/adv **downwards** adv **downbeat** adj Inf gloomy **downcast** adj dejected; looking down **downfall** n sudden loss of position **downpour** n heavy fall of rain **downright** adj straightforward ~adv quite, thoroughly **down-and-out** adj/n destitute, homeless (person)

down[2] n soft underfeathers, hair; fluff **downy** adj

downs pl n open high land

dowry n property wife brings to husband

doyen n (fem **doyenne**) senior, respected member of group

doze v/n sleep, nap **dozy** adj

———— THESAURUS ————

weakness

double adj coupled, doubled, dual, duplicate, in pairs, paired, twice, twin, twofold ~v duplicate, enlarge, fold, grow, increase, magnify, multiply, plait, repeat

double-cross betray, cheat, defraud, hoodwink, mislead, swindle, trick

doubt v discredit, distrust, fear, misgive, mistrust, query, question, suspect; be dubious, be uncertain, demur, fluctuate, hesitate, scruple, vacillate, waver ~n apprehension, disquiet, distrust, fear, incredulity, misgiving, mistrust, qualm, scepticism, suspicion

doubtful hesitating, irresolute, perplexed, sceptical, suspicious, tentative, uncertain, unconvinced, undecided, unresolved, unsettled, unsure, vacillating, wavering; ambiguous, debatable, dodgy Brit, Aust, & NZ inf, dubious, equivocal, hazardous, iffy Inf, indefinite, obscure, problematic, questionable, unclear, unconfirmed, unsettled, vague

doubtless assuredly, certainly, clearly, of course, precisely, surely, truly, unquestionably; apparently, most likely, ostensibly, presumably, probably, seemingly

dour dismal, dreary, forbidding, gloomy, grim, morose, sour, sullen, unfriendly

dowdy dingy, drab, old-fashioned, shabby, unfashionable

down adj blue, dejected, depressed, disheartened, downcast, low, miserable, sad, unhappy

downcast cheerless, dejected, depressed, despondent, disconsolate, discouraged, disheartened, dismayed, dispirited, miserable, sad, unhappy

downfall breakdown, collapse, debacle, descent, destruction, disgrace, fall, overthrow, ruin, undoing

downpour cloudburst, deluge, flood, inundation, rainstorm

downward adj declining, descending, earthward, heading down, slipping

doze v catnap, drowse, kip Brit sl, nap, nod, sleep, slumber, zizz Brit inf

dozen *n* (set of) twelve

Dr. Doctor; Drive

drab *adj* dull, monotonous

draconian *adj* very harsh, cruel

draft[1] *n* sketch; rough copy of document; order for money; detachment of troops; ~*v* make sketch of; make rough copy of; send detached party

draft[2] *v US* select for compulsory military service

drag *v* dragging, dragged pull along with difficulty; trail; sweep with net; protract; lag, trail; be tediously protracted ~*n* check on progress; checked motion

dragon *n* mythical fire-breathing monster **dragonfly** *n* long-bodied insect with gauzy wings

dragoon *n* cavalryman ~*v* coerce

drain *v* draw off (liquid) by pipes, ditches etc.; dry; empty; exhaust; flow off or away ~*n* channel; sewer; depletion; strain **drainage** *n*

drake *n* male duck

dram *n* small draught of strong drink

drama *n* stage play; art or literature of plays; playlike series of events **dramatic** *adj* of drama; striking or effective **dramatist** *n* writer of plays **dramatize** *v* adapt for acting

drape *v* cover, adorn with cloth **draper** *n* dealer in cloth, linen etc. **drapery** *n*

drastic *adj* extreme; severe

draught *n* current of air; act of drawing; act of drinking; quantity drunk at once; *pl* game played on chessboard with flat round pieces ~*adj* for drawing; drawn **draughty** *adj* full of air currents **draughtsman** *n* one who makes drawings, plans etc. **draughtsmanship** *n*

draw *v* drawing, drew, drawn portray with pencil etc.; pull, haul; attract; come (near); entice; take from (well, barrel etc.); receive (money); get by lot; make, admit current of air; (of game) tie ~*n* act of drawing; casting of lots; tie **drawer** *n* one who or that which draws; sliding box in table or chest **drawing** *n* art of depicting in line; sketch so done **drawback** *n* snag **drawbridge** *n* hinged bridge to pull up **drawing room** living room, sitting room **draw up** arrange in order; stop

drawl *v* speak slowly ~*n* such speech

——————— **THESAURUS** ———————

drab cheerless, colourless, dingy, dismal, dreary, dull, flat, gloomy, grey, lacklustre, shabby, sombre, uninspired

draft *n* outline, plan, rough, sketch, version ~*v* compose, design, draw, draw up, formulate, outline, plan, sketch

drag draw, hale, haul, lug, pull, tow, trail, tug, yank

drain *v* bleed, draw off, dry, empty, milk, remove, tap, withdraw; consume, deplete, dissipate, empty, exhaust, sap, strain, tax, use up, weary ~*n* channel, conduit, culvert, ditch, duct, outlet, pipe, sewer, sink, trench, watercourse; depletion, drag, exhaustion, reduction, sap, strain,

withdrawal

drama play, show; acting, dramaturgy, stagecraft, theatre; crisis, excitement, scene, spectacle, theatrics, turmoil

dramatic theatrical; breathtaking, electrifying, emotional, exciting, melodramatic, sensational, startling, sudden, tense, thrilling

dramatist playwright, scriptwriter

dramatize act, overdo, overstate, play-act

drastic desperate, dire, extreme, forceful, harsh, radical, severe, strong

draught *of air* current, flow, movement; cup, dose, drench, drink, potion, quantity

draw *v* drag, haul, pull, tow, tug; al-

drawn *adj* haggard

dread *v* fear greatly ~*n* awe, terror ~*adj* feared, awful **dreadful** *adj* disagreeable, shocking or bad **dreadfully** *adv*

dream *n* vision during sleep; fancy, reverie, aspiration ~*v* **dreaming**, **dreamt** *or* **dreamed** have dreams; see, imagine in dreams; think of as possible **dreamer** *n* **dreamy** *adj*

dreary *adj* dismal, dull **drearily** *adv*

dredge *v* bring up mud etc. from sea bottom ~*n* scoop **dredger** *n* boat with machinery for dredging

dregs *pl n* sediment, grounds

drench *v* wet thoroughly, soak

dress *v* put on clothes; array for show; prepare; put dressing on (wound) ~*n* one-piece garment for woman; clothing; evening wear **dresser** *n* one who dresses; kitchen sideboard **dressing** *n* something applied, as sauce to food, ointment to wound etc. **dressing-down** *n Inf* severe scolding **dressing gown** robe worn before dressing **dressy** *adj* stylish

dressage *n* method of training horse

drey *n* squirrel's nest

dribble *v* flow in drops, trickle; run at the mouth ~*n* trickle, drop

drift *v* be carried as by current of air, water ~*n* process of being driven by current; tendency; meaning; wind-heaped mass of snow, sand etc. **drift-**

lure, attract, bring forth, elicit, engage, entice, evoke, induce, influence, invite, persuade; depict, design, map out, mark out, outline, paint, portray, sketch, trace ~*n Inf* attraction, enticement, lure; dead heat, stalemate, tie

drawback defect, difficulty, disadvantage, downside, fault, flaw, handicap, hindrance, hitch, impediment, nuisance, obstacle, snag, stumbling block, trouble

drawing cartoon, depiction, illustration, outline, picture, portrayal, representation, sketch, study

drawn fatigued, fraught, harassed, harrowed, pinched, sapped, strained, stressed, taut, tense, tired, worn

draw up compose, draft, formulate, frame, prepare, write out

dread *v* fear, quail, shrink from, shudder, tremble ~*n* alarm, apprehension, aversion, awe, dismay, fear, fright, horror, terror, trepidation

dreadful alarming, appalling, awful, distressing, fearful, formidable, frightful, ghastly, hideous, horrible, monstrous, shocking, terrible, tragic

dream *n* daydream, delusion, fantasy, illusion, imagination, reverie, speculation, trance, vision; ambition, aspiration, design, desire, goal, hope, notion, wish ~*v* daydream, envisage, fancy, imagine, stargaze, think, visualize

dreamer daydreamer, fantasist, fantasizer, idealist, utopian, visionary

dreamy chimerical, fantastic, misty, shadowy, unreal

dreary bleak, cheerless, comfortless, depressing, dismal, doleful, downcast, drear, forlorn, funereal, gloomy, glum, lonely, melancholy, mournful, sad, solitary, sombre, sorrowful, wretched; boring, drab, dull, ho-hum *Inf*, mind-numbing, monotonous, routine, tedious

dregs deposit, dross, grounds, residue, scum, sediment, trash, waste

drench drown, flood, inundate, saturate, soak, souse, steep, wet

dress *v* attire, change, clothe, don, garb, put on, robe; bandage, bind up, plaster, treat ~*n* costume, ensemble, frock, garment, gown, outfit, robe, suit; attire, clothes, clothing, costume, garb, garments, guise

dribble drip, drop, leak, ooze, run,

er n **driftwood** n wood washed ashore by sea

drill[1] n boring tool; exercise of soldiers; routine teaching ~v bore hole; exercise in routine; practise routine

drill[2] v/n (machine to) sow seed in furrows

drink v drinking, drank, drunk swallow liquid ~n liquid for drinking; intoxicating liquor **drinkable** adj **drinker** n

drip v dripping, dripped fall or let fall in drops ~n Med intravenous administration of solution; Inf insipid person **dripping** n melted fat from roasting meat ~adj very wet **drip-dry** adj (of fabric) drying free of creases if hung up while wet

drive v driving, drove, driven urge in some direction; make move and steer (vehicle, animal etc.); be conveyed in vehicle; hit with force ~n act, action of driving; journey in vehicle; united effort, campaign; energy; forceful stroke **driver** n

drivel v -elling, -elled run at the mouth; talk nonsense ~n foolish

nonsense

drizzle v/n rain in fine drops

droll adj funny, odd

dromedary n one-humped camel

drone n male bee; lazy idler; deep humming ~v hum; talk in monotonous tone

drool v slaver, drivel

droop v hang down; wilt, flag ~n **droopy** adj

drop n globule of liquid; very small quantity; fall, descent; distance to fall ~v dropping, dropped (let) fall; utter casually; set down; discontinue; come or go casually **droplet** n **dropout** n person who fails to complete course of study or one who rejects conventional society **droppings** pl n dung of rabbits, sheep, birds etc.

dropsy n disease causing watery fluid to collect in the body

dross n scum of molten metal; impurity, refuse

drought n long spell of dry weather

drove n herd, flock, esp. in motion **drover** n driver of cattle etc.

——————— T H E S A U R U S ———————

seep, trickle

drift coast, float, meander, stray, waft, wander

drill n bit, borer, gimlet; discipline, exercise, practice, preparation, repetition, training ~v bore, pierce, puncture, sink in; exercise, instruct, practise, rehearse, teach, train

drink v drain, gulp, guzzle, imbibe, partake of, quaff, sip, suck, sup, swallow, swig Inf, swill, wash down ~n beverage, liquid, potion, refreshment; alcohol, liquor, spirits

drip v drop, exude, filter, splash, sprinkle, trickle

drive v herd, hurl, impel, propel, push, send, urge; direct, go, guide, handle, manage, motor, operate, ride, steer, travel ~n excursion, jaunt, journey, outing, ride, run, trip, turn;

effort, energy, enterprise, initiative, vigour

drizzle v rain, shower, spray, sprinkle ~n fine rain, Scotch mist

droll amusing, comic, comical, diverting, eccentric, entertaining, funny, humorous, jocular, whimsical

droop bend, drop, fall down, hang (down), sag, sink

drop n bead, drip, globule, pearl, tear; dab, dash, nip, pinch, sip, taste, tot, trace; decline, decrease, downturn, fall-off, reduction ~v abandon, cease, desert, discontinue, forsake, give up, leave, relinquish, terminate; decline, depress, descend, diminish, dive, droop, fall, lower, plunge, sink, tumble

drought dry spell, dry weather

drove collection, company, crowd,

drown v die or be killed by immersion in liquid; make sound inaudible by louder sound

drowsy adj half-asleep; lulling; dull **drowsiness** n **drowse** v

drub v **drubbing, drubbed** thrash, beat **drubbing** n beating

drudge v work at menial or distasteful tasks ~n one who drudges **drudgery** n

drug n medical substance; narcotic ~v **drugging, drugged** mix drugs with; administer drug to

druid n (also with cap.) member of ancient order of Celtic priests

drum n percussion instrument of skin stretched over round hollow frame; thing shaped like drum ~v **drumming, drummed** play drum; tap, thump continuously **drummer** n **drum major** leader of military band **drumstick** n stick for beating drum; lower joint of cooked fowl's leg

drunk adj/n (person) overcome by strong drink **drunkard** n **drunken** adj **drunkenness** n

dry adj **drier** or **dryer**, **driest** or **dryest** without moisture; not yielding liquid; unfriendly; caustically witty; uninteresting; lacking sweetness ~v **drying**, **dried** remove water, moisture; become dry; evaporate **dryer, drier** n person or thing that dries; apparatus for removing moisture **dryly, drily** adv **dry-clean** v clean clothes with solvent **dry-cleaner** n **dry-cleaning** n

dual adj twofold

dub v **dubbing, dubbed** confer knighthood on; give title to; provide film with soundtrack

dubious adj causing doubt

duchess n duke's wife or widow

duck n (masc **drake**) common swimming bird ~v plunge (someone) under water; bob down; Inf avoid **duckling** n young duck

duct n channel, tube

dud n futile, worthless person or thing ~adj worthless

due adj owing; proper; expected; timed for ~adv (with points of compass) exactly ~n person's right; (usu. pl) charge, fee etc. **duly** adj properly; punctually **due to** attributable to; caused by

flock, gathering, herd, horde, mob, multitude, press, swarm, throng

drown deluge, drench, engulf, flood, go down, go under, immerse, inundate, sink, submerge, swamp

drudge factotum, hack, menial, plodder, servant, slave, toiler, worker

drudgery chore, hack work, hard work, labour, slavery, slog, toil

drug n medicine, physic, poison, remedy; narcotic, opiate ~v dose, medicate, treat

drum v beat, pulsate, rap, reverberate, tap, tattoo, throb

drunk adj blitzed Sl, blotto Sl, drunken, fuddled, inebriated, intoxicated, legless Inf, merry Inf, paralytic Inf, tipsy, well-oiled Sl ~n drunkard, inebriate, sot, toper

drunkenness alcoholism, dipsomania, insobriety, intemperance, intoxication, tipsiness

dry adj arid, barren, dehydrated, dried up, parched, sapless, thirsty, torrid, waterless ~v dehydrate, desiccate, drain, make dry, parch, sear

dual coupled, double, duplicate, matched, paired, twin, twofold

dubious doubtful, hesitant, uncertain, unconvinced, undecided, unsure, wavering

duck v bend, bow, crouch, dodge, drop, lower, stoop; Inf avoid, dodge, escape, evade, shirk, sidestep

due adj outstanding, owed, owing, payable, unpaid; appropriate, becoming, bounden, deserved, fit, fitting, just, justified, merited, obliga-

duel *n* arranged fight with deadly weapons, between two persons ~*v* **duelling, duelled** fight in duel

duet *n* piece of music for two performers

duffel, duffle *n* coarse woollen cloth; coat of this

duffer *n* stupid inefficient person

dugout *n* covered excavation to provide shelter; canoe of hollowed-out tree; *Sport* covered bench for players when not on the field

duke *n* peer of rank next below prince **dukedom** *n*

dulcet *adj* (of sounds) sweet, melodious

dulcimer *n* stringed instrument played with hammers

dull *adj* stupid; sluggish; tedious; overcast ~*v* make or become dull **dullard** *n* **dully** *adj*

dumb *adj* incapable of speech; silent; *Inf* stupid **dumbbell** *n* weight for exercises **dumbfound** *v* confound into silence

dummy *n* tailor's or dressmaker's model; imitation object; baby's dummy teat ~*adj* sham, bogus

dump *v* throw down in mass; deposit; unload ~*n* rubbish heap; temporary depot of stores; *Inf* squalid place; *pl* low spirits **dumpling** *n* small round pudding of dough **dumpy** *adj* short, stout

dunce *n* stupid pupil

dune *n* sandhill

dung *n* excrement of animals

dungarees *pl n* overalls made of coarse cotton fabric

dungeon *n* underground cell for prisoners

dunk *v* dip bread etc. into liquid before eating it

duo *n* (*pl* **duos**) pair of performers

duodenum *n* upper part of small intestine **duodenal** *adj*

dupe *n* victim of delusion or sharp practice ~*v* deceive

duplicate *v* make exact copy of ~*adj* double ~*n* exact copy **duplication** *n* **duplicator** *n* **duplicity** *n* deceitfulness, double-dealing

durable *adj* lasting, resisting wear **durability** *n*

tory, proper, right, rightful, suitable; expected, expected to arrive, scheduled ~*adv* dead, direct, directly, exactly, straight

duel affair of honour, single combat

dull dense, dim, dozy *Brit inf,* slow, stupid, thick; apathetic, blank, dead, empty, heavy, indifferent, lifeless, listless, slow, sluggish; boring, commonplace, dreary, dry, flat, hohum *Inf,* mind-numbing, plain, prosaic, tedious, tiresome, uninteresting; cloudy, dim, gloomy, overcast

duly accordingly, befittingly, correctly, deservedly, fittingly, properly, rightfully, suitably; on time, punctually

dumb inarticulate, mute, silent, soundless, speechless, tongue-tied, voiceless, wordless

dummy *n* figure, form, model; copy, counterfeit, duplicate, imitation, sham, substitute ~*adj* artificial, bogus, fake, false, imitation, mock, sham, simulated

dump *v* deposit, drop, fling down, let fall, throw down ~*n* junkyard, refuse heap, rubbish tip; *Inf* hovel, mess, pigsty, shack, shanty, slum

dungeon cage, cell, lockup, prison

duplicate *v* copy, double, echo, photocopy, repeat, reproduce ~*adj* corresponding, identical, matched, twin, twofold ~*n* carbon copy, copy, double, likeness, match, mate, replica, reproduction, twin

durable abiding, constant, dependable, enduring, fast, firm, hard-

duration *n* time things last

duress *n* compulsion

during *prep* throughout, in the time of, in the course of

dusk *n* darker stage of twilight **dusky** *adj*

dust *n* fine particles, powder of earth or other matter; ashes of the dead ~*v* sprinkle with powder; rid of dust **duster** *n* cloth for removing dust **dusty** *adj* covered with dust **dustbin** *n* container for household rubbish

Dutch *adj* pert. to the Netherlands, its inhabitants, its language

duty *n* moral or legal obligation; that which is due; tax on goods **duteous** *adj* **dutiful** *adj*

duvet *n* quilt filled with down or artificial fibre

dwarf *n* (*pl* **dwarfs, dwarves**) very undersized person; mythological, small, manlike creature ~*adj* unusually small ~*v* make seem small; make stunted

dwell *v* **dwelling, dwelt** *or* **dwelled** live, make one's home (in); think, speak at length (on) **dwelling** *n* house

dwindle *v* waste away

dye *v* **dyeing, dyed** impregnate (cloth etc.) with colouring matter; colour thus ~*n* colouring matter in solution

dyke *n* embankment to prevent flooding; ditch

dynamics *pl n* (with *sing v*) branch of physics dealing with force as producing or affecting motion **dynamic** *adj* energetic and forceful

dynamite *n* high explosive mixture ~*v* blow up with this

dynamo *n* (*pl* **-mos**) machine to convert mechanical into electrical energy, generator of electricity

dynasty *n* line, family of hereditary rulers

dysentery *n* infection of intestine causing severe diarrhoea

dysfunction *n* abnormal, impaired functioning

dyslexia *n* impaired ability to read **dyslexic** *adj*

dyspepsia *n* indigestion **dyspeptic** *adj/n*

dystrophy *n* wasting of bodily tissues, esp. muscles

———— THESAURUS ————

wearing, persistent, reliable, resistant, sound, stable, strong, sturdy, substantial, tough

dusk dark, evening, nightfall, sundown, sunset, twilight

dusky dark, dark-hued, sable, swarthy

dust *n* grime, grit, particles, powder

dusty dirty, grubby, sooty, unclean, undusted, unswept

dutiful compliant, conscientious, devoted, docile, obedient, punctilious, respectful, submissive

duty business, calling, charge, engagement, function, mission, obligation, office, onus, responsibility, role, service, task, work; customs, excise, impost, levy, tariff, tax, toll

dwarf *n* bantam, midget, pygmy *or* pigmy ~*adj* baby, diminutive, minia-

ture, petite, pocket, small, teensy-weensy, tiny, undersized ~*v* dominate, overshadow, tower above or over

dwell abide, inhabit, live, lodge, remain, reside, rest, settle, sojourn, stay, stop

dwelling abode, domicile, establishment, habitation, home, house, pad *Sl*, quarters, residence

dye *v* colour, pigment, stain, tincture, tinge, tint ~*n* colour, colouring, pigment, stain, tinge, tint

dynamic active, driving, energetic, forceful, go-ahead, high-powered, lively, powerful, vigorous, vital

dynasty ascendancy, dominion, empire, government, house, regime, rule, sovereignty, sway

E e

E East; Eastern; English

each *adj/pron* every one taken separately

eager *adj* having a strong wish; keen, impatient

eagle *n* large bird of prey

ear¹ *n* organ of hearing; sense of hearing; sensitiveness to sounds; attention **earache** *n* pain in ear **eardrum** *n* thin piece of skin inside the ear **earmark** *v* assign for definite purpose **earphone** *n* receiver for radio etc. held or put in ear **earring** *n* ornament for lobe of the ear **earshot** *n* hearing distance **earwig** *n* small insect with pincer-like tail

ear² *n* spike, head of corn

earl *n* British nobleman

early *adj/adv* before expected or usual time; in first part, near beginning

earn *v* obtain by work or merit; gain **earnings** *pl n*

earnest *adj* serious, sincere

earth *n* planet we live on; ground; soil; electrical connection to earth ~*v* cover, connect with earth **earthly** *adj* possible **earthy** *adj* of earth; uninhibited **earthenware** *n* (vessels of) baked clay **earthquake** *n* convulsion of earth's surface **earthworm** *n*

ease *n* comfort; freedom from constraint, awkwardness or trouble; idleness ~*v* reduce burden; give ease to; slacken; (cause to) move carefully **easily** *adv* **easy** *adj* not difficult; free from pain, care, or anxiety; compliant; comfortable **easy-going** *adj* not fussy; indolent

easel *n* frame to support picture etc.

east *n* part of horizon where sun rises; eastern lands, orient ~*adj* on, in, or near, east; coming from east ~*adv* from, or to, east **easterly** *adj/adv* **eastern** *adj* **eastward** *adj/adv* **eastwards** *adv*

Easter *n* festival of the Resurrection of Christ

easy *see* EASE

THESAURUS

each *adj* every ~*pron* every one, one and all

eager agog, anxious, ardent, athirst, earnest, enthusiastic, fervent, greedy, hungry, intent, keen, longing, raring, zealous

early *adj* forward, premature, untimely ~*adv* beforehand, in advance, in good time, prematurely, too soon

earn deserve, merit, rate, warrant, win; collect, draw, gain, get, gross, make, net, obtain, procure, reap, receive

earnest close, constant, determined, firm, fixed, grave, intent, resolute, serious, sincere, solemn, stable, staid, steady

earnings gain, income, pay, proceeds, profits, receipts, remuneration, return, reward, salary, stipend, wages

earth globe, orb, planet, sphere, world; clay, dirt, ground, land, loam, sod, soil, topsoil, turf

earthenware ceramics, crockery, crocks, pots, pottery, terra cotta

ease *n* affluence, calmness, comfort, contentment, enjoyment, happiness, leisure, peace, quiet, relaxation, repose, rest, serenity, tranquillity ~*v* abate, allay, alleviate, assuage, calm, comfort, lessen, lighten, moderate, pacify, quiet, relax, relent, relieve, soothe, still

easily comfortably, effortlessly, readily, simply, smoothly, with ease

easy child's play, clear, effortless, facile, light, no bother, no trouble, pain-

eat *v* eating, ate, eaten chew and swallow; destroy; gnaw; wear away **eatable** *adj*

eau de Cologne *Fr* light perfume

eaves *pl n* overhanging edges of roof **eavesdrop** *v* -dropping, -dropped listen secretly

ebb *v* flow back; decay ~*n* flowing back of tide; decline, decay

ebony *n/adj* (made of) hard black wood

ebullient *adj* exuberant **ebullience** *n*

eccentric *adj* odd, unconventional; irregular; not placed centrally ~*n* odd, unconventional person **eccentricity** *n*

echo *n* (*pl* echoes) repetition of sounds by reflection; imitation ~*v* echoing, echoed repeat as echo; imitate; resound; be repeated

éclair *n* finger-shaped iced cake filled with cream

eclectic *adj* selecting from various sources

eclipse *n* blotting out of sun, moon etc. by another heavenly body; obscurity ~*v* obscure; surpass

ecology *n* science of plants and animals in relation to their environment **ecological** *adj* **ecologist** *n*

economy *n* careful management of resources to avoid unnecessary expenditure; system of interrelationship of money, industry and employment **economic** *adj* **economical** *adj* frugal **economics** *pl n* (*with sing v*) study of economies of nations; (*used as pl*) financial aspects **economist** *n* **economize** *v*

ecstasy *n* exalted state of feeling **ecstatic** *adj*

eczema *n* skin disease

──────── **THESAURUS** ────────

less, simple, smooth, straightforward, uncomplicated, undemanding

easy-going amenable, calm, carefree, casual, even-tempered, flexible, laid-back *Inf,* lenient, liberal, mild, moderate, placid, relaxed, serene, tolerant, uncritical, undemanding

eat chew, consume, devour, munch, scoff *Sl,* swallow

eavesdrop listen in, monitor, overhear, spy

ebb *v* abate, fall away, flow back, go out, recede, retire, retreat, sink, subside, wane, withdraw; decay, decline, decrease, degenerate, deteriorate, diminish, drop, dwindle, fade away, flag, lessen, peter out, shrink, weaken

eccentric abnormal, anomalous, bizarre, capricious, erratic, idiosyncratic, irregular, odd, peculiar, queer *Inf,* strange, uncommon, unconventional, weird

eccentricity abnormality, anomaly, caprice, foible, idiosyncrasy, irregularity, nonconformity, oddity, pecul-

arity, quirk, singularity, strangeness, weirdness

echo *n* answer, repetition, reverberation; copy, imitation, parallel, reflection, reproduction, ringing ~*v* repeat, resound, reverberate

eclipse *v* blot out, cloud, darken, dim, obscure, overshadow, shroud, veil ~*n* dimming, extinction, shading

economic productive, profitable, profit-making, solvent, viable; business, commercial, financial, industrial, mercantile, trade

economical careful, frugal, prudent, thrifty

economize cut back, retrench, save, scrimp, tighten one's belt

economy frugality, husbandry, parsimony, providence, prudence, restraint, saving, thrift

ecstasy bliss, delight, elation, euphoria, exaltation, fervour, frenzy, joy, rapture

ecstatic blissful, delirious, elated, enthusiastic, euphoric, fervent, fren-

eddy *n* small whirl in water, smoke etc. ~*v* eddying, eddied move in whirls

edge *n* border, boundary; cutting side of blade; sharpness; advantage ~*v* sharpen; give edge or border to; move gradually edgy *adj* irritable on edge nervy; excited

edible *adj* eatable

edict *n* order, decree

edifice *n* building

edify *v* -fying, -fied improve morally, instruct

edit *v* prepare book, film, tape etc. edition *n* form in which something is published; number of copies editor *n* editorial *adj* ~*n* article stating opin-

ion of newspaper etc.

educate *v* provide schooling for, teach; train education *n* educational *adj*

eel *n* snakelike fish

eerie *adj* weird, uncanny

efface *v* wipe or rub out

effect *n* result; impression; condition of being operative *pl* property; lighting, sounds etc. ~*v* bring about effective *adj* useful; in force effectual *adj*

effeminate *adj* womanish, unmanly, womanish

effervesce *v* give off bubbles effervescent *adj*

efficient *adj* capable, competent efficiency *n*

—————— THESAURUS ——————

zied, joyful, joyous, overjoyed, raptured

eddy *n* swirl, vortex, whirlpool ~*v* swirl, whirl

edge border, bound, boundary, brim, brink, fringe, limit, line, lip, margin, outline, perimeter, rim, side, threshold, verge; bite, force, incisiveness, interest, keenness, point, pungency, sharpness, sting, urgency, zest

edible eatable, fit to eat, good, harmless, palatable, wholesome

edict act, command, decree, dictate, dictum, fiat, injunction, law, mandate, manifesto, order, pronouncement, regulation, ruling, statute

edify educate, elevate, enlighten, guide, improve, inform, instruct, nurture, school, teach, uplift

edit adapt, annotate, censor, check, condense, correct, emend, polish, revise, rewrite

edition copy, impression, issue, number, printing, version, volume

educate civilize, coach, cultivate, develop, discipline, drill, edify, enlighten, exercise, foster, improve, inform, instruct, school, teach, train

education breeding, civilization, cul-

tivation, culture, development, discipline, edification, enlightenment, erudition, improvement, indoctrination, instruction, knowledge, scholarship, training, tutoring

eerie creepy *Inf*, frightening, ghostly, mysterious, scary *Inf*, spectral, spooky *Inf*, strange, uncanny, unearthly, weird

effect *n* conclusion, consequence, event, fruit, issue, outcome, result, upshot ~*v* accomplish, achieve, bring about, carry out, cause, complete, create, execute, fulfil, give rise to, initiate, make, perform, produce

effective able, active, capable, competent, effectual, efficient, energetic, operative, productive, serviceable, useful; active, current, in force, in operation, operative, real

effervesce ferment, fizz, foam, sparkle

effervescent bubbling, bubbly, foaming, foamy, frothing, sparkling

efficiency adeptness, capability, competence, economy, effectiveness, power, skill

efficient able, adept, businesslike, capable, competent, economic, pro-

effigy *n* image, likeness

effluent *n* liquid discharged as waste

effort *n* exertion, endeavour, attempt or something achieved **effortless** *adj*

effrontery *n* impudence

e.g. for example

egalitarian *adj* believing that all people should be equal

egg[1] *n* oval or round object from which young emerge

egg[2] *v* **egg on** urge

ego *n* (*pl* **egos**) the self **egotism, egoism** *n* selfishness; self-conceit **egotist, egoist** *n* **egotistic, -ical** *adj* **egocentric** *adj* self-centred

egregious *adj* blatant

eider *n* Arctic duck **eiderdown** *n* its breast feathers; quilt

eight *adj/n* cardinal number one above seven **eighteen** *adj/n* eight more than ten **eighteenth** *adj/n* **eighth** *adj/n* **eightieth** *adj/n* **eighty** *adj/n* ten times eight

either *adj/n* one or the other; one of two; each ~*adv/conj* bringing in first of alternatives

ejaculate *v* eject (semen); exclaim

ejaculation *n*

eject *v* throw out; expel **ejection** *n* **ejector** *n*

eke out make (supply) last

elaborate *adj* detailed; complicated ~*v* expand (upon); work out in detail **elaboration** *n*

élan *n* style and vigour

elapse *v* (of time) pass

elastic *adj* springy; flexible ~*n* tape containing strands of rubber **elasticity** *n*

elation *n* high spirits **elate** *v* (*usu. passive*) make happy

elbow *n* joint between fore and upper parts of arm; part of sleeve covering this ~*v* shove with elbow **elbowroom** *n* room to move

elder[1] *adj* older, senior ~*n* person of greater age; official of certain churches **elderly** *adj* **eldest** *adj* oldest

elder[2] *n* tree with black berries

elect *v* choose by vote; choose ~*adj* appointed but not yet in office; chosen **election** *n* **elective** *adj* appointed by election **elector** *n* **electoral** *adj* **electorate** *n* body of electors

——————— THESAURUS ———————

ductive, proficient, ready, skilful, workmanlike

effort endeavour, energy, exertion, force, labour, power, striving, struggle, toil, trouble, work

effortless easy, facile, painless, simple, smooth, uncomplicated, undemanding

egocentric egotistic, self-centred, selfish

eject discharge, dislodge, dismiss, get rid of, oust, throw out; cast out, discharge, disgorge, emit, expel, throw out

elaborate *adj* careful, detailed, exact, intricate, laboured, minute, painstaking, precise, skilful, thorough; complex, complicated, detailed, fussy, involved, ornamented, showy

~*v* add detail, amplify, decorate, develop, devise, enhance, enlarge, expand upon, garnish, improve, polish, refine

elapse go, go by, lapse, pass, pass by, slip away

elastic flexible, plastic, pliable, resilient, rubbery, springy, supple, yielding

elbow *n* angle, bend, corner, joint, turn ~*v* bump, crowd, hustle, jostle, knock, nudge, push, shoulder, shove

elder *adj* ancient, first-born, older, senior ~*n* older person, senior

elect appoint, choose, decide upon, determine, opt for, pick, pick out, prefer, select, settle on, vote

election choice, choosing, decision, judgment, preference, selection, vote

electricity *n* form of energy; electric current **electric** *adj* of, transmitting or powered by electricity **electrical** *adj* **electrician** *n* one trained in installation etc. of electrical devices **electrify** *v* **-fying, -fied electrification** *n*

electro- *comb. form* by, caused by electricity, as in **electrotherapy**

electrocute *v* kill by electricity **electrocution** *n*

electrode *n* conductor of electric current

electron *n* one of fundamental components of atom, charged with negative electricity **electronic** *adj* **electronics** *pl n* (*with sing v*) technology of electronic devices and circuits

elegant *adj* graceful; tasteful; refined **elegance** *n*

elegy *n* lament for the dead in poem **elegiac** *adj*

element *n* substance which cannot be separated by ordinary chemical techniques; component part; trace; heating wire in electric kettle etc.; proper sphere; *pl* powers of atmosphere; rudiments **elemental** *adj* **elementary** *adj* rudimentary, simple

elephant *n* huge animal with ivory tusks and long trunk

elevate *v* raise, exalt **elevation** *n* raising; height, esp. above sea level; drawing of one side of building etc. **elevator** *n* US lift

eleven *adj/n* number next above 10 **eleventh** *adj*

elf *n* (*pl* **elves**) fairy **elfin, elvish** *adj*

elicit *v* draw out

eligible *adj* qualified; desirable **eligibility** *n*

eliminate *v* remove, get rid of, set aside **elimination** *n*

elite *n* the pick or best part of society

elixir *n* remedy

elk *n* large deer

ellipse *n* oval **elliptical** *adj*

elm *n* tree with serrated leaves

elocution *n* art of public speaking

elongate *v* lengthen

elope *v* run away from home with lover **elopement** *n*

eloquence *n* fluent, powerful use of

elector constituent, voter

electric charged, dynamic, rousing, stimulating, stirring, tense, thrilling

electrify amaze, animate, astonish, astound, excite, fire, invigorate, jolt, rouse, shock, startle, stimulate, stir, thrill

elegance beauty, dignity, gentility, grace, gracefulness, grandeur, polish, refinement

elegant artistic, beautiful, chic, choice, cultivated, delicate, exquisite, fashionable, fine, genteel, graceful, handsome, luxurious, refined, stylish, sumptuous, tasteful

element basis, component, constituent, factor, feature, ingredient, member, part, section, unit

elementary clear, easy, facile, plain, rudimentary, simple, straightforward, uncomplicated

elevate heighten, hoist, lift, lift up, raise, uplift, upraise; advance, aggrandize, exalt, prefer, promote, upgrade

elevation altitude, height

elicit bring out, call forth, cause, derive, draw out, educe, evoke, evolve, exact, extort, extract, obtain, wrest

eligible fit, preferable, proper, qualified, suitable, suited, worthy

eliminate cut out, dispose of, do away with, exterminate, get rid of, remove, stamp out, take out

elite aristocracy, best, cream, elect, gentry, high society, nobility, upper class

elocution articulation, delivery, diction, enunciation, oratory, public speaking, rhetoric, speech, utterance

language **eloquent** *adj* **eloquently** *adv*
else *adv* besides, instead; otherwise **elsewhere** *adv* in or to some other place
elucidate *v* explain
elude *v* escape; baffle **elusive** *adj* difficult to catch
emaciated *adj* abnormally thin
emanate *v* issue, proceed from **emanation** *n*
emancipate *v* set free **emancipation** *n*
emasculate *v* castrate; enfeeble, weaken **emasculation** *n*
embalm *v* preserve corpse
embankment *n* artificial mound carrying road, railway, or to dam water
embargo *n* (*pl* -goes) order stopping movement of ships; ban ~ *v* -goes, -going, -goed put under embargo; requisition

embark *v* board ship, aircraft etc.; (*with* on *or* upon) commence new project etc.
embarrass *v* disconcert; abash; confuse **embarrassment** *n*
embassy *n* office or official residence of ambassador
embattled *adj* having many difficulties
embed *v* -bedding, -bedded fix fast (in)
embellish *v* adorn, enrich **embellishment** *n*
ember *n* glowing cinder
embezzle *v* misappropriate (money in trust etc.) **embezzlement** *n* **embezzler** *n*
embitter *v* make bitter
emblem *n* symbol; badge **emblematic** *adj*
embody *v* **embodying, embodied**

─────────── T H E S A U R U S ───────────

elope abscond, bolt, decamp, disappear, escape, leave, run away, run off, slip away, steal away
eloquence expressiveness, fluency, oratory, persuasiveness, rhetoric
eloquent articulate, fluent, forceful, graceful, moving, persuasive, well-expressed
elsewhere abroad, absent, away, not here, somewhere else
elucidate clarify, clear up, explain, expound, gloss, illuminate, make plain, spell out, unfold
elude avoid, dodge, escape, evade, flee, shirk, shun
elusive shifty, slippery, tricky
emaciated attenuated, cadaverous, gaunt, haggard, lank, lean, meagre, pinched, thin, wasted
emanate arise, derive, emerge, flow, issue, originate, proceed, spring, stem
emancipate deliver, discharge, enfranchise, free, liberate, release, set free, unshackle

emancipation deliverance, enfranchisement, freedom, liberation, liberty
embargo ban, bar, boycott, check, interdict, prohibition, restraint, restriction
embark board ship, go aboard, take ship (*with* on *or* upon) begin, broach, commence, engage, initiate, launch, plunge into, set about, set out, start, take up, undertake
embarrass chagrin, discompose, disconcert, distress, fluster, mortify
embarrassment awkwardness, bashfulness, chagrin, confusion, distress, humiliation, mortification, shame
embellish adorn, beautify, bedeck, deck, decorate, dress up, elaborate, embroider, enhance, enrich, garnish, gild, grace, ornament
embezzle abstract, appropriate, filch, misapply, misappropriate, misuse, peculate, pilfer, purloin, steal
embitter anger, disaffect, disillusion,

represent, include, be expression of **embodiment** *n*

embolism *n* *Med* obstruction of artery

emboss *v* carve in relief

embrace *v* clasp in arms, hug; accept; comprise ~*n* hug

embrocation *n* lotion for rubbing limbs etc. to relieve pain

embroider *v* ornament with needlework **embroidery** *n*

embroil *v* involve (someone) in problems

embryo *n* (*pl* **-bryos**) undeveloped offspring, germ **embryonic** *adj*

emend *v* to remove errors from, correct **emendation** *n*

emerald *n* bright green gem

emerge *v* come up, out; rise to notice **emergence** *n*

emergency *n* sudden unforeseen

event needing prompt action

emery *n* hard mineral used for polishing

emigrate *v* go and settle in another country **emigrant** *n* **emigration** *n*

eminent *adj* distinguished **eminently** *adv* **eminence** *n*

emissary *n* agent, representative sent on mission

emit *v* **emitting, emitted** give out, put forth **emission** *n*

emollient *adj* softening, soothing ~*n* ointment

emotion *n* excited state of feeling, as joy, fear etc. **emotional** *adj* **emotive** *adj* arousing emotion

empathy *n* understanding of another's feelings

emperor *n* (*fem* **empress**) ruler of an empire

emphasis *n* (*pl* **-ses**) importance at-

———————— THESAURUS ————————

envenom, poison, sour

emblem badge, crest, device, figure, image, insignia, mark, representation, sign, symbol, token, type

embrace *v* clasp, cuddle, encircle, enfold, grasp, hold, hug, seize, squeeze; accept, adopt, espouse, grab, receive, seize, take up, welcome ~*n* clasp, cuddle, hug, squeeze

embroil complicate, confound, confuse, enmesh, entangle, implicate, incriminate, involve, mire, mix up

embryo germ, nucleus, root

emend amend, correct, edit, improve, revise

emerge appear, arise, come forth, come out, come up, emanate, issue, proceed, rise, spring up, surface

emergency crisis, danger, difficulty, extremity, necessity, pass, pinch, plight, predicament, quandary, strait

emigrate migrate, move, move abroad, remove

eminence celebrity, dignity, distinction, esteem, fame, greatness, impor-

tance, notability, note, prestige, rank, renown, reputation, repute, superiority

eminent celebrated, distinguished, esteemed, exalted, famous, illustrious, important, notable, noted, outstanding, prestigious, renowned, well-known

emission diffusion, discharge, ejection, exhalation, issuance, issue, radiation

emit diffuse, discharge, eject, emanate, exhale, exude, give off, give out, issue, radiate, send out, shed, throw out, transmit, utter, vent

emotion ardour, excitement, feeling, fervour, passion, sensation, sentiment, warmth

emotional demonstrative, excitable, hot-blooded, passionate, sensitive, susceptible, temperamental, tender, warm

emotive affecting, emotional, heartwarming, moving, pathetic, poignant, sentimental, tear-jerking *Inf,*

tached; stress on words **emphasize** *v* **emphatic** *adj* forceful

emphysema *n* disease of lungs, causing breathlessness

empire *n* group of states under supreme leader

empirical *adj* relying on experiment or experience

emplacement *n* position for gun

employ *v* **employing, employed** provide work for in return for money; keep busy; use **employee** *n* **employer** *n* **employment** *n* employing, being employed; work; occupation

empower *v* authorize

empress *see* EMPEROR

empty *adj* containing nothing; unoccupied; senseless ~*v* **emptying, emp-**

tied make, become devoid of content; discharge (contents) into **empties** *pl n* empty bottles etc. **emptiness** *n*

emu *n* large Aust. flightless bird

emulate *v* strive to equal or excel; imitate **emulation** *n*

emulsion *n* light-sensitive coating of film; liquid with oily particles in suspension; paint in this form **emulsifier** *n*

enable *v* make able

enact *v* make law; act part

enamel *n* glasslike coating applied to metal etc.; coating of teeth; any hard coating ~*v* **-elling, -elled** cover with this

enamour *v* inspire with love

——— THESAURUS ———

touching

emphasis accent, attention, force, importance, insistence, intensity, moment, priority, prominence, significance, strength, stress, weight

emphasize accent, dwell on, highlight, insist on, play up, press home, stress, underline, underscore, weight

emphatic absolute, certain, decided, definite, distinct, earnest, forceful, forcible, important, impressive, insistent, marked, positive, powerful, resounding, significant, striking, strong, telling, vigorous

empire commonwealth, domain, kingdom, realm

employ engage, enlist, hire, retain, take on; engage, fill, occupy, spend, take up, use up

employee hand, staff member, wage-earner, worker, workman

employer boss *Inf,* business, company, establishment, firm, organization, owner, patron, proprietor

employment application, exercise, exertion, use; engagement, enlistment, hire; business, calling, craft, employ, job, line, métier, occupation,

profession, pursuit, service, trade, vocation, work

empower allow, authorize, commission, delegate, enable, entitle, license, permit, qualify, sanction, warrant

emptiness bareness, blankness, desolation, vacancy, vacuum, void, waste

empty *adj* bare, blank, clear, deserted, desolate, hollow, unfurnished, uninhabited, unoccupied, vacant, void, waste; aimless, banal, frivolous, fruitless, futile, hollow, inane, ineffective, meaningless, silly, unreal, vain, valueless, worthless ~*v* clear, consume, deplete, discharge, drain, evacuate, exhaust, pour out, unburden, unload, use up, vacate, void

enable allow, authorize, commission, empower, fit, license, permit, prepare, qualify, sanction, warrant

enact authorize, command, decree, legislate, ordain, order, pass, proclaim, ratify, sanction

enamour bewitch, charm, enchant, endear, enrapture, entrance, fascinate

encapsulate *v* summarize; enclose

enchant *v* bewitch, delight **enchantment** *n*

encircle *v* surround; enfold

enclave *n* part of country entirely surrounded by foreign territory

enclose *v* shut in; surround; place in with letter **enclosure** *n*

encompass *v* surround, contain

encore *interj* again ~*n* (call for) repetition of song etc.

encounter *v* meet unexpectedly; meet in conflict ~*n* encountering

encourage *v* inspire with hope; embolden **encouragement** *n*

encroach *v* intrude (on) **encroachment** *n*

encrust *v* cover with layer

encumber *v* hamper; burden **encumbrance** *n*

encyclopedia, encyclopaedia *n* book, set of books of information on one or all subjects **encyclopedic, -paedic** *adj*

end *n* limit; extremity; conclusion; fragment; latter part; death; event; aim ~*v* put an end to; come to an end, finish **ending** *n* **endless** *adj*

endanger *v* put in danger

endear *v* make beloved **endearment** *n* loving word

endeavour *v* try, strive after ~*n* attempt

endorse *v* sanction; confirm; sign

————————— THESAURUS —————————

enchant beguile, bewitch, captivate, charm, delight, enamour, enrapture, enthral, fascinate, hypnotize, spellbind

enclose bound, cover, encase, encircle, encompass, fence, hedge, hem in, pen, shut in, wall in, wrap; include, insert, put in, send with

encompass circle, encircle, enclose, envelop, girdle, hem in, ring, surround

encounter *v* chance upon, come upon, confront, experience, face, meet, run across, run into *Inf*; attack, combat, contend, engage, fight, grapple with, strive, struggle ~*n* brush, confrontation, meeting

encourage buoy up, cheer, comfort, console, embolden, hearten, incite, inspire, rally, reassure, rouse, stimulate

encouragement aid, boost, cheer, consolation, favour, help, inspiration, reassurance, stimulation, stimulus, succour, support, urging

encroach impinge, infringe, intrude, invade, make inroads, overstep, trench, trespass, usurp

end *n* boundary, edge, extent, extremity, limit, terminus; close, closure, completion, conclusion, consequence, culmination, denouement, ending, expiry, finale, finish, outcome, resolution, result, stop, termination, upshot; death, demise, destruction, dissolution, doom, extinction, ruin, ruination; aim, aspiration, design, drift, goal, intention, object, objective, point, purpose, reason ~*v* cease, close, complete, conclude, culminate, dissolve, expire, finish, resolve, stop, terminate, wind up

endanger compromise, hazard, imperil, jeopardize, put at risk, risk, threaten

endeavour *v* aim, aspire, attempt, essay, strive, struggle, try, undertake ~*n* aim, attempt, effort, enterprise, essay, go *Inf,* trial, try, venture

ending close, completion, conclusion, denouement, finale, finish, resolution, termination

endless ceaseless, constant, continual, eternal, everlasting, immortal, incessant, infinite, interminable, perpetual, unbounded, unbroken, undying, unlimited; continuous, unbroken, undivided, whole

back of; record conviction on driving licence **endorsement** *n*

endow *v* provide permanent income for; furnish (with) **endowment** *n*

endure *v* undergo; tolerate, bear; last **endurable** *adj* **endurance** *n*

enema *n* medicine, liquid injected into rectum

enemy *n* hostile person; opponent; armed foe

energy *n* vigour, force, activity; source of power, as oil, coal etc.; capacity of machine, battery etc. for work **energetic** *adj* **energize** *v*

enervate *v* weaken

enfeeble *v* weaken

enfold *v* cover by wrapping something around

enforce *v* compel obedience to; impose (action) upon **enforceable** *adj* **enforcement** *n*

enfranchise *v* give right of voting to; give parliamentary representation to; set free

engage *v* participate; involve; employ; bring into operation; begin conflict **engaged** *adj* pledged to be married; in use **engagement** *n* appointment; pledge of marriage **engaging** *adj* charming

engender *v* give rise to

engine *n* any machine to convert energy into mechanical work; railway locomotive **engineer** *n* one who is in charge of engines, machinery etc.; one who originates, organizes ~*v* construct as engineer; contrive **engineering** *n*

———————— THESAURUS ————————

endorse advocate, affirm, approve, authorize, back, champion, confirm, favour, O.K. *or* okay *Inf*, ratify, recommend, sanction, support, sustain, warrant

endowment award, benefaction, bequest, bestowal, boon, donation, fund, gift, grant, income, largess, legacy, presentation, property, provision, revenue

endurance bearing, fortitude, patience, perseverance, resignation, resolution, stamina, staying power, strength, submission, sufferance, tenacity, toleration

endure bear, brave, cope with, experience, go through, stand, suffer, support, sustain, undergo, weather, withstand; abide, allow, bear, brook, countenance, permit, stand, stick *Sl*, stomach, suffer, swallow, take patiently, tolerate

enemy adversary, antagonist, competitor, foe, opponent, rival

energetic active, brisk, dynamic, forceful, forcible, indefatigable, lively, potent, powerful, spirited, strenuous, strong, tireless, vigorous

energy activity, ardour, drive, efficiency, élan, exertion, fire, force, intensity, life, liveliness, power, spirit, stamina, strength, verve, vigour, vitality, vivacity, zeal, zest

enforce apply, carry out, coerce, compel, constrain, exact, execute, impose, insist on, oblige, prosecute, reinforce, require, urge

enfranchise give the vote to; emancipate, free, liberate, manumit, release, set free

engage absorb, busy, engross, grip, involve, occupy, preoccupy, tie up; appoint, commission, employ, enlist, enrol, hire, retain, take on; activate, apply, energize, set going, switch on; assail, attack, combat, fall on, fight with, meet, take on

engaged affianced, pledged, promised, spoken for

engagement appointment, commitment, date, meeting; betrothal, bond, compact, contract, oath, obligation, pact, pledge, promise, vow, word

engine machine, mechanism, motor

engrave *v* cut in lines on metal for printing; carve, incise; impress deeply **engraving** *n*

engross *v* absorb (attention); occupy wholly

engulf *v* swallow up

enhance *v* intensify value or attractiveness of **enhancement** *n*

enigma *n* puzzling thing or person **enigmatic** *adj*

enjoy *v* delight in; have benefit of **enjoy oneself** be happy **enjoyable** *adj* **enjoyment** *n*

enlarge *v* make bigger; grow bigger; talk in greater detail **enlargement** *n*

enlighten *v* give information to enlightenment *n*

enlist *v* engage as soldier or helper

enliven *v* animate

enmesh *v* entangle

enmity *n* ill will, hostility

enormous *adj* very big, vast **enormity** *n* gross offence

enough *adj/n/adv* as much as need be

enquire *see* INQUIRE

enrich *v* make rich; add to

enrol *v* **-rolling, -rolled** write name of on roll; enlist; become member

en route *Fr* on the way

ensemble *n* all parts taken together; woman's complete outfit; *Mus* group of soloists performing together

————————— THESAURUS —————————

engineer *n* contriver, designer, deviser, director, inventor, manipulator, originator, planner, schemer ~*v* bring about, cause, concoct, contrive, control, create, devise, effect, manage, mastermind, originate, plan, plot, scheme

engrave carve, chase, chisel, cut, etch, inscribe

enigma conundrum, mystery, problem, puzzle, riddle

enigmatic cryptic, Delphic, inscrutable, mysterious, obscure, perplexing, puzzling

enjoy appreciate, delight in, like, rejoice in, relish, revel in, take joy in; experience, own, possess, use

enjoyable agreeable, amusing, delicious, delightful, entertaining, pleasant, pleasing, pleasurable, satisfying

enjoyment amusement, delight, entertainment, fun, gladness, gratification, gusto, happiness, indulgence, joy, pleasure, recreation, relish, satisfaction, zest

enlarge add to, augment, broaden, diffuse, dilate, distend, elongate, expand, extend, grow, heighten, increase, inflate, lengthen, magnify, multiply, stretch, swell, widen

enlighten advise, apprise, civilize, counsel, edify, educate, inform, instruct, make aware, teach

enlist engage, enrol, gather, join, join up, muster, obtain, procure, recruit, register, secure, sign up

enliven brighten, buoy up, cheer up, excite, exhilarate, fire, gladden, hearten, inspire, inspirit, invigorate, quicken, rouse, spark, stimulate, vitalize, wake up

enmity animosity, animus, antagonism, antipathy, aversion, bad blood, bitterness, hate, hatred, hostility, ill will, malevolence, malice, rancour, spite, venom

enormity atrocity, depravity, disgrace, evilness, turpitude, viciousness, villainy, wickedness

enormous astronomic, colossal, gigantic, gross, huge, immense, jumbo *Inf,* mammoth, massive, monstrous, prodigious, tremendous, vast

enough *adj* abundant, adequate, ample, plenty, sufficient ~*adv* abundantly, adequately, amply, fairly, moderately, passably, reasonably, satisfactorily, sufficiently, tolerably

en route in transit, on the way

ensemble costume, get-up *Inf,* outfit,

enshrine v preserve with sacred affection

ensign n naval or military flag; badge

enslave v make into slave

ensnare v trap; entangle

ensue v follow, happen after

ensure v make certain

entail v necessitate

entangle v ensnare; perplex

entente n friendly understanding between nations

enter v go, come into; penetrate; join; write in; begin **entrance** n going, coming in; door, passage; right to enter; fee **entrant** n one who enters entry n

enterprise n bold undertaking; bold spirit; business **enterprising** adj

entertain v amuse, receive as guest; consider **entertainer** n **entertainment** n

enthral v -thralling, -thralled captivate

enthusiasm n ardent eagerness **enthuse** v **enthusiast** n **enthusiastic** adj

entice v allure, attract

entire adj whole, complete **entirely** adv **entirety** n

entitle v qualify; name **entitlement** n

———— T H E S A U R U S ————

suit; band, cast, chorus, company, group, troupe

ensue arise, attend, be consequent on, befall, come after, derive, flow, follow, issue, proceed, result, stem, succeed, supervene

entail bring about, call for, cause, demand, give rise to, impose, involve, lead to, necessitate, occasion, require, result in

entangle catch, embroil, enmesh, ensnare, implicate, involve, knot, mix up, snag, snare, tangle, trap; complicate, confuse, mix up, muddle, perplex, puzzle, snarl, twist

enter arrive, come or go in or into, insert, introduce, penetrate, pierce; begin, commence, embark upon, enlist, enrol, join, sign up, start, take up; list, log, note, record, register, set down, take down, write down

enterprise adventure, effort, endeavour, essay, operation, plan, programme, project, undertaking, venture; activity, daring, dash, drive, energy, enthusiasm, initiative, readiness, resource, spirit, vigour, zeal; business, company, concern, establishment, firm, operation

enterprising active, adventurous, bold, daring, dashing, eager, go-ahead, intrepid, keen, ready, resourceful, vigorous, zealous

entertain amuse, charm, cheer, delight, divert, occupy, please

entertainment amusement, cheer, distraction, diversion, enjoyment, fun, good time, play, pleasure, recreation, satisfaction, sport, treat

enthusiasm ardour, eagerness, earnestness, excitement, fervour, frenzy, interest, keenness, passion, relish, vehemence, warmth, zeal, zest

enthusiast admirer, aficionado, buff Inf, devotee, fan, fanatic, fiend Inf, follower, freak Inf, lover, zealot

enthusiastic ardent, avid, devoted, eager, earnest, ebullient, excited, fervent, fervid, hearty, keen, lively, spirited, unstinting, vigorous, warm, wholehearted, zealous

entice allure, attract, beguile, cajole, coax, decoy, draw, inveigle, lead on, lure, persuade, seduce, tempt, wheedle

entire complete, full, total, whole

entirely absolutely, altogether, completely, fully, perfectly, thoroughly, totally, unreservedly, utterly, wholly, without exception, without reservation

entitle allow, authorize, empower, enable, fit for, license, permit, qualify for, warrant; call, christen, designate,

entity n thing's being or existence; reality

entomology n study of insects

entourage n group of people assisting important person

entrails pl n intestines

entrance¹ See ENTER

entrance² v delight

entreat v ask earnestly; beg, implore **entreaty** n

entrench v establish firmly

entrepreneur n businessman who attempts to profit by risk and initiative

entrust v commit, charge with

entwine v plait, interweave

enumerate v mention one by one

enunciate v state clearly

envelop v wrap up, surround

envelope n cover of letter

environment n surroundings; conditions of life or growth **environmental** adj

environs pl n outskirts

envisage v visualize

envoy n diplomat

envy v **envying, envied** grudge another's good fortune ~n (object of) this feeling **enviable** adj **envious** adj

enzyme n any of group of proteins produced by living cells and acting as catalysts

epaulette n shoulder ornament on uniform

ephemeral adj short-lived

epic n long poem telling of achievements of hero ~adj on grand scale

epicentre n point immediately above origin of earthquake

epicure n one delighting in eating and drinking **epicurean** adj/n

epidemic adj (esp. of disease) prevalent and spreading rapidly ~n serious outbreak

———————— THESAURUS ————————

dub, label, name, style, term, title

entity being, body, creature, individual, object, organism, presence, thing

entrance¹ n access, door, doorway, entry, gate, inlet, opening, passage, way in; arrival, entry, ingress, introduction; access, admission, admittance, entrée, entry, ingress

entrance² v bewitch, captivate, charm, delight, enchant, enthral, fascinate, ravish, transport

entrant candidate, competitor, contestant, entry, participant, player

entrust assign, charge, commend, commit, confide, consign, delegate, deliver, hand over, invest, trust

entry access, door, doorway, entrance, gate, inlet, opening, passageway, portal, way in; access, admission, entrance, entrée; attempt, candidate, competitor, contestant, effort, entrant, participant, player, submission

envelop blanket, cloak, conceal, cover, embrace, encase, enclose, enfold, engulf, hide, obscure, sheathe, shroud, surround, swathe, veil, wrap

envelope case, casing, coating, cover, covering, jacket, sheath, shell, skin, wrapping

enviable blessed, desirable, favoured, fortunate, lucky, privileged

envious covetous, grudging, jaundiced, jealous, malicious, resentful, spiteful

environment atmosphere, background, conditions, context, element, habitat, locale, medium, milieu, scene, setting, situation, surroundings

envoy agent, ambassador, courier, delegate, diplomat, emissary, intermediary, messenger, minister, representative

envy v begrudge, be jealous (of), covet, grudge, resent ~n covetousness, grudge, hatred, ill will, jealousy, malice, resentment, spite

epidemic adj general, prevailing, rampant, rife, sweeping, widespread

epidermis *n* outer skin

epidural *n* spinal anaesthetic

epigram *n* witty saying

epigraph *n* quotation at start of book; inscription

epilepsy *n* disorder of nervous system causing fits **epileptic** *n/adj*

epilogue *n* closing speech

episcopal *adj* of, ruled by bishop

episode *n* incident; section of (serialized) book etc. **episodic** *adj*

epistle *n* letter

epitaph *n* inscription on tomb

epithet *n* descriptive word

epitome *n* typical example **epitomize** *v*

epoch *n* period, era

equable *adj* even-tempered, placid

equal *adj* the same in number, size, merit etc.; fit ~*n* one equal to another ~*v* **equalling, equalled** be equal to

equally *adv* **equality** *n* **equalize** *v*

equanimity *n* composure

equate *v* make equal **equation** *n* equating of two mathematical expressions

equator *n* imaginary circle round earth equidistant from the poles

equestrian *adj* of horse-riding

equilateral *adj* having equal sides

equilibrium *n* (*pl* -**riums, -ria**) state of steadiness

equinox *n* time when sun crosses equator and day and night are equal

equip *v* **equipping, equipped** supply, fit out **equipment** *n*

equitable *adj* fair, reasonable, just **equity** *n*

equivalent *adj* equal in value

equivocal *adj* of double or doubtful meaning **equivocate** *v*

era *n* period of time

———— THESAURUS ————

~*n* outbreak, plague, rash, spread, wave

epigram bon mot, quip, witticism

epilogue coda, conclusion, postscript

episode adventure, affair, event, experience, happening, incident, matter, occurrence; chapter, instalment, part, passage, scene, section

epistle communication, letter, message, missive, note

epitome embodiment, essence, exemplar, personification, type

equable agreeable, calm, composed, easy-going, even-tempered, placid, serene, unflappable *Inf*

equal *adj* alike, commensurate, equivalent, identical, like, proportionate, tantamount, uniform; able, adequate, capable, competent, fit, ready, suitable, up to ~*n* brother, compeer, equivalent, fellow, match, mate, peer, rival, twin

equality balance, egalitarianism, equivalence, evenness, fairness, identity, likeness, parity, sameness, simi-

larity, uniformity

equate agree, balance, compare, correspond with, liken, match, offset, pair, square, tally

equation agreement, balancing, comparison, correspondence, equivalence, likeness, match, pairing, parallel

equilibrium balance, counterpoise, equipoise, evenness, rest, stability, steadiness

equip accoutre, arm, array, attire, endow, fit out, furnish, kit out, outfit, prepare, provide, rig, stock, supply

equipment accoutrements, apparatus, baggage, furnishings, gear, outfit, stuff, supplies, tackle, tools

equivalent alike, commensurate, comparable, corresponding, equal, even, interchangeable, of a kind, same, similar, synonymous, tantamount

equivocal ambiguous, ambivalent, doubtful, dubious, evasive, indefinite, indeterminate, misleading, ob-

eradicate *v* wipe out

erase *v* rub out; remove

ere *prep/conj Poet* before

erect *adj* upright ~*v* set up; build **erection** *n*

ermine *n* stoat in northern regions

erode *v* wear away; eat into **erosion** *n*

erotic *adj* of sexual pleasure

err *v* make mistakes; be wrong; sin **erratic** *adj* irregular **erratum** *n (pl* -ta) error, esp. in printing **erroneous** *adj* wrong **error** *n* mistake

errand *n* short journey for simple business

errant *adj* wandering

erstwhile *adj* former

erudite *adj* learned

erupt *v* burst out **eruption** *n*

escalate *v* increase, be increased, in extent, intensity etc. **escalation** *n*

escalator *n* moving staircase

escape *v* get free; get off safely; find way out; elude; leak ~*n* escaping **escapade** *n* wild adventure **escapism** *n* taking refuge in fantasy

escarpment *n* steep hillside

eschew *v* avoid, shun

escort *n* person accompanying another to guard, guide etc. ~*v* accompany

esoteric *adj* obscure

—————— THESAURUS ——————

scure, questionable, suspicious, uncertain

era age, cycle, date, day *or* days, epoch, generation, period, stage, time

eradicate annihilate, destroy, efface, eliminate, erase, expunge, extinguish, obliterate, remove, root out, stamp out, uproot, weed out, wipe out

erect *adj* firm, raised, rigid, standing, stiff, straight, upright, vertical ~*v* build, construct, lift, mount, pitch, put up, raise

erode consume, corrode, destroy, deteriorate, eat away, grind down, spoil

erotic carnal, erogenous, seductive, sensual, sexy *Inf,* titillating, voluptuous

err be inaccurate, be incorrect, blunder, go wrong, make a mistake, miscalculate, misjudge, mistake

errand charge, commission, job, message, mission, task

erratic aberrant, abnormal, capricious, changeable, desultory, fitful, inconsistent, irregular, shifting, unreliable, unstable, variable, wayward

erroneous amiss, fallacious, false, inaccurate, incorrect, inexact, invalid, mistaken, spurious, untrue, wrong

error bloomer *Brit inf,* blunder, boob

Brit sl, delusion, erratum, fallacy, fault, flaw, inaccuracy, miscalculation, mistake, oversight, slip, solecism

erudite cultivated, educated, knowledgeable, learned, lettered, literate, scholarly, well-educated, well-read

erupt belch forth, blow up, break out, burst forth, burst out, discharge, explode, flare up, gush, pour forth *or* out, spit out, spout, throw off, vent, vomit

eruption discharge, ejection, explosion, flare-up, outbreak, outburst

escalate ascend, be increased, enlarge, expand, extend, grow, heighten, increase, intensify, mount, raise, rise

escapade adventure, antic, caper, fling, mischief, spree, stunt, trick

escape *v* bolt, break free, decamp, flee, fly, get away, run away *or* off, skedaddle *Inf,* skip, slip away; avoid, dodge, duck, elude, evade, pass, shun, slip; drain, emanate, flow, gush, issue, leak, seep, spurt ~*n* break, break-out, flight, getaway

escort *n* bodyguard, company, convoy, cortege, entourage, guard, protection, retinue, safeguard, train ~*v* accompany, conduct, convoy, guard,

ESP extrasensory perception
especial *adj* pre-eminent; particular **especially** *adv*
espionage *n* spying
esplanade *n* promenade
espouse *v* support; *Obs* marry **espousal** *n*
espy *v* **espying, espied** catch sight of
Esq. Esquire, title used on letters
essay *n* prose composition; attempt ~*v* **essaying, essayed** try
essence *n* all that makes thing what it is; extract got by distillation **essential** *adj* vitally important; basic ~*n* essential thing
establish *v* set up; settle; prove **establishment** *n*
estate *n* landed property; person's property; area of property develop-

ment **estate agent** one who values, leases and sells property
esteem *v/n* regard, respect
ester *n Chem* organic compound
estimate *v/n* (form) approximate idea of (amounts, measurements etc.) **estimable** *adj* worthy of regard **estimation** *n* opinion
estranged *adj* no longer living with one's spouse
estuary *n* mouth of river
etc. et cetera
et cetera *Lat* and the rest, and others, and so on
etch *v* make engraving on metal plate with acids etc. **etching** *n*
eternal *adj* everlasting **eternity** *n*
ether *n* colourless liquid used as anaesthetic; clear sky **ethereal** *adj* airy;

———— T H E S A U R U S ————

guide, lead, partner, protect, squire, usher
especially chiefly, conspicuously, exceptionally, extraordinarily, mainly, markedly, notably, principally, remarkably, specially, strikingly, supremely, uncommonly, unusually
essay article, composition, discourse, disquisition, dissertation, paper, piece, tract
essence being, core, entity, heart, kernel, life, lifeblood, nature, pith, principle, soul, spirit, substance; concentrate, distillate, extract, spirits, tincture
essential *adj* crucial, important, indispensable, necessary, needed, requisite, vital; basic, cardinal, fundamental, inherent, innate, intrinsic, key, main, principal ~*n* basic, fundamental, must, necessity, requisite, rudiment
establish base, constitute, create, decree, enact, entrench, fix, form, found, ground, implant, inaugurate, install, institute, plant, root, secure, settle, set up, start

establishment business, company, concern, enterprise, firm, house, institution, organization, outfit *Inf*, set-up *Inf*, structure, system
estate area, domain, holdings, lands, manor, property
esteem *v* admire, be fond of, cherish, honour, like, love, prize, respect, revere, reverence, treasure, value ~*n* credit, good opinion, honour, regard, respect, reverence
estimate *v* assess, calculate roughly, evaluate, gauge, guess, judge, number, reckon, value ~*n* approximate calculation, assessment, evaluation, guess, judgment, reckoning, valuation
estuary creek, firth, fjord, inlet, mouth,
et cetera and others, and so forth, and so on, and the like, and the rest
eternal abiding, ceaseless, constant, deathless, endless, everlasting, immortal, infinite, interminable, never-ending, perennial, perpetual, timeless, unceasing, undying, unending, without end

heavenly

ethics *pl n* (science of) morals **ethical** *adj*

ethnic *adj* of race or relating to classification of humans into different groups

ethos *n* distinctive spirit of people, culture etc.

etiquette *n* conventional code of conduct

étude *n* short musical composition, exercise

etymology *n* tracing, account of word's origin, development

eucalyptus, eucalypt *n* Aust. tree, providing timber and gum

Eucharist *n* Christian sacrament of the Lord's Supper

eugenics *pl n* (*with sing v*) science of improving the human race by selective breeding

eulogy *n* praise **eulogize** *v*

eunuch *n* castrated man

euphemism *n* substitution of mild term for offensive one **euphemistic** *adj*

euphoria *n* sense of elation **euphoric** *adj*

eureka *interj* exclamation of triumph

euthanasia *n* painless putting to death to relieve suffering

evacuate *v* empty; withdraw from **evacuation** *n* **evacuee** *n*

evade *v* avoid; elude **evasion** *n* **evasive** *adj*

evaluate *v* find or judge value of **evaluation** *n*

evangelical *adj* of, or according to, gospel teaching **evangelism** *n* **evangelist** *n*

evaporate *v* turn into vapour **evaporation** *n*

evasion *See* EVADE

eve *n* evening before; time just before **evensong** *n* evening service

even *adj* flat, smooth; uniform, equal; divisible by two; impartial ~*v* smooth; equalize ~*adv* equally; simply; notwithstanding

evening *n* close of day

event *n* happening; notable occurrence; result; any one contest in

——— **THESAURUS** ———

ethical correct, fitting, good, honest, honourable, just, moral, principled, proper, right, upright

ethics conscience, moral code, morality, moral philosophy, moral values, principles, standards

ethnic cultural, folk, indigenous, national, native, racial, traditional

etiquette civility, code, convention, courtesy, customs, decorum, manners, politeness, propriety, protocol, rules, usage

evacuate abandon, clear, decamp, depart, desert, forsake, leave, move out, pull out, quit, relinquish, remove, vacate, withdraw

evade avoid, circumvent, decline, dodge, duck, elude, escape, shirk, shun, sidestep

evaluate appraise, assay, assess, esti-

mate, gauge, judge, rank, rate, reckon, size up *Inf*, value, weigh

evaporate dry, dry up, vaporize; dematerialize, disappear, disperse, dissipate, dissolve, fade away, melt, vanish

evasion avoidance, cunning, dodge, equivocation, escape, evasiveness, excuse, prevarication, ruse, shift, shuffling, sophistry, subterfuge, trickery

evasive cagey *Inf*, cunning, devious, elusive, equivocating, indirect, misleading, oblique, prevaricating, shifty

eve day before, night before, vigil

even *adj* flat, flush, level, plane, plumb, smooth, steady, straight, true, uniform; balanced, disinterested, dispassionate, equitable, fair, impartial, just, unbiased, unprejudiced

sporting programme **eventful** *adj* full of exciting events **eventual** *adj* resulting in the end **eventuality** *n* possible event

ever *adv* always; at any time **evergreen** *n/adj* (tree or shrub) bearing foliage throughout the year **evermore** *adv* for all time to come

every *adj* each of all; all possible **everybody** *n* **everyday** *adj* usual, ordinary **everyone** *n* **everything** *n* **everywhere** *adv* in all places

evict *v* expel by legal process, turn out **eviction** *n*

evidence *n* ground of belief; sign; testimony ~*v* indicate, prove **evident** *adj* plain, obvious

evil *adj/n* (what is) bad or harmful

evoke *v* call to mind; bring about **evocation** *n* **evocative** *adj*

evolve *v* (cause to) develop gradually; undergo slow changes **evolution** *n* development of species from earlier forms

ewe *n* female sheep

ex- *comb. form* out from, from, out of, formerly, as in **exclaim, exodus**

exacerbate *v* aggravate, make worse

~*adv* all the more, much, still, yet

event affair, business, circumstance, episode, experience, fact, happening, incident, matter, milestone, occasion, occurrence

eventful active, busy, critical, crucial, decisive, exciting, fateful, full, historic, important, lively, memorable, momentous, notable, significant

eventual concluding, consequent, ensuing, final, future, later, resulting, ultimate

eventuality case, chance, contingency, event, likelihood, possibility, probability

ever always, at all times, constantly, continually, endlessly, eternally, incessantly, perpetually, relentlessly, unceasingly; at all, at any period, at any point, at any time, in any case, on any occasion

evermore always, eternally, ever, for ever, *in perpetuum,* to the end of time

every all, each, each one, the whole number

everyday accustomed, common, commonplace, conventional, dull, familiar, frequent, habitual, informal, mundane, ordinary, routine, stock, usual, wonted

evict boot out *Inf,* chuck out *Inf,* dislodge, dispossess, eject, expel, kick out *Inf,* oust, put out, remove, show the door (to), throw on to the streets, throw out, turf out *Inf,* turn out

evidence affirmation, confirmation, data, declaration, demonstration, grounds, indication, mark, proof, sign, substantiation, testimony, token, witness

evident apparent, clear, incontestable, indisputable, manifest, noticeable, obvious, patent, perceptible, plain, visible

evil *adj* bad, base, corrupt, depraved, malicious, malignant, sinful, vicious, vile, villainous, wicked, wrong; calamitous, catastrophic, destructive, dire, harmful, hurtful, injurious, mischievous, painful, pernicious, ruinous, sorrowful, unfortunate, unlucky, woeful ~*n* badness, baseness, corruption, immorality, vice, villainy, wickedness, wrong, wrongdoing

evoke arouse, awaken, call, excite, induce, recall, stimulate, stir up, summon up; bring about, call forth, elicit, produce, provoke

evolution development, enlargement, expansion, growth, increase, progress, unrolling

evolve develop, disclose, educe, elaborate, enlarge, expand, grow, increase, mature, open, progress, un-

exact *adj* precise, strictly correct ~*v* demand, extort **exacting** *adj* making rigorous demands **exactly** *adv*

exaggerate *v* magnify beyond truth, overstate **exaggeration** *n*

exalt *v* raise up; praise

exam *n* examination

examine *v* investigate; look at closely; ask questions of; test knowledge of **examination** *n* **examiner** *n*

example *n* specimen; model

exasperate *v* irritate **exasperation** *n*

excavate *v* hollow out; dig; unearth **excavator** *n*

exceed *v* be greater than; go beyond **exceedingly** *adv* very

excel *v* -**celling, -celled** surpass; be very good **excellence** *n* **excellent** *adj* very good

except *prep* not including ~*v* exclude **exception** *n* thing not included in a rule; objection **exceptional** *adj* above

———————— THESAURUS ————————

fold, unroll, work out

exact *adj* accurate, careful, correct, definite, explicit, faithful, faultless, identical, literal, methodical, orderly, particular, precise, right, specific, true, unequivocal, unerring, veracious, very; careful, meticulous, painstaking, punctilious, rigorous, scrupulous, severe, strict ~*v* call for, claim, command, compel, demand, extort, extract, force, impose, insist upon, require

exactly accurately, carefully, correctly, definitely, explicitly, faithfully, faultlessly, literally, precisely, severely, strictly, truly, truthfully, veraciously

exaggerate amplify, embroider, emphasize, enlarge, exalt, inflate, magnify, overdo, overestimate, overstate

exaggeration embellishment, emphasis, enlargement, excess, hyperbole, inflation, overstatement, pretension, pretentiousness

exalt advance, dignify, elevate, ennoble, honour, promote, raise, upgrade

examination analysis, catechism, checkup, exploration, inquiry, inquisition, inspection, interrogation, investigation, once-over *Inf*, perusal, probe, questioning, quiz, review, scrutiny, search, study, survey, test, trial

examine analyse, appraise, check out, consider, explore, inspect, inves-

tigate, look over, peruse, ponder, probe, review, scan, scrutinize, sift, study, survey, test, vet, weigh

example case, illustration, instance, sample, specimen

exasperate anger, annoy, enrage, exacerbate, gall, get *Inf*, incense, inflame, infuriate, irk, irritate, madden, pique, provoke, rankle, vex

exasperation anger, annoyance, fury, irritation, passion, pique, rage, vexation, wrath

excavate burrow, delve, dig, dig out, dig up, gouge, hollow, mine, quarry, scoop, trench, tunnel, uncover, unearth

exceed beat, better, cap *Inf*, eclipse, excel, outdistance, outdo, outreach, outrun, outshine, outstrip, overtake, pass, surmount, surpass, top, transcend

excel beat, be superior, better, cap *Inf*, eclipse, exceed, go beyond, outdo, outrival, outshine, pass, surmount, surpass, top, transcend

excellence distinction, eminence, goodness, greatness, high quality, merit, perfection, superiority, supremacy, virtue, worth

excellent admirable, capital, champion, choice, cracking *Brit inf*, distinguished, exemplary, exquisite, fine, first-class, first-rate, good, great, meritorious, outstanding, prime, select, superb, superior, superlative,

average

excerpt n passage from book etc.

excess n too great amount; intemperance **excessive** adj

exchange v give (something) in return for something else; barter ~n giving one thing and receiving another; thing given; building where merchants meet for business; central telephone office **exchangeable** adj

exchequer n government department in charge of revenue

excise[1] n duty charged on home goods

excise[2] v cut away

excite v arouse to strong emotion, stimulate; set in motion **excitable** adj **excitement** n **exciting** adj

exclaim v speak suddenly, cry out **exclamation** n **exclamation mark** punctuation mark (!), used after exclamations

exclude v shut out; debar from; reject, not consider **exclusion** n **exclusive** adj excluding; select **exclusiveness, exclusivity** n

excommunicate v cut off from sacraments of the Church **excommunication** n

excrement n waste matter from bow-

——————————————— T H E S A U R U S ———————————————

top-notch Inf, worthy

except, except for apart from, bar, barring, besides, but, excepting, excluding, exclusive of, omitting, other than

exception anomaly, deviation, freak, irregularity, oddity, peculiarity, quirk, special case

exceptional excellent, extraordinary, marvellous, outstanding, phenomenal, prodigious, remarkable, special, superior

excess n glut, leftover, overdose, overflow, plethora, remainder, superfluity, surfeit, surplus, too much; debauchery, dissipation, dissoluteness, extravagance, intemperance, overindulgence, prodigality

excessive enormous, exaggerated, extravagant, extreme, inordinate, needless, overdone, overmuch, prodigal, profligate, superfluous, too much, undue, unreasonable

exchange v bandy, barter, change, commute, swap Inf, switch, trade, truck ~n barter, dealing, substitution, swap Inf, switch, trade, traffic, truck

excitable edgy, hasty, highly strung, hot-headed, nervous, passionate, sensitive, temperamental, testy,

touchy, violent, volatile

excite agitate, arouse, awaken, disturb, evoke, fire, foment, galvanize, incite, inflame, inspire, move, provoke, quicken, rouse, stimulate, stir up, thrill, waken

excitement action, ado, adventure, animation, commotion, elation, ferment, kicks Inf, passion, thrill, tumult, warmth

exciting exhilarating, inspiring, intoxicating, moving, provocative, riproaring Inf, rousing, sensational, stimulating, stirring, thrilling

exclaim call, call out, cry, cry out, declare, proclaim, shout, utter, yell

exclamation call, cry, expletive, interjection, outcry, shout, utterance, yell

exclude ban, bar, blackball, debar, disallow, forbid, interdict, keep out, ostracize, prohibit, proscribe, refuse, shut out, veto; eliminate, except, ignore, leave out, omit, pass over, preclude, reject, repudiate, rule out

exclusive aristocratic, chic, choice, clannish, closed, elegant, fashionable, limited, narrow, posh Inf, chiefly Brit, private, restricted, select, selfish, snobbish

excommunicate anathematize, ban,

els **excrete** v discharge from the system **excretion** n **excretory** adj

excruciating adj unbearably painful

excursion n trip for pleasure

excuse v overlook; try to clear from blame; gain exemption; set free ~n that which serves to excuse; apology **excusable** adj

execrable adj hatefully bad

execute v inflict capital punishment on, kill; carry out, perform; make **execution** n **executioner** n **executive** n/adj (of) person in administrative position; (of) branch of government enforcing laws **executor** n (fem **executrix**) person appointed to carry out provisions of a will

exemplary adj serving as example

exemplify v -**fying**, -**fied** serve as example of

exempt v free from; excuse ~adj freed from, not liable for **exemption** n

exercise n use of limbs for health; practice; task; use ~v use; carry out; take exercise

exert v make effort **exertion** n

exhale v breathe out

exhaust v tire out; use up; empty ~n waste gases from engine; passage for this **exhaustible** adj **exhaustion** n state of extreme fatigue **exhaustive** adj comprehensive

exhibit v show, display ~n thing

———————— THESAURUS ————————

banish, cast out, denounce, eject, exclude, expel, proscribe, remove, repudiate, unchurch

excursion airing, day trip, expedition, jaunt, journey, outing, pleasure trip, tour, trip

excuse v absolve, acquit, bear with, exculpate, exonerate, forgive, indulge, overlook, pardon, pass over, tolerate, wink at; absolve, discharge, exempt, free, let off, liberate, release, relieve, spare ~n apology, defence, explanation, grounds, justification, mitigation, plea, pretext, reason, vindication

execute behead, electrocute, guillotine, hang, kill, put to death, shoot

execution capital punishment, hanging, killing; accomplishment, achievement, administration, carrying out, completion, discharge, effect, enactment, enforcement, implementation, performance, prosecution, realization, rendering

executive n administrator, director, manager, official; administration, directorate, directors, government, leadership, management ~adj administrative, controlling, decision-

making, directing, governing, managerial

exemplary admirable, commendable, correct, estimable, excellent, good, ideal, laudable, meritorious, model, praiseworthy, sterling

exemplify demonstrate, depict, display, embody, evidence, exhibit, illustrate, instance, represent, show

exempt v absolve, discharge, except, excuse, exonerate, free, let off, liberate, release, relieve, spare ~adj absolved, clear, discharged, excused, favoured, free, immune, liberated, not liable, not subject, privileged, released, spared

exercise n action, activity, discipline, drill, drilling, effort, labour, toil, training, work, work-out; drill, lesson, practice, problem, schooling, task, work ~v apply, bring to bear, employ, enjoy, exert, practise, put to use, use, utilize, wield; drill, inure, practise, train, work out

exert bring into play, bring to bear, employ, exercise, expend, use, utilize, wield

exertion action, application, attempt, effort, industry, strain, stretch, strug-

shown **exhibition** *n* display; public show **exhibitionist** *n* one with compulsive desire to attract attention **exhibitor** *n*

exhilarate *v* enliven, gladden **exhilaration** *n*

exhort *v* urge

exhume *v* dig up (corpse etc.)

exigency *n* urgent need

exile *n* banishment, expulsion from one's own country; one banished ~*v* banish

exist *v* be, have being, live **existence** *n* **existent** *adj*

exit *n* way out; going out ~*v* go out

exodus *n* departure

exonerate *v* free, declare free, from

blame

exorbitant *adj* excessive

exorcize *v* cast out (evil spirits) by invocation **exorcism** *n* **exorcist** *n*

exotic *adj* foreign; unusual

expand *v* increase, spread out **expandable** *adj* **expanse** *n* wide space

expansion *n* **expansive** *adj* extensive; friendly

expatiate *v* speak or write at great length (on)

expatriate *adj/n* (one) living in exile

expect *v* regard as probable; look forward to **expectant** *adj* **expectation** *n*

expedient *adj* fitting; politic; convenient ~*n* something suitable, useful **expediency** *n*

———— T H E S A U R U S ————

gle, toil, trial, use

exhaust bankrupt, cripple, debilitate, disable, drain, enervate, fatigue, impoverish, prostrate, sap, tire, weaken, wear out; consume, deplete, dissipate, expend, finish, run through, spend, squander, use up, waste; drain, dry, empty, strain, void

exhibit *v* display, expose, express, indicate, manifest, offer, parade, present, put on view, reveal, show ~*n* display, exhibition, model, show

exhort advise, beseech, bid, call upon, encourage, entreat, goad, incite, persuade, spur, urge, warn

exile *n* banishment, expatriation, expulsion, ostracism, proscription, separation; émigré, expatriate, outcast, refugee ~*v* banish, deport, drive out, eject, expel, oust, proscribe

exist abide, be, be living, be present, breathe, endure, happen, last, live, occur, prevail, remain, stand, survive

existence actuality, animation, being, breath, continuance, continuation, duration, endurance, life, subsistence, survival

exit door, egress, gate, outlet, passage out, vent, way out

exotic alien, foreign, imported, introduced, not native; bizarre, colourful, curious, different, extraordinary, outlandish, peculiar, strange, striking, unfamiliar, unusual

expand amplify, augment, bloat, blow up, broaden, develop, dilate, distend, enlarge, extend, fatten, fill out, grow, heighten, increase, inflate, lengthen, magnify, multiply, prolong, protract, swell, thicken, wax, widen

expanse area, breadth, extent, field, plain, range, space, stretch, sweep, tract

expansive affable, communicative, effusive, free, friendly, garrulous, genial, loquacious, open, outgoing, sociable, talkative, warm

expect assume, believe, calculate, conjecture, forecast, foresee, imagine, presume, reckon, suppose, surmise, think, trust; anticipate, await, contemplate, envisage, hope for, look ahead to, look for, look forward to, predict, watch for

expectation assumption, assurance, belief, calculation, confidence, conjecture, forecast, likelihood, presumption, probability, supposition,

expedite v help on, hasten **expedition** n journey for definite purpose; people, equipment comprising expedition

expel v **-pelling, -pelled** drive out; exclude **expulsion** n

expend v spend, pay out; use up **expendable** adj likely to be used up **expenditure** n **expense** n cost; pl charges incurred **expensive** adj

experience n observation of facts as source of knowledge; being affected by event; the event; knowledge, skill gained ~v undergo, suffer, meet with **experienced** adj

experiment n/v test to discover or prove something **experimental** adj

expert n/adj (one) skilful, knowledgeable, in something **expertise** n

expiate v make amends for

expire v come to an end; die; breathe out **expiry** n end

——————————— THESAURUS ———————————

surmise, trust

expedient advantageous, advisable, appropriate, beneficial, convenient, desirable, effective, fit, helpful, meet, opportune, politic, practical, pragmatic, profitable, proper, prudent, suitable, useful, worthwhile

expedition enterprise, excursion, exploration, journey, mission, quest, safari, tour, trek, trip, undertaking, voyage

expel cast out, discharge, dislodge, drive out, eject, remove, throw out; ban, banish, bar, discharge, dismiss, evict, exclude, exile, oust, proscribe, throw out

expend consume, disburse, dissipate, employ, exhaust, go through, lay out Inf, pay out, shell out Inf, spend, use (up)

expendable inessential, replaceable, unimportant

expenditure charge, cost, disbursement, expense, outgoings, outlay, output, payment, spending, use

expense charge, cost, disbursement, loss, outlay, output, payment, sacrifice, spending, toll, use

expensive costly, dear, excessive, exorbitant, overpriced, rich, steep Inf, stiff

experience n contact, doing, evidence, exposure, familiarity, knowledge, observation, participation, practice, proof, training, trial, under-

standing; affair, encounter, episode, event, happening, incident, ordeal, test, trial ~v behold, encounter, endure, face, feel, go through, have, know, live through, meet, observe, perceive, sample, sense, suffer, sustain, taste, try, undergo

experienced accomplished, adept, capable, competent, expert, familiar, knowledgeable, practised, professional, qualified, seasoned, skilful, tested, trained, tried, veteran, well-versed

experiment n assay, attempt, investigation, procedure, proof, research, test, trial, trial run, venture ~v examine, investigate, research, sample, test, try, verify

experimental empirical, exploratory, pilot, preliminary, provisional, speculative, tentative, test, trial

expert n ace Inf, adept, authority, buff Inf, dab hand Brit inf, master, past master, professional, specialist, virtuoso, whiz Inf, wizard ~adj able, adept, adroit, apt, clever, deft, experienced, handy, knowledgeable, masterly, practised, proficient, qualified, skilful, trained

expertise aptness, cleverness, command, deftness, dexterity, facility, judgment, knack, knowledge, mastery, proficiency, skilfulness, skill

expire cease, close, come to an end, conclude, end, finish, lapse, run out,

explain *v* make clear, intelligible; account for **explanation** *n* **explanatory** *adj*

expletive *n* exclamation; oath

explicable *adj* explainable

explicit *adj* clearly stated

explode *v* (make) burst violently; (of population) increase rapidly; discredit **explosion** *n* **explosive** *adj/n*

exploit *n* brilliant feat, deed ~*v* turn to advantage; make use of for one's own ends **exploitation** *n*

explore *v* investigate; examine (country etc.) by going through it **exploration** *n* **exploratory** *adj* **explorer** *n*

exponent *see* EXPOUND

export *v* send (goods) out of the country ~*n* exporting; product sold abroad

expose *v* display; reveal (scandalous) truth; leave unprotected **exposure** *n*

exposé *n* bringing of scandal, crime etc, to public notice.

expound *v* explain, interpret **exponent** *n* one who expounds or promotes (idea, cause etc.); performer **exposition** *n* explanation; exhibition of goods etc.

express *v* put into words; make known or understood; *adj* definitely stated; specially designed; speedy ~*adv* with speed ~*n* express train; rapid parcel delivery service **expression** *n* expressing; word, phrase; look **expressive** *adj*

expropriate *v* dispossess

——————— THESAURUS ———————

stop, terminate; depart, die, pass away *or* on, perish

explain clarify, clear up, define, demonstrate, describe, disclose, elucidate, expound, interpret, resolve, solve, teach, unfold

explanation elucidation, exposition, interpretation, resolution; account, answer, cause, excuse, meaning, motive, reason, sense, vindication

explicit categorical, certain, clear, definite, direct, distinct, exact, express, frank, open, patent, plain, positive, precise, specific, stated, unqualified, unreserved

explode blow up, burst, detonate, discharge, go off, set off, shatter, shiver; debunk, discredit, disprove, invalidate, refute, repudiate

exploit *n* achievement, adventure, attainment, deed, feat, stunt ~*v* abuse, manipulate, misuse, play on *or* upon, take advantage of

exploration examination, inquiry, inspection, investigation, probe, research, scrutiny, search, study

explore analyse, examine, inquire into, inspect, investigate, look into,

probe, prospect, research, scrutinize, search

explosion bang, blast, burst, clap, crack, detonation, discharge, outburst, report

explosive unstable, volatile

exponent advocate, backer, champion, defender, promoter, spokesman, supporter, upholder

expose display, exhibit, manifest, present, put on view, reveal, show, uncover, unveil; air, betray, bring to light, denounce, detect, disclose, divulge, lay bare, let out, make known, reveal, show up, uncover, unmask

exposure baring, display, manifestation, publicity, revelation, showing, uncovering, unveiling; airing, denunciation, detection, disclosure, divulgence, revelation, unmasking

expound describe, elucidate, explain, illustrate, interpret, spell out

express *v* articulate, assert, asseverate, communicate, couch, declare, phrase, pronounce, put, say, speak, state, tell, utter, voice, word ~*adj* clearcut, especial, particular, singular, special; direct, fast, high-speed,

expunge *v* delete, blot out

expurgate *v* remove objectionable parts (from book etc.)

exquisite *adj* of extreme beauty or delicacy

extempore *adj/adv* without previous preparation **extemporary** *adj* **extemporize** *v*

extend *v* stretch out; prolong; widen; accord, grant; reach; cover area; have range or scope **extension** *n* extending; additional part **extensive** *adj* wide **extent** *n* space; scope; size

extenuate *v* make less blameworthy;

lessen; mitigate

exterior *n* outside ~*adj* outer, external

exterminate *v* destroy completely **extermination** *n*

external *adj* outside, outward **externally** *adv*

extinct *adj* having died out; quenched **extinction** *n*

extinguish *v* put out, quench; wipe out

extol *v* -tolling, -tolled praise highly

extort *v* get by force or threats **extortion** *n* **extortionate** *adj* excessive

———— THESAURUS ————

nonstop, quick, rapid, speedy, swift

expression assertion, communication, declaration, mention, pronouncement, speaking, statement, utterance; idiom, locution, phrase, remark, term, turn of phrase, word; air, appearance, countenance, face, look

expulsion banishment, discharge, dismissal, ejection, eviction, exclusion, exile, proscription, removal

exquisite beautiful, dainty, delicate, elegant, fine, lovely, precious

extend carry on, continue, drag out, draw out, lengthen, prolong, protract, spin out, spread out, stretch, unfurl, unroll; add to, augment, broaden, develop, dilate, enhance, enlarge, expand, increase, spread, widen

extension addendum, addition, adjunct, annexe, branch, supplement, wing

extensive broad, capacious, commodious, comprehensive, far-flung, far-reaching, general, great, huge, large, lengthy, long, prevalent, protracted, spacious, sweeping, thorough, universal, vast, wholesale, wide, widespread

extent bounds, compass, play, range, reach, scope, sphere, sweep; amount,

amplitude, area, breadth, bulk, degree, duration, expanse, expansion, length, magnitude, measure, quantity, size, stretch, term, time, volume, width

exterior *n* appearance, aspect, coating, covering, façade, face, finish, outside, shell, skin, surface ~*adj* external, outer, outermost, outside, outward, superficial, surface

exterminate abolish, annihilate, destroy, eliminate, eradicate, extirpate

external apparent, exterior, outer, outermost, outside, outward, superficial, surface, visible

extinct dead, defunct, gone, lost, vanished

extinction abolition, annihilation, death, dying out, excision, extermination, obliteration, oblivion

extinguish blow out, douse, put out, quench, smother, snuff out, stifle; abolish, destroy, eliminate, end, expunge, exterminate, kill, obscure, remove, suppress, wipe out

extol acclaim, applaud, celebrate, commend, eulogize, exalt, glorify, laud, praise

extort blackmail, bleed *Inf,* bully, exact, extract, force, squeeze, wrest, wring

extortionate excessive, exorbitant,

extra *adj* additional; more than usual ~*adv* additionally; more than usually ~*n* extra person or thing; something charged as additional

extra- *comb. form* beyond, as in **extradition, extramural**

extract *v* take out, esp. by force; get by distillation etc.; derive; quote ~*n* passage from book, film etc.; concentrated solution **extraction** *n* extracting; ancestry

extradition *n* delivery of foreign fugitive **extradite** *v*

extramural *adj* outside normal courses etc. of university or college

extraneous *adj* not essential; added from without

extraordinary *adj* very unusual **extraordinarily** *adv*

extrapolate *v* make inference from known facts

extrasensory *adj* of perception apparently gained without use of known senses

extravagant *adj* wasteful; exorbitant **extravagance** *n* **extravaganza** *n* elaborate entertainment

extreme *adj* of high or highest degree; severe; going beyond moderation; outermost ~*n* utmost degree; thing at either end **extremely** *adv* **extremist** *n* ~*adj* (one) favouring immoderate methods **extremity** *n* end; *pl* hands and feet

─────── T H E S A U R U S ───────

immoderate, inflated, inordinate, outrageous, preposterous, sky-high, unreasonable

extra *adj* accessory, added, additional, auxiliary, fresh, further, more, new, other, supplemental, supplementary ~*adv* especially, exceptionally, extraordinarily, extremely, particularly, remarkably, uncommonly, unusually ~*n* addendum, addition, appurtenance, attachment, bonus, complement, extension, supernumerary, supplement

extract *v* draw, pluck out, pull, pull out, remove, take out, uproot, withdraw; derive; draw, elicit, evoke, exact, gather, get, glean, obtain, reap, wrest, wring ~*n* abstract, citation, clipping, cutting, excerpt, passage, quotation, selection

extraordinary amazing, bizarre, curious, exceptional, fantastic, odd, outstanding, particular, peculiar, phenomenal, rare, remarkable, singular, special, strange, surprising, uncommon, unfamiliar, unheard-of, unique, unprecedented, unusual, unwonted, weird, wonderful

extravagance improvidence, lavish-

ness, overspending, prodigality, profligacy, profusion, squandering, waste

extravagant excessive, improvident, imprudent, lavish, prodigal, profligate, spendthrift, wasteful; costly, excessive, exorbitant, expensive, extortionate, inordinate, overpriced, steep *Inf*, unreasonable

extreme *adj* acute, great, greatest, high, highest, intense, maximum, severe, supreme, ultimate, utmost, uttermost, worst; faraway, far-off, farthest, final, last, outermost, remotest, terminal, ultimate, utmost ~*n* acme, apex, boundary, climax, depth, edge, end, excess, extremity, height, limit, maximum, minimum, nadir, pinnacle, pole, termination, top, ultimate, zenith

extremely acutely, awfully *Inf*, exceedingly, exceptionally, excessively, extraordinarily, greatly, highly, inordinately, intensely, markedly, quite, severely, uncommonly, unusually, utterly, very

extremity acme, apex, apogee, border, bound, boundary, brim, brink, edge, end, frontier, limit, margin,

extricate *v* disentangle

extrovert *n* lively, outgoing person

extrude *v* squeeze, force out

exuberant *adj* high-spirited **exuberance** *n*

exude *v* ooze out; give off

exult *v* rejoice, triumph **exultant** *adj* **exultation** *n*

eye *n* organ of sight; look, glance; attention; aperture; thing resembling eye ~*v* look at; observe **eyebrow** *n* fringe of hair above eye **eyelash** *n* hair fringing eyelid **eyelet** *n* small hole **eyelid** *n* **eye shadow** coloured cosmetic worn on upper eyelids **eyesore** *n* ugly object **eyetooth** *n* canine tooth **eyewitness** *n* one who was present at an event

eyrie *n* nest of bird of prey, esp. eagle

——————————————— THESAURUS ———————————————

maximum, minimum, nadir, pinnacle, pole, rim, terminal, tip, top, ultimate, verge, zenith

extricate clear, deliver, disengage, disentangle, free, get out, liberate, release, relieve, remove, rescue, withdraw

exuberance cheerfulness, eagerness, ebullience, effervescence, energy, enthusiasm, excitement, exhilaration, high spirits, life, liveliness, pep, spirit, sprightliness, vigour, vitality, vivacity, zest

exuberant animated, buoyant, cheerful, chirpy *Inf*, eager, ebullient, effervescent, elated, energetic, enthusiastic, excited, exhilarated, high-spirited, lively, sparkling, spirited, sprightly, vigorous, vivacious, zestful

exult be delighted, be elated, be joyful, be jubilant, be overjoyed, celebrate, jubilate, make merry, rejoice

eye *n* eyeball; appreciation, discernment, discrimination, judgment, perception, recognition, taste ~*v* contemplate, gaze at, inspect, look at, peruse, regard, scan, scrutinize, stare at, study, survey, view, watch

eyesore atrocity, blemish, blight, blot, disgrace, horror, mess, monstrosity, sight *Inf*

eyewitness looker-on, observer, onlooker, spectator, viewer, witness

F f

F Fahrenheit

f *Mus* forte

fable *n* short story with moral **fabulous** *adj* amazing; *Inf* extremely good

fabric *n* cloth; structure **fabricate** *v* construct; invent (lie etc.)

façade *n* front of building; outward appearance

face *n* front of head; distorted expression; outward appearance; chief side of anything; dignity ~*v* look or front towards; meet (boldly); give a covering surface; turn **faceless** *adj* anonymous **face-lift** *n* operation to remove wrinkles **face-saving** *adj* maintaining dignity **facet** *n* one side of cut gem; one aspect **face value** apparent worth **facial** *n* cosmetic treatment for face ~*adj* of face

facetious *adj* given to joking

facia *see FASCIA*

facile *adj* easy; superficial **facilitate** *v* make easy **facility** *n* easiness; dexterity; *pl* opportunities, good conditions; means, equipment for doing something

facsimile *n* exact copy

fact *n* thing known to be true; reality **factual** *adj*

faction *n* (dissenting) minority group; dissension

factor *n* something contributing to a result; one of numbers which multiplied together give a given number; agent

factory *n* building where things are manufactured

faculty *n* inherent power; ability; apti-

THESAURUS

fable allegory, legend, myth, parable, story, tale

fabric cloth, material, stuff, textile, web; constitution, framework, make-up, organization, structure

fabulous amazing, astounding, breathtaking, fictitious, inconceivable, incredible, legendary, phenomenal, unbelievable

face *n* countenance, features, physiognomy, visage; appearance, aspect, expression, frown, grimace, look, pout, scowl, smirk ~*v* be opposite, front onto, look onto, overlook; brave, confront, deal with, defy, encounter, experience, meet, oppose

facet angle, aspect, face, part, phase, plane, side, slant, surface

facetious amusing, comical, droll, flippant, frivolous, funny, humorous, jesting, jocular, merry, playful, waggish, witty

facile adept, adroit, easy, effortless, fluent, light, quick, ready, simple, skilful, smooth, uncomplicated

facilitate ease, expedite, forward, further, help, make easy, promote, speed up

facility ability, adroitness, dexterity, ease, efficiency, effortlessness, fluency, knack, proficiency, quickness, readiness, skilfulness, skill, smoothness

facsimile copy, duplicate, photocopy, print, replica, reproduction, transcript

fact act, deed, event, happening, incident, occurrence, performance; actuality, certainty, reality, truth

faction bloc, cabal, camp, caucus, clique, coalition, confederacy, division, lobby, minority, party, pressure group, schism, section, set, splinter group

factor aspect, cause, circumstance, component, consideration, element, influence, item, part, point, thing

factory mill, plant, works

tude; department of university
fad *n* short-lived fashion
fade *v* lose colour, strength; cause to fade
faeces *pl n* excrement
fag *n Inf* boring task; *Sl* cigarette ~*v* **fagging, fagged** *Inf* (*esp. with* **out**) tire
faggot *n* ball of chopped liver; bundle of sticks
Fahrenheit *adj* measured by thermo-metric scale with freezing point of water 32°, boiling point 212°
fail *v* be unsuccessful; stop working; (judge to) be below the required standard; disappoint, give no help to;

be insufficient; become bankrupt; ne-glect, forget to do **failing** *n* deficien-cy; fault ~*prep* in default of **failure** *n* **without fail** certainly
faint *adj* feeble, dim, pale; weak; dizzy ~*v* lose consciousness temporarily
fair[1] *adj* just; according to rules; blond; beautiful; of moderate quality or amount; favourable ~*adv* honestly **fairly** *adv* **fairness** *n* **fairway** *n* smooth area on golf course between tee and green
fair[2] *n* travelling entertainment with sideshows etc.; trade exhibition **fair-ground** *n*
fairy *n* imaginary small creature with

———————— THESAURUS ————————

factual accurate, authentic, close, correct, credible, exact, faithful, genuine, literal, objective, precise, real, sure, true, true-to-life, un-adorned, unbiased, veritable
faculty department, discipline, pro-fession, school, teaching staff
fad affectation, craze, fancy, fashion, mania, mode, rage, trend, vogue, whim
fade blanch, bleach, blench, dim, dis-colour, dull, grow dim, pale, wash out; decline, die out, dim, disperse, dissolve, droop, dwindle, ebb, fail, fall, flag, melt away, perish, shrivel, vanish, waste away, wilt, wither
fail be defeated, be unsuccessful, break down, come to grief, come to naught, fall short, founder, go astray, go down, miscarry, misfire, miss, run aground; abandon, desert, disap-point, forget, forsake, let down, ne-glect, omit
failing *n* blemish, blind spot, defect, deficiency, drawback, error, failure, fault, flaw, imperfection, lapse, mis-fortune, shortcoming, weakness
failure breakdown, collapse, defeat, downfall, fiasco, miscarriage, over-throw, wreck; default, neglect, negli-

gence, nonsuccess, omission, remiss-ness, shortcoming; bankruptcy, crash, downfall, insolvency, ruin
faint *adj* delicate, dim, distant, dull, faltering, feeble, hazy, hushed, ill-defined, indistinct, light, low, muted, soft, subdued, thin, vague, whis-pered; feeble, remote, slight, weak; dizzy, drooping, exhausted, fatigued, giddy, lethargic, light-headed, muz-zy, vertiginous, weak ~*v* black out, collapse, fade, fail, languish, pass out, weaken
fair[1] *adj* above board, clean, disinter-ested, dispassionate, equal, even-handed, honest, honourable, impar-tial, just, lawful, legitimate, objective, proper, unbiased, upright; blond, light; beautiful, comely, handsome, lovely, pretty, well-favoured; ad-equate, all right, average, decent, me-diocre, middling, moderate, not bad, O.K. *or* okay, passable, reasonable, respectable, satisfactory, tolerable
fair[2] *n* bazaar, carnival, festival, fête, gala, market, show
fairly deservedly, equitably, honestly, justly, objectively, properly; ad-equately, moderately, pretty well, quite, rather, reasonably, somewhat,

powers of magic ~*adj* of fairies; delicate, imaginary

faith *n* trust; belief (without proof); religion; loyalty **faithful** *adj* constant, true **faithfully** *adv* **faithless** *adj*

fake *v* touch up; counterfeit ~*n/adj* fraudulent (thing or person)

falcon *n* small bird of prey

fall *v* falling, fell, fallen drop; become lower; hang down; cease to stand; perish; collapse; be captured; become; happen ~*n* falling; amount that falls; decrease; collapse; drop; (*oft. pl*) cascade; yielding to temptation; *US* autumn **fallout** *n* radioactive

particles spread as result of nuclear explosion

fallacy *n* incorrect opinion or argument **fallacious** *adj* **fallible** *adj* liable to error

fallow *adj* ploughed but left without crop

false *adj* wrong; deceptive; faithless; artificial **falsely** *adv* **falsehood** *n* **falsify** *v*-fying, -fied alter fraudulently

falsetto *n* (*pl* -tos) forced voice above natural range

falter *v* hesitate; waver; stumble

fame *n* renown **famed** *adj* **famous** *adj* widely known **famously** *adv* *Inf*

———————— THESAURUS ————————

tolerably

fairness decency, equity, impartiality, justice, legitimacy, rightfulness, uprightness

fairy brownie, elf, hob, sprite

faith assurance, confidence, conviction, credence, credit, reliance, trust; allegiance, constancy, faithfulness, fealty, fidelity, loyalty, truth, truthfulness

faithful constant, dependable, devoted, loyal, reliable, staunch, steadfast, true, trusty, truthful, unwavering

faithless disloyal, doubting, false, fickle, inconstant, perfidious, traitorous, treacherous, unbelieving, unfaithful, unreliable, untrue, untrustworthy, untruthful

fake *v* copy, counterfeit, fabricate, feign, forge, pretend, put on, sham, simulate ~*n* charlatan, copy, forgery, fraud, hoax, imitation, impostor, mountebank, phoney *or* phony *Inf*, reproduction, sham

fall *v* cascade, collapse, crash, descend, dive, drop, drop down, keel over, nose-dive, pitch, plummet, plunge, settle, sink, stumble, subside, topple, trip, trip over, tumble; abate, decline, decrease, depreciate, diminish, drop, dwindle, ebb, fall off, flag,

go down, lessen, slump, subside; capitulate, give in *or* up, give way, go out of office, resign, succumb, surrender, yield ~*n* cut, decline, decrease, dip, drop, dwindling, falling off, lessening, lowering, reduction, slump; descent, dive, drop, plummet, plunge, slip, spill, tumble

fallacy deceit, deception, delusion, error, falsehood, flaw, illusion, misconception, sophism

fallible erring, frail, ignorant, imperfect, mortal, uncertain, weak

fallow dormant, idle, inert, resting, uncultivated, undeveloped

false concocted, erroneous, faulty, fictitious, improper, inaccurate, incorrect, inexact, invalid, mistaken, unfounded, unreal, wrong; lying, mendacious, unreliable, unsound, untrue, untrustworthy, untruthful; artificial, bogus, feigned, forged, imitation, mock, pretended, sham

falsehood deceit, deception, dishonesty, mendacity, perjury, prevarication; fib, fiction, lie, story, untruth

falsify alter, belie, counterfeit, distort, doctor, fake, forge, misrepresent, pervert

falter hesitate, shake, stammer, stutter, tremble, waver

excellently

familiar *adj* well-known; customary; intimate; acquainted; impertinent ~*n* friend; demon **familiarity** *n* **familiarize** *v*

family *n* parents and children, relatives; group of allied objects

famine *n* extreme scarcity of food; starvation **famished** *adj* very hungry

fan[1] *n* instrument for producing current of air; folding object of paper etc., for cooling the face ~*v* **fanning, fanned** blow or cool with fan; spread out

fan[2] *n Inf* devoted admirer

fanatic *adj/n* (person) filled with abnormal enthusiasm **fanatical** *adj* **fanaticism** *n*

fancy *adj* **-cier, -ciest** ornamental; *n* whim; liking; imagination; mental image ~*v* **-cying, -cied** imagine; be inclined to believe; *Inf* have a liking for **fancier** *n* one with special interest in something **fanciful** *adj*

fanfare *n* flourish of trumpets; ostentatious display

fang *n* snake's tooth, injecting poison; long, pointed tooth

fantasy *n* power of imagination; mental image; fanciful invention **fantasize** *v* **fantastic** *adj* quaint, extremely fanciful, wild; *Inf* very good; *Inf* very large

far *adv* **farther** *or* **further, farthest** *or* **furthest** at or to a great distance or a remote time; by very much ~*adj* distant; more distant **far-fetched** *adj* incredible

fame celebrity, credit, eminence, glory, honour, name, prominence, renown, reputation, repute, stardom

familiar common, conventional, customary, domestic, everyday, frequent, household, mundane, ordinary, recognizable, repeated, routine, stock, well-known; amicable, close, confidential, cordial, easy, free, friendly, informal, intimate, near, open, relaxed, unreserved

familiarity acquaintance, awareness, experience, grasp; closeness, ease, fellowship, freedom, friendliness, intimacy, naturalness, openness, sociability

family brood, children, household, issue, kin, offspring, people, progeny, relations, relatives

famine dearth, hunger, scarcity, starvation

famous celebrated, conspicuous, eminent, glorious, honoured, illustrious, legendary, notable, noted, prominent, remarkable, renowned, well-known

fan[1] *v* air-condition, air-cool, blow, cool, refresh, ventilate ~*n* air conditioner, blade, blower, propeller, vane, ventilator

fan[2] adherent, admirer, aficionado, buff *Inf,* devotee, enthusiast, follower, lover, supporter, zealot

fanatic *n* addict, bigot, buff *Inf,* devotee, enthusiast, extremist, visionary, zealot

fanciful capricious, chimerical, curious, extravagant, fabulous, fairy-tale, fantastic, ideal, imaginary, imaginative, mythical, poetic, romantic, unreal, visionary, whimsical, wild

fancy *adj* decorated, elaborate, elegant, intricate, ornamental, ornate ~*v* believe, conceive, guess, imagine, infer, reckon, suppose, surmise, think, think likely; crave, desire, dream of, long for, relish, wish for, would like, yearn for

fantastic eccentric, exotic, fanciful, freakish, grotesque, imaginative, odd, peculiar, quaint, queer, rococo, strange, unreal, weird, whimsical

far *adv* afar, a good way, a great distance, a long way, deep; consider-

farce n comedy of boisterous humour; absurd and futile proceeding **farcical** adj

fare n charge for transport; passenger; food ~v get on; happen **farewell** interj goodbye ~n leave-taking

farm n tract of land for cultivation or rearing livestock ~v cultivate (land); rear livestock (on farm) **farmer** n **farmhouse** n **farmyard** n

fart Vulg n (audible) emission of gas from anus ~v break wind

farther adv/adj further; comparative of FAR **farthest** adv/adj furthest; superlative of FAR

farthing n formerly, coin worth a quarter of a penny

fascia, facia n (pl -ciae) flat surface above shop window; dashboard

fascinate v attract and delight **fascination** n

fascism n authoritarian political system opposed to democracy and liberalism **fascist** adj/n

fashion n (latest) style, esp. of dress etc.; manner; type ~v shape, make **fashionable** adj

fast[1] adj (capable of) moving quickly; ahead of true time; Obs dissipated; firm, steady ~adv rapidly; tightly **fast food** food, esp. hamburgers etc., served very quickly

fast[2] v go without food ~n fasting **fasting** n

fasten v attach, fix, secure; become joined **fastener, fastening** n

fastidious adj hard to please

fat n oily animal substance; fat part

——————— T H E S A U R U S ———————

ably, decidedly, extremely, greatly, incomparably, much ~adj distant, long, outlying, remote, removed

farce buffoonery, comedy, satire, slapstick; absurdity, joke, mockery, nonsense, parody, sham, travesty

fare n charge, price, ticket money, transport cost; diet, eatables, food, meals, menu, provisions, rations ~v do, get along, get on, make out, manage, prosper

farewell adieu, departure, goodbye, parting, valediction

far-fetched doubtful, dubious, improbable, incredible, preposterous, strained, unbelievable, unconvincing, unlikely, unnatural, unrealistic

farm n grange, holding, homestead, land, plantation, smallholding ~v cultivate, operate, plant, work

fascinate absorb, allure, beguile, bewitch, captivate, charm, delight, enchant, engross, enthral, entrance, hypnotize, rivet, transfix

fascination allure, attraction, charm, enchantment, glamour, lure, magic, magnetism, pull, sorcery, spell

fashion n convention, craze, custom, fad, latest, latest style, look, mode, rage, style, trend, usage, vogue; attitude, demeanour, manner, method, mode, style, way ~v construct, contrive, create, design, forge, form, make, manufacture, mould, shape, work

fashionable à la mode, chic, current, customary, genteel, happening Inf, in vogue, latest, modern, modish, popular, prevailing, smart, stylish, up-to-date, usual

fast[1] adj brisk, fleet, flying, hasty, hurried, nippy Brit inf, quick, quickie Inf, rapid, speedy, swiftly, winged; dissipated, dissolute, intemperate, licentious, loose, profligate, promiscuous, wild ~adv quickly, rapidly, speedily, swiftly

fast[2] v abstain, deny oneself, go hungry, go without food, practise abstention ~n abstinence, fasting

fasten affix, anchor, attach, bind, bolt, chain, connect, fix, grip, join, lace, link, lock, make fast, make firm, seal, secure, tie, unite

~*adj* **fatter, fattest** having too much fat; greasy; profitable **fatten** *v* **fatty** *adj*

fate *n* power supposed to predetermine events; destiny; person's appointed lot; death or destruction **fatal** *adj* ending in death **fatality** *n* death **fatally** *adv* **fated** *adj* destined **fateful** *adj*

father *n* male parent; ancestor; (*with cap.*) God; originator; priest ~*v* beget; originate **fatherhood** *n* **father-in-law** *n* husband's or wife's father **fatherland** *n* native country

fathom *n* measure of six feet of water ~*v* sound (water); understand

fatigue *v* tire ~*n* weariness; toil; weakness of metals etc.

fatuous *adj* very silly, idiotic

fault *n* defect; misdeed; blame ~*v* find fault in; (cause to) commit fault **faultily** *adv* **faultless** *adj* **faulty** *adj*

faun *n* mythological woodland being with tail and horns

fauna *n* (*pl* **-nas, -nae**) animals of region collectively

faux pas *n* social blunder or indiscretion

favour *n* goodwill; approval; especial kindness; partiality ~*v* regard or treat with favour; oblige; treat with partiality; support **favourable** *adj* **favourite** *n* favoured person or thing ~*adj* chosen, preferred **favouritism** *n* practice of showing undue preference

fawn[1] *n* young deer ~*adj* light yellow-

——————— THESAURUS ———————

fat *n* beef *Inf*, blubber, bulk, corpulence, flesh, obesity, overweight, paunch ~*adj* corpulent, fleshy, gross, heavy, obese, overweight, plump, podgy, portly, rotund, solid, stout, tubby

fatal deadly, final, incurable, killing, lethal, malignant, mortal, pernicious

fate chance, destiny, divine will, fortune, predestination, providence; end, future, issue, outcome, upshot

fated destined, doomed, foreordained, marked down, predestined, preordained, sure, written

fateful critical, crucial, decisive, important, significant

father *n* begetter, pater, patriarch, sire; ancestor, forebear, forefather, predecessor, progenitor; abbé, confessor, curé, pastor, priest ~*v* beget, get, procreate, sire

fatigue *v* drain, exhaust, jade, overtire, tire, weaken, wear out, weary ~*n* debility, heaviness, languor, lethargy, tiredness

fault *n* blemish, defect, demerit, drawback, failing, flaw, imperfection, lack, shortcoming, snag, weakness,

weak point; lapse, misconduct, misdeed, misdemeanour, offence, sin, trespass, wrong

faultless accurate, classic, correct, exemplary, faithful, foolproof, impeccable, model, perfect; above reproach, blameless, guiltless, immaculate, impeccable, innocent, pure, sinless, spotless, stainless

faulty bad, broken, damaged, defective, erroneous, impaired, imperfect, inaccurate, incorrect, invalid, malfunctioning, unsound, weak, wrong

favour *n* approval, backing, bias, esteem, good opinion, goodwill, grace, kindness, partiality, patronage, support; benefit, boon, courtesy, good turn, indulgence, kindness, service ~*v* be partial to, esteem, indulge, pamper, reward, smile upon, spoil, value

favourable advantageous, appropriate, auspicious, beneficial, convenient, fair, fit, good, helpful, hopeful, opportune, promising, propitious, suitable, timely

favourite *n* choice, darling, dear, idol, pet, pick, preference ~*adj* best-

ish brown

fawn² v (*oft. with* **on** *or* **upon**) cringe, court favour servilely

fax n facsimile ~v send by telegraphic facsimile system

FBI US Federal Bureau of Investigation

fear n unpleasant emotion caused by coming danger ~v be afraid; regard with fear **fearful** adj **fearless** adj **fearsome** adj

feasible adj able to be done **feasibility** n

feast n banquet; religious anniversary ~v eat banquet; entertain with feast; delight

feat n notable deed

feather n one of the barbed shafts which form covering of birds; anything resembling this ~v provide with feathers; grow feathers **feathery** adj

feature n (*usu. pl*) part of face; notable part of anything; main or special item ~v portray; be prominent (in) **featureless** adj without striking features

Feb. February

February n second month

feckless adj ineffectual, irresponsible

federal adj of the government of states which are united but retain internal independence **federalism** n **federalist** n **federate** v form into, become, a federation **federation** n league; federal union

fee n payment for services

feeble adj weak; not effective or convincing

feed v **feeding, fed** give food to; supply, support; take food ~n feeding; fodder **feedback** n response **fed up** Inf bored, dissatisfied

loved, choice, dearest, esteemed, preferred

fawn¹ adj beige, buff, neutral

fawn² v (*oft. with* **on** *or* **upon**) be obsequious, be servile, court, crawl, creep, cringe, flatter, grovel, kneel, kowtow, pander to, toady

fear n alarm, awe, dread, fright, horror, panic, qualms, terror, trepidation ~v dare not, dread, shudder at, take fright, tremble at

fearful afraid, alarmed, anxious, apprehensive, diffident, frightened, hesitant, intimidated, nervous, panicky, scared, shrinking, tense, timid, timorous, uneasy

fearless bold, brave, confident, courageous, daring, gallant, heroic, indomitable, intrepid, plucky, unafraid, valiant, valorous

feasible attainable, likely, possible, practicable, reasonable, viable, workable

feast n banquet, carousal, dinner, entertainment, junket, repast, revels, treat

feat achievement, act, attainment, deed, exploit, performance

feature n aspect, attribute, characteristic, facet, factor, hallmark, mark, peculiarity, point, property, quality, trait; article, column, comment, item, piece, report, story ~v accentuate, emphasize, headline, play up, present, promote, set off, spotlight, star

federation alliance, amalgamation, association, coalition, combination, confederacy, entente, federacy, league, syndicate, union

fee account, bill, charge, compensation, emolument, pay, payment, remuneration, reward, toll

feeble delicate, doddering, effete, enervated, enfeebled, exhausted, failing, faint, frail, infirm, languid, powerless, puny, sickly, weak, weakened

feed v cater for, nourish, provide for, supply, sustain, victual; devour, eat, fare, graze, live on, nurture, pasture,

feel *v* **feeling, felt** touch; experience; find (one's way) cautiously; be sensitive to; show emotion (for); believe, consider *~n* feeling; impression perceived by feeling; sense of touch **feeler** *n* **feeling** *n* sense of touch; sensation; emotion; sympathy; opinion *pl* susceptibilities **feel like** have an inclination for

feet *see* FOOT

feign *v* pretend, sham

feint *n* sham attack; pretence *~v* make feint

felicity *n* great happiness; apt wording **felicitations** *pl n* congratulations **felicitous** *adj*

feline *adj* of cats; catlike

fell[1] *v* knock down; cut down (tree) **feller** *n*

fell[2] *n* mountain, moor

fellow *n* *Inf* man, boy; associate; counterpart; member (of society, college etc.) *~adj* of the same class, associated **fellowship** *n*

felon *n* one guilty of felony **felony** *n* serious crime

felt *n* soft, matted fabric *~v* make into, or cover with, felt; become matted **felt-tip pen** pen with writing point of pressed fibres

female *adj* of sex which bears offspring; relating to this sex *~n* one of this sex

feminine *adj* of women; womanly **feminism** *n* advocacy of equal rights for women **feminist** *n/adj* **femininity** *n*

fen *n* tract of marshy land

fence *n* structure of wire, wood etc. enclosing an area; *Sl* dealer in stolen property *~v* erect fence; fight with swords; *Sl* deal in stolen property **fencing** *n* art of swordplay

fend *v* ward off; repel; provide (for oneself etc.) **fender** *n* low metal frame in front of fireplace

fennel *n* fragrant plant

feral *adj* wild

ferment *n* substance causing thing to ferment; excitement *~v* (cause to) undergo chemical change with effervescence and alteration of properties **fermentation** *n*

fern *n* plant with feathery fronds

———————— THESAURUS ————————

subsist

feel *v* caress, finger, fondle, handle, manipulate, maul, paw, stroke, touch; be aware of, endure, enjoy, experience, go through, have, know, notice, observe, perceive, suffer, undergo; explore, fumble, grope, sound, test, try; believe, consider, deem, hold, judge, think

feeling feel, perception, sensation, sense, sense of touch, touch; consciousness, hunch, idea, impression, inkling, notion, presentiment, sense, suspicion; inclination, instinct, opinion, view

fell *v* cut, cut down, demolish, flatten, floor, hew, knock down, level, raze

fellow *n* boy, character, individual, man, person; associate, colleague,

companion, compeer, comrade, co-worker, equal, friend, member, partner, peer

fellowship brotherhood, camaraderie, communion, familiarity, intercourse, intimacy, kindliness, sociability

feminine delicate, gentle, girlish, graceful, ladylike, modest, soft, tender, womanly

fen bog, marsh, morass, quagmire, slough, swamp

fence *n* barricade, barrier, defence, guard, hedge, paling, palisade, railings, rampart, shield, stockade, wall *v* (*oft. with* in *or* off) bound, confine, coop, defend, enclose, guard, hedge, pen, pound, protect, restrict, secure, separate, surround

ferocious adj fierce, savage, cruel **ferocity** n

ferret n tamed animal like weasel ~v drive out with ferrets; search about

ferric, ferrous adj pert. to, containing, iron

ferry n boat etc. for transporting people, vehicles, across water ~v **-rying, -ried** carry, travel, by ferry

fertile adj (capable of) producing offspring, bearing crops etc.; producing abundantly **fertility** n **fertilize** v make fertile **fertilization** n **fertilizer** n

fervent, fervid adj ardent, intense **fervour** n

fester v (cause to) form pus; rankle; become embittered

festival n day, period of celebration; organized series of events, performances etc. **festive** adj joyous, merry

festivity n gaiety; rejoicing; pl festive proceedings

festoon n loop of flowers, ribbons etc. ~v form, adorn with festoons

fetch v go and bring; draw forth; be sold for **fetching** adj attractive

fete, fête n gala, bazaar etc., esp. one held out of doors ~v honour with festive entertainment

fetid, foetid adj stinking

fetish n object believed to have magical powers; object, activity, to which excessive devotion is paid

fetter n chain for feet; check; pl captivity ~v chain up; restrain

fettle n state of health

fetus, foetus n fully developed embryo **fetal, foetal** adj

feud n long bitter hostility ~v carry on feud

———————————— THESAURUS ————————————

ferment v boil, brew, bubble, concoct, foam, froth, heat, leaven, rise, seethe, work; agitate, boil, excite, fester, foment, heat, incite, inflame, provoke, rouse, seethe, smoulder, stir up ~n agitation, commotion, excitement, fever, frenzy, glow, heat, stew, stir, tumult, turmoil, unrest, uproar

ferocious fierce, predatory, rapacious, ravening, savage, violent, wild

ferocity brutality, cruelty, inhumanity, rapacity, ruthlessness, savagery, wildness

ferry n ferryboat, packet ~v carry, convey, ship, shuttle, transport

fertile abundant, fat, fecund, flowering, fruitful, luxuriant, plentiful, productive, prolific, rich, teeming, yielding

fertility abundance, fecundity, fruitfulness, productiveness, richness

fervent, fervid ardent, devout, eager, earnest, emotional, enthusiastic, excited, fiery, flaming, heartfelt, impassioned, intense, vehement, warm

fervour ardour, eagerness, earnest-

ness, enthusiasm, excitement, intensity, passion, vehemence, warmth, zeal

festival commemoration, feast, fête, fiesta, holiday, saint's day; carnival, celebration, festivities, fête, field day, gala, jubilee, treat

festive back-slapping, carnival, celebratory, cheery, convivial, festal, gala, gay, happy, hearty, holiday, jolly, jovial, joyful, jubilant, lighthearted, merry, mirthful, sportive

festoon array, bedeck, deck, decorate, drape, garland, hang, swathe, wreathe

fetch bring, carry, conduct, convey, deliver, escort, get, go for, lead, obtain, retrieve, transport; draw forth, elicit, give rise to, produce; bring in, earn, go for, make, realize, sell for, yield

feud n argument, bad blood, broil, conflict, disagreement, discord, dissension, enmity, faction, grudge, hostility, quarrel, rivalry, strife, vendetta ~v bicker, brawl, clash, contend, dis-

fever n condition of illness with high body temperature; intense nervous excitement **fevered** adj **feverish** adj

few adj not many ~pron small number

fez n (pl **fezzes**) red, brimless cap with tassel

fiancé n (fem **fiancée**) person engaged to be married

fiasco n (pl **-cos**) breakdown, total failure

fib n/v **fibbing, fibbed** (tell) trivial lie

fibre n filament forming part of animal or plant tissue; substance that can be spun **fibrous** adj **fibreglass** n material made of fine glass fibres

fickle adj changeable

fiction n literary works of the imagination **fictional** adj **fictitious** adj false; imaginary

fiddle n violin; Inf fraudulent arrangement ~v play fiddle; fidget; Sl cheat

fiddling adj trivial **fiddly** adj small, awkward to handle

fidelity n faithfulness

fidget v move restlessly ~n (oft. pl) restless mood; one who fidgets **fidgety** adj

field n area of (farming) land; tract of land rich in specified product; players in a game or sport collectively; battlefield; sphere of knowledge ~v Cricket etc. stop and return ball; send player, team, on to sports field **fielder** n **field day** exciting occasion **fieldwork** n investigation made away from classroom or laboratory

fiend n devil; person addicted to something **fiendish** adj

fierce adj savage, wild, violent; intense **fiercely** adv

fiery adj **fierier, fieriest** consisting of, or like, fire; irritable **fierily** adv

————————— THESAURUS —————————

pute, duel, fall out, quarrel, row, squabble, war

fever agitation, delirium, ecstasy, excitement, ferment, fervour, flush, frenzy, heat, passion, turmoil, unrest

few adj inconsiderable, infrequent, insufficient, meagre, negligible, rare, scant, scanty, scarce, scattered, sparse, sporadic, thin ~pron handful, scarcely any, scattering, small number, some

fiasco catastrophe, cock-up Brit sl, debacle, disaster, failure, mess, rout, ruin

fib n fiction, lie, prevarication, story, untruth, white lie

fibre pile, staple, strand, texture, thread

fickle capricious, changeable, faithless, fitful, flighty, inconstant, irresolute, mercurial, temperamental, unfaithful, unstable, unsteady, vacillating, volatile

fiction fable, fantasy, legend, myth, novel, romance, story, tale, urban

legend

fictitious apocryphal, artificial, assumed, bogus, false, fanciful, feigned, imaginary, imagined, improvised, invented, made-up, mythical, spurious, unreal, untrue

fidelity constancy, devotion, faithfulness, integrity, loyalty, staunchness, trustworthiness

fidget bustle, chafe, fret, squirm, twitch, worry

fidgety impatient, jerky, nervous, on edge, restive, restless, uneasy

field n grassland, green, meadow, pasture ~v catch, pick up, retrieve, return, stop

fiend demon, devil, evil spirit; addict, enthusiast, fanatic

fierce brutal, cruel, dangerous, feral, ferocious, menacing, murderous, passionate, savage, threatening, truculent, uncontrollable, untamed, vicious, wild

fiercely frenziedly, furiously, menacingly, passionately, savagely, tempes-

fiesta *n* carnival

fifteen, fifth, fifty *see* FIVE

fig *n* soft, pear-shaped fruit; tree bearing this

fight *v* fighting, fought contend with in battle; maintain against opponent; settle by combat ~*n* fighting **fighter** *n* person or aircraft that fights

figment *n* imaginary thing

figure *n* numerical symbol; amount, number; (bodily) shape; (conspicuous) appearance; space enclosed by lines; diagram, illustration ~*v* calculate; (*oft. with* **in**) show **figurative** *adj* (of language) symbolic **figurine** *n* statuette **figurehead** *n* nominal leader

filament *n* fine wire; threadlike body

filch *v* steal, pilfer

file¹ *n* (box, folder etc. holding) papers for reference; orderly line ~*v* arrange (papers etc.) and put them away for reference; march in file **filing** *n*

file² *n/v* (use) roughened tool for smoothing or shaping **filing** *n* scrap of metal removed by file

filial *adj* of, befitting, son or daughter

filibuster *v* obstruct legislation by making long speeches ~*n* filibustering

filigree *n* fine tracery or openwork of metal

fill *v* make full; occupy completely; discharge duties of; stop up; satisfy; fulfil; become full ~*n* full supply; as much as desired **filling** *n/adj*

fillet *n* boneless slice of meat, fish; narrow strip ~*v* cut into fillets, bone **filleted** *adj*

fillip *n* stimulus

filly *n* young female horse

film *n* sequence of images projected on screen, creating illusion of movement; sensitized celluloid roll used in photography, cinematography; thin skin or layer ~*adj* connected with cinema ~*v* photograph with cine camera; make cine film of; cover, become covered, with film **filmy** *adj* gauzy

filter *n* device permitting fluids to pass but retaining solid particles; anything similar ~*v* act as filter, or as if passing through filter; pass slowly (through)

filth *n* disgusting dirt; obscenity **filthi-**

————————————— THESAURUS —————————————

tuously, tigerishly, viciously

fight *v* assault, battle, box, brawl, clash, close, combat, conflict, contend, engage, feud, grapple, joust, row, spar, struggle, tilt, tussle, war, wrestle; contest, defy, dispute, oppose, resist, strive, struggle, withstand ~*n* altercation, battle, bout, brawl, brush, clash, combat, conflict, contest, dispute, duel, encounter, engagement, fracas, fray, hostilities, joust, melee, riot, row, scuffle, skirmish, struggle, tussle, war

fighter fighting man, soldier, warrior

figure *n* character, cipher, digit, number, numeral, symbol; amount, cost, price, sum, total, value; form, outline, shadow, shape, silhouette; body, build, frame, physique, proportions,

shape, torso

figurehead cipher, dummy, mouthpiece, name, nonentity, puppet

file¹ *n* case, data, documents, dossier, folder, information, portfolio ~*v* enter, record, register, slot in *Inf*

file² *v* abrade, burnish, furbish, polish, rasp, refine, rub, rub down, scrape, shape, smooth

fill brim over, cram, crowd, furnish, glut, gorge, pack, pervade, replenish, sate, satiate, satisfy, stock, store, stuff, supply, swell

filling *n* contents, insides, padding, stuffing, wadding ~*adj* ample, heavy, satisfying, square, substantial

film *n* motion picture, movie *US inf*; coating, covering, gauze, layer, membrane, scum, skin, tissue ~*v* photo-

ness *n* filthy *adj*

fin *n* propelling organ of fish; anything like this

final *adj* at the end; conclusive ~*n* game, heat, examination etc., coming at end of series **finale** *n* closing part of musical composition **finalist** *n* competitor in a final **finalize** *v* **finally** *adv*

finance *n* management of money; (*also pl*) money resources ~*v* find capital for **financial** *adj* **financier** *n*

finch *n* one of family of small singing birds

find *v* finding, found come across; experience, discover; *Law* give verdict ~*n* (valuable) thing found **finding** *n* conclusion from investigation

fine[1] *adj* of high quality; not rainy; delicate; subtle; pure; in small particles; *Inf* healthy, at ease; satisfactory **finery** *n* showy dress **finesse** *n* skilful management **fine art** art produced for its aesthetic value **fine-tune** *v* make small adjustments

fine[2] *n* sum fixed as penalty ~*v* punish by fine

——————————— THESAURUS ———————————

graph, shoot, take

filter *n* gauze, mesh, riddle, sieve, strainer ~*v* clarify, filtrate, purify, refine, screen, sieve, sift, strain, winnow

filth contamination, crap *Sl*, dirt, dung, excrement, excreta, faeces, filthiness, foulness, garbage, grime, muck, nastiness, ordure, pollution, refuse, sewage, shit *Taboo sl*; corruption, dirty-mindedness, impurity, indecency, obscenity, pornography, smut, vileness, vulgarity

filthy dirty, faecal, feculent, foul, nasty, polluted, putrid, slimy, squalid, unclean, vile; begrimed, black, blackened, grimy, grubby, miry, mucky, muddy, smoky, sooty, unwashed; bawdy, coarse, corrupt, depraved, foul, impure, indecent, lewd, licentious, obscene, pornographic, smutty, suggestive

final closing, end, eventual, last, latest, terminating, ultimate; absolute, conclusive, decided, decisive, definite, definitive, determinate, finished, incontrovertible, irrevocable, settled

finalize agree, complete, conclude, decide, settle, tie up, work out

finally at last, at length, in the end, lastly, ultimately

finance *n* accounts, banking, business, commerce, economics, investment, money ~*v* back, float, fund, guarantee, pay for, subsidize, support, underwrite

financial budgeting, economic, fiscal, monetary, money, pecuniary

find *v* chance upon, come across, descry, discover, encounter, espy, expose, ferret out, hit upon, locate, meet, recognize, spot, turn up, uncover, unearth ~*n* acquisition, asset, bargain, catch, discovery, good buy

fine[1] *adj* admirable, beautiful, choice, excellent, exceptional, exquisite, first-class, first-rate, great, magnificent, masterly, ornate, outstanding, rare, select, skilful, splendid, sterling, superior, supreme, world-class; balmy, bright, clear, cloudless, dry, fair, pleasant, sunny; dainty, delicate, elegant, exquisite, fragile; abstruse, acute, critical, fastidious, hairsplitting, intelligent, keen, minute, precise, quick, refined, sensitive, sharp, subtle, tasteful, tenuous; clear, pure, refined, solid, sterling, unadulterated, unalloyed, unpolluted; acceptable, agreeable, all right, convenient, good, O.K. *or* okay, satisfactory, suitable

fine[2] *v* mulct, penalize, punish ~*n* damages, forfeit, penalty, punishment

finger *n* one of the jointed branches of the hand; various things like this ~*v* touch with fingers **fingerprint** *n* impression of tip of finger

finicky *adj* fussy

finish *v* bring, come to an end, conclude; complete; perfect ~*n* end; way in which thing is finished; final appearance

finite *adj* bounded, limited

fiord *see* FJORD

fir *n* coniferous tree

fire *n* state of burning; mass of burning fuel; destructive burning; device for heating a room etc.; shooting of guns; ardour ~*v* discharge (firearm); *Inf* dismiss from employment; bake; make burn; inspire; explode; begin to burn; become excited **firearm** *n* gun, rifle, pistol etc. **fire brigade** organized body to put out fires **fire engine** vehicle with apparatus for extinguishing fires **fire escape** means, esp. stairs, for escaping from burning buildings

firefly *n* beetle that glows in dark **fireguard** *n* protective grating in front of fire **fireman** *n* member of fire brigade **fireplace** *n* recess in room for fire **fire station** building housing fire-fighting vehicles and equipment **firework** *n* device to give spectacular effects by explosions and coloured sparks; *pl* outburst of temper **firing squad** group of soldiers ordered to execute offender

firm *adj* solid, fixed, stable ~*v* make, become firm ~*n* commercial enterprise

first *adj* earlier in time or order; foremost in rank or position ~*n* beginning; first occurrence of something ~*adv* before others in time, order etc. **firstly** *adv* **first aid** help given to injured person before arrival of doctor **first-class** *adj* of highest quality **firsthand** *adj* obtained directly from original source **first-rate** *adj* of highest class or quality

———————— THESAURUS ————————

finesse adroitness, artfulness, cleverness, craft, delicacy, diplomacy, discretion, polish, quickness, savoir-faire, skill, subtlety, tact

finger *v* feel, handle, manipulate, maul, meddle with, touch, toy with

finish *v* accomplish, achieve, cease, close, complete, conclude, deal with, discharge, do, end, execute, finalize, fulfil, get done, round off, settle, stop, terminate; elaborate, perfect, polish, refine ~*n* cessation, close, closing, completion, conclusion, culmination, dénouement, end, ending, finale; appearance, grain, lustre, patina, polish, shine, smoothness, surface, texture

finite bounded, conditioned, limited, restricted, terminable

fire *n* blaze, combustion, conflagration, flames, inferno; barrage, hail, salvo, shelling, sniping, volley; ar-

dent, eager, enthusiastic, excited, inspired, passionate ~*v* ignite, kindle, light, set ablaze, set aflame, set alight, set fire to, set on fire; detonate, discharge, eject, explode, hurl, launch, let off, loose, set off, shell, shoot

firm[1] *adj* compact, compressed, concentrated, dense, hard, inelastic, inflexible, rigid, set, solid, solidified, stiff, unyielding; braced, embedded, fast, fastened, fixed, immovable, motionless, riveted, robust, rooted, secure, secured, stable, stationary, steady, strong, sturdy, taut, tight, unshakable; adamant, constant, definite, fixed, immovable, inflexible, obdurate, resolute, resolved, set on, settled, stalwart, staunch, steadfast, strict, true, unflinching, unwavering, unyielding

firm[2] *n* association, business, company, concern, corporation, enterprise,

fiscal *adj* of government finances

fish *n* (*pl* **fish, fishes**) vertebrate cold-blooded animal with gills, living in water ~*v* (attempt to) catch fish; try to get information indirectly **fishy** *adj* of, like, or full of fish; *Inf* suspicious **fisherman** *n* **fishmonger** *n* seller of fish

fissure *n* cleft, split **fission** *n* splitting; reproduction by division of living cells; splitting of atomic nucleus

fist *n* clenched hand **fisticuffs** *pl n* fighting

fit¹ *v* **fitting, fitted** be suited to; be properly adjusted; adjust; supply ~*adj* **fitter, fittest** well-suited; proper; in good health ~*n* way anything fits

fitness *n* **fitter** *n* **fitting** *adj* appropriate ~*n* attachment; action of fitting

fit² *n* seizure with convulsions; passing state, mood **fitful** *adj* spasmodic

five *adj/n* cardinal number after four **fifth** *adj* ordinal number **fifteen** *adj/n* ten plus five **fifteenth** *adj* **fiftieth** *adj* **fifty** *adj/n* five tens

fix *v* fasten, make firm; determine; repair; *Inf* influence unfairly ~*n* difficult situation; position of ship, aircraft ascertained by radar, observation etc.; *Sl* dose of narcotic drug **fixation** *n* obsession **fixed** *adj* **fixture** *n* thing fixed in position; (date for) sporting event

fizz *v* hiss ~*n* hissing noise; efferves-

house, organization, partnership

first *adj* earliest, initial, maiden, opening, original, premier, primitive, primordial, pristine; chief, foremost, head, highest, leading, pre-eminent, prime, principal, ruling ~*adv* beforehand, firstly, initially

first-rate admirable, cracking *Brit inf*, elite, excellent, exceptional, first class, outstanding, prime, sovereign, superb, superlative, world-class

fissure breach, break, chink, crack, cranny, crevice, fault, fracture, gap, hole, opening, rent, rift, rupture, slit, split

fit¹ *v* accord, agree, belong, concur, conform, correspond, dovetail, go, interlock, join, match, meet, suit, tally; adapt, adjust, alter, arrange, dispose, fashion, modify, place, position, shape ~*adj* able, adequate, apposite, appropriate, apt, becoming, capable, competent, convenient, correct, deserving, equipped, expedient, good enough, prepared, proper, qualified, ready, right, seemly, suitable, trained, worthy; hale, healthy, robust, strapping, toned up, trim, well

fit² *n* attack, bout, convulsion, paroxysm, seizure, spasm; caprice, fancy, humour, mood, whim

fitful broken, desultory, erratic, fluctuating, haphazard, impulsive, inconstant, intermittent, irregular, spasmodic, sporadic, variable

fitness adaptation, applicability, appropriateness, aptness, competence, eligibility, pertinence, preparedness, propriety, qualifications, readiness, seemliness, suitability; good condition, good health, health, robustness, strength, vigour

fitting *adj* appropriate, becoming, correct, decent, decorous, desirable, proper, right, seemly, suitable ~*n* attachment, component, connection, part, piece, unit

fix *v* attach, bind, cement, connect, couple, fasten, glue, link, pin, secure, stick, tie; anchor, embed, establish, implant, install, locate, place, plant, position, root, set, settle; agree on, appoint, arrange, arrive at, conclude, decide, define, determine, establish, limit, name, resolve, set, settle, specify ~*n Inf* difficulty, dilemma, embarrassment, hot water *Inf*, mess, plight,

cent liquid **fizzy** *adj*
fizzle *v* splutter weakly **fizzle out** *Inf* fail
fjord, fiord *n* (esp. in Norway) long, narrow inlet of sea
flabbergast *v* overwhelm with astonishment
flabby *adj* limp; too fat; weak and lacking purpose **flabbiness** *n*
flag[1] *n* banner, piece of bunting as standard or signal ~*v* **flagging, flagged** inform by flag signals **flag-pole, flagstaff** *n* pole for flag **flagship** *n* admiral's ship; most important item
flag[2] *n* flat slab of stone **flagstone** *n*
flag[3] *v* **flagging, flagged** lose vigour
flagon *n* large bottle
flagrant *adj* blatant
flail *n* instrument for threshing corn by hand ~*v* beat with, move as, flail
flair *n* natural ability; elegant style
flak *n* anti-aircraft fire; *Inf* adverse criticism
flake *n* small, thin piece; piece chipped off ~*v* (cause to) peel off in flakes **flaky** *adj*
flambé *v* **flambéing, flambéed** cook in flaming brandy

flamboyant *adj* showy **flamboyance** *n*
flame *n* burning gas, esp. above fire ~*v* give out flames
flamenco *n* (*pl* **-cos**) rhythmical Spanish dance
flamingo *n* (*pl* **-gos**) large pink bird with long neck and legs
flammable *adj* liable to catch fire
flan *n* open sweet or savoury tart
flange *n* projecting rim
flank *n* part of side between hips and ribs; side of anything ~*v* be at, move along either side of
flannel *n* soft woollen fabric; small piece of cloth for washing face
flap *v* **flapping, flapped** move (wings, arms etc.) as bird flying ~*n* act of flapping; broad piece of anything hanging from one side; *Inf* state of panic
flapjack *n* chewy biscuit
flare *v* blaze with unsteady flame; spread outwards ~*n* instance of flaring; signal light
flash *n* sudden burst of light or flame; very short time ~*v* break into sudden flame; move very fast; (cause to) gleam **flash, flashy** *adj* showy, sham

————— THESAURUS —————

predicament, quandary, spot *Inf*, tight spot
fixed attached, established, immovable, made fast, permanent, rigid, rooted, secure, set; agreed, arranged, decided, definite, established, planned, resolved, settled
flag[1] banner, colours, ensign, jack, pennant, pennon, standard, streamer
flag[2] *v* abate, decline, die, droop, ebb, fade, fail, faint, fall, fall off, languish, pine, sag, sink, slump, succumb, wane, weaken, weary, wilt
flagrant awful, barefaced, blatant, bold, brazen, crying, dreadful, egregious, enormous, flaunting, glaring, immodest, infamous, notorious,

open, ostentatious, outrageous, scandalous, shameless
flail *v* beat, thrash, thresh, windmill
flair ability, aptitude, faculty, feel, genius, gift, knack, mastery, talent; chic, dash, discernment, elegance, panache, style, stylishness, taste
flamboyant elaborate, florid, ornate, rich, rococo, showy, theatrical
flame *n* blaze, fire, light ~*v* blaze, burn, flare, flash, glare, glow, shine
flap *v* agitate, beat, flail, flutter, shake, swing, swish, thrash, thresh, vibrate, wag, wave ~*n* apron, cover, fly, fold, lapel, skirt, tab, tail
flare blaze, burn up, dazzle, flicker, flutter, glare, waver

flashback *n* break in narrative to introduce what has taken place previously

flask *n* type of bottle

flat[1] *adj* **flatter, flattest** level; at full length; smooth; downright; dull; *Mus* below true pitch; (of tyre) deflated; (of battery) dead ~*n* what is flat; *Mus* note half tone below natural pitch **flatly** *adv* **flatten** *v* **flatfish** *n* type of fish with broad, flat body **flat rate** the same in all cases **flat out** at, with maximum speed or effort

flat[2] *n* suite of rooms in larger building

flatter *v* praise insincerely; gratify **flatterer** *n* **flattery** *n*

flatulent *adj* suffering from, generating (excess) gases from intestines **flatulence** *n*

flaunt *v* show off

flavour *n* distinctive taste, savour ~*v* give flavour to **flavouring** *n*

flaw *n* defect, blemish **flawless** *adj*

flax *n* plant grown for its fibres, spun into linen thread **flaxen** *adj* of flax; light yellow

flay *v* strip skin off; criticize severely

flea *n* small, wingless, jumping, blood-sucking insect

fleck *n/v* (make) small mark(s)

fledgling, fledgeling *n* young bird; inexperienced person

flee *v* **fleeing, fled** run away from

fleece *n* sheep's wool ~*v* rob **fleecy** *adj*

fleet[1] *n* number of warships organized as unit; number of ships, cars etc.

fleet[2] *adj* swift; nimble **fleeting** *adj* passing quickly

flesh *n* soft part, muscular substance, between skin and bone; in plants, pulp; fat; sensual appetites **fleshy** *adj* plump; pulpy **in the flesh** in person,

flash *n* blaze, burst, dazzle, flare, flicker, gleam, ray, shaft, shimmer, spark, sparkle, streak, twinkle; instant, moment, second, shake, split second, trice, twinkling ~*v* blaze, flare, flicker, glare, gleam, glint, glisten, glitter, light, shimmer, sparkle, twinkle; bolt, dart, fly, race, shoot, speed, sprint, streak, sweep, zoom

flat[1] even, horizontal, level, levelled, low, plane, smooth, unbroken; laid low, outstretched, prone, prostrate, reclining, recumbent, supine; boring, dead, dull, ho-hum *Inf*, insipid, lacklustre, lifeless, monotonous, prosaic, spiritless, stale, tedious, uninteresting, vapid, watery, weak

flat[2] apartment, rooms

flatly absolutely, categorically, completely, positively, unhesitatingly

flatten compress, even out, iron out, level, plaster, raze, roll, squash, trample

flatter blandish, butter up, cajole, compliment, court, fawn, humour, inveigle, pander to, praise, puff, wheedle

flattery blandishment, cajolery, fawning, obsequiousness, servility

flavour *n* aroma, essence, extract, odour, piquancy, relish, savour, seasoning, smack, tang, taste, zest ~*v* imbue, infuse, lace, leaven, season, spice

flaw blemish, defect, failing, fault, imperfection, speck, spot, weakness, weak spot

flawless faultless, impeccable, perfect, spotless, unblemished, unsullied

flee avoid, bolt, decamp, depart, do a runner *Sl*, escape, fly, get away, leave, shun, take flight, vanish

fleet *n* armada, flotilla, navy, squadron, task force, vessels, warships

fleeting brief, ephemeral, flying, fugitive, momentary, passing, short, short-lived, temporary, transient, transitory

actually present

flex *n* flexible insulated electric cable ~*v* bend, be bent **flexible** *adj* easily bent; manageable; adaptable **flexibility** *n*

flick *v* strike lightly, jerk ~*n* light blow; jerk; *pl Sl* cinema

flicker *v* burn, shine, unsteadily ~*n* unsteady light or movement; slight trace

flight[1] *n* act or manner of flying through air; group of flying birds or aircraft; power of flying; stairs between two landings **flighty** *adj* frivolous **flight recorder** electronic device in aircraft storing information about its flight

flight[2] *n* running away

flimsy *adj* delicate; weak, thin

flinch *v* draw back, wince

fling *v* **flinging, flung** throw, send, move with force ~*n* throw; spell of

indulgence; vigorous dance

flint *n* hard steel-grey stone

flip *v* **flipping, flipped** flick lightly; turn over **flippant** *adj* treating serious things lightly **flipper** *n* limb, fin for swimming

flirt *v* play with another's affections ~*n* person who flirts **flirtation** *n* **flirtatious** *adj*

flit *v* **flitting, flitted** pass lightly and rapidly

float *v* rest on surface of liquid; be suspended freely; in commerce, get (company) started; obtain loan ~*n* anything small that floats; small delivery vehicle; motor vehicle carrying tableau etc.; sum of money used to provide change **floating** *adj* moving about, changing **flotation** *n*

flock *n* number of animals of one kind together; religious congregation ~*v* gather in a crowd

———————— THESAURUS ————————

flesh body, brawn, fatness, food, meat, tissue, weight; body, human nature, sensuality

flexibility adaptability, complaisance, elasticity, resilience, springiness

flexible ductile, elastic, limber, lissom(e), lithe, plastic, pliable, springy, stretchy, supple; amenable, biddable, docile, gentle, manageable, responsive, tractable; adaptable, adjustable, open, variable

flicker *v* flutter, quiver, vibrate, waver ~*n* flare, flash, gleam, glimmer, spark; breath, drop, glimmer, spark, trace, vestige

flight[1] mounting, soaring, winging; journey, trip, voyage; cloud, flock, formation, squadron, swarm, unit, wing

flight[2] escape, exit, exodus, fleeing, getaway, retreat

flimsy delicate, fragile, frail, insubstantial, makeshift, rickety, shaky, shallow, slight, superficial, unsub-

stantial; feeble, frivolous, implausible, inadequate, pathetic, poor, thin, transparent, trivial, unconvincing, unsatisfactory, weak

flinch baulk, blench, cower, cringe, duck, flee, quail, recoil, retreat, shirk, shrink, start, swerve, wince, withdraw

fling *v* cast, heave, hurl, jerk, pitch, precipitate, propel, send, shy, sling, throw, toss

flippant disrespectful, frivolous, glib, impertinent, impudent, irreverent, pert, rude

flirt *v* coquet, dally, make advances, philander ~*n* coquette, heartbreaker, philanderer, tease

float *v* be buoyant, hang, hover, poise; bob, drift, glide, move gently, sail, slide, slip along; launch, promote, set up

floating fluctuating, free, migratory, movable, unattached, uncommitted, variable, wandering

floe *n* floating ice

flog *v* **flogging, flogged** beat with whip, stick etc.; *Sl* sell

flood *n* inundation, overflow of water; rising of tide; outpouring ~*v* inundate; cover, fill with water; arrive, move etc. in great numbers **floodlight** *n* broad, intense beam of artificial light **floodlit** *adj*

floor *n* lower surface of room; set of rooms on one level; (right to speak in) legislative hall ~*v* supply with floor; knock down; confound **flooring** *n* material for floors

flop *v* **flopping, flopped** bend, fall, collapse loosely; fall flat on water etc.; *Inf* fail ~*n* flopping movement or sound; *Inf* failure **floppy** *adj* **floppy disk** *Computers* flexible magnetic disk that stores information

flora *n* (*pl* **-ras, -rae**) plants of a region **floral** *adj* of flowers **florist** *n* dealer in flowers

floret *n* small flower

florid *adj* with red, flushed complex-ion; ornate

floss *n* mass of fine, silky fibres

flotilla *n* fleet of small vessels; group of destroyers

flotsam *n* floating wreckage

flounce[1] *v* go, move abruptly and impatiently ~*n* fling, jerk of body or limb

flounce[2] *n* ornamental gathered strip on woman's garment

flounder[1] *v* plunge and struggle, esp. in water or mud

flounder[2] *n* flatfish

flour *n* powder prepared by sifting and grinding wheat etc.

flourish *v* thrive; brandish; wave about ~*n* ornamental curve; showy gesture; fanfare

flout *v* show contempt for

flow *v* glide along as stream; circulate, as the blood; hang loose; be present in abundance ~*n* act, instance of flowing; quantity that flows; rise of tide

flower *n* brightly coloured part of

———————— THESAURUS ————————

flock *n* drove, flight, gaggle, herd, skein; collection, company, congregation, convoy, crowd, gathering, group, herd, host, mass, multitude, throng ~*v* collect, congregate, converge, crowd, gather, group, herd, huddle, mass, throng, troop

flog beat, chastise, flay, lash, scourge, thrash, trounce, whack, whip

flood *n* deluge, downpour, flash flood, inundation, overflow, spate, tide, torrent; abundance, flow, glut, outpouring, profusion, rush, stream, torrent ~*v* engulf, flow, gush, inundate, overwhelm, rush, surge, swarm, sweep; deluge, drown, immerse, overflow, submerge, swamp

floor *n* level, stage, storey, tier ~*v* baffle, beat, bewilder, confound, conquer, defeat, discomfit, disconcert, dumbfound, faze, nonplus, over-throw, perplex, puzzle, stump

flop *v* collapse, dangle, droop, drop, fall, hang limply, sag, slump, topple, tumble; *Inf* close, come to nothing, fail, fall flat, fall short, founder, misfire ~*n* *Inf* debacle, disaster, failure, fiasco, loser, nonstarter, washout *Inf*

florid flushed, high-coloured, rubicund, ruddy; baroque, busy, embellished, flamboyant, flowery, fussy, high-flown, ornate

flounder *v* blunder, fumble, grope, muddle, plunge, struggle, stumble, toss, tumble, wallow

flourish *v* bear fruit, be successful, bloom, blossom, boom, burgeon, develop, flower, increase, prosper, succeed, thrive ~*n* dash, display, fanfare, parade, shaking, show, twirling, wave

flow circulate, course, glide, gush, move, pour, purl, ripple, roll, run,

plant from which fruit is developed; bloom, blossom; choicest part ~*v* produce flowers; come to prime condition **flowery** *adj* **flowerbed** *n* ground for growing flowers

fl. oz. fluid ounce

flu *n* short for INFLUENZA

fluctuate *v* vary, rise and fall, undulate **fluctuation** *n*

flue *n* chimney

fluent *adj* speaking, writing easily and well **fluency** *n*

fluff *n* soft, feathery stuff ~*v* make or become soft, light; *Inf* make mistake **fluffy** *adj*

fluid *adj* flowing easily; flexible ~*n* gas or liquid **fluid ounce** unit of capacity 1/20 of pint

fluke *n* stroke of luck

flummox *v* bewilder, perplex

flunky, flunkey liveried manservant; servile person

fluorescent *adj* giving off a special type of bright light

fluoride *n* salt containing fluorine **fluorine** *n* nonmetallic element, yellowish gas

flurry *n* gust; bustle; fluttering ~*v* -rying, -ried agitate

flush[1] *v* blush; flow suddenly or violently; be excited; cleanse (e.g. toilet) by rush of water; excite ~*n* blush; rush of water; excitement; freshness

flush[2] *adj* level with surrounding surface; overflowing

fluster *v* make or become nervous, agitated ~*n* agitation

flute *n* wind instrument with blowhole in side; groove; *v* play on flute; make grooves in

flutter *v* flap (as wings) rapidly; quiver; be or make agitated ~*n* flapping movement; agitation; *Inf* modest wager

rush, slide, surge, sweep, swirl, whirl

flower *n* bloom, blossom, efflorescence; best, cream, elite, freshness, height, pick, vigour ~*v* bloom, blossom, burgeon, effloresce, flourish, mature, open, unfold

flowery embellished, fancy, figurative, florid, ornate, rhetorical

fluctuate alternate, change, hesitate, oscillate, seesaw, shift, swing, undulate, vacillate, vary, veer, waver

fluency assurance, command, control, ease, facility, glibness, slickness, smoothness

fluent articulate, easy, effortless, facile, flowing, natural, ready, smooth, voluble

fluid *adj* flowing, liquefied, liquid, melted, molten, runny, watery; adaptable, adjustable, changeable, flexible, floating, indefinite, mercurial, mobile, mutable, shifting ~*n* liquid, liquor, solution

flurry agitation, bustle, commotion,

disturbance, excitement, ferment, flap, fluster, flutter, furore, fuss, hurry, stir, to-do, tumult, whirl

flush[1] *v* blush, burn, colour, colour up, crimson, flame, glow, go red, redden, suffuse ~*n* bloom, blush, colour, freshness, glow, redness, rosiness

flush[2] *adj* even, flat, level, plane, square, true; abundant, affluent, full, generous, lavish, liberal, overflowing, prodigal

fluster *v* agitate, bother, bustle, confound, confuse, disturb, excite, flurry, heat, hurry, perturb, ruffle, unnerve, upset ~*n* bustle, commotion, disturbance, dither *chiefly Brit,* flurry, flutter, furore, ruffle, turmoil

flutter *v* agitate, beat, flap, flicker, fluctuate, hover, palpitate, quiver, ripple, ruffle, shiver, tremble, vibrate, waver ~*n* palpitation, quiver, shiver, shudder, tremble, tremor, twitching, vibration

flux *n* discharge; constant succession of changes; substance mixed with metal in soldering etc.

fly[1] *v* **flying, flew, flown** move through air on wings or in aircraft; pass quickly; float loosely; run away; operate aircraft; cause to fly; set flying ~*n* (zip or buttons fastening) opening in trousers **flyer, flier** *n* small advertising leaflet; aviator **flying** *adj* hurried, brief **flying colours** conspicuous success **flying saucer** unidentified disc-shaped flying object **flying squad** special detachment of police, soldiers etc., ready to act quickly **flying start** very good start **flyover** *n* road passing over another by bridge **flywheel** *n* heavy wheel regulating speed of machine

fly[2] *n* (*pl* **flies**) two-winged insect, esp. common housefly

foal *n* young of horse

foam *n* collection of small bubbles on liquid; light cellular solid ~*v* (cause to) produce foam **foamy** *adj*

fob *v* **fobbing, fobbed** (*with* **off**) ignore, dismiss in offhand manner

focus *n* (*pl* **-cuses, -ci**) point at which rays meet; state of optical image when it is clearly defined; point on which interest, activity is centred ~*v* **-cusing, -cused** bring to focus; concentrate **focal** *adj*

fodder *n* bulk food for livestock

foe *n* enemy

fog *n* thick mist ~*v* **fogging, fogged** cover in fog; puzzle **foggy** *adj* **foghorn** *n* large horn to warn ships

fogey *n* old-fashioned person

foible *n* minor weakness, slight peculiarity of character

foil[1] *v* baffle, frustrate ~*n* blunt sword for fencing

foil[2] *n* metal in thin sheet; anything which sets off another thing to advantage

foist *v* (*usually with* **on**) force, impose on

fold[1] *v* double up, bend part of; interlace (arms); clasp (in arms); *Cookery* mix gently; become folded; admit of being folded; *Inf* fail ~*n* folding; line made by folding **folder** *n* binder, file for loose papers

fold[2] *n* enclosure for sheep

foliage *n* leaves collectively

—————— THESAURUS ——————

fly *v* flit, flutter, hover, mount, sail, soar, take wing, wing; aviate, control, manoeuvre, operate, pilot; elapse, flit, glide, pass, pass quickly, roll on, run its course, slip away; display, float, show, wave; bolt, career, dart, dash, hasten, hurry, race, rush, scamper, scoot, shoot, speed, sprint, tear

flying *adj* brief, fleeting, hasty, hurried, rushed

foam *n* bubbles, froth, head, lather, spray, spume, suds ~*v* boil, bubble, effervesce, fizz, froth, lather

focus *n* centre, core, cynosure, headquarters, heart, hub, meeting place, target

foe adversary, antagonist, enemy, opponent, rival

fog *n* gloom, miasma, mist, murk, murkiness, smog

foggy blurred, cloudy, dim, grey, hazy, indistinct, misty, murky, nebulous, obscure, vaporous

foil[1] *v* baffle, balk, check, counter, defeat, elude, frustrate, nullify, outwit, stop, thwart

foil[2] antithesis, background, complement, contrast, setting

fold *v* bend, crease, crumple, double, gather, intertwine, overlap, pleat, tuck, turn under; do up, enclose, enfold, entwine, envelop, wrap, wrap up ~*n* bend, crease, furrow, layer, overlap, pleat, turn, wrinkle

folder binder, envelope, file, portfolio

folio *n* (*pl* **-lios**) sheet of paper folded in half to make two leaves of book; book of largest common size

folk *n* people in general; family, relative; race of people **folksy** *adj* simple, unpretentious **folklore** *n* tradition, customs, beliefs popularly held

follicle *n* small sac

follow *v* go or come after; accompany; keep to; be a consequence of; take as guide; grasp meaning of; have keen interest in **follower** *n* disciple, supporter **following** *adj* about to be mentioned ~*n* body of supporters

folly *n* foolishness

foment *v* foster, stir up

fond *adj* tender, loving **fondness** *n*

fond of having liking for

fondant *n* flavoured paste of sugar and water

fondle *v* caress

font *n* bowl for baptismal water

fontanelle *n* soft, membraneous gap between bones of baby's skull

food *n* solid nourishment; what one eats

fool[1] *n* silly, empty-headed person; *Hist* jester ~*v* delude; dupe; act as fool **foolhardy** *adj* foolishly adventurous **foolish** *adj* silly; unwise **foolishness** *n* **foolproof** *adj* unable to fail **foolscap** *n* size of paper

fool[2] *n* dessert made from fruit and cream

——————— THESAURUS ———————

folk clan, family, kin, people, race, tribe

follow succeed, supersede, supplant; accompany, attend, escort, tag along; comply, conform, heed, mind, note, obey, observe, regard, watch

follower adherent, admirer, apostle, backer, believer, convert, devotee, disciple, fan, fancier, habitué, partisan, pupil, supporter, votary, worshipper

following *adj* consequent, ensuing, later, next, specified, subsequent, succeeding, successive ~*n* audience, entourage, fans, public, supporters

folly absurdity, foolishness, idiocy, imbecility, imprudence, indiscretion, irrationality, lunacy, madness, nonsense, recklessness, silliness, stupidity

fond adoring, affectionate, amorous, caring, devoted, doting, indulgent, loving, tender, warm

fondle caress, cuddle, dandle, pat, pet, stroke

fondness attachment, fancy, liking, love, partiality, penchant, predilection, preference, soft spot, taste, weakness

food board, bread, cooking, cuisine, diet, edibles, fare, feed, foodstuffs, larder, meat, menu, nourishment, nutrition, provisions, rations, refreshment, stores, sustenance, table

fool *n* ass, berk *Brit sl*, charlie *Brit inf*, dolt, dunce, dunderhead, halfwit, idiot, ignoramus, illiterate, jackass, jerk *Sl, chiefly US & Canad*, lamebrain *Inf*, loon, moron, nerd *or* nurd *Sl*, nitwit, numskull *or* numbskull, silly, simpleton, wally *Sl*; buffoon, clown, comic, harlequin, jester, motley, pierrot ~*v* beguile, bluff, cheat, deceive, delude, dupe, hoax, hoodwink, mislead, take in, trick

foolhardy bold, hot-headed, impetuous, imprudent, incautious, irresponsible, madcap, precipitate, rash, reckless, venturesome, venturous

foolish brainless, crackpot *Inf*, crazy, doltish, fatuous, half-witted, harebrained, idiotic, imbecilic, inane, ludicrous, mad, ridiculous, senseless, silly, simple, stupid, weak, witless; absurd, ill-considered, inane, nonsensical, short-sighted, unwise

foolishness absurdity, folly, idiocy, imprudence, inanity, indiscretion,

foot *n* (*pl* **feet**) lowest part of leg, from ankle down; lower part of anything, base, stand; end of bed etc.; measure of twelve inches ~*v* pay cost of **footage** *n* amount of film used **footing** *n* basis, foundation **football** *n* game played with large blown-up ball; the ball **footballer** *n* **foothills** *pl n* hills at foot of mountain **foothold** *n* place giving secure grip for the foot **footlights** *pl n* lights across front of stage **footloose** *adj* free from ties **footman** *n* male servant in livery **footnote** *n* note of reference or explanation printed at foot of page **footprint** *n* mark left by foot **footstep** *n* step in walking; sound made by walking **footwear** *n* anything worn to cover feet **footwork** *n* skilful use of the feet in football etc.

footle *v* *Inf* loiter aimlessly **footling** *adj* trivial

for *prep* directed to; because of; instead of; towards; on account of; in favour of; respecting; during; in search of; in payment of; in the character of; in spite of ~*conj* because

forage *n* food for cattle and horses ~*v* collect forage; make roving search

foray *n* raid, inroad

forbear *v* **forbearing, forbore, forborne** (*esp. with* **from**) cease; refrain (from); be patient **forbearance** *n*

forbid *v* **forbidding, forbade, forbidden** prohibit; refuse to allow **forbidden** *adj* **forbidding** *adj* uninviting, threatening

force *n* strength, power; compulsion; that which tends to produce a change in a physical system; body of troops, police etc.; group of people organized for particular task; validity; vigour ~*v* compel; produce by effort, strength; break open; hasten maturity of **forced** *adj* compulsory; unnatural **forceful** *adj* powerful, persuasive **forcible** *adj* done by force

forceps *pl n* surgical pincers

irresponsibility, silliness, stupidity, weakness

foolproof certain, guaranteed, infallible, safe, unassailable

footing basis, establishment, foothold, foundation, ground, groundwork, installation, settlement

footstep footmark, footprint, trace, track; footfall, step, tread

forage *n* feed, fodder, food, foodstuffs, provender

forbear abstain, avoid, cease, decline, desist, eschew, omit, pause, refrain, stop, withhold

forbearance indulgence, leniency, lenity, mildness, moderation, patience, resignation, restraint, self-control, temperance, tolerance

forbid ban, debar, disallow, exclude, hinder, inhibit, outlaw, preclude, prohibit, proscribe, rule out, veto

forbidden banned, outlawed, prohibited, proscribed, taboo, vetoed

force *n* energy, impact, impulse, life, might, muscle, potency, power, pressure, stimulus, strength, stress, vigour; coercion, compulsion, constraint, duress, enforcement, pressure, violence; bite, cogency, effect, effectiveness, efficacy, influence, power, strength, validity, weight; drive, emphasis, fierceness, intensity, persistence, vehemence, vigour ~*v* coerce, compel, constrain, dragoon, drive, impel, impose, make, necessitate, obligate, oblige, overcome, press, press-gang, pressure, pressurize, railroad *Inf*, urge; blast, break open, prise, propel, push, thrust, use violence on, wrench, wrest

forced compulsory, involuntary, mandatory, obligatory, slave, unwilling; affected, artificial, contrived, false, insincere, laboured, stiff, strained,

ford *n* shallow place where river may be crossed ~*v* cross river

fore *adj* in front ~*n* front part

forearm *n* arm between wrist and elbow ~*v* arm beforehand

forebear *n* ancestor

forebode *v* indicate in advance **foreboding** *n* anticipation of evil

forecast *v* estimate beforehand (esp. weather) ~*n* prediction

forecastle *n* forward raised part of ship

foreclose *v* take away power of redeeming (mortgage)

forecourt *n* open space in front of building

forefather *n* ancestor

forefinger *n* finger next to thumb

forefront *n* most active or prominent position

foregoing *adj* going before, preceding **foregone** *adj* determined beforehand

foreground *n* part of view nearest observer

forehand *adj* (of stroke in racket games) made with inner side of wrist leading

forehead *n* part of face above eyebrows and between temples

foreign *adj* not of, or in, one's own country; relating to other countries; strange **foreigner** *n*

foreman *n* one in charge of work; leader of jury

foremost *adj/adv* first in time, place, importance etc.

forensic *adj* connected with a court of law **forensic medicine** application of medical knowledge in legal matters

forerunner *n* one who goes before, precursor

foresee *v* **-seeing, -saw, -seen** see beforehand

foreshadow *v* show, suggest beforehand

foresight *n* foreseeing; care for future

——————— THESAURUS ———————

unnatural, wooden

forceful cogent, compelling, convincing, dynamic, effective, pithy, potent, powerful, telling, vigorous, weighty

forcible active, cogent, compelling, effective, efficient, energetic, forceful, impressive, mighty, potent, powerful, strong, telling, valid, weighty

forebear ancestor, father, forefather, forerunner, predecessor, progenitor

foreboding anxiety, apprehension, apprehensiveness, chill, dread, fear, misgiving, premonition, presentiment

forecast *v* augur, calculate, divine, estimate, foresee, foretell, plan, predict, prophesy ~*n* anticipation, conjecture, foresight, forethought, guess, outlook, planning, prediction, prognosis, projection, prophecy

forefather ancestor, father, forebear, forerunner, predecessor

foregoing above, antecedent, former, preceding, previous, prior

foreign alien, borrowed, distant, exotic, external, imported, outlandish, outside, overseas, remote, strange, unfamiliar, unknown

foreigner alien, immigrant, incomer, newcomer, outlander, stranger

foremost chief, first, front, highest, initial, leading, pre-eminent, principal, supreme

forerunner ancestor, envoy, forebear, foregoer, harbinger, herald, precursor, predecessor, progenitor, prototype

foresee anticipate, divine, envisage, forebode, forecast, foretell, predict, prophesy

foreshadow augur, betoken, bode, forebode, imply, indicate, portend, predict, presage, promise, signal

foresight anticipation, care, caution,

foreskin n skin that covers the tip of the penis

forest n area with heavy growth of trees **forestry** n

forestall v prevent, guard against in advance

foretaste n experience of something to come

foretell v -telling, -told prophesy

forethought n thoughtful consideration of future events

forever adv always; eternally; Inf for a long time

forewarn v warn, caution in advance

foreword n preface

forfeit n thing lost by crime or fault; penalty, fine ~adj lost by crime or fault ~v lose by penalty

forge¹ n place where metal is worked, smithy ~v shape (metal) by heating and hammering; counterfeit **forger** n **forgery** n counterfeiting; counterfeit thing

forge² v advance steadily

forget v -getting, -got, -gotten lose memory of, neglect, overlook **forgetful** adj liable to forget **forget-me-not** n plant with small blue flowers

forgive v cease to blame or hold resentment against; pardon **forgiveness** n

forgo v -going, -went, -gone go without; give up

fork n pronged instrument used for eating food; pronged tool for digging or lifting; division into branches ~v branch; dig, lift, throw, with fork; make fork-shaped

forlorn adj forsaken; desperate

form n shape, visible appearance; structure; nature; species; kind; regularly drawn up document; condition; class in school; customary way of doing things; bench ~v shape, organize; conceive; make part of; come into existence or shape **formation** n forming; thing formed **formative** adj

formal adj ceremonial, according to

forethought, precaution, preparedness, prescience, provision

foretell adumbrate, augur, forecast, foreshadow, forewarn, portend, predict, presage, prophesy, signify

forethought anticipation, precaution, providence, provision, prudence

forewarn admonish, advise, alert, caution, tip off

forfeit n damages, fine, loss, penalty ~v be deprived of, be stripped of, give up, lose, relinquish, surrender

forge coin, copy, counterfeit, fake, falsify, feign, imitate

forget lose sight of, omit, overlook

forgetful absent-minded, apt to forget, careless, dreamy, heedless, inattentive, lax, neglectful, negligent, oblivious, slapdash, slipshod, unmindful

forgive absolve, acquit, condone, excuse, exonerate, pardon, remit

forgo, forego abandon, cede, do without, give up, relinquish, renounce, resign, sacrifice, surrender, waive, yield

forlorn abandoned, cheerless, comfortless, deserted, desolate, destitute, disconsolate, helpless, homeless, hopeless, lonely, lost, miserable, pathetic, pitiable, pitiful, unhappy, wretched

form n appearance, cast, cut, fashion, formation, model, mould, pattern, shape, stamp, structure; format, framework, harmony, order, orderliness, organization, plan, proportion, structure, symmetry; application, document, paper, sheet ~v assemble, bring about, build, concoct, construct, contrive, create, devise, establish, fabricate, fashion, forge, found, invent, make, model, mould, produce, set up, shape, stamp; arrange,

rule; of outward form; stiff **formality** *n* observance required by custom; condition of being formal **formalize** *v* make official **formally** *adv*

format *n* size and shape of book etc.

former *adj* earlier in time; of past times; first named **~pron** first named thing or person or fact **formerly** *adv* previously

Formica *n Trademark* material used for heat-resistant surfaces

formidable *adj* to be feared; overwhelming; likely to be difficult

formula *n* (*pl* **-las, -lae**) set form of words, rule; *Science, Maths* rule, fact expressed in symbols and figures **formulate** *v*

fornication *n* sexual intercourse outside marriage

forsake *v* **-saking, -sook, -saken** abandon, desert; give up

forswear *v* **-swearing, -swore, -sworn** renounce, deny; perjure

fort *n* stronghold

forte[1] *n* one's strong point, that in which one excels

forte[2] *adv Mus* loudly

forth *adv* onwards, into view **forthcoming** *adj* about to come; ready when wanted; willing to talk **forthwith** *adv* at once

forthright *adj* outspoken

fortify *v* **-fying, -fied** strengthen **fortification** *n*

———————— T H E S A U R U S ————————

combine, design, dispose, draw up, frame, organize, pattern, plan

formal approved, ceremonial, explicit, express, fixed, lawful, legal, methodical, official, prescribed, regular, rigid, ritualistic, set, solemn, strict

formality ceremony, convention, custom, gesture, procedure, red tape, rite, ritual; correctness, decorum, etiquette, protocol

formation accumulation, composition, development, establishment, evolution, generation, genesis, manufacture, organization, production; arrangement, configuration, design, disposition, figure, grouping, pattern, rank, structure

former ancient, bygone, departed, of yore, old, old-time, past; above, aforesaid, foregoing, preceding

formerly already, before, lately, once, previously

formidable daunting, dreadful, fearful, frightful, horrible, intimidating, menacing, shocking, terrifying, threatening; arduous, challenging, colossal, difficult, onerous, overwhelming, toilsome

formula blueprint, method, precept,

prescription, principle, procedure, recipe, rule, way

formulate codify, define, detail, express, frame, specify, systematize

forsake abandon, cast off, desert, disown, jilt, kick *Inf*, leave, quit, repudiate, throw over

fort blockhouse, camp, castle, citadel, fortress, garrison, redoubt, station, stronghold

forthcoming approaching, coming, expected, future, imminent, impending, prospective, upcoming; chatty, communicative, expansive, free, informative, open, sociable, talkative, unreserved

forthright above-board, blunt, candid, direct, downright, frank, open, outspoken, straightforward, upfront *Inf*

forthwith at once, directly, immediately, instantly, quickly, right away, straightaway

fortification bulwark, castle, citadel, defence, fastness, fort, fortress, keep, protection, stronghold

fortify brace, cheer, confirm, embolden, encourage, hearten, invigorate, reassure, stiffen, strengthen, sustain

fortitude *n* endurance

fortnight *n* two weeks

fortress *n* fortified place

fortuitous *adj* accidental

fortune *n* good luck; wealth; chance **fortunate** *adj* **fortunately** *adv*

forty *see* FOUR

forum *n* (place or medium for) meeting, discussion or debate

forward *adj* lying in front of; onward; presumptuous; advanced; relating to the future ~*n* player in various team games ~*adv* towards the future; towards the front, to the front, into view ~*v* help forward; send, dispatch **forwards** *adv*

fossil *n* remnant or impression of animal or plant, preserved in earth **fossilize** *v* turn into fossil; petrify

foster *v* promote development of; bring up child, esp. not one's own

foul *adj* loathsome, offensive; stinking;

dirty; unfair; obscene ~*n* act of unfair play; breaking of a rule ~*v* make, become foul; jam; collide with

found[1] *v* establish; lay base of; base **foundation** *n* basis; lowest part of building; founding; endowed institution etc. **founder** *n*

found[2] *v* melt and run into mould; cast **foundry** *n* place for casting

founder *v* collapse; sink

foundling *n* deserted infant

fount *n* fountain; source

fountain *n* jet of water, esp. ornamental one; spring; source

four *n/adj* cardinal number next after three **fourth** *adj* ordinal number **fourteen** *n/adj* four plus ten **fourteenth** *adj* **forty** *n/adj* four tens **fortieth** *adj* **foursome** *n* group of four people

fowl *n* domestic cock or hen; bird, its flesh

fox *n* red bushy-tailed animal; its fur;

———— THESAURUS ————

fortress castle, citadel, fort, redoubt

fortunate bright, favoured, golden, happy, jammy *Brit sl*, lucky, prosperous, rosy, successful, well-off

fortunately by good luck, happily, luckily, providentially

fortune accident, chance, destiny, fate, hazard, kismet, luck, providence; affluence, gold mine, possessions, property, prosperity, riches, treasure, wealth

forward *adj* advanced, early, onward, precocious, premature, progressive, well-developed *adv* (*also* **forwards**) ahead, forth, on, onward ~*v* advance, aid, assist, back, encourage, expedite, favour, foster, further, hasten, help, hurry, promote, speed, support

foster cultivate, encourage, feed, nurture, promote, stimulate, support, uphold; bring up, mother, nurse, raise, rear, take care of

foul *adj* contaminated, dirty, disgusting, fetid, filthy, impure, loathsome,

nasty, nauseating, offensive, polluted, putrid, rank, repulsive, revolting, rotten, squalid, stinking, sullied, tainted, unclean ~*v* besmear, besmirch, contaminate, defile, dirty, pollute, smear, smirch, soil, stain, sully, taint

found constitute, construct, create, endow, erect, establish, fix, inaugurate, institute, organize, originate, plant, raise, settle, set up, start

foundation base, basis, bedrock, bottom, footing, substructure, underpinning; endowment, establishment, inauguration, institution, settlement

founder[1] author, beginner, benefactor, builder, designer, establisher, father, framer, generator, initiator, inventor, maker, organizer, originator, patriarch

founder[2] *v* be lost, go down, go to the bottom, sink, submerge

fountain fount, jet, reservoir, spout, spray, spring, well

cunning person ~v perplex; act craftily **foxy** adj **foxglove** n tall flowering plant **foxtrot** n (music for) ballroom dance

foyer n entrance hall in theatres, hotels etc.

fracas n noisy quarrel

fraction n numerical quantity not an integer; fragment

fractious adj irritable

fracture n breakage; breaking of bone ~v break

fragile adj breakable; delicate **fragility** n

fragment n piece broken off ~v shatter **fragmentary** adj

fragrant adj sweet-smelling **fragrance** n

frail adj fragile; in weak health **frailty** n

frame n that in which thing is set, as square of wood round picture etc.; structure; build of body ~v make; put into words; put into frame; bring false charge against **framework** n supporting structure

franc n monetary unit in France, Switzerland etc.

franchise n right of voting; citizenship; privilege or right

frank adj candid, outspoken; sincere ~n official mark on letter either cancelling stamp or ensuring delivery without stamp ~v mark letter thus

frankfurter n smoked sausage

frankincense n aromatic gum resin burned as incense

frantic adj distracted with rage, grief, joy etc.; frenzied **frantically** adv

——————— THESAURUS ———————

foyer anteroom, entrance hall, lobby, vestibule

fracas brawl, disturbance, fight, melee, quarrel, riot, row, rumpus, scrimmage, scuffle, shindig *Inf,* shindy *Inf,* trouble, uproar

fractious awkward, captious, crabby, cross, fretful, irritable, peevish, recalcitrant, testy, touchy, unruly

fracture n breach, break, cleft, crack, fissure, gap, opening, rent, rift, rupture, schism, split ~v break, crack, rupture, splinter, split

fragile breakable, brittle, dainty, delicate, feeble, fine, flimsy, frail, infirm, slight, weak

fragment bit, chip, fraction, morsel, oddment, part, piece, portion, remnant, scrap, shiver, sliver

fragmentary bitty, broken, disconnected, discrete, disjointed, incoherent, incomplete, partial, piecemeal

fragrance aroma, balm, bouquet, perfume, scent, smell

fragrant aromatic, balmy, odorous, perfumed, sweet-scented, sweet-smelling

frail breakable, brittle, decrepit, delicate, feeble, flimsy, fragile, infirm, insubstantial, puny, slight, tender, unsound, vulnerable, weak

frailty feebleness, puniness, susceptibility, weakness

frame n mount, mounting, setting; casing, fabric, form, scheme, shell, structure, system; anatomy, body, build, physique, skeleton ~v assemble, build, constitute, construct, fabricate, fashion, forge, form, institute, invent, make, model, mould, set up; compose, contrive, devise, draft, draw up, form, formulate, hatch, plan, shape, sketch; case, enclose, mount, surround

framework core, fabric, foundation, groundwork, plan, schema, shell, skeleton, structure

frank artless, blunt, candid, direct, downright, forthright, free, honest, open, outright, outspoken, plain, sincere, straightforward, transparent, truthful, unconcealed, undisguised, unreserved, unrestricted, upfront *Inf*

frantic berserk, desperate, distracted,

fraternal *adj* of brother, brotherly **fraternity** *n* brotherliness; brotherhood **fraternize** *v* associate; make friends

fraud *n* criminal deception; impostor **fraudulent** *adj*

fraught *Inf* v filled (with), involving

fray[1] *n* fight; noisy quarrel

fray[2] *v* make, become ragged at edge

frazzle *Inf* v make or become exhausted ~*n* exhausted state

freak *n/adj* abnormal (person or thing)

freckle *n* light brown spot on skin, esp. caused by sun

free *adj* freer, freest able to act at will, not under compulsion or restraint; self-ruling; not restricted or affected by; not subject to cost or tax; not in use; (of person) not occupied; loose, not fixed ~*v* freeing, freed set at liberty; remove (obstacles, pain etc.); rid (of) **freedom** *n* **free-for-all** *n* brawl **freehold** *n* tenure of land without obligation of service or rent **freelance** *adj/n* (of) self-employed person **freeloader** *n* *Sl* scrounger **free-range** *adj* kept, produced in natural, nonintensive conditions **free speech** right to express opinions publicly **freewheel** *v* travel downhill on bicycle without pedalling

freeze *v* freezing, froze, frozen change

——————— THESAURUS ———————

distraught, frenetic, frenzied, furious, hectic, mad, overwrought, raging, raving, wild

fraternity association, brotherhood, circle, clan, club, companionship, company, comradeship, fellowship, guild, kinship, league, order, set, sodality, union

fraud artifice, cheat, chicanery, craft, deceit, deception, double-dealing, duplicity, guile, hoax, humbug, imposture, scam *Sl*, spuriousness, stratagems, swindling, treachery, trickery; bluffer, charlatan, cheat, counterfeit, double-dealer, fake, forgery, hoax, hoaxer, impostor, mountebank, pretender, quack, sham, swindler

fraudulent crafty, criminal, deceitful, deceptive, dishonest, false, knavish, sham, spurious, swindling, treacherous

fray v chafe, fret, rub, wear, wear away, wear thin

freak *n* aberration, abnormality, anomaly, malformation, monster, oddity ~*adj* aberrant, abnormal, atypical, bizarre, erratic, exceptional, fortuitous, odd, queer, unexpected, unforeseen, unpredictable, unusual

free *adj* at large, at liberty, footloose, independent, liberated, loose, uncommitted, unconstrained, unfettered, unrestrained; autarchic, autonomous, democratic, emancipated, independent, self-governing, self-ruling, sovereign; complimentary, for nothing, gratis, gratuitous, unpaid; able, allowed, clear, disengaged, loose, open, permitted, unattached, unhampered, unimpeded, unobstructed, unregulated, unrestricted, untrammelled; available, empty, extra, idle, not tied down, spare, unemployed, uninhabited, unoccupied, unused, vacant ~*v* deliver, discharge, emancipate, let go, let out, liberate, loose, manumit, release, turn loose, unbridle, uncage, unchain, unfetter, unleash, untie; clear, cut loose, deliver, disengage, disentangle, exempt, extricate, ransom, redeem, relieve, rescue, rid, unburden, undo

freedom autonomy, deliverance, emancipation, home rule, independence, liberty, release, self-government; exemption, immunity, impunity, privilege; ability, carte blanche, discretion, elbowroom, fa-

(by reduction of temperature) from liquid to solid, as water to ice; preserve (food etc.) by extreme cold; fix (prices etc.); feel very cold; become rigid **freezer** *n* insulated cabinet for long-term storage of perishable foodstuffs

freight *n* commercial transport (esp. by railway, ship); cost of this; goods so carried ~*v* send as or by freight **freighter** *n*

French *n* language spoken by people of France ~*adj* of, pert. to France **French dressing** salad dressing **French fries** potato chips **French horn** musical wind instrument

frenetic *adj* frenzied

frenzy *n* violent mental derangement; wild excitement **frenzied** *adj*

frequent *adj* happening often; common; numerous ~*v* go often to **frequency** *n* rate of occurrence; in radio etc., cycles per second of alternating current

fresco *n* (*pl* **-coes**) (method of) painting on wet plaster

fresh *adj* not stale; new; additional; different; recent; inexperienced; pure; not pickled, frozen etc.; not faded; not tired; (of wind) strong **freshen** *v* **freshman, fresher** *n* first-year student

fret[1] *v* **fretting, fretted** be irritated, worry ~*n* irritation **fretful** *adj*

fret[2] *n* repetitive geometrical pattern ~*v* **fretting, fretted** ornament with carved pattern **fretwork** *n*

friable *adj* easily crumbled

friar *n* member of religious order

fricassee *n* dish of stewed pieces of meat

friction *n* rubbing; resistance met with by body moving over another; clash of wills etc.

Friday *n* sixth day of the week

fridge *n Inf* refrigerator

friend *n* one well known to another and regarded with affection and loyalty **friendly** *adj* kind; favourable **friendship** *n*

cility, flexibility, free rein, latitude, leeway, licence, opportunity, play, power, range, scope

freeze benumb, chill, congeal, glaciate, harden, ice over *or* up, stiffen; fix, hold up, inhibit, peg, stop, suspend

freight *n* bales, bulk, burden, cargo, consignment, contents, goods, haul, lading, load, merchandise, payload, tonnage

frenzied agitated, convulsive, distracted, distraught, excited, frantic, frenetic, furious, hysterical, mad, maniacal, rabid, uncontrolled, wild

frequent *adj* common, constant, continual, customary, everyday, familiar, habitual, numerous, persistent, recurrent, repeated, usual ~*v* attend, be found at, haunt, patronize, resort, visit

fresh added, additional, extra, further, more, other, renewed; different, latest, modern, new, novel, original, recent, unusual, up-to-date ; artless, callow, green, inexperienced, natural, new, raw, untrained, untried, youthful; bracing, bright, brisk, clean, clear, cool, crisp, invigorating, pure, refreshing, sparkling, stiff, sweet; blooming, clear, fair, florid, glowing, good, hardy, healthy, rosy, wholesome

freshen enliven, liven up, refresh, restore, revitalize, rouse, spruce up, titivate

fret affront, agonize, anguish, annoy, brood, chagrin, goad, grieve, harass, irritate, provoke, ruffle, torment, worry

friction abrasion, erosion, fretting, grating, irritation, resistance, rub-

frieze *n* ornamental band, strip (on wall)

frigate *n* fast warship

fright *n* sudden fear; shock; alarm; grotesque or ludicrous person or thing **frighten** *v* cause fear, fright in **frightening** *adj* **frightful** *adj* terrible, calamitous; shocking; *Inf* very great, very large **frightfully** *adv*

frigid *adj* formal; (sexually) unfeeling; cold

frill *n* strip of fabric gathered at one edge; ruff of hair, feathers around neck of dog, bird etc.; unnecessary words; superfluous thing; adornment **frilly** *adj*

fringe *n* ornamental edge of hanging threads, tassels etc.; hair cut in front and falling over brow; edge ~*adj* (of theatre etc.) unofficial

frisk *v* move, leap, playfully; *Inf* search (person) **frisky** *adj*

frisson *n* shiver of excitement

fritter[1] *v* waste

fritter[2] *n* piece of food fried in batter

frivolous *adj* not serious, unimportant; flippant **frivolity** *n*

frizz *v* crisp, curl into small curls ~*n* frizzed hair **frizzy** *adj*

frock *n* woman's dress; various similar garments

frog *n* tailless amphibious animal de-

——————— THESAURUS ———————

bing, scraping

friend chum, companion, comrade, confidant, crony, familiar, intimate, pal, partner, playmate, soul mate

friendly affectionate, amiable, amicable, attentive, beneficial, benevolent, benign, close, companionable, comradely, convivial, cordial, familiar, favourable, fond, genial, good, helpful, intimate, kind, kindly, neighbourly, outgoing, peaceable, propitious, receptive, sociable, sympathetic, welcoming, well-disposed

friendship affection, affinity, alliance, amity, attachment, benevolence, closeness, concord, familiarity, fondness, good-fellowship, good will, harmony, intimacy, love, rapport, regard

fright alarm, apprehension, dismay, dread, fear, horror, panic, quaking, scare, shock, terror, trepidation

frighten alarm, appal, cow, daunt, dismay, intimidate, petrify, scare, shock, startle, terrify, terrorize, unman, unnerve

frightening alarming, appalling, dismaying, dreadful, fearful, fearsome, hair-raising, horrifying, intimidating, menacing, shocking, terrifying, unnerving

frightful appalling, awful, dire, dreadful, fearful, ghastly, grim, grisly, gruesome, harrowing, hideous, horrible, lurid, macabre, petrifying, shocking, terrible, terrifying, traumatic, unnerving, unspeakable

frigid aloof, austere, forbidding, formal, icy, lifeless, passionless, passive, repellent, rigid, stiff, unapproachable, unbending, unfeeling, unloving, unresponsive; arctic, chill, cold, cool, frost-bound, frosty, frozen, gelid, glacial, hyperborean, icy, Siberian, wintry

fringe binding, border, edging, hem, tassel, trimming; borderline, edge, limits, march, marches, margin, outskirts, perimeter, periphery

frisky bouncy, frolicsome, full of beans *Inf*, high-spirited, in high spirits, kittenish, lively, playful, rollicking, romping, spirited, sportive

frivolity childishness, flippancy, folly, fun, gaiety, giddiness, jest, levity, lightness, nonsense, puerility, shallowness, silliness, superficiality, trifling, triviality

frivolous childish, dizzy, emptyheaded, flighty, flippant, foolish, giddy, idle, juvenile, puerile, silly,

veloped from tadpole **frogman** *n* underwater swimmer with rubber suit

frolic *n* merrymaking ~*v* **-icking**, **-icked** behave playfully

from *prep* expressing point of departure, source, distance, cause, change of state etc.

frond *n* plant organ consisting of stem and foliage

front *n* fore part; position directly before or ahead; seaside promenade; outward aspect; *Inf* thing serving as respectable cover ~*v* look, face; *Inf* be a cover for ~*adj* of, at the front **frontal** *adj* **frontage** *n* façade of building; extent of front **frontier** *n* part of country which borders on another **frontispiece** *n* illustration facing title page of book

frost *n* frozen dew or mist; act or state of freezing ~*v* cover, be covered with frost or something similar in appearance **frosted** *adj* (of glass) opaque

frosty *adj* accompanied by frost; cold; unfriendly **frostbite** *n* destruction of tissue by cold

froth *n* collection of small bubbles, foam ~*v* (cause to) foam **frothy** *adj*

frown *v* wrinkle brows; (*with* **on**) disapprove of ~*n* expression of disapproval

frugal *adj* sparing; thrifty, economical; meagre

fruit *n* seed and its envelope, esp. edible one; vegetable product; (*usu.* pl) result, benefit ~*v* bear fruit **fruitful** *adj* **fruition** *n* enjoyment; realization of hopes **fruitless** *adj* **fruity** *adj*

frump *n* dowdy woman **frumpy** *adj*

frustrate *v* thwart; disappoint **frustration** *n*

fry[1] *v* **frying, fried** cook with fat; be cooked thus

fry[2] *pl n* young fishes

ft. feet; foot

fuchsia *n* shrub with purple-red flowers

superficial

frolic *n* amusement, fun, gaiety, high jinks, sport ~*v* caper, cavort, cut capers, frisk, gambol, lark, make merry, play, rollick, romp, sport

front *n* exterior, façade, face, facing, foreground, fore part, frontage, obverse; beginning, fore, forefront, head, lead, top, van, vanguard; blind, cover, cover-up, disguise, façade, mask, pretext, show ~*v* face (onto), look over *or* onto, overlook ~*adj* first, foremost, head, headmost, lead, leading, topmost

frontier borderland, borderline, bound, boundary, confines, edge, limit, marches, perimeter, verge

frosty chilly, cold, frozen, icy, parky *Brit inf*, rimy, wintry; discouraging, frigid, standoffish, unfriendly, unwelcoming

frown glare, glower, lour *or* lower,

scowl (*with* **on**) disapprove of, discourage, dislike

frugal abstemious, careful, economical, meagre, niggardly, parsimonious, prudent, saving, sparing, thrifty

fruit crop, harvest, produce, product, yield; advantage, benefit, consequence, effect, outcome, profit, result, return, reward

fruitful fecund, fertile; abundant, copious, flush, plenteous, plentiful, productive, profuse, prolific, rich, spawning

fruitless abortive, barren, futile, idle, ineffectual, in vain, pointless, profitless, unavailing, unproductive, unprofitable, unsuccessful, useless, vain

frustrate baffle, balk, block, check, confront, counter, defeat, disappoint, foil, forestall, inhibit, neutralize, nullify, stymie, thwart

fuddle *v* (cause to) be intoxicated, confused

fuddy-duddy *n Inf* (elderly) dull person

fudge[1] *n* soft, variously flavoured sweet

fudge[2] *v* avoid definite decision

fuel *n* material for burning as source of heat or power ~*v* **fuelling, fuelled** provide with fuel

fugitive *n* one who flees, esp. from arrest ~*adj* elusive

fugue *n* musical composition in which themes are repeated in different parts

fulcrum *n* (*pl* **-crums, -cra**) point on which a lever is placed for support

fulfil *v* **-filling, -filled** satisfy; carry out **fulfilment** *n*

full *adj* containing as much as possible; abundant; complete; ample; plump ~*adv* very; quite; exactly **fully**

adv **full-blooded** *adj* vigorous, enthusiastic **full-blown** *adj* fully developed **full stop** punctuation mark (.) at end of sentence

fulminate *v* (*esp. with* **against**) criticize harshly

fulsome *adj* insincerely excessive

fumble *v* grope about; handle awkwardly ~*n* awkward attempt

fume *v* be angry; emit smoke or vapour ~*n* smoke; vapour **fumigate** *v* apply fumes or smoke to, esp. for disinfection

fun *n* anything enjoyable, amusing etc. **funny** *adj* comical; odd **funnily** *adv* **funfair** *n* entertainment with rides and stalls

function *n* work a thing is designed to do; (large) social event; duty; profession ~*v* operate, work **functional** *adj*

fund *n* stock or sum of money; supply;

──────── **T H E S A U R U S** ────────

fuel ammunition, encouragement, fodder, food, incitement, material, means, nourishment, provocation

fugitive runaway

fulfil accomplish, achieve, answer, carry out, complete, conclude, conform to, discharge, effect, execute, fill, finish, keep, meet, obey, observe, perfect, perform, realize, satisfy

fulfilment accomplishment, achievement, attainment, completion, consummation, crowning, discharge, end, implementation, observance, perfection, realization

full brimful, complete, entire, filled, gorged, intact, loaded, replete, sated, satiated, satisfied, saturated, stocked, sufficient; abundant, ample, broad, comprehensive, copious, detailed, exhaustive, extensive, generous, maximum, plenary, plenteous, plentiful, thorough, unabridged

fully absolutely, altogether, completely, entirely, intimately, perfectly, positively, thoroughly, totally,

utterly, wholly; abundantly, adequately, amply, enough, plentifully, satisfactorily, sufficiently

fulsome adulatory, excessive, extravagant, fawning, gross, ingratiating, inordinate, insincere, nauseating, saccharine, sickening, sycophantic, unctuous

fumble botch, bungle, make a hash of *Inf*, mess up, mishandle, mismanage, muff, spoil

fume boil, chafe, rage, rant, rave, see red *Inf*, seethe, smoulder, storm

fumigate cleanse, disinfect, purify, sterilize

fun amusement, cheer, distraction, diversion, enjoyment, entertainment, frolic, gaiety, good time, jollity, joy, merriment, mirth, pleasure, recreation, romp, sport, treat

function *n* activity, business, capacity, charge, concern, duty, employment, exercise, job, mission, occupation, office, operation, part, post, province, purpose, responsibility,

pl money resources ~*v* provide or obtain funds

fundamental *adj* of, affecting, or serving as, the base; essential, primary ~*n* basic rule or fact **fundamentalism** *n* strict interpretation of religion **fundamentalist** *n/adj*

funeral *n* (ceremony associated with) burial or cremation of dead **funereal** *adj* like a funeral; dark; gloomy

fungus *n* (*pl* -**gi**, -**guses**) plant without leaves, flowers, or roots, as mushroom, mould **fungicide** *n* substance that destroys fungi

funk *n* style of dance music **funky** *adj*

funnel *n* cone-shaped vessel or tube; chimney of locomotive or ship ~*v* -**nelling**, -**nelled** (cause to) move as through funnel

funny *adj see* FUN

fur *n* soft hair of animal; garment of this **furry** *adj*

furious *adj* extremely angry; violent

furl *v* roll up and bind

furlong *n* eighth of mile

furnace *n* apparatus for applying great heat to metals

furnish *v* fit up house with furniture; supply **furnishings** *pl n* **furniture** *n*

furore *n* very angry or excited reaction to something

furrow *n* trench; groove ~*v* make furrows in

further *adv* more; in addition; at or to a greater distance or extent ~*adj* more distant; additional; *comparative of* FAR ~*v* promote **furthermore** *adv* besides **furthermost** *adj* **furthest** *adj/adv superlative of* FAR

furtive *adj* stealthy, sly, secret

role, situation, task; affair, do *Inf*, gathering, reception, social occasion ~*v* act, behave, do duty, go, officiate, operate, perform, run, serve, work

functional practical, serviceable, useful, utilitarian, utility, working

fund *n* hoard, mine, repository, reserve, reservoir, source, storehouse, treasury, vein; capital, endowment, foundation, kitty, pool, reserve, stock, store, supply ~*v* capitalize, endow, finance, float, pay for, promote, stake, subsidize, support

fundamental *adj* basic, cardinal, central, crucial, elementary, essential, first, important, indispensable, integral, intrinsic, key, necessary, prime, principal, radical, underlying, vital

funeral burial, interment, obsequies

funny absurd, amusing, comic, comical, diverting, droll, entertaining, facetious, farcical, hilarious, humorous, jocular, jolly, laughable, ludicrous, rich, ridiculous, riotous, risible, silly, slapstick, waggish, witty;

curious, dubious, mysterious, odd, peculiar, perplexing, puzzling, queer, remarkable, rum *Brit sl*, strange, suspicious, unusual, weird

furious angry, beside oneself, boiling, enraged, frantic, frenzied, fuming, incensed, infuriated, mad, maddened, raging, wrathful

furnish appoint, decorate, equip, fit out, fit up, outfit, provide, purvey, rig, stock, store, supply; afford, bestow, endow, give, grant, hand out, offer, present, provide, reveal, supply

furniture appointments, chattels, effects, equipment, fittings, furnishings, goods, household goods, possessions

furrow channel, crease, fluting, groove, hollow, line, rut, seam, trench, wrinkle

further *adv* additionally, also, as well as, besides, furthermore, in addition, moreover, on top of, what's more, yet ~*adj* additional, extra, fresh, more, new, other, supplementary ~*v* advance, aid, assist, champion, encour-

fury *n* wild rage, violence

fuse *v* blend by melting; melt with heat; (cause to) fail as a result of blown fuse ~*n* soft wire used as safety device in electrical systems; device for igniting bomb etc. **fusion** *n*

fuselage *n* body of aircraft

fuss *n* needless bustle or concern; complaint; objection ~*v* make fuss **fussy** *adj*

fusty *adj* mouldy; smelling of damp; old-fashioned

futile *adj* useless, ineffectual, trifling **futility** *n*

futon *n* Japanese padded quilt

future *n* time to come; what will happen ~*adj* that will be; of, relating to, time to come **futuristic** *adj* appearing to belong to some future time

fuzz *n* fluff; frizzed hair; blur; *Sl* police **fuzzy** *adj*

age, expedite, facilitate, forward, foster, hasten, help, patronize, promote, push, speed, succour, work for

furthermore additionally, as well, besides, in addition, moreover, to boot, too

furthest extreme, farthest, most distant, outermost, outmost, remotest, ultimate, uttermost

furtive clandestine, cloaked, covert, hidden, secret, secretive, skulking, slinking, sly, sneaking, sneaky, stealthy, surreptitious, underhand

fury anger, frenzy, ire, madness, passion, rage, wrath; ferocity, force, intensity, power, savagery, severity, turbulence, vehemence, violence

fuss *n* ado, agitation, bother, bustle, commotion, confusion, excitement, fidget, flurry, fluster, flutter, hurry, stir, to-do, upset, worry; argument, bother, complaint, difficulty, display, furore, objection, row, squabble, trouble, unrest, upset ~*v* bustle, fidget, fret, fume

fussy choosy, difficult, exacting, faddy, fastidious, finicky, particular, pernickety, picky *Inf*

futile abortive, barren, bootless, empty, forlorn, fruitless, hollow, ineffectual, nugatory, profitless, sterile, unavailing, unproductive, unprofitable, unsuccessful, useless, vain, valueless, worthless

future *n* expectation, hereafter, outlook, prospect, time to come ~*adj* approaching, coming, destined, eventual, expected, fated, forthcoming, impending, later, prospective, subsequent, to come

G g

g gram

gabardine, gaberdine *n* fine twill cloth like serge

gabble *v* gabbling, gabbled talk, utter inarticulately or too fast

gable *n* triangular upper part of wall at end of ridged roof

gad *v* gadding, gadded (*esp. with about*) go around in search of pleasure

gadget *n* small mechanical device

gaffe *n* tactless remark

gaffer *n* old man; *Inf* foreman, boss

gag[1] *v* gagging, gagged stop up (person's mouth); *Sl* retch, choke ~*n* cloth etc. tied across mouth

gag[2] *n* joke, funny story

gaggle *n* flock of geese

gain *v* obtain (as profit); earn; reach; increase, improve; get nearer ~*n*

profit; increase, improvement

gainsay *v* gainsaying, gainsaid deny, contradict

gait *n* manner of walking

gala *n* festive occasion; show; sporting event

galaxy *n* system of stars **galactic** *adj*

gale *n* strong wind; *Inf* outburst, esp. of laughter

gall[1] *n* *Inf* impudence; bitterness **gall bladder** sac for bile

gall[2] *v* make sore by rubbing; irritate

gallant *adj* fine, stately, brave; chivalrous **gallantry** *n*

galleon *n* large sailing ship

gallery *n* projecting upper floor in church, theatre etc.; place for showing works of art

galley *n* one-decked vessel with sails and oars; kitchen of ship or aircraft

---

THESAURUS

gadget appliance, contrivance, device, gimmick, invention, novelty, tool

gaffe blunder, boob *Brit sl*, clanger *Inf*, faux pas, howler, indiscretion

gag[1] *v* curb, muffle, muzzle, quiet, silence, stifle, suppress, throttle

gag[2] crack *Sl*, funny *Inf*, hoax, jest, joke, wisecrack *Inf*, witticism

gaiety blitheness, cheerfulness, elation, glee, good humour, high spirits, *joie de vivre,* jollity, joviality, joyousness, liveliness, merriment, mirth, vivacity

gaily blithely, cheerfully, gleefully, happily, joyfully, light-heartedly, merrily

gain *v* achieve, acquire, advance, attain, capture, collect, gather, get, glean, harvest, increase, net, obtain, pick up, procure, profit, realize, reap, secure, win, win over; acquire, bring in, clear, earn, get, make, net, obtain,

produce, realize, win, yield ~*n* acquisition, advance, advantage, attainment, benefit, dividend, earnings, emolument, growth, headway, improvement, income, increase, increment, proceeds, produce, profit, return, rise, winnings, yield

gait bearing, carriage, pace, step, stride, tread, walk

gala carnival, celebration, festival, festivity, fête, jamboree, pageant, party

gale blast, hurricane, squall, storm, tempest, tornado, typhoon

gallant *adj* bold, brave, courageous, daring, dashing, doughty, fearless, heroic, honourable, intrepid, manly, noble, plucky, valiant, valorous; attentive, chivalrous, courteous, courtly, gentlemanly, gracious, magnanimous, noble, polite

gallantry audacity, boldness, bravery, courage, daring, fearlessness, heroism, manliness, mettle, nerve, pluck,

gallivant *v* gad about

gallon *n* liquid measure of eight pints (4.55 litres)

gallop *n* horse's fastest pace; ride at this pace ~*v* go, ride at gallop; move fast

gallows *n* structure for hanging criminals

galore *adv* in plenty

galoshes *pl n* waterproof overshoes

galvanize *v* stimulate to action; coat (iron etc.) with zinc

gambit *n* opening move, comment etc. intended to secure an advantage

gamble *v* play games of chance to win money; act on expectation of ~*n* risky undertaking; bet **gambler** *n* **gambling** *n*

gambol *v* **-bolling, -bolled** skip, jump playfully

game[1] *n* pastime; jest; contest for amusement; scheme; animals or birds hunted; their flesh ~*adj* brave; willing **gaming** *n* gambling **game-keeper** *n* man employed to breed game, prevent poaching

game[2], **gammy** *adj* lame

gammon *n* cured or smoked ham

gamut *n* whole range or scale

gander *n* male goose

gang *n* (criminal) group; organized group of workmen ~*v* (*esp. with* to-gether) form gang

gangling *adj* lanky

gangplank *n* portable bridge for boarding or leaving vessel

gangrene *n* death or decay of body tissue as a result of disease or injury

gangster *n* member of criminal gang

gangway *n* bridge from ship to shore; anything similar; passage be-tween rows of seats

gannet *n* predatory sea bird

gantry *n* structure to support crane, railway signals etc.

gaol *n* see JAIL

gap *n* opening, interval

gape *v* stare in wonder; open mouth wide; be, become wide open

garage *n* (part of) building to house cars; refuelling and repair centre for cars

garb *n/v* dress

garbage *n* rubbish

————————— THESAURUS —————————

prowess, spirit, valiance, valour

gallop bolt, career, dart, dash, fly, hasten, hurry, race, run, rush, shoot, speed, sprint

gamble *v* back, bet, game, play, punt, stake, wager; back, chance, hazard, risk, speculate, stake, venture ~*n* chance, lottery, risk, speculation, un-certainty, venture; bet, flutter *Inf,* punt, wager

gambol caper, cavort, frisk, frolic, hop, jump, prance, rollick, skip

game *n* amusement, distraction, di-version, entertainment, frolic, fun, jest, joke, merriment, pastime, play, recreation, romp, sport; contest, event, match, meeting, round; chase, prey, quarry ~*adj* bold, brave, coura-geous, dogged, fearless, gallant, hero-

ic, intrepid, persistent, plucky, reso-lute, spirited, valiant

gang band, circle, clique, club, com-pany, coterie, crew *Inf,* crowd, group, herd, horde, lot, mob, pack, party, ring, set, shift, squad, team, troupe

gangster bandit, brigand, crook *Inf,* desperado, hoodlum *chiefly US,* rack-eteer, robber, ruffian, thug, tough

gap blank, breach, break, chink, cleft, crack, cranny, crevice, divide, hiatus, hole, intermission, interruption, in-terstice, interval, lacuna, lull, open-ing, pause, recess, rent, rift, space, void

gape gawk, goggle, stare, wonder; crack, open, split, yawn

garbage debris, detritus, junk, litter,

garble v jumble or distort story, account etc.

garden n ground for cultivation ~v cultivate garden **gardener** n **gardening** n

gargantuan adj immense

gargle v wash throat with liquid kept moving by the breath ~n gargling; preparation for this purpose

gargoyle n grotesque carving on church etc.

garish adj showy; gaudy

garland n wreath of flowers as decoration

garlic n (bulb of) plant with strong smell and taste, used in cooking and seasoning

garment n article of clothing

garner v store up, collect

garnet n red semiprecious stone

garnish v decorate (esp. food) ~n material for this

garret n attic

garrison n troops stationed in town, fort etc.; fortified place ~v occupy with garrison

garrotte v execute by strangling

garrulous adj talkative

garter n band worn round leg to hold up sock or stocking

gas n (pl **gases**) airlike substance; fossil fuel in form of gas; gaseous anaesthetic; gaseous poison or irritant; Inf, esp. US petrol ~v **gassing**, **gassed** poison with gas; talk idly, boastfully **gaseous** adj of, like gas

gash n gaping wound, slash ~v cut deeply

gasket n seal between metal faces, esp. in engines

gasp v catch breath as in exhaustion or surprise ~n gasping

gastric adj of stomach

gastroenteritis n inflammation of stomach and intestines **gastronomy** n art of good eating

gate n opening in wall, fence etc.; barrier for closing it; any entrance or way out **gate-crash** v enter social function etc. uninvited **gateway** n entrance with gate; means of access

gâteau n (pl **-eaux**) elaborate, rich cake

gather v (cause to) assemble; increase gradually; draw together; collect; learn, understand **gathering** n assembly

gaudy adj showy in tasteless way

rubbish, scraps

garble confuse, jumble, mix up; distort, doctor, falsify, misquote, misreport, misrepresent, mistranslate, slant, tamper with, twist

garish brassy, cheap, flash Inf, flashy, gaudy, glaring, glittering, loud, showy, tacky Inf, tasteless, vulgar

garland bays, chaplet, crown, festoon, honours, laurels, wreath

garner accumulate, amass, assemble, collect, deposit, gather, hoard, put by, reserve, save, stockpile, store

garnish adorn, beautify, bedeck, deck, decorate, embellish, enhance, grace, ornament, set off, trim

garrison armed force, command, detachment, troops, unit; base, camp, encampment, fort, fortification, fortress, post, station, stronghold

gash n cleft, cut, incision, laceration, rent, slash, slit, split, tear, wound ~v cleave, cut, incise, lacerate, rend, slash, slit, split, tear, wound

gasp v blow, choke, gulp, pant, puff ~n blow, ejaculation, exclamation, gulp, pant, puff

gate access, barrier, door, doorway, egress, entrance, exit, passage, portal

gather accumulate, amass, assemble, collect, congregate, convene, flock, garner, group, heap, hoard, marshal, mass, muster, pile up, round up, stack up, stockpile; collect, crop, cull,

gauge *n* standard measure, as of diameter of wire etc.; distance between rails of railway; instrument for measuring ~*v* measure; estimate

gaunt *adj* lean, haggard

gauntlet *n* (armoured) glove covering part of arm

gauze *n* thin transparent fabric of silk, wire etc.

gavel *n* auctioneer's mallet

gay *adj* homosexual; merry; bright **gaiety** *n* **gaily** *adv*

gaze *v* look fixedly ~*n* fixed look

gazebo *n* (*pl* -**bos**) summerhouse

gazelle *n* small graceful antelope

gazette *n* official newspaper for announcements **gazetteer** *n* geographical dictionary

GB Great Britain

GBH grievous bodily harm

GC George Cross

GCE General Certificate of Education

GCSE General Certificate of Secondary Education

gear *n* set of wheels working together, esp. by engaging cogs; equipment; clothing; *Sl* drugs ~*v* adapt (one thing) so as to conform with another

gearbox *n* case protecting gearing of bicycle, car etc.

geese *pl of* GOOSE

geezer *n Inf* (old or eccentric) man

geisha *n* in Japan, professional female companion for men

gel *n* jelly-like substance

gelatine, gelatin *n* substance prepared from animal bones etc., producing edible jelly

geld *v* castrate **gelding** *n* castrated horse

gelignite *n* powerful explosive consisting of dynamite in gelatine form

gem *n* precious stone, esp. when cut and polished

gen *n Inf* information

gender *n* sex, male or female

gene *n* biological factor determining inherited characteristics

genealogy *n* study or account of descent from ancestors

──────── THESAURUS ────────

garner, glean, harvest, pick, pluck, reap, select; assume, conclude, deduce, draw, hear, infer, learn, make, surmise, understand

gathering assembly, company, conclave, concourse, congregation, congress, convention, crowd, flock, group, knot, meeting, muster, party, rally, throng, turnout

gaudy bright, flash *Inf*, flashy, florid, garish, gay, glaring, loud, ostentatious, raffish, showy, tacky *Inf*, tasteless, tawdry, vulgar

gauge *v* ascertain, calculate, check, compute, count, determine, measure, weigh; adjudge, appraise, assess, estimate, evaluate, guess, judge, rate, reckon, value ~*n* basis, example, guide, indicator, measure, meter, model, pattern, rule, sample, standard, test, yardstick

gaunt angular, bony, cadaverous, emaciated, haggard, lank, lean, meagre, pinched, rawboned, scraggy, scrawny, skinny, spare, thin, wasted

gay animated, blithe, carefree, cheerful, debonair, glad, gleeful, happy, hilarious, jolly, jovial, joyful, joyous, lively, merry, sparkling, sunny, vivacious; bright, brilliant, colourful, flamboyant, flashy, fresh, garish, gaudy, rich, showy, vivid

gaze *v* contemplate, gape, look, regard, stare, view, watch, wonder ~*n* fixed look, look, stare

gear cog, cogwheel, toothed wheel; accessories, accoutrements, apparatus, equipment, harness, instruments, outfit, rigging, supplies, tackle, tools, trappings; apparel, attire, clothes, dress, garb, outfit

gem jewel, precious stone, stone

general *adj* widespread; not particular or specific; usual; miscellaneous ~*n* army officer of rank above colonel **generally** *adv* **generalize** *v* draw general conclusions **general practitioner** doctor serving local area

generate *v* bring into being; produce **generation** *n* bringing into being; all persons born about same time; time between generations (about 30 years) **generator** *n* apparatus for producing (steam, electricity etc.)

generous *adj* free in giving; abundant **generosity** *n*

genesis *n* (*pl* -**eses**) origin; mode of formation

genetics *pl n* (*with sing v*) scientific study of heredity **genetic** *adj*

genial *adj* cheerful; mild

genie *n* in fairy tales, servant appearing by, and working, magic

genital *adj* relating to sexual organs or reproduction **genitals** *pl n* sexual organs

genius *n* (person with) exceptional power or ability

genocide *n* murder of entire race of people

genre *n* style of literary work

gent *Inf n* gentleman **gents** *n* men's public lavatory

genteel *adj* well-bred; affectedly proper **gentility** *n* respectability

gentile *adj n*; (person) of race other than Jewish

gentle *adj* mild, not rough or severe; moderate; well-born **gently** *adv* **gentleness** *n* quality of being gentle **gentleman** *n* chivalrous well-bred man; man (used as a mark of politeness)

gentry *n* people just below nobility in

──────── T H E S A U R U S ────────

general accepted, broad, common, extensive, popular, prevailing, prevalent, public, universal, widespread; approximate, ill-defined, imprecise, inaccurate, indefinite, inexact, loose, undetailed, unspecific, vague; accustomed, conventional, customary, everyday, habitual, normal, ordinary, regular, typical, usual

generally almost always, as a rule, by and large, conventionally, customarily, habitually, mainly, normally, ordinarily, regularly, typically, usually; commonly, extensively, popularly, publicly, universally, widely

generate beget, breed, cause, create, engender, form, initiate, make, originate, procreate, produce, propagate, spawn

generation begetting, breeding, creation, formation, genesis, procreation, production, propagation, reproduction; age, day, days, epoch, era, period, time, times

generosity benevolence, bounty, charity, kindness, liberality

generous benevolent, bounteous, bountiful, charitable, free, hospitable, kind, lavish, liberal, princely, ungrudging, unstinting

genial affable, agreeable, amiable, cheerful, cheery, convivial, cordial, easygoing, friendly, happy, hearty, jolly, jovial, kind, kindly, pleasant, sunny, warm

genius adept, expert, maestro, master, virtuoso, whiz *Inf*; ability, aptitude, bent, brilliance, capacity, endowment, faculty, flair, gift, inclination, knack, talent, turn

genteel aristocratic, civil, courteous, courtly, cultured, elegant, fashionable, formal, gentlemanly, ladylike, mannerly, polished, polite, refined, respectable, stylish, urbane, well-mannered

gentility civility, courtesy, culture, decorum, elegance, etiquette, formality, good manners, polish, politeness, propriety, refinement, respectability

social rank

genuine adj real; sincere

genus n (pl **genera**) class, order, group (esp. of insects, animals etc.) with common characteristics

geography n science of earth's form, physical features, climate, population etc. **geographer** n **geographical** adj

geology n science of earth's crust, rocks, strata etc. **geological** adj **geologist** n

geometry n science of properties and relations of lines, surfaces etc. **geometrical, -metric** adj

geranium n plant with red, pink or white flowers

gerbil n desert rodent of Asia and Africa

geriatrics n science of old age and its diseases **geriatric** adj/n old (person)

germ n microbe, esp. causing disease; rudiment

German n language spoken by people of Germany ~adj of, pert. to Germany **German measles** contagious disease accompanied by red spots

germinate v (cause to) sprout or begin to grow

gestation n carrying of young in womb

gesticulate v use expressive movements of hands and arms when speaking

gesture n/v (make) movement to convey meaning

get v getting, got obtain; catch; cause to go or come; bring into position or state; induce; be in possession of, have (to do); become

geyser n hot spring throwing up spout of water; water heater

ghastly adj deathlike; Inf horrible ~adv sickly

gherkin n small pickled cucumber

ghetto n (pl **-tos**) densely populated (esp. by one racial group) slum area **ghetto blaster** Inf large portable cassette recorder

ghost n dead person appearing again; spectre; faint trace **ghostly** adj

——————— T H E S A U R U S ———————

gentle amiable, benign, bland, humane, kind, kindly, lenient, meek, merciful, mild, peaceful, placid, quiet, soft, tender; balmy, calm, clement, easy, light, low, mild, moderate, muted, placid, quiet, serene, slight, smooth, soft, soothing, temperate, tranquil, untroubled

genuine actual, authentic, honest, legitimate, natural, original, pure, real, sound, sterling, true, veritable

germ bug Inf, microbe, microorganism, virus; beginning, bud, cause, embryo, origin, root, rudiment, seed, source, spark

germinate bud, develop, grow, originate, shoot, sprout, swell

gesture n action, indication, motion, sign, signal ~v indicate, motion, sign, signal, wave

get achieve, acquire, attain, bring, come by, earn, fetch, gain, glean, inherit, make, net, obtain, pick up, procure, realize, reap, receive, secure, succeed to, win; arrest, capture, catch, collar Inf, grab, nab Inf, nail Inf, seize, take, trap; arrive, come, reach; arrange, contrive, fix, manage, succeed; coax, convince, induce, influence, persuade, sway, wheedle, win over; become, come to be, grow, turn, wax

ghastly ashen, cadaverous, deathlike, dreadful, frightful, grim, grisly, gruesome, hideous, horrible, livid, loathsome, pale, pallid, repellent, shocking, spectral, terrible, terrifying, wan

ghost apparition, phantom, revenant, soul, spectre, spirit, spook Inf, wraith

ghostly eerie, illusory, insubstantial, phantom, spectral, spooky Inf, supernatural, uncanny, unearthly, weird

ghoul *n* malevolent spirit; person with morbid interests **ghoulish** *adj*

giant *n* mythical being of superhuman size; very tall person, plant etc. ~*adj* huge **gigantic** *adj* enormous, huge

gibber *v* make meaningless sounds with mouth **gibberish** *n* meaningless speech or words

gibbon *n* type of ape

gibe, jibe *v/n* jeer

giblets *pl n* internal edible parts of fowl

giddy *adj* dizzy; liable to cause dizziness; flighty

gift *n* thing given, present; faculty, power **gifted** *adj* talented

gig *n* performance by pop or jazz musicians

gigantic *see* GIANT

giggle *v* laugh nervously, foolishly ~*n* such a laugh

gild *v* **gilding, gilded, gilt** *or* **gilded** put thin layer of gold on **gilt** *n* thin layer of gold put on **gilt-edged** *adj* guaranteed

gill[1] *n* (*usu. pl*) breathing organ in fish

gill[2] *n* liquid measure, quarter of pint (0.142 litres)

gimmick *n* stratagem etc., esp. designed to attract attention or publicity

gin *n* spirit flavoured with juniper berries

ginger *n* plant with hot-tasting spicy root; the root ~*v* stimulate **gingerbread** *n* cake flavoured with ginger

gingerly *adv* cautiously

gingham *n* cotton cloth, usu. checked

gingivitis *n* inflammation of gums

ginseng *n* plant root used as tonic

Gipsy *see* GYPSY

giraffe *n* Afr. animal with very long neck

gird *v* **girding, girded** *or* **girt** put belt round; prepare (oneself) **girder** *n* large beam

girdle *n* corset; waistband

girl *n* female child; young (unmarried) woman **girlfriend** *n* man's female companion

giro *n* system operated by banks and post offices for the transfer of money

girth *n* measurement round thing;

──────── T H E S A U R U S ────────

giant *n* colossus, leviathan, monster, titan ~*adj* colossal, elephantine, enormous, gargantuan, gigantic, huge, immense, large, mammoth, monstrous, prodigious, vast

gibberish babble, balderdash, double talk, drivel, garbage *Inf*, gobbledegook *Inf*, jabber, jargon, mumbo jumbo, nonsense, twaddle

gibe, jibe *n* barb, crack *Sl*, derision, dig, jeer, mockery, ridicule, sarcasm, scoffing, sneer, taunt

giddy dizzy, faint, light-headed, reeling, unsteady, vertiginous

gift benefaction, bequest, bounty, contribution, donation, grant, gratuity, hand-out, legacy, offering, present; ability, aptitude, attribute, bent, capability, capacity, faculty, flair, ge-

nius, knack, power, talent

gifted able, accomplished, adroit, brilliant, capable, clever, expert, ingenious, intelligent, masterly, skilled, talented

gigantic colossal, elephantine, enormous, gargantuan, giant, huge, immense, mammoth, monstrous, prodigious, stupendous, tremendous, vast

giggle *v/n* chortle, chuckle, laugh, snigger, titter

gimmick contrivance, device, dodge, gadget, gambit, ploy, scheme, stratagem, stunt, trick

gird belt, bind, girdle

girdle band, belt, cummerbund, fillet, sash, waistband

girl bird *Sl*, damsel, daughter, female child, lass, lassie *Inf*, maid, maiden,

band put round horse to hold saddle etc.

gist *n* substance, main point (of remarks etc.)

give *n* giving, **gave**, **given** make present of; deliver; assign; utter; yield, give way ~*n* yielding, elasticity

glacé *adj* crystallized; iced

glacier *n* slow-moving river of ice **glacial** *adj*

glad *adj* pleased; happy **gladden** *v* make glad **gladly** *adv*

glade *n* grassy space in forest

gladiator *n* trained fighter in Roman arena

gladiolus *n* (*pl* -**li**) kind of iris, with sword-shaped leaves

glamour *n* alluring charm, fascination **glamorous** *adj*

glance *v* look rapidly or briefly; glide

off something struck ~*n* brief look

gland *n* organ controlling different bodily functions by chemical means **glandular** *adj*

glare *v* look fiercely; shine intensely ~*n* glaring **glaring** *adj* conspicuous

glass *n* hard transparent substance; things made of it; tumbler; its contents; *pl* spectacles **glassy** *adj* like glass; expressionless

glaucoma *n* eye disease

glaze *v* furnish with glass; cover with glassy substance; become glassy ~*n* transparent coating; substance used for this **glazier** *n* one who glazes windows

gleam *n*/*v* (give out) slight or passing beam of light

glean *v* pick up; gather

glee *n* mirth, merriment **gleeful** *adj*

———————— THESAURUS ————————

miss, wench

girth bulk, measure, size

gist core, drift, essence, force, idea, import, marrow, meaning, nub, pith, point, sense, substance

give accord, administer, allow, award, bestow, commit, confer, consign, contribute, deliver, donate, entrust, furnish, grant, permit, present, provide, supply; allow, cede, concede, devote, grant, hand over, lend, relinquish, surrender, yield

glad cheerful, chuffed *Sl*, contented, delighted, gay, gleeful, gratified, happy, jocund, jovial, joyful, overjoyed, pleased, willing

gladden cheer, delight, enliven, exhilarate, hearten, please, rejoice

gladly cheerfully, freely, gaily, gleefully, happily, joyfully, merrily, readily, willingly

glamorous alluring, attractive, beautiful, captivating, charming, dazzling, elegant, enchanting, entrancing, exciting, fascinating, glittering, glossy, lovely, prestigious, smart

glamour allure, appeal, attraction, beauty, charm, enchantment, fascination, prestige

glance *v* gaze, glimpse, look, peep, scan, view ~*n* dekko *Sl*, gander *Inf*, glimpse, look, peek, peep, quick look, squint, view

glare *v* frown, glower, lower, scowl; blaze, dazzle, flame, flare ~*n* black look, dirty look, frown, glower, lower, scowl; blaze, brilliance, dazzle, flame, glow

glaring audacious, blatant, conspicuous, flagrant, gross, manifest, obvious, open, outstanding, overt, patent, rank, visible

glassy clear, glossy, icy, shiny, slick, slippery, smooth, transparent

glaze *v* burnish, coat, enamel, gloss, lacquer, polish, varnish ~*n* coat, enamel, finish, gloss, lacquer, lustre, patina, polish, shine, varnish

gleam *n* beam, flash, glow, ray, sparkle ~*v* flare, flash, glance, glimmer, glint, glisten, glitter, glow, shimmer, shine, sparkle

glen *n* narrow valley

glib *adj* fluent but insincere or superficial

glide *v* pass smoothly and continuously ~*n* smooth, silent movement

glider *n* aircraft without engine

glimmer *v* shine faintly ~*n* faint light

glimpse *n* brief view ~*v* catch glimpse of

glint *v/n* flash

glisten *v* gleam by reflecting light

glitter *v* shine with bright quivering light, sparkle ~*n* lustre; sparkle

gloat *v* regard with smugness or malicious satisfaction

globe *n* sphere with map of earth or stars; ball **global** *adj* relating to whole world; total, comprehensive

globule *n* small round drop

glockenspiel *n* percussion instrument played with hammers

gloom *n* darkness; melancholy **gloomy** *adj*

glory *n* renown; splendour; heavenly

———————— THESAURUS ————————

glee cheerfulness, delight, elation, exultation, fun, gaiety, gladness, hilarity, jollity, joy, joyfulness, liveliness, merriment, mirth, triumph, verve

gleeful cheerful, chirpy *Inf,* cock-a-hoop, delighted, elated, exuberant, exultant, gay, happy, jovial, joyful, jubilant, merry, overjoyed

glib artful, easy, fluent, plausible, quick, ready, slick, smooth, suave, voluble

glide coast, drift, float, flow, fly, roll, run, sail, skate, skim, slide, slip, soar

glimmer *v* blink, flicker, gleam, glisten, glitter, glow, shimmer, shine, sparkle, twinkle ~*n* blink, flicker, gleam, glow, shimmer, sparkle, twinkle

glimpse *n* brief view, gander *Inf,* glance, look, peek, peep, quick look, sight, sighting ~*v* espy, sight, spot, spy, view

glint *v* flash, gleam, glimmer, glitter, shine, sparkle, twinkle ~*n* flash, gleam, glimmer, glitter, shine, sparkle

glisten flash, gleam, glimmer, glint, glitter, shimmer, shine, sparkle, twinkle

glitter *v* coruscate, flare, flash, gleam, glimmer, glint, glisten, scintillate, shimmer, shine, sparkle, twinkle ~*n* beam, brightness, flash, glare, gleam, lustre, radiance, sheen, shimmer, shine, sparkle

gloat crow, exult, glory, relish, revel in, rub it in *Inf,* triumph, vaunt

global international, planetary, universal, worldwide; all-inclusive, all-out, comprehensive, encyclopedic, exhaustive, general, thorough, total, unbounded, unlimited

globe ball, earth, orb, planet, round, sphere, world

globule bead, bubble, drop, droplet, particle

gloom blackness, cloud, cloudiness, dark, darkness, dimness, dullness, dusk, murk, murkiness, obscurity, shade, shadow, twilight; blues, dejection, depression, despair, despondency, low spirits, melancholy, misery, sadness, sorrow, unhappiness, woe

gloomy black, dark, dim, dismal, dreary, dull, dusky, murky, obscure, overcast, shadowy, sombre; bad, black, cheerless, depressing, disheartening, dispiriting, dreary, joyless, sad, sombre; blue, cheerless, dejected, despondent, dispirited, down, downcast, downhearted, glum, melancholy, miserable, moody, morose, pessimistic, sad

glorify adorn, augment, dignify, elevate, enhance, ennoble, illuminate, immortalize, lift up, magnify, raise; celebrate, eulogize, extol, hymn, laud, lionize, magnify, praise

bliss ~*v* **glorying, gloried** take pride (in) **glorify** *v* **-ifying, -ified** make glorious; praise **glorious** *adj* illustrious; splendid; *Inf* delightful **gloriously** *adv*

gloss[1] *n* surface shine, lustre ~*v* put gloss on; (*esp. with* **over**) (try to) cover up, pass over (fault, error) **glossy** *adj* smooth, shiny

gloss[2] *n* interpretation of word; comment ~*v* interpret; comment **glossary** *n* dictionary of special words

glove *n* covering for the hand ~*v* cover as with glove

glow *v* give out light and heat without flames; be or look hot ~*n* shining heat **glow-worm** *n* insect giving out light

glower *v*/*n* scowl

glucose *n* type of sugar found in fruit etc.

glue *n*/*v* (fasten with) sticky substance

gluey *adj*

glum *adj* sullen, gloomy

glut *n* surfeit, excessive amount ~*v* **glutting, glutted** feed, gratify to the full or to excess

glutton *n* greedy person; one with great liking or capacity for something **gluttonous** *adj* **gluttony** *n*

glycerine, glycerol *n* colourless sweet liquid

GMT Greenwich Mean Time

gnarled *adj* knobby, twisted

gnash *v* grind (teeth) together as in anger or pain

gnat *n* small, biting fly

gnaw *v* bite or chew steadily

gnome *n* legendary creature like small old man

gnu *n* oxlike antelope

go *v* **going, went, gone** move along; depart; function; fare; fail; elapse; be

——————————— THESAURUS ———————————

glorious celebrated, distinguished, elevated, eminent, excellent, famed, famous, grand, honoured, illustrious, magnificent, majestic, noble, noted, renowned, sublime, triumphant; *Inf* delightful, enjoyable, excellent, fine, great, heavenly *Inf*, marvellous, pleasurable, splendid, wonderful

glory *n* celebrity, dignity, distinction, eminence, exaltation, fame, honour, immortality, kudos, praise, prestige, renown; grandeur, greatness, magnificence, majesty, nobility, pageantry, pomp, splendour, sublimity, triumph ~*v* boast, crow, exult, gloat, relish, revel, triumph

gloss[1] *n* brightness, brilliance, burnish, gleam, lustre, polish, sheen, shine, varnish, veneer ~*v* camouflage, conceal, cover up, disguise, hide, mask, veil

gloss[2] annotation, commentary, explanation, footnote, note, scholium, translation

glossy bright, brilliant, burnished,

glassy, glazed, lustrous, polished, shining, shiny, sleek, smooth

glow *v* brighten, burn, gleam, glimmer, redden, shine, smoulder; blush, colour, fill, flush, radiate, thrill, tingle ~*n* brightness, brilliance, burning, effulgence, gleam, glimmer, light, radiance, splendour, vividness

glower frown, glare, lour *or* lower, scowl

glue *n* adhesive, cement, gum, paste ~*v* affix, cement, fix, gum, paste, seal, stick

glum crestfallen, crusty, dejected, doleful, down, gloomy, gruff, grumpy, ill-humoured, low, moody, morose, saturnine, sour, sulky, sullen

glut excess, oversupply, saturation, superfluity, surfeit, surplus

glutton gannet *Sl*, gobbler, gorger, gormandizer, gourmand, pig *Inf*

gluttony greed, piggishness, rapacity, voraciousness, voracity

gnaw bite, chew, munch, nibble, worry

able to be put; become ~*n* going; energy; attempt; turn **go-between** *n* intermediary

goad *n* spiked stick for driving cattle; anything that urges to action ~*v* urge on; torment

goal *n* end of race; object of effort; posts through which ball is to be driven in football etc.; the score so made

goat *n* animal with long hair, horns and beard **goatee** *n* small pointed beard

gobble[1] *v* eat hastily, noisily or greedily

gobble[2] *n/v* (make) cry of turkey

gobbledegook, gobbledygook *n* unintelligible language

goblet *n* drinking cup

goblin *n Folklore* small, usu. malevolent being

god *n* (*fem* **goddess**) superhuman being worshipped as having supernatural power; object of worship, idol; (*with cap.*) the Supreme Being, creator and ruler of universe **godly** *adj* devout, pious **godfather** *n* (*fem* **godmother**) sponsor at baptism **godforsaken** *adj* desolate, dismal **godsend** *n* something unexpected but welcome

goggle *v* (of eyes) bulge; stare ~*pl n* protective spectacles

go-kart *or* **go-cart** *n* miniature, low-powered racing car

gold *n* yellow precious metal; coins of this; colour of gold ~*adj* of, like gold **golden** *adj* **golden wedding** fiftieth wedding anniversary **goldfinch** *n* bird with yellow feathers **goldfish** *n* any of various ornamental pond or aquarium fish

golf *n* outdoor game in which small ball is struck into holes **golfer** *n*

gondola *n* Venetian canal boat **gondolier** *n* rower of gondola

gong *n* metal plate which sounds when struck with soft mallet

good *adj* **better, best** commendable; right; beneficial; well-behaved; virtuous; sound; valid ~*n* benefit; well-being; profit; *pl* property; wares **goodly** *adj* large, considerable **goodness** *n* **goodwill** *n* kindly feeling

go *v* advance, decamp, depart, journey, leave, move, pass, proceed, repair, set off, travel, withdraw; function, move, operate, perform, run, work; develop, eventuate, fall out, fare, happen, proceed, result, turn out, work out; elapse, expire, flow, lapse, pass, slip away ~*n* attempt, bid, effort, essay, shot *Inf*, stab *Inf*, try, turn, whack *Inf*

goad *n* impetus, incentive, incitement, irritation, motivation, pressure, spur, stimulation, stimulus, urge ~*v* annoy, arouse, drive, egg on, exhort, harass, hound, impel, incite, instigate, irritate, lash, prick, prod, prompt, propel, spur, stimulate, sting, urge, worry

goal aim, ambition, design, destination, end, intention, limit, mark, object, objective, purpose, target

gobble bolt, cram, devour, gorge, gulp, guzzle, stuff, swallow, wolf

go-between agent, broker, dealer, factor, intermediary, liaison, mediator

godforsaken abandoned, backward, bleak, deserted, desolate, dismal, dreary, forlorn, gloomy, lonely, remote

godly devout, god-fearing, good, holy, pious, religious, righteous, saintly

godsend blessing, windfall

golden blond *or* blonde, bright, brilliant, flaxen, shining, yellow

good *adj* admirable, capital, choice, commendable, excellent, fine, first-

goodbye *interj/n* form of address on parting

gooey *adj Inf* sticky, soft

goose *n* (*pl* **geese**) web-footed bird; its flesh; simpleton

gooseberry *n* thorny shrub; its hairy fruit

gore[1] *n* (dried) blood from wound **gory** *adj*

gore[2] *v* pierce with horns

gorge *n* ravine; disgust, resentment ~*v* feed greedily

gorgeous *adj* splendid, showy

gorilla *n* largest anthropoid ape, found in Africa

gormless *adj Inf* stupid

gorse *n* prickly shrub

gosling *n* young goose

gospel *n* unquestionable truth; (*with cap.*) any of first four books of New Testament

gossamer *n* filmy substance like spider's web

gossip *n* idle (malicious) talk about other persons; one who talks thus ~*v* engage in gossip

gouge *v* scoop out; force out ~*n* chisel with curved cutting edge

goulash *n* stew seasoned with paprika

gourd *n* large fleshy fruit; its rind as vessel

gourmand *n* glutton

gourmet *n* connoisseur of wine, food; epicure

gout *n* disease with inflammation, esp. of joints

govern *v* rule, control; determine **governess** *n* woman teacher, esp. in private household **government** *n* exercise of political authority in directing a people, state etc.; system by which community is ruled; governing group; control **governor** *n* one who governs; chief administrator of an institution; member of committee responsible for an organization or institution

gown *n* loose flowing outer garment;

——————— **THESAURUS** ———————

class, first-rate, great, pleasant, pleasing, splendid, superior, valuable, worthy; decorous, dutiful, mannerly, obedient, orderly, polite, proper, seemly, well-behaved; admirable, estimable, ethical, exemplary, honest, honourable, moral, praiseworthy, right, righteous, upright, virtuous, worthy; able, accomplished, adept, adroit, capable, clever, competent, dexterous, efficient, expert, first-rate, proficient, reliable, satisfactory, serviceable, skilled, sound, suitable, talented, thorough, useful; authentic, bona fide, dependable, genuine, honest, legitimate, proper, real, reliable, sound, true, trustworthy, valid ~*n* advantage, avail, behalf, benefit, gain, interest, profit, service, use, usefulness, welfare, wellbeing, worth

goodbye adieu, farewell, parting

goodness excellence, merit, quality,

superiority, value, worth; benevolence, friendliness, generosity, good will, graciousness, kindness, mercy; honesty, honour, integrity, merit, morality, probity, rectitude, uprightness, virtue

gorge[1] *n* canyon, cleft, defile, fissure, pass, ravine ~*v* bolt, cram, devour, feed, fill, glut, gobble, gulp, guzzle, overeat, surfeit, swallow, wolf

gorgeous beautiful, brilliant, dazzling, elegant, glittering, grand, luxuriant, magnificent, opulent, ravishing, showy, splendid, stunning *Inf,* sumptuous, superb

gossip *n* chitchat, hearsay, idle talk, prattle, scandal, small talk, tittle-tattle; blether, busybody, chatterbox *Inf,* scandalmonger, tattler, telltale ~*v* blether, chat, gabble, prate, prattle, tattle

govern administer, command, con-

woman's (long) dress; official robe

GP General Practitioner

grab v **grabbing, grabbed** grasp suddenly; snatch ~n sudden clutch; quick attempt to seize

grace n charm, elegance; goodwill, favour; sense of propriety; postponement granted; short thanksgiving for meal ~v add grace to, honour **graceful** adj **gracious** adj kind; condescending

grade n step, stage; class; rating; slope ~v arrange in classes; assign grade to **gradation** n series of steps; each of them

gradient n (degree of) slope

gradual adj taking place by degrees; slow and steady; not steep **gradually** adv

graduate v take university degree; divide into degrees ~n holder of university degree **graduation** n

graffiti pl n (oft. obscene) writing, drawing on walls

graft[1] n shoot of plant set in stalk of another; the process; surgical transplant of skin, tissue ~v insert (shoot) in another stalk; transplant (living tissue in surgery)

graft[2] n Inf hard work; self-

duct, control, direct, guide, hold sway, lead, manage, order, oversee, pilot, reign, rule, steer, supervise

government administration, authority, dominion, law, rule, sovereignty, state, statecraft; administration, executive, ministry, regime; authority, command, control, direction, domination, guidance, management, regulation, restraint, supervision, sway

governor administrator, chief, commander, controller, director, executive, head, leader, manager, overseer, ruler, supervisor

gown costume, dress, frock, garb, garment, habit, robe

grab bag, capture, catch, clutch, grasp, grip, pluck, seize, snap up, snatch

grace n beauty, charm, ease, elegance, finesse, loveliness, pleasantness, poise, polish, refinement; benefaction, beneficence, benevolence, favour, generosity, goodness, good will, kindness; cultivation, decency, decorum, etiquette, manners, propriety, tact; charity, clemency, compassion, forgiveness, indulgence, leniency, mercy, pardon, quarter, reprieve; benediction, blessing, prayer, thanks, thanksgiving ~v adorn, beautify, be-

deck, deck, decorate, dignify, distinguish, elevate, embellish, enhance, enrich, favour, garnish, glorify, honour, ornament, set off

graceful agile, beautiful, becoming, charming, comely, easy, elegant, fine, flowing, natural, pleasing, smooth, tasteful

gracious affable, amiable, beneficent, benevolent, benign, charitable, chivalrous, civil, compassionate, considerate, cordial, courteous, friendly, hospitable, indulgent, kind, lenient, loving, merciful, mild, obliging, pleasing, polite, well-mannered

grade n brand, category, class, condition, degree, echelon, group, level, mark, notch, order, place, position, quality, rank, rung, size, stage, station, step ~v arrange, brand, class, classify, evaluate, group, order, range, rank, rate, sort, value

gradient bank, grade, hill, incline, rise, slope

gradual even, gentle, graduated, moderate, piecemeal, progressive, regular, slow, steady, unhurried

gradually bit by bit, by degrees, evenly, gently, moderately, piecemeal, progressively, slowly, steadily

graduate v calibrate, grade, mark off,

advancement, profit by unfair means

grain n (seed, fruit of) cereal plant; small hard particle; very small unit of weight; arrangement of fibres; any very small amount

gram, gramme n one thousandth of a kilogram

grammar n science of structure and usages of language; use of words **grammatical** adj **grammar school** state-maintained secondary school providing academic education

gramophone n record player

gran, granny n Inf grandmother

granary n storehouse for grain

grand adj magnificent; noble; splendid; eminent **grandeur** n nobility; magnificence; dignity **grandiose** adj imposing; affectedly grand **grandchild** n child of one's child **grandson, granddaughter** n **grandparent** n parent of parent **grandfather, grandmother** n **grandstand** n structure with tiered seats for spectators

granite n hard crystalline rock

grant v consent to fulfil (request); permit; admit ~n sum of money provided for specific purpose, esp. education; gift; allowance, concession

granule n small grain

grape n small fruit, used to make wine **grapevine** n grape-bearing plant; Inf unofficial way of spreading news

grapefruit n subtropical citrus fruit

graph n drawing depicting relation of different numbers, quantities etc.

graphic adj vividly descriptive; of writing, drawing, painting etc. ~pl n diagrams etc. used on television, computer screen etc.

graphite n form of carbon (used in pencils)

grapple v wrestle; struggle

grasp v (try, struggle to) seize hold; understand ~n grip; comprehension **grasping** adj greedy, avaricious

grass n common type of plant with

measure out, proportion, regulate

grain cereals, corn; grist, kernel, seed

grand ambitious, august, dignified, elevated, eminent, exalted, fine, glorious, great, haughty, illustrious, imposing, impressive, lofty, lordly, luxurious, magnificent, majestic, noble, opulent, palatial, pompous, princely, regal, splendid, stately

grandeur dignity, greatness, importance, loftiness, magnificence, majesty, nobility, pomp, splendour, state

grandiose affected, ambitious, bombastic, extravagant, flamboyant, pompous, pretentious, showy

grant v accede to, accord, acknowledge, admit, agree to, allocate, allot, allow, assign, award, bestow, cede, concede, confer, consent to, donate, give, impart, permit, present, yield ~n admission, allocation, allotment, allowance, award, bequest, bounty,

concession, donation, endowment, gift, present, subsidy

graphic clear, descriptive, detailed, explicit, expressive, forcible, illustrative, lively, lucid, picturesque, striking, telling, vivid, well-drawn; diagrammatic, drawn, illustrative, pictorial, representational, seen, visible, visual

grasp v catch, clasp, clinch, clutch, grab, grapple, grip, hold, lay or take hold of, seize, snatch; comprehend, follow, realize, see, take in, understand ~n clasp, clutches, embrace, grip, hold, possession, tenure; comprehension, knowledge, mastery, perception, realization, understanding

grasping acquisitive, avaricious, close-fisted, covetous, greedy, mean, miserly, niggardly, penny-pinching Inf, rapacious, selfish, stingy, tight-

jointed stems and long narrow leaves; such plants grown as lawn; pasture; *Sl* marijuana; *Sl* informer **grassy** *adj* **grasshopper** *n* jumping, chirping insect **grass roots** ordinary members of group

grate¹ *n* framework of metal bars for holding fuel in fireplace **grating** *n* framework of bars covering opening

grate² *v* rub into small bits on rough surface; rub with harsh noise; irritate **grater** *n* utensil with rough surface for reducing substance to small particles **grating** *adj* harsh; irritating

grateful *adj* thankful; appreciative; pleasing **gratefully** *adv* **gratitude** *n* sense of being thankful

gratify *v* **-ifying, -ified** satisfy; please **gratification** *n*

gratis *adv/adj* free, for nothing

gratuitous *adj* given free; uncalled for **gratuity** *n* gift of money for services rendered, tip

grave¹ *n* hole dug to bury corpse **graveyard** *n*

grave² *adj* serious; solemn

grave³ *n* accent (`) over letter

gravel *n* small stones; coarse sand **gravelly** *adj*

graven *adj* carved, engraved

gravitate *v* move by gravity; tend (towards) centre of attraction; sink, settle down

gravity *n* force of attraction of one body for another, esp. of objects to the earth; heaviness; importance; seriousness

gravy *n* juices from meat in cooking; sauce made from these

graze¹ *v* feed on grass, pasture

graze² *v* touch lightly in passing, scratch, scrape ~*n* grazing; abrasion

grease *n* soft melted fat of animals; thick oil as lubricant ~*v* apply grease to **greasy** *adj* **greasepaint** *n* theatrical make-up

great *adj* large; important; preeminent; *Inf* excellent ~*comb. form* one degree further removed in relationship, as in **great-grandfather** **greatly** *adv*

greed *n* excessive consumption of,

———— THESAURUS ————

fisted, venal

grate creak, grind, rasp, rub, scrape, scratch; annoy, chafe, exasperate, fret, gall, irk, irritate, jar, nettle, peeve, rankle, vex

grateful appreciative, indebted, obliged, thankful

gratify delight, favour, fulfil, give pleasure, gladden, humour, indulge, pander to, please, recompense, thrill

gratitude appreciation, indebtedness, obligation, recognition, thanks

gratuitous free, unasked-for, unpaid, unrewarded, voluntary

gratuity benefaction, bonus, bounty, donation, gift, largess *or* largesse, present, reward, tip

grave¹ crypt, mausoleum, pit, sepulchre, tomb, vault

grave² acute, critical, crucial, danger-

ous, hazardous, important, momentous, perilous, pressing, serious, severe, threatening, vital, weighty; dignified, dour, dull, earnest, gloomy, muted, quiet, serious, sober, solemn, sombre, staid, subdued, thoughtfu

graveyard burial ground, cemetery, churchyard, necropolis

gravity acuteness, exigency, importance, moment, seriousness, severity, significance, urgency, weightiness

greasy fatty, oily, slick, slimy, slippery

great big, bulky, colossal, enormous, extensive, gigantic, huge, immense, large, mammoth, stupendous, tremendous, vast, voluminous; consequential, critical, crucial, grave, important, momentous, serious, significant, weighty; celebrated, distin-

desire for, food, wealth **greedy** *adj*

green *adj* of colour between blue and yellow; grass-coloured; unripe; inexperienced; envious *~n* colour; area of grass, esp. for playing bowls etc; *pl* green vegetables **greenery** *n* vegetation **greenfly** *n* aphid, small green garden pest **greengrocer** *n* dealer in vegetables and fruit **greenhouse** *n* glass building for rearing plants

greet *v* meet with expressions of welcome; salute; receive **greeting** *n*

gregarious *adj* sociable

gremlin *n* imaginary being blamed for mechanical malfunctions

grenade *n* bomb thrown by hand or shot from rifle **grenadier** *n* soldier in Grenadier Guards

grenadine *n* syrup made from pomegranate juice, for sweetening and colouring drinks

grey *adj* between black and white; clouded; turning white; aged; intermediate, indeterminate *~n* grey colour

greyhound *n* swift slender dog

grid *n* network of horizontal and vertical lines, bars etc.; any interconnecting system of links

griddle *n* flat iron plate for cooking

gridiron *n* frame of metal bars for grilling

grief *n* deep sorrow **grievance** *n* real or imaginary cause for complaint

grieve *v* feel grief; cause grief to **grievous** *adj* painful, oppressive; very serious

grill *n* device on cooker to radiate heat

———————— **THESAURUS** ————————

guished, eminent, exalted, excellent, famed, famous, glorious, illustrious, notable, outstanding, pre-eminent, prominent, remarkable, renowned; admirable, cracking *Brit inf*, excellent, fantastic *Inf*, fine, first-rate, good, marvellous *Inf*, superb, terrific *Inf*, tremendous *Inf*, wonderful

greatly abundantly, by much, considerably, enormously, exceedingly, extremely, highly, hugely, immensely, mightily, much, notably, powerfully, remarkably, vastly, very much

greed gluttony, hunger, piggishness, ravenousness, voracity; avidity, covetousness, cupidity, desire, eagerness, longing, rapacity, selfishness

greedy gluttonous, hungry, insatiable, piggish, ravenous, voracious; acquisitive, avaricious, avid, covetous, craving, desirous, eager, grasping, hungry, impatient, rapacious, selfish

green *adj* blooming, budding, fresh, grassy, leafy, new, undecayed, verdant; fresh, immature, new, raw, recent, unripe *~n* common, grassplot,

lawn, sward, turf

greet accost, address, hail, meet, receive, salute, welcome

greeting address, hail, reception, salute, welcome

grey ashen, bloodless, colourless, livid, pale, pallid, wan; cheerless, clouded, cloudy, dark, depressing, dim, dismal, drab, dreary, dull, foggy, gloomy, misty, murky, overcast, sunless; aged, ancient, elderly, mature, old, venerable

grief agony, anguish, bereavement, dejection, distress, grievance, heartache, heartbreak, misery, mourning, pain, regret, remorse, sadness, sorrow, suffering, trial, tribulation, woe

grievance complaint, damage, distress, gripe *Inf*, hardship, injury, injustice, resentment, sorrow, trial, tribulation, trouble, wrong

grieve ache, bemoan, bewail, complain, deplore, lament, mourn, regret, rue, sorrow, suffer, wail, weep; afflict, agonize, crush, distress, hurt, injure, pain, sadden, wound

grievous calamitous, damaging, dis-

downwards; food cooked under grill;
gridiron ~v cook (food) under grill;
subject to severe questioning

grille n grating

grim adj stern; relentless; joyless

grimace n/v (pull) wry face

grime n ingrained dirt, soot **grimy** n

grin v/n **grinning, grinned** (give)
broad smile

grind v **grinding, ground** crush to
powder; make sharp, smooth; grate
~n Inf hard work; action of grinding

grip n firm hold; mastery; handle;
travelling bag ~v **gripping, gripped**
hold tightly; hold attention of

gripe v Inf complain (persistently) ~n
intestinal pain (esp. in infants); Inf
complaint

grisly adj causing terror

grist n corn to be ground

gristle n cartilage, tough flexible tis-

sue found in meat

grit n rough particles of sand; courage
~v **gritting, gritted** clench (teeth)

grizzle v Inf whine

grizzled adj grey (haired)

grizzly n large Amer. bear

groan v/n (make) low, deep sound of
grief or pain

grocer n dealer in foodstuffs **gro-
ceries** pl n commodities sold by a
grocer **grocery** n trade, premises of
grocer

grog n spirit (esp. rum) and water

groggy adj Inf shaky, weak

groin n fold where legs meet abdomen

groom n person caring for horses;
bridegroom ~v tend or look after;
brush or clean (esp. horse); train

groove n narrow channel; routine ~v
cut groove in

——————— T H E S A U R U S ———————

tressing, dreadful, grave, harmful,
heavy, hurtful, injurious, lamentable,
oppressive, painful, severe; deplorable, dreadful, flagrant, glaring, heinous, intolerable, lamentable, monstrous, offensive, outrageous, shameful, shocking, unbearable

grim cruel, ferocious, fierce, forbidding, formidable, frightful, ghastly,
grisly, gruesome, harsh, hideous,
horrible, horrid, merciless, morose,
relentless, resolute, ruthless, severe,
shocking, sinister, stern, sullen, surly,
terrible

grimace face, frown, mouth, scowl,
sneer, wry face

grime dirt, filth, smut, soot

grimy begrimed, besmeared, be-
smirched, dirty, filthy, foul, grubby,
smutty, soiled, sooty, unclean

grind v crush, granulate, grate, mill,
pound, powder, pulverize; gnash,
grate, grit, scrape ~n chore, drudgery, hard work, labour, task, toil

grip n clasp, purchase; control, domi-

nation, grasp, hold, influence, mastery, perception, possession, power,
tenure, understanding ~v clasp,
clutch, grasp, hold, seize; absorb,
catch up, compel, engross, enthral,
entrance, fascinate, hold, involve,
mesmerize, rivet, spellbind

grisly abominable, appalling, awful,
dreadful, frightful, ghastly, grim,
gruesome, hideous, horrid, macabre,
terrible

grit dust, gravel, sand; backbone,
courage, fortitude, gameness, guts
Inf, mettle, nerve, perseverance,
pluck, resolution, spirit, tenacity,
toughness

groan v cry, grumble, moan, sigh,
whine ~n cry, moan, sigh, whine

groggy confused, dazed, dizzy, faint,
muzzy, punch-drunk, reeling, shaky,
stunned, unsteady, weak, woozy Inf

groom n stableboy, stableman ~v
clean, dress, smarten up, spruce up,
tidy, turn out; coach, drill, educate,
make ready, nurture, prepare, prime,

grope v feel about, search blindly

gross adj very fat; total, not net; coarse; flagrant ~n twelve dozen

grotesque adj (horribly) distorted; ugly or repulsive

grotto n (pl **-oes**) cave

grotty adj Inf nasty, in bad condition

grouch Inf n persistent grumbler; discontented mood ~v grumble

ground n surface of earth; soil, earth; reason; special area; pl dregs; enclosed land round house ~v establish; instruct; place on ground; run ashore **grounded** adj (of aircraft) unable or not permitted to fly **grounding** n basic knowledge of subject **groundless** adj without reason **groundwork** n preliminary work

group n number of persons or things together; small musical band; class ~v place, fall into group

grouse¹ n (pl **grouse**) game bird; its flesh

grouse² v grumble, complain ~n complaint

grout n thin fluid mortar ~v fill up with grout

grove n small group of trees

grovel v **-elling, -elled** abase oneself; lie face down

grow v **growing, grew, grown** develop naturally; increase; be produced; become by degrees; produce by cultivation **growth** n growing; increase; what has grown or is growing **grown-up** adj/n adult

growl v/n (make) low guttural sound of anger

——————— T H E S A U R U S ———————

ready, train

groove channel, cutting, flute, furrow, gutter, hollow, rut, score, trench

grope feel, finger, fish, flounder, fumble, grabble, search

gross adj big, bulky, corpulent, fat, great, heavy, hulking, large, massive, obese, overweight; aggregate, entire, total, whole; coarse, crude, improper, impure, indecent, indelicate, lewd, low, obscene, offensive, ribald, rude, sensual, unseemly, vulgar

grotesque bizarre, deformed, distorted, fantastic, freakish, incongruous, malformed, misshapen, odd, outlandish, ridiculous, strange, unnatural, weird

ground n clod, dirt, dry land, dust, earth, field, land, mould, sod, soil, terra firma, terrain, turf (oft. pl) area, country, district, domain, estate, fields, gardens, land, property, realm, terrain, tract ~v base, establish, fix, found, set, settle

groundless baseless, empty, false, idle, imaginary, uncalled-for, unfounded, unjustified, unsupported,

unwarranted

groundwork base, basis, footing, foundation, fundamentals, preliminaries, preparation, spadework

group n association, band, batch, bevy, bunch, category, circle, class, clique, clump, cluster, collection, company, coterie, crowd, faction, formation, gang, gathering, organization, pack, party, set, troop ~v arrange, assemble, associate, assort, bracket, class, classify, dispose, gather, marshal, order, organize, put together, range, sort

grovel abase oneself, bow and scrape, cower, crawl, creep, cringe, demean oneself, fawn, flatter, humble oneself, kowtow, pander to, toady

grow develop, flourish, shoot, spring up, sprout, vegetate; develop, enlarge, expand, extend, fill out, heighten, increase, multiply, spread, stretch, swell, thicken, widen; breed, cultivate, farm, produce, raise

grown-up adult, fully-grown, mature

growth development, enlargement, evolution, expansion, extension,

grub v grubbing, grubbed dig; root up; rummage ~n short, legless larva of certain insects; *Sl* food

grubby adj dirty

grudge v be unwilling to give, allow ~n ill will

gruel n food of oatmeal etc., boiled in milk or water

gruelling adj exhausting

gruesome adj horrible, grisly

gruff adj rough-voiced, surly

grumble v complain; rumble ~n complaint

grumpy adj ill-tempered, surly

grunt v/n (make) sound characteristic of pig

G-string n very small covering for genitals

guarantee n formal assurance (esp. in writing) that product etc. will meet certain standards ~v **guaranteeing, guaranteed** give guarantee; secure (against risk etc.) **guarantor** n

guard v protect, defend; take precautions (against) ~n person, group that protects; sentry; official in charge of train; protection **guarded** adj cautious, noncommittal **guardian** n keeper, protector; person having custody of infant etc.

guava n tropical tree with fruit used to make jelly

guerrilla, guerilla n member of irregular armed force

guess v estimate; conjecture; *US* think ~n conclusion reached by guessing

———————— THESAURUS ————————

growing, increase, multiplication; crop, cultivation, development, produce, shooting, sprouting, vegetation

grubby dirty, filthy, grimy, messy, mucky, scruffy, seedy, shabby, slovenly, smutty, soiled, sordid, squalid, unkempt, untidy, unwashed

grudge v begrudge, complain, covet, envy, mind, resent, stint ~n antipathy, aversion, bitterness, dislike, enmity, grievance, hate, ill will, malevolence, malice, pique, rancour, resentment, spite, venom

gruelling arduous, brutal, crushing, demanding, difficult, fierce, grinding, hard, harsh, laborious, punishing, severe, stiff, strenuous, taxing, tiring, trying

gruesome abominable, awful, fearful, ghastly, grim, grisly, horrendous, horrific, horrifying, macabre, repugnant, repulsive, shocking, terrible

gruff bearish, blunt, brusque, churlish, crabbed, crusty, curt, discourteous, grumpy, ill-humoured, ill-natured, impolite, rough, rude, sour, sullen, surly, uncivil, ungracious, unmannerly

grumble v beef *Sl*, bitch *Sl*, carp, complain, find fault, gripe *Inf*, grouse, moan, whine ~n beef *Sl*, complaint, grievance, gripe *Inf*, grouse, moan, objection

guarantee n assurance, bond, certainty, covenant, earnest, pledge, promise, security, surety, undertaking, warranty, word ~v answer for, assure, certify, insure, maintain, pledge, promise, protect, secure, swear, vouch for, warrant

guard v cover, defend, escort, keep, mind, oversee, patrol, police, protect, safeguard, save, screen, secure, shelter, shield, tend, watch, watch over ~n custodian, defender, lookout, picket, sentinel, sentry, warder, watch, watchman; buffer, bulwark, bumper, defence, pad, protection, rampart, safeguard, screen, security, shield

guardian champion, curator, custodian, defender, escort, guard, keeper, preserver, protector, trustee, warden, warder

guess v conjecture, estimate, fathom, predict, solve, speculate, work out ~n

guest *n* one entertained at another's house; one living in hotel

guffaw *n/v* (make) burst of boisterous laughter

guide *n* one who shows the way; adviser; book of instruction or information ~*v* lead, act as guide to **guidance** *n* **guideline** *n* set principle

guild *n* organization for mutual help, or with common object

guile *n* cunning, deceit

guillotine *n* machine for beheading; machine for cutting paper ~*v* use guillotine on

guilt *n* fact, state of having done wrong; responsibility for offence **guiltless** *adj* innocent **guilty** *adj* having committed an offence

guinea *n* formerly, sum of 21 shillings **guinea pig** rodent originating in S

Amer; *Inf* person or animal used in experiments

guise *n* external appearance, esp. one assumed

guitar *n* stringed instrument played by plucking or strumming **guitarist** *n*

gulf *n* large inlet of the sea; chasm; large gap

gull *n* long-winged web-footed sea bird

gullet *n* food passage from mouth to stomach

gullible *adj* easily imposed on, credulous

gully *n* channel or ravine worn by action of water

gulp *v/n* swallow; gasp

gum¹ *n* firm flesh in which teeth are set

gum² *n* sticky substance issuing from

——————— THESAURUS ———————

conjecture, feeling, hypothesis, judgment, notion, prediction, reckoning, speculation, supposition, surmise, suspicion, theory

guest boarder, company, lodger, visitor

guidance advice, conduct, control, counsel, direction, government, help, instruction, intelligence, leadership, management, teaching

guide *n* adviser, attendant, conductor, counsellor, director, escort, leader, mentor, monitor, pilot, steersman, teacher; catalogue, directory, handbook, instructions, key, manual ~*v* accompany, attend, conduct, convoy, direct, escort, lead, pilot, shepherd, steer, usher; advise, counsel, educate, govern, influence, instruct, regulate, rule, superintend, supervise, sway, teach, train

guild brotherhood, club, company, corporation, fellowship, fraternity, league, lodge, order, society, union

guile art, artifice, cleverness, craft, craftiness, cunning, deceit, decep-

tion, duplicity, knavery, ruse, treachery, trickery

guilt blame, delinquency, iniquity, misconduct, responsibility, sinfulness, wickedness, wrong, wrongdoing; bad conscience, contrition, disgrace, dishonour, infamy, regret, remorse, self-reproach, shame, stigma

guiltless blameless, clean *Sl*, clear, impeccable, innocent, irreproachable, pure, sinless, spotless, untainted, untarnished

guilty at fault, convicted, criminal, culpable, delinquent, erring, evil, felonious, offending, responsible, sinful, to blame, wicked, wrong

gulf bay, bight, sea inlet; abyss, breach, chasm, cleft, gap, rent, rift, split, void

gullible credulous, foolish, green, innocent, naive, silly, simple, trusting, unsophisticated, unsuspecting

gulp *v* bolt, devour, gobble, guzzle, knock back *Inf*, quaff, swallow, swig *Inf*, swill, toss off, wolf ~*n* draught,

certain trees; adhesive; chewing gum ~*v* **gumming, gummed** stick with gum **gumboots** *pl n* boots of rubber **gumtree** *n* any species of eucalypt

gumption *n* resourcefulness; shrewdness, sense

gun *n* weapon with metal tube from which missiles are discharged by explosion; cannon, pistol etc. ~*v* shoot; pursue vigorously **gunner** *n* **gunpowder** *n* explosive mixture of saltpetre, sulphur, charcoal **gunshot** *n* shot or range of gun ~*adj* caused by missile from gun

gunge *n Inf* any sticky, unpleasant substance

gunwale, gunnel *n* upper edge of ship's side

guppy *n* small colourful aquarium fish

gurgle *n/v* (make) bubbling noise

guru *n* spiritual teacher, esp. in India

gush *v* flow out suddenly and copiously, spurt ~*n* sudden and copious flow

gusset *n* triangle or diamond-shaped piece of material let into garment

gust *n* sudden blast of wind; burst of rain, anger, passion etc.

gusto *n* enjoyment, zest

gut *n* (*oft. pl*) intestines; material made from guts of animals, e.g. for violin strings etc. *pl Inf* courage ~*v* remove guts from (fish etc.); remove, destroy contents of (house)

gutter *n* shallow trough for carrying off water from roof or side of street

guttural *adj* harsh-sounding, as if produced in the throat

guy[1] *n* effigy of Guy Fawkes burnt on Nov. 5th; *Inf* person (usu. male) ~*v* make fun of; ridicule

guy[2] *n* rope, chain to steady, secure something, e.g. tent

guzzle *v* eat or drink greedily

gym *n short for* GYMNASIUM *or* GYMNASTICS

gymkhana *n* competition or display of horse riding

gymnasium *n* (*pl* -nasiums, -nasia) place equipped for muscular exercises, athletic training **gymnastics** *pl n* muscular exercises **gymnast** *n*

gynaecology *n* branch of medicine dealing with functions and diseases of women **gynaecologist** *n*

gypsum *n* chalklike mineral, used for making plaster

Gypsy *n* one of wandering race orig. from NW India

gyrate *v* move in circle, spiral

gyroscope *n* disc rotating on axis that can turn in any direction

———— THESAURUS ————

mouthful, swallow

gum adhesive, cement, exudate, glue, mucilage, paste, resin

gumption ability, acumen, common sense, enterprise, initiative, resourcefulness, sagacity, savvy *Sl*, shrewdness, spirit, wit(s)

gurgle *n* murmur, ripple ~*v* babble, bubble, burble, crow, lap, murmur, plash, purl, ripple, splash

gush *v* burst, cascade, flood, flow, jet, pour, run, rush, spout, spurt, stream ~*n* burst, cascade, flood, flow, jet, outburst, outflow, rush, spout, spurt, stream, torrent

gust blast, blow, breeze, flurry, gale, puff, rush, squall

gusto appetite, brio, delight, enjoyment, enthusiasm, fervour, liking, pleasure, relish, verve, zeal, zest

gutter channel, conduit, ditch, drain, duct, pipe, sluice, trench, trough

guttural deep, gravelly, gruff, hoarse, husky, low, rasping, rough, thick, throaty

guy *n Inf* bloke *Brit inf*, chap, fellow, lad, man, person, youth

guzzle bolt, cram, devour, drink, gobble, gorge, quaff, stuff (oneself), swill, wolf

H h

haberdasher *n* dealer in articles of dress, ribbons, pins, needles etc. **haberdashery** *n*

habit *n* settled tendency or practice; customary apparel, esp. of nun or monk **habitual** *adj* formed or acquired by habit; usual, customary

habitable *adj* fit to live in **habitat** *n* natural home (of animal etc.) **habitation** *n* abode

hack¹ *v* cut, chop (at) violently; *Inf* utter harsh, dry cough ~*n* violent blow **hacker** *n Sl* computer enthusiast who breaks into computer system of company or government

hack² *n* horse for ordinary riding; inferior writer

hackles *pl n* hairs on back of neck of dog and other animals which are raised in anger

hackneyed *adj* (of words etc.) stale, trite because of overuse

hacksaw *n* handsaw for cutting metal

haddock *n* large, edible sea fish

haemoglobin *n* colouring and oxygen-bearing matter of red blood corpuscles

haemophilia *n* illness in which blood does not clot **haemophiliac** *n*

haemorrhage *n* profuse bleeding

haemorrhoids *pl n* swollen veins in rectum

hag *n* ugly old woman; witch

haggard *adj* anxious, careworn

haggis *n* Scottish dish made from sheep's offal, oatmeal etc.

haggle *v* bargain over price

hail¹ *n* (shower of) pellets of ice; barrage ~*v* pour down as shower of hail **hailstone** *n*

hail² *v* greet; acclaim; call

hair *n* filament growing from skin of animal, as covering of man's head; such filaments collectively **hairy** *adj* **hairdo** *n* (*pl* -os) way of dressing hair **hairdresser** *n* one who cuts and styles hair **hairgrip** *n* small, tightly bent metal hairpin **hairpin** *n* pin for keeping hair in place **hairpin bend** U-shaped turn of road

hale *adj* robust, healthy

half *n* (*pl* halves) either of two equal

THESAURUS

habit bent, custom, disposition, manner, practice, propensity, quirk, tendency, way; custom, mode, practice, routine, rule, second nature, tradition, usage, wont; dress, garb, garment, riding dress

habitation abode, domicile, dwelling, home, house, lodging, pad *Sl*, quarters, residence

habitual accustomed, common, customary, familiar, fixed, natural, normal, ordinary, regular, routine, standard, traditional, usual

hack¹ chop, cut, gash, hew, kick, lacerate, mangle, mutilate, notch, slash

hack² penny-a-liner, scribbler

hackneyed banal, common, commonplace, overworked, stale, stereotyped, stock, threadbare, timeworn, tired, trite, unoriginal, worn-out

hag crone, fury, harridan, shrew, virago, vixen, witch

haggard careworn, drawn, emaciated, gaunt, pinched, shrunken, thin, wan, wasted

haggle bargain, barter

hail¹ *n* barrage, pelting, rain, shower, storm, volley ~*v* barrage, batter, pelt, rain, shower, storm, volley

hail² acclaim, acknowledge, applaud, cheer, exalt, glorify, greet, honour, salute, welcome

hair locks, mane, mop, shock, tresses

parts of thing ~*adj* forming half ~*adv*
to the extent of half **half-baked** *adj*
Inf poorly planned **half-breed, half-caste** *n* person with parents of differ-ent races **half-brother, -sister** *n* broth-er (or sister) by one parent only **half-hearted** *adj* unenthusiastic **halfwit** *n*
feeble-minded person

halibut *n* large edible flatfish

halitosis *n* bad-smelling breath

hall *n* (entrance) passage; large room
or building used for esp. public as-sembly

hallelujah *n/interj* exclamation of
praise to God

hallmark *n* mark used to indicate
standard of tested gold and silver;
mark of excellence; distinguishing
feature

hallo *interj see* HELLO

hallowed *adj* holy

hallucinate *v* suffer illusions **halluci-nation** *n* **hallucinatory** *adj*

halo *n* (*pl* **-loes**) circle of light

halt *n* interruption or end to progress
etc. (esp. as command to stop
marching) ~*v* (cause to) stop **halting**
adj hesitant, lame

halter *n* rope with headgear to fasten
horse; low-cut dress style with strap

passing behind neck; noose for hang-ing person

halve *v* cut in half; reduce to half;
share

ham *n* meat (esp. salted or smoked)
from thigh of pig; actor adopting ex-aggerated style; amateur radio enthu-siast **ham-fisted** *adj* clumsy

hamburger *n* fried cake of minced
beef

hamlet *n* small village

hammer *n* tool usu. with heavy head
at end of handle, for beating, driving
nails etc. ~*v* strike as with hammer

hammock *n* bed of canvas etc., hung
on cords

hamper[1] *n* large covered basket

hamper[2] *v* impede, obstruct

hamster *n* type of rodent, sometimes
kept as pet

hamstring *n* tendon at back of knee

hand *n* extremity of arm beyond
wrist; side; style of writing; cards
dealt to player; manual worker; help;
pointer of dial; applause ~*v* pass; de-liver; hold out **handful** *n* (*pl* **-fuls**)
small quantity; *Inf* person, thing
causing problems **handiness** *n* dex-terity; state of being near, available
handy *adj* convenient; clever with

———————— THESAURUS ————————

hale blooming, fit, flourishing,
healthy, hearty, robust, sound,
strong, vigorous

half *n* division, equal part, fifty per
cent, fraction, portion, section ~*adj*
divided, fractional, halved, incom-plete, limited, moderate, partial ~*adv*
all but, barely, inadequately, incom-pletely, in part, partially, partly,
slightly

half-hearted cool, indifferent, list-less, lukewarm, perfunctory, spirit-less, uninterested

hall corridor, entry, foyer, lobby, pas-sage, vestibule; auditorium, cham-ber, meeting place

halt *n* arrest, break, close, end, pause,
stand, standstill, stop, stoppage, ter-mination ~*v* break off, cease, close
down, desist, draw up, pull up, rest,
stand still, stop, wait

halting awkward, faltering, hesitant,
laboured, stumbling, stuttering

halve bisect, cut in half, divide equal-ly, split in two

hammer *v* bang, beat, drive, hit,
knock, strike

hamper *v* bind, cramp, curb, embar-rass, encumber, fetter, frustrate,
handicap, hinder, hold up, impede,
obstruct, prevent, restrict, slow
down, thwart

hands **handbag** *n* woman's bag **handbook** *n* small instruction book **handcuff** *n* fetter for wrist, usu. joined in pair ~*v* secure thus **handicraft** *n* manual occupation or skill **handiwork** *n* thing done by particular person **handkerchief** *n* small square of fabric for wiping nose etc. **hand-out** *n* thing given free; written information given out at talk etc. **handwriting** *n* way person writes **handyman** *n* man employed to do various tasks

handicap *n* something that hampers or hinders; race, contest in which chances are equalized; any physical disability ~*v* **-capping, -capped** hamper, impose handicaps on

handle *n* part of thing to hold it by ~*v* touch, feel with hands; manage; deal with; trade **handler** *n* person who controls animal **handlebars** *pl n* curved metal bar to steer cycle

handsome *adj* of fine appearance; generous; ample

hang *v* **hanging, hung** suspend; attach, set up (wallpaper, doors etc.); be suspended, cling; *(past hanged)* kill by suspension by neck **hanger** *n* frame on which clothes etc. can be hung **hangdog** *adj* sullen, dejected **hang-glider** *n* glider with light frame from which pilot hangs in harness **hangman** *n* person who executes people by hanging **hangover** *n* aftereffects of too much drinking **hang-up** *n* *Inf* emotional or psychological problem

hangar *n* large shed for aircraft

hanker *v* crave

hanky *n* *Inf* handkerchief

haphazard *adj* random, careless

hapless *adj* unlucky

happen *v* come about, occur; chance to do **happening** *n* occurrence, event

————— THESAURUS —————

hand *n* fist, palm; aid, assistance, help, support ~*v* deliver, pass; aid, assist, conduct, convey, give, guide, help, lead, present, transmit

handbook guide, instruction book, manual

handcuff fetter, manacle, shackle

handful few, small number, small quantity, smattering, sprinkling

handicap barrier, block, disadvantage, drawback, encumbrance, hindrance, impediment, limitation, obstacle, restriction, shortcoming; advantage, edge, head start, odds, penalty, upper hand; defect, disability, impairment

handcraft art, craft, handiwork, skill, workmanship

handiwork achievement, artefact, craft, creation, design, invention, product, production, result

handle *n* grip, haft, helve, hilt, knob, stock ~*v* feel, finger, fondle, grasp, hold, maul, poke, touch; control, direct, guide, manage, manipulate, manoeuvre, operate, steer, use, wield; administer, conduct, cope with, deal with, manage, supervise, treat

hand-out alms, charity, dole; bulletin, circular, leaflet

handsome admirable, attractive, becoming, comely, elegant, fine, good-looking, graceful

handwriting calligraphy, fist, hand, longhand, scrawl, script

handy accessible, available, close, convenient, near, nearby, within reach; convenient, helpful, manageable, neat, practical, serviceable, useful; adept, adroit, clever, deft, dexterous, expert, nimble, ready, skilful, skilled

hang dangle, depend, droop, incline, suspend; attach, cover, deck, decorate, drape, fasten, fix, furnish; adhere, cling, hold, rest, stick

happen appear, arise, come about, come to pass, develop, ensue, follow,

happy *adj* glad, content; lucky **happily** *adv* **happiness** *n*

harangue *n* vehement speech; tirade ~*v* address vehemently

harass *v* worry, torment **harassment** *n*

harbour *n* shelter for ships ~*v* give shelter; maintain (secretly)

hard *adj* firm, resisting pressure; solid; difficult to do, understand; unfeeling; heavy ~*adv* vigorously; persistently; close **harden** *v* **hardly** *adv* unkindly,

harshly; scarcely, not quite; only just **hardship** *n* ill luck; severe toil, suffering; instance of this **hard-headed** *adj* shrewd **hard-hearted** *adj* unfeeling **hard shoulder** motorway verge for emergency stops **hardware** *n* tools, implements; *Computers* mechanical and electronic parts **hardwood** *n* wood from deciduous trees

hardy *adj* robust, vigorous; bold; (of plants) able to grow in the open all the year round

——————— THESAURUS ———————

materialize, occur, result, transpire; chance, fall out, pan out *Inf,* supervene, turn out

happening accident, adventure, affair, case, chance, episode, event, experience, incident, occurrence, phenomenon

happily agreeably, contentedly, delightedly, enthusiastically, freely, gladly, heartily, willingly, with pleasure; auspiciously, favourably, fortunately, luckily, propitiously

happiness bliss, cheer, cheerfulness, contentment, delight, ecstasy, elation, enjoyment, gaiety, gladness, high spirits, joy, jubilation, merriment, satisfaction

happy blessed, blithe, cheerful, cock-a-hoop, content, contented, delighted, ecstatic, elated, glad, gratified, jolly, joyful, jubilant, merry, overjoyed, pleased, rapt, thrilled

harass annoy, badger, bait, bother, disturb, exasperate, exhaust, fatigue, harry, hound, perplex, persecute, pester, plague, tease, tire, torment, trouble, vex, weary, worry

harbour *n* destination, haven, port ~*v* conceal, hide, lodge, protect, provide refuge, relieve, secrete, shelter, shield

hard *adj* compact, dense, firm, inflexible, rigid, rocklike, solid, stiff, stony, strong, tough, unyielding; arduous, backbreaking, exacting, exhausting,

fatiguing, formidable, laborious, rigorous, strenuous, tough, uphill, wearying; baffling, complex, complicated, difficult, intricate, involved, knotty, perplexing, puzzling, tangled, thorny; callous, cold, cruel, exacting, grim, harsh, implacable, obdurate, pitiless, ruthless, severe, stern, strict, stubborn, unkind ~*adv* energetically, fiercely, forcefully, forcibly, heavily, intensely, powerfully, severely, sharply, strongly, vigorously, violently; assiduously, determinedly, diligently, doggedly, earnestly, industriously, intently, persistently, steadily, strenuously

harden bake, cake, freeze, set, solidify, stiffen; brace, buttress, fortify, gird, indurate, nerve, reinforce, steel, strengthen, toughen

hardly almost not, barely, by no means, faintly, infrequently, just, not at all, not quite, no way, only, only just, scarcely, with difficulty

hardship adversity, affliction, austerity, burden, calamity, destitution, difficulty, fatigue, grievance, labour, misery, misfortune, need, suffering, toil, torment, tribulation, trouble, want

hardy firm, fit, hale, healthy, hearty, lusty, robust, rugged, sound, stalwart, stout, strong, sturdy, tough, vigorous

hare n animal like large rabbit **harebell** n round-leaved bell-shaped flower **harebrained** adj rash, wild **harelip** n fissure of upper lip

harem n women's part of Muslim dwelling; one man's wives

hark v listen

harlequin n masked clown in diamond-patterned costume

harlot n whore, prostitute

harm n/v damage **harmful** adj **harmless** adj unable or unlikely to hurt

harmony n agreement; combination of notes to make chords; melodious sound **harmonic** adj of harmony **harmonica** n mouth organ **harmonious** adj **harmonium** n small organ **harmonize** v bring into harmony; cause to agree; reconcile; be in harmony

harness n equipment for attaching horse to cart, plough etc. ~v put on, in harness; utilize energy or power of

harp n musical instrument of strings played by hand ~v play on harp; dwell on continuously **harpsichord** n stringed instrument like piano

harpoon n/v (use) barbed spear for catching whales

harrier n hound used in hunting hares; falcon

harrow n implement for smoothing, levelling or stirring up soil ~v draw harrow over; distress greatly **harrowing** adj distressful

harry v **harrying, harried** harass; ravage

harsh adj rough, discordant; severe; unfeeling **harshly** adv

harvest n (season for) gathering grain; gathering; crop ~v reap and gather in **harvester** n

has third person sing. of HAVE **has-been** n Inf one who is no longer successful

hash n dish of chopped meat etc.; mess ~v cut up small, chop; mix up

hashish, hasheesh n resinous extract of Indian hemp, esp. used as hallucinogen

hassle ~n Inf quarrel; a lot of bother, trouble ~v bother

hassock n kneeling cushion

haste n speed, hurry ~v hasten **hasten** v (cause to) hurry **hastily** adv **hasty** adj

————————— THESAURUS —————————

harm n abuse, damage, detriment, hurt, ill, impairment, injury, loss, mischief, misfortune ~v abuse, blemish, damage, hurt, ill-treat, ill-use, impair, injure, maltreat, mar, molest, ruin, spoil, wound

harmful baleful, baneful, destructive, detrimental, evil, hurtful, injurious, noxious, pernicious

harmless gentle, innocent, innocuous, inoffensive, safe

harmonious agreeable, compatible, concordant, congruous, coordinated, dulcet, euphonious, matching, melodious, musical, tuneful

harmony accord, agreement, amicability, amity, assent, compatibility, concord, conformity, cooperation, friendship, like-mindedness, peace, rapport, sympathy, unity; euphony, melody, tune, tunefulness

harness n equipment, gear, tack, tackle, trappings ~v couple, hitch up, saddle, yoke; apply, channel, control, employ, exploit, utilize

harsh coarse, croaking, crude, discordant, dissonant, glaring, grating, guttural, jarring, rasping, raucous, rough, strident; abusive, austere, bitter, bleak, brutal, cruel, dour, grim, hard, relentless, ruthless, severe, sharp, stern, unfeeling, unkind, unpleasant

harvest ingathering, reaping; crop, produce, yield

hash hotchpotch, jumble, mess, mixup, muddle, pig's ear Inf, shambles

haste briskness, celerity, dispatch, ex-

hat *n* head covering usu. with brim **hat trick** set of three achievements

hatch[1] *v* (of young birds etc.) (cause to) emerge from egg; contrive, devise **hatchery** *n*

hatch[2] *n* hatchway; trapdoor over it; opening in wall, to facilitate service of meals etc. **hatchback** *n* car with lifting rear door **hatchway** *n* opening in deck of ship etc.

hatchet *n* small axe

hate *v* dislike strongly; bear malice towards ~*n* this feeling; that which is hated **hateful** *adj* detestable **hatred** *n*

haughty *adj* proud, arrogant **haughtily** *adv*

haul *v* pull, drag with effort ~*n* hauling; quantity of something obtained

haulage *n* **haulier** *n*

haunch *n* human hip or fleshy hindquarter of animal

haunt *v* visit regularly; visit in form of ghost; recur to ~*n* place frequently visited **haunted** *adj* frequented by ghosts; worried **haunting** *adj* extremely beautiful or sad

have *v* (*present tense I, we, you, they* **have**, *he, she* **has**; *present participle* **having**; *past tense and past participle* **had**) hold, possess; be affected with; be obliged (to do); cheat; obtain; contain; allow; cause to be done; give birth to; as auxiliary, forms perfect and other tenses

haven *n* place of safety

haversack *n* canvas bag for provi-

pedition, fleetness, quickness, rapidity, speed, swiftness, urgency; bustle, hurry, hustle, impetuosity, rashness, recklessness, rush

hasten bolt, dash, fly, haste, race, run, rush, scurry, scuttle, speed, sprint

hastily apace, fast, promptly, quickly, rapidly, speedily; hurriedly, impetuously, impulsively, rashly, recklessly, too quickly

hasty brisk, eager, fast, fleet, hurried, prompt, rapid, speedy, swift, urgent; foolhardy, headlong, heedless, impetuous, impulsive, precipitate, rash, reckless

hatch breed, brood, incubate; conceive, concoct, contrive, design, devise, manufacture, plan, plot, project, scheme

hate *v* abhor, abominate, despise, detest, dislike, execrate, ~*n* abhorrence, abomination, antagonism, antipathy, aversion, detestation, dislike, enmity, execration, hatred, hostility, loathing, odium

hateful abominable, despicable, detestable, disgusting, execrable, foul,

horrible, loathsome, obnoxious, odious, offensive, repellent, repugnant, repulsive, revolting, vile

hatred animosity, animus, antagonism, antipathy, aversion, detestation, dislike, enmity, execration, hate, ill will, odium, repugnance, revulsion

haughty arrogant, conceited, disdainful, high, imperious, lofty, overweening, proud, scornful, snobbish, supercilious

haul *v* drag, draw, hale, heave, lug, pull, tow, trail, tug ~*n* booty, catch, find, gain, harvest, loot, spoils, takings, yield

haunt *v* frequent, repair, resort, visit; beset, come back, obsess, plague, possess, prey on, recur, torment, trouble ~*n* rendezvous, resort

haunting eerie, evocative, nostalgic, poignant, unforgettable

have hold, keep, obtain, occupy, own, possess, retain; endure, enjoy, experience, feel, meet with, suffer, sustain, undergo **have to** be bound, be compelled, be forced, be obliged, must, ought, should

sions etc. carried on back

havoc n devastation, ruin; *Inf* confusion, chaos

hawk[1] n bird of prey smaller than eagle; advocate of warlike policies

hawk[2] v offer (goods) for sale, esp. in street **hawker** n

hawthorn n thorny shrub or tree

hay n grass mown and dried **hay fever** allergic reaction to pollen, dust etc. **haystack** n large pile of hay **haywire** *adj* crazy; disorganized

hazard n chance; risk, danger ~v expose to risk; run risk of **hazardous** *adj* risky

haze n mist; obscurity **hazy** *adj* misty; vague

hazel n bush bearing nuts ~*adj* light brown

he *pron* (*third person masc*) person, animal already referred to; *comb. form* male, as in **he-goat**

head n upper part of body, containing mouth, sense organs and brain; upper part of anything; chief of or-

ganization, school etc.; chief part; aptitude, capacity; crisis; person, animal considered as unit ~*adj* chief, principal; (of wind) contrary ~v be at the top; lead; provide with head; hit (ball) with head; make for; form a head **heading** n title **heady** *adj* apt to intoxicate or excite **headache** n continuous pain in head **headland** n area of land jutting into sea **headlight** n powerful lamp on front of vehicle etc. **headline** n news summary, in large type in newspaper **headlong** *adv* in rush **headphones** *pl* n two small loudspeakers strapped against ears **headquarters** *pl* n centre of operations **head start** advantage **headstrong** *adj* self-willed **headway** n progress

heal v make or become well **health** n soundness of body; condition of body; toast drunk in person's honour **healthy** *adj* **health food** vegetarian food etc., eaten for dietary value

heap n pile; great quantity ~v pile,

————————— THESAURUS —————————

haven asylum, refuge, retreat, sanctuary, shelter

havoc damage, desolation, destruction, devastation, ravages, ruin, slaughter, waste, wreck; chaos, confusion, disorder, disruption, mayhem, shambles

hazardous dangerous, difficult, insecure, perilous, precarious, risky, unsafe

haze cloud, film, fog, mist, obscurity, smokiness, steam, vapour

hazy blurry, cloudy, dim, dull, faint, foggy, misty, nebulous, obscure, overcast, smoky, veiled; fuzzy, indefinite, indistinct, loose, muddled, nebulous, uncertain, unclear, vague

head n pate, skull; apex, crest, crown, height, peak, pitch, summit, tip, top, vertex; captain, chief, chieftain, commander, director, leader, manager,

master, principal, supervisor; ability, aptitude, brain, capacity, faculty, flair, intellect, mind, talent, thought ~*adj* arch, chief, first, foremost, front, highest, leading, main, premier, prime, principal, supreme, topmost ~v be *or* go first, cap, crown, lead, precede, top; command, control, direct, govern, guide, lead, manage, rule, run, supervise

heading caption, headline, name, rubric, title

headlong hastily, heedlessly, helter-skelter, hurriedly, pell-mell, precipitately, rashly, wildly

headstrong contrary, heedless, impulsive, intractable, obstinate, perverse, rash, reckless, self-willed, stiff-necked, stubborn, ungovernable, unruly, wilful

headway advance, improvement,

load with

hear v **hearing, heard** perceive sound by ear; listen to; *Law* try (case); heed; learn **hearing** n ability to hear; earshot; judicial examination **hearsay** n rumour

hearken v listen

hearse n funeral carriage for coffin

heart n organ which makes blood circulate; seat of emotions and affections; mind, soul, courage; central part; suit at cards **hearten** v make, become cheerful **heartless** adj unfeeling **hearty** adj friendly; vigorous; in good health; satisfying **heart attack** sudden severe malfunction of heart **heartbeat** n single pulsation of heart

heartbreak n intense grief **heartfelt** adj felt sincerely **heart-rending** adj agonizing **by heart** by memory

hearth n part of room where fire is made; home

heat n hotness; sensation of this; hot weather; warmth of feeling, anger etc.; sexual excitement in female animals; one of many eliminating races etc. ~v make, become hot **heated** adj angry **heater** n

heath n tract of waste land

heathen adj/n (pl **heathens, heathen**) (one) not adhering to a religious system; pagan

heather n shrub growing on heaths and mountains

———— THESAURUS ————

progress, way

heal cure, make well, mend, remedy, restore, treat

health fitness, robustness, soundness, strength, vigour, wellbeing

healthy active, blooming, fit, flourishing, hale, hardy, robust, sound, strong, sturdy, vigorous, well

heap n accumulation, collection, hoard, lot, mass, mound, mountain, pile, stack, store ~v accumulate, amass, augment, bank, collect, gather, hoard, increase, mound, pile, stack, stockpile, store

hear attend, catch, eavesdrop, hark, heed, listen to, overhear; *Law* examine, investigate, judge, try; ascertain, be informed, discover, find out, gather, learn, pick up, understand

hearing audition, ear, perception; audience, audition, interview; inquiry, investigation, review, trial

hearsay buzz, gossip, report, rumour, talk

heart affection, benevolence, compassion, concern, humanity, love, pity, tenderness, understanding; boldness, bravery, courage, mettle, mind, nerve, pluck, purpose, resolution,

spirit, will; centre, core, crux, essence, hub, kernel, marrow, middle, nucleus, pith, quintessence, root

heartfelt ardent, cordial, deep, devout, earnest, fervent, genuine, honest, profound, sincere, unfeigned, warm

heartless brutal, callous, cold, cruel, hard, harsh, inhuman, merciless, pitiless, uncaring, unfeeling, unkind

hearty affable, ardent, cordial, eager, effusive, friendly, generous, genial, jovial, unreserved, warm; active, energetic, hale, hardy, healthy, robust, sound, strong, vigorous, well

heat n fever, sultriness, swelter, torridity, warmness, warmth; agitation, ardour, excitement, fervour, fever, fury, intensity, passion, vehemence, violence, warmth, zeal ~v flush, glow, grow hot, make hot, reheat, warm up

heated angry, bitter, excited, fierce, fiery, frenzied, furious, intense, passionate, raging, stormy, vehement, violent

heathen adj godless, heathenish, idolatrous, infidel, irreligious, pagan ~n idolater, infidel, pagan, unbeliever

heave *v* lift (and throw) with effort; utter (sigh); swell, rise; feel nausea ~*n* act of heaving

heaven *n* abode of God; place of bliss; (*also pl*) sky **heavenly** *adj*

heavy *adj* weighty; dense; sluggish; severe; sorrowful; serious; dull **heavily** *adv*

heckle *v* interrupt (speaker) by questions, taunts etc.

hectare *n* one hundred ares or 10,000 square metres (2,471 acres)

hectic *adj* rushed, busy

hedge *n* fence of bushes ~*v* surround with hedge; be evasive; secure against loss **hedgehog** *n* small animal covered with spines

hedonism *n* pursuit of pleasure **hedonist** *n*

heed *v* take notice of **heedless** *adj* careless

heel¹ *n* hind part of foot; part of shoe supporting this; *Sl* undesirable person ~*v* supply with heel

heel² *v* lean to one side

hefty *adj* bulky; weighty; strong

heifer *n* young cow

height *n* measure from base to top; quality of being high; elevation; highest degree; (*oft. pl*) hilltop **heighten** *v* make higher; intensify

heinous *adj* atrocious, extremely wicked, detestable

heir *n* (*fem* **heiress**) person entitled to inherit property or rank **heirloom** *n* thing that has been in family for generations

helicopter *n* aircraft lifted by rotating blades

helium *n* very light, nonflammable gaseous element

helix *n* (*pl* **helices, helixes**) spiral

hell *n* abode of the damned; abode of the dead generally; place of torture **hellish** *adj* **hell-bent** *adj* intent

hello *also* **hallo** *interj* expression of

——————— THESAURUS ———————

heave drag, elevate, haul, hoist, lever, lift, pull, raise, tug; cast, fling, hurl, pitch, send, sling, throw, toss

heaven bliss, dreamland, ecstasy, enchantment, happiness, paradise, rapture, transport, utopia

heavenly *Inf* beautiful, blissful, delightful, entrancing, exquisite, glorious, lovely, rapturous, ravishing, sublime, wonderful

heavy bulky, massive, ponderous, portly, weighty; apathetic, drowsy, dull, inactive, indolent, inert, listless, slow, sluggish, stupid, torpid, wooden; burdensome, difficult, grievous, hard, harsh, intolerable, laborious, onerous, oppressive, severe, tedious, vexatious, wearisome

heckle boo, disrupt, interrupt, jeer, pester, shout down, taunt

hectic boisterous, chaotic, excited, fevered, feverish, flurrying, frantic, frenetic, frenzied, heated, riotous, turbulent, wild

hedge *n* hedgerow, quickset ~*v* border, edge, enclose, fence, surround; dodge, duck, equivocate, evade, flannel *Brit inf*, prevaricate, quibble, sidestep, temporize

heed attend, consider, follow, listen to, mark, mind, note, obey, observe, regard

heedless careless, imprudent, inattentive, negligent, oblivious, rash, reckless, thoughtless

height altitude, elevation, highness, loftiness, stature; apex, apogee, crest, crown, hill, mountain, peak, pinnacle, summit, top, vertex, zenith; acme, dignity, eminence, exaltation, grandeur, loftiness, prominence

heighten add to, aggravate, amplify, augment, enhance, improve, increase, intensify, magnify, sharpen, strengthen

hell abyss, infernal regions, inferno,

greeting or surprise

helm *n* tiller, wheel for turning ship's rudder

helmet *n* defensive or protective covering for head

help *v/n* aid; support; remedy **helper** *n* **helpful** *adj* **helping** *n* single portion of food **helpless** *adj* incompetent; unaided; unable to help

helter-skelter *adv/adj/n* (in) hurry and confusion ~*n* high spiral slide at fairground

hem *n* edge of cloth, folded and sewn down ~*v* **hemming, hemmed** sew thus; confine, shut in

hemisphere *n* half sphere; half of the earth

hemlock *n* poisonous plant

hemp *n* Indian plant; its fibre used for rope etc.; any of several narcotic drugs

hen *n* female of domestic fowl and others **henpecked** *adj* (of man) dominated by wife

hence *adv* from this point; for this reason **henceforward, henceforth** *adv*

from now onwards

henchman *n* trusty follower

henna *n* flowering shrub; reddish dye made from it

hepatitis *n* inflammation of the liver

heptagon *n* figure with seven angles

her *pron* object of SHE ~*adj* of, belonging to her **hers** *pron* of her **herself** *pron* emphatic or reflexive form of SHE

herald *n* messenger, envoy ~*v* announce **heraldic** *adj* **heraldry** *n* study of (right to have) heraldic bearings

herb *n* plant used in cookery or medicine **herbaceous** *adj* of, like herbs; perennial flowering **herbal** *adj* **herbicide** *n* chemical which destroys plants **herbivore** *n* animal that feeds on plants **herbivorous** *adj*

herd *n* company of animals feeding together ~*v* crowd together; tend (herd) **herdsman** *n*

here *adv* in this place; at or to this point **hereabouts** *adv* near here **hereafter** *adv* in time to come ~*n* future existence **hereby** *adv* as a result of this **herein** *adv* in this place **herewith**

———— T H E S A U R U S ————

underworld; agony, anguish, martyrdom, misery, nightmare, ordeal, suffering, torment, trial, wretchedness

hellish damnable, damned, devilish, diabolical, fiendish, infernal

help *v* abet, aid, assist, back, befriend, cooperate, encourage, promote, relieve, save, second, serve, stand by, succour, support; alleviate, ameliorate, cure, ease, facilitate, heal, improve, mitigate, relieve, remedy, restore ~*n* advice, aid, assistance, avail, benefit, cooperation, guidance, service, support, use, utility

helper aide, ally, assistant, attendant, collaborator, colleague, deputy, helpmate, mate, partner, second, supporter

helpful beneficial, constructive, favourable, fortunate, practical, pro-

ductive, profitable, serviceable, timely, useful; beneficent, benevolent, caring, friendly, kind, supportive, sympathetic

helping *n* piece, plateful, portion, ration, serving

helpless disabled, feeble, impotent, incapable, incompetent, infirm, paralysed, powerless, unfit, weak

hem border, edge, fringe, margin, trimming

herald *n* crier, messenger ~*v* advertise, announce, broadcast, proclaim, publish, trumpet

herd *n* collection, crowd, crush, drove, flock, horde, mass, mob, multitude, press, swarm, throng ~*v* assemble, associate, collect, congregate, flock, gather, huddle, muster, rally

adv with this

heredity *n* tendency of organism to transmit its nature to its descendants **hereditary** *adj* descending by inheritance or heredity

heresy *n* unorthodox opinion or belief **heretic** *n* **heretical** *adj*

heritage *n* what may be or is inherited

hermaphrodite *n* person or animal with characteristics, or reproductive organs, of both sexes

hermetic *adj* sealed so as to be airtight **hermetically** *adj*

hermit *n* one living in solitude **hermitage** *n* hermit's dwelling

hernia *n* projection of organ through lining

hero *n* (*pl* **heroes**, *fem* **heroine**) one greatly regarded for achievements or qualities; principal character in story **heroic** *adj* **heroism** *n*

heroin *n* highly addictive drug

heron *n* long-legged wading bird

herring *n* important food fish

hertz *n* (*pl* **hertz**) SI unit of frequency

hesitate *v* hold back; feel, or show indecision; be reluctant **hesitancy**,

hesitation *n* **hesitant** *adj*

hessian *n* coarse jute cloth

heterogeneous *adj* composed of diverse elements **heterogeneity** *n*

heterosexual *n/adj* (person) sexually attracted to members of the opposite sex

hew *v* **hewing, hewed, hewed** or **hewn** chop, cut with axe; carve

hexagon *n* figure with six angles **hexagonal** *adj*

hey *interj* expression of surprise or for catching attention

heyday *n* bloom, prime

hiatus *n* (*pl* **hiatuses, hiatus**) break or gap

hibernate *v* pass the winter, esp. in a torpid state **hibernation** *n*

hiccup, hiccough *n/v* (have) spasm of the breathing organs with an abrupt sound

hickory *n* N Amer. nut-bearing tree; its tough wood

hide¹ *v* **hiding, hid, hidden** or **hid** put, keep out of sight; conceal oneself

hide² *n* skin of animal **hiding** *n Sl* thrashing **hidebound** *adj* restricted; narrow-minded

————————————— THESAURUS —————————————

hereafter after this, from now on, henceforth, in future

hereditary family, genetic, inborn, inbred, inheritable

heresy apostasy, error, impiety, schism, unorthodoxy

heretic apostate, dissenter, renegade, sectarian, separatist

heritage bequest, birthright, endowment, estate, inheritance, legacy, lot, patrimony, portion, share, tradition

hermit anchorite, eremite, monk, recluse, solitary

hero celebrity, champion, exemplar, great man, idol, star, superstar, victor; leading man, male lead, protagonist

heroic bold, brave, courageous, dar-

ing, doughty, fearless, gallant, intrepid, undaunted, valiant

heroism boldness, bravery, courage, daring, fearlessness, fortitude, gallantry, prowess, spirit, valour

hesitant diffident, doubtful, half-hearted, halting, irresolute, reluctant, sceptical, shy, timid, uncertain, unsure, vacillating, wavering

hesitate be uncertain, delay, dither *chiefly Brit,* doubt, pause, vacillate, wait, waver

hew axe, chop, cut, hack, lop, split; carve, fashion, form, make, model, sculpt, sculpture, shape, smooth

heyday bloom, flowering, pink, prime, salad days

hide cache, conceal, hole up, lie low,

hideous *adj* repulsive, revolting

hierarchy *n* system of persons or things arranged in graded order **hierarchical** *adj*

hieroglyphic *adj* of picture writing, as used in ancient Egypt ~*n* symbol representing object, concept or sound

hi-fi *adj* short for HIGH-FIDELITY ~*n* high-fidelity equipment

high *adj* tall, lofty; far up; (of sound) acute in pitch; expensive; of great importance, quality, or rank; *Inf* in state of euphoria ~*adv* at, to a height **highly** *adv* **highness** *n* quality of being high; (with cap.) title of royal person **highbrow** *n/adj* intellectual **high-fidelity** *adj* of high-quality sound reproducing equipment **high-handed** *adj* domineering **highlands** *pl n* area of relatively high ground **highlight** *n*

outstanding feature ~*v* emphasize **highly strung** excitable, nervous **high-rise** *adj* of building that has many storeys **high-tech** *adj* using sophisticated technology **high time** latest possible time **highway** *n* main road; ordinary route **highwayman** *n* formerly, horseman who robbed travellers

hijack *v* divert or wrongfully take command of a vehicle (esp. aircraft) **hijacker** *n*

hike *v* walk a long way (for pleasure) in country; pull (up), hitch **hiker** *n*

hilarity *n* cheerfulness, gaiety **hilarious** *adj*

hill *n* natural elevation, small mountain; mound **hillock** *n* little hill **hilly** *adj*

hilt *n* handle of sword etc.

him *pron* object of HE **himself** *pron* em-

secrete, stash *Inf,* take cover; bury, cloak, conceal, cover, disguise, eclipse, mask, obscure, screen, shelter, shroud, veil

hidebound conventional, narrow-minded, rigid, set

hideous ghastly, grim, grisly, grotesque, gruesome, monstrous, repulsive, revolting, ugly, unsightly

hiding *n* beating, caning, drubbing, flogging, spanking, thrashing, whipping

high *adj* elevated, lofty, soaring, steep, tall, towering; arch, chief, eminent, exalted, important, influential, leading, notable, powerful, prominent, ruling, significant, superior; acute, penetrating, piercing, piping, sharp, shrill, soprano, strident, treble; costly, dear, expensive, high-priced ~*adv* aloft, at great height, far up, way up

highbrow *n* aesthete, intellectual, mastermind, savant, scholar ~*adj* bookish, cultivated, cultured, deep

high-handed arbitrary, autocratic,

despotic, domineering, imperious, oppressive, overbearing

highlight *n* climax, feature, focus, peak ~*v* accent, emphasize, feature, set off, show up, spotlight, stress, underline

highly decidedly, eminently, extraordinarily, extremely, greatly, immensely, supremely, tremendously, vastly, very, very much

hijack commandeer, expropriate, seize, skyjack, take over

hike *v* back-pack, ramble, tramp, walk ~*n* march, ramble, tramp, trek, walk

hilarious amusing, comical, convivial, entertaining, funny, gay, happy, humorous, jolly, jovial, joyful, merry, noisy

hilarity amusement, cheerfulness, exhilaration, exuberance, gaiety, glee, high spirits, jollity, joyousness, laughter, merriment, mirth

hill elevation, eminence, fell, height, knoll, mound, mount, prominence, tor

phatic form of HE

hind[1] *n* female of deer

hind[2] *adj* at the back, posterior

hinder *v* obstruct, impede, delay **hindrance** *n*

hinge *n* movable joint, as that on which door hangs ~*v* attach with hinge; depend on

hint *n* slight indication; piece of advice; small amount ~*v* give hint

hinterland *n* district lying behind coast, port etc.

hip *n* either side of body below waist and above thigh; fruit of rose

hippie *n* person who rejects conventional dress and lifestyle

hippopotamus *n* (*pl* **-muses, -mi**) large Afr. animal living in rivers

hire *v* obtain temporary use of by payment; engage for wage ~*n* hiring or being hired; payment for use of thing

hire-purchase *n* purchase of goods by instalments

hirsute *adj* hairy

his *pron/adj* belonging to him

hiss *v* make sharp sound of letter *s*; express disapproval thus ~*n* hissing

history *n* (record of) past events; study of these **historian** *n* **historic** *adj* **historical** *adj*

histrionic *adj* excessively theatrical, insincere, artificial in manner **histrionics** *pl n* behaviour like this

hit *v* **hitting, hit** strike with blow or missile; affect injuriously; find; light (upon) ~*n* blow; success **hit man** hired assassin

hitch *v* fasten with loop etc.; raise with jerk; be caught or fastened ~*n* difficulty; knot; jerk **hitchhike** *v* travel by begging free rides **hitchhiker** *n*

hither *adv* to this place **hitherto** *adv*

——————— THESAURUS ———————

hinder arrest, check, debar, delay, deter, encumber, hamper, handicap, impede, interrupt, obstruct, oppose, prevent, retard, stop, thwart

hindrance bar, barrier, block, check, deterrent, difficulty, drag, drawback, encumbrance, handicap, hitch, impediment, limitation, obstacle, snag, stoppage

hinge *v* depend, hang, pivot, rest, turn

hint *n* clue, implication, indication, inkling, innuendo, intimation, mention, reminder, suggestion, tip-off; advice, help, pointer, suggestion, tip; breath, dash, *soupçon*, speck, suggestion, suspicion, taste, tinge, touch, trace, whiff, whisper ~*v* allude, cue, imply, indicate, intimate, mention, prompt, suggest, tip off

hire *v* charter, engage, lease, let, rent; appoint, employ, engage, sign up, take on ~*n* charge, cost, fee, price, rent, rental

hiss *v* rasp, shrill, sibilate, wheeze,

whirr, whistle, whiz; boo, catcall, condemn, damn, decry, deride, hoot, jeer, mock, revile, ridicule ~*n* buzz, hissing, sibilance; boo, catcall, contempt, derision, jeer

historic celebrated, extraordinary, famous, momentous, notable, outstanding, remarkable, significant

history account, annals, chronicle, memoirs, narration, narrative, recital, record, relation, saga, story

hit *v* bang, batter, beat, cuff, deck *Sl*, flog, knock, lay one on *Sl*, lob, punch, slap, smack, sock *Sl*, strike, swat, thump, whack ~*n* blow, bump, clash, cuff, impact, knock, rap, shot, slap, smack, stroke; *Inf* sellout, sensation, success, triumph, winner

hitch *v* attach, connect, couple, fasten, harness, join, make fast, tether, tie, unite, yoke ~*n* catch, check, delay, difficulty, drawback, hassle *Inf*, hindrance, hold-up, impediment, mishap, obstacle, problem, snag, stoppage, trouble

up to now

HIV human immunodeficiency virus

hive *n* structure in which bees live **hive off** transfer

hives *pl n* eruptive skin disease

HM His (*or* Her) Majesty

HMS His (*or* Her) Majesty's Service *or* Ship

hoard *n* store, esp. hidden ~*v* amass and hide

hoarding *n* large board for displaying advertisements

hoarse *adj* sounding husky

hoary *adj* grey with age; greyish-white; very old **hoarfrost** *n* frozen dew

hoax *n* practical joke ~*v* play trick upon

hob *n* top area of cooking stove

hobble *v* walk lamely; tie legs together ~*n* limping gait

hobby *n* favourite occupation as pastime **hobbyhorse** *n* favourite topic; toy horse

hobgoblin *n* mischievous fairy

hobnob *v* -nobbing, -nobbed drink together; be familiar (with)

hobo *n* (*pl* -bos) *US & Canad* shiftless, wandering person

hock[1] *n* backward-pointing joint on leg of horse etc.

hock[2] *n* dry white wine

hockey *n* team game played on a field with ball and curved sticks; *US & Canad* ice hockey

hod *n* small trough for carrying bricks etc.; coal scuttle

hoe *n* tool for weeding, breaking ground etc. ~*v* **hoeing, hoed** work with hoe

hog *n* pig; greedy person ~*v* **hogging, hogged** *Inf* eat, use (something) selfishly

hoist *v* raise aloft, raise with tackle etc.

hold[1] *v* **holding, held** keep in hands; maintain in position; contain; occupy; carry on; detain; be in force; occur ~*n* grasp; influence **holdall** *n* large travelling bag **holder** *n* **holding** *n* (*oft. pl*) property **hold-up** *n* armed robbery; delay

hold[2] space in ship or aircraft for cargo

———— THESAURUS ————

hitherto heretofore, previously, so far, thus far, till now, until now, up until now

hoard *n* cache, fund, heap, mass, pile, reserve, stockpile, store, supply ~*v* accumulate, amass, buy up, cache, collect, deposit, garner, gather, hive, lay up, put by, save, stockpile, store, treasure

hoarse croaky, grating, gravelly, growling, gruff, guttural, harsh, husky, rasping, raucous, rough, throaty

hoax cheat, deception, fraud, imposture, joke, practical joke, prank, ruse, swindle, trick

hobby activity, diversion, pastime, relaxation, sideline

hoist elevate, erect, heave, lift, raise, rear, upraise

hold *v* adhere, clasp, cleave, clinch, cling, clutch, cradle, embrace, enfold, grasp, grip, stick; have, keep, maintain, occupy, own, possess, retain; accommodate, comprise, contain, seat, take; assemble, call, carry on, celebrate, conduct, convene, have, run; arrest, bind, check, confine, curb, detain, imprison, pound, restrain, stay, stop, suspend ~*n* clasp, clutch, grasp, grip; authority, control, dominance, influence, sway

holder bearer, custodian, incumbent, keeper, occupant, owner, possessor, proprietor, purchaser

hold-up bottleneck, delay, difficulty, hitch, obstruction, setback, snag, stoppage, trouble, wait

hole *n* hollow place; perforation; opening; *Inf* unattractive place **holey** *adj*

holiday *n* day(s) of rest from work etc., esp. spent away from home

holistic *adj* considering the complete person, esp. in treatment of disease

hollow *adj* having a cavity, not solid; empty; insincere ~*n* cavity, hole, valley ~*v* make hollow; excavate

holly *n* evergreen shrub with prickly leaves and red berries

hollyhock *n* tall plant bearing many large flowers

holocaust *n* great destruction of life, esp. by fire

hologram *n* three-dimensional photographic image

holster *n* leather case for pistol, hung from belt etc.

holy *adj* belonging, devoted to God; free from sin; divine; consecrated **holily** *adv* **holiness** *n*

homage *n* tribute, respect

home *n* dwelling-place; residence ~*adj* of home; native; in home ~*adv* to, at one's home; to the point ~*v* direct or be directed onto a point or target **homeless** *adj* **homelessness** *n* **homely** *adv* unpretentious; domesti-

cated **homeward** *adj/adv* **homewards** *adv* **home-made** *adj* **homesick** *adj* depressed by absence from home **homesickness** *n* **homespun** *adj* domestic; simple **homestead** *n* house with outbuildings, esp. on farm **homework** *n* school work done at home

homeopathy *n* treatment of disease by small doses of drug that produces symptoms of the disease in healthy people **homeopathic** *adj*

homicide *n* killing of human being; killer **homicidal** *adj*

homily *n* sermon

homogeneous *adj* formed of uniform parts; similar **homogeneity** *n* **homogenize** ~*v* break up fat globules in milk and cream to distribute them evenly

homonym *n* word of same form as another, but of different sense

homosexual *n/adj* (person) sexually attracted to members of the same sex **homosexuality** *n*

hone *v* sharpen (on whetstone)

honest *adj* not cheating, lying, stealing etc.; genuine **honestly** *adv* **honesty** *n*

honey *n* sweet fluid made by bees

———————— THESAURUS ————————

hole breach, break, crack, fissure, gap, opening, outlet, puncture, rent, split, tear, vent

holiday break, leave, recess, time off, vacation

holiness devoutness, divinity, godliness, piety, purity, sanctity, spirituality

hollow *adj* empty, unfilled, vacant, void; concave, depressed, indented, sunken; empty, fruitless, futile, pointless, useless, vain, worthless ~*n* basin, bowl, cave, cavern, cavity, crater, cup, dent, depression, hole, indentation, pit, trough; bottom, dale, dell, dingle, glen, valley

holy devout, divine, faithful, godly, hallowed, pious, pure, religious, righteous, saintly, sublime, virtuous

home abode, dwelling, habitation, house, pad *Sl*, residence

homespun artless, coarse, homely, inelegant, plain, rough, rude, rustic, unpolished

homicidal deadly, lethal, mortal, murderous

homicide bloodshed, killing, manslaughter, murder, slaying

homogeneous akin, alike, cognate, comparable, consistent, identical, kindred, similar, uniform, unvarying

honest decent, ethical, high-minded,

honeycomb *n* wax structure in hexagonal cells ~*v* fill with cells or perforations **honeymoon** *n* holiday taken by newly wedded pair **honeysuckle** *n* climbing plant

honk *n* call of wild goose; sound of motor-horn ~*v* make this sound

honour *n* personal integrity; renown; reputation ~*v* respect highly; confer honour on; accept or pay (bill etc.) when due **honourable** *adj* **honorary** *adj* conferred for the sake of honour only

hood *n* covering for head and neck; hoodlike thing **hoodwink** ~*v* deceive

hoodlum *n* gangster

hoof *n* (*pl* **hoofs** or **hooves**) horny casing of foot of horse etc.

hook *n* bent piece of metal etc., for catching hold, hanging up etc.; something resembling hook in shape or function ~*v* grasp, catch, hold, as with hook **hooked** *adj* shaped like hook; caught; *Sl* addicted

hooligan *n* violent, irresponsible (young) person **hooliganism** *n*

hoop *n* rigid circular band of metal, wood etc.

hooray *interj see* HURRAH

hoot *n* owl's cry or similar sound; cry of derision; *Inf* funny person or thing ~*v* utter hoot **hooter** *n* device (e.g. horn) to emit hooting sound

Hoover *n Trademark* vacuum cleaner ~*v* (*without cap.*) vacuum

hop[1] *v* **hopping, hopped** spring on one foot ~*n* leap, skip

hop[2] *n* climbing plant with bitter cones used to flavour beer etc.; *pl* the cones

hope *n* expectation of something desired; thing that gives, or object of,

honourable, law-abiding, reliable, reputable, scrupulous, trustworthy, trusty, truthful, upright, veracious, virtuous; candid, direct, forthright, frank, genuine, open, outright, plain, sincere, upfront *Inf*

honestly by fair means, cleanly, ethically, honourably, in good faith, lawfully, legally, legitimately; candidly, frankly, in all sincerity, in plain English, plainly, straight (out), to one's face, truthfully

honesty fidelity, honour, integrity, morality, probity, rectitude, trustworthiness, uprightness, virtue

honour *n* decency, fairness, goodness, integrity, morality, probity, rectitude, uprightness; credit, dignity, distinction, eminence, esteem, fame, glory, prestige, rank, renown, reputation, repute ~*v* admire, adore, appreciate, esteem, exalt, glorify, hallow, prize, respect, revere, reverence, value, venerate, worship

honourable ethical, fair, honest, just, moral, principled, true, trustworthy, trusty, upright, upstanding, virtuous; eminent, great, illustrious, noble, notable, noted, prestigious, renowned, venerable

hoodwink befool, cheat, cozen, delude, dupe, fool, hoax, impose, kid *Inf*, mislead, swindle, trick

hook *n* catch, clasp, fastener, hasp, holder, link, lock, peg; noose, snare, springe, trap ~*v* catch, clasp, fasten, fix, hasp, secure

hooligan delinquent, rowdy, ruffian, tough, vandal

hoop band, circlet, girdle, loop, ring, wheel

hoot *n* call, cry, toot; boo, catcall, hiss, jeer, yell ~*v* cry, scream, shout, shriek, toot, whoop, yell; boo, catcall, condemn, decry, denounce, hiss, howl down, jeer, yell at

hop *v* bound, caper, dance, jump, leap, skip, spring, trip, vault ~*n* bounce, bound, jump, leap, skip, spring, step, vault

this feeling ~*v* feel hope (for) **hopeful** *adj* **hopefully** *adv* **hopeless** *adj*

hopper *n* one who hops; device for feeding material into mill

hopscotch *n* children's game of hopping in pattern drawn on ground

horde *n* large crowd

horizon *n* line where earth and sky seem to meet **horizontal** *adj* parallel with horizon, level

hormone *n* substance secreted from gland which stimulates organs of the body

horn *n* hard projection on heads of certain animals; various things made of, or resembling it; wind instrument; device (esp. in car) emitting sound **horny** *adj* **hornpipe** *n* sailor's lively dance

hornet *n* large insect of wasp family

horoscope *n* telling of person's fortune by studying positions of planets etc. at his or her birth

horrendous *adj* horrific

horror *n* terror; loathing, fear of; its cause **horrible** *adj* exciting horror, hideous, shocking; disagreeable **horribly** *adv* **horrid** *adj* unpleasant, repulsive; *Inf* unkind **horrific** *adj* particularly horrible **horrify** *v* **-ifying, -ified** cause horror (in); shock

hors d'oeuvre *n* small dish served before main meal

horse *n* four-footed animal used for riding; cavalry; frame for support etc. **horsy** *adj* devoted to horses; like a horse **horse chestnut** tree with white or pink flowers and large nuts **horsefly** *n* large bloodsucking fly **horseman** *n* (*fem* **horsewoman**) rider on horse **horsepower** *n* unit of power of engine etc. **horseradish** *n* plant with pungent root **horseshoe** *n* protective U-shaped piece of iron nailed to horse's hoof

horticulture *n* art or science of gardening

hose *n* flexible tube for conveying liquid or gas; stockings ~*v* water with hose **hosiery** *n* stockings

hospice *n* home for care of the terminally ill

———————— THESAURUS ————————

hope *n* ambition, anticipation, assumption, belief, confidence, desire, dream, expectancy, faith, longing ~*v* anticipate, aspire, await, believe, desire, expect, foresee, long, rely, trust

hopeful assured, buoyant, confident, expectant, optimistic, sanguine; auspicious, bright, cheerful, encouraging, heartening, promising, propitious, reassuring, rosy

hopefully confidently, expectantly, optimistically, sanguinely; conceivably, expectedly, feasibly, probably

hopeless forlorn, futile, impossible, impracticable, pointless, unattainable, useless, vain

horde band, crew, crowd, drove, gang, host, mob, multitude, pack, press, swarm, throng, troop

horizon skyline, vista

horrible abominable, appalling, awful, dreadful, fearful, frightful, ghastly, grim, grisly, gruesome, heinous, hideous, horrid, repulsive, revolting, shameful, shocking, terrible; awful, cruel, disagreeable, dreadful, horrid, mean, nasty, terrible, unkind, unpleasant

horrid awful, disgusting, dreadful, horrible, nasty, offensive, terrible, unpleasant

horrify alarm, frighten, intimidate, petrify, scare, terrify; appal, disgust, dismay, gross out *US sl,* outrage, shock, sicken

horror alarm, apprehension, awe, consternation, dismay, dread, fear, fright, panic, terror; aversion, disgust, hatred, loathing, repugnance, revulsion

hospital *n* institution for care of sick **hospitalize** *v* send or admit to hospital

hospitality *n* friendly and liberal reception of strangers or guests **hospitable** *adj*

host[1] *n* (*fem* **hostess**) one who entertains another; innkeeper; compere of show ~*v* act as a host

host[2] *n* large number

hostage *n* person taken or given as pledge or security

hostel *n* building providing accommodation at low cost for students etc.

hostile *adj* antagonistic; warlike; of an enemy **hostility** *n* enmity; *pl* acts of warfare

hot *adj* **hotter, hottest** of high temperature; angry; new; spicy **hotly** *adv* **hot air** *Inf* empty talk **hotbed** *n* bed of heated earth for young plants; any place encouraging growth **hot-blooded** *adj* excitable **hot dog** hot sausage in split bread roll **hotfoot** *v/adv* (go) quickly **hothead** *n* intemperate person **hothouse** *n* heated greenhouse **hotline** *n* direct telephone link for emergency use **hotplate** *n* heated plate on electric cooker

hotchpotch *n* medley; dish of many ingredients

hotel *n* commercial establishment providing lodging and meals **hotelier** *n*

hound *n* hunting dog ~*v* chase, urge, pursue

hour *n* twenty-fourth part of day; sixty minutes; appointed time; *pl* fixed periods for work etc. **hourly** *adv/adj* **hourglass** *n* timing device in which sand trickles between two glass compartments

house *n* building for human habitation; legislative assembly; family; business firm ~*v* give or receive shelter, lodging, or storage; cover or contain **housing** *n* (providing of) houses; part designed to cover, protect, contain **houseboat** *n* boat used as home **household** *n* inmates of house collectively **housekeeper** *n* person managing affairs of household **housekeeping** *n* (money for) running household **housewife** *n* woman who runs her own household

hovel *n* lowly dwelling

——————— T H E S A U R U S ———————

hospitable amicable, bountiful, cordial, friendly, generous, genial, gracious, kind, liberal, sociable, welcoming

hospitality cheer, conviviality, cordiality, friendliness, hospitableness, sociability, warmth, welcome

host[1] entertainer, innkeeper, landlord, proprietor

host[2] army, array, drove, horde, legion, multitude, myriad, swarm, throng

hostage captive, gage, pawn, pledge, prisoner, security, surety

hostile antagonistic, contrary, inimical, malevolent, opposed, unkind, warlike

hostility animosity, antagonism, an-

tipathy, aversion, detestation, enmity, hatred, ill will, malevolence, malice, opposition

hot boiling, burning, fiery, flaming, heated, roasting, scalding, scorching, searing, steaming, sultry, sweltering, torrid, warm; acrid, biting, peppery, piquant, pungent, sharp, spicy

hot air bombast, bunkum *or* buncombe *chiefly US,* rant, verbiage, wind

hotchpotch hash, jumble, medley, *mélange,* mess, mishmash, mixture, potpourri

hothead daredevil, desperado, tearaway

hound *v* chase, drive, give chase, hunt, hunt down, pursue

hover v hang in the air; loiter; be in state of indecision **hovercraft** n type of craft which can travel over both land and sea on a cushion of air

how adv in what way; by what means; in what condition; to what degree **however** conj nevertheless ~adv in whatever way, degree; all the same

howl v/n (utter) long loud cry **howler** n Inf stupid mistake

HP hire-purchase

HQ headquarters

HRH His (or Her) Royal Highness

hub n middle part of wheel; central point of activity

hubbub n confused noise

huddle n crowded mass; Inf impromptu conference ~v heap, crowd together; hunch

hue n colour

huff n passing mood of anger ~v make or become angry; blow

hug v **hugging, hugged** clasp tightly in the arms; keep close to ~n fond embrace

huge adj very big **hugely** adv very much

hulk n body of abandoned vessel; large, unwieldy person or thing **hulking** adj

hull n frame, body of ship; calyx of strawberry etc. ~v remove shell, hull from (fruit, seeds)

hullabaloo n uproar; clamour

hum v **humming, hummed** make low continuous sound; sing with closed lips ~n humming sound **humming-bird** n very small Amer. bird whose wings make humming noise

human adj of man; relating to, characteristic of, man's nature **humane** adj kind; merciful **humanism** n belief in human effort rather than religion **humanitarian** n philanthropist ~adj

———————— THESAURUS ————————

house n abode, building, dwelling, edifice, home, pad Sl, residence; family, household, ménage; business, company, concern, establishment, firm, organization ~v accommodate, billet, board, domicile, harbour, lodge, put up, quarter, take in

household n family, home, house, ménage

housing dwellings, homes, houses

hovel cabin, den, hole, hut, shack, shanty, shed

hover drift, float, flutter, fly, hang, poise; linger

however after all, anyhow, but, even though, nevertheless, nonetheless, notwithstanding, still, though, yet

howl v bellow, cry, cry out, lament, roar, scream, shout, shriek, wail, weep, yell, yelp ~n bay, bellow, clamour, cry, groan, hoot, outcry, roar, scream, shriek, wail, yelp

howler blunder, error, malapropism, mistake

huddle n crowd, disorder, heap, jumble, mass, mess, muddle; conference, discussion, meeting ~v cluster, converge, crowd, flock, gather, press, throng

hue colour, dye, shade, tincture, tinge, tint, tone

hug v clasp, cuddle, embrace, enfold, hold close, squeeze; cherish, cling, hold onto, nurse, retain ~n clasp, clinch Sl, embrace, squeeze

huge colossal, elephantine, enormous, gargantuan, giant, gigantic, great, immense, large, massive, prodigious, stupendous, tremendous, vast

hulk derelict, frame, hull, shell, shipwreck, wreck

hull n body, casing, covering, frame, framework, skeleton; husk, peel, pod, rind, shell, shuck, skin

hum buzz, drone, mumble, murmur, purr, sing, throb, thrum, vibrate, whir

philanthropic **humanity** n human nature; human race; kindliness; pl study of literature, philosophy, the arts **humanize** v

humble adj lowly, modest ~v humiliate **humbly** adv

humbug n imposter; sham, nonsense; sweet of boiled sugar

humdrum adj commonplace, dull

humid adj moist, damp **humidifier** n device for increasing amount of water vapour in air in room etc. **humidity** n

humiliate v lower dignity of, abase, mortify **humiliation** n

humility n state of being humble; meekness

hummock n low knoll, hillock

humour n faculty of saying or perceiving what excites amusement; amusing speech, writing etc.; state of mind, mood ~v gratify, indulge **humorist** n person who acts, speaks, writes humorously **humorous** adj

hump n normal or deforming lump, esp. on back ~v make hump-shaped; Sl carry or heave **humpback** n person with hump

humus n decayed vegetable and animal mould

hunch n Inf intuition; hump ~v bend into hump **hunchback** n humpback

hundred n/adj cardinal number, ten times ten **hundredth** adj ordinal number **hundredweight** n weight of 112 lbs (50.8 kg), 20th part of ton

hunger n/v (have) discomfort from lack of food; (have) strong desire **hungrily** adv **hungry** adj having keen appetite

hunk n thick piece

human fleshly, manlike, mortal

humane benign, charitable, clement, compassionate, forbearing, forgiving, gentle, good, kind, lenient, merciful, mild, sympathetic, tender, understanding

humanity flesh, man, mankind, men, mortality, people

humble meek, modest, submissive, unostentatious; common, commonplace, insignificant, low, low-born, lowly, mean, modest, obscure, ordinary, poor, simple

humbug charlatan, cheat, fraud, impostor, phoney or phony Inf, quack, swindler, trickster; bluff, cheat, deceit, dodge, feint, fraud, hoax, ruse, sham, swindle, trick, trickery, wile

humdrum banal, boring, dreary, dull, ho-hum Inf, mind-numbing, mundane, ordinary, repetitious, routine, tedious, tiresome, unvaried

humid clammy, damp, dank, moist, muggy, steamy, sticky, sultry, wet

humiliate abase, bring low, chagrin, chasten, crush, debase, degrade, discomfit, disgrace, embarrass, humble, shame, subdue

humility diffidence, lowliness, meekness, modesty, servility, submissiveness

humorist card Inf, comedian, comic, droll, jester, joker, wag, wit

humorous amusing, comic, comical, entertaining, facetious, farcical, funny, hilarious, laughable, ludicrous, merry, playful, pleasant, witty

humour n amusement, comedy, drollery, facetiousness, fun, funniness, jocularity, wit; comedy, farce, jesting, jests, jokes, joking, pleasantry, wit, wittiness; mood, spirits, temper ~v accommodate, cosset, favour, flatter, gratify, indulge, mollify, pamper, pander to, spoil

hump bulge, bump, knob, mound, projection, swelling

hunch feeling, idea, impression, inkling, intuition, premonition, presentiment, suspicion

hunger n appetite, emptiness, famine, ravenousness, starvation, voracity;

hunt *v* seek out to kill or capture for sport or food; search (for) ~*n* chase, search; (party organized for) hunting **hunter** *n*

hurdle *n* portable frame of bars for temporary fences or for jumping over; obstacle ~*v* race over hurdles

hurdy-gurdy *n* mechanical musical instrument

hurl *v* throw violently

hurly-burly *n* loud confusion

hurrah, hooray *interj* exclamation of joy or applause

hurricane *n* very strong, violent wind or storm

hurry *v* **hurrying, hurried** (cause to) move or act in great haste ~*n* undue haste; eagerness **hurriedly** *adv*

hurt *v* **hurting, hurt** injure, damage, give pain to; feel pain ~*n* wound, injury, harm **hurtful** *adj*

hurtle *v* rush violently

husband *n* married man ~*v* econo-mize; use to best advantage **husbandry** *n* farming; economy

hush *v* make or be silent ~*n* stillness; quietness

husk *n* dry covering of certain seeds and fruits ~*v* remove husk from

husky *adj* rough in tone; hoarse, throaty

husky *n* Arctic sledge dog

hussy *n* cheeky young woman

hustings *pl n* political campaigning

hustle *v* push about, jostle, hurry ~*n* lively activity

hut *n* small house or shelter

hutch *n* cage for rabbits etc.

hyacinth *n* bulbous plant with bell-shaped flowers

hybrid *n* offspring of two plants or animals of different species ~*adj* crossbred

hydrangea *n* ornamental shrub

hydrant *n* water-pipe with nozzle for hose

———————————— T H E S A U R U S ————————————

appetite, craving, desire, itch, lust, yearning ~*v* crave, desire, hanker, itch, long, pine, starve, thirst, want, wish, yearn

hungry empty, famishing, hollow, ravenous, starved, starving, voracious

hunk block, chunk, lump, mass, piece, slab, wedge

hunt *v* chase, hound, pursue, stalk, track, trail; forage, look, scour, search, seek ~*n* chase, hunting, investigation, pursuit, quest, search

hurdle *n* barricade, barrier, block, fence, hedge, wall; barrier, block, difficulty, hindrance, impediment, obstacle, snag

hurl cast, fire, fling, heave, launch, pitch, project, propel, send, shy, sling, throw, toss

hurricane cyclone, gale, storm, tempest, tornado, typhoon, windstorm

hurry *v* dash, fly, rush, scurry; accelerate, expedite, goad, hasten, hustle, push on, quicken, urge ~*n* bustle, celerity, commotion, dispatch, flurry, haste, quickness, rush, speed, urgency

hurt *v* bruise, damage, disable, harm, impair, injure, mar, spoil, wound; afflict, aggrieve, annoy, distress, grieve, pain, sadden, sting, upset, wound; ache, be sore, burn, pain, smart, sting, throb ~*n* bruise, sore, wound; discomfort, distress, pain, pang, soreness, suffering

hush *v* mute, quieten, silence, still, suppress ~*n* calm, peace, quiet, silence, stillness, tranquillity

husky croaking, croaky, gruff, guttural, harsh, hoarse, rasping, raucous, rough, throaty

hustle bustle, crowd, elbow, force, haste, hasten, hurry, impel, jog, jostle, push, rush, shove, thrust

hut cabin, den, hovel, lean-to, refuge, shanty, shed, shelter

hydraulic *adj* concerned with, operated by, pressure transmitted through liquid in pipe

hydrochloric acid strong colourless acid

hydroelectric *adj* pert. to generation of electricity by use of water

hydrofoil *n* fast, light vessel with hull raised out of water at speed

hydrogen *n* colourless gas which combines with oxygen to form water **hydrogen bomb** atom bomb of enormous power **hydrogen peroxide** colourless liquid used as antiseptic and bleach

hydrophobia *n* aversion to water, esp. as symptom of rabies

hyena *n* wild animal related to dog

hygiene *n* (study of) principles and practice of health and cleanliness **hygienic** *adj*

hymen *n* membrane partly covering vagina of virgin

hymn *n* song of praise, esp. to God ~*v* praise in song

hype *n* intensive publicity ~*v* publicize

hyperbole *n* rhetorical exaggeration

hypermarket *n* huge self-service store

hypertension *n* abnormally high blood pressure

hyphen *n* short line (-) indicating that two words or syllables are to be connected **hyphenate** *v* **hyphenated** *adj*

hypnosis *n* (*pl* **-ses**) induced state like deep sleep in which subject acts on external suggestion **hypnotic** *adj* **hypnotism** *n* **hypnotize** *v* affect with hypnosis

hypochondria *n* morbid depression without cause, about one's own health **hypochondriac** *adj/n*

hypocrisy *n* assuming of false appearance of virtue; insincerity **hypocrite** *n* **hypocritical** *adj*

hypodermic *adj* introduced, injected beneath the skin ~*n* hypodermic syringe or needle

hypotenuse *n* side of right-angled triangle opposite the right angle

hypothermia *n* condition of having body temperature reduced to dangerously low level

hypothesis *n* (*pl* **-eses**) suggested explanation of something; assumption as basis of reasoning **hypothetical** *adj*

hysterectomy *n* surgical operation for removing uterus

hysteria *n* mental disorder with emotional outbursts; fit of crying or laughing **hysterical** *adj* **hysterics** *pl n* fits of hysteria

———————————— THESAURUS ————————————

hygiene cleanliness, sanitation

hygienic aseptic, clean, germ-free, healthy, pure, sanitary, sterile

hypnotic mesmeric, mesmerizing, narcotic, sleep-inducing, soporific, spellbinding

hypnotize entrance, fascinate, magnetize, mesmerize, spellbind

hypocrisy cant, deceit, deception, dissembling, duplicity, falsity, insincerity, pharisaism, pretence, twofacedness

hypocrite charlatan, deceiver, dissembler, fraud, impostor, pharisee,

phoney *or* phony *Inf,* pretender

hypocritical deceitful, deceptive, duplicitous, false, fraudulent, hollow, insincere, phoney *or* phony *Inf,* sanctimonious, two-faced

hypothesis assumption, postulate, premise, proposition, theory, thesis

hypothetical academic, assumed, conjectural, imaginary, putative

hysteria agitation, delirium, frenzy, hysterics, madness, panic, unreason

hysterical berserk, convulsive, crazed, distracted, distraught, frantic, frenzied, mad, raving

I i

I *pron* the pronoun of the first person singular

ibis *n* storklike bird

ice *n* frozen water; ice cream ~*v* cover, become covered with ice; cool with ice; cover with icing **icicle** *n* hanging spike of ice **icing** *n* mixture of sugar and water etc. used to decorate cakes **icy** *adj* covered with ice; cold; unfriendly **iceberg** *n* large floating mass of ice **ice cream** sweet creamy frozen dessert **ice hockey** team game played on ice with puck **ice skate** boot with steel blade for gliding over ice **ice-skate** *v*

icon *n* religious image **iconoclast** *n* one who attacks established ideas

idea *n* notion; conception; plan, aim **ideal** *n* idea of perfection; perfect person or thing ~*adj* perfect **idealism** *n*

tendency to seek perfection in everything **idealist** *n* one who strives after the ideal; impractical person **idealistic** *adj* **idealization** *n* **idealize** *v* portray as ideal **ideally** *adv*

identity *n* individuality; state of being exactly alike **identical** *adj* very same **identifiable** *adj* **identification** *n* recognition; identifying document **identify** *v* identifying, identified establish identity of; associate (oneself) with; treat as identical

ideology *n* body of ideas, beliefs of group, nation etc. **ideological** *adj*

idiom *n* expression peculiar to a language or group **idiomatic** *adj*

idiosyncrasy *n* peculiarity of mind

idiot *n* mentally deficient person; stupid person **idiocy** *n* **idiotic** *adj* utterly stupid

---
THESAURUS
---

icy arctic, biting, bitter, chilly, cold, freezing, frosty, frozen over, ice-cold, parky *Brit inf*, raw

idea belief, conviction, doctrine, interpretation, notion, opinion, teaching, view, viewpoint; conception, conclusion, fancy, impression, judgment, perception, thought, understanding

ideal *n* archetype, criterion, epitome, example, exemplar, last word, model, paradigm, paragon, pattern, perfection, prototype, standard ~*adj* classic, complete, model, perfect, quintessential, supreme

idealist *n* romantic, visionary

identical alike, duplicate, equal, equivalent, indistinguishable, interchangeable, like, selfsame, the same, twin

identification cataloguing, labelling, naming, pinpointing, recognition; credentials, ID, identity card, papers

identify catalogue, classify, diagnose, label, make out, name, pick out, pinpoint, place, recognize, spot, tag

identity distinctiveness, existence, individuality, oneness, particularity, personality, self, selfhood, singularity, uniqueness

idiocy fatuity, fatuousness, foolishness, imbecility, insanity, lunacy

idiom expression, locution, phrase

idiosyncrasy characteristic, eccentricity, habit, mannerism, peculiarity, quirk, trick

idiot ass, berk *Brit sl*, cretin, dunderhead, fool, halfwit, imbecile, jerk *Sl, chiefly US & Canad*, moron, nerd *or* nurd *Sl*, nitwit *Inf*, numskull *or* numbskull, prat *Sl*, simpleton, twit *Inf, chiefly Brit*, wally *Sl*

idiotic asinine, crackpot *Inf*, crazy, fatuous, foolish, halfwitted, imbecile, insane, lunatic, moronic, senseless, stupid

idle *adj* unemployed; lazy; useless; groundless ~*v* be idle; run slowly in neutral gear **idleness** *n* **idler** *n* **idly** *adv*

idol *n* image worshipped as deity; object of excessive devotion **idolatry** *n* **idolize** *v* love or admire to excess

idyll *n* (poem describing) picturesque or charming scene or episode **idyllic** *adj* delightful

i.e. that is

if *conj* on condition or supposition that; whether; although

igloo *n* (*pl* **-loos**) domed house made of snow

ignite *v* (cause to) burn **ignition** *n* act of kindling or setting on fire; car's electrical firing system

ignoble *adj* mean, base; of low birth

ignominy *n* public disgrace; shameful act **ignominious** *adj*

ignore *v* disregard, leave out of account **ignoramus** *n* ignorant person **ignorance** *n* lack of knowledge **ignorant** *adj* lacking knowledge; uneducated

iguana *n* large tropical American lizard

ill *adj* not in good health; bad, evil; harmful ~*n* evil, harm ~*adv* badly; hardly **illness** *n* **ill-advised** *adj* imprudent **ill-disposed** *adj* unsympathetic **ill-fated** *adj* unfortunate **ill-gotten** *adj* obtained dishonestly **ill-treat** *v* treat cruelly **ill will** hostility

illegal *adj* against the law

idle *adj* dead, empty, inactive, jobless, out of work, redundant, stationary, unemployed, unoccupied, unused, vacant; indolent, lazy, shiftless, slothful, sluggish ~*v* coast, drift, mark time, shirk, slack, slow down, vegetate

idleness inaction, inactivity, leisure, unemployment; lazing, loafing, pottering, time-wasting, trifling

idol deity, god, graven image, image, pagan symbol

idolize admire, adore, deify, dote upon, exalt, glorify, hero-worship, look up to, love, revere, venerate, worship

ignite burn, catch fire, fire, inflame, kindle, light, set fire to

ignominious abject, disgraceful, dishonourable, disreputable, humiliating, indecorous, inglorious, scandalous, shameful, sorry, undignified

ignorance benightedness, blindness, illiteracy, unenlightenment, unintelligence

ignorant benighted, blind to, inexperienced, innocent, oblivious, unaware, unconscious, unenlightened, uninformed, unknowing, unwitting; green, illiterate, naive, unaware, uneducated, unlettered, unread, untaught, untrained, untutored

ignore cold-shoulder, discount, disregard, neglect, overlook, pass over, reject

ill *adj* ailing, diseased, indisposed, infirm, off-colour, queasy, queer, sick, unwell; bad, damaging, evil, foul, harmful, injurious, ruinous, unfortunate, unlucky, vile, wicked, wrong ~*n* abuse, badness, cruelty, damage, destruction, evil, malice, mischief, suffering, wickedness; affliction, hardship, harm, hurt, injury, misery, misfortune, pain, trial, tribulation, trouble, unpleasantness, woe ~*adv* badly, hard, poorly, unfavourably, unfortunately, unluckily

ill-advised foolish, impolitic, imprudent, inappropriate, incautious, indiscreet, misguided, overhasty, rash, reckless, unseemly, unwise

illegal banned, black-market, bootleg, criminal, felonious, forbidden, illicit, lawless, outlawed, prohibited, proscribed, unauthorized, unconstitu-

illegible *adj* unable to be read
illegitimate *adj* born to unmarried parents; irregular **illegitimacy** *n*
illicit *adj* illegal; prohibited, forbidden
illiterate *adj* unable to read or write ~*n* illiterate person **illiteracy** *n*
illogical *adj* not logical
illuminate *v* light up; clarify; decorate with lights or colours **illumination** *n*

illusion *n* deceptive appearance or belief **illusionist** *n* conjuror **illusory** *adj*
illustrate *v* provide with pictures or examples; explain by examples **illustration** *n* picture, diagram; example
illustrious *adj* famous; glorious
image *n* likeness; optical counterpart; double, copy; general impression; word picture **imagery** *n* images collectively

───────────── THESAURUS ─────────────

tional, under-the-table, unlawful, unlicensed, unofficial, wrongful
illegible faint, indecipherable, obscure, scrawled, unreadable
illegitimate bastard, fatherless, natural; illegal, illicit, improper, unconstitutional, under-the-table, unlawful
ill-fated blighted, doomed, hapless, ill-omened, luckless, unfortunate, unhappy, unlucky
illicit bootleg, contraband, criminal, felonious, illegal, prohibited, unlawful, unlicensed; forbidden, furtive, guilty, immoral, improper, wrong
illiterate benighted, ignorant, uncultured, uneducated
illness affliction, ailment, attack, complaint, disability, disease, disorder, indisposition, infirmity, malady, malaise, poor health, sickness
illogical absurd, fallacious, faulty, inconsistent, incorrect, invalid, irrational, meaningless, senseless, specious, spurious, unreasonable, unsound
ill-treat abuse, damage, harass, harm, harry, injure, maltreat, mishandle, misuse, oppress, wrong
illuminate brighten, light, light up; clarify, clear up, elucidate, enlighten, explain, instruct, make clear
illumination awareness, clarification, enlightenment, perception, revelation, understanding
illusion chimera, daydream, fantasy, hallucination, mirage, mockery, phantasm, semblance

illusory apparent, beguiling, deceitful, delusive, fallacious, false, misleading, mistaken, sham, unreal, untrue
illustrate adorn, decorate, depict, draw, picture, sketch; bring home, clarify, demonstrate, elucidate, emphasize, exhibit, explain, interpret, show
illustration adornment, decoration, figure, picture, plate, sketch; analogy, case, clarification, demonstration, elucidation, example, explanation, instance, specimen
illustrious brilliant, celebrated, distinguished, eminent, famous, glorious, great, noble, notable, noted, prominent, remarkable, renowned, signal, splendid
ill will acrimony, animosity, antagonism, antipathy, aversion, dislike, enmity, envy, grudge, hatred, hostility, malice, rancour, resentment, spite, unfriendliness, venom
image appearance, effigy, figure, icon, idol, likeness, picture, portrait, reflection, statue; conceit, concept, figure, idea, impression, perception
imaginable conceivable, credible, likely, plausible, possible, thinkable
imaginary assumed, dreamlike, fanciful, fictional, ideal, illusive, illusory, imagined, invented, legendary, made-up, mythological, nonexistent, shadowy, supposed, unreal, unsub-

imagine v picture to oneself; think; conjecture **imaginable** adj **imaginary** adj existing only in fantasy **imagination** n faculty of making mental images of things not present; fancy **imaginative** adj

imbalance n lack of balance in emphasis or proportion

imbecile n idiot ~adj idiotic

imbibe v drink (in)

imbue v instil, fill

imitate v take as model; copy **imitation** n act of imitating; copy; counterfeit ~adj synthetic **imitative** adj

immaculate adj spotless; pure

immaterial adj unimportant; not consisting of matter

immature adj not fully developed; lacking wisdom because of youth

immediate adj occurring at once; closest **immediately** adv

immense adj huge, vast **immensely** adv **immensity** n

immerse v submerge in liquid; involve; engross **immersion** n

immigrant n settler in foreign country **immigration** n

imminent adj liable to happen soon **imminence** n

immobile adj unable to move **immobility** n **immobilize** v

immolate v kill, sacrifice

stantial, visionary

imagination creativity, enterprise, fancy, ingenuity, insight, inspiration, inventiveness, originality, vision, wit

imaginative clever, creative, dreamy, enterprising, fanciful, ingenious, inspired, inventive, original, poetical, visionary, vivid

imagine conceive, conjure up, create, devise, envisage, frame, invent, jerk, picture, plan, project, scheme, think of, think up, visualize

imitate affect, ape, burlesque, copy, counterfeit, duplicate, echo, emulate, follow, impersonate, mimic, mirror, mock, parody, personate, repeat, simulate

imitation n fake, forgery, impersonation, impression, mockery, parody, reflection, reproduction, sham, substitution, travesty; aping, copy, counterfeit, echoing, likeness, mimicry, resemblance, simulation ~adj artificial, dummy, ersatz, mock, reproduction, sham, simulated, synthetic

immaculate clean, impeccable, neat, spotless, spruce, squeaky-clean, trim; faultless, flawless, guiltless, impeccable, incorrupt, innocent, perfect, pure, sinless, squeaky-clean, stain-less, unpolluted, unsullied, untarnished, virtuous

immaterial extraneous, impertinent, inapposite, inconsequential, inessential, insignificant, irrelevant, trifling, trivial, unimportant

immature adolescent, crude, green, premature, raw, undeveloped, unformed, unripe, unseasonable, untimely, young; callow, childish, inexperienced, infantile, jejune, juvenile, puerile

immediate instant, instantaneous; adjacent, close, direct, near, nearest, next, recent

immediately at once, directly, forthwith, instantly, now, posthaste, promptly, right away, this instant, unhesitatingly, without delay

immense colossal, enormous, extensive, giant, gigantic, great, huge, infinite, large, mammoth, massive, monumental, prodigious, titanic, tremendous, vast

immigrant incomer, newcomer, settler

imminent at hand, close, coming, forthcoming, gathering, impending, looming, menacing, near, threatening

immoral *adj* corrupt; promiscuous **immorality** *n*

immortal *adj* deathless; famed for all time ~*n* person living forever **immortality** *n* **immortalize** *v*

immune *adj* protected (against a disease etc.); exempt **immunity** *n* **immunization** *n* process of making immune to disease **immunize** *v*

imp *n* little devil; mischievous child

impact *n* collision; profound effect **impacted** *adj* wedged

impair *v* weaken, damage **impairment** *n*

impala *n* S Afr. antelope

impale *v* pierce with sharp instrument

impart *v* communicate; give

impartial *adj* unbiased; fair **impartiality** *n*

impassable *adj* blocked

impasse *n* deadlock

impassioned *adj* full of feeling, ardent

impassive *adj* showing no emotion; calm

impatient *adj* irritable; restless **impatience** *n*

impeach *v* charge, esp. with treason or crime in office; denounce **impeachable** *adj* **impeachment** *n*

impeccable *adj* faultless

impede *v* hinder **impediment** *n* ob-

——————— THESAURUS ———————

immobile fixed, frozen, immovable, motionless, rigid, riveted, rooted, stable, static, stationary, stiff, still, unmoving

immobilize cripple, disable, freeze, halt, paralyse, stop, transfix

immoral abandoned, bad, corrupt, debauched, degenerate, depraved, evil, impure, indecent, sinful, unchaste, unethical, vile, wicked, wrong

immorality corruption, debauchery, depravity, dissoluteness, evil, licentiousness, profligacy, sin, vice, wickedness

immortal *adj* abiding, constant, deathless, endless, enduring, eternal, everlasting, indestructible, perennial, perpetual, timeless, undying, unfading ~*n* god, goddess; hero

immortality deathlessness, endlessness, eternity, perpetuity; celebrity, fame, glorification, greatness, renown

immune clear, exempt, free, invulnerable, proof (against), protected, resistant, safe, unaffected

immunity amnesty, charter, exemption, franchise, freedom, indemnity, liberty, prerogative, privilege, release, right

immunize inoculate, protect, safe-

guard, vaccinate

impact bang, blow, bump, collision, contact, crash, force, jolt, knock, shock, smash, stroke, thump

impair blunt, damage, deteriorate, diminish, enfeeble, harm, hinder, injure, lessen, mar, reduce, spoil, undermine, weaken, worsen

impartial detached, disinterested, equal, equitable, even-handed, fair, just, neutral, objective, open-minded, unbiased, unprejudiced

impartiality detachment, disinterest, dispassion, equality, equity, fairness, neutrality, objectivity

impasse deadlock, stalemate

impassioned ardent, blazing, excited, fervent, fiery, furious, glowing, heated, inflamed, inspired, intense, passionate, rousing, stirring, violent, vivid, warm

impatient abrupt, brusque, curt, demanding, edgy, hasty, intolerant, irritable, sudden, testy; eager, fretful, headlong, impetuous, restless

impeach accuse, arraign, blame, censure, charge, denounce, indict, tax

impeccable exact, exquisite, faultless, flawless, incorrupt, innocent, perfect, precise, pure, sinless, stain-

struction; defect
impel *v* **-pelling, -pelled** induce; drive
impending *adj* imminent
imperative *adj* necessary; peremptory; *Grammar* expressing command **~n** *Grammar* imperative mood
imperfect *adj* having faults; not complete **imperfection** *n*
imperial *adj* of empire, or emperor; majestic; denoting weights and measures formerly official in Brit. **imperialism** *n* policy of acquiring empire
imperil *v* **-illing, -illed** endanger
imperious *adj* domineering
impersonal *adj* objective
impersonate *v* pretend to be **impersonation** *n* **impersonator** *n*

impertinent *adj* insolent, rude **impertinence** *n*
imperturbable *adj* calm, not excitable
impervious *adj* impossible to penetrate; unaffected by
impetigo *n* contagious skin disease
impetuous *adj* rash **impetuosity** *n*
impetus *n* incentive; momentum
impinge *v* encroach (upon)
impious *adj* irreverent
implacable *adj* not to be placated
implant *v* insert firmly
implement *n* tool, instrument **~v** carry out
implore *v* entreat earnestly
imply *v* **implying, implied** hint; mean

———————————— THESAURUS ————————————

less, unblemished
impediment bar, barrier, block, check, clog, curb, defect, difficulty, hindrance, obstacle, snag
impel drive, force, incite, induce, influence, instigate, motivate, move, oblige, power, prod, prompt, propel, push, require, spur, stimulate, urge
impending approaching, coming, gathering, imminent, looming, menacing, near, nearing, threatening, upcoming
imperative compulsory, crucial, essential, insistent, obligatory, pressing, urgent, vital
imperfect broken, damaged, defective, faulty, flawed, immature, impaired, incomplete, inexact, limited, partial, patchy, sketchy, unfinished
imperfection blemish, defect, deficiency, failing, fault, flaw, frailty, infirmity, shortcoming, stain, taint, weakness
imperial kingly, majestic, princely, queenly, regal, royal, sovereign
imperil endanger, expose, hazard, jeopardize, risk
impersonal cold, detached, dispassionate, formal, inhuman, neutral,

objective, remote
impersonate act, ape, enact, imitate, mimic, personate
impetuous ardent, eager, fierce, furious, hasty, headlong, impulsive, precipitate, rash, spontaneous, unplanned, unthinking, vehement, violent
impetus goad, impulse, incentive, push, spur, stimulus; energy, force, momentum, power
implant inculcate, infix, infuse, instil, sow
implement *n* apparatus, appliance, device, gadget, instrument, tool **~v** bring about, carry out, complete, effect, enforce, execute, fulfil, perform, realize
implicate associate, compromise, concern, embroil, entangle, imply, include, incriminate, involve, mire
implication inference, innuendo, meaning, overtone, presumption, significance, signification, suggestion
implicit contained, implied, inferred, inherent, latent, tacit, understood, unspoken
implore beg, beseech, crave, entreat, importune, plead with, pray, solicit,

implicate *v* involve **implication** *n* something implied **implicit** *adj* implied; absolute

import *v* bring in ~*n* thing imported; meaning **importation** *n* **importer** *n*

important *adj* of great consequence; eminent, powerful **importance** *n*

impose *v* place (upon); take advantage (of) **imposing** *adj* impressive **imposition** *n*

impossible *adj* not possible; unreasonable **impossibility** *n* **impossibly** *adv*

impostor *n* one who assumes false identity

impotent *adj* powerless; (of males) unable to perform sexual intercourse

impotence *n*

impound *v* seize legally

impoverish *v* make poor or weak

impractical *adj* not sensible

impregnable *adj* proof against attack

impregnate *v* saturate; make pregnant

impresario *n* (*pl* **-ios**) organizer of public entertainment; manager of opera, ballet etc.

impress *v* affect deeply, usu. favourably; imprint, stamp **impression** *n* effect; notion, belief; imprint; comic impersonation **impressionable** *adj* susceptible **impressive** *adj* making deep impression

imprint *n* mark made by pressure ~*v*

———————————— THESAURUS ————————————

supplicate

imply connote, hint, insinuate, intimate, signify, suggest; betoken, denote, entail, evidence, import, include, indicate, involve, mean, point to, presuppose

import *v* bring in, introduce, land ~*n* bearing, drift, gist, implication, intention, meaning, message, purport, sense, significance, thrust

importance concern, consequence, import, interest, moment, significance, substance, value, weight; distinction, eminence, esteem, influence, mark, pre-eminence, prestige, prominence, standing, status, worth

important far-reaching, grave, large, material, momentous, primary, salient, serious, signal, significant, substantial, urgent, weighty; eminent, foremost, high-level, high-ranking, influential, leading, notable, noteworthy, outstanding, powerful, pre-eminent, prominent, seminal

impose decree, establish, exact, fix, institute, introduce, lay, levy, ordain, place, promulgate, put, set

imposing august, commanding, dignified, effective, grand, impressive,

majestic, stately, striking

imposition application, decree, laying on, levying, promulgation; encroachment, intrusion, liberty, presumption

impossible hopeless, impracticable, inconceivable, unattainable, unobtainable, unthinkable

impostor charlatan, cheat, deceiver, fake, fraud, hypocrite, phoney *or* phony *Inf*, pretender, quack, rogue, sham, trickster

impotence disability, feebleness, frailty, inability, inadequacy, incapacity, incompetence, ineffectiveness, infirmity, paralysis, powerlessness, uselessness, weakness

impotent disabled, feeble, frail, helpless, incapable, ineffective, infirm, nerveless, paralysed, powerless, unable, weak

impoverish bankrupt, beggar, break, ruin; deplete, diminish, drain, exhaust, reduce, sap

impractical impossible, unrealistic, unserviceable, unworkable, visionary, wild

impress affect, excite, influence, inspire, move, stir, strike, sway, touch

stamp; fix in mind

imprison v put in prison **imprisonment** n

improbable adj unlikely

impromptu adv/adj without preparation ~n improvisation

improper adj indecent; incorrect **impropriety** n

improve v make or become better **improvement** n

improvident adj thriftless

improvise v make use of materials at hand; perform, speak without prepa-

ration **improvisation** n

impudent adj impertinent **impudence** n

impugn v call in question, challenge

impulse n sudden inclination to act; impetus **impulsive** adj rash

impunity n exemption from consequences

impure adj having unwanted substances mixed in; immoral, obscene **impurity** n

impute v attribute to **imputation** n reproach

———————— THESAURUS ————————

impression effect, feeling, impact, influence, reaction, sway; belief, concept, conviction, fancy, feeling, hunch, idea, memory, notion, opinion, sense, suspicion; imitation, impersonation, parody

impressive exciting, forcible, moving, powerful, stirring, striking, touching

imprint n impression, mark, print, sign, stamp ~v engrave, establish, etch, fix, impress, print, stamp

imprison confine, constrain, detain, immure, jail, lock up, put away

imprisonment confinement, custody, detention, duress, incarceration

improbability doubt, dubiety, uncertainty, unlikelihood

improbable doubtful, dubious, fanciful, far-fetched, implausible, questionable, unbelievable, unlikely

impromptu ad-lib, extempore, improvised, offhand, spontaneous, unprepared, unrehearsed, unscripted

improper impolite, indecent, indecorous, indelicate, risqué, smutty, suggestive, unfitting, unseemly, untoward, vulgar; abnormal, false, inaccurate, incorrect, irregular, wrong

impropriety bad taste, indecency, vulgarity; bloomer Brit inf, blunder, faux pas, gaffe, gaucherie, mistake, slip, solecism

improve advance, amend, augment, better, correct, help, mend, polish, rectify, touch up, upgrade; develop, enhance, increase, pick up, progress, rally, reform, rise

improvement amelioration, amendment, betterment, correction, gain, rectification; advance, development, enhancement, increase, progress, rally, recovery, rise, upswing

improvise concoct, contrive, devise, make do; ad-lib, busk, extemporize, invent, vamp, wing it Inf

impudent audacious, bold, boldfaced, brazen, forward, impertinent, insolent, presumptuous, rude

impulse force, impetus, momentum, movement, pressure, push, stimulus, surge, thrust

impulsive emotional, hasty, headlong, impetuous, instinctive, intuitive, passionate, precipitate, quick, rash

impure adulterated, alloyed, debased, mixed, unrefined; contaminated, defiled, dirty, filthy, foul, infected, polluted, sullied, tainted, unclean

impurity adulteration, mixture; contamination, defilement, dirtiness, filth, foulness, infection, pollution, taint, uncleanness

imputation accusation, attribution, blame, censure, charge, insinuation,

in *prep* expresses inclusion within limits of space, time, circumstance, sphere etc. ~*adv* in or into some state, place etc.; *Inf* in vogue etc. ~*adj Inf* fashionable

inability *n* lack of means or skill to do something

inaccurate *adj* not correct **inaccuracy** *n*

inadequate *adj* not enough; incapable **inadequacy** *n*

inane *adj* foolish

inanimate *adj* lifeless

inappropriate *adj* not suitable

inarticulate *adj* unable to express oneself clearly

inaugurate *v* initiate; admit to office **inaugural** *adj* **inauguration** *n* formal initiation (to office etc.)

inauspicious *adj* unlucky

inborn *adj* existing from birth

incalculable *adj* beyond calculation; very great

incandescent *adj* glowing; produced by glowing filament

incantation *n* magic spell

incapable *adj* helpless

incapacitate *v* disable; disqualify

incarcerate *v* imprison

incarnate *adj* in human form; typified **incarnation** *n*

incendiary *adj* designed to cause fires; inflammatory ~*n* fire-bomb

incense¹ *v* enrage

incense² *n* gum, spice giving perfume when burned; its smoke

incentive *n* something that stimulates effort

inception *n* beginning

incessant *adj* unceasing

——————— THESAURUS ———————

reproach, slander, slur

inability impotence, inadequacy, incapability, incapacity, incompetence, ineptitude, powerlessness

inaccurate careless, defective, faulty, imprecise, incorrect, in error, inexact, mistaken, out, unfaithful, unreliable, unsound, wild, wrong

inadequate defective, deficient, faulty, imperfect, incomplete, insubstantial, insufficient, meagre, niggardly, scant, scanty, short, sketchy, skimpy, sparse; inapt, incapable, incompetent, unequal, unfitted, unqualified

inane empty, fatuous, frivolous, futile, idiotic, mindless, puerile, senseless, silly, stupid, trifling, vacuous, vain, vapid, worthless

inanimate cold, dead, defunct, extinct, inactive, inert, lifeless, quiescent, soulless, spiritless

inappropriate ill-suited, ill-timed, improper, incongruous, malapropos, tasteless, unbecoming, unbefitting, unfit, unfitting, unseemly, unsuit-

able, untimely

inarticulate faltering, halting, hesitant, poorly spoken

inaugurate begin, commence, initiate, institute, introduce, launch, originate, set in motion, set up; induct, install, instate, invest

inauguration initiation, institution, launch, launching, opening

incalculable boundless, countless, enormous, immense, inestimable, infinite, limitless, measureless, numberless, untold, vast

incapable feeble, incompetent, ineffective, inept, insufficient, unfit, unfitted, unqualified, weak

incapacitate cripple, disable, disqualify, immobilize, paralyse, prostrate

incentive bait, encouragement, goad, impetus, impulse, inducement, lure, motivation, motive, spur, stimulus

incessant ceaseless, constant, continuous, endless, eternal, everlasting, interminable, perpetual, persistent, relentless, unending, unrelenting,

incest *n* sexual intercourse between close relatives **incestuous** *adj*

inch *n* one twelfth of a foot, or 0.0254 metre ~*v* move very slowly

incident *n* event or occurrence; public disturbance **incidence** *n* extent or frequency of occurrence **incidental** *adj* occurring as a minor, inevitable, or chance accompaniment **incidentally** *adv* by chance; by the way **incidentals** *pl n* accompanying items

incinerate *v* burn up completely **incinerator** *n*

incipient *adj* beginning

incise *v* cut into **incision** *n* **incisive** *adj* sharp **incisor** *n* cutting tooth

incite *v* urge, stir up

inclement *adj* severe

incline *v* lean, slope; (cause to) be dis-posed ~*n* slope **inclination** *n* liking, tendency; degree of deviation

include *v* have as (part of) contents; add in **inclusion** *n* **inclusive** *adj* including (everything)

incognito *adv/adj* under an assumed identity ~*n* (*pl* **-tos**) assumed identity

incoherent *adj* lacking clarity; inarticulate **incoherence** *n*

income *n* money received from salary, investments etc.

incoming *adj* coming in; about to come into office; next

incomparable *adj* beyond comparison

incompatible *adj* inconsistent, conflicting

incompetent *adj* lacking necessary ability **incompetence** *n*

———————— THESAURUS ————————

unremitting

incident adventure, circumstance, episode, event, fact, happening, matter, occurrence; brush, clash, commotion, mishap, scene, skirmish

incidental accidental, casual, chance, fortuitous, odd, random

incipient beginning, developing, embryonic, inceptive, inchoate, starting

incision cut, gash, slash, slit

incisive acute, keen, piercing, sharp, trenchant

incite animate, drive, egg on, encourage, excite, goad, impel, inflame, instigate, prod, prompt, provoke, rouse, spur, stimulate, urge

inclement bitter, boisterous, foul, harsh, intemperate, rigorous, rough, severe, stormy, tempestuous

inclination affection, aptitude, bent, bias, desire, disposition, fancy, fondness, leaning, liking, partiality, penchant, predilection, proclivity, propensity, stomach, taste, tendency, turn, wish

incline *v* bend, bevel, cant, deviate, diverge, heel, lean, slant, slope, tend, tilt, tip, veer; be disposed, bias, influence, persuade, prejudice, sway, tend, turn ~*n* ascent, descent, dip, grade, gradient, ramp, rise, slope

include comprehend, comprise, contain, cover, embody, embrace, encompass, incorporate, involve, take in

inclusion incorporation, insertion

inclusive all in, all together, blanket, comprehensive, full, general, overall, sweeping, umbrella

incoherent confused, disjointed, inarticulate, inconsistent, loose, muddled, rambling, uncoordinated, unintelligible, wandering, wild

income earnings, gains, interest, means, pay, proceeds, profits, receipts, revenue, salary, takings, wages

incomparable inimitable, matchless, paramount, peerless, superlative, supreme, unequalled, unmatched, unrivalled

incompatible antipathetic, conflicting, contradictory, discordant, disparate, incongruous, inconsistent, mismatched, uncongenial, unsuitable

inconceivable *adj* impossible to imagine

inconclusive *adj* not giving a final decision

incongruous *adj* not appropriate **incongruity** *n*

inconsequential *adj* trivial; haphazard

incontinent *adj* not able to control bladder or bowels

incontrovertible *adj* undeniable

inconvenience *n* trouble, difficulty **inconvenient** *adj*

incorporate *v* include; form into corporation

incorrigible *adj* beyond correction or reform

increase *v* make or become greater in size, number etc. ~*n* growth, enlarge-

ment **increasingly** *adv* more and more

incredible *adj* unbelievable; *Inf* amazing **incredibly** *adv*

incredulous *adj* unbelieving **incredulity** *n*

increment *n* increase

incriminate *v* imply guilt of

incubate *v* provide eggs, bacteria etc. with heat for development; develop in this way **incubation** *n* **incubator** *n* apparatus for hatching eggs or rearing premature babies

inculcate *v* fix in the mind

incumbent *n* holder of office

incur *v* **-curring, -curred** bring upon oneself **incursion** *n* invasion

indebted *adj* owing gratitude or money

———— THESAURUS ————

incompetent cowboy *Inf*, incapable, ineffectual, inept, inexpert, insufficient, unable, unfit, unfitted, unskilful, useless

inconceivable impossible, incredible, unbelievable, unheard-of, unimaginable, unknowable, unthinkable

inconclusive ambiguous, indecisive, indeterminate, open, uncertain, undecided, unsettled, vague

incongruous absurd, conflicting, contradictory, contrary, discordant, extraneous, improper, inapt, incoherent, inconsistent, unbecoming, unsuitable, unsuited

inconvenience *n* annoyance, awkwardness, bother, difficulty, disadvantage, disruption, disturbance, drawback, fuss, hassle *Inf*, hindrance, nuisance, trouble, uneasiness, upset

inconvenient annoying, awkward, bothersome, disturbing, embarrassing, inopportune, tiresome, troublesome, unsuitable, untimely

incorporate absorb, amalgamate, assimilate, blend, coalesce, combine, consolidate, embody, fuse, include,

integrate, meld, merge, mix, unite

incorrigible hardened, hopeless, incurable, intractable, inveterate

increase *v* add to, advance, amplify, augment, boost, build up, develop, dilate, enhance, enlarge, escalate, expand, extend, grow, heighten, inflate, intensify, magnify, mount, multiply, proliferate, prolong, raise, spread, strengthen, swell ~*n* addition, boost, development, enlargement, escalation, expansion, extension, gain, growth, increment, intensification, rise, upsurge, upturn

incredible absurd, beyond belief, far-fetched, implausible, impossible, improbable, inconceivable, preposterous, unbelievable, unimaginable, unthinkable

incredulous disbelieving, doubtful, doubting, dubious, sceptical, suspicious, unbelieving

incriminate accuse, arraign, blame, charge, impeach, implicate, indict, involve

incur arouse, contract, draw, earn, gain, induce, meet with, provoke

indecent *adj* offensive; unseemly

indeed *adv* really; in fact *~interj* denoting surprise, doubt etc.

indefatigable *adj* untiring

indefensible *adj* not justifiable

indefinite *adj* without exact limits

indelible *adj* that cannot be blotted out **indelibly** *adv*

indelicate *adj* coarse, embarrassing

indemnity *n* compensation; security against loss **indemnify** *v* indemnifying, indemnified give indemnity to

indent *v* set in (from margin etc.); notch; order by indent *~n* notch; requisition **indentation** *n*

independent *adj* not subject to others; self-reliant; free; valid in itself **independence** *n* being independent; self-reliance; self-support

indescribable *adj* beyond description

indeterminate *adj* uncertain

index *n* (*pl* **indexes, indices**) alphabetical list of references; indicator; *Maths* exponent; forefinger *~v* provide with, insert in index

indicate *v* point out; state briefly; signify **indication** *n* **indicative** *adj* pointing to; *Grammar* stating fact **indicator** *n*

indict *v* accuse, esp. by legal process **indictment** *n*

indifferent *adj* uninterested; mediocre **indifference** *n*

indigenous *adj* native

indigent *adj* poor, needy

———————————— THESAURUS ————————————

indebted beholden, grateful, obligated, obliged

indecent blue, coarse, crude, dirty, filthy, foul, gross, improper, impure, indelicate, lewd, licentious, pornographic, salacious, scatological, smutty, vile

indeed actually, certainly, doubtlessly, positively, really, strictly, truly, undeniably, undoubtedly, verily, veritably

indefensible inexcusable, unforgivable, unpardonable, wrong

indefinite confused, doubtful, equivocal, evasive, general, imprecise, indeterminate, indistinct, inexact, loose, obscure, uncertain, unclear, undetermined, unfixed, unknown, unlimited, unsettled, vague

indelible enduring, indestructible, ineffaceable, ineradicable, permanent

indelicate blue, coarse, crude, embarrassing, gross, immodest, improper, indecent, low, obscene, offcolour, offensive, risqué, rude, suggestive, tasteless, vulgar

independence autarchy, autonomy, freedom, home rule, liberty, self-government, self-rule, sovereignty

independent absolute, free, liberated, separate, unconnected, uncontrolled, unrelated

indescribable ineffable, inexpressible, unutterable

index director, forefinger, hand, indicator, needle, pointer

indicate betoken, denote, evince, imply, manifest, point to, reveal, show, signify, suggest

indication clue, evidence, explanation, hint, index, manifestation, mark, note, omen, portent, sign, signal, symptom, warning

indicator display, gauge, guide, index, mark, marker, meter, pointer, sign, signal, signpost, symbol

indictment accusation, allegation, charge, impeachment, prosecution, summons

indifferent aloof, apathetic, callous, careless, cold, cool, detached, distant, heedless, inattentive, regardless, unconcerned, unimpressed, unresponsive; average, fair, mediocre, middling, moderate, ordinary, passable, perfunctory, undistinguished,

indigestion n (discomfort caused by) poor digestion

indignant adj angered by injury or injustice **indignation** n **indignity** n humiliation, insult, slight

indigo n (pl **-gos**) blue dye obtained from plant; the plant ~adj deep blue

indirect adj done, caused by someone or something else; not by straight route

indiscreet adj tactless in revealing secrets **indiscretion** n

indiscriminate adj lacking discrimination; jumbled

indispensable adj essential

indisposed adj unwell; disinclined

indisputable adj without doubt

indissoluble adj permanent

individual adj single; distinctive ~n single person or thing **individuality** n distinctive personality **individually** adv singly

indoctrinate v implant beliefs in the mind of

indolent adj lazy **indolence** n

indoor adj within doors; under cover **indoors** adv

indubitable adj beyond doubt

induce v persuade; bring on **inducement** n incentive

induct v install in office **induction** n inducting; general inference from particular inferences; production of electric or magnetic state by proximity

indulge v gratify; pamper **indulgence** n indulging; extravagance; favour, privilege **indulgent** adj

———————— THESAURUS ————————

uninspired

indignant angry, annoyed, disgruntled, exasperated, furious, heated, incensed, irate, resentful, riled, scornful, wrathful

indignation anger, fury, rage, resentment, scorn, umbrage, wrath

indirect circuitous, crooked, devious, meandering, oblique, rambling, roundabout, tortuous, wandering, winding, zigzag

indiscreet foolish, hasty, ill-advised, ill-considered, ill-judged, imprudent, naive, rash, reckless, tactless, unwise

indiscriminate aimless, careless, desultory, general, random, sweeping, wholesale

indispensable crucial, essential, imperative, key, necessary, needed, needful, requisite, vital

indisposed ailing, ill, sick, unwell

indisputable absolute, beyond doubt, certain, evident, incontrovertible, positive, sure, undeniable

individual adj characteristic, discrete, distinct, exclusive, identical, own, particular, peculiar, personal, proper, respective, separate, several, single, singular, special, specific, unique ~n being, character, creature, mortal, party, person, soul, type, unit

individuality character, distinction, originality, uniqueness

indubitable certain, evident, incontrovertible, indisputable, obvious, sure, undeniable

induce actuate, convince, draw, encourage, get, impel, incite, influence, move, persuade, press, prompt

inducement attraction, bait, cause, consideration, encouragement, impulse, incentive, incitement, influence, lure, motive, reward, spur, stimulus, urge

indulge cater to, feed, give way to, gratify, pander to, regale, satiate, satisfy, yield to

indulgence excess, fondness, intemperance, kindness, leniency, partiality, profligacy, spoiling

indulgent compliant, easy-going, favourable, fond, forbearing, gentle, kind, lenient, liberal, mild, permissive, tender, tolerant

industry n manufacture, processing etc. of goods; branch of this; diligence **industrial** adj of industries, trades **industrialize** v **industrious** adj diligent

inebriated adj drunk

inedible adj not eatable

ineffable adj unutterable

ineligible adj not fit or qualified (for something)

inept adj absurd; out of place; clumsy **ineptitude** n

inert adj without power of motion; sluggish; unreactive **inertia** n inactivity; tendency to continue at rest or in uniform motion

inescapable adj unavoidable

inestimable adj immeasurable

inevitable adj unavoidable; sure to happen **inevitability** n

inexorable adj relentless

inexplicable adj impossible to explain

infallible adj not liable to fail or err

infamous adj notorious; shocking **infamy** n

infant n very young child **infancy** n babyhood; early stage of development **infantile** adj childish

infantry n foot soldiers

infatuated adj foolishly enamoured **infatuation** n

infect v affect (with disease); contaminate **infection** n **infectious** adj catching

infer v **-ferring, -ferred** deduce, con-

————— THESAURUS —————

industrious active, busy, diligent, energetic, hard-working, productive, tireless

industry business, commerce, manufacturing, production, trade; activity, application, assiduity, determination, diligence, effort, labour, perseverance, persistence, toil, vigour, zeal

ineligible disqualified, ruled out, unacceptable, undesirable, unfit, unqualified, unsuitable

inept awkward, bungling, clumsy, gauche, maladroit, unskilful

inert dead, dormant, dull, idle, immobile, inactive, inanimate, leaden, lifeless, motionless, passive, quiescent, slack, sluggish, static, still, torpid, unresponsive

inertia apathy, deadness, drowsiness, dullness, idleness, immobility, laziness, lethargy, listlessness, passivity, sloth, stillness, stupor, torpor

inescapable certain, destined, fated, inevitable, inexorable, sure

inevitable assured, certain, decreed, destined, fixed, necessary, ordained, settled, sure, unavoidable

inexplicable baffling, enigmatic, in-

scrutable, insoluble, mysterious, strange, unaccountable

infallible faultless, impeccable, perfect, unerring

infamous base, disgraceful, dishonourable, disreputable, heinous, ignominious, loathsome, monstrous, nefarious, notorious, odious, outrageous, scandalous, shameful, shocking, villainous, wicked

infancy babyhood, early childhood; beginnings, cradle, dawn, early stages, emergence, inception, origins, outset, start

infant n baby, child, toddler, tot

infantile babyish, childish, immature, puerile, tender, weak, young

infatuated beguiled, besotted, bewitched, captivated, enraptured, fascinated, inflamed, intoxicated, obsessed, possessed, spellbound

infect blight, contaminate, corrupt, defile, influence, poison, pollute, taint, touch

infection contagion, contamination, corruption, poison, pollution

infectious catching, communicable, contagious, contaminating, corrupt-

clude **inference** n

inferior adj of poor quality; lower ~n one lower (in rank etc.) **inferiority** n

infernal adj devilish; hellish; Inf irritating, confounded

inferno n (pl -nos) intense, raging fire; hell

infertile adj barren, not productive

infest v inhabit or overrun in dangerously or unpleasantly large numbers

infidelity n unfaithfulness; religious disbelief **infidel** n unbeliever

infiltrate v trickle through; gain access surreptitiously

infinite adj boundless **infinitely** adv exceedingly **infinitesimal** adj extremely small **infinity** n unlimited extent

infinitive n form of verb without tense, person, or number

infirm adj physically or mentally weak; **infirmary** n hospital, sick quarters **infirmity** n

inflame v rouse to anger, excitement; cause inflammation in **inflammable** adj easily set on fire; excitable **inflammation** n painful infected swelling **inflammatory** adj

inflate v blow up with air, gas; swell; raise price, esp. artificially **inflatable** adj **inflation** n increase in prices and fall in value of money

inflection, inflexion n modification of word; modulation of voice

inflexible adj incapable of being bent; stubborn

inflict v impose, deliver forcibly **infliction** n

influence n power to affect other people, events etc.; person, thing possessing such power ~v sway; induce; affect **influential** adj

——————— THESAURUS ———————

ing, infective, pestilential, poisoning, virulent

infer conclude, conjecture, deduce, derive, gather, presume, understand

inference assumption, conclusion, conjecture, consequence, corollary, deduction, presumption, surmise

inferior junior, lesser, lower, menial, minor, secondary, subordinate, subsidiary, underneath

inferiority imperfection, inadequacy, meanness, mediocrity, shoddiness

infertile barren, sterile, unfruitful

infest beset, flood, invade, overrun, ravage, swarm, throng

infiltrate creep in, penetrate, percolate, permeate, pervade

infinite adj absolute, all-embracing, boundless, eternal, immense, inestimable, inexhaustible, interminable, limitless, measureless, numberless, perpetual, total, unbounded, uncounted, untold, vast, wide, without end

infinity boundlessness, endlessness, eternity, immensity, vastness

infirm decrepit, doddering, doddery, failing, feeble, frail, lame, weak

inflame anger, arouse, enrage, excite, fire, heat, ignite, incense, infuriate, kindle, madden, provoke, rile, rouse, stimulate

inflammable combustible, flammable, incendiary

inflate amplify, balloon, blow up, boost, dilate, distend, enlarge, escalate, exaggerate, expand, increase, swell

inflation blowing up, distension, enlargement, escalation, expansion, increase, rise, spread, swelling

inflection accentuation, intonation, modulation; Grammar conjugation, declension

inflexible adamant, firm, fixed, immovable, implacable, intractable, obdurate, relentless, resolute, rigorous, set, steadfast, strict, stringent, stubborn

inflict apply, deliver, exact, impose,

influenza *n* contagious viral disease

influx *n* flowing in; inflow

inform *v* give information (about) **informant** *n* one who tells **information** *n* what is told, knowledge **informative** *adj* **informer** *n*

informal *adj* relaxed and friendly; appropriate for everyday use **informally** *adv* **informality** *n*

infrared *adj* below visible spectrum

infrastructure *n* basic structure or fixed capital items of an organization or economic system

infringe *v* transgress, break

infuriate *v* enrage

infuse *v* soak to extract flavour etc.; instil **infusion** *n* infusing; extract obtained

ingenious *adj* clever at contriving; cleverly contrived **ingenuity** *n*

ingenuous *adj* frank; innocent

ingot *n* block of cast metal, esp. gold

ingrained *adj* deep-rooted; inveterate

ingratiate *v* get (oneself) into favour

ingredient *n* component part of a mixture

inhabit *v* dwell in **inhabitant** *n*

inhale *v* breathe in (air etc.) **inhalation** *n* **inhaler** *n* container with medical preparation inhaled to help breathing

inherent *adj* existing as an inseparable part

inherit *v* receive, succeed as heir; derive from parents **inheritance** *n*

inhibit *v* restrain; hinder **inhibition** *n* repression of emotion, instinct

inhospitable *adj* unfriendly; harsh

————— THESAURUS —————

levy, visit, wreak

influence *n* agency, authority, control, credit, direction, domination, effect, guidance, mastery, power, pressure, rule, spell, sway, weight ~*v* affect, arouse, control, count, direct, dispose, guide, impel, impress, induce, instigate, manipulate, modify, move, persuade, predispose, prompt, rouse, sway

inform acquaint, advise, apprise, communicate, enlighten, instruct, notify, teach, tell, tip off

informal casual, easy, familiar, natural, relaxed, simple

information advice, counsel, data, facts, instruction, intelligence, knowledge, latest *Inf*, material, message, news, notice, report, tidings, word

informer accuser, betrayer, sneak, stool pigeon

infringe break, contravene, disobey, transgress, violate

infuriate anger, enrage, exasperate, gall, incense, irritate, madden, provoke, rile

ingenious adroit, bright, brilliant, clever, crafty, creative, dexterous, fertile, inventive, masterly, original, ready, resourceful, shrewd, skilful, subtle

ingenuous artless, candid, childlike, frank, honest, innocent, naive, open, plain, simple, sincere, trustful, unsophisticated

ingredient component, constituent, element, part

inhabit abide, dwell, live, lodge, occupy, people, populate, possess, reside, tenant

inhabitant citizen, denizen, inmate, native, occupant, occupier, resident, tenant

inherit accede to, be left, fall heir to, succeed to

inheritance bequest, birthright, heritage, legacy, patrimony

inhibit arrest, bar, bridle, check, constrain, curb, debar, discourage, forbid, frustrate, hinder, impede, obstruct, prevent, restrain, stop

inhibition bar, check, embargo, hindrance, interdict, obstacle, prohibi-

inhuman *adj* cruel, brutal; not human

inhumane *adj* cruel, brutal **inhumanity** *n*

inimical *adj* unfavourable, hostile

inimitable *adj* defying imitation

iniquity *n* gross injustice; sin **iniquitous** *adj*

initial *adj* of, occurring at the beginning ~*n* initial letter, esp. of person's name ~*v* **-tialling, -tialled** mark, sign with one's initials **initially** *adv*

initiate *v* originate; admit into closed society; instruct **initiation** *n* **initiative** *n* lead; ability to act independently

inject *v* put (fluid, medicine etc.) into body with syringe; introduce (new element) **injection** *n*

injunction *n* (judicial) order

injury *n* physical damage; wrong **injure** *v* do harm or damage to

injustice *n* want of justice; wrong; unjust act

ink *n* fluid used for writing or printing ~*v* mark, cover with ink **inky** *adj*

inkling *n* hint, vague idea

inland *adj/adv* in, towards the interior; away from the sea

in-law *n* relative by marriage

inlay *v* **inlaying, inlaid** embed; decorate with inset pattern ~*n* inlaid piece or pattern

inlet *n* entrance; mouth of creek; piece inserted

inmate *n* occupant, esp. of prison, hospital, etc.

inmost *adj* most inward, deepest

inn *n* public house providing food and accommodation; hotel **innkeeper** *n*

innards *pl n Inf* internal parts, esp. of body

innate *adj* inborn; inherent

inner *adj* lying within **innermost** *adj*

innings *n Sport* player's or side's turn

——————— THESAURUS ———————

tion, reserve, restraint, restriction, reticence, shyness

inhospitable unfriendly, ungenerous, unwelcoming; bare, barren, bleak, desolate, empty, godforsaken, harsh, hostile, lonely

inhuman animal, barbaric, bestial, brutal, cruel, heartless, merciless, pitiless, ruthless, savage, unfeeling, vicious

inhumane brutal, cruel, heartless, pitiless, unfeeling, unkind

initial *adj* beginning, early, first, inaugural, introductory, opening, primary

initially at first, at *or* in the beginning, first, firstly, originally, primarily

initiate begin, break the ice, inaugurate, institute, kick-start, launch, open, originate, pioneer, start; indoctrinate, induct, instate, instruct, introduce, invest, teach, train

initiative advantage, beginning, first move, first step, lead

inject inoculate, vaccinate; infuse, insert, instil, interject, introduce

injunction command, dictate, mandate, order, precept, ruling

injure abuse, blemish, blight, break, damage, deface, disable, harm, hurt, impair, maltreat, mar, ruin, spoil, tarnish, undermine, weaken, wound

injury abuse, damage, evil, grievance, harm, hurt, ill, injustice, mischief, ruin, wound, wrong

injustice bias, favouritism, inequality, oppression, partiality, partisanship, prejudice, unfairness, unlawfulness, wrong

inland interior, internal, upcountry

inlet arm (of the sea), bay, bight, cove, creek, entrance

inmost basic, buried, central, deep, deepest, essential, intimate, personal, private, secret

innate congenital, essential, inborn, inbred, inherent, instinctive, intrinsic, intuitive, native, natural

of batting; turn

innocent *adj* guiltless; without experience of evil ~*n* innocent person **innocence** *n*

innocuous *adj* harmless

innovate *v* introduce new things **innovation** *n*

innuendo *n* (*pl* -**does**) indirect accusation

innumerable *adj* countless

inoculate *v* immunize by injecting vaccine **inoculation** *n*

inoperable *adj Med* not able to be operated on **inoperative** *adj* not operative

inordinate *adj* excessive

inorganic *adj* not organic; not containing carbon

input *n* material, data, current etc. fed into a system

inquest *n* coroner's inquiry into cause of death; detailed inquiry

inquire, enquire *v* seek information **inquirer, enquirer** *n* **inquiry, enquiry** *n* question; investigation

inquisition *n* searching investigation; *Hist* (*with cap.*) tribunal for suppression of heresy **inquisitor** *n*

inquisitive *adj* curious; prying

insane *adj* mentally deranged; crazy **insanely** *adv* madly; excessively **insanity** *n*

insatiable *adj* incapable of being satisfied

inscribe *v* write, engrave (in or on something) **inscription** *n* words inscribed

inscrutable *adj* enigmatic; incomprehensible

insect *n* small, usu. winged animal with six legs **insecticide** *n* preparation for killing insects

insecure *adj* not safe or firm; anxious

inseminate *v* implant semen into

——————————— THESAURUS ———————————

inner central, essential, inside, interior, internal, intestinal, inward, middle

innocence blamelessness, faultlessness, guiltlessness, righteousness; artlessness, gullibility, naiveté, simplicity

innocent blameless, clear, faultless, guiltless, honest; artless, childlike, credulous, frank, guileless, gullible, ingenuous, naive, open, simple

innovation change, departure, introduction, novelty, variation

innuendo aspersion, hint, implication, insinuation, suggestion, whisper

innumerable countless, incalculable, infinite, many, myriad, untold

inordinate excessive, exorbitant, extravagant, unreasonable

inquest inquiry, inquisition, investigation, probe

inquire examine, explore, inspect, investigate, make inquiries, probe, scrutinize, search

inquisition cross-examination, examination, inquest, inquiry, investigation, question

inquisitive curious, inquiring, intrusive, peering, probing, prying, questioning

insane barking mad *Sl*, crackpot *Inf*, crazed, crazy, demented, deranged, mad, unhinged

insanity dementia, frenzy, madness, mental illness

insatiable greedy, intemperate, rapacious, ravenous, voracious

inscribe address, dedicate, write; carve, cut, engrave, etch, impress, imprint

inscription dedication, engraving, label, legend, lettering, saying, words

inscrutable blank, deadpan, enigmatic; hidden, incomprehensible, mysterious, unintelligible

insecure flimsy, frail, insubstantial, loose, precarious, rickety, rocky, shaky, unreliable, unsound, unstable,

insensible *adj* unconscious; without feeling; not aware **insensibly** *adv* imperceptibly

insensitive *adj* unaware of other people's feelings

insert *v* put into or between ~*n* something inserted **insertion** *n*

inset *n* something extra inserted **inset** *v* **-setting, -set**

inshore *adv/adj* near shore

inside *n* inner part; *pl Inf* stomach, entrails ~*adj/adv/prep* in, on, into the inside

insidious *adj* unseen but deadly

insight *n* discernment

insignia *pl n* badges, emblems

insignificant *adj* having little or no importance **insignificance** *n*

insincere *adj* pretending what one does not feel **insincerity** *n*

insinuate *v* hint; introduce subtly **insinuation** *n*

insipid *adj* dull, tasteless

insist *v* demand persistently; maintain; emphasize **insistence** *n* **insistent** *adj*

insole *n* inner sole of shoe or boot

insolent *adj* impudent **insolence** *n*

insoluble *adj* incapable of being solved; incapable of being dissolved

insolvent *adj* unable to pay one's debts **insolvency** *n*

insomnia *n* inability to sleep **insomniac** *adj/n*

——————— THESAURUS ———————

unsteady, weak; afraid, anxious, uncertain, unsure

insensible dull, inert, numbed, stupid, torpid

insensitive callous, crass, indifferent, obtuse, tactless, thick-skinned, unfeeling

insert enter, interpolate, interpose, introduce, place, put, set, stick in, tuck in

insertion addition, implant, inclusion, inset, introduction

inside *n* contents, inner part, interior; (*oft. pl*) *Inf* belly, bowels, entrails, gut, guts, stomach ~*adj* inner, innermost, interior, internal, inward ~*adv* indoors, under cover, within

insidious artful, crafty, cunning, deceptive, duplicitous, slick, sly, smooth, stealthy, subtle, tricky, wily

insight awareness, discernment, intuition, judgment, observation, perception, understanding, vision

insignia badge, crest, emblem, ensign, symbol

insignificant flimsy, irrelevant, meaningless, minor, negligible, paltry, petty, scanty, trifling, trivial, unimportant

insincere devious, dishonest, double-dealing, duplicitous, evasive, false, hollow, hypocritical, lying, two-faced, unfaithful, untrue

insinuate allude, hint, imply, indicate, intimate, suggest; infiltrate, infuse, inject, instil, introduce

insinuation allusion, aspersion, hint, implication, innuendo, slur, suggestion

insist be firm, demand, persist, require; aver, claim, contend, hold, maintain, reiterate, repeat, swear, urge, vow

insistence assertion, contention, emphasis, reiteration, stress, urging

insistent demanding, dogged, emphatic, exigent, forceful, incessant, unrelenting, urgent

insolence abuse, audacity, boldness, disrespect, effrontery, front, gall, impertinence, impudence, insubordination, rudeness

insolent abusive, bold, contemptuous, impertinent, impudent, insubordinate, insulting, pert, rude, uncivil

insoluble baffling, inexplicable, mysterious, mystifying, obscure, unfathomable

inspect v examine (closely or officially) **inspection** n **inspector** n

inspire v arouse creatively; give rise to **inspiration** n good idea; creative influence

install v place in position; formally place (person) in position or rank **installation** n act of installing; equipment installed

instalment n part payment; one of a series of parts

instance n example ~v cite

instant n moment ~adj immediate; (of foods) requiring little preparation **instantaneous** adj happening in an instant **instantly** adv at once

instead adv in place (of)

instep n top of foot between toes and ankle

instigate v incite, urge **instigation** n **instigator** n

instil v **-stilling, -stilled** implant; inculcate

instinct n inborn impulse; unconscious skill **instinctive** adj

institute v establish; set going ~n society for promoting science etc. **institution** n setting up; establishment for care or education; established custom, law etc. **institutional** adj of institutions; routine

instruct v teach; inform; order **in-**

insolvent bankrupt, failed, ruined

insomnia sleeplessness, wakefulness

inspect check, check out Inf, examine, investigate, look over, oversee, scan, scrutinize, search, supervise, survey, vet

inspection check, examination, investigation, review, scan, scrutiny, search, supervision, surveillance, survey

inspector censor, checker, critic, examiner, investigator, overseer, scrutineer, supervisor

inspiration arousal, awakening, encouragement, influence, muse, spur, stimulus

inspire animate, encourage, enliven, galvanize, hearten, imbue, influence, infuse, inspirit, instil, rouse, spark off, spur, stimulate

install fix, lay, lodge, place, position, put in, set up, station; establish, induct, institute, introduce, invest, set up

installation inauguration, induction, investiture; equipment, machinery, plant; system

instalment chapter, division, episode, part, portion, repayment, section

instance n case, example, illustration, occasion, occurrence, precedent, situation, time ~v adduce, cite, mention, name, quote, specify

instant n flash, moment, second, split second, trice, twinkling ~adj direct, immediate, instantaneous, prompt, quick, quickie Inf, urgent

instantaneous direct, immediate, instant, on-the-spot

instantly at once, directly, forthwith, immediately, instantaneously, now, without delay

instead alternatively, preferably, rather

instigate actuate, encourage, get going, impel, incite, influence, initiate, kick-start, kindle, move, prompt, provoke, rouse, set off, set on, spur, start, stimulate, stir up, trigger

instil engender, implant, impress, infix, infuse, insinuate

instinct aptitude, faculty, feeling, gift, impulse, intuition, knack, proclivity, talent, tendency, urge

instinctive inborn, inherent, innate, intuitional, intuitive, natural, reflex

institute v appoint, begin, enact, establish, fix, found, induct, initiate, install, introduce, invest, ordain, or-

struction n teaching, order; pl directions **instructive** adj informative **instructor** n

instrument n thing used to make, do, measure etc.; mechanism for producing musical sound **instrumental** adj acting as instrument or means; produced by musical instruments

insubordinate adj mutinous, rebellious **insubordination** n

insufferable adj unbearable

insular adj of an island; narrow-minded

insulate v prevent or reduce transfer of electricity, heat, sound etc.; isolate, detach **insulation** n **insulator** n

insulin n hormone used in treatment of diabetes

insult v behave rudely to; offend ~n affront **insulting** adj

insuperable adj not able to be overcome

insure v contract for payment in event of loss, death etc.; make safe (against) **insurance** n

insurrection n revolt

intact adj untouched; uninjured

intake n thing, amount taken in; opening

integer n whole number

integral adj essential **integrate** v combine into one whole **integration** n

———————————— THESAURUS ————————————

ganize, pioneer, settle, set up, start ~n academy, college, conservatory, foundation, guild, school, seminary, society

institution creation, establishment, foundation, investiture; academy, college, foundation, hospital, institute, school, seminary, society, university; custom, fixture, law, practice, ritual, rule, tradition

instruct coach, discipline, drill, educate, ground, guide, inform, school, teach, train, tutor, bid, charge, direct, enjoin, order, tell

instruction coaching, discipline, drilling, education, grounding, guidance, information, lesson(s), schooling, teaching, training, tuition

instructor adviser, coach, guide, master, mentor, pedagogue, teacher, trainer, tutor

instrument appliance, contrivance, device, gadget, implement, mechanism, tool, utensil

instrumental active, assisting, auxiliary, conducive, grounding, helpful, involved, subsidiary, useful

insubordinate defiant, disobedient, disorderly, rebellious, riotous, seditious, turbulent, undisciplined, un-

governable, unruly

insubordination defiance, disobedience, indiscipline, insurrection, mutiny, rebellion, revolt, sedition

insufferable detestable, impossible, intolerable, outrageous, unbearable, unendurable

insular blinkered, closed, limited, narrow, parochial, petty, provincial

insulate close off, cut off, isolate, protect

insult v abuse, injure, offend, outrage, put down, revile, slander, slight ~n abuse, indignity, insolence, outrage, put-down, rudeness, slight, snub

insurance cover, guarantee, indemnity, protection, provision, safeguard, security, warranty

insure assure, cover, guarantee, indemnify, underwrite, warrant

intact complete, entire, perfect, sound, together, unbroken, undamaged, unharmed, unhurt, untouched, virgin, whole

integral basic, component, constituent, essential

integrate accommodate, assimilate, blend, coalesce, combine, fuse, harmonize, join, knit, merge, unite

integration amalgamation, assimila-

integrity *n* honesty

intellect *n* power of thinking and reasoning **intellectual** *adj* of, appealing to intellect; having good intellect ~*n* intellectual person

intelligent *adj* clever **intelligence** *n* intellect; information, esp. military **intelligible** *adj* understandable

intemperate *adj* drinking alcohol to excess; immoderate

intend *v* propose, mean

intense *adj* very strong or acute; emotional **intensify** *v* intensifying, intensified increase **intensity** *n* **intensive** *adj*

intent *n* purpose ~*adj* concentrating (on); resolved **intention** *n* purpose, aim **intentional** *adj*

inter *v* interring, interred bury **interment** *n*

inter- *comb. form* between, among, mutually, as in **interglacial, interrelation**

interact *v* act on each other **interaction** *n* **interactive** *adj*

intercede *v* plead in favour of, mediate **intercession** *n*

intercept *v* cut off; seize, stop in transit **interception** *n*

interchange *v* (cause to) exchange

———— THESAURUS ————

tion, blending, combining, fusing, harmony, incorporation, mixing, unification

integrity goodness, honesty, honour, rectitude, righteousness, virtue

intellect brains *Inf*, intelligence, judgment, mind, reason, sense, understanding

intellectual *adj* bookish, highbrow, intelligent, mental, rational, scholarly, studious, thoughtful ~*n* academic, highbrow

intelligence acumen, alertness, brightness, capacity, cleverness, discernment, intellect, mind, perception, quickness, reason, understanding; advice, data, disclosure, facts, findings, information, knowledge, news, notice, report, rumour, tidings, tip-off, word

intelligent acute, alert, apt, bright, clever, discerning, knowing, perspicacious, quick, rational, sharp, smart

intelligible clear, distinct, lucid, open, plain, understandable

intend aim, contemplate, determine, mean, meditate, plan, propose, purpose, scheme

intense acute, close, concentrated, deep, drastic, extreme, fierce, forceful, great, harsh, powerful, profound,

protracted, severe, strained; ardent, burning, eager, earnest, emotional, fanatical, fervent, fierce, heightened, impassioned, keen, passionate, vehement

intensify add to, aggravate, augment, boost, concentrate, deepen, emphasize, enhance, heighten, increase, magnify, quicken, reinforce, set off, sharpen, strengthen

intensity ardour, concentration, depth, emotion, energy, excess, fervour, fire, force, keenness, passion, potency, power, severity, strength, vehemence, vigour

intensive all-out, concentrated, demanding, exhaustive, thorough

intent absorbed, alert, attentive, committed, concentrated, determined, eager, earnest, fixed, occupied, preoccupied, rapt, resolute, resolved, steadfast, steady, watchful, wrapped up

intention aim, design, end, goal, idea, object, objective, point, purpose, scope, target, view

intentional deliberate, designed, meant, planned, premeditated, purposed, studied

intercept arrest, block, catch, check, cut off, deflect, head off, stop, take

places ~*n* motorway junction **interchangeable** able to be exchanged in position or use

inter-city *adj* denoting fast rail service between main towns

intercom *n* internal communication system

intercontinental *adj* connecting continents; (of missile) able to reach one continent from another

intercourse *n* act of having sex; communications or dealings between individuals or groups

interdict *n* formal prohibition ~*v* prohibit

interest *n* concern, curiosity; thing exciting this; sum paid for borrowed money; advantage; right, share ~*v* excite, cause to feel interest **interested** *adj* **interesting** *adj*

interface *adj* area, surface, boundary linking two systems

interfere *v* meddle, intervene; clash **interference** *n* act of interfering; *Radio* atmospherics

interim *n* meantime ~*adj* temporary

interior *adj* inner; inland; indoors ~*n* inside; inland region

interject *v* interpose (remark etc.) **interjection** *n* exclamation; interjected remark

interlock *v* lock together firmly

interloper *n* intruder

interlude *n* interval; something filling an interval

intermarry *v* (of families, races, religions) become linked by marriage; marry within one's family **intermarriage** *n*

intermediate *adj* coming between; interposed **intermediary** *n*

interminable *adj* endless

intermission *n* interval **intermittent** *adj* occurring at intervals

intern *v* confine to special area or camp **internment** *n*

internal *adj* inward; interior; within (a country, organization)

international *adj* of relations between nations ~*n* game or match be-

─────────── T H E S A U R U S ───────────

interchangeable equivalent, identical, reciprocal, synonymous, the same

intercourse association, commerce, communion, connection, contact, converse, dealings, trade, traffic, truck; carnal knowledge, coitus, copulation, sex, sexual intercourse

interest *n* affection, attention, attraction, concern, curiosity, notice, regard, suspicion, sympathy; activity, diversion, hobby, pastime, pursuit, relaxation; advantage, benefit, gain, good, profit ~*v* amuse, attract, divert, engross, excite, fascinate; affect, concern, engage, involve

interested affected, attentive, attracted, curious, drawn, excited, fascinated, intent, into *Inf,* keen, moved, stimulated

interesting absorbing, compelling,

engaging, engrossing, entertaining, gripping, intriguing, stimulating

interfere butt in, intervene, intrude, meddle, tamper

interference intervention, intrusion, meddling

interior *adj* inner, inside, internal, inward; *Geog* central, inland, remote ~*n Geog* centre, heartland, upcountry

interlude break, delay, episode, halt, hiatus, intermission, interval, pause, respite, rest, spell, stop, stoppage, wait

intermediate halfway, intervening, mean, mid, middle, midway

intermittent broken, discontinuous, fitful, irregular, occasional, periodic, punctuated, recurrent, spasmodic, sporadic

internal inner, inside, interior, intimate, private

tween teams of different countries

internecine *adj* mutually destructive; deadly

interplanetary *adj* of, linking planets

interplay *n* action and reaction of things upon each other

interpolate *v* insert new matter; interject

interpose *v* insert; say as interruption

interpret *v* explain; translate, esp. orally; represent **interpretation** *n* **interpreter** *n*

interrogate *v* question, esp. closely or officially **interrogation** *n* **interrogative** *n* word used in asking question **interrogator** *n*

interrupt *v* break in (upon); stop; block **interruption** *n*

intersect *v* divide by passing across or through; meet and cross **intersection** *n*

intersperse *v* sprinkle among or in

interstellar *adj* between stars

interstice *n* slit, crevice

intertwine *v* twist together

interval *n* intervening time or space; pause, break; difference (of pitch)

intervene *v* come into a situation in order to change it; be, come between or among; occur in the meantime; interpose **intervention** *n*

interview *n* meeting, esp. one involving questioning ~*v* have interview with **interviewee** *n* **interviewer** *n*

intestate *adj* not having made a will

intestine *n* (*usu. pl*) lower part of alimentary canal between stomach and anus **intestinal** *adj*

intimate¹ *adj* closely acquainted, familiar; private; having cosy atmosphere ~*n* intimate friend **intimacy** *n*

intimate² *v* announce; imply in indirect way **intimation** *n*

intimidate *v* frighten into submission

——————— T H E S A U R U S ———————

international cosmopolitan, global, intercontinental, universal, worldwide

interpose insert, interject, introduce; interfere, intervene, intrude, step in

interpret adapt, clarify, construe, decipher, decode, define, elucidate, explain, expound, paraphrase, read, render, solve, take, translate

interpretation analysis, diagnosis, elucidation, explanation, meaning, performance, reading, rendering, sense, translation, version

interpreter annotator, exponent, scholiast, translator

interrogate ask, cross-examine, enquire, examine, inquire, investigate, pump, question, quiz

interrogation cross-examination, cross-questioning, enquiry, examination, inquisition, probing, questioning

interrupt break in, butt in, disturb, divide, heckle, hinder, hold up, in-

trude, obstruct, separate, sever, stay, stop, suspend

interruption break, disconnection, disruption, disturbance, division, halt, hiatus, hitch, impediment, intrusion, obstacle, obstruction, pause, stop, stoppage

intersection crossing, crossroads, interchange, junction

interval break, delay, gap, interlude, intermission, meantime, meanwhile, opening, pause, period, playtime, respite, rest, season, space, spell, term, time, wait

intervene arbitrate, intercede, interfere, intrude, mediate

intervention agency, interference, intrusion, mediation

interview *n* audience, conference, consultation, dialogue, meeting, talk ~*v* examine, interrogate, question, talk to

intimacy closeness, confidence, familiarity, understanding

intimidation n

into prep expresses motion to a point within; indicates change of state; indicates coming up against, encountering; indicates arithmetical division

intolerable adj more than can be endured

intolerant adj narrow-minded

intone v chant intonation n accent

intoxicate v make drunk

intractable adj difficult

intransigent adj uncompromising

intravenous adj into a vein

intrepid adj fearless, undaunted

intricate adj complex intricacy n

intrigue n underhand plot; secret love affair; v carry on intrigue; interest, puzzle

intrinsic adj inherent, essential

introduce v make acquainted; present; bring in; insert introduction n introducing; preliminary part of book etc. introductory adj preliminary

introvert n Psychoanalysis one who looks inward introverted adj

intrude v thrust (oneself) in intruder n intrusion n intrusive adj

intuition n instinctive knowledge or

———————— THESAURUS ————————

intimate[1] adj bosom, cherished, close, confidential, dear, friendly, near, warm; personal, private, privy, secret; comfy, cosy, friendly, informal, snug ~n bosom friend, companion, comrade, confidant, crony, familiar, friend, pal

intimate[2] v allude, communicate, declare, hint, impart, imply, indicate, insinuate, remind, state, suggest, warn

intimidate alarm, appal, bully, coerce, dishearten, dismay, frighten, overawe, scare, subdue, terrify, terrorize, threaten

intimidation browbeating, bullying, fear, menaces, pressure, terror, threat

intolerable excruciating, impossible, insufferable, painful, unbearable, unendurable

intolerant chauvinistic, fanatical, narrow, narrow-minded, one-sided, prejudiced, small-minded

intrepid bold, brave, courageous, daring, doughty, fearless, gallant, have-a-go Inf, heroic, plucky, resolute, stalwart, unafraid, unflinching, valiant, valorous

intricate complex, complicated, difficult, elaborate, fancy, involved, knotty, obscure, perplexing, tangled, tortuous

intrigue n collusion, conspiracy, double-dealing, knavery, manipulation, manoeuvre, plot, ruse, scheme, stratagem, trickery, wile; affair, amour, liaison, romance ~v connive, conspire, machinate, plot, scheme; attract, charm, fascinate, interest, rivet, titillate

intrinsic basic, built-in, central, congenital, essential, genuine, inborn, inbred, inherent, native, natural, real, true

introduce acquaint, familiarize, make known, present; begin, bring in, commence, establish, found, inaugurate, initiate, institute, launch, organize, pioneer, set up, start, usher in

introduction baptism, debut, inauguration, induction, initiation, institution, launch, presentation; foreword, lead-in, opening, overture, preamble, preface, prelude, proem, prologue

introductory early, elementary, first, inaugural, initial, opening, preliminary, preparatory

intrude encroach, infringe, interfere, interrupt, obtrude, trespass, violate

intruder burglar, interloper, invader, prowler, raider, thief, trespasser

intrusion infringement, interruption, invasion, trespass, violation

belief intuitive *adj*

inundate *v* flood; overwhelm **inundation** *n*

inured *adj* hardened

invade *v* enter by force; overrun **invader** *n* **invasion** *n*

invalid[1] *n* one suffering from ill health ~*v* retire because of illness etc.

invalid[2] *adj* having no legal force **invalidate** *v*

invaluable *adj* priceless

invasion *see* INVADE

invective *n* bitter verbal attack

inveigle *v* entice

invent *v* devise, originate; fabricate **invention** *n* that which is invented; ability to invent **inventive** *adj* resourceful; creative **inventor** *n*

inventory *n* detailed list

invert *v* turn upside down; reverse **inverse** *adj* inverted; opposite **inversion** *n*

invertebrate *n/adj* (animal) without backbone

invest *v* lay out (money, time, effort etc.) for profit or advantage; install; endow **investiture** *n* formal installation in office or rank **investment** *n* investing; money invested; stocks and shares bought **investor** *n*

investigate *v* inquire into; examine **investigation** *n* **investigative** *adj* **investigator** *n*

inveterate *adj* deep-rooted; confirmed

invidious *adj* likely to cause ill will

invigilate *v* supervise examination candidates **invigilator** *n*

——————— THESAURUS ———————

intuition hunch, insight, instinct, perception, presentiment

invade assail, assault, attack, burst in, encroach, infringe, occupy, raid, violate

invader aggressor, attacker, plunderer, raider, trespasser

invalid[1] *adj* ailing, disabled, feeble, frail, ill, infirm, sick, sickly

invalid[2] *adj* baseless, false, ill-founded, illogical, irrational, null and void, unfounded, unsound, untrue, void, worthless

invaluable costly, inestimable, precious, priceless, valuable

invasion assault, attack, foray, incursion, inroad, irruption, offensive, onslaught, raid

invent coin, conceive, contrive, create, design, devise, discover, formulate, imagine, improvise, manufacture, originate, think up

invention contraption, contrivance, creation, design, development, device, discovery, gadget

inventive creative, fertile, gifted, ground-breaking, imaginative, ingenious, resourceful

inventor author, coiner, creator, designer, father, maker, originator

inventory *n* account, catalogue, list, record, register, roll, roster, schedule

inverse *adj* contrary, inverted, opposite, reverse, transposed

invert capsize, overturn, reverse, transpose, upset, upturn

invest advance, devote, lay out, put in, sink, spend; endow, endue, provide, supply

investigate consider, enquire into, examine, explore, inspect, probe, scrutinize, search, sift, study

investigation analysis, enquiry, examination, exploration, hearing, inquest, inquiry, inspection, probe, recce, research, review, scrutiny, search, study, survey

investigator examiner, inquirer, (private) detective, researcher, reviewer, sleuth

investment asset, speculation, transaction, venture

inveterate chronic, confirmed, entrenched, established, hardened, in-

invigorate *v* give vigour to

invincible *adj* unconquerable

inviolable *adj* not to be violated **inviolate** *adj* not violated

invisible *adj* not able to be seen

invite *v* request the company of; ask courteously; ask for; attract, call forth **invitation** *n*

invoice *n* list of goods or services sold, with prices ~*v* make, present an invoice

invoke *v* call on; appeal to; ask earnestly for; summon **invocation** *n*

involuntary *adj* unintentional; instinctive

involve *v* include; entail; implicate (person); concern; entangle **involved** *adj* complicated; concerned (in)

inward *adj* internal; situated within; mental ~*adv* (*also* **inwards**) towards the inside; into the mind **inwardly** *adv* in the mind; internally

iodine *n* nonmetallic element found in seaweed

ion *n* electrically charged atom

IOU *n* signed paper acknowledging debt

IQ intelligence quotient

IRA Irish Republican Army

ire *n* anger **irascible** *adj* hot-tempered **irate** *adj* angry

iridescent *adj* exhibiting changing colours

iris *n* circular membrane of eye containing pupil; plant with sword-shaped leaves and showy flowers

irk *v* irritate, vex **irksome** *adj* tiresome

iron *n* common metallic element; tool etc. of this metal; appliance used to smooth cloth; metal-headed golf club; *pl* fetters ~*adj* of, like, iron; unyielding; robust ~*v* press **ironmonger** *n* dealer in hardware

irony *n* use of words to mean the op-

——————— THESAURUS ———————

corrigible, long-standing

invigorate brace, energize, enliven, exhilarate, fortify, galvanize, harden, quicken, refresh, rejuvenate, stimulate, strengthen

invincible indestructible, unassailable, unbeatable

invisible indiscernible, out of sight, unseen; concealed, disguised, hidden, inconspicuous

invitation asking, begging, bidding, call, request, solicitation, summons; coquetry, enticement, incitement, inducement, overture, provocation, temptation

invite ask, beg, bid, call, request, solicit, summon; allure, attract, bring on, court, draw, encourage, entice, lead, provoke, solicit, tempt, welcome

invocation appeal, entreaty, petition, prayer, supplication

invoke adjure, beg, beseech, call upon, conjure, entreat, implore, peti-

tion, pray, solicit, supplicate

involuntary compulsory, forced, obligatory, reluctant, unwilling

involve entail, imply, mean, necessitate, presuppose, require; affect, associate, concern, connect, draw in, implicate, incriminate, inculpate, touch

involvement association, commitment, concern, connection, interest, responsibility

inward *adj* entering, incoming, ingoing, penetrating; confidential, hidden, inmost, innermost, inside, interior, internal, personal, private, secret

irksome annoying, boring, burdensome, disagreeable, exasperating, tedious, tiresome, troublesome, unwelcome, vexatious, vexing, wearisome

iron *adj* adamant, cruel, hard, heavy, immovable, implacable, inflexible, obdurate, rigid, steel, strong, tough, unbending, unyielding

posite of what is said; event, situation opposite of that expected **ironic, ironical** *adj* of, using, irony
irradiate *v* treat with light or beams of particles; shine upon **irradiation** *n*
irrational *adj* not based on logic
irregular *adj* not regular or even; unconventional **irregularity** *n*
irrelevant *adj* not connected with the matter in hand **irrelevance** *n*
irreparable *adj* not able to be repaired or remedied
irresistible *adj* too strong to resist; enchanting, seductive
irrespective *adj* without taking account (of)
irreverence *n* lack of respect **irreverent** *adj*
irrevocable *adj* not able to be

changed or undone
irrigate *v* water by artificial channels, pipes etc. **irrigation** *n*
irritate *v* annoy; inflame **irritable** *adj* easily annoyed **irritant** *adj/n* (person or thing) causing irritation **irritation** *n*
is *third person sing. of* BE
Islam *n* Muslim faith or world **Islamic** *adj*
island *n* piece of land surrounded by water; anything like this **islander** *n* inhabitant of island
isle *n* island **islet** *n* little island
isobar *n* line on map connecting places of equal mean barometric pressure
isolate *v* place apart or alone **isolation** *n*

──────── THESAURUS ────────

irony mockery, sarcasm, satire; incongruity, paradox
irrational absurd, crackpot *Inf,* crazy, foolish, illogical, silly, unreasonable, unsound, unthinking, unwise
irregular asymmetrical, broken, bumpy, craggy, crooked, jagged, lopsided, pitted, ragged, rough, unequal, uneven; eccentric, erratic, fitful, fluctuating, fragmentary, haphazard, inconstant, intermittent, occasional, patchy, random, shifting, spasmodic, sporadic, unsteady, variable, wavering
irregularity asymmetry, bumpiness, crookedness, lopsidedness, patchiness, raggedness, roughness, spottiness, unevenness; aberration, anomaly, breach, deviation, eccentricity, freak, malfunction, malpractice, oddity, peculiarity
irrelevant extraneous, immaterial, impertinent, inapplicable, inappropriate, unrelated
irreparable beyond repair, irretrievable, irreversible
irresistible compelling, imperative,

overpowering, overwhelming, potent, urgent; alluring, enchanting, fascinating, ravishing, seductive, tempting
irreverent derisive, disrespectful, flippant, impertinent, mocking
irrevocable changeless, fated, fixed, irreversible, predestined, settled
irrigate flood, inundate, moisten, water, wet
irritable bad-tempered, cantankerous, choleric, crabbed, cross, dyspeptic, edgy, exasperated, ill-tempered, irascible, peevish, petulant, prickly, testy, touchy
irritate anger, annoy, bother, enrage, exasperate, fret, gall, harass, incense, infuriate, nettle, offend, pester, provoke; aggravate, chafe, fret, inflame, intensify, pain, rub
irritation anger, annoyance, displeasure, exasperation, impatience, indignation, irritability, resentment
isolate cut off, detach, disconnect, divorce, insulate, quarantine, segregate, separate, set apart
isolation aloofness, detachment, exile, loneliness, quarantine, seclusion,

isomer *n* substance with same molecules as another but different atomic arrangement

isometric *adj* having equal dimensions; relating to muscular contraction without movement **isometrics** *pl n* (with *sing v*) system of isometric exercises

isosceles *adj* (of triangle) having two sides equal

isotope *n* atom having different atomic weight from other atoms of same element

issue *n* topic of discussion or dispute; edition of newspaper etc.; offspring; outcome ~*v* go out; result in; arise (from); give, send out; publish

isthmus *n* narrow strip of land between two seas

it *pron* neuter pronoun of the third person **its** *adj* belonging to it **it's** it is **itself** *pron emphatic form of* IT

italic *adj* (of type) sloping **italics** *pl n* this type, used for emphasis etc. **italicize** *v* put in italics

itch *v/n* (feel) irritation in the skin **itchy** *adj*

item *n* single thing; piece of information; entry **itemize** *v*

itinerant *adj* travelling from place to place **itinerary** *n* plan of journey; route

ivory *n* hard white substance of the tusks of elephants etc.

ivy *n* climbing evergreen plant

———————— THESAURUS ————————

separation, solitude, withdrawal

issue *n* affair, argument, concern, matter, point, problem, question, subject, topic; copy, edition, instalment, number ~*v* arise, emanate, emerge, flow, originate, proceed, rise, spring, stem; announce, broadcast, circulate, deliver, distribute, emit, give out, promulgate, publish, release

itch *v* irritate, prickle, tickle, tingle ~*n* irritation, prickling, tingling

item account, article, bulletin, dispatch, feature, note, paragraph, piece, report; article, aspect, component, consideration, detail, entry, matter, particular, point, thing

itinerary circuit, journey, line, programme, route, schedule, timetable, tour

Jj

jab *v* **jabbing, jabbed** poke roughly; thrust, stab ~*n* poke; *Inf* injection

jabber *v* chatter; talk incoherently

jack *n* device for lifting heavy weight, esp. motorcar; lowest court card; *Bowls* ball aimed at; socket and plug connection in electronic equipment; small flag, esp. national, at sea ~*v* (*usu. with* up) lift with a jack

jackal *n* doglike scavenging animal of Asia and Africa

jackass *n* male ass; blockhead

jackboot *n* large military boot

jackdaw *n* small kind of crow

jacket *n* outer garment, short coat; outer casing, cover

jackknife *n* (*pl* **-knives**) clasp knife ~*v* angle sharply, esp. the parts of an articulated lorry

jackpot *n* large prize, accumulated stake, as pool in poker

Jacuzzi *n* *Trademark* bath with device that swirls water

jade *n* ornamental semiprecious stone, usu. dark green; this colour ~*adj* of this colour

jaded *adj* tired; off colour

jagged *adj* having sharp points

jaguar *n* large S Amer. cat

jail *n* building for confinement of criminals or suspects ~*v* send to, confine in prison **jailer** *n*

jam *v* **jamming, jammed** pack together; (cause to) stick and become unworkable; *Radio* block (another station) ~*n* fruit preserved by boiling with sugar; crush; hold-up of traffic; awkward situation

jamb *n* side post of door, fireplace etc.

jamboree *n* large gathering or rally of Scouts

Jan. January

jangle *v* (cause to) sound harshly, as bell; (of nerves) be irritated

janitor *n* caretaker

January *n* first month

jar¹ *n* round vessel of glass, earthenware etc.; *Inf* glass of esp. beer

jar² *v* **jarring, jarred** grate, jolt; have distressing effect on ~*n* jarring sound; shock etc.

jargon *n* special vocabulary for par-

--- THESAURUS ---

jab *v/n* dig, lunge, nudge, poke, prod, punch, stab, tap, thrust

jacket case, casing, coat, covering, envelope, folder, sheath, skin, wrapper

jackpot award, bonanza, kitty, pool, pot, prize, reward, winnings

jaded exhausted, fatigued, spent, tired, weary

jagged barbed, broken, craggy, pointed, ragged, ridged, rough, serrated, spiked, toothed, uneven

jail *n* nick *Brit sl*, prison, slammer *Sl* ~*v* confine, detain, impound, imprison, incarcerate, lock up

jailer captor, guard, keeper, warder

jam *v* cram, crowd, crush, force, pack,

press, squeeze, stuff, throng, wedge; block, clog, congest, halt, obstruct, stall, stick ~*n* crowd, crush, horde, mass, mob, multitude, pack, press, swarm, throng; bind, dilemma, hot water, plight, predicament, quandary, strait, tight spot, trouble

jangle *v* chime, clank, clash, rattle, vibrate ~*n* clang, clangour, clash, din, dissonance, jar, racket, rattle

janitor caretaker, concierge, custodian, doorkeeper, porter

jar¹ *n* crock, flagon, jug, pitcher, pot, urn, vase, vessel

jar² *v* agitate, disturb, grate, irritate, jolt, rasp, rock, shake, vibrate; annoy, clash, gall, grate, grind, irk, irritate,

ticular subject; pretentious language

jasmine n shrub with sweet-smelling flowers

jaundice n disease marked by yellowness of skin **jaundiced** adj prejudiced, bitter etc.

jaunt n/v (make) short pleasure excursion

jaunty adj sprightly; brisk

javelin n spear, esp. for throwing in sporting events

jaw n one of bones in which teeth are set; pl mouth; gripping part of vice etc.

jay n noisy bird of brilliant plumage

jazz n syncopated music and dance ~v (with **up**) make more lively **jazzy** adj flashy, showy

jealous adj envious; suspiciously watchful **jealousy** n

jeans pl n casual trousers, esp. of denim

Jeep n Trademark light four-wheel-drive motor vehicle

jeer v/n scoff, taunt

jell v congeal; Inf assume definite form

jelly n sweet, preserve etc. becoming softly stiff as it cools; anything of similar consistency **jellyfish** n small jelly-like sea animal

jemmy n short steel crowbar

jeopardy n danger **jeopardize** v endanger

jerk n sharp push or pull; Sl stupid person ~v move or throw with a jerk **jerky** adj uneven; spasmodic

jerkin n sleeveless jacket

jersey n knitted jumper; machine-knitted fabric

jest n/v joke **jester** n joker; Hist professional fool at court

jet[1] n aircraft driven by jet propulsion; stream of liquid, gas etc.; spout, nozzle ~v **jetting, jetted** throw out; shoot forth **jet lag** fatigue caused by crossing time zones in aircraft **jet propulsion** propulsion by jet of gas or liquid **jet-propelled** adj

jet[2] n hard black mineral **jet-black** adj glossy black

jetsam n goods thrown overboard **jettison** v abandon; throw overboard

——— T H E S A U R U S ———

nettle

jargon argot, cant, dialect, idiom, parlance, patois, slang, tongue, usage

jaunt airing, excursion, expedition, outing, ramble, stroll, tour, trip

jaunty airy, breezy, buoyant, carefree, gay, high-spirited, lively, perky, smart, sprightly, spruce, trim

jealous covetous, desirous, envious, green, grudging, intolerant, resentful, rival

jealousy covetousness, distrust, envy, ill-will, mistrust, resentment, spite, suspicion

jeer v banter, barrack, deride, flout, gibe, heckle, hector, mock, ridicule, scoff, sneer, taunt

jeopardize chance, endanger, gamble, hazard, imperil, risk, stake, venture

jeopardy danger, exposure, hazard, peril, pitfall, risk, venture

jerk n/v jolt, lurch, pull, throw, thrust, tug, tweak, twitch, wrench, yank

jest n banter, bon mot, fun, hoax, jape, joke, play, prank, quip, sally, sport, witticism ~v banter, chaff, deride, gibe, jeer, joke, mock, quip, scoff, sneer, tease

jester comedian, comic, humorist, joker, wag, wit; buffoon, clown, fool, madcap

jet[1] n flow, fountain, gush, spout, spray, spring, stream; nozzle, rose, spout, sprinkler ~v flow, gush, issue, rush, shoot, spout, squirt, stream, surge

jet[2] black, ebony, inky, raven, sable

jettison abandon, discard, dump, eject, expel, heave, scrap, unload

jetty *n* small pier, wharf

Jew *n* one of Hebrew religion or ancestry **Jewish** *adj*

jewel *n* precious stone; ornament containing one; precious thing **jeweller** *n* dealer in jewels **jewellery** *n*

jib *n* triangular sail set forward of mast; arm of crane ~*v* **jibbing, jibbed** (of horse, person) stop and refuse to go on

jibe *see* GIBE

jig *n* lively dance; music for it; guide for cutting etc. ~*v* **jigging, jigged** dance jig; make jerky up-and-down movements **jigsaw** *n* machine fret saw **jigsaw puzzle** picture cut into pieces, which the user tries to fit together again

jilt *v* reject (lover)

jingle *n* light metallic noise; catchy rhythmic verse, song etc. ~*v* (cause to) make jingling sound

jingoism *n* aggressive nationalism

jinks *pl n* **high jinks** boisterous merrymaking

jinx *n* force, person, thing bringing bad luck ~*v* cause bad luck

jitters *pl n* worried nervousness, anxiety **jittery** *adj* nervous

jive *n* (dance performed to) popular music, esp. of 1950s ~*v* do this dance

job *n* piece of work, task; post; *Inf* difficult task **jobbing** *adj* doing single, particular jobs for payment **jobless** *adj/pl n* unemployed (people)

jockey *n* (*pl* **jockeys**) rider in horse races ~*v* **jockeying, jockeyed** (*esp. with* **for**) manoeuvre

jockstrap *n* belt with pouch to support genitals

jocular *adj* joking; given to joking **jocularity** *n*

jodhpurs *pl n* tight-legged riding breeches

jog *v* **jogging, jogged** run slowly, trot, esp. for exercise; nudge; stimulate ~*n* jogging **jogger** *n* **jogging** *n*

join *v* fasten, unite; become a member (of); become connected; (*with* **up**) enlist; take part (in) ~*n* (place of) joining **joiner** *n* maker of finished woodwork **joinery** *n* joiner's work

joint *n* arrangement by which two things fit together; place of this; meat for roasting, oft. with bone; *Sl* disreputable bar or nightclub; *Sl* marijuana cigarette ~*adj* shared ~*v* connect by joints; divide at the joints **jointly** *adv* **out of joint** dislocated; disorganized

jetty breakwater, dock, mole, pier, quay, wharf

jewel brilliant, ornament, precious stone, trinket; charm, gem, paragon, pearl, prize, rarity, wonder

jig *v* bounce, caper, prance, shake, skip, twitch, wobble

jingle *n* clang, clink, rattle, ringing, tinkle; chorus, ditty, doggerel, melody, song, tune ~*v* chime, clatter, clink, rattle, ring, tinkle

jinx *n* curse, evil eye, hoodoo *Inf*, plague, voodoo ~*v* bewitch, curse

job affair, charge, chore, concern, duty, errand, function, pursuit, responsibility, role, stint, task, undertaking, venture, work; business, calling, capacity, career, craft, employment, function, livelihood, métier, occupation, office, position, post, profession, situation, trade, vocation

jocular amusing, comical, droll, facetious, funny, humorous, jolly, jovial, playful, roguish, sportive, teasing, waggish, witty

jog canter, lope, run, trot; arouse, nudge, prod, prompt, push, remind, shake, stimulate, stir, suggest

join accompany, add, adhere, annex, append, attach, cement, combine, connect, couple, fasten, knit, link, marry, splice, tie, unite, yoke; enlist,

joist *n* beam supporting floor or ceiling

joke *n* thing said or done to cause laughter; ridiculous thing ~*v* make jokes **joker** *n* one who jokes; *Sl* fellow; extra card in pack **jokey** *adj*

jolly *adj* jovial; merry ~*v* **jollying, jollied** make person, occasion happier **jollification** *n* **jollity** *n*

jolt *n/v* jerk; jar; shock

joss stick incense stick

jostle *v* knock or push

jot *n* small amount ~*v* **jotting, jotted** note **jotter** *n* notebook

joule *n Electricity* unit of work or energy

journal *n* newspaper or other periodical; daily record **journalism** *n* editing, writing in periodicals **journalist** *n*

journey *n* going to a place, excursion; distance travelled ~*v* travel

journeyman *n* qualified craftsman

jovial *adj* convivial, merry **joviality** *n*

jowl *n* (flesh hanging over) lower jaw

joy *n* gladness, pleasure, delight; cause of this **joyful** *adj* **joyous** *adj* extremely happy **joy ride** trip, esp. in stolen car

joystick *n* control column of aircraft; control device for video game

JP Justice of the Peace

jubilant *adj* exultant **jubilation** *n*

jubilee *n* time of rejoicing, esp. 25th or 50th anniversary

judder *v* shake, vibrate ~*n* vibration

judge *n* officer appointed to try cases in law courts; one who decides in a dispute, contest etc.; one able to form a reliable opinion ~*v* act as judge (of, for) **judgment, judgement** *n* faculty of judging; sentence of

——————— T H E S A U R U S ———————

enrol, enter, sign up

joint *n* connection, hinge, junction, knot, nexus, node, seam, union ~*adj* collective, combined, communal, concerted, cooperative, joined, mutual, shared, united

joke *n* frolic, fun, jape, jest, lark, play, prank, pun, quip, quirk, sally, sport, witticism, yarn ~*v* banter, frolic, gambol, jest, mock, quip, ridicule, taunt, tease

jolly carefree, cheerful, funny, gay, hilarious, jocund, jovial, joyful, jubilant, merry, mirthful, playful

jolt *n* bump, jar, jerk, jump, quiver, shake, start; blow, bombshell, reversal, setback, shock, surprise ~*v* jar, jerk, knock, push, shake, shove; astonish, disturb, perturb, shock, stagger, startle, stun, surprise, upset

jostle bump, butt, crowd, elbow, jog, jolt, press, push, shove, squeeze, throng, thrust

journal daily, gazette, magazine, monthly, newspaper, paper, periodical, record, register, review, tabloid, weekly; diary, log, record

journalist broadcaster, columnist, commentator, contributor, correspondent, hack, newspaperman, pressman, reporter

journey excursion, expedition, jaunt, odyssey, outing, passage, pilgrimage, tour, travel, trek, trip, voyage

jovial airy, blithe, buoyant, cheery, convivial, cordial, gay, glad, happy, jolly, jubilant, merry

joy bliss, delight, ecstasy, elation, exultation, gaiety, gladness, glee, pleasure, rapture, satisfaction

joyful blithesome, delighted, glad, gratified, happy, jubilant, light-hearted, merry, pleased, satisfied

jubilant cock-a-hoop, elated, enraptured, excited, exuberant, exultant, glad, joyous, overjoyed, rejoicing, thrilled, triumphant

jubilation celebration, ecstasy, elation, excitement, exultation, joy, triumph

jubilee carnival, celebration, festival, festivity, fête, gala

court; opinion **judgmental, judge-mental** *adj*

judicial *adj* of, by a court or judge **judiciary** *n* judges collectively **judicious** *adj* well-judged, sensible

judo *n* modern sport derived from jujitsu

jug *n* vessel for liquids, with handle and small spout; its contents

juggernaut *n* large heavy lorry; irresistible, destructive force

juggle *v* keep several objects in the air simultaneously; manipulate to deceive **juggler** *n*

jugular vein one of three large veins of the neck returning blood from the head

juice *n* liquid part of vegetable, fruit or meat; *Inf* electric current; *Inf* petrol **juicy** *adj* succulent; interesting

jujitsu, jujutsu *n* Japanese art of wrestling and self-defence

jukebox *n* automatic, coin-operated record player

July *n* seventh month

jumble *v* mix in confused heap ~*n* confused heap or state **jumble sale** sale of miscellaneous, usu. second-hand, items

jumbo *n* (*pl* **jumbos**) *Inf* elephant; anything very large

jump *v* (cause to) spring, leap (over); move hastily; pass or skip (over); rise steeply; start (with astonishment etc.) ~*n* act of jumping; obstacle to be jumped; distance, height jumped; sudden rise **jumper** *n* sweater, pullover **jumpy** *adj* nervous

junction *n* place where routes meet; point of connection

juncture *n* state of affairs

June *n* sixth month

jungle *n* equatorial forest; tangled mass; condition of intense competition

junior *adj* younger; of lower standing ~*n* junior person

juniper *n* evergreen shrub

judge *n* justice, magistrate; adjudicator, arbiter, moderator, referee, umpire; arbiter, assessor, authority, connoisseur, critic, evaluator, expert ~*v* adjudge, adjudicate, arbitrate, ascertain, conclude, decide, determine, discern, mediate, referee, umpire; appreciate, assess, consider, criticize, esteem, estimate, evaluate, examine, review, value

judicial judiciary, legal, official

judicious acute, astute, careful, cautious, circumspect, considered, diplomatic, discerning, discreet, expedient, informed, politic, prudent, rational, sage, sane, sensible, shrewd, skilful, sober, sound, thoughtful, wise

jug carafe, crock, ewer, jar, pitcher, urn, vessel

juice fluid, liquid, liquor, nectar, sap

juicy lush, moist, succulent, watery; colourful, interesting, racy, risqué,

sensational, spicy *Inf,* suggestive, vivid

jumble *v* confound, confuse, disarrange, dishevel, disorder, disorganize, entangle, mix, muddle, shuffle, tangle ~*n* chaos, clutter, confusion, disarray, disorder, litter, medley, *mélange,* mess, miscellany, mixture, muddle

jump *v* bounce, bound, caper, clear, gambol, hop, hurdle, leap, skip, spring, vault; avoid, digress, evade, miss, omit, overshoot, skip, switch ~*n* bound, caper, hop, leap, skip, spring, vault; advance, boost, increase, increment, rise, upsurge, upturn

jumpy agitated, anxious, fidgety, jittery, nervous, restless, tense, twitchy *Inf*

junction alliance, combination, connection, coupling, joint, juncture,

junk[1] *n* useless objects **junkie** *n Sl* drug addict **junk food** food of low nutritional value **junk mail** unsolicited mail

junk[2] *n* Chinese sailing vessel

junket *n* flavoured curdled milk; excursion

junta *n* group holding power in country

jurisdiction *n* authority; territory covered by it

jury *n* body of persons sworn to render verdict in court of law; judges of competition **juror** *n*

just *adj* fair; upright; honest; right,

equitable ~*adv* exactly; barely; at this instant; merely; really **justice** *n* moral or legal fairness; judge, magistrate **justice of the peace** person who can act as judge in local court **justify** *v* **-ifying, -ified** prove right; vindicate **justifiable** *adj* **justification** *n*

jut *v* **jutting, jutted** project, stick out, protrude

jute *n* plant fibre used for rope, canvas etc.

juvenile *adj* of, for young children; immature ~*n* young person, child

juxtapose *v* put side by side **juxtaposition** *n*

──────── THESAURUS ────────

linking, seam, union

junior inferior, lesser, lower, minor, secondary, subordinate, younger

junk clutter, debris, leavings, litter, oddments, refuse, rubbish, rummage, scrap, trash, waste

jurisdiction authority, command, control, dominion, influence, power, prerogative, rule, say, sway

just *adj* blameless, decent, equitable, fair, good, honest, honourable, impartial, lawful, pure, right, righteous, unbiased, upright, virtuous; appropriate, apt, deserved, due, fitting, justified, merited, proper, reasonable, right, suitable ~*adv* absolutely, completely, entirely, exactly, perfectly, precisely; barely, hardly, lately, only

now, recently, scarcely

justice equity, fairness, honesty, impartiality, integrity, justness, law, legality, legitimacy, rectitude, right

justifiable acceptable, defensible, excusable, fit, lawful, legitimate, proper, right, sound, tenable, valid, warrantable, well-founded

justification apology, approval, defence, excuse, explanation, plea, vindication

justify absolve, acquit, approve, confirm, defend, establish, excuse, exonerate, explain, legalize, maintain, substantiate, support, sustain, uphold, validate, vindicate, warrant

juvenile adolescent, boy, child, girl, infant, minor, youth

K k

kaftan *n* woman's long, loose dress with sleeves

kaleidoscope *n* optical toy producing changing patterns; any complex pattern **kaleidoscopic** *adj*

kamikaze *n* Japanese suicide pilot ~*adj* (of action) certain to kill or injure the doer

kangaroo *n* Aust. marsupial with strong hind legs for jumping

karaoke *n* entertainment involving singing over prerecorded backing tape

karate *n* Japanese system of unarmed combat

karma *n* person's actions affecting fate for next incarnation

kasbah *n* citadel of N Afr. town

kayak *n* Inuit canoe; any similar canoe

kebab *n* dish of small pieces of meat, tomatoes etc. grilled on skewers; grilled minced lamb served in split slice of unleavened bread

kedgeree *n* dish of fish cooked with rice, eggs etc.

keel *n* lowest longitudinal support on which ship is built **keel over** turn upside down; *Inf* collapse suddenly

keen *adj* sharp; acute; eager; shrewd; (of price) competitive

keep *v* **keeping, kept** retain possession of, not lose; hold; (cause to) remain; maintain; remain good; continue ~*n* maintenance; central tower of castle

keeper *n* **keeping** *n* harmony; care, charge **keepsake** *n* gift treasured for sake of the giver

keg *n* small barrel; container for beer

kelp *n* large seaweed

ken *n* range of knowledge

kennel *n* shelter for dog

kerb *n* stone edging to footpath

kernel *n* inner seed of nut or fruit stone; central, essential part

kerosene *n* paraffin oil

kestrel *n* small falcon

ketchup *n* sauce of vinegar, tomatoes etc.

kettle *n* metal vessel with spout and handle, esp. for boiling water **kettledrum** *n* musical instrument made of membrane stretched over copper hemisphere

key *n* instrument for operating lock, winding clock etc.; explanation, means of achieving an end etc.; *Mus* set of related notes; operating lever of typewriter, piano, organ etc. ~*adj* most important **keyboard** *n* set of

---

THESAURUS

keen ardent, avid, eager, earnest, enthusiastic, fervid, fierce, intense, zealous; acid, acute, biting, caustic, cutting, incisive, sardonic, satirical, sharp, vitriolic

keep *v* conserve, control, hold, maintain, possess, preserve, retain; amass, carry, deal in, deposit, furnish, garner, heap, hold, pile, place, stack, stock, store; care for, defend, guard, look after, maintain, manage, mind, operate, protect, safeguard, shelter, shield, tend, watch over ~*n* board,

food, livelihood, living, maintenance, means, nourishment, subsistence, support

keeper attendant, caretaker, curator, custodian, defender, governor, guard, jailer, steward, warden, warder

keeping care, charge, custody, patronage, possession, protection, safekeeping, trust

keepsake emblem, favour, memento, relic, remembrance, reminder, souvenir, symbol, token

keys on piano, computer etc. **keyhole** *n* opening for key **keynote** *n* dominant idea

kg kilogram

khaki *adj* dull, yellowish-brown ~*n* khaki cloth; military uniform

kibbutz *n* (*pl* **kibbutzim**) communal agricultural settlement in Israel

kick *v* strike (out) with foot; recoil; resist; *Inf* free oneself of (habit etc.) ~*n* blow with foot; thrill; strength (of flavour, alcoholic drink etc.); recoil **kick off** start (a game of football) **kick out** dismiss or expel forcibly

kid *n* young goat; leather of its skin; *Inf* child ~*v* **kidding, kidded** *Inf* tease, deceive; behave, speak in fun

kidnap *v* -**napping, -napped** seize and hold to ransom **kidnapper** *n*

kidney *n* (*pl* -**neys**) either of the pair of organs which secrete urine; animal kidney used as food

kill *v* deprive of life; put an end to; pass (time) ~*n* act of killing; animals etc. killed **killer** *n* **killing** *adj Inf* very tiring; very funny

kiln n furnace, oven

kilo *n short for* KILOGRAM

kilo- *comb. form* one thousand, as in **kilometre, kilowatt**

kilogram, kilogramme *n* 1000 grams

kilohertz *n* 1000 cycles per second

kilt *n* pleated tartan skirt worn orig. by Scottish Highlanders

kimono *n* (*pl* -**nos**) loose Japanese robe

kin *n* relatives **kindred** *n* relatives ~*adj* similar; related **kinsman** *n* (*fem* **kinswoman**)

kind *n* sort, type, class ~*adj* considerate; gentle **kindly** *adj* kind, genial ~*adv* gently **kindness** *n* **kind-hearted** *adj*

kindergarten *n* class, school for children of about four to six years old

kindle *v* set alight; arouse; catch fire **kindling** *n* small wood to kindle fires

———— THESAURUS ————

key *n* latchkey, opener; answer, clue, cue, explanation, guide, interpretation, lead, means, pointer, sign, solution ~*adj* basic, chief, crucial, decisive, essential, fundamental, important, leading, main, major, pivotal, principal

keynote centre, core, essence, gist, kernel, marrow, substance

kick *v* boot, punt ~*n* force, intensity, pep, power, punch, pungency, sparkle, strength, tang, verve, vitality, zest

kid *n* baby, bairn, boy, child, girl, infant, lad, teenager, youngster, youth ~*v* bamboozle, fool, hoax, hoodwink, jest, mock, pretend, ridicule, tease, trick

kidnap abduct, capture, hijack, remove, seize, skyjack, steal

kill annihilate, assassinate, butcher, destroy, execute, exterminate, massacre, murder, slaughter, slay; cancel, cease, deaden, defeat, halt, quash, quell, ruin, scotch, smother, stifle, stop, suppress, veto

killer assassin, butcher, executioner, gunman, murderer, slaughterer, slayer

killing bloodshed, carnage, fatality, homicide, manslaughter, massacre, murder, slaughter, slaying

kin affinity, blood, connection, extraction, kinship, lineage, relationship, stock

kind *n* brand, breed, class, family, genus, race, set, sort, species, stamp, variety ~*adj* affectionate, amiable, beneficent, benevolent, benign, bounteous, charitable, compassionate, congenial, considerate, cordial, courteous, friendly, generous, gentle, good, gracious, humane, indulgent, lenient, loving, mild, neighbourly, obliging, thoughtful

kinetic *adj* relating to motion

king *n* male ruler; chess piece; highest court card; *Draughts* crowned piece **kingdom** *n* state ruled by king; realm; sphere **kingpin** *n Inf* chief thing or person **king-size** *adj Inf* very large

kingfisher *n* small brightly-coloured bird

kink *n* tight twist in rope, wire, hair etc. ~*v* make, become kinked **kinky** *adj* full of kinks; *Inf* deviant

kiosk *n* small, sometimes movable booth; public telephone box

kip *n/v* **kipping, kipped** *Inf* sleep

kipper *n* smoked herring

kirk *n* in Scotland, church

kismet *n* fate, destiny

kiss *n* touch or caress with lips; light touch ~*v* touch with lips **kiss of life** mouth-to-mouth resuscitation

kit *n* outfit, equipment; personal effects, esp. of traveller; set of pieces of equipment sold ready to be assembled ~*v* (*with* **out**) provide with kit **kitbag** *n* bag for soldier's or traveller's kit

kitchen *n* room used for cooking

kite *n* light papered frame flown in wind; large hawk

kitsch *n* vulgarized, pretentious art

kitten *n* young cat **kittenish** *adj* playful

kitty *n* in some card games; pool; communal fund

kiwi *n* (*pl* **kiwis**) NZ flightless bird; *Inf* New Zealander **kiwi fruit** edible fruit with green flesh

klaxon *n* loud horn

kleptomania *n* compulsion to steal **kleptomaniac** *n*

km kilometre

knack *n* acquired facility or dexterity; trick; habit

knacker *n* buyer of worn-out horses etc. for killing **knackered** *adj Sl* exhausted

knapsack *n* haversack

knave *n* jack at cards; *Obs* rogue **knavish** *adj*

knead *v* work into dough; massage

knee *n* joint between thigh and lower leg **kneecap** *n* bone in front of knee **kneejerk** *adj* (of reaction) automatic and predictable **knees-up** *n Inf* party

kneel *v* **kneeling, knelt** fall, rest on knees

knell *n/v* (ring) death bell

knickers *pl n* woman's undergarment

——————— T H E S A U R U S ———————

kindle fire, ignite, inflame, light, set fire to

kindly *adj* affable, benevolent, compassionate, cordial, favourable, genial, gentle, good-natured, hearty, helpful, kind, mild, pleasant, polite, sympathetic, warm ~*adv* agreeably, graciously, politely, tenderly, thoughtfully

kindness affection, benevolence, charity, compassion, fellow-feeling, generosity, goodness, grace, humanity, indulgence, tenderness, tolerance, understanding

king emperor, majesty, monarch, overlord, prince, ruler, sovereign

kingdom dominion, dynasty, empire,

monarchy, realm, reign, sovereignty

kink bend, coil, knot, tangle, twist, wrinkle

kiosk bookstall, booth, counter, newsstand, stall, stand

kiss *v* greet, osculate, salute

kit apparatus, effects, equipment, gear, outfit, rig, supplies, tackle, tools

knack ability, aptitude, bent, capacity, dexterity, expertise, flair, forte, genius, gift, ingenuity, skill, talent, trick

kneel bow, curtsey, genuflect, kowtow, stoop

knell *n* chime, peal, toll ~*v* chime, herald, peal, resound, ring, sound, toll

for lower half of body

knick-knack *n* trinket

knife *n* (*pl* **knives**) cutting blade, esp. one in handle, used as implement or weapon ~*v* cut or stab with knife

knight *n* man of rank below baronet; member of medieval order of chivalry; piece in chess ~*v* confer knighthood on **knighthood** *n*

knit *v* **knitting, knitted** *or* **knit** form (garment etc.) by linking loops of yarn; draw together; unite **knitter** *n* **knitting** *n* knitted work; act of knitting

knob *n* rounded lump **knobbly** *adj*

knock *v* strike, hit; *Inf* disparage; rap audibly; (of engine) make metallic noise ~*n* blow, rap **knocker** *n* appliance for knocking on door **knock back** *Inf* drink quickly; reject **knock-kneed** *adj* having incurved legs **knock out** render unconscious; *Inf* overwhelm, amaze **knockout** *n*

knoll *n* small hill

knot *n* fastening of strands by looping and pulling tight; cluster; hard lump, esp. in timber; nautical miles per hour ~*v* **knotting, knotted** tie with

knot, in knots **knotty** *adj* full of knots; puzzling, difficult

know *v* **knowing, knew, known** be aware (of), have information (about); be acquainted with; understand; feel certain **knowing** *adj* shrewd **knowingly** *adv* shrewdly; deliberately **knowledge** *n* knowing; what one knows; learning **knowledgable, knowledgeable** *adj* well-informed

knuckle *n* bone at finger joint **knuckle down** get down (to work) **knuckle-duster** *n* metal appliance on knuckles to add force to blow **knuckle under** submit

KO knockout

koala *n* marsupial Aust. animal, native bear

kohl *n* cosmetic powder

Koran *n* sacred book of Muslims

kosher *adj* conforming to Jewish dietary law; *Inf* legitimate, authentic

kowtow *v* prostrate oneself; be obsequious

krypton *n* rare atmospheric gas

kudos *n* fame; credit

kung fu *n* Chinese martial art

———————————————— THESAURUS ————————————————

knickers bloomers, briefs, drawers, panties, smalls, underwear

knife blade, cutter, cutting tool

knit affix, ally, bind, connect, contract, fasten, heal, intertwine, join, link, loop, mend, secure, tie, unite, weave

knob bump, knot, lump, projection, protrusion, snag, stud, swelling, tumour

knock *v* belt *Inf*, clap, cuff, hit, punch, rap, slap, smack, strike, thump, thwack ~*n* belt *Inf*, blow, box, clip, clout *Inf*, cuff, hammering, rap, slap, smack, thump

knot *n* bond, bow, braid, connection, joint, ligature, loop, tie ~*v* bind, entangle, knit, loop, secure, tether, tie,

weave

know apprehend, experience, fathom, feel certain, learn, notice, perceive, realize, recognize, see, undergo, understand; be familiar with, have dealings with, have knowledge of, recognize

knowing astute, clever, competent, discerning, experienced, expert, intelligent, qualified, skilful, well-informed

knowledge ability, cognition, consciousness, discernment, grasp, judgment, recognition, understanding; enlightenment, erudition, instruction, intelligence, learning, scholarship, science, tuition, wisdom

L l

l litre

lab *n Inf short for* LABORATORY

label *n* slip of paper, metal etc., giving information; descriptive phrase ~*v* **-elling, -elled** give label

laboratory *n* place for scientific investigations or for manufacture of chemicals

labour *n* exertion of body or mind; workers collectively; process of childbirth ~*v* work hard; strive; move with difficulty; stress to excess **laboured** *adj* uttered, done, with difficulty **labourer** *n* manual worker **laborious** *adj* tedious

labrador *n* breed of large, smooth-coated retriever dog

laburnum *n* tree with yellow hanging flowers

labyrinth *n* maze; perplexity

lace *n* patterned openwork fabric; cord, usu. one of pair, to draw edges together ~*v* fasten with laces; flavour with spirit **lacy** *adj* fine, like lace

lacerate *v* tear, mangle

lachrymose *adj* tearful

lack *n* deficiency ~*v* need, be short of

lackadaisical *adj* languid

lackey *n* (*pl* **-eys**) servile follower; footman

lacklustre *adj* lacking brilliance or vitality

laconic *adj* terse

lacquer *n* hard varnish ~*v* coat with this

lacrosse *n* ball game played with long-handled racket

lad *n* boy, young fellow

ladder *n* frame with rungs, for climbing; line of torn stitches, esp. in stockings

laden *adj* heavily loaded

ladle *n* spoon with long handle and large bowl ~*v* serve out liquid with a ladle

lady *n* female counterpart of gentleman; polite term for a woman; title of some women of rank **ladybird** *n* small red beetle with black spots **ladylike** *adj* polite and refined

lag[1] *v* **lagging, lagged** go too slowly, fall behind **laggard** *n* one who lags

lag[2] *v* **lagging, lagged** wrap boiler, pipes etc. with insulating material **lagging** *n* this material

lag[3] *n Sl* convict

THESAURUS

label *n* flag, marker, sticker, tag, tally, ticket ~*v* flag, mark, stamp, sticker, tag, tally

labour *n* industry, toil, work; employees, hands, labourers, workers, work force, workmen; childbirth, contractions, delivery, labour pains, pains, throes ~*v* dwell on, elaborate, overdo, overemphasize, strain

laboured awkward, difficult, forced, heavy, stiff, strained

labourer blue-collar worker, drudge, hand, labouring man, manual worker, worker, workman

lacerate cut, gash, jag, maim, rend,

rip, slash, tear, wound

lack *n* absence, dearth, deficiency, deprivation, destitution, need, scantiness, scarcity, shortage, want ~*v* miss, need, require, want

lackey creature, hanger-on, instrument, minion, parasite, sycophant, toady, tool, yes man; attendant, flunky, footman, manservant, valet

lacklustre boring, drab, dry, dull, flat, leaden, lifeless, prosaic, vapid

lad boy, fellow, juvenile, kid *Inf,* schoolboy, youngster, youth

laden burdened, charged, full, hampered, loaded, oppressed, taxed,

lager *n* light-bodied beer

lagoon *n* saltwater lake, enclosed by atoll or sandbank

laid *See* LAY² **laid-back** *adj Inf* relaxed

lair *n* den of animal

laird *n* Scottish landowner

laissez-faire *n* principle of nonintervention

laity *n* people not belonging to clergy

lake *n* expanse of inland water

lama *n* Buddhist priest in Tibet or Mongolia

lamb *n* young of the sheep; its meat; innocent or helpless creature ~*v* give birth to lamb

lambast, lambaste *v* beat, thrash; reprimand severely

lame *adj* crippled in leg; limping; unconvincing ~*v* cripple

lamé *n/adj* (fabric) interwoven with gold or silver thread

lament *v* express sorrow (for) ~*n* expression of grief; song of grief **lamentable** *adj* deplorable, disappointing, **lamentation** *n*

laminate *v* make (sheet of material) by bonding together two or more thin sheets; cover with thin sheet ~*n* laminated sheet **lamination** *n*

lamp *n* appliance (esp. electrical) that produces, light, heat etc. **lamppost** *n* post supporting lamp in street

lampoon *n/v* (make subject of) a satire

lamprey *n* fish like an eel

lance *n* horseman's spear ~*v* pierce with lance or lancet **lancet** *n* pointed two-edged surgical knife **lance corporal** lowest noncommissioned army rank

land *n* solid part of earth's surface; ground; country; estate ~*v* come to land; disembark; arrive on ground; bring to land; *Inf* obtain; catch; *Inf* strike **landed** *adj* possessing, consisting of lands **landing** *n* act of landing; platform between flights of stairs **landlocked** *adj* completely surrounded by land **landlord** *n* (*fem* **landlady**) person who lets land or houses etc.; master or mistress of inn, boarding house etc. **landlubber** *n* person ignorant of the sea and ships **landmark** *n* conspicuous object; event, decision etc. considered as important stage in development of something **landscape** *n* piece of inland scenery; picture of this ~*v* create, arrange garden, park etc. **landslide** *n* falling of soil, rock etc. down mountainside; overwhelming election victory

lane *n* narrow road or street; specified

—————————— **THESAURUS** ——————————

lag dawdle, delay, idle, linger, loiter, saunter, straggle, tarry, trail

laid-back at ease, casual, easy-going, relaxed, unhurried

lame crippled, disabled, game, hobbling, limping; feeble, flimsy, inadequate, pathetic, poor, thin, unconvincing, weak

lament *v* bemoan, bewail, complain, deplore, grieve, mourn, regret, sorrow, wail, weep ~*n* complaint, moan, moaning, plaint, wail, wailing

lamentable deplorable, disappointing, low, meagre, mean, miserable, pitiful, poor, wretched

lampoon *n* burlesque, parody, satire, skit, squib ~*v* burlesque, caricature, make fun of, mock, parody, ridicule, satirize

land *n* earth, ground, terra firma; dirt, ground, loam, soil; country, district, nation, province, region, territory, tract; acres, estate, grounds, property, realty ~*v* alight, arrive, berth, debark, disembark, dock, touch down

landlord host, hotelier, hotel-keeper, innkeeper

landmark feature, monument; crisis, milestone, turning point, watershed

air, sea route; area of road for one stream of traffic

language *n* system of sounds, symbols etc. for communicating thought; style of speech or expression

languish *v* be or become weak or faint; droop, pine **languid** *adj* lacking energy, spiritless **languor** *n* lack of energy; tender mood **languorous** *adj*

lank *adj* lean; limp **lanky** *adj*

lantern *n* transparent case for lamp or candle

lap[1] *n* the part between waist and knees of a person when sitting; single circuit of track; stage or part of journey ~*v* **lapping, lapped** enfold, wrap round; overtake opponent to be one or more circuits ahead

lap[2] *v* **lapping, lapped** drink by scooping up with tongue; (of waves etc.) beat softly

lapel *n* part of front of coat folded back towards shoulders

lapse *n* fall (in standard, condition, virtue etc.); slip; passing (of time etc.) ~*v* fall away; end, esp. through disuse

lapwing *n* type of plover

larceny *n* theft

larch *n* deciduous conifer tree

lard *n* prepared pig's fat ~*v* insert strips of bacon in (meat); intersperse

larder *n* storeroom for food

large *adj* great in size, number etc. ~*adv* in a big way **largely** *adv* **largesse** *n* generosity; gift **at large** free; in general **large-scale** *adj* wide-ranging, extensive

largo *adv/n Mus* (passage played) in slow and dignified manner

lark[1] *n* small, brown singing bird; skylark

lark[2] *n* frolic, spree ~*v* indulge in lark

larva *n* (*pl* **-vae**) immature insect **larval** *adj*

larynx *n* (*pl* **larynges**) part of throat containing vocal cords **laryngitis** *n* inflammation of this

lasagne *n* pasta formed in wide, flat sheets

lascivious *adj* lustful

laser *n* device for concentrating electromagnetic radiation in an intense, narrow beam

———————— THESAURUS ————————

landscape countryside, outlook, panorama, prospect, scene, scenery, view, vista

language conversation, discourse, expression, parlance, speech, talk; dialect, idiom, speech, tongue, vernacular, vocabulary; diction, expression, phrasing, style, wording

languid drooping, faint, feeble, limp, pining, sickly, weak, weary; dull, inactive, lazy, lethargic, listless, sluggish, spiritless

languish decline, droop, fade, fail, faint, flag, sicken, waste, weaken, wilt, wither

lank dull, lifeless, limp, long, straggling

lanky angular, bony, gaunt, rangy, spare, tall, thin

lap[1] *n* circle, circuit, course, loop, orbit, round, tour ~*v* cover, enfold, fold, swathe, turn, twist, wrap

lap[2] drink, lick, sip, sup; ripple, slap, splash, swish, wash

lapse *n* error, failing, fault, indiscretion, mistake, omission, oversight, slip ~*v* decline, drop, fail, fall, sink, slide, slip; end, expire, run out, stop, terminate

large big, bulky, enormous, giant, great, huge, immense, king-size, massive, monumental, sizable, substantial, vast

largely chiefly, generally, mainly, mostly, predominantly, primarily, principally, widely

lark antic, caper, fling, frolic, fun, gambol, game, jape, mischief, prank,

lash¹ n stroke with whip; flexible part of whip; eyelash ~v strike with whip etc.; dash against; attack verbally, ridicule; flick, wave sharply to and fro; (*with* out) hit, kick

lash² v fasten or bind tightly

lashings pl n Inf abundance

lass, lassie n girl

lassitude n weariness

lasso n (pl **-sos, -soes**) rope with noose for catching cattle etc. ~v **-soing, -soed** catch with this

last¹ adj/adv after all others; most recent(ly) ~adj only remaining ~n last person or thing **lastly** adv finally **last-ditch** adj done as final resort **last straw** small irritation that, coming after others, is too much to bear **last word** final comment in argument; most recent or best example

last² v continue, hold out

last³ n model of foot on which shoes are made, repaired

latch n fastening for door ~v fasten with latch; (*with* **onto**) become attached to

late adj **later, latest, last** coming after the appointed time; recent; recently dead ~adv after proper time; recent-ly; at, till late hour **lately** adv not long since

latent adj existing but not developed; hidden

lateral adj of, at, from the side

latex n sap or fluid of plants, esp. of rubber tree

lath n thin strip of wood

lathe n machine for turning and shaping

lather n soapy froth; frothy sweat ~v make frothy

Latin n language of ancient Romans ~adj of ancient Romans or their language

latitude n angular distance in degrees N or S of equator; scope; pl regions

latrine n in army etc., lavatory

latter adj second of two; later; more recent **latterly** adv **latter-day** adj modern

lattice n network of strips of wood, metal etc.; window so made

laud v praise **laudable** adj praiseworthy

laudanum n sedative from opium

laugh v/n (make) sound of amusement, merriment or scorn **laughable** adj ludicrous **laughter** n **laughing**

———————————— THESAURUS ————————————

romp, spree

lash¹ n blow, hit, stripe, stroke ~v beat, birch, flog, horsewhip, lambast(e), thrash, whip

lash² bind, fasten, join, make fast, rope, secure, strap, tie

lass damsel, girl, maid, maiden, miss, young woman

last¹ adj aftermost, hindmost, rearmost; latest, most recent ~adv after, behind

last² v abide, continue, endure, keep, persist, remain, survive, wear

latch bar, bolt, catch, clamp, fastening, hasp, hook, lock

late behind, belated, delayed, overdue, slow, tardy, unpunctual; ad-vanced, fresh, modern, new, recent; dead, deceased, defunct, departed

lately just now, latterly, of late, recently

lateral edgeways, flanking, side, sideways

lather bubbles, foam, froth, soap, soapsuds, suds

latitude breadth, compass, extent, range, room, scope, space, span, spread, sweep, width

latter closing, concluding, last, later, latest, modern, recent, second

lattice fretwork, grating, grid, grille, mesh, network, trellis, web

laudable admirable, creditable, excellent, meritorious, praiseworthy,

stock object of general derision

launch[1] v set afloat; set in motion; begin; propel (missile, spacecraft) into space

launch[2] n large power-driven boat

laundry n place for washing clothes; clothes etc. for washing **launder** v wash and iron **Launderette** n Trademark shop with coin-operated washing, drying machines

laureate adj crowned with laurels **poet laureate** poet with appointment to Royal Household

laurel n glossy-leaved shrub, bay tree; pl its leaves, emblem of victory or merit

lava n molten matter thrown out by volcano

lavatory n toilet, water closet

lavender n shrub with fragrant, pale-lilac flowers; this colour

lavish adj plentiful, rich; very generous ~v spend, bestow, profusely

law n rule binding on community; system of such rules; legal science; general principle deduced from facts **lawful** adj allowed by law **lawless** adj ignoring laws; violent **lawyer** n professional expert in law **lawsuit** n prosecution of claim in court

lawn n tended turf in garden etc.

lawyer see LAW

lax adj not strict; slack **laxative** adj/n (substance) having loosening effect on bowels **laxity, laxness** n

lay[1] past tense of LIE **layabout** n lazy person, loafer

lay[2] v laying, laid deposit, set, cause to lie; devise (plan); attribute (blame); place (bet); (of animal) produce eggs **layer** n single thickness as stratum or coating ~v form layer **lay-by** n stopping place for traffic beside road **lay off** v dismiss staff during slack period **lay-off** n **layout** n arrangement

lay[3] adj not clerical or professional **layman** n ordinary person

lay[4] n narrative poem

worthy

laugh v chortle, chuckle, giggle, guffaw, snigger, titter ~n chortle, chuckle, giggle, guffaw, snigger, titter

laughter amusement, glee, hilarity, merriment, mirth

launch cast, discharge, dispatch, fire, project, propel, throw; begin, commence, embark upon, inaugurate, initiate, instigate, introduce, open, start

lavatory bathroom, convenience, loo, powder room, (public) convenience, toilet, washroom, water closet

lavish copious, exuberant, lush, opulent, plentiful, profuse, prolific, sumptuous; bountiful, free, generous, liberal, munificent, openhanded

law act, code, commandment, covenant, decree, edict, enactment, order, ordinance, rule, statute

lawful allowable, authorized, constitutional, just, legal, legalized, legitimate, licit, permissible, proper, rightful, valid

lawless anarchic, chaotic, disorderly, insubordinate, insurgent, mutinous, rebellious, reckless, riotous, seditious, unruly, wild

lawsuit action, argument, case, cause, contest, dispute, litigation, proceedings, prosecution, suit, trial

lawyer advocate, attorney, barrister, legal adviser, solicitor

lay[1] deposit, establish, leave, place, plant, posit, put, set, set down, settle, spread; arrange, dispose, locate, organize, position, set out; concoct, contrive, design, devise, hatch, plan, plot, prepare, work out; bet, gamble, hazard, risk, stake, wager

lay[2] secular; amateur, inexpert

layabout good-for-nothing, idler, lag-

layette *n* clothes for newborn child

lazy *adj* averse to work **laze** *v* be lazy **lazily** *adv*

lb. pound

lbw *Cricket* leg before wicket

lead[1] *v* **leading, led** guide, conduct; persuade; direct; be, go, play first; spend (one's life); result; give access to ~*n* that which leads or is used to lead; example; front or principal place, role etc.; cable bringing current to electrical instrument **leader** *n* one who leads; editorial article in newspaper **leadership** *n*

lead[2] *n* soft, heavy grey metal; graphite in pencil; plummet **leaded** *adj* (of windows) made from small panes held together by lead strips **leaden** *adj* sluggish; dull grey; made from lead

leaf *n* (*pl* **leaves**) organ of photosynthesis in plants, consisting of a flat, usu. green blade on stem; two pages of book etc.; thin sheet ~*v* turn through (pages etc.) cursorily **leaflet** *n* small leaf; single printed and folded sheet, handbill **leafy** *adj*

league[1] *n* agreement for mutual help; parties to it; federation of clubs etc.; *Inf* class, level

league[2] *n* former measure of distance, about 3 miles

leak *n* defect that allows escape or entrance of liquid, gas, radiation etc.; disclosure ~*v* let fluid etc. in or out; (of fluid etc.) find its way through leak; (allow to) become known little by little **leakage** *n* leaking; gradual escape or loss **leaky** *adj*

lean[1] *adj* lacking fat; thin; meagre; *n* lean part of meat

lean[2] *v* **leaning, leaned** *or* **leant** rest against; incline; tend (towards); rely (on) **leaning** *n* tendency **lean-to** *n* room, shed built against existing wall

leap *v* **leaping, leapt** *or* **leaped** spring,

———— THESAURUS ————

gard, loafer, lounger, shirker, vagrant, wastrel

layer bed, ply, row, seam, stratum, thickness, tier

layman amateur, lay person, nonprofessional, outsider

lay off discharge, dismiss, drop, let go, oust, pay off

layout arrangement, design, draft, outline, plan

lazy idle, inactive, indolent, inert, slack, slothful, slow

lead *v* conduct, escort, guide, pilot, precede, steer, usher; cause, dispose, draw, incline, induce, influence, persuade, prevail, prompt; command, direct, govern, head, manage, supervise; be ahead (of), exceed, excel, outdo, outstrip, surpass, transcend; have, live, pass, spend, undergo ~*n* advantage, edge, first place, margin, precedence, priority, start, supremacy, van; direction, example, guid-

ance, leadership, model; leading role, principal, protagonist, star part

leader captain, chief, chieftain, commander, conductor, director, guide, head, principal, ruler, superior

leadership direction, domination, guidance, management, running; authority, command, control, influence, initiative, pre-eminence, supremacy, sway

leaf *n* blade, flag, needle, pad; folio, page, sheet

leaflet bill, booklet, circular, handbill, pamphlet

league alliance, association, coalition, compact, confederacy, fellowship, fraternity, guild, order, partnership, union

leak *n* chink, crack, crevice, fissure, hole, opening, puncture; drip, leakage, percolation, seepage; disclosure, divulgence ~*v* discharge, drip, escape, exude, pass, percolate, seep,

jump; spring over ~*n* jump **leapfrog**
n/v vault over person bending down
leap year year with extra day
learn *v* **learning, learnt** *or* **learned** gain
skill, knowledge; memorize; find out
learned *adj* showing much learning
learner *n* **learning** *n* knowledge got
by study
lease *n* contract by which land or
property is rented ~*v* let, rent by
lease **leasehold** *adj* held on lease
leash *n* lead for dog
least *adj* smallest; *superlative of* LITTLE
~*n* smallest one ~*adv* in smallest degree
leather *n* prepared skin of animal
leathery *adj* like leather, tough
leave[1] *v* **leaving, left** go away; allow to
remain; entrust; bequeath
leave[2] *n* permission, esp. to be absent
from duty; period of such absence;
formal parting

leaven *n* yeast ~*v* raise with leaven
lecherous *adj* full of lust; lascivious
lecher *n* lecherous man **lechery** *n*
lectern *n* reading desk
lecture *n* instructive discourse;
speech of reproof ~*v* deliver discourse; reprove **lecturer** *n*
ledge *n* narrow shelf sticking out from
wall, cliff etc.; ridge below surface of
sea
ledger *n* book of debit and credit accounts
lee *n* shelter; side, esp. of ship, away
from wind **leeward** *adj/adv/n* (on, towards) lee side **leeway** *n* leeward
drift of ship; room for movement
within limits
leech *n* species of bloodsucking worm
leek *n* plant like onion with long bulb
and thick stem
leer *v/n* glance with malign or lascivious expression

—————— THESAURUS ——————

spill, trickle; disclose, divulge
lean[1] *adj* bony, emaciated, gaunt,
lank, rangy, skinny, slender, slim,
spare, thin, wiry; bare, barren, meagre, pitiful, poor, scanty, sparse
lean[2] *v* be supported, prop, recline,
repose, rest; bend, incline, slant,
slope, tilt, tip
leaning aptitude, bent, bias, inclination, liking, partiality, penchant,
taste, tendency
leap *v* bounce, bound, caper, cavort,
frisk, gambol, hop, jump, skip, spring
~*n* bound, caper, frisk, hop, jump,
skip, spring, vault
learn acquire, attain, grasp, imbibe,
master, pick up; get off pat, learn by
heart, memorize; detect, discern, discover, find out, gain, gather, hear,
understand
learned academic, cultured, erudite,
expert, highbrow, literate, scholarly,
skilled, versed, well-read
learner beginner, disciple, novice, pu-

pil, scholar, student, trainee, tyro
lease *v* charter, hire, let, loan, rent
least fewest, last, lowest, meanest,
minimum, poorest, smallest, tiniest
leave[1] *v* abandon, abscond, decamp,
depart, desert, disappear, exit, forsake, go, move, quit, relinquish, retire, withdraw; abandon, cease, desert, desist, drop, give up, relinquish,
renounce, stop; allot, assign, cede,
commit, consign, entrust, refer; bequeath, transmit, will
leave[2] *n* allowance, concession, consent, freedom, liberty, permission,
sanction; furlough, holiday, sabbatical, time off, vacation
lecture *n* address, discourse, harangue, instruction, lesson, speech,
talk; censure, chiding, rebuke, reprimand, reproof, scolding ~*v* address,
discourse, expound, harangue, speak,
spout, talk, teach; admonish, castigate, censure, chide, reprimand, reprove, scold

lees *pl n* sediment; dregs

left[1] *adj* on or to the west; opposite to the right; radical, socialist ~*adv* on or towards the left ~*n* the left hand or part; *Politics* reforming or radical party; (*also* **left wing**) **leftist** *n/adj* (person) of the political left

left[2] *past tense past participle of* LEAVE[1]

leftover *n* unused portion

leg *n* of limbs on which person or animal walks, runs, stands; part of garment covering leg; support, as leg of table; stage **leggings** *pl n* covering of leather or other material (for legs) **leggy** *adj* long-legged **legless** *adj* without legs; *Sl* very drunk

legacy *n* bequest; thing handed down to successor

legal *adj* in accordance with law **legality** *n* **legalize** *v* make legal **legally** *adv*

legate *n* messenger, representative

legatee *n* recipient of legacy

legato *adv Mus* smoothly

legend *n* traditional story; notable person or event; inscription **legendary** *adj*

legible *adj* readable **legibility** *n*

legion *n* various military bodies; association of veterans; large number ~*adj* countless **legionary** *adj/n* **legionnaire** *n* member of legion **legionnaire's disease** serious bacterial disease similar to pneumonia

legislate *v* make laws **legislation** *n* act of legislating; laws which are made **legislative** *adj*

legislator *n* **legislature** *n* body that makes laws

legitimate *adj* born in wedlock; lawful, regular ~*v* make lawful **legitimacy** *n* **legitimize** *v*

legume *n* pod

leisure *n* spare time **leisurely** *adj* unhurried ~*adv* slowly

lemming *n* rodent of arctic regions

lemon *n* pale yellow fruit; its colour; *Sl* useless person or thing **lemonade** *n* drink made from lemon juice **lemon**

——————— THESAURUS ———————

leeway latitude, margin, play, room, scope, space

left *adj* larboard *Naut*, left-hand, port, sinistral; communist, leftist, left-wing, socialist

leftover *pl* leavings, oddments, odds and ends, remains, remnants, scraps

leg limb, member; brace, prop, support, upright; lap, part, portion, section, segment, stage, stretch

legacy bequest, estate, gift, heirloom, inheritance; heritage, tradition

legal allowed, authorized, lawful, legalized, legitimate, licit, permissible, proper, rightful, sanctioned, valid

legalize allow, approve, license, permit, sanction, validate

legend fable, fiction, folk tale, myth, narrative, saga, story, tale

legendary fabled, fabulous, fanciful, fictitious, mythical, romantic, traditional

legible clear, distinct, neat, plain, readable

legion *n* army, brigade, company, division, force, troop; drove, horde, host, mass, multitude, myriad, number, throng ~*adj* countless, myriad

legislate enact, establish, ordain, prescribe

legislation enactment, prescription, regulation; act, bill, charter, law, measure

legislative *adj* congressional, judicial, ordaining, parliamentary

legitimate authentic, genuine, kosher *Inf*, lawful, legal, licit, proper, real, rightful, sanctioned, statutory, true

leisure ease, freedom, holiday, liberty, opportunity, pause, quiet, recreation, relaxation, respite, rest, retirement, spare time, vacation

leisurely comfortable, easy, gentle,

curd creamy spread made of lemons, butter etc.

lemur *n* nocturnal animal like monkey

lend *v* **lending, lent** give temporary use of; let out at interest; bestow **lender** *n*

length *n* measurement from end to end; duration; extent; piece of a certain length **lengthen** *v* make, become, longer **lengthy** *adj* very long

lenient *adj* not strict **leniency** *n*

lens *n* (*pl* **lenses**) glass etc. shaped to converge or diverge light rays

Lent *n* period of fasting from Ash Wednesday to Easter Eve

lent *see* LEND

lentil *n* edible seed of leguminous plant

leopard *n* (*fem* **leopardess**) large, spotted, carnivorous cat

leotard *n* tight-fitting garment covering most of body

leper *n* one ill with leprosy; person shunned **leprosy** *n* ulcerous skin disease

leprechaun *n* mischievous Irish elf

lesbian *n* homosexual woman ~*adj* (of woman) homosexual

lesion *n* harmful sore on bodily organ

less *adj comparative of* LITTLE not so much ~*n* smaller part, quantity; a lesser amount ~*adv* to a smaller extent ~*prep* minus **lessen** *v* diminish; reduce **lesser** *adj* smaller; minor

lesson *n* instalment of course of instruction; content of this; experience that teaches; portion of Scripture read in church

lest *conj* for fear that

let[1] *v* **letting, let** allow, enable, cause; rent; be leased **let down** disappoint; lower; deflate **let off** excuse; fire, explode; emit **let up** *v* diminish, stop

let[2] *n* hindrance; in some games, minor infringement or obstruction

lethal *adj* deadly

lethargy *n* apathy, lack of energy **lethargic** *adj*

letter *n* alphabetical symbol; written

———————— THESAURUS ————————

lazy, relaxed, restful, slow, unhurried

lend advance, loan; add, afford, bestow, confer, contribute, furnish, give, grant, hand out, impart, present, provide, supply

length *of linear extent* distance, extent, measure, reach, span; *of time* duration, period, space, span, stretch, term

lengthen continue, draw out, elongate, expand, extend, increase, prolong, protract, stretch

lengthy diffuse, extended, interminable, long, prolix, tedious, verbose

leniency, lenience clemency, forbearance, gentleness, indulgence, mercy, mildness, tolerance

lenient forbearing, forgiving, gentle, indulgent, kind, merciful, mild, tender, tolerant

less *adj* shorter, slighter, smaller; inferior, minor, secondary, subordinate ~*adv* barely, little, meagrely

lessen abate, abridge, contract, curtail, decrease, diminish, ease, impair, lighten, lower, moderate, narrow, reduce, relax, shrink, slacken, weaken

lesser inferior, lower, minor, secondary, slighter, subordinate

lesson class, coaching, instruction, period, schooling, teaching, tutoring; deterrent, example, exemplar, message, model, moral, precept

let *v* allow, authorize, give leave, grant, permit, sanction, tolerate, warrant; hire, lease, rent

lethal baneful, deadly, destructive, devastating, fatal, mortal, murderous, pernicious, virulent

lethargic apathetic, comatose, drowsy, dull, heavy, inactive, inert, languid, lazy, listless, sleepy, slothful,

message; strict meaning, interpretation; *pl* literature *~v* mark with, in, letters

lettuce *n* salad plant

leukaemia *n* progressive blood disease

level *adj* horizontal; even, flat *~n* horizontal line or surface; instrument for establishing horizontal plane; position on scale; grade *~v* **-elling, -elled** make, become level; knock down; aim (gun, accusation etc.) **level crossing** point where railway and road cross **level-headed** *adj* not apt to be carried away by emotion

lever *n* rigid bar pivoted about a fulcrum to transfer a force with mechanical advantage; operating handle *~v* prise, move, with lever **leverage** *n* action, power of lever; influence

leveret *n* young hare

leviathan *n* sea monster; anything huge or formidable

levitation *n* raising of solid body into the air supernaturally **levitate** *v* (cause to) do this

levity *n* (undue) frivolity

levy *v* **levying, levied** impose (tax); raise (troops) *~n* (*pl* **levies**) imposition or collection of taxes

lewd *adj* lustful; indecent

lexicon *n* dictionary

liable *adj* answerable; exposed (to); subject (to); likely (to) **liability** *n* state of being liable; debt; hindrance, disadvantage; *pl* debts

liaison *n* union; connection; secret relationship **liaise** *v*

liar *n* *see* LIE[2]

lib *n* *Inf short for* LIBERATION

libel *n* published statement falsely damaging person's reputation *~v* **-belling, -belled** defame falsely **libellous** *adj* defamatory

———————— THESAURUS ————————

slow, sluggish, torpid

let off absolve, discharge, excuse, exempt, exonerate, forgive, pardon, release, spare; discharge, emit, explode, fire, give off, leak, release

letter character, sign, symbol; acknowledgment, answer, communication, dispatch, epistle, line, message, missive, note, reply

let up abate, decrease, diminish, moderate, relax, slacken, stop, subside

level *adj* even, flat, horizontal, plain, plane, smooth, uniform; balanced, comparable, equal, equivalent, even, flush, in line, on a par, proportionate *~n* bed, floor, layer, storey, stratum; altitude, elevation, height *~v* flatten, plane, smooth; bulldoze, demolish, destroy, flatten, raze, smooth, wreck

level-headed balanced, calm, collected, composed, cool, dependable, reasonable, sane, sensible, steady

lever *n* bar, crowbar, handle *~v* force, move, prise, purchase, raise

levy *v* charge, collect, demand, exact, gather, impose, tax *~n* assessment, collection, exaction, gathering, imposition

lewd bawdy, blue, dirty, indecent, libidinous, licentious, loose, obscene, pornographic, salacious, smutty, vile, vulgar

liability accountability, duty, obligation, onus, responsibility; arrear, debit, debt, obligation; burden, disadvantage, drag, drawback, encumbrance, handicap, hindrance, impediment, millstone, nuisance

liable accountable, answerable, bound, responsible; exposed, open, subject, susceptible, vulnerable

liaison communication, connection, contact, go-between, interchange; affair, amour, intrigue, romance

liar fibber, perjurer, prevaricator

libel *n* aspersion, defamation, slander, smear *~v* blacken, defame, malign,

liberal *adj* (*also with cap.*) of political party favouring democratic reforms and individual freedom; generous; tolerant; abundant ~*n* one who has liberal ideas or opinions **liberality** *n* generosity **liberalize** *v* make (laws etc.) less restrictive **liberally** *adv*

liberate *v* set free **liberation** *n* **liberator** *n*

libertine *n* morally dissolute person ~*adj* dissolute

liberty *n* freedom **libertarian** *n/adj* (person) believing in freedom of thought and action **at liberty** free; having the right **take liberties** be presumptuous

libido *n* psychic energy; sexual drive **libidinous** *adj* lustful

library *n* room, building where books are kept; collection of books, records etc. **librarian** *n* keeper of library

libretto *n* (*pl* **-tos**, **-ti**) words of opera **librettist** *n*

lice *n pl of* LOUSE

licence *n* permit; permission; excessive liberty; dissoluteness **license** *v* grant licence to **licensee** *n* holder of licence

licentious *adj* dissolute

lichen *n* small flowerless plants on rocks, trees etc.

licit *adj* lawful

lick *v* pass tongue over; touch slightly; *Sl* defeat ~*n* act of licking; small amount (esp. of paint etc.); *Sl* speed **licking** *n Sl* beating

licorice *n see* LIQUORICE

lid *n* movable cover; eyelid

lido *n* (*pl* **-dos**) pleasure centre with swimming and boating

lie[1] *v* **lying, lay, lain** be horizontal, at rest; be situated; be in certain state; exist ~*n* state (of affairs etc.) **lie in** remain in bed late **lie-in** *n*

lie[2] *v* **lying, lied** make false statement ~*n* deliberate falsehood **liar** *n* person who tells lies

lieu *n* **in lieu of** in place of

——————— T H E S A U R U S ———————

revile, slander, slur, smear, traduce, vilify

libellous aspersive, defamatory, derogatory, false, injurious, malicious, scurrilous, slanderous, traducing, untrue

liberal libertarian, progressive, radical, reformist; altruistic, bountiful, charitable, generous, kind, open-handed, prodigal; abundant, ample, bountiful, copious, handsome, lavish, munificent, plentiful, profuse, rich

liberalize broaden, ease, expand, extend, loosen, moderate, relax, slacken, soften, stretch

liberate deliver, discharge, emancipate, free, redeem, release, rescue, set free

liberation deliverance, emancipation, freedom, release

liberty autonomy, emancipation, freedom, immunity, independence,

release, self-determination, sovereignty

libidinous carnal, debauched, lascivious, lecherous, loose, lustful, prurient, randy *Inf, chiefly Brit,* salacious, wanton, wicked

licence *n* authority, carte blanche, certificate, charter, dispensation, entitlement, exemption, immunity, leave, liberty, permission, permit, privilege, right, warrant; abandon, anarchy, disorder, excess, indulgence, lawlessness

license *v* accredit, allow, authorize, certify, commission, empower, entitle, permit, sanction, warrant

licentious abandoned, debauched, dissolute, immoral, impure, lascivious, lewd, profligate, sensual, wanton

lick brush, lap, taste, tongue, touch, wash

lie[1] *v* be prone, lounge, recline, re-

lieutenant *n* deputy; junior army or navy officer

life *n* (*pl* **lives**) active principle of existence; time that it lasts; story of a person's life; way of living; vigour, vivacity **lifeless** *adj* dead; insensible; dull **lifelike** *adj* **lifelong** *adj* lasting a lifetime **life belt, jacket** buoyant device to keep person afloat **lifeline** *n* means of help; rope thrown to person in danger **lifestyle** *n* particular habits, attitudes etc. of person or group **lifetime** *n* time person, animal or object lives or functions

lift *v* move upwards in position, status, mood, volume etc.; take up and remove; *Inf* steal; disappear ~*n* cage in vertical shaft for raising and lowering people or goods; act of lifting; ride in car etc., as passenger; boost **liftoff** *n* moment rocket leaves the ground

ligament *n* band of tissue joining bones **ligature** *n* anything which binds; thread for tying up artery

light¹ *adj* of, or bearing, little weight; not severe; easy; trivial; not clumsy; not serious or profound; (of industry) producing small, usu. consumer goods, using light machinery ~*adv* in light manner ~*v* **lighted, lit** come by chance (upon) **lighten** *v* reduce, remove (load etc.) **lightly** *adv* **lights** *pl n* lungs of animal **light-fingered** *adj* likely to steal **light-headed** *adj* dizzy, delirious **light-hearted** *adj* carefree **lightweight** *n/adj* (person) of little weight or importance

light² *n* electromagnetic radiation by which things are visible; source of this, lamp; window; means or act of setting fire to; understanding; *pl* traffic lights ~*adj* bright; pale; not dark ~*v* **lighting, lighted** *or* **lit** set on fire; give light to; brighten **lighten** *v* give light to **lighting** *n* apparatus for supplying artificial light **lightning** *n* visible discharge of electricity in atmosphere **lighthouse** *n* tower with a light to guide ships **light year** distance light travels in one year

—————— T H E S A U R U S ——————

pose, rest, sprawl, stretch out; be located, belong, be placed, be situated, exist, extend, remain

lie² *v* equivocate, fabricate, falsify, fib, invent, misrepresent, perjure, prevaricate ~*n* deceit, fabrication, falsehood, fib, fiction, invention, mendacity, prevarication, untruth

life being, breath, entity, growth, vitality; being, career, course, duration, existence, span, time; autobiography, biography, career, confessions, history, memoirs, story

lifeless cold, dead, deceased, defunct, extinct, inanimate, inert

lifelike authentic, exact, faithful, natural, real, realistic, vivid

lifelong constant, enduring, lasting, long-lasting, long-standing, perennial, permanent, persistent

lift *v* elevate, hoist, pick up, raise, rear,

upheave, uplift, upraise; annul, cancel, end, relax, remove, rescind, revoke, stop, terminate; ascend, be dispelled, climb, disappear, disperse, dissipate, mount, rise, vanish ~*n* car ride, drive, ride, run, transport

light¹ *adj* airy, delicate, easy, flimsy, portable, slight; easy, effortless, manageable, moderate, simple; minute, scanty, slight, small, thin, tiny, trifling, trivial; agile, airy, graceful, lithe, nimble; entertaining, frivolous, funny, pleasing, superficial, trifling, trivial, witty

light² *n* blaze, brilliance, flash, glare, gleam, glint, glow, illumination, radiance, ray, shine, sparkle; beacon, bulb, candle, flare, lamp, lantern, star, taper, torch; flame, lighter, match ~*adj* aglow, bright, glowing, shining, sunny ~*v* fire, ignite, in-

lighter n device for lighting cigarettes etc.; flat-bottomed boat for unloading ships

like[1] adj resembling; similar; characteristic of ~adv in the manner of ~pron similar thing **likelihood** n probability **likely** adj probable; promising ~adv probably **liken** v compare **likeness** n resemblance; portrait **likewise** adv in like manner

like[2] v find agreeable, enjoy, love **likeable** adj **liking** n fondness; inclination, taste

lilac n shrub bearing pale mauve or white flowers

lilt n rhythmical swing **lilting** adj

lily n bulbous flowering plant **lily of the valley** small garden plant with fragrant white flowers

limb n arm or leg; wing; branch of tree

limber adj pliant, lithe **limber up** loosen stiff muscles by exercise

limbo[1] n (pl -bos) region between Heaven and Hell for the unbaptized; indeterminate place or state

limbo[2] n (pl -bos) West Indian dance in which dancers lean backwards to pass under a bar

lime[1] n calcium compound used in fertilizer, cement ~v treat (land) with lime **limelight** n glare of publicity **limestone** n sedimentary rock used in building

lime[2] n small acid fruit like lemon **lime-green** adj greenish-yellow

lime[3] n tree

limerick n humorous verse of five lines

limit n utmost extent or duration; boundary ~v restrict, restrain, bound **limitation** n **limited company** one whose shareholders' liability is restricted

limousine n large, luxurious car

limp[1] adj without firmness or stiffness

——————— THESAURUS ———————

flame, kindle; brighten, clarify, illuminate, irradiate, put on, switch on, turn on

lighten[1] ease, unload; alleviate, assuage, ease, lessen, mitigate, reduce, relieve

lighten[2] brighten, flash, gleam, illuminate, irradiate, make bright, shine

lightweight adj insignificant, paltry, petty, slight, trifling, trivial, unimportant, worthless

like[1] adj akin, alike, allied, analogous, corresponding, identical, relating, resembling, same, similar

like[2] v delight in, enjoy, love, relish, revel in; admire, appreciate, approve, cherish, esteem, prize

likelihood chance, liability, likeliness, possibility, probability, prospect

likely adj anticipated, apt, disposed, expected, inclined, liable, possible, probable, prone, tending ~adv doubtlessly, no doubt, presumably, probably

likeness affinity, resemblance, similarity; copy, depiction, effigy, facsimile, image, model, picture, portrait, replica, study

liking affection, appreciation, attraction, bias, desire, fondness, love, penchant, preference, stomach, taste, tendency, weakness

limb appendage, arm, extension, extremity, leg, member, part, wing

limelight attention, fame, prominence, publicity, public eye, recognition, stardom, the spotlight

limit n bound, deadline, end, termination, ultimate, utmost; ceiling, check, curb, maximum, restraint, restriction ~v bound, check, confine, curb, fix, hinder, ration, restrain, restrict, specify, straiten

limitation block, check, condition, constraint, control, curb, drawback, impediment, qualification, restraint,

limp² *v* walk lamely ~*n* limping walk

limpet *n* shellfish that sticks tightly to rocks

limpid *adj* clear; translucent

linchpin *n* pin to hold wheel on its axle; essential person or thing

linctus *n* syrupy cough medicine

line *n* long narrow mark; row; series, course; telephone connection; progeny; province of activity; shipping company; railway track; any class of goods; cord; approach, policy ~*v* cover inside; mark with lines; bring into line **lineage** *n* descent from, descendants of an ancestor **lineament** *n* feature **linear** *adj* of, in lines **liner** *n* large ship or aircraft of passenger line **linesman** *n* sporting official who helps referee **line-up** *n* people or things assembled for particular purpose

linen *adj* made of flax ~*n* linen cloth; linen articles collectively

linger *v* delay, loiter; remain long

lingerie *n* women's underwear or nightwear

linguist *n* one skilled in languages or language study **linguistic** *adj* of languages or their study **linguistics** *pl n* (*with sing v*) study, science of language

liniment *n* embrocation

lining *n* covering for inside of garment etc.

link *n* ring of chain; connection ~*v* join with, as with, link; intertwine **linkage** *n*

links *pl n* golf course

linnet *n* songbird of finch family

lino *n short for* LINOLEUM

linoleum *n* floor covering of powdered cork, linseed oil etc. backed with hessian

linseed *n* seed of flax plant

lint *n* soft material for dressing wounds

lintel *n* top piece of door or window

lion *n* (*fem* **lioness**) large animal of cat family

lip *n* either edge of the mouth; edge or margin; *Sl* impudence **lip-reading** *n* method of understanding speech by interpreting lip movements **lip service** insincere tribute or respect **lipstick** *n* cosmetic for colouring lips

liqueur *n* alcoholic liquor flavoured and sweetened

liquid *adj* fluid, not solid or gaseous; flowing smoothly; (of assets) easily converted into money ~*n* substance

————————— THESAURUS —————————

restriction, snag

limp¹ *adj* drooping, flabby, flaccid, floppy, lax, loose, relaxed, slack, soft

limp² *v* falter, hobble, hop, shamble, shuffle

line *n* band, bar, channel, groove, mark, rule, score, streak, stripe, stroke; column, file, procession, queue, rank, row, sequence, series; ancestry, family, lineage, race, succession; activity, area, business, calling, department, employment, field, forte, interest, job, occupation, profession, pursuit, trade, vocation; axis, course, direction, path, route, track; cable, cord, filament, rope, strand,

string, thread, wire ~*v* crease, cut, draw, furrow, inscribe, mark, rule, score, trace; border, bound, edge, fringe, rank, rim, skirt, verge

line-up arrangement, array, row, selection, team

linger loiter, remain, stay, stop, tarry, wait; abide, continue, endure, persist, remain, stay

link *n* component, element, member, part, piece; affiliation, affinity, association, attachment, bond, connection, joint, knot, tie ~*v* attach, bind, connect, couple, fasten, join, tie, unite, yoke; associate, bracket, connect, identify

in liquid form **liquefy** v **-fying, -fied** make or become liquid **liquidity** n state of being able to meet debts **liquidize** v **liquidizer** n

liquidate v pay (debt); arrange affairs of, and dissolve (company); wipe out, kill **liquidation** n clearing up of financial affairs; bankruptcy **liquidator** n official appointed to liquidate business

liquor n alcoholic liquid

liquorice n black substance used in medicine and as a sweet

lira n (pl **-re, -ras**) monetary unit of Italy and Turkey

lisp v/n (speak with) faulty pronunciation of s and z

lissom, lissome adj supple, agile

list[1] n inventory, register; catalogue ~v place on list

list[2] v (of ship) lean to one side ~n inclination of ship

listen v try to hear, attend to **listener** n

listless adj indifferent, languid

litany n prayer with responses

literal adj according to the strict meaning of the words, not figurative; actual, true **literally** adv

literate adj able to read and write; educated **literacy** n

literature n books and writings of a country, period or subject **literary** adj

lithe adj supple, pliant

lithium n metallic chemical element

lithography n method of printing using the antipathy of grease and water **lithograph** n print so produced ~v print thus

litigation n lawsuit

litmus n blue dye turned red by acids and restored to blue by alkali

litre n measure of volume of fluid, one cubic decimetre, about 1.75 pints

litter n untidy refuse; young of animal produced at one birth; kind of stretcher for wounded ~v strew with litter; give birth to young

lip brim, brink, edge, margin, rim

liquid adj fluid, melted, molten, running, runny, thawed, wet; of assets convertible, negotiable ~n fluid, juice, liquor

liquidate clear, discharge, pay, settle, square; abolish, annul, cancel, dissolve, terminate; annihilate, destroy, dispatch, eliminate, exterminate, kill, murder

liquor alcohol, drink, intoxicant, spirits, strong drink

list[1] n catalogue, directory, file, index, inventory, invoice, register, roll, schedule, tally ~v bill, book, catalogue, enrol, enter, enumerate, file, index, itemize, note, record, register, schedule

list[2] v cant, heel over, incline, lean, tilt, tip ~n cant, slant, tilt

listen attend, hark, hear

listless apathetic, heavy, indolent, inert, languid, lethargic, limp, sluggish, supine, torpid

literal close, exact, faithful, strict, verbatim; actual, genuine, plain, real, simple, true

literally actually, exactly, faithfully, plainly, precisely, really, simply, strictly, truly, verbatim

literary bookish, erudite, formal, learned, literate, well-read

literate cultivated, educated, erudite, informed, learned, lettered, scholarly

literature letters, lore, writings

lithe flexible, lissom(e), pliable, pliant, supple

litigation action, case, contending, disputing, lawsuit, process

litter n debris, fragments, muck, refuse, rubbish, shreds; brood, family, offspring, progeny, young; palanquin, stretcher ~v clutter, derange, disorder, scatter, strew

little *adj* **less, least** small, not much; young ~*n* small quantity ~*adv* slight-ly

liturgy *n* prescribed form of public worship **liturgical** *adj*

live¹ *v* have life; pass one's life; continue in life; continue, last; dwell **living** *n* action of being in life; people now alive; means of living; church benefice ~*adj* alive **living room** room in house for relaxation and entertainment

live² *adj* living, alive, active, vital; flaming; (of electrical conductor) carrying current; (of broadcast) transmitted during the actual performance **liveliness** *n* **lively** *adj* brisk, active, vivid **liven** *v* (*esp. with* up) make (more) lively

livelihood *n* means of living

liver *n* organ secreting bile; animal liver as food **liverish** *adj* unwell, as from liver upset; touchy, irritable

livery *n* distinctive dress, esp. servant's

livestock *n* farm animals

livid *adj Inf* angry, furious; discoloured, as by bruising

lizard *n* four-footed reptile

llama *n* woolly animal of S America

load *n* something carried; quantity carried; burden; amount of power used ~*v* put load on or into; charge (gun); weigh down **loaded** *adj* carrying a load; (of dice) dishonestly weighted; (of question) containing hidden trap or implication; (of weapon) charged with ammunition; *Sl* wealthy; *Sl* drunk

loaf¹ *n* (*pl* **loaves**) mass of baked bread; shaped mass of food

loaf² *v* idle, loiter **loafer** *n* idler

loam *n* fertile soil

loan *n* act of lending; thing lent; money borrowed at interest ~*v* lend

loath, loth *adj* unwilling **loathe** *v* feel

——————— THESAURUS ———————

little *adj* diminutive, dwarf, elfin, mini, miniature, minute, petite, pygmy *or* pigmy, short, slender, small, teeny-weeny, tiny, wee; infant, junior, undeveloped, young ~*adv* barely, hardly, slightly; rarely, scarcely, seldom

live¹ *v* be, breathe, exist, have life; endure, fare, feed, lead, pass, remain, subsist, survive; last, persist, prevail; abide, dwell, inhabit, lodge, occupy, reside, settle

live² *adj* alive, animate, breathing, existent, living, vital; active, burning, current, hot, pressing, prevalent, topical, unsettled, vital

livelihood job, living, maintenance, means, occupation, subsistence, work

liveliness activity, brio, dynamism, energy, gaiety, spirit, vitality, vivacity

lively active, agile, alert, brisk, chirpy *Inf*, energetic, keen, nimble, perky, quick, sprightly, spry, upbeat *Inf*, vigorous; bright, colourful, exciting, forceful, invigorating, racy, refreshing, stimulating, vivid

livid; enraged, fuming, furious, incensed, indignant; angry, black-and-blue, bruised, contused, discoloured

living *n* being, existence, life, subsistence; job, livelihood, maintenance, occupation, subsistence, sustenance, work ~*adj* active, alive, breathing, existing, strong, vigorous, vital

load *n* bale, cargo, freight, lading, shipment; burden, millstone, onus, oppression, pressure, trouble, weight, worry ~*v* cram, fill, freight, heap, lade, pack, pile, stack, stuff; charge, prime; burden, hamper, oppress, trouble, weigh down, worry

loaded burdened, charged, full, laden, weighted; biased, distorted, weighted; charged, primed; *Sl* affluent, moneyed, rich, wealthy, well off,

strong disgust for **loathing** *n* disgust **loathsome** *adj*

lob *n* in tennis etc., shot pitched high in air ~*v* **lobbing, lobbed** throw, pitch shots thus

lobby *n* corridor into which rooms open; group which tries to influence legislature ~*v* try to enlist support (of)

lobe *n* soft, hanging part of ear; rounded segment **lobotomy** *n* surgical incision into lobe of brain

lobelia *n* garden plant with lobed flowers

lobster *n* shellfish with long tail and claws, turning red when boiled

local *adj* of, existing in particular place; confined to particular place ~*n* person from district; *Inf* (nearby) pub **locale** *n* scene of event **locality** *n* neighbourhood **localize** *v* assign, restrict to definite place **locally** *adv*

locate *v* find; situate **location** *n* placing; situation; site of film production away from studio

loch *n* Scottish lake or long narrow bay

lock[1] *n* appliance for fastening door, lid etc.; arrangement for moving boats from one level of canal to another; extent to which vehicle's front

wheels will turn; block, jam ~*v* fasten, make secure with lock; place in locked container; join firmly; jam; embrace closely **locker** *n* small cupboard with lock **lockjaw** *n* tetanus **lockout** *n* exclusion of workers by employers as means of coercion **locksmith** *n* one who makes and mends locks **lockup** *n* garage, storage area away from main premises

lock[2] *n* tress of hair

locket *n* small hinged pendant for portrait etc.

locomotive *n* engine for pulling carriages on railway tracks **locomotion** *n* action, power of moving

locum *Lat* substitute, esp. for doctor or clergyman

locus *n* (*pl* **loci**) curve traced by all points satisfying specified mathematical condition

locust *n* destructive winged insect

lodge *n* house, cabin used seasonally or occasionally, e.g. for hunting, skiing; gatekeeper's house; branch of Freemasons etc. ~*v* house; deposit; bring (a charge etc.); live in another's house at fixed charge; come to rest (in, on) **lodger** *n* **lodgings** *pl n* rented accommodation in another person's house

——————————— THESAURUS ———————————

well-to-do

loan *n* advance, credit, mortgage

loath, loth against, averse, disinclined, indisposed, opposed, reluctant, resisting, unwilling

loathing abhorrence, antipathy, aversion, disgust, hatred, horror, odium, repugnance, repulsion, revulsion

loathsome abhorrent, disgusting, execrable, hateful, horrible, nasty, odious, offensive, repugnant, revolting, vile

lobby *n* corridor, foyer, hall, hallway, passage, porch, vestibule; pressure group ~*v* campaign for, influence,

persuade, pressure, promote

local *adj* community, district, parish, regional; confined, limited, narrow, parish, parochial, provincial, restricted ~*n* inhabitant, native, resident

locality area, district, region, vicinity

localize circumscribe, concentrate, confine, contain, delimit, limit, restrain, restrict

locate detect, discover, find, pinpoint, unearth

location bearings, locale, place, point, site, situation, spot, venue

lock[1] *n* bolt, clasp, padlock ~*v* bolt, close, fasten, latch, seal, secure, shut

loft *n* space under roof **loftily** *adv*
haughtily **lofty** *adj* of great height; elevated; haughty

log[1] *n* trimmed portion of felled tree;
record of voyages of ship, aircraft etc.
~*v* logging, logged enter in a log; record; cut logs **logbook** *n*

log[2] *n* logarithm

loganberry *n* purplish-red fruit

logarithm *n* one of series of
arithmetical functions tabulated for
use in calculation

loggerheads *pl n* **at loggerheads**
quarrelling, disputing

logic *n* science of reasoning; reasoned
thought or argument; coherence of
various facts, events etc. **logical** *adj* of
logic; according to reason; reasonable; apt to reason correctly

logistics *pl n* (*with sing or pl v*) the
handling of supplies and personnel
logistical *adj*

logo *n* company emblem or similar
device

loin *n* part of body between ribs and
hip; cut of meat from this; *pl* hips and
lower abdomen **loincloth** *n* garment
covering loins only

loiter *v* dawdle, hang about; idle **loi-
terer** *n*

loll *v* sit, lie lazily; (esp. of the tongue)
hang out

lollipop *n* sweet on small wooden
stick

lolly *n Inf* lollipop or ice lolly; *Sl* money

lone *adj* solitary **loneliness** *n* **lonely**
adj sad because alone; unfrequented;
solitary **loner** *n* one who prefers to be
alone **lonesome** *adj*

long[1] *adj* having length, esp. great
length, in space or time; extensive;
protracted ~*adv* for a long time
long-distance *adj* going between
places far apart **longhand** *n* words
written in full **long-range** *adj* into the
future; able to travel long distances
without refuelling; (of weapons) designed to hit distant target **long shot**
competitor, undertaking, bet etc.
with small chance of success **long-
sighted** *adj* able to see distant objects
in focus but not nearby ones **long-
standing** *adj* existing for a long time
long-suffering *adj* enduring trouble
or unhappiness without complaint

——————————— T H E S A U R U S ———————————

lock[2] curl, ringlet, strand, tress

lodge *n* cabin, chalet, cottage, gate-
house, house, hut, shelter; association, branch, club, group, society ~*v*
accommodate, billet, board, entertain, harbour, put up, shelter, stay,
stop; catch, imbed, implant, stick

lodger boarder, guest, paying guest,
resident, tenant

lofty high, raised, soaring, tall, towering; distinguished, elevated, grand,
illustrious, imposing, majestic, noble,
stately, superior

log *n* block, chunk, stump, trunk; account, chart, journal, listing, record,
tally ~*v* book, chart, note, record,
register, tally

logic reason, sense, sound judgment;

link, rationale, relationship

logical clear, cogent, coherent, consistent, rational, relevant, sound, valid

loiter dally, dawdle, delay, idle, lag,
linger, loaf, stroll

loll flop, lean, loaf, lounge, recline, relax, slouch, slump, sprawl; dangle,
droop, drop, flop, hang, hang loosely, sag

lone isolated, one, only, separate, single, sole, unaccompanied

loneliness desolation, isolation, seclusion, solitude

lonely abandoned, estranged, forlorn,
forsaken, friendless, outcast; deserted, remote, secluded, solitary, unfrequented, uninhabited; alone, apart,

long-winded *adj* tediously loquacious

long² *v* have keen desire, yearn (for) **longing** *n* yearning

longevity *n* long life

longitude *n* distance east or west from standard meridian

loo *n Inf* lavatory

look *v* direct eyes (at); face; seem; search (for); hope (for); (*with* **after**) take care of ~*n* looking; view; search; (*oft. pl*) appearance **lookalike** *n* person who is double of another **lookout** *n* watchman; place for watching; prospect

loom¹ *n* machine for weaving

loom² *v* appear dimly; seem ominously close

loony *n/adj Sl* foolish or insane (person)

loop *n* figure made by curved line crossing itself ~*v* form loop **loophole** *n* means of evading rule without infringing it

loose *adj* slack; not fixed or restrained; vague; dissolute ~*v* free; unfasten; slacken; (*with* **off**) shoot, let fly **loosen** *v* make loose **loose-leaf** *adj* allowing addition or removal of pages

loot *n/v* plunder

lop *v* lopping, lopped cut away twigs and branches; chop off

lope *v* run with long, easy strides

lopsided *adj* with one side lower than the other

loquacious *adj* talkative

lord *n* British nobleman; ruler; (*with cap.*) God ~*v* domineer **lordly** *adj* imperious; fit for a lord **lordship** *n*

——————— THESAURUS ———————

single, solitary, withdrawn

long¹ *adj* expanded, extended, lengthy, stretched

long² *v* covet, crave, desire, hanker, hunger, itch, lust, pine, want, yearn

longing ambition, aspiration, coveting, craving, desire, hungering, itch, thirst, urge, wish

long-standing enduring, established, fixed, time-honoured

long-suffering easygoing, patient, resigned, stoical, tolerant

long-winded garrulous, lengthy, rambling, verbose, wordy

look *v* consider, contemplate, examine, eye, gaze, glance, inspect, observe, peep, regard, scan, scrutinize, see, study, survey, view, watch; appear, display, evidence, exhibit, present, seem, show ~*n* gander *Inf,* gaze, glance, glimpse, inspection, observation, review, sight, survey, view; air, appearance, aspect, bearing, cast, complexion, demeanour, effect, expression, face, fashion, guise, manner

lookout guard, sentinel, sentry; beacon, citadel, post, watchtower

loom appear, bulk, emerge, hover, impend, menace, take shape, threaten

loop *n* bend, circle, coil, curl, curve, eyelet, kink, noose, ring, spiral, twirl, twist ~*v* bend, circle, coil, connect, curl, encircle, fold, join, knot, roll, turn, twist

loophole avoidance, escape, evasion, excuse, plea, pretext

loose *adj* baggy, easy, relaxed, slack, sloppy; floating, free, insecure, movable, released, unattached, unfastened, unsecured, untied, wobbly; diffuse, ill-defined, imprecise, inaccurate, indefinite, inexact, rambling, random, vague ~*v* detach, disengage, ease, free, release, slacken, unbind, unbridle, undo, unfasten, unloose, untie

loosen detach, separate, slacken, undo, unstick, untie

loot booty, goods, haul, plunder, prize, spoils

lopsided askew, awry, crooked, off balance, squint, tilting, unbalanced, uneven

lore *n* learning; body of facts and traditions

lorry *n* motor vehicle for heavy loads, truck

lose *v* **losing, lost** be deprived of, fail to retain or use; fail to get; (of clock etc.) run slow; be defeated in **loser** *n* **loss** *n* act of losing; what is lost **lost** *adj* unable to be found; unable to find one's way; bewildered; not won; not utilized

lot *pron* great number; ~*n* collection; large quantity; share; fate; item at auction; object used to make decision by chance; area of land; *pl Inf* great numbers or quantity **a lot** *Inf* a great deal

lotion *n* liquid for washing wounds, improving skin etc.

lottery *n* method of raising funds by selling tickets that win prizes by chance; gamble

lotus *n* legendary plant whose fruits induce forgetfulness

loud *adj* strongly audible; noisy; *Fig* garish **loudly** *adv* **loudspeaker** *n* instrument for converting electrical signals into sound audible at a distance

lounge *v* recline, move at ease ~*n* living room of house; public room, area for sitting **lounge suit** man's suit for daytime wear

lour *see* LOWER

louse *n* (*pl* **lice**) parasitic insect **lousy** *adj Sl* bad; *Sl* nasty; having lice

lout *n* crude, oafish person

louvre *n* one of set of slats slanted to admit air but not rain

love *n* warm affection; benevolence; sexual passion; sweetheart; *Tennis etc.* score of nothing ~*v* admire passionately; delight in **lovable** *adj* **lovelorn** *adj* pining for a lover **lovely** *adj* beautiful, delightful **lover** *n* **loving** *adj* affectionate; tender **make love** (**to**) have sexual intercourse (with)

——————————— THESAURUS ———————————

lord earl, noble, nobleman, peer, viscount; commander, governor, leader, master, potentate, prince, ruler, seigneur, sovereign, superior

lore beliefs, doctrine, folk-wisdom, teaching, wisdom

lose displace, drop, forget, mislay, misplace, miss; be defeated

loser also-ran, failure, underdog

loss deprivation, failure, losing, misfortune, privation, waste; cost, damage, defeat, destruction, detriment, harm, hurt, injury, ruin

lost disappeared, forfeited, mislaid, misplaced, missing, strayed, vanished, wayward; adrift, astray, at sea, disoriented, off-course; baffled, bewildered, confused, helpless, ignorant, mystified, perplexed, puzzled

lot batch, collection, crowd, group, quantity, set; accident, chance, destiny, doom, fate, fortune, hazard, plight, portion; allowance, parcel, part, piece, portion, quota, ration, share **lots** abundance, heap(s), numbers, piles *Inf*, plenty, scores

lotion balm, cream, liniment, solution

lottery draw, raffle, sweepstake; chance, gamble, hazard, risk

loud blaring, deafening, ear-piercing, noisy, piercing, resounding, stentorian, strident, thundering; brash, brassy, flamboyant, flashy, garish, gaudy, glaring, lurid, ostentatious, showy, tacky *Inf*, tasteless, vulgar

lounge *v* laze, loaf, loiter, recline, relax, saunter, sprawl

lout bear, boor, clod, dolt, oaf

lovable amiable, attractive, charming, cuddly, cute, delightful, enchanting, endearing, lovely, pleasing, sweet, winning

love *n* adulation, affection, ardour, devotion, fondness, friendship, infatuation, liking, passion, rapture, regard, tenderness, warmth ~*v* cherish,

low[1] *adj* not tall, high or elevated; humble; vulgar; unwell; below what is usual; not loud **lower** *v* cause, allow to move down; diminish, degrade ~*adj* below; at an early stage, period **lowly** *adj* modest, humble **lowbrow** *n/adj* nonintellectual (person) **lowdown** *n Inf* inside information **low-down** *adj Inf* mean, shabby **lower case** small letters **low-key** *adj* not intense **lowland** *n* low-lying country

low[2] *v/n* (utter) cry, bellow of cattle

lower, lour *v* (of sky) look threatening; scowl

loyal *adj* faithful, true to allegiance **loyalist** *n* **loyalty** *n*

lozenge *n* small sweet or tablet of medicine; diamond shape

LP long-playing record

L-plate *n* sign on car driven by learner driver

LSD lysergic acid diethylamide (hallucinogenic drug); pounds, shillings, and pence

lubricate *v* oil, grease; make slippery **lubricant** *n* substance used for this **lubrication** *n*

lucerne *n* fodder plant

lucid *adj* clear; easily understood; sane **lucidity** *n*

luck *n* chance, whether good or bad; good fortune **luckily** *adv* fortunately **luckless** *adj* having bad luck **lucky** *adj* having good luck

lucrative *adj* very profitable

ludicrous *adj* ridiculous

lug[1] *v* **lugging, lugged** drag with effort

hold dear, idolize, prize, treasure, worship; appreciate, delight in, desire, enjoy, fancy, like, relish, savour

lovely attractive, beautiful, charming, comely, exquisite, graceful, handsome, pretty, sweet; agreeable, delightful, enjoyable, gratifying, nice, pleasant

lover admirer, beau, beloved, boyfriend, girlfriend, mistress, paramour, suitor, sweetheart

loving affectionate, ardent, cordial, dear, devoted, doting, fond, friendly, kind, tender, warm

low little, short, small, squat, stunted; deep, shallow, subsided, sunken; humble, lowborn, lowly, meek, obscure, plain, plebeian, poor, simple; coarse, common, crude, disgraceful, dishonourable, disreputable, gross, obscene, rough, rude, unrefined, vulgar; abject, base, dastardly, degraded, depraved, despicable, ignoble, mean, nasty, sordid, unworthy, vile, vulgar; gentle, hushed, muffled, muted, quiet, soft, subdued, whispered

lower *v* depress, drop, fall, sink, sub-

merge; abase, belittle, debase, degrade, deign, demean, devalue, disgrace, humiliate ~*adj* inferior, junior, lesser, minor, secondary, smaller, subordinate

loyal attached, constant, dependable, devoted, dutiful, faithful, immovable, staunch, steadfast, true, trustworthy

loyalty allegiance, faithfulness, fidelity, patriotism

lubricate grease, oil, smear

lucid clear, distinct, evident, explicit, intelligible, limpid, obvious, plain, transparent; *compos mentis,* rational, sane

luck accident, chance, destiny, fate, fortune; advantage, blessing, fluke, prosperity, stroke, success, windfall

luckily favourably, fortunately, happily, opportunely

lucky blessed, charmed, favoured, fortunate, jammy *Brit sl,* prosperous, successful

lucrative fat, fruitful, gainful, paying, productive, profitable, remunerative, well-paid

ludicrous absurd, burlesque, comic,

lug[2] *n* projection, serving as handle or support; *Inf* ear

luggage *n* traveller's baggage

lugubrious *adj* doleful

lukewarm *adj* tepid; indifferent

lull *v* soothe, sing to sleep; calm; subside ~*n* quiet spell **lullaby** *n* lulling song, esp. for children

lumbago *n* rheumatism of the lower part of the back

lumber[1] *n* disused articles, useless rubbish; sawn timber ~*v Inf* burden with something unpleasant **lumberjack** *n US & Canad* man who fells trees and prepares logs

lumber[2] *v* move heavily

luminous *adj* shedding light; glowing **luminary** *n* famous person **luminescence** *n* emission of light without heat

lump[1] *n* shapeless piece or mass; swelling; large sum ~*v* throw together **lumpy** *adj* full of lumps; uneven

lump[2] *v Inf* tolerate

lunar *adj* relating to the moon

lunatic *adj/n* foolish or irresponsible (person); insane (person) **lunacy** *n*

lunch *n* meal taken in middle of day ~*v* eat, entertain to lunch **luncheon** *n* lunch **luncheon meat** tinned ground mixture of meat and cereal

lung *n* one of the two organs of respiration in vertebrates

lunge *v* thrust with sword etc. ~*n* thrust; sudden movement of body, plunge

lupin *n* leguminous plant with spikes of flowers

lurch *n* sudden roll to one side ~*v* stagger **leave in the lurch** leave in difficulties

lure *n* bait; power to attract ~*v* entice; attract

lurid *adj* sensational; garish

lurk *v* lie hidden **lurking** *adj* (of suspicion) not definite

luscious *adj* sweet, juicy; extremely attractive

———————————— THESAURUS ————————————

crazy, funny, laughable, odd, preposterous, ridiculous, silly

luggage baggage, bags, cases, gear, suitcases, trunks

lull *v* allay, calm, compose, hush, pacify, quell, quiet, soothe, still, subdue ~*n* calm, calmness, hush, pause, quiet, respite, silence

lumber clump, plod, shamble, shuffle, stump, trudge, trundle

luminous bright, brilliant, glowing, lighted, lit, lustrous, radiant, resplendent, shining, vivid

lump *n* ball, bunch, cake, chunk, gob, group, hunk, mass, piece, spot, wedge; bulge, bump, growth, hump, protrusion, protuberance, swelling, tumour ~*v* bunch, collect, combine, group, mass, pool, unite

lunacy absurdity, craziness, folly, foolishness, idiocy, madness, stupidity

lunatic *adj* barking mad *Sl,* crackpot *Inf,* crazy, daft, demented, deranged, insane, irrational, loopy *Inf,* mad, unhinged ~*n* headcase *Inf,* madman, maniac, psychopath

lunge *v* bound, charge, cut, dash, dive, jab, leap, poke, stab, thrust ~*n* charge, cut, jab, pass, spring, stab, swing, swipe, thrust

lure *n* attraction, bait, decoy, magnet, temptation ~*v* attract, beckon, decoy, draw, ensnare, entice, inveigle, invite, lead on, seduce, tempt

lurid graphic, melodramatic, sensational, shock-horror *Facetious,* shocking, startling, unrestrained, vivid

lurk crouch, hide, prowl, skulk, slink, sneak, snoop

luscious appetizing, delectable, delicious, honeyed, juicy, mouthwatering, palatable, rich, savoury, succulent, sweet

lush *adj* (of plant growth) luxuriant; luxurious

lust *n* strong desire for sexual gratification; any strong desire ~*v* have passionate desire **lustful** *adj* **lusty** *adj* vigorous, healthy

lustre *n* gloss, sheen; renown; metallic pottery glaze **lustrous** *adj* shining

lute *n* old stringed musical instrument played like a guitar

luxury *n* possession and use of costly, choice things for enjoyment; enjoyable, comfortable surroundings; enjoyable but not essential thing **luxuriance** *n* abundance **luxuriant** *adj* growing thickly; abundant **luxuriate** *v*

indulge in luxury; flourish profusely; take delight (in) **luxurious** *adj* fond of luxury; self-indulgent; sumptuous

lychee *n* Chinese fruit

Lycra *n Trademark* fabric used for tight-fitting garments

lymph *n* colourless body fluid, mainly white blood cells **lymphatic** *adj*

lynch *v* put to death without trial

lynx *n* animal of cat family

lyre *n* instrument like harp

lyric *n* songlike poem expressing personal feelings; *pl* words of popular song **lyrical** *adj* expressed in this style; enthusiastic **lyricist** *n*

———————— T H E S A U R U S ————————

lush abundant, dense, green, lavish, prolific, rank, teeming, verdant

lust *n* carnality, lechery, lewdness, libido, salaciousness, sensuality; appetite, avidity, craving, cupidity, desire, greed, longing, passion, thirst ~*v* covet, crave, desire, need, want, yearn

lustre burnish, gleam, glint, glitter, gloss, glow, sheen, shimmer, shine, sparkle; distinction, fame, glory, honour, prestige, renown

lusty hale, healthy, hearty, powerful, robust, stalwart, stout, strapping, strong, sturdy, vigorous, virile

luxurious comfortable, costly, expensive, lavish, opulent, rich, splendid, sumptuous

luxury affluence, opulence, richness, splendour; comfort, delight, enjoyment, gratification, indulgence, pleasure, satisfaction, wellbeing; extra, extravagance, treat

M m

m metre
MA Master of Arts
mac n Inf mackintosh
macabre adj gruesome, ghastly
macaroni n pasta in thin tubes
macaroon n biscuit containing almonds
macaw n kind of parrot
mace[1] n staff of office
mace[2] n spice made of nutmeg shell
machete n broad, heavy knife
Machiavellian adj (politically) unprincipled, crafty
machination n (usu. pl) plotting, intrigue
machine n apparatus with several parts to apply mechanical force; controlling organization; mechanical appliance ~v shape etc. with machine **machinery** n machines or machine parts; procedures by which system functions **machinist** n **machine gun** automatic gun firing repeatedly
macho adj exhibiting exaggerated pride in masculinity **machismo** n strong, exaggerated masculinity
mackerel n edible sea fish
mackintosh n waterproof raincoat
macramé n ornamental work of knotted cord
macrocosm n the universe; any large system
mad adj suffering from mental disease, foolish; enthusiastic (about); excited; Inf furious **madden** v make mad **madness** n
madam n polite title for a woman
madcap adj/n reckless (person)
made past tense and past participle of MAKE
Madonna n Virgin Mary
madrigal n unaccompanied part song
maelstrom n great whirlpool
maestro n (pl **-tros**, **-tri**) outstanding musician, conductor; master of any art
magazine n periodical publication; appliance for supplying cartridges to gun; storehouse for arms etc.
magenta adj/n (of) deep purplish-red
maggot n grub, larva **maggoty** adj
magic n art of supposedly invoking supernatural powers to influence events etc.; witchcraft, conjuring; fascinating quality or power ~adj of, using magic **magical** adj **magician** n wizard, conjuror
magistrate n civil officer administer-

THESAURUS

machine apparatus, appliance, contraption, device, engine, instrument, tool; agency, organization, party, structure, system
machinery apparatus, equipment, gear, tackle, tools, works; agency, channels, organization, procedure, system
mad crazed, delirious, demented, deranged, insane, lunatic, psychotic, raving, unhinged; absurd, foolhardy, foolish, imprudent, inane, irrational, ludicrous, preposterous, unsound, wild

madden aggravate, annoy, craze, enrage, exasperate, infuriate, provoke, upset, vex
madness delusion, dementia, derangement, insanity, lunacy, mania, mental illness, psychosis; absurdity, folly, foolishness, idiocy, nonsense
magazine journal, pamphlet, paper, periodical
magic n enchantment, occultism, sorcery, spell, witchcraft; conjuring, illusion, trickery; allurement, charm, enchantment, fascination, glamour, magnetism, power adj also **magical**

ing law **magisterial** *adj* of magistrate; authoritative

magnanimous *adj* generous, not petty **magnanimity** *n*

magnate *n* influential person

magnesium *n* metallic element **magnesia** *n* white powder used in medicine

magnet *n* piece of iron, steel having properties of attracting iron, steel **magnetic** *adj* of magnet; exerting powerful attraction **magnetism** *n* **magnetize** *v* **magneto** *n* (*pl* -tos) apparatus for ignition in internal-combustion engine **magnetic tape** coated plastic strip for recording sound or video signals

magnificent *adj* splendid; imposing; excellent **magnificence** *n*

magnify *v* -fying, -fied increase apparent size of, as with lens; exaggerate

magnification *n*

magnitude *n* importance; size

magnolia *n* tree with white, sweet-scented flowers

magnum *n* large wine bottle

magpie *n* black-and-white bird

maharajah *n* (*fem* **maharanee**) former title of some Indian princes

mahogany *n* tree yielding reddish-brown wood

maiden *n Lit* young unmarried woman ~*adj* unmarried; first **maid** *n* woman servant; *Lit* maiden **maiden name** woman's surname before marriage

mail[1] *n* letters etc. transported and delivered by the post office; postal system; train etc. carrying mail ~*v* send by mail

mail[2] *n* armour of interlaced rings

maim *v* cripple, mutilate

——————— T H E S A U R U S ———————

charming, enchanting, entrancing, fascinating, magnetic, marvellous, miraculous

magician conjurer, conjuror, enchanter, illusionist, sorcerer, warlock, witch, wizard

magistrate judge, justice

magnanimous big, charitable, free, generous, handsome, kind, munificent, noble, selfless, ungrudging, unselfish

magnate baron, chief, leader, mogul, plutocrat, tycoon

magnetic alluring, attractive, captivating, charming, enchanting, entrancing, hypnotic, irresistible, seductive

magnetism allure, appeal, attraction, charisma, charm, draw, enchantment, fascination, magic, power, pull, spell

magnificent brilliant, elevated, exalted, excellent, glorious, gorgeous, grand, imposing, impressive, lavish, noble, opulent, princely, regal, rich,

splendid, stately, sumptuous, superb, superior

magnify amplify, augment, boost, deepen, dilate, enlarge, expand, heighten, increase, intensify; blow up, dramatize, enhance, exaggerate

magnitude consequence, eminence, grandeur, greatness, importance, mark, moment, note, significance, weight; amount, amplitude, bulk, capacity, dimensions, expanse, extent, hugeness, immensity, largeness, mass, measure, quantity, size, space, strength, volume

maid housemaid, servant; damsel, girl, maiden, miss, wench

maiden *n* damsel, girl, maid, miss, nymph, virgin, wench ~*adj* chaste, intact, pure, virgin; first, initial, introductory

mail *n* letters, packages, parcels, post; post, postal service ~*v* dispatch, forward, post, send

maim cripple, disable, hurt, incapacitate, injure, mutilate, wound

main *adj* chief, principal *~n* principal pipe, line carrying water etc.; *Obs* sea **mainframe** *n* high-speed general-purpose computer; central processing unit of computer **mainland** *n* stretch of land which forms main part of a country **mainstay** *n* chief support **mainstream** *n* prevailing cultural trend

maintain *v* carry on; support; assert; support by argument **maintenance** *n* maintaining; means of support; upkeep of buildings etc.

maisonette *n* part of house fitted as self-contained dwelling

maize *n* type of corn

majesty *n* stateliness; sovereignty **majestic** *adj*

major *n* army officer above captain; scale in music *~adj* greater in number, extent etc. **majority** *n* greater number; coming of age

make *v* **making, made** construct; produce; create; establish; appoint; amount to; cause to do; reach; earn; tend; contribute *~n* brand, type **maker** *n* **making** *n* **make-believe** *n* fantasy, pretence **make do** manage with inferior alternative **make it** *Inf* be successful **makeshift** *adj* serving as temporary substitute **make-up** *n* cosmetics; characteristics; layout

——————— THESAURUS ———————

main *adj* central, chief, critical, crucial, essential, foremost, head, leading, paramount, pre-eminent, primary, prime, principal, special, supreme, vital *~n* cable, channel, conduit, duct, line, pipe

mainstay anchor, backbone, bulwark, linchpin, pillar, prop

maintain conserve, continue, finance, keep, look after, nurture, perpetuate, preserve, prolong, provide, retain, supply, support, sustain, uphold; affirm, allege, assert, asseverate, aver, avow, claim, contend, declare, hold, insist, profess, state; back, champion, defend, justify, plead for, uphold, vindicate

maintenance care, conservation, continuation, nurture, preservation, provision, repairs, supply, support, upkeep

majestic awesome, elevated, exalted, grand, imperial, imposing, impressive, lofty, magnificent, monumental, noble, princely, regal, royal, splendid, stately, sublime, superb

majesty dignity, glory, grandeur, kingliness, magnificence, nobility, pomp, royalty, splendour, state, sublimity

major better, bigger, chief, elder, greater, head, higher, larger, lead, leading, main, most, senior, superior, supreme

majority best part, bulk, mass, more, most, plurality, preponderance, superiority; manhood, maturity, seniority

make *v* assemble, build, compose, constitute, construct, create, fabricate, fashion, forge, form, frame, manufacture, originate, produce, shape, synthesize; accomplish, beget, cause, create, effect, generate, occasion, produce; appoint, assign, create, designate, elect, install, invest, nominate, ordain; draw up, enact, establish, fix, form, frame, pass; cause, coerce, compel, constrain, dragoon, drive, force, impel, induce, oblige, press, railroad *Inf,* require *~n* brand, build, construction, cut, designation, form, kind, mark, model, shape, sort, style, type, variety

make do cope, improvise, manage

maker author, builder, director, framer, manufacturer, producer

makeshift expedient, provisional, stopgap, substitute, temporary

make-up cosmetics, powder; ar-

mal-, male- *comb. form* ill, badly, as in **malformation, malfunction**

maladjusted *adj* badly adjusted, as to society

malady *n* disease

malaise *n* vague feeling of discomfort

malapropism *n* ludicrous misuse of word

malaria *n* infectious disease transmitted by mosquitoes

malcontent *adj/n* discontented (person)

male *adj* of sex that fertilizes female; of men or male animals ~*n* male person or animal

malevolent *adj* full of ill will **malevolence** *n*

malice *n* ill will; spite **malicious** *adj* spiteful

malign *adj* causing evil ~*v* slander **malignancy** *n* **malignant** *adj* feeling ill will; (of disease) resistant to therapy

malinger *v* feign illness to escape duty

mall *n* shopping centre

mallard *n* wild duck

malleable *adj* capable of being hammered into shape; adaptable

mallet *n* (wooden) hammer

malnutrition *n* inadequate nutrition

malodorous *adj* evil-smelling

malpractice *n* immoral, illegal or unethical conduct

malt *n* grain used for brewing

maltreat *v* treat badly

mammal *n* animal of type that suckles its young **mammalian** *adj*

mammary *adj* of, relating to breast

mammon *n* wealth regarded as source of evil

mammoth *n* extinct animal like an elephant ~*adj* colossal

man *n* (*pl* **men**) human being; human race; adult male; piece used in chess etc. ~*v* **manning, manned** supply with men **manful** *adj* brave **manly** *adj* **manhandle** *v* treat roughly **manhole** *n* opening through which man may pass to a sewer etc. **mankind** *n* human beings **manslaughter** *n* unintentional homicide

———————— THESAURUS ————————

rangement, assembly, composition, configuration, constitution, construction, format, formation, layout, organization, structure

maladjusted disturbed, neurotic, unstable

malady ailment, complaint, disease, illness, infirmity, sickness

malcontent agitator, complainer, grumbler, rebel, troublemaker

male manlike, manly, masculine, virile

malevolent baleful, evil-minded, hostile, malicious, malignant, pernicious, spiteful, vengeful, vicious, vindictive

malice animosity, bitterness, enmity, hate, hatred, rancour, spite, venom, vindictiveness

malicious baleful, bitter, hateful, injurious, malevolent, pernicious, rancorous, resentful, spiteful, vengeful, vicious

malign *adj* bad, baleful, baneful, evil, harmful, hostile, hurtful, pernicious, vicious, wicked ~*v* abuse, defame, denigrate, disparage, knock *Inf*, libel, revile, slag (off) *Sl*, slander, smear

malignant baleful, bitter, harmful, hostile, hurtful, malevolent, malicious, pernicious, spiteful, vicious

malpractice misbehaviour, misconduct, misdeed, offence

maltreat abuse, damage, harm, hurt, injure, mistreat

man *n* adult, being, body, human being, individual, one, person, personage, somebody, soul; humanity, human race, mankind, mortals, people; gentleman, male ~*v* crew, fill, garri-

manacle n/v fetter

manage v be in charge of; succeed in doing; control; handle **manageable** adj **management** n those who manage; administration **manager** n **managerial** adj

mandarin n small orange; high-ranking bureaucrat

mandate n command of, or commission to act for, another; instruction from electorate to representative or government **mandatory** adj compulsory

mandible n lower jawbone

mandolin n stringed musical instrument

mane n long hair on neck of horse, lion etc.

manganese n metallic element

mange n skin disease of dogs etc. **mangy** adj

manger n eating trough in stable

mangle¹ n machine for rolling clothes etc. to remove water ~v press in

mangle

mangle² v mutilate

mango n (pl **-goes, -gos**) tropical fruit

mangrove n tropical tree which grows on muddy river banks

mania n madness; prevailing craze **maniac** adj/n mad (person) **maniacal, manic** adj affected by mania

manicure n treatment and care of fingernails and hands ~v treat, care for hands

manifest adj clear, undoubted ~v make manifest **manifestation** n **manifesto** n (pl **-tos**) declaration of policy by political party etc.

manifold adj numerous and varied ~n in engine, pipe with several outlets

manila, manilla n fibre used for ropes; tough paper

manipulate v handle skilfully; manage; falsify **manipulation** n

manna n nourishment; unexpected

———————— THESAURUS ————————

son, occupy, people, staff

manage administer, command, concert, conduct, direct, govern, handle, oversee, rule, run, supervise; accomplish, arrange, contrive, cut it *Inf*, deal with, effect, engineer, succeed; control, guide, handle, influence, manipulate, operate, pilot, ply, steer, train, use, wield

manageable compliant, controllable, docile, easy, handy, submissive, tractable, wieldy

management administration, board, directorate, employers

manager conductor, controller, director, executive, governor, head, organizer, proprietor, supervisor

mandate authority, bidding, charge, command, decree, directive, edict, fiat, instruction, order, sanction, warrant

mandatory binding, compulsory, ob-

ligatory, required, requisite

mangle butcher, crush, cut, deform, destroy, distort, hack, maim, mar, mutilate, spoil, tear, trash *Sl*, wreck

mangy dirty, mean, scruffy, seedy, shabby, shoddy, squalid

manhandle maul, pull, push

mania craziness, delirium, derangement, disorder, frenzy, insanity, lunacy, madness

maniac headbanger *Inf*, headcase *Inf*, lunatic, madman, psychopath

manifest adj apparent, blatant, clear, distinct, evident, glaring, noticeable, obvious, open, patent, plain, visible

manifestation disclosure, display, exhibition, exposure, instance, mark, materialization, revelation, show, sign, symptom, token

manifold abundant, assorted, diverse, many, multiple, numerous, varied, various

gift

mannequin *n* woman who models clothes

manner *n* way, style; bearing; sort, kind; *pl* social behaviour **mannered** *adj* affected **mannerism** *n* person's distinctive habit

manoeuvre *n* complicated, perhaps deceptive plan or action ~*v* employ stratagems; (cause to) perform manoeuvres

manor *n* large country house with land

manse *n* house of minister in some religious denominations

mansion *n* large house

mantelpiece *n* shelf at top of fireplace

mantle *n* loose cloak; covering ~*v* cover

mantra *n* sacred word or syllable in Hinduism and Buddhism

manual *adj* done with the hands; by human labour, not automatic ~*n*

handbook

manufacture *v* make (materials) into finished articles; concoct ~*n* making of articles, esp. in large quantities **manufacturer** *n*

manure *n* dung or chemical fertilizer used to enrich land

manuscript *n* book etc. written by hand; copy for printing

many *adj* more, most numerous ~*n* large number

map *n* flat representation of the earth ~*v* **mapping, mapped** make map of; (*with* **out**) plan

maple *n* tree of sycamore family

mar *v* **marring, marred** spoil

Mar. March

maraca *n* shaken percussion instrument

marathon *n* long-distance race; endurance contest

maraud *v* raid; plunder **marauder** *n*

marble *n* kind of limestone; small ball used in children's game

manipulate employ, handle, operate, ply, use, wield, work

mankind humanity, human race, man, people

manly bold, brave, courageous, daring, fearless, gallant, hardy, heroic, male, masculine, noble, powerful, resolute, robust, strong, valiant, valorous, vigorous, virile

manner approach, custom, genre, habit, line, method, mode, practice, process, routine, style, tenor, usage, way, wont; air, appearance, aspect, bearing, behaviour, conduct, demeanour, deportment, look, presence, tone

mannerism foible, habit, peculiarity, quirk, trait, trick

manoeuvre *n* action, artifice, dodge, intrigue, machination, move, plan, plot, ploy, ruse, scheme, subterfuge, tactic, trick ~*v* contrive, devise, engi-

neer, intrigue, manage, plan, plot, scheme; direct, drive, guide, handle, navigate, pilot, steer

mansion abode, dwelling, habitation, hall, manor, residence, seat, villa

manual *adj* hand-operated, human, physical ~*n* bible, guide, handbook, instructions

manufacture *v* assemble, build, compose, construct, create, forge, form, make, mould, process, produce, shape, think up, trump up ~*n* assembly, construction, fabrication, production

manure compost, droppings, dung, muck, ordure

many *adj* abundant, copious, countless, frequent, manifold, myriad, numerous, profuse, sundry, varied, various

mar blemish, blight, blot, damage, deface, harm, hurt, injure, ruin, scar,

March *n* third month

march *v* walk with military step; go, progress ~*n* action of marching; distance marched; marching tune

marchioness *n* wife, widow of marquis

mare *n* female horse

margarine *n* butter substitute made from vegetable fats

margin *n* border, edge; space round printed page; amount allowed beyond what is necessary **marginal** *adj*

marigold *n* plant with yellow flowers

marijuana, marihuana *n* dried flowers and leaves of hemp plant, used as narcotic

marina *n* mooring facility for pleasure boats

marinade *n* liquid in which food is soaked before cooking **marinate** *v* soak in marinade

marine *adj* of the sea or shipping ~*n* soldier trained for land or sea combat; fleet **mariner** *n* sailor

marionette *n* puppet

marital *adj* of marriage

maritime *adj* of seafaring; near the sea

mark[1] *n* dot, scar etc.; sign, token; letter, number showing evaluation of schoolwork etc.; indication; target ~*v* make mark on; distinguish; notice; assess; stay close to sporting opponent **marked** *adj* noticeable **marker** *n* **marksman** *n* skilled shot

mark[2] *n* German currency unit

market *n* place for buying and selling; demand for goods ~*v* offer for sale **marketable** *adj* **market garden** place where fruit and vegetables are grown for sale

marmalade *n* preserve made of oranges, lemons etc.

marmoset *n* small bushy-tailed monkey

maroon[1] *adj/n* (of) brownish-crimson colour

maroon[2] *v* leave on deserted island etc.; isolate

marquee *n* large tent

marquetry *n* inlaid work, wood mosaic

marquis, marquess *n* nobleman of rank below duke

———————— THESAURUS ————————

spoil, stain, taint, tarnish, vitiate

march *v* file, pace, parade, stalk, stride, strut, tramp, tread, walk ~*n* demonstration, parade, procession

margin border, bound, brim, brink, confine, edge, limit, rim, side, verge; allowance, extra, latitude, leeway, play, room, scope, space

marginal borderline, peripheral

marine maritime, nautical, naval, oceanic, seafaring

mariner hand, sailor, salt, seafarer, seaman, tar

marital conjugal, married, matrimonial, nuptial, wedded

maritime marine, nautical, naval, oceanic, sea, seafaring

mark *n* blot, bruise, dent, impression, line, nick, scar, scratch, smirch,

smudge, spot, stain, streak; badge, blaze, brand, emblem, evidence, feature, hallmark, indication, label, note, print, proof, seal, sign, stamp, symbol, symptom, token ~*v* blemish, blot, blotch, brand, bruise, dent, impress, imprint, nick, scar, scratch, smirch, smudge, stain, streak; attend, mind, note, notice, observe, regard, remark, watch

marked apparent, blatant, clear, conspicuous, decided, distinct, evident, manifest, notable, noted, obvious, patent, remarkable, signal, striking

market *n* bazaar, fair, mart ~*v* retail, sell, vend

maroon abandon, cast away, desert, leave, strand

marriage match, matrimony, wed-

marrow *n* fatty substance inside bones; vital part; plant with long, green-striped fruit, eaten as vegetable

marry *v* **marrying, married** join as husband and wife; unite closely **marriage** *n* being married; wedding

marsh *n* low-lying wet land **marshy** *adj*

marshal *n* high officer of state; *US* law enforcement officer; high-ranking officer in the army, air force ~*v* **-shalling, -shalled** arrange; conduct with ceremony

marshmallow *n* spongy pink or white sweet

marsupial *n* animal that carries its young in pouch

marten *n* weasel-like animal

martial *adj* of war; warlike

martin *n* species of swallow

martinet *n* strict disciplinarian

martyr *n* one who suffers or dies for his beliefs ~*v* make martyr of

marvel *v* **-velling, -velled** wonder ~*n* wonderful thing **marvellous** *adj*

marzipan *n* paste of almonds, sugar etc.

mascara *n* cosmetic for darkening eyelashes

mascot *n* thing supposed to bring luck

masculine *adj* relating to males; manly

mash *n/v* (crush into) soft mass or pulp

mask *n* covering for face; disguise, pretence ~*v* disguise

masochism *n* abnormal condition where pleasure (esp. sexual) is derived from pain **masochist** *n*

mason *n* worker in stone **masonry** *n* stonework

masquerade *n* masked ball ~*v* appear in disguise

Mass *n* service in R.C. Church

mass *n* quantity of matter; *Physics* amount of matter in body; large quantity ~*v* form into mass **massive** *adj* large and heavy **mass-market** *adj* appealing to many people **mass-produce** *v* produce standardized articles in large quantities

massacre *n* indiscriminate, large-scale killing ~*v* kill indiscriminately

ding, wedlock

marrow core, cream, essence, gist, heart, kernel, pith, quick, substance

marry espouse, wed; ally, bond, join, knit, link, match, merge, tie, unite, yoke

marsh bog, fen, quagmire, slough, swamp

marshal align, arrange, array, assemble, collect, deploy, dispose, gather, group, muster, order, rank

marshy boggy, miry, spongy, swampy, wet

marvel *v* gape, gaze, goggle, wonder ~*n* genius, miracle, phenomenon, portent, prodigy, wonder

marvellous amazing, astounding, breathtaking, brilliant, extraordinary, miraculous, prodigious, remarkable,

sensational *Inf*, stupendous, wondrous

masculine male, manful, manlike, manly, virile; bold, brave, gallant, hardy, powerful, resolute, robust, strong, vigorous

mask *n* false face, visor; camouflage, cloak, cover, cover-up, disguise, façade, front, guise, screen, veil, veneer ~*v* camouflage, cloak, conceal, cover, disguise, hide, obscure, screen, veil

mass *n* block, chunk, hunk, lump, piece; bulk, dimension, magnitude, size ~*v* accumulate, assemble, collect, forgather, gather, mob, muster, rally, swarm, throng ~*adj* extensive, large-scale, popular, wholesale, widespread

massage *n* rubbing and kneading of muscles etc. as curative treatment ~*v* perform massage **masseur** *n* (*fem* **masseuse**) one who practises massage

mast *n* pole for supporting ship's sails; tall support for aerial etc.

mastectomy *n* surgical removal of breast

master *n* one in control; employer; owner; document etc. from which copies are made; expert; teacher ~*adj* expert, skilled ~*v* overcome; acquire skill in **masterful** *adj* expert, skilled; domineering **masterly** *adj* showing great skill **mastery** *n* understanding (of); expertise; victory **mastermind** *v* plan, direct ~*n* one who directs complex operation **masterpiece** *n* outstanding work

masticate *v* chew

mastiff *n* large dog

masturbate *v* fondle genital organs **masturbation** *n*

mat¹ *n* small rug; piece of fabric to protect another surface; thick tangled mass ~*v* **matting, matted** form into such mass

mat², matt *adj* dull, lustreless

matador *n* man who kills bull in bullfights

match¹ *n* contest, game; equal; person, thing corresponding to another; marriage ~*v* get something corresponding to; oppose, put in competition (with); correspond **matchmaker** *n* person who schemes to bring about marriage

match² *n* small stick with head which ignites when rubbed **matchbox** *n* **matchstick** *n*

mate *n* comrade; husband, wife; one of pair; officer in merchant ship ~*v* marry; pair **matey** *adj Inf* friendly

massacre *n* butchery, carnage, killing, murder, slaughter ~*v* butcher, exterminate, kill, murder, slaughter, slay

massage *n* manipulation, rub-down ~*v* manipulate, rub down

massive big, bulky, enormous, extensive, gigantic, great, heavy, huge, hulking, immense, substantial, vast, weighty

master *n* captain, chief, commander, controller, director, employer, governor, head, lord, manager, overlord, overseer, owner, principal, ruler; adept, expert, genius, maestro, virtuoso, wizard ~*adj* adept, expert, masterly, proficient, skilful, skilled ~*v* bridle, check, conquer, curb, defeat, overcome, quash, quell, subdue, subjugate, suppress, tame, vanquish; acquire, grasp, learn

masterful adept, adroit, clever, deft, expert, first-rate, skilful, skilled, superior, supreme; arrogant, dictator-ial, domineering, high-handed

masterly adept, adroit, clever, fine, first-rate, skilful, superior

mastermind *v* conceive, devise, direct, manage, organize, plan ~*n* brain(s) *Inf*, brainbox, director, engineer, genius, intellect, manager, organizer, planner

masterpiece classic, jewel, *tour de force*

mastery command, familiarity, grasp, knowledge, understanding; ability, attainment, expertise, prowess, skill

match *n* bout, contest, game, head-to-head, test, trial; equal, peer, rival; affiliation, alliance, combination, couple, duet, marriage, pair, pairing, partnership, union ~*v* ally, combine, couple, join, link, marry, mate, pair, unite, yoke; compare, contend, equal, oppose, pit against, rival, vie; adapt, agree, blend, correspond, fit, go with, harmonize, suit, tally

material *n* substance from which thing is made; cloth; information on which piece of work is based *~adj* of body; affecting physical wellbeing; important **materialism** *n* excessive interest in money and possessions; doctrine that nothing but matter exists **materialistic** *adj* **materialize** *v* come into existence or view **materially** *adv* appreciably

maternal *adj* of mother **maternity** *n* motherhood

mathematics *pl n* (*with sing v*) science of number, quantity, shape and space **mathematical** *adj* **mathematician** *n*

maths *n Inf* mathematics

matinée *n* afternoon performance in theatre

matins *pl n* morning service

matriarch *n* mother as head of family **matriarchal** *adj*

matriculate *v* enrol, be enrolled in college or university

matrimony *n* marriage **matrimonial** *adj*

matrix *n* (*pl* **matrices**) substance, situation in which something originates, is enclosed; mould

matron *n* married woman; woman who superintends domestic arrangements of public institution; *former name for* NURSING OFFICER

matter *n* substance of which thing is made; affair; business; trouble; pus *~v* be of importance

mattress *n* stuffed flat (sprung) case used as part of bed

mature *adj* ripe, completely developed; grown-up *~v* bring, come to maturity **maturity** *n*

maudlin *adj* weakly sentimental

maul *v* handle roughly

mausoleum *n* (*pl* **-leums, -lea**) stately building as a tomb

mauve *adj/n* pale purple

maverick *n* independent, unorthodox person

maw *n* stomach

mawkish *adj* maudlin; sickly

maxim *n* general truth; rule of conduct

———————— THESAURUS ————————

mate *n* colleague, companion, comrade, fellow-worker; husband, partner, significant other *US inf*, spouse, wife *~v* marry, match, wed; breed, copulate, couple, pair

material *n* body, element, matter, stuff, substance; cloth, fabric, stuff; data, evidence, facts, information, notes, work *~adj* bodily, concrete, fleshly, physical, substantial, tangible, worldly

materialize appear, happen, occur, turn up

materially appreciably, considerably, essentially, gravely, greatly, much, seriously, significantly, substantially

matrimonial conjugal, marital, married, nuptial, wedding

matrimony marriage, nuptials, wedlock

matter *n* body, stuff, substance; affair, business, concern, episode, event, incident, occurrence, question, situation, subject, topic *~v* signify

mature *adj* adult, fit, grown, matured, mellow, of age, perfect, prepared, ready, ripe, seasoned *~v* age, bloom, blossom, develop, mellow, perfect, ripen, season

maturity adulthood, experience, fullness, majority, manhood, perfection, ripeness, wisdom

maudlin lachrymose, sentimental, tearful

maul abuse, ill-treat, manhandle, molest, paw

maxim adage, aphorism, axiom, byword, dictum, motto, proverb, rule, saw, saying

maximum *adj/n* (*pl* -mums, -ma) greatest (size or number) **maximize** *v* increase to maximum

May *n* fifth month; (*without cap.*) hawthorn or its flowers **mayfly** *n* short-lived aquatic insect

may *v* (*past tense* **might**) expresses possibility, permission, opportunity etc. **maybe** *adv* perhaps; possibly

Mayday *n* international distress signal

mayhem *n* violent destruction

mayonnaise *n* creamy sauce, esp. for salads

mayor *n* head of municipality **mayoress** *n* mayor's wife; lady mayor

maze *n* labyrinth; network of paths, lines; state of confusion

MBE Member of the Order of the British Empire

MD Doctor of Medicine

me *pron object of* I

mead *n* alcoholic drink made from honey

meadow *n* piece of grassland

meagre *adj* lean, scanty

meal¹ *n* occasion when food is served and eaten; the food

meal² *n* grain ground to powder **mealy-mouthed** *adj* not outspoken enough

mean¹ *v* **meaning**, **meant** intend; signify; have a meaning; have the intention of behaving **meaning** *n* **meaningful** *adj* of great significance

mean² *adj* ungenerous, petty; miserly; callous; shabby

mean³ *n* middle point; *pl* that by which thing is done; money; resources ~*adj* intermediate; average **meantime**, **meanwhile** *adv/n* (during) time between one happening and another

meander *v* flow windingly; wander aimlessly ~*n* wandering course

measles *n* infectious disease producing rash of red spots **measly** *adj* Inf meagre

———————— THESAURUS ————————

maximum *adj* greatest, highest, most, topmost, utmost ~*n* ceiling, crest, extremity, height, most, peak, pinnacle, summit, top, utmost, zenith

maybe perchance, perhaps, possibly

mayhem chaos, commotion, confusion, destruction, disorder, fracas, havoc, trouble, violence

maze intricacy, labyrinth, meander; imbroglio, perplexity, puzzle, snarl, tangle, web

meadow field, grassland, pasture

meagre deficient, inadequate, little, measly, paltry, pathetic, poor, puny, scanty, short, slender, slight, small, spare, sparse

mean¹ *v* convey, denote, express, imply, indicate, purport, represent, say, signify, spell, suggest, symbolize; aim, aspire, design, desire, intend, plan, propose, purpose, set out, want, wish

mean² *adj* beggarly, close, mercenary, miserly, parsimonious, stingy, tight, ungenerous; abject, base, callous, contemptible, degraded, despicable, ignoble, shabby, shameful, sordid, vile, wretched

mean³ *n* average, balance, median, middle, mid-point, norm ~*adj* average, intermediate, medial, median, medium, middle, standard

meander *v* ramble, snake, stray, stroll, turn, wander, wind ~*n* bend, coil, curve, loop, turn, twist, zigzag

meaning drift, explanation, gist, implication, import, interpretation, message, purport, sense, significance, substance, upshot, value; aim, design, end, goal, idea, intention, object, plan, point, purpose, trend

meaningful important, material, purposeful, relevant, serious, signifi-

measure *n* size, quantity; unit, system of measuring; course of action; law ~*v* ascertain size, quantity of; be (so much) in size or quantity; indicate measurement of **measurable** *adj* **measured** *adj* slow and steady; carefully considered **measurement** *n* measuring; size

meat *n* animal flesh as food; food **meaty** *adj*

mechanic *n* one who works with machinery; *pl* scientific theory of motion **mechanical** *adj* of, by machine; acting without thought

mechanism *n* structure of machine; piece of machinery; process, technique **mechanization** *n* **mechanize** *v* equip with machinery; make automatic

medal *n* piece of metal with inscription etc. used as reward or memento **medallion** *n* (design like) large medal

meddle *v* interfere

media *n pl of* MEDIUM used esp. of the mass media, radio, television etc.

median *adj/n* middle (point or line)

mediate *v* intervene to reconcile **mediation** *n* **mediator** *n*

medic *n Inf* doctor or medical student

medicine *n* drug or remedy for treating disease; science of preventing, curing disease **medical** *adj* **medicate** *v* impregnate with medicinal substances **medication** *n* (treatment with) medicinal substance **medicinal** *adj* curative

medieval, mediaeval *adj* of Middle Ages

mediocre *adj* ordinary, middling; second-rate **mediocrity** *n* state of being mediocre; mediocre person

meditate *v* reflect deeply, esp. on spiritual matters; think about, plan **meditation** *n*

medium *adj* between two qualities, degrees etc. ~*n* (*pl* **mediums, media**) middle quality; means; agency of communicating news etc. to public;

cant, valid

measurable determinable, material, perceptible, quantifiable, significant

measure *n* allowance, amount, amplitude, capacity, degree, extent, proportion, quantity, quota, range, ration, reach, scope, share, size; gauge, metre, rule, scale; method, standard, system; act, action, course, deed, expedient, means, procedure, step; act, bill, enactment, law, resolution, statute ~*v* assess, calculate, calibrate, compute, determine, estimate, evaluate, gauge, judge, quantify, rate, size, sound, survey, value, weigh

measurement assessment, calculation, calibration, estimation, evaluation, mensuration, survey, valuation

mechanical automatic; cold, cursory, dead, habitual, impersonal, instinctive, lacklustre, lifeless, perfunctory, routine, unconscious, unfeeling, un-

thinking

mechanism apparatus, appliance, contrivance, device, instrument, structure, system, tool; agency, execution, means, medium, method, operation, performance, procedure, system, technique

meddle interfere, intervene, intrude, pry

mediate arbitrate, conciliate, intercede, intervene, reconcile, referee, resolve, settle, umpire

medicine cure, drug, physic, remedy

medieval antiquated, archaic, old-fashioned, primitive

mediocre average, indifferent, inferior, mean, middling, ordinary, passable, pedestrian, tolerable, undistinguished, uninspired

meditate cogitate, consider, contemplate, deliberate, muse, ponder, reflect, study, think

surroundings

medley *n* (*pl* **-leys**) mixture

meek *adj* submissive, humble

meet *v* **meeting, met** come face to face (with); satisfy; pay; converge; assemble; come into contact **meeting** *n*

megabyte *n* *Computers* 1 048 576 bytes

megalith *n* great stone

megalomania *n* desire for, delusions of grandeur, power etc. **megalomaniac** *adj/n*

megaphone *n* cone-shaped instrument to amplify voice

megaton *n* explosive power of 1 000 000 tons of TNT

melancholy *n* sadness, dejection ~*adj* gloomy, dejected

melanin *n* dark pigment found in hair, skin etc.

mêlée *n* confused fight

mellifluous *adj* (of sound) smooth, sweet

mellow *adj* ripe; softened by age, experience; not harsh; genial ~*v* make, become mellow

melodrama *n* play full of sensational situations **melodramatic** *adj*

melody *n* series of musical notes which make tune; sweet sound **melodic** *adj* **melodious** *adj*

melon *n* large, fleshy, juicy fruit

melt *v* **melting, melted, melted** *or* **molten** (cause to) become liquid by heat; dissolve; soften; disappear

member *n* individual making up body or society; limb; any part of complex whole **membership** *n*

membrane *n* thin flexible tissue in plant or animal body

memento *n* (*pl* **-tos**) reminder, souvenir

medium *adj* average, fair, intermediate, mean, mediocre, middle ~*n* average, centre, mean, middle; agency, avenue, channel, form, instrument, means, mode, organ, vehicle, way

medley jumble, miscellany, mishmash, mixture, pastiche, patchwork

meek deferential, docile, gentle, humble, mild, modest, patient, peaceful, soft, submissive, yielding

meet confront, contact, encounter, find; answer, comply, discharge, equal, fulfil, gratify, handle, match, perform, satisfy; connect, converge, cross, intersect, join, touch, unite; assemble, collect, come together, gather, muster, rally

meeting assignation, encounter, engagement, introduction, rendezvous; concourse, confluence, convergence, crossing, intersection, junction, union; assembly, audience, company, conference, congregation, congress, convention, gathering, rally, reunion, session

melancholy *n* dejection, depression, despondency, gloom, sadness, sorrow, unhappiness, woe ~*adj* gloomy, glum, joyless, low, lugubrious, miserable, mournful, pensive, sad, sombre, sorrowful, unhappy

mellow *adj* delicate, juicy, mature, perfect, rich, ripe, soft, sweet; dulcet, full, melodious, rich, rounded, smooth, sweet, tuneful; cheerful, cordial, elevated, expansive, genial, happy, jolly, jovial, relaxed ~*v* develop, improve, mature, perfect, ripen, season, soften, sweeten

melodious dulcet, musical, silvery, sweet-sounding, tuneful

melodramatic extravagant, histrionic, overdramatic, theatrical

melody air, descant, music, refrain, song, strain, theme, tune

melt diffuse, dissolve, flux, fuse, liquefy, soften, thaw

member fellow, representative; arm, component, constituent, element, leg, limb, organ, part, portion

memo *n* short for MEMORANDUM

memoir *n* autobiography, personal history

memory *n* faculty of recalling to mind; recollection; thing remembered; commemoration **memorable** *adj* worthy of remembrance **memorandum** *n* (*pl* **-dums**, **-da**) note to help the memory etc.; informal letter **memorial** *n* thing which serves to keep in memory ~*adj* serving as a memorial **memorize** *v* commit to memory

men *n pl of* MAN

menace *n* threat ~*v* threaten

ménage *n* household

menagerie *n* collection of wild animals

mend *v* repair; correct, put right; improve ~*n* repaired breakage

menial *adj* requiring little skill; servile ~*n* servant

meningitis *n* inflammation of the membranes of the brain

menopause *n* final cessation of menstruation

menstruation *n* monthly discharge of blood from womb **menstrual** *adj* **menstruate** *v*

mensuration *n* measuring

mental *adj* of, by the mind; *Inf* mad **mentality** *n* way of thinking

menthol *n* substance found in peppermint

mention *v* refer to briefly ~*n* acknowledgment; reference to

mentor *n* wise adviser

menu *n* list of dishes served

mercantile *adj* of trade

mercenary *adj* influenced by greed; working merely for reward ~*n* hired soldier

merchant *n* one engaged in trade; wholesale trader **merchandise** *n* trader's wares **merchant navy** ships engaged in a nation's commerce

———————— THESAURUS ————————

memoir account, biography, essay, journal, life, narrative

memorable celebrated, distinguished, famous, historic, illustrious, important, notable, remarkable, significant, striking, unforgettable

memorial *n* monument, plaque, record, souvenir ~*adj* commemorative, monumental

memorize learn, learn by heart, learn by rote, remember

memory recall, recollection, reminiscence; commemoration, honour, remembrance

menace *n* scare, threat, warning ~*v* alarm, browbeat, bully, frighten, impend, intimidate, loom, terrorize, threaten

mend *v* cure, darn, fix, heal, patch, rectify, refit, reform, remedy, renew, repair, restore; amend, better, correct, emend, improve, rectify, reform, revise ~*n* darn, patch, repair, stitch

menial *adj* boring, dull, humdrum, routine, unskilled

mental cerebral, intellectual

mentality attitude, disposition, outlook, personality, way of thinking

mention *v* adduce, broach, cite, communicate, declare, disclose, divulge, impart, intimate, name, recount, refer to, report, reveal, state, tell, touch upon ~*n* acknowledgment, citation, recognition, tribute; allusion, indication, reference, remark

mercenary *adj* avaricious, covetous, grasping, greedy, sordid, venal; bought, hired, paid, venal ~*n* soldier of fortune

merchandise goods, produce, stock, wares

merchant broker, dealer, purveyor, retailer, salesman, seller, shopkeeper, supplier, trader, tradesman, trafficker, vendor, wholesaler

mercury *n* silvery metal, liquid at ordinary temperature **mercurial** *adj* lively, changeable

mercy *n* refraining from infliction of suffering by one who has right, power to inflict it; fortunate occurrence **merciful** *adj*

mere *adj* only; nothing but **merely** *adv*

merge *v* (cause to) lose identity or be absorbed **merger** *n* combination esp. of business firms

meridian *n* circle of the earth passing through poles; highest point

meringue *n* baked mixture of white of eggs and sugar

merit *n* excellence, worth; quality of deserving reward ~*v* deserve

mermaid *n* imaginary sea creature half woman, half fish

merry *adj* joyous, cheerful **merriment**

n **merry-go-round** *n* roundabout

mesh *n* (one of the open spaces of, or wires etc. forming) network, net ~*v* (cause to) entangle, engage

mesmerize *v* hypnotize

mess *n* untidy confusion; trouble; (place where) group regularly eat together ~*v* potter (about); muddle **messy** *adj*

message *n* communication sent; meaning, moral **messenger** *n*

Messiah *n* promised saviour; Christ

met *past tense past participle of* MEET

metabolism *n* chemical process of living body **metabolic** *adj*

metal *n* mineral substance, malleable and capable of conducting heat and electricity **metallic** *adj* **metallurgist** *n* **metallurgy** *n* scientific study of metals

metamorphosis *n* (*pl* -phoses)

————————————— THESAURUS —————————————

merciful compassionate, forbearing, forgiving, generous, gracious, humane, kind, lenient, liberal, soft, sparing, sympathetic

mercy charity, clemency, compassion, favour, forbearance, forgiveness, grace, kindness, pity, quarter; boon, godsend, piece of luck, relief

mere *adj* absolute, bare, common, entire, plain, pure, sheer, simple, stark, unmixed, utter

merge amalgamate, blend, combine, fuse, join, meet, mingle, mix, unite

merger amalgamation, coalition, fusion, incorporation, union

merit *n* asset, excellence, good, goodness, integrity, quality, talent, value, virtue, worth, worthiness; claim, credit, desert, due, right ~*v* deserve, earn, incur, warrant

merriment amusement, conviviality, festivity, frolic, fun, gaiety, laughter, mirth, revelry, sport

merry blithe, carefree, cheerful, convivial, festive, gay, glad, gleeful, hap-

py, jolly, joyful, joyous, light-hearted, rollicking, vivacious

mesh *n* net, network, web ~*v* catch, ensnare, entangle, net, snare, tangle, trap; combine, connect, dovetail, engage, harmonize, knit

mess *n* botch, chaos, clutter, cock-up *Brit sl*, confusion, disarray, disorder, hotchpotch, jumble, litter, shambles, state, untidiness; difficulty, hot water *Inf*, muddle, perplexity, plight, predicament, spot *Inf*, tight spot, trouble *v* (*often with* up) botch, bungle, clutter, dirty, disarrange, dishevel, foul, litter, muddle, pollute, scramble

message bulletin, communication, dispatch, letter, missive, note, notice, tidings, word; idea, import, moral, point, theme

messenger agent, bearer, carrier, courier, emissary, envoy, go-between, herald, runner

messy chaotic, cluttered, confused, dirty, dishevelled, disordered, disorganized, grubby, littered, muddled

change of shape, character etc.

metaphor *n* figure of speech in which term is transferred to something it does not literally apply to **metaphorical** *adj*

metaphysical *adj* philosophical; abstract, abstruse

mete *v* **mete out** distribute; allot

meteor *n* small, fast-moving celestial body, visible as streak of incandescence if it enters earth's atmosphere **meteoric** *adj* of meteor; brilliant but short-lived **meteorite** *n* fallen meteor

meteorology *n* study of climate, weather **meteorological** *adj* **meteorologist** *n*

meter *n* instrument for recording, measuring

methane *n* flammable gas, compound of carbon and hydrogen

method *n* way, manner; technique; orderliness **methodical** *adj* orderly

meths *n Inf* methylated spirits

methylated spirits alcoholic mixture used as fuel etc.

meticulous *adj* particular about details

metre *n* unit of length in decimal system; SI unit of length; rhythm of poem **metric** *adj* of system of weights and measures in which metre is a unit **metrical** *adj* of measurement; of poetic metre

metronome *n* instrument which marks musical time by means of ticking pendulum

metropolis *n* (*pl* **-lises**) chief city of a region **metropolitan** *adj*

mettle *n* courage, spirit

mew *n/v* (utter) cry of cat

mews *pl n* (*with sing or pl v*) yard, street orig. of stables, now oft. converted to houses

mezzanine *n* intermediate storey, balcony between two main storeys

mezzo-soprano *n* (*pl* **-nos**) voice, singer between soprano and contralto

mg milligram

miasma *n* (*pl* **-mata, -mas**) unwholesome atmosphere

mica *n* mineral found as glittering scales, plates

microbe *n* minute organism; disease germ

microchip *n* small wafer of silicon containing electronic circuits

microcosm *n* miniature representation of larger system

microfiche *n* microfilm in sheet form

microfilm *n* miniaturized recording of manuscript, book on roll of film

microphone *n* instrument for amplifying, transmitting sounds

microprocessor *n* integrated circuit acting as central processing unit in small computer

microscope *n* instrument by which very small body is magnified **microscopic** *adj* very small

microwave *n* electromagnetic wave with wavelength of a few centimetres, used in radar, cooking etc.; oven

———— T H E S A U R U S ————

metaphor allegory, analogy, image, symbol

mete *v* administer, allot, assign, deal, dispense, distribute, divide, dole, measure, portion, ration, share

method approach, course, fashion, form, manner, mode, plan, practice, procedure, programme, routine, rule, scheme, style, system, technique, way; design, form, order, pattern,

planning, structure

methodical businesslike, deliberate, disciplined, efficient, meticulous, neat, organized, planned, precise, regular, tidy

meticulous detailed, exact, fastidious, painstaking, precise, scrupulous, strict, thorough

microscopic imperceptible, infinitesimal, teensy-weensy, teeny-weeny,

using microwaves

mid *adj* intermediate **midday** *n* noon **midnight** *n* twelve o'clock at night **midway** *adj/adv* halfway

middle *adj* equidistant from two extremes ~*n* middle point or part **midding** *adj* mediocre; moderate **middle age** period of life between youth and old age **middle class** social class of businessmen, professional people etc. **middleman** *n* trader between producer and consumer **middle-of-the-road** *adj* moderate

midge *n* gnat or similar insect

midget *n* very small person or thing

midriff *n* middle part of body

midst *prep* in the middle of ~*n* middle

midwife *n* trained person who assists at childbirth **midwifery** *n*

mien *n* person's manner or appearance

might[1] *past tense of* MAY

might[2] *n* power, strength **mightily** *adv* **mighty** *adj*

migraine *n* severe headache

migrate *v* move from one place to another **migrant** *n/adj* **migration** *n*

mike *n Inf* microphone

mild *adj* not strongly flavoured; gentle; temperate **mildly** *adv*

mildew *n* destructive fungus on plants or things exposed to damp

mile *n* measure of length, 1760 yards, 1.609 km **mileage** *n* travelling expenses per mile; miles travelled (per gallon of petrol) **mileometer** *n* device that records miles travelled by vehicle **milestone** *n* significant event

milieu *n* (*pl* **-lieux**) environment

militant *adj* aggressive, vigorous in support of cause; prepared to fight **militancy** *n*

military *adj* of, for, soldiers, armies or war ~*n* armed forces **militarism** *n* enthusiasm for military force and methods **militia** *n* military force of citizens for home service

militate *v* (*esp. with* **against**) have strong influence, effect on

milk *n* white fluid with which mammals feed their young; fluid in some plants ~*v* draw milk from **milky** *adj*

mill *n* factory; machine for grinding, pulverizing corn, paper etc. ~*v* put through mill; cut fine grooves across edges of (e.g. coins); move in con-

———————— THESAURUS ————————

tiny, wee *Inf*

midday noon, noonday, twelve o'clock

middle *adj* central, halfway, inner, inside, mean, medial, median, medium, mid ~*n* centre, focus, heart, inside, mean, midpoint, midst, thick

midget dwarf, gnome, pygmy *or* pigmy, teeny-weeny

midst bosom, centre, core, depths, heart, hub, interior, middle, thick

might ability, capability, efficacy, energy, force, potency, power, prowess, strength, sway, valour, vigour

mighty forceful, hardy, potent, powerful, robust, stalwart, stout, strong, sturdy, vigorous

migrant drifter, gypsy, itinerant, no-

mad, rover, tinker, transient, vagrant, wanderer

migrate journey, move, roam, rove, shift, travel, trek, wander

migration journey, movement, roving, shift, travel, trek, voyage

mild amiable, balmy, bland, calm, docile, easy, forbearing, forgiving, gentle, indulgent, kind, meek, mellow, merciful, moderate, peaceable, placid, pleasant, serene, smooth, soft, temperate, tender, tranquil, warm

militant active, aggressive, assertive, combative; belligerent, fighting

military *adj* armed, martial, soldierly, warlike ~*n* armed forces, army, forces, services

milk *v* drain, express, extract, press,

fused manner **miller** *n* **millstone** *n* flat circular stone for grinding

millennium *n* (*pl* -iums, -ia) period of a thousand years; period of peace, happiness

millet *n* cereal grass

milli- *comb. form* thousandth part of, as in **milligram, millilitre, millimetre**

milliner *n* maker of women's hats

million *n* 1000 thousands **millionaire** *n* owner of a million pounds, dollars etc. **millionth** *adj/n*

millipede, millepede *n* small animal with many pairs of legs

mime *n* acting without words ~*v* perform mime

mimic *v* mimicking, mimicked imitate, esp. for satirical effect ~*n* one who does this **mimicry** *n*

mimosa *n* plant with fluffy, yellow flowers

minaret *n* tall slender tower of mosque

mince *v* cut, chop small; soften (words etc.) ~*n* minced meat **mincer** *n* **mincing** *adj* affected in manner **mincemeat** *n* mixture of currants, spices, suet etc. **mince pie** pie containing mincemeat

mind *n* intellectual faculties; memory; intention; taste; sanity ~*v* take offence at; care for; attend to; heed **minder** *n* Sl bodyguard **mindful** *adj* heedful **mindless** *adj* stupid; requiring no thought; careless

mine[1] *pron* belonging to me

mine[2] *n* deep hole for digging out coal, metals etc.; hidden deposit of explosive to blow up ship etc.; profitable source ~*v* dig from mine; place explosive mines in, on **miner** *n* **minefield** *n* area of land or sea containing mines **minesweeper** *n* ship for clearing mines

mineral *n/adj* (of) naturally occurring inorganic substance **mineralogy** *n* science of minerals **mineral water** water containing dissolved mineral salts

minestrone *n* soup containing vegetables and pasta

mingle *v* mix, blend; mix socially

mini *n* something small or miniature; short skirt ~*adj* small

miniature *n* small painted portrait; anything on small scale ~*adj* on small scale **miniaturize** *v* make to very small scale

siphon, tap

mill *n* factory, foundry, plant, shop, works; crusher, grinder

mime *n* dumb show, gesture ~*v* gesture, represent, simulate

mimic *v* ape, caricature, imitate, impersonate, parody ~*n* caricaturist, imitator, impersonator, parodist, parrot

mind *n* intellect, mentality, reason, sense, spirit, understanding, wits; brain, head, imagination, psyche; memory, recollection, remembrance; bent, desire, disposition, fancy, inclination, intention, leaning, notion, purpose, tendency, urge, will, wish ~*v* care, disapprove, dislike, object,

resent; guard, look after, take care of, tend, watch

mindful alert, attentive, aware, careful, chary, cognizant, conscious, heedful, wary, watchful

mine *n* colliery, deposit, lode, pit, shaft, vein; fund, hoard, reserve, source, stock, store, supply ~*v* delve, excavate, extract, hew, quarry, unearth

mingle alloy, blend, combine, compound, intermix, join, marry, merge, mix, unite; associate, circulate, fraternize, hobnob, socialize

miniature *adj* baby, diminutive, dwarf, little, midget, pocket, pygmy *or* pigmy, reduced, small, toy

minibus *n* small bus

minim *n* *Mus* note half the length of semibreve

minimum *n* (*pl* -mums, -ma) lowest size or quantity ~*adj* least possible **minimal** *adj* **minimize** *v* reduce to minimum

minion *n* servile dependant

minister *n* person in charge of department of State; diplomatic representative; clergyman ~*v* take care of **ministerial** *adj* **ministration** *n* rendering help **ministry** *n* office of clergyman; government department

mink *n* variety of weasel; its fur

minnow *n* small freshwater fish

minor *adj* lesser; under age ~*n* person below age of legal majority; scale in music **minority** *n* lesser number, group; state of being a minor

minster *n* cathedral, large church

minstrel *n* medieval singer, musician, poet

mint¹ *n* place where money is coined ~*adj* brand-new ~*v* coin, invent

mint² *n* aromatic plant

minuet *n* stately dance

minus *prep/adj* less; lacking; negative ~*n* the sign of subtraction (-)

minuscule *adj* very small

minute¹ *adj* very small; precise

minute² *n* 60th part of hour or degree; *pl* record of proceedings of meeting etc.

minx *n* bold, flirtatious woman

miracle *n* supernatural event; marvel **miraculous** *adj*

mirage *n* deceptive image in atmosphere

mire *n* swampy ground, mud

mirror *n* glass or polished surface reflecting images ~*v* reflect in or as if in mirror

mirth *n* merriment, gaiety

mis- *comb. form* wrong, bad

misadventure *n* unlucky chance

misanthrope, misanthropist *n* hater of mankind

misapprehension *n* misunderstanding

misappropriate *v* put to dishonest use; embezzle

——— THESAURUS ———

minimal least, littlest, nominal, slightest, smallest, token

minimum *n* bottom, depth, least, lowest, nadir, slightest ~*adj* least, lowest, slightest, smallest

minister *n* ambassador, delegate, diplomat, envoy, executive, officeholder, official; churchman, clergyman, cleric, ecclesiastic, parson, pastor, preacher, priest, vicar ~*v* attend, tend

ministry administration, cabinet, council, government, holy orders

minor inconsiderable, inferior, junior, lesser, light, paltry, petty, secondary, slight, small, subordinate, trivial, younger

mint *adj* brand-new, excellent, first-class, fresh, perfect ~*v* cast, coin, make, produce, stamp, strike

minute¹ *adj* fine, little, slender, small, teensy-weensy, teeny-weeny, tiny

minute² *n* flash, instant, moment, second

minx coquette, flirt, hoyden, hussy, jade, tomboy, wanton

miracle marvel, prodigy, wonder

miraculous amazing, astonishing, astounding, extraordinary, incredible, magical, marvellous, phenomenal, supernatural, wonderful

mirage illusion, phantasm

mire bog, marsh, morass, quagmire, swamp

mirror *n* glass, reflector ~*v* copy, depict, echo, emulate, follow, reflect, represent, show

mirth amusement, cheerfulness, festivity, frolic, fun, gaiety, glee, laughter, levity, merriment, pleasure, re-

miscarry *v* expel fetus prematurely; fail **miscarriage** *n*

miscellaneous *adj* mixed **miscellany** *n* medley

mischief *n* annoying behaviour; inclination to tease; harm, annoyance **mischievous** *adj*

misconception *n* wrong idea

misconduct *n* unethical behaviour

miscreant *n* evildoer

misdemeanour *n* minor offence

miser *n* hoarder of money

miserable *adj* very unhappy; causing misery; worthless; squalid **misery** *n*

misfire *v* fail to fire, start etc.

misfit *n* person not suited to environment

misfortune *n* (piece of) bad luck

misgiving *n* (*oft. pl*) feeling of fear, doubt etc.

misguided *adj* foolish

mishap *n* minor accident

misjudge *v* judge wrongly

mislay *v* put in place which cannot later be remembered

mislead *v* **misleading, misled** give false information to

mismanage *v* organize badly

——————— THESAURUS ———————

joicing, revelry, sport

misappropriate embezzle, misapply, misuse, pocket, steal, swindle

miscellaneous assorted, diverse, indiscriminate, jumbled, manifold, many, mingled, mixed, motley, promiscuous, sundry, varied, various

mischief devilment, impishness, misbehaviour, naughtiness, roguery, trouble, waywardness; damage, detriment, disruption, evil, harm, hurt, injury, trouble

mischievous arch, bad, impish, naughty, playful, puckish, teasing; bad, damaging, destructive, evil, harmful, hurtful, injurious, malignant, pernicious, sinful, spiteful, wicked

misconception delusion, error, misunderstanding

misconduct delinquency, immorality, impropriety, malpractice, misbehaviour, transgression, wrongdoing

misdemeanour fault, misconduct, offence, peccadillo, transgression

miser niggard, skinflint

miserable afflicted, crestfallen, dejected, depressed, despondent, dismal, distressed, downcast, forlorn, gloomy, melancholy, mournful, sorrowful, unhappy, woebegone, wretched; abject, bad, contemptible,

despicable, disgraceful, low, mean, pathetic, piteous, pitiable, shabby, shameful, sordid, sorry, squalid, vile, worthless, wretched

misery agony, anguish, depression, desolation, despair, discomfort, distress, gloom, grief, hardship, melancholy, sadness, sorrow, suffering, torment, torture, unhappiness, woe; affliction, burden, calamity, curse, disaster, hardship, load, misfortune, ordeal, sorrow, trial, tribulation, trouble, woe

misfire fail, fall through, miscarry

misfit eccentric, nonconformist

misfortune bad luck, infelicity; accident, adversity, affliction, blow, calamity, disaster, hardship, harm, loss, misadventure, misery, reverse, setback, tragedy, trouble

misgiving anxiety, distrust, doubt, hesitation, reservation, suspicion, uncertainty, unease, worry

misguided deluded, foolish, ill-advised, imprudent, misled, misplaced, mistaken, unreasonable, unwise

mishap accident, adversity, bad luck, hard luck, misadventure, misfortune

misjudge miscalculate, overestimate, overrate, underestimate, underrate

mislay lose, lose track of, misplace,

misnomer n wrong name or term

misogyny n hatred of women **misogynist** n

misprint n printing error

Miss n title of unmarried woman; (*without cap.*) girl

miss v fail to hit, reach, catch etc.; not be in time for; notice or regret absence of; avoid; omit **~n** fact, instance of missing **missing** adj lost, absent

missal n book containing prayers, rites etc.

missile n that which may be thrown, shot etc. to damage or destroy

mission n specific duty; delegation; those sent **missionary** n one sent to a place, society to spread religion

missive n letter

mist n water vapour in fine drops

misty adj

mistake n error **~v** fail to understand; take (person or thing) for another **mistaken** adj

mister n (*abbrev* **Mr.**) title of courtesy to man

mistletoe n evergreen parasitic plant

mistress n illicit lover of married man; woman with mastery or control; title formerly given to married woman

mistrust v not trust **~n** lack of trust

misunderstand v fail to understand properly **misunderstanding** n

misuse n incorrect use **~v** use wrongly; treat badly

mite n very small insect; anything very small

mitigate v make less severe **mitigation** n

——————— THESAURUS ———————

miss

mislead beguile, bluff, deceive, delude, fool, hoodwink, misdirect, misguide, misinform

mismanage botch, bungle, maladminister, misdirect, misgovern, mishandle

miss[1] v avoid, blunder, err, escape, evade, fail, forego, lack, lose, miscarry, mistake, omit, overlook, skip, slip, trip; need, pine for, want, wish **~n** blunder, error, failure, fault, loss, mistake, omission, oversight, want

miss[2] damsel, girl, maid, spinster

missile projectile, rocket, weapon

missing absent, astray, gone, lacking, lost, mislaid, misplaced

mission aim, assignment, business, calling, charge, duty, errand, goal, job, office, operation, purpose, pursuit, quest, task, trust, undertaking, vocation, work; delegation, deputation, task force

missionary converter, evangelist, preacher

mist cloud, dew, drizzle, film, fog,

haze, smog, spray, steam, vapour

mistake n blunder, error, fault, gaffe, oversight, slip, solecism **~v** misconceive, misconstrue, misjudge, misread, misunderstand

mistaken fallacious, false, faulty, inaccurate, incorrect, misguided, misinformed, unfounded, wrong

mistress concubine, girlfriend, kept woman, lover, paramour

mistrust v beware, doubt, fear, suspect **~n** doubt, fear, misgiving, scepticism, suspicion, uncertainty

misty bleary, cloudy, dark, dim, foggy, hazy, indistinct, obscure, vague

misunderstand misconceive, misconstrue, mishear, misinterpret, misjudge, mistake

misunderstanding error, misconstruction, misjudgment, misreading, mistake, mix-up

misuse n abuse, corruption, malapropism, perversion, profanation, solecism, waste **~v** abuse, corrupt, desecrate, dissipate, misapply, pervert, profane, prostitute, squander,

mitre *n* bishop's headdress; right-angled joint

mitt *n* covering for hand

mitten *n* glove with two compartments for thumb and fingers

mix *v* put together, combine, blend; be mixed; associate **mixed** *adj* of different elements, races etc. **mixer** *n* **mixture** *n* **mix-up** *n* confused situation

ml millilitre

mm millimetre

mnemonic *n* something to help the memory

moan *v/n* (utter) low murmur, usually of pain

moat *n* deep wide ditch, esp. round castle

mob *n* disorderly crowd ~*v* **mobbing, mobbed** attack in mob, hustle

mobile *adj* capable of movement;

easily changed ~*n* hanging structure designed to move in air currents **mobility** *n*

mobilize *v* prepare, esp. for military service **mobilization** *n*

moccasin *n* Amer. Indian soft shoe, usu. of deerskin

mocha *n* strong dark coffee; flavouring of coffee and chocolate

mock *v* ridicule; mimic ~*adj* sham **mockery** *n* derision; travesty

mode *n* manner; prevailing fashion **modish** *adj* fashionable

model *n* miniature representation; pattern; one worthy of imitation; person employed to pose, or display clothing ~*adj* made as (miniature) copy; exemplary ~*v* **-elling, -elled** make model of; mould; display (clothing)

modem *n* device for connecting two

waste

mitigate abate, allay, appease, assuage, blunt, calm, check, dull, ease, extenuate, lessen, lighten, modify, mollify, pacify, palliate, placate, soften, soothe, subdue, temper

mix alloy, amalgamate, blend, coalesce, combine, compound, cross, fuse, incorporate, intermingle, join, meld, merge, mingle, unite; associate, consort, fraternize, join, mingle, socialize

mixed alloyed, amalgamated, blended, combined, composite, compound, fused, incorporated, joint, mingled, united; assorted, diverse, motley, varied

mixture alloy, amalgam, association, assortment, blend, brew, combine, compound, concoction, conglomeration, cross, fusion, medley, meld, miscellany, mix, union, variety

mix-up confusion, disorder, jumble, mess, mistake, muddle

moan *v* bewail, deplore, grieve,

groan, lament, mourn, sigh, sob, whine ~*n* groan, lament, sigh, sob, sough, wail, whine

mob *n* body, collection, crowd, drove, flock, gang, gathering, herd, horde, host, mass, pack, press, swarm, throng

mobile itinerant, migrant, movable, peripatetic, portable, travelling, wandering

mobilize call up, marshal, muster, organize, prepare, rally, ready

mock *v* chaff, deride, flout, insult, jeer, ridicule, scoff, scorn, sneer, taunt, tease ~*adj* artificial, bogus, counterfeit, dummy, fake, false, feigned, forged, fraudulent, imitation, pretended, sham, spurious

mockery contempt, contumely, derision, disdain, jeering, ridicule, scorn; burlesque, caricature, deception, farce, imitation, lampoon, mimicry, parody, pretence, sham, travesty

model *n* copy, facsimile, image, imitation, mock-up, replica, representa-

computers by telephone line

moderate *adj* not going to extremes
~*n* person of moderate views ~*v*
make, become less excessive; preside
over **moderation** *n* **moderator** *n* arbitrator

modern *adj* of present or recent
times; in, of current fashion **modernity** *n* **modernize** *v* bring up to date

modest *adj* not overrating one's qualities or achievements; moderate, decent **modesty** *n*

modicum *n* small quantity

modify *v* **-fying, -fied** change slightly
modification *n*

modulate *v* regulate; vary in tone
modulation *n*

module *n* (detachable) component
with specific function

mogul *n* powerful person

mohair *n* cloth of goat's hair

moist *adj* slightly wet **moisten** *v* **mois-**

ture *n* liquid, esp. diffused or in
drops

molar *n/adj* (tooth) for grinding

molasses *n* syrup, by-product of sugar refining

mole[1] *n* small dark spot on skin

mole[2] *n* small burrowing animal

molecule *n* simplest freely existing
chemical unit **molecular** *adj*

molest *v* pester, interfere with so as to
annoy or injure

moll *n Sl* gangster's female accomplice

mollify *v* **-fying, -fied** calm down, placate **mollification** *n*

mollusc *n* soft-bodied, usu. hardshelled animal, e.g. snail

mollycoddle *v* pamper

molten *see* MELT

moment *n* short space of, (present)
point in, time **momentarily** *adv* **momentary** *adj* lasting only a moment

———————— T H E S A U R U S ————————

tion; archetype, design, epitome, example, exemplar, gauge, ideal,
mould, norm, original, paradigm,
paragon, pattern, prototype, standard, type; poser, sitter, subject ~*adj*
copy, dummy, facsimile, imitation,
miniature; archetypal, exemplary,
ideal, illustrative, paradigmatic, perfect, standard, typical ~*v* base, carve,
cast, design, fashion, form, mould,
pattern, plan, sculpt, shape, stamp;
display, show off, wear

moderate *adj* calm, cool, deliberate,
equable, gentle, limited, mild, modest, peaceable, reasonable, restrained, sober, steady, temperate ~*v*
abate, allay, appease, calm, control,
curb, decrease, diminish, mitigate,
pacify, quiet, restrain, soften, subdue, tame, temper

moderation calmness, composure,
coolness, equanimity, fairness, justice, mildness, reasonableness, restraint, sedateness, temperance

modern contemporary, current,
fresh, late, latest, new, novel, present, recent

modernize rejuvenate, remake, remodel, renew, renovate, revamp, update

modest bashful, coy, demure, discreet, humble, meek, quiet, reserved,
reticent, retiring, shy, simple; fair,
limited, moderate, ordinary, small

modesty demureness, diffidence, humility, meekness, propriety, reserve,
reticence, shyness, timidity

modify adapt, adjust, alter, change,
convert, recast, reform, reorganize,
reshape, revise, transform, vary

moist clammy, damp, dank, dewy,
drizzly, humid, rainy, wet, wettish

moisten damp, soak, water, wet

moisture damp, dew, humidity, liquid, sweat, water

molest abuse, afflict, annoy, badger,
bother, disturb, harass, harry, hector,
irritate, persecute, pester, torment,

momentous *adj* of great importance

momentum *n* (*pl* -**ta**, -**tums**) force of a moving body; impetus gained from motion

monarch *n* sovereign ruler **monarchist** *n* supporter of monarchy **monarchy** *n* state ruled by sovereign; government by sovereign

monastery *n* house occupied by religious order **monastic** *adj*

Monday *n* second day of the week

money *n* (*pl* -**eys**, -**ies**) banknotes, coins etc., used as medium of exchange **monetary** *adj* **moneyed, monied** *adj* rich

mongoose *n* (*pl* -**gooses**) small animal of Asia and Africa

mongrel *n/adj* (animal) of mixed breed; hybrid

monitor *n* person or device which checks, controls, warns, records; pupil assisting teacher with odd jobs; type of large lizard ~*v* watch, check on

monk *n* one of a religious community

of men living apart under vows

monkey *n* long-tailed primate; mischievous child ~*v* meddle with

mono- *comb. form* single, as in **monosyllabic**

monochrome *adj* of one colour

monocle *n* single eyeglass

monogamy *n* custom of being married to one person at a time

monogram *n* design of letters interwoven

monograph *n* short book on single subject

monolith *n* large upright block of stone **monolithic** *adj*

monologue *n* long speech by one person

monopoly *n* exclusive possession of trade, privilege etc. **monopolize** *v* claim, take exclusive possession of

monotone *n* speech on one note **monotonous** *adj* lacking variety, dull **monotony** *n*

monsoon *n* seasonal wind of SE Asia; very heavy rainfall season

───────── T H E S A U R U S ─────────

upset, vex, worry

moment flash, instant, minute, second, twinkling; hour, instant, juncture, point, stage, time

momentous critical, crucial, decisive, fateful, grave, historic, important, serious, significant, vital

momentum drive, energy, force, impetus, power, push, thrust

monarch king, potentate, prince, princess, queen, ruler, sovereign

monastery abbey, cloister, convent, friary, house, nunnery, priory

monastic ascetic, austere, cloistered, recluse, secluded, withdrawn

monetary capital, cash, financial, fiscal

money banknotes, brass *N Eng dial,* capital, cash, coin, currency, dosh *Brit & Aust sl,* funds, hard cash, legal tender

mongrel *n* cross, crossbreed, hybrid ~*adj* crossbred, half-breed, hybrid

monitor *n* guide, overseer, supervisor, watchdog ~*v* check, follow, observe, record, scan, supervise, survey, watch

monk brother, monastic, religious

monkey *n* primate, simian; devil, imp, rascal, rogue, scamp ~*v* fool, interfere, meddle, mess, play, tamper, tinker, trifle

monologue harangue, lecture, sermon, speech

monopolize control, corner, dominate, engross, take up

monotonous boring, colourless, droning, dull, flat, ho-hum *Inf,* humdrum, mind-numbing, plodding, repetitious, repetitive, soporific, tedious, tiresome, toneless, unchanging, wearisome

monster *n* fantastic imaginary beast; huge or misshapen person, animal or thing ~*adj* huge **monstrosity** *n* monstrous being; deformity **monstrous** *adj* horrible; shocking; enormous

month *n* one of twelve periods into which the year is divided **monthly** *adj/adv* once a month

monument *n* anything that commemorates, esp. a building or statue **monumental** *adj*

mooch *v Sl* loaf, slouch

mood¹ *n* state of mind and feelings; sulk **moody** *adj* gloomy; changeable in mood

mood² *n Grammar* form indicating function of verb

moon *n* satellite which revolves round earth; any secondary planet ~*v* go about dreamily **moonlight** *n*

moor¹ *n* tract of open uncultivated

land **moorhen** *n* small black water bird

moor² *v* secure (ship) with chains or ropes **moorings** *pl n* ropes etc. for mooring

moose *n* N Amer. deer

moot *adj* debatable

mop *n* yarn, cloth etc. on end of stick, used for cleaning; tangle (of hair etc.) ~*v* **mopping, mopped** clean, wipe as with mop

mope *v* be gloomy, apathetic

moped *n* light motorized bicycle

moral *adj* pert. to right and wrong conduct; of good conduct ~*n* practical lesson, e.g. of fable; *pl* habits with respect to right and wrong **morality** *n* good moral conduct; moral goodness or badness **moralize** *v* write, think about moral aspect of things

morale *n* degree of confidence, hope

———————— THESAURUS ————————

monster *n* barbarian, beast, brute, demon, devil, fiend, ghoul, ogre, savage, villain ~*adj* colossal, enormous, giant, huge, immense, massive, tremendous

monstrous abnormal, dreadful, fiendish, freakish, frightful, grotesque, gruesome, hellish, hideous, horrible, obscene, terrible, unnatural; atrocious, cruel, diabolical, disgraceful, evil, fiendish, foul, horrifying, infamous, inhuman, loathsome, odious, satanic, scandalous, shocking, vicious, villainous; colossal, enormous, giant, gigantic, great, huge, immense, massive, prodigious, stupendous, tremendous, vast

monument cairn, gravestone, mausoleum, memorial, obelisk, pillar, shrine, statue, tombstone

monumental awesome, classic, enduring, enormous, historic, immortal, important, lasting, majestic, memorable, outstanding, prodigious, unforgettable

mood disposition, humour, spirit, temper, tenor, vein; blues, depression, doldrums, melancholy, sulk

moody angry, broody, crabbed, crestfallen, cross, crusty, curt, dismal, doleful, dour, downcast, gloomy, glum, ill-tempered, irritable, lugubrious, melancholy, miserable, morose, pensive, petulant, sulky, sullen, temperamental, touchy

moon *n* satellite ~*v* daydream, idle, languish

moor¹ heath, moorland

moor² anchor, berth, dock, fasten, fix, lash, secure

moral *adj* ethical; blameless, chaste, decent, good, honest, innocent, just, noble, principled, proper, pure, right, righteous, upright, virtuous ~*n* lesson, meaning, message, point, significance

morale confidence, heart, mettle, spirit, temper

morality chastity, decency, goodness, honesty, integrity, justice, principle,

morass *n* marsh; mess

moratorium *n* (*pl* **-ria**) authorized postponement of payments etc.

morbid *adj* unduly interested in death; gruesome; diseased

mordant *adj* biting; corrosive

more *adj/pron* greater or additional (amount or number); *comparative of* MANY *and* MUCH ~*adv* to a greater extent; in addition **moreover** *adv* besides

mores *pl n* customs and conventions of society

morgue *n* mortuary

moribund *adj* dying; without force or vitality

morning *n* early part of day until noon **morn** *n Poet* morning

moron *n* mentally deficient person

morose *adj* sullen, moody

morphine, morphia *n* extract of opium used to relieve pain

morrow *n Poet* next day

Morse *n* telegraphic signalling in which letters are represented by dots and dashes

morsel *n* small piece

mortal *adj* subject to death; causing death ~*n* mortal creature **mortality** *n* state of being mortal; death rate; great loss of life

mortar *n* mixture of lime, sand and water for holding bricks together; small cannon; vessel in which substances are pounded **mortarboard** *n* square academic cap

mortgage *n* conveyance of property as security for debt ~*v* pledge as security

mortify *v* **-fying, -fied** humiliate; subdue by self-denial; (of flesh) be affected with gangrene **mortification** *n*

mortise *n* hole in piece of wood etc. to receive the tongue (tenon) and end of another piece

mortuary *n* building where corpses are kept before burial

mosaic *n* picture or pattern of small bits of coloured stone, glass etc.

mosque *n* Muslim temple

mosquito *n* **-toes, -tos** flying, biting insect

moss *n* small plant growing in masses on moist surfaces **mossy** *adj*

———— THESAURUS ————

righteousness, virtue

morbid brooding, funereal, gloomy, grim, pessimistic, sick, sombre, unhealthy, unwholesome; dreadful, ghastly, grisly, gruesome, hideous, horrid, macabre

more *adj* added, extra, fresh, further, new, other, spare, supplementary ~*adv* better, further, longer

moreover additionally, also, besides, further

morning dawn, daybreak, forenoon, sunrise

moron ass, berk *Brit sl,* blockhead, cretin, dolt, dunce, fool, halfwit, idiot, imbecile, nitwit *Inf,* numbskull, simpleton, thickhead, twit *Inf,* wally *Sl*

morose crabbed, cross, depressed, dour, down, gloomy, glum, gruff, ill-tempered, low, melancholy, moody, mournful, perverse, pessimistic, sulky, sullen, surly, taciturn

morsel bit, bite, crumb, fraction, fragment, grain, mouthful, piece, scrap, segment, slice, *soupçon,* taste

mortal *adj* earthly, ephemeral, human, temporal, transient, worldly; deadly, destructive, fatal, killing, lethal, murderous ~*n* being, body, earthling, human, individual, man, person, woman

mortality humanity, transience; bloodshed, carnage, death, destruction, fatality, killing

mortify abase, abash, annoy, chasten, confound, crush, disappoint, displease, embarrass, humble, shame,

most *adj/n* (of) greatest number, amount or degree; *superlative of* MUCH *and* MANY ~*adv* in the greatest degree **mostly** *adv* generally

MOT Ministry of Transport

motel *n* roadside hotel for motorists

moth *n* usu. nocturnal insect like butterfly **mothball** *n* small ball of chemical to repel moths from stored clothing etc. ~*v* store, postpone **moth-eaten** *adj* damaged by grub of moth; scruffy

mother *n* female parent; head of religious community of women ~*adj* inborn ~*v* act as mother to **motherhood** *n* **motherly** *adj* **mother-in-law** *n* mother of one's wife or husband **mother of pearl** iridescent lining of certain shells

motif *n* dominating theme

motion *n* process or action or way of moving; proposal in meeting ~*v* direct by sign

motive *n* that which makes person act

in particular way **motivate** *v* incite **motivation** *n*

motley *adj* varied; multicoloured

motocross *n* motorcycle race over rough course

motor *n* that which imparts movement; machine to supply power to move ~*v* travel by car **motorist** *n* **motorize** *v* equip with a motor or motor transport **motorbike**, **motorcycle** *n* **motorcar** *n* **motorway** *n* main road for fast-moving traffic

mottled *adj* marked with blotches

motto *n* -toes, -tos saying adopted as rule of conduct

mould[1] *n* hollow object in which metal etc. is cast; character; shape ~*v* shape **moulding** *n* ornamental edging

mould[2] *n* fungoid growth caused by dampness **mouldy** *adj*

mould[3] *n* loose or surface earth **moulder** *v* decay

moult *v* cast or shed fur, feathers etc. ~*n* moulting

───────── THESAURUS ─────────

vex

mostly chiefly, customarily, generally, largely, mainly, particularly, predominantly, principally, usually

mother *n* dam, mater ~*adj* inborn, innate, native, natural ~*v* bear, produce; cherish, nurse, nurture, protect, raise, rear, tend

motherly affectionate, caring, fond, gentle, kind, loving, maternal, tender

motion *n* action, change, flow, move, movement, passage, progress, travel; proposal, proposition, submission, suggestion ~*v* beckon, direct, gesture, nod, signal, wave

motionless calm, frozen, halted, immobile, lifeless, static, stationary, still, unmoving

motivate actuate, arouse, bring, cause, draw, drive, impel, induce, inspire, instigate, lead, move, persuade, prod, prompt, stimulate, stir

motivation ambition, desire, drive, hunger, inspiration, interest, wish

motive *n* cause, design, ground(s), incentive, inducement, influence, inspiration, intention, occasion, purpose, reason, spur, stimulus

motley assorted, dissimilar, diversified, mingled, mixed, unlike, varied

mottled blotchy, chequered, dappled, flecked, marbled, piebald, pied, speckled, stippled, streaked, variegated

motto adage, cry, dictum, maxim, proverb, rule, saw, saying, slogan

mould *n* cast, die, form, pattern, shape, stamp; brand, build, cut, design, fashion, form, format, frame, kind, line, make, pattern, shape, stamp, style ~*v* carve, cast, construct, create, fashion, forge, form, make, model, sculpt, shape, stamp, work

mouldy bad, decaying, rotten,

mound n heap; small hill

mount v rise; increase; get on (horse); frame (picture); set up ~n support; horse; hill

mountain n hill of great size **mountaineer** n one who lives among or climbs mountains **mountainous** adj **mountain bike** bicycle with straight handlebars and heavy-duty tyres

mountebank n charlatan, fake

mourn v feel, show sorrow (for) **mourner** n **mournful** adj sad; dismal **mourning** n grieving; clothes of mourner

mouse n (pl **mice**) small rodent **mousy** adj like mouse, esp. in colour

mousse n dish of flavoured cream

moustache n hair on upper lip

mouth n opening in head for eating, speaking etc.; opening; entrance ~v form (words) with lips without speaking **mouth organ** small musical instrument **mouthpiece** n end of anything placed between lips

move v change position, place; (cause to) be in motion; stir emotions of; incite; propose; change one's dwelling etc. ~n a moving; motion **movement** n moving; moving parts; group with common aim; division of piece of music **movie** n Inf film

mow v **mowing**, **mown** cut (grass etc.) **mower** n

MP Member of Parliament; Military Police

mph miles per hour

Mr. mister

Mrs. title of married woman

Ms. title used instead of Miss or Mrs.

much adj **more**, **most** existing in quantity ~n large amount; important matter ~adv in a great degree; nearly

muck n dung; dirt **mucky** adj

mucus n fluid secreted by mucous

——————— THESAURUS ———————

spoiled, stale

mound heap, pile, stack; bank, dune, hill, hillock, knoll, rise

mount v arise, ascend, rise, soar, tower; build, grow, increase, intensify, multiply, pile up, swell; bestride, jump on; display, frame, set ~n backing, base, fixture, foil, frame, mounting, setting, stand, support; horse

mountain alp, elevation, eminence, height, mount, peak

mountainous alpine, high, highland, rocky, soaring, steep, towering, upland

mourn bewail, deplore, grieve, lament, miss, rue, sorrow, wail, weep

mournful afflicting, distressing, grievous, harrowing, lamentable, melancholy, painful, piteous, plaintive, sad, sorrowful, tragic, unhappy, woeful

mourning grief, lamentation, weeping, woe

mouth n jaws, lips; door, entrance, gateway, inlet, opening, orifice, rim

move v carry, change, shift, switch, transfer, transport, transpose; advance, budge, drift, go, march, proceed, progress, shift, stir, walk; affect, agitate, cause, excite, incite, induce, influence, inspire, lead; advocate, propose, recommend, suggest, urge; leave, migrate, quit, relocate, remove ~n act, action, deed, measure, motion, ploy, shift, step, stratagem, stroke, turn

movement act, action, activity, advance, agitation, change, exercise, flow, gesture, motion, operation, progress, shift, steps, stir, stirring, transfer; campaign, crusade, drive, faction, front, group, party; Mus division, part, passage, section

mow crop, cut, scythe, shear, trim

much adj abundant, ample, considerable, copious, great, plenteous, substantial ~adv a lot, considerably, decidedly, exceedingly, frequently, greatly, indeed, often, regularly

membranes

mud *n* wet and soft earth **muddy** *adj* **mudguard** *n* cover over wheel **mud-pack** *n* cosmetic paste to improve complexion

muddle *v* (*esp. with* up) confuse; bewilder; mismanage ~*n* confusion

muesli *n* mixture of grain, nuts, dried fruit etc.

muff¹ *n* tube-shaped covering to keep hands warm

muff² *v* bungle, fail in

muffin *n* light round yeast cake

muffle *v* wrap up, esp. to deaden sound **muffler** *n* scarf

mug¹ *n* drinking cup

mug² *n* *Sl* face; *Sl* fool, simpleton ~*v* **mugging, mugged** rob violently **mugger** *n*

mug³ *v* **mugging, mugged** *Inf* (*esp. with* up) study hard

muggy *adj* damp and stifling

mulberry *n* tree whose leaves are used to feed silkworms

mulch *n* straw, leaves etc. spread as protection for roots of plants ~*v* protect thus

mule *n* cross between horse and ass; hybrid **mulish** *adj* obstinate

mull *v* heat (wine) with sugar and spices; think (over)

multi- *comb. form* many, as in **multi-storey**

multifarious *adj* of various kinds or parts

multiple *adj* having many parts ~*n* quantity which contains another an exact number of times **multiplication** *n* **multiplicity** *n* variety, greatness in number **multiply** *v* **-plying, -plied** (cause to) increase; combine (two numbers) by multiplication; increase by reproduction

multitude *n* great number

mum *n* *Inf* mother

mumble *v* speak indistinctly

mummy¹ *n* embalmed body **mummify** *v* **-fying, -fied**

mummy² *n* *Inf* mother

mumps *pl* *n* infectious disease marked by swelling in neck

munch *v* chew vigorously

mundane *adj* ordinary, everyday; earthly

municipal *adj* belonging to affairs of city or town **municipality** *n* city or town with local self-government

munificent *adj* very generous **munificence** *n*

munition *n* (*usu. pl*) military stores

——————— THESAURUS ———————

mud clay, dirt, mire, ooze, silt, slime, sludge

muddle *v* confuse, disorder, mess, scramble, spoil, tangle; bewilder, confound, confuse, daze, perplex, stupefy ~*n* chaos, clutter, confusion, daze, disarray, disorder, hotchpotch, mess, mix-up, tangle

muddy boggy, dirty, marshy, soiled

muffle cloak, conceal, cover, disguise, envelop, hood, mask, shroud

mug¹ beaker, cup, flagon, jug, pot, tankard

mug² *n* charlie *Brit inf*, chump *Inf*, soft touch *Sl*, fool, muggins *Brit sl*, simpleton, sucker *Sl* ~*v* assail, assault, attack, beat up, duff up *Brit sl*, hold up, rob, set about

muggy close, damp, humid, sticky, stuffy, sultry

multiple collective, many, several, sundry, various

multiply augment, breed, expand, extend, increase, reproduce, spread

multitude army, assembly, collection, congregation, crowd, horde, host, legion, lot, mass, mob, myriad, sea, swarm, throng

mundane banal, everyday, humdrum, ordinary, prosaic, routine, workaday

municipal borough, city, civic, com-

mural *n* painting on wall

murder *n* unlawful premeditated killing of human being ~*v* kill thus **murderer** *n* **murderous** *adj*

murk *n* darkness **murky** *adj*

murmur *n* low, indistinct sound ~*v* make, utter such a sound; complain

muscle *n* part of body which produces movement by contracting; system of muscles **muscular** *adj* strong; of muscle

muse *v* ponder; be lost in thought ~*n* musing; reverie; goddess inspiring creative artist

museum *n* (place housing) collection of historical etc. objects

mush *n* soft pulpy mass **mushy** *adj*

mushroom *n* fungoid growth, typically with stem and cap ~*v* shoot up rapidly

music *n* art form using harmonious combination of notes; composition in this art **musical** *adj* of, like, interested in music ~*n* show, film in which music plays essential part **musician** *n*

musk *n* scent obtained from gland of deer **musky** *adj* **muskrat** *n* N Amer. rodent found near water; its fur

musket *n Hist* infantryman's gun

Muslim, Moslem *n* follower of religion of Islam ~*adj* of Islam

muslin *n* fine cotton fabric

mussel *n* bivalve shellfish

must *v* be obliged to, or certain to ~*n* necessity

mustang *n* wild horse

mustard *n* powder made from the seeds of a plant, used in paste as a condiment

muster *v* assemble ~*n* assembly, esp. for exercise, inspection

musty *adj* mouldy, stale

mutate *v* (cause to) undergo mutation **mutant** *n* mutated animal, plant etc. **mutation** *n* change, esp. genetic change causing divergence from kind or racial type

mute *adj* dumb; silent ~*n* dumb person; *Mus* contrivance to soften tone of instruments **muted** *adj* muffled;

──────── THESAURUS ────────

munity, public, town, urban

murder *n* assassination, bloodshed, butchery, carnage, homicide, killing, manslaughter, massacre, slaying ~*v* assassinate, butcher, destroy, dispatch, kill, massacre, slaughter

murderer assassin, butcher, cutthroat, killer, slayer

murderous barbarous, bloodthirsty, bloody, brutal, cruel, deadly, fatal, lethal, savage

murky cheerless, cloudy, dark, dim, dreary, dull, dusky, foggy, gloomy, grey, misty, obscure, overcast

murmur *n* babble, drone, humming, mumble, muttering, purr, rumble, undertone, whisper ~*v* babble, buzz, drone, hum, mumble, mutter, purr, rumble, whisper

muscle sinew, tendon, thew; brawn, force, might, potency, power, stamina, strength, weight

muscular athletic, lusty, powerful, robust, sinewy, stalwart, strapping, strong, vigorous

muse brood, cogitate, deliberate, dream, meditate, ponder, reflect, ruminate, speculate, think, weigh

musical dulcet, lilting, lyrical, melodious, tuneful

must *n* duty, essential, imperative, necessity, obligation, requirement, requisite, *sine qua non*

muster *v* assemble, call up, collect, congregate, convene, convoke, enrol, gather, group, marshal, meet, mobilize, rally, summon ~*n* assembly, collection, concourse, congregation, convention, gathering, meeting, rally

musty airless, dank, decayed, frowsty, fusty, mildewed, mouldy, old, smelly, stale, stuffy

subdued

mutilate v deprive of a limb etc.; damage

mutiny n rebellion against authority, esp. against officers of disciplined body **~v** mutinying, mutinied commit mutiny **mutineer** n **mutinous** adj

mutter v speak, utter indistinctly; grumble **~n** muttered sound

mutton n flesh of sheep used as food

mutual adj done, possessed etc. by each of two with respect to the other; Inf common

muzzle n mouth and nose of animal; cover for these to prevent biting; open end of gun **~v** put muzzle on

muzzy adj indistinct, confused

my adj belonging to me **myself** pron emphatic or reflexive form of I

mynah n Indian bird related to starling

myopia n short-sightedness **myopic** adj

myriad adj innumerable **~n** large number

myrrh n aromatic gum, formerly used as incense

myrtle n flowering evergreen shrub

myself SEE MY

mystery n obscure or secret thing; anything strange or inexplicable **mysterious** adj

mystic n one who seeks divine, spiritual knowledge, esp. by prayer, contemplation etc. **mystical** adj

mystify v **-fying, -fied** bewilder, puzzle

mystique n aura of mystery, power etc.

myth n tale with supernatural characters or events; imaginary person or object **mythical** adj **mythology** n myths collectively

myxomatosis n contagious, fatal disease of rabbits

———————— THESAURUS ————————

mute adj dumb, silent, speechless, unspoken, wordless

mutilate butcher, cripple, damage, disable, disfigure, dismember, hack, injure, lacerate, lame, maim, mangle

mutinous disobedient, insubordinate, rebellious, refractory, revolutionary, seditious, subversive, unruly

mutiny n disobedience, insubordination, insurrection, rebellion, resistance, revolt, revolution, riot, rising, strike, uprising **~v** disobey, rebel, resist, revolt, strike

mutter complain, mumble, murmur, rumble

mutual common, interactive, joint, reciprocal, returned, shared

muzzle censor, choke, curb, restrain, silence, stifle, suppress

mysterious abstruse, arcane, baffling, concealed, cryptic, curious, dark, furtive, hidden, inexplicable, inscrutable, obscure, recondite, secret, strange, uncanny, unknown, weird

mystery conundrum, enigma, problem, puzzle, question, riddle, secrecy, secret

mystify baffle, bewilder, confound, confuse, escape, flummox, nonplus, perplex, puzzle, stump

myth allegory, fable, fiction, legend, parable, saga, story, tradition

mythical fabled, fairy-tale, legendary; fabricated, fanciful, fictitious, invented, unreal, untrue

mythology folklore, legend, stories, tradition

N n

nadir n lowest point

naff adj Sl inferior or useless

nag[1] v **nagging, nagged** scold or trouble constantly ~n nagging; one who nags

nag[2] n Inf horse

nail n horny shield at ends of fingers, toes; small metal spike for fixing wood etc. ~v fix with nails

naive, naïve adj simple, unaffected, ingenuous **naiveté, naivety** n

naked adj without clothes; exposed, bare; undisguised

name n word by which person, thing etc. is denoted; reputation ~v give name to; call by name; appoint; mention **nameless** adj without a name; unknown; indescribable **namely** adv that is to say **namesake** n person with same name as another

nanny n child's nurse **nanny goat** she-goat

nap[1] v **napping, napped** take short sleep ~n short sleep

nap[2] n downy surface on cloth made by projecting fibres

nape n back of neck

napkin n cloth, paper for wiping fingers or lips at table; nappy

nappy n towelling cloth to absorb baby's excrement

narcissism n abnormal admiration for oneself

narcissus n (pl **-cissi**) genus of bulbous plants including daffodil, esp. one with white flowers

narcotic n/adj (drug) producing numbness and stupor

nark v Sl annoy, irritate

narrate v tell (story) **narration** n **narrative** n account, story **narrator** n

narrow adj of little breadth; limited ~v make, become narrow **narrow-minded** adj illiberal; bigoted

---

THESAURUS

nadir bottom, depths, zero

nag v annoy, badger, chivvy, goad, harass, harry, hassle Inf, henpeck, pester, plague, provoke, scold, vex, worry ~n harpy, scold, shrew, termagant, virago

nail v attach, beat, fasten, fix, hammer, join, pin, secure, tack

naive artless, candid, childlike, guileless, ingenuous, innocent, open, simple, trusting, unsophisticated

naked bare, divested, exposed, nude, stripped, undressed; defenceless, helpless, unarmed, unguarded, unprotected, vulnerable

name n denomination, designation, epithet, nickname, sobriquet, term, title; credit, reputation ~v baptize, call, christen, dub, entitle, label, style, term; appoint, choose, commission, designate, identify, nominate, select, specify

nameless anonymous, untitled; incognito, obscure, unsung; horrible, indescribable, unmentionable, unspeakable

namely specifically, to wit, viz.

narcissism egotism, self-admiration, self-love, vanity

narrate describe, detail, recite, recount, rehearse, relate, repeat, report, tell

narration description, explanation, reading, recital, relation, storytelling

narrative account, chronicle, detail, history, report, statement, story, tale

narrator author, bard, chronicler, commentator, reporter, storyteller

narrow adj close, confined, cramped, limited, meagre, near, pinched, restricted, scanty, straitened, tight ~v diminish, limit, reduce, simplify,

nasal *adj* of nose ~*n* sound partly produced in nose

nasturtium *n* garden plant with red or orange flowers

nasty *adj* foul, unpleasant; spiteful

nation *n* people or race organized as a state **national** *adj* of, characteristic of, a nation ~*n* citizen **nationalism** *n* devotion to one's country; movement for independence **nationalist** *n/adj* **nationality** *n* fact of belonging to a particular nation **nationalization** *n* acquisition and management of industries by the state **nationalize** *v* **National Health Service** system of medical services financed mainly by taxation **national service** compulsory military service

native *adj* inborn; born in particular place ~*n* native person, animal or plant

nativity *n* birth; (*with cap.*) birth of Christ

NATO North Atlantic Treaty Organization

natter *Inf v* talk idly ~*n* idle talk

natty *adj* neat and smart

nature *n* innate qualities of person or thing; class, sort; (*oft. with cap.*) power underlying all phenomena; natural unspoilt scenery **natural** *adj* of nature; inborn; normal; unaffected ~*n* something, somebody well suited for something; *Mus* character used to remove effect of sharp or flat preceding it **naturalist** *n* one who studies animals and plants **naturalize** *v* admit to citizenship **naturally** *adv*

naturism *n* nudism

naughty *adj* disobedient; *Inf* mildly indecent

nausea *n* feeling that precedes vomiting **nauseate** *v* sicken **nauseous** *adj*

nautical *adj* of seamen or ships **nautical mile** 1852 metres

nave *n* main part of church

——————— THESAURUS ———————

straiten, tighten

narrow-minded biased, bigoted, hidebound, insular, intolerant, parochial, petty, strait-laced

nasty dirty, disagreeable, disgusting, filthy, foul, horrible, nauseating, obnoxious, odious, offensive, repellent, repugnant, sickening, unpleasant, vile; abusive, despicable, malicious, mean, spiteful, unpleasant, vicious, vile

nation community, country, people, race, realm, society, state

national civil, countrywide, governmental, public, state; domestic, internal, social

nationalism allegiance, chauvinism, loyalty, patriotism

nationality birth, race

native *adj* congenital, endemic, hereditary, indigenous, inherited, innate, instinctive; domestic, home, home-made, indigenous, local ~*n*

aborigine, citizen, countryman, dweller, inhabitant

natural characteristic, essential, inborn, inherent, innate, instinctive, intuitive; common, everyday, logical, normal, ordinary, regular, typical, usual; artless, candid, frank, genuine, ingenuous, open, real, simple, spontaneous, unaffected, unpretentious

nature character, complexion, essence, features, make-up, quality, traits; disposition, humour, mood, outlook, temper, temperament; category, description, kind, sort, species, style, type, variety; creation, earth, environment, universe, world; country, landscape

naughty bad, disobedient, impish, misbehaved, mischievous, wayward

nausea biliousness, qualm(s), sickness, vomiting

nauseate disgust, horrify, offend, repel, repulse, revolt, sicken

navel *n* small depression in abdomen where umbilical cord was attached

navigate *v* direct, plot path of ship etc.; travel **navigable** *adj* **navigation** *n* **navigator** *n*

navvy *n* labourer employed on roads, railways etc.

navy *n* fleet; warships of country with their crews ~*adj* navy-blue **naval** *adj* of the navy **navy-blue** *adj* very dark blue

nay *adv Obs* no

NB note well

near *prep* close to ~*adv* at or to a short distance ~*adj* close at hand; closely related; stingy ~*v* approach **nearby** *adj* adjacent **nearly** *adv* closely; almost **nearside** *n* side of vehicle nearer kerb

neat *adj* tidy, orderly; deft; undiluted

nebulous *adj* vague

necessary *adj* that must be done; inevitable ~*n* what is needed **necessarily** *adv* **necessitate** *v* make necessary **necessity** *n* something needed; constraining power; compulsion; poverty

neck *n* part of body joining head to shoulders; narrow part of anything **neckerchief** *n* cloth tied round the neck **necklace** *n* ornament round the neck

nectar *n* honey of flowers

nectarine *n* variety of peach

née, nee *adj* indicating maiden name of married woman

need *v* want, require ~*n* (state, instance of) want; requirement; necessity; poverty **needful** *adj* necessary **needless** *adj* unnecessary **needy** *adj* poor, in want

———————— T H E S A U R U S ————————

nautical maritime, naval, seafaring, yachting

naval marine, maritime, nautical

navigable clear, negotiable, passable, unobstructed

navigate cross, cruise, direct, drive, guide, handle, journey, manoeuvre, pilot, plan, plot, sail, steer, voyage

navigation cruising, pilotage, sailing, seamanship, steering, voyaging

navy fleet, flotilla, warships

near *adj* adjacent, adjoining, alongside, beside, bordering, close, contiguous, nearby, neighbouring, nigh, touching; akin, allied, attached, connected, dear, familiar, intimate, related

nearby adjacent, adjoining, convenient, handy, neighbouring

nearly about, all but, almost, approaching, approximately, closely, not quite, practically, roughly, virtually, well-nigh

neat accurate, dainty, fastidious, methodical, nice, orderly, shipshape, smart, spruce, straight, systematic,

tidy, trim; adept, adroit, agile, apt, clever, deft, dexterous, efficient, effortless, elegant, expert, graceful, handy, nimble, precise, skilful, stylish; *of alcoholic drinks* pure, straight, undiluted, unmixed

necessarily automatically, by definition, certainly, compulsorily, consequently, inevitably, inexorably, naturally, of course, perforce, willy-nilly

necessary compulsory, essential, imperative, mandatory, needful, obligatory, required, vital

necessitate call for, coerce, compel, constrain, demand, entail, force, oblige, require

necessity demand, exigency, need, requirement; fundamental, need, prerequisite, requirement, requisite, *sine qua non,* want

need *v* call for, demand, entail, lack, miss, necessitate, require, want ~*n* longing, requisite, want, wish; obligation, urgency, want; destitution, distress, extremity, inadequacy, lack, neediness, paucity, penury, poverty,

needle *n* thin pointed piece of metal for sewing, knitting; stylus for record player; leaf of fir tree ~*v Inf* goad, provoke **needlework** *n* sewing, embroidery

nefarious *adj* wicked

negate *v* deny, nullify **negation** *n*

negative *adj* expressing denial or refusal; lacking enthusiasm; not positive; of electrical charge having the same polarity as the charge of an electron ~*n* negative word or statement; *Photog* picture in which lights and shades are reversed

neglect *v* take no care of; fail to do ~*n* fact of neglecting or being neglected

negligee, negligée *v* woman's light dressing gown

negligence *n* carelessness **negligent** *adj* **negligible** *adj* very small or unimportant

negotiate *v* discuss with view to mutual settlement; arrange by conference; transfer (bill, cheque etc.); get over (obstacle) **negotiable** *adj* **negotiation** *n* **negotiator** *n*

neigh *n/v* (utter) cry of horse

neighbour *n* one who lives near another **neighbourhood** *n* district; people of district **neighbouring** *adj* nearby **neighbourly** *adj* friendly; helpful

neither *adj/pron* not the one or the other ~*adv* not on the one hand; not either ~*conj* nor yet

nemesis *n* (*pl* -**ses**) retribution, vengeance

neologism *n* newly-coined word or phrase

neon *n* inert gas in the atmosphere, used to illuminate signs and lights

———————— THESAURUS ————————

privation, shortage

needful essential, indispensable, necessary, needed, required, requisite, stipulated, vital

needless dispensable, excessive, expendable, groundless, pointless, redundant, superfluous, unwanted, useless

needy deprived, destitute, impoverished, penniless, poor, underprivileged

negate annul, cancel, invalidate, neutralize, nullify, obviate, repeal, rescind, retract, reverse, revoke, void, wipe out

negation antithesis, contrary, converse, denial, disavowal, disclaimer, inverse, opposite, rejection, reverse

negative *adj* contrary, denying, dissenting, opposing, refusing, resisting; antagonistic, contrary, cynical, gloomy, jaundiced, neutral, pessimistic, unenthusiastic, unwilling, weak; invalidating, neutralizing, nullifying ~*n* denial, refusal

neglect *v* disdain, disregard, ignore, overlook, rebuff, scorn, slight, spurn; be remiss, evade, forget, omit, procrastinate, shirk, skimp ~*n* disdain, disregard, disrespect, indifference, slight, unconcern; carelessness, default, failure, forgetfulness, laxity, oversight, slackness

negligent careless, forgetful, heedless, inadvertent, inattentive, indifferent, offhand, regardless, remiss, slack, slapdash, slipshod, thoughtless, unthinking

negligible insignificant, minor, minute, petty, small, trifling, trivial, unimportant

negotiate arbitrate, arrange, bargain, confer, consult, contract, deal, debate, discuss, handle, manage, mediate, parley, settle, transact, work out

negotiation arbitration, bargaining, debate, diplomacy, discussion

neighbourhood community, district, environs, locality, precincts, proximity, quarter, region, vicinity

neighbouring adjacent, adjoining, bordering, near, nearby, nearest,

nephew *n* brother's or sister's son

nepotism *n* undue favouritism towards one's relations

nerve *n* bundle of fibres carrying feeling, impulses to motion etc. to and from brain; assurance; coolness in danger; audacity; *pl* sensitiveness to fear, annoyance etc. ~*v* give courage to **nervous** *adj* excitable; apprehensive **nervy** *adj* nervous, jumpy **nerve-racking** *adj* very distressing

nest *n* place in which bird lays and hatches its eggs; animal's breeding place; snug retreat ~*v* make, have a nest **nest egg** (fund of) money in reserve

nestle *v* settle comfortably close to something

net[1] *n* openwork fabric of meshes of cord etc. ~*v* **netting, netted** cover with, or catch in, net **netting** *n* string or wire net **netball** *n* game in which ball has to be thrown through high net

net[2], **nett** *adj* left after all deductions ~*v* **netting, netted** gain, yield as clear profit

nether *adj* lower

nettle *n* plant with stinging hairs ~*v* irritate

network *n* system of intersecting lines, roads etc.; interconnecting group; linked broadcasting stations

neural *adj* of the nerves

neuralgia *n* pain in, along nerves

neurosis *n* (*pl* -**ses**) relatively mild mental disorder **neurotic** *adj*/*n*

neuter *adj* neither masculine nor feminine ~*v* castrate (animals)

neutral *adj* taking neither side in war, dispute etc.; without marked qualities ~*n* neutral nation or subject of one; position of disengaged gears **neutrality** *n* **neutralize** *v* make ineffective

neutron *n* electrically neutral particle of nucleus of an atom

never *adv* at no time **nevertheless** *adv* for all that

new *adj* not existing before, fresh; unfamiliar ~*adv* newly **newly** *adv* recently, freshly **newcomer** *n* recent arrival **newfangled** *adj* objectionably or unnecessarily modern

next, surrounding

nerve bravery, courage, daring, fearlessness, firmness, fortitude, mettle, pluck, resolution, spirit, vigour, will; *Inf* audacity, boldness, brazenness, chutzpah *US & Canad inf*, effrontery, gall, impertinence, impudence, insolence

nervous agitated, anxious, apprehensive, edgy, fidgety, hysterical, jumpy, neurotic, shaky, tense, timid, twitchy *Inf*, uneasy, weak, worried

nest breeding-ground, den; den, haunt, refuge, resort, retreat

nestle cuddle, huddle, snuggle

net[1] *n* lattice, mesh, tracery, web ~*v* bag, capture, catch, enmesh, ensnare, entangle, trap

net[2], **nett** *adj* clear, final, take-home

~*v* clear, earn, gain, make, realize, reap

network arrangement, channels, complex, grid, grill, maze, mesh, organization, structure, system, web

neurosis abnormality, deviation, instability, obsession, phobia

neurotic abnormal, anxious, compulsive, disordered, disturbed, nervous, unstable

neuter *v* castrate, geld, spay

neutral disinterested, dispassionate, impartial, unaligned, unbiased, uncommitted, undecided, unprejudiced

neutralize cancel, counteract, frustrate, nullify, offset, undo

nevertheless but, (even) though, however, notwithstanding, regardless, still, yet

news *n* report of recent happenings; interesting fact not previously known **newsagent** *n* shopkeeper selling newspapers, magazines etc. **newsflash** *n* brief news item, oft. interrupting programme **newspaper** *n* periodical publication containing news **newsprint** *n* inexpensive paper **newsreel** *n* film giving news

newt *n* small, tailed amphibian

newton *n* unit of force

next *adj/adv* nearest; immediately following **next-of-kin** *n* closest relative

NHS National Health Service

nib *n* (split) pen point

nibble *v* take little bites of ~*n* little bite

nice *adj* pleasant; friendly; kind; subtle, fine; careful, exact **nicely** *adv* **nicety** *n* minute distinction or detail

niche *n* recess in wall

nick *v* make notch in, indent; *Sl* steal ~*n* notch; *Inf* condition; *Sl* prison

nickel *n* silver-white metal much used in alloys and plating; *US & Canad* five cent piece

nickname *n* familiar name

nicotine *n* poisonous oily liquid in tobacco

niece *n* brother's or sister's daughter

nifty *adj Inf* smart; quick

niggard *n* mean, stingy person **niggardly** *adj/adv*

niggle *v* find fault continually; annoy

nigh *adj/adv/prep Obs or poet* near

night *n* time of darkness between sunset and sunrise **nightie, nighty** *n* nightdress **nightly** *adj/adv* (happening, done) every night **nightcap** *n* drink taken before bedtime **nightclub** *n* place for dancing, music etc., open late at night **nightdress** *n* woman's loose robe worn in bed **nightingale** *n* small bird which sings at night **nightmare** *n* very bad dream; terrifying experience **nightshade** *n* various plants of potato family, some with very poisonous berries **night-time** *n*

———————— THESAURUS ————————

new advanced, contemporary, current, different, fresh, happening *Inf*, latest, modern, newfangled, novel, original, recent, topical, up-to-date

newcomer alien, arrival, beginner, foreigner, incomer, novice, outsider

newfangled contemporary, modern, new, new-fashioned, novel, recent

newly anew, freshly, just, lately, latterly, recently

news account, bulletin, dispatch, exposé, gossip, hearsay, information, intelligence, latest *Inf*, leak, release, report, revelation, rumour, scandal, statement, story, tidings, word

next *adj* adjacent, adjoining, closest, nearest, neighbouring; consequent, ensuing, following, later, subsequent, succeeding ~*adv* afterwards, closely, following, later, subsequently, thereafter

nibble *v* bite, eat, gnaw, munch, nip,

pick at ~*n* bite, crumb, morsel, snack, *soupçon,* taste, titbit

nice agreeable, amiable, attractive, charming, courteous, friendly, good, kind, likable *or* likeable, pleasant, polite, refined, well-mannered; dainty, fine, neat, tidy, trim; accurate, careful, critical, delicate, exact, fastidious, fine, meticulous, precise, rigorous, scrupulous, strict, subtle

niche alcove, corner, hollow, nook, opening, recess

nick chip, cut, damage, dent, mark, notch, scar, score, scratch

nickname diminutive, epithet, label, moniker *or* monicker *Sl,* pet name, sobriquet

niggardly close, covetous, frugal, grudging, mean, mercenary, miserly, parsimonious, penurious, sparing, stingy, tightfisted

niggle carp, cavil, criticize, find fault,

nil *n* nothing, zero

nimble *adj* agile, quick, dexterous

nimbus *n* (*pl* **-bi, -buses**) rain or storm cloud; halo

nincompoop *n* *Inf* stupid person

nine *adj/n* cardinal number next above eight **ninth** *adj* ordinal number **nineteen** *adj/n* nine more than ten **nineteenth** *adj* **ninetieth** *adj* **ninety** *adj/n* nine tens

nip *v* **nipping, nipped** pinch sharply; detach by pinching, bite; check growth (of plants) thus; *Inf* hurry ~*n* pinch; sharp coldness of weather; short drink **nipper** *n* thing that nips; *Inf* small child **nippy** *adj* *Inf* cold; quick

nipple *n* point of breast, teat; anything like this

nit *n* egg of louse or other parasite; *Inf* nitwit **nit-picking** *adj* *Inf* overconcerned with insignificant detail **nitwit** *n* *Inf* fool

nitrogen *n* one of the gases making up air **nitrate** *n* compound of nitric acid and an alkali **nitric** *adj* **nitroglyc-**

erine *n* explosive liquid

no *adj* not any, not a; not at all ~*adv* expresses negative reply ~*n* (*pl* **noes**) refusal; denial; negative vote or voter **no-one, no one** nobody

no. number

noble *adj* of the nobility; having high moral qualities; impressive ~*n* member of the nobility **nobility** *n* class holding special rank; being noble **nobleman** *n* (*fem* **noblewoman**) **nobly** *adv*

nobody *n* no person; person of no importance

nocturnal *adj* of, in, by, night

nod *v* **nodding, nodded** bow head slightly and quickly in assent, command etc.; let head droop with sleep ~*n* act of nodding

node *n* knot or knob

nodule *n* little knot; rounded irregular mineral mass

noise *n* any sound, esp. disturbing one ~*v* rumour **noisy** *adj*

nomad *n* member of wandering tribe; wanderer **nomadic** *adj*

——————— THESAURUS ———————

fuss; annoy, irritate, rankle, worry

night dark, night-time

nightmare hallucination; horror, ordeal, torment, trial, tribulation

nil duck, love, none, nothing, zero

nimble active, agile, alert, brisk, deft, lively, prompt, quick, ready, smart, sprightly, spry, swift

nip *v* bite, catch, clip, grip, pinch, snag, snap, snip, tweak, twitch ~*n* dram, draught, drop, finger, portion, sip, *soupçon*, taste

nippy biting, chilly, sharp, stinging

nobility aristocracy, elite, lords, nobles, peerage; dignity, eminence, excellence, grandeur, greatness, majesty, nobleness, superiority, worthiness

noble *adj* aristocratic, highborn, lordly; generous, honourable, upright, virtuous, worthy; august, dignified,

distinguished, elevated, eminent, grand, great, imposing, impressive, lofty, splendid, stately ~*n* lord, nobleman, peer

nobody no-one; cipher, menial, nonentity

nocturnal night, nightly, night-time

nod *v* bow, dip, duck, gesture, indicate, salute, signal; agree, assent, concur; doze, droop, drowse, kip *sl*, nap, sleep, slump ~*n* beck, gesture, greeting, salute, sign, signal

noise babble, blare, clamour, clatter, commotion, cry, din, fracas, hubbub, outcry, pandemonium, racket, row, tumult, uproar

noisy boisterous, chattering, deafening, loud, piercing, riotous, strident, uproarious, vociferous

nomad drifter, migrant, rambler, rov-

nomenclature *n* system of names

nominal *adj* in name only; (of fee etc.) small

nominate *v* propose as candidate; appoint to office **nomination** *n* **nominee** *n* candidate

non- *comb. form* indicates the negative of a word

nonchalant *adj* casually unconcerned, indifferent

noncommissioned officer *Mil* subordinate officer, risen from the ranks

noncommittal *adj* avoiding definite preference or pledge

nonconformist *n* dissenter, esp. from Established Church

nondescript *adj* lacking distinctive characteristics

none *pron* no-one, not any **~adv** in no way **nonetheless** *adv* despite that, however

nonentity *n* insignificant person, thing

nonevent *n* disappointing or insignificant occurrence

nonflammable *adj* not easily set on fire

nonpareil *n/adj* (person or thing) unequalled or unrivalled

nonplussed *adj* disconcerted

nonsense *n* absurd language; absurdity; silly conduct

non sequitur statement with little relation to what preceded it

noodle *n* strip of pasta served in soup etc.

nook *n* sheltered corner

noon *n* midday, twelve o'clock

noose *n* loop on end of rope; snare

nor *conj* and not

norm *n* average level; standard **normal** *adj* ordinary; usual; conforming to type **normality** *n* **normally** *adv*

north *n* direction to the right of per-

———————— THESAURUS ————————

er, vagabond, wanderer

nomadic itinerant, migrant, roaming, roving, travelling, vagrant, wandering

nominal formal, ostensible, pretended, professed, puppet, self-styled, so-called, supposed, theoretical, titular

nominate appoint, assign, choose, designate, elect, elevate, name, present, propose, recommend, select, submit, suggest, term

nomination appointment, choice, election, proposal, selection, suggestion

nominee aspirant, candidate, contestant, entrant, runner

nonchalant airy, apathetic, calm, careless, casual, collected, cool, detached, indifferent, offhand, unconcerned

noncommittal careful, cautious, discreet, evasive, guarded, indefinite, neutral, politic, reserved, tactful, vague, wary

nonconformist dissenter, eccentric, heretic, maverick, protester, radical, rebel

nondescript characterless, dull, ordinary, undistinguished, uninspiring, uninteresting, unremarkable

none nil, nobody, no-one, nothing, not one, zero

nonentity cipher, mediocrity, nobody

nonetheless despite that, even so, however, nevertheless, yet

nonsense absurdity, balderdash, bilge *Inf*, bunkum, drivel, folly, garbage *Inf*, gibberish, inanity, jest, poppycock *Inf*, rot, rubbish, stupidity, trash, twaddle

nook alcove, cavity, corner, cranny, crevice, niche, opening, recess, retreat

norm average, criterion, mean, model, par, pattern, rule, standard, type

normal accustomed, average, common, natural, ordinary, popular,

son facing the sunset *~adv/adj* from, towards or in the north **northerly** *adj* *~n* wind from the north **northern** *adj* **northwards** *adv*

nose *n* organ of smell, used also in breathing; any projection resembling a nose *~v* (cause to) move forward slowly and carefully; touch with nose; smell, sniff; pry **nosy** *adj Inf* inquisitive **nose dive** sudden drop

nosh *Sl n* food *~v* eat

nostalgia *n* longing for past events **nostalgic** *adj*

nostril *n* one of the two external openings of the nose

not *adv* expressing negation, refusal, denial

notable *adj/n* remarkable (person) **notably** *adv*

notary *n* person authorized to draw up deeds, contracts

notation *n* representation of numbers, quantities by symbols

notch *n/v* (make) V-shaped cut

note *n* brief comment or record; short letter; banknote; symbol for musical sound; single tone; fame; notice *~v* observe, record; heed **noted** *adj* well-known **notebook** *n* small book with blank pages for writing

nothing *n* no thing; not anything, nought *~adv* not at all, in no way

notice *n* observation; attention; warning, announcement *~v* observe, mention; give attention to

notify *v* **-fying, -fied** give notice of or to

notion *n* concept; opinion; whim

notorious *adj* known for something bad **notoriety** *n*

notwithstanding *prep* in spite of *~adv* all the same *~conj* although

nougat *n* chewy sweet containing nuts, fruit etc.

regular, routine, run-of-the-mill, standard, typical, usual

nostalgia homesickness, longing, yearning

nostalgic homesick, longing, regretful

notable *adj* celebrated, distinguished, eminent, famous, manifest, marked, memorable, noteworthy, noticeable, pre-eminent, pronounced, rare, remarkable, renowned, striking, uncommon, unusual, well-known *~n* celebrity, dignitary, personage

notation characters, code, script, signs, symbols, system

notch cleft, cut, incision, mark, nick, score

note *n* comment, epistle, gloss, letter, memo, message, minute, record, remark, reminder; indication, mark, sign, symbol, token; heed, notice, observation, regard *~v* designate, indicate, mark, mention, notice, observe, record, register, remark, see

noted acclaimed, celebrated, distinguished, eminent, famous, illustrious, prominent, recognized, wellknown

nothing cipher, naught, nonentity, nonexistence, nought, void, zero

notice *n* heed, note, observation, regard; advice, announcement, instruction, intelligence, intimation, news, order, warning *~v* detect, discern, distinguish, heed, mark, mind, note, observe, perceive, remark, see, spot

notify acquaint, advise, alert, announce, declare, inform, tell, warn

notion belief, concept, idea, impression, inkling, judgment, knowledge, opinion, view; caprice, desire, fancy, impulse, whim, wish

notoriety dishonour, disrepute, scandal

notorious disreputable, infamous, scandalous

notwithstanding although, despite, (even) though, however, neverthe-

nought *n* nothing; figure 0

noun *n* word used as name of person, idea or thing

nourish *v* feed; nurture **nourishment** *n.*

Nov. November

novel[1] *n* fictitious tale in book form **novelist** *n*

novel[2] *adj* new, recent; strange **novelty** *n* newness; something new; small trinket

November *n* eleventh month

novice *n* beginner

now *adv* at the present time; immediately; recently ~*conj* seeing that, since **nowadays** *adv* in these times

nowhere *adv* not in any place or state

noxious *adj* poisonous, harmful

nozzle *n* pointed spout, esp. at end of hose

nuance *n* delicate shade of difference

nub *n* small lump; main point

nubile *adj* sexually attractive; marriageable

nucleus *n* (*pl* **-clei**) centre, kernel;

core of atom **nuclear** *adj* of, pert. to atomic nucleus **nuclear energy** energy released by nuclear fission **nuclear fission** disintegration of atom

nude *n/adj* naked (person) **nudism** *n* practice of nudity **nudist** *n* **nudity** *n*

nudge *v* touch slightly with elbow ~*n* such touch

nugget *n* lump of gold

nuisance *n* something or someone annoying

nuke *v Sl* attack or destroy with nuclear weapons

null *adj* of no effect, void **nullify** *v* -**fy**-**ing, -fied** cancel; make useless

numb *adj* deprived of feeling ~*v* make numb

number *n* sum or aggregate; word or symbol saying how many; single issue of a paper etc.; company, collection; identifying number ~*v* count; class, reckon; give a number to **numberless** *adj* countless

numeral *n* sign or word denoting a number **numeracy** *n* ability to use

less, nonetheless, though, yet

nought naught, nil, nothing, zero

nourish attend, feed, nurse, nurture, supply, sustain, tend

nourishment diet, food, nutrition, sustenance

novel[1] fiction, romance, story, tale

novel[2] different, fresh, groundbreaking, new, original, rare, singular, strange, uncommon, unfamiliar, unusual

novelty freshness, newness, oddity, strangeness, surprise; bauble, curiosity, gadget, gimmick, memento, souvenir, trifle, trinket

novice amateur, apprentice, beginner, learner, newcomer, proselyte, pupil, trainee, tyro

now at once, immediately, instantly, promptly, straightaway

nucleus basis, centre, core, heart,

kernel, pivot

nude bare, disrobed, exposed, naked, stripped, unclothed, undressed

nudge *v* bump, dig, elbow, jog, poke, prod, push, shove, touch

nudity bareness, nakedness, undress

nugget chunk, clump, hunk, lump

nuisance bore, bother, drag *Inf,* hassle *Inf,* irritation, offence, pest, plague, problem, trouble

numb *adj* dead, deadened, frozen, insensible, paralysed, stupefied, torpid ~*v* benumb, deaden, dull, freeze, paralyse, stun, stupefy

number *n* count, digit, figure, integer, numeral, sum, total, unit; copy, edition; amount, collection, company, crowd, horde, many, multitude, quantity ~*v* account, add, calculate, compute, count, reckon, tell, total

numberless countless, endless, infi-

numbers in calculations **numerate**
adj **numerator** *n* top part of fraction
numerical *adj* of numbers **numerous**
adj many
numskull *n* dolt, dunce
nun *n* woman living (in convent) under religious vows **nunnery** *n* convent
of nuns
nuptial *adj* of marriage **nuptials** *pl n*
wedding
nurse *n* person trained for care of sick
or injured ~*v* act as nurse to; suckle
nursery *n* room for children; rearing
place for plants **nursing home** private
hospital or home for old people **nursing officer** administrative head of
nursing staff of hospital
nurture *n* bringing up; rearing ~*v*
bring up; educate; nourish

nut *n* fruit consisting of hard shell and
kernel; hollow metal collar into
which a screw fits; *Inf* head; *Sl* crank,
maniac **nutty** *adj* **nutmeg** *n* aromatic
seed of Indian tree
nutrient *adj* nourishing ~*n* something
nutritious
nutrition *n* receiving foods; act of
nourishing **nutritional, nutritious, nu-
tritive** *adj*
nuzzle *v* burrow, press with nose; nestle
nylon *n* synthetic material used for
fabrics etc. *pl* stockings of this
nymph *n* legendary spirit of sea,
woods etc.
nymphomaniac *n* woman with abnormally intense sexual desire

———————————— T H E S A U R U S ————————————

nite, untold
numeral character, cipher, digit, figure, integer, number, symbol
numerous abundant, copious, many,
plentiful, profuse, several
nurse *v* tend, treat; feed, nourish,
nurture, suckle

nurture *n* rearing ~*v* feed, nourish,
nurse, support, sustain, tend; bring
up, develop, educate, instruct, rear,
school, train
nutrition food, nourishment, sustenance

O o

oaf *n* lout; dolt

oak *n* common deciduous tree

OAP old age pensioner

oar *n* wooden lever with broad blade worked by the hands to propel boat

oasis *n* (*pl* **-ses**) fertile spot in desert

oat *n* (*usu. pl*) grain of cereal plant; the plant **oatmeal** *n*

oath *n* confirmation of truth of statement by naming something sacred; curse

obdurate *adj* stubborn, unyielding

OBE Officer of the Order of the British Empire

obedience *n* submission to authority **obedient** *adj*

obelisk *n* tapering rectangular stone column

obese *adj* very fat **obesity** *n*

obey *v* do the bidding of; do as ordered

obituary *n* notice, record of death; biographical sketch of deceased person

object[1] *n* material thing; that to which feeling or action is directed; end or aim; *Grammar* word dependent on verb or preposition

object[2] *v* express or feel dislike or reluctance to something **objection** *n* **objectionable** *adj*

objective *adj* external to the mind; impartial ~*n* thing or place aimed at

oblige *v* compel; do favour for (someone) **obligate** *v* bind, esp. by legal contract **obligation** *n* binding duty, promise; debt of gratitude **obligatory** *adj* required; binding **obliging** *adj* ready to serve others, helpful

oblique *adj* slanting; indirect

THESAURUS

---

oasis haven, island, refuge, retreat, sanctuary

oath affirmation, avowal, bond, pledge, promise, vow, word; curse, expletive, profanity

obedience acquiescence, agreement, compliance, deference, docility, duty, observance, respect

obedient acquiescent, amenable, biddable, compliant, docile, duteous, dutiful, regardful, respectful, submissive

obese corpulent, fat, heavy, plump, podgy, portly, rotund, stout, tubby

obey comply, conform, discharge, execute, follow, fulfil, heed, keep, mind, observe, perform, respond, serve

object[1] *n* article, body, fact, item, reality, thing; design, end, goal, idea, intent, motive, objective, point, purpose, reason

object[2] *v* demur, expostulate, oppose, protest

objection cavil, censure, demur, doubt, exception, opposition, protest, remonstrance, scruple

objectionable deplorable, distasteful, insufferable, intolerable, obnoxious, offensive, regrettable, repugnant, undesirable, unpleasant

objective *adj* detached, dispassionate, fair, impartial, impersonal, just, unprejudiced ~*n* aim, ambition, aspiration, design, end, goal, mark, object, purpose, target

obligation burden, charge, compulsion, duty, liability, must, onus, requirement, responsibility, trust

obligatory binding, compulsory, essential, imperative, mandatory, necessary, required

oblige bind, compel, force, impel, make, require; accommodate, benefit, favour, gratify, indulge, please, serve

obliterate v blot out, efface; destroy completely

oblivion n forgetting or being forgotten **oblivious** adj forgetful; unaware

oblong adj rectangular, with adjacent sides unequal ~n oblong figure

obnoxious adj offensive, odious

oboe n woodwind instrument

obscene adj indecent, repulsive **obscenity** n

obscure adj unclear; indistinct ~v make unintelligible; dim; conceal **obscurity** n indistinctness; lack of intel-

ligibility; obscure place or position

obsequious adj servile, fawning

observe v notice, remark; watch; note systematically; keep, follow **observance** n keeping of custom; ritual, ceremony **observant** adj quick to notice **observation** n **observatory** n place for watching stars etc. **observer** n

obsess v haunt, fill the mind **obsession** n

obsolete adj disused, out of date **obsolescent** adj going out of use

———————————— THESAURUS ————————————

obliging agreeable, amiable, civil, considerate, cooperative, courteous, helpful, kind, polite, willing

oblique angled, aslant, inclined, slanted, slanting, sloped, sloping

obliterate cancel, delete, destroy, efface, eradicate, erase, wipe out

oblivious blind, careless, deaf, forgetful, heedless, ignorant, neglectful, regardless, unaware

obnoxious abominable, detestable, disgusting, foul, insufferable, nasty, odious, offensive, repellent, repulsive, revolting, unpleasant

obscene bawdy, blue, coarse, dirty, disgusting, filthy, foul, gross, indecent, lewd, offensive, pornographic, salacious, suggestive

obscure adj ambiguous, arcane, confusing, cryptic, deep, doubtful, esoteric, hazy, hidden, involved, mysterious, occult, opaque, unclear, vague; blurred, cloudy, dim, dusky, faint, gloomy, indistinct, murky, shadowy, shady, sombre, tenebrous, unlit, veiled ~v blur, cloak, cloud, darken, dim, dull, eclipse, mask, overshadow, shade, shroud; conceal, cover, disguise, hide, screen, veil

obscurity darkness, dimness, dusk, gloom, haze, murkiness, shadows; ambiguity, complexity, vagueness; insignificance, lowliness,

unimportance

observance attention, celebration, discharge, notice, observation, performance; ceremonial, custom, fashion, form, practice, rite, ritual, tradition

observant alert, attentive, heedful, mindful, perceptive, quick, vigilant, watchful

observation attention, consideration, examination, experience, information, inspection, knowledge, notice, review, scrutiny, study, surveillance

observe detect, discern, discover, espy, note, notice, perceive, see, spot, witness; check out *Inf*, monitor, regard, scrutinize, study, survey, view, watch; comply, follow, fulfil, heed, honour, keep, mind, obey, respect; keep, remember, solemnize; comment, declare, mention, note, opine, remark, say, state

observer commentator, eyewitness, onlooker, spectator, viewer, witness

obsession complex, fetish, fixation, hang-up *Inf*, infatuation, mania, phobia, preoccupation

obsolescent ageing, declining, waning

obsolete ancient, antiquated, archaic, bygone, dated, *démodé,* extinct, old, outmoded, outworn, passé

obstacle *n* obstruction

obstetrics *pl n* (*with sing v*) branch of medicine concerned with childbirth **obstetrician** *n*

obstinate *adj* stubborn; hard to overcome or cure **obstinacy** *n*

obstreperous *adj* unruly, noisy

obstruct *v* block up; hinder; impede **obstruction** *n* **obstructive** *adj*

obtain *v* get; acquire; be customary **obtainable** *adj*

obtrude *v* thrust forward unduly **obtrusive** *adj*

obtuse *adj* dull of perception; stupid; greater than right angle; not pointed

obverse *n* complement; principal side of coin, medal etc.

obviate *v* remove, make unnecessary

obvious *adj* clear, evident **obviously** *adv* **obviousness** *n*

occasion *n* time when thing happens; reason, need; opportunity; special event ~*v* cause **occasional** *adj* happening, found now and then **occasionally** *adv*

Occident *n* the West **Occidental** *adj*

occult *adj* secret, mysterious; supernatural

occupy *v* **-pying, -pied** inhabit, fill; employ; take possession of **occupancy** *n* fact of occupying **occupant** *n* **occupation** *n* employment, pursuit; tenancy; military control of country by foreign power **occupational** *adj* **occupier** *n*

occur *v* **-curring, -curred** happen; come to mind **occurrence** *n* happening

——————— T H E S A U R U S ———————

obstacle bar, barrier, block, check, hindrance, hitch, hurdle, interruption, obstruction, snag

obstinate determined, dogged, firm, immovable, inflexible, intractable, opinionated, perverse, recalcitrant, self-willed, stubborn, tenacious

obstruct arrest, bar, block, bung, check, choke, clog, curb, cut off, frustrate, hamper, hamstring, hide, hinder, impede, inhibit, interrupt, mask, obscure, prevent, restrict, stop

obstruction bar, barrier, block, blockage, check, hindrance, impediment, obstacle, snag, stop, stoppage

obstructive awkward, preventative, restrictive, unhelpful

obtain achieve, acquire, earn, gain, get, procure, secure

obtrusive forward, meddling, nosy, officious, prying

obvious apparent, blatant, clear, conspicuous, distinct, evident, manifest, open, overt, palpable, patent, perceptible, plain, pronounced, recognizable, self-evident, straightforward, transparent, unmistakable, unsubtle, visible

occasion chance, incident, moment, occurrence, opening, time; call, cause, excuse, ground(s), motive, prompting, provocation, reason; affair, event, experience, occurrence

occasional casual, desultory, incidental, infrequent, irregular, odd, rare, sporadic

occupant holder, indweller, inhabitant, inmate, lessee, occupier, resident, tenant, user

occupation activity, business, calling, craft, employment, job, post, profession, pursuit, trade, vocation, work; control, holding, occupancy, possession, residence, tenancy, tenure, use; conquest, invasion

occupy (*oft. passive*) absorb, amuse, busy, divert, employ, engage, engross, entertain, immerse, interest, involve, monopolize, preoccupy; capture, hold, invade, keep, seize

occur arise, befall, betide, chance, eventuate, happen, materialize, result

occurrence affair, circumstance, episode, event, happening, incident,

ocean *n* great body of water; large division of this; the sea

ochre *n* earth used as yellow or brown pigment

o'clock *adv* by the clock

Oct. October

octagon *n* figure with eight angles **octagonal** *adj*

octane *n* chemical found in petrol

octave *n* in *Mus* eighth note above or below given note; this space

octet *n* (music for) group of eight

October *n* tenth month

octopus *n* mollusc with eight arms covered with suckers

odd *adj* strange, queer; incidental, random; left over or additional; not even; not part of a set **oddity** *n* odd person or thing; quality of being odd **oddments** *pl n* things left over **odds** *pl n* advantage conceded in betting; likelihood **odds and ends** odd fragments or scraps

ode *n* lyric poem

odium *n* hatred, widespread dislike

odious *adj*

odour *n* smell **odorous** *adj* fragrant; scented

odyssey *n* long eventful journey

oesophagus *n* (*pl* **-gi**) passage between mouth and stomach

of *prep* denotes removal, separation, ownership, attribute, material, quality

off *adv* away **~prep** away from **~adj** not operative; cancelled or postponed; bad, sour etc. **offhand** *adj/adv* without previous thought; curt **off-licence** *n* place where alcoholic drinks are sold for consumption elsewhere **offset** *v* counterbalance, compensate **offspring** *n* children, issue

offal *n* edible entrails of animal; refuse

offend *v* hurt feelings of, displease; do wrong; disgust **offence** *n* wrong; crime; insult **offender** *n* **offensive** *adj* causing displeasure; aggressive **~n** position or movement of attack

offer *v* present for acceptance or refusal; tender; propose; attempt **~n** of-

proceeding

odd abnormal, bizarre, curious, deviant, different, eccentric, freak, irregular, peculiar, quaint, queer, remarkable, rum *Brit sl*, singular, strange, uncommon, unusual, weird, whimsical; lone, remaining, single, solitary, spare, unpaired

oddity abnormality, anomaly, freak, irregularity, peculiarity, phenomenon, quirk, rarity

odds edge, lead, superiority; balance, chances, likelihood, probability

odious abominable, detestable, disgusting, execrable, foul, hateful, horrible, loathsome, offensive, repellent, repugnant, repulsive, revolting, unpleasant

odour aroma, bouquet, essence, fragrance, perfume, scent, smell, stink

off *adj* absent, cancelled, finished,

gone, inoperative, postponed, unavailable; bad, decomposed, high, mouldy, rancid, rotten, sour, turned

offence crime, fault, lapse, misdeed, misdemeanour, peccadillo, sin, transgression, trespass, wrong

offend affront, annoy, displease, fret, gall, insult, irritate, outrage, pain, pique, provoke, rile, slight, snub, upset, vex, wound

offender criminal, culprit, lawbreaker, malefactor, miscreant, transgressor, villain

offensive *adj* disagreeable, disgusting, loathsome, nasty, obnoxious, odious, repellent, revolting, sickening, unpleasant, unsavoury, vile, abusive, aggressive, annoying, detestable, displeasing, insolent, insulting, irritating, rude, uncivil **~n** attack, drive, onslaught

fering, bid

office n room(s), building, in which business, clerical work etc. is done; commercial or professional organization; official position; service; duty; form of worship; pl task; service **offic-er** n one in command in army, navy, ship etc.; official

official adj with, by, authority ~n one holding office

officiate v perform duties of office, ceremony

officious adj importunate in offering service; interfering

offside adj/adv Sport illegally forward

oft adv Poet often

often adv many times

ogle v stare, look (at) amorously ~n this look

ogre n man-eating giant; monster

oh interj exclamation of surprise, pain etc.

ohm n unit of electrical resistance

oil n any viscous liquid with smooth, sticky feel; petroleum ~v lubricate with oil **oily** adj **oilskin** n cloth treated with oil to make it waterproof

ointment n greasy preparation for healing or beautifying the skin

O.K., okay Inf adj/adv/interj all right ~v agree to, endorse

old adj aged, having lived or existed long; belonging to earlier period **old-en** adj old **old-fashioned** adj in style of earlier period, out of date; fond of old ways

olfactory adj of smelling

oligarchy n government by small group

olive n evergreen tree; its oil-yielding fruit; its wood ~adj greyish-green

ombudsman n official who investigates complaints against government organizations

omelette n dish of eggs beaten and fried

omen n prophetic happening **ominous** adj boding evil, threatening

———————— THESAURUS ————————

offer v bid, extend, give, proffer, tender; advance, extend, move, propose, submit, suggest; afford, furnish, present, provide, show ~n attempt, bid, essay, overture, proposal, suggestion, tender

offhand abrupt, aloof, brusque, careless, casual, cavalier, curt, glib, perfunctory

office appointment, business, capacity, charge, commission, duty, employment, obligation, occupation, place, post, responsibility, role, service, situation, station, trust, work

officer agent, bureaucrat, executive, representative

official adj authentic, authoritative, bona fide, certified, formal, legitimate, licensed, proper ~n agent, bureaucrat, executive, representative

officiate chair, conduct, manage, preside, serve

officious bustling, forward, impertinent, interfering, intrusive, meddlesome, obtrusive, opinionated, overzealous

offset counteract, counterbalance, counterpoise, countervail, neutralize

often frequently, generally, much, repeatedly

oil v grease, lubricate

old aged, ancient, decrepit, elderly, grey, mature, senile, venerable; antiquated, antique, cast-off, crumbling, dated, decayed, done, obsolete, old-fashioned, outdated, passé, stale, timeworn, unoriginal, worn-out; antique, archaic, bygone, early, immemorial, original, primeval, primitive, pristine, remote

old-fashioned ancient, antiquated, archaic, dated, dead, obsolescent, past

omen augury, foreboding, indication,

omit *v* omitting, omitted leave out, leave undone **omission** *n*

omnibus *n* book etc. containing several works; bus ~*adj* serving, containing several objects

omnipotent *adj* all-powerful

omniscient *adj* knowing everything

omnivorous *adj* eating both animals and plants **omnivore** *n*

on *prep* above and touching, at, near, towards etc.; attached to; concerning; performed upon; during; taking regularly ~*adj* operating; taking place ~*adv* so as to be on; forwards; continuously etc.; in progress **oncoming** *adj* approaching from the front **on-going** *adj* in progress, continuing

once *adv* one time; formerly; ever **at once** immediately; simultaneously **once-over** *n Inf* quick examination

one *adj* lowest cardinal number; single; united; only, without others; identical ~*n* number or figure 1; unity; single specimen ~*pron* particular but not stated person; any person **oneself** *pron* **one-sided** *adj* partial; uneven

onerous *adj* burdensome

onion *n* vegetable with edible bulb of pungent flavour

onlooker *n* person who watches without taking part

only *adj* being the one specimen ~*adv* solely, merely, exclusively ~*conj* but then; excepting that

onset *n* beginning

onslaught *n* attack

onto *prep* on top of

onus *n* responsibility, burden

onward *adj* advanced or advancing ~*adv* in advance, ahead, forward **onwards** *adv*

onyx *n* variety of quartz

ooze *v* pass slowly out, exude ~*n* sluggish flow; wet mud

opal *n* glassy gemstone displaying variegated colours

opaque *adj* not transparent

open *adj* not shut or blocked up; without lid or door; bare; undisguised; not enclosed, covered or exclusive; spread out, accessible; frank ~*v* make or become open; begin ~*n* clear space, unenclosed country **opening** *n* hole, gap; beginning; opportunity ~*adj* first; initial **openly** *adv* without concealment **open-minded** *adj* unprejudiced

portent, presage, sign

ominous dark, fateful, menacing, portentous, sinister, threatening

omission default, failure, gap, lack, leaving out, neglect, oversight

omit disregard, drop, eliminate, exclude, fail, forget, miss (out), neglect, overlook, skip

omnipotent all-powerful, supreme

once long ago, previously **at once** directly, forthwith, immediately, instantly, now, right away

one-sided biased, coloured, lopsided, partial, partisan, prejudiced, unfair, unjust

onlooker bystander, eyewitness, observer, spectator, witness

only *adj* exclusive, individual, lone, single, sole, solitary, unique ~*adv* exclusively, just, merely, purely

ooze bleed, discharge, drain, drop, emit, escape, filter, leach, leak, seep, strain, sweat, weep

opaque cloudy, dim, dull, filmy, hazy, muddied, murky

open *adj* agape, ajar, extended, gaping, revealed, uncovered, unfastened, unlocked, yawning; airy, bare, clear, exposed, extensive, free, navigable, passable, rolling, spacious, sweeping, wide; accessible, available, free, general, public, unoccupied, vacant; artless, candid, fair, frank, guileless, honest, innocent, natural, sincere ~*v*

opera *n* musical drama **operatic** *adj* **operetta** *n* light opera

operation *n* working, way things work; act of surgery; military campaign **operate** *v* cause to function; work; produce an effect; perform act of surgery **operative** *adj* working *~n* worker **operator** *n*

ophthalmic *adj* of eyes

opinion *n* what one thinks about something; belief, judgment **opinionated** *adj* stubborn in one's opinions

opium *n* narcotic drug made from poppy **opiate** *n* drug containing opium

opossum *n* small Amer. and Aust. marsupial

opponent *n* adversary, antagonist

opportune *adj* seasonable, well-timed **opportunist** *n* one who grasps opportunities regardless of principle **opportunity** *n* favourable time or condition; good chance

oppose *v* resist, set against **opposite** *adj* contrary; facing *~n* the contrary *~prep/adv* facing; on the other side **opposition** *n* resistance; hostility; group opposing another

oppress *v* govern by tyranny; weigh down **oppression** *n* **oppressive** *adj* tyrannical; hard to bear; (of weather) hot and tiring

———————— T H E S A U R U S ————————

clear, crack, uncover, undo, unfasten, unlock, unseal, untie; begin, commence, inaugurate, initiate, launch, start

opening *n* aperture, breach, break, cleft, crack, gap, hole, rent, rupture, slot, space, split, vent; beginning, birth, dawn, inception, initiation, launch, onset, outset, start *~adj* beginning, early, first, inaugural, initial, introductory, primary

openly candidly, forthrightly, frankly, overtly, plainly; blatantly, brazenly, publicly, shamelessly

open-minded dispassionate, enlightened, free, impartial, liberal, reasonable, tolerant, unbiased, unprejudiced

operate act, function, go, perform, run, work

operation action, affair, course, exercise, motion, movement, procedure, process, use, working; assault, campaign, exercise, manoeuvre

operator conductor, driver, handler, mechanic, technician, worker

opinion assessment, belief, conjecture, feeling, idea, judgment, mind, notion, persuasion, sentiment, theory, view

opinionated bigoted, doctrinaire, dogmatic, inflexible, obstinate, prejudiced, stubborn

opponent adversary, antagonist, challenger, competitor, contestant, disputant, enemy, foe, rival

opportune appropriate, apt, auspicious, convenient, favourable, fitting, lucky, seasonable, suitable, timely

opportunity chance, hour, moment, occasion, opening, scope, time

oppose bar, block, check, combat, counter, defy, face, fight, hinder, obstruct, prevent, resist, take on, withstand

opposite *adj* adverse, conflicting, contradictory, contrary, hostile, inimical, irreconcilable, opposed, reverse, unlike; corresponding, facing, fronting *~n* antithesis, contradiction, contrary, converse, inverse, reverse

opposition antagonism, competition, disapproval, hostility, prevention, resistance; antagonist, foe, other side, rival

oppress abuse, crush, harry, maltreat, overpower, persecute, subdue, subjugate, suppress, wrong

oppression abuse, brutality, cruelty, harshness, injury, injustice, misery,

opt *v* make a choice

optic *adj* of eye or sight **optical** *adj* **optician** *n* maker of, dealer in spectacles, optical instruments

optimism *n* disposition to look on the bright side **optimist** *n* **optimistic** *adj*

optimum *adj/n* (*pl* **-ma, -mums**) the best, the most favourable

option *n* choice; thing chosen **optional** *adj* leaving to choice

optometrist *n* person testing eyesight, prescribing corrective lenses

opulent *adj* rich; copious **opulence** *n*

opus *n* work; musical composition

or *conj* introducing alternatives; if not

oracle *n* divine utterance, prophecy given at shrine of god; the shrine; wise adviser

oral *adj* spoken; by mouth ~*n* spoken examination

orange *adj* reddish-yellow ~*n* reddish-yellow citrus fruit

orang-utan, orang-utang *n* large reddish-brown ape

orator *n* maker of speech; skilful speaker **oration** *n* formal speech **oratory** *n* speeches; eloquence

orb *n* globe

orbit *n* track of planet, satellite, comet etc. around any other heavenly body; field of influence ~*v* move in, or put into, an orbit

orchard *n* (area for) fruit trees

orchestra *n* band of musicians; place for such band in theatre etc. **orchestral** *adj* **orchestrate** *v* arrange (music) for orchestra; organize (something) to particular effect

orchid *n* genus of various flowering plants

ordain *v* confer holy orders upon; decree, enact

ordeal *n* severe, trying experience

order *n* regular, proper or peaceful arrangement or condition; class; species; command; request for something to be supplied; monastic society ~*v* command; request (something) to be supplied; arrange **orderly** *adj* tidy; well-behaved ~*n* hospital attendant

persecution, severity, tyranny

oppressive brutal, cruel, despotic, grinding, harsh, heavy, onerous, repressive, severe, tyrannical, unjust; airless, close, heavy, stifling, stuffy, sultry, torrid

optimistic assured, bright, buoyant, cheerful, confident, expectant, hopeful, positive

optimum *adj* best, highest, ideal, peak, perfect, superlative

option alternative, choice, election, preference, selection

optional extra, open, possible, voluntary

oracle divination, prediction, prognostication, prophecy, revelation, vision; prophet, seer, sibyl, soothsayer

oral spoken, verbal, viva voce, vocal

orator declaimer, lecturer, rhetori-cian, speaker

oratory declamation, eloquence, rhetoric

orbit *n* circle, course, cycle, path, revolution, rotation, track, trajectory; compass, course, domain, influence, range, reach, scope, sphere, sweep ~*v* circle, encircle, revolve around

ordain anoint, appoint, call, consecrate, destine, elect, frock, invest, nominate; decree, dictate, enact, enjoin, establish, fix, lay down, order, prescribe, rule, set, will

ordeal affliction, agony, anguish, hardship, suffering, test, torture, trial

order *n* calm, control, discipline, law, peace; arrangement, method, pattern, plan, regularity, symmetry, system; caste, class, degree, grade, hierarchy, position, rank, status; breed,

ordinal number number showing position in series

ordinance *n* decree, rule

ordinary *adj* usual, normal; commonplace **ordinarily** *adv*

ordnance *n* artillery; military stores **ordnance survey** official geographical survey of Britain

ore *n* mineral which yields metal

oregano *n* aromatic herb

organ *n* musical wind instrument of pipes and stops, played with keys; member of animal or plant with particular function; medium of information **organist** *n* organ player

organism *n* plant, animal **organic** *adj* of, derived from, living organisms; of bodily organs; *Chem* of compounds formed from carbon; organized, systematic

organize *v* give definite structure; arrange; unite in a society **organization** *n* act of organizing; structure; association, group **organizer** *n*

orgasm *n* sexual climax

orgy *n* drunken or licentious revel; unrestrained bout

orient *n* (*with cap.*) East ~*v* determine (one's) position (*also* **orientate**) **oriental** *adj/n* **orientation** *n*

orifice *n* opening, mouth

origami *n* art of paper folding

origin *n* beginning; source; parentage **original** *adj* earliest; new, not copied; thinking or acting for oneself ~*n* thing from which another is copied **originality** *n* **originally** *adv* **originate** *v* come or bring into existence, begin; create, pioneer

ornament *n* any object used to adorn

cast, class, family, genre, genus, ilk, kind, sort, species, tribe; application, booking, commission, request, reservation; brotherhood, community, company, fraternity, guild, league, lodge, sect, sisterhood, society, union ~*v* bid, charge, command, decree, direct, enact, enjoin, instruct, ordain, prescribe, require; book, call for, engage, prescribe, request, reserve; adjust, align, arrange, catalogue, class, classify, conduct, control, dispose, group, manage, marshal, neaten, organize, regulate, systematize, tabulate, tidy

orderly *adj* businesslike, methodical, neat, shipshape, systematic, tidy; controlled, decorous, disciplined, law-abiding, restrained, well-behaved

ordinarily commonly, customarily, generally, habitually, normally, usually

ordinary accustomed, common, customary, established, everyday, mundane, normal, prevailing, regular, routine, settled, standard, stock, typi-

cal, usual; average, commonplace, fair, indifferent, inferior, pedestrian, unremarkable

organ element, member, part, process, structure, unit; agency, channel, forum, medium, mouthpiece, newspaper, publication, vehicle, voice

organism animal, being, body, creature, entity

organization assembly, construction, disposal, formation, management, regulation, running, standardization; arrangement, chemistry, composition, constitution, design, format, framework, grouping, make-up, method, organism, pattern, plan, structure, system, unity, whole; association, body, combine, company, concern, consortium, group, institution, league, society, syndicate, union

organize arrange, catalogue, classify, codify, constitute, construct, coordinate, dispose, establish, form, frame, group, marshal, pigeonhole, set up, shape

orgy debauch, revelry; bout, excess,

or decorate ~*v* adorn **ornamental** *adj*

ornate *adj* highly decorated or elaborate

ornithology *n* science of birds

orphan *n* child whose parents are dead **orphanage** *n* institution for care of orphans

orthodox *adj* holding accepted views; conventional **orthodoxy** *n*

orthopaedic *adj* for curing deformity, disorder of bones

oscillate *v* swing to and fro; waver

osmosis *n* movement of liquid through membrane from higher to lower concentration

osprey *n* fishing hawk

ossify *v* -**fying**, -**fied** turn into bone;

grow rigid

ostensible *adj* apparent; professed

ostentation *n* show, pretentious display **ostentatious** *adj*

osteopathy *n* art of treating disease by manipulation of bones **osteopath** *n*

ostracize *n* exclude, banish from society **ostracism** *n*

ostrich *n* large flightless bird

other *adj* not this; not the same; alternative ~*pron* other person or thing **otherwise** *adv* differently ~*conj* or else, if not

otter *n* furry aquatic fish-eating mammal

ouch *interj* exclamation of sudden

———— T H E S A U R U S ————

indulgence, spree, surfeit

origin beginning, birth, dawning, emergence, foundation, genesis, inauguration, inception, launch, outset, start; base, cause, derivation, fount, fountain, occasion, roots, source, spring

original *adj* earliest, first, initial, introductory, opening, primary, pristine, rudimentary, starting; archetypal, authentic, first, genuine, master, primary; creative, fertile, fresh, ground-breaking, ingenious, inventive, new, novel, resourceful, untried, unusual ~*n* archetype, master, model, pattern, precedent, prototype, standard, type

originality boldness, creativeness, creative spirit, creativity, daring, freshness, imagination, individuality, ingenuity, innovation, inventiveness, novelty

originate arise, begin, come, derive, emerge, flow, issue, result, rise, spring, start, stem; conceive, create, discover, evolve, formulate, generate, initiate, institute, introduce, invent, launch, pioneer, produce

ornament adornment, bauble, deco-

ration, frill, garnish, trinket

ornamental attractive, decorative, showy

ornate busy, decorated, elaborate, elegant, fancy, florid, rococo

orthodox accepted, approved, conformist, conventional, doctrinal, established, official, received, traditional

ostensible alleged, apparent, manifest, outward, plausible, professed, seeming, specious

ostentation affectation, boasting, display, exhibitionism, flourish, parade, pomp, pretentiousness, show

ostentatious boastful, conspicuous, extravagant, flamboyant, gaudy, loud, pompous, pretentious, showy, vulgar

ostracize blackball, blacklist, boycott, cast out, cold-shoulder, exclude, expel, give (someone) the cold shoulder, reject, send to Coventry, shun, snub

other *adj* different, dissimilar, distinct, diverse, remaining, separate; added, alternative, extra, further, more, spare, supplementary

otherwise if not, or else, or then

pain

ought *v* expressing obligation or advisability or probability

ounce *n* unit of weight, sixteenth of pound (28.4 grams)

our *adj* belonging to us **ours** *pron* **ourselves** *pron emphatic or reflexive form of* WE

oust *v* put out, expel

out *adv/adj* from within, away; wrong; not burning; not allowed; *Sport* dismissed **outer** *adj* away from the inside **outermost, outmost** *adj* on extreme outside **outing** *n* pleasure excursion **outward** *adj/adv*

outboard *adj* (of boat's engine) mounted on, outside stern

outbreak *n* sudden occurrence

outburst *n* sudden expression of emotion

outcast *n* rejected person

outcome *n* result

outcry *n* expression of widespread protest

outdoors *adv* in the open air **outdoor** *adj*

outfit *n* equipment; clothes and accessories; *Inf* group or association regarded as a unit

outgoing *adj* leaving; sociable **outgoings** *pl n* expenses

outlandish *adj* queer, extravagantly strange

outlaw *n* one beyond protection of the law ~*v* make (someone) an outlaw; ban

outlay *n* expenditure

outlet *n* means of release or escape; market

outline *n* rough sketch; general plan; lines enclosing visible figure ~*v* sketch; summarize

outlook *n* point of view; probable outcome

outlying *adj* remote

outmoded *adj* no longer fashionable or accepted

outpatient *n* patient who does not

——————— THESAURUS ———————

out *adj* impossible, ruled out, unacceptable; abroad, absent, away, elsewhere, gone, not at home, outside

outbreak burst, explosion, flare-up, flash, outburst, rash, spasm

outcast *n* castaway, exile, leper, pariah, refugee, untouchable, wretch

outcome aftermath, consequence, end, issue, result, upshot

outcry clamour, complaint, cry, howl, noise, outburst, protest, scream, screech, uproar, yell

outdoor alfresco, open-air, outside

outer exposed, exterior, external, outside, outward, peripheral, remote, superficial, surface

outfit clothes, costume, ensemble, garb, gear *Inf*, kit, suit, trappings

outgoing departing, former, last, leaving, past, retiring

outgoings costs, expenditure, expenses, outlay, overheads

outing excursion, jaunt, trip

outlandish alien, barbarous, eccentric, exotic, foreign, grotesque, queer, strange, weird

outlaw *n* bandit, brigand, highwayman, marauder, robber ~*v* ban, banish, bar, condemn, forbid, prohibit, proscribe

outlay *n* cost, expenses, investment, outgoings

outlet avenue, channel, opening, release, vent

outline *n* draft, drawing, frame, layout, plan, rough, skeleton, sketch, tracing; résumé, rundown, summary, synopsis; contour, figure, form, profile, shape, silhouette ~*v* adumbrate, delineate, draft, plan, summarize, trace

outlook angle, attitude, perspective, slant, viewpoint, views; forecast, future, prospect

stay in hospital overnight

outpost *n* outlying settlement

output *n* quantity produced; *Computers* information produced

outrage *n* violation of others' rights; shocking act; anger arising from this ~*v* commit outrage **outrageous** *adj* shocking; offensive

outright *adj* complete; definite ~*adv* completely

outset *n* beginning

outside *n* exterior ~*adv* not inside ~*adj* on exterior; unlikely; greatest possible **outsider** *n* person outside specific group; contestant thought unlikely to win

outsize, outsized *adj* larger than normal

outskirts *pl n* outer areas, districts,

esp. of city

outspoken *adj* frank, candid

outstanding *adj* excellent; remarkable; unsettled, unpaid

outweigh *v* be more important than

outwit *v* get the better of by cunning

oval *adj/n* egg-shaped, elliptical (thing)

ovary *n* female egg-producing organ **ovarian** *adj*

ovation *n* enthusiastic burst of applause

oven *n* heated chamber for baking

over *adv* above; beyond; in excess; finished; in repetition; across; downwards ~*prep* above; upon; more than; along ~*n Cricket* delivery of six balls from one end

over- *comb. form* too, too much, in

———— T H E S A U R U S ————

output manufacture, production, yield

outrage *n* abuse, affront, indignity, injury, insult, offence, shock, violation, violence; atrocity, enormity, evil, inhumanity; anger, fury, hurt, indignation, resentment, shock, wrath ~*v* affront, incense, offend, scandalize, shock

outrageous atrocious, beastly, flagrant, horrible, infamous, inhuman, scandalous, shocking, villainous, violent, wicked; disgraceful, offensive, over the top *Sl*, scandalous, shocking

outright *adj* absolute, arrant, complete, perfect, pure, thorough, total, undisputed, utter, wholesale; definite, direct, flat ~*adv* absolutely, completely, explicitly, openly, overtly, straightforwardly, thoroughly

outset beginning, inception, opening, start

outside *n* exterior, façade, face, front, skin, surface, topside ~*adj* exterior, external, extramural, extreme, outdoor, outer, outward, surface; distant, faint, marginal, negligible, re-

mote, slight, slim, small, unlikely

outskirts borders, boundary, edge, environs, suburbs, vicinity

outspoken abrupt, blunt, candid, direct, downright, explicit, frank, free, open, round

outstanding celebrated, distinguished, eminent, excellent, exceptional, great, important, impressive, special, superior, well-known; arresting, conspicuous, marked, memorable, notable, prominent, remarkable, salient, striking; due, open, owing, payable, pending, unpaid, unsettled

outward *adj* apparent, evident, exterior, external, obvious, ostensible, outer, outside, perceptible, superficial, surface, visible

outweigh compensate for, eclipse, override, predominate

outwit cheat, deceive, defraud, dupe, outjockey, outmanoeuvre, swindle

ovation acclaim, applause, cheers, plaudits, tribute

over *adv* above, aloft, on high, overhead ~*prep* above, on, on top of,

excess, above

overall n (*also pl*) loose garment worn as protection against dirt etc. ~*adj* total

overbearing *adj* domineering

overboard *adv* from a boat into water **go overboard** go to extremes

overcast *adj* cloudy

overcome *v* conquer; surmount; make incapable or powerless

overdose *n/v* (take) excessive dose of drug

overdraft *n* withdrawal of more money than is in bank account

overdrive *n* very high gear in motor vehicle

overgrown *adj* thickly covered with plants

overhaul *v* examine and set in order ~*n* examination and repair

overhead *adj/adv* over one's head, above

overland *adj/adv* by land

overlap *v* share part of same space or period of time ~*n* area overlapping

overlook *v* fail to notice; disregard

overseas *adj/adv* foreign; from or to a place over the sea

overseer *n* supervisor **oversee** *v* supervise

overshadow *v* reduce significance of

oversight *n* failure to notice; mistake

overt *adj* open, unconcealed

overtake *v* move past; catch up

overthrow *v* overturn; defeat ~*n* ruin; fall

overtime *n* time at work, outside normal working hours; payment for this time

overtone *n* additional meaning

overture *n Mus* orchestral introduction; opening of negotiations

overwhelm *v* crush; submerge **overwhelming** *adj* irresistible

———— T H E S A U R U S ————

upon; above, exceeding, in excess of, more than

overall *adj* blanket, complete, general, inclusive, umbrella

overbearing arrogant, despotic, dogmatic, domineering, lordly, officious, oppressive, overweening, peremptory, superior

overcast clouded, darkened, dismal, dreary, dull, grey, hazy, lowering, murky, sombre, threatening

overcome beat, best, conquer, crush, defeat, master, overpower, prevail, subdue, subjugate, surmount, vanquish

overhaul *v* check, do up *Inf*, examine, inspect, recondition, re-examine, repair, restore, service, survey ~*n* checkup, examination, inspection, service

overhead *adj* overhanging, roof, upper ~*adv* above, skyward, up above, upward

overlook disregard, forget, ignore,

miss, neglect, omit, pass, slight; condone, disregard, excuse, forgive

overshadow dominate, dwarf, eclipse, excel, outshine, surpass

oversight blunder, error, fault, lapse, laxity, mistake, neglect, omission, slip

overt apparent, blatant, manifest, obvious, open, patent, plain, unconcealed, undisguised, visible

overtake outdistance, outdo, outstrip, overhaul, pass

overthrow *v* demolish, destroy, level, overturn, raze, ruin, subvert, upend, upset; abolish, conquer, defeat, depose, dethrone, oust, overwhelm, topple, unseat ~*n* defeat, displacement, dispossession, downfall, end, fall, ousting, rout, ruin, undoing

overture (*oft. pl*) advance, approach, invitation, offer, proposal, signal, tender

overwhelm bury, crush, deluge, engulf, flood, inundate, submerge,

overwrought *adj* overexcited

owe *v* be bound to repay, be indebted for **owing** *adj* owed, due **owing to** caused by, as result of

owl *n* night bird of prey

own *adj* emphasizes possession ~*v* possess; acknowledge; confess **owner** *n* **ownership** *n* possession

ox *n* (*pl* **oxen**) castrated bull

oxide *n* compound of oxygen and one other element

oxygen *n* gas in atmosphere essential to life

oyster *n* edible mollusc

oz. ounce

ozone *n* form of oxygen with pungent odour

——————— THESAURUS ———————

swamp

overwhelming crushing, devastating, overpowering, shattering, stunning

overwrought agitated, distracted, excited, frantic, keyed up, on edge, tense, wired *Sl*

owe be beholden to, be in arrears, be in debt, be indebted, be under an obligation to

owing *adj* due, outstanding, overdue, owed, payable, unpaid, unsettled

own *adj* individual, particular, personal, private ~*v* enjoy, have, hold, keep, possess, retain; acknowledge, admit, allow, avow, concede, confess, disclose, grant, recognize

owner holder, landlord, lord, master, mistress, possessor, proprietor

ownership dominion, possession, proprietorship, title

P p

p page; pence; penny; *Mus* piano (softly)

pace *n* step; rate of movement ~*v* step; set speed for; measure **pacemaker** *n* electronic device to regulate heartbeat; person who sets speed for race

pacify *v* -ifying, -ified calm **pacifism** *n* **pacifist** *n* advocate of abolition of war; one who refuses to help in war

pack *n* bundle; band of animals; large set of people or things ~*v* put together in suitcase etc.; make into a bundle; cram; fill **package** *n* parcel; set of items offered together ~*v* put into packages **packet** *n* small parcel; small container (and contents)

pact *n* covenant, agreement

pad *n* soft stuff used as a cushion, protection etc.; block of sheets of paper; foot or sole of various animals ~*v* **padding, padded** make soft, fill in, protect etc., with pad; walk with soft step

paddle[1] *n* short oar with broad blade ~*v* move by, as with, paddles

paddle[2] *v* walk with bare feet in shallow water

paddock *n* small grass enclosure

paddy field field where rice is grown

padlock *n/v* (fasten with) detachable lock with hinged hoop

paediatrics *pl n* (*with sing v*) branch of medicine dealing with diseases of children **paediatrician** *n*

paella *n* Spanish dish of rice, chicken, shellfish etc.

pagan *adj/n* heathen

page[1] *n* one side of leaf of book etc.

page[2] *n* boy attendant ~*v* summon by loudspeaker announcement or electronic device **pager** *n* small portable electronic signalling device

pageant *n* show of persons in costume in procession, dramatic scenes etc.

pagoda *n* pyramidal temple of Chinese or Indian type

pail *n* bucket

pain *n* bodily or mental suffering; *pl* trouble ~*v* inflict pain upon **painful** *adj* **painkiller** *n* drug that reduces pain **painstaking** *adj* careful

paint *n* colouring matter spread on a

THESAURUS

---

pace *n* gait, measure, step, stride, tread, walk; progress, rate, speed, tempo, time, velocity ~*v* march, patrol, pound, stride; count, mark out, measure, step

pack *n* bale, bundle, load, package, packet, parcel; band, bunch, collection, company, crew, crowd, gang, group, lot, mob, troop ~*v* bundle, load, package, store, stow; compact, compress, cram, fill, jam, press, ram, stuff

package *n* box, carton, container, parcel; combination, unit, whole ~*v* box, pack, wrap

packet bag, carton, container, package, parcel

pact agreement, alliance, bargain, bond, contract, covenant, deal, treaty

pad *n* buffer, cushion, protection, stuffing, wad; jotter, notepad, tablet, writing pad; foot, paw, sole ~*v* cushion, pack, protect, stuff

paddle[1] *v* oar, propel, pull, row

paddle[2] *n* dabble, plash, wade

page[1] folio, leaf, sheet, side

page[2] *n* footboy, pageboy, squire ~*v* call, summon

pageant display, parade, procession, show, spectacle, tableau

pain *n* ache, hurt, pang, spasm, throb, twinge; affliction, agony, distress,

surface ~*v* colour, coat, or make picture of, with paint **painter** *n* **painting** *n*

pair *n* set of two ~*v* arrange in twos

pal *n Inf* friend

palace *n* residence of king, bishop etc.; stately mansion **palatial** *adj*

palate *n* roof of mouth; sense of taste **palatable** *adj* agreeable to eat

palaver *n* fuss

pale *adj* wan, whitish ~*v* whiten; lose superiority

palette *n* artist's flat board for mixing colours on

palindrome *n* word etc., that is the same when read backwards or forwards

paling *n* upright plank in fence

pall¹ *n* cloth spread over a coffin **pallbearer** *n* one carrying coffin at funeral

pall² *v* become tiresome; cloy

pallet *n* portable platform for storing and moving goods

palliate *v* relieve without curing; excuse **palliative** *adj/n*

pallid *adj* pale **pallor** *n*

palm *n* inner surface of hand; tropical tree; its leaf as symbol of victory

palmistry *n* fortune-telling from lines on palm of hand

palomino *n* (*pl* **-nos**) golden horse with white mane and tail

palpable *adj* obvious

palpitate *v* throb

palsy *n* paralysis

paltry *adj* worthless

pamper *v* overindulge, spoil

pamphlet *n* thin unbound book

pan- *comb. form* all, as in **panAmerican**

pan¹ *n* broad, shallow vessel; bowl of lavatory; depression in ground ~*v* **panning, panned** *Inf* criticize harshly

pan² *v* **panning, panned** move film camera slowly while filming

panacea *n* universal remedy ·

panache *n* dashing style

panama *n* straw hat

pancake *n* thin cake of batter fried in pan

pancreas *n* digestive gland behind stomach

panda *n* large black and white bearlike mammal of China

pandemonium *n* din and uproar

pander *v* (*esp. with* **to**) give gratification to ~*n* pimp

——————— THESAURUS ———————

grief, heartache, misery, suffering, torment, torture ~*v* chafe, hurt, smart, sting, throb; afflict, aggrieve, distress, grieve, hurt, sadden, torment, torture, wound

painful disagreeable, distasteful, grievous, unpleasant; agonizing, inflamed, raw, smarting, sore, tender

painkiller anaesthetic, analgesic, drug, sedative

painstaking assiduous, careful, conscientious, diligent, meticulous, scrupulous, thorough

paint *n* colour, colouring, dye, emulsion, pigment, stain, tint ~*v* delineate, depict, draw, picture, portray, represent, sketch; apply, coat, colour,

cover, daub

pair *n* brace, couple, duo ~*v* couple, join, marry, match, mate, team, twin, wed

pale anaemic, ashen, bleached, colourless, faded, light, pallid, pasty, wan, white

pamper baby, coddle, cosset, indulge, pet, spoil

pamphlet booklet, brochure, circular, leaflet, tract

pan *n* container, pot, saucepan, vessel ~*v* censure, criticize, knock *Inf,* slate *Inf*

panache dash, élan, flamboyance, flourish, style

pandemonium bedlam, din, hulla-

pane *n* sheet of glass

panegyric *n* speech of praise

panel *n* compartment of surface, usu. raised or sunk, e.g. in door; team in quiz game etc.; list of jurors, doctors etc. ~*v* **-elling, -elled** adorn with panels

pang *n* sudden pain

panic *n* sudden and infectious fear ~*v* **-icking, -icked** (cause to) feel panic **panicky** *adj*

pannier *n* basket carried by beast of burden, bicycle etc.

panoply *n* magnificent array

panorama *n* wide view

pansy *n* flower, species of violet; *Inf* effeminate man

pant *v/n* gasp

pantechnicon *n* large van, esp. for carrying furniture

panther *n* variety of leopard

pantomime *n* theatrical show, usu. at Christmas time, often founded on a fairy tale

pantry *n* room for storing food or utensils

pants *pl n* undergarment for lower trunk; *US* trousers

pap *n* soft food

papacy *n* office of Pope **papal** *adj* of the Pope

paper *n* material made by pressing pulp of rags, wood etc., into thin sheets; sheet of paper; newspaper; es-

say; *pl* documents etc. ~*v* cover with paper **paperback** *n* book with flexible covers

papier-mâché *n* paper pulp mixed with paste, shaped and dried hard

paprika *n* red pepper

papyrus *n* (*pl* **papyri**) species of reed; paper made from this

par *n* equality of value or standing; face value; *Golf* estimated standard score **parity** *n* equality; analogy

parable *n* allegory, story with moral lesson

parachute *n* apparatus extending like umbrella used to slow the descent of falling body ~*v* drop by parachute

parade *n* display; muster of troops ~*v* march; display

paradise *n* Heaven; state of bliss; Garden of Eden

paradox *n* statement that seems self-contradictory **paradoxical** *adj*

paraffin *n* waxlike or liquid hydrocarbon mixture used as fuel, solvent, etc.

paragon *n* pattern or model of excellence

paragraph *n* section of chapter or book ~*v* arrange in paragraphs

parakeet *n* small parrot

parallel *adj/n* (line or lines) continuously at equal distances; (thing) precisely corresponding ~*v* represent as similar **parallelogram** *n* four-sided

———————— THESAURUS ————————

baloo, racket, uproar

pang pain, spasm, stab, sting, twinge

panic alarm, consternation, fear, fright, scare, terror

panorama prospect, scenery, view, vista

pant blow, gasp, heave, huff, puff

paper *n* (*oft. pl*) certificate, deed, documents, record

par *n* average, level, mean, norm, standard, usual

parable allegory, fable, moral tale

parade *n* display, ostentation, show, spectacle; array, cavalcade, ceremony, march, pageant, procession, review, spectacle ~*v* display, exhibit, flaunt, show, show off *Inf*, strut, swagger

paradise bliss, delight, heaven

paradox ambiguity, contradiction, enigma, puzzle

paragon exemplar, ideal, model, nonpareil, pattern

paragraph clause, item, part, pas-

figure with opposite sides parallel

paralysis *n* (*pl* -yses) incapacity to move or feel **paralyse** *v* affect with paralysis; make immobile **paralytic** *adj/n*

paramedic *n* person working in support of medical profession

parameter *n* limiting factor

paramilitary *adj* organized on military lines

paramount *adj* supreme

paranoia *n* mental disease with delusions of persecution etc. **paranoid** *adj/n*

parapet *n* low wall along edge of bridge etc.

paraphernalia *pl n* (*used as sing*) belongings; equipment

paraphrase *v* express in other words

paraplegia *n* paralysis of lower body **paraplegic** *n/adj*

parasite *n* animal or plant living in or on another **parasitic** *adj*

parasol *n* sunshade

paratroops, -troopers *pl n* troops trained to descend by parachute

parboil *v* boil until partly cooked

parcel *n* packet ~*v* -celling, -celled

wrap up; divide into parts

parch *v* make, become hot and dry

parchment *n* sheep, goat, calf skin prepared for writing

pardon *v* forgive, excuse ~*n* forgiveness; release from punishment

pare *v* peel, trim; decrease

parent *n* father or mother **parentage** *n* descent, extraction **parental** *adj* **parenthood** *n*

parenthesis *n* word(s) inserted in passage **parentheses** *pl n* round brackets, (), used to mark this

pariah *n* social outcast

parish *n* district under one clergyman **parishioner** *n* inhabitant of parish

parity *see* PAR

park *n* large area of land in natural state for recreational use ~*v* leave for short time; manoeuvre (car) into suitable space

parka *n* warm waterproof coat

parlance *n* particular way of speaking

parley *v/n* (hold) discussion about terms

parliament *n* law-making assembly of country **parliamentary** *adj*

parlour *n* sitting room

sage, portion, section, subdivision

parallel *adj* analogous, like, matching, similar ~*n* counterpart, equivalent, match, twin; analogy, comparison, likeness, resemblance, similarity

paralyse cripple, disable, incapacitate, lame; arrest, freeze, halt, immobilize, petrify

parameter framework, guideline, limit, limitation, restriction

paramount chief, first, foremost, greatest, highest, pre-eminent, prime, principal, top

paraphernalia apparatus, belongings, effects, gear, stuff, tackle, trappings

paraphrase rephrase, restate, reword

parasite hanger-on, leech, scrounger,

sponger *Inf*

parcel *n* bundle, carton, package *v* (*oft. with* up) do up, pack, package, tie up, wrap

parch dehydrate, desiccate, dry up, shrivel, wither

pardon *v* absolve, acquit, condone, excuse, exonerate, forgive, let off *Inf*, overlook, reprieve ~*n* absolution, acquittal, amnesty, forgiveness, release, remission, reprieve

parentage ancestry, birth, descent, family, line, lineage, origin, pedigree, race, stock

park estate, garden, grounds, parkland

parliament assembly, congress, council, senate

parochial *adj* narrow, provincial; of a parish

parody *n/v* **-odying, -odied** (write) satirical, amusing imitation of a work

parole *n* release of prisoner on condition of good behaviour *~v* release on parole

paroxysm *n* sudden attack of pain, rage, laughter

parquet *n* flooring of wooden blocks

parrot *n* brightly coloured bird which can imitate speaking *~v* **parroting, parroted** repeat words without thinking

parry *v* **parrying, parried** ward off, turn aside

parsimony *n* stinginess **parsimonious** *adj*

parsley *n* herb used for seasoning, garnish etc.

parsnip *n* root vegetable

parson *n* clergyman

part *n* portion; role; duty; region; component *~v* divide; separate **parting** *n* division of hair on head; separa-

tion; leave-taking **partly** *adv* in part

partake *v* **partaking, partook** take or have share in; take food or drink

partial *adj* not complete; prejudiced; fond of **partially** *adv* partly

participate *v* share in; take part **participant** *n* **participation** *n*

participle *n* *Grammar* verbal adjective

particle *n* minute portion

particular *adj* relating to one; distinct; fussy *~n* detail, item; *pl* items of information **particularly** *adv*

partisan *n* adherent of a party; guerilla *~adj* adhering to faction; prejudiced

partition *n* division; interior dividing wall *~v* divide into sections

partner *n* ally or companion; spouse **partnership** *n*

partridge *n* game bird

party *n* social assembly; group of persons organized together, esp. with common political aim; person

pass *v* go by, beyond, through etc.;

──────── T H E S A U R U S ────────

parlour front room, lounge, sitting room

parody *n* burlesque, caricature, lampoon, satire, send-up *Brit inf*, skit, spoof *Inf*, takeoff *Inf* *~v* burlesque, caricature, lampoon, satirize, send up *Brit inf*, travesty

part *n* bit, fraction, fragment, piece, portion, scrap, section, slice; capacity, duty, function, place, role, task, work; component, constituent, element, ingredient, member, unit *~v* break, cleave, come apart, detach, divide, separate, split, tear

partake (*with* in) engage, participate, share, take part

partial incomplete, limited, uncompleted, unfinished; biased, one-sided, partisan, prejudiced, unfair, unjust

participate enter into, join in, share, take part

particle atom, bit, crumb, grain, jot, piece, scrap, shred, speck

particular *adj* distinct, exact, peculiar, precise, special, specific; choosy *Inf*, demanding, discriminating, exacting, fastidious, finicky, fussy, pernickety *Inf*

parting adieu, farewell, goodbye; breaking, division, separation, split

partisan *n* adherent, backer, devotee, supporter, upholder *~adj* biased, one-sided, partial, prejudiced, sectarian

partition *n* division, segregation, separation; barrier, screen, wall *~v* apportion, cut up, divide, separate, share, split up, subdivide

partner ally, associate, colleague, helper, mate, team-mate; consort, helpmate, husband, mate, spouse, wife

exceed; transfer; spend; elapse; undergo examination successfully; bring a law into force ~*n* way, esp. through mountains; permit; successful result **passable** *adj* (just) acceptable **passing** *adj* transitory; casual **pass away** die **pass out** faint

passage *n* opening; corridor; part of book etc.; voyage, fare

passé *adj* out-of-date

passenger *n* traveller, esp. by public conveyance

passion *n* ardent desire; any strong emotion; great enthusiasm **passionate** *adj*

passive *adj* submissive; inactive

passport *n* official document granting permission to travel abroad etc.

password *n* secret word to ensure admission etc.

past *adj* ended; gone by; elapsed ~*n* bygone times ~*adv* by; along ~*prep* beyond; after

pasta *n* any of several preparations of dough, e.g. spaghetti

paste *n* soft mixture; adhesive ~*v* fasten with paste **pasting** *n* *Sl* defeat; strong criticism **pasty** *adj* like paste; white; sickly

pastel *n* coloured crayon; drawing with crayons; pale, delicate colour ~*adj* (of colour) pale

pasteurize *v* sterilize by heat

pastiche *n* work of art that mixes or copies styles

pastille *n* lozenge

pastime *n* recreation

pastor *n* clergyman **pastoral** *adj* of rural life; of pastor

pastry *n* article of food made chiefly

party celebration, do *Inf*, festivity, function, knees-up *Brit inf*, reception, social; alliance, cabal, camp, clique, coalition, confederacy, league, set, side

pass *v* flow, go, move, proceed, roll, run; exceed, excel, go beyond, outdo, outstrip, surmount, surpass; convey, deliver, give, hand, send, transfer; get through, graduate, qualify, succeed; accept, approve, decree, ratify ~*n* authorization, identification, licence, passport, permission, permit, ticket, warrant

passable acceptable, adequate, all right, so-so *Inf*, tolerable

passage alley, avenue, channel, lane, thoroughfare, way; corridor, hall, lobby, vestibule; excerpt, extract, paragraph, piece, quotation, reading, section; crossing, journey, tour, trek, trip, voyage

passing *adj* brief, ephemeral, fleeting, momentary, short, transient, transitory; casual, cursory, quick, short, slight, superficial

passion ardour, emotion, feeling, fervour, fire, heat, intensity, spirit, zeal; ardour, desire, love, lust; bug *Inf*, craze, enthusiasm, fascination, infatuation, mania, obsession

passionate amorous, ardent, erotic, hot, loving, lustful, sensual; ardent, emotional, fervent, fierce, impassioned, intense, strong, vehement, wild

passive compliant, docile, inactive, inert, quiescent, submissive

past *adj* completed, done, elapsed, ended, finished, gone, over; ancient, bygone, erstwhile, former, late, olden, previous ~*n* background, experience, history, life

pastel delicate, light, pale, soft

pastiche blend, hotchpotch, medley, *mélange,* miscellany, mixture

pastime activity, amusement, diversion, entertainment, game, hobby, recreation, sport

pastoral *adj* rural, rustic, simple; clerical, ecclesiastical, ministerial, priestly

of flour, fat and water

pasture *n* ground on which cattle graze ~*v* (cause to) graze

pasty *n* small pie of meat and crust, baked without a dish

pat¹ *v* **patting, patted** tap ~*n* tap; small mass, as of butter

pat² *adv* exactly; fluently

patch *n* piece of cloth sewed on garment; spot; plot of ground ~*v* mend; repair clumsily **patchy** *adj* of uneven quality **patchwork** *n* needlework of different pieces sewn together

pate *n* head; top of head

pâté *n* spread of finely minced liver etc.

patent *n* exclusive right to invention ~*adj* open; evident ~*v* secure a patent **patently** *adv* obviously

paternal *adj* fatherly; of a father **paternity** *n* fatherhood

path *n* way, track; course of action

pathetic *adj* moving to pity

pathology *n* science of diseases **pathological** *adj* **pathologist** *n*

pathos *n* power of exciting tender emotions

patient *adj* bearing troubles calmly

~*n* person under medical treatment

patience *n*

patio *n* (*pl* **-tios**) paved area adjoining house

patriarch *n* father and ruler of family

patrician *n/adj* (one) of noble birth

patriot *n* person that loves his or her country **patriotic** *adj* **patriotism** *n*

patrol *n* regular circuit by guard; person, small group patrolling ~*v* **-trolling, -trolled** go round on guard

patron *n* one who aids artists, charities etc.; regular customer; guardian saint **patronage** *n* support given by patron **patronize** *v* assume air of superiority towards; be regular customer

patter *n* quick succession of taps; *Inf* glib, rapid speech ~*v* make quick tapping noise

pattern *n* arrangement of repeated parts; design; plan for cutting cloth etc.; model ~*v* (*with* **on** *or* **after**) model

paunch *n* belly

pauper *n* very poor person

pause *v/n* stop, rest

pave *v* form surface with stone **pave-**

──────── THESAURUS ────────

pat *v* dab, slap, stroke, tap ~*n* clap, dab, light blow, slap, stroke, tap

patch *n* bit, scrap, shred, spot; area, ground, land, plot, tract

patent *adj* apparent, clear, conspicuous, downright, evident, manifest, obvious, open, unmistakable ~*n* copyright, licence

path footway, track, trail; avenue, course, direction, passage, road, route, way

pathetic affecting, moving, pitiable, poignant, sad, touching

pathos pitifulness, poignancy, sadness

patience forbearance, sufferance, tolerance, toleration

patient *adj* long-suffering, philo-

sophical, resigned, stoical, uncomplaining

patron advocate, backer, benefactor, champion, friend, helper, sponsor, supporter; buyer, client, customer, shopper

patronage aid, assistance, backing, encouragement, help, promotion, sponsorship, support

patronize look down on, talk down to; frequent, shop at

pattern *n* arrangement, decoration, design, device, figure, motif; design, diagram, guide, instructions, plan, template; example, guide, model, norm, original, prototype, sample, specimen, standard ~*v* form, model, mould, shape, style

ment *n* paved footpath

pavilion *n* clubhouse on playing field etc.; building for exhibition etc.; large tent

paw *n* foot of animal ~*v* scrape with forefoot; maul

pawn¹ *v* deposit (article) as security for money borrowed **pawnbroker** *n* lender of money on goods deposited

pawn² *n* piece in chess; person used as mere tool

pay *v* **paying, paid** give money etc., for goods or services; give; be profitable to; (*with* **out**) spend ~*n* wages **payable** *adj* justly due **payee** *n* person to whom money is paid or due **payment** *n*

PC personal computer; Police Constable; Privy Councillor

PE physical education

pea *n* edible seed, growing in pods, of climbing plant; the plant

peace *n* freedom from war; harmony; calm **peaceable** *adj* disposed to peace **peaceful** *adj*

peach *n* fruit of delicate flavour

peacock *n* male bird with fanlike tail

peak *n* pointed end of anything, esp.

hilltop; highest point

peal *n* (succession of) loud sound(s) ~*v* sound loudly

peanut *n* pea-shaped nut; *pl Inf* trifling amount of money

pear *n* tree yielding sweet, juicy fruit; the fruit **pear-shaped** *adj* shaped like a pear, heavier at the bottom than the top

pearl *n* hard, lustrous structure found esp. in oyster and used as jewel

peasant *n* member of low social class, esp. in rural district

peat *n* decomposed vegetable substance

pebble *n* small roundish stone

peccadillo *n* (*pl* **-los, -loes**) slight offence; petty crime

peck *v* strike with or as with beak; nibble at; *Inf* kiss quickly ~*n* pecking movement **peckish** *adj Inf* hungry

pectoral *adj* of the breast

peculiar *adj* strange; particular; belonging to **peculiarity** *n* oddity; characteristic; distinguishing feature

pedal *n* foot lever ~*v* **-alling, -alled** propel bicycle by using its pedals; use pedal

pause *v* break, cease, desist, discontinue, halt, interrupt, rest ~*n* break, breather *Inf*, gap, halt, interlude, intermission, interval, let-up *Inf*, lull, respite, rest

pawn *n* cat's-paw, instrument, puppet, stooge *Sl*, tool

pay *v* clear, compensate, discharge, foot, give, honour, meet, reimburse, requite, reward, settle; bestow, give, grant, hand out, present ~*n* earnings, fee, income, remuneration, salary, wages

payment discharge, paying, remittance, settlement; fee, remuneration, wage

peace armistice, conciliation, treaty, truce; accord, agreement, concord,

harmony; calm, calmness, quiet, silence, stillness, tranquillity

peaceful amicable, friendly, nonviolent; calm, placid, quiet, restful, serene, still, tranquil, undisturbed

peak *n* apex, crest, pinnacle, point, summit, tip, top; climax, crown, culmination, zenith

peal *n* chime, clang, clap, crash, ring, rumble ~*v* chime, crash, resonate, resound, ring, roll, rumble, toll

peasant countryman, hick *Inf, chiefly US & Canad*, rustic, yokel

peculiar abnormal, bizarre, curious, eccentric, funny, odd, quaint, queer, strange, uncommon, unusual, weird

peculiarity abnormality, eccentricity, foible, mannerism, oddity, quirk

pedant *n* one who insists on petty details of book-learning, grammatical rules etc. **pedantic** *adj*

peddle *v* go round selling goods

pedestal *n* base of column

pedestrian *n* one who walks on foot ~*adj* going on foot; commonplace; dull **pedestrian crossing** place marked where pedestrians may cross road

pedigree *n* register of ancestors; genealogy

pedlar *n* one who sells; hawker

peek *v/n* peep, glance

peel *v* strip off skin, rind or covering; flake off, as skin, rind ~*n* rind, skin

peep *v* look slyly or quickly ~*n* such a look

peer[1] *n* (*fem* **peeress**) nobleman; one of the same rank **peerage** *n* **peerless** *adj* without match or equal **peer group** group of people of similar age, status etc.

peer[2] *v* look closely

peeved *adj Inf* sulky, irritated

peevish *adj* fretful; irritable

peewit *n* lapwing

peg *n* pin for joining, fastening, marking etc.; (mark of) level, standard etc. ~*v* **pegging, pegged** fasten with pegs; stabilize (prices); (*with* **away**) persevere

pejorative *adj* (of words etc.) with disparaging connotation

pelican *n* waterfowl with large pouch beneath its bill **pelican crossing** road crossing with pedestrian-operated traffic lights

pellet *n* little ball

pelmet *n* ornamental drapery or board, concealing curtain rail

pelt[1] *v* throw missiles; rain persistently; rush

pelt[2] *n* raw hide or skin

pelvis *n* bony cavity at base of human trunk **pelvic** *adj*

pen[1] *n* instrument for writing ~*v* **penning, penned** compose; write **pen friend** friend with whom one corresponds without meeting **penknife** *n* small knife with folding blade

pen[2] *n/v* **penning, penned** (put in) enclosure

penal *adj* of punishment **penalize** *v* impose penalty on **penalty** *n* punishment; forfeit; *Sport* handicap

penance *n* suffering submitted to as expression of penitence

pence *n pl of* PENNY

penchant *n* inclination, decided taste

pedantic academic, fussy, hair-splitting, nit-picking *Inf*, particular, pompous, precise, punctilious

pedestal base, foot, plinth, stand, support

pedigree ancestry, blood, breed, descent, family, genealogy, heritage, line, lineage, race, stock

peel flake off, pare, scale, skin, strip off

peer[1] *n* aristocrat, noble, nobleman; equal, fellow

peer[2] *v* gaze, inspect, scan

peerless incomparable, matchless, unequalled, unrivalled

peevish cantankerous, cross, crotchety *Inf*, fractious, grumpy, irritable, querulous, snappy, testy, touchy

pelt batter, bombard, cast, hurl, shower, sling, throw

pen *n* cage, coop, enclosure, fold, hutch, sty ~*v* cage, coop up, enclose, fence in

penal corrective, disciplinary, punitive

penalize discipline, handicap, punish

penalty fine, forfeit, handicap, price, punishment

penance atonement, reparation

penchant bent, bias, fondness, inclination, leaning, liking, partiality, propensity, taste, tendency

pencil *n* instrument, esp. of graphite, for writing etc. ~*v* -cilling, -cilled draw; mark with pencil

pendant *n* hanging ornament **pendent** *adj* hanging

pending *prep* during, until ~*adj* awaiting settlement; imminent

pendulous *adj* hanging, swinging **pendulum** *n* suspended weight swinging to and fro

penetrate *v* enter into; pierce; arrive at meaning of **penetrating** *adj* sharp; easily heard; quick to understand **penetration** *n*

penguin *n* flightless bird

penicillin *n* antibiotic drug

peninsula *n* portion of land nearly surrounded by water **peninsular** *adj*

penis *n* male organ of copulation and urination

penitent *adj* affected by sense of guilt ~*n* one that repents **penitence** *n* sorrow for sin **penitentiary** *adj* ~*n* US prison

pennant *n* long narrow flag

pennon *n* small pointed flag

penny *n* (*pl* **pence, pennies**) Brit. bronze coin, 100th part of pound **penniless** *adj* having no money

pension *n* regular payment to old people, soldiers etc. ~*v* grant pension to **pensioner** *n*

pensive *adj* thoughtful

pent *adj* shut up, kept in

pentacle, pentagram *n* five-pointed star

pentagon *n* figure with five angles

penthouse *n* apartment, flat on top of building

penultimate *adj* next before the last

penury *n* extreme poverty

peony *n* plant with showy red, pink, or white flowers

people *pl n* persons generally, nation; race; family ~*v* populate

pep *n Inf* vigour; energy ~*v* **pepping, pepped** give energy, enthusiasm **pep talk** *Inf* talk designed to increase confidence, enthusiasm etc.

pepper *n* pungent aromatic spice; slightly pungent vegetable ~*v* season with pepper; sprinkle; pelt with missiles **peppermint** *n* plant noted for aromatic pungent liquor distilled from it; sweet flavoured with this

per *prep* for each; by; in manner of

perambulate *v* walk through or over; walk about **perambulator** *n* pram

per annum *Lat* by the year

per capita *Lat* for each person

perceive *v* obtain knowledge of through senses; understand **perceptible** *adj* **perception** *n* **perceptive** *adj*

percentage *n* proportion or rate per hundred **per cent** in each hundred

perch[1] *n* freshwater fish

———— THESAURUS ————

penetrate bore, enter, go through, pierce, stab

penitent *adj* apologetic, contrite, regretful, remorseful, repentant, sorry

penniless broke *Inf*, destitute, down and out, impoverished, indigent, poor, poverty-stricken, skint *Brit sl*

pension allowance, annuity, benefit, superannuation

pensive contemplative, dreamy, meditative, musing, preoccupied, reflective, thoughtful

people *pl n* humanity, mankind, persons; citizens, clan, community, family, folk, nation, population, public, race, tribe ~*v* colonize, inhabit, occupy, populate, settle

perceive discern, discover, note, notice, observe, recognize, remark, see, spot

perceptible apparent, appreciable, clear, detectable, discernible, evident, noticeable, observable, recognizable, visible

perception awareness, consciousness, discernment, feeling, idea, im-

perch[2] *n* resting place, as for bird ~*v* place, as on perch; alight on branch etc.; balance on

perchance *adv Obs* perhaps

percolate *v* pass through fine mesh as liquor; filter **percolator** *n* coffeepot with filter

percussion *n* striking of one thing against another

peregrine *n* type of falcon

peremptory *adj* imperious

perennial *adj* lasting through the years; perpetual ~*n* plant lasting more than two years

perfect *adj* complete; unspoilt; correct, precise; excellent ~*v* improve; make skilful **perfection** *n* **perfectionist** *n* one who demands highest standards **perfectly** *adv*

perfidy *n* treachery, disloyalty **perfidious** *adj*

perforate *v* make holes in, penetrate **perforation** *n*

perform *v* fulfil; function; act part; play, as on musical instrument

performance *n*

perfume *n* agreeable scent ~*v* imbue with an agreeable odour

perfunctory *adj* done indifferently

perhaps *adv* possibly

peril *n* danger; exposure to injury **perilous** *adj*

perimeter *n* outer boundary of area; length of this

period *n* particular portion of time; series of years; single occurrence of menstruation; full stop ~*adj* (of furniture, dress etc.) belonging to a particular time in history **periodic** *adj* recurring at regular intervals **periodical** *adj* periodic ~*n* publication issued at regular intervals **periodic table** *Chem* chart showing relationship of elements to each other

peripatetic *adj* travelling about

periphery *n* circumference; outside **peripheral** *adj* unimportant

periscope *n* instrument used for giving view of objects on different level

perish *v* die; rot **perishable** *adj* that

———————— THESAURUS ————————

pression, insight, recognition, sensation, sense, understanding

perceptive acute, alert, astute, discerning, observant, quick, sharp

perch *v* alight, balance, land, rest, roost, settle, sit on

perennial abiding, constant, continual, enduring, incessant, lasting, persistent, recurrent

perfect *adj* absolute, complete, consummate, finished, full, sheer, utter, whole; faultless, flawless, ideal, immaculate, impeccable, pure, spotless, unspoilt, untarnished ~*v* develop, hone, improve, polish, refine

perfection achievement, completion, consummation, fulfilment; completeness, exactness, faultlessness, purity, wholeness

perform accomplish, achieve, act, carry out, complete, discharge, do,

effect, execute, fulfil, function, work; act, play

performance accomplishment, achievement, act, carrying out, completion, discharge, execution, fulfilment; acting, appearance, gig *Inf,* play, portrayal, production, show

perfume aroma, bouquet, fragrance, odour, scent, smell

perfunctory careless, cursory, indifferent, negligent, offhand, superficial

perhaps maybe, perchance *Arch,* possibly

peril danger, hazard, jeopardy, menace, risk

perimeter border, boundary, bounds, circumference, confines, edge, limit, margin

period interval, season, space, spell, term, time, while

periodical *n* journal, magazine, pa-

will not last long **perishing** adj Inf very cold

perjure v be guilty of perjury **perjury** n crime of false testimony on oath

perk n incidental benefit from employment

perky adj lively, cheerful

perm n long-lasting curly hairstyle ~v give a perm

permanent adj continuing in same state; lasting **permanence** n

permeate v pervade; pass through pores of **permeable** adj

permit v -mitting, -mitted allow; give leave to ~n warrant or licence to do something **permissible** adj **permission** n **permissive** adj (too) tolerant, esp. sexually

permutation n Maths arrangement of a number of quantities in every possible order

pernicious adj wicked; harmful

pernickety adj Inf fussy

peroxide n short for HYDROGEN PEROXIDE

perpendicular adj/n (line) at right angles to another; (something) exactly upright

perpetrate v perform or be responsible for (something bad)

perpetual adj continuous; lasting forever **perpetuate** v make perpetual; not to allow to be forgotten **perpetuity** n

perplex v puzzle; bewilder **perplexity** n

persecute v oppress because of race, religion etc. **persecution** n

persevere v persist, maintain effort **perseverance** n

persist v continue in spite of obstacles or objections **persistence** n **persistent** adj

person n individual (human) being; body of human being; Grammar classification of pronouns and verb forms according to the person speaking,

———————— T H E S A U R U S ————————

per, publication, serial

perish be killed, die, expire, lose one's life, pass away; decay, decompose, rot, waste

perjury false statement, forswearing, oath breaking

permanent abiding, constant, durable, enduring, eternal, everlasting, fixed, immutable, invariable, lasting, perpetual, persistent, stable, unchanging

permeate fill, impregnate, penetrate, pervade, saturate

permissible acceptable, allowable, all right, authorized, lawful, legal, legitimate, O.K. or okay Inf, permitted

permission assent, authorization, consent, freedom, go-ahead Inf, green light, leave, licence, permit, sanction

permissive free, lax, liberal, tolerant

permit v agree, allow, authorize, consent, give leave or permission, let, li-

cense, sanction ~n licence, pass, passport, warrant

perpetrate carry out, commit, do, execute, perform

perpetual abiding, endless, enduring, eternal, everlasting, immortal, lasting, perennial, permanent

perpetuate maintain, preserve, sustain

perplex baffle, bewilder, confound, confuse, mystify, puzzle, stump

persecute harass, ill-treat, maltreat, oppress, torment, victimize

perseverance dedication, determination, doggedness, persistence, resolution, tenacity

persevere carry on, continue, go on, keep going, maintain, persist

persist continue, persevere; carry on, continue, keep up, last, remain

persistence doggedness, endurance, perseverance, tenacity

persistent determined, dogged, per-

spoken to, or of **personable** *adj* pleasant in looks and personality **personal** *adj* individual, private; of grammatical person **personality** *n* distinctive character; celebrity **personally** *adv* independently; in one's own opinion **personal computer** small computer for word processing or computer games **personal stereo** portable cassette player with headphones

persona *n* (*pl* **-nae**) someone's personality as presented to others

personify *v* **-fying, -fied** represent as person; typify **personification** *n*

personnel *n* staff employed in organization

perspective *n* mental view; method of drawing on flat surface to give effect of relative distances and sizes

Perspex *n* *Trademark* transparent acrylic substitute for glass

perspicacious *adj* having quick mental insight

perspire *v* sweat **perspiration** *n*

persuade *v* make (one) do something

by argument, charm etc.; convince **persuasion** *n* art, act of persuading; belief **persuasive** *adj*

pert *adj* forward, saucy

pertain *v* belong, relate, have reference (to)

pertinacious *adj* persistent

pertinent *adj* to the point **pertinence** *n* relevance

perturb *v* disturb; alarm

peruse *v* read in careful or leisurely manner **perusal** *n*

pervade *v* spread through **pervasive** *adj*

pervert *v* turn to wrong use; lead astray ~*n* one who practises sexual perversion **perverse** *adj* obstinately or unreasonably wrong; wayward **perversion** *n* sexual act considered abnormal; corruption **perversity** *n*

peseta *n* Spanish monetary unit

pessimism *n* tendency to see worst side of things **pessimist** *n* **pessimistic** *adj*

pest *n* troublesome or harmful thing,

——————— T H E S A U R U S ———————

severing, pertinacious, tenacious

person being, body, human, individual, soul

personal individual, own, particular, private, special

personality character, disposition, make-up, nature, temperament; celebrity, household name, star

personification embodiment, epitome, incarnation, representation

personify embody, epitomize, represent, symbolize, typify

personnel employees, people, staff, workers

perspective angle, attitude, context, outlook, way of looking

persuade coax, entice, induce, influence, prompt, sway, urge, win over

persuasive cogent, compelling, convincing, forceful, logical, moving, sound, telling, weighty

pertain apply, befit, belong, concern, regard, relate

pertinent apposite, appropriate, apt, fit, fitting, germane, material, relevant

perturb agitate, alarm, disquiet, disturb, fluster, trouble, unsettle, upset, vex

pervade fill, imbue, infuse, penetrate, permeate, spread through, suffuse

perverse contrary, obstinate, pigheaded, stiff-necked, stubborn, wayward

perversion aberration, abnormality, deviation, kink *Brit inf*, kinkiness *Sl*

pervert *v* distort, misuse, twist, warp; corrupt, debase, debauch, degrade, deprave, lead astray ~*n* degenerate, deviant

pessimism cynicism, gloom, hopelessness

person or insect **pesticide** n chemical
for killing pests, esp. insects

pester v vex; harass

pestilence n epidemic disease

pestle n instrument with which things
are pounded

pet n animal or person kept or regarded with affection ~adj favourite ~v
petting, petted make pet of; Inf fondle

petal n white or coloured leaflike part
of flower

peter v **peter out** Inf lose power
gradually

petite adj small, dainty

petition n request, esp. to sovereign
or parliament ~v present petition to

petrel n sea bird

petrify v **-fying, -fied** turn to stone;
make motionless with fear

petroleum n mineral oil **petrol** n refined petroleum as used in motorcars
etc.

petticoat n woman's underskirt

pettifogging adj overconcerned with
unimportant detail

petty adj unimportant; small-minded
petty cash cash kept to pay minor ex-

penses **petty officer** noncommissioned officer in navy

petulant adj irritable; peevish

petunia n garden plant

pew n fixed seat in church

pewter n greyish alloy of tin and lead

phallus n (pl **-luses, -li**) penis; symbol
of it used in primitive rites **phallic** adj

phantom n apparition; ghost

Pharaoh n title of ancient Egyptian
kings

pharmaceutical adj of drugs or
pharmacy **pharmacist** n person qualified to dispense drugs **pharmacology**
n study of drugs **pharmacy** n preparation and dispensing of drugs; dispensary

phase n distinct stage in development
phase in, out introduce or discontinue gradually

PhD Doctor of Philosophy

pheasant n game bird

phenomenon n (pl **phenomena**)
anything observed; remarkable person or thing **phenomenal** adj

phial n small bottle

philanthropy n practice of doing
good to one's fellow men **philan-**

———————————— T H E S A U R U S ————————————

pessimist cynic, defeatist, wet blanket Inf, worrier

pessimistic bleak, cynical, gloomy,
glum, hopeless

pest annoyance, bother, drag Inf, irritation, nuisance; bane, blight, curse,
plague

pester aggravate Inf, annoy, badger,
bother, bug Inf, harass, nag, plague,
torment

pet n darling, favourite ~adj favourite,
preferred, special ~v coddle, cosset,
pamper, spoil; caress, fondle, pat,
stroke

petition n appeal, entreaty, plea,
prayer, request, supplication ~v adjure, appeal, ask, beg, beseech, entreat, plead, pray

petty inconsiderable, insignificant,
negligible, paltry, slight, small, trifling, trivial, unimportant; cheap,
mean, shabby, small-minded, ungenerous

petulant bad-tempered, cross, huffy,
irritable, moody, peevish, querulous,
sulky, sullen

phantom apparition, ghost, phantasm, spectre, spirit

phase chapter, juncture, period,
point, stage, step, time

phenomenal extraordinary, marvellous, miraculous, outstanding, prodigious, remarkable, sensational

phenomenon marvel, prodigy, rarity, sensation, wonder

philanthropist altruist, benefactor,

thropic *adj* philanthropist *n*

philately *n* stamp collecting philatelist *n*

philistine *n/adj* ignorant (person)

philosophy *n* study of realities and general principles; system of theories on nature of things or on conduct philosopher *n* philosophical *adj* of, like philosophy; wise, learned; calm, stoical

phlegm *n* thick yellowish substance formed in throat phlegmatic *adj* not easily agitated

phobia *n* fear or aversion

phoenix *n* legendary bird

phone *n* telephone; telephone call; *v* telephone phonecard *n* card used to operate some public telephones

phonetic *adj* of vocal sounds phonetics *pl n* (*with sing v*) science of vocal sounds

phoney *Inf adj* sham; suspect ~*n* phoney person or thing

phosphorus *n* nonmetallic element which appears luminous in the dark phosphate *n* compound of phosphorus phosphorescence *n* faint glow in the dark

photo *n Inf* photograph

photocopy *n* photographic reproduction ~*v* make photocopy of

photogenic *adj* tending to look attractive when photographed

photograph *n* picture made by chemical action of light on sensitive film ~*v* take photograph of photographer *n* photographic *adj* photography *n*

photosynthesis *n* process by which green plant uses sun's energy to make carbohydrates

phrase *n* group of words; expression ~*v* express in words phraseology *n* choice of words

physics *pl n* (*with sing v*) science of properties of matter and energy physical *adj* bodily, as opposed to mental; material physician *n* qualified medical practitioner physicist *n* one skilled in, or student of, physics

physiognomy *n* face

physiology *n* science of living things

physiotherapy *n* therapeutic use of physical means, as massage etc. physiotherapist *n*

physique *n* bodily structure, constitution

pi *n* (*pl* pis) *Maths* ratio of circumference of circle to its diameter

piano *n* (*pl* pianos) musical instrument with keyboard ~*adj/adv Mus* softly pianist *n* performer on piano

piazza *n* square

pic *n* (*pl* pics, pix) *Inf* photograph or

humanitarian

philistine *n* boor, ignoramus, lout, lowbrow ~*adj* anti-intellectual, boorish, crass, ignorant, lowbrow, tasteless, uncultured, unrefined

philosophical calm, collected, composed, cool, imperturbable, resigned, stoical, unruffled

philosophy knowledge, reason, reasoning, thinking, thought, wisdom

phobia aversion, detestation, dread, fear, hatred, horror, loathing, revulsion, terror

phoney *adj* bogus, counterfeit, fake, false, forged, imitation, pseudo *Inf*, sham ~*n* counterfeit, fake, forgery, fraud, humbug, impostor, pretender, sham

photograph *n* photo *Inf*, picture, shot, slide, snap *Inf*, snapshot ~*v* film, record, shoot, snap *Inf*

phrase *n* expression, idiom, saying ~*v* couch, express, frame, put, put into words, say, word

physical bodily, corporal, corporeal, fleshly; material, real, solid, substantial, tangible

physique body, build, figure, form,

illustration

picador *n* mounted bullfighter with lance

piccalilli *n* pickle of vegetables in mustard sauce

piccolo *n* (*pl* **-los**) small flute

pick[1] *v* choose, select carefully; pluck, gather; find occasion for ~*n* act of picking; choicest part **pick on** find fault with **pickpocket** *n* thief who steals from someone's pocket **pick up** lift; obtain; collect; get better; accelerate **pick-up** *n* small truck; device for conversion of mechanical energy into electric signals

pick[2] tool with curved iron crossbar **pickaxe** *n* pick

picket *n* pointed stake; party of trade unionists posted to deter would-be workers during strike ~*v* post as picket

pickle *n* food preserved in brine, vinegar etc.; awkward situation ~*v* preserve in pickle

picnic *n* pleasure excursion including meal out of doors ~*v* **picnicking, picnicked** take part in picnic

picture *n* drawing or painting; mental image; film, movie; *pl* cinema ~*v* represent in, or as in, a picture **pictorial**

adj of, in, with pictures ~*n* newspaper with pictures **picturesque** *adj* visually striking, vivid

pidgin *n* language made up of two or more other languages

pie *n* baked dish of meat, fruit etc. usu. with pastry crust

piebald *adj* irregularly marked with black and white **pied** *adj* piebald; variegated

piece *n* bit, part, fragment; single object; literary or musical composition etc. ~*v* mend, put together **piecemeal** *adv* by, in, or into pieces, a bit at a time

pier *n* structure running into sea; piece of solid upright masonry

pierce *v* make hole in; make a way through **piercing** *adj* shrill; alert, probing

piety *n* godliness; devoutness

pig *n* wild or domesticated mammal killed for pork, ham, bacon; *Inf* greedy, dirty person **piggish, piggy** *adj* **pig-headed** *adj* obstinate

pigeon *n* bird of wild and domesticated varieties **pigeonhole** *n* compartment for papers in desk etc. ~*v* defer; classify

piggyback *n* ride on the back

—————— THESAURUS ——————

frame, shape

pick *v* choose, decide upon, opt for, select, single out; collect, gather, harvest, pluck, pull ~*n* choice, option, preference, selection; cream, elect, elite

pick on bait, bully, tease, torment

pick up hoist, lift, raise, take up, uplift; buy, obtain, purchase; call for, collect, get

picture *n* drawing, illustration, image, likeness, painting, photograph, portrait, print, representation, sketch; account, depiction, description, image; film, movie ~*v* see, visualize

picturesque attractive, beautiful,

charming, pretty, scenic, striking, vivid

piebald black and white, dappled, pied

piece bit, chunk, division, fraction, fragment, morsel, part, portion, scrap, section, segment, shred, slice; article, composition, item, study, work

pierce bore, drill, enter, penetrate, puncture, stab, transfix

piercing *usu. of sound* ear-splitting, high-pitched, penetrating, sharp, shrill, alert, keen, penetrating, sharp, shrewd

piety devotion, faith, godliness, holi-

pigment *n* colouring matter, paint or dye

pigmy *see* PYGMY

pigtail *n* plait of hair on either side of head

pike¹ *n* predatory freshwater fish

pike² *n* long-handled spear

pilau, pilaf *n* Oriental dish of meat or fowl boiled with rice, spices etc.

pilchard *n* small sea fish like herring

pile¹ *v* heap (up); (*with* **in, out, off** *etc.*) crowd ~*n* heap **pile-up** *n Inf* traffic accident with several vehicles

pile² *n* beam driven into the ground, esp. as foundation

pile³ *n* nap of cloth

piles *pl n* haemorrhoids

pilfer *v* steal small items

pilgrim *n* one who journeys to sacred place **pilgrimage** *n*

pill *n* small ball of medicine swallowed whole **the pill** oral contraceptive

pillage *v/n* plunder

pillar *n* upright support; strong supporter **pillar box** red pillar-shaped letter box

pillion *n* seat behind rider of motorcycle or horse

pillory *n* frame with holes for head and hands in which offender was confined ~*v* **pillorying, pilloried** expose to ridicule and abuse

pillow *n* cushion for the head, esp. in bed **pillowcase** *n* removable cover for pillow

pilot *n* person qualified to fly an aircraft or spacecraft; one qualified to take charge of ship entering or leaving harbour etc.; guide ~*adj* experimental and preliminary ~*v* act as pilot to; steer **pilot light** small flame lighting main one in gas appliance

pimento *or* **pimiento** *n* (*pl* **-tos**) allspice; sweet red pepper

pimp *n* one who solicits for prostitute ~*v* act as pimp

pimpernel *n* plant with small scarlet, blue, or white flowers

pimple *n* small pus-filled spot on skin **pimply** *adj*

pin *n* piece of stiff wire with point and head, for fastening; wooden or metal peg or rivet ~*v* **pinning, pinned** fasten with pin; seize and hold fast **pinpoint** *v* identify exactly **pinstripe** *n* very narrow stripe in fabric **pin-up** *n* picture of sexually attractive person

pinafore *n* apron; dress with bib top

pincers *pl n* tool for gripping; claws of lobster etc.

pinch *v* nip, squeeze; stint; *Inf* steal; *Inf* arrest ~*n* nip; small amount; emergency

pine¹ *n* evergreen coniferous tree; its wood

pine² *v* yearn; waste away with grief,

——————————— T H E S A U R U S ———————————

ness, religion, reverence, veneration

pig-headed inflexible, obstinate, perverse, self-willed, stiff-necked, stubborn, unyielding, wilful

pigment colour, dye, paint, stain, tint

pile *n* accumulation, heap, mass, mound, mountain, stack ~*v* accumulate, amass, heap, mass, stack

pile-up accident, collision, crash, smash

pill capsule, pellet, tablet

pillage *v* loot, plunder, raid, ransack, sack, strip ~*n* plunder, sack

pillar column, post, prop, shaft, support, upright; mainstay, rock, supporter, upholder

pilot *n* airman, aviator, helmsman, steersman ~*adj* model, test, trial ~*v* control, direct, drive, fly, guide, handle, manage, operate, steer

pimple boil, pustule, spot, zit *Sl*

pin *v* affix, attach, fasten, fix, secure; fix, hold fast, immobilize, pinion

pinch *v* nip, press, squeeze ~*n* nip, squeeze; dash, jot, mite, *soupçon*, speck; crisis, difficulty, emergency,

longing etc.

pineapple *n* tropical plant bearing large edible fruit

pinion *n* bird's wing *~v* confine by binding wings, arms etc.

pink *n* pale red colour; garden plant; best condition *~adj* of the colour pink *~v* pierce; cut indented edge; (of engine) knock

pinnacle *n* highest point; mountain peak; pointed turret

pint *n* liquid measure; 1/8 gallon (.568 litre)

pioneer *n* explorer; early settler; originator *~v* act as pioneer

pious *adj* devout; self-righteous

pip[1] *n* seed in fruit

pip[2] *n* high-pitched sound as time signal on radio; spot on cards, dice etc.; *Inf* star on junior officer's shoulder showing rank

pipe *n* tube of metal or other material; tube with small bowl at end for smoking tobacco; musical instrument; *pl* bagpipes *~v* play on pipe; utter in shrill tone; convey by pipe; ornament with piping **piper** *n* **piping** *n* system of pipes; decoration of icing on cake; fancy edging on clothes **pipeline** *n* long pipe for transporting oil, water etc.

piquant *adj* pungent

pique *n* feeling of injury *~v* hurt pride of; irritate

piranha *n* fierce tropical Amer. fish

pirate *n* sea robber; publisher etc. who infringes copyright; person broadcasting illegally *~v* use or re-produce (artistic work etc.) illicitly **piracy** *n*

pirouette *n/v* (perform) act of spinning round on toe

pistachio *n* (*pl* **-os**) small hard-shelled, sweet-tasting nut

piste *n* ski slope

pistol *n* small firearm for one hand

piston *n* in engine, cylindrical part propelled to and fro in hollow cylinder

pit *n* deep hole in ground; mine or its shaft; depression; part of theatre occupied by orchestra; servicing area on motor-racing track *~v* **pitting**, **pitted** set to fight, match; mark with small dents **pitfall** *n* hidden danger

pitch[1] *v* throw; set up; set the key of (a tune); fall headlong *~n* act of pitching; degree, height, intensity; slope; degree of highness or lowness of sound; *Sport* field of play **pitchfork** *n* fork for lifting hay etc. *~v* throw with, as with, pitchfork

pitch[2] *n* dark sticky substance obtained from tar or turpentine

———— **THESAURUS** ————

plight, predicament

pine (*oft. with* **for**) ache, crave, eat one's heart out over, hanker, hunger for, long, yearn; decline, fade, languish, waste

pinnacle apex, crest, crown, height, peak, summit, top, zenith

pinpoint define, distinguish, identify, locate

pioneer *n* colonist, explorer, settler; developer, founder, originator *~v* create, develop, establish, initiate, institute, invent, originate

pious devout, God-fearing, godly,

holy, religious, righteous, saintly

pipe *n* conduit, duct, hose, line, main, tube

pique *n* huff, hurt feelings, offence, resentment, umbrage, wounded pride *~v* affront, annoy, irk, mortify, nettle, offend, sting, wound

pirate *v* copy, crib *Inf*, plagiarize, poach, reproduce, steal

pit abyss, cavity, chasm, crater, hole, hollow, pothole

pitch *v* cast, chuck *Inf*, fling, heave, hurl, sling, throw, toss; erect, put up, set up *~n* degree, height, level, point,

pitcher *n* large jug

pith *n* tissue in stems and branches of certain plants; essential part **pithy** *adj* terse, concise; consisting of pith

pittance *n* small amount of money

pituitary *adj* of, pert. to, endocrine gland at base of brain

pity *n* sympathy for others' suffering; regrettable fact ~*v* pitying, pitied feel pity for **piteous** *adj* **pitiful** *adj* woeful; contemptible **pitiless** *adj* feeling no pity; hard, merciless

pivot *n* shaft or pin on which thing turns ~*v* furnish with pivot; hinge on one

pixie *n* fairy

pizza *n* baked disc of dough covered with savoury topping

pizzicato *adv/adj Mus* played by plucking strings with finger

pl. place; plate; plural

placard *n* notice for posting up or carrying poster

placate *v* pacify, appease

place *n* locality, spot; position; duty; town, village, residence, buildings; employment; seat, space ~*v* put in particular place; identify; make (order, bet etc.)

placebo *n* (*pl* **-bos, -boes**) inactive substance given to patient in place of active drug

placenta *n* (*pl* **-tas, -tae**) organ formed in uterus during pregnancy, providing nutrients for fetus; afterbirth

placid *adj* calm

plagiarism *n* presenting another's ideas, writing etc. as one's own **plagiarize** *v*

plague *n* highly contagious disease; *Inf* nuisance ~*v* trouble, annoy

plaice *n* flat fish

plaid *n* long Highland cloak or shawl; tartan pattern

plain *adj* flat, level; not intricate; clear, simple; candid, forthright; ordinary; without decoration; not beau-

——————— **THESAURUS** ———————

summit; angle, dip, gradient, incline, slope, tilt

piteous affecting, distressing, heartbreaking, heart-rending, moving, pathetic, pitiable, pitiful, poignant, sad

pitfall catch, danger, hazard, peril, snag, trap

pitiful distressing, heartbreaking, heart-rending, pathetic, piteous, pitiable, sad, wretched; contemptible, despicable, insignificant, low, mean, miserable, paltry, sorry, worthless

pitiless callous, cold-blooded, coldhearted, cruel, hardhearted, harsh, heartless, merciless, ruthless, unmerciful

pittance chicken feed *Sl*, peanuts *Sl*, slave wages

pity *n* clemency, compassion, condolence, sympathy, understanding ~*v* commiserate with, feel for, feel sorry for

pivot *n* axis, axle, fulcrum, swivel ~*v* revolve, rotate, spin, swivel, turn

placate appease, assuage, calm, mollify, pacify, propitiate

place *n* area, location, point, position, site, spot, station; district, hamlet, locale, locality, neighbourhood, quarter, region, vicinity; grade, position, rank, station, status; duty, function, responsibility, right, role; appointment, job, position, post ~*v* deposit, establish, fix, install, lay, locate, plant, position, put, rest, set, settle, situate, stand

placid calm, collected, composed, cool, equable, even-tempered, quiet, unexcitable, unruffled

plague *n* disease, epidemic, infection, pestilence; *Inf* bother, hassle *Inf*, irritant, nuisance, pest, problem ~*v* annoy, badger, bother, harass, hassle *Inf*, pester, tease, torment, trouble

tiful ~*n* tract of level country ~*adv* clearly

plaintiff *n Law* one who sues in court

plaintive *adj* sad, mournful

plait *n* braid of hair, straw etc. ~*v* weave into plaits

plan *n* scheme; way of proceeding; project; drawing; map ~*v* **planning**, **planned** make plan of; arrange beforehand

plane[1] *n* smooth surface; level; tool for smoothing wood ~*v* make smooth with plane ~*adj* perfectly flat or level

plane[2] *n* aeroplane

plane[3] *n* tree with broad leaves

planet *n* heavenly body revolving round sun **planetary** *adj*

planetarium *n* (*pl* **-iums**, **-ia**) apparatus that shows movement of sun, moon, stars and planets by projecting lights on inside of dome

plank *n* long flat piece of timber

plankton *n* minute animal and vegetable organisms floating in ocean

plant *n* living organism without power of locomotion; building and equipment for manufacturing purposes ~*v* set in ground to grow; establish; *Sl* hide

plantation *n* estate for cultivation of tea, tobacco etc.; wood of planted trees

plaque *n* ornamental tablet; plate of brooch; deposit on teeth

plasma *n* clear, fluid portion of blood

plaster *n* mixture of lime, sand etc. for coating walls etc.; adhesive dressing for cut, wound etc. ~*v* apply plaster to; apply like plaster **plastered** *adj Sl* drunk

plastic *n* synthetic substance, easily moulded and extremely durable ~*adj* made of plastic; easily moulded **plastic surgery** repair, reconstruction of part of body for medical or cosmetic reasons

Plasticine *n Trademark* modelling material like clay

plate *n* shallow round dish; flat thin sheet of metal, glass etc.; utensils of gold or silver; device for printing illustration in book; device to straighten children's teeth; *Inf* denture ~*v* cover with thin coating of metal

plateau *n* (*pl* **-eaus**, **-eaux**) tract of level high land; period of stability

platform *n* raised level surface, stage; raised area in station from which passengers board trains

platinum *n* white heavy malleable metal

platitude *n* commonplace remark

——————— T H E S A U R U S ———————

plain *adj* apparent, clear, distinct, evident, manifest, obvious, patent, unambiguous, unmistakable; artless, blunt, candid, direct, downright, forthright, frank, honest, open, outspoken, straightforward; common, commonplace, ordinary, simple, workaday; austere, bare, basic, severe, simple, stark, unadorned, unembellished; ugly, unattractive

plaintive *adj* doleful, grief-stricken, melancholy, mournful, pathetic, piteous, sad, sorrowful, woebegone, woeful

plan *n* design, method, plot, procedure, programme, project, proposal, proposition, scheme, strategy, system; blueprint, chart, diagram, drawing, map, representation, sketch ~*v* arrange, contrive, design, devise, draft, formulate, organize, outline, plot, scheme, think out

plane *adj* even, flat, flush, horizontal, level, regular, smooth

plant *v* scatter, seed, set out, sow, transplant

plaster *v* coat, cover, smear, spread

plastic *adj* flexible, mouldable, pliable, pliant, soft, supple

plate dish, platter; layer, panel, sheet

platform dais, podium, rostrum,

platonic *adj* (of love) purely spiritual, friendly

platoon *n* body of soldiers employed as unit

platter *n* flat dish

platypus *also* **duck-billed platypus** *n* Aust. egg-laying amphibious mammal

plaudit *n* act of applause

plausible *adj* apparently reasonable; persuasive

play *v* amuse oneself; contend with in game; take part in (game); trifle; act the part of; perform (music); perform on (instrument) ~*n* dramatic piece or performance; sport; amusement; activity; free movement; gambling **player** *n* **playful** *adj* lively **playboy** *n* rich man who lives for pleasure **playing card** one of set of 52 cards **playing fields** extensive piece of ground for open-air games **playwright** *n* author of plays

plaza *n* open space or square

plc public limited company

plea *n* entreaty; statement of prisoner

or defendant; excuse **plead** *v* **pleading, pleaded** *or US, Scots* **pled** make earnest appeal; address court of law; bring forward as excuse or plea

please *v* be agreeable to; gratify; delight; be willing ~*adv* word of request **pleasant** *adj* pleasing, agreeable **pleasantry** *n* joke, humour **pleased** *adj* pleasing *adj* **pleasurable** *adj* giving pleasure **pleasure** *n* enjoyment; satisfaction

pleat *n* fold made by doubling material ~*v* make into pleats

plebeian *adj/n* (one) of the common people

plectrum *n* (*pl* **-trums, -tra**) small implement for plucking strings of guitar etc.

pledge *n* solemn promise; thing given as security ~*v* promise, swear

plenary *adj* complete

plenipotentiary *adj/n* (envoy) having full powers

plenitude *n* abundance

plenty *n* abundance; quite enough **plenteous** *adj* ample **plentiful** *adj*

———— T H E S A U R U S ————

stage, stand

platter dish, plate, salver, tray

plausible believable, credible, glib, likely, persuasive, reasonable

play *v* challenge, compete, participate, take on, take part; act, perform, portray, represent ~*n* comedy, drama, dramatic piece, entertainment, performance, show, stage show, tragedy; fun, humour, jest, sport; amusement, diversion, entertainment, fun, game, pastime, recreation

playboy lady-killer *Inf,* philanderer, rake, womanizer

player competitor, contestant, participant; instrumentalist, musician, performer

playful frisky, frolicsome, gay, lively, merry, mischievous

plea appeal, entreaty, petition, prayer,

request, supplication

plead ask, beg, beseech, crave, entreat, implore, petition

pleasant agreeable, delightful, enjoyable, fine, nice, pleasurable, satisfying; affable, agreeable, amiable, charming, congenial, friendly, genial, likable, nice

please charm, content, delight, gladden, gratify, humour, indulge, rejoice, satisfy, suit

pleasure bliss, comfort, contentment, delight, enjoyment, gladness, gratification, happiness, joy, satisfaction

pledge *n* assurance, covenant, oath, promise, undertaking, vow; bail, bond, collateral, deposit, guarantee, security ~*v* contract, engage, promise, swear, undertake, vow

plentiful abundant, ample, bountiful,

plethora *n* oversupply

pleurisy *n* inflammation of membrane lining chest and covering lungs

pliable *adj* easily bent or influenced **pliant** *adj* pliable

pliers *pl n* tool with hinged arms and jaws for gripping

plight¹ *n* distressing state

plight² *v* promise

plimsolls *pl n* rubber-soled canvas shoes

plinth *n* slab as base of column etc.

plod *v* **plodding, plodded** walk or work doggedly

plonk¹ *v* put down heavily and carelessly

plonk² *n* Inf cheap inferior wine

plop *n* sound of object falling into water without splash ~*v* fall with this sound

plot¹ *n* secret plan, conspiracy; essence of story, play etc. ~*v* **plotting, plotted** plan secretly; mark position of; make map of

plot² *n* small piece of land

plough *n* implement for turning up soil ~*v* turn up with plough, furrow; work at slowly **ploughman** *n*

plover *n* shore bird with straight bill and long pointed wings

ploy *n* manoeuvre designed to gain advantage

pluck *v* pull, pick off; strip from; sound strings of (guitar etc.) with fingers, plectrum ~*n* courage; sudden pull or tug **plucky** *adj* brave

plug *n* thing fitting into and filling hole; *Electricity* device connecting appliance to electricity supply; *Inf* favourable mention of product etc. intended to promote it ~*v* **plugging, plugged** stop with plug; *Inf* advertise product etc. by frequently mentioning it

plum *n* fruit with stone; tree bearing it; choicest part, piece, position etc. ~*adj* choice

plumb *n* ball of lead attached to string used for sounding, finding the perpendicular etc. ~*adj* perpendicular ~*adv* exactly; perpendicularly ~*v* find depth of; equip with, connect to plumbing system **plumber** *n* worker who attends to water and sewage systems **plumbing** *n* trade of plumber; system of water and sewage pipes **plumb line** cord with plumb attached

plume *n* feather; ornament of feathers etc. ~*v* furnish with plumes; pride oneself **plumage** *n* bird's feathers

———————— THESAURUS ————————

copious, generous, lots *Inf*, mass, masses, oodles *Inf*, quantity

pliable bendy, flexible, malleable, plastic, pliant, supple; impressionable, pliant, susceptible, tractable, yielding

plight *n* difficulty, dilemma, jam *Inf*, pickle *Inf*, predicament, scrape *Inf*, spot *Inf*, trouble

plod tramp, tread, trudge

plot¹ *n* cabal, conspiracy, intrigue, plan, scheme, stratagem; outline, story, subject, theme ~*v* collude, conspire, intrigue, plan, scheme; calculate, chart, draft, draw, locate, map, mark

plot² *n* allotment, area, ground, lot, patch

plough *v* cultivate, dig, till, turn over

pluck *v* catch, jerk, tug, tweak, yank ~*n* boldness, bravery, courage, grit, guts *Inf*, nerve

plucky bold, brave, courageous, daring, game, gutsy *Sl*

plug *n* bung, stopper; mention, publicity, puff, push ~*v* bung, close, cork, seal, stop, stop up; *Inf* advertise, mention, publicize, puff, push, write up

plumb *n* lead, weight ~*v* fathom, gauge, measure, sound

plummet *v* plunge headlong ~*n* plumb line

plump¹ *adj* fat, rounded ~*v* make, become plump

plump² *v* drop, fall abruptly; choose

plunder *v* take by force; rob ~*n* booty, spoils

plunge *v* put forcibly, throw (into); descend suddenly ~*n* dive **plunger** *n* suction cap to unblock drains **plunging** *adj* (of neckline) cut low

plural *adj* of, denoting more than one ~*n* word in its plural form **plurality** *n* majority

plus *prep* with addition of (usu. indicated by the sign +) ~*adj* positive

plush *n* fabric with long nap ~*adj* luxurious

ply¹ *v* **plying, plied** wield; work at; supply insistently; go to and fro regularly

ply² *n* fold or thickness; strand of yarn **plywood** *n* board of thin layers of wood glued together

PM prime minister

p.m. after noon

PMT premenstrual tension

pneumatic *adj* of, worked by, inflated with wind or air

pneumonia *n* inflammation of the lungs

PO Post Office

poach¹ *v* take (game) illegally; encroach **poacher** *n*

poach² *v* simmer (eggs, fish etc.) gently in water etc.

pocket *n* small bag inserted in garment; cavity, pouch or hollow; isolated group or area ~*v* put into one's pocket; appropriate ~*adj* small **pocket money** small allowance, esp. for children

pod *n* long seed vessel, as of peas, beans etc.

podgy *adj* short and fat

podium *n* (*pl* **-diums, -dia**) small raised platform

poem *n* imaginative composition in rhythmic lines **poet** *n* writer of poems **poetic** *adj* **poetry** *n* art or work of poet, verse

poignant *adj* moving; keen **poignancy** *n*

point *n* dot; punctuation mark; detail; unit of value, scoring; degree, stage; moment; gist; purpose; special quality; sharp end; headland; direction mark on compass; movable rail changing train to other rails; power point ~*v* show direction or position by extending finger; direct; sharpen; fill up joints with mortar **pointed** *adj* sharp; direct **pointer** *n* indicating rod etc. used for pointing; indication; breed of gun dog **pointless** *adj* futile **point-blank** *adj* at short range; blunt, direct ~*adv* bluntly

poise *n* composure; self-possession;

plump buxom, chubby, fat, podgy, roly-poly, rotund, round, tubby

plunder *v* loot, pillage, raid, ransack, rob, sack, strip ~*n* booty, loot, pillage, spoils

plunge *v* cast, descend, dive, drop, fall, immerse, nose-dive, pitch, plummet, throw ~*n* descent, dive, drop, fall

plus *prep* added to, and, with ~*adj* added, additional, extra, positive

poach encroach, infringe, intrude,

steal, trespass

pocket *n* bag, compartment, pouch, receptacle, sack

podgy chubby, dumpy, fat, plump, roly-poly, rotund, tubby

poignant affecting, moving, pathetic, sad, touching

point *n* dot, full stop, period, stop; condition, degree, extent, stage; instant, juncture, moment, time; location, place, position, site, spot, stage; aim, design, end, goal, intent, inten-

balance **poised** *adj* ready; showing poise

poison *n* substance harmful or fatal to living organism ~*v* give poison to; infect **poisonous** *adj*

poke *v* push, thrust with finger, stick etc.; thrust forward; pry ~*n* act of poking **poker** *n* metal rod for poking fire **poky** *adj* small, confined, cramped

poker *n* card game

pole[1] *n* long, rounded piece of wood etc.

pole[2] *n* each of the ends of axis of earth or celestial sphere; each of opposite ends of magnet, electric cell etc. **polar** *adj* **polarize** *v* (cause to) form into groups with opposite views **polar bear** white bear that lives around North Pole

poleaxe *v* stun with heavy blow

polecat *n* small animal of weasel family

police *n* civil force which maintains public order ~*v* keep in order **police-man** *n* (*fem* **policewoman**) member of police force

policy[1] *n* course of action adopted, esp. in state affairs

policy[2] *n* insurance contract

polio *also* **poliomyelitis** *n* disease affecting spinal cord, often causing paralysis

polish *v* make smooth and glossy; refine ~*v* shine; polishing; substance for polishing; refinement

polite *adj* showing regard for others in manners, speech etc.; refined, cultured

politics *pl n* art of government; political affairs **politic** *adj* wise, shrewd **political** *adj* of the state or its affairs **politician** *n* one engaged in politics

polka *n* lively dance; music for it **pol-**

———————————————— T H E S A U R U S ————————————————

tion, motive, object, purpose, reason; aspect, attribute, characteristic, peculiarity, quality; apex, prong, spike, spur, summit, tip ~*v* direct, indicate, show, signify

point-blank *adj* abrupt, blunt, direct, downright, plain ~*adv* bluntly, frankly, openly, plainly, straight

pointed acute, barbed, sharp; biting, cutting, direct, incisive, pertinent, sharp

pointer hand, indicator, needle; advice, hint, recommendation, suggestion, tip

pointless aimless, futile, meaningless, senseless, useless, vain, worthless

poise aplomb, assurance, calmness, composure, cool *Sl*, sang-froid, self-possession

poised all set, prepared, ready, standing by, waiting; calm, collected, composed, self-confident, self-possessed

poison *n* bane, toxin, venom ~*v* con-

taminate, infect, pollute

poisonous noxious, toxic, venomous, virulent

poke *v/n* butt, dig, hit, jab, nudge, prod, push, shove, thrust

poky confined, cramped, narrow, small, tiny

pole mast, post, rod, shaft, staff, stick

police *n* constabulary, fuzz *Sl*, the law *Inf* ~*v* control, guard, patrol, protect, watch

policeman bobby *Inf*, constable, cop *Sl*, copper *Sl*, officer

policy action, approach, course, custom, practice, programme

polish *v* brighten, buff, burnish, clean, rub, shine, smooth; brush up, refine ~*n* brightness, brilliance, finish, gloss, lustre, sheen; class *Inf*, finesse, refinement, style, suavity, urbanity

polite civil, courteous, gracious, mannerly, respectful, well-behaved, well-mannered

ka dot one of pattern of bold spots on fabric etc.

poll *n* voting; counting of votes; number of votes recorded; survey of opinion ~*v* receive (votes); take votes of; vote **polling booth** voting place

pollen *n* fertilizing dust of flower **pollinate** *v*

pollute *v* make foul; corrupt **pollution** *n*

polo *n* game like hockey played on horseback **polo neck** (sweater with) tight turned-over collar

poltergeist *n* spirit believed to move furniture, throw objects around etc.

polyester *n* synthetic material

polygamy *n* custom of being married to several persons at a time **polygamist** *n*

polygon *n* figure with many angles or sides

polystyrene *n* synthetic material used esp. as rigid foam for packing etc.

polythene *n* tough light plastic material

polyunsaturated *adj* pert. to fats that do not form cholesterol in blood

polyurethane *n* synthetic material used esp. in paints

pomegranate *n* tree; its fruit with thick rind containing many seeds in red pulp

pommel *n* front of saddle; knob of sword hilt

pomp *n* splendid display or ceremony

pompom *n* decorative tuft of ribbon, wool, feathers etc.

pompous *adj* self-important; ostentatious; (of language) inflated, stilted

pond *n* small body of still water

ponder *v* muse, think over

ponderous *adj* heavy, unwieldy; boring

pong *n/v Inf* (give off) strong unpleasant smell

pontiff *n* Pope; bishop **pontificate** *v* speak dogmatically

pontoon[1] *n* flat-bottomed boat or metal drum for use in supporting temporary bridge

pontoon[2] *n* gambling card game

pony *n* horse of small breed **ponytail** *n* long hair tied at back of head

poodle *n* pet dog with long curly hair

pool[1] *n* small body of still water; deep place in river or stream; puddle; swimming pool

pool[2] *n* common fund or resources; group of people, e.g. typists, shared by several employers; collective stakes in various games ~*v* put in common fund

poop *n* ship's stern

poor *adj* having little money; unproductive; inadequate; inferior; miserable, pitiful **poorly** *adj* not in good health ~*adv* in poor manner

——————— T H E S A U R U S ———————

poll *n* ballot, canvass, census, count, survey

pollute contaminate, dirty, foul, infect, poison, soil, taint; besmirch, corrupt, debase, defile, desecrate, profane, sully

pollution contamination, corruption, impurity, taint, uncleanness

pompous affected, arrogant, grandiose, ostentatious, pretentious, showy

ponder cogitate, consider, contemplate, deliberate, meditate, mull over,

muse, reflect, think

pool *n* bank, funds, kitty, pot; collective, consortium, group, syndicate ~*v* amalgamate, combine, merge, share

poor broke *Inf*, destitute, hard up *Inf*, impecunious, impoverished, indigent, needy, penniless, poverty-stricken, skint *Brit sl*, stony-broke *Brit sl*; deficient, inadequate, insufficient, meagre, measly, miserable, niggardly, scanty, skimpy, sparse; inferior, low-grade, rotten *Inf*, rub-

pop[1] v popping, popped (cause to) make small explosive sound; put or place suddenly ~n small explosive sound **popcorn** n maize that puffs up when roasted

pop[2] n/adj (music) of general appeal, esp. to young people

Pope n bishop of Rome and head of R.C. Church

poplar n tall slender tree

poplin n corded fabric, usu. of cotton

poppadom n thin round crisp Indian bread

poppy n bright-flowered plant yielding opium

populace n the common people

popular adj finding general favour; of, by the people **popularity** n **popularize** v

populate v fill with inhabitants **population** n (number of) inhabitants **populous** adj thickly populated

porcelain n fine earthenware, china

porch n covered approach to entrance of building

porcupine n rodent covered with long, pointed quills

pore[1] v study closely

pore[2] n minute opening, esp. in skin

porous adj allowing liquid to soak through; full of pores

pork n pig's flesh as food

pornography n indecent literature, films etc. **pornographic** adj

porpoise n blunt-nosed sea mammal like dolphin

porridge n soft food of oatmeal etc. boiled in water

port[1] n (town with) harbour

port[2] n left side of ship

port[3] n strong red wine

port[4] n opening in side of ship **porthole** n small opening or window in side of ship

portable adj easily carried

portcullis n grating above gateway that can be lowered to block entrance

portend v foretell; be an omen of **portent** n omen

porter n person employed to carry luggage etc.; doorkeeper

portfolio n (pl -os) flat portable case for loose papers; collection of work, shares etc.

portico n (pl -coes) porch, covered walkway

portion n part, share, helping; destiny, lot ~v divide into shares

———————————— THESAURUS ————————————

bishy, sorry, substandard, unsatisfactory

pop v bang, burst, explode, go off; insert, push, put, shove, slip, stick, thrust ~n bang, burst, explosion

populace crowd, general public, hoi polloi, masses, multitude, people

popular approved, fashionable, favourite, in, in demand, in favour, liked, sought-after, well-liked; common, current, general, prevailing, public, universal

populate colonize, inhabit, occupy, settle

population community, folk, inhabitants, natives, people, residents

pore[1] v brood, dwell on, examine, pe-

ruse, ponder, read, scrutinize, study

pore[2] n hole, opening, orifice, outlet

pornographic blue, dirty, filthy, indecent, lewd, obscene, salacious, smutty

pornography dirt, filth, indecency, obscenity, porn Inf, smut

port anchorage, harbour, haven

portable handy, light, manageable, movable

portend augur, betoken, bode, foreshadow, foretell, herald, indicate, omen, predict

portent augury, forewarning, indication, omen, premonition, sign, threat, warning

porter bearer, carrier; caretaker, con-

portly *adj* bulky, stout

portmanteau *n* (*pl* -teaus, -teaux) leather suitcase, esp. one opening into two compartments

portray *v* make pictures of, describe **portrait** *n* likeness of (face of) individual **portraiture** *n* **portrayal** *n* act of portraying

pose *v* place in attitude; put forward; assume attitude; affect or pretend to be a certain character ~*n* attitude, esp. one assumed for effect

poser *n* puzzling question

posh *adj* luxurious; upper-class

position *n* place; situation; attitude; status; employment ~*v* place in position

positive *adj* sure; definite; assertive; constructive; not negative ~*n* something positive

possess *v* own; have mastery of **possession** *n* act of possessing; ownership; *pl* things a person possesses **possessive** *adj* of, indicating possession; with excessive desire to possess, control

possible *adj* that can, or may be, exist, happen or be done; worthy of consideration **possibility** *n* feasibility; chance **possibly** *adv* perhaps

possum *see* OPOSSUM

post[1] *n* upright pole to support or mark something ~*v* display; stick up (on notice board etc.) **poster** *n* large advertisement

post[2] *n* official carrying of letters or parcels; collection or delivery of these; office; situation; place of duty; fort ~*v* put into official box for carriage by post; station (soldiers etc.) in

——————————— T H E S A U R U S ———————————

cierge, doorman, gatekeeper

portion bit, part, piece, section, segment; allocation, allotment, allowance, lot, quota, ration, share; helping, piece

portrait image, likeness, painting, photograph, picture, representation

portray depict, draw, illustrate, paint, picture, represent, sketch; characterize, depict, describe

pose *v* arrange, position, sit; advance, present, propound, put, set, state, submit (*oft. with* **as**) affect, impersonate, masquerade as, sham; posture, show off *Inf* ~*n* attitude, position, posture, stance; act, air, façade, front, masquerade, pretence

poser enigma, problem, puzzle, question, riddle

position *n* area, location, place, point, post, site, situation, spot, whereabouts; angle, attitude, outlook, point of view, stance, standpoint, view, viewpoint; prestige, rank, reputation, status; duty, employment, job, occupation, office,

place, post, situation ~*v* arrange, fix, lay out, locate, place, put, set, settle, stand

positive assured, certain, confident, convinced, sure; absolute, actual, categorical, certain, clear-cut, conclusive, concrete, definite, firm, real; beneficial, constructive, helpful, practical, productive, useful

possess have, hold, own; control, dominate, hold, occupy

possession control, custody, hold, occupation, ownership; *pl* assets, belongings, chattels, effects, property, things

possessive controlling, dominating, domineering, jealous

possibility feasibility, likelihood, plausibility, workableness; chance, hope, liability, odds, prospect, risk

possible conceivable, credible, likely, potential; attainable, feasible, practicable, realizable, viable, workable; hopeful, likely, potential, promising

possibly maybe, perchance *Arch*, perhaps

particular spot **postage** *n* charge for carrying letter **postal** *adj* **postal order** written order for payment of sum of money **postcard** *n* stamped card sent by post **postman** *n* (*fem* **postwoman**) person who collects and delivers post **postmark** *n* official mark stamped on letters **post office** place where postal business is conducted

post- *comb. form* after, later than, as in **postwar**

posterior *adj* later, hind ~*n* buttocks

posterity *n* later generations; descendants

posthaste *adv* with great speed

posthumous *adj* occurring after death

postmortem *n* medical examination of dead body

postpone *v* put off to later time, defer

postscript *n* addition to letter, book

postulate *v* take for granted ~*n* something postulated

posture *n* attitude, position of body ~*v* pose

posy *n* bunch of flowers

pot *n* round vessel; cooking vessel ~*v* **potting, potted** put into, preserve in pot **potluck** *n* whatever is available

potassium *n* white metallic element

potato *n* (*pl* **-toes**) plant with tubers grown for food; one of these tubers

potent *adj* powerful, influential **potency** *n*

potentate *n* ruler

potential *adj* that might exist or act but does not now ~*n* possibility

pothole *n* hole in surface of road; underground cave

potion *n* dose of medicine or poison

potpourri *n* fragrant mixture of dried flower petals; medley

potter[1] *n* maker of earthenware vessel **pottery** *n* earthenware; where it is made; art of making it

potter[2] *v* work, act in unsystematic way

potty[1] *adj Inf* crazy, silly

potty[2] *n* bowl used by small child as toilet

pouch *n* small bag; pocket ~*v* put into pouch

poultice *n* soft composition of mustard, kaolin etc., applied hot to sore or inflamed parts of body

poultry *n* domestic fowls

pounce *v* spring (upon) suddenly, swoop (upon) ~*n* swoop, sudden descent

——————— THESAURUS ———————

post[1] *n* column, picket, pillar, pole, shaft, stake, support, upright

post[2] *n* collection, delivery, mail; appointment, employment, job, office, place, position, situation ~*v* dispatch, mail, send, transmit; assign, establish, locate, place, position, put, situate, station

poster advertisement, bill, notice, placard

postpone adjourn, defer, delay, put back, shelve, suspend

postscript addition, afterthought, P.S.

posture *n* attitude, bearing, carriage, set, stance ~*v* affect, pose, show off

Inf, try to attract attention

potent forceful, mighty, powerful, strong

potential *adj* future, hidden, latent, likely, possible, promising ~*n* ability, capability, capacity, possibility

potion brew, concoction, dose, draught, elixir, mixture

potter dabble, footle *Inf,* mess about, tinker

pottery ceramics, earthenware, stoneware, terra cotta

pouch bag, container, pocket, purse, sack

pounce *v* attack, drop, jump, spring, strike, swoop ~*n* attack, bound,

pound[1] *v* beat, thump; crush to pieces or powder; walk, run heavily

pound[2] *n* British monetary unit; unit of weight equal to 0.454 kg

pound[3] *n* enclosure for stray animals or officially removed vehicles

pour *v* come out in a stream, crowd etc.; flow freely; rain heavily ~*v* give out thus

pout *v* thrust out lips to look sulky ~*n* act of pouting

poverty *n* state of being poor; lack of, scarcity

POW prisoner of war

powder *n* solid matter in fine dry particles; medicine in this form; gunpowder; face powder etc. ~*v* apply powder to; reduce to powder **powdery** *adj*

power *n* ability to do or act; strength; authority; control; person or thing having authority; mechanical energy; electricity supply **powerful** *adj* **powerless** *adj*

pp pages

PR proportional representation; public relations

practical *adj* given to action rather than theory; sensible, realistic; skilled

practicable *adj* that can be done, used etc. **practically** *adv* all but; sensibly **practical joke** trick intended to make someone look foolish

practise *v* do repeatedly, work at to gain skill; do habitually; put into action; exercise profession **practice** *n* habit; exercise of art or profession; action, not theory

pragmatic *adj* concerned with practical consequences

prairie *n* large treeless tract of grassland

praise *n* commendation; fact of praising; expression of thanks to God ~*v*

——————— THESAURUS ———————

jump, leap, spring, swoop

pound[1] batter, beat, clobber *Sl*, hammer, strike, thump; crush, powder, pulverize

pound[2] *n* compound, enclosure, pen, yard

pour course, flow, gush, run, rush, spout, stream; bucket down *Inf*, pelt (down), teem

poverty beggary, destitution, hardship, insolvency, penury, privation, want; dearth, deficiency, insufficiency, lack, scarcity, shortage

powder *v* dredge, dust, scatter, sprinkle; crush, granulate, grind, pound, pulverize

power ability, capability, capacity, faculty, potential; energy, force, intensity, might, muscle, potency, strength; authority, authorization, licence, prerogative, right, warrant; authority, command, control, dominion, influence, mastery, rule, sovereignty, sway

powerful mighty, potent, strapping, strong, sturdy, vigorous; authoritative, commanding, dominant, influential

powerless feeble, frail, helpless, impotent, incapable, incapacitated, ineffectual, weak

practicable achievable, attainable, doable, feasible, possible, viable, workable

practical applied, empirical, functional, pragmatic, realistic; businesslike, down-to-earth, hard-headed, realistic, sensible

practically all but, almost, just about, nearly, virtually, well-nigh; rationally, realistically, sensibly

practice custom, habit, method, routine, system, tradition, usage, way, wont; drill, exercise, preparation, rehearsal, training, work-out

practise drill, go over, prepare, rehearse, study, train; apply, carry out, do, follow, observe, perform; carry

precede *v* go, come before in rank, order, time etc. precedence *n* priority in position, rank, time etc. precedent *n* previous case or occurrence taken as rule

pram *n* carriage for baby

prance *v/n* swagger; caper

prank *n* mischievous trick

prattle *v* talk like child

prawn *n* edible sea shellfish like shrimp

pray *v* ask earnestly; entreat; offer prayers, esp. to God prayer *n* action, practice of praying to God; earnest entreaty

pre- *comb. form* before, as in prerecord, preshrunk

preach *v* deliver sermon; give moral, religious advice; advocate preacher *n*

preamble *n* introductory part of story etc.

precarious *adj* insecure, unstable, perilous

precaution *n* previous care to prevent evil or secure good

precept *n* rule for conduct

precinct *n* enclosed, limited area; *pl* environs

precious *adj* beloved, cherished; of great value

precipice *n* very steep cliff or rock face

precipitate *v* hasten happening of; throw headlong; *Chem* cause to be deposited in solid form from solution ~*adj* too sudden; rash ~*n* substance chemically precipitated precipitation *n* rain, snow etc.

precipitous *adj* steep; rash, hurried

précis *n* (*pl* précis) summary ~*v* summarize

precise *adj* definite; exact; careful in observance precisely *adv* precision *n*

──────── THESAURUS ────────

on, engage in, pursue, undertake

praise *n* acclaim, acclamation, accolade, applause, approval, commendation, compliment, plaudit, tribute; adoration, glory, thanks, worship ~*v* acclaim, applaud, approve, compliment, congratulate, extol, laud; adore, glorify, worship

praiseworthy admirable, commendable, creditable, laudable, meritorious

prance bound, caper, cavort, dance, frisk, gambol, skip

prank caper, escapade, jape, lark *Inf*, practical joke, trick

prattle babble, blether, chatter, gabble, jabber, rabbit (on) *Brit inf*, waffle *Inf, chiefly Brit,* witter *Inf*

pray ask, beg, beseech, entreat, implore, petition, plead, request

prayer devotion, litany, orison; appeal, entreaty, petition, plea, request

preach lecture, moralize, sermonize

preacher clergyman, evangelist, minister, missionary, parson

precarious dangerous, dicey *Inf, chiefly Brit*, dodgy *Brit, Aust, & NZ inf*, hazardous, insecure, perilous, risky, shaky, tricky, unsafe

precaution insurance, protection, safeguard

precede antedate, come first, go before, introduce, lead, preface

precedence primacy, priority, rank, seniority, superiority

precedent *n* antecedent, criterion, example, instance, model, pattern, standard

precinct area, district, quarter, section, sector, zone

precious adored, beloved, cherished, darling, dear, loved, prized, treasured, valued; costly, dear, invaluable, priceless, valuable

precise absolute, accurate, clear-cut, correct, definite, exact, literal, par-

preclude *v* prevent

precocious *adj* developed, matured early or too soon

preconceive *v* form an idea beforehand **preconception** *n*

precursor *n* forerunner

predatory *adj* preying on other animals **predator** *n*

predecessor *n* one who precedes another in office or position

predestined *adj* decreed beforehand **predestination** *n*

predicament *n* difficult situation

predict *v* foretell, prophesy **predictable** *adj* **prediction** *n*

predispose *v* incline, influence; make susceptible

predominate *v* be main or controlling element **predominance** *n* **predominant** *adj*

pre-eminent *adj* excelling all others **pre-eminence** *n*

pre-empt *v* do in advance of or to exclusion of others

preen *v* trim (feather) with beak;

smarten oneself

prefabricated *adj* (of building) manufactured in shaped sections for rapid assembly

preface *n* introduction to book etc. ~*v* introduce

prefect *n* person put in authority; schoolchild in position of limited authority over others

prefer *v* **-ferring, -ferred** like better; promote **preferable** *adj* more desirable **preference** *n* **preferential** *adj* special, privileged **preferment** *n* promotion

prefix *n* group of letters put at beginning of word ~*v* put as introduction; put as prefix

pregnant *adj* carrying fetus in womb; full of meaning, significant **pregnancy** *n*

prehistoric *adj* before period in which written history begins

prejudice *n* preconceived opinion; unreasonable or unfair dislike ~*v* influence; bias; injure **prejudicial** *adj*

—————————————— THESAURUS ——————————————

ticular, specific, strict

precision accuracy, correctness, exactness, meticulousness

precocious advanced, ahead, developed, forward

preconception bias, predisposition, prejudice, presupposition

predecessor antecedent, forerunner, precursor

predicament corner, fix *Inf,* jam *Inf,* mess, scrape *Inf,* situation, spot *Inf*

predict forecast, foretell, prophesy

prediction forecast, prognosis, prophecy

predispose dispose, incline, influence, lead, prompt

predominant chief, dominant, leading, main, prevailing, principal, ruling

pre-eminent excellent, foremost, outstanding, peerless, predominant,

superior, supreme, unrivalled, unsurpassed

preen *of birds* clean, plume; doll up *Sl,* dress up, spruce up, titivate

preface *n* foreword, introduction, preamble, prelude, prologue ~*v* begin, introduce, open, precede, prefix

prefer be partial to, choose, elect, fancy, favour, incline towards, opt for, pick, select

preference choice, favourite, first choice, option, partiality, pick, selection

preferential better, favoured, privileged, special, superior

pregnant expectant, expecting *Inf,* in the club *Brit sl,* in the family way *Inf,* preggers *Brit inf,* with child; charged, expressive, loaded, meaningful, pointed, significant, telling

prehistoric earliest, early, primeval,

preliminary *adj/n* preparatory, introductory (action, statement)

prelude *n* Mus introductory movement; performance, event etc. serving as introduction

premature *adj* happening, done before proper time

premeditated *adj* planned beforehand

premier *n* prime minister ~*adj* chief, foremost; first

première *n* first performance of play etc.

premise *n* Logic proposition from which inference is drawn

premises *pl n* house, building with its belongings

premium *n* (*pl* **-iums**) bonus; sum paid for insurance; excess over nominal value; great value or regard

premonition *n* presentiment

preoccupy *v* **-pying, -pied** occupy to exclusion of other things **preoccupation** *n*

preordained *adj* determined in advance

prepare *v* make, get ready; concoct, make **preparation** *n* making ready beforehand; something prepared, as a medicine **preparatory** *adj* serving to prepare; introductory **prepared** *adj* ready; willing

preponderate *v* be of greater weight or power **preponderance** *n*

preposition *n* word marking relation between noun or pronoun and other words

prepossessing *v* impressive

preposterous *adj* utterly absurd, foolish

prerequisite *n/adj* (something) required as prior condition

prerogative *n* peculiar power or right, esp. as vested in sovereign

prescribe *v* set out rules for; order use of (medicine) **prescription** *n* prescribing; thing prescribed; written statement of it

———————— T H E S A U R U S ————————

primitive, primordial

prejudice *n* preconception, prejudgment; bigotry, chauvinism, discrimination, intolerance, racism, sexism, unfairness ~*v* bias, colour, distort, influence, slant, sway; damage, harm, injure, spoil, undermine

preliminary *adj* first, initial, introductory, opening, preparatory, prior ~*n* beginning, groundwork, introduction, opening, preamble, preface, prelude, start

prelude beginning, introduction, overture, preamble, preface, prologue, start

premature early, immature, undeveloped, unripe, untimely; hasty, impulsive, overhasty, precipitate, rash

premeditated calculated, considered, deliberate, intentional, planned

premium bonus, fee, remuneration, reward

premonition feeling, foreboding, hunch, idea, intuition, presentiment

preparation development, getting ready groundwork; anticipation, foresight, precaution, provision, readiness, safeguard

preparatory introductory, opening, prefatory, preliminary

prepare arrange, fit, make ready, prime; assemble, concoct, construct, contrive, fashion, make, produce

prepared in order, in readiness, ready, set; disposed, inclined, predisposed, willing

preposterous absurd, crazy, foolish, impossible, incredible, insane, laughable, ludicrous, ridiculous, senseless, unthinkable

prerequisite *n* condition, must, necessity, precondition, qualification, requirement ~*adj* essential, indispensable, mandatory, necessary, obliga-

present¹ *adj* that is here; now existing or happening ~*n* present time or tense **presence** *n* being present; appearance, bearing **presently** *adv* soon; *US* at present

present² *v* introduce formally; show; give ~*n* gift **presentable** *adj* fit to be seen **presentation** *n* **presenter** *n*

presentiment *n* sense of something about to happen

preserve *v* keep from harm, injury or decay ~*n* special area; fruit preserved by cooking in sugar; place where game is kept for private fishing, shooting **preservation** *n* **preservative** *n* preserving agent ~*adj* preserving

preside *v* be in charge **presidency** *n* **president** *n* head of society, company, republic etc. **presidential** *adj*

press *v* subject to push or squeeze; smooth; urge; throng; hasten ~*n* machine for pressing, esp. printing machine; printing house; newspapers and journalists collectively; crowd **pressing** *adj* urgent; persistent

pressure *n* act of pressing; compelling force; *Physics* thrust per unit area

prestige *n* reputation; influence depending on it **prestigious** *adj*

presto *adv Mus* very quickly

presume *v* take for granted; take liberties **presumably** *adv* **presumption** *n* forward, arrogant opinion or conduct; strong probability **presumptive** *adj* that may be assumed is true or valid until contrary is proved **presumptuous** *adj* forward, impudent

presuppose *v* assume or take for

————————— T H E S A U R U S —————————

tory, required, vital

prescribe decree, define, dictate, direct, lay down, ordain, rule, set, specify, stipulate

prescription drug, medicine, mixture, preparation, remedy

presence attendance, existence, occupancy, residence; air, appearance, aspect, aura, bearing, demeanour

present¹ *adj* at hand, available, here, ready, there, to hand; contemporary, current, existing, immediate, instant ~*n* here and now, the time being, today

present² *v* acquaint with, introduce; advance, declare, extend, offer, put forward, state, submit, suggest, tender; display, exhibit, give, mount, put on, show, stage ~*n* donation, endowment, gift, grant, gratuity, hand-out, largess, offering

presentable acceptable, decent, fit to be seen, O.K. *or* okay *Inf,* passable, respectable, satisfactory, suitable

presentation award, bestowal, conferral, offering; demonstration, display, exhibition, performance, production, show

presently anon *Arch,* before long, by and by, shortly, soon

preservation conservation, maintenance, protection, safekeeping, safety

preserve *v* care for, conserve, guard, keep, protect, safeguard, save, shelter

preside administer, control, direct, govern, head, lead, manage, run

press *v* crush, depress, jam, mash, push, squeeze, stuff; flatten, iron, smooth; beg, entreat, exhort, implore, plead, urge *n* **the press** Fleet Street, fourth estate, journalism, news media, newspapers, the papers

pressing crucial, high-priority, imperative, important, serious, urgent, vital

pressure compression, crushing, force, squeezing, weight; coercion, compulsion, constraint, force, influence

prestige credit, honour, importance, influence, kudos, renown, reputation, standing, status

presumably apparently, it would

granted beforehand **presupposition** *n*

pretend *v* claim or allege (something untrue); make believe; lay claim (to) **pretence** *n* simulation **pretender** *n* claimant (to throne) **pretension** *n* **pretentious** *adj* making claim to special merit or importance; given to outward show

pretext *n* excuse; pretence

pretty *adj* appealing in a delicate way ~*adv* moderately

prevail *v* gain mastery; be generally established **prevalent** *adj* widespread; predominant

prevaricate *v* tell lies or speak evasively **prevaricator** *n*

prevent *v* stop, hinder **prevention** *n*

preventive *adj/n*

preview *n* advance showing

previous *adj* preceding; happening before **previously** *adv*

prey *n* animal hunted by another for food; victim ~*v* (*with* on) treat as prey; worry, obsess

price *n* that for which thing is bought or sold; cost ~*v* fix, ask price for **priceless** *adj* invaluable **pricey** *adj Inf* expensive

prick *v* pierce slightly; cause to feel sharp pain ~*n* slight hole made by pricking; sting **prickle** *n* thorn, spike ~*v* feel pricking sensation **prickly** *adj* thorny; stinging; touchy

pride *n* too high an opinion of oneself;

———— THESAURUS ————

seem, probably, seemingly

presume assume, believe, conjecture, guess *Inf, chiefly US & Canad,* infer, suppose, surmise, take for granted, take it, think

presumption audacity, cheek *Inf,* effrontery, gall *Inf,* impudence, insolence, nerve *Inf,* temerity

presuppose assume, postulate, presume, take as read, take for granted, take it

pretence acting, charade, feigning, sham, simulation

pretend affect, allege, assume, fake, falsify, feign, impersonate, profess, sham, simulate; imagine, play, suppose

pretension aspiration, assumption, claim, profession; affectation, airs, conceit, pomposity, pretentiousness, self-importance, show, snobbery, vanity

pretentious affected, conceited, extravagant, grandiloquent, grandiose, ostentatious, pompous, showy, snobbish

pretext cloak, cover, excuse, guise, mask, ploy, pretence, ruse, semblance, show

pretty *adj* attractive, beautiful, bonny, comely, fair, good-looking, lovely

prevail be victorious, overcomee, succeed, triumph, win

prevalent common, current, customary, established, fashionable, general, ordinary, popular, usual, widespread

prevaricate dodge, equivocate, evade, flannel *Brit inf,* hedge, lie

prevent avert, bar, block, check, frustrate, hamper, hinder, impede, inhibit, obstruct, restrain, stop, thwart

prevention bar, check, hindrance, impediment, interruption, obstacle, obstruction, stoppage

previous antecedent, earlier, erstwhile, former, past, preceding, prior

previously before, beforehand, earlier, formerly, hitherto, once

prey game, kill, quarry; dupe, target, victim

price *n* amount, assessment, charge, cost, expense, fee, figure, outlay, payment, rate, valuation, value, worth; consequences, cost, penalty, toll ~*v* assess, cost, estimate, evaluate, rate, value

priceless costly, dear, expensive, invaluable

worthy self-esteem; great satisfaction; something causing this; best part of something **pride oneself** take pride

priest *n* (*fem* **priestess**) official minister of religion **priesthood** *n*

prig *n* smug self-righteous person **priggish** *adj*

prim *adj* formal and prudish

primacy *n* supremacy

prima donna female opera singer

primary *adj* chief; earliest; elementary

primate[1] *n* one of order of mammals including monkeys and man

primate[2] *n* archbishop

prime *adj* fundamental; original; chief; best ~*n* first, best part of anything ~*v* prepare for use **primer** *n* paint for preliminary coating **Prime**

Minister leader of government

primeval *adj* of earliest age of the world

primitive *adj* of an early undeveloped kind; crude

primrose *n* pale yellow spring flower; this colour ~*adj* of this colour

prince *n* male member of royal family; ruler, chief **princely** *adj* generous; magnificent **princess** *n* female member of royal family

principal *adj* chief in importance ~*n* person for whom another is agent; head of institution, esp. school or college; sum of money lent and yielding interest **principality** *n* territory of prince

principle *n* moral rule; settled reason

———————— THESAURUS ————————

prick *v* jab, lance, perforate, pierce, puncture, stab; prickle, smart, sting, tingle ~*n* hole, perforation, pinhole, puncture, wound

prickle barb, needle, point, spike, spine, spur, thorn

prickly barbed, spiny, thorny; itchy, scratchy, sharp, smarting, stinging, tingling; bad-tempered, cantankerous, grumpy, irritable, peevish, snappish, tetchy, touchy

pride *n* arrogance, conceit, egotism, loftiness, pretension, pretentiousness, self-importance, snobbery, superciliousness, vanity; dignity, honour, self-esteem, self-respect, self-worth; delight, gratification, joy, pleasure, satisfaction ~*v* boast, brag, congratulate oneself, exult, glory in

priest clergyman, cleric, curate, divine, ecclesiastic, father, minister, padre *Inf*, pastor, vicar

prig goody-goody *Inf*, prude, puritan

priggish goody-goody *Inf*, holier-than-thou, prim, prudish, puritanical

prim demure, formal, fussy, precise, priggish, prissy *Inf*, proper, prudish, puritanical, strait-laced

prima donna diva, leading lady, star

primary cardinal, chief, first, greatest, highest, leading, main, paramount, prime, principal; basic, elemental, elementary, essential, fundamental

prime *adj* basic, fundamental, original, underlying; chief, leading, main, predominant, pre-eminent, principal, ruling; best, capital, choice, excellent, first-class, first-rate, highest, select, superior, top ~*n* bloom, flower, height, heyday, peak, zenith ~*v* get ready, make ready, prepare

primeval, primaeval ancient, early, first, old, prehistoric, primal, primitive, primordial

primitive earliest, early, elementary, first, primeval, primordial; crude, rough, rude, rudimentary, simple, uncivilized, unrefined

prince monarch, ruler, sovereign

princely bounteous, generous, lavish, liberal, munificent, rich

principal *adj* cardinal, chief, essential, first, foremost, highest, key, leading, main, paramount, pre-eminent, primary, prime ~*n* dean, head *Inf*, headmaster, headmistress, master, rector

of action; uprightness; fundamental truth

print v reproduce (words, pictures etc.) by pressing inked types on blocks of paper etc.; write in imitation of this; *Photog* produce pictures from negatives; stamp (fabric) with design ~n printed matter; photograph; impression left by something pressing; printed cotton fabric **printer** n

prior adj . earlier ~n (fem **prioress**) leader of religious house or order **priority** n precedence, something given special attention **priory** n monastery, nunnery under prior, prioress **prior to** before

prise v force open by levering

prism n transparent solid, usu. with triangular ends and rectangular sides, used to disperse light into spectrum

prison n jail **prisoner** n one kept in prison; captive

pristine adj completely new and pure

private adj secret, not public; not general, individual; personal; secluded; denoting soldier of lowest rank

~n private soldier **privacy** n **privatize** v transfer (service etc.) from public to private ownership

privation n lack of comforts or necessities

privet n bushy evergreen shrub used for hedges

privilege n right, advantage granted or belonging only to few **privileged** adj enjoying privilege

privy adj admitted to knowledge of secret ~n lavatory

prize n reward given for success in competition; thing striven for; thing won, e.g. in lottery etc. ~adj winning or likely to win prize ~v value highly

pro- comb. form in favour of; instead of

pro¹ adj/adv in favour of **pros and cons** arguments for and against

pro² n professional

probable adj likely **probability** n likelihood; anything probable **probably** adv

probate n proving of authenticity of will; certificate of this

probation n system of dealing with

principle axiom, canon, criterion, doctrine, dogma, law, maxim, precept, rule; belief, code, ethic, tenet; conscience, integrity, morals, rectitude, scruples, uprightness

print v engrave, impress, imprint, issue, publish, stamp ~n copy, engraving, photo *Inf*, photograph, picture, reproduction

priority precedence, preference, rank, seniority, superiority, supremacy

priory abbey, convent, monastery, nunnery

prison confinement, cooler *Sl*, dungeon, gaol, jail, jug *Sl*, lockup, nick *Brit sl*, penitentiary *US*

prisoner convict, jailbird, lag *Sl*; captive, detainee, hostage, internee

privacy isolation, retirement, retreat,

seclusion, solitude

private confidential, in camera, secret; exclusive, individual, own, personal, special; isolated, secluded, secret, separate, sequestered

privilege advantage, birthright, claim, concession, due, entitlement, prerogative, right

prize n accolade, award, honour, trophy; aim, ambition, goal; jackpot, purse, stakes, winnings ~adj award-winning, best, champion, first-rate, outstanding, top ~v cherish, esteem, hold dear, treasure, value

probability chance(s), expectation, likelihood, likeliness, odds, prospect

probable credible, feasible, likely, presumable, reasonable

probably likely, maybe, perchance

lawbreakers by placing them under supervision; trial period **probationer** *n* person on probation

probe *v* search into, examine, question closely ~*n* that which probes, or is used to probe; thorough inquiry

probity *n* honesty, integrity

problem *n* matter etc. difficult to deal with or solve; question set for solution **problematical** *adj*

proceed *v* go forward, continue; be carried on; arise from; go to law **procedure** *n* act, manner of proceeding **proceeding** *n* act or course of action; *pl* minutes of meeting; legal action **proceeds** *pl n* profit

process *n* series of actions or changes; method of operation; state of going on; action of law ~*v* handle,

treat, prepare by special method of manufacture etc. **procession** *n* train of persons in formal order

proclaim *v* announce publicly, declare **proclamation** *n*

procrastinate *v* put off, delay **procrastination** *n*

procreate *v* produce offspring **procreation** *n*

procure *v* obtain, acquire; bring about; act as pimp **procurement** *n* **procurer** *n* (*fem* **procuress**) one who procures; pimp

prod *v* **prodding, prodded** poke ~*n* prodding; pointed instrument

prodigal *adj* wasteful ~*n* spendthrift

prodigy *n* person with some marvellous gift; thing causing wonder **prodigious** *adj* very great; extraordinary

——————— THESAURUS ———————

Arch, perhaps, possibly, presumably

probation apprenticeship, test, trial, trial period

probe *v* examine, explore, go into, investigate, look into, scrutinize, search, sift; explore, feel around, poke, prod ~*n* examination, exploration, inquiry, investigation, research, scrutiny, study

problem *n* complication, difficulty, dilemma, dispute, predicament, quandary, trouble; conundrum, enigma, poser, puzzle, question, riddle

procedure action, conduct, course, custom, method, modus operandi, policy, practice, process, routine, strategy, system

proceed advance, carry on, continue, go ahead, go on, move on, progress; arise, come, emanate, ensue, flow, issue, originate, result, spring, stem

proceeding *pl n* business, dealings, doings, minutes, records, report, transactions

proceeds earnings, gain, income, profit, returns, revenue, takings

process *n* action, course, means,

measure, method, mode, operation, performance, practice, procedure, system, transaction; advance, course, development, evolution, movement, progress, progression

procession cavalcade, column, file, parade, train

proclaim advertise, announce, circulate, declare, make known, profess, promulgate, publish

proclamation announcement, declaration, decree, edict, notice, notification, promulgation, pronouncement, publication

procrastinate adjourn, defer, delay, postpone, put off, stall, temporize

procure acquire, appropriate, come by, find, gain, get, obtain, pick up, secure

prod *v* dig, jab, nudge, poke, push, shove ~*n* dig, jab, nudge, poke, push, shove; goad, spur

prodigal *adj* extravagant, immoderate, improvident, profligate, reckless, spendthrift, wasteful ~*n* profligate, spendthrift

prodigy genius, talent, whiz *Inf,* wiz-

produce v bring into existence; yield; bring forward; manufacture; present on stage, film, television ~n that which is yielded or made **producer** n **product** n thing produced; consequence **production** n producing; staging of play etc. **productive** adj fertile; creative **productivity** n

Prof. Professor

profane adj irreverent, blasphemous; not sacred ~v treat irreverently **profanity** n profane talk

profess v affirm belief in; claim, pretend **profession** n calling or occupation, esp. learned, scientific or artis- tic; professing **professional** adj engaged in a profession; taking part in sport, music etc. for money; skilled ~n paid player **professor** n teacher of highest rank in university

proffer v offer

proficient adj skilled; expert **proficiency** n

profile n outline, esp. of face, as seen from side; brief biographical sketch

profit n money gained; benefit obtained ~v benefit; earn **profitable** adj **profiteer** n one who makes excessive profits at public's expense ~v profit thus

ard; marvel, miracle, phenomenon, sensation, wonder

produce v bear, beget, breed, bring forth, deliver, give, render, yield; bring about, cause, effect, generate, give rise to, occasion, provoke, set off; compose, construct, create, develop, invent, make, manufacture, turn out; direct, present, put on, show, stage ~n crop, harvest, product, yield

producer director, impresario; farmer, grower, maker, manufacturer

product artefact, commodity, creation, goods, merchandise, produce, work; consequence, effect, fruit, outcome, result, spin-off, upshot, yield

production construction, creation, fabrication, manufacture, origination; direction, management, presentation, staging

productive creative, fertile, fruitful, inventive, plentiful, prolific

productivity output, production, work rate, yield

profane adj blasphemous, disrespectful, impious, irreligious, irreverent, sacrilegious ~v abuse, debase, defile, desecrate, misuse, pervert, violate

profanity blasphemy, curse, foul language, impiety, malediction, obscen- ity, sacrilege, swearing, swearword

profess affirm, announce, assert, aver, avow, confirm, declare, maintain, proclaim, state

profession business, calling, career, line, occupation, sphere, vocation; affirmation, assertion, avowal, claim, declaration, statement, testimony, vow

professional adj adept, competent, efficient, expert, masterly, polished, practised, proficient, qualified, skilled

proficiency ability, accomplishment, competence, expertise, facility, knack, know-how Inf, mastery, skill, talent

proficient able, accomplished, adept, capable, competent, efficient, expert, gifted, masterly, skilful, talented

profile n contour, figure, form, outline, portrait, shape, silhouette, sketch; biography, characterization, sketch

profit n (oft. pl) earnings, gain, proceeds, return, revenue, takings, winnings, yield; advantage, avail, benefit, gain, good, use, value ~v aid, avail, benefit, gain, help, serve; clear, earn, gain, make money

profitable cost-effective, lucrative,

profligate *adj* recklessly extravagant; depraved, immoral

profound *adj* very learned; deep; heartfelt **profundity** *n*

profuse *adj* abundant **profusion** *n*

progeny *n* children **progenitor** *n* ancestor

prognosis *n* (*pl* -noses) forecast

programme *n* plan of intended proceedings; broadcast on radio or television **program** *n* instructions for computer ~*v* -gramming, -grammed feed program into (computer); arrange program

progress *n* onward movement; sequence ~*v* go forward; improve **progression** *n* moving forward; improve-

ment **progressive** *adj* progressing by degrees; favouring political or social reform

prohibit *v* forbid **prohibition** *n* act of forbidding; ban on sale or drinking of alcohol **prohibitive** *adj* tending to forbid or exclude; (of cost) too high to be afforded

project *n* plan, scheme ~*v* plan; throw; cause to appear on distant background; stick out **projectile** *n* heavy missile **projection** *n* bulge; forecast **projector** *n* apparatus for projecting photographic images

proletariat *n* working class **proletarian** *adj/n*

proliferate *v* grow or reproduce rap-

———————————— THESAURUS ————————————

money-making, paying; advantageous, beneficial, fruitful, productive, rewarding, useful, valuable, worthwhile

profound abstruse, deep, erudite, learned, sagacious, serious, wise; abysmal, bottomless, cavernous, deep, fathomless, yawning; extreme, great, heartfelt, intense

profuse abundant, ample, copious, plentiful, prolific, teeming

profusion abundance, excess, glut, multitude, quantity, surplus, wealth

programme *n* design, plan, procedure, project, scheme; broadcast, performance, presentation, production, show ~*v* arrange, bill, book, engage, line up, plan, schedule

progress *n* advance, course, movement, passage, way ~*v* advance, continue, make headway, move on, proceed, travel; advance, develop, grow, improve, increase

progression advance, advancement, furtherance, headway; advance, development, growth, headway, improvement, increase

progressive advancing, continuing, developing, growing, increasing, in-

tensifying; avant-garde, forward-looking, liberal, radical, reformist, revolutionary

prohibit ban, debar, disallow, forbid, outlaw, proscribe, veto

prohibition exclusion, prevention, restriction; ban, bar, boycott, embargo, injunction, interdict, proscription, veto

prohibitive forbidding, repressive, restrictive, suppressive; *esp. of prices* excessive, exorbitant, extortionate, steep *Inf*

project *n* activity, assignment, enterprise, job, plan, programme, proposal, scheme, task, undertaking, venture, work ~*v* contrive, design, devise, draft, frame, outline, plan, propose, scheme; cast, fling, hurl, launch, propel, shoot, throw; bulge, extend, jut, overhang, protrude, stick out

projectile bullet, missile, rocket, shell

projection bulge, protrusion, protuberance, ridge; calculation, computation, estimate, estimation, forecast, reckoning

proletariat commoners, hoi polloi, labouring classes, the common peo-

idly **proliferation** n
prolific adj fruitful; producing much
prologue n preface
prolong v lengthen
promenade n leisurely walk; place
made or used for this ~v take leisurely walk
prominent adj sticking out; conspicuous; distinguished **prominence**
n
promiscuous adj indiscriminate,
esp. in sexual relations **promiscuity** n
promise v give undertaking or assurance; be likely to ~n undertaking to
do or not to do something; potential

promising adj showing good signs,
hopeful; likely to succeed
promontory n high land jutting out
into sea
promote v help forward; move up to
higher rank or position; encourage
sale of **promoter** n **promotion** n
prompt adj done at once; punctual
~adv punctually ~v urge; suggest;
help (actor or speaker) by suggesting
next words ~n cue, reminder
promulgate v proclaim, publish
prone adj lying face downwards; inclined (to)
prong n one spike of fork or similar

———— T H E S A U R U S ————

ple, the masses, wage-earners, working class
prolific bountiful, copious, fertile,
fruitful, luxuriant, productive, profuse, rich, teeming
prologue foreword, introduction,
preamble, preface, prelude
prolong continue, drag out, draw
out, extend, lengthen, perpetuate,
spin out, stretch
promenade n constitutional, saunter, stroll, turn, walk; esplanade, parade, prom, walkway ~v perambulate, saunter, stroll, walk
prominence distinction, eminence,
fame, greatness, importance, prestige, rank, reputation, standing
prominent bulging, jutting, protruding, standing out; conspicuous, eye-
catching, noticeable, obtrusive, obvious, salient, striking; chief, distinguished, eminent, famous, foremost,
important, leading, main, notable,
renowned, top, well-known
promiscuous abandoned, dissolute,
fast, immoral, lax, licentious, loose,
wanton, wild
promise v assure, give one's word,
guarantee, pledge, swear, undertake,
vouch, vow; augur, betoken, denote,
indicate, suggest ~n assurance, bond,

commitment, guarantee, oath,
pledge, undertaking, vow, word; aptitude, flair, potential, talent
promising auspicious, bright, encouraging, favourable, hopeful, likely, rosy; gifted, likely, rising, talented
promote advance, aid, assist, back,
boost, develop, encourage, forward,
foster, help, support; aggrandize, dignify, elevate, exalt, raise, upgrade;
advertise, hype, plug Inf, push, sell
promotion advancement, aggran-
dizement, elevation, preferment,
upgrading; advertising, hype, propaganda, publicity
prompt adj immediate, instant, punctual, quick, rapid, speedy, swift,
timely, unhesitating ~adv Inf exactly,
on the dot, punctually, sharp ~v impel, incite, induce, inspire, motivate,
move, provoke, spur, stimulate, urge;
cue, prod, remind ~n cue, help, hint,
prod, reminder, spur, stimulus
promptly at once, directly, immediately, on the dot, on time, punctually, quickly, speedily, swiftly, unhesitatingly
prone face down, flat, horizontal,
prostrate, recumbent; apt, disposed,
given, inclined, liable, subject, susceptible

instrument

pronoun *n* word used to replace noun

pronounce *v* utter (formally); give opinion **pronounced** *adj* strongly marked **pronouncement** *n* declaration **pronunciation** *n* way word etc. is pronounced

proof *n* evidence; thing which proves; test, demonstration; trial impression from type or engraved plate; standard of strength of alcoholic drink ~*adj* giving impenetrable defence against

prop¹ *n/v* propping, propped support

prop² *n* object used on set of film, play etc.

propaganda *n* organized dissemination of information to assist or damage political cause etc.

propagate *v* reproduce, breed; spread **propagation** *n*

propel *v* -pelling, -pelled cause to

move forward **propeller** *n* revolving shaft with blades for driving ship or aircraft **propulsion** *n* act of driving forward

propensity *n* inclination; tendency

proper *adj* appropriate; correct; conforming to etiquette; strict; (of noun) denoting individual person or place **properly** *adv*

property *n* that which is owned; land, real estate; quality, attribute

prophet *n* (*fem* **prophetess**) inspired teacher or revealer of God's word; foreteller of future **prophecy** *n* prediction, prophetic utterance **prophesy** *v* foretell **prophetic** *adj*

proponent *n* one who argues in favour of something

proportion *n* relative size or number; due relation between connected things or parts; share; *pl* dimensions ~*v* arrange proportions of **propor-**

—————— THESAURUS ——————

prong point, spike, tine

pronounce articulate, enunciate, say, sound, speak, utter, voice; affirm, announce, declare, proclaim

pronounced conspicuous, decided, definite, distinct, marked, noticeable, obvious, striking

pronouncement announcement, declaration, proclamation, statement

pronunciation accent, articulation, diction, elocution, enunciation, inflection, intonation, stress

proof *n* authentication, confirmation, corroboration, demonstration, evidence, substantiation, testimony, verification ~*adj* impenetrable, impervious, repellent, resistant

prop *n* brace, buttress, mainstay, stay, support ~*v* bolster, brace, buttress, support, sustain, uphold

propaganda advertising, disinformation, hype, promotion, publicity

propagate breed, engender, increase, multiply, procreate, produce, prolif-

erate, reproduce; broadcast, circulate, disseminate, promulgate, publicize, publish, spread, transmit

propel drive, force, push, send, shoot, shove, thrust

proper appropriate, apt, becoming, befitting, fit, fitting, right, suitable, suited; accepted, conventional, correct, established, exact, formal, orthodox, precise; decent, decorous, genteel, gentlemanly, ladylike, mannerly, polite, refined, seemly

property assets, belongings, capital, chattels, effects, estate, goods, holdings, means, possessions, resources; estate, freehold, holding, land, real estate; attribute, characteristic, feature, hallmark, quality, trait, virtue

prophecy divination, forecast, prediction, prognosis, second sight

prophesy divine, forecast, foresee, foretell, predict

prophet clairvoyant, forecaster, oracle, seer, sibyl, soothsayer

tional, proportionate *adj* in due proportion

propose *v* put forward for consideration; intend; offer marriage **proposal** *n* **proposition** *n* offer; statement

propound *v* put forward for consideration

proprietor *n* (*fem* **proprietress**) owner

propriety *n* properness, correct conduct

propulsion *see* PROPEL

prosaic *adj* commonplace, unromantic

proscribe *v* outlaw, condemn

prose *n* speech or writing not in verse

prosecute *v* carry on, bring legal proceedings against **prosecution** *n* **prosecutor** *n*

prospect *n* expectation, chance for

success; view **prospective** *adj* anticipated; future **prospector** *n* **prospectus** *n* booklet giving details of university, company etc.

prosper *v* be successful **prosperity** *n* **prosperous** *adj* successful; well-off

prostate *n* gland around neck of male bladder

prostitute *n* one who offers sexual intercourse in return for payment ~*v* make a prostitute of; put to unworthy use **prostitution** *n*

prostrate *adj* lying flat; overcome ~*v* throw flat on ground; reduce to exhaustion

protagonist *n* leading character in story; proponent

protect *v* keep from harm **protection** *n* **protective** *adj* **protector** *n*

protégé *n* (*fem* **protégée**) one under

proportion ratio, relationship, relative amount; agreement, balance, congruity, correspondence, harmony, symmetry; amount, part, percentage, quota, segment, share; *pl* amplitude, breadth, bulk, capacity, dimensions, expanse, extent, size, volume

proposal bid, motion, offer, plan, presentation, programme, project, recommendation, scheme, suggestion, tender

propose advance, present, proffer, propound, put forward, submit, suggest, tender; aim, intend, mean, plan, purpose, scheme

proposition motion, offer, recommendation, suggestion

propriety aptness, correctness, fitness, rightness; courtesy, decency, decorum, etiquette, manners, politeness, respectability, seemliness

propulsion drive, impetus, impulse, power, push, thrust

prosecute arraign, indict, litigate, sue, try

prospect *n* anticipation, expectation,

future, hope, odds, outlook, probability, promise; landscape, panorama, scene, sight, spectacle, view, vista

prospective anticipated, coming, destined, expected, future, imminent, intended, likely, potential

prospectus catalogue, list, programme, syllabus, synopsis

prosper do well, flourish, get on, succeed, thrive

prosperity affluence, plenty, prosperousness, riches, success, wealth

prosperous booming, flourishing, prospering, successful, thriving; affluent, moneyed, opulent, rich, wealthy, well-off, well-to-do

prostitute *n* call girl, courtesan, harlot, hooker, streetwalker, strumpet, tart *Inf*, trollop, whore ~*v* cheapen, debase, degrade, demean

prostrate *adj* flat, horizontal, prone; drained, exhausted, overcome, spent, worn out

protect care for, defend, guard, harbour, keep, look after, safeguard,

another's patronage

protein *n* any of group of organic compounds which form essential part of food of living creatures

protest *n* declaration or demonstration of objection ~*v* object; make declaration against; assert formally **protestation** *n* strong declaration

Protestant *adj* relating to Christian church split from R.C. church ~*n* member of Protestant church

protocol *n* diplomatic etiquette

proton *n* positively charged particle in nucleus of atom

prototype *n* original, model, after which thing is copied

protract *v* lengthen; prolong **protractor** *n* instrument for measuring angles

protrude *v* stick out, project **protrusion** *n*

protuberant *adj* bulging out

proud *adj* pleased, satisfied; arrogant, haughty

prove *v* **proving, proved, proved** or **proven** establish validity of; demonstrate, test; turn out to be **proven** *adj* proved

proverb *n* short, pithy saying in common use **proverbial** *adj*

provide *v* make preparation; supply, equip **provided that** on condition that

provident *adj* thrifty; showing foresight **providence** *n* kindly care of God or nature; foresight; economy

province *n* division of country; sphere of action; *pl* any part of country outside capital **provincial** *adj* of a province; narrow in outlook ~*n* unsophisticated person; inhabitant of province

provision *n* providing, esp. for the future; thing provided; *pl* food ~*v* sup-

save, screen, shelter, shield, stick up for *Inf*, watch over

protection care, charge, custody, defence, safeguard, safekeeping, safety, security; armour, barrier, cover, guard, screen, shelter, shield

protector bodyguard, champion, defender, guard, guardian, patron

protest *n* complaint, dissent, objection, outcry, remonstrance ~*v* complain, demonstrate, demur, disagree, disapprove, object, oppose

protocol decorum, etiquette, manners, propriety

prototype model, original, pattern, type

protrude bulge, come through, extend, jut, project, stand out, stick out

proud; appreciative, content, glad, gratified, pleased, satisfied; arrogant, conceited, disdainful, haughty, lordly, self-satisfied, snobbish, supercilious

prove authenticate, confirm, demonstrate, determine, establish, justify, show, substantiate, verify; analyse, assay, check, experiment, test, try; end up, result, turn out

proverb adage, dictum, maxim, saying

proverbial axiomatict, famed, famous, legendary, traditional, typical, well-known

provide cater, equip, furnish, outfit, purvey, stock up, supply

providence destiny, fate, fortune; care, caution, foresight, prudence

provident careful, cautious, farseeing, prudent, shrewd, thrifty, well-prepared, wise

province colonyt, district, division, patch, region, section, tract, zone; area, business, capacity, concern, duty, field, function, line, responsibility, role, sphere, turf *US sl*

provincial *adj* insular, inwardlooking, limited, narrow, narrowminded, parochial, small-minded,

ply with food **provisional** *adj* temporary

proviso *n* (*pl* **-os**) condition

provoke *v* anger; arouse; cause **provocation** *n* **provocative** *adj*

prow *n* bow of vessel

prowess *n* bravery; skill

prowl *v* roam stealthily, esp. in search of prey or booty ~*n* prowling **prowler** *n*

proximity *n* nearness

proxy *n* authorized agent or substitute; writing authorizing one to act as this

prude *n* one who is excessively modest or proper **prudish** *adj*

prudent *adj* careful, discreet; sensible; thrifty **prudence** *n*

prune¹ *n* dried plum

prune² *v* cut out dead parts, excessive branches etc.; shorten, reduce

pry *v* **prying, pried** make furtive or impertinent inquiries

PS postscript

psalm *n* sacred song

pseudo- *comb. form* false

pseudonym *n* false, fictitious name; pen name

psychic *adj* of soul or mind; sensitive to phenomena lying outside range of normal experience **psychiatric** *adj* of psychiatry **psychiatrist** *n* **psychiatry** *n* medical treatment of mental diseases **psychoanalysis** *n* method of studying and treating mental disorders **psychoanalyse** *v* **psychoanalyst** *n* **psychological** *adj* of psychology; of the mind **psychologist** *n* **psychology** *n* study of mind; *Inf* person's mental make-up **psychopath** *n* person afflicted with severe mental disorder **psychopathic** *adj* **psychosis** *n* severe mental disorder **psychosomatic** *adj* (of a physical disorder) thought to have psychological causes **psychotherapy** *n* treatment of disease by psychological, not physical, means

PTO please turn over

———— THESAURUS ————

small-town *US*

provision catering, equipping, furnishing, providing, supplying; arrangement, plan, precaution, preparation; *pl* food, rations, supplies

provocation cause, grounds, incitement, motivation, reason; affront, annoyance, grievance, offence, taunt

provocative annoying, goading, offensive, provoking

provoke anger, annoy, enrage, exasperate, infuriate, irk, irritate, madden, offend, rile, vex; cause, elicit, evoke, inspire, produce, rouse, stir

prowess adeptness, expertise, genius, mastery, skill, talent

prowl move stealthily, skulk, slink, stalk

proximity closeness, nearness, vicinity

proxy agent, delegate, deputy, representative, substitute

prudence care, caution, common sense, discretion, judgment, wisdom; foresight, planning, precaution, providence, thrift

prudent careful, cautious, discreet, judicious, politic, sensible, shrewd, wise; canny, careful, economical, far-sighted, provident, sparing, thrifty

prudish old-maidish *Inf*, priggish, prim, prissy *Inf*, proper, puritanical, schoolmarmish *Brit inf*, starchy *Inf*, strait-laced, stuffy, Victorian

prune clip, cut, snip, trim

pry intrude, meddle, peep, peer, poke

psalm chant, hymn

pseudonym alias, assumed name, incognito, pen name

psychiatrist analyst, psychoanalyst, psychologist

psychic extrasensory, mystic, occult, supernatural, telepathic

pub *n* public house, building with bar and licence to sell alcoholic drinks

puberty *n* sexual maturity

pubic *adj* of the lower abdomen

public *adj* of or concerning the community as a whole; not private ~*n* the community or its members **publican** *n* keeper of public house **public house** *see* PUB **public school** *Brit* private fee-paying school

publicity *n* process of attracting public attention; attention thus gained **publicize** *v* advertise

publish *v* prepare and issue for sale (books, music etc.); make generally known; proclaim **publication** *n* **publisher** *n*

puck *n* rubber disc used instead of ball in ice hockey

pucker *v* gather into wrinkles ~*n* crease, fold

pudding *n* sweet, cooked dessert, often made from suet, flour etc.; sweet course of meal; soft savoury dish with pastry or batter; kind of sausage

puddle *n* small muddy pool

puerile *adj* childish

puff *n* short blast of breath, wind etc.; type of pastry; laudatory notice or advertisement ~*v* blow abruptly; breathe hard; send out in a puff; inflate; advertise; smoke hard **puffy** *adj* swollen

puffin *n* sea bird with large brightly-coloured beak

pug *n* small snub-nosed dog

pugnacious *adj* given to fighting **pugnacity** *n*

pull *v* exert force on object to move it towards source of force; remove; strain or stretch; attract ~*n* act of pulling; force exerted by this; *Inf* influence

pulley *n* wheel with groove in rim for cord, used to raise weights

pullover *n* jersey, sweater without fastening, to be pulled over head

pulmonary *adj* of lungs

pulp *n* soft, moist, vegetable or animal matter; flesh of fruit; any soft soggy mass ~*v* reduce to pulp

pulpit *n* (enclosed) platform for

———————————— THESAURUS ————————————

psychopath headbanger *Inf*, headcase *Inf*, lunatic, madman, maniac

pub *also* **public house** bar, inn, tavern

puberty adolescence, teenage, teens

public *adj* civic, common, general, national, popular, social, state, universal, widespread; accessible, communal, open, unrestricted; acknowledged, known, open, plain ~*n* citizens, community, nation, people, populace, society

publication brochure, handbill, leaflet, magazine, newspaper, pamphlet, periodical, title

publicity attention, boost, press, promotion

publicize advertise, broadcast, make known, promote, push

publish issue, print, produce, put out; advertise, announce, broadcast, circulate, declare, disclose, divulge, leak, proclaim, promulgate, publicize, reveal, spread

puerile babyish, childish, immature, juvenile

puff *n* blast, breath, draught, gust, whiff ~*v* blow, breathe, exhale, gasp, gulp, pant, wheeze (*usu. with* **up**) bloat, dilate, distend, expand, inflate, swell

puffy bloated, distended, enlarged, puffed up, swollen

pull *v* drag, draw, haul, jerk, tow, trail, tug, yank; dislocate, rip, sprain, strain, stretch, tear, wrench *Inf* attract, draw, entice, lure ~*n* jerk, tug, twitch, yank; attraction, force, influence, lure, magnetism, power *Inf* influence, muscle, weight

preacher

pulse[1] n movement of blood in arteries corresponding to heartbeat, discernible to touch, e.g. in wrist; any regular beat or vibration **pulsate** v throb, quiver **pulsation** n

pulse[2] n edible seed of pod-bearing plant

pulverize v reduce to powder

puma n large Amer. feline carnivore, cougar

pumice n light porous variety of lava

pummel v -melling, -melled strike repeatedly

pump[1] n appliance for raising water, or putting in or taking out air or liquid etc. ~v raise, put in, take out etc. with pump; work like pump

pump[2] n light shoe

pumpkin n edible gourd

pun n play on words ~v **punning, punned** make pun

punch[1] n tool for perforating or stamping; blow with fists; *Inf* vigour ~v stamp, perforate with punch; strike with fist

punch[2] n drink of spirits or wine with fruit juice etc.

punctilious adj making much of details of etiquette; very exact, particular

punctual adj in good time, not late **punctuality** n

punctuate v put in punctuation marks; interrupt at intervals **punctuation** n marks put in writing to assist in making sense clear

puncture n small hole made by sharp object, esp. in tyre ~v prick hole in, perforate

pundit n expert who speaks publicly on subject

pungent adj acrid, bitter

punish v cause to suffer for offence; inflict penalty on; use or treat roughly **punishable** adj **punishing** adj harsh, difficult **punishment** n **punitive** adj inflicting or intending to inflict punishment

punnet n small basket for fruit

punt n flat-bottomed square-ended boat, propelled by pushing with pole ~v propel thus

punter n person who bets; member of public

puny adj small and feeble

pup n young of certain animals, e.g. dog, seal

pulp n flesh, soft part; mash, mush, paste ~v crush, mash, squash

pulsate beat, throb, vibrate

pulse n beat, beating, rhythm, throb, vibration

pump v drive, force, inject, pour, push, send

punch n blow, hit, knock, thump; *Inf* bite, drive, forcefulness, impact, verve, vigour ~v bore, cut, drill, pierce, puncture, stamp; belt *Inf,* hit, slam, smash, strike

punctual exact, precise, prompt, timely

punctuate break, interrupt, pepper, sprinkle

puncture n hole, leak, nick, opening, slit ~v bore, cut, nick, penetrate, perforate, pierce, prick

pungent acid, acrid, bitter, hot, peppery, piquant, sharp, sour, spicy, strong, tart

punish beat, chastise, correct, discipline, flog, penalize, scourge, whip

punishing arduous, backbreaking, exhausting, gruelling, strenuous, taxing, tiring, wearing

punishment chastisement, correction, discipline, penalty, penance, retribution

punt n bet, gamble, stake, wager ~v bet, gamble, lay, stake, wager

puny diminutive, feeble, frail, little, pygmy *or* pigmy, sickly, stunted, tiny,

pupa n (pl **pupae**) stage between larva and adult in metamorphosis of insect

pupil n person being taught; opening in iris of eye

puppet n small doll controlled by operator's hand; *Fig* stooge, pawn

puppy n young dog

purchase v buy ~n buying; what is bought; leverage, grip

pure adj unmixed, untainted; simple; faultless; innocent; concerned with theory only **purely** adv **purification** n

purify v -ifying, -ified make, become pure, clear or clean **purist** n person obsessed with strict obedience to tradition **purity** n state of being pure

purée n pulp of cooked fruit or vegetables ~v reduce to pulp

purgatory n place or state of torment, pain or distress, esp. temporary

purge v make clean, purify; remove, get rid of; clear out ~n act, process of

purging **purgative** adj/n

puritan n person with strict moral and religious principles ~adj strictly moral **puritanical** adj

purl n stitch that forms ridge in knitting ~v knit in purl

purloin v steal; pilfer

purple n/adj (of) colour between crimson and violet

purport v claim to be (true etc.); signify, imply ~n meaning; apparent meaning

purpose n reason, object; design; aim, intention; determination ~v intend **on purpose** intentionally **purposely** adv

purr n pleased noise which cat makes ~v utter this

purse n small bag for money; resources; money as prize ~v pucker **purser** n ship's officer who keeps accounts

pursue v chase; engage in; continue

weak, weakly

pupil disciple, learner, scholar, schoolboy, schoolgirl, student, trainee

puppet doll, marionette; instrument, mouthpiece, pawn, stooge, tool

purchase v acquire, buy, get, invest in, obtain, pay for, pick up, procure, score *Sl* ~n asset, buy, investment, possession, property

pure unadulterated, uncontaminated, unpolluted, untainted, wholesome; genuine, natural, perfect, real, simple, straight, unalloyed, unmixed; blameless, chaste, honest, impeccable, innocent, maidenly, virtuous

purely absolutely, completely, entirely, merely, only, simply, solely, wholly

purge v absolve, cleanse, clear, exonerate, forgive, pardon, purify; eradicate, expel, exterminate, kill, liquidate, oust, remove ~n cleanup, elimi-

nation, eradication, liquidation, removal, witch hunt

purify clarify, clean, cleanse, disinfect, filter, wash; absolve, cleanse, exonerate, redeem, sanctify

purist formalist, pedant, stickler

puritanical ascetic, austere, intolerant, narrow-minded, prudish, rigid, severe, strait-laced, strict

purpose n aim, design, end, goal, intention, object, plan, target; determination, resolution, resolve, tenacity, will **on purpose** deliberately, intentionally, knowingly ~v aim, aspire, decide, design, determine, intend, mean, plan, propose, resolve

purposely consciously, deliberately, intentionally, knowingly, wilfully, with intent

purse pouch, wallet; exchequer, funds, means, money, resources, treasury, wealth; award, gift, prize, reward

pursuer n **pursuit** n pursuing; occupation

purvey v supply (provisions)

pus n yellowish matter produced by suppuration

push v move, try to move away by pressure; drive or impel; make thrust; advance with steady effort ~n thrust; persevering self-assertion; big military advance **pusher** n seller of illegal drugs **pushy** adj assertive, ambitious **pushchair** n collapsible chair-shaped carriage for baby

puss also **pussy** n cat

pustule n pimple containing pus

put v **putting, put** place; set; express; throw (esp. shot) ~n throw **put off** postpone; disconcert; repel **put up** erect; accommodate

putrid adj decomposed; rotten **putrefy** v **-efying, -efied** make or become rotten

putt v strike (golf ball) along ground **putter** n golf club for putting

putty n paste used by glaziers

puzzle v perplex or be perplexed ~n bewildering, perplexing question, problem or toy

PVC polyvinyl chloride

pygmy, pigmy n abnormally undersized person; (with cap.) member of one of dwarf peoples of Equatorial Africa ~adj very small

pyjamas pl n sleeping suit of trousers and jacket

pylon n tower-like erection, esp. to carry electric cables

pyramid n solid figure or structure with sloping sides meeting at apex, esp. in ancient Egypt

pyre n pile of wood for burning dead body

pyromania n urge to set things on fire **pyromaniac** n

pyrotechnics n (with sing v) manufacture, display of fireworks

python n large nonpoisonous snake that crushes its prey

——————— T H E S A U R U S ———————

pursue chase, dog, follow, hound, hunt, hunt down, run after, shadow, stalk, tail Inf, track; adhere to, carry on, continue, maintain, persist in, proceed

pursuit chase, hunt, quest, search, trailing; activity, hobby, interest, occupation, pastime, pleasure

push v drive, press, propel, ram, shove, thrust; elbow, jostle, move, shoulder, shove ~n butt, jolt, nudge, shove, thrust; Inf ambition, determination, drive, dynamism, enterprise, initiative; Inf advance, assault, attack, charge, offensive, thrust

put bring, deposit, lay, place, position, rest, set, settle, situate

put off defer, delay, postpone, put on the back burner Inf, take a rain check on US & Canad inf; confuse, discom-

fit, disconcert, faze, nonplus, unsettle

putrefy corrupt, decay, decompose, go bad, rot, spoil

putrid bad, corrupt, decayed, decomposed, off, putrefied, rancid, rotten, spoiled

put up build, construct, erect, raise; accommodate, board, house, lodge

puzzle v baffle, bewilder, mystify, perplex, stump; brood, muse, ponder, think hard, wonder ~n conundrum, enigma, mystery, paradox, poser, problem, question, riddle

puzzlement bafflement, bewilderment, confusion, mystification, perplexity

pygmy, pigmy adj baby, diminutive, dwarf, midget, miniature, small, stunted, teeny-weeny, tiny, undersized

Q q

QC *Brit* Queen's Counsel

quack *n* harsh cry of duck; pretender to medical or other skill ~*v* (of duck) utter cry

quadrangle *n* four-sided figure; four-sided courtyard in a building

quadrant *n* quarter of circle

quadrilateral *adj/n* four-sided (figure)

quadruped *n* four-footed animal

quadruple *adj* fourfold ~*v* make, become four times as much

quadruplet *n* one of four offspring born at one birth

quaff *v* drink heartily or in one draught

quagmire *n* bog, swamp

quail[1] *n* small bird of partridge family

quail[2] *v* flinch; cower

quaint *adj* interestingly old-fashioned or odd; curious

quake *v* shake, tremble

qualify *v* **-fying, -fied** make (oneself) competent; moderate; ascribe quality to **qualification** *n* skill needed for activity; modifying or limiting condition **qualified** *adj* fully trained; conditional, restricted

quality *n* attribute; (degree of) excellence

qualm *n* misgiving; sudden feeling of sickness

quandary *n* state of perplexity, dilemma

quango *n* (*pl* **-gos**) partly independent official body, set up by government

quantify *v* **-fying, -fied** discover or express the quantity of

quantity *n* (specified or considerable) amount

quarantine *n/v* (place in) isolation to prevent spreading of infection

quarrel *n* angry dispute; argument ~*v* **-relling, -relled** argue; find fault with **quarrelsome** *adj*

THESAURUS

---

quack *n* charlatan, fake, fraud, humbug, impostor, pretender

quagmire bog, fen, marsh, mire, quicksand, slough, swamp

quaint curious, eccentric, fanciful, old-fashioned, peculiar, queer, rum *Brit sl*, singular, strange, unusual, whimsical

quake move, quiver, rock, shake, shudder, throb, tremble, vibrate, waver

qualification ability, aptitude, capability, capacity, eligibility, fitness, skill, suitability; allowance, caveat, condition, exception, limitation, modification, requirement, reservation, rider, stipulation

qualified able, adept, capable, certificated, competent, efficient, equipped, experienced, expert, fit, practised, proficient, skilful, talented, trained; bounded, conditional, limited, modified, provisional, reserved, restricted

qualify certify, commission, condition, empower, endow, equip, fit, ground, permit, prepare, ready, sanction, train; abate, adapt, assuage, diminish, ease, lessen, limit, moderate, reduce, regulate, restrain, restrict, soften, temper, vary

quality aspect, attribute, condition, feature, mark, property, trait; calibre, distinction, excellence, grade, merit, position, rank, standing, status, superiority, value, worth

quandary difficulty, dilemma, doubt, impasse, plight, strait, uncertainty

quantity allotment, amount, lot, number, part, sum, total

quarry[1] *n* object of hunt or pursuit; prey

quarry[2] *n* excavation where stone etc. is dug for building etc. ~*v* **-rying, -ried** get from quarry

quart *n* liquid measure, quarter of gallon

quarter *n* fourth part; region, district; mercy; *pl* lodgings ~*v* divide into quarters; lodge **quarterly** *adj* happening, due etc. each quarter of year

quartermaster *n* officer responsible for stores

quartet *n* (music for) group of four musicians

quartz *n* hard glossy mineral

quash *v* annul; reject

quasi- *comb. form* not really, as in **quasi-religious**

quaver *v* say or sing in quavering tones; tremble, shake, vibrate ~*n* mu-sical note half length of crotchet

quay *n* solid, fixed landing stage; wharf

queasy *adj* inclined to, or causing, sickness

queen *n* female sovereign; king's wife; piece in chess; fertile female bee, wasp etc.; court card

queer *adj* odd, strange

quell *v* crush, put down; allay

quench *v* slake; extinguish

querulous *adj* peevish, whining

query *n/v* **-ried** question

quest *n/v* search

question *n* sentence seeking for an-swer; problem; point at issue; doubt ~*v* ask questions of; dispute; doubt **questionable** *adj* doubtful **question-naire** *n* formal list of questions **question mark** punctuation mark (?) writ-ten at end of questions

quarrel *n* affray, argument, breach, controversy, disagreement, discord, dispute, dissension, feud, fight, row, squabble, tiff ~*v* argue, bicker, brawl, clash, differ, disagree, dispute, fight, row, wrangle

quarrelsome argumentative, com-bative, disputatious, fractious, iras-cible, irritable, peevish, petulant, querulous

quarry aim, game, goal, objective, prey, prize, victim

quarter *n* area, district, locality, neighbourhood, part, place, point, position, province, region, territory; favour, forgiveness, leniency, mercy, pity ~*v* accommodate, billet, board, house, install, lodge, place, post, sta-tion

quash annul, cancel, invalidate, nulli-fy, overrule, overthrow, rescind, re-verse, revoke

queen consort, monarch, ruler, sover-eign

queer abnormal, curious, droll, extraordinary, funny, odd, peculiar, remarkable, rum *Brit sl,* singular, strange, uncanny, uncommon, un-natural, weird

quench check, crush, douse, end, ex-tinguish, put out, smother, stifle, suppress

query *n* demand, doubt, hesitation, inquiry, objection, problem, ques-tion, suspicion ~*v* ask, enquire, ques-tion; challenge, disbelieve, dispute, distrust, doubt, mistrust, suspect

question *n* inquiry, investigation; ar-gument, contention, controversy, de-bate, difficulty, dispute, doubt, mis-giving, problem, query; issue, mo-tion, point, proposal, proposition, subject, theme, topic ~*v* ask, cross-examine, enquire, examine, interro-gate, interview, probe, quiz; chal-lenge, disbelieve, dispute, doubt, mistrust, oppose, query, suspect

questionable controversial, debat-able, dodgy *Brit, Aust, & NZ inf,* doubtful, equivocal, iffy *Inf,* moot,

queue *n* line of waiting persons, vehicles ~*v* wait in queue

quibble *n/v* (make) trivial objection

quiche *n* savoury flan

quick *adj* fast; lively; hasty ~*n* sensitive flesh ~*adv* rapidly **quicken** *v* make, become faster or more lively **quickly** *adj* **quicksand** *n* loose wet sand that engulfs heavy objects **quicksilver** *n* mercury **quickstep** *n* fast ballroom dance

quiet *adj* with little noise; undisturbed; not showy or obtrusive ~*n* quietness ~*v* make, become quiet **quieten** *v*

quiff *n* tuft of brushed-up hair

quill *n* large feather; pen made from feather; spine of porcupine

quilt *n* padded coverlet ~*v* stitch (two pieces of cloth) with pad between

quinine *n* drug used to treat fever and as tonic

quintessence *n* most perfect representation of a quality **quintessential** *adj*

quintet *n* (music for) group of five musicians

quintuplet *n* one of five offspring born at one birth

quip *n/v* **quipping, quipped** (utter) witty saying

quirk *n* individual peculiarity of character; unexpected twist

quit *v* **quitting, quit** stop doing (something); leave; give up

quite *adv* completely; somewhat ~*interj* expression of agreement

quiver[1] *v/n* shake, tremble

quiver[2] *n* case for arrows

quiz *n* (*pl* **quizzes**) entertainment in which knowledge of players is tested by questions; examination, interrogation ~*v* **quizzing, quizzed** question, interrogate **quizzical** *adj* questioning; mocking

quoit *n* ring for throwing at peg as a

—————— THESAURUS ——————

problematical, suspect, uncertain

queue chain, file, line, order, sequence, series, string, train

quibble *n* cavil, complaint, criticism, evasion, objection ~*v* carp, cavil

quick active, brief, brisk, express, fast, fleet, hasty, headlong, hurried, prompt, quickie *Inf,* rapid, speedy, swift; agile, alert, animated, energetic, flying, lively, nimble, spirited, spry, vivacious

quicken accelerate, expedite, hasten, hurry, impel, speed; arouse, excite, incite, inspire, revive, stimulate

quickly abruptly, apace, briskly, fast, hastily, hurriedly, promptly, pronto *Inf,* rapidly, soon, speedily, swiftly

quiet *adj* dumb, hushed, inaudible, low, peaceful, silent, soft, soundless; calm, contented, gentle, mild, pacific, peaceful, placid, restful, serene, smooth, tranquil; modest, plain, restrained, simple, sober, subdued, unobtrusive ~*n* calmness, ease, peace, quietness, repose, rest, serenity, silence, tranquillity

quieten allay, appease, blunt, calm, deaden, dull, hush, lull, muffle, mute, quell, quiet, silence, soothe, stifle, still, stop, subdue

quip *n* gibe, jest, joke, pleasantry, repartee, retort, witticism

quirk aberration, caprice, characteristic, eccentricity, fancy, fetish, foible, habit, idiosyncrasy, kink, mannerism, oddity, peculiarity, singularity, trait, vagary, whim

quit cease, discontinue, drop, end, halt, stop, suspend; abandon, decamp, depart, desert, exit, go, leave, resign, retire, step down *Inf,* surrender, withdraw

quite completely, entirely, fully, largely, totally, wholly; fairly, rather, somewhat

quiver *v* oscillate, palpitate, pulsate,

game; *pl* (*with sing v*) this game

quorum *n* least number that must be present to make meeting valid **quorate** *adj*

quota *n* share to be contributed or received

quote *v* repeat passages from; state price for **quotation** *n*

quotient *n* number resulting from dividing one number by another

———————————— T H E S A U R U S ————————————

shiver, shudder, tremble, vibrate

quiz *n* questioning, test ~*v* ask, examine, investigate, question

quota allowance, assignment, part, portion, ration, share, slice

quotation cutting, excerpt, extract, passage, reference; *Commerce* charge, cost, estimate, figure, price, rate, tender

quote attest, cite, detail, instance, name, proclaim, recall, recite, recollect, refer to, repeat, retell

R r

R King; Queen; river

rabbi (*pl* **rabbis**) *n* Jewish learned man, spiritual leader

rabbit *n* small burrowing mammal

rabble *n* crowd of vulgar, noisy people

rabid *adj* of, having rabies; fanatical

rabies *n* infectious disease transmitted by dogs etc.

raccoon *n* small N Amer. mammal

race¹ *n* contest of speed; rivalry; strong current; *pl* meeting for horse racing ~*v* (cause to) run, move swiftly **racer** *n*

race² *n* group of people of common ancestry with distinguishing physical features; species **racial** *adj* **racism, racialism** *n* belief in superiority of particular race; antagonism towards members of different race based on this **racist, racialist** *adj/n*

rack *n* framework for displaying or holding things; instrument of torture ~*v* torture

racket¹ *n* uproar; occupation by which money is made illegally **racketeer** *n*

racket², racquet *n* bat used in tennis etc.; *pl* ball game

raconteur *n* skilled storyteller

racquet *see* RACKET²

racy *adj* lively; piquant

radar *n* device for locating objects by radio waves, which reflect back to their source

radial *SEE* RADIUS

radiate *v* emit, be emitted in rays; spread out from centre **radiance** *n* brightness; splendour **radiation** *n* transmission of heat, light etc. from one body to another; particles, rays emitted in nuclear decay **radiator** *n* heating apparatus for rooms; cooling apparatus of car engine

radical *adj* fundamental; extreme; of root ~*n* person of extreme (political) views

radio *n* use of electromagnetic waves for broadcasting, communication etc.; device for receiving, amplifying radio signals; broadcasting of radio programmes ~*v* transmit message etc. by radio

radioactive *adj* emitting invisible rays that penetrate matter **radioactivity** *n*

THESAURUS

---

rabble crowd, herd, horde, mob, swarm, throng

rabid berserk, crazed, fanatical, frantic, furious, mad, raging

race¹ *n* chase, contest, dash, pursuit, rivalry ~*v* career, compete, contest, dart, dash, fly, gallop, hurry, run, speed, tear

race² blood, breed, clan, family, folk, house, issue, kin, kindred, line, nation, offspring, people, progeny, stock, tribe, type

racial ethnic, ethnological, folk, genealogical, genetic, national, tribal

rack *n* frame, framework, stand, structure

racket clamour, din, fuss, noise, outcry, row, shouting, tumult, uproar; fraud, scheme

racy animated, buoyant, energetic, entertaining, exciting, heady, lively, sparkling, spirited

radiate diffuse, emit, gleam, pour, scatter, send out, shed, shine, spread

radical *adj* basic, deep-seated, essential, fundamental, innate, native, natural, profound; complete, drastic, entire, excessive, extreme, extremist, fanatical, severe, sweeping, thorough, violent ~*n* extremist, fanatic, militant

radiography *n* production of image on film by radiation

radiology *n* science of use of rays in medicine

radiotherapy *n* diagnosis and treatment of disease by X-rays

radish *n* pungent root vegetable

radium *n* radioactive metallic element

radius *n* (*pl* **radii, radiuses**) straight line from centre to circumference of circle **radial** *adj*

RAF Royal Air Force

raffia *n* prepared palm fibre for making mats etc.

raffle *n* lottery in which article is won by one of those buying tickets ~*v* dispose of by raffle

raft *n* floating structure of logs, planks etc.

rafter *n* main beam of roof

rag *n* fragment of cloth; torn piece; *pl* tattered clothing **ragged** *adj* **ragtime** *n* style of jazz piano music

ragamuffin *n* ragged, dirty person, esp. child

rage *n* violent anger; fury ~*v* speak, act with fury; proceed violently, as storm

raglan *adj* (of sleeve) continuing in one piece to the neck

raid *n* attack; foray ~*v* make raid on

rail[1] *n* horizontal bar **railing** *n* fence, barrier made of rails supported by posts **railway** *n* track of iron rails on which trains run

rail[2] *v* utter abuse; scold

rain *n* moisture falling in drops from clouds ~*v* pour down as, like rain **rainy** *adj* **rainbow** *n* arch of colours in sky **rainforest** *n* dense forest in tropics

raise *v* lift up; set up; build; increase; heighten, as voice; breed; collect; propose, suggest

raisin *n* dried grape

rake[1] *n* tool with long handle and teeth for gathering leaves etc. ~*v* gather, smooth with rake; search over; sweep with shot

rake[2] *n* dissolute man

rakish *adj* dashing; speedy

rally *v* **rallying, rallied** bring together, esp. what has been scattered; come together; regain health or strength ~*n* assembly, esp. outdoor; *Tennis* lively exchange of strokes

ram *n* male sheep; hydraulic machine; battering engine ~*v* **ramming, rammed** force, drive; strike against with force; stuff

———— T H E S A U R U S ————

rage *n* anger, frenzy, fury, ire, madness, obsession, rampage, violence, wrath ~*v* blow a fuse *Sl*, fly off the handle *Inf*, fret, fume, go up the wall *Sl*, rave, seethe, storm

ragged mean, poor, rent, shabby, threadbare, torn, unkempt, worn-out

raid *n* attack, foray, incursion, inroad, invasion, sally, seizure, sortie ~*v* assault, attack, foray, invade, pillage, plunder, rifle, sack

rain *n* deluge, downpour, drizzle, fall, showers ~*v* drizzle, fall, pelt (down), pour, shower, teem

raise build, elevate, erect, exalt, heave, hoist, lift, promote, rear, uplift; advance, aggravate, amplify, boost, enhance, enlarge, heighten, increase, inflate, intensify, magnify, strengthen

rake[1] *v* collect, gather, remove; harrow, hoe, scour, scrape, scratch, smooth

rake[2] *n* lech *or* letch *Inf*, lecher, libertine, playboy, profligate, roué

rally *v* reassemble, re-form, regroup, reorganize, unite; assemble, collect, convene, gather, marshal, mobilize, muster, organize, round up, summon, unite; improve, pick up, recover, recuperate, revive ~*n* congress, convention, convocation, gathering,

ramble *v* walk without definite route; talk incoherently ~*n* rambling walk

ramify *v* **-ifying, -ified** spread in branches; become complex **ramification** *n*

ramp *n* gradual slope joining two level surfaces

rampage *v* dash about violently ~*n* angry or destructive behaviour

rampant *adj* violent; rife; rearing

rampart *n* wall for defence

ramshackle *adj* rickety

ran *past tense of* RUN

ranch *n* Amer. cattle farm

rancid *adj* smelling or tasting offensively, like stale fat

rancour *n* bitter hate

random *adj* by chance, without plan

randy *adj* Sl sexually aroused

rang *past tense of* RING²

range *n* limits; row; scope, distance missile can travel; place for shooting practice; kitchen stove ~*v* set in row; extend; roam; fluctuate **ranger** *n* official patrolling park etc. **rangy** *adj* with long, slender limbs

rank¹ *n* row, line; place where taxis wait; order; status; relative position; *pl (also* **rank and file**) common soldiers; great mass of people ~*v* draw up in rank; have rank, place

rank² *adj* growing too thickly; rancid; flagrant

rankle *v* continue to cause anger or bitterness

ransack *v* search thoroughly; pillage

ransom *n* release from captivity by payment; amount paid ~*v* pay ransom for

rant *v* rave in violent language

——— THESAURUS ———

meeting, muster

ram butt, crash, dash, drive, force, hit, impact, smash, strike

ramble *v* drift, range, roam, rove, saunter, straggle, stray, stroll, walk, wander; chatter, digress, maunder, waffle *Inf, chiefly Brit*, wander ~*n* excursion, hike, saunter, stroll, tour, trip, walk

ramification branch, division, extension, offshoot; complication, consequence, development, result, sequel, upshot

rampage *v* rage, storm ~*n* fury, rage, storm, tempest, tumult, uproar, violence

rampant aggressive, flagrant, outrageous, raging, riotous, unbridled, wanton, wild

rampart bastion, bulwark, defence, fence, fort, guard, security, wall

ramshackle crumbling, decrepit, derelict, flimsy, rickety, shaky, unsafe

rancid bad, fetid, foul, off, putrid, rank, rotten, sour, tainted

random accidental, aimless, casual, chance, fortuitous, haphazard, hit or miss, incidental, spot

range *n* area, bounds, distance, extent, field, latitude, limits, orbit, province, radius, reach, scope, span, sphere, sweep ~*v* align, arrange, array, dispose, line up, order; cruise, explore, ramble, roam, rove, stray, stroll, sweep, wander

rank¹ *n* column, file, group, line, range, row, series, tier; caste, class, degree, dignity, division, grade, level, order, position, quality, sort, station, status, type ~*v* align, arrange, array, class, classify, grade, locate, marshal, order, range, sort

rank² dense, lush, productive, profuse, vigorous; bad, fetid, foul, fusty, musty, off, putrid, rancid

ransack explore, rake, scour, search; despoil, gut, loot, pillage, plunder, raid, ravage, rifle, sack, strip

ransom *n* liberation, redemption, release, rescue; money, payment, payoff, price ~*v* deliver, liberate, redeem, release, rescue

rap v **rapping, rapped** give smart slight blow to; utter abruptly; perform monologue to music ~n smart slight blow; punishment; monologue set to music

rapacious adj greedy; grasping

rape[1] v force (woman) to submit to sexual intercourse ~n act of raping **rapist** n

rape[2] n plant with oil-yielding seeds

rapid adj quick, swift ~n (esp. pl) part of river with fast, turbulent current

rapier n fine-bladed sword

rapport n harmony, agreement

rapt adj engrossed **rapture** n ecstasy

rare[1] adj uncommon; of exceptionally high quality **rarely** adv seldom **rarity** n

rare[2] adj (of meat) lightly cooked

rarefy v **-fying, -fied** make, become thin or less dense

raring adj enthusiastically willing, ready

rascal n rogue; naughty (young) person

rash[1] adj hasty, reckless

rash[2] n skin eruption; outbreak

rasher n slice of bacon

rasp n harsh, grating noise; coarse file ~v scrape with rasp; make scraping noise; irritate

raspberry n red, edible berry; plant which bears it

Rastafarian n (oft. shortened to **Rasta**) member of Jamaican cult ~adj of this cult

rat n small rodent ~v **ratting, ratted** inform (on); betray; desert **ratty** adj Inf irritable **rat race** continual hectic competitive activity

ratchet n set of teeth on bar or wheel allowing motion in one direction only

rate n proportion between two things; charge; degree of speed etc.; pl local tax on business property ~v value

rather adv to some extent; preferably; more willingly

ratify v **-ifying, -ified** confirm **ratification** n

rating n valuing; classification; (also **naval rating**) sailor

ratio n (pl **-tios**) proportion; relation

rant bluster, cry, declaim, rave, roar, shout, yell

rape v ravish, sexually assault, violate ~n sexual assault, violation

rapid brisk, express, fast, fleet, flying, hasty, hurried, prompt, quick, swift

rapt absorbed, engrossed, enthralled, gripped, held, intent, spellbound

rapture bliss, delight, ecstasy, exaltation, happiness, joy, spell, transport

rare few, infrequent, scarce, singular, sparse, strange, uncommon, unusual; choice, extreme, fine, great, peerless, superb

rarely hardly, little, seldom

rarity curio, find, gem, pearl, treasure; infrequency, shortage

rascal blackguard, devil, disgrace, imp, rake, rogue, scamp, scoundrel, villain, wastrel

rash[1] brash, careless, foolhardy, hasty, heedless, hot-headed, ill-advised, impetuous, imprudent, impulsive, reckless

rash[2] eruption, outbreak; flood, outbreak, plague, series, spate, wave

rate n degree, proportion, ratio, scale, standard; charge, cost, dues, duty, fee, figure, hire, price, tariff, tax; measure, pace, speed, tempo, time ~v appraise, assess, class, consider, count, estimate, evaluate, grade, measure, rank, reckon, regard, value, weigh

rather a bit, a little, fairly, moderately, quite, relatively, slightly, somewhat, to some degree, to some extent; instead, preferably, sooner

ratify affirm, approve, bind, confirm, corroborate, endorse, establish, sanc-

ration n fixed allowance of food etc.
~v supply with, limit to certain
amount

rational adj reasonable, capable of
reasoning **rationale** n reason for decision **rationalize** v justify by plausible
reasoning; reorganize to improve efficiency etc.

rattle v (cause to) give out succession
of short sharp sounds ~n such sound;
instrument for making it; set of horny
rings in rattlesnake's tail **rattlesnake**
n poisonous snake

raucous adj hoarse

raunchy adj Sl earthy, sexy

ravage v plunder ~n destruction

rave v talk wildly in delirium or enthusiasm ~n wild talk; large-scale
party with electronic music **raving**
adj delirious; Inf exceptional

raven n black bird ~adj jet-black

ravenous adj very hungry

ravine n narrow steep-sided valley

ravioli pl n small squares of pasta with
filling

ravish v enrapture; rape **ravishing** adj

lovely

raw adj uncooked; not manufactured
or refined; skinned; inexperienced;
chilly

ray[1] n narrow beam of light, heat etc.;
any of set of radiating lines

ray[2] n marine flatfish

rayon n synthetic fibre

raze v destroy completely

razor n sharp instrument for shaving

razzle-dazzle also **razzmatazz** n
showy activity

RC Roman Catholic

RE religious education

re prep concerning

re- comb. form again

reach v arrive at; extend; touch ~n act
of reaching; grasp; range

react v act in return, opposition or towards former state **reaction** n counter
or backward tendency; response;
chemical or nuclear change **reactionary** n/adj (person) opposed to
change, esp. in politics etc. **reactive**
adj chemically active **reactor** n apparatus to produce nuclear energy

——————————— THESAURUS ———————————

tion, sign, uphold

ratio fraction, percentage, proportion,
rate, relation

ration n allotment, allowance, dole,
helping, measure, part, portion, provision, quota, share ~v allocate, allot,
deal, distribute, dole, give out, issue,
mete; budget, conserve, control, limit, restrict, save

rational enlightened, intelligent, logical, lucid, realistic, reasonable, sane,
sensible, sound, wise

rationalize excuse, justify, vindicate;
downsize, restructure

rattle v bang, clatter; bounce, jar, jolt,
shake, vibrate

raucous grating, harsh, hoarse,
husky, loud, noisy, rasping, rough,
strident

ravage demolish, despoil, destroy,

devastate, loot, pillage, plunder, ransack, ruin, sack, spoil

rave fume, go mad Inf, rage, rant,
roar, splutter, storm, thunder

ravenous famished, starved

ravine canyon, defile, flume, gorge,
gully, pass

raw fresh, natural, uncooked, undressed, unprepared; basic, coarse,
crude, green, natural, organic, rough,
unprocessed, unrefined, unripe;
chafed, grazed, open, skinned, sore,
tender

ray bar, beam, flash, gleam, shaft

reach v arrive at, attain, drop, fall,
move, rise, sink; contact, extend to,
grasp, stretch to, touch ~n ambit, capacity, command, compass, distance,
extension, extent, grasp, influence,
jurisdiction, mastery, power, range,

read v **reading, read** understand written matter; learn by reading; read and utter; study; understand any indicating instrument **reader** n one who reads; university lecturer; school textbook **reading** n

ready adj prepared for action; willing **readiness** n

real adj happening; actual; genuine **realism** n regarding things as they are **realist** n **realistic** adj **reality** n real existence **really** adv **real estate** landed property

realize v grasp significance of; make real; convert into money

realm n kingdom

ream n twenty quires of paper; pl Inf large quantity of written matter

reap v cut and gather harvest

rear[1] n back part **rear admiral** high-ranking naval officer

rear[2] v care for and educate (children); breed; rise on hind feet

reason n motive; ability to think; sanity; sensible thought ~v think logically; persuade by logical argument **reasonable** adj sensible; suitable; logical

reassure v restore confidence to

rebate n discount, refund

rebel v **-belling, -belled** resist lawful

——————— THESAURUS ———————

scope

react answer, reply, respond; act, behave, function, operate, proceed, work

reaction recoil; answer, feedback, reply, response

reactionary n die-hard, obscurantist, rightist ~adj blimpish, conservative

read comprehend, construe, decipher, discover, interpret, see, understand; look at, peruse, pore over, scan, study; announce, declaim, deliver, recite, speak, utter

readily eagerly, freely, gladly, promptly, quickly, willingly; easily, effortlessly, quickly, smoothly, speedily, unhesitatingly

reading lecture, lesson, recital, rendering, sermon

ready arranged, completed, fit, organized, prepared, primed, ripe, set; agreeable, apt, disposed, eager, glad, happy, inclined, keen, prone, willing

real absolute, actual, authentic, certain, factual, genuine, honest, intrinsic, positive, right, rightful, sincere, true, unfeigned, valid, veritable

realistic common-sense, level-headed, matter-of-fact, practical, real, sensible, sober; authentic, faithful, genuine, lifelike, natural, true,

truthful

reality actuality, fact, realism, truth, validity, verity

realize appreciate, comprehend, conceive, grasp, imagine, recognize, understand; accomplish, bring off, complete, consummate, do, effect, fulfil, perform; acquire, clear, earn, gain, get, make, net, obtain, produce

reap acquire, collect, cut, derive, gain, garner, gather, get, harvest, win

rear[1] n back, end, rearguard, stern, tail, tail end

rear[2] v breed, cultivate, educate, foster, grow, nurse, nurture, raise, train

reason n aim, basis, cause, design, end, goal, grounds, impetus, incentive, inducement, intention, motive, object, purpose; brains, intellect, judgment, logic, mentality, mind, sanity, sense(s), soundness, understanding ~v conclude, deduce, infer, make out, ratiocinate, resolve, solve, think, work out

reasonable arguable, believable, credible, intelligent, logical, plausible, practical, sane, sensible, sober, sound, tenable, wise; average, equitable, fair, fit, honest, inexpensive, just, moderate, modest

reassure comfort, encourage, heart-

authority ~*n* one who rebels ~*adj* rebelling **rebellion** *n* organized open resistance to authority **rebellious** *adj*

rebound *v* spring back; misfire, esp. so as to hurt perpetrator ~*n* recoiling

rebuff *n/v* repulse, snub

rebuke *n/v* reprimand

rebut *v* **-butting, -butted** refute, disprove **rebuttal** *n*

recalcitrant *adj* wilfully disobedient

recall *v* remember; call back; restore ~*n* summons; ability to remember

recant *v* withdraw statement, opinion etc.

recap *v* **-capping, -capped** recapitulate ~*n* recapitulation

recapitulate *v* state again briefly **recapitulation** *n*

recede *v* go back; slope backward

receipt *n* written acknowledgment of money received; receiving

receive *v* accept, experience; greet (guests) **receiver** *n* officer appointed to take public money; one who knowingly takes stolen goods; equipment in telephone etc. to convert electrical signals into sound etc.

recent *adj* lately happened; new **recently** *adv*

receptacle *n* vessel to contain anything

reception *n* receiving; formal party; area for receiving guests etc.; in broadcasting, quality of signals received **receptionist** *n* person who receives clients etc.

receptive *adj* quick, willing to receive new ideas

recess *n* alcove; hollow; suspension of business

recession *n* period of reduction in trade; act of receding **recessive** *adj*

———————— T H E S A U R U S ————————

en, inspirit, restore confidence to

rebel *v* mutiny, resist, revolt; defy, disobey, dissent ~*n* insurgent, revolutionary, revolutionist, secessionist; apostate, dissenter, heretic, schismatic ~*adj* insurgent, rebellious

rebellion mutiny, resistance, revolt, revolution, rising, uprising

rebellious defiant, disloyal, disobedient, disorderly, insurgent, mutinous, rebel, revolutionary, unruly

rebound *v* bounce, recoil, return; backfire, boomerang, misfire, recoil ~*n* bounce, kickback, return, ricochet

rebuff *n* check, defeat, denial, discouragement, knock-back *Sl*, opposition, refusal, rejection, repulse, slight, snub ~*v* cold-shoulder, cut, decline, deny, discourage, refuse, reject, repulse, resist, slight, snub, spurn

rebuke *n* blame, censure, lecture, reprimand, reproach, reproof ~*v* admonish, blame, castigate, censure,

chide, lecture, reprehend, reproach, reprove, scold

recall *v* evoke, recollect, remember; annul, cancel, countermand, repeal, retract, revoke, withdraw ~*n* cancellation, repeal, retraction, withdrawal; memory, remembrance

recede abate, ebb, fall back, regress, retire, retreat, return, subside, withdraw

receipt stub, voucher; acceptance, delivery, receiving, reception

receive accept, acquire, collect, derive, get, obtain, pick up, take; accommodate, admit, entertain, greet, meet, take in, welcome

recent current, fresh, late, latter, modern, new, novel, young

reception admission, receipt; function, levee, party, soirée

receptive alert, bright, perceptive, responsive, sensitive

recess alcove, bay, corner, hollow, niche, nook, oriel; break, closure, holiday, intermission, interval, res-

receding
recipe *n* directions for cooking food
recipient *n* one that receives
reciprocal *adj* complementary; mutual; moving backwards and forwards
reciprocate *v* give and receive mutually
recite *v* repeat aloud, esp. to audience **recital** *n* musical performance, usu. by one person; narration **recitation** *n*
reckless *adj* incautious
reckon *v* count; include; think
reclaim *v* make fit for cultivation; bring back; reform; demand the return of
recline *v* sit, lie back

recluse *n* hermit
recognize *v* identify again; treat as valid; notice **recognition** *n*
recoil *v* draw back in horror; rebound ~*n* recoiling
recollect *v* remember **recollection** *n*
recommend *v* advise; praise; make acceptable **recommendation** *n*
recompense *v* reward; compensate ~*n* reward; compensation
reconcile *v* bring back into friendship; adjust, harmonize **reconciliation** *n*
reconnoitre *v* make survey of **reconnaissance** *n* survey, esp. for military purposes

——————— T H E S A U R U S ———————

pite, rest, vacation
recession decline, depression, drop, slump
recipe ingredients, instructions
reciprocate barter, exchange, reply, requite, respond, return, swap, trade
recital account, narrative, performance, reading, rehearsal, rendering, statement, story, tale, telling
recite declaim, deliver, describe, detail, itemize, narrate, perform, recount, repeat, speak, tell
reckless careless, hasty, headlong, heedless, imprudent, indiscreet, mindless, precipitate, rash, thoughtless, wild
reckon add up, compute, count, figure, number, tally, total; assume, believe, imagine, suppose, surmise, think
reclaim recapture, recover, redeem, reform, regain, reinstate
recline lean, loll, lounge, repose, rest, sprawl
recluse anchoress, anchorite, ascetic, hermit, monk, solitary
recognition discovery, recall, remembrance; acceptance, admission, allowance, appreciation, avowal, concession, confession, notice, per-

ception, respect
recognize identify, know, notice, place, recall, recollect, remember, spot; accept, admit, allow, avow, concede, confess, grant, own, perceive, realize, respect, see, take on board, understand
recoil *v* draw back, falter, quail, shrink; backfire, misfire, rebound ~*n* backlash, kick, reaction, rebound, repercussion
recollect place, recall, remember, summon up
recollection impression, memory, recall, reminiscence
recommend advance, advise, advocate, counsel, enjoin, exhort, prescribe, propose, put forward, suggest, urge
recommendation advice, counsel, proposal; advocacy, approval, blessing, endorsement, praise, reference, sanction, testimonial
reconcile appease, conciliate, propitiate, reunite; adjust, compose, harmonize, rectify, resolve, settle, square; accept, resign, submit, yield
reconnaissance exploration, observation, patrol, scan, survey
reconnoitre case *Sl*, explore, inspect,

reconstitute *v* restore (food) to former state, esp. by addition of water

record *n* document that records; disc with indentations which can be transformed into sound; best achievement; known facts ~*v* put in writing; preserve (sound etc.) on magnetic tape etc. for reproduction on playback device **recorder** *n* one that records; type of flute; judge in certain courts **record player** instrument for reproducing sound on records

recount *v* tell in detail

recoup *v* recover what has been expended or lost

recourse *n* (resorting to) source of help

recover *v* get back; become healthy again **recovery** *n*

recreation *n* agreeable relaxation, amusement

recrimination *n* mutual abuse and blame

recruit *n* newly-enlisted soldier; one newly joining ~*v* enlist **recruitment** *n*

rectangle *n* oblong four-sided figure with four right angles **rectangular** *adj*

rectify *v* **-fying, -fied** correct

rectitude *n* honesty

rector *n* clergyman with care of parish; head of academic institution **rectory** *n* rector's house

rectum *n* (*pl* **-ta**) final section of large intestine

recumbent *adj* lying down

recuperate *v* restore, be restored from illness etc.

recur *v* **-curring, -curred** happen again; go or come back in mind **recurrence** *n* **recurrent** *adj*

recycle *v* reprocess substance for use again

red *adj/n* (of) colour of blood; *Inf* communist **redden** *v* **reddish** *adj* **red-blooded** *adj Inf* vigorous; virile **red carpet** special welcome for important guest **red-handed** *adj Inf* (caught) in the act **red herring** topic introduced to divert attention **red-hot** *adj* extremely hot; very keen **red tape** excessive adherence to rules

redwood *n* giant coniferous tree of

———————— T H E S A U R U S ————————

investigate, observe, patrol, scan, scout, spy out, survey

record *n* account, chronicle, diary, entry, file, journal, log, memoir, minute, register, report; album, disc, recording, release, single; background, career, history, performance ~*v* document, enrol, enter, inscribe, log, minute, note, register, report, transcribe

recount depict, detail, enumerate, narrate, portray, recite, rehearse, relate, repeat, report, tell

recover recapture, reclaim, redeem, regain, repair, repossess, restore, retrieve; convalesce, get better, get well, heal, improve, mend, rally, recuperate, revive

recovery healing, improvement, mending, rally, revival; betterment, improvement, rally, restoration, revival, upturn

recreation amusement, diversion, enjoyment, exercise, fun, hobby, pastime, play, pleasure, relaxation, relief, sport

recruit *n* apprentice, beginner, convert, helper, initiate, learner, novice, trainee ~*v* draft, enlist, enrol, impress, levy, mobilize, muster, raise; engage, procure

rectify adjust, amend, correct, emend, fix, improve, mend, redress, reform, remedy, repair, right, square

recuperate convalesce, improve, mend, recover

recur come again, happen again, persist, reappear, repeat, return, revert

recurrent continued, frequent, habitual, periodic

California

redeem v buy back; set free; free from sin; make up for **redemption** n

redolent adj smelling strongly; reminiscent (of)

redouble v increase, intensify

redoubtable adj dreaded, formidable

redress v make amends for ~n compensation

reduce v lower; lessen; bring by necessity to some state; slim; simplify **reduction** n

redundant adj superfluous; (of worker) deprived of job because no longer needed **redundancy** n

reed n various water plants; tall straight stem of one; Mus vibrating strip of certain wind instruments

reef n ridge of rock or coral near surface of sea; part of sail which can be rolled up to reduce area

reek v/n (emit) strong unpleasant smell

reel n spool on which film, thread etc. is wound; Cinema portion of film; lively dance ~v wind on reel; draw (in) by means of reel; stagger

refectory n room for meals in college etc.

refer v -ferring, -ferred relate (to); send to for information; ascribe to; submit for decision **reference** n act of referring; citation; appeal to judgment of another; testimonial; one to whom inquiries as to character etc. may be made

referee n arbitrator; umpire ~v act as referee

referendum n (pl -dums, -da) submitting of question to electorate

refill v fill again ~n subsequent filling; replacement supply

refine v purify **refined** adj cultured, polite; purified **refinement** n subtlety; elaboration; fineness of taste or manners **refinery** n place where sugar, oil etc. is refined

reflect v throw back, esp. light; cast (discredit etc.) upon; meditate **reflection** n reflecting; image of object given back by mirror etc.; thought; expression of thought **reflective** adj

———— T H E S A U R U S ————

red cardinal, carmine, cherry, coral, crimson, rose, ruby, scarlet, titian, vermilion, wine

redeem reclaim, recover, regain, repossess, repurchase, retrieve, win back; deliver, emancipate, free, liberate, ransom

redress make amends

reduce abate, abridge, curtail, decrease, dilute, diminish, impair, lessen, lower, moderate, shorten, truncate, weaken; cheapen, cut, discount, lower, slash; bring, conquer, drive, force, master, overpower, subdue, vanquish

redundant excessive, superfluous, supernumerary, surplus, unwanted

reek v smell, stink ~n odour, smell, stench, stink

reel revolve, spin, swim, swirl, twirl, whirl; lurch, pitch, rock, roll, stagger, sway

refer advert, allude, cite, hint, invoke, mention; direct, guide, point, recommend, send; apply, consult, go, turn to

referee n arbiter, arbitrator, judge, umpire ~v adjudicate, arbitrate, judge, mediate, umpire

reference allusion, citation, mention, note, quotation, remark; character, recommendation, testimonial

refine clarify, cleanse, distil, filter, process, purify, rarefy

refined civilized, courtly, cultivated, elegant, gracious, ladylike, polished, polite, urbane

refinement fine point, nicety, nuance, subtlety; breeding, civility, courtesy, cultivation, culture, gentil-

reflector *n*

reflex *n* involuntary action ~*adj* (of muscular action) involuntary; bent back **reflexive** *adj Grammar* describes verb denoting agent's action on himself

reform *v* improve; abandon evil practices ~*n* improvement **reformation** *n*

refract *v* change course of light etc. passing from one medium to another **refraction** *n*

refractory *adj* unmanageable

refrain[1] *v* abstain (from)

refrain[2] *n* chorus

refresh *v* revive; renew; brighten **refreshment** *n* that which refreshes, esp. food, drink

refrigerate *v* freeze; cool **refrigerant** *n/adj* **refrigeration** *n* **refrigerator** *n* apparatus in which foods, drinks are kept cool

refuge *n* shelter, sanctuary **refugee** *n* one who seeks refuge, esp. in foreign country

refund *v* pay back ~*n* repayment

refurbish *v* renovate and brighten up

refuse[1] *v* decline, deny, reject **refusal** *n*

refuse[2] *n* rubbish

refute *v* disprove **refutation** *n*

regain *v* get back, recover; reach again

regal *adj* of, like a king **regalia** *pl n* insignia of royalty; emblems of high office

regale *v* give pleasure to; feast

regard *v* look at; consider; relate to ~*n* look; attention; particular respect; esteem; *pl* expression of good will **regardless** *adj* heedless ~*adv* in spite of everything

regatta *n* meeting for boat races

regenerate *v* reform; re-create; reorganize **regeneration** *n*

———— THESAURUS ————

ity, polish

reflect echo, mirror, reproduce, return, throw back; cogitate, consider, meditate, muse, ponder, ruminate, think, wonder

reflection echo, image; cogitation, consideration, idea, meditation, musing, observation, opinion, pondering, study, thinking, view

reform *v* amend, correct, emend, improve, mend, rebuild, reclaim, regenerate, remodel, renovate, repair, restore ~*n* amendment, betterment, improvement, rehabilitation

refrain *v* abstain, avoid, cease, desist, forbear, kick *Inf*, renounce, stop

refresh brace, cheer, cool, enliven, freshen, reinvigorate, revitalize, revive, revivify, stimulate; prompt, renew, stimulate

refreshment enlivenment, freshening, renewal, repair, revival, stimulation; *pl* drinks, snacks, titbits

refuge asylum, harbour, haven, hide-out, resort, retreat, shelter

refugee émigré, escapee, exile, fugitive, runaway

refund *v* pay back, reimburse, repay, restore, return ~*n* repayment, return

refusal denial, rebuff, rejection, repudiation

refuse *v* decline, deny, reject, repel, repudiate, withhold

regain recapture, recoup, recover, repossess, retake, retrieve

regard *v* behold, check, check out *Inf*, clock *Brit sl*, eye, mark, notice, observe, remark, view, watch; adjudge, believe, consider, deem, esteem, hold, imagine, rate, see, suppose, think, treat, value, view ~*n* attention, heed, interest, mind, notice; affection, care, concern, deference, esteem, honour, love, note, repute, respect, store, sympathy, thought

regardless *adj* heedless, inconsiderate, indifferent, neglectful, rash, reckless, remiss, unmindful ~*adv* anyway,

regent *n* ruler of kingdom during absence, minority etc. of its monarch **regency** *n*

reggae *n* popular music with strong beat

regime *n* system of government

regiment *n* organized body of troops ~*v* discipline (too) strictly **regimental** *adj*

region *n* area, district; part; sphere **regional** *adj*

register *n* list; catalogue; device for registering; range of voice or instrument ~*v* show, be shown on meter, face etc.; enter in register; record **registrar** *n* keeper of a register; senior hospital doctor **registration** *n* **registry** *n* registering; place where registers are kept

regress *v* revert to former place, condition etc. **regression** *n*

regret *v* -gretting, -gretted feel sorry, distressed for loss of or on account of ~*n* feeling of sorrow **regretful** *adj* **regrettable** *adj*

regular *adj* normal; habitual; according to rule; periodical; straight ~*n* soldier in standing army **regularity** *n*

regulate *v* adjust; arrange; govern **regulation** *n*

regurgitate *v* vomit; bring back (swallowed food) into mouth

rehabilitate *v* help (person) to readjust to society after illness, imprisonment etc.; restore to former position **rehabilitation** *n*

rehash *n* old materials presented in new form ~*v* rework

rehearse *v* practise (play etc.); repeat; train **rehearsal** *n*

reign *n* period of sovereign's rule ~*v* rule

———————— THESAURUS ————————

nevertheless, nonetheless

regime government, leadership, management, reign, rule, system

region area, country, district, expanse, land, locality, part, patch, place, quarter, section, sector, territory, tract, zone

regional district, local, parochial, provincial, sectional, zonal

register *n* archives, catalogue, chronicle, diary, file, ledger, list, log, record, roll, roster, schedule ~*v* betray, display, exhibit, express, indicate, manifest, mark, read, record, reflect, reveal, say, show; catalogue, chronicle, enlist, enrol, enter, inscribe, list, note, record, take down

regret *v* bemoan, bewail, deplore, grieve, lament, miss, mourn, repent, rue ~*n* bitterness, compunction, contrition, disappointment, penitence, remorse, repentance, ruefulness, sorrow

regrettable disappointing, distressing, lamentable, pitiable, sad, shameful, unfortunate

regular common, customary, daily, everyday, habitual, normal, ordinary, routine, typical, usual; consistent, constant, even, fixed, ordered, periodical, set, stated, steady, systematic, uniform; balanced, even, flat, level, smooth, straight, symmetrical, uniform

regulate adjust, arrange, balance, conduct, control, direct, fit, govern, guide, handle, manage, monitor, order, rule, run, settle, supervise, tune

regulation *n* decree, dictate, direction, edict, law, order, precept, procedure, requirement, rule, statute; adjustment, control, direction, government, management, supervision, tuning

rehearsal drill, practice, preparation, reading

rehearse act, drill, practise, prepare, ready, recite, repeat, run through, study, train, try out

reign *n* command, control, dominion,

reimburse *v* pay back

rein *n* strap attached to bit to guide horse; instrument for governing

reincarnation *n* rebirth of soul in successive bodies

reindeer *n* (*pl* **-deer, -deers**) deer of cold regions

reinforce *v* strengthen with new support, material, force **reinforcement** *n*

reinstate *v* replace, restore

reiterate *v* repeat again

reject *v* refuse to accept; put aside; discard; renounce ~*n* person or thing rejected **rejection** *n*

rejig *v* **-jigging, -jigged** re-equip; rearrange

rejoice *v* make or be joyful

rejoin *v* reply **rejoinder** *n*

rejuvenate *v* restore to youth

relapse *v* fall back into evil, illness etc. ~*n* relapsing

relate *v* narrate; establish relation between; have reference to; (*with* **to**) form sympathetic relationship

relation *n* relative condition; connection by blood or marriage; connection between things; narrative **relationship** *n* **relative** *adj* dependent on relation to something else; having reference (to) ~*n* one connected by blood or marriage

relax *v* make, become loose or slack; ease up; make, become less strict **relaxation** *n* recreation; abatement

relay *n* fresh set of people or animals relieving others; *Radio, Television* broadcasting station receiving programmes from another station ~*v* **relaying, relayed** pass on, as message **relay race** race between teams of

——————————— THESAURUS ———————————

empire, influence, monarchy, power, rule, sway ~*v* administer, command, govern, influence, rule

reinforce bolster, emphasize, fortify, harden, increase, prop, stiffen, strengthen, stress, support, toughen, underline

reinforcement enlargement, fortification, increase, strengthening, supplement; brace, buttress, prop, shore, stay, support

reinstate recall, rehabilitate, replace, restore, return

reject *v* decline, deny, despise, discard, jettison, rebuff, refuse, renounce, repel, scrap, spurn, throw away *or* out, turn down, veto ~*n* castoff, discard, failure, second

rejection dismissal, exclusion, knock-back *Sl*, rebuff, refusal, repudiation, veto

rejoice celebrate, delight, exult, glory, joy, revel, triumph

relapse *v* degenerate, fail, lapse, regress, revert, weaken; deteriorate, fade, fail, sicken, sink, weaken, worsen ~*n* lapse, regression, retrogression, reversion; deterioration, weakening, worsening

relate describe, detail, narrate, present, recite, rehearse, report, tell; apply, concern, pertain, refer

relation affinity, kindred, kinship; kin, kinsman, relative; bearing, bond, comparison, connection, link, pertinence, reference, regard, similarity

relationship affair, affinity, bond, conjunction, connection, exchange, kinship, liaison, link, proportion, similarity, tie-up

relative *adj* allied, connected, contingent, dependent, reciprocal, related, respective; applicable, apposite, appropriate, appurtenant, apropos, germane, pertinent, relevant ~*n* kinsman

relax abate, ease, ebb, lessen, let up, loosen, lower, moderate, reduce, relieve, slacken, weaken; calm, chill out *Sl, chiefly US*, laze, soften, unwind

relaxation enjoyment, fun, leisure, pleasure, recreation, refreshment,

which each runner races part of distance

release *v* set free; permit showing of (film etc.) ~*n* releasing; permission to show publicly; film, record etc. newly issued

relegate *v* put in less important position; demote **relegation** *n*

relent *v* become less severe **relentless** *adj*

relevant *adj* having to do with the matter in hand **relevance** *n*

reliable, reliance *SEE* RELY

relic *n* thing remaining

relief *n* alleviation of pain etc.; money, food given to victims of disaster; release from duty; one who relieves another; bus, plane etc. operating when a scheduled service is full; free-

ing of besieged city; projection of carved design from surface; prominence **relieve** *v*

religion *n* system of belief in, worship of a supernatural power or god **religious** *adj* of religion; pious; scrupulous

relinquish *v* give up

relish *v* enjoy ~*n* liking; savoury taste; sauce; pickle

relocate *v* move to new place, esp. to work

reluctant *adj* unwilling **reluctance** *n*

rely *v* **relying, relied** depend (on); trust **reliability** *n* **reliable** *adj* **reliance** *n* trust; confidence

remain *v* be left behind; continue; last **remainder** *n* **remains** *pl n* relics; dead body

———— T H E S A U R U S ————

rest

relay *n* relief, shift, turn; dispatch, message, transmission ~*v* broadcast, carry, hand on, pass on, send, spread, transmit

release *v* deliver, discharge, drop, extricate, free, liberate, loose, set free, unchain, undo, unfasten, untie; circulate, distribute, issue, launch, present, publish, put out, unveil ~*n* acquittal, delivery, discharge, freedom, liberty, relief

relent be merciful, capitulate, forbear, melt, soften, unbend, yield

relentless cruel, fierce, grim, hard, harsh, pitiless, remorseless

relevant admissible, apposite, appropriate, apt, fitting, material, pertinent, proper, related, significant, suited

reliable dependable, faithful, honest, predictable, regular, responsible, safe, sound, stable, staunch, sure, true

relic fragment, keepsake, memento, remnant, scrap, token, trace, vestige

relief balm, comfort, cure, deliver-

ance, ease, mitigation, release, remedy, solace; aid, assistance, help, succour, support; break, diversion, remission, respite, rest

relieve allay, alleviate, appease, assuage, calm, comfort, console, cure, dull, ease, mitigate, mollify, relax, soften, solace, soothe; aid, assist, help, succour, support, sustain; stand in for, substitute for

religious devotional, devout, faithful, godly, holy, pious, pure, reverent, righteous, sacred, spiritual

relish *v* delight in, enjoy, fancy, like, prefer, savour, taste ~*n* appreciation, enjoyment, fancy, fondness, gusto, liking, love, partiality, penchant, taste; flavour, savour, smack, spice, tang, taste, trace; condiment, sauce, seasoning

reluctant disinclined, grudging, hesitant, loath, slow, unwilling

rely bank, bet, count, depend, lean, reckon, trust

remain abide, cling, continue, delay, dwell, endure, last, linger, persist, prevail, rest, stand, stay, survive,

remand v send back, esp. into custody **on remand** in custody

remark v/n (make) casual comment (on) **remarkable** adj unusual

remedy n means of curing ~v **-edying, -edied** put right **remedial** adj

remember v retain in, recall to memory **remembrance** n

remind v cause to remember **reminder** n

reminisce v talk, write of past times, experiences etc. **reminiscence** n **reminiscent** adj

remiss adj careless

remit v **-mitting, -mitted** send money for goods etc.; refrain from exacting; give up; return; slacken ~n area of authority **remission** n abatement; reduction of prison term; pardon **remittance** n sending of money; money sent

remnant n fragment

remonstrate v protest

remorse n regret and repentance **remorseful** adj **remorseless** adj pitiless

remote adj distant; aloof; slight **remote control** control of apparatus from distance by electrical device

remove v take, go away; transfer; withdraw **removal** n

————————— THESAURUS —————————

tarry, wait

remainder balance, excess, leavings, residue, residuum, rest, surplus, trace

remains balance, crumbs, debris, dregs, fragments, leftovers, pieces, relics, remnants, residue, rest, scraps, traces, vestiges

remark v comment, declare, mention, observe, pass comment, reflect, say, state ~n comment, declaration, reflection, statement, thought, utterance, word

remarkable distinguished, extraordinary, famous, impressive, notable, outstanding, phenomenal, preeminent, rare, signal, singular, strange, striking, surprising, uncommon, unusual, wonderful

remedy n cure, medicine, nostrum, panacea, relief, treatment ~v alleviate, assuage, control, cure, ease, heal, help, relieve, restore, soothe, treat

remember call up, commemorate, recall, recognize, recollect, reminisce, retain

remind call up, prompt

reminiscence anecdote, memoir, recall, review

reminiscent remindful, similar, suggestive

remission abatement, alleviation, lull, moderation, reduction, relaxation, respite, suspension; absolution, amnesty, discharge, excuse, exemption, exoneration, forgiveness, pardon, release, reprieve

remit v dispatch, forward, mail, post, send, transmit; cancel, desist, forbear, halt, refrain, repeal, rescind, stop ~n brief, guidelines, instructions, orders

remorse anguish, compassion, compunction, contrition, grief, guilt, pity, regret, shame

remorseless inexorable, relentless; callous, cruel, hard, harsh, inhumane, merciless, pitiless

remote distant, far, inaccessible, isolated, secluded; abstracted, aloof, cold, detached, distant, removed, reserved, standoffish, withdrawn

removal dislodgment, dismissal, dispossession, ejection, elimination, eradication, expulsion, extraction, stripping, subtraction, taking off, withdrawal; departure, move, relocation, transfer

remove abolish, delete, depose, detach, discharge, dismiss, displace, doff, efface, eject, eliminate, erase, excise, expel, extract, move, oust,

remunerate v reward, pay **remuneration** n **remunerative** adj

renaissance n revival, rebirth

renal adj of the kidneys

rend v rending, rent tear apart; burst

render v submit; give in return; cause to become; represent; melt down; plaster

rendezvous n (pl -vous) meeting place; appointment

rendition n performance; translation

renegade n deserter

renege v go back on (promise etc.)

renew v begin again; make valid again; make new; restore; replenish **renewal** n

renounce v give up, disown; resign, as claim **renunciation** n

renovate v restore, repair **renovation** n

renown n fame

rent[1] n payment for use of land, buildings etc. ~v hire

rent[2] n tear

reorganize v organize in new, more efficient way

rep n short for REPERTORY or REPRESENTATIVE

repair[1] v make whole again ~n repaired part **reparation** n compensation

repair[2] v go (to)

repartee n witty retort; interchange of them

repatriate v send (someone) back to his or her own country **repatriation** n

repay v repaying, repaid pay back; make return for **repayment** n

repeal v cancel ~n cancellation

repeat v say, do again; recur ~n act, instance of repeating **repetition** n act of repeating; thing repeated **repetitive** adj

repel v -pelling, -pelled drive back; be repulsive to **repellent** adj/n

repent v feel regret for deed or omis-

---

purge, relegate, shed, transfer, transport, unseat, withdraw; depart, move away, quit, relocate, shift, transfer, vacate

render deliver, furnish, give, hand out, pay, present, provide, show, submit, supply, tender, turn over, yield; exchange, give, return, swap, trade; act, depict, do, give, interpret, perform, play, portray, present, represent

renew continue, extend, mend, modernize, overhaul, reaffirm, recreate, refit, refurbish, rejuvenate, renovate, reopen, repair, replace, restore, transform

renounce abjure, abstain from, cast off, decline, deny, discard, disown, forgo, forsake, forswear, quit, recant, reject, relinquish, renege, repudiate, resign, retract, spurn, waive

renovate modernize, overhaul, recondition, refit, reform, renew, repair, restore

rent n fee, hire, lease, payment, rental, tariff ~v charter, hire, lease, let

repair v fix, heal, mend, patch, patch up, recover, rectify, redress, renew, renovate, restore ~n darn, mend, overhaul, patch

repay compensate, refund, reimburse, requite, restore, square

repeal v abolish, annul, cancel, invalidate, nullify, recall, reverse, revoke, withdraw ~n abolition, annulment, invalidation, rescindment, withdrawal

repeat v echo, iterate, quote, recite, rehearse, reiterate, relate, renew, replay, reproduce, restate, retell ~n duplicate, echo, reiteration, repetition, replay, reproduction, reshowing

repel check, confront, decline, fight, oppose, parry, rebuff, refuse, reject, repulse, resist; disgust, nauseate, offend, revolt, sicken

sion **repentance** v **repentant** adj

repercussion n indirect effect, oft. unpleasant

repertoire n stock of plays, songs etc. that player or company can give **repertory** n repertoire

repetition See REPEAT

replace v substitute for; put back **replacement** n

replay n reshowing on TV of sporting incident, esp. in slow motion; second sports match, esp. following earlier draw ~v play (match, recording etc.) again

replenish v fill up again

replete adj filled, gorged

replica n exact copy **replicate** v make or be copy of

reply n/v **replying, replied** answer

report n account; written statement of child's progress at school; rumour; repute; bang ~v announce; give account of; complain about; make report; present oneself (to) **reporter** n

repose n; peace; composure; sleep ~v rest **repository** n place where valuables are deposited for safekeeping

repossess v take back property from one who is behind with payments

reprehensible adj deserving censure; unworthy

represent v stand for; deputize for; act; symbolize; make out to be; describe **representation** n **representative** n one chosen to stand for group; salesman ~adj typical

———— THESAURUS ————

repent atone, deplore, regret, relent, rue, sorrow

repentant ashamed, chastened, contrite, rueful, sorry

repercussion backlash, consequence, echo, rebound, recoil, result, sequel

repetition echo, recital, recurrence, rehearsal, reiteration, relation, renewal, repeat, replication, restatement, return, tautology

replace follow, oust, re-establish, reinstate, restore, substitute, succeed, supersede, supplant, supply

replacement double, proxy, substitute, successor, surrogate, understudy

replenish fill, furnish, provide, refill, reload, replace, restore, supply, top up

replica carbon copy, copy, duplicate, facsimile, imitation, model, reproduction

reply n answer, counter, counterattack, echo, reaction, rejoinder, response, retort, return ~v answer, counter, echo, react, reciprocate, rejoin, respond, retaliate, retort, return

report n account, announcement, article, declaration, description, detail, dispatch, message, news, note, paper, piece, statement, story, tale, tidings, word, write-up; gossip, hearsay, rumour, talk; bang, blast, boom, crack, crash, detonation, discharge, explosion, noise, sound ~v air, broadcast, circulate, cover, declare, describe, detail, document, inform of, mention, narrate, note, pass on, proclaim, publish, recite, record, recount, relate, relay, state, tell; appear, arrive, come, turn up

reporter correspondent, journalist, newspaperman, pressman, writer

reprehensible bad, culpable, delinquent, disgraceful, errant, ignoble, remiss, shameful, unworthy

represent act for, be, betoken, express, mean, serve as, speak for, stand for, symbolize; embody, epitomize, exemplify, personify, symbolize, typify; act, enact, exhibit, perform, produce, put on, show, stage; denote, depict, describe, evoke, outline, picture, portray, render, reproduce, show, sketch

repress v keep down or under **repression** n **repressive** adj

reprieve v suspend execution of (condemned person) ~n postponement or cancellation of punishment; respite

reprimand n/v rebuke

reprisal n retaliation

reproach v blame, rebuke ~n scolding; thing bringing discredit **reproachful** adj

reprobate adj/n depraved (person)

reproduce v produce copy of; bring new individuals into existence **reproduction** n **reproductive** adj

reprove v censure, rebuke **reproof** n

reptile n cold-blooded, air breathing vertebrate, as snake

republic n state without monarch governed by elected representatives **republican** adj/n

repudiate v reject authority or validity of

repugnant adj offensive; distasteful; contrary

repulse v drive back; rebuff; repel **repulsion** n **repulsive** adj disgusting

repute v consider ~n reputation **reputable** adj of good repute **reputation** n estimation in which person is held; character; good name

request n asking; thing asked for ~v ask

Requiem n Mass for the dead

require v need; demand **requirement**

──────── THESAURUS ────────

representation account, description, illustration, image, likeness, model, picture, portrait, portrayal, relation, sketch

representative n agent, councillor, delegate, deputy, member, proxy; agent, rep, salesman, traveller ~adj archetypal, characteristic, illustrative, symbolic, typical

repress chasten, check, control, crush, curb, inhibit, master, overpower, quash, quell, restrain, silence, stifle, subdue, suppress

reprieve v abate, allay, alleviate, mitigate, palliate, relieve, respite ~n amnesty, deferment, pardon, postponement, remission, suspension

reprimand n blame, censure, rebuke, reprehension, reproach, reproof, row ~v blame, censure, check, chide, rebuke, reproach, scold, tear into Inf, upbraid

reproach v blame, censure, chide, condemn, criticize, discredit, find fault with, rebuke, reprimand, reprove, scold ~n abuse, blemish, censure, contempt, disgrace, disrepute, scorn, shame, slight, slur, stain, stigma

reproduce copy, echo, imitate, match, mirror, print, recreate, repeat; breed, multiply, proliferate, propagate, spawn

reproduction copy, duplicate, facsimile, imitation, picture, print, replica; generation, increase, multiplication

repugnant abhorrent, abominable, disgusting, distasteful, foul, hateful, horrid, loathsome, nauseating, objectionable, obnoxious, odious, offensive, repellent, revolting, sickening, vile

repulsive abominable, disagreeable, distasteful, foul, hateful, hideous, objectionable, odious, revolting, sickening, ugly, vile

reputable creditable, excellent, good, honourable, legitimate, reliable, respectable, trustworthy, upright, worthy

reputation credit, eminence, esteem, fame, honour, name, opinion, stature

request n appeal, asking, begging, call, demand, desire, petition, prayer, suit ~v ask (for), beg, beseech, demand, desire, entreat, petition, pray, seek, solicit

n

requisite *adj/n* essential

requisition *n* formal demand, e.g. for materials ~*v* demand (supplies); press into service

require *v* repay

rescind *v* cancel

rescue *v* -cuing, -cued save, extricate ~*n* rescuing

research *n* investigation to gather or discover facts ~*v* investigate

resemble *v* be like; look like **resemblance** *n*

resent *v* show, feel indignation at **resentful** *adj* **resentment** *n*

reserve *v* hold back, set aside ~*n* (*also pl*) something, esp. troops, kept for emergencies; (*also* **reservation**) area of land reserved for particular purpose or group; reticence ~*adj* auxiliary, substitute **reservation** *n* reserving; thing reserved; doubt; limitation **reserved** *adj* booked; not showing one's feelings

reservoir *n* enclosed area for storage of water; receptacle for liquid, gas etc.

reshuffle *n* reorganization ~*v* reorganize

reside *v* dwell permanently **residence** *n* home **resident** *adj/n* **residential** *adj*

residue *n* remainder **residual** *adj*

resign *v* give up (esp. office, job); reconcile (oneself) to **resignation** *n*

———————— THESAURUS ————————

require crave, desire, lack, miss, need, want, wish; ask, beg, bid, command, compel, constrain, demand, direct, enjoin, exact, insist upon, oblige, order

requirement demand, essential, lack, must, need, precondition, stipulation, want

rescue *v* deliver, free, get out, liberate, recover, redeem, release, salvage, save ~*n* deliverance, liberation, recovery, release, relief, salvage, saving

research *n* examination, exploration, probe, study ~*v* analyse, examine, experiment, explore, investigate, probe, scrutinize, study, work over

resemblance comparison, correspondence, facsimile, image, kinship, likeness, semblance

resemble duplicate, echo, look like, remind one of, take after

resent begrudge, dislike, grudge, take exception to

resentful angry, bitter, incensed, indignant, irate, jealous, piqued

resentment anger, bitterness, displeasure, fury, grudge, hurt, ire, malice, pique, rage, umbrage, wrath

reservation condition, doubt, rider, scepticism, scruple, stipulation

reserve *v* hoard, hold, husband, keep, preserve, put by, retain, save, stockpile, store, withhold; book, engage, prearrange, retain, secure ~*n* backlog, cache, capital, fall-back, fund, hoard, reservoir, savings, stock, store, supply; park, preserve, reservation, sanctuary, tract; coolness, formality, restraint, reticence, shyness, silence ~*adj* auxiliary, extra, fall-back, spare, substitute

reserved booked, engaged, held, kept, retained, taken; cautious, cold, cool, demure, modest, restrained, reticent, secretive, shy, silent

reside abide, dwell, inhabit, live, lodge, remain, settle, sojourn, stay

residence domicile, dwelling, flat, habitation, home, house, lodging, place, quarters

resident citizen, inhabitant, local, lodger, occupant, tenant

resign abandon, abdicate, cede, forgo, forsake, hand over, leave, quit, relinquish, renounce, step down *Inf*, surrender, turn over, vacate, yield

resignation abdication, departure, notice, retirement, surrender; acqui-

resilient *adj* elastic; (of person) recovering quickly from shock etc. **resilience** *n*

resin *n* sticky substance from plants, esp. firs and pines

resist *v* withstand, oppose **resistance** *n* resisting; opposition **resistant** *adj* **resistor** *n* component of electrical circuit producing resistance to current

resit *v* retake (exam) ~*n* exam to be retaken

resolute *adj* determined **resolution** *n* resolving; firmness; thing resolved; decision; vote

resolve *v* decide; vote; separate component parts of; make clear ~*n* absolute determination

resonance *n* echoing, esp. in deep tone **resonant** *adj* **resonate** *v*

resort *v* have recourse ~*n* place of recreation, e.g. beach; recourse

resound *v* echo, go on sounding

resource *n* ingenuity; that to which one resorts for support; expedient; *pl* stock that can be drawn on; funds **resourceful** *adj*

respect *n* esteem; aspect; reference ~*v* treat with esteem; show consideration for **respectability** *n* **respectable** *adj* worthy of respect; fairly good **respectful** *adj* **respecting** *prep* concerning **respective** *adj* relating separately to each; separate **respectively** *adv*

respiration *n* breathing **respirator** *n*

escence, compliance, endurance, fortitude, passivity, patience, submission, sufferance

resilient buoyant, hardy, irrepressible, quick to recover, strong, tough

resist battle, check, combat, confront, curb, defy, dispute, hinder, oppose, refuse, repel, thwart, weather, withstand

resolute bold, constant, determined, dogged, firm, fixed, immovable, obstinate, relentless, set, staunch, steadfast, stubborn, undaunted

resolution boldness, courage, dedication, determination, doggedness, earnestness, firmness, fortitude, purpose, resolve, sincerity, steadfastness, tenacity, willpower; aim, decision, declaration, intent, intention, judgment, motion, purpose, resolve, verdict

resolve *v* agree, conclude, decide, determine, fix, intend, purpose, settle, undertake; analyse, break down, clear, disintegrate ~*n* boldness, courage, determination, firmness, resoluteness, willpower

resort *v* employ, exercise, look to, turn to, use, utilize ~*n* haunt, refuge, retreat, spot, tourist centre

resound echo, re-echo, resonate, reverberate, ring

resource ability, capability, cleverness, ingenuity, initiative, talent; hoard, reserve, source, stockpile, supply

resourceful able, bright, capable, clever, creative, ingenious, inventive, quick-witted, sharp, talented

respect *n* admiration, consideration, deference, esteem, honour, recognition, regard, veneration; aspect, detail, feature, matter, particular, point, sense, way; bearing, connection, reference, regard, relation ~*v* admire, adore, appreciate, defer to, esteem, honour, look up to, recognize, regard, value, venerate; abide by, adhere to, attend, follow, heed, honour, notice, obey, observe, regard

respectable decent, decorous, dignified, estimable, good, honest, proper, upright, venerable, worthy; ample, appreciable, decent, fair, goodly, presentable, reasonable, sizable, substantial, tolerable

apparatus worn over mouth and breathed through **respiratory** *adj*

respite *n* pause, interval; reprieve

resplendent *adj* brilliant, shining

respond *v* answer; react **respondent** *adj* replying ~*n* one who answers; defendant **response** *n* **responsive** *adj* readily reacting

responsible *adj* in charge; liable to answer for; dependable; involving responsibility **responsibility** *n*

rest¹ *n* repose; freedom from exertion etc.; pause; support ~*v* take, give rest; support, be supported **restful**

adj **restless** *adj* unable to rest or be still

rest² *n* remainder ~*v* remain

restaurant *n* commercial establishment serving food

restitution *n* giving back; compensation

restive *adj* restless

restore *v* repair, renew; give back **restoration** *n* **restorative** *adj/n*

restrain *v* hold back; prevent **restraint** *n* self-control; anything that restrains

restrict *v* confine to limits **restriction**

——————————— THESAURUS ———————————

respective individual, own, particular, personal, relevant, several, specific, various

respite break, cessation, halt, interval, lull, pause, recess, relaxation, relief, rest

respond answer, counter, react, reciprocate, rejoin, reply, retort, return

response answer, counterattack, feedback, reaction, rejoinder, reply, retort, return, riposte

responsibility answerability, care, charge, duty, liability, obligation, onus, trust; authority, importance, power; blame, burden, fault, guilt

responsible in charge, in control; accountable, answerable, bound, chargeable, duty-bound, liable, subject; at fault, culpable, guilty, to blame

rest¹ *n* calm, doze, kip *Brit sl*, leisure, nap, relaxation, relief, repose, siesta, sleep, slumber, stillness, tranquillity; break, cessation, halt, holiday, interlude, intermission, interval, lull, pause, respite, stop, time off, vacation; base, holder, prop, shelf, stand, support, trestle ~*v* doze, drowse, kip *Brit sl*, nap, relax, sit down, sleep, slumber; lay, lean, lie, prop, recline, repose, sit, stand

rest² balance, excess, others, remain-

der, remnants, residue, rump, surplus

restful calm, calming, pacific, peaceful, placid, quiet, relaxed, serene, sleepy, tranquil

restive agitated, edgy, fidgety, fretful, impatient, jumpy, nervous, uneasy, unquiet, unruly

restless agitated, disturbed, edgy, fidgety, fitful, fretful, jumpy, nervous, restive, sleepless, troubled, uneasy, unquiet

restore fix, mend, recover, refurbish, renew, renovate, repair, retouch, touch up; give back, hand back, recover, reinstate, replace, return, send back

restrain bridle, check, confine, contain, control, curb, curtail, debar, govern, hamper, hinder, hold, hold back, inhibit, keep, limit, prevent, rein, repress, restrict, subdue, suppress

restrained calm, controlled, mild, moderate, muted, reticent, soft, steady

restraint compulsion, constraint, control, curtailment, grip, hindrance, hold, inhibition, moderation, self-control, self-discipline, suppression; ban, bridle, check, curb, embargo, interdict, limit, limitation, rein

n **restrictive** *adj*

result *v* follow as consequence; happen; end ~*n* outcome **resultant** *adj*

resume *v* begin again **résumé** *n* summary **resumption** *n*

resurgence *n* rising again **resurgent** *adj*

resurrect *v* restore to life, use **resurrection** *n*

resuscitate *v* restore to consciousness **resuscitation** *n*

retail *n* sale in small quantities ~*adv* by retail ~*v* sell, be sold, retail; recount **retailer** *n*

retain *v* keep; engage services of **retainer** *n* fee to retain esp. barrister; *Hist* follower of nobleman etc. **retention** *n* **retentive** *adj*

retaliate *v* repay in kind **retaliation** *n*

retard *v* make slow; impede development of **retarded** *adj*

retch *v* try to vomit

reticent *adj* reserved; uncommunicative **reticence** *n*

retina *n* (*pl* **-nas, -nae**) light-sensitive membrane at back of eye

retinue *n* band of followers

retire *v* give up office or work; go away; go to bed **retirement** *n* **retiring** *adj* unobtrusive, shy

retort *v* reply; retaliate ~*n* vigorous reply; vessel with bent neck used for distilling

retrace *v* go back over

retract *v* draw in or back; withdraw statement **retraction** *n*

retreat *v* move back ~*n* withdrawal; place to which anyone retires; refuge

restrict bound, confine, contain, hamper, handicap, hem in, impede, inhibit, limit, regulate, restrain

restriction check, condition, containment, control, handicap, inhibition, limitation, regulation, restraint, rule

result *v* appear, arise, derive, develop, emanate, ensue, flow, follow, happen, issue, spring, stem, turn out ~*n* consequence, decision, development, effect, end, event, fruit, issue, outcome, product, reaction, sequel, upshot

resume begin again, carry on, continue, go on, proceed, reopen, restart

resurrect bring back, reintroduce, renew, revive

resurrection reappearance, rebirth, renaissance, renewal, restoration, resurgence, resuscitation, return, revival

retain absorb, contain, grasp, grip, hold, hold back, keep, maintain, preserve, reserve, restrain, save; employ, engage, hire, pay, reserve

retainer advance, deposit, fee; attendant, domestic, flunky, footman,

lackey, servant, supporter, valet, vassal

retaliate give tit for tat, hit back, reciprocate, strike back, take revenge

retaliation reprisal, retribution, revenge, vengeance

retard arrest, brake, check, clog, decelerate, defer, delay, detain, encumber, handicap, hinder, hold back *or* up, impede, obstruct, set back, slow down, stall

reticent mum, quiet, reserved, secretive, silent

retire give up work, stop working; depart, exit, go away, leave, remove, withdraw

retiring coy, demure, diffident, humble, meek, modest, quiet, reserved, reticent, shy, timid, unassuming

retract pull back, sheathe; cancel, deny, disavow, disclaim, disown, recall, recant, renege, repeal, repudiate, reverse, revoke, take back, unsay, withdraw

retreat *v* depart, draw back, ebb, fall back, go back, leave, pull back, recede, recoil, retire, shrink, turn tail,

retrench v reduce expenditure

retribution n recompense, esp. for evil

retrieve v fetch back again; regain **retrieval** n **retriever** n dog trained to retrieve game

retroactive adj applying to the past

retrograde adj going backwards, reverting

retrospect n survey of past **retrospective** adj

return v go, come back; give, send back; report officially; elect ~n returning; profit; report **returning officer** one conducting election

reunion n gathering of people who have been apart **reunite** v bring, come together again

rev n Inf revolution (of engine)

Rev. Reverend

revalue v adjust exchange value of currency upwards

revamp v renovate, restore

reveal v make known; show **revelation** n

reveille n morning bugle call etc. to waken soldiers

revel v -elling, -elled take pleasure (in); make merry ~n (usu. pl) merry-making **revelry** n

revenge n retaliation for wrong done ~v avenge; make retaliation for

revenue n income, esp. of state

reverberate v echo, resound **reverberation** n

revere v hold in great regard or religious respect **reverence** n **reverend** adj (esp. as prefix to clergyman's name) worthy of reverence **reverent** adj

——————————— THESAURUS ———————————

withdraw ~n ebb, flight, retirement, withdrawal

retribution compensation, justice, reckoning, redress, repayment, reprisal, requital, retaliation, revenge, reward, satisfaction, vengeance

retrieve recall, recapture, recoup, recover, redeem, regain, repair, rescue, restore, salvage, save, win back

retrospect hindsight, review, survey

return v come back, go back, reappear, rebound, recur, repair, retreat, revert, turn back; convey, give back, put back, re-establish, reinstate, remit, render, replace, restore, send, take back, transmit; give back, pay back, refund, reimburse, repay, requite; choose, elect, pick, vote in ~n homecoming, rebound, recoil, recurrence, retreat, returning, reversion

reveal betray, blow wide open Sl, broadcast, disclose, divulge, give away, give out, impart, leak, let on, let out, let slip, proclaim, publish, tell; bare, display, exhibit, manifest,

open, show, uncover, unearth, unmask, unveil

revel v (with in) delight, gloat, indulge, joy, lap up, luxuriate, rejoice, relish, savour, wallow; carouse, celebrate n (oft. pl) carousal, celebration, debauch, festivity, gala, jollification, party, rave Brit sl, rave-up Brit sl

revelation disclosure, discovery, display, exhibition, exposition, giveaway, leak, news, publication, telling

revenge n reprisal, retaliation, retribution, satisfaction ~v avenge, hit back, repay, requite, retaliate

revenue gain, income, proceeds, profits, receipts, returns, rewards, yield

reverberate echo, rebound, recoil, re-echo, resound, ring, vibrate

revere adore, defer to, exalt, honour, respect, reverence, venerate, worship

reverence admiration, adoration, awe, deference, devotion, homage, honour, respect, worship

reverent adoring, awed, deferential, devout, humble, loving, meek, pious,

reverie *n* daydream

reverse *v* move (vehicle) backwards; turn other way round; change completely ~*n* opposite; side opposite; defeat ~*adj* opposite **reversal** *n*

revert *v* return to former state, subject **reversion** *n*

review *v* examine; reconsider; hold, make, write review of ~*n* survey; critical notice of book etc.; periodical with critical articles; *Mil* inspection of troops

revile *v* abuse viciously

revise *v* look over and correct; study

again (work done previously); change **revision** *n*

revive *v* bring, come back to life, vigour, use etc. **revival** *n*

revoke *v* withdraw; cancel **revocation** *n*

revolt *n* rebellion ~*v* rise in rebellion; feel disgust; affect with disgust **revolting** *adj* disgusting

revolve *v* turn round; be centred on; rotate **revolution** *n* violent overthrow of government; great change; complete rotation **revolutionary** *adj/n* **revolutionize** *v*

──────────── T H E S A U R U S ────────────

respectful, solemn

reverse *v* back, go backwards, move backwards, retreat; invert, transpose, turn back, turn over, turn round, turn upside down, upend; alter, annul, cancel, change, invalidate, overrule, overturn, quash, repeal, rescind, retract, revoke, undo ~*n* contrary, converse, inverse, opposite; adversity, affliction, blow, check, defeat, failure, hardship, mishap, repulse, reversal, setback, trial ~*adj* backward, contrary, inverted, opposite

review *v* assess, criticize, examine, inspect, judge, study, weigh; reassess, reconsider, re-examine, rethink, revise, think over ~*n* examination, report, scrutiny, study, survey; commentary, criticism, critique, evaluation, judgment, notice, study; journal, magazine, periodical; *Mil* display, inspection, march past, parade, procession

revise alter, amend, change, correct, edit, emend, review, rework, rewrite, update; go over, memorize, reread, run through, study

revision amendment, change, correction, emendation, modification, review, rewriting; homework, rereading, studying

revival reawakening, rebirth, recru-

descence, renaissance, renewal, restoration, resurgence, resuscitation

revive awaken, bring round, cheer, comfort, invigorate, quicken, rally, reanimate, recover, refresh, rekindle, renew, renovate, restore, resuscitate, rouse

revoke abrogate, annul, cancel, countermand, disclaim, invalidate, negate, nullify, quash, recall, recant, renege, renounce, repeal, repudiate, rescind, retract, reverse, withdraw

revolt *n* insurgency, insurrection, rebellion, revolution, rising, uprising ~*v* defect, mutiny, rebel, resist, rise; disgust, nauseate, offend, repel, sicken

revolting abhorrent, disgusting, foul, horrible, nasty, nauseating, obnoxious, obscene, offensive, repugnant, repulsive, shocking, sickening

revolution coup, insurgency, mutiny, rebellion, revolt, rising, uprising; innovation, reformation, shift, transformation, upheaval; circle, circuit, cycle, gyration, lap, orbit, rotation, spin, turn

revolutionary *adj* extremist, insurgent, radical, rebel, subversive; different, drastic, experimental, fundamental, ground-breaking, innovative, new, novel, progressive, radical ~*n*

revolver *n* pistol with revolving magazine

revue *n* entertainment with sketches and songs

revulsion *n* repugnance or abhorrence

reward *n* thing given in return for service, conduct etc. ~*v* give reward **rewarding** *adj*

rewind *v* run (tape, film etc.) back to earlier point

rewire *v* provide (house, engine etc.) with new wiring

rhapsody *n* enthusiastic (musical) piece or utterance **rhapsodic** *adj* **rhapsodize** *v*

rhesus *n* small, long-tailed monkey **rhesus factor** feature distinguishing different types of human blood

rhetoric *n* art of effective speaking or writing; exaggerated language **rhetorical** *adj* (of question) not requiring an answer

rheumatism *n* painful inflammation of joints or muscles **rheumatic** *adj/n*

rhinoceros *n* (*pl* **-oses, -os**) large animal with one or two horns on nose

rhododendron *n* evergreen flower-

ing shrub

rhombus *n* (*pl* **-buses, -bi**) diamond-shaped figure

rhubarb *n* garden plant with edible fleshy stalks

rhyme *n* identity of final sounds in words; word or syllable identical in final sound to another; verse marked by rhyme ~*v* (of words) have identical final sounds

rhythm *n* measured beat of words, music etc. **rhythmic, -ical** *adj*

rib *n* one of curved bones springing from spine and forming framework of upper part of body; raised series of rows in knitting etc. ~*v* **ribbing, ribbed** mark with ribs; knit to form a rib pattern

ribald *adj* irreverent, scurrilous

ribbon *n* narrow band of fabric; long strip of anything

rice *n* Eastern cereal plant; its seeds as food

rich *adj* wealthy; fertile; abounding; valuable; containing much fat or sugar; mellow; amusing **riches** *pl n* wealth **richly** *adv* elaborately; fully

rick[1] *n* stack of hay etc.

———— T H E S A U R U S ————

insurgent, mutineer, rebel

revolve circle, gyrate, orbit, rotate, spin, turn, twist, wheel, whirl

revulsion abhorrence, abomination, aversion, disgust, distaste, loathing, repugnance

reward *v* honour, pay, recompense, repay ~*n* benefit, bonus, bounty, gain, honour, merit, payment, premium, prize, profit, return, wages

rewarding edifying, enriching, fulfilling, gainful, gratifying, pleasing, productive, profitable, satisfying, valuable

rhetoric eloquence, oratory; bombast, hyperbole, rant, verbosity, wordiness

rhyme *n* ode, poem, poetry, song,

verse ~*v* harmonize, sound like

rhythm accent, beat, cadence, flow, lilt, metre, movement, pattern, pulse, swing, tempo, time

rich affluent, moneyed, opulent, prosperous, wealthy, well-off; abounding, abundant, ample, copious, exuberant, fertile, fruitful, full, lush, luxurious, plentiful, productive, prolific; costly, elaborate, elegant, expensive, exquisite, fine, gorgeous, lavish, palatial, precious, priceless, splendid, superb, valuable; creamy, delicious, juicy, luscious, savoury, spicy, succulent, sweet, tasty

riches affluence, assets, fortune, gold, money, plenty, property, resources, substance, treasure, wealth

rick² *v/n* sprain, wrench

rickets *n* disease of children marked by softening of bones **rickety** *adj* shaky, unstable

rickshaw *n* two-wheeled man-drawn Asian vehicle

ricochet *v* (of bullet) rebound or be deflected ~*n* rebound

rid *v* **ridding, rid** relieve of; free **riddance** *n*

ridden *past participle of* RIDE ~*adj* afflicted, as in **disease-ridden**

riddle¹ *n* question made puzzling to test one's ingenuity; puzzling thing, person

riddle² *v* pierce with many holes ~*n* coarse sieve

ride *v* **riding, rode, ridden** sit on and control or propel; be carried on or across; go on horseback or in vehicle; lie at anchor ~*n* journey on horse, in vehicle **rider** *n* one who rides; supplementary clause; addition to document

ridge *n* long narrow hill; line of meeting of two sloping surfaces ~*v* form into ridges

ridiculous *adj* deserving to be laughed at, absurd **ridicule** *v* laugh at, deride ~*n* derision

rife *adj* prevalent, common

riff *n* short repeated musical phrase

riffraff *n* rabble

rifle *v* search and rob ~*n* firearm with long barrel

rift *n* crack, split

rig *v* **rigging, rigged** provide (ship) with ropes etc.; equip; arrange in dishonest way ~*n* apparatus for drilling for oil **rigging** *n* ship's spars and ropes

right *adj* just; in accordance with truth and duty; true; correct; proper; of side that faces east when front is turned to north; *Politics* conservative; straight ~*v* make, become right ~*n* claim, title etc. allowed or due; what is right; conservative political party ~*adv* straight; properly; very; on or to right side **rightful** *adj* **right angle** angle of 90 degrees **right-hand man** most valuable assistant

——————— THESAURUS ———————

rid clear, deliver, disburden, disencumber, free, make free, purge, relieve, unburden

riddle brain-teaser *Inf,* conundrum, enigma, mystery, poser, problem, puzzle

ride *v* control, handle, manage, sit on; float, go, journey, move, progress, sit, travel ~*n* drive, jaunt, journey, lift, outing, trip

ridicule *v* banter, caricature, deride, humiliate, jeer, lampoon, mock, parody, pooh-pooh, satirize, scoff, sneer, taunt ~*n* banter, derision, gibe, irony, jeer, laughter, mockery, sarcasm, satire

ridiculous absurd, comical, derisory, farcical, foolish, funny, incredible, laughable, outrageous, risible, silly, stupid

rift breach, break, chink, cleft, crack, crevice, fault, fissure, flaw, gap, space, split; breach, disagreement, division, quarrel, schism, separation, split

rig *v* equip, fit out, furnish, provision, supply, turn out; arrange, engineer, fake, falsify, gerrymander, juggle, manipulate ~*n* apparatus, equipment, fittings, fixtures, gear, machinery, outfit, tackle

right *adj* equitable, ethical, fair, good, honest, just, lawful, moral, proper, true, virtuous; accurate, admissible, authentic, correct, exact, factual, genuine, precise, sound, true, unerring, valid; appropriate, becoming, convenient, deserved, desirable, done, due, favourable, fit, ideal, proper, propitious, seemly, suitable

righteous *adj* virtuous; good **righteousness** *n*

rigid *adj* inflexible; stiff **rigidity** *n*

rigmarole *n* long, complicated procedure; nonsense

rigor mortis stiffening of body after death

rigour *n* severity; hardship **rigorous** *adj*

rile *v* anger

rim *n* edge

rind *n* outer coating of fruits etc.

ring¹ *n* circular band, esp. for finger; circle of persons; enclosed area ~*v* put ring round **ringer** *n Inf* identical thing or person **ringleader** *n* instigator of mutiny, riot etc. **ringlet** *n* curly lock of hair **ring road** main road that bypasses a town (centre) **ringworm** *n* skin disease

ring² *v* **ringing, rang, rung** (cause to)

give out resonant sound like bell; telephone ~*n* resonant sound

rink *n* sheet of ice for skating

rinse *v* remove soap from by applying water; wash lightly ~*n* rinsing; liquid to tint hair

riot *n/v* (engage in) tumult, disorder **riotous** *adj*

RIP rest in peace

rip *v/n* **ripping, ripped** cut, slash **ripcord** *n* cord pulled to open parachute **rip off** *Sl* cheat by overcharging

ripe *adj* ready to be harvested, eaten etc. **ripen** *v*

riposte *n* verbal retort; counterattack ~*v* make riposte

ripple *n* slight wave; soft sound ~*v* form into little waves; (of sounds) rise and fall gently

rise *v* **rising, rose, risen** get up; move upwards; reach higher level; increase;

——————— THESAURUS ———————

~*adv* directly, promptly, quickly, straight; ethically, fairly, honestly, justly, morally, properly; absolutely, completely, entirely, perfectly, quite, thoroughly, totally, utterly, wholly ~*v* correct, fix, rectify, redress, repair, settle, sort out ~*n* business, claim, due, freedom, interest, liberty, licence, permission, power, prerogative, privilege, title; equity, good, goodness, honour, integrity, justice, lawfulness, legality, morality, propriety, reason, truth, virtue

rigid austere, exact, fixed, harsh, inflexible, rigorous, set, severe, stern, stiff, strict, unalterable, uncompromising

rigorous challenging, demanding, exacting, firm, hard, harsh, inflexible, severe, stern, strict, tough; bad, bleak, extreme, harsh, inclement, severe

rigour austerity, hardship, inflexibility, ordeal, sternness, suffering, trial

rim border, brim, brink, edge, lip,

margin, verge

rind crust, husk, integument, outer layer, peel, skin

ring¹ *n* band, circle, circuit, halo, hoop, loop, round; association, band, cartel, clique, combine, coterie, gang, group, mob, syndicate; arena, circus, enclosure, rink ~*v* encircle, enclose, gird, girdle, hem in, surround

ring² *v* chime, clang, peal, reverberate, sound, toll; call, phone, telephone ~*n* chime, knell, peal; call, phone call

rinse *v* bathe, clean, cleanse, dip, splash, wash, wash out, wet ~*n* bath, dip, splash, wash, wetting

riot *n* anarchy, confusion, disorder, fray, lawlessness, quarrel, row, strife, tumult, turmoil, upheaval, uproar ~*v* rampage, run riot

riotous disorderly, lawless, rebellious, rowdy, unruly, violent

ripe fully developed, mature, mellow, ready, seasoned

ripen burgeon, develop, mature, prepare, season

rebel; have its source ~*n* rising;
upslope; increase **rising** *n* revolt

risk *n* chance of disaster or loss ~*v* put
in jeopardy; take chance of **risky** *adj*

risotto *n* (*pl* **-tos**) dish of rice with
vegetables, meat etc.

risqué *adj* suggestive of indecency

rissole *n* cake of minced meat coated
with breadcrumbs

rite *n* formal practice or custom, esp.
religious **ritual** *n* prescribed order of
rites; stereotyped behaviour ~*adj*
concerning rites

rival *n* one that competes with another ~*adj* in position of rival ~*v* **-valling,
-valled** vie with **rivalry** *n*

river *n* large natural stream of water

rivet *n* bolt for fastening metal plates,
the end being put through holes and

then beaten flat ~*v* fasten firmly **riv-
eting** *adj* very interesting

rivulet *n* small stream

RN Royal Navy

roach *n* freshwater fish

road *n* track, way prepared for passengers, vehicles etc.; direction, way;
street **roadblock** *n* barricade across
road to stop traffic for inspection
roadworks *pl n* repairs to road

roam *v* wander about, rove

roar *v/n* (utter) loud deep hoarse
sound

roast *v* cook in oven or over open fire;
make, be very hot ~*n* roasted joint
~*adj* roasted

rob *v* **robbing, robbed** steal from **robber** *n* **robbery** *n*

robe *n* long outer garment ~*v* dress;

———— T H E S A U R U S ————

rise *v* get up, stand up, surface; ascend, climb, enlarge, go up, grow,
improve, increase, intensify, lift,
mount, soar, swell, wax; advance,
progress, prosper; appear, crop up,
emanate, emerge, eventuate, flow,
happen, issue, occur, originate,
spring; mutiny, rebel, resist, revolt
~*n* ascent, incline, upward slope; increment, pay increase; advance,
climb, improvement, increase,
upsurge, upturn

risk *n* chance, danger, gamble, hazard,
jeopardy, peril, pitfall, speculation,
uncertainty, venture ~*v* chance, dare,
endanger, gamble, hazard, imperil,
jeopardize, venture

ritual *n* ceremonial, ceremony, liturgy, mystery, observance, rite, sacrament, service, solemnity; convention,
custom, form, formality, habit, ordinance, practice, prescription, procedure, protocol, red tape, routine,
stereotype, tradition, usage ~*adj* ceremonial, ceremonious, conventional,
customary, formal, habitual, prescribed, procedural, routine

rival *n* adversary, challenger, competitor, contender, contestant, opponent
~*adj* competing, conflicting, opposed
~*v* come up to, compare with, compete, contend, equal, match, oppose,
vie with

rivalry antagonism, competition, conflict, contention, contest, duel, opposition

road avenue, course, highway, lane,
motorway, path, pathway, roadway,
route, street, thoroughfare, track,
way

roam prowl, ramble, range, rove,
stray, stroll, travel, walk, wander

roar *v* bawl, bay, bellow, clamour,
crash, cry, howl, rumble, shout, yell
~*n* bellow, clamour, crash, cry, howl,
outcry, rumble, shout, thunder, yell

rob burgle, cheat, defraud, despoil,
dispossess, gyp *Sl*, hold up, loot, pillage, plunder, raid, ransack, rifle,
sack, skin *Sl*, strip, swindle

robber bandit, brigand, burglar,
cheat, fraud, highwayman, pirate,
plunderer, raider, stealer, thief

robbery burglary, fraud, hold-up, lar-

put on robes

robin *n* small brown bird with red breast

robot *n* automated machine, esp. performing functions in human manner

robust *adj* sturdy; strong

rock¹ *n* stone; mass of stone; hard sweet in sticks **rockery** *n* mound of stones in garden **rocky** *adj*

rock² *v* (cause to) sway to and fro ~*n* popular music with heavy beat **rocker** *n* curved piece of wood etc. on which thing may rock; rocking chair **rock and roll** style of popular music

rocket *n* self-propelling device powered by burning of explosive contents ~*v* move fast, esp. upwards, as rocket

rod *n* slender straight bar, stick; cane

rodent *n* gnawing animal

rodeo *n* (*pl* **-deos**) *US & Canad* display of bareback riding, cattle handling etc.

roe¹ *n* small species of deer

roe² *n* mass of eggs in fish

rogue *n* scoundrel; mischief-loving person or child

role, rôle *n* actor's part; specific task or function

roll *v* move by turning over and over; wind round; smooth out with roller; move, sweep along; undulate ~*n* act of rolling; anything rolled up; list; small round piece of baked bread; continuous sound, as of drums, thunder etc. **roller** *n* cylinder of wood, stone, metal etc.; long wave of sea **roller coaster** narrow undulating railway at funfair **roller skate** skate with wheels instead of runner **rolling pin** cylindrical roller for pastry **rolling stock** locomotives, carriages etc. of railway

rollicking *adj* boisterously jovial and merry

roly-poly *n* pudding of suet pastry ~*adj* round, plump

ROM *Computers* read only memory

Roman *adj* of Rome or Church of Rome **Roman Catholic** member of that section of Christian Church which acknowledges supremacy of the Pope **Roman numerals** letters used to represent numbers

romance *n* love affair; mysterious or exciting quality; tale of chivalry; tale remote from ordinary life ~*v* exaggerate, fantasize **romantic** *adj* characterized by romance; of love; (of litera-

──────── THESAURUS ────────

ceny, pillage, plunder, raid, rapine, stealing, swindle, theft

robe *n* costume, gown, habit ~*v* attire, clothe, drape, dress, garb

robot android, automaton, machine, mechanical man

rock¹ boulder, stone

rock² lurch, pitch, reel, roll, sway, swing, toss

rocky craggy, rough, rugged, stony; firm, flinty, hard, rugged, solid, steady, tough

rod bar, baton, birch, cane, mace, pole, sceptre, shaft, staff, stick, wand

rogue charlatan, cheat, fraud, rascal, reprobate, scally *NW Eng dial*, scamp, scoundrel, swindler, villain

role character, part, portrayal, representation; capacity, duty, function, job, part, position, post, task

roll *v* flow, go round, gyrate, pass, pivot, reel, revolve, rock, rotate, run, spin, swivel, trundle, turn, twirl, wheel, whirl; bind, coil, curl, enfold, entwine, envelop, furl, swathe, twist, wind, wrap; flatten, level, press, smooth, spread ~*n* cycle, reel, revolution, rotation, run, spin, turn, twirl, wheel, whirl; annals, catalogue, census, chronicle, directory, index, inventory, list, record, register, schedule, scroll, table; boom, growl, grumble, resonance, reverberation, roar, rumble, thunder

ture etc.) displaying passion and imagination ~*n* romantic person

Romany *n/adj* Gypsy

romp *v* run, play wildly ~*n* spell of romping **rompers** *pl n* child's overalls

roof *n* outside upper covering of building ~*v* put roof on, over

rook *n* bird of crow family

rookie *n Inf* new recruit

room *n* space; division of house; scope; *pl* lodgings **roomy** *adj* spacious

roost *n/v* perch **rooster** *n US* domestic cock

root *n* underground part of plant; source, origin; *Anat* embedded portion of tooth, hair etc.; *pl* person's sense of belonging ~*v* (cause to) take root; pull by roots; dig, burrow

rope *n* thick cord ~*v* secure, mark off with rope

rosary *n* series of prayers; string of beads for counting these prayers

rose *n* shrub usu. with prickly stems

and fragrant flowers; the flower; pink colour **rosette** *n* rose-shaped bunch of ribbon **rosy** *adj* flushed; promising **rose-coloured** *adj* having colour of rose; unjustifiably optimistic **rosehip** *n* berry-like fruit of rose plant

rosé *n* pink wine

rosemary *n* evergreen fragrant flowering shrub

roster *n* list of turns of duty

rostrum *n* (*pl* **-trums, -tra**) platform, stage

rot *v* **rotting, rotted** decompose, decay; deteriorate physically or mentally ~*n* decay; any disease producing decomposition of tissue; *Inf* nonsense

rotten *adj* decomposed; very bad; corrupt **rotter** *n Inf* despicable person

rota *n* roster, list

rotary *adj* (of movement) circular **rotate** *v* (cause to) move round centre; (cause to) follow set sequence **rotation** *n*

rote *n* mechanical repetition

———————— THESAURUS ————————

romance affair, amour, attachment, intrigue, liaison, passion, relationship; charm, colour, excitement, fascination, glamour, mystery, sentiment; fantasy, fiction, idyll, legend, melodrama, novel, story, tale

romantic *adj* colourful, exciting, exotic, fascinating, glamorous, mysterious, nostalgic, picturesque; amorous, fond, loving, passionate, sentimental, tender; dreamy, high-flown, idealistic, quixotic, utopian, visionary, whimsical ~*n* dreamer, idealist, sentimentalist, visionary

room area, capacity, compass, expanse, extent, leeway, margin, play, range, scope, space, territory, volume; apartment, chamber, office; chance, occasion, scope

root *n* rhizome, stem, tuber; base, bottom, cause, core, crux, derivation, foundation, fundamental, germ,

heart, nucleus, occasion, origin, seat, seed, source; *pl* birthplace, cradle, family, heritage, home, origins ~*v* anchor, embed, entrench, establish, fasten, fix, ground, implant, moor, set, stick

rope *n* cable, cord, hawser, line, strand ~*v* bind, fasten, hitch, lash, lasso, moor, pinion, tether, tie

roster agenda, catalogue, list, register, roll, rota, scroll, table

rosy blooming, blushing, flushed, fresh, glowing, radiant, reddish, ruddy; auspicious, bright, cheerful, encouraging, favourable, hopeful, optimistic, promising, sunny

rot *v* corrupt, crumble, decay, decompose, deteriorate, go bad, moulder, perish, putrefy, spoil, taint; decline, deteriorate, waste away ~*n* blight, canker, corruption, decay, mould, putrefaction

rotor n revolving portion of dynamo motor or turbine

Rottweiler n large dog with black and tan coat

rotund adj round; plump

rouge n red powder, cream used to colour cheeks

rough adj not smooth; violent, stormy; rude; approximate; in preliminary form ~v make rough; plan ~n rough state or area; sketch **roughen** v **roughage** n unassimilated portion of food **rough it** live without usual comforts etc.

roulette n gambling game played with revolving wheel

round adj spherical, circular, curved; plump; complete; roughly correct; considerable ~adv with circular course ~n thing round in shape; recurrent duties; stage in competition; customary course; game (of golf); period in boxing match etc.; cartridge for firearm ~prep about; on all sides of ~v make, become round; move round **rounders** pl n ball game **roundly** adv thoroughly **roundabout** n revolving circular platform on which people ride for amusement; road junction at which traffic passes round central island ~adj not straightforward **round trip** journey out and back again **round up** drive (cattle) together

rouse v wake up, stir up, excite; waken

rout n overwhelming defeat, disorderly retreat ~v put to flight

route n road, chosen way

routine n regularity of procedure ~adj ordinary, regular

rove v wander, roam

——————————— THESAURUS ———————————

rotate go round, gyrate, pivot, reel, revolve, spin, swivel, turn, wheel; alternate, interchange, switch

rotation orbit, reel, revolution, spin, spinning, turn, turning, wheel; cycle, sequence, succession, switching

rotten bad, corrupt, crumbling, decayed, decomposed, festering, fetid, foul, mouldy, perished, putrid, rank, sour, stinking, tainted, unsound; bad, deplorable, disappointing, regrettable, unfortunate, unlucky; corrupt, deceitful, degenerate, dishonest, disloyal, faithless, immoral, perfidious, treacherous, venal, vicious

rough adj broken, bumpy, craggy, irregular, jagged, rocky, stony, uneven; bristly, bushy, coarse, disordered, tangled, uncut, unshorn; boisterous, choppy, squally, stormy, turbulent, wild; basic, crude, cursory, hasty, imperfect, incomplete, quick, raw, rudimentary, shapeless, sketchy, unpolished

round adj circular, curved, cylindrical, disc-shaped, globular, rotund, rounded, spherical; ample, fleshy, full, full-fleshed, plump, rotund ~n ball, band, circle, disc, globe, orb, ring, sphere; bout, cycle, sequence, series, session, succession; division, lap, level, period, session, stage, turn; ambit, beat, circuit, compass, course, routine, schedule, series, tour, turn; bullet, discharge, shell, shot ~v bypass, circle, encircle, flank, go round, skirt, turn

rouse agitate, anger, animate, disturb, excite, incite, inflame, instigate, move, prod, provoke, startle, stimulate, stir, whip up; awaken, call, rise, wake, waken, wake up

rout n beating, debacle, defeat, drubbing, overthrow, pasting Sl, ruin, shambles, thrashing ~v beat, chase, clobber Sl, conquer, crush, defeat, destroy, dispel, overpower, overthrow, thrash

route beat, circuit, course, direction, itinerary, journey, passage, path,

row[1] *n* number of things in a straight line

row[2] *v* propel boat by oars ~*n* spell of rowing

row[3] *Inf n* dispute; disturbance ~*v* quarrel noisily

rowan *n* tree producing bright red berries, mountain ash

rowdy *adj/n* disorderly, noisy (person)

rowlock *n* device to hold oar on gunwale of boat

royal *adj* of king or queen **royalist** *n* supporter of monarchy **royalty** *n* royal power; royal persons; payment for right, use of invention or copyright

rpm revolutions per minute

RSVP please reply

rub *v* **rubbing, rubbed** apply pressure to with circular or backwards-and-forwards movement; clean, polish, dry thus; abrade, chafe; remove by friction; become frayed or worn by friction ~*n* rubbing

rubber *n* elastic dried sap of certain tropical trees; synthetic material resembling this; piece of rubber etc. used for erasing ~*adj* made of rubber **rubbery** *adj*

rubbish *n* refuse; anything worthless; nonsense ~*v Inf* criticize

rubble *n* fragments of stone

rubella *n* mild contagious viral disease, German measles

ruby *n* precious red gem; its colour ~*adj* of this colour

ruck[1] *n* crowd; common herd

ruck[2] *n/v* crease

rucksack *n* pack carried on back, knapsack

ruction *n Inf* noisy disturbance

rudder *n* steering device for boat, aircraft

ruddy *adj* of healthy red colour

rude *adj* impolite; coarse; vulgar; roughly made

rudiments *pl n* elements, first principles **rudimentary** *adj*

—————————— THESAURUS ——————————

road, round, run, way

routine *n* custom, formula, groove, method, order, pattern, practice, programme, usage, way ~*adj* customary, everyday, familiar, habitual, normal, ordinary, standard, typical, usual, workaday

row[1] bank, column, file, line, queue, range, rank, sequence, series, string, tier

row[2] *n* brawl, dispute, disturbance, fray, fuss, noise, quarrel, racket, rumpus, squabble, tiff, trouble, tumult, uproar ~*v* argue, brawl, dispute, fight, spar, wrangle

rowdy disorderly, loud, noisy, rough, unruly, uproarious, wild

royal imperial, kingly, princely, queenly, regal, sovereign

rub *v* caress, chafe, clean, fray, grate, massage, polish, scour, scrape, shine, smooth, stroke, wipe; apply, put,

smear, spread ~*n* caress, massage, polish, shine, stroke, wipe

rubbish debris, dregs, dross, garbage, junk *Inf*, litter, lumber, offal, refuse, scrap, trash, waste; drivel, gibberish, hot air *Inf*, nonsense, piffle *Inf*, rot, tripe *Inf*, twaddle

ruddy blooming, blushing, florid, flushed, fresh, glowing, healthy, radiant, red, reddish, rosy, rosy-cheeked, sanguine, sunburnt

rude abrupt, abusive, blunt, brusque, cheeky, curt, discourteous, ill-mannered, impertinent, impolite, impudent, insolent, insulting, offhand, short, unmannerly; boorish, brutish, coarse, crude, graceless, loutish, oafish, rough, savage, uncivilised, uncouth, uncultured, vulgar; artless, crude, inartistic, inelegant, makeshift, primitive, raw, rough, simple

rudiments basics, beginnings, el-

rue v grieve for; regret **rueful** adj

ruff n frilled collar; natural collar of feathers, fur etc. on some birds and animals **ruffle** v rumple, annoy, frill ~n frilled trimming

ruffian n violent, lawless person

rug n small floor mat; woollen coverlet

rugby n form of football in which the ball may be carried

rugged adj rough; strong-featured

ruin n destruction; downfall; fallen or broken state; loss of wealth etc.; pl ruined buildings etc. ~v bring or come to ruin **ruinous** adj

rule n principle; government; what is usual; measuring stick ~v govern; decide; mark with straight lines **ruler** n one who governs; stick for measuring or ruling lines **ruling** n formal decision

rum n spirit distilled from sugar cane

rumba n lively ballroom dance

rumble v/n (make) noise as of distant thunder

ruminate v chew cud; ponder over **ruminant** adj/n cud-chewing (animal)

rummage v search thoroughly

rummy n card game

rumour n hearsay, unproved statement ~v put around as rumour

rump n tail end; buttocks

rumple v make untidy, dishevelled

rumpus n disturbance

run v running, ran, run move with more rapid gait than walking; go quickly; flow; flee; compete in race, contest, election; cross by running; expose oneself (to risk etc.); cause to run; manage; operate ~n act, spell of running; rush; tendency; course; enclosure for domestic fowls; ride in

——————— THESAURUS ———————

ements, essentials, first principles, foundation, fundamentals

ruffle derange, disarrange, discompose, disorder, rumple, tousle, wrinkle; agitate, annoy, confuse, disquiet, disturb, fluster, harass, hassle Inf, irritate, nettle, perturb, stir, torment, trouble, unnerve, unsettle, upset, worry

rugged broken, bumpy, craggy, difficult, jagged, ragged, rocky, rough, stark, uneven; furrowed, lined, rough-hewn, weathered, worn, wrinkled

ruin n bankruptcy, breakdown, collapse, crash, damage, decay, defeat, destruction, devastation, disrepair, downfall, failure, fall, wreckage ~v bankrupt, break, bring down, crush, defeat, demolish, destroy, devastate, impoverish, lay waste, overthrow, raze, shatter, smash, wreck

rule n axiom, canon, decree, direction, guideline, law, maxim, order, ordinance, precept, principle, regula-

tion, standard; ascendancy, authority, command, control, direction, domination, empire, government, influence, leadership, mastery, power, regime, reign, supremacy, sway; condition, convention, custom, form, habit, practice, procedure, routine, tradition, wont; course, formula, method, policy, procedure, way ~v administer, command, control, direct, dominate, govern, guide, hold sway, lead, manage, preside over, regulate, reign; decide, decree, determine, establish, find, judge, lay down, pronounce, resolve, settle

ruler commander, controller, emperor, empress, governor, king, leader, lord, monarch, potentate, prince, princess, queen, sovereign; measure, rule, straight edge, yardstick

ruling adjudication, decision, decree, finding, judgment, pronouncement, resolution, verdict

rumour buzz, gossip, hearsay, news, report, story, talk, tidings, whisper,

car; unravelled stitches; score of one
at cricket **runner** *n* racer; messenger;
curved piece of wood on which sleigh
slides; stem of plant forming new
roots; strip of cloth, carpet **running**
adj continuous; consecutive; flowing
~*n* act of moving or flowing quickly;
ride in car; continuous period or sequence **runny** *adj* **rundown** *n* summary **run-down** *adj* exhausted; decrepit, broken-down **run down** stop
working; reduce; exhaust; denigrate
run-of-the-mill *adj* ordinary **run out**
be completely used up **runway** *n* level
stretch where aircraft take off and
land

rune *n* character of old Germanic alphabet

rung *n* crossbar in ladder

runt *n* unusually small animal

rupture *n* breaking, breach; hernia ~*v*
break; burst, sever

rural *adj* of the country; rustic

ruse *n* stratagem, trick

rush[1] *v* hurry or cause to hurry; move
violently or rapidly ~*n* rushing ~*adj*
done with speed **rush hour** period
when many people travel to or from
work

rush[2] *n* marsh plant with slender pithy
stem

rusk *n* kind of biscuit

russet *n/adj* reddish-brown (colour)

rust *n* reddish-brown coating formed
on iron; disease of plants ~*v* affect
with rust **rusty** *adj* corroded;
reddish-brown; out of practice

rustic *adj* simple, homespun; rural;

——————— THESAURUS ———————

word

run *v* bolt, career, dart, dash, gallop,
hare *Brit inf,* hasten, hotfoot, hurry,
jog, race, rush, scamper, scramble,
scurry, speed, sprint; discharge, flow,
go, gush, leak, spill, spout, stream;
abscond, bolt, decamp, depart, do a
runner *Sl,* escape, flee; challenge,
compete, contend, stand, take part;
administer, carry on, conduct, control, coordinate, direct, handle, head,
lead, manage, operate, oversee, own,
regulate, supervise; function, go, operate, perform, tick, work ~*n* dash,
gallop, jog, race, rush, sprint, spurt;
drive, excursion, jaunt, journey, lift,
outing, ride, round; course, cycle,
passage, period, round, season, sequence, series, spell, stretch, string

run down curtail, cut, cut back, decrease, drop, reduce, trim; exhaust,
tire, weaken; belittle, decry, defame,
disparage, put down, revile, rubbish
Inf, slag (off) *Sl*

run-down below par, debilitated,
drained, enervated, exhausted, unhealthy, weak, weary, worn-out;

broken-down, decrepit, dilapidated,
dingy, ramshackle, seedy, shabby,
worn-out

running *adj* constant, continuous, incessant, perpetual, together, unbroken, uninterrupted; flowing, moving,
streaming ~*n* charge, conduct, control, direction, leadership, management, organization, regulation,
supervision

run-of-the-mill average, common,
fair, mediocre, middling, ordinary,
passable, tolerable, undistinguished

rupture *n* breach, break, burst, cleavage, cleft, crack, rent, split, tear ~*v*
break, burst, cleave, crack, fracture,
puncture, rend, separate, sever, split,
tear

rural agrarian, agricultural, bucolic,
country, pastoral, rustic, sylvan

rush *v* bolt, career, dart, dash, fly,
hasten, hurry, press, push, quicken,
race, run, scramble, scurry, shoot,
speed, sprint, stampede, tear ~*n*
charge, dash, expedition, haste, hurry, race, scramble, speed, stampede,
surge, swiftness, urgency

uncouth. boorish ~*n* countryman
rustle[1] *v/n* (make) sound as of blown
dead leaves etc.
rustle[2] *v US* steal (cattle) **rustler** *n*

rut *n* furrow made by wheel; settled
habit
ruthless *adj* merciless
rye *n* grain; plant bearing it

——————————— THESAURUS ———————————

rust *n* corrosion, oxidation; blight,
mildew, mould, must, rot ~*v* corrode, oxidize
rustic *adj* artless, homespun, plain,
simple, unaffected, unpolished;
country, pastoral, rural, sylvan; awkward, boorish, churlish, clownish,
coarse, crude, loutish, rough, uncouth ~*n* boor, bumpkin, clod,
countryman, peasant, yokel

rustle *v* crackle, whisper ~*n* crackle,
rustling, whisper
rut furrow, gouge, groove, indentation, score, track, wheelmark; dead
end, groove, habit, pattern, routine,
system
ruthless brutal, callous, cruel, ferocious, fierce, hard, harsh, heartless,
inhuman, merciless, pitiless, relentless, savage, stern, unmerciful

S s

Sabbath *n* day of worship and rest, observed on Saturday in Judaism, on Sunday by Christians **sabbatical** *adj/n* (pert. to) leave for study

sabotage *n* intentional damage done to roads, machines etc., esp. secretly in war ~*v* damage intentionally **saboteur** *n*

sabre *n* curved cavalry sword

sac *n* pouchlike structure in animal or plant

saccharin *n* artificial sweetener

sachet *n* small envelope or bag, esp. one holding liquid

sack *n* large bag, esp. of coarse material; pillaging; *Inf* dismissal ~*v* pillage (captured town); *Inf* dismiss **sackcloth** *n* coarse fabric used for sacks

sacrament *n* one of certain ceremonies of Christian Church

sacred *adj* dedicated, regarded as holy; revered; inviolable

sacrifice *n* giving something up for sake of something else; thing so given up; making of offering to a god; thing offered ~*v* offer as sacrifice; give up

sacrificial *adj*

sacrilege *n* misuse, desecration of something sacred **sacrilegious** *adj*

sacrosanct *adj* preserved by religious fear against desecration or violence

sad *adj* sorrowful; unsatisfactory, deplorable **sadden** *v* make sad **sadness** *n*

saddle *n* rider's seat on horse, bicycle etc.; joint of meat ~*v* put saddle on; lay burden on

sadism *n* love of inflicting pain **sadist** *n* **sadistic** *adj*

safari *n* (*pl* **-ris**) expedition to hunt or observe wild animals, esp. in Africa

safe *adj* secure, protected; uninjured, out of danger; not involving risk; trustworthy; sure ~*n* strong lockable container **safely** *adv* **safety** *n* **safeguard** *n* protection ~*v* protect **safety pin** pin with guard over the point when closed

saffron *n* crocus; orange-coloured flavouring obtained from it; orange colour ~*adj* orange

sag *v* **sagging**, **sagged** sink in middle; curve downwards under pressure;

THESAURUS

sabotage *n* damage, destruction, wrecking ~*v* damage, destroy, disable, vandalize, wreck

sack *v* discharge, dismiss

sacred; holy, religious; blessed, divine, hallowed, holy, revered, sanctified, venerable; inviolable, sacrosanct

sacrifice *n* loss, renunciation, surrender ~*v* give up, lose, surrender

sacrilege blasphemy, desecration, impiety, violation

sad depressed, dismal, doleful, down, melancholy, mournful, sorrowful, unhappy, woebegone; bad, deplorable, lamentable, regrettable, serious, sorry

sadden deject, depress, grieve

sadistic barbarous, brutal, cruel, vicious

sadness depression, gloominess, grief, melancholy, misery, sorrow, unhappiness

safe *adj* guarded, protected, secure; intact, undamaged, unharmed, unhurt; dependable, reliable, sure, trustworthy ~*n* coffer, safe-deposit box, strongbox

safeguard *n* defence, protection, shield ~*v* defend, preserve, protect, shield

safety protection, refuge, sanctuary, security, shelter

hang loosely ~*n* droop

saga *n* legend of Norse heroes; any long (heroic) story

sage¹ *n* very wise man ~*adj* wise

sage² *n* aromatic herb

sago *n* starchy cereal from powdered pith of palm tree

said *past tense and past participle of* SAY

sail *n* piece of fabric stretched to catch wind for propelling ship etc.; act of sailing; arm of windmill ~*v* travel by water; move smoothly; begin voyage **sailor** *n* seaman; one who sails

saint *n* person recognized as having gained a special place in heaven; exceptionally good person

sake *n* cause, account; end, purpose **for the sake of** on behalf of; to please or benefit

salad *n* mixed raw vegetables or fruit used as food

salami *n* variety of highly-spiced sausage

salary *n* fixed regular payment to persons employed usu. in nonmanual work

sale *n* selling; selling of goods at unusually low prices; auction **salesman** *n* shop assistant; one travelling to sell goods

salient *adj* prominent, noticeable; jutting out

saline *adj* containing, consisting of a chemical salt, esp. common salt; salty

saliva *n* liquid which forms in mouth, spittle

sallow *adj* of unhealthy pale or yellowish colour

sally *n* (*pl* -**lies**) rushing out, esp. by troops; witty remark ~*v* -**lying**, -**lied** rush; set out

salmon *n* large silvery fish with orange-pink flesh valued as food; colour of its flesh ~*adj* of this colour

salmonella *n* (*pl* -**lae**) bacterium causing food poisoning

salon *n* (reception room for) guests in fashionable household; commercial premises of hairdressers, beauticians etc.

saloon *n* public room, esp. on passenger ship; car with fixed roof **saloon bar** first-class bar in hotel etc.

salt *n* white powdery or crystalline substance consisting mainly of sodium chloride, used to season or preserve food; chemical compound of acid and metal ~*v* season, sprinkle with, preserve with salt ~*adj* preserved in salt **salty** *adj* of, like salt **saltcellar** *n* small vessel for salt at table

salubrious *adj* favourable to health, beneficial

salutary *adj* producing beneficial result

salute *v* greet with words or sign; acknowledge with praise; perform military salute ~*n* word, sign by which one greets another; motion of arm as mark of respect to military superior; firing of guns as military greeting of honour

salvage *n* act of saving ship or other property from danger of loss; proper-

sail *v* navigate, pilot, steer, voyage; drift, float, glide, scud, skim; embark, set sail

sailor marine, mariner, salt, sea dog, seafarer, seaman

sake account, behalf, good, interest, profit, welfare

salary earnings, emolument income, pay, remuneration

sale deal, transaction

sallow pale, pasty, peely-wally *Scot*, sickly, wan, yellowish

salt *n* flavour, relish, seasoning ~*adj* brackish, briny, saline, salty

salute *v* address, greet, hail; acknowledge, honour, recognize ~*n* address,

ty so saved ~*v* save

salvation *n* fact or state of being saved, esp. of soul

salve *n* healing ointment ~*v* anoint with such, soothe

salver *n* (silver) tray for presentation of food, letters etc.

salvo *n* (*pl* **-vos**, **-voes**) simultaneous discharge of guns etc.

same *adj* identical, not different, unchanged; uniform; just mentioned previously

sample *n* specimen ~*v* take, give sample of; try **sampler** *n* beginner's exercise in embroidery

sanatorium *n* (*pl* **-riums**, **-ria**) hospital, esp. for chronically ill; health resort

sanctify *v* **-fying**, **-fied** set apart as holy; free from sin **sanctity** *n* sacredness **sanctuary** *n* holy place; place of refuge; nature reserve

sanctimonious *adj* making affected show of piety

sanction *n* permission, authorization; penalty for breaking law; *pl* boycott or other coercive measure, esp. by one state against another ~*v* allow, authorize

sand *n* substance consisting of small grains of rock or mineral, esp. on

beach or in desert; *pl* stretches or banks of this ~*v* polish, smooth with sandpaper; cover, mix with sand **sandy** *adj* like sand; sand-coloured; consisting of, covered with sand

sandbag *n* bag filled with sand or earth as protection against gunfire, floodwater etc. and as weapon ~*v* beat, hit with sandbag **sandpaper** *n* paper with sand stuck on it for scraping or polishing **sandpiper** *n* shore bird with long bill **sandstone** *n* rock composed of sand

sandal *n* shoe consisting of sole attached by straps

sandwich *n* two slices of bread with meat or other substance between ~*v* insert between two other things

sane *adj* of sound mind; sensible, rational **sanity** *n*

sang *past tense of* SING

sanguine *adj* cheerful, confident; ruddy in complexion

sanitary *adj* helping protection of health against dirt etc. **sanitation** *n* measures, apparatus for preservation of public health

sap¹ *n* moisture which circulates in plants; *Inf* foolish person **sapling** *n* young tree

sap² *v* **sapping**, **sapped** undermine;

——— T H E S A U R U S ———

greeting, salutation

salvage *v* recover, rescue, retrieve, save

salvation deliverance, redemption, rescue, saving

same *adj* duplicate, equal, identical, twin; aforementioned, aforesaid

sample *n* example, illustration, instance, specimen ~*v* experience, taste, test, try

sanctify bless, consecrate, hallow, set apart

sanctimonious hypocritical, pious, self-satisfied, smug

sanction *n* approval, authority, en-

dorsement, support; (*oft. pl*) ban, boycott, embargo, penalty ~*v* allow, approve, authorize, endorse, permit, support

sanctuary altar, church, shrine, temple; asylum, haven, refuge, retreat, shelter

sane lucid, mentally sound, rational; balanced, judicious, level-headed, reasonable, sensible

sanitary clean, germ-free, healthy, hygienic

sanity rationality, reason, stability; good sense, level-headedness, rationality, sense

weaken

sapphire n (usu. blue) precious stone; deep blue ~adj of deep blue colour

sarcasm n bitter or wounding ironic remark; (use of) such remarks **sarcastic** adj

sarcophagus n (pl -gi, -guses) stone coffin

sardine n small fish of herring family

sardonic adj characterized by irony, mockery or derision

sari, saree n long garment worn by Hindu women

sartorial adj of tailor, tailoring, or men's clothes

sash n decorative belt, ribbon, wound around the body

Satan n the devil **satanic** adj devilish

satchel n small bag, esp. for school books

satellite n celestial body or man-made projectile orbiting planet; person, country etc. dependent on another

satin n fabric (of silk, rayon etc.) with glossy surface on one side

satire n use of ridicule or sarcasm to expose vice and folly **satirical** adj **satirize** v make object of satire

satisfy v -fying, -fied please, meet wishes of; fulfil, supply adequately; convince **satisfaction** n **satisfactory** adj

satsuma n kind of small orange

saturate v soak thoroughly **saturation** n act, result of saturating

Saturday n seventh day of the week

satyr n woodland deity, part man, part goat; lustful man

sauce n liquid added to food to enhance flavour ~v add sauce to **saucy** adj impudent **saucepan** n cooking pot with long handle

saucer n curved plate put under cup; shallow depression

sauerkraut n dish of shredded cabbage fermented in brine

sauna n steam bath

saunter v walk in leisurely manner, stroll ~n leisurely walk or stroll

sausage n minced meat enclosed in thin tube of animal intestine or synthetic material **sausage roll** pastry cylinder filled with sausage

sauté v fry quickly

savage adj wild; ferocious; brutal; uncivilized, primitive ~n member of savage tribe, barbarian ~v attack ferociously

save v rescue, preserve; keep for future; prevent need of; lay by money

——————— THESAURUS ———————

sarcasm cynicism, derision, irony, mockery, satire

sarcastic cynical, ironical, mocking, sardonic, satirical

Satan Beelzebub, Lord of the Flies, Lucifer, Mephistopheles, Old Nick *Inf*, Prince of Darkness, The Devil

satanic devilish, diabolic, evil, fiendish, hellish, wicked

satire burlesque, irony, lampoon, parody, ridicule

satirical biting, caustic, cutting, incisive, ironical, mocking

satisfaction content, contentment, enjoyment, happiness, pleasure; assuaging, fulfilment, gratification

satisfactory acceptable, adequate, all right, average, fair, passable, sufficient

satisfy assuage, content, feed, fill, gratify, please, sate, slake; do, fulfil, meet, serve, suffice; assure, convince, persuade, reassure

saturate drench, soak, souse, steep

saunter v amble, meander, ramble, stroll ~n amble, promenade, ramble, stroll, walk

savage adj rough, untamed; wild; barbarous, bloody, brutal, cruel, ferocious, fierce, murderous, vicious;

~*n Sport* act of preventing goal etc.
~*prep* except **saving** *adj* redeeming
~*prep* excepting ~*n* economy; *pl*
money put by for future use
saviour *n* person who rescues another; (*with cap.*) Christ
savour *n* characteristic taste or smell
~*v* have particular taste or smell; give
flavour to; have flavour of; enjoy **savoury** *adj* attractive to taste or smell;
not sweet
saw[1] *n* tool with toothed edge for cutting wood etc. ~*v* **sawing, sawed,
sawed** *or* **sawn** cut with saw; make
movements of sawing **sawdust** *n* fine
wood fragments made in sawing
saw[2] *past tense of* SEE
saxophone *n* keyed wind instrument
say *v* **saying, said** speak; pronounce;
state; express; take as example or as
near enough; form and deliver opinion ~*n* what one has to say; chance of
saying it; share in decision **saying** *n*
maxim, proverb
scab *n* crust formed over wound; skin
disease; disease of plants
scabbard *n* sheath for sword or dagger
scaffold *n* temporary platform for
workmen; gallows **scaffolding** *n* (material for building) scaffold
scald *v* burn with hot liquid or steam;
heat (liquid) almost to boiling point

~*n* injury by scalding
scale[1] *n* one of the thin, overlapping
plates covering fishes and reptiles;
thin flake; crust which forms in ket-
tles etc. ~*v* remove scales from; come
off in scales
scale[2] *n* (*usu. pl*) weighing instrument
scale[3] *n* graduated table or sequence
of marks at regular intervals used as
reference in making measurements;
series of musical notes; ratio of size
between a thing and a model or map
of it; (relative) degree, extent ~*v*
climb ~*adj* proportionate
scallop *n* edible shellfish; edging in
small curves like scallop shell ~*v*
shape like scallop shell
scalp *n* skin and hair of top of head ~*v*
cut off scalp of
scalpel *n* small surgical knife
scamp *n* mischievous person
scamper *v* run about; run hastily ~*n*
scampering
scampi *pl n* large prawns
scan *v* **scanning, scanned** look at carefully; examine, search using radar or
sonar beam; glance over quickly; (of
verse) conform to metrical rules ~*n*
scanning **scanner** *n* device, esp. electronic, which scans
scandal *n* something disgraceful; malicious gossip **scandalize** *v* shock
scandalous *adj*

———————— THESAURUS ————————

primitive, uncivilized ~*v* attack, maul
save deliver, free, liberate, recover,
redeem, rescue, salvage; guard, keep
safe, preserve, protect, screen, shield;
economize, hoard, husband, lay by,
put by, reserve, set aside, store
saving *adj* qualifying, redeeming
savour *n* flavour, relish, smack, taste
~*v* appreciate, enjoy, relish
savoury delectable, delicious, luscious, palatable, tasty
say *v* announce, declare, mention,
pronounce, remark, speak, state,

utter, voice; communicate, convey,
express ~*n* authority, influence, power, sway, weight
saying adage, aphorism, axiom, dictum, maxim, proverb
scale *n* gradation, graduation, hierarchy, ladder, series, steps; proportion,
ratio; degree, extent, range, scope
scamper dash, fly, hurry, run, scoot
scan check, check out *Inf*, examine,
glance over, scrutinize, search, skim,
survey, sweep
scandal crime, disgrace, offence, sin,

scant *adj* barely sufficient or not sufficient **scanty** *adj*

scapegoat *n* person bearing blame due to others

scar *n* mark left by healed wound, burn or sore; change resulting from emotional distress ~*v* **scarring, scarred** mark, heal with scar

scarce *adj* hard to find; existing or available in insufficient quantity; uncommon **scarcely** *adv* only just; not quite; definitely or probably not **scarcity, scarceness** *n*

scare *v* frighten ~*n* fright, sudden panic **scary** *adj* **scarecrow** *n* thing set up to frighten birds from crops; badly dressed person

scarf *n* (*pl* **scarves** *or* **scarfs**) long narrow strip of material to put round neck, head etc.

scarlet *n* brilliant red colour ~*adj* of this colour; immoral, esp. unchaste **scarlet fever** infectious fever with scarlet rash

scathing *adj* harshly critical

scatter *v* throw in various directions; put here and there; sprinkle; disperse **scatterbrain** *n* empty-headed person

scavenge *v* search for (anything usable), esp. among discarded material **scavenger** *n* person who scavenges; animal, bird which feeds on refuse

scenario *n* (*pl* **-rios**) summary of plot of play or film; imagined sequence of future events

scene *n* place of action of novel, play etc.; place of any action; subdivision of play; view; episode; display of strong emotion **scenery** *n* natural features of district; constructions used on stage to represent scene of action **scenic** *adj* picturesque

scent *n* distinctive smell, esp. pleasant one; trail; perfume ~*v* detect or track (by smell); sense; fill with fragrance

sceptic *n* one who maintains doubt or disbelief **sceptical** *adj* **scepticism** *n*

sceptre *n* ornamental staff as symbol of royal power

schedule *n* plan of procedure for project; list; timetable ~*v* enter into schedule; plan to occur at certain time

scheme *n* plan, design; project; outline ~*v* devise, plan, esp. in under-

———————————— THESAURUS ————————————

wrongdoing; dirt, gossip, rumours, slander, talk

scandalous atrocious, disgraceful, monstrous, outrageous, shameful, shocking, unseemly; defamatory, libellous, scurrilous

scanty bare, deficient, inadequate, meagre, poor, short, thin

scar *n* injury, mark ~*v* damage, disfigure, mark

scarce deficient, few, infrequent, insufficient, rare, uncommon, unusual

scare *v* alarm, frighten, intimidate, shock, startle, terrify ~*n* alarm, fright, panic, shock, start

scathing biting, caustic, critical, cutting, harsh, scornful

scatter diffuse, disseminate, fling,

shower, spread, sprinkle, strew; disband, dispel, disperse, dissipate

scene backdrop, location, set, setting; area, locality, place, position, setting, site, spot; landscape, panorama, prospect, view, vista; exhibition, fuss, performance, row, to-do, upset

scenery landscape, surroundings, view, vista

scent *n* aroma, bouquet, fragrance, odour, perfume, smell; spoor, track, trail ~*v* detect, discern, sense, smell

sceptic cynic, disbeliever, doubter

sceptical cynical, doubtful, dubious, incredulous

schedule *n* agenda, calendar, plan, programme, timetable ~*v* appoint, arrange, book, organize, plan, pro-

hand manner **scheming** *adj*

schism *n* (group resulting from) division in political party, church etc.

schizophrenia *n* mental disorder involving deterioration of, confusion about personality **schizophrenic** *adj/n*

school¹ *n* institution for teaching children or for giving instruction in any subject; buildings of such institution; group of thinkers, writers, artists etc. with principles or methods in common ~*v* educate; bring under control, train **scholar** *n* learned person; one taught in school **scholarly** *adj* learned **scholarship** *n* learning; prize, grant to student for payment of school or college fees **scholastic** *adj* of schools or scholars

school² *n* shoal (of fish, whales etc.)

schooner *n* fore-and-aft rigged vessel with two or more masts; tall glass

science *n* systematic study and knowledge of natural or physical phenomena; any branch of study concerned with observed material facts; skill, technique **scientific** *adj* of the principles of science; systematic **scientist** *n* **science fiction** stories making imaginative use of scientific knowledge

scimitar *n* curved oriental sword

scintillating *adj* sparkling; animated, witty, clever

scissors *pl n* (*esp.* **pair of scissors**) cutting instrument of two blades pivoted together

scoff¹ *v* express derision for

scoff² *v Sl* eat rapidly

scold *v* find fault; reprimand

scone *n* small plain cake baked on griddle or in oven

scoop *n* shovel-like tool for ladling, hollowing out etc.; news story reported in one newspaper before its rivals ~*v* use scoop

scooter *n* child's vehicle propelled by pushing on ground with one foot; light motorcycle (*also* **motor scooter**)

scope *n* range of activity or application; room, opportunity

scorch *v* burn, be burnt, on surface ~*n* slight burn

score *n* points gained in game, competition; group of 20; (*esp. pl*) a lot; musical notation; mark or notch, part. to keep tally; reason, account; grievance ~*v* gain points in game; mark; cross out; arrange music (for); keep tally of points

scorn *n* contempt, derision ~*v* despise

———————— T H E S A U R U S ————————

gramme, time

scheme *n* design, plan, programme, project, proposal, strategy, system, tactics; blueprint, chart, diagram, draft, layout, outline, pattern ~*v* conspire, devise, intrigue, plan, plot

scheming calculating, conniving, cunning, sly, underhand

scholar academic, intellectual; learner, pupil, schoolboy, schoolgirl, student

scholarship book-learning, education, erudition, knowledge, learning; bursary, fellowship

school *n* academy, college, institution, seminary ~*v* coach, discipline,

drill, educate, instruct, prepare, prime, train, tutor

scientific accurate, controlled, exact, precise, systematic

scoff belittle, deride, jeer, mock, pooh-pooh, ridicule, scorn, sneer

scold *v* berate, castigate, chide, lecture, rebuke, reprimand, reproach, reprove, tear into *Inf*, tear (someone) off a strip *Brit inf*

scope area, capacity, extent, freedom, latitude, liberty, opportunity, orbit, range, reach, room, space, sphere

scorch blacken, burn, char, sear, singe

score *n* grade, mark, outcome, points,

scornful *adj*

scorpion *n* small lobster-shaped animal with sting at end of jointed tail

scotch *v* put an end to

scot-free *adj* without harm or loss

scoundrel *n* villain, blackguard

scour[1] *v* clean, polish by rubbing; clean or flush out **scourer** *n* rough pad for cleaning pots and pans

scour[2] *v* move rapidly along or over (territory) in search of something

scourge *n* whip, lash; severe affliction ~*v* flog; punish severely

scout *n* one sent out to reconnoitre ~*v* act as scout

scowl *v/n* (make) gloomy or sullen frown

scrabble *v* scrape at with hands, claws in disorderly manner

scrag *n* lean person or animal; lean end of a neck of mutton **scraggy** *adj* thin, bony

scram *v* **scramming, scrammed** *Inf* go away hastily

scramble *v* move along or up by crawling, climbing etc.; struggle with others (for); mix up; cook (eggs) beaten up with milk ~*n* scrambling; rough climb; disorderly proceeding

scrap *n* small piece or fragment; leftover material; *Inf* fight; *pl* leftover food ~*v* **scrapping, scrapped** break up, discard as useless; *Inf* fight **scrappy** *adj* unequal in quality; badly finished **scrapbook** *n* book in which newspaper cuttings or pictures are stuck

scrape *v* rub with something sharp; clean, smooth thus; grate; scratch; rub with harsh noise ~*n* act, sound of scraping **scraper** *n* instrument for scraping

scratch *v* score, make narrow surface mark or wound with something sharp; scrape (skin) with nails to relieve itching; remove, withdraw from list, race etc. ~*n* wound, mark or sound made by scratching

scrawl *v* write, draw untidily ~*n* thing scrawled

——————— THESAURUS ———————

result, total; account, cause, grounds, reason; grievance, grudge, injury ~*v* achieve, gain, win; cut, graze, scrape, scratch, slash; (*with* **out** *or* **through**) cancel, cross out, delete, strike out

scorn *n* contempt, derision, disdain, mockery ~*v* be above, disdain, reject, scoff at, slight, spurn

scornful contemptuous, derisive, disdainful, mocking, sneering

scoundrel bastard *Offens,* blackguard, good-for-nothing, heel *Sl,* rascal, reprobate, rogue, son-of-a-bitch *Sl, chiefly US & Canad,* villain

scour[1] buff, clean, polish, scrub

scour[2] comb, hunt, ransack, search

scourge *n* lash, switch, thong, whip; affliction, bane, curse, plague, torment ~*v* beat, cane, flog, horsewhip, lash, leather, thrash, whip

scowl *v* frown, glower, lour *or* lower

~*n* black look, frown, glower

scramble *v* climb, crawl; contend, struggle, strive, vie ~*n* climb, trek; melee, race, rush, struggle, tussle

scrap *n* atom, bit, crumb, fragment, grain, morsel, part, particle, piece, portion; junk, off cuts, waste; *pl* bits, leavings, leftovers, remains ~*v* abandon, chuck *Inf,* discard, drop, jettison, write off

scrape *v* bark, graze, scratch, scuff, skin; clean, rub, scour; grate, grind, rasp, scratch

scrappy bitty, disjointed, fragmentary, piecemeal, sketchy, thrown together

scratch *v* claw, grate, graze, mark, score, scrape; cancel, eliminate, withdraw ~*n* graze, laceration, mark, scrape

scrawl doodle, scratch, scribble,

scrawny *adj* thin, bony

scream *v* utter piercing cry, esp. of fear, pain etc.; utter in a scream ~*n* shrill, piercing cry

screech *v/n* scream

screed *n* long (tedious) letter, passage or speech

screen *n* device to shelter from heat, light, draught, observation etc.; blank surface on which photographic images are projected; windscreen ~*v* shelter, hide; show (film); examine (group of people) for political motives or for presence of disease, weapons etc.

screw *n* metal pin with spiral thread, twisted into materials to pin or fasten; anything resembling a screw in shape ~*v* fasten with screw; twist around **screwdriver** *n* tool for turning screws

scribble *v* write, draw carelessly; make meaningless marks with pen or pencil ~*n* something scribbled

scribe *n* writer; copyist ~*v* scratch a line with pointed instrument

scrimp *v* make too small or short; treat meanly

script *n* (system or style of) handwriting; written text of film, play, radio or television programme

scripture *n* sacred writings; the Bible

scroll *n* roll of parchment or paper;

ornament shaped thus

scrotum *n* (*pl* **-ta, -tums**) pouch of skin containing testicles

scrounge *v Inf* get without cost, by begging **scrounger** *n*

scrub[1] *v* **scrubbing, scrubbed** clean with hard brush and water; scour; *Inf* delete, cancel ~*n* scrubbing

scrub[2] *n* stunted trees; brushwood

scruff *n* nape of neck

scruffy *adj* unkempt, shabby

scrum, scrummage *n Rugby* restarting of play in which opposing packs of forwards push against each other to gain possession of the ball; disorderly struggle

scruple *n* doubt or hesitation about what is morally right ~*v* hesitate **scrupulous** *adj* extremely conscientious; thorough

scrutiny *n* close examination; critical investigation **scrutinize** *v* examine closely

scuba diving sport of swimming under water using self-contained breathing apparatus

scud *v* **scudding, scudded** run fast; run before wind

scuff *v* drag, scrape with feet in walking; graze ~*n* act, sound of scuffing

scuffle *v* fight in disorderly manner; shuffle ~*n* scuffling

scull *n* oar used in stern of boat; short

writing

scream *v/n* screech, shriek, squeal

screen *n* canopy, cover, guard, shade, shelter, shield ~*v* cloak, conceal, cover, hide, mask, shade, veil; defend, guard, protect, shelter, shield; examine, filter, scan, vet

screw *v* tighten, turn, twist

scribble *v* dash off, jot, scrawl

script book, copy, dialogue, lines, text, words

scrounge beg, cadge, sponge *Inf*

scrounger cadger, parasite, sponger

scrub *v* clean, cleanse, rub, scour; *Inf* call off, cancel, delete, drop, give up

scruffy ragged, shabby, slovenly, tattered, untidy

scrupulous careful, exact, meticulous, precise, punctilious, rigorous, strict

scrutinize examine, inspect, peruse, scan, study

scrutiny examination, inspection, perusal, study

scuffle *n* brawl, fight, scrimmage, shindig *Inf*, shindy *Inf*, tussle

oar used in pairs ~v propel, move by means of sculls

scullery n place for washing dishes etc.

sculpture n art of forming solid figures; product of this art ~v represent by sculpture **sculptor** n (fem **sculptress**)

scum n froth or other floating matter on liquid; waste part of anything; vile people **scummy** adj

scurrilous adj coarse, indecently abusive

scurry v **-rying, -ried** run hastily ~n bustling haste; flurry

scurvy n disease caused by lack of vitamin C

scuttle[1] n fireside container for coal

scuttle[2] v rush away; run hurriedly ~n hurried run

scuttle[3] v make hole in ship to sink it

scythe n manual implement with long curved blade for cutting grass ~v cut with scythe

sea n mass of salt water covering greater part of earth; broad tract of this; waves; vast expanse ~adj of the sea **seagull** n gull **sea horse** fish with bony-plated body and horselike head **sea lion** kind of large seal **seaman** n sailor **seasick** adj **seasickness** n nausea caused by motion of ship **seaweed** n plant growing in sea **seaworthy** adj in fit condition to put to sea

seal[1] n piece of metal or stone engraved with device for impression on wax etc.; impression thus made (on letters etc.); device, material preventing passage of water, air, oil etc. ~v affix seal to ratify, authorize; mark with stamp as evidence of some quality; keep close or secret; settle; make watertight, airtight etc.

seal[2] n amphibious furred carnivorous mammal with flippers as limbs

seam n line of junction of two edges, e.g. of two pieces of cloth; thin layer, stratum ~v mark with furrows or wrinkles **seamless** adj **seamy** adj sordid

seance n meeting at which people attempt to communicate with the dead

sear v scorch

search v look over or through to find something ~n act of searching; quest **searching** adj thorough

season n one of four divisions of year; period during which thing happens etc. ~v flavour with salt, herbs etc.; make reliable or ready for use; make experienced **seasonable** adj appropriate for the season; opportune **seasonal** adj varying with seasons **seasoning** n flavouring

seat n thing for sitting on; buttocks; base; right to sit (e.g. in council etc.); place where something is located, centred; locality of disease, trouble etc.; country house ~v make to sit; provide sitting accommodation for **seat belt** belt worn in vehicle to pre-

———————————— THESAURUS ————————————

scurry v dash, hurry, race, scamper, scoot, scuttle

sea n main, ocean, the deep, the waves; expanse, mass, multitude ~adj marine, ocean, saltwater

seal n insignia, stamp ~v bung, plug, stop, stopper, waterproof; ratify, stamp, validate; clinch, finalize, settle

seam n layer, lode, stratum, vein

search v comb, examine, ferret, in-

quire, inspect, investigate, look, probe, ransack, rummage through, scour ~n examination, hunt, inquiry, inspection, investigation, rummage

searching adj close, intent, keen, probing, thorough

season n period, spell, term, time ~v accustom, harden, mature, prepare, toughen, train

seasoning condiment, flavouring

vent injury in crash

secateurs *pl n* small pruning shears

secede *v* withdraw formally from federation, Church etc. **secession** *n*

seclude *v* guard from, remove from sight, view, contact with others **secluded** *adj* remote; private **seclusion** *n*

second[1] *adj* next after first; alternate, additional; of lower quality ~*n* person or thing coming second; attendant; sixtieth part of minute ~*v* support **second-class** *adj* inferior **second-hand** *adj* bought after use by another; not original **second sight** supposed ability to predict events

second[2] *v* transfer (employee, officer) temporarily

secondary *adj* of less importance; developed from something else; *Education* after primary stage

secret *adj* kept, meant to be kept from knowledge of others; hidden ~*n* thing kept secret **secrecy** *n* keeping or

being kept secret **secretive** *adj* given to having secrets

secretary *n* one employed to deal with papers and correspondence, keep records etc.; head of a state department **secretariat** *n* body of secretaries

secrete *v* hide; conceal; (of gland etc.) collect and supply particular substance in body **secretion** *n*

sect *n* group of people (within religious body etc.) with common interest; faction **sectarian** *adj*

section *n* division; portion; distinct part; cutting; drawing of anything as if cut through

sector *n* part or subdivision

secular *adj* worldly; lay, not religious

secure *adj* safe; firmly fixed; certain ~*v* gain possession of; make safe; make firm **security** *n* state of safety; protection; anything given as bond or pledge

sedate[1] *adj* calm, serious

———————————— THESAURUS ————————————

seat *n* bench, chair, pew, stool; base, bottom, cause, foundation, ground; capital, centre, cradle, heart, hub, site, source, station ~*v* fix, install, locate, place, set, settle, sit; accommodate, cater for, contain, hold, take

secluded cloistered, cut off, isolated, lonely, private, remote, sheltered

second *adj* following, next, subsequent, succeeding; additional, alternative, extra, further, other; inferior, lesser, lower ~*n* backer, helper, supporter ~*v* aid, assist, back, endorse, help, promote, support

secondary lesser, lower, minor, subordinate; backup, extra, reserve, subsidiary, supporting

second-hand nearly new, used

secret concealed, disguised, furtive, hidden, underground, undisclosed, unknown, unseen; hidden, private, secluded

secretive close, cryptic, deep, enigmatic

secretly furtively, privately, quietly, stealthily, surreptitiously

sect camp, denomination, division, faction, group, party, schism, splinter group, wing

sectarian exclusive, insular, limited, parochial, partisan

section division, fraction, instalment, part, passage, piece, portion, segment

secular earthly, lay, profane, temporal, worldly

secure *adj* immune, protected, safe, unassailable; fast, fastened, firm, fixed, immovable, stable, steady, tight; assured, certain, sure ~*v* acquire, gain, get, obtain, procure; fasten, fix, lash, moor, tie up

security asylum, refuge, retreat, safety; defence, protection, surveillance;

sedate[2] *v* make calm by sedative **sedation** *n* **sedative** *adj* having soothing or calming effect ~*n* sedative drug

sediment *n* matter which settles to the bottom of liquid

sedition *n* stirring up of rebellion

seduce *v* persuade to commit some (wrong) deed, esp. sexual intercourse **seducer** *n* (*fem* **seductress**) **seduction** *n* **seductive** *adj* alluring

see[1] *v* **seeing, saw, seen** perceive with eyes or mentally; watch; find out; interview; make sure; accompany; consider **seeing** *conj* in view of the fact that

see[2] *n* diocese, office of bishop

seed *n* reproductive germs of plants; one grain of this; such grains saved or used for sowing; sperm; origin ~*v* sow with seed; produce seed **seedling** *n* young plant raised from seed **seedy** *adj* shabby; full of seed

seek *v* **seeking, sought** make search

or enquiry (for)

seem *v* appear (to be or to do) **seemly** *adj* becoming and proper

seep *v* trickle through slowly

seesaw *n* plank on which children sit at opposite ends and swing up and down ~*v* move up and down

seethe *v* **seething, seethed** boil, foam; be very agitated; be in constant movement (as large crowd etc.)

segment *n* piece cut off; section ~*v* divide into segments

segregate *v* set apart from rest **segregation** *n*

seize *v* grasp; lay hold of; capture; (of machine part) stick tightly through overheating **seizure** *n* act of taking; sudden onset of disease

seldom *adv* not often, rarely

select *v* pick out, choose ~*adj* choice, picked; exclusive **selection** *n* option; assortment **selective** *adj* **selector** *n*

self *n* (*pl* **selves**) one's own person or

collateral, guarantee, insurance, pledge

sedate calm, collected, composed, cool, quiet, serious, sober, solemn

sedative *adj* calming, relaxing, soothing ~*n* narcotic, opiate, tranquilliser

sediment deposit, dregs, grounds, lees, residue

seduce corrupt, deprave, dishonour; beguile, entice, lure, mislead, tempt

seductive alluring, bewitching, enticing, inviting, tempting

see *v* behold, discern, distinguish, espy, glimpse, look, mark, note, notice, observe, perceive, regard, sight, spot, view, witness; follow, get, grasp, know, realize, understand; ascertain, determine, discover, find out, learn; consider, decide, deliberate, judge; confer with, consult, interview, meet, speak to

seed germ, grain, kernel, pip; beginning, germ, nucleus, origin, source,

start

seedy dilapidated, old, run-down, shabby, worn

seek hunt, pursue, search for

seem appear, look, pretend

seemly becoming, befitting, decent, decorous, fit, fitting, proper, suitable

seethe boil, bubble, foam, froth; be alive with, swarm, teem

segment bit, division, part, piece, portion, section, slice, wedge

segregate dissociate, isolate, separate, set apart

seize clutch, grab, grasp, grip, lay hands on; catch, get, nab *Inf*, nail *Inf*; annex, arrest, capture, commandeer, confiscate, impound

seizure arrest, capture, commandeering, grabbing, taking; attack, convulsion, fit, paroxysm, spasm

seldom infrequently, not often, occasionally, rarely

select *v* choose, pick ~*adj* choice, ex-

individuality **selfish** *adj* unduly concerned with personal profit or pleasure; greedy **selfless** *adj* unselfish

self- *comb. form* of oneself or itself

self-assured *adj* confident

self-conscious *adj* unduly aware of oneself

self-contained *adj* containing everything needed

self-made *adj* having achieved wealth, status etc. by one's own efforts

self-possessed *adj* calm

self-respect *n* proper sense of one's own dignity and integrity

self-righteous *adj* smugly sure of one's own virtue

selfsame *adj* very same

self-service *adj* (of shop or restaurant) letting customers serve themselves

self-sufficient *adj* independent

sell *v* **selling, sold** hand over for a price; stock, have for sale; make someone accept; *Inf* betray, cheat; find purchasers **seller** *n*

Sellotape *n Trademark* type of adhesive tape ~*v* (*without cap.*) stick with Sellotape

semaphore *n* system of signalling by human or mechanical arms

semblance *n* (false) appearance; image, likeness

semen *n* fluid carrying sperm of male animals; sperm

semi- *comb. form* half, partly, not completely, as in semicircle

semibreve *n* musical note equal to four crotchets

semicircle *n* half of circle

semicolon *n* punctuation mark (;)

semiconductor *n* substance whose electrical conductivity increases with temperature, used in transistors, circuits etc.

semidetached *adj* (of house) joined to another by one side only

semifinal *n* match, round etc. before final

seminal *adj* capable of developing; influential; of semen or seed

seminar *n* meeting of group (of students) for discussion

semiprecious *adj* (of gemstones) having less value than precious stones

semolina *n* hard grains left after sifting of flour, used for puddings etc.

senate *n* upper council of state, university etc. **senator** *n*

send *v* **sending, sent** cause to go or be conveyed; despatch; transmit (by radio)

senile *adj* showing weakness of old

———————— THESAURUS ————————

cellent, first-rate, hand-picked, picked, prime, special, superior

selection choice, choosing, option, pick; assortment, choice, collection, medley, range, variety

selective discerning, discriminating, particular

self-conscious awkward, bashful, embarrassed, ill at ease, insecure, nervous

selfish egoistic, egotistical, greedy, mean, self-seeking, ungenerous

selfless altruistic, generous, self-denying, self-sacrificing, unselfish

self-possessed collected, confident, cool, poised, self-assured, unruffled

self-respect dignity, pride, self-esteem

self-righteous complacent, priggish, sanctimonious, self-satisfied, smug, superior

sell barter, exchange, trade; deal in, market, peddle, stock, trade in, traffic in

seller agent, dealer, merchant, purveyor, rep, retailer, salesman, shopkeeper, supplier, tradesman, vendor

send consign, convey, despatch, di-

age **senility** n

senior adj superior in rank or standing; older ~n superior; elder person **seniority** n

sensation n operation of sense, feeling, awareness; excited feeling, state of excitement; exciting event **sensational** adj producing great excitement **sensationalism** n deliberate use of sensational material

sense n any of bodily faculties of perception or feeling; ability to perceive; consciousness; meaning; coherence; sound practical judgment ~v perceive **senseless** adj

sensible adj reasonable, wise; aware **sensibility** n ability to feel, esp. emotional or moral feelings

sensitive adj open to, acutely affected by, external impressions; easily affected or altered; easily upset by criticism; responsive to slight changes **sensitivity, sensitiveness** n **sensitize** v make sensitive

sensor n device that detects or measures the presence of something

sensory adj relating to senses

sensual adj of senses only and not of mind; given to pursuit of pleasures of sense

sensuous adj stimulating, or apprehended by, senses, esp. in aesthetic manner

sentence n combination of words expressing a thought; judgment passed on criminal by court or judge ~v pass sentence on, condemn

sentient adj capable of feeling

sentiment n tendency to be moved by feeling rather than reason; mental feeling; opinion **sentimental** adj given to indulgence in sentiment and in its expression **sentimentality** n

sentinel n sentry

sentry n soldier on watch

separate v part; divide ~adj disconnected, distinct, individual **separable** adj **separation** n disconnection; living

rect, forward, transmit

senile decrepit, doting, failing

senior adj elder, higher ranking, older, superior

seniority precedence, priority, rank, superiority

sensation consciousness, feeling, impression, perception, sense; agitation, commotion, excitement, furore, scandal, stir, surprise, thrill

sensational amazing, astounding, dramatic, electrifying, exciting, thrilling

sense n faculty, feeling, sensation; atmosphere, aura, feel, impression; drift, gist, implication, import, meaning; (sometimes pl) brains Inf, cleverness, discernment, discrimination, intelligence, judgment, mother wit, reason, understanding, wisdom ~v appreciate, discern, divine, feel, grasp, notice, observe, perceive, pick

up, realize, understand

senseless absurd, crazy, foolish, idiotic, inane, mad, mindless, nonsensical, stupid; cold, out, stunned, unconscious

sensible down-to-earth, intelligent, judicious, practical, prudent, rational, realistic, shrewd, sound, wise

sensitive acute, delicate, fine, keen, perceptive, responsive, susceptible

sensual animal, bodily, carnal, fleshly, physical; erotic, lascivious, lustful, sexual

sentence n decision, decree, judgment, order, ruling, verdict

sentiment emotion, sensibility, tenderness; (oft. pl) feeling, idea, opinion, view, way of thinking

sentimental emotional, impressionable, nostalgic, romantic, softhearted, tender, touching

sentimentality nostalgia, romanti-

apart of married couple

sepia *n* reddish-brown pigment ~*adj* of this colour

Sept. September

September *n* ninth month

septet *n* (music for) group of seven musicians

septic *adj* (of wound) infected; of, caused by pus-forming bacteria

septicaemia *n* blood poisoning

sepulchre *n* tomb; burial vault

sequel *n* consequence; continuation, e.g. of story

sequence *n* arrangement of things in successive order

sequin *n* small ornamental metal disc on dresses etc.

seraph *n* (*pl* **seraphim, seraphs**) angel

serenade *n* sentimental song addressed to woman by lover, esp. at evening ~*v* sing serenade (to someone)

serendipity *n* gift of making fortunate discoveries by accident

serene *adj* calm, tranquil; unclouded **serenity** *n*

serf *n* one of class of medieval labour-

ers bound to, and transferred with, land

sergeant *n* noncommissioned officer in army; police officer above constable **sergeant major** highest noncommissioned officer in regiment

series *n* (*pl* **series**) sequence; succession, set (e.g. of radio, TV programmes) **serial** *n* story or play produced in successive episodes **serialize** *v*

serious *adj* thoughtful, solemn; earnest, sincere; of importance; giving cause for concern

sermon *n* discourse of religious instruction or exhortation; any similar discourse

serpent *n* snake **serpentine** *adj* twisting, winding like a snake

serrated *adj* having notched, sawlike edge

serum *n* (*pl* **-rums, -ra**) watery animal fluid, esp. thin part of blood as used for inoculation or vaccination

serve *v* work for, under another; attend (to customers) in shop etc.; provide; help to (food etc.); present

———— THESAURUS ————

cism, tenderness

separate *v* break up, divorce, estrange, part, split up; isolate, segregate, single out; come away, detach, disconnect, divide, remove, sever, split, sunder ~*adj* apart, detached, disconnected, divided, divorced, isolated; distinct, independent, individual, particular, single, solitary

separation break, disconnection, dissociation, division, segregation, severance; break-up, divorce, parting, split

septic festering, infected, poisoned, suppurating

sequel continuation, follow-up; conclusion, end, outcome, result, upshot

sequence arrangement, chain, course, cycle, series, succession

serene calm, composed, peaceful, placid, tranquil, undisturbed, unruffled, untroubled; clear, cloudless, fair

serenity calm, calmness, composure, peace, peacefulness, peace of mind, placidity, quietness, stillness, tranquillity; brightness, clearness, fairness

series chain, course, run, sequence, set, string, succession

serious grave, sober, solemn, unsmiling; earnest, genuine, in earnest, sincere; crucial, important, momentous, pressing, significant, urgent, weighty; acute, critical, dangerous, grave, severe

sermon address, homily; harangue, lecture

servant attendant, domestic, maid,

(food etc.) in particular way; be member of military unit; spend time doing; be useful, suitable enough **servant** n personal or domestic attendant **service** n act of serving; system organized to provide for needs of public; maintenance of vehicle; use; department of State employment; set of dishes etc.; form, session of public worship; pl armed forces ~v overhaul **serviceable** adj in working order, usable; durable **serviceman** n member of armed forced **service station** place supplying fuel, oil, maintenance for motor vehicles

serviette n table napkin

servile adj slavish, without independence; fawning

servitude n bondage, slavery

sesame n plant whose seeds and oil are used in cooking

session n meeting of court etc.; continuous series of such meetings; any period devoted to an activity

set v setting, set put or place in specified position or condition; make ready; become firm or fixed; estab-

lish; prescribe, allot; put to music; (of sun) go down ~adj fixed, established; deliberate; unvarying ~n act or state of being set; bearing, posture; Radio, Television complete apparatus for reception or transmission; Theatre, Cinema organized settings and equipment to form ensemble of scene; number of associated things, persons **setback** n anything that hinders or impedes **set up** establish

sett n badger's burrow

settee n couch

setter n gun dog

setting n background; surroundings; scenery and other stage accessories; decorative metalwork holding precious stone etc. in position; tableware and cutlery for (single place at) table; music for song

settle v arrange; establish; decide upon; end (dispute etc.); pay; make calm or stable; come to rest; subside; become clear; take up residence **settlement** n act of settling; place newly inhabited; money bestowed legally **settler** n colonist

——————————— THESAURUS ———————————

retainer, slave, vassal

serve aid, assist, help, minister to, wait on, work for; act, do, fulfil, officiate, perform; deal, dish up, distribute, provide, purvey, supply; be acceptable, be adequate, do, suffice, suit

service n assistance, benefit, help, use; check, maintenance, overhaul; business, duty, labour, office, work; ceremony, function, observance, rite, worship ~v check, go over, maintain, overhaul, repair, tune (up)

session assembly, conference, congress, hearing, period, sitting, term

set v aim, direct, fasten, fix, lay, locate, place, plant, put, rest, seat, situate; allocate, appoint, arrange, assign, decide, determine, establish,

fix, schedule, settle, specify; congeal, harden, solidify, thicken; allot, impose, ordain, prescribe ~adj agreed, appointed, arranged, decided, definite, firm, fixed, prescribed, scheduled, settled; hidebound, inflexible, rigid, stubborn ~n band, circle, clique, company, coterie, crowd, gang, group; assortment, collection, compendium

setback blow, check, hitch, hold-up, misfortune

setting backdrop, background, location, scene, scenery, set, site, surroundings

settle arrange, order, straighten out, work out; clear up, complete, conclude, decide, reconcile, resolve; clear, discharge, pay; allay, calm,

seven *adj/n* cardinal number next after six **seventh** *adj* ordinal number **seventeen** *adj/n* ten plus seven **seventeenth** *adj* **seventieth** *adj* **seventy** *adj/n* ten times seven

sever *v* separate, divide; cut off **severance** *n*

several *adj* some, a few; separate; individual ~*pron* indefinite small number

severe *adj* strict; harsh; austere; extreme **severity** *n*

sew *v* **sewing, sewed, sewn** join with needle and thread; make by sewing **sewing** *n*

sewage *n* refuse, waste matter, excrement conveyed in sewer **sewer** *n* underground drain

sex *n* state of being male or female; males or females collectively; sexual intercourse ~*adj* concerning sex ~*v* ascertain sex of **sexism** *n* discrimination on basis of sex **sexist** *n/adj* **sex-ual** *adj* **sexy** *adj* **sexual intercourse** act of procreation in which male's penis is inserted into female's vagina

sextet *n* (composition for) six musicians

shabby *adj* faded, worn; poorly dressed; mean, dishonourable

shack *n* rough hut

shackle *n* metal ring or fastening for prisoner's wrist or ankle ~*v* fasten with shackles; hamper

shade *n* partial darkness; shelter, place sheltered from light, heat etc.; darker part of anything; depth of colour; screen; *US* window blind ~*v* screen from light, darken; represent shades in drawing **shady** *adj* shielded from sun; *Inf* dishonest

shadow *n* dark figure projected by anything that intercepts rays of light; patch of shade; slight trace ~*v* cast shadow over; follow and watch closely **shadowy** *adj*

pacify, quell, quieten, reassure, relieve, soothe; alight, descend, land, light; decline, fall, sink, subside; colonize, people, pioneer, populate

settlement agreement, arrangement, conclusion, resolution; colony, community, encampment, outpost

settler colonist, immigrant, pioneer

set up arrange, begin, establish, found, institute, organize; back, finance, subsidize

several *adj* many, some, sundry, various; different, distinct, individual, single

severe cruel, hard, harsh, oppressive, pitiless, relentless, strict, unrelenting; austere, classic, plain, restrained, simple, unfussy; acute, critical, dangerous, extreme, intense

sex gender; *Inf* coition, coitus, copulation, (sexual) intercourse, intimacy, lovemaking

sexual carnal, erotic, intimate, sexy

sexual intercourse carnal knowledge, coition, coitus, copulation, coupling, mating, union

sexy erotic, naughty, provocative, seductive, sensual, suggestive, titillating, voluptuous

shabby dilapidated, frayed, ragged, tattered, tatty, threadbare, worn-out; contemptible, despicable, dirty, dishonourable, low, mean, shameful, shoddy

shade *n* dimness, dusk, gloom, obscurity, shadow; colour, hue, tint, tone; blind, canopy, cover, curtain, screen, shield, veil ~*v* cloud, conceal, cover, dim, hide, protect, screen, shadow, veil

shadow *n* cover, darkness, dimness, protection, shade, shelter; hint, suggestion, suspicion, trace ~*v* screen, shade, shield; follow, stalk, trail

shadowy dark, dim, indistinct, obscure, shaded; dim, nebulous, ob-

shaft *n* straight rod, stem, handle; arrow; ray, beam (of light); revolving rod for transmitting power

shag *n* long-napped cloth; coarse shredded tobacco **shaggy** *adj* covered with rough hair; unkempt

shake *v* **shaking, shook, shaken** (cause to) move with quick vibrations; tremble; grasp the hand (of another) in greeting; upset; wave, brandish ~*n* act of shaking; vibration; jolt; *Inf* short period of time **shaky** *adj* unsteady, insecure; questionable

shale *n* flaky fine-grained rock

shall *v* (*past tense* **should**) makes compound tenses or moods to express obligation, command, condition or intention

shallow *adj* not deep; superficial ~*n* shallow place

sham *adj/n* imitation, counterfeit ~*v* **shamming, shammed** pretend, feign

shamble *v* walk in shuffling, awkward way

shambles *pl n* messy, disorderly thing or place

shame *n* emotion caused by consciousness of guilt or dishonour in one's conduct or state; cause of disgrace; pity, hard luck ~*v* cause to feel shame; disgrace; force by shame (into) **shameful** *adj* **shameless** *adj* with no sense of shame; indecent **shamefaced** *adj* ashamed

shampoo *n* preparation of liquid soap for washing hair, carpets etc.; this process ~*v* use shampoo to wash

shamrock *n* clover leaf, esp. as Irish emblem

shandy *n* drink of beer and lemonade

shanty[1] *n* temporary wooden building; crude dwelling

shanty[2] *n* sailor's song

shape *n* external form or appearance; mould, pattern; *Inf* condition ~*v* **shaping, shaped** form, mould; develop **shapeless** *adj* **shapely** *adj* well-proportioned

———— T H E S A U R U S ————

scure, undefined, vague

shady cool, dim, leafy, shaded; *Inf* crooked, disreputable, dodgy *Brit, Aust, & NZ inf*, dubious, shifty, slippery, suspect

shaft handle, pole, rod, stem; beam, gleam, ray, streak

shaggy hairy, hirsute, long-haired, unkempt, unshorn

shake *v* quake, rock, shiver, shudder, totter, tremble, vibrate, waver; distress, disturb, frighten, intimidate, shock, unnerve, upset; brandish, flourish, wave ~*n* agitation, quaking, shiver, shudder, trembling, tremor, vibration

shaky insecure, precarious, quivery, rickety, trembling, unstable, unsteady; dubious, questionable, suspect

shallow empty, foolish, frivolous, idle, simple, slight, superficial, sur-

face, trivial

sham *adj* artificial, bogus, counterfeit, false, feigned, imitation, mock, phoney *or* phony *Inf*, pretended, simulated ~*n* forgery, fraud, hoax, humbug, imitation, impostor, phoney *or* phony *Inf*, pretence ~*v* affect, assume, fake, feign, pretend, put on, simulate

shame *n* blot, disgrace, disrepute, infamy, scandal, smear; abashment, humiliation, ignominy ~*v* abash, embarrass, humble; blot, disgrace, dishonour, smear, stain

shameful base, disgraceful, low, mean, scandalous; degrading, humiliating, shaming

shameless audacious, brash, brazen, flagrant, immodest, improper, indecent, wanton

shape *n* build, configuration, contours, cut, figure, form, lines, outline, profile; frame, model, mould, pat-

shard *n* broken piece of pottery

share *n* portion; quota; lot; unit of ownership in public company ~*v* give, take a share; join with others in doing, using, something **shareholder** *n*

shark *n* large usu. predatory sea fish; person who cheats others

sharp *adj* having keen cutting edge or fine point; not gradual or gentle; brisk; clever; harsh; dealing cleverly but unfairly; shrill; strongly marked, esp. in outline; sour ~*adv* promptly **sharpen** *v* make sharp **sharpshooter** *n* marksman

shatter *v* break in pieces; ruin (plans etc.); disturb (person) greatly **shattered** *adj Inf* completely exhausted

shave *v* **shaving, shaved, shaved** *or* **shaven** cut close, esp. hair of face or head; pare away; graze; reduce ~*n* shaving **shavings** *pl n* parings

shawl *n* piece of fabric to cover woman's shoulders or wrap baby

she *pron* (*third person fem*) person, animal already referred to; *comb. form* female, as in **she-wolf**

sheaf *n* (*pl* **sheaves**) bundle, esp. of corn; loose leaves of paper

shear *v* **shearing, sheared, sheared** *or* **shorn** clip hair, wool from; cut through; fracture **shears** *pl n* large pair of scissors

sheath *n* close-fitting cover, esp. for knife or sword **sheathe** *v* put into sheath

shed[1] *n* roofed shelter used as store or workshop

shed[2] *v* **shedding, shed** (cause to) pour forth (e.g. tears, blood); cast off

sheen *n* gloss

sheep *n* ruminant animal bred for wool or meat **sheepish** *adj* embarrassed, shy **sheepdog** *n* dog used for herding sheep

sheer *adj* perpendicular; (of material) very fine, transparent; absolute, unmitigated

sheet *n* large piece of cotton etc. to cover bed; broad piece of any thin material; large expanse

sheikh *n* Arab chief

shelf *n* (*pl* **shelves**) board fixed horizontally (on wall etc.) for holding things; ledge

shell *n* hard outer case (esp. of egg, nut etc.); explosive projectile; outer part of structure left when interior is removed ~*v* take shell from; take out of shell; fire at with shells **shellfish** *n*

———— T H E S A U R U S ————

tern; condition, fettle, health, state, trim ~*v* create, fashion, form, make, model, mould, produce; adapt, develop, devise, frame, plan

shapeless amorphous, formless, nebulous, undeveloped, unstructured

share *n* allotment, allowance, contribution, lot, part, portion, quota, ration ~*v* distribute, divide, partake, participate, split

sharp *adj* acute, jagged, keen, pointed, serrated, spiky; abrupt, marked, sudden; alert, astute, bright, clever, observant, perceptive, quick, ready; caustic, cutting, harsh, hurtful, scathing, trenchant; clear, clear-cut, crisp, distinct, well-defined; acerbic, acid, sour, tart, vinegary ~*adv* exactly, on time, on the dot, precisely, promptly, punctually

shatter break, burst, crush, demolish, explode, smash; blast, demolish, destroy, ruin, torpedo, wreck; crush, devastate

shed *v* cast, emit, give, give forth, radiate, scatter, shower, spill; cast off, discard, moult, slough

sheer abrupt, precipitous, steep; complete, downright, pure, total, unqualified, utter

sheet area, expanse, stretch, sweep; blanket, coat, covering, film, layer,

mollusc; crustacean

shelter *n* place, structure giving protection; refuge ~*v* give protection to; take shelter

shelve *v* put on a shelf; put off; slope gradually

shepherd *n* (*fem* **shepherdess**) one who tends sheep ~*v* guide, watch over **shepherd's pie** dish of minced meat and potato

sherbet *n* fruit-flavoured effervescent powder

sheriff *n* US law enforcement officer; in England and Wales, chief executive officer of the crown in a county; in Scotland, chief judge of a district; *Canad* municipal officer who enforces court orders etc.

sherry *n* fortified wine

shield *n* piece of armour carried on arm; any protection used to stop blows, missiles etc. ~*v* cover, protect

shift *v* (cause to) move, change position ~*n* move, change of position; relay of workers; time of their working; woman's underskirt or dress **shiftless** *adj* lacking in resource or character **shifty** *adj* evasive, of dubious character

shilling *n* former Brit. coin, now 5p

shimmer *v* shine with quivering light

~*n* such light

shin *n* front of lower leg ~*v* climb with arms and legs

shine *v* **shining, shone** give out, reflect light; excel; polish ~*n* brightness, lustre; polishing **shiny** *adj*

shingle *n* mass of pebbles

shingles *n* disease causing rash of small blisters

ship *n* large seagoing vessel ~*v* **shipping, shipped** put on or send (esp. by ship) **shipment** *n* act of shipping; goods shipped **shipping** *n* freight transport business; ships collectively **shipshape** *adj* orderly, neat **shipwreck** *n* destruction of ship ~*v* cause shipwreck of **shipyard** *n* place for building and repair of ships

shire *n* county **shire horse** large powerful breed of horse

shirk *v* evade, try to avoid (duty etc.)

shirt *n* garment with sleeves and collar for upper part of body

shirty *adj Inf* annoyed

shiver[1] *v* tremble, usu. with cold or fear ~*n* act, state of shivering

shiver[2] *v/n* splinter

shoal[1] *n* large number of fish swimming together

shoal[2] *n* stretch of shallow water; sandbank

———————— T H E S A U R U S ————————

panel, piece, plate, slab

shell *n* case, husk, pod; frame, framework, hull ~*v* blitz, bomb, bombard

shelter *n* asylum, cover, haven, protection, refuge, retreat, safety, sanctuary ~*v* cover, harbour, protect, safeguard, shield

shelve defer, postpone, put on the back burner *Inf,* take a rain check on *US & Canad inf*

shield *n* cover, defence, guard, protection, safeguard, screen, shelter ~*v* cover, defend, guard, protect, safeguard, screen, shelter

shift *v* budge, change, displace, move,

relocate, reposition, switch, transfer, transpose ~*n* change, move, shifting, switch, transfer

shifty devious, evasive, furtive, slippery, sly, tricky, underhand, untrustworthy

shimmer dance, gleam, glisten, twinkle

shine *v* beam, flash, glare, gleam, glisten, glitter, glow, radiate, sparkle, twinkle; be conspicuous, excel, stand out ~*n* brightness, glare, gleam, light, radiance, shimmer, sparkle

shiny bright, gleaming, glistening, glossy, lustrous

shock¹ v horrify, scandalize ~n violent or damaging blow; emotional disturbance; state of weakness, illness, caused by physical or mental shock; paralytic stroke; collision; effect on sensory nerves of electric discharge **shocking** adj causing horror, disgust or astonishment; Inf very bad

shock² n mass of hair

shoddy adj worthless, trashy

shoe n (pl **shoes**) covering for foot, not enclosing ankle; metal rim put on horse's hoof; various protective plates or undercoverings ~v **shoeing, shod** protect, furnish with shoe(s)

shoo interj go away!

shoot v **shooting, shot** wound, kill with missile fired from weapon; discharge weapon; send, slide, push rapidly; photograph, film; hunt; sprout ~n young branch, sprout; hunting expedition

shop n place for retail sale of goods and services; workshop, works building ~v **shopping, shopped** visit shops to buy **shoplifter** n one who steals from shop **shopsoiled** adj damaged from being displayed in shop

shore¹ n edge of sea or lake

shore² v prop (up)

short adj not long; not tall; brief; not enough; lacking; abrupt ~adv abruptly; without reaching end ~n drink of spirits; short film; pl short trousers

shortage n deficiency **shorten** v

shortly adv soon; briefly **shortbread, shortcake** n crumbly biscuit made with butter **short circuit** Electricity connection, often accidental, of low resistance between two parts of circuit **shortcoming** n failing **short cut** quicker route or method **shorthand** n method of rapid writing **short list** list of candidates from which final choice will be made **short-sighted** adj unable to see faraway things clearly; lacking in foresight

shot n act of shooting; small lead pellets; marksman; Inf attempt; photograph; dose; Inf injection **shotgun** n gun for firing shot at short range **shot put** contest in which athletes throw heavy metal ball

should past tense of SHALL

shoulder n part of body to which arm or foreleg is attached; anything resembling shoulder; side of road ~v undertake; put on one's shoulder;

shirk avoid, dodge, evade

shock v disgust, gross out US sl, horrify, nauseate, offend, outrage, revolt, shake, sicken, stagger ~n blow, bombshell, collapse, distress, stupor, trauma, upset

shocking appalling, atrocious, disgraceful, dreadful, ghastly, hideous, horrible, offensive, outrageous, revolting, scandalous, sickening

shoddy inferior, poor, second-rate, slipshod, trashy

shoot v bag, hit, open fire, pick off; emit, fire, fling, hurl, launch, project, propel; bolt, charge, dart, dash, fly, hurtle, race, rush, speed, tear ~n branch, bud, sprig, sprout

shore beach, coast, sands, seashore

short adj dumpy, little, low, small, squat; brief, fleeting, momentary; brief, concise, laconic, pithy, succinct, summary, terse; (oft. with of) deficient, lacking, limited, meagre, poor, scant, scanty, scarce, tight, wanting ~adv abruptly, by surprise, suddenly, unaware

shortage dearth, deficit, lack, poverty, scarcity, want

shortcoming defect, failing, fault, flaw, imperfection, weakness

shorten abbreviate, cut, decrease, diminish, dock, lessen, reduce, trim

shot n Inf attempt, chance, effort, endeavour, essay, go Inf, opportunity,

make way by pushing

shout *n/v* (utter) loud cry

shove *v/n* push

shovel *n* instrument for scooping earth etc. ~*v* -elling, -elled lift, move (as) with shovel

show *v* showing, showed, shown *or* showed expose to view; point out; explain; prove; guide; appear; be noticeable ~*n* display; entertainment; ostentation; pretence **showy** *adj* gaudy; ostentatious **show business** the entertainment industry **showcase** *n* glass case to display objects; situation in which thing is displayed to best advantage **showdown** *n* confrontation **showman** *n* one skilled at presenting anything effectively **show off** exhibit to invite admiration; behave in this way **show-off** *n* **showroom** *n* room in which goods for sale are displayed

shower *n* short fall of rain; anything falling like rain; kind of bath in which person stands under water spray ~*v* bestow liberally; take bath in shower

shrapnel *n* shell splinters

shred *n* fragment, torn strip ~*v* shredding, **shredded** *or* **shred** cut, tear to shreds

shrew *n* animal like mouse; bad-tempered woman

shrewd *adj* astute; crafty

shriek *n/v* (utter) piercing cry

shrill *adj* piercing, sharp in tone

shrimp *n* small edible crustacean; *Inf* undersized person

shrine *n* place of worship, usu. associated with saint

shrink *v* shrinking, shrank, shrunk *or* shrunken become smaller; recoil; make smaller **shrinkage** *n*

shrivel *v* -elling, -elled shrink and wither

shroud *n* wrapping for corpse; anything which envelops like a shroud ~*v* put shroud on; veil

shrub *n* bush **shrubbery** *n*

shrug *v* shrugging, shrugged raise (shoulders) as sign of indifference, ignorance etc. ~*n* shrugging

shudder *v* shake, tremble violently ~*n* shuddering

shuffle *v* move feet without lifting them; mix (cards) ~*n* shuffling; rearrangement

——————————— THESAURUS ———————————

stab *Inf*, try, turn

shoulder *v* accept, assume, bear, be responsible for, carry, take on; elbow, jostle, push, shove, thrust

shout *n/v* bawl, bellow, call, cry, roar, scream, yell

shove *v* drive, elbow, impel, jostle, propel, push, thrust

show *v* disclose, display, divulge, exhibit, indicate, manifest, present, register, reveal; demonstrate, explain, instruct, prove, teach; conduct, escort, guide, lead ~*n* demonstration, display, exhibition, sight, spectacle, view; appearance, display, illusion, ostentation, pose, pretence, profession, semblance

shower *n* deluge, rain, stream, torrent, volley ~*v* deluge, heap, lavish, load, pour, rain, spray

show off advertise, display, exhibit, flaunt, parade; boast, brag

shred *n* bit, fragment, piece, rag, scrap, tatter

shrewd astute, canny, clever, crafty, cunning, discerning, keen, knowing, perceptive, sharp, smart

shrill high, penetrating, piercing, screeching, sharp

shrink contract, decrease, diminish, dwindle, lessen, shorten; cower, cringe, draw back, flinch, quail, recoil

shrivel desiccate, dwindle, shrink, wither

shudder *v* quake, quiver, shake, shiv-

shun v **shunning, shunned** keep away from

shunt v push aside; move (train) from one line to another

shut v **shutting, shut** close; forbid entrance to **shutter** n movable window screen; device in camera admitting light as required

shuttle n bobbin-like device to hold thread in weaving, sewing etc.; plane, bus etc. travelling to and fro

shuttlecock n cone with feathers, struck to and fro in badminton

shy¹ adj timid, bashful; lacking ~v **shying, shied** start back in fear; show sudden reluctance ~n start of fear by horse

shy² n/v **shying, shied** throw

Siamese twins twins born joined to each other

sibilant adj/n hissing (sound)

sibling n brother or sister

sick adj inclined to vomit; not well or healthy; Inf macabre; Inf bored; Inf disgusted **sicken** v make, become sick; disgust **sickly** adj unhealthy; inducing nausea **sickness** n

sickle n reaping hook

side n one of the surfaces of object that is to right or left; aspect; faction

~adj at, in the side; subordinate ~v (usu. with **with**) take up cause of **siding** n short line of rails from main line

sideboard n piece of dining room furniture **sideburns** pl n man's side whiskers **side effect** additional undesirable effect **sidekick** n Inf close associate **sidelong** adj not directly forward ~adv obliquely **sidestep** v avoid **sidetrack** v divert from main topic **sideways** adv to or from the side

sidle v move in furtive or stealthy manner; move sideways

siege n besieging of town

siesta n rest, sleep in afternoon

sieve n device with perforated bottom ~v sift; strain

sift v separate coarser portion from finer

sigh v/n (utter) long audible breath

sight n faculty of seeing; thing seen; glimpse; device for guiding eye; spectacle ~v catch sight of; adjust sights on gun etc. **sightseeing** n visiting places of interest

sign n mark, gesture etc. to convey some meaning; (board bearing) notice etc.; symbol; omen ~v put one's signature to; make sign or gesture

signal n sign to convey order or infor-

———————— THESAURUS ————————

er, tremble ~n quiver, spasm, tremor

shuffle confuse, disarrange, disorder, mix, rearrange, shift

shun avoid, eschew, evade

shut bar, close, draw to, fasten, seal, secure

shy bashful, coy, diffident, modest, nervous, retiring, shrinking, timid

sick ill, nauseated, queasy; ailing, diseased, indisposed, unwell; Inf black, ghoulish, macabre, morbid, sadistic

sicken ail, fall ill, take sick; disgust, gross out US sl, nauseate, repel, revolt

sickly ailing, delicate, faint, feeble, infirm, peaky, unhealthy, weak

sickness nausea, vomiting; affliction, ailment, bug Inf, complaint, disease, disorder, illness, infirmity, lurgi Inf, malady

side n border, edge, limit, margin, perimeter, rim, verge; aspect, face, facet, flank, part, surface, view; camp, faction, party, sect, team

sidetrack deflect, distract, divert

sift filter, separate, sieve

sight n eye, eyes, seeing, vision; display, exhibition, scene, show, spectacle, vista ~v observe, perceive, see, spot

sign n clue, evidence, gesture, hint, indication, proof, signal, symptom,

mation; *Radio etc.* sequence of electrical impulses transmitted or received ~*adj* remarkable ~*v* **-nalling, -nalled** make signals to; give orders etc. by signals

signatory *n* one of those who signs agreements, treaties

signature *n* person's name written by himself **signature tune** tune used to introduce television or radio programme

signet *n* small seal

significant *adj* revealing; designed to make something known; important **significance** *n*

signify *v* **-fying, -fied** mean; indicate; imply; be of importance

silage *n* fodder crop stored in state of partial fermentation

silence *n* absence of noise; refraining from speech ~*v* make silent; put a stop to **silencer** *n* device to reduce noise of engine exhaust, gun etc. **silent** *adj*

silhouette *n* outline of object seen against light ~*v* show in silhouette

silica *n* naturally occurring dioxide of silicon

silicon *n* brittle metal-like element found in sand, clay, stone **silicon chip**

tiny wafer of silicon used in electronics

silk *n* fibre made by silkworms; thread, fabric made from this **silky** *adj* **silkworm** *n* larva of certain moth

sill *n* ledge beneath window

silly *adj* foolish; trivial

silo *n* (*pl* **-los**) pit, tower for storing fodder

silt *n* mud deposited by water ~*v* fill, be choked with silt

silver *n* white precious metal; silver coins; cutlery ~*adj* made of silver; resembling silver or its colour **silvery** *adj*

similar *adj* resembling, like **similarity** *n* likeness

simile *n* comparison of one thing with another

simmer *v* keep or be just below boiling point; be in state of suppressed rage

simper *v* smile, utter in silly or affected way

simple *adj* not complicated; plain; not complex; ordinary; stupid **simpleton** *n* foolish person **simplicity** *n* **simplify** *v* **-fying, -fied** make simple, plain or easy **simply** *adv*

simulate *v* make pretence of; repro-

———————— T H E S A U R U S ————————

token; board, notice, placard; badge, device, emblem, ensign, logo, mark, symbol; augury, auspice, omen, portent, warning ~*v* autograph, endorse, initial; beckon, gesticulate, gesture, indicate, signal

signal *n* beacon, cue, gesture, indication, mark, sign ~*v* beckon, gesture, indicate, motion, sign

significance force, import, meaning, message, point; consequence, importance, relevance, weight

significant expressive, indicative, meaningful; critical, important, momentous, vital, weighty

silence *n* calm, hush, peace, quiet,

stillness; dumbness, muteness, reticence, taciturnity ~*v* cut off, cut short, gag, muffle, quieten, still

silent hushed, quiet, soundless, still; dumb, mute, speechless, taciturn, voiceless, wordless

silhouette *n* form, outline, profile, shape

silly absurd, asinine, fatuous, foolhardy, foolish, idiotic, inane, irresponsible, stupid

similar alike, comparable, resembling, uniform

similarity affinity, closeness, correspondence, likeness, resemblance

simple clear, easy, easy-peasy *Sl,* in-

duce simulation *n*

simultaneous *adj* occurring at the same time

sin *n* breaking of divine or moral law ~*v* **sinning, sinned** commit sin **sinful** *adj* **sinner** *n*

since *prep* during period of time after ~*conj* from time when; because ~*adv* from that time

sincere *adj* not hypocritical; genuine **sincerity** *n*

sine *n* in a right-angled triangle, ratio of opposite side to hypotenuse

sinew *n* tough, fibrous cord joining muscle to bone

sing *v* **singing, sang, sung** utter (sounds, words) with musical modulation; hum, ring; celebrate in song **singer** *n*

singe *v* **singeing, singed** burn surface of

single *adj* one only; unmarried; for one; denoting ticket for outward journey only ~*n* single thing ~*v* pick (out) **single file** persons in one line **single-handed** *adj* without assistance **single-minded** *adj* having one aim

only

singlet *n* sleeveless undervest

singular *adj* remarkable; unique; denoting one person or thing

sinister *adj* threatening; evil-looking; wicked

sink *v* **sinking, sank, sunk** *or* **sunken** become submerged; drop; decline; penetrate (into); cause to sink; make by digging out; invest ~*n* fixed basin with waste pipe

sinuous *adj* curving

sinus *n* cavity in bone, esp. of skull

sip *v* **sipping, sipped** drink in very small portions ~*n* amount sipped

siphon, syphon *n/v* (device to) draw liquid from container

sir *n* polite term of address for man

sire *n* male parent, esp. of horse or domestic animal ~*v* father

siren *n* device making loud wailing noise

sirloin *n* prime cut of beef

sissy *adj/n* weak, cowardly (person)

sister *n* daughter of same parents; woman fellow-member; senior nurse **sister-in-law** *n* sister of husband or

———— T H E S A U R U S ————

telligible, lucid, plain, uncomplicated, understandable; natural, plain, unfussy; elementary, pure, single, uncombined, unmixed; brainless, dense, feeble, foolish, obtuse, slow, stupid, thick

simplicity clarity, clearness, ease; naturalness, plainness, purity

simultaneous at the same time, coinciding, concurrent, contemporaneous

sin *n* crime, evil, guilt, iniquity, misdeed, offence, trespass, unrighteousness, wickedness ~*v* err, fall, lapse, offend, transgress

sincere artless, candid, earnest, frank, genuine, guileless, honest, open, real, true, unaffected

sincerity candour, frankness, genu-

ineness, honesty, truth

sinful bad, corrupt, guilty, immoral, iniquitous, unrighteous, wicked

sing chant, croon, trill, warble

single individual, lone, one, sole, solitary; free, unattached, unmarried, unwed

single-minded dedicated, determined, dogged, fixed, steadfast

singular exceptional, notable, noteworthy, outstanding, remarkable, unparalleled; individual, separate, single

sinister menacing, ominous, threatening

sink *v* decline, descend, dip, disappear, drop, ebb, fall, lower, plunge, submerge, subside; decay, decline, die, diminish, dwindle, fade, lessen

wife; brother's wife

sit *v* **sitting, sat** rest on buttocks; thighs; perch; pose for portrait; hold session; remain; take examination; keep watch over baby etc.

sitar *n* stringed musical instrument of India

site *n* place, space for building ~*v* provide with site

situate *v* place **situation** *n* position; state of affairs; employment

six *adj/n* cardinal number one more than five **sixth** *adj* ordinal number **sixteen** *n/adj* six and ten **sixteenth** *adj* **sixtieth** *adj* **sixty** *n/adj* six times ten

size[1] *n* dimensions; one of series of standard measurements ~*v* arrange according to size **sizable** *adj* quite large **size up** *v Inf* assess

size[2] *n* gluelike sealer, filler

sizzle *v/n* (make) hissing, spluttering sound as of frying

skate[1] *n* steel blade attached to boot ~*v* glide as on skates **skateboard** *n* small board mounted on roller-skate wheels

skate[2] *n* large marine ray

skein *n* quantity of yarn, wool etc. in loose knot

skeleton *n* bones of animal; framework ~*adj* reduced to a minimum

sketch *n* rough drawing; short humorous play ~*v* make sketch (of) **sketchy** *adj*

skew *adj/v* (make) slanting or crooked

skewer *n* pin to fasten meat

ski *n* (*pl* **skis**) long runner fastened to foot for sliding over snow or water ~*v* **skiing, skied** slide on skis

skid *v* **skidding, skidded** slide (sideways) ~*n* instance of this

skill *n* practical ability, cleverness, dexterity **skilful** *adj* **skilled** *adj*

skim *v* **skimming, skimmed** remove floating matter from surface of liquid; glide over lightly and rapidly; read quickly

skimp *v* give short measure; do imperfectly **skimpy** *adj* scanty

skin *n* outer covering of body; animal hide; fruit rind ~*v* **skinning, skinned** remove skin of **skinless** *adj* **skinny** *adj* thin **skinflint** *n* miser

skint *adj Sl* having no money

skip[1] *v* **skipping, skipped** leap lightly; jump over rope; pass over, omit ~*n* act of skipping

skip[2] *n* large open container for build-

———————————— T H E S A U R U S ————————————

sit perch, rest, settle; assemble, convene, meet

site *n* ground, location, place, position, spot

situation location, place, position, setting, site, spot; case, circumstances, condition, plight, state; employment, job, place, position, post

size amount, bulk, dimensions, extent, mass, proportions, volume

sketch *n* design, draft, drawing, outline, plan ~*v* draft, draw, outline, plot, rough out

sketchy bitty, incomplete, rough, scrappy, skimpy, superficial, vague

skilful able, adept, adroit, expert, masterly, professional, proficient, skilled

skill ability, adroitness, competence, craft, dexterity, expertise, knack, talent

skilled able, expert, masterly, professional, proficient, skilful

skim coast, fly, glide, sail; (*usu. with* **through**) glance, run one's eye over, scan, skip *Inf,* thumb *or* leaf through

skimp be mean with, be niggardly, be sparing with, cut corners, scamp, stint

skin *n* hide, pelt; casing, coating, husk, peel, rind ~*v* bark, flay, graze, peel, scrape

ers' rubbish etc.

skipper *n* captain of ship

skirmish *n* small battle; ~*v* fight briefly

skirt *n* woman's garment hanging from waist; lower part of dress, coat etc. ~*v* border; go round **skirting board** narrow board round bottom of wall

skit *n* satire, esp. theatrical

skittish *adj* frisky, frivolous

skittles *n* game in which players try to knock over bottle-shaped objects

skive *v* evade work

skivvy *n* servant who does menial work

skulduggery *n Inf* trickery

skulk *v* sneak out of the way

skull *n* bony case enclosing brain

skunk *n* small N Amer. animal which emits evil-smelling fluid

sky *n* (*pl* **skies**) expanse extending upwards from the horizon; outer space **skylark** *n* bird that sings while soaring at great height **skylight** *n* window in roof or ceiling **skyscraper** *n* very tall building

slab *n* thick, broad piece

slack *adj* loose; careless; not busy ~*n* loose part ~*v* be idle or lazy **slacken** *v* become looser; become slower

slacks *pl n* casual trousers

slag *n* refuse of smelted metal

slake *v* satisfy (thirst)

slalom *n* skiing race over winding course

slam *v* **slamming, slammed** shut noisily; bang ~*n* (noise of) this action

slander *n/v* (utter) false or malicious statement about person **slanderous** *adj*

slang *n* colloquial language

slant *v* slope; write, present (news etc.) with bias ~*n* slope; point of view **slanting** *adj*

slap *n* blow with open hand or flat instrument ~*v* **slapping, slapped** strike thus; *Inf* put down carelessly **slapdash** *adj* careless, hasty **slapstick** *n* boisterous knockabout comedy

slash *v/n* gash; cut

slat *n* narrow strip

slate *n* stone which splits easily in flat sheets; piece of this for covering roof ~*v* cover with slates; abuse

slaughter *n* killing ~*v* kill **slaughter-**

————— T H E S A U R U S —————

skinny lean, thin

skip *v* caper, dance, frisk, gambol, hop, prance

skirmish *n* battle, brush, clash, combat, conflict, fracas, incident, tussle

skirt *v* border, edge, flank

slab chunk, lump, piece, portion, slice, wedge

slack *adj* baggy, limp, loose, relaxed; idle, inactive, inattentive, lax, lazy, neglectful, negligent, slapdash, slipshod; inactive, quiet, slow, slow-moving, sluggish ~*n* excess, leeway, room

slam *v/n* bang, crash, smash

slander *n* calumny, libel, misrepresentation, scandal, smear ~*v* decry, defame, disparage, libel, malign, slur,

smear, vilify

slanderous abusive, damaging, defamatory, libellous, malicious

slant *v* bend, cant, heel, incline, lean, list, slope, tilt; angle, bias, colour, distort, twist ~*n* camber, gradient, incline, pitch, slope, tilt; angle, bias, emphasis, one-sidedness, prejudice

slanting angled, bent, inclined, oblique, sloping, tilted, tilting

slap *n/v* clout, cuff, smack, spank, whack

slapdash careless, hasty, hurried, perfunctory, slipshod

slash *v* cut, gash, hack, lacerate, rip, score, slit ~*n* cut, gash, incision, laceration, rip, slit

slate *v* berate, censure, criticize,

house *n* place where animals are killed for food

slave *n* captive, person without freedom or personal rights ~*v* work like slave **slavery** *n* **slavish** *adj* servile

slaver *v/n* (dribble) saliva from mouth

slay *v* **slaying, slew, slain** kill

sleazy *adj* sordid

sledge[1], **sled** *n* carriage on runners for sliding on snow; toboggan ~*v* move on sledge

sledge[2], **sledgehammer** *n* heavy hammer with long handle

sleek *adj* glossy, smooth, shiny

sleep *n* unconscious state regularly occurring in man and animals; slumber, repose ~*v* **sleeping, slept** take rest in sleep **sleeper** *n* one who sleeps; beam supporting rails; railway sleeping car **sleepless** *adj* **sleepy** *adj*

sleet *n* rain and snow falling together

sleeve *n* part of garment which covers arm

sleigh *n* sledge

sleight *n* **sleight of hand** (manual dexterity in) conjuring

slender *adj* slim, slight; small in amount

sleuth *n* detective

slice *n* thin flat piece cut off; share ~*v* cut into slices

slick *adj* smooth; glib; skilful ~*v* make glossy, smooth ~*n* slippery area; patch of oil on water

slide *v* **sliding, slid** slip smoothly along; glide; pass ~*n* sliding; track for sliding; glass mount for object to be viewed under microscope; photographic transparency

slight *adj* small, trifling; slim ~*v* disregard ~*n* act of discourtesy **slightly** *adv*

slim *adj* **slimmer, slimmest** thin; slight ~*v* **slimming, slimmed** reduce weight by diet and exercise

slime *n* thick, liquid mud **slimy** *adj* of, like, covered in slime; insincerely pleasant

sling *n* loop for hurling stone; bandage for supporting wounded limb; rope for hoisting weights ~*v* **slinging, slung** throw

slink *v* **slinking, slunk** move stealthily, sneak

— THESAURUS —

scold, tear into *Inf*

slaughter *n* bloodshed, butchery, carnage, killing, massacre, murder, slaying ~*v* butcher, destroy, kill, massacre, murder, slay

slave *n* drudge, serf, servant, skivvy *chiefly Brit* ~*v* drudge, slog, toil

slavery bondage, captivity, serfdom, servitude

sleep *n* doze, kip *Brit sl,* nap, repose, siesta, slumber(s) ~*v* catnap, doze, drowse, kip *Brit sl,* slumber

sleepless restless, wakeful

sleepy drowsy, dull, heavy, inactive, lethargic, sluggish, torpid

slender lean, narrow, slight, slim, willowy; inadequate, insufficient, little, meagre, scant, scanty, small

slice *n* cut, piece, portion, segment, share, sliver, wedge ~*v* carve, cut, divide, sever

slick glib, plausible, smooth; adroit, deft, dextrous, polished, skilful

slide *v* coast, glide, skim, slip, slither

slight *adj* insignificant, meagre, minor, paltry, scanty, small, superficial, trivial, unimportant; delicate, fragile, lightly-built, slim, small, spare ~*v* affront, disparage, ignore, insult, put down, scorn, snub ~*n* affront, discourtesy, disdain, disrespect, insult, rebuff, snub

slightly a little, somewhat

slim *adj* lean, narrow, slender, slight, thin, trim; faint, poor, remote, slender, slight

slimy glutinous, miry, muddy, viscous; creeping, ingratiating, obsequi-

slip *v* **slipping, slipped** (cause to) move smoothly; pass out of (mind etc.); lose balance by sliding; fall from person's grasp; (*usu. with* up) make mistake; put on or take off easily, quickly ~*n* act or occasion of slipping; mistake; petticoat; small piece of paper **slipshod** *adj* slovenly, careless **slipstream** *n* stream of air forced backwards by fast-moving object

slipper *n* light shoe for indoors

slippery *adj* so smooth as to cause slipping or to be difficult to hold; unreliable

slit *v* **slitting, slit** make long straight cut in ~*n* long straight cut

slither *v* slide unsteadily (down slope etc.)

sliver *n* splinter

slob *n Inf* lazy, untidy person

slobber *v/n* slaver

slog *v* **slogging, slogged** hit vigorously; work doggedly ~*n* struggle

slogan *n* distinctive phrase

slop *v* **slopping, slopped** spill, splash ~*n* liquid spilt; liquid food; *pl* liquid refuse **sloppy** *adj* careless, untidy

slope *v* be, place at slant ~*n* slant

slot *n* narrow hole; slit for coins; place in series ~*v* **slotting, slotted** put in slot; *Inf* place in series

sloth *n* S Amer. animal; sluggishness **slothful** *adj*

slouch *v* walk, sit etc. in drooping manner ~*n* drooping posture

slovenly *adj* dirty, untidy

slow *adj* lasting a long time; moving at low speed; dull ~*v* slacken speed (of) **slowly** *adv*

sludge *n* thick mud

slug[1] *n* land snail with no shell; bullet **sluggish** *adj* slow, inert; not functioning well

slug[2] *v* **slugging, slugged** hit, slog ~*n* heavy blow; portion of spirits

sluice *n* gate, door to control flow of water

slum *n* squalid street or neighbourhood

slumber *v/n* sleep

slump *v* fall heavily; relax ungracefully; decline suddenly ~*n* sudden decline

slur *v* **slurring, slurred** pass over light-

———————— THESAURUS ————————

ous, oily, sycophantic, unctuous

slink creep, prowl, skulk, slip, sneak, steal

slip *v* glide, slide, slither; creep, sneak, steal; fall, skid; (*sometimes with* up) blunder, err, miscalculate ~*n* blunder, error, indiscretion, mistake, omission, oversight

slippery glassy, greasy, icy, smooth; crafty, cunning, devious, dishonest, evasive, false, tricky, unreliable

slit *v* cut (open), gash, rip, slash ~*n* cut, gash, incision, opening, split, tear

slither *v* glide, slide, slip

slog *v* labour, plod, plough through, slave, toil, trudge, work ~*n* effort, exertion, labour, struggle, tramp, trudge

slogan catchphrase, motto

slope *v* drop away, fall, incline, lean, pitch, rise, slant, tilt ~*n* gradient, incline, rise, slant, tilt

sloppy *Inf* careless, inattentive, messy, slipshod, slovenly, unkempt, untidy

slot *n* aperture, groove, hole, slit, vent *Inf* place, position, space, time, vacancy

slouch *v* droop, loll, slump, stoop

slow gradual, lingering, prolonged, protracted; deliberate, easy, leisurely, measured, unhurried; dense, dim, dozy *Brit inf,* dull, dull-witted, obtuse, stupid, thick

sluggish dull, heavy, inactive, inert, lethargic, slow, torpid

slump *v* collapse, crash, deteriorate,

ly; run together (words); disparage ~*n* slight

slurp *Inf v* eat or drink noisily ~*n* slurping sound

slurry *n* muddy liquid mixture

slush *n* watery, muddy substance

slut *n* dirty (immoral) woman

sly *adj* cunning; deceitful

smack[1] *n* taste, flavour ~*v* taste (of); suggest

smack[2] *v* slap; open and close (lips) loudly ~*n* slap; such sound; loud kiss ~*adv Inf* squarely

small *adj* little; unimportant; short ~*n* small slender part, esp. of the back **smallholding** *n* small area of farmland **smallpox** *n* contagious disease

smart *adj* astute; clever; well-dressed ~*v* feel, cause pain ~*n* sharp pain **smarten** *v* make or become smart

smash *v* break; ruin; destroy ~*n* heavy blow; collision **smashing** *adj Inf* excellent

smattering *n* slight superficial knowledge

smear *v* rub with grease etc.; smudge; slander ~*n* greasy mark; slander

smell *v* **smelling, smelt** *or* **smelled** perceive by nose; give out odour ~*n* faculty of perceiving odours; anything detected by sense of smell **smelly** *adj* having nasty smell

smelt *v* extract metal from ore

smile *n* curving or parting of lips in pleased or amused expression ~*v* give smile

smirk *n* smile expressing scorn, smugness ~*v* give smirk

smite *v* **smiting, smote, smitten** strike; afflict

smith *n* worker in iron, gold etc. **smithy** *n* blacksmith's workshop

smithereens *pl n* shattered fragments

smock *n* loose, outer garment

smog *n* mixture of smoke and fog

smoke *n* cloudy mass that rises from fire etc. ~*v* give off smoke; inhale and expel tobacco smoke; expose to smoke **smoker** *n* **smoky** *adj* **smoke screen** thing intended to hide truth

smooth *adj* not rough, even; calm; unctuous ~*v* make smooth

smother *v* suffocate

———————— THESAURUS ————————

fall, fall off, plunge, sink ~*n* collapse, crash, decline, depression, downturn, drop, fall, low, recession

slur *n* blot, discredit, disgrace, insult, smear, stain, stigma

slut scrubber *Brit & Aust sl*, tart, trollop

sly *adj* artful, crafty, cunning, devious, furtive, scheming, secret, shifty, stealthy, subtle, underhand

smack *v* clap, cuff, hit, slap ~*n* blow, crack, slap

small diminutive, little, miniature, minute, petite, pygmy *or* pigmy, slight, tiny, undersized, wee; insignificant, minor, negligible, paltry, petty, trifling, trivial, unimportant

smart *adj* acute, astute, bright, canny, clever, intelligent, keen, quick,

shrewd; chic, elegant, neat, snappy, spruce, stylish, trim ~*v* hurt, pain, sting, tingle

smash *v* break, collide, crash, crush, demolish, shatter; defeat, destroy, lay waste, ruin, trash *Sl*, wreck ~*n* accident, collision, crash

smear *v* bedaub, blur, coat, cover, daub, smirch, smudge, spread over, stain, sully; blacken, sully, tarnish ~*n* blot, blotch, daub, smirch, smudge, splotch, streak; calumny, libel, slander

smell *v* scent, sniff; niff *Brit sl*, reek, stink ~*n* aroma, fragrance, odour, perfume, scent, whiff

smooth *adj* even, flat, flush, horizontal, level; glossy, polished, shiny, silky, sleek; calm, glassy, peaceful, se-

smoulder *v* burn slowly; (of feelings) be suppressed

smudge *v/n* (make) smear, stain (on)

smug *adj* self-satisfied, complacent

smuggle *v* import, export without paying customs duties **smuggler** *n*

smut *n* piece of soot; obscene talk etc. **smutty** *adj*

snack *n* light, hasty meal

snag *n* difficulty; sharp protuberance; hole, loop in fabric *~v* **snagging, snagged** catch, damage on snag

snail *n* slow-moving mollusc with shell

snake *n* long scaly limbless reptile *~v* move like snake

snap *v* **snapping, snapped** break suddenly; make cracking sound; bite (at) suddenly; speak suddenly, angrily *~n* act of snapping; fastener; card game; *Inf* snapshot *~adj* sudden, unplanned **snappy** *adj* irritable; *Sl* quick; *Sl* fashionable **snapshot** *n* photograph

snare *n/v* trap

snarl *n* growl of angry dog; tangle *~v* utter snarl

snatch *v* make quick grab (at); seize, catch *~n* grab; fragment

sneak *v* move about furtively; act in underhand manner *~n* petty informer **sneaking** *adj* secret; slight but persistent

sneer *n* scornful, contemptuous expression or remark *~v* give sneer

sneeze *v* emit breath through nose with sudden involuntary spasm and noise *~n* act of sneezing

snide *adj* malicious, supercilious

sniff *v* inhale through nose with sharp hiss; smell; (*with* at) express disapproval etc. *~n* act of sniffing **sniffle** *v* sniff noisily, esp. when suffering from a cold

snigger *n* sly, disrespectful laugh, esp. partly stifled *~v* produce snigger

snip *v* **snipping, snipped** cut with quick stroke *~n* quick cut; *Inf* bargain **snippet** *n* small piece

snipe *n* wading bird *~v* shoot at enemy from cover; (*with* at) criticize **sniper** *n*

snivel *v* **-elling, -elled** sniffle to show distress; whine

snob *n* one who pretentiously judges others by social rank etc. **snobbery** *n* **snobbish** *adj*

snooker *n* game played on table with balls and cues

snoop *v* pry, meddle; peer into

snooty *adj* *Sl* haughty

snooze *v/n* (take) nap

snore *v* breathe noisily when asleep

───── T H E S A U R U S ─────

rene, tranquil, undisturbed, unruffled; glib, persuasive, silky, slick, suave, unctuous *~v* flatten, iron, level, plane, press

smug complacent, conceited, superior

snack bite, light meal, refreshment(s), titbit

snap *v* break, crack, separate; click, crackle, pop *~adj* immediate, instant, sudden

snare *v* catch, net, seize, trap

snatch *v* clutch, grab, grasp, grip, pluck, pull, seize, take *~n* bit, fragment, part, piece, snippet

sneak *v* lurk, sidle, skulk, slink, slip, steal *~n* informer, telltale

sneaking hidden, private, secret; nagging, persistent

sneer *n* derision, gibe, jeer, mockery, ridicule, scorn *~v* gibe, jeer, laugh, mock, ridicule, scoff, scorn

sniff *v* breathe, inhale, smell, snuffle

snigger giggle, laugh, titter

snip *v* clip, crop, cut, dock, trim *~n* bit, clipping, fragment, piece, scrap, shred; *Inf* bargain, giveaway, good buy, steal *Inf*

snoop interfere, poke one's nose in *Inf*, pry, spy

~n sound of snoring

snorkel *n* tube for breathing underwater

snort *v* make (contemptuous) noise by driving breath through nostrils **~n** act of snorting

snout *n* animal's nose

snow *n* frozen vapour which falls in flakes **~v** fall, sprinkle as snow **snowy** *adj* **snowball** *n* snow pressed into hard ball for throwing **~v** increase rapidly **snowdrift** *n* bank of deep snow **snowdrop** *n* small, white, bell-shaped spring flower **snowman** *n* figure shaped out of snow **snowplough** *n* vehicle for clearing away snow **snowshoes** *pl n* racket-shaped shoes for travelling on snow

snub *v* **snubbing, snubbed** insult (esp. by ignoring) intentionally **~n** snubbing **~adj** short and blunt **snub-nosed** *adj*

snuff[1] *n* powdered tobacco

snuff[2] *v* extinguish (esp. candle)

snuffle *v* breathe noisily

snug *adj* warm, comfortable

snuggle *v* lie close to, nestle

so *adv* to such an extent; in such a manner; very **~conj** therefore; in order that; with the result that **~interj** well! **so-and-so** *n* *Inf* person whose name is not specified; unpleasant person **so-called** *adj* called by but doubtfully deserving that name

soak *v* steep; absorb; drench **soaking** *n/adj*

soap *n* compound of alkali and oil used in washing **~v** apply soap to **soapy** *adj* **soap opera** television, radio serial dealing with domestic themes

soar *v* fly high; increase rapidly

sob *v* **sobbing, sobbed** catch breath, esp. in weeping **~n** sobbing

sober *adj* not drunk; temperate; subdued; dull; solemn **~v** make, become sober **sobriety** *n*

soccer *n* game of football, with spherical ball

sociable *adj* friendly; convivial

social *adj* living in communities; relating to society; sociable **~n** informal gathering **socialize** *v*

socialism *n* political system which advocates public ownership of means of production **socialist** *n/adj*

society *n* living associated with others; those so living; companionship; association; fashionable people collectively

———— THESAURUS ————

snooze *v* catnap, doze, nap **~n** catnap, doze, nap, siesta

snub *v* cold-shoulder, rebuff, slight **~n** affront, insult

snug comfortable, cosy, homely, warm

snuggle cuddle, nestle, nuzzle

soak drench, immerse, infuse, penetrate, permeate, saturate, steep

soaking drenched, dripping, saturated, sodden, sopping, water logged, wringing wet

soar ascend, fly, rise, wing; climb, escalate, rise, rocket, shoot up

sober abstemious, abstinent, moderate, temperate; calm, composed,

cool, dispassionate, grave, rational, reasonable, serious, solemn, steady, unexcited, unruffled

so-called alleged, professed, self-styled, supposed

sociable affable, companionable, convivial, friendly, gregarious, outgoing, social

social *adj* collective, communal, community, group, public

socialize fraternize, get about *or* around, get together, go out, mix

society civilization, culture, mankind, people, the community, the public; companionship, company, fellowship, friendship; association, club,

sociology *n* study of societies **sociological** *adj*

sock[1] *n* cloth covering for foot

sock[2] *Sl v* hit ~*n* blow

socket *n* hole or recess for something to fit into

sod *n* lump of earth with grass

soda *n* compound of sodium; **soda water** water charged with carbon dioxide

sodden *adj* soaked

sodium *n* metallic alkaline element **sodium bicarbonate** compound used in baking powder

sodomy *n* anal intercourse

sofa *n* upholstered seat with back and arms

soft *adj* yielding easily to pressure; not hard; mild; easy; subdued; quiet; gentle; (too) lenient **soften** *v* make, become soft or softer **softly** *adv* **soft drink** nonalcoholic drink **software** *n* computer programs

soggy *adj* damp and heavy

soil[1] *n* earth, ground

soil[2] *v* make, become dirty

solace *n/v* comfort in distress

solar *adj* of the sun

solarium *n* (*pl* **-lariums, -laria**) place with beds and ultraviolet lights for acquiring artificial suntan

solder *n* easily-melted alloy used for joining metal ~*v* join with it

soldier *n* one serving in army ~*v* serve in army; (*with* on) persist doggedly

sole[1] *adj* one and only **solely** *adv* alone; only; entirely

sole[2] *n* underside of foot; underpart of boot etc. ~*v* fit with sole

sole[3] *n* small edible flatfish

solemn *adj* serious; formal **solemnity** *n* **solemnize** *v* celebrate, perform

solicit *v* request; accost **solicitor** *n* lawyer who prepares documents, advises clients **solicitous** *adj* anxious; eager **solicitude** *n*

solid *adj* not hollow; composed of one substance; firm; reliable ~*n* body of three dimensions; substance not liquid or gas **solidarity** *n* unity **solidify** *v* **-fying, -fied** harden

soliloquy *n* (esp. in drama) thoughts spoken by person while alone

solitary *adj* alone, single **solitaire** *n* game for one person; single precious stone set by itself **solitude** *n* state of being alone

solo *n* (*pl* **-los**) music for one perform-

——— THESAURUS ———

fellowship, fraternity, group, guild, institute, league, union; gentry, high society, upper classes

soft pulpy, spongy, squashy, yielding; elastic, flexible, plastic, pliable, supple; balmy, mild, temperate; dim, low, subdued; faint, gentle, low, muted, quiet; compassionate, gentle, kind, sensitive, sentimental, sympathetic, tender

soften ease, lessen, lighten, mitigate, moderate, temper; abate, allay, appease, calm, soothe, still

soil[1] *n* clay, dirt, earth, ground, loam

soil[2] *v* defile, dirty, foul, pollute, smear, smirch, stain, sully, tarnish

soldier fighter, man-at-arms, service-

man, squaddie *or* squaddy *Brit sl*, trooper, warrior

sole alone, individual, one, single, solitary

solemn grave, serious, sober; ceremonial, formal, grand, stately

solid *adj* compact, concrete, dense, hard; firm, stable, strong, sturdy, unshakable; dependable, genuine, pure, reliable, sound

solidarity accord, concordance, harmony, team spirit, unanimity, unity

solidify cake, coagulate, congeal, harden, jell, set

solitary alone, lone, single, sole

solitude isolation, loneliness, privacy, seclusion

er ~*adj* unaccompanied, alone **soloist** *n*

solstice *n* shortest (winter) or longest (summer) day

solve *v* work out; find answer to **soluble** *adj* capable of being dissolved in liquid; able to be solved **solution** *n* answer; dissolving; liquid with something dissolved in it **solvable** *adj* **solvency** *n* **solvent** *adj* able to meet financial obligations ~*n* liquid with power of dissolving

sombre *adj* dark, gloomy

sombrero *n* (*pl* -ros) wide-brimmed hat

some *adj* denoting an indefinite number, amount or extent; one or another; certain ~*pron* portion, quantity **somebody** *pron* some person ~*n* important person **somehow** *adv* by some means **someone** *pron* somebody **something** *pron* thing not clearly defined **sometime** *adv* at some unspecified time ~*adj* former **sometimes** *adv* occasionally **somewhat** *adv* rather **somewhere** *adv* at some unspecified place

somersault *n* tumbling head over heels

son *n* male child **son-in-law** *n* daughter's husband

sonar *n* device for detecting underwater objects

sonata *n* piece of music in several movements

song *n* singing; poem etc. for singing

sonic *adj* pert. to sound waves

sonnet *n* fourteen-line poem with definite rhyme scheme

sonorous *adj* giving out (deep) sound, resonant

soon *adv* in a short time; before long; early, quickly

soot *n* black powdery substance formed by burning of coal etc. **sooty** *adj*

soothe *v* make calm, tranquil; relieve (pain etc.)

sop *n* piece of bread etc. soaked in liquid; bribe ~*v* **sopping**, **sopped** steep in water etc.; soak (up) **soppy** *adj Inf* oversentimental

sophisticated *adj* worldly wise; complex, refined **sophistication** *n*

soporific *adj* causing sleep

soprano *n* (*pl* -pranos) highest voice in women and boys

sorbet *n* (fruit-flavoured) water ice

sorcerer *n* (*fem* **sorceress**) magician **sorcery** *n*

sordid *adj* mean, squalid; base

sore *adj* painful; causing annoyance

——— **THESAURUS** ———

solution answer, explanation, key, resolution, result; blend, compound, mix, mixture

solve answer, clear up, crack, decipher, disentangle, explain, resolve, suss (out) *Sl*

sombre dark, dim, drab, dull, gloomy, grave, shadowy, shady, sober

sometimes at times, occasionally

soon before long, in the near future, shortly

soothe allay, alleviate, appease, assuage, calm, ease, hush, lull, pacify, quiet, relieve, settle, still

sophisticated cultivated, cultured, refined, urbane, worldly; advanced, complex, complicated, elaborate, intricate, subtle

sophistication poise, savoir-faire, urbanity, worldliness, worldly wisdom

soppy corny *Sl*, mawkish, overemotional, schmaltzy *Sl*, sentimental, slushy *Inf*

sorcerer enchanter, magician, sorceress, warlock, witch, wizard

sorcery black art, black magic, magic, necromancy, witchcraft, wizardry

sordid dirty, filthy, foul, mean, seedy,

~n sore place **sorely** adv greatly

sorrow n/v (feel) grief, sadness **sorrowful** adj

sorry adj feeling pity or regret; miserable, wretched

sort n kind, class ~v classify

sortie n sally by besieged forces

SOS n international code signal of distress; call for help

so-so adj Inf mediocre

soufflé n dish of eggs beaten to froth, flavoured and baked

soul n spiritual and immortal part of human being; person; sensitivity; type of Black music **soulful** adj

sound[1] n what is heard; noise ~v make sound; give impression of; utter **soundproof** adj

sound[2] adj in good condition; solid; of good judgment; thorough; deep **soundly** adv thoroughly

sound[3] v find depth of, as water; ascertain views of; probe

sound[4] n channel; strait

soup n liquid food made by boiling meat, vegetables etc.

sour adj acid; gone bad; peevish; disagreeable ~v make, become sour

source n origin, starting point; spring

south n point opposite north; region, part of country etc. lying to that side ~adj/adv from, towards or in the south **southerly** adj ~n wind from the south **southern** adj **southward** adj **southwards** adv

souvenir n keepsake, memento

sou'wester n seaman's waterproof headgear

sovereign n king, queen; former gold coin worth 20 shillings ~adj supreme; efficacious **sovereignty** n

sow[1] v sowing, sowed, sown or sowed scatter, plant seed

sow[2] n female adult pig

soya n plant yielding edible beans **soya bean** edible bean used for food

———————— THESAURUS ————————

squalid, unclean; base, low, shabby, shameful

sore painful, raw, sensitive, tender; annoying, troublesome

sorrow n anguish, distress, grief, heartache, misery, mourning, sadness, unhappiness, woe

sorrowful dejected, depressed, dismal, melancholy, miserable, mournful, sad, unhappy, woebegone, woeful, wretched

sorry contrite, penitent, regretful, remorseful, repentant; abject, base, deplorable, distressing, mean, miserable, pathetic, pitiful, poor, sad, wretched

sort n brand, breed, category, character, class, kind, make, nature, order, race, species, style, type, variety ~v arrange, categorize, class, classify, divide, group, order, rank

soul essence, life, mind, psyche, spirit; being, creature, individual, mortal, person

sound[1] n din, noise, tone ~v echo, resound, reverberate

sound[2] adj complete, entire, firm, fit, hale, healthy, intact, perfect, robust, solid, whole; correct, rational, reasonable, reliable, responsible, right, sensible, trustworthy, valid, well-founded, wise

sound[3] v fathom, plumb, probe

sour acid, bitter, sharp, tart; cynical, disagreeable, embittered, grudging, ill-natured, peevish, tart, waspish

source beginning, cause, derivation, fount, origin, spring, wellspring

souvenir keepsake, memento, relic, reminder

sovereign n chief, emperor, empress, king, monarch, potentate, prince, queen, ruler, shah, tsar

sovereignty ascendancy, domination, kingship, primacy, supremacy, supreme power, sway

and oil **soy sauce** sauce made from fermented soya beans

spa *n* medicinal spring; place, resort with one

space *n* extent; room; period; empty place; area; expanse; region beyond earth's atmosphere ~*v* place at intervals **spacious** *adj* roomy, extensive **spacecraft, spaceship** *n* vehicle for travel beyond earth's atmosphere **spaceman** *n* astronaut

spade¹ *n* tool for digging

spade² *n* suit at cards

spaghetti *n* pasta in long strings

span *n* extent, space; stretch of arch etc.; space from thumb to little finger ~*v* **spanning, spanned** stretch over; measure with hand

spangle *n* small shiny metallic ornament ~*v* decorate with spangles

spaniel *n* breed of dog with long ears and silky hair

spank *v* slap with flat of hand, esp. on buttocks ~*n* spanking

spanner *n* tool for gripping nut or bolt head

spar¹ *n* pole, beam, esp. as part of ship's rigging

spar² *v* **sparring, sparred** box; dispute, esp. in fun ~*n* sparring

spare *v* leave unhurt; show mercy; do without; give away ~*adj* additional; in reserve; thin; lean ~*n* reserve copy **sparing** *adj* economical, careful

spark *n* small glowing or burning particle; flash of light produced by electrical discharge; trace ~*v* emit sparks; kindle

sparkle *v* glitter; effervesce ~*n* glitter; vitality **sparkling** *adj* glittering; (of wines) effervescent

sparrow *n* small brownish bird **sparrowhawk** *n* hawk that hunts small birds

sparse *adj* thinly scattered

spartan *adj* strict, austere

spasm *n* sudden convulsive (muscular) contraction; sudden burst of activity etc. **spasmodic** *adj*

spastic *adj* affected by spasms; suffering cerebral palsy ~*n* person with cerebral palsy

spate *n* rush, outpouring; flood

spatial *adj* of, in space

spatter *v* splash, cast drops over; be scattered in drops ~*n* spattering

spatula *n* utensil with broad, flat blade for various purposes

spawn *n* eggs of fish or frog ~*v* (of fish or frog) cast eggs

spay *v* remove ovaries from (female animal)

speak *v* **speaking, spoke, spoken** utter words; converse; express; communicate in; give speech **speaker** *n* one who speaks; speech maker; loudspeaker

spear *n* long pointed weapon ~*v*

——— THESAURUS ———

space capacity, expanse, leeway, margin, room, scope; blank, gap, interval

spacious ample, broad, commodious, expansive, extensive, huge, large, roomy, sizable, vast

span *n* extent, length, reach, spread, stretch ~*v* bridge, cross, link, traverse

spank *v* slap, smack

spare *v* be merciful to, have mercy on, pardon, release; allow, bestow, give, grant; afford , dispense with, part with, relinquish ~*adj* additional,

extra, free, leftover, odd, superfluous, surplus; gaunt, lean, meagre, slender, slight, slim

sparing careful, economical, frugal, prudent, saving, thrifty

spark flare, flash, flicker, gleam, glint

sparkle *v* beam, dance, flash, gleam, glint, glitter, shimmer, shine, twinkle ~*n* flash, gleam, glint, glitter, twinkle; dash, élan, gaiety, life, spirit, vitality

spasm convulsion, paroxysm; burst, fit, frenzy, outburst, seizure

pierce with spear **spearhead** *n* leading force in attack *~v* lead attack

spearmint *n* type of mint

special *adj* beyond the usual; particular **specialist** *n* one who devotes himself to special subject **speciality** *n* special product, skill, characteristic etc. **specialization** *n* **specialize** *v* be specialist; make special

species *n* (*pl* -cies) group of plants or animals that are closely related

specific *adj* exact in detail; characteristic **specification** *n* detailed description of something **specify** *v* -fying, -fied state definitely or in detail

specimen *n* part typifying whole; individual example

specious *adj* deceptively plausible, but false

speck *n* small spot, particle *~v* mark with spots **speckle** *n/v* speck

spectacle *n* show; thing exhibited; strange, interesting, or ridiculous

sight; *pl* pair of lenses for correcting defective sight **spectacular** *adj* impressive; showy **spectate** *v* **spectator** *n* one who looks on

spectre *n* ghost; image of something unpleasant

spectrum *n* (*pl* -tra) band of colours into which light can be decomposed, e.g. by prism

speculate *v* guess, conjecture; engage in (risky) commercial transactions **speculation** *n* **speculative** *adj* **speculator** *n*

speech *n* act, faculty of speaking; words, language; (formal) talk given before audience **speechless** *adj* dumb; at a loss for words

speed *n* swiftness; rate of progress *~v* **speeding, sped** *or* **speeded** move quickly; drive vehicle at high speed; further **speeding** *n* driving at high speed, esp. over legal limit **speedy** *adj* **speedometer** *n* instrument to

———————— THESAURUS ————————

speak articulate, converse, discourse, express, pronounce, say, state, talk, tell, utter, voice

speaker lecturer, orator, public speaker, spokesman

special especial, exceptional, extraordinary, important, significant, unique, unusual; appropriate, certain, distinctive, individual, particular, peculiar

specialist *n* authority, buff *Inf*, connoisseur, consultant, expert, master, professional

speciality bag *Sl*, forte, métier

species category, class, group, kind, sort, type, variety

specific definite, exact, explicit, particular, precise; characteristic, especial, peculiar, special

specification detail, particular, requirement, stipulation

specify define, designate, detail, enumerate, indicate, mention

specimen copy, example, individual, instance, model, proof, sample, type

speck blemish, blot, dot, fleck, mark, speckle, spot, stain; atom, bit, grain, iota, jot, mite, particle

spectacle display, event, pageant, parade, performance, show, sight

spectacular dazzling, dramatic, grand, impressive, magnificent, splendid, striking

spectator bystander, eyewitness, looker-on, observer, onlooker, viewer, watcher, witness

speculate conjecture, guess, suppose, surmise, theorize; gamble, hazard, risk

speech communication, conversation, dialogue, discussion, talk; address, discourse, homily, lecture, oration

speechless dumb, inarticulate, mute, silent, wordless; aghast, amazed, astounded

show speed of vehicle **speedwell** n plant with small blue flowers

spell[1] v spelling, spelt or spelled give letters of in order; indicate, result in **spelling** n

spell[2] n magic formula; enchantment **spellbound** adj enchanted; entranced

spell[3] n (short) period of time, work

spend v spending, spent pay out; pass (time); use up completely **spendthrift** n wasteful person

sperm n male reproductive cell; semen

spew v vomit

sphere n ball, globe; field of action **spherical** adj

spice n aromatic or pungent vegetable substance; spices collectively; anything that adds relish, interest etc. ~v season with spices **spicy** adj

spick-and-span adj neat, smart, new-looking

spider n small eight-legged creature which spins web to catch prey **spidery** adj thin and angular

spike n sharp point; long cluster with flowers attached directly to stalk ~v pierce, fasten with spike; render ineffective **spiky** adj

spill v spilling, spilt or spilled (cause to) pour from, flow over, fall out, esp. unintentionally ~n fall; amount

spilt **spillage** n

spin v spinning, spun (cause to) revolve rapidly; twist into thread; prolong ~n spinning **spinning** n act, process of drawing out and twisting into threads **spin-dryer** n machine in which clothes are spun to remove excess water **spin-off** n incidental benefit

spinach n dark green leafy vegetable

spindle n rod, axis for spinning **spindly** adj long and slender

spine n backbone; thin spike, esp. on fish etc.; ridge; back of book **spinal** adj **spineless** adj lacking in spine; cowardly

spinster n unmarried woman

spiral n continuous curve drawn at ever increasing distance from fixed point; anything resembling this ~adj shaped like spiral

spire n pointed part of steeple

spirit n life principle animating body; disposition; liveliness; courage; essential character or meaning; soul; ghost; pl emotional state; strong alcoholic drink ~v carry away mysteriously **spirited** adj lively **spiritual** adj given to, interested in things of the spirit ~n sacred song orig. sung by Black slaves in America **spiritualism** n belief that spirits of the dead communi-

———————————— THESAURUS ————————————

speed n haste, hurry, quickness, rapidity, swiftness, velocity ~v career, gallop, hasten, hurry, race, rush, sprint, tear, zoom; advance, aid, assist, expedite, facilitate, further, help

speedy express, fast, hasty, headlong, hurried, immediate, precipitate, prompt, quick, rapid, summary, swift

spell[1] n charm, incantation

spell[2] n bout, course, interval, period, season, stint, stretch, term, time, turn

spend disburse, expend; fill, occupy, pass, while away; consume, drain,

empty, exhaust, run through, use up

sphere ball, globe, orb; capacity, domain, field, function, patch, province, range, realm, scope, territory, turf US sl

spherical globe-shaped, globular, rotund, round

spice colour, excitement, pep, piquancy, zest

spike n barb, point, prong, spine ~v impale, spear

spill disgorge, overflow, overturn, slop over, run over, upset

spin v revolve, rotate, turn, twirl,

cate with the living **spiritualist** *n* **spirituality** *n*

spit[1] *v* **spitting, spat** eject saliva (from mouth) ~*n* spitting, saliva **spittle** *n* saliva

spit[2] *n* sharp rod to put through meat for roasting; sandy point projecting into the sea ~*v* **spitting, spitted** thrust through

spite *n* malice ~*v* thwart spitefully **spiteful** *adj* **in spite of** *prep* regardless of; notwithstanding

splash *v* scatter liquid about or on, over something; print (story, photo) prominently in newspaper ~*n* sound of splashing liquid; patch, esp. of colour; (effect of) extravagant display

splatter *v/n* spatter

splay *adj* spread out; turned outwards ~*v* spread out; twist outwards

spleen *n* organ in the abdomen **splenetic** *adj* spiteful, irritable

splendid *adj* magnificent, excellent **splendour** *n*

splice *v* join by interweaving strands ~*n* spliced joint

splint *n* rigid support for broken limb etc.

splinter *n* thin fragment ~*v* break into fragments

split *v* **splitting, split** break asunder; separate; divide ~*n* crack; division **split second** very short period of time

splutter *v* make hissing, spitting sounds; utter incoherently with spitting sounds ~*n* spluttering

spoil *v* **spoiling, spoilt** *or* **spoiled** damage, injure; damage manners or behaviour of (esp. child) by indulgence; go bad **spoils** *pl n* booty **spoilsport** *n* person who spoils others' enjoyment

spoke *n* radial bar of a wheel

spokesman *n* one deputed to speak for others

sponge *n* marine animal; its skeleton, or a synthetic substance like it, used to absorb liquids; type of light cake ~*v* wipe with sponge; live at the ex-

———————— THESAURUS ————————

twist, wheel, whirl

spirit *n* life, soul, vital spark; attitude, character, disposition, outlook, temper, temperament; energy, enthusiasm, fire, force, liveliness, mettle, sparkle, vigour, zest; essence, intent, intention, meaning, purpose, sense; apparition, ghost, phantom, spectre; *pl* feelings, mood, morale

spirited animated, energetic, feisty *Inf, chiefly US & Canad,* high-spirited, lively, mettlesome, vivacious

spite malice, rancour, spitefulness, spleen, venom **in spite of** despite, (even) though, notwithstanding, regardless of

spiteful ill-natured, malicious, venomous, vindictive

splash *v* shower, slop, spatter, spray, sprinkle, wet ~*n* burst, dash, patch, splodge, touch

splendid brilliant, glorious, grand,

magnificent, outstanding, superb, supreme

splendour brilliance, glory, grandeur, magnificence

splinter *n* chip, flake, fragment ~*v* fracture, shatter, split

split *v* break, burst, cleave, crack, open, part, separate; disband, disunite, part, separate; branch, diverge, fork; divide, halve, parcel out, partition, share out ~*n* breach, crack, division, fissure; breach, break-up, disunion, division, estrangement, rift, schism

spoil damage, destroy, harm, injure, mar, mess up, ruin, undo, upset, wreck; indulge, overindulge, pamper; curdle, decay, go bad, putrefy, rot, turn

spoilsport damper, dog in the manger, kill-joy, misery *Brit inf,* wet blanket *Inf*

pense of others **spongy** *adj* sponge-like; wet and soft

sponsor *n* one promoting something; one who agrees to give money to charity on completion of a specified activity by another; godparent ~*v* act as sponsor **sponsorship** *n*

spontaneous *adj* voluntary; natural **spontaneity** *n*

spoof *n* mildly satirical parody

spook *n Inf* ghost **spooky** *adj*

spool *n* reel, bobbin

spoon *n* implement with shallow bowl at end of handle for carrying food to mouth etc. ~*v* lift with spoon **spoonful** *n* **spoon-feed** *v* give (someone) too much help

sporadic *adj* intermittent; scattered

spore *n* minute reproductive body of some plants

sporran *n* pouch worn in front of kilt

sport *n* game, activity for pleasure, competition, exercise; enjoyment; cheerful person, good loser ~*v* wear (esp. ostentatiously); frolic; play (sport) **sporting** *adj* of sport; behaving with fairness, generosity **sports car** fast low-built car **sportsman** *n* (*fem* **sportswoman**) one who engages in sport; good loser

spot *n* small mark, stain; blemish; pimple; place; (difficult) situation; *Inf* small quantity ~*v* **spotting, spotted** mark with spots; detect; observe **spotless** *adj* unblemished; pure **spotty** *adj* with spots; uneven **spotlight** *n* powerful light illuminating small area; centre of attention

spouse *n* husband or wife

spout *v* pour out ~*n* projecting tube or lip for pouring liquids; copious discharge

sprain *v/n* wrench, twist

sprat *n* small sea fish

sprawl *v* lie or sit about awkwardly; spread in rambling, unplanned way ~*n* sprawling

spray[1] *n* (device for producing) fine drops of liquid ~*v* sprinkle with shower of fine drops

spray[2] *n* branch, twig with buds, flowers etc.; ornament like this

spread *v* **spreading, spread** extend; stretch out; open out; scatter; distribute; unfold; cover ~*n* extent; increase; ample meal; food which can be spread on bread etc. **spread-eagled** *adj* with arms and legs outstretched

spree *n* session of overindulgence; romp

sprig *n* small twig

—————————— THESAURUS ——————————

sponsor *n* backer, patron, promoter ~*v* back, finance, fund, promote, subsidize

spontaneous free, impulsive, instinctive, natural, unforced, unprompted, voluntary

sport *n* amusement, diversion, game, pastime, play, recreation

spot *n* blemish, blot, blotch, flaw, mark, smudge, speck, stain; location, place, position, scene, site; *Inf* difficulty, hot water *Inf*, mess, plight, predicament, quandary ~*v* detect, discern, observe, recognize, see, sight

spotless clean, flawless, immaculate, impeccable, pure, unblemished, unstained, unsullied, untarnished

spouse consort, mate, partner, significant other *US inf*

spout *v* discharge, emit, erupt, gush, jet, shoot, stream

sprawl *v* flop, loll, lounge, slouch, slump, spread

spray *v* scatter, shower, sprinkle

spread *v* broaden, expand, extend, open, sprawl, stretch, unfold, unfurl, unroll, widen ~*n* extent, reach, span, stretch; advance, development, escalation, expansion, increase

spree bender *Inf*, binge *Inf*, carousal,

sprightly *adj* lively, brisk

spring *v* **springing, sprang, sprung** leap; shoot up or forth; come into being; appear; grow; become bent or spilt; produce unexpectedly; set off (trap) ~*n* leap; recoil; piece of coiled or bent metal with much resilience; flow of water from earth; first season of year **springy** *adj* elastic **spring-clean** *v* clean (house) thoroughly

springbok *n* S Afr. antelope

sprinkle *v* scatter small drops on, strew **sprinkler** *n* **sprinkling** *n* small quantity or number

sprint *v* run short distance at great speed ~*n* such run, race **sprinter** *n*

sprite *n* elf

sprocket *n* toothed wheel, attached to chain

sprout *v* put forth shoots, spring up ~*n* shoot

spruce[1] *n* variety of fir

spruce[2] *adj* neat in dress **spruce up** make neat and smart

spry *adj* nimble, vigorous

spur *n* pricking instrument attached to horseman's heel; incitement; stimulus ~*v* **spurring, spurred** urge on

spurious *adj* not genuine

spurn *v* reject with scorn

spurt *v* send, come out in jet; rush suddenly ~*n* jet; short sudden effort

spy *n* one who watches (esp. in rival countries, companies etc.) and reports secretly ~*v* **spying, spied** act as spy; catch sight of

squabble *v/n* (engage in) petty, noisy quarrel

squad *n* small party, esp. of soldiers **squadron** *n* division of cavalry regiment, fleet or air force

squalid *adj* mean and dirty **squalor** *n*

squall *n* harsh cry; sudden gust of wind; short storm ~*v* yell

squander *v* spend wastefully

square *n* equilateral rectangle; area of this shape; in town, open space (of this shape); product of a number multiplied by itself; instrument for drawing right angles ~*adj* square in form; honest; straight, even; level, equal ~*v* make square; find square of; pay; fit, suit

squash *v* crush flat; pulp; suppress ~*n* juice of crushed fruit; crowd; game played with rackets and ball in walled court

———— THESAURUS ————

carouse, fling, orgy

sprightly active, brisk, lively, spirited, spry

spring *v* bounce, bound, jump, leap, vault (*oft. with* from) arise, come, emerge, grow, originate, start, stem (*with* up) appear, develop, grow, mushroom, shoot up ~*n* bound, jump, leap, vault

sprinkle dredge, dust, pepper, powder, scatter

sprout *v* bud, develop, grow, shoot, spring

spur *n* goad, prick; impetus, impulse, incentive, inducement, motive, stimulus ~*v* drive, goad, impel, incite, prompt, stimulate, urge

spurious artificial, bogus, fake, false, forged, imitation, mock, phoney *or* phony *Inf*, pretended, sham

spurn disdain, rebuff, reject, scorn, slight, snub

spy *v* descry, espy, glimpse, notice, observe, spot

squabble *v* argue, bicker, fight, quarrel, row ~*n* argument, disagreement, fight, row, tiff

squad band, company, crew, force, team, troop

squalid dirty, filthy, seedy, slummy, sordid, unclean

squalor filth, meanness, squalidness

squander fritter away, lavish, misspend, misuse, spend, waste

squat v **squatting, squatted** sit on heels; occupy unused premises illegally ~adj short and thick **squatter** n

squawk n short harsh cry, esp. of bird ~v utter this

squeak v/n (make) short shrill sound

squeal n long piercing squeak ~v make one

squeamish adj easily made sick; easily shocked

squeeze v press; wring; force; hug ~n act of squeezing

squelch v/n (make) wet sucking sound

squid n type of cuttlefish

squiggle n wavy line

squint v have the eyes turn in different directions; glance sideways ~n this eye disorder; glance

squire n country gentleman

squirm v wriggle; be embarrassed ~n squirming

squirrel n small graceful bushy-tailed tree animal

squirt v (of liquid) force, be forced through narrow opening ~n jet of liquid

St. Saint; Street

st. stone (weight)

stab v **stabbing, stabbed** pierce, strike (at) with pointed weapon ~n blow, wound so inflicted; sudden sensation, e.g. of fear; attempt

stabilize v make or become stable **stabilizer** n device to maintain stability of ship, aircraft etc.

stable[1] n building for horses; racehorses of particular owner, establishment; such establishment ~v put into stable

stable[2] adj firmly fixed; steadfast, resolute **stability** n steadiness; ability to resist change

staccato adj/adv Mus with the notes sharply separated

stack n ordered pile, heap; chimney; v pile in stack

stadium n (pl **-diums, -dia**) open-air arena for athletics etc.

staff n body of officers or workers; pole ~v supply with personnel

stag n male deer

stage n period, division of development; (platform of) theatre; stopping-place on road, distance between two of them ~v put (play) on stage; arrange, bring about

stagger v walk unsteadily; astound; arrange in overlapping or alternating positions, times; distribute over a period

———————— THESAURUS ————————

squash v compress, crush, distort, flatten, pulp; crush, humiliate, quell, silence, suppress

squeak v peep, pipe, squeal

squeamish queasy, sick; delicate, fastidious, prudish, scrupulous, strait-laced

squeeze v compress, crush, press, squash; clasp, cuddle, embrace, hug ~n clasp, embrace, hug; crush, jam, press, squash

squirm twist, wriggle, writhe

stab v cut, injure, jab, knife, pierce, stick, thrust, wound ~n gash, jab, puncture, thrust, wound; pang, prick, twinge; attempt, endeavour, essay, try

stable enduring, established, fast, firm, fixed, immovable, lasting, permanent, reliable, secure, sound, steady, strong, sturdy, well-founded

stack n heap, mound, mountain, pile ~v bank up, heap up, load, pile

staff n employees, personnel, workers, work force; cane, pole, rod, sceptre, stave

stage division, leg, length, level, period, phase, point, step

stagger lurch, reel, sway, waver, wobble; amaze, astonish, astound,

stagnate v cease to flow or develop **stagnant** adj sluggish; not flowing; foul, impure **stagnation** n

staid adj of sober and quiet character, sedate

stain v spot, mark; apply liquid colouring to (wood etc.) ~n discoloration or mark; moral blemish **stainless** adj **stainless steel** rustless steel alloy

stairs pl n set of steps, esp. as part of house **staircase, stairway** n structure enclosing stairs; stairs

stake n sharpened stick or post; bet; investment ~v secure, mark out with stakes; wager, risk

stalactite n lime deposit hanging from roof of cave

stalagmite n lime deposit sticking up from floor of cave

stale adj old, lacking freshness; lacking energy, interest through monotony **stalemate** n deadlock

stalk[1] n plant's stem; anything like this

stalk[2] v follow stealthily; walk in stiff and stately manner

stall n compartment in stable etc.; erection for display and sale of goods; front seat in theatre etc. ~v (of motor engine) unintentionally stop; delay

stallion n uncastrated male horse, esp. for breeding

stalwart adj strong, brave; staunch ~n stalwart person

stamina n power of endurance

stammer v speak, say with repetition of syllables ~n habit of so speaking

stamp v put down foot with force; impress mark on; affix postage stamp ~n stamping with foot; imprinted mark; appliance for marking; piece of gummed paper printed with device as evidence of postage etc.

stampede n sudden frightened rush, esp. of herd of cattle, crowd ~v rush

stance n manner, position of standing; attitude

stanch See STAUNCH[1]

stanchion n upright bar used as support

stand v **standing, stood** have, take, set in upright position; be situated; remain firm or stationary; endure; offer oneself as a candidate; be symbol etc. of; Inf provide free, treat to ~n holding firm; position; something on which thing may be placed; structure from which spectators can watch sport etc. **standing** n reputation, status; duration ~adj erect; lasting; stagnant **standoffish** adj reserved or haughty

─────── T H E S A U R U S ───────

overwhelm, stun, stupefy, surprise

staid quiet, sedate, serious, sober

stain v blemish, blot, dirty, discolour, mark, smirch, soil, spot, tarnish ~n blemish, spot; blemish, disgrace, dishonour, shame, slur, smirch, stigma

stake n concern, interest, investment, involvement, share ~v bet, gamble, hazard, risk, venture, wager

stale decayed, fetid, flat, fusty, insipid, musty, old, tasteless

stalk v follow, hunt, pursue, shadow, track

stamina energy, force, power, strength, vigour

stammer v falter, stumble, stutter

stamp v crush, trample; impress, imprint, mark, print ~n brand, hallmark, imprint, mark, mould, signature

stance bearing, carriage, deportment, posture; attitude, position, stand, standpoint, viewpoint

stand v be upright, erect, mount, place, position, put, rise, set; continue, exist, halt, hold, pause, prevail, remain, rest, stay, stop; abide, allow, bear, countenance, endure, experience, handle, stomach, suffer, take, tolerate, undergo, weather, withstand

standard *n* accepted example of something against which others are judged; degree, quality; flag ~*adj* usual; of recognized authority, accepted as correct **standardize** *v* regulate by a standard

standpipe *n* tap attached to water main to provide public water supply

standpoint *n* point of view

standstill *n* complete halt

stanza *n* group of lines of verse

staple *n* U-shaped piece of metal used to fasten; main product ~*adj* principal ~*v* fasten with staple **stapler** *n*

star *n* celestial body, seen as twinkling point of light; asterisk (*); celebrated player, actor ~*v* **starring, starred** adorn with stars; mark (with asterisk); feature as star performer ~*adj* most important **stardom** *n* **starry** *adj* covered with stars **starfish** *n* small star-shaped sea creature

starboard *n* right-hand side of ship

starch *n* substance forming the main food element in bread, potatoes etc., and used mixed with water, for stiffening linen etc. ~*v* stiffen thus **starchy** *adj* containing starch; stiff

stare *v* look fixedly (at) ~*n* staring gaze

stark *adj* blunt, bare; desolate; absolute; *adv* completely

starling *n* glossy black speckled songbird

start *v* begin; set going; make sudden movement ~*n* beginning; abrupt movement; advantage of a lead in a race **starter** *n* first course of meal; electric motor starting car engine; competitor in race; supervisor of start of race

startle *v* give a fright to

starve *v* (cause to) suffer or die from hunger **starvation** *n*

stash *v Inf* store in secret place

state *n* condition; politically organized people; government; pomp ~*v* express in words **stately** *adj* dignified, lofty **statement** *n* expression in words; account **statesman** *n* (*fem* **stateswoman**) respected political leader **statesmanship** *n*

static *adj* motionless, inactive ~*n* electrical interference in radio reception

station *n* place where thing stops or is placed; stopping place for railway

———————————— THESAURUS ————————————

~*n* attitude, opinion, position, stance

standard *n* criterion, example, guide, measure, model, norm, par, sample, type ~*adj* average, basic, customary, normal, regular, typical, usual

standpoint angle, position, post, stance, station

star *n* celebrity, lead, luminary, megastar *Inf* ~*adj* leading, major, principal, prominent, well-known

stare *v* gape, gawk, gaze, look

stark *adj* absolute, bare, blunt, downright, pure, sheer, utter; austere, bare, barren, bleak, desolate, plain, severe, unadorned ~*adv* absolutely, altogether, completely, entirely

start *v* arise, begin, commence, de-

part, originate, set off, set out; activate, initiate, kick-start, open, originate, trigger, turn on ~*n* beginning, birth, dawn, foundation, initiation, onset, outset; advantage, edge, lead

startle agitate, frighten, scare, shock

state *n* case, circumstances, condition, position, shape, situation; commonwealth, country, federation, kingdom, land, nation, republic, territory ~*v* affirm, assert, declare, explain, express, put, report, say, specify

stately august, dignified, lofty, majestic, noble

statement account, communiqué, declaration, explanation, proclama-

trains; local office for police force, fire brigade etc.; place equipped for radio or television transmission; bus garage; post; position in life ~v put in position **stationary** adj not moving; not changing

stationer n dealer in writing materials etc. **stationery** n

statistics pl n (with sing v) science of classifying and interpreting numerical information **statistic** n systematically collected fact **statistical** adj **statistician** n expert in statistics

statue n solid carved or cast image **statuesque** adj like statue; dignified **statuette** n small statue

stature n bodily height; greatness

status n position, rank; prestige; relation to others **status quo** existing state of affairs

statute n law **statutory** adj

staunch¹ v stop flow (of blood) from

staunch² adj trustworthy, loyal

stave n strip of wood in barrel ~v **staving, stove** or **staved** break hole in; ward (off)

stay¹ v remain; reside; endure; stop; postpone ~n remaining, residing; postponement

stay² n support, prop

stead n place in stead in place (of)

steady adj steadier, steadiest firm; regular; temperate ~v **steadying, steadied** make steady **steadily** adv **steadfast** adj firm, unyielding

steak n thick slice of meat

steal v stealing, stole, stolen take without right or permission; move silently

stealth n secret or underhand procedure, behaviour **stealthy** adj

steam n vapour of boiling water ~v give off steam; move by steam power; cook or treat with steam **steamer** n steam-propelled ship **steam engine** engine worked by steam **steamroller** n steam-powered vehicle with heavy rollers, used to level road surfaces

steed n Lit horse

steel n hard and malleable metal made by mixing carbon in iron ~v harden

steep¹ adj sloping abruptly; (of prices) very high

steep² v soak, saturate

steeple n church tower with spire **steeplechase** n race with obstacles to jump **steeplejack** n one who builds,

———— THESAURUS ————

tion, report

station n base, depot, headquarters, location, place, position, post, situation; appointment, business, calling, employment, grade, position, post, rank, situation, standing, status ~v establish, install, locate, post, set

stationary fixed, motionless, parked, standing

status condition, position, prestige, rank, standing

stay v abide, continue, delay, halt, linger, loiter, pause, remain, reside, stand, stop, wait ~n sojourn, stop, stopover, visit

steadfast constant, faithful, fast, firm, loyal, persevering, resolute,

staunch, steady, unswerving, unwavering

steady adj firm, fixed, safe, stable; consistent, constant, even, regular, unbroken, uninterrupted, unvarying; balanced, calm, equable, imperturbable, level-headed, sensible, temperate ~v balance, brace, stabilize

steal appropriate, embezzle, filch, nick Sl, chiefly Brit, pilfer, purloin, take, thieve; creep, slink, slip, sneak

stealth secrecy, slyness, surreptitiousness

stealthy clandestine, furtive, secret, secretive, sly, sneaking, surreptitious

steep adj abrupt, precipitous, sheer; Inf exorbitant, extortionate, high, un-

repairs chimneys etc.

steer[1] *v* guide, direct course of vessel, motor vehicle etc.; direct one's course

steer[2] *n* castrated male ox

stellar *adj* of stars

stem[1] *n* stalk, trunk; part of word to which inflections are added

stem[2] *v* **stemming**, **stemmed** check, dam up

stench *n* foul smell

stencil *n* thin sheet pierced with pattern which is brushed over with paint or ink, leaving pattern on surface under it; the pattern ~*v* **-cilling**, **-cilled** make pattern thus

step *v* **stepping**, **stepped** move and set down foot; proceed (in this way); measure in paces ~*n* stepping; series of foot movements forming part of dance; measure, act, stage in proceeding; board, rung etc. to put foot on; degree in scale **stepladder** *n* folding portable ladder with supporting frame

stepchild *n* child of husband or wife by former marriage **stepbrother** *n* **stepfather** *n* **stepmother** *n* **stepsister** *n*

stereophonic *adj* (of sound) giving effect of coming from many directions **stereo** *n* stereophonic sound, record player etc. ~*adj* stereophonic

stereotype *n* something (monotonously) familiar, conventional ~*v* form stereotype of

sterile *adj* unable to produce fruit, crops, young etc.; free from (harmful) germs **sterility** *n* **sterilize** *v* render sterile

sterling *adj* genuine, true; of solid worth; in British money ~*n* British money

stern[1] *adj* severe, strict

stern[2] *n* rear part of ship

sternum *n* (*pl* **-na**, **-nums**) breast bone

steroid *n* organic compound, oft. used to increase body strength

stethoscope *n* instrument for listening to action of heart, lungs etc.

stew *n* food cooked slowly in closed vessel ~*v* cook slowly

steward *n* (*fem* **stewardess**) one who manages another's property; official managing race meeting, assembly etc.; attendant on ship or aircraft

stick *n* long, thin piece of wood; anything shaped like a stick ~*v* **sticking**, **stuck** pierce, stab; place, fasten, as by pins, glue; protrude; adhere; come to stop; jam; remain **sticker** *n* adhesive label, poster **sticky** *adj* covered with, like adhesive substance; (of weather) warm, humid; *Inf* awkward, tricky

stickleback *n* small fish with sharp

——————— THESAURUS ———————

reasonable

steer conduct, control, direct, govern, guide, handle, pilot

stem[1] *n* branch, shoot, stalk, trunk

stem[2] *v* check, contain, curb, dam, staunch, stop

step *v* move, pace, tread, walk ~*n* footfall, footstep, gait, pace, stride, walk; act, action, deed, measure, move; degree, level, rank

stereotype *n* formula, mould, pattern ~*v* categorize, typecast

sterile barren, empty, fruitless, un-

fruitful, unproductive; aseptic, disinfected, germ-free, sterilized

sterilize disinfect, fumigate, purify

stern forbidding, grim, hard, harsh, inflexible, rigid, serious, severe, strict, unyielding

stick *v* dig, jab, penetrate, pierce, poke, prod, spear, stab, thrust; adhere, affix, attach, bond, cement, cling, fasten, fix, glue, paste (with out, up, etc.) bulge, extend, jut, project, protrude; catch, clog, jam, lodge, stop

spines on back

stickler *n* person who insists on something

stiff *adj* not easily bent or moved; difficult; thick, not fluid; formal; strong or fresh, as breeze **stiffen** *v* **stiffness** *n*

stifle *v* smother, suppress

stigma *n* (*pl* **-mas, -mata**) mark of disgrace **stigmatize** *v*

stile *n* arrangement of steps for climbing a fence

still¹ *adj* motionless, noiseless ~*v* quiet ~*adv* to this time; yet; even ~*n* photograph, esp. of film scene **stillness** *n* **stillborn** *adj* born dead

still² *n* apparatus for distilling

stilt *n* pole with footrests for walking raised from ground; long post supporting building etc. **stilted** *adj* stiff in manner, pompous

stimulus *n* (*pl* **-li**) something that rouses to activity; incentive **stimulant** *n* drug etc. acting as stimulus **stimulate** *v* rouse up, spur **stimulation** *n*

sting *v* **stinging, stung** thrust sting into; cause sharp pain to; feel sharp pain ~*n* (wound, pain, caused by) sharp pointed organ, often poisonous, of certain creatures

stingy *adj* mean; niggardly

stink *v* **stinking, stank, stunk** give out strongly offensive smell; *Sl* be abhorrent

stint *v* be frugal, miserly ~*n* allotted amount of work or time; limitation, restriction

stipulate *v* specify in making a bargain **stipulation** *n* proviso; condition

stir *v* **stirring, stirred** (begin to) move; rouse; excite ~*n* commotion, disturbance

stirrup *n* loop for supporting foot of rider on horse

stitch *n* movement of needle in sewing etc.; its result in the work; sharp pain in side; least fragment (of clothing) ~*v* sew

stoat *n* small mammal with brown coat and black-tipped tail

stock *n* goods, material stored, esp. for sale or later use; financial shares in, or capital of, company etc.; standing, reputation; farm animals, livestock; plant, stem from which cuttings are taken; handle of gun, tool etc.; liquid broth produced by boiling meat etc.; flowering plant; lineage ~*adj* kept in stock; standard; hack-

sticky adhesive, gluey, gummy, tacky, viscous; awkward, difficult, embarrassing, nasty, tricky, unpleasant

stiff firm, hard, inelastic, inflexible, rigid, unbending, unyielding; chilly, cold, formal, standoffish

stiffen congeal, harden, jell, set, solidify, thicken

stifle choke, smother, suffocate; check, curb, prevent, repress, smother, stop, suppress

still *adj* calm, hushed, inert, motionless, peaceful, placid, quiet, serene, silent, stationary, tranquil ~*v* calm, hush, pacify, quieten, silence, soothe, subdue ~*adv* but, however, nevertheless, notwithstanding, yet

stilted artificial, forced, stiff, unnatural, wooden

stimulate arouse, fire, goad, impel, incite, instigate, provoke, rouse, spur, urge

sting smart, tingle

stipulate agree, contract, covenant, require, settle, specify

stipulation agreement, clause, condition, provision, qualification, requirement, restriction, rider, specification, term

stir *v* (*oft. with* **up**) arouse, excite, incite, inflame, prompt, provoke, raise, rouse, spur, stimulate, urge ~*n* agitation, commotion, disorder, flurry, fuss, to-do

neyed ~v keep, store; supply with livestock, fish etc. **stockist** n dealer who stocks a particular product **stocky** adj thickset **stockbroker** n agent for buying, selling shares in companies **stock exchange** institution for buying and selling shares **stockpile** v acquire and store large quantity of (something) **stocktaking** n examination, counting and valuing of goods in a shop etc.

stockade n enclosure of stakes, barrier

stocking n close-fitting covering for leg and foot

stodgy adj heavy, dull

stoic adj capable of much self-control, great endurance without complaint ~n stoical person **stoical** adj **stoicism** n

stoke v feed, tend fire or furnace **stoker** n

stole n long scarf or shawl

stolid adj hard to excite

stomach n sac forming chief digestive organ in any animal; appetite ~v put up with

stomp v tread heavily

stone n (piece of) rock; gem; hard seed of fruit; hard deposit formed in kidneys, bladder; unit of weight, 14 pounds ~v throw stones at; free (fruit) from stones **stony** adj of, like stone; hard; cold **stone-deaf** adj completely deaf

stooge n person taken advantage of

stool n backless chair

stoop v lean forward or down; abase, degrade oneself ~n stooping posture

stop v **stopping, stopped** bring, come to halt; prevent; desist from; fill up an opening; cease; stay ~n place where something stops; stopping or becoming stopped; punctuation mark, esp. full stop; set of pipes in organ having tones of a distinct quality **stoppage** n **stopper** n plug for closing bottle etc. **stopcock** n valve to control flow of fluid in pipe **stopwatch** n watch which can be stopped for exact timing of race

store v stock, keep ~n shop; abundance; stock; place for keeping goods; warehouse; pl stocks of goods, provisions **storage** n

storey n horizontal division of a building

stork n large wading bird

———— T H E S A U R U S ————

stock n array, choice, fund, goods, hoard, range, selection, stockpile, store, supply, variety, wares; capital, funds, investment, property ~adj banal, conventional, customary, ordinary, regular, routine, set, standard, trite, usual, worn-out v (with **up**) amass, buy up, gather, hoard, save; deal in, keep, sell, supply, trade in

stocky dumpy, stubby, thickset

stomach n belly, pot, tummy Inf; appetite, desire, inclination, taste ~v abide, bear, endure, swallow, take, tolerate

stony blank, chilly, expressionless, frigid, hard, hostile, icy

stoop v bend, bow, crouch, duck, incline, lean

stop v cease, conclude, cut short, desist, discontinue, end, finish, halt, pause, put an end to, quit, refrain, terminate; arrest, bar, block, break, check, close, hinder, hold back, impede, intercept, interrupt, obstruct, plug, prevent, restrain, seal, silence, staunch, stem, suspend ~n cessation, conclusion, end, finish, halt, standstill

store v hoard, keep, put aside, put by, reserve, save, stockpile ~n emporium, shop, supermarket; cache, fund, hoard, provision, reserve, stock, supply; repository, storeroom, warehouse

storm *n* violent weather with wind, rain etc.; assault on fortress; violent outbreak ~*v* assault; take by storm; rage **stormy** *adj* like storm

story *n* account, tale; newspaper report

stout *adj* fat; sturdy, resolute ~*n* strong dark beer

stove *n* apparatus for cooking, heating etc.

stow *v* pack away **stowaway** *n* person who hides in ship to obtain free passage

straddle *v* bestride; spread legs wide

straggle *v* stray, get dispersed, linger **straggler** *n*

straight *adj* without bend; honest; level; in order; in continuous succession; (of spirits) undiluted; (of face) expressionless ~*n* straight state or part ~*adv* direct **straighten** *v*

straightaway *adv* at once, immediately **straightforward** *adj* open, frank; simple

strain¹ *v* stretch tightly; stretch to excess; filter; make great effort ~*n* stretching force; violent effort; injury from being strained; great demand; (condition caused by) overwork, worry etc. **strained** *adj* **strainer** *n* filter, sieve

strain² *n* breed or race; trace

strait *n* channel of water connecting two larger areas of water; *pl* position of difficulty or distress **straitjacket** *n* jacket to confine arms of violent person **strait-laced** *adj* prudish

strand¹ *v* run aground; leave, be left in difficulties

strand² *n* single thread of string, wire etc.

strange *adj* odd; unaccustomed; for-

——————— T H E S A U R U S ———————

storm *n* blizzard, hurricane, squall, tempest, tornado, whirlwind; commotion, disturbance, furore, outburst, tumult; assault, attack, onslaught, rush ~*v* assail, assault, charge, rush; fume, rage, rant, rave

stormy blustery, inclement, raging, rough, turbulent, wild, windy

story account, anecdote, legend, narrative, romance, tale; urban legend, yarn; article, feature, news item, report

stout big, burly, fat, plump, portly, tubby; brawny, hardy, robust, stalwart, strapping, strong, sturdy; bold, brave, courageous, fearless, plucky, resolute, valiant

straight *adj* direct, near, short; erect, even, horizontal, level, plumb, right, smooth, upright, vertical; in order, neat, orderly, organized, shipshape, tidy; consecutive, continuous, nonstop, solid, successive; neat, pure, unadulterated, undiluted, unmixed ~*adv* at once, directly, immediately,

instantly

straightaway at once, directly, immediately, instantly, now, right away

straighten arrange, neaten, put in order, tidy (up)

straightforward candid, direct, forthright, honest, open, upfront *Inf*; easy, easy-peasy *Sl*, elementary, simple, uncomplicated

strain *v* distend, stretch, tauten, tighten; pull, sprain, tear, twist, wrench; filter, separate, sieve, sift; bend over backwards *Inf*, break one's neck *Inf*, knock oneself out *Inf*, labour, strive, struggle ~*n* tautness, tension; effort, exertion, struggle; injury, pull, sprain, wrench; anxiety, pressure, stress, tension

strained artificial, awkward, difficult, false, forced, stiff, tense, uneasy, unnatural

strait-laced prim, proper, prudish, puritanical

strand *n* fibre, filament, length, string, thread

eign **strangeness** *n* **stranger** *n* unknown person; foreigner; one unaccustomed (to)

strangle *v* kill by squeezing windpipe; suppress **strangulation** *n* strangling **stranglehold** *n*

strap *n* strip, esp. of leather ~*v* **strapping, strapped** fasten, beat with strap **strapping** *adj* tall and well-made

strategy *n* overall plan; art of war **stratagem** *n* plan, trick **strategic** *adj* **strategist** *n*

stratosphere *n* layer of atmosphere high above the earth

stratum *n* (*pl* **strata**) layer, esp. of rock; class in society **stratification** *n* **stratify** *v* -**fying**, -**fied** form, deposit in layers

straw *n* stalks of grain; long, narrow tube used to suck up liquid **strawberry** *n* creeping plant producing red, juicy fruit; the fruit

stray *v* wander; digress; get lost ~*adj* strayed; occasional; scattered ~*n* stray animal

streak *n* long line or band; element ~*v* mark with streaks; move fast; run naked in public **streaker** *n* **streaky** *adj*

stream *n* flowing body of water or other liquid; steady flow ~*v* flow; run with liquid **streamer** *n* (paper) ribbon, narrow flag

streamlined *adj* (of car, plane etc.) built so as to offer least resistance to air **streamlining** *n*

street *n* road in town or village, usu. lined with houses **streetwise** *adj* adept at surviving in dangerous environment

strength *n* quality of being strong; power **strengthen** *v*

strenuous *adj* energetic; earnest

stress *n* emphasis; tension ~*v* emphasize

stretch *v* extend; exert to utmost; tighten, pull out; reach; have elasticity ~*n* stretching, being stretched; expanse; spell **stretcher** *n* person, thing that stretches; appliance on which disabled person is carried

strew *v* **strewing, strewed, strewed**

————————— THESAURUS —————————

strange bizarre, curious, eccentric, extraordinary, odd, off-the-wall *Sl*, peculiar, queer, rare, rum *Brit sl*, uncanny, weird; alien, exotic, foreign

stranger alien, foreigner, incomer, newcomer

strangle choke, throttle; inhibit, repress, stifle, suppress

strategy approach, plan, policy, programme

stray *v* drift, range, roam, rove, wander; deviate, digress, diverge, ramble ~*adj* abandoned, homeless, lost

streak *n* band, layer, line, slash, strip, stripe; dash, element, strain, touch, trace, vein

stream *n* brook, burn, course, current, flow, river, rush, surge, tide, torrent, tributary ~*v* cascade, course, flood, flow, gush, issue, pour, run, shed, spill, spout

street avenue, lane, road, row, terrace

strength brawn, fortitude, might, muscle, robustness, stamina, stoutness, sturdiness, toughness; energy, force, intensity, potency, power

strengthen brace up, fortify, hearten, invigorate, toughen; augment, bolster, brace, reinforce, steel, support

strenuous arduous, demanding, hard, laborious, taxing, tough; determined, earnest, resolute, spirited, strong, tireless

stress *n* emphasis, force, importance, significance, urgency, weight; anxiety, pressure, strain, tension, worry ~*v* accentuate, dwell on, emphasize, rub in, underline

stretch *v* extend, put forth, reach,

or **strewn** scatter over surface, spread

stricken *adj* seriously affected by disease, grief etc.

strict *adj* stern, not lax or indulgent; precisely defined; without exception

stricture *n* critical remark

stride *v* **striding, strode, stridden** walk with long steps ~*n* single step; length of step

strident *adj* harsh, loud **stridently** *adv* **stridency** *n*

strife *n* conflict; quarrelling

strike *v* **striking, struck** hit (against); ignite; attack; sound (time), as bell in clock etc.; affect; enter mind of; cease work as protest or to make demands ~*n* act of striking **striker** *n* **striking** *adj* noteworthy, impressive

string *n* (length of) thin cord or other material; series; fibre in plants; *pl* conditions ~*v* **stringing, strung** provide with, thread on string; form in line, series **stringed** *adj* (of musical instruments) furnished with strings **stringy** *adj* like string; fibrous

stringent *adj* strict, binding **stringency** *n*

strip *v* **stripping, stripped** lay bare, take covering off; undress ~*n* long, narrow piece **stripper** *n* **striptease** *n* cabaret or theatre in which person undresses

stripe *n* narrow mark, band **striped, stripy** *adj* marked with stripes

strive *v* **striving, strove, striven** try hard, struggle

strobe *also* **stroboscope** *n* instrument producing bright flashing light

stroke *n* blow; sudden action, occurrence; apoplexy; chime of clock; mark made by pen, brush etc.; style, method of swimming; act of stroking ~*v* pass hand lightly over

stroll *v* walk in leisurely or idle manner ~*n* leisurely walk

strong *adj* powerful, robust, healthy; difficult to break; noticeable; intense; emphatic; not diluted; having a certain number **strongly** *adv* **stronghold** *n* fortress **strongroom** *n* room for keeping valuables

stroppy *adj* *Sl* angry or awkward

structure *n* (arrangement of parts in) construction, building etc.; form ~*v*

——————— THESAURUS ———————

spread; distend, draw out, elongate, expand, lengthen, pull, strain, tighten ~*n* area, distance, expanse, extent, spread

strict firm, rigid, rigorous, severe, stern, stringent; accurate, exact, faithful, meticulous, precise, scrupulous, true

strike *v* beat, buffet, cuff, hit, knock, punch, slap, smack, thump; assail, assault, attack, hit, set upon; come to, hit, occur to, seem; down tools, walk out

striking conspicuous, dazzling, impressive, memorable, noticeable, outstanding

string *n* cord, fibre, twine; chain, line, procession, row, sequence, series, succession

strip *v* bare, denude, divest, peel, skin; disrobe, unclothe, undress ~*n* band, belt, ribbon, shred, slip

strive attempt, bend over backwards *Inf*, break one's neck *Inf*, endeavour, fight, give it one's best shot *Inf*, knock oneself out *Inf*, labour, strain, struggle, toil

stroke *n* blow, hit, knock, rap, thump; apoplexy, attack, fit, seizure ~*v* caress, fondle, pet, rub

stroll *v* amble, ramble, saunter, wander ~*n* promenade, ramble, walk

strong athletic, brawny, muscular, powerful, stout, strapping, sturdy, tough; hale, hardy, healthy, robust, sound; durable, hard-wearing, sturdy, tough, unyielding; deep, fervent, fierce, firm, intense, keen; concen-

give structure to **structural** adj

struggle v contend; fight; proceed, work, move with difficulty and effort ~n struggling

strum v **strumming, strummed** strike notes of guitar etc.

strut v **strutting, strutted** walk affectedly or pompously ~n rigid support; strutting walk

strychnine n poisonous drug

stub n remnant of anything, e.g. pencil; counterfoil ~v **stubbing, stubbed** strike (toes) against fixed object; extinguish by pressing against surface **stubby** adj short, broad

stubble n stumps of cut grain after reaping; short growth of beard

stubborn adj unyielding, obstinate

stucco n plaster

stud[1] n nail with large head; removable double-headed button ~v **studding, studded** set with studs

stud[2] n set of horses kept for breeding

studio n (pl **-dios**) workroom of artist, photographer etc.; building, room where film, television or radio shows are made, broadcast

study v **studying, studied** be engaged in learning; make study of; scrutinize ~n effort to acquire knowledge; subject of this; room to study in; book, report etc. produced as result of study; sketch **student** n one who studies **studied** adj carefully designed, premeditated **studious** adj fond of study; painstaking; deliberate

stuff v pack, cram, fill (completely); eat large amount; fill with seasoned mixture; fill (animal's skin) with material to preserve lifelike form ~n material; any substance; belongings **stuffing** n material for stuffing **stuffy** adj lacking fresh air; Inf dull, conventional

stultify v **-fying, -fied** make dull by boring routine

stumble v trip and nearly fall; falter ~n stumbling

stump n remnant of tree, tooth etc., when main part has been cut away; one of uprights of wicket in cricket ~v confuse, puzzle; walk heavily, noisily **stumpy** adj short and thickset

stun v **stunning, stunned** knock senseless; amaze **stunning** adj

stunt[1] v stop growth of

trated, pure, undiluted

structure n arrangement, conformation, design, form, formation, makeup, organization; building, construction, edifice, erection ~v arrange, assemble, build up, design, organize, shape

struggle v bend over backwards Inf, break one's neck Inf, knock oneself out Inf, labour, strain, strive, toil, work; battle, compete, contend, fight, wrestle ~n effort, exertion, labour, pains, toil, work; battle, combat, conflict, contest, tussle

stubborn dogged, inflexible, intractable, obdurate, obstinate, pigheaded, unyielding

student apprentice, disciple, learner, pupil, scholar, undergraduate

studious academic, bookish, diligent, earnest, scholarly, serious

study v consider, contemplate, examine, learn, pore over, read, read up; analyse, examine, investigate, peruse, research, scrutinize, survey ~n analysis, contemplation, inquiry, investigation, perusal, review, scrutiny, survey

stuff v cram, crowd, fill, force, jam, pack, push, ram, shove, wedge ~n essence, matter, substance; belongings, effects, equipment, gear, kit, tackle, things

stuffy airless, close, heavy, muggy, oppressive, stale, stifling, unventilated; dull, staid, stodgy

stumble fall, lurch, stagger, trip

stunt² *n* feat of dexterity or daring

stupefy *v* **-fying, -fied** make insensitive, lethargic; astound **stupefaction** *n*

stupendous *adj* astonishing; amazing; huge

stupid *adj* slow-witted; silly **stupidity** *n*

stupor *n* dazed state

sturdy *adj* robust, strongly built; vigorous

sturgeon *n* fish yielding caviare

stutter *v* speak with difficulty; stammer **~***n* tendency to stutter

sty *n* place to keep pigs in

stye *n* inflammation on eyelid

style *n* design; manner of writing, doing etc.; fashion; elegance **~***v* design **stylish** *adj* fashionable **stylist** *n* one cultivating style; designer

stylus *n* (*pl* **-li, -luses**) (in record player) tiny point running in groove of record

suave *adj* smoothly polite

sub *n* short for SUBMARINE, SUBSCRIPTION, SUBSTITUTE

subconscious *adj* acting, existing without one's awareness **~***n Psychology* part of human mind unknown, or only partly known, to possessor

subdivide *v* divide again **subdivision** *n*

subdue *v* overcome **subdued** *adj* cowed, quiet; not bright

subject *n* person or thing being dealt with or studied; person under rule of government or monarch **~***adj* owing allegiance; dependent; liable (to) **~***v* cause to undergo; subdue **subjection** *n* act of bringing, or state of being, under control **subjective** *adj* based on personal feelings, not impartial; existing in the mind **subjectivity** *n*

subjugate *v* force to submit; conquer

stun astonish, astound, knock out, overcome, overpower, stagger, stupefy

stunning dazzling, marvellous, sensational *Inf,* spectacular, striking, wonderful

stunt *n* act, deed, exploit, feat, trick

stupendous amazing, astounding, breathtaking, colossal, enormous, gigantic, huge, marvellous, sensational *Inf,* staggering, superb, vast, wonderful

stupid brainless, dense, dim, dull, half-witted, moronic, obtuse, simple, simple-minded, slow, slow-witted, thick, witless; asinine, idiotic, inane, ludicrous, mindless, senseless, unintelligent

stupidity brainlessness, denseness, dimness, dullness, imbecility, obtuseness, slowness, thickness; folly, idiocy, inanity, lunacy, madness, silliness

sturdy athletic, brawny, durable, firm, hardy, hearty, muscular, powerful, robust, secure, solid, substantial, vigorous, well-built

style *n* cut, design, form , manner; approach, manner, method, mode, way; fashion, mode, rage, trend, vogue; chic, dash, elegance, flair, panache, polish, smartness, sophistication **~***v* adapt, arrange, cut, design, fashion, shape

stylish chic, dapper, fashionable, modish, polished, smart

subconscious *adj* hidden, inner, latent, subliminal

subdue break, conquer, crush, defeat, overcome, overpower, quell, vanquish

subject *n* affair, business, issue, matter, object, question, theme, topic; dependent, subordinate **~***adj* answerable, bound by, dependent, inferior, subordinate; conditional, contingent, dependent; disposed, liable, open, prone, susceptible **~***v* expose, lay open, submit, treat

subjugation n
sublet v -letting, -let rent out property rented from someone else
sublime adj elevated; inspiring awe; exalted
subliminal adj relating to mental processes of which the individual is not aware
submarine n craft which can travel below surface of sea and remain submerged for long periods ~adj below surface of sea
submerge v place, go under water **submersion** n
submit v -mitting, -mitted surrender; put forward for consideration; defer **submission** n **submissive** adj meek, obedient
subnormal adj below normal
subordinate n/adj (one) of lower rank or less importance ~v make, treat as subordinate **subordination** n
subscribe v pay, promise to pay (contribution); give support, approval **subscription** n money paid

subsequent adj later, following or coming after in time
subservient adj submissive, servile
subside v abate; sink **subsidence** n
subsidiary adj/n secondary (person or thing)
subsidize v help financially; pay grant to **subsidy** n money granted
subsist v exist, sustain life **subsistence** n the means by which one supports life
substance n (particular kind of) matter; essence; wealth **substantial** adj considerable; of real value; really existing **substantiate** v bring evidence for, prove
substitute v put, serve in place of ~n thing, person put in place of another ~adj serving as a substitute **substitution** n
subsume v incorporate in larger group
subterfuge n trick, lying excuse used to evade something
subterranean adj underground

———————— THESAURUS ————————

subjective biased, emotional, personal, prejudiced
submerge dip, duck, engulf, flood, immerse, overflow, plunge, sink, swamp
submission capitulation, surrender, yielding
submissive acquiescent, compliant, docile, meek, obedient, passive, pliant, tractable, unresisting, yielding
submit accede, bend, bow, capitulate, defer, give in, succumb, surrender, yield; hand in, present, tender
subordinate n inferior, junior, second, underling ~adj inferior, junior, lesser, lower, minor, secondary
subscribe contribute, donate, give, pledge, promise
subscription donation, dues, gift, membership fee
subsequent after, ensuing, follow-

ing, later, succeeding, successive
subside abate, decrease, diminish, dwindle, ebb, lessen, recede, wane
subsidiary ancillary, assistant, auxiliary, lesser, minor, secondary, subordinate, supplementary
subsidize finance, fund, promote, sponsor, support
subsidy aid, allowance, assistance, grant, support
substance fabric, material, stuff; essence, gist, import, matter, meaning, significance, subject, theme; assets, means, property, resources, wealth
substantial big, important, large, significant, sizable, worthwhile
substitute v change, exchange, interchange, replace, switch ~n agent, deputy, locum, makeshift, replacement, reserve, stopgap, sub ~adj acting, alternative, replacement, reserve,

subtitle *n* secondary title of book; *pl* translation superimposed on foreign film ~*v* provide with subtitle or subtitles

subtle *adj* not immediately obvious; ingenious; crafty; making fine distinctions **subtlety** *n* **subtly** *adv*

subtract *v* take away, deduct **subtraction** *n*

suburb *n* residential area on outskirts of city **suburban** *adj* **suburbia** *n* suburbs and their inhabitants

subvert *v* overthrow; corrupt **subversion** *n* **subversive** *adj*

subway *n* underground passage; *US* underground railway

succeed *v* accomplish purpose; turn out satisfactorily; follow; take place of **success** *n* favourable accomplishment, attainment, issue or outcome; successful person or thing **successful** *adj* **succession** *n* following; series; succeeding **successive** *adj* following in order; consecutive **successor** *n*

succinct *adj* brief and clear

succour *v/n* help in distress

succulent *adj* juicy; (of plant) having thick, fleshy leaves ~*n* such plant

succulence *n*

succumb *v* give way

such *adj* of the kind or degree mentioned; so great, so much

suck *v* draw into mouth; hold in mouth; draw in ~*n* sucking **sucker** *n* person, thing that sucks; shoot coming from root or base of stem of plant; *Inf* one who is easily deceived

suckle *v* feed from the breast **suckling** *n* unweaned infant

suction *n* drawing or sucking of air or fluid; force produced by difference in pressure

sudden *adj* done, occurring unexpectedly; abrupt **suddenly** *adv*

suds *pl n* froth of soap and water

sue *v* **suing, sued** prosecute; seek justice from; make application or entreaty

suede *n* leather with soft, velvety finish

suet *n* hard animal fat

suffer *v* undergo; tolerate **suffering** *n*

suffice *v* be adequate, satisfactory (for) **sufficiency** *n* adequate amount **sufficient** *adj* enough, adequate

suffix *n* group of letters added to end

surrogate, temporary

subtle faint, implied, indirect, slight; deep, delicate, ingenious, profound, sophisticated; artful, crafty, cunning, shrewd, wily

subtlety delicacy, nicety, refinement, sophistication; craftiness, cunning, guile, wiliness

subtract deduct, diminish, remove, take away

subversive destructive, overthrowing, riotous, seditious

succeed crack it *Inf*, flourish, make good, prosper, triumph, work; come next, ensue, follow

success fortune, luck, prosperity, triumph

successful flourishing, fruitful, lucrative, profitable, prosperous, thriving, unbeaten, victorious

succession chain, course, order, progression, run, sequence, series, train

successive consecutive, following

succinct brief, concise, laconic, pithy, terse

succulent juicy, luscious, lush

succumb capitulate, submit, surrender, yield

sudden abrupt, quick, rapid, swift, unexpected

sue charge, indict, prosecute, summon

suffer bear, endure, experience, feel, sustain, tolerate, undergo

suffering *n* affliction, agony, anguish, distress, hardship, misery, ordeal,

of word

suffocate v kill, be killed by deprivation of oxygen; smother **suffocation** n

suffrage n vote or right of voting

suffuse v well up and spread over

sugar n sweet crystalline substance ~v sweeten, make pleasant (with sugar) **sugary** adj

suggest v propose; call up the idea of **suggestible** adj easily influenced **suggestion** n hint; proposal; insinuation of impression, belief etc. into mind **suggestive** adj containing suggestions, esp. of something indecent

suicide n act of killing oneself; one who does this **suicidal** adj

suit n set of clothing; garment worn for particular event, purpose; one of four sets in pack of cards; action at law ~v make, be fit or appropriate for; be acceptable to (someone) **suitability** n **suitable** adj fitting, convenient **suitcase** n flat rectangular travelling case

suite n matched set of furniture; set of rooms; retinue

suitor n wooer; one who sues

sulk v be silent, resentful ~n this mood **sulky** adj

sullen adj unwilling to talk or be sociable, morose

sully v -lying, -lied stain, tarnish

sulphur n pale yellow nonmetallic element **sulphuric** adj **sulphurous** adj

sultan n ruler of Muslim country

sultana n kind of raisin

sultry adj (of weather) hot, humid; (of person) looking sensual

sum n amount, total; problem in arithmetic ~v **summing, summed** add up; make summary of main parts

summary n brief statement of chief points of something ~adj done quickly **summarily** adv speedily; abruptly **summarize** v make summary of

summer n second, warmest season

summit n top, peak

summon v demand attendance of; bid witness appear in court; gather up (energies etc.) **summons** n call; authoritative demand

sumo n Japanese style of wrestling

———————————— THESAURUS ————————————

pain, torment

sufficient adequate, enough

suffocate asphyxiate, choke, smother, stifle

suggest advise, move, prescribe, propose, recommend; hint, imply, insinuate, intimate

suggestion motion, plan, proposal, proposition; breath, hint, intimation, trace, whisper

suggestive bawdy, blue, improper, indecent, racy, ribald, risqué, rude, smutty, titillating

suit n costume, dress, ensemble, habit, outfit; Law action, case, cause, lawsuit, proceeding, prosecution, trial ~v accommodate, adapt, adjust, fashion, fit, modify, tailor; do, gratify, please, satisfy; agree, answer, become, befit, match, harmonize, tally

suitable applicable, appropriate, apt, becoming, befitting, due, fit, fitting, pertinent, proper, relevant, right; convenient, opportune

sulk brood, look sullen, pout

sulky churlish, cross, huffy, ill-humoured, moody, petulant, resentful, sullen

sullen brooding, gloomy, heavy, moody, morose, surly, unsociable

sultry close, humid, oppressive, sticky, stuffy

sum aggregate, amount, quantity, tally, total, whole

summarize encapsulate, epitomize, outline, sum up

summary digest, outline, précis, résumé, review, rundown, synopsis

summit apex, crown, head, height, peak, pinnacle, top, zenith

sumptuous *adj* lavish, magnificent **sumptuousness** *n*

sun *n* luminous body round which earth and other planets revolve; its rays ~*v* **sunning, sunned** expose to sun's rays **sunless** *adj* **sunny** *adj* like the sun; warm; cheerful **sunbathe** *n* lie in sunshine **sunbeam** *n* ray of sun **sunburn** *n* inflammation of skin due to excessive exposure to sun **sundown** *n* sunset **sunflower** *n* plant with large golden flowers **sunrise** *n* appearance of sun above the horizon **sunset** *n* disappearance of sun below the horizon **sunshine** *n* light and warmth from sun **sunstroke** *n* illness caused by prolonged exposure to hot sun

sundae *n* ice cream topped with fruit etc.

Sunday *n* first day of the week **Sunday school** school for religious instruction of children

sunder *v* separate, sever

sundry *adj* several, various **sundries** *pl n* odd items, not mentioned in detail

sup *v* **supping, supped** take by sips; take supper ~*n* mouthful of liquid

super *adj Inf* very good

super- *comb. form* above, greater, exceedingly, as in **superhuman, supertanker**

superannuation *n* pension given on retirement; contribution by employee to pension

superb *adj* extremely good or impressive

supercharger *n* device that increases power of engine **supercharged** *adj*

supercilious *adj* displaying arrogant pride, scorn

superficial *adj* of or on surface; not careful or thorough; without depth, shallow

superfluous *adj* extra, unnecessary **superfluity** *n*

superhuman *adj* beyond normal human ability or experience

superimpose *v* place on or over something else

superintend *v* have charge of; overlook; supervise **superintendent** *n* senior police officer

superior *adj* greater in quality or quantity; upper, higher in position, rank or quality; showing consciousness of being so ~*n* supervisor, manager **superiority** *n*

superlative *adj* of, in highest degree

—————— T H E S A U R U S ——————

summon bid, call, convene, convoke, rally

sumptuous grand, lavish, luxurious, opulent, rich, splendid, superb

sunny bright, brilliant, clear, fine, summery, unclouded; blithe, cheerful, genial, happy, pleasant

superb excellent, fine, first-rate, grand, magnificent, marvellous, splendid, superior, unrivalled, world-class

superficial exterior, external, shallow, skin-deep, slight, surface; casual, cursory, perfunctory, sketchy, slapdash

superfluous excess, extra, left over, needless, redundant, remaining, spare, surplus, uncalled-for, unnecessary, unrequired

superintendent chief, controller, director, governor, manager, overseer, supervisor

superior *adj* better, grander, greater, higher, paramount; choice, de luxe, excellent, exceptional, first-class, first-rate, surpassing, unrivalled; condescending, disdainful, haughty, lofty, lordly, patronizing, snobbish ~*n* boss *Inf*, chief, director, manager, senior, supervisor

superiority advantage, excellence, lead, supremacy

or quality; surpassing; *Grammar* denoting form of adjective, adverb meaning *most*

supermarket *n* large self-service store

supernatural *adj* being beyond the powers or laws of nature; miraculous

supernumerary *adj* exceeding the required or regular number

superpower *n* extremely powerful nation

supersede *v* take the place of

supersonic *adj* denoting speed greater than that of sound

superstition *n* religion, opinion or practice based on belief in luck or magic **superstitious** *adj*

superstructure *n* structure above foundations; part of ship above deck

supervise *v* oversee; direct; inspect and control **supervision** *n* **supervisor** *n* **supervisory** *adj*

supine *adj* lying on back with face upwards

supper *n* (light) evening meal

supplant *v* take the place of

supple *adj* pliable; flexible **supply** *adv*

supplement *n* thing added to fill up, supply deficiency, esp. extra part added to book etc. ~*v* add to; supply deficiency **supplementary** *adj*

supplicate *v* beg humbly, entreat **supplicant** *n* **supplication** *n*

supply *v* -plying, -plied furnish; make available; provide ~*n* (*pl* -plies) stock, store; food, materials needed for journey etc.

support *v* hold up; sustain; assist ~*n* supporting, being supported; means of support **supporter** *n* adherent **supporting** *adj* (of role in film etc.) less important **supportive** *adj*

suppose *v* assume as theory; take for granted; accept as likely **supposed** *adj* assumed; expected, obliged; permitted **supposedly** *adv* **supposition** *n* assumption; belief without proof; conjecture

———— T H E S A U R U S ————

supernatural miraculous, mystic, occult, paranormal, psychic, uncanny, unearthly

supervise administer, conduct, control, direct, look after, manage, oversee, run, superintend

supervision administration, charge, control, direction, guidance, management

supervisor administrator, chief, foreman, manager, overseer

supple elastic, flexible, limber, lithe, pliable, pliant

supplement *n* addition, appendix, codicil, extra, insert, pull-out ~*v* add, augment, extend, fill out, reinforce, top up

supplementary additional, auxiliary, extra, secondary

supply *v* afford, contribute, endow, furnish, give, grant, provide, stock, yield ~*n* fund, quantity, reserve,

source, stock, store; (*usu. pl*) equipment, provisions, rations, stores

support *v* bear, brace, buttress, carry, hold, prop, reinforce, sustain, uphold; finance, fund, keep, maintain, provide for, sustain; aid, assist, back, champion, defend, help, promote, second, side with ~*n* aid, approval, assistance, backing, blessing, encouragement, help, patronage, promotion; brace, foundation, pillar, post, prop, stay

supporter adherent, advocate, champion, fan, follower, patron, sponsor, well-wisher

suppose assume, conjecture, expect, imagine, infer, judge, presume, surmise, think; believe, conceive, conjecture, consider, fancy, imagine, pretend

supposition conjecture, guess, hypothesis, idea, presumption, specula-

suppress *v* put down, restrain; keep or withdraw from publication **suppression** *n*

suppurate *v* fester, form pus

supreme *adj* highest in authority or rank; utmost **supremacy** *n* position of being supreme **supremo** *n* person in overall authority

surcharge *v/n* (make) additional charge

sure *adj* certain; trustworthy; without doubt *~adv Inf* certainly **surely** *adv* **surety** *n* person, thing acting as guarantee for another's obligations

surf *n* waves breaking on shore *~v* ride surf **surfer** *n* **surfing** *n* sport of riding over surf **surfboard** *n* board used in surfing

surface *n* outside face of object; plane; top; superficial appearance *~adj* involving the surface only *~v* come to surface

surfeit *n* excess; disgust caused by excess *~v* feed to excess

surge *n* wave; sudden increase *~v* move in large waves; swell

surgeon *n* medical expert who performs operations **surgery** *n* medical treatment by operation; doctor's, dentist's consulting room **surgical** *adj*

surly *adj* cross and rude

surmise *v/n* guess, conjecture

surmount *v* get over, overcome

surname *n* family name

surpass *v* go beyond; excel; outstrip **surpassing** *adj* excellent

surplus *n* what remains over in excess *~adj* spare, superfluous

surprise *n* something unexpected; emotion aroused by being taken unawares *~v* cause surprise to; astonish; take, come upon unexpectedly

surrealism *n* incongruous combination of images **surreal** *adj*

surrender *v* hand over, give up; yield; cease resistance *~n* act of surrendering

surreptitious *adj* done secretly or stealthily; furtive

surrogate *n* substitute **surrogate**

———————— THESAURUS ————————

tion, surmise, theory

suppress check, conquer, crush, extinguish, overpower, quash, quell, quench, stop, subdue

suppression check, clampdown, crackdown, prohibition, quashing

supremacy ascendancy, dominance, mastery, predominance, primacy, sovereignty, sway

supreme chief, first, foremost, greatest, head, highest, leading, paramount, pre-eminent, prime, principal, top, ultimate, utmost

sure certain, confident, convinced, decided, definite, positive; accurate, dependable, foolproof, indisputable, infallible, precise, trustworthy, undeniable, undoubted, unerring, unfailing; guaranteed, inescapable, inevitable, irrevocable

surface *n* covering, exterior, face, outside, plane, side, top, veneer

surfeit *n* excess, glut, plethora, superfluity *~v* cram, fill, glut, gorge, overfeed, stuff

surge gush, heave, rise, rush, swell

surly churlish, cross, morose, sulky, sullen, uncivil, ungracious

surpass beat, eclipse, exceed, excel, outdo, outshine, outstrip, transcend

surplus *n* balance, excess, remainder, surfeit *~adj* excess, extra, remaining, spare, superfluous, unused

surprise *n* bombshell, jolt, revelation, shock; amazement, astonishment, incredulity, wonder *~v* amaze, astonish, astound

surrender *v* abandon, cede, concede, give up, part with, relinquish, renounce, waive, yield; capitulate, give in, give way, submit, succumb, yield *~n* capitulation, resignation, submis-

mother woman who bears child on behalf of childless couple

surround v be, come all round, encompass; encircle ~n border, edging **surroundings** pl n conditions, scenery etc. around a person, place, environment

surveillance n close watch, supervision

survey v view, scrutinize; inspect, examine; measure, map (land) ~n act of surveying; inspection; report incorporating results of survey **surveyor** n

survive v continue to live or exist; outlive **survival** n continuation of existence **survivor** n one who survives

susceptible adj yielding readily (to); capable (of); impressionable **susceptibility** n

suspect v doubt innocence of; have impression of existence or presence of; be inclined to believe that ~adj of suspicious character ~n suspected

person

suspend v hang up; cause to cease for a time; keep inoperative; sustain in fluid **suspenders** pl n straps for supporting stockings

suspense n state of uncertainty, esp. while awaiting news, an event etc.; anxiety, worry **suspension** n state of being suspended; springs on axle of body of vehicle

suspicion n suspecting, being suspected; slight trace **suspicious** adj

sustain v keep, hold up; endure; keep alive; confirm **sustenance** n food

svelte adj gracefully slim

swab n mop; pad of surgical wool etc. for cleaning; taking specimen etc. ~v **swabbing, swabbed** clean with swab

swag n Sl stolen property

swagger v strut; boast ~n strutting gait; boastful manner

swallow[1] v cause, allow to pass down gullet; suppress ~n act of swallowing

swallow[2] n migratory bird with

—————— THESAURUS ——————

sion, yielding

surreptitious covert, furtive, secret, sly, stealthy, underhand

surround encircle, enclose, encompass, envelop, ring

surroundings background, location, milieu, setting

surveillance inspection, scrutiny, supervision, watch

survey v contemplate, examine, eye up, inspect, observe, scan, scrutinize, study, view; appraise, assess, estimate, size up ~n examination, inquiry, inspection, overview, review, scrutiny, study

survive endure, exist, last, live, live on, outlast, outlive, remain alive

susceptible (usu. with **to**) disposed, given, inclined, liable, prone, subject; easily moved, impressionable, sensitive, suggestible

suspect v distrust, doubt, mistrust;

believe, conjecture, consider, fancy, guess, speculate, suppose, surmise ~adj doubtful, dubious, iffy Inf, questionable

suspend dangle, hang; arrest, cease, cut short, defer, delay, discontinue, interrupt, postpone, put off, shelve

suspense anxiety, apprehension, doubt, insecurity, tension, uncertainty

suspicion distrust, doubt, misgiving, mistrust, scepticism, wariness; glimmer, hint, shade, suggestion, tinge, touch, trace

suspicious doubtful, sceptical, unbelieving, wary; dodgy Brit, Aust, & NZ inf, doubtful, dubious, funny, queer, questionable

sustain bear, carry, support, uphold; bear, endure, experience, suffer, withstand; approve, confirm, maintain, ratify

forked tail

swamp *n* bog ~*v* entangle in swamp; overwhelm; flood

swan *n* large, web-footed water bird with curved neck

swap *v* swapping, swapped exchange; barter ~*n* exchange

swarm¹ *n* large cluster of insects; vast crowd ~*v* (of bees) be on the move in swarm; gather in large numbers

swarm² *v* climb (rope etc.) by grasping with hands and knees

swarthy *adj* dark-complexioned

swashbuckler *n* daredevil adventurer **swashbuckling** *adj*

swastika *n* symbol of cross with arms bent at right angles

swat *v* swatting, swatted hit smartly; kill, esp. insects

swathe *v* cover with wraps or bandages

sway *v* swing unsteadily; (cause to) vacillate in opinion etc. ~*n* control; power; swaying motion

swear *v* swearing, swore, sworn promise on oath; cause to take an oath; declare; curse **swearword** *n* word considered obscene or blasphemous

sweat *n* moisture oozing from, forming on skin; *Inf* state of anxiety ~*v* (cause to) exude sweat; toil **sweaty** *adj* **sweatshirt** *n* long-sleeved cotton jersey

sweater *n* woollen jersey

swede *n* variety of turnip

sweep *v* sweeping, swept clean with broom; pass quickly or magnificently; extend in continuous curve; carry away suddenly ~*n* act of cleaning with broom; sweeping motion; wide curve; one who cleans chimneys **sweeping** *adj* wide-ranging; without limitations **sweepstake** *n* lottery with stakes of participants as prize

sweet *adj* tasting like sugar; agreeable; kind, charming; fragrant; tuneful; dear, beloved ~*n* small piece of sweet food; sweet course served at end of meal **sweeten** *v* **sweetener** *n* sweetening agent; *Sl* bribe **sweetness** *n* **sweet corn** type of maize with sweet yellow kernels **sweetheart** *n* lover **sweet pea** plant of pea family with bright flowers **sweet-talk** *v* *Inf* coax, flatter

swell *v* swelling, swelled, swollen *or* swelled expand; be greatly filled with pride, emotion ~*n* act of swelling or being swollen; wave of sea **swelling** *n*

———————— THESAURUS ————————

swallow absorb, consume, devour, drink, eat, gulp

swamp *n* bog, fen, marsh, morass, quagmire ~*v* drench, engulf, flood, inundate, overwhelm, submerge

swap, swop *v* barter, exchange, interchange, switch, trade, traffic

swarm *n* army, crowd, drove, flock, herd, horde, host, mass, multitude, shoal, throng ~*v* crowd, flock, throng (*with* **with**) abound, crawl, teem

sway *v* lurch, rock, roll, swing, wave; affect, control, govern, influence, persuade ~*n* authority, command, control, influence, jurisdiction, power, rule, sovereignty

swear affirm, assert, attest, avow, declare, promise, testify, vow; blaspheme, curse

sweaty clammy, perspiring, sticky

sweep *v* brush, clean, clear, remove ~*n* arc, bend, curve, stroke, swing

sweeping all-embracing, all-inclusive, broad, comprehensive, global, wide; blanket, indiscriminate, unqualified, wholesale

sweet *adj* cloying, honeyed, sweetened, treacly; affectionate, agreeable, amiable, appealing, charming, cute, engaging, kind, likable *or* likeable, lovable

sweetheart beloved, boyfriend, dar-

enlargement of part of body, caused by injury or infection

swelter v be oppressed by heat

swerve v swing round, change direction during motion; turn aside (from duty etc.) ~n swerving

swift adj rapid, quick ~n bird like a swallow

swig n large swallow of drink ~v **swigging, swigged** drink thus

swill v drink greedily; pour water over or through ~n liquid pig food; rinsing

swim v swimming, swam, swum support and move oneself in water; float; be flooded; have feeling of dizziness ~n spell of swimming **swimmer** n **swimmingly** adv successfully

swindle n/v cheat **swindler** n

swine n (pl **swine**) pig; contemptible person

swing v swinging, swung (cause to) move to and fro; (cause to) pivot, turn; hang; be hanged; hit out (at) ~n act, instance of swinging; seat hung to swing on; fluctuation (esp. in voting pattern)

swingeing adj punishing, severe

swipe v strike with wide, sweeping or glancing blow

swirl v (cause to) move with eddying motion ~n such motion

swish v (cause to) move with hissing

sound ~n the sound

switch n mechanism to complete or interrupt electric circuit etc.; abrupt change; flexible stick or twig; tress of false hair ~v change abruptly; exchange; affect (current etc.) with switch **switchboard** n installation for connecting telephone calls

swivel n mechanism of two parts which can revolve the one on the other ~v -**elling, -elled** turn (on swivel)

swoop v dive, as hawk ~n act of swooping

sword n weapon with long blade **swordfish** n fish with elongated sharp upper jaw

swot Inf v swotting, swotted study hard ~n one who works hard at lessons

sycamore n tree related to maple

sycophant n one using flattery to gain favours **sycophantic** adj

syllable n division of word as unit for pronunciation

syllabus n (pl -**buses, -bi**) outline of course of study

syllogism n form of logical reasoning consisting of two premises and conclusion

symbol n sign; thing representing or typifying something **symbolic** adj **symbolism** n **symbolize** v

———————— **THESAURUS** ————————

ling, dear, girlfriend, love, lover

swell v balloon, billow, bloat, bulge, distend, enlarge, expand, grow, increase, rise

swelling n bulge, bump, enlargement, lump, protuberance

swerve v bend, deflect, deviate, diverge, stray, swing, turn, turn aside, veer

swift fast, fleet, prompt, quick, rapid, speedy, sudden

swindle n deception, fraud, racket, scam Sl, sting Inf, trickery ~v cheat, deceive, defraud, dupe, fleece, over-

charge, skin Sl, sting Inf, trick

swindler charlatan, cheat, fraud, impostor, mountebank, trickster

swing v fluctuate, oscillate, sway, vary, veer; dangle, hang, suspend ~n fluctuation, stroke, sway

swirl v churn, eddy, twist

switch n alteration, change, exchange, reversal, shift, substitution ~v change, deflect, deviate, exchange, shift, substitute, trade

swoop v descend, dive, pounce, stoop, sweep ~n drop, pounce, rush

syllabus course, course of study,

symmetry *n* proportion between parts **symmetrical** *adj*

sympathy *n* feeling for another in pain etc.; compassion, pity; sharing of emotion etc. **sympathetic** *adj* **sympathize** *v*

symphony *n* composition for full orchestra

symposium *n* (*pl* -**siums**, -**sia**) conference

symptom *n* change in body indicating disease; sign **symptomatic** *adj*

synagogue *n* Jewish place of worship

sync *n Inf* synchronization

synchromesh *adj* (of gearbox) having device that synchronizes speeds of gears before they engage

synchronize *v* make agree in time; happen at same time **synchronization** *n*

syncopate *v* accentuate weak beat in bar of music **syncopation** *n*

syndicate *n* body of persons associated for some enterprise ~*v* form syndicate; publish in many newspapers at the same time

syndrome *n* combination of several symptoms in disease

synod *n* church council

synonym *n* word with same meaning as another **synonymous** *adj*

synopsis *n* summary, outline

syntax *n* arrangement of words in sentence

synthesis *n* (*pl* -**ses**) putting together, combination **synthesize** *v* make artificially **synthesizer** *n* electronic keyboard instrument reproducing wide range of musical sounds **synthetic** *adj* artificial; of synthesis

syphilis *n* contagious venereal disease

syringe *n* instrument for drawing in liquid and forcing it out in fine spray ~*v* spray, cleanse with syringe

syrup *n* thick solution obtained in process of refining sugar; any liquid like this

system *n* complex whole; method; classification **systematic** *adj* methodical

———— THESAURUS ————

curriculum

symbol badge, emblem, figure, image, representation, sign, token

symbolize denote, mean, personify, represent, signify, stand for, typify

symmetrical balanced, proportional, regular

symmetry balance, evenness, harmony, proportion

sympathetic caring, compassionate, concerned, kind, kindly, pitying, supportive

sympathize commiserate, feel for, pity

sympathy compassion, pity, tenderness, understanding; affinity, agreement, harmony, rapport, union

symptom indication, mark, sign, token, warning

synthetic artificial, fake, man-made, mock

system method, practice, procedure, routine, technique; arrangement, classification, organization, scheme, structure

systematic efficient, methodical, orderly, organized

T t

ta *interj Inf* thank you

tab *n* tag, label, short strap

Tabasco *n Trademark* hot red pepper sauce

tabby *n/adj* (cat) with stripes on lighter background

table *n* flat board supported by legs; facts, figures arranged in lines or columns ~*v* submit (motion etc.) for discussion **tablespoon** *n* spoon for serving food

tableau *n* (*pl* **-leaux**) group of persons representing some scene

tablet *n* pill of compressed powdered medicine; cake of soap etc.; inscribed slab of stone, wood etc.

table tennis ball game played on table

tabloid *n* small-sized newspaper with many photographs and usu. sensational style

taboo *adj* forbidden ~*n* prohibition resulting from social conventions etc.

tabulate *v* arrange (figures etc.) in tables

tacit *adj* implied but not spoken

taciturn *adj* habitually silent

tack¹ *n* small nail; long loose stitch; *Naut* course of ship obliquely to windward; approach, method ~*v* nail with tacks; stitch lightly; append; sail to windward

tack² *n* riding harness for horses

tackle *n* equipment, esp. for lifting; *Sport* physical challenge of opponent ~*v* undertake; challenge

tacky¹ *adj* sticky; not quite dry

tacky² *adj* vulgar, tasteless

tact *n* skill in dealing with people or situations **tactful** *adj* **tactless** *adj*

tactics *pl n* art of handling troops, ships in battle; methods, plans **tactical** *adj* **tactician** *n*

tactile *adj* of sense of touch

tadpole *n* immature frog

taffeta *n* stiff silk fabric

tag¹ *n* label identifying or showing price of (something); hanging end ~*v* **tagging, tagged** add (on)

tag² *n* children's game where one chased becomes the chaser upon being touched ~*v* **tagging, tagged** touch

tail *n* flexible appendage at animal's rear; hindmost, lower or inferior part of anything; *pl* reverse side of coin ~*v*

THESAURUS
---

table *n* chart, diagram, graph, index, list ~*v* move, propose, put forward, submit, suggest

taboo *adj* banned, forbidden, outlawed, prohibited, proscribed, unmentionable ~*n* anathema, ban, prohibition, proscription

tacit implicit, implied, silent, understood, unspoken, unstated

taciturn quiet, reserved, reticent, silent, unforthcoming

tack *n* nail, pin; approach, bearing, course, direction, line, method, path, way ~*v* affix, attach, fasten, fix, nail, pin

tackle *n* apparatus, equipment, gear, tools, trappings; block, challenge, stop ~*v* attempt, essay, have a stab at *Inf,* undertake; block, bring down, challenge, halt, stop

tact delicacy, diplomacy, discretion, judgment

tactful careful, considerate, delicate, diplomatic, discreet, sensitive, thoughtful

tactical artful, clever, cunning, shrewd, smart

tactless careless, clumsy, gauche, inconsiderate, indiscreet, insensitive, thoughtless, unfeeling

remove tail of; *Inf* follow closely **tail-back** *n* queue of traffic stretching back from obstruction **tailboard** *n* hinged rear board on lorry etc. **tail coat** man's evening dress jacket **tail off** diminish gradually **tailspin** *n* spinning dive of aircraft **tailwind** *n* wind coming from rear

tailor *n* maker of clothing, esp. for men **tailor-made** *adj* well-fitting

taint *v* affect or be affected by pollution etc. ~*n* defect; contamination

take *v* **taking, took, taken** grasp; get; receive; understand; consider; use; capture; steal; accept; bear; consume; assume; carry; accompany; subtract; require; contain, hold; be effective; please ~*n* (recording of) scene filmed without break **takings** *pl n* earnings, receipts **take after** resemble in face or character **takeaway** *n* shop, restaurant selling meals for eating elsewhere; meal bought at this

place **take in** understand; include; make (garment etc.) smaller; deceive **take off** remove; (of aircraft) leave ground; *Inf* go away; *Inf* mimic **take-off** *n* **takeover** *n* act of taking control of company by buying large number of its shares

talc *also* **talcum powder** *n* powder, usu. scented, to absorb body moisture

tale *n* story, narrative

talent *n* natural ability **talented** *adj* gifted

talisman *n* object supposed to have magic power

talk *v* express, exchange ideas etc. in words; discuss ~*n* lecture; conversation; rumour; discussion **talkative** *adj*

tall *adj* high; of great stature

tally *v* **tallying, tallied** correspond one with the other; count ~*n* record, account

talon *n* claw

taint *v* contaminate, corrupt, dirty, foul, infect, pollute, spoil ~*n* defect, disgrace, dishonour, fault, flaw, smear, smirch, stain

take clutch, grasp, grip, seize; acquire, get, obtain, receive, secure, win; appropriate, filch, nick *Sl, chiefly Brit,* pocket, purloin, steal; accept, book, buy, engage, hire, lease, purchase, rent; abide, bear, endure, stand, stomach, suffer, swallow, tolerate; consume, drink, eat, ingest, inhale, swallow; bear, bring, carry, convey, fetch, transport; accompany, bring, conduct, escort, guide, lead; deduct, remove, subtract

take in absorb, assimilate, comprehend, digest, grasp, understand; cheat, deceive, fool, hoodwink, swindle, trick

take off discard, doff, drop, peel off, remove, strip off; *Inf* caricature, imitate, lampoon, mimic, mock, parody,

satirize

tale account, anecdote, fable, fiction, legend, saga, story, urban legend

talent ability, aptitude, faculty, flair, genius, gift

talented able, artistic, brilliant, gifted

talk *v* chat, chatter, converse, gossip, say, speak, utter; confer, discuss, have a confab *Inf,* hold discussions, negotiate ~*n* address, discourse, lecture, oration, sermon, speech; chat, chatter, chitchat, conversation; gossip, hearsay, rumour; conference, congress, consultation, dialogue, discussion, meeting, seminar, symposium

talkative chatty, garrulous, long-winded, loquacious, verbose, voluble, wordy

tall big, giant, high, lanky, lofty

tally *v* accord, agree, correspond, match, square; count, mark, reckon, total ~*n* count, mark, reckoning,

tambourine *n* flat half-drum with jingling discs of metal attached

tame *adj* not wild, domesticated; uninteresting ~*v* make tame

tamper *v* interfere (with)

tampon *n* plug of cotton wool inserted into vagina during menstruation

tan *adj/n* (of) brown colour of skin after exposure to sun etc. ~*v* **tanning, tanned** (cause to) go brown; (of animal hide) convert to leather **tannin** *n* vegetable substance used as tanning agent

tandem *n* bicycle for two

tandoori *adj* (of Indian food) cooked in a clay oven

tang *n* strong pungent taste or smell **tangy** *adj*

tangent *n* line that touches a curve **tangential** *adj*

tangerine *n* (fruit of) Asian citrus tree

tangible *adj* that can be touched; real **tangibility** *n*

tangle *n* confused mass or situation ~*v* confuse

tango *n* (*pl* **-gos**) dance of S Amer. origin

tank *n* storage vessel for liquids or gases; armoured motor vehicle on tracks **tanker** *n* ship, lorry for carrying liquid

tankard *n* large drinking cup

Tannoy *n* *Trademark* type of public-address system

tantalize *v* torment by appearing to offer something

tantamount *adj* equivalent, equal (to)

tantrum *n* outburst of temper

tap¹ *v* **tapping, tapped** strike lightly but with some noise ~*n* **tapping tap dance** dance in which the feet beat out elaborate rhythms

tap² *n* valve with handle, plug etc. to regulate or stop flow of fluid ~*v* **tapping, tapped** draw off with tap; use, draw on; make secret connection to telephone wire to overhear conversation on it

tape *n* narrow strip of fabric, paper etc.; magnetic recording ~*v* record (speech, music etc.) **tape measure** tape marked off in centimetres, inches etc. **tape recorder** apparatus for recording sound on magnetized tape **tapeworm** *n* long flat parasitic worm

taper *v* become gradually thinner ~*n* thin candle

tapestry *n* fabric decorated with woven designs

tapioca *n* beadlike starch made from cassava root

tar *n* thick black liquid distilled from coal etc. ~*v* **tarring, tarred** coat, treat with tar

tarantula *n* (*pl* **-las, -lae**) large (poisonous) hairy spider

tardy *adj* slow, late

——————— THESAURUS ———————

score, total

tame *adj* cultivated, disciplined, docile, obedient; bland, boring, dull, flat, insipid ~*v* break in, domesticate, pacify, train

tamper interfere, meddle, muck about *Brit slf*, tinker

tangle *n* coil, confusion, knot, mass, mesh, snarl; complication, labyrinth, maze, mess, mix-up ~*v* coil, knot, mat, mesh, snarl

tantalize taunt, tease, torment, torture

tantrum fit, ill humour, outburst, storm, temper

tap¹ *v/n* beat, knock, pat, rap, touch

tap² *n* spigot, spout, stopcock, valve ~*v* draw on, exploit, milk, mine, use, utilize

tape *n* band, ribbon, strip ~*v* record, video

taper come to a point, narrow, thin

target *n* thing aimed at; victim

tariff *n* tax levied on imports etc.; list of charges

Tarmac *n Trademark* mixture of tar etc. giving hard, smooth surface to road

tarn *n* small mountain lake

tarnish *v* (cause to) become stained or sullied ~*n* discoloration, blemish

tarot *n* pack of cards used in fortune-telling

tarpaulin *n* (sheet of) heavy hard-wearing waterproof fabric

tarragon *n* aromatic herb

tarry *v* **tarrying, tarried** linger, delay; stay behind

tart[1] *n* small pie or flan filled with fruit, jam etc.; loose woman

tart[2] *adj* sour; sharp; bitter

tartan *n* woollen cloth woven in pattern of coloured checks

tartar *n* crust deposited on teeth

task *n* piece of work (esp. unpleasant or difficult) set or undertaken **taskmaster** *n* overseer

tassel *n* ornament of fringed knot of threads etc.; tuft

taste *n* sense by which flavour, quality of substance is detected by the tongue; (brief) experience of something; small amount; liking; power of discerning, judging ~*v* observe or distinguish the taste of a substance; take small amount into mouth; experience; have specific flavour **tasteful** *adj* with, showing good taste **tasteless** *adj* bland, insipid; showing bad taste **tasty** *adj* pleasantly flavoured **taste bud** small organ of taste on tongue

tattered *adj* ragged **tatters** *pl n* ragged pieces

tattle *v/n* gossip, chatter

tattoo[1] *n* beat of drum and bugle call; military spectacle

tattoo[2] *v* **tattooing, tattooed** mark skin in coloured patterns etc. by pricking ~*n* pattern made thus

tatty *adj* shabby, worn out

taunt *v* provoke with insults etc. ~*n* scornful remark

taupe *adj* brownish-grey

taut *adj* drawn tight; under strain

tavern *n* inn, public house

—————————— T H E S A U R U S ——————————

target aim, end, goal, intention, mark, object, objective; butt, quarry, scapegoat, victim

tariff duty, excise, levy, rate, tax, toll

tarnish dim, dull, rust, smirch, stain, sully, taint

tart[1] harlot, loose woman, prostitute, scrubber *Brit & Aust sl*, slag *Brit sl*, slut, strumpet, trollop, whore

tart[2] acid, bitter, pungent, sharp, sour, tangy; biting, caustic, sharp, short, snappish

task *n* assignment, chore, duty, job, mission

taste *n* flavour, relish, savour, smack; bit, bite, dash, drop, morsel, mouthful, sample, sip, swallow; appetite, bent, desire, fancy, inclination, leaning, liking, penchant, preference; appreciation, cultivation, culture, discernment, discrimination, judgment, refinement, sophistication, style ~*v* sample, savour, sip, test, try

tasteful beautiful, charming, cultivated, elegant, exquisite, polished, refined, smart, stylish

tasteless bland, boring, dull, flat, insipid, thin, uninteresting, vapid, weak; cheap, coarse, crass, crude, flashy, gross, improper, indelicate, low, naff *Brit sl*, rude, tacky *Inf*, tawdry, uncouth, vulgar

tasty appetizing, delectable, delicious, luscious, palatable

taunt *v* deride, insult, jeer, mock, ridicule, tease ~*n* dig, gibe, insult, jeer, ridicule

taut rigid, strained, stretched, tense,

tawdry *adj* showy, but cheap

tawny *adj/n* (of) light yellowish-brown colour

tax *n* compulsory payments imposed by government to raise revenue; heavy demand on something ~*v* impose tax on; strain **taxation** *n* levying of taxes **tax return** statement of income for tax purposes

taxi *also* **taxicab** *n* (*pl* **taxis**) motor vehicle for hire with driver ~*v* **taxiing**, **taxied** (of aircraft) run along ground

taxidermy *n* art of stuffing animal skins **taxidermist** *n*

TB tuberculosis

tea *n* dried leaves of plant cultivated esp. in Asia; infusion of it as beverage; meal eaten in afternoon or early evening **tea bag** small porous bag of tea leaves **teapot** *n* container for making and serving tea **teaspoon** *n* small spoon for stirring tea etc. **tea towel** towel for drying dishes

teach *v* **teaching**, **taught** instruct; educate; train **teacher** *n*

teak *n* (hard wood from) E Indian tree

team *n* set of animals, players of game etc. ~*v* (*usu. with* **up**) (cause to) make a team **teamwork** *n* cooperative

work by team

tear[1] *n* drop of fluid falling from eye **tearful** *adj* inclined to weep; involving tears **teardrop** *n* **tear gas** irritant gas causing temporary blindness

tear[2] *v* **tearing, tore, torn** pull apart; become torn; rush ~*n* hole or split **tearaway** *n* wild or unruly person

tease *v* tantalize, torment, irritate ~*n* one who teases

teat *n* nipple of breast; rubber nipple of baby's bottle

technical *adj* of, specializing in industrial, practical or mechanical arts; belonging to particular art or science; according to letter of the law **technicality** *n* point of procedure **technician** *n* one skilled in technique of an art **technique** *n* method of performance in an art; skill required for mastery of subject

Technicolor *n* *Trademark* colour photography, esp. in cinema

technology *n* application of practical, mechanical sciences; technical skills, knowledge **technological** *adj*

teddy *also* **teddy bear** *n* child's soft toy bear

tedious *adj* causing fatigue or boredom **tedium** *n* monotony

——————— THESAURUS ———————

tight

tax *n* charge, customs, duty, excise, levy, rate, tariff, toll, tribute ~*v* charge, impose; burden, drain, exhaust, load, overburden, push, sap, strain, stretch, try

teach advise, coach, direct, educate, guide, inform, instruct, school, show, train, tutor

teacher coach, guide, instructor, lecturer, master, mentor, mistress, professor, schoolmaster, schoolmistress, trainer, tutor

team *n* band, body, bunch, company, crew, gang, group, side, squad, troupe *v* (*usu. with* **up**) cooperate,

couple, get together, join, link, unite, work together

tear *v* claw, rend, rip, scratch, shred ~*n* hole, rent, rip, rupture, scratch

tearful crying, sobbing, weeping

tease annoy, badger, bait, chaff, goad, mock, needle *Inf*, pester, provoke, taunt, torment, wind up *Brit sl*

technique fashion, means, method, mode, procedure, style, system, way; art, artistry, craft, knack, proficiency, skill, touch

tedious banal, boring, dreary, dull, ho-hum *Inf*, laborious, mind-numbing, monotonous, unexciting, uninteresting, wearisome

tee *n Golf* place from which first stroke of hole is made; small peg supporting ball for first stroke

teem *v* abound with; swarm; rain heavily

teens *pl n* years of life from 13 to 19 **teenage** *adj* **teenager** *n* young person between 13 and 19

teeter *v* seesaw, wobble

teeth *n pl of* TOOTH

teethe *v* (of baby) grow first teeth **teething troubles** problems, difficulties at first stage of something

teetotal *adj* pledged to abstain from alcohol **teetotaller** *n*

Teflon *n Trademark* substance used for nonstick coatings on saucepans etc.

telecommunications *pl n* (*with sing v*) communications by telephone, television etc.

telegram *n* formerly, message sent by telegraph

telegraph *n* formerly, electrical apparatus for transmitting messages over distance ~*v* send by telegraph

telepathy *n* action of one mind on another at a distance **telepathic** *adj*

telephone *n* apparatus for communicating sound to hearer at a distance ~*v* communicate, speak by telephone **telephonist** *n* person operating telephone switchboard

telephoto *adj* (of lens) producing magnified image

teleprinter *n* apparatus for sending and receiving typed messages by wire

telescope *n* optical instrument for magnifying distant objects ~*v* slide together **telescopic** *adj*

teletext *n* electronic system which shows information, news on subscribers' television screens

television *n* system of producing on screen images of distant objects, events etc. by electromagnetic radiation; device for receiving this; programmes etc. viewed on television set **televise** *v* transmit by television; make, produce as television programme

telex *n* international communication service ~*v* send by telex

tell *v* **telling, told** let know; order; narrate, make known; discern; distinguish; give account; be of weight, importance **teller** *n* narrator; bank cashier **telling** *adj* effective, striking **tell off** reprimand **telltale** *n* sneak ~*adj* revealing

telly *n Inf* television (set)

temerity *n* boldness, audacity

temp *n Inf* one employed on temporary basis

temper *n* frame of mind; angry state; calmness, composure ~*v* restrain, moderate; harden (metal)

temperament *n* natural disposition; emotional mood **temperamental** *adj* moody; erratic

———— THESAURUS ————

tedium banality, boredom, dreariness, dullness, monotony, routine, tediousness

teem abound, brim, bristle, overflow, swarm

telepathy mind-reading, sixth sense, thought transference

telephone *v* call, call up, phone, ring *Inf, chiefly Brit*

tell announce, communicate, confess, disclose, divulge, express, impart, in-

form, notify, proclaim, reveal, say, speak, state; bid, command, direct, instruct, order; depict, describe, narrate, recount, relate, report

temper *n* attitude, disposition, humour, mood, nature, vein; anger, annoyance, fury, heat, irritability, petulance, rage, tantrum

temperament bent, character, constitution, humour, make-up, nature, personality

temperate *adj* (of climate) mild; not extreme; showing moderation **temperance** *n* moderation; abstinence, esp. from alcohol

temperature *n* degree of heat or coldness; *Inf* high body temperature

tempest *n* violent storm **tempestuous** *adj* stormy; violent

template *n* pattern used to cut out shapes accurately

temple¹ *n* building for worship

temple² *n* flat part on either side of forehead

tempo *n* (*pl* **-pos, -pi**) rate, rhythm

temporal *adj* of time; of this life or world

temporary *adj* lasting only a short time

tempt *v* try to persuade, entice, esp. to something wrong or unwise **temptation** *n* **tempter** *n* (*fem* **temptress**) **tempting** *adj* attractive, inviting

ten *n/adj* cardinal number after nine **tenth** *adj* ordinal number

tenable *adj* able to be held, defended, maintained

tenacious *adj* holding fast; retentive; stubborn **tenacity** *n*

tenant *n* one who holds lands, house etc. on rent or lease **tenancy** *n*

tench *n* freshwater fish

tend¹ *v* be inclined; be conducive; make in direction of **tendency** *n* inclination **tendentious** *adj* controversial

tend² *v* take care of

tender¹ *adj* not tough; easily injured; gentle, loving; delicate

tender² *v* offer; make offer or estimate ~*n* offer or estimate for contract to undertake specific work **legal tender** currency that must, by law, be accepted as payment

tendon *n* sinew attaching muscle to bone etc.

———————— THESAURUS ————————

temperamental emotional, excitable, moody, passionate, sensitive, touchy, volatile; erratic, unreliable

temperance moderation, restraint, self-control, self-restraint; abstinence, teetotalism

temperate balmy, fair, mild, pleasant; calm, mild, moderate, reasonable, sensible, stable

tempestuous blustery, inclement, raging, squally, stormy, turbulent; emotional, heated, impassioned, intense, passionate, stormy, turbulent, uncontrolled, violent, wild

temple church, sanctuary, shrine

temporary brief, ephemeral, fleeting, interim, momentary, passing, provisional, transient

tempt allure, attract, coax, draw, entice, invite, lure, seduce

temptation allurement, attraction, coaxing, draw, inducement, invitation, lure, pull, seduction

tempting alluring, attractive, enticing, inviting, seductive

tenable defendable, defensible, justifiable, maintainable, plausible, rational, reasonable, sound, viable

tenacious clinging, fast, firm, immovable, strong, tight; determined, dogged, firm, immovable, inflexible, obstinate, persistent, resolute, stiffnecked, stubborn, unyielding

tenancy holding, lease, occupancy, possession, residence

tenant holder, inhabitant, leaseholder, lessee, occupier, resident

tend¹ gravitate, incline, lean

tend² cultivate, keep, look after, maintain, nurse

tendency inclination, leaning, partiality, penchant, predilection, predisposition, propensity

tender aching, bruised, delicate, inflamed, irritated, painful, raw, sensitive, smarting, sore; affectionate, amorous, caring, fond, gentle, kind, loving, warm

tendril *n* slender curling stem by which climbing plant clings

tenement *n* building divided into separate flats

tenet *n* belief

tennis *n* game in which ball is struck with racket by players on opposite sides of net

tenor *n* male voice between alto and bass; general course, meaning

tenpin bowling game in which players try to knock over ten skittles with ball

tense¹ *n* form of verb showing time of action

tense² *adj* stretched tight; taut; emotionally strained ~*v* make, become tense **tensile** *adj* of, relating to tension **tension** *n* stretching; strain when stretched; emotional strain; suspense; *Electricity* voltage

tent *n* portable shelter of canvas

tentacle *n* flexible organ of some animals (e.g. octopus) used for grasping, feeding etc.

tentative *adj* experimental; cautious

tenterhooks *pl n* **on tenterhooks** in anxious suspense

tenuous *adj* flimsy; thin

tenure *n* (length of time of) possession of office etc.

tepee *n* N Amer. Indian cone-shaped tent

tepid *adj* moderately warm

tequila *n* Mexican alcoholic drink

term *n* word, expression; limited period of time; period during which schools are open; *pl* conditions; relationship ~*v* name

terminal *adj* at, forming an end; (of disease) ending in death ~*n* terminal part or structure; point where current enters, leaves battery etc.; device permitting operation of computer at distance

terminate *v* bring, come to an end

termination *n*

terminology *n* set of technical terms or vocabulary

terminus *n* (*pl* **-ni, -nuses**) finishing point; railway station etc. at end of line

termite *n* wood-eating insect

tern *n* sea bird like gull

terpsichorean *adj* of dancing

terrace *n* raised level place; row of houses built as one block; (*oft. pl*) unroofed tiers for spectators at sports stadium ~*v* form into terrace

terracotta *n/adj* (made of) hard unglazed pottery; (of) brownish-red colour

terrain *n* area of ground, esp. with reference to its physical character

terrapin *n* type of aquatic tortoise

terrestrial *adj* of the earth; of, living

———— THESAURUS ————

tense rigid, strained, stretched, taut, tight; edgy, fidgety, jumpy, keyed up, nervous, restless, strained, twitchy *Inf*, wired *Sl*; stressful, worrying

tension stiffness, stress, tautness, tightness; pressure, strain, stress, unease

tentative experimental, indefinite, provisional, speculative; cautious, diffident, hesitant, timid, uncertain, unsure

term *n* denomination, designation, expression, name, phrase, title, word; period, season, space, spell, time; course, session ~*v* call, denominate, designate, dub, entitle, label, name, style

terminal *adj* deadly, fatal, incurable, killing, lethal, mortal

terminate axe *Inf*, cease, close, conclude, cut off, discontinue, end, expire, finish, lapse, run out, stop, wind up

termination cessation, close, conclusion, discontinuation, end, ending, expiry, finish

on land

terrible *adj* serious; *Inf* very bad; causing fear **terribly** *adv*

terrier *n* small dog of various breeds

terrific *adj* very great; *Inf* good; awe-inspiring

terrify *v* frighten greatly **terrifying** *adj*

territory *n* region; geographical area, esp. a sovereign state **territorial** *adj* **Territorial Army** reserve army

terror *n* great fear; *Inf* troublesome person or thing **terrorism** *n* use of violence to achieve ends **terrorist** *n/adj* **terrorize** *v* oppress by violence; terrify

terse *adj* concise; abrupt

tertiary *adj* third in degree, order etc.

Terylene *n Trademark* synthetic yarn; fabric made of it

test *v* try, put to the proof; carry out examination on ~*n* examination; means of trial **testing** *adj* difficult **test case** lawsuit viewed as means of establishing precedent **test match** international sports contest, esp. one of series **test tube** tubelike glass vessel

testament *n Law* will; (*with cap.*) one of the two main divisions of the Bible

testate *adj* (of dead person) having left a valid will

testicle *also* **testis** *n* either of two male reproductive glands

testify *v* **-fying, -fied** declare; bear witness (to)

testimony *n* affirmation; evidence **testimonial** *n* certificate of character etc.; gift expressing regard for recipient

testy *adj* irritable

tetanus *n* (*also called* **lockjaw**) acute infectious disease

tête-à-tête *n* private conversation

tether *n* rope for fastening (grazing) animal ~*v* tie up with rope

tetrahedron *n* solid contained by four plane faces

text *n* (actual words of) book, passage etc.; passage of Bible **textual** *adj* **textbook** *n* book of instruction on particular subject

textile *n* any fabric or cloth, esp. woven

texture *n* structure, appearance; consistency

than *conj* introduces second part of

——————————— THESAURUS ———————————

terrible bad, dangerous, extreme, serious, severe; *Inf* abysmal, awful, bad, dire, dreadful, frightful, godawful *Sl*; awful, dreadful, fearful, frightful, gruesome, horrible, horrifying, monstrous, shocking

terrific enormous, extreme, great, huge, intense, tremendous; *Inf* amazing, breathtaking, brilliant, cracking *Brit inf*, excellent, fine, marvellous, mean *Sl*, outstanding, superb, wonderful

terrify frighten, intimidate, petrify, shock, terrorize

territory area, country, district, land, patch, province, region, turf *US sl*, zone

terror fear, fright, horror, intimida-

tion, panic, shock

terrorize browbeat, bully, intimidate, menace, oppress, threaten

terse brief, clipped, concise, crisp, laconic, pithy, short, succinct; abrupt, brusque, curt, short

test *v* analyse, check, experiment, investigate, prove, research, try, verify ~*n* analysis, check, examination, investigation, research, trial

testify affirm, assert, attest, bear witness, certify, corroborate, declare, state, swear, vouch

testimonial certificate, commendation, endorsement, tribute

testimony affidavit, attestation, corroboration, deposition, evidence, statement

comparison

thank v express gratitude to; say thanks **thankful** adj grateful **thankless** adj unrewarding or unappreciated **thanks** pl n words of gratitude

that adj refers to thing already mentioned; refers to thing further away ~pron refers to particular thing; introduces relative clause ~conj introduces noun or adverbial clause

thatch n reeds, straw etc. used as roofing material ~v build roof with this

thaw v melt; (cause to) unfreeze ~n melting (of frost etc.)

the adj the definite article

theatre n place where plays etc. are performed; dramatic works generally; hospital operating room **theatrical** adj of, for the theatre; exaggerated

thee pron Obs object of THOU

theft n stealing

their adj of, belonging to them **theirs** pron belonging to them

them pron object of THEY **themselves** pron emphatic or reflexive form of THEY

theme n main topic of book etc.; subject of composition; recurring melody **thematic** adj **theme park** leisure area designed round one subject

then adv at that time; next; that being so

thence adv Obs from that place or time

theology n systematic study of religion and religious beliefs **theologian** n **theological** adj

theorem n proposition which can be demonstrated

theory n supposition to account for something; system of rules and principles, esp. distinguished from practice **theoretical** adj based on theory; speculative

therapy n healing treatment **therapeutic** adj of healing; serving to improve health **therapist** n

there adv in that place; to that point **thereby** adv by that means **therefore** adv that being so **thereupon** adv immediately

therm n unit of measurement of heat **thermal** adj

thermodynamics pl n (with sing v) science that deals with interrelationship of different forms of energy

thermometer n instrument to measure temperature

Thermos n Trademark vacuum flask

thermostat n apparatus for regulating temperature

thesaurus n (pl **-ruses**) book containing lists of synonyms

these pron pl of THIS

thesis n (pl **theses**) written work sub-

———————— T H E S A U R U S ————————

text body, matter, wording, words

texture consistency, feel, grain, structure, surface, tissue

thankful appreciative, grateful, indebted, obliged

thanks acknowledgment, appreciation, credit, gratefulness, gratitude, recognition, thanksgiving

thaw v defrost, melt, warm

theatrical affected, artificial, camp Inf, dramatic, exaggerated, histrionic, mannered, overdone, showy, stagy

theft fraud, larceny, pilfering, robbery, stealing

theme idea, keynote, matter, subject, topic

theoretical abstract, academic, impractical, notional, speculative

theory assumption, guess, hypothesis, speculation, surmise

therapeutic corrective, curative, healing, remedial

therapy cure, healing, remedial treatment, remedy, treatment

therefore accordingly, consequently, ergo, so, thus

mitted for degree, diploma; theory maintained in argument

thespian *adj* of the theatre ~*n* actor, actress

they *pron* pronoun of the third person plural

thick *adj* fat, broad, not thin; dense; crowded; viscous; (of voice) throaty; *Inf* stupid ~*n* busiest part **thicken** *v* make, become thick; become complicated **thickness** *n* dimension through an object; layer **thickset** *adj* sturdy, stocky

thicket *n* thick growth of trees

thief *n* (*pl* **thieves**) one who steals **thieve** *v* steal

thigh *n* upper part of leg

thimble *n* cap protecting end of finger when sewing

thin *adj* of little thickness; slim; of little density; sparse; fine; not close-packed ~*v* **thinning, thinned** make, become thin

thing *n* (material) object; fact, idea

think *v* **thinking, thought** have one's mind at work; reflect, meditate; reason; deliberate; believe

third *adj* of number three in a series ~*n* third part **third degree** violent interrogation **third party** *Law, Insurance etc.* person involved by chance in legal proceedings etc.

thirst *n* desire to drink; feeling caused by lack of drink; craving ~*v* have thirst **thirsty** *adj*

thirteen *adj/n* three plus ten **thirteenth** *adj*

thirty *adj/n* three times ten **thirtieth** *adj*

this *adj/pron* denotes thing, person near or just mentioned

thistle *n* prickly plant

thither *adv Obs* to or towards that place

thong *n* narrow strip of leather, strap

thorax *n* part of body between neck and belly

thorn *n* prickle on plant; bush noted for its thorns **thorny** *adj*

thorough *adj* careful, methodical; complete **thoroughly** *adv* **thoroughbred** *n* pure-bred animal, esp. horse **thoroughfare** *n* road or passage; right of way

———————————— THESAURUS ————————————

thesis composition, dissertation, essay, paper, treatise; hypothesis, idea, line of argument, opinion, theory, view

thick broad, deep, fat, solid, wide; compact, dense, heavy, opaque; bristling, bursting, chock-a-block, chock-full, covered, crawling, crowded, full, packed, swarming, teeming; dense, heavy, soupy, viscous; guttural, hoarse, husky, throaty; *Inf* brain-dead *Inf*, brainless, dense, dozy *Brit inf*, dull, obtuse, slow, stupid, thick-headed

thicken cake, clot, condense, congeal

thin *adj* fine, narrow; bony, lanky, lean, meagre, skinny, slender, slight, slim, spare; diluted, runny, watery, weak; deficient, meagre, scanty,

scarce, skimpy, sparse; delicate, filmy, fine, flimsy, sheer, unsubstantial

thing article, entity, item, object; affair, aspect, detail, facet, fact, factor, feature, idea, item, matter, point

think brood, cogitate, consider, deliberate, meditate, muse, ponder, reason, reflect; believe, conceive, conclude, consider, deem, esteem, estimate, guess *Inf, chiefly US & Canad,* imagine, judge, reckon, regard, suppose

thirst *n* dryness, thirstiness; appetite, craving, longing, passion, yearning

thorough careful, complete, conscientious, exhaustive, full, intensive, painstaking, scrupulous; absolute, complete, deep-dyed *usu derog,*

those *pron pl of* THAT

thou *pron Obs* the second person singular pronoun

though *conj* even if *~adv* nevertheless

thought *n* process, product of thinking; what one thinks; meditation **thoughtful** *adj* considerate; showing careful thought; reflective **thoughtless** *adj* inconsiderate; careless

thousand *n/adj* ten hundred **thousandth** *adj*

thrash *v* beat; defeat soundly; move in wild manner

thread *n* yarn; ridge cut on screw; theme *~v* put thread into; fit film etc. into machine; put on thread; pick (one's way etc.) **threadbare** *adj* worn, shabby; hackneyed

threat *n* declaration of intention to harm, injure etc.; dangerous person or thing **threaten** *v* make or be threat to

three *adj/n* one more than two **three-dimensional** *adj* having height, width and depth **three-ply** *adj* having three

layers or strands **threesome** *n* group of three

thresh *v* beat to separate grain from husks; thrash

threshold *n* bar of stone forming bottom of doorway; entrance; starting point

thrice *adv* three times

thrift *n* saving, economy **thrifty** *adj* economical

thrill *n* sudden sensation of excitement and pleasure *~v* (cause to) feel a thrill; tremble **thriller** *n* suspenseful book, film etc. **thrilling** *adj*

thrive *v* **thriving, throve** *or* **thrived, thriven** *or* **thrived** grow well; prosper

throat *n* front of neck; passage from mouth to stomach **throaty** *adj* hoarse; deep, guttural

throb *v* **throbbing, throbbed** quiver strongly, pulsate *~n* pulsation

throes *pl n* violent pangs, pain etc. **in the throes of** in the process of

thrombosis *n* clot in blood vessel or heart

downright, perfect, pure, sheer, total, utter

though *conj* allowing, even if, notwithstanding, tho' *US or poet,* while

thought cogitation, consideration, contemplation, deliberation, meditation, musing, reflection; belief, concept, idea, judgment, opinion, thinking, view

thoughtful attentive, caring, considerate, kind, solicitous; contemplative, meditative, musing, pensive, rapt, reflective, serious

thoughtless inconsiderate, insensitive, selfish, tactless; careless, foolish, heedless, mindless, silly, stupid, unthinking

thrash beat, belt *Inf,* birch, cane, clobber *Sl,* flog, leather, lick *Inf,* spank, whip; beat, clobber *Brit sl,* crush, defeat, lick *Inf,* run rings

around *Inf,* trounce

threadbare down at heel, frayed, old, shabby, worn, worn-out

threat intimidation, menace, warning

threaten endanger, jeopardize; browbeat, bully, cow, intimidate, menace

threshold door, doorway, entrance; beginning, brink, dawn, opening, outset, start

thrift carefulness, economy, saving

thrifty careful, economical, frugal, provident, saving, sparing

thrill *v* arouse, electrify, excite, move, stimulate, stir

thrilling exciting, gripping, sensational, stimulating, stirring

thrive bloom, boom, flourish, grow, increase, prosper, succeed

throb *v* beat, pound, pulsate, thump *~n* beat, pounding, pulsation, pulse, thumping

throne *n* ceremonial seat; power of sovereign

throng *n/v* crowd

throttle *n* device controlling amount of fuel entering engine ~*v* strangle; restrict

through *prep* from end to end; in consequence of; by means of ~*adv* from end to end; to the end ~*adj* completed; *Inf* finished; continuous; (of transport, traffic) not stopping **throughout** *adv/prep* in every part (of) **throughput** *n* quantity of material processed

throw *v* **throwing, threw, thrown** fling, cast; move, put abruptly, carelessly; cause to fall ~*n* act or distance of throwing **throwaway** *adj* designed to be discarded after use; done, said casually **throwback** *n* person, thing that reverts to earlier type

thrush *n* songbird

thrust *v* **thrusting, thrust** push, drive; stab ~*n* lunge, stab; propulsive force or power

thud *n* dull heavy sound ~*v* **thudding, thudded** make thud

thug *n* violent person

thumb *n* shortest, thickest finger of hand ~*v* handle with thumb; signal for lift in vehicle

thump *n* (sound of) dull heavy blow ~*v* strike heavily

thunder *n* loud noise accompanying lightning ~*v* make noise of or like thunder **thunderbolt, thunderclap** *n* lightning followed by thunder; anything unexpected

Thursday *n* fifth day of the week

thus *adv* in this way; therefore

thwart *v* foil, frustrate

thy *adj Obs* of or associated with you **thyself** *pron emphatic or reflexive form of* THOU

thyme *n* aromatic herb

thyroid gland gland controlling body growth

tiara *n* coronet

tibia *n* (*pl* **tibiae, tibias**) shinbone

tic *n* spasmodic twitch in muscles, esp. of face

tick[1] *n* slight tapping sound, as of watch movement; small mark (✓); *Inf* moment ~*v* mark with tick; make slight tapping sound

tick[2] *n* small insect-like parasite living on blood

ticket *n* card, paper entitling holder to admission, travel etc.; label ~*v* attach label to

tickle *v* touch, stroke (person etc.) to produce laughter etc.; amuse; itch ~*n* act, instance of this **ticklish** *adj* sensitive to tickling; requiring care

tiddler *n Inf* very small fish **tiddly** *adj* tiny; *Inf* slightly drunk

———————— THESAURUS ————————

through *prep* between, during, in, in the middle of, throughout; by means of, by way of, using, via ~*adj Inf* completed, done, ended, finished

throughout everywhere, the whole time

throw *v* cast, heave, hurl, pitch, send, shy, sling, toss ~*n* cast, fling, heave, pitch, shy, sling, toss

thrust *v* drive, force, jam, plunge, propel, push, ram, shove; jab, lunge, pierce, stab, stick ~*n* lunge, push, shove, stab; impetus, momentum

thug heavy *Sl*, hooligan, ruffian, tough

thump *n* bang, blow, knock, smack, thud, whack ~*v* bang, batter, beat, hit, knock, pound, strike

thunder *n* boom, crash, pealing, rumble, rumbling ~*v* boom, crash, peal, resound, reverberate, roar, rumble

thus like this, so; accordingly, consequently, ergo, hence, then, therefore

tick *n* click, tap; dash, mark, stroke ~*v* choose, indicate, mark, select; click, tap

ticket card, coupon, pass, slip, token,

tiddlywinks *pl n* game of trying to flip small plastic discs into cup

tide *n* rise and fall of sea happening twice each day **tidal** *adj* **tidal wave** great wave, esp. produced by earthquake **tide over** help someone for a while

tidings *pl n* news

tidy *adj* orderly, neat ~*v* put in order

tie *v* **tying, tied** fasten, bind; restrict; equal (score of) ~*n* that with which anything is bound; restraint; piece of material worn knotted round neck; connecting link; contest with equal scores; match, game in eliminating competition **tied** *adj* (of public house) selling beer etc. of only one brewer; (of cottage etc.) rented to tenant employed by owner

tier *n* row, rank, layer

tiff *n* petty quarrel

tiger *n* (*fem* **tigress**) large carnivorous feline animal

tight *adj* taut, tense; closely fitting; secure, firm; not allowing passage of water etc.; cramped; *Inf* mean; *Inf* drunk **tighten** *v* **tights** *pl n* one-piece clinging garment covering body from waist to feet **tightrope** *n* taut rope on

which acrobats perform

tile *n* flat piece of ceramic, plastic etc. used for roofs, floors etc. ~*v* cover with tiles

till[1] *prep/conj* until

till[2] *v* cultivate

till[3] *n* drawer for money in shop counter; cash register

tiller *n* lever to move rudder of boat

tilt *v* slope, slant; take part in medieval combat with lances; thrust (at) ~*n* slope; *Hist* combat for mounted men with lances

timber *n* wood for building etc.; trees

timbre *n* distinctive quality of voice or sound

time *n* past, present and future as continuous whole; hour; duration; period; point in duration; opportunity; occasion; leisure ~*v* choose time for; note time taken by **timeless** *adj* changeless, everlasting **timely** *adj* at appropriate time **timer** *n* person, device for recording or indicating time **time bomb** bomb designed to explode at prearranged time **time-lag** *n* period between cause and effect **timetable** *n* plan showing times of arrival and departure etc.

———— T H E S A U R U S ————

voucher; card, label, slip, sticker, tag

tide course, current, ebb, flow

tidy *adj* methodical, neat, orderly, shipshape, spruce, trim, well-ordered ~*v* neaten, order, straighten

tie *v* attach, bind, connect, fasten, join, rope, secure; bind, confine, hamper, hinder, limit, restrain ~*n* band, bond, cord, fastening, link, rope, string; affiliation, affinity, bond, connection, kinship, relationship; dead heat, deadlock, draw, stalemate

tier bank, rank, row, series

tight rigid, stretched, taut, tense; close, compact, snug; fast, firm, fixed, secure; impervious, proof,

sealed, sound, watertight; constricted, cramped, narrow; *Inf* close, mean, miserly stingy

tighten stretch, tense; fasten, screw, secure; close, cramp, narrow

till cultivate, dig, plough, work

tilt *v* cant, heel, lean, slant, slope, tip ~*n* angle, cant, incline, pitch, slant, slope

timber beams, boards, logs, planks, trees, wood

time *n* age, date, epoch, era, generation, hour, interval, period, season, spell, stretch, term; allotted span, day, duration, life, season ~*v* schedule, set; clock, count, measure

timeless abiding, ageless, changeless,

timid *adj* easily frightened; shy **timorous** *adj* timid; indicating fear

timpani, tympani *pl n* set of kettle-drums

tin *n* malleable metal; container made of tin ~*v* **tinning, tinned** put in tin, esp. for preserving **tinny** *adj* (of sound) thin, metallic **tinpot** *adj* Inf worthless

tinder *n* dry easily-burning material used to start fire

tinge *n* slight trace ~*v* colour, flavour slightly

tingle *v/n* (feel) thrill or pricking sensation

tinker *n* formerly, travelling mender of pots and pans ~*v* fiddle, meddle (with)

tinkle *v* (cause to) give out sounds like small bell ~*n* this sound or action

tinsel *n* glittering decorative metallic substance

tint *n* (shade of) colour; tinge ~*v* give tint to

tiny *adj* very small, minute

tip[1] *n* slender or pointed end of anything; small piece forming an extremity ~*v* **tipping, tipped** put a tip on

tip[2] *n* small present of money given for service rendered; helpful piece of information; *also* **tip-off** warning, hint ~*v* **tipping, tipped** reward with money; *also* **tip off** give tip to

tip[3] *v* **tipping, tipped** tilt, upset; touch lightly; topple over ~*n* place where rubbish is dumped

tipple *v* drink (alcohol) habitually ~*n* drink

tipsy *adj* (slightly) drunk

tiptoe *v* walk on ball of foot and toes; walk softly

tiptop *adj* of the best quality or condition

tirade *n* long angry speech or denunciation

tire *v* reduce energy of, weary; bore; become tired, bored **tired** *adj* weary; hackneyed **tireless** *adj* not tiring easily **tiresome** *adj* irritating, tedious **tiring** *adj*

tissue *n* substance of animal body, plant; soft paper handkerchief

tit *n* small bird

titanic *adj* huge, epic

titanium *n* light metallic element

titbit *n* tasty morsel of food; scrap (of

———— **THESAURUS** ————

deathless, endless, enduring, eternal, everlasting, immortal, lasting, permanent, undying

timely convenient, opportune, prompt, punctual, seasonable

timetable curriculum, list, programme, schedule

timid afraid, bashful, cowardly, fearful, nervous, retiring, shy

tingle *v* itch, prickle, sting, tickle ~*n* itch, itching, prickling, stinging, tickling

tinker *v* dabble, meddle, play, toy

tint *n* cast, colour, hue, shade, tone ~*v* colour, dye, rinse, stain

tiny diminutive, little, minute, pygmy *or* pigmy, slight, small, teensy-weensy, teeny-weeny, wee

tip[1] apex, crown, end, head, peak, point, top

tip[2] *n* hint, pointer, suggestion *also* **tip-off** forecast, hint, warning, word ~*v* remunerate, reward *also* **tip off** advise, caution, warn

tip[3] *v* cant, incline, lean, slant, spill, tilt, upset

tire drain, exhaust, fail, flag, weary

tired drained, drowsy, exhausted, fatigued, sleepy, spent, weary, worn out

tireless determined, energetic, industrious, resolute, vigorous

tiresome dull, exasperating, flat, laborious, tedious, trying, wearing, wearisome

tiring arduous, fatiguing, strenuous,

scandal etc.)

tithe *n* (esp. formerly) tenth part of income, paid to church as tax ~*v* exact tithes from

titillate *v* stimulate agreeably

title *n* name of book; heading; name, esp. denoting rank; legal right or document proving it; *Sport* championship

titter *v/n* snigger, giggle

titular *adj* pert. to title; nominal

TNT *see* TRINITROTOLUENE

to *prep* denoting direction, destination; introducing comparison, indirect object, infinitive etc. ~*adv* to fixed position **to and fro** back and forth

toad *n* animal like large frog **toady** *n* servile flatterer ~*v* be ingratiating **toadstool** *n* fungus like mushroom

toast *n* slice of bread browned on both sides by heat; tribute, proposal of health etc. marked by people drinking together; person or thing so toasted ~*v* make (bread etc.) crisp and brown; drink toast to; warm at fire **toaster** *n* electrical device for toasting bread

tobacco *n* (*pl* **-cos**) plant with leaves used for smoking **tobacconist** *n* one who sells tobacco products

toboggan *n* sledge for sliding down slope of snow

today *n* this day ~*adv* on this day; nowadays

toddle *v* walk with unsteady short steps **toddler** *n* young child beginning to walk

to-do *n* (*pl* **-dos**) *Inf* fuss, commotion

toe *n* digit of foot; anything resembling this **toe the line** conform

toffee *n* chewy sweet made of boiled sugar etc.

toga *n* garment worn in ancient Rome

together *adv* in company; simultaneously

toggle *n* small peg fixed crosswise on cord etc. and used for fastening

toil *n* heavy work or task ~*v* labour

toilet *n* lavatory; process of washing, dressing; articles used for this **toiletries** *pl n* objects, cosmetics used for cleaning or grooming

token *n* sign, symbol; disc used as money; gift card, voucher exchangeable for goods ~*adj* nominal

——————— THESAURUS ———————

tough, wearing

titbit dainty, delicacy, goody, juicy bit, morsel, snack, treat

title *n* caption, heading, label; name; designation, epithet, name, nickname, pseudonym, term; claim, entitlement, ownership, privilege, right

toady *n* hanger-on, lackey, parasite, sycophant, yes man ~*v* crawl, creep, flatter, grovel

together closely, in concert, in unison, jointly, mutually; concurrently, en masse, in unison, simultaneously

toil *n* drudgery, effort, exertion, hard work, industry, labour, pains, slog, sweat ~*v* break one's neck *Inf,* drudge, labour, slave, slog, strive, struggle, work

toilet bathroom, can *US & Canad sl,* closet, convenience, john *Sl, chiefly US & Canad,* latrine, lavatory, loo, outhouse, privy, urinal, washroom, W.C.; ablutions, bathing, dressing, grooming, toilette

token *n* badge, mark, proof, sign, symbol ~*adj* nominal, superficial, symbolic

tolerable acceptable, bearable, endurable, supportable; acceptable, adequate, average, fair, middling, O.K. *or* okay *Inf,* ordinary, unexceptional

tolerance charity, magnanimity, patience, sympathy; endurance, fortitude, resilience, resistance, stamina, toughness

tolerant charitable, fair, liberal,

tolerate *v* put up with; permit **tolerable** *adj* bearable; fair **tolerance** *n* **tolerant** *adj* forbearing; broad-minded **toleration** *n*

toll¹ *v* ring (bell) slowly at regular intervals ~*n* ringing

toll² *n* tax, esp. for use of bridge or road; loss, damage

tom *n* male cat

tomahawk *n* fighting axe of N Amer. Indians

tomato *n* (*pl* **-toes**) plant with red fruit; the fruit

tomb *n* grave; monument over one **tombstone** *n*

tombola *n* lottery with tickets drawn from revolving drum

tomboy *n* girl who acts, dresses like boy

tome *n* large book

tomfoolery *n* foolish behaviour

tomorrow *adv/n* (on) the day after today

tom-tom *n* drum beaten with hands

ton *n* (*also* **long ton**) measure of weight, 1016 kg (2240 lbs.); *US* (*also* **short ton**) measure of weight, 907 kg (2000 lbs.) **tonnage** *n* carrying capacity of ship

tone *n* quality of musical sound, voice, colour etc.; general character ~*v* blend, harmonize (with) **tone-**

deaf *adj* unable to perceive subtle differences in pitch

tongs *pl n* apparatus for handling coal, sugar etc.

tongue *n* organ inside mouth, used for speech, taste etc.; language, speech

tonic *n* medicine etc. with invigorating effect; *Mus* first note of scale ~*adj* invigorating, restorative **tonic water** mineral water oft. containing quinine

tonight *n* this (coming) night ~*adv* on this night

tonne *n* metric ton, 1000 kg

tonsil *n* gland in throat **tonsillitis** *n* inflammation of tonsils

tonsure *n* shaving of part of head as religious practice; part shaved

too *adv* also, in addition; overmuch

tool *n* implement or appliance for mechanical operations; means to an end ~*v* work on with tool

toot *n* short sound of horn, trumpet etc.

tooth *n* (*pl* **teeth**) bonelike projection in gums of upper and lower jaws of vertebrates; prong, cog **toothless** *adj* **toothpaste** *n* paste used to clean teeth **toothpick** *n* small stick for removing food from between teeth

top¹ *n* highest part, summit; highest rank; first in merit; garment for upper

——————— THESAURUS ———————

open-minded, patient, unbigoted, unprejudiced; indulgent, lenient, permissive, soft

tolerate abide, bear, endure, stand, stomach, suffer, swallow, take; accept, allow, permit, stand for

toll¹ *v/n* chime, clang, knell, peal, ring

toll² *n* charge, customs, duty, fee, levy, payment, rate, tariff, tax; cost, damage, inroad, loss

tomb crypt, grave, sepulchre, vault

tombstone gravestone, headstone, memorial, monument

tone *n* modulation, pitch, sound, tim-

bre; air, aspect, attitude, character, manner, mood, note, quality, spirit, style, temper, vein; cast, colour, hue, shade, tinge, tint ~*v* blend, go well with, harmonize, match, suit

tongue dialect, idiom, language, speech, talk, vernacular

tonic cordial, refresher, stimulant

too also, as well, besides, further, likewise, moreover, to boot; excessively, extremely, unduly

tool *n* appliance, contrivance, device, gadget, implement, instrument, utensil; agent, means, medium,

part of body; lid, stopper of bottle etc. ~*adj* highest in position, rank ~*v* **topping, topped** cut off, pass, reach, surpass top; provide top for **topmost** *adj* highest **topping** *n* sauce or garnish for food **top brass** important officials **top hat** man's tall cylindrical hat **top-heavy** *adj* unbalanced **top-notch** *adj* excellent, first-class **topsoil** *n* surface layer of soil

top² *n* toy which spins on tapering point

topaz *n* precious stone of various colours

topiary *n* trimming trees, bushes into decorative shapes

topic *n* subject of discourse, conversation etc. **topical** *adj* up-to-date, having news value

topography *n* (description of) surface features of a place **topographic** *adj*

topple *v* (cause to) fall over

topsy-turvy *adj* in confusion

tor *n* high rocky hill

torch *n* portable hand light containing electric battery; burning wooden shaft; any apparatus burning with hot flame

toreador *n* bullfighter

torment *v* torture in body or mind; afflict; tease ~*n* suffering, agony of body or mind; pest **tormentor, -er** *n*

tornado *n* (*pl* **-does, -dos**) whirlwind; violent storm

torpedo *n* (*pl* **-does**) self-propelled underwater missile with explosive warhead ~*v* strike with torpedo

torpid *adj* sluggish, apathetic **torpor** *n* torpid state

torrent *n* rushing stream; downpour **torrential** *adj*

torrid *adj* parched; highly emotional

torsion *n* twist, twisting

torso *n* (*pl* **-sos**) (statue of) body without head or limbs

tortilla *n* thin Mexican pancake

tortoise *n* four-footed reptile covered with shell of horny plates **tortoise-shell** *n* mottled brown shell of turtle

tortuous *adj* winding, twisting; involved, not straightforward

torture *n* infliction of severe pain ~*v* inflict severe pain

Tory *n* member of conservative political party

toss *v* throw up, about; be thrown, fling oneself about ~*n* tossing

———————— T H E S A U R U S ————————

vehicle

top *n* apex, crest, crown, head, height, peak, pinnacle, summit, vertex; head, lead; cap, cork, cover, lid ~*v* beat, best, better, outdo, surpass ~*adj* crowning, highest, superior, topmost, upper; best, chief, elite, finest, first, greatest, head, lead, prime, principal, ruling, sovereign, superior

topic issue, matter, point, subject, theme

topical current, popular, up-to-date

topple fall, fall headlong, fall over, keel over, knock down, overbalance, overturn, tip over, upset

topsy-turvy chaotic, confused, disorderly, inside-out, jumbled, messy, untidy

torment *v* agonize, distress, harrow, pain, rack, torture; aggravate *Inf*, annoy, harass, hassle *Inf*, persecute, pester, trouble ~*n* agony, anguish, distress, hell, misery, pain, suffering, torture; hassle *Inf*, nuisance, pest, plague, scourge, trouble

tornado cyclone, gale, typhoon, whirlwind

torrent flood, flow, gush, rush, spate, stream

torture *v* agonize, distress, pain, persecute, torment ~*n* agony, anguish, distress, hell, misery, pain, suffering, torment

toss *v* cast, fling, hurl, pitch, shy,

tot¹ *n* very small child; small quantity, esp. of drink

tot² *v* **totting, totted** add (up); amount to

total *n* whole amount; sum ~*adj* complete, absolute ~*v* **totalling, totalled** amount to; add up **totality** *n* **totally** *adv*

totalitarian *adj* of dictatorial, one-party government

totem *n* tribal badge or emblem **totem pole** carved post of Amer. Indians

totter *v* walk unsteadily; begin to fall

toucan *n* large-billed tropical Amer. bird

touch *v* come into contact with; put hand on; reach; affect emotions of; deal with; (*with* on) refer to ~*n* sense by which qualities of object etc. are perceived by touching; touching; characteristic manner or ability; slight contact, amount etc. **touching**

adj emotionally moving ~*prep* concerning **touchy** *adj* easily offended **touch down** (of aircraft) land **touchline** *n* side line of pitch in some games **touchstone** *n* criterion

touché *interj* acknowledgment that remark or blow has struck target

tough *adj* strong; able to bear hardship, strain; strict; difficult; needing effort to chew; violent ~*n Inf* rough, violent person **toughen** *v*

toupee *n* wig

tour *n* travelling round; journey to one place after another ~*v* make tour **tourism** *n* **tourist** *n*

tournament *n* competition, contest usu. with several stages

tourniquet *n* bandage, surgical instrument to stop bleeding

tousled *adj* ruffled

tout *v* solicit custom ~*n* person who sells tickets at inflated prices

tow *v* drag along behind, esp. at end

———————— THESAURUS ————————

sling, throw ~*n* cast, fling, pitch, shy, throw

tot *v* add up, calculate, count up, reckon, tally, total

total *n* all, amount, entirety, mass, sum, whole ~*adj* all-out, complete, consummate, deep-dyed *usu derog*, downright, entire, full, outright, perfect, sheer, thorough, unqualified, utter ~*v* add up, amount to, reach, reckon

totally absolutely, completely, entirely, fully, perfectly, quite, thoroughly, unconditionally, utterly, whole-heartedly, wholly

totter stagger, stumble, sway, teeter, walk unsteadily

touch *v* brush, caress, feel, finger, fondle, handle, stroke; affect, melt, move, soften, stir ~*n* feel, feeling; brush, caress, contact, pat, stroke; approach, manner, method, style, way; ability, adroitness, artistry, flair,

knack, mastery, skill, virtuosity; bit, dash, drop, hint, jot, pinch, speck, spot, taste, trace

touching affecting, melting, moving, stirring

touchy bad-tempered, cross, easily offended, grouchy *Inf*, grumpy, irascible, irritable, oversensitive, quick-tempered, ratty *Brit & NZ inf*, testy

tough *adj* durable, firm, hard, leathery, solid, stiff, strong, sturdy; brawny, hardy, stout, strong, sturdy; firm, resolute, severe, stern, strict, unbending; difficult, hard, knotty, thorny, uphill; rough, ruffianly, vicious, violent ~*n Inf* brute, heavy *Sl*, ruffian, thug

tour *n* excursion, journey, outing, trip; circuit, course, round ~*v* explore, holiday in, journey, sightsee, visit

tourist holiday-maker, sightseer, traveller

of rope ~*n* towing or being towed
towpath *n* path beside canal or river
towards *prep* (*also* **toward**) in direction of; with regard to; as contribution to
towel *n* cloth for wiping off moisture after washing
tower *n* tall strong structure, esp. part of church etc.; fortress ~*v* stand very high; loom (over)
town *n* collection of dwellings etc. larger than village and smaller than city **township** *n* small town
toxic *adj* poisonous; due to poison **toxicity** *n* strength of a poison **toxin** *n* poison
toy *n* something designed to be played with ~*adj* very small ~*v* trifle **toy boy** much younger lover of older woman
trace *n* track left by anything; indication; minute quantity ~*v* follow course of; find out; make plan of; draw or copy exactly **tracing paper** transparent paper placed over drawing, map etc. to enable exact copy to be taken
trachea *n* (*pl* **tracheae**) windpipe
track *n* mark left by passage of anything; path; rough road; course; rail-

way line; jointed metal band as on tank etc.; separate song, piece on record ~*v* follow trail or path of **track events** athletic sports held on running track **track record** past accomplishments **tracksuit** *n* loose-fitting suit worn by athletes etc.
tract[1] *n* wide expanse, area
tract[2] *n* pamphlet, esp. religious one
traction *n* action of pulling
tractor *n* motor vehicle for hauling, pulling etc.
trade *n* commerce, business; skilled craft; exchange ~*v* engage in trade **trader** *n* **trade-in** *n* used article given in part payment for new **trademark**, **trade name** *n* distinctive legal mark on maker's goods **trade-off** *n* exchange made as compromise **tradesman** *n* dealer; skilled worker **trade union** society of workers for protection of their interests
tradition *n* unwritten body of beliefs, facts etc. handed down from generation to generation; custom, practice of long standing **traditional** *adj*
traffic *n* vehicles passing to and fro in street, town etc.; (illicit) trade ~*v* **trafficking, trafficked** trade **traffic**

——————— THESAURUS ———————

tow *v* drag, haul, lug, pull, trail, tug
towards almost, nearing, nearly; about, concerning, for, regarding; for, to
tower *n* castle, citadel, fort, keep, refuge, stronghold ~*v* loom, overlook, rear, rise, soar, top
toxic harmful, noxious, poisonous, septic
trace *n* evidence, mark, record, remnant, sign, token; bit, dash, drop, hint, shadow, suggestion, touch ~*v* detect, determine, discover, find, follow, pursue, seek, track, trail, unearth; chart, copy, draw, map, outline, sketch
track *n* footmark, footprint, footstep,

mark, path, scent, trace, trail, wake; course, line, path, pathway, road, track, way ~*v* chase, dog, follow, pursue, trace, trail
trade *n* barter, business, commerce, dealing, exchange, traffic, truck; business, calling, craft, job, line, occupation, profession, skill; deal, exchange, swap ~*v* bargain, barter, deal, exchange, peddle, traffic; exchange, swap, switch
tradesman dealer, merchant, purveyor, seller, shopkeeper, supplier, vendor; craftsman, workman
tradition custom, customs, habit, institution, ritual
traditional conventional, customary,

lights set of coloured lights at road junctions etc.
tragedy *n* sad event; dramatic, literary work dealing with serious, sad topic **tragedian** *n* actor in, writer of tragedies **tragic** *adj* of, in manner of tragedy; disastrous; appalling
trail *v* drag behind one; lag behind; track, pursue ~*n* track or trace; rough path **trailer** *n* vehicle towed by another vehicle
train *v* educate, instruct, cause to grow in particular way; follow course of training; aim (gun etc.) ~*n* line of railway vehicles joined to locomotive; succession, esp. of thoughts etc.; procession; trailing part of dress **trainee** *n* one training to be skilled worker **trainer** *n* **training** *n*
traipse *v* walk wearily
trait *n* characteristic feature
traitor *n* one who is guilty of treason **traitorous** *adj*
trajectory *n* line of flight

tram *n* vehicle running on rails laid on roadway
tramp *v* travel on foot; walk heavily ~*n* (homeless) person who travels about on foot; walk; cargo ship without fixed route
trample *v* tread on and crush under foot
trampoline *n* tough canvas sheet stretched horizontally with elastic cords etc. to frame
trance *n* unconscious or dazed state; state of ecstasy or total absorption
tranche *n* portion
tranquil *adj* calm, quiet; serene **tranquillity** *n* **tranquillize** *v* make calm **tranquillizer** *n* drug which induces calm state
trans- *comb. form* across, through, beyond
transact *v* carry through; negotiate **transaction** *n* performing of business; single sale or purchase; *pl* proceedings

——————— THESAURUS ———————

established, fixed
traffic *n* transport, vehicles; barter, business, commerce, dealing, exchange, trade, truck ~*v* barter, deal, exchange, market, peddle, trade
tragedy affliction, calamity, disaster, misfortune
tragic appalling, awful, catastrophic, dire, disastrous, dreadful, grievous, miserable, pathetic, sad, shocking, unfortunate, woeful, wretched
trail *v* drag, draw, haul, pull, tow; dawdle, follow, lag, loiter, straggle; chase, follow, hunt, pursue, trace, track ~*n* footsteps, mark, path, scent, trace, track, wake; beaten track, footpath, path, road, route, track, way
train *v* coach, educate, guide, instruct, school, teach, tutor; aim, direct, level, point ~*n* chain, course, order, series, set, string; caravan, convoy, procession

training discipline, education, guidance, instruction, tuition, upbringing; exercise, practice, preparation
trait attribute, feature, mannerism, quality, quirk
traitor betrayer, deceiver, informer, quisling, turncoat
tramp *v* hike, march, slog, trek, walk; march, plod, stamp, toil, trudge ~*n* bag lady *chiefly US*, bum *Inf*, vagabond, vagrant; hike, march, slog, trek
trample crush, squash, stamp, tread
trance daze, dream, rapture, reverie, spell, stupor
tranquil calm, composed, peaceful, placid, quiet, restful, serene, still
tranquillity calm, calmness, composure, peace, peacefulness, placidity, quiet, quietness, restfulness, serenity, stillness
transaction affair, bargain, business, deal, deed, matter, proceeding,

transcend v rise above; surpass **transcendence** n **transcendent** adj **transcendental** adj surpassing experience; supernatural; abstruse **transcendentalism** n

transcribe v copy out; record for later broadcast **transcript** n copy

transfer v -ferring, -ferred move, send from one person, place etc. to another ~n removal of person or thing from one place to another **transference** n transfer

transfigure v alter appearance of

transfix v astound, stun; pierce through

transform v change shape, character of **transformation** n **transformer** n Electricity apparatus for changing voltage

transfuse v convey from one to another, esp. blood from healthy to ill person **transfusion** n

transgress v break (law); sin **transgression** n

transient adj fleeting, not permanent

transistor n Electronics small, semiconducting device used to amplify electric currents; portable radio using transistors

transit n passage, crossing **transition** n change from one state to another **transitive** adj (of verb) requiring direct object **transitory** adj not lasting long

translate v turn from one language into another; interpret **translation** n **translator** n

translucent adj letting light pass through, semitransparent

transmit v -mitting, -mitted send, cause to pass to another place, person etc.; send out (signals) by means of radio waves **transmission** n transmitting; gears by which power is communicated from engine to road wheels

transmute v change in form, properties or nature

transparent adj letting light pass without distortion; that can be seen through **transparency** n quality of being transparent; photographic slide

transpire v become known; Inf happen; (of plants) give off water vapour through leaves

transplant v move and plant again in another place; transfer organ surgically ~n surgical transplanting of

———— T H E S A U R U S ————

undertaking

transcend eclipse, exceed, excel, go above, go beyond, leave behind, outdo, outshine, outstrip, surpass

transcribe copy, reproduce, rewrite

transfer v carry, change, convey, move, shift, transport, turn over ~n change, handover, move, shift

transform alter, change, make over, remodel

transformation change, conversion

transient brief, fleeting, momentary, passing, short, temporary

transit n carriage, crossing, passage, shipment, travel

transition change, conversion, passage, passing, shift

transitional changing, fluid, passing

translate convert, decode, transcribe; explain, interpret, paraphrase, simplify

translation decoding, gloss, paraphrase, version; paraphrase, simplification

transmission broadcasting, relaying, sending, showing; broadcast, programme

transmit broadcast, radio, relay, send, send out

transparent clear, diaphanous, filmy, limpid, translucent; apparent, evident, manifest, obvious, patent, plain, visible

transpire Inf arise, befall, chance,

organ
transport v convey from one place to
another; deport ~n system of conveyance; vehicle used for this **transporta-
tion** n transporting; *Hist* deportation
to penal colony
transpose v change order of; put music into different key
transverse adj lying across; at right
angles
transvestite n person who wears
clothes of opposite sex
trap n device for catching game etc.;
anything planned to deceive, betray
etc.; arrangement of pipes to prevent
escape of gas; movable opening ~v
trapping, trapped catch; trick **trapper**
n one who traps animals for their fur
trapdoor n door in floor or roof
trapeze n horizontal bar suspended
from two ropes for acrobatics etc.
trapezium n four-sided figure with
two parallel sides of unequal length
trappings pl n equipment, ornaments
trash n rubbish; nonsense
trauma n emotional shock; injury,
wound **traumatic** adj **traumatize** v
travail v/n labour, toil

travel v -elling, -elled go, move from
one place to another ~n act of travelling; pl (account of) travelling **traveller** n **travelogue** n film etc. about
travels
traverse v cross, go through or over
~n traversing; path across
travesty n grotesque imitation ~v
-estying, -estied make, be a travesty
of
trawl v fish at deep levels with net
dragged behind boat **trawler** n trawl-
ing boat
tray n flat board, usu. with rim, for
carrying things
treachery n deceit, betrayal **treacherous** adj disloyal; unsafe
treacle n thick syrup produced when
sugar is refined
tread v treading, trod, trodden or trod
walk; trample (on) ~n treading; fashion of walking; upper surface of step;
part of tyre which makes contact with
ground **treadmill** n dreary routine
treadle n lever worked by foot to turn
wheel
treason n violation by subject of allegiance to sovereign or state; treachery

———————— THESAURUS ————————

happen, occur
transport v bear, bring, carry, convey, fetch, move, ship, take, transfer;
banish, deport, exile ~n conveyance,
vehicle; carriage, conveyance, shipment, shipping
transpose change, exchange, reor-
der, swap *Inf,* switch
trap n ambush, net, pitfall, snare; device, ruse ~v ambush, catch, corner,
ensnare, snare; deceive, dupe, ensnare, trick
trappings adornments, dress, equipment, finery, fittings, fixtures, gear
trash garbage, junk *Inf,* litter, refuse,
rubbish; balderdash, bosh *Inf,* bunkum *or* buncombe *chiefly US,* crap *Sl,*
drivel, garbage *Inf,* hogwash, hot air

Inf, nonsense, rot, rubbish, tripe *Inf,*
twaddle
traumatic damaging, disturbing,
painful, scarring, shocking, upset-
ting, wounding
travel go, journey, move, proceed,
progress, tour, voyage
traveller explorer, gypsy, nomad,
tourist, voyager, wayfarer
treacherous deceitful, disloyal, faithless, false, perfidious, unfaithful, unreliable, untrue; dangerous, hazardous, perilous, risky, tricky, unsafe
treachery betrayal, disloyalty, duplicity, infidelity
tread v pace, plod, stamp, step,
tramp, walk; squash, trample ~n
footstep, gait, pace, step, walk

treasure n riches; valued person or thing ~v prize, cherish **treasurer** n official in charge of funds **treasury** n place for treasure; government department in charge of finance **treasure-trove** n treasure found with no evidence of ownership

treat n pleasure, entertainment given ~v deal with, act towards; give medical treatment to; provide with treat **treatment** n method of counteracting disease; act or mode of treating

treatise n formal essay

treaty n signed contract between states etc.

treble adj threefold; Mus high-pitched ~n soprano voice ~v increase threefold

tree n large perennial plant with woody trunk

trek n long difficult journey ~v **trekking, trekked** make trek

trellis n lattice or grating of light bars

tremble v quiver, shake; feel fear ~n involuntary shaking

tremendous adj vast, immense; Inf exciting; Inf excellent

tremor n quiver; shaking

tremulous adj quivering slightly

trench n long narrow ditch **trench coat** double-breasted waterproof coat

trenchant adj cutting, incisive

trend n direction, tendency; fashion **trendy** adj Inf consciously fashionable

trepidation n fear, anxiety

trespass v intrude on property etc. of another ~n wrongful entering on another's land; wrongdoing **trespasser** n

tress n long lock of hair

trestle n board fixed on pairs of spreading legs

trews pl n close-fitting tartan trousers

tri- comb. form three

trial n test, examination; Law investigation of case before judge; thing, person that strains endurance or patience

triangle n figure with three angles

——————— THESAURUS ———————

treasure n gold, jewels, riches, valuables ~v adore, cherish, esteem, love, prize, value

treasury bank, cache, hoard, store, vault

treat n banquet, entertainment, feast, party; delight, enjoyment, fun, joy, pleasure ~v deal with, handle, manage, use; attend to, care for, doctor, nurse; buy for, give, lay on, pay for, provide, regale

treatise dissertation, essay, paper, study, thesis, tract, work

treatment care, cure, healing, medicine, remedy; conduct, dealing, handling, reception, usage

treaty agreement, alliance, compact, concordat, contract, covenant, pact

trek n hike, journey, march, slog, tramp ~v hike, journey, march, plod, slog, tramp

tremble v quake, quiver, shake, shiver, shudder, teeter, totter, vibrate ~n quake, quiver, shake, shiver, shudder, trembling, tremor, vibration

tremendous colossal, enormous, great, huge, immense, monstrous, towering, vast; Inf amazing, brilliant, excellent, exceptional, great, incredible, marvellous, sensational Inf, super, wonderful

tremor quaking, quiver, shaking, shiver, trembling, vibration

trench channel, ditch, drain, furrow, gutter, pit

trend bias, course, current, drift, leaning, tendency; craze, fashion, mode, rage, style, thing, vogue

trespass v encroach, intrude ~n encroachment, intrusion

trial n audition, check, experiment, probation, proof, test, testing; con-

triangular *adj*

tribe *n* race; subdivision of race of people **tribal** *adj*

tribulation *n* trouble, affliction

tribunal *n* lawcourt; body appointed to inquire into specific matter

tributary *n* stream flowing into another

tribute *n* sign of honour; tax paid by one state to another

trice *n* moment, instant

trick *n* deception; prank; feat of skill or cunning; knack; cards played in one round ~*v* deceive, cheat **trickery** *n* **trickster** *n* **tricky** *adj* difficult

trickle *v* (cause to) run, flow, move in thin stream or drops ~*n* trickling flow

tricolour *n* three-coloured striped flag

tricycle *n* three-wheeled cycle

trident *n* three-pronged spear

trifle *n* insignificant thing or matter; small amount; pudding of sponge cake, whipped cream etc. ~*v* toy (with)

trigger *n* catch which releases spring, esp. to fire gun ~*v* (*oft. with* **off**) set in action etc. **trigger-happy** *adj* tending to be irresponsible

trigonometry *n* branch of mathematics dealing with relations of sides and angles of triangles

trilby *n* man's soft felt hat

trill *v/n* (sing, play with) rapid alternation between two close notes

trillion *n* one million million, 10^{12}; *Obs* one million million million, 10^{18}

trilogy *n* series of three related (literary) works

trim *adj* neat, smart; slender; in good order ~*v* **trimming, trimmed** shorten slightly by cutting; prune; decorate; adjust ~*n* decoration; order, state of being trim **trimming** *n* (*oft. pl*) decoration, addition

trinitrotoluene *n* powerful explosive

trinity *n* the state of being threefold; (*with cap.*) state of God as three persons, Father, Son and Holy Spirit

trinket *n* small ornament

trio *n* (*pl* **trios**) group of three; music for three parts

trip *n* (short) journey for pleasure; stumble; *Inf* hallucinatory experience caused by drug ~*v* **tripping, tripped** (cause to) stumble; (cause to) make mistake; run lightly

——————— THESAURUS ———————

test, hearing, litigation, tribunal; adversity, affliction, burden, hardship, load, ordeal, pain, suffering, tribulation, trouble; bother, drag *Inf*, irritation, nuisance, pest, vexation

tribe blood, clan, class, family, people, race, stock

tribute acknowledgment, applause, compliment, honour, praise, recognition, respect; charge, homage, offering, payment, tax

trick *n* artifice, deceit, deception, device, dodge, fraud, ploy, ruse, scam *Sl*, stratagem, swindle, trap; hoax, jape, joke, prank, stunt; art, gift, knack, secret, skill, technique ~*v* cheat, deceive, delude, dupe, fool, hoax, mislead, trap

trickery cheating, con *Inf*, deceit, deception, double-dealing, fraud, hoax, swindling

trickle *v* drip, drop, exude, ooze, seep ~*n* dribble, drip, seepage

tricky complicated, delicate, difficult

trifle *n* nothing, triviality; bit, jot, little, spot, touch, trace ~*v* amuse oneself, play, toy

trim *adj* dapper, neat, orderly, smart, spruce, tidy, well turned-out; fit, shapely, sleek, slender, slim, streamlined ~*v* clip, crop, cut, pare, prune, tidy; adorn, array, bedeck, decorate, dress, embellish, garnish, ornament

trimming adornment, decoration, embellishment; *pl* accessories, extras, frills, garnish, trappings

tripe *n* stomach of cow as food; *Inf* nonsense

triple *adj* threefold ~*v* treble **triplet** *n* one of three offspring born at one birth

triplicate *adj* threefold ~*n* state of being triplicate; one of set of three copies

tripod *n* stool, stand etc. with three feet

trite *adj* hackneyed, banal

triumph *n* great success; victory; exultation ~*v* achieve great success or victory; rejoice over victory **triumphal** *adj* **triumphant** *adj*

trivia *pl n* petty, unimportant things **trivial** *adj* of little consequence **triviality** *n*

troll *n* giant or dwarf in Scandinavian mythology and folklore

trolley *n* small wheeled table for food and drink; wheeled cart for moving goods etc.; *US* tram

trollop *n* promiscuous woman

trombone *n* deep-toned brass instrument **trombonist** *n*

troop *n* group of persons; *pl* soldiers ~*v* move in troop **trooper** *n* cavalry soldier

trophy *n* prize, award

tropic *n* either of two lines of latitude N and S of equator; *pl* area of earth's surface between these lines **tropical** *adj* pert. to, within tropics; (of climate) very hot

trot *v* trotting, trotted (of horse) move at medium pace; (of person) run easily with short strides ~*n* trotting, jog **trotter** *n* horse trained to trot in race; foot of pig etc.

troubadour *n* medieval travelling poet and singer

trouble *n* state or cause of mental distress, pain, inconvenience etc.; care ~*v* be trouble to; be inconvenienced, be agitated; take pains **troublesome** *adj* **troubleshooter** *n* person employed to deal with problems

——————— T H E S A U R U S ———————

trip *n* excursion, expedition, jaunt, journey, outing, run, tour, travel, voyage ~*v* blunder, err, fall, lapse, slip, stumble, tumble

trite banal, commonplace, hackneyed, routine, stale, stock, tired

triumph *n* accomplishment, achievement, attainment, coup, feat, success, victory; exultation, joy, rejoicing ~*v* celebrate, exult, gloat, glory, rejoice, revel

triumphant conquering, dominant, successful, victorious

trivia details, minutiae, petty details, trivialities

trivial inconsequential, inconsiderable, insignificant, little, meaningless, minor, negligible, paltry, petty, slight, small, trifling, unimportant

troop *n* band, body, company, crowd, gang, group, horde, multitude, squad, team, unit; *pl* armed forces,

army, men, military, soldiers ~*v* crowd, flock, march, parade, stream, swarm

trophy award, cup, laurels, prize

tropical hot, humid, steamy, sultry, torrid

trot *v* canter, jog, lope, run ~*n* brisk pace, canter, jog, lope

trouble *n* anxiety, distress, hardship, misfortune, pain, sorrow, suffering, vexation, woe, worry; discord, disorder, disturbance, hassle *Inf,* row, strife, tumult; ailment, complaint, defect, disease, disorder, illness; danger, difficulty, dilemma, mess, problem, spot *Inf,* tight spot; bother, care, effort, exertion, labour, pains, work ~*v* afflict, annoy, bother, distress, disturb, fret, harass, hassle *Inf,* pain, perturb, pester, plague, torment, upset, vex, worry; bother, burden, incommode, inconvenience, put out

trough n long open vessel, esp. for animals' food or water; hollow between waves

trounce v beat thoroughly, thrash

troupe n company of performers **trouper** n

trousers pl n garment covering legs

trousseau n bride's outfit of clothing

trout n freshwater fish

trowel n small tool like spade

truant n one absent without leave **truancy** n

truce n temporary cessation of fighting

truck¹ n wheeled (motor) vehicle for moving goods

truck² n dealing, esp. in **have no truck with**

truculent adj aggressive, defiant

trudge v walk laboriously ~n tiring walk

true adj in accordance with facts; faithful; correct; genuine **truism** n self-evident truth **truly** adv **truth** n state of being true; something that is true **truthful** adj accustomed to speak the truth; accurate

truffle n edible underground fungus; sweet flavoured with chocolate

trump n card of suit ranking above others ~v play trump **trump up** invent, concoct

trumpet n metal wind instrument like horn ~v blow trumpet; make sound like one; proclaim **trumpeter** n

truncate v cut short

truncheon n short thick club

trundle v move heavily, as on small wheels

trunk n main stem of tree; person's body excluding head and limbs; box for clothes etc.; elephant's snout; pl man's swimming costume **trunk call** long-distance telephone call **trunk road** main road

truss v fasten up, tie up ~n support; medical supporting device

trust n confidence; firm belief; reliance; combination of business firms; care; property held for another ~v rely on; believe in; expect, hope; consign for care **trustee** n one legally holding property for another **trustful**, **trusting** adj **trustworthy** adj **trusty** adj

try v **trying**, **tried** attempt; test, sample; afflict; examine in court of law ~n attempt, effort; *Rugby* score gained by touching ball down over opponent's goal line **tried** adj proved **trying** adj troublesome

tryst n arrangement to meet, esp.

——————— THESAURUS ———————

troublesome annoying, bothersome, difficult, hard, taxing, tiresome, wearisome; disorderly, rowdy, turbulent, uncooperative, undisciplined, unruly, violent

truce armistice, break, ceasefire, interval, lull, respite

trudge v plod, slog, stump, tramp ~n footslog, haul, slog, tramp

true adj accurate, actual, authentic, bona fide, correct, exact, factual, genuine, precise, real, right, valid, veracious, veritable; devoted, faithful, loyal, staunch, steady, trusty

trunk body, torso; box, case, chest, coffer; proboscis, snout

trust n belief, certainty, confidence, faith, hope, reliance; care, charge, custody ~v believe, rely upon; assume, believe, expect, hope, presume, surmise; commit, consign, entrust, give

trusty dependable, faithful, reliable, staunch, true, trustworthy

truth accuracy, exactness, genuineness, legitimacy, reality, veracity; axiom, fact, law, maxim, reality, truism

truthful candid, honest, reliable, sincere; accurate, correct, exact, faithful, honest, literal, precise, realistic,

secretly

Tsar *see CZAR*

T-shirt, tee-shirt *n* informal (short-sleeved) sweater

tub *n* open wooden vessel like bottom half of barrel; small round container; bath **tubby** *adj* short and fat

tuba *n* valved brass wind instrument of low pitch

tube *n* long, narrow hollow cylinder; flexible cylinder with cap to hold pastes; underground electric railway **tubular** *adj*

tuber *n* fleshy underground stem of some plants

tuberculosis *n* communicable disease, esp. of lung **tubercular** *adj* **tuberculin** *n* bacillus used to treat tuberculosis

tuck *v* push, fold into small space; gather, stitch in folds ~*n* stitched fold; *Inf* food

Tuesday *n* third day of the week

tuft *n* bunch of feathers etc.

tug *v* **tugging, tugged** pull hard or violently ~*n* violent pull; ship used to tow other vessels **tug-of-war** *n* contest in which two teams pull against one another on rope

tuition *n* teaching, esp. private

tulip *n* plant with bright cup-shaped flowers

tumble *v* (cause to) fall or roll, twist etc.; rumple ~*n* fall **tumbler** *n* stemless drinking glass; acrobat **tumbledown** *adj* dilapidated **tumble dryer** machine that dries laundry by rotating it in warm air

tummy *n Inf* stomach

tumour *n* abnormal growth in or on body

tumult *n* violent uproar, commotion **tumultuous** *adj*

tuna *n (pl* **-na, nas)** large marine food and game fish

tundra *n* vast treeless zone between ice cap and timber line

tune *n* melody; quality of being in pitch; adjustment of musical instrument ~*v* put in tune; adjust machine to obtain efficient running; adjust radio to receive broadcast **tuneful** *adj* **tuner** *n*

tungsten *n* greyish-white metal

tunic *n* close-fitting jacket forming part of uniform; loose hip-length garment

tunnel *n* underground passage, esp. as track for railway line ~*v* **-nelling, -nelled** make tunnel (through)

———————— T H E S A U R U S ————————

reliable

try *v* aim, attempt, bend over backwards *Inf*, break one's neck *Inf*, endeavour, essay, give it one's best shot *Inf*, make an all-out effort *Inf*, strive; examine, inspect, sample, test; adjudge, adjudicate, examine, hear ~*n* attempt, effort, endeavour, essay, go *Inf*, stab *Inf*

tuck *v* fold, gather, insert, push ~*n* fold, gather, pinch, pleat

tug *v/n* drag, haul, heave, jerk, pull, tow, yank

tuition education, instruction, lessons, schooling, teaching, training

tumble *v* drop, fall, pitch, plummet,

roll, topple ~*n* collapse, drop, fall, plunge, roll, spill

tumult bedlam, brawl, commotion, din, disorder, riot, row, strife, turmoil, uproar

tune *n* air, melody, strain, theme; concert, concord, harmony, unison ~*v* adapt, adjust, attune, pitch, regulate

tuneful catchy, harmonious, melodic, melodious, musical

tuneless cacophonous, discordant, dissonant, unmelodic, unmelodious, unmusical

tunnel *n* burrow, channel, hole, passage, shaft ~*v* burrow, dig, excavate,

turban *n* headdress made by coiling length of cloth round head

turbine *n* rotary engine driven by steam, gas, water or air playing on blades

turbocharger *n* propulsion unit driven by turbine

turbot *n* large flatfish

turbulent *adj* in commotion; swirling; riotous **turbulence** *n*

tureen *n* serving dish for soup

turf *n* (*pl* **turfs, turves**) short grass with earth bound to it by matted roots ~*v* lay with turf **turf accountant** bookmaker **turf out** *Inf* throw out

turgid *adj* swollen, inflated; bombastic

turkey *n* large bird reared for food

Turkish *adj* of Turkey **Turkish bath** steam bath **Turkish delight** jelly-like sweet coated with icing sugar

turmoil *n* confusion, commotion

turn *v* move around, rotate; change, alter position or direction (of); (*oft. with* **into**) change in nature; make, shape on lathe ~*n* turning; inclination etc.; period; short walk; (part of) rotation; performance **turning** *n* road, path leading off main rout **turncoat** *n* person who deserts party,

cause etc. to join another **turn down** reduce volume or brightness of; refuse **turnout** *n* number of people appearing for some purpose **turnover** *n* total sales made by business; rate at which staff leave and are replaced **turnstile** *n* revolving gate for controlling admission of people **turntable** *n* revolving platform **turn up** *v* appear

turnip *n* plant with edible root

turpentine *n* oil from certain trees used in paints etc. **turps** *n Inf* turpentine

turquoise *n* bluish-green precious stone; this colour

turret *n* small tower; revolving armoured tower on tank etc.

turtle *n* sea tortoise

tusk *n* long pointed side tooth of elephant etc.

tussle *n/v* fight, wrestle, struggle

tutor *n* one teaching individuals or small groups ~*v* teach **tutorial** *n* period of instruction

tutu *n* skirt worn by ballerinas

tuxedo *n* (*pl* **-dos**) *US* dinner jacket

TV television

twang *n* vibrating metallic sound; nasal speech ~*v* (cause to) make such sounds

——————— T H E S A U R U S ———————

mine, scoop out

turbulence agitation, commotion, disorder, roughness, storm, turmoil

turbulent agitated, rough, swirling, unsettled, unstable; riotous, rowdy, unruly, violent, wild

turmoil agitation, bedlam, chaos, disorder, strife, tumult, upheaval, violence

turn *v* circle, gyrate, pivot, revolve, roll, rotate, spin, swivel, twirl, twist, wheel, whirl; go back, return, reverse, shift, switch, veer, wheel; alter, become, change, convert, mutate, transfigure, transform ~*n* circle, curve, gyration, spin, twist, whirl;

bend, curve, departure, deviation, shift; chance, go, opportunity, shift, spell, stint, try; act, action, deed, service

turn down diminish, lessen, lower, quieten, reduce the volume of; decline, rebuff, refuse, reject, say no to, spurn

turning side road, turn, turn-off

turn up appear, arrive, attend, come, show *Inf*; discover, find, unearth

tutor *n* coach, guide, instructor, lecturer, master, mentor, schoolmaster, teacher ~*v* coach, direct, educate, guide, instruct, lecture, school, teach, train

tweak v pinch and twist or pull ~n tweaking

twee adj Inf oversentimental

tweed n rough-surfaced cloth used for clothing

tweet n/v chirp

tweezers pl n small forceps or tongs

twelve adj/n two more than ten **twelfth** adj ordinal number

twenty adj/n twice ten **twentieth** adj ordinal number

twerp, twirp n Inf stupid person

twice adv two times

twiddle v fiddle; twist

twig n small branch, shoot

twilight n soft light after sunset

twill n fabric with surface of parallel ridges

twin n one of two children born together ~v **twinning, twinned** pair, be paired

twine v twist, coil round ~n string, cord

twinge n momentary sharp pain; qualm

twinkle v shine with dancing light, sparkle ~n twinkling; flash

twirl v turn or twist round quickly; whirl; twiddle

twist v make, become spiral, by turning with one end fast; distort, change; wind ~n twisting

twit n Inf foolish person ~v **twitting, twitted** taunt

twitch v give momentary sharp pull or jerk (to) ~n such pull; spasmodic jerk

twitter v (of birds) utter tremulous sounds ~n tremulous sound

two n/adj one more than one **two-faced** adj deceitful

tycoon n powerful, influential businessman

type n class; sort; model; pattern; characteristic build; specimen; block bearing letter used for printing ~v print with typewriter **typecast** v repeatedly cast (actor, actress) in similar roles **typescript** n typewritten document **typewriter** n keyed writing machine **typist** n one who operates typewriter

typhoid fever acute infectious disease, esp. of intestines

typhoon n violent tropical storm

typhus n infectious feverish disease

typical adj true to type; characteristic **typically** adv

typify v -fying, -fied serve as model of

typography n art of printing; style of printing

tyrant n oppressive or cruel ruler **ty-**

——————— T H E S A U R U S ———————

twilight n dusk, evening, half-light

twin n counterpart, double, fellow, match, mate ~adj double, dual, identical, matching, paired

twine v braid, knit, plait, twist, weave; coil, curl, loop, spiral, twist, wind, wrap ~n cord, string, yarn

twirl v gyrate, revolve, rotate, spin, turn, twist, whirl, wind

twist v coil, curl, wind, wring; contort, distort ~n coil, curl, spin, wind; arc, bend, convolution, curve, turn

twitch v jerk, pluck, pull, snatch, tug, yank ~n jerk, jump, pull, spasm, tic

tycoon industrialist, magnate, mogul,

potentate

type category, class, form, group, kind, order, sort, species, strain, variety; example, model, norm, pattern, personification, standard

typical average, characteristic, classic, normal, orthodox, standard, usual

typify embody, epitomize, exemplify, illustrate, personify

tyrannical autocratic, cruel, despotic, dictatorial, domineering, high-handed, oppressive, overbearing, ruthless, severe

tyranny authoritarianism, autocracy, cruelty, despotism, dictatorship, op-

rannical *adj* despotic; ruthless **tyrannize** *v* exert ruthless or tyrannical authority (over) **tyrannous** *adj* tyran-

ny *n* despotism
tyre *n* (inflated) rubber ring over rim of wheel of road vehicle

pression, reign of terror
tyrant autocrat, despot, dictator, op-

pressor, slave-driver

U u

ubiquitous *adj* everywhere at once
udder *n* milk-secreting organ of cow etc.
UFO unidentified flying object
ugly *adj* unpleasant to see, hideous; threatening
ukulele *n* small four-stringed guitar
ulcer *n* open sore on skin
ulterior *adj* lying beneath, beyond what is revealed
ultimate *adj* last; highest; fundamental **ultimatum** *n* (*pl* -**tums**, -**ta**) final terms
ultra- *comb. form* beyond, excessively, as in **ultramodern**
ultraviolet *adj* (of electromagnetic radiation) beyond limit of visibility at violet end of spectrum
umbilical cord cordlike structure connecting fetus with placenta of mother
umbrage *n* offence, resentment
umbrella *n* folding circular cover of nylon etc. on stick, carried in hand to protect against rain

umpire *n* person chosen to decide question, or to enforce rules in game ~*v* act as umpire
umpteen *adj* *Inf* very many
un- *comb. form* indicating not, reversal of an action
unaccountable *adj* that cannot be explained
unanimous *adj* in complete agreement **unanimity** *n*
unassuming *adj* modest
unaware *adj* not aware **unawares** *adv* unexpectedly
uncanny *adj* weird, mysterious
unceremonious *adj* without ceremony; abrupt, rude
uncertain *adj* not able to be known; changeable **uncertainty** *n*
uncle *n* brother of father or mother, husband of aunt
unconscious *adj* insensible; not aware ~*n* set of thoughts, memories etc. of which one is not normally aware
uncouth *adj* clumsy, boorish

--- THESAURUS ---

ugly no oil painting *Inf*, plain, unattractive, unprepossessing, unsightly; frightful, hideous, horrid, monstrous, repugnant, repulsive, shocking, vile; baleful, dangerous, menacing, ominous, threatening
ulterior concealed, covert, hidden, secret
ultimate end, eventual, final, furthest, last; extreme, greatest, highest, paramount, superlative, supreme, utmost
umpire *n* arbiter, arbitrator, judge, referee ~*v* adjudicate, judge, referee
unanimous agreed, common, likeminded, of one mind, united
unassuming humble, modest, quiet, reserved, retiring

unaware heedless, ignorant, unconscious, uninformed, unsuspecting
unawares by surprise, off guard, suddenly, unexpectedly
uncanny eerie, mysterious, queer, strange, supernatural, unnatural, weird
uncertain doubtful, dubious, iffy *Inf*, questionable, risky, speculative; hazy, irresolute, unclear, unconfirmed, undecided, unsettled, unsure, vague
uncertainty ambiguity, confusion, doubt, hesitancy, indecision
unconscious insensible, numb, out, senseless, stunned; heedless, ignorant, oblivious, unaware, unknowing
uncouth awkward, boorish, clumsy, coarse, crude, graceless, gross, lout-

unction *n* anointing **unctuous** *adj* excessively polite

under *prep* below, beneath; included in; less than; subjected to ~*adv* in lower place or condition ~*adj* lower

under- *comb. form* beneath, below, lower, as in **underground**

underarm *adj* from armpit to wrist; *Sport* with hand swung below shoulder level

undercarriage *n* aircraft's landing gear; framework supporting body of vehicle

undercurrent *n* current that is not apparent at surface; underlying opinion, emotion

undercut *v* charge less than (another trader)

underdog *n* person, team unlikely to win

undergo *v* **-going, -went, -gone** experience, endure, sustain

undergraduate *n* student member of university

underground *adj* under the ground; secret ~*adv* secretly ~*n* secret but organized resistance to government in power; railway system under the ground

undergrowth *n* small trees, bushes growing beneath taller trees

underhand *adj* secret, sly

underlie *v* lie, be placed under; be the foundation, cause, or basis of

underline *v* put line under; emphasize

underling *n* subordinate

undermine *v* wear away base, support of; weaken insidiously

underneath *adv* below ~*prep* under ~*adj* lower ~*n* lower surface

underpants *pl n* man's underwear for lower part of body

underpass *n* road that passes under another road or railway line

underpin *v* give strength, support to

understand *v* **-standing, -stood** know and comprehend; realize; infer; take for granted

understudy *n* one prepared to take over theatrical part ~*v* act as understudy

undertake *v* **-taking, -took, -taken** make oneself responsible for; enter upon; promise **undertaker** *n* one who arranges funerals **undertaking** *n*

———————— THESAURUS ————————

ish, rough, rude, uncultivated, vulgar

under *prep* below, beneath, underneath , governed by, secondary to, subject to, subservient to ~*adv* below, beneath, down

undercurrent riptide, undertow; feeling, flavour, hint, sense, suggestion, tendency, tinge, undertone, vibes *Sl*

undergo bear, endure, experience, stand, suffer, sustain, withstand

underground *adj* buried, covered, subterranean; clandestine, concealed, covert, hidden, secret

underhand deceitful, dishonest, fraudulent, furtive, secret, sly, sneaky, stealthy

underline mark, underscore; accen-

tuate, emphasize, highlight, stress

undermine sabotage, sap, subvert, threaten, weaken

understand appreciate, comprehend, fathom, follow, get, grasp, know, make out, perceive, realize, recognize, see, take in; assume, believe, conclude, gather, hear, infer, learn, presume, suppose, think

understudy *n* replacement, reserve, sub, substitute

undertake agree, bargain, contract, guarantee, pledge, promise; attempt, begin, commence, endeavour, tackle, try

undertaking assurance, pledge, promise, vow, word; affair, attempt, business, enterprise, operation, proj-

undertone *n* dropped tone of voice; underlying suggestion

underwear *n* (*also* **underclothes**) garments worn next to skin

underworld *n* criminals and their associates; *Myth* abode of the dead

underwrite *v* **-writing, -wrote, -written** agree to pay; accept liability in insurance policy **underwriter** *n*

undo *v* **-doing, -done, -did** untie, unfasten; reverse; cause downfall of

undulate *v* move up and down like waves

unearth *v* dig up; discover

uneasy *adj* anxious; uncomfortable

unemployed *adj* having no paid employment, out of work **unemployment** *n*

unexceptionable *adj* beyond criticism

unfold *v* open, spread out; reveal

ungainly *adj* awkward, clumsy

uni- *comb. form* one, as in **unicycle**

unicorn *n* mythical horselike animal with single long horn

uniform *n* identifying clothes worn by members of same group, e.g. soldiers, nurses etc. ~*adj* not changing; regular **uniformity** *n*

unify *v* **-fying, -fied** make or become one **unification** *n*

unilateral *adj* one-sided; (of contract) binding one party only

union *n* joining into one; state, result of being joined; federation; trade union **unionize** *v* organize (workers) into trade union

unique *adj* being only one of its kind; unparalleled

unison *n Mus* singing etc. of same notes as others; agreement

unit *n* single thing or person; group or individual being part of larger whole; standard quantity

unite *v* join into one; associate; become one; combine **unity** *n* state of

ect, task, venture

undertone murmur, whisper; feeling, flavour, hint, tinge, touch, trace

underwear lingerie, underclothes, underthings, undies, unmentionables *Humorous*

underworld criminals, gangsters, Hades, hell, the inferno

undo loose, open, unbutton, unfasten, untie, unwrap; annul, cancel, neutralize, offset, reverse; defeat, destroy, ruin, shatter, upset, wreck

unearth dig up, excavate, exhume; discover, expose, find, reveal, uncover

uneasy anxious, edgy, nervous, twitchy *Inf*, worried; awkward, insecure, precarious, shaky, strained, tense, uncomfortable

unemployed idle, jobless, laid off, redundant

unfold open, undo, unfurl, unravel, unroll, unwrap

ungainly awkward, clumsy, gawky, inelegant, lumbering, uncouth

uniform *n* costume, dress, garb, habit, livery, outfit, regalia, suit ~*adj* consistent, even, regular, smooth, unchanging

uniformity consistency, evenness, homogeneity, regularity, sameness

union amalgamation, blend, combination, conjunction, fusion, mixture, uniting; accord, agreement, concord, harmony, unison, unity; alliance, association, coalition, confederacy, federation, league

unique lone, only, single, solitary; incomparable, inimitable, matchless, peerless, unequalled, unmatched, unparalleled, unrivalled

unison accord, agreement, concert, concord, harmony

unit entity, group, section, whole; item, member, part, portion, section, segment

being one; harmony; agreement

universe *n* all existing things considered as constituting systematic whole; the world **universal** *adj* relating to all things or all people

university *n* educational institution that awards degrees

unkempt *adj* untidy

unless *conj* if not, except

unlike *adj* dissimilar, different ~*prep* not typical of **unlikely** *adj* improbable

unravel *v* -elling, -elled undo, untangle

unrest *n* discontent

unruly *adj* badly behaved, disorderly

unsavoury *adj* distasteful

unscathed *adj* not harmed

unsightly *adj* ugly

unthinkable *adj* out of the question; inconceivable; unreasonable

until *conj* to the time that; (with a negative) before ~*prep* up to the time of

unto *prep* Obs to

untoward *adj* awkward, inconvenient

unwell *adj* not well, ill

unwieldy *adj* awkward; bulky

unwind *v* slacken, undo, unravel; become relaxed

unwitting *adj* not knowing; not intentional

up *prep* from lower to higher position; along ~*adv* in or to higher position, source, activity etc.; indicating completion **upward** *adj/adv* **upwards** *adv* **upbeat** ~*adj Inf* cheerful **up-to-date** *adj* modern, fashionable

upbringing *n* rearing and education of children

update *v* bring up to date

upfront *adj Inf* open, frank

upgrade *v* promote to higher position; improve

upheaval *n* sudden or violent disturbance

uphold *v* -holding, -held maintain, support etc.

——————— THESAURUS ———————

unite amalgamate, blend, combine, couple, fuse, join, link, merge, unify; ally, associate, band, close ranks, cooperate

unity singleness, undividedness, union, wholeness; accord, agreement, assent, concord, consensus, harmony, peace, solidarity, unison

universal common, general, widespread, worldwide

universe cosmos, creation, nature

unlike different, dissimilar, distinct, diverse

unlikely doubtful, faint, improbable, remote, slight

unravel disentangle, free, undo, unwind

unrest agitation, discontent, dissension, rebellion, sedition, strife

unruly disobedient, lawless, mutinous, rebellious, rowdy, wayward, wild, wilful

unsightly hideous, horrid, repulsive, ugly, unattractive

unthinkable implausible, inconceivable, incredible, unimaginable

unwell ailing, ill, sick, sickly, unhealthy

unwieldy awkward, cumbersome, inconvenient, unmanageable

unwind uncoil, undo, unreel, unroll; relax, take it easy

unwitting ignorant, innocent, unaware, unknowing, unsuspecting; accidental, chance, involuntary, unintended, unplanned

upbringing breeding, education, rearing, training

upgrade advance, better, enhance, improve, promote, raise

upheaval disorder, disruption, revolution, turmoil

uphold aid, back, champion, defend, maintain, stick up for *Inf*, support

upholster v fit springs, coverings on chairs etc. **upholstery** n

upkeep n act, cost of keeping something in good repair

upon prep on

upper adj situated above; of superior quality, status etc. ~n upper part of boot or shoe **upper case** capital letters **upper hand** position of control

upright adj erect; honest; just ~adv vertically ~n thing standing upright, e.g. post in framework

uprising n rebellion, revolt

uproar n tumult, disturbance

uproot v pull up, as by roots; displace from usual surroundings

upset v -setting, -set overturn; distress; disrupt ~n unexpected defeat; confusion ~adj disturbed; emotionally troubled

upshot n outcome, end

upside down turned over completely; Inf confused

upstage v overshadow

upstart n one suddenly raised to wealth, power etc.

uptight adj Inf tense; repressed

uranium n white radioactive metallic element

urban adj relating to town or city

urbane adj elegant, sophisticated

urchin n mischievous, unkempt child

urge v exhort earnestly; entreat; drive on ~n strong desire **urgency** n **urgent** adj needing attention at once

urine n fluid excreted by kidneys to bladder and passed as waste from body **urinal** n place for urinating **urinate** v discharge urine

urn n vessel like vase; large container with tap

us pron object of WE

use v employ; exercise; exploit; consume ~n employment; need to employ; serviceableness; profit; habit **usable** adj fit for use **usage** n act of

upkeep keep, maintenance, running, subsistence; expenditure, outlay, overheads

upper high, higher, top, topmost

upper hand advantage, edge, mastery, supremacy

upright erect, straight, vertical; ethical, good, honest, just, principled, righteous, virtuous

uprising insurgence, insurrection, mutiny, rebellion, revolt, revolution, rising

uproar commotion, disturbance, furore, mayhem, racket, riot

upset v capsize, overturn, spill; agitate, bother, disconcert, dismay, distress, disturb, fluster, trouble, unnerve; disorder, disrupt, disturb, spoil ~n agitation, bother, confusion, distress, disturbance, shock, trouble, worry ~adj ill, queasy, sick; agitated, bothered, dismayed, distressed, disturbed, hurt, troubled, worried

upshot end, end result, finale, outcome, result

upside down inverted, overturned, upturned; confused, disordered, muddled, topsy-turvy

urban city, civic, metropolitan, municipal, town

urchin brat, gamin, ragamuffin, waif

urge v beg, beseech, entreat, exhort, implore, plead; drive, encourage, force, impel, incite, induce, press, push, spur, stimulate ~n desire, drive, impulse, longing, wish, yearning

urgency importance, necessity, need, pressure, stress

urgent critical, crucial, imperative, immediate, important, pressing

usable functional, practical, serviceable, valid, working

usage control, employment, management, operation, running; convention, custom, habit, practice, rule,

using; custom **used** *adj* second-hand; accustomed **useful** *adj* **useless** *adj* having no practical use; *Inf* inept

usher *n* (*fem* **usherette**) doorkeeper, one showing people to seats etc. *~v* introduce, announce

usual *adj* habitual, ordinary **usually** *adv* as a rule

usurp *v* seize wrongfully

utensil *n* vessel, implement, esp. in domestic use

uterus *n* (*pl* **uteri**) womb

utility *n* usefulness; benefit; useful thing *~adj* made for practical purposes **utilitarian** *adj* useful rather than beautiful **utilize** *v*

utmost *adj* to the highest degree; extreme, furthest *~n* greatest possible amount

Utopia *n* imaginary ideal state

utter[1] *v* express, say **utterance** *n*

utter[2] *adj* complete, total **utterly** *adv*

—————— THESAURUS ——————

tradition

use *v* apply, employ, exercise, operate, practise, utilize; exploit, manipulate; consume, exhaust, expend, run through, spend *~n* application, employment, exercise, operation, practice, usage; advantage, benefit, good, help, profit, service, value, worth; custom, habit, practice

used cast-off, second-hand, shop-soiled, worn

useful advantageous, effective, fruitful, helpful, practical, profitable, valuable, worthwhile

useless disadvantageous, fruitless, futile, ineffective, pointless, profitless,

unproductive, vain, valueless, worthless *Inf* hopeless, ineffectual, inept

usual common, customary, everyday, general, normal, ordinary, routine, standard, stock, typical

utmost *adj* chief, extreme, greatest, highest, maximum, paramount, supreme; extreme, final, furthest, last, remotest

utter[1] *v* articulate, express, pronounce, say, speak, voice

utter[2] *adj* absolute, complete, deep-dyed *usu derog*, downright, outright, sheer, stark, total, unqualified

utterly absolutely, entirely, extremely, fully, thoroughly, totally

V v

vacant *adj* empty, unoccupied **vacancy** *n* untaken job, room etc.

vacate *v* quit, leave empty **vacation** *n* time when universities and law courts are closed; *US* holidays

vaccinate *v* inoculate with vaccine **vaccination** *n* **vaccine** *n* any substance used for inoculation against disease

vacillate *v* waver; move to and fro **vacillation** *n*

vacuous *adj* not expressing intelligent thought

vacuum *n* (*pl* **vacuums, vacua**) place, region containing no matter and from which all or most air, gas has been removed **vacuum cleaner** apparatus for removing dust by suction **vacuum flask** double-walled flask with vacuum between walls, for keeping contents hot or cold

vagabond *n* person with no fixed home; wandering beggar or thief

vagaries *pl n* unpredictable changes

vagina *n* passage from womb to exterior

vagrant *n* vagabond, tramp **vagrancy** *n*

vague *adj* indefinite or uncertain; indistinct; not clearly expressed

vain *adj* conceited; worthless; unavailing

vale *n Poet* valley

valentine *n* (one receiving) card, gift, expressing affection, on Saint Valentine's day

valet *n* gentleman's personal servant

valiant *adj* brave, courageous

valid *adj* sound; of binding force in law **validate** *v* make valid **validity** *n*

Valium *n Trademark* drug used as tranquillizer

valley *n* low area between hills; river basin

valour *n* bravery

value *n* cost; worth; usefulness; importance; *pl* principles, standards ~*v* estimate value of; prize **valuable** *adj* precious; worthy ~*n* (*usu. pl*) valuable thing **valuation** *n* estimated worth **value-added tax** tax on difference between cost of basic materials and cost of article made from them

valve *n* device to control passage of fluid etc. through pipe; *Anat* part of body allowing one-way passage of fluids

vampire *n* (in folklore) corpse that rises from dead to drink blood of the living **vampire bat** bat that sucks

---

THESAURUS

vacancy job, position, post, situation

vacant available, empty, free, unfilled, untenanted

vacuum emptiness, gap, space, void

vague dim, doubtful, hazy, ill-defined, imprecise, indefinite, indistinct, obscure, shadowy, uncertain, unclear, unknown, unspecified, woolly

vain arrogant, conceited, egotistical, proud, swaggering, vainglorious; empty, fruitless, futile, idle, pointless, unproductive, unprofitable, useless, worthless

valiant bold, brave, heroic, plucky, stouthearted, worthy

valid authentic, bona fide, genuine, lawful, legal, legitimate, official

valuable *adj* costly, dear, precious; esteemed, important, prized, treasured, useful, valued, worthy

value *n* cost, rate; advantage, benefit, importance, merit, use, worth; *pl* ethics, principles, standards ~*v* account, assess, estimate, price; esteem, prize, regard highly, respect

blood of animals

van[1] *n* covered vehicle, esp. for goods; railway carriage for goods and use of guard

van[2] *n short for* VANGUARD

vandal *n* one who wantonly and deliberately damages or destroys **vandalism** *n* **vandalize** *v*

vane *n* weathercock; blade of propeller

vanguard *n* leading, foremost group, position etc.

vanilla *n* tropical climbing orchid; its seed pod; essence of this for flavouring

vanish *v* disappear

vanity *n* excessive pride or conceit

vanquish *v* conquer, overcome

vantage *n* advantage **vantage point** position that gives overall view

vapid *adj* flat, dull, insipid

vapour *n* gaseous form of a substance; steam; mist **vaporize** *v* convert into, pass off in, vapour **vaporizer** *n*

variable *see* VARY

varicose *adj* (of vein) swollen, twisted

variegated *adj* having patches of different colours

variety *n* state of being varied or various; diversity; varied assortment; sort or kind

various *adj* diverse, of several kinds

varnish *n* resinous solution put on surface to make it hard and shiny ~*v* apply varnish to

vary *v* **varying, varied** (cause to) change, diversify, differ **variability** *n* **variable** *adj* changeable; unsteady or fickle ~*n* something subject to variation **variance** *n* state of discord, discrepancy **variant** *adj* different ~*n* alternative form **variation** *n* alteration; extent to which thing varies; modification **varied** *adj* diverse; modified

vase *n* vessel, jar as ornament or for holding flowers

Vaseline *n Trademark* jelly-like petroleum product

vast *adj* very large

VAT value-added tax

vat *n* large tub, tank

vault[1] *n* arched roof; cellar; burial chamber; secure room for storing valuables

vault[2] *v* spring, jump over with the hands resting on something ~*n* such jump

VDU visual display unit

veal *n* calf flesh as food

vector *n Maths* quantity that has size and direction

veer *v* change direction; change one's mind

vegan *n* one who eats no meat, eggs,

—————— THESAURUS ——————

vanguard forefront, front rank, leaders, spearhead, trendsetters, van

vanish disappear, evaporate, fade

vanity conceit, egotism, vainglory

vapour fog, fumes, haze, mist, smoke, steam

variation alteration, change, departure, deviation, difference, diversity

variety change, difference, diversity, variation; assortment, collection, medley, mixture, range; brand, breed, category, class, kind, make, sort, species, strain, type

various assorted, different, diverse, miscellaneous, sundry

varnish *v* adorn, decorate, gild, glaze, gloss

vary alter, change, depart, fluctuate, modify

vault[1] *n* arch, ceiling, roof; cellar, crypt; depository, strongroom

vault[2] *v* bound, clear, hurdle, jump, leap, spring

veer be deflected, change, change course, change direction, sheer, shift, swerve, tack, turn

or dairy products

vegetable *n* plant, esp. edible one ~*adj* of, from, concerned with plants

vegetarian *n* one who does not eat meat or fish ~*adj* suitable for vegetarians

vegetate *v* (of plants) grow, develop; (of people) live dull, unproductive life **vegetation** *n* plants collectively

vehement *adj* marked by intensity of feeling

vehicle *n* means of conveying

veil *n* light material to cover face or head ~*v* cover with, as with, veil

vein *n* tube in body taking blood to heart; fissure in rock filled with ore **veined** *adj*

Velcro *n Trademark* fabric with tiny hooked threads that adheres to coarse surface

velocity *n* rate of motion in given direction; speed

velvet *n* silk or cotton fabric with thick, short pile **velvety** *adj* of, like velvet; soft and smooth

vend *v* sell **vendor** *n* **vending machine** machine that dispenses goods automatically

vendetta *n* prolonged quarrel

veneer *n* thin layer of fine wood; superficial appearance ~*v* cover with veneer

venerable *adj* worthy of reverence

venerate *v* look up to, respect, revere **veneration** *n*

venereal *adj* (of disease) transmitted by sexual intercourse

Venetian blind window blind made of thin horizontal slats

vengeance *n* revenge **vengeful** *adj*

venison *n* flesh of deer as food

venom *n* poison; spite **venomous** *adj*

vent *n* small hole or outlet ~*v* give outlet to; utter

ventilate *v* supply with fresh air **ventilation** *n* **ventilator** *n*

ventricle *n* cavity of heart or brain

ventriloquist *n* one who can so speak that the sounds seem to come from some other person or place **ventriloquism** *n*

venture *v* expose to hazard; risk; dare; have courage to do something or go somewhere ~*n* risky undertaking

venue *n* meeting place; location

veracious *adj* truthful **veracity** *n*

verandah, veranda *n* open or partly enclosed porch on outside of house

verb *n* part of speech used to express action or being **verbal** *adj* of, by, or relating to words spoken rather than written **verbatim** *adj/adv* word for word

verbose *adj* long-winded

verdant *adj* green and fresh

———— THESAURUS ————

vegetate idle, moulder, stagnate

vehement eager, earnest, fervent, fierce, forceful, intense, passionate, strong, violent

veil *n* cloak, cover, curtain, disguise, film, mask, screen, shade ~*v* cloak, conceal, cover, disguise, hide, mask, screen, shield

vein course, current, seam, streak, stripe; dash, hint, strain, streak, thread

vendetta feud, quarrel

veneer *n* appearance, façade, front,

gloss, pretence

vengeance reprisal, retaliation, retribution, revenge

venom poison, toxin; acrimony, bitterness, hate, malice, rancour, spite, spleen

vent *n* aperture, duct, hole, outlet ~*v* air, emit, express, release, utter, voice

venture *v* chance, hazard, risk, speculate, stake, wager ~*n* chance, endeavour, enterprise, gamble, hazard, risk

verbal literal, oral, spoken

verbatim exactly, precisely, word for

verdict *n* decision of jury; opinion reached after examination of facts

verge *n* edge; brink; grass border along road ~*v* come close to; be on the border of

verger *n* church caretaker

verify *v* -ifying, -ified prove, confirm truth of; test accuracy of **verification** *n*

veritable *adj* actual, true

vermilion *adj/n* (of) bright red colour

vermin *pl n* harmful animals, parasites etc.

vernacular *n* commonly spoken language or dialect of particular country or place ~*adj* of vernacular; native

verruca *n* (*pl* -cae, -cas) wart, esp. on the foot

versatile *adj* capable of, adapted to many different uses, skills etc. **versatility** *n*

verse *n* stanza or short subdivision of poem or the Bible; poetry **versed in** skilled in

version *n* description from certain point of view; translation; adaptation

versus *prep* against

vertebra *n* (*pl* **vertebrae**) single section of backbone **vertebrate** *n/adj* (animal) with backbone

vertical *adj* at right angles to the horizon; upright; overhead

vertigo *n* giddiness

verve *n* enthusiasm; vigour

very *adv* extremely, to great extent ~*adj* exact, ideal; absolute

vespers *pl n* evening church service

vessel *n* any object used as a container, esp. for liquids; ship, large boat; tubular structure conveying liquids (e.g. blood) in body

vest *n* undergarment for upper body ~*v* place; confer **vestment** *n* robe or official garment

vestibule *n* entrance hall, lobby

vestige *n* small trace, amount

vestry *n* room in church for keeping vestments, holding meetings etc.

vet *n* short for VETERINARY SURGEON ~*v* **vetting, vetted** check suitability of

veteran *n* one who has served a long time, esp. in fighting services ~*adj* long-serving

veterinary *adj* of, concerning the health of animals **veterinary surgeon** one qualified to treat animal ailments

veto *n* (*pl* -toes) power of rejecting piece of legislation; any prohibition ~*v* enforce veto against

vex *v* annoy; distress **vexation** *n* cause

———— THESAURUS ————

word

verdict conclusion, decision, finding, judgment, opinion

verge *n* border, brim, brink, edge ~*v* approach, border

verification authentication, confirmation, proof

verify attest, authenticate, check, confirm, prove, support, validate

vernacular *n* dialect, idiom, parlance, patois, speech ~*adj* common, informal, local, native, popular, vulgar

versatile adaptable, flexible, resourceful

version account, portrayal, reading,

rendering, translation

vertical erect, on end, upright

very absolutely, decidedly, exceedingly, extremely, greatly, highly, particularly, really, truly

vessel container, pot, receptacle, utensil; boat, craft, ship

vet *v* appraise, check, examine, investigate, look over, review, scan, scrutinize

veteran *adj* expert, long-serving, proficient, seasoned

veto *n* ban, boycott, embargo, interdict, prohibition ~*v* ban, boycott, forbid, prohibit, reject, rule out, turn down

of irritation; state of distress

VHF very high frequency

via *prep* by way of

viable *adj* practicable; able to live and grow independently

viaduct *n* bridge over valley for road or railway

vibrate *v* (cause to) move to and fro rapidly and continuously; give off (light or sound) by vibration; oscillate; quiver **vibrant** *adj* throbbing; vibrating; appearing vigorous **vibration** *n*

vicar *n* clergyman in charge of parish **vicarage** *n* vicar's house

vicarious *adj* obtained, enjoyed or undergone by imagining another's experiences

vice[1] *n* evil or immoral habit or practice; criminal immorality, esp. prostitution; fault, imperfection

vice[2] *n* appliance with screw mechanism for holding things while working on them

vice[3] *adj* serving in place of

viceroy *n* ruler acting for king in province or dependency

vice versa *Lat* conversely, the other way round

vicinity *n* neighbourhood

vicious *adj* wicked, cruel; ferocious, dangerous **vicious circle** sequence of

problems and solutions which always leads back to original problem

victim *n* person or thing killed, injured etc. as result of another's deed, or accident, circumstances etc.; person cheated; sacrifice **victimization** *n* **victimize** *v* punish unfairly; make victim of

victor *n* conqueror; winner **victorious** *adj* winning; triumphant **victory** *n* winning of battle etc.

video *adj* relating to or used in transmission or production of television image ~*n* video cassette recorder; cassette containing video tape ~*v* **videoing, videoed** record on video **video cassette recorder** tape recorder for recording and playing back TV programmes and films on cassette **video tape** magnetic tape used to record TV programmes

vie *v* **vying, vied** (*with* **with** *or* **for**) contend, compete against or for someone, something

view *n* survey by eyes or mind; range of vision; picture; scene; opinion; purpose ~*v* look at; survey; consider **viewer** *n* one who views; one who watches television; optical device to assist viewing of photographic slides **viewfinder** *n* window on camera showing what will appear in photo-

——————— T H E S A U R U S ———————

vex agitate, annoy, bother, distress, exasperate, get on one's nerves *Inf,* harass, hassle *Inf,* irritate, pester, plague, provoke, rile, tease, torment, trouble, upset, worry

viable feasible, operable, practicable, usable, workable

vibrant alive, animated, colourful, dynamic, sparkling, spirited, vivacious, vivid

vibrate pulsate, quiver, shake, shiver, throb, tremble

vibration pulse, quiver, shaking, throb, trembling, tremor

vice corruption, depravity, evil, evil-doing, immorality, iniquity, sin, turpitude, wickedness

vicious bad, cruel, fiendish, foul, monstrous, savage, vile, violent, wicked; cruel, malicious, mean, spiteful, vindictive

victim casualty, fatality, martyr, scapegoat, sufferer; dupe

victimize persecute, pick on

victor champion, conqueror, winner

victorious champion, successful, triumphant, winning

victory conquest, laurels, success,

graph **viewpoint** *n* way of regarding subject; position commanding view of landscape

vigil *n* keeping awake, watch **vigilance** *n* **vigilant** *adj* watchful, alert

vigilante *n* person who takes it upon himself or herself to enforce the law

vignette *n* concise description of typical features

vigour *n* force, strength; energy, activity **vigorous** *adj* strong; energetic; flourishing

vile *adj* very wicked, shameful; disgusting; despicable

vilify *v* -**fying**, -**fied** unjustly attack the character of

villa *n* large, luxurious country house; detached or semidetached suburban house

village *n* small group of houses in country area

villain *n* wicked person **villainous** *adj*

vindicate *v* clear of charges; justify **vindication** *n*

vindictive *adj* revengeful; inspired by resentment

vine *n* climbing plant bearing grapes **vineyard** *n* plantation of vines

vinegar *n* acid liquid obtained from wine and other alcoholic liquors

vintage *n* gathering of the grapes; the yield; wine of particular year; time of origin ~*adj* best and most typical **vintner** *n* dealer in wine

vinyl *n* plastic material with variety of domestic and industrial uses; record made of vinyl

viola *n see* VIOLIN

violate *v* break (law, agreement etc.); rape; outrage, desecrate **violation** *n*

———————— THESAURUS ————————

triumph, win

view *n* sight, vision; outlook, panorama, picture, prospect, scene, vista (*sometimes pl*) attitude, belief, feeling, opinion, sentiment, thought ~*v* behold, check out *Inf,* examine, eye, get a load of *Inf,* inspect, look at, observe, regard, scan, survey, take a dekko at *Brit sl,* watch; consider, deem, judge, regard, think about

viewer observer, onlooker, spectator, watcher

viewpoint angle, perspective, position, slant, stance, standpoint, vantage point, view

vigilant alert, attentive, watchful

vigorous active, brisk, energetic, flourishing, forceful, intense, lively, lusty, powerful, spirited, strong, vital

vigour activity, animation, dash, dynamism, energy, force, gusto, liveliness, might, power, spirit, strength, verve, vitality

vile bad, base, contemptible, corrupt, debased, degrading, depraved, evil, impure, loathsome, low, mean, per-

verted, shocking, sinful, ugly, vicious, wicked; disgusting, foul, horrid, loathsome, nasty, repellent, repugnant, repulsive, sickening

villain blackguard, criminal, reprobate, rogue, scoundrel, wretch

villainous bad, base, criminal, debased, evil, fiendish, mean, sinful, vicious, wicked

vindicate absolve, acquit, clear, defend, excuse, exonerate, justify

vindication defence, excuse, justification, plea, support

vindictive malicious, revengeful, spiteful, vengeful

vintage *n* crop, era, harvest, origin, year ~*adj* best, choice, prime, select, superior

violate break, disobey, disregard, infringe, transgress; abuse, assault, debauch, defile, desecrate, dishonour, invade, outrage

violation abuse, breach, contravention, infringement, transgression, trespass; defilement, desecration, profanation, sacrilege, spoliation

violent *adj* marked by, due to, extreme force, passion or fierceness; using excessive force; intense **violence** *n*

violet *n* plant with small bluish-purple or white flowers; bluish-purple colour ~*adj* of this colour

violin *n* small four-stringed musical instrument **viola** *n* large violin with lower range **violinist** *n*

VIP very important person

viper *n* poisonous snake

viral *adj see* VIRUS

virgin *n* one who has not had sexual intercourse ~*adj* without experience of sexual intercourse; uncorrupted; (of land) untilled **virginal** *adj* **virginity** *n*

virile *adj* (of male) capable of copulation or procreation; strong, forceful **virility** *n*

virtual *adj* so in effect, though not in appearance or name **virtually** *adv* practically, almost

virtue *n* moral goodness; good quality; merit **virtuous** *adj* morally good

virtuoso *n* (*pl* **-sos**, **-si**) one with special skill, esp. in music ~*adj* showing great skill **virtuosity** *n*

virulent *adj* very infectious, poisonous etc.; malicious

virus *n* infecting agent that causes disease **viral** *adj*

visa *n* endorsement on passport permitting bearer to travel into country of issuing government

visage *n* face

vis-à-vis *prep* in relation to, regarding

viscount *n* (*fem* **viscountess**) Brit. nobleman ranking below earl and above baron

viscous *adj* thick and sticky

visible *adj* that can be seen **visibility** *n* degree of clarity of vision

vision *n* sight; insight; dream; hallucination **visionary** *adj* marked by vision; impractical ~*n* mystic; impractical person

visit *v* go, come and see; stay temporarily with (someone) ~*n* stay; call at person's home etc. **visitation** *n* formal visit or inspection; affliction or plague **visitor** *n*

visor, vizor *n* movable front part of

────────── THESAURUS ──────────

violence bloodshed, brutality, cruelty, ferocity, force, frenzy, fury, passion, savagery, wildness

violent brutal, cruel, fierce, flaming, furious, passionate, powerful, raging, rough, savage, strong, tempestuous, vehement, vicious, wild; devastating, powerful, raging, strong, tempestuous, tumultuous, turbulent, wild

virgin chaste, fresh, immaculate, maidenly, pure, undefiled, untouched

virtually as good as, effectually, in effect, nearly, practically

virtue excellence, goodness, incorruptibility, integrity, morality, rectitude, uprightness; advantage, asset, attribute, credit, merit, strength

virtuoso *n* artist, genius, maestro, master ~*adj* brilliant, dazzling, masterly

virtuous blameless, good, honest, incorruptible, moral, pure, righteous, squeaky-clean, upright

visible apparent, clear, detectable, discernible, evident, manifest, noticeable, observable, obvious, perceivable, plain, unconcealed

vision eyes, eyesight, perception, seeing, sight, view; discernment, foresight, imagination, insight; concept, daydream, dream, fantasy, idea, image

visionary *adj* idealistic, romantic ~*n* dreamer, idealist, mystic, prophet, ʹseer

visit *v* inspect, stay with ~*n* call, sojourn, stay, stop

helmet; eyeshade, esp. on car; peak on cap

vista n extensive view

visual adj of sight; visible **visualize** v form mental image of

vital adj necessary to, affecting life; lively; animated; essential **vitality** n life, vigour

vitamin n any of group of substances occurring in foodstuffs and essential to health

viva interj long live

vivacious adj lively, sprightly **vivacity** n

vivid adj bright, intense; true to life

vivisection n dissection of, or operating on, living animals

vixen n female fox

vizor see VISOR

vocabulary n list of words, usu. in alphabetical order; stock of words used in particular language or subject

vocal adj of, with, or giving out voice; outspoken, articulate **vocalist** n singer **vocals** pl n singing part

vocation n (urge, inclination, predisposition to) particular career, profession etc. **vocational** adj

vociferous adj shouting, noisy

vodka n spirit distilled from potatoes or grain

vogue n fashion, style; popularity

voice n sound given out by person in speaking, singing etc.; quality of the sound; expressed opinion; (right to) share in discussion ~v give utterance to, express

void adj empty; destitute; not legally binding ~n empty space ~v make ineffectual or invalid; empty out

vol. volume

volatile adj evaporating quickly; lively; changeable

volcano n (pl **-noes, -nos**) hole in earth's crust through which lava, ashes, smoke etc. are discharged; mountain so formed **volcanic** adj

vole n small rodent

volition n exercise of will

volley n simultaneous discharge of weapons or missiles; rush of oaths, questions etc.; Sport kick, stroke etc. at moving ball before it touches ground ~v discharge; kick, strike etc.

——————————— THESAURUS ———————————

visitor caller, company, guest

visual optic, optical; discernible, observable, perceptible, visible

visualize envisage, imagine, picture

vital animated, dynamic, energetic, forceful, lively, spirited, vivacious, zestful; basic, essential, indispensable, requisite

vitality animation, energy, life, liveliness, sparkle, vivacity

vivacious lively, spirited, vital

vivid bright, brilliant, glowing, intense, rich; clear, distinct, graphic, lifelike, memorable, powerful, strong

vocabulary dictionary, glossary, language, lexicon, wordbook, words

vocal adj clamorous, eloquent, expressive, forthright, frank, noisy, outspoken, strident

vocation business, calling, career, job, post, profession, trade

vociferous loud, noisy, shouting, strident

vogue craze, custom, fashion, mode, style, trend, way; currency, favour, popularity, prevalence, use

voice n language, sound, tone, utterance, words; decision, part, say, view, vote ~v air, articulate, assert, declare, enunciate, express, utter

void adj empty, free, unfilled, unoccupied, vacant; invalid, useless, worthless ~n blank, emptiness, gap, space, vacuum ~v discharge, drain, emit, empty, evacuate

volatile changeable, erratic, fickle, inconstant, mercurial, temperamental, unsettled, unstable, unsteady, up and

in volley **volleyball** n game where ball is hit over high net

volt n unit of electric potential **voltage** n electric potential difference expressed in volts

voluble adj talking easily and at length

volume n space occupied; mass; amount; power, fullness of voice or sound; book; part of book bound in one cover **voluminous** adj bulky, copious

voluntary adj having, done by free will; done without payment; supported by free-will contributions **volunteer** n one who offers service, joins force etc. of his or her own free will ~v offer oneself or one's services

voluptuous adj of, contributing to pleasures of the senses; sexually alluring because of full, shapely figure

vomit v eject (contents of stomach) through mouth ~n matter vomited

voodoo n religion involving ancestor worship and witchcraft

voracious adj greedy, ravenous **voracity** n

vortex n (pl **-texes, -tices**) whirling;

whirling motion

vote n formal expression of choice; individual pronouncement; right to give it; result of voting ~v express, declare opinion, choice, preference etc. by vote

vouch v (usu. with **for**) guarantee **voucher** n document to establish facts; ticket as substitute for cash

vow n solemn promise, esp. religious one ~v promise, threaten by vow

vowel n any speech sound pronounced without stoppage or friction of the breath; letter standing for such sound, as a, e, i, o, u

voyage n journey, esp. long one, by sea or air ~v make voyage

vulcanize v treat (rubber) with sulphur at high temperature to increase its durability **vulcanization** n

vulgar adj offending against good taste; common **vulgarity** n

vulnerable adj capable of being physically or emotionally wounded or hurt; exposed, open to attack, persuasion etc. **vulnerability** n

vulture n large bird which feeds on carrion

————— THESAURUS —————

down Inf, variable

volley n barrage, burst, discharge, hail, salvo, shower

volume amount, body, bulk, capacity, mass, quantity, total; book, publication, title, tome, treatise

voluntary free, intentional, spontaneous, unforced, unpaid, willing

volunteer v advance, offer, present, proffer, propose, suggest

vomit v be sick, chuck (up) Sl, chiefly US, disgorge, heave, regurgitate, retch

voracious devouring, gluttonous, greedy, hungry, ravenous

vote n ballot, franchise, poll, referendum, suffrage ~v ballot, elect, opt

vouch (usu. with **for**) answer for,

back, certify, confirm, guarantee, support, uphold

vow n oath, pledge, promise ~v affirm, dedicate, devote, pledge, promise, swear

voyage n crossing, cruise, journey, passage, travels, trip

vulgar boorish, coarse, common, crude, dirty, gross, ill-bred, impolite, improper, indecent, indelicate, low, nasty, ribald, rude, tasteless, unmannerly, unrefined

vulgarity bad taste, coarseness, crudeness, grossness, indelicacy, rudeness

vulnerable assailable, defenceless, exposed, susceptible, weak, wide open

W w

wacky *adj Inf* eccentric, funny

wad *n* small pad of fibrous material; thick roll of banknotes ~*v* **wadding**, **wadded** pad, stuff etc. with wad

waddle *v* walk like duck ~*n* this gait

wade *v* walk through something that hampers movement, esp. water **wader** *n* person or bird that wades

wafer *n* thin, crisp biscuit

waffle[1] *n/v Inf* (use) long-winded and meaningless language

waffle[2] *n* kind of pancake

waft *v* convey smoothly through air or water ~*n* breath of wind; odour, whiff

wag *v* **wagging, wagged** (cause to) move rapidly from side to side ~*n* instance of wagging; *Inf* witty person **wagtail** *n* small bird with long tail

wage *n* (*oft. pl*) payment for work done ~*v* carry on

wager *n/v* bet

waggle *v/n* wag

wagon, waggon *n* four-wheeled vehicle for heavy loads; railway freight truck

waif *n* homeless person, esp. child

wail *v/n* cry, lament

waist *n* part of body between hips and ribs; various narrow central parts

waistcoat *n* sleeveless garment worn under jacket or coat

wait *v* stay in one place, remain inactive in expectation (of something); be prepared (for something); delay; serve in restaurant etc. ~*n* act or period of waiting **waiter** *n* (*fem* **waitress**) attendant on guests at hotel, restaurant etc.

waive *v* forgo; not insist on **waiver** *n* (written statement of) this act

wake[1] *v* **waking, woke, woken** rouse from sleep; stir up ~*n* vigil; watch beside corpse **waken** *v* wake

wake[2] *n* track or path left by anything that has passed

walk *v* (cause, assist to) move, travel on foot at ordinary pace; cross, pass through by walking; escort, conduct by walking ~*n* act, instance of walking; path or other place or route for walking **walking stick** stick used as

---

THESAURUS

wade ford, paddle, splash

wag *v* bob, flutter, nod, quiver, rock, shake, stir, wave ~*n* bob, flutter, nod, oscillation, quiver, shake, toss, wave

wage *n also* **wages** allowance, compensation, earnings, fee, hire, pay, payment, remuneration, reward, stipend

wager *n* bet, gamble, stake ~*v* bet, chance, gamble, hazard, lay, punt *chiefly Brit,* risk, stake

wail *v* bawl, bemoan, cry, grieve, howl, lament, weep ~*n* complaint, cry, grief, howl, lament, moan, weeping

wait *v* abide, dally, delay, hang fire, hold back, linger, pause, remain, rest, stay, tarry ~*n* delay, halt, interval, pause, rest, stay

waiter, waitress attendant, server, steward, stewardess

waive abandon, defer, forgo, give up, postpone, put off, relinquish, remit, renounce, resign, surrender

wake[1] *v* arise, bestir, get up, rouse, stir; activate, animate, arouse, awaken, enliven, excite, fire, galvanize, kindle, provoke, quicken, rouse, stimulate, stir up

wake[2] *n* backwash, path, slipstream, track, trail, train, wash, waves

waken activate, arouse, enliven, fire, galvanize, get up, kindle, quicken, rouse, stimulate, stir

support when walking **Walkman** *n*
Trademark small portable cassette
player with headphones **walkover** *n*
Inf easy victory

wall *n* structure of brick, stone etc.
serving as fence, side of building etc.;
surface of one; anything resembling
this ~*v* enclose with wall; block up
with wall **wallflower** *n* garden plant
wallpaper *n* paper, usu. patterned, to
cover interior walls

wallaby *n* Aust. marsupial similar to
and smaller than kangaroo

wallet *n* small folding case, esp. for
paper money, documents etc.

wallop *Inf v* beat soundly; strike hard
~*n* stroke or blow

wallow *v* roll (in liquid or mud); revel
(in) ~*n* wallowing

walnut *n* large nut with crinkled
shell; tree it grows on; its wood

walrus *n* large sea mammal with long
tusks

waltz *n* ballroom dance; music for it
~*v* perform waltz

wan *adj* pale, pallid

wand *n* stick, esp. as carried by magician etc.

wander *v* roam, ramble; go astray,
deviate ~*n* wandering

wane *v/n* decline; (of moon) decrease
in size

wangle *v Inf* get by devious methods

want *v* desire; lack ~*n* desire; need;
deficiency **wanted** *adj* being sought,
esp. by police **wanting** *adj* lacking;
below standard

wanton *adj* dissolute; without motive; unrestrained

war *n* fighting between nations; state
of hostility; conflict, contest ~*v* **war-
ring, warred** make war **warlike** *adj* of,
for war; fond of war **warrior** *n* fighter
warfare *n* hostilities **warhead** *n* part
of missile etc. containing explosives

warble *v* sing with trills **warbler** *n* any

——————————— T H E S A U R U S ———————————

walk *v* advance, go, hike, move, pace,
promenade, saunter, step, stride,
stroll, tramp, trek, trudge; accompany, convoy, escort, take ~*n* hike,
march, promenade, ramble, saunter,
stroll, tramp, trek, trudge, turn; alley,
avenue, footpath, lane, path, pathway, pavement, promenade, side-
walk, trail

wall divider, enclosure, panel, partition, screen; barrier, block, impediment, obstacle

wallet case, holder, notecase, pouch,
purse

wallow lie, splash around, tumble,
welter; bask, delight, glory, luxuriate,
relish, revel

wand baton, rod, stick, twig

wander *v* cruise, drift, meander, ramble, range, roam, rove, straggle, stray,
stroll; depart, digress, diverge, err,
lapse, veer ~*n* meander, ramble

wane *v* abate, decline, decrease, dim,

drop, dwindle, ebb, fade, fail, lessen,
sink, subside, weaken, wind down,
wither

want *v* covet, crave, desire, eat one's
heart out over, need, require, wish,
yearn for; be short of, be without, call
for, demand, lack, miss, need, require ~*n* appetite, craving, demand,
desire, fancy, hankering, hunger,
longing, need, thirst, wish; destitution, need, penury, poverty; absence,
dearth, deficiency, famine, lack, scarcity, shortage

wanting absent, incomplete, lacking,
less, missing, short, shy; defective,
faulty, imperfect, patchy, poor,
sketchy, substandard, unsound

wanton *adj* abandoned, dissolute,
fast, immoral, lewd, libertine, licentious, loose, shameless, unchaste;
cruel, evil, gratuitous, malicious, mo-
tiveless, needless, senseless, spiteful,
unjustified, unprovoked, vicious,

of various kinds of small songbirds

ward *n* division of city, hospital etc.; minor under care of guardian **warder** *n* (*fem* **wardress**) jailer **ward off** avert, repel

warden *n* person in charge of building, college etc.

wardrobe *n* piece of furniture for hanging clothes in; person's supply of clothes

ware *n* goods; articles collectively; *pl* goods for sale **warehouse** *n* storehouse for goods

warm *adj* moderately hot; serving to maintain heat; affectionate; enthusiastic ~*v* make, become warm **warmth** *n* mild heat; cordiality; intensity of emotion **warm up** *v* make

or become warmer; do preliminary exercises

warn *v* put on guard; caution; give advance information to **warning** *n*

warp *v* (cause to) twist (out of shape); pervert or be perverted

warrant *n* authority; document giving authority ~*v* guarantee; authorize, justify **warranty** *n* guarantee of quality of goods; security

warren *n* (burrows inhabited by) colony of rabbits

warrior *n see* WAR

wart *n* small hard growth on skin **wart hog** kind of Afr. wild pig

wary *adj* watchful, cautious, alert

was *past tense, first and third person sing. of* BE

———————— THESAURUS ————————

wicked, wilful

war *n* battle, bloodshed, combat, conflict, contest, enmity, fighting, hostilities, strife, struggle, warfare

ward *n* area, district, division, precinct, quarter, zone; charge, minor, protégé, pupil

warden administrator, caretaker, curator, guardian, janitor, keeper, ranger, steward, warder, watchman

warder, wardress gaoler, guard, jailer, keeper, prison officer

ward off avert, avoid, block, deflect, forestall, parry, repel, thwart

wardrobe closet, clothes cupboard; apparel, attire, clothes, outfit

warehouse depository, depot, stockroom, store, storehouse

warfare arms, battle, blows, combat, conflict, contest, discord, fighting, hostilities, strife, struggle, war

warlike aggressive, belligerent, combative, hawkish, hostile, jingoistic, martial, militaristic, pugnacious, warmongering

warm *adj* balmy, pleasant, sunny; affable, affectionate, amiable, amorous, cheerful, congenial, cordial, friendly,

genial, happy, hearty, kindly, likable *or* likeable, loving, pleasant, tender ~*v* heat, melt, thaw

warmth heat, warmness; affability, affection, cordiality, happiness, heartiness, kindliness, love, tenderness

warn admonish, advise, alert, caution, forewarn, inform, notify, tip off

warning *n* admonition, advice, alarm, alert, caution, hint, notice, notification, omen, premonition, sign, signal, threat, tip

warrant *n* assurance, authority, authorization, commission, guarantee, licence, permission, permit, pledge, sanction, security ~*v* affirm, assure, attest, avouch, certify, declare, guarantee, pledge, underwrite, uphold; approve, authorize, commission, demand, deserve, empower, entitle, excuse, justify, license, permit, require, sanction

warrior combatant, fighter, soldier

wary alert, attentive, careful, cautious, chary, distrustful, guarded, heedful, prudent, suspicious, vigilant, watchful

wash v clean (oneself, clothes etc.) with water, soap etc.; be washable; move, be moved by water; flow, sweep over, against ~n act of washing; clothes washed at one time; sweep of water, esp. set up by moving ship **washable** adj capable of being washed without damage **washer** n one who, that which, washes; ring put under nut **washing** n clothes to be washed **washout** n Inf complete failure **wash up** wash dishes and cutlery after meal

wasp n striped stinging insect resembling bee

waste v expend uselessly; fail to take advantage; dwindle; pine away ~n act of wasting; rubbish; desert ~adj worthless, useless; desert; wasted **wasteful** adj extravagant

watch v observe closely; guard; wait expectantly (for); be on watch ~n portable timepiece for wrist, pocket etc.; state of being on the lookout; spell of duty **watchful** adj **watchdog** n dog kept to guard property; person or group guarding against inefficiency or illegality **watchman** n man

guarding building etc., esp. at night **watchword** n password; rallying cry

water n transparent, colourless, odourless, tasteless liquid, substance of rain, river etc.; body of water; urine ~v put water on or into; irrigate or provide with water; salivate; (of eyes) fill with tears **watery** adj wet; weak **water closet** sanitary convenience flushed with water **watercolour** n paint thinned with water; painting in this **watercress** n plant growing in clear ponds and streams **waterfall** n vertical descent of waters of river **water lily** plant that floats on surface of fresh water **waterlogged** adj saturated, filled with water **watermark** n faint translucent design in sheet of paper **watermelon** n melon with green skin and red flesh **water polo** team game played by swimmers with ball **waterproof** adj not letting water through ~v make waterproof ~n waterproof garment **watershed** n line separating two river systems; divide **water-skiing** n sport of riding over water on skis towed by speedboat **watertight** adj preventing water from

wash v bath, bathe, clean, cleanse, launder, moisten, rinse, scrub, shower, wet; (with away) carry off, erode, move, sweep away, wash off ~n ablution, bath, cleaning, rinse, scrub, shampoo, shower, washing; flow, roll, surge, sweep, swell, wave

washout disappointment, disaster, failure, fiasco, mess

waste v dissipate, lavish, misuse, squander; consume, corrode, crumble, decay, decline, disable, drain, dwindle, exhaust, fade, gnaw, perish, sink, undermine, wane, wither ~n extravagance, loss, misapplication, misuse, prodigality, squandering, wastefulness; debris, dregs, dross, garbage, leavings, litter, offal, refuse, rubbish,

scrap, trash; desert, void, wilderness ~adj superfluous, unused, worthless; bare, barren, desolate, empty, unproductive

wasteful extravagant, lavish, prodigal, ruinous, spendthrift, thriftless, uneconomical

watch v check out Inf, contemplate, eye, get a load of Inf, look, mark, note, observe, regard, see, stare at, view; guard, keep, look after, mind, protect, tend ~n chronometer, timepiece; eye, lookout, notice, surveillance, vigil, vigilance

watchful alert, attentive, guarded, heedful, observant, suspicious, vigilant, wary, wide awake

watchman caretaker, custodian,

entering or escaping; with no weak
points

watt *n* unit of electric power

wave *v* move to and fro, as hand in
greeting or farewell; signal by waving;
give, take shape of waves (as hair
etc.) ~*n* ridge and trough on water
etc.; act, gesture of waving; vibration,
as in radio waves; prolonged spell;
upsurge; wavelike shapes in hair etc.
wavy *adj* **wavelength** *n* distance between the same points of two successive waves

waver *v* hesitate, be irresolute; be, become unsteady

wax[1] *n* yellow, soft, pliable material
made by bees; this or similar substance used for sealing, making can-
dles etc.; waxy secretion of ear ~*v* put

wax on **waxy** *adj* like wax

wax[2] *v* grow, increase

way *n* manner; method; direction;
path; passage; progress; state or condition; room for activity **wayfarer** *n*
traveller, esp. on foot **waylay** *v* **-lay-
ing, -laid** lie in wait for and accost, attack **wayside** *n/adj* (by) side or edge
of road **wayward** *adj* capricious, perverse, wilful

WC water closet

we *pron* first person plural pronoun

weak *adj* lacking strength; irresolute;
(of sound) faint; (of argument) unconvincing; unprotected, vulnerable;
lacking flavour **weaken** *v* **weakling** *n*
feeble creature **weakly** *adj* weak;
sickly ~*adv* in weak manner **weakness** *n*

——————— THESAURUS ———————

guard, security man

water *n* aqua, H_2O ~*v* dampen,
drench, flood, hose, irrigate, moisten,
soak, spray, sprinkle

waterfall cascade, cataract, fall

watertight sound, waterproof; airtight, firm, flawless, foolproof, impregnable, sound, unassailable

watery adulterated, diluted, insipid,
runny, tasteless, thin, washy, weak

wave *v* beckon, direct, gesture, indicate, sign, signal; brandish, flourish,
flutter, oscillate, quiver, ripple,
shake, stir, sway, swing, undulate,
wag ~*n* billow, breaker, ripple, roller,
sea surf, swell; current, drift, flood,
movement, outbreak, rush, stream,
surge, sweep, tendency, trend,
upsurge

waver dither *chiefly Brit,* falter, hesitate, seesaw, vacillate; flicker, fluctuate, quiver, reel, shake, sway, undulate, vary, wave, weave, wobble

way approach, fashion, manner,
means, method, mode, plan, practice, procedure, process, scheme, system, technique; access, avenue,

channel, course, direction, lane,
path, road, route, street, track, trail;
advance, approach, journey, march,
passage, progress

wayward contrary, disobedient,
headstrong, incorrigible, mulish, obdurate, obstinate, perverse, rebellious, self-willed, stubborn, ungovernable, unruly, wilful

weak anaemic, debilitated, delicate,
exhausted, faint, feeble, fragile, frail,
infirm, puny, shaky, sickly, spent,
tender, unsteady, wasted; cowardly,
impotent, indecisive, ineffectual, infirm, irresolute, pathetic, powerless,
soft, spineless; feeble, flimsy, hollow,
invalid, lame, pathetic, shallow,
slight, unconvincing, unsatisfactory;
defenceless, exposed, helpless, unprotected, unsafe, untenable, vulnerable, wide open; diluted, insipid,
tasteless, thin, watery

weaken abate, diminish, dwindle, enervate, fade, fail, flag, impair, invalidate, lessen, lower, reduce, sap, tire,
undermine, wane; cut, debase, dilute, thin

weal n streak left on flesh by blow of stick or whip

wealth n riches; abundance **wealthy** adj

wean v accustom to food other than mother's milk; win over, coax away from

weapon n implement to fight with

wear v **wearing, wore, worn** have on the body; show; (cause to) become impaired by use; harass or weaken; last ~n act of wearing; things to wear; damage caused by use; ability to resist effect of constant use

weary adj tired, exhausted, jaded; tiring; tedious ~v **-rying, -ried** make, become weary **weariness** n

weasel n small carnivorous mammal with long body and short legs

weather n day-to-day meteorological conditions, esp. temperature etc. of a place ~v affect by weather; endure;

resist; come safely through **weathercock** n revolving object to show which way wind blows

weave v **weaving, wove, woven** form into texture or fabric by interlacing, esp. on loom; construct; (past tense **weaved**) make one's way, esp. with side to side motion

web n woven fabric; net spun by spider; membrane between toes of waterfowl, frogs etc.

wed v **wedding, wedded** marry; unite closely **wedding** n marriage ceremony **wedlock** n marriage

wedge n piece of wood, metal etc. tapering to a thin edge ~v fasten, split with wedge; stick by compression or crowding

Wednesday n fourth day of the week

wee adj small; little

weed n plant growing where undesired ~v clear of weeds **weedy** adj full

weakling doormat Sl, drip Inf, milksop, sissy, wimp Inf

weakness faintness, feebleness, frailty, impotence, infirmity, powerlessness, vulnerability; blemish, defect, deficiency, failing, fault, flaw, imperfection, shortcoming

wealth affluence, assets, capital, cash, estate, fortune, funds, means, money, opulence, possessions, property, resources, riches, substance; abundance, bounty, plenty, profusion, richness

wealthy affluent, comfortable, opulent, prosperous, rich, well-off

wear v clothe oneself, don, have on, put on, sport Inf; display, exhibit, show; abrade, corrode, deteriorate, erode, fray, grind, rub; annoy, drain, get on one's nerves Inf, harass, irk, pester, tax, vex, weaken, weary ~n apparel, attire, clothes, costume, dress, garments, gear Inf, habit, outfit; abrasion, attrition, damage, erosion, use; employment, mileage Inf, service, use, utility

weariness drowsiness, exhaustion, fatigue, lassitude, lethargy, tiredness

weary adj dead beat Inf, drained, drowsy, exhausted, fatigued, flagging, sleepy, spent, tired, wearied, worn out; arduous, laborious, taxing, tiring, wearing ~v burden, drain, enervate, fatigue, sap, tax, tire, wear out

weather n climate, conditions ~v endure, overcome, stand, suffer, surmount, survive, withstand

weave blend, braid, entwine, intermingle, intertwine, knit, plait, twist; build, construct, contrive, create, fabricate, make, spin; wind, zigzag

web cobweb; lattice, mesh, net, network, weave

wed join, make one, marry, unite

wedding marriage, nuptials, wedlock

wedge n block, chunk, lump ~v cram, force, jam, lodge, pack, squeeze, stuff

of weeds; weak

week *n* period of seven days **weekly** *adj/adv* happening, done, published etc. once a week **weekday** *n* any day of the week except Saturday or Sunday **weekend** *n* Saturday and Sunday

weep *v* **weeping, wept** shed tears (for); grieve

weigh *v* find weight of; consider; have weight; be burdensome **weight** *n* measure of the heaviness of an object; quality of heaviness; heavy mass; object of known mass for weighing; importance, influence ~*v* add weight to **weighting** *n* extra allowance paid in special circumstances

weir *n* river dam

weird *adj* unearthly, uncanny; strange, bizarre

welcome *adj* received gladly; freely permitted ~*n* kindly greeting ~*v* **-coming, -comed** greet with pleasure; receive gladly

weld *v* unite metal by softening with heat; unite closely ~*n* welded joint

welder *n*

welfare *n* wellbeing **welfare state** system in which government takes responsibility for wellbeing of citizens

well[1] *adv* **better, best** in good manner or degree; suitably; intimately; fully; favourably; kindly; to a considerable degree ~*adj* in good health; satisfactory ~*interj* exclamation of surprise, interrogation etc. **wellbeing** *n* state of being well, happy, or prosperous **well-disposed** *adj* inclined to be friendly **well-mannered** *adj* having good manners **well-off** *adj* fairly rich **well-read** *adj* having read much

well[2] *n* hole sunk into the earth to reach water, gas, oil etc.; spring ~*v* spring, gush

wellies *pl n Inf* wellingtons

wellingtons *pl n* high waterproof boots

welter *v* roll or tumble ~*n* turmoil, disorder

wench *n* young woman

wend *v* go, travel

——————— THESAURUS ———————

weep bemoan, bewail, cry, lament, mourn, snivel, sob, whimper

weigh consider, contemplate, evaluate, examine, eye up, ponder, study; burden, oppress, prey

weight *n* burden, gravity, heaviness, load, mass, pressure, tonnage; ballast, load, mass; authority, consequence, consideration, emphasis, impact, importance, influence, power, substance, value ~*v* ballast, charge, freight, load

weird bizarre, eerie, freakish, ghostly, grotesque, mysterious, odd, queer, strange, uncanny, unearthly, unnatural

welcome *adj* acceptable, agreeable, desirable, gratifying, wanted ~*n* acceptance, greeting, hospitality, reception ~*v* embrace, greet, hail, meet, receive

welfare advantage, benefit, good, happiness, health, interest, profit, prosperity, success, wellbeing

well[1] *adv* agreeably, nicely, pleasantly, satisfactorily, smoothly, splendidly, successfully; ably, adeptly, admirably, effectively, efficiently, expertly, proficiently, skilfully; correctly, easily, fairly, fittingly, justly, properly, readily, rightly, suitably; abundantly, amply, completely, considerably, fully, greatly, heartily, highly, substantially, thoroughly, very much ~*adj* able-bodied, fit, hale, healthy, hearty, robust, sound, strong

well[2] *n* bore, hole, pit, shaft; pool, source, spring ~*v* exude, flow, gush, ooze, pour, rise, run, seep, spout, spring, spurt, stream, surge, trickle

well-off comfortable, flourishing, fortunate, lucky, successful, thriving

went *past tense of* GO

were *past tense of* BE *(used with you, we and they)*

werewolf *n* in folklore, person who can turn into a wolf

west *n* part of sky where sun sets; part of country etc. lying to this side ~*adj* that is toward or in this region ~*adv* to the west **westerly** *adj/adv* **western** *adj* **westernize** *v* adapt to customs and culture of the West **westward** *adj/adv* **westwards** *adv*

wet *adj* **wetter, wettest** having water or other liquid on a surface or being soaked in it; rainy; (of paint, ink etc.) not yet dry ~*v* **wetting, wetted** make wet ~*n* moisture, rain **wet suit** close-fitting rubber suit worn by divers etc.

whack *v* strike with sharp resounding sound ~*n* such blow

whale *n* large fish-shaped sea mammal

wharf *n* (*pl* **wharves**) platform at harbour, on river etc. for loading and unloading ships

what *pron* which thing; that which; request for statement to be repeated ~*adj* which; as much as; how great, surprising etc. ~*adv* in which way **whatever** *pron* anything which; of what kind it may be **whatsoever** *adj* at all

wheat *n* cereal plant yielding grain from which bread is chiefly made

wheedle *v* coax, cajole

wheel *n* circular frame or disc revolving on axle; anything like a wheel in shape or function; act of turning ~*v* (cause to) turn as if on axis; (cause

to) move on or as if on wheels; (cause to) change course, esp. in opposite direction **wheelbarrow** *n* barrow with one wheel **wheelchair** *n* chair mounted on large wheels, used by invalids

wheeze *v* breathe with whistling noise ~*n* this sound

whelk *n* edible shellfish

when *adv* at what time ~*conj* at the time that; although; since ~*pron* at which time **whenever** *adj/conj* at whatever time

whence *adv/conj Obs* from what place or source

where *adv/conj* at what place; at or to the place in which **whereabouts** *adv/conj* in what, which place ~*n* present position **whereas** *conj* considering that; while, on the contrary **whereby** *conj* by which **whereupon** *conj* at which point **wherever** *adv* at whatever place **wherewithal** *n* necessary funds, resources etc.

whet *v* **whetting, whetted** sharpen; stimulate

whether *conj* introduces the first of two alternatives

whey *n* watery part of milk left after cheese making

which *adj* used in requests for a selection from alternatives ~*pron* person or thing referred to **whichever** *pron*

whiff *n* brief smell or suggestion of; puff of air

while *conj* in the time that; in spite of the fact that, although; whereas ~*v* pass (time) idly ~*n* period of time

whilst *conj* while

whim *n* sudden, passing fancy **whim-**

———————— THESAURUS ————————

wet *adj* damp, dank, dripping, moist, saturated, soaking, sodden, soggy, sopping, waterlogged ~*v* drizzling, misty, pouring, raining, rainy, showery, teeming ~*v* damp, dip, drench, irrigate, moisten, saturate, soak, splash, spray, sprinkle, steep ~*n*

dampness, humidity, liquid, moisture

wheeze *v/n* cough, gasp, hiss, rasp, whistle

whereabouts location, position, site, situation

whet edge, file, grind, hone, sharpen

whiff aroma, breath, draught, hint,

sy, whimsey n fanciful mood **whimsical** adj fanciful; full of whims

whimper v cry or whine softly; complain in this way ~n such cry or complaint

whine n high-pitched plaintive cry; peevish complaint ~v utter this

whinge v complain ~n complaint

whinny v -nying, -nied neigh softly ~n soft neigh

whip n lash attached to handle for urging or punishing ~v **whipping, whipped** strike with whip; beat (cream, eggs) to a froth; pull, move quickly

whippet n dog like small greyhound

whirl v swing rapidly round; move rapidly in a circular course; drive at high speed ~n whirling movement; confusion, bustle, giddiness **whirlpool** n circular current, eddy **whirlwind** n wind whirling round while moving forwards ~adj very quick

whirr, whir v whirring, whirred (cause to) fly, spin etc. with buzzing sound ~n this sound

whisk v brush, sweep, beat lightly; move, remove quickly; beat to a froth ~n light brush; egg-beating implement

whisker n any of the long stiff hairs at side of mouth of cat or other animal; pl hair on a man's face

whisky n (Irish, Canad, US **whiskey**) spirit distilled from fermented cereals

whisper v speak in soft, hushed tones, without vibration of vocal cords; rustle ~n such speech; trace or suspicion; rustle

whist n card game

whistle v produce shrill sound by forcing breath through rounded, nearly closed lips; make similar sound; utter, summon etc. by whistle ~n such sound; any similar sound; instrument to make it

white adj of the colour of snow; pale; light in colour; having a light-coloured skin ~n colour of snow; white pigment; white part; clear fluid round yolk of egg; (with cap.) white person **whiten** v **whitewash** n substance for whitening walls etc. ~v apply this; cover up, gloss over

whither adv Obs to what place; to which

whittle v cut, carve with knife; pare away

whizz, whiz n loud hissing sound ~v **whizzing, whizzed** move with such sound, or make it

who pron what or which person or

————— THESAURUS —————

odour, scent, smell, sniff

whim caprice, craze, fancy, impulse, notion, quirk, urge

whimper v/n cry, moan, snivel, sob, whine

whimsical capricious, eccentric, fanciful, freakish, funny, odd, peculiar, quaint, queer, unusual, weird

whine n cry, moan, sob, wail ~v cry, moan, sob, wail; bleat, complain, grouch Inf, grouse, grumble

whip n birch, cane, crop, horsewhip, lash, scourge, switch ~v beat, cane, flog, lash, scourge, strap, thrash

whirl v circle, pirouette, pivot, revolve, rotate, spin, turn, twirl, twist, wheel ~n circle, pirouette, revolution, rotation, spin, turn, twist, wheel; confusion, daze, flurry, giddiness, spin

whirlwind adj hasty, lightning, quick, rapid, speedy, swift

whisper v breathe, murmur; hiss, murmur, rustle, sigh ~n low voice, murmur, undertone; breath, fraction, hint, shadow, suggestion, suspicion, tinge, trace; hiss, murmur, rustle, sigh, sighing

white ashen, bloodless, pale, pasty, wan

persons; that **whoever** *pron* who, any one or every one that

whodunnit *n Inf* detective story

whole *adj* containing all elements or parts; not defective or imperfect; healthy *~n* complete thing or system **wholly** *adv* **wholehearted** *adj* sincere; enthusiastic **wholesale** *n* sale of goods in large quantities to retailers *~adj* dealing by wholesale; extensive **wholesome** *adj* producing good effect, physically or morally

whom *pron objective form of* WHO

whoop *n/v* (make) shout or cry expressing excitement etc.

whooping cough infectious disease marked by convulsive coughing with loud whoop or drawing in of breath

whopper *n Inf* unusually large thing **whopping** *adj*

whore *n* prostitute

whose *pron* of whom or which

why *adv* for what cause or reason

wick *n* strip of thread feeding flame of lamp of candle with oil, grease etc.

wicked *adj* evil, sinful; very bad

wicker *adj* made of woven cane

wicket *n* set of cricket stumps; small gate

wide *adj* having a great extent from side to side, broad; having considerable distance between; spacious; vast; far from the mark; opened fully; *adv* to the full extent; far from the intended target **widen** *v* **width** *n* breadth **widespread** *adj* extending over a wide area

widow *n* woman whose husband is dead and who has not married again *~v* make a widow of **widower** *n* man whose wife is dead and who has not married again

wield *v* hold and use

wife *n* (*pl* **wives**) man's partner in

———— T H E S A U R U S ————

whitewash *v* conceal, suppress

whole *adj* complete, entire, full, total; intact, perfect, sound, unbroken, unimpaired, uninjured, unscathed, untouched; able-bodied, fit, hale, healthy, robust, sound, strong, well *~n* aggregate, all, everything, lot, sum total, total, totality; entity, unit

wholehearted committed, dedicated, determined, devoted, earnest, enthusiastic, genuine, real, sincere, true, unreserved, unstinting

wholesale *adj* broad, extensive, indiscriminate, mass, sweeping

wholesome beneficial, good, health-giving, healthy, nourishing, nutritious; clean, decent, honourable, moral, pure, respectable, righteous, virtuous, worthy

wholly all, altogether, completely, comprehensively, entirely, fully, heart and soul, in every respect, one hundred per cent *Inf*, perfectly, thoroughly, totally, utterly

whore call girl, harlot, hooker *US sl*, loose woman, prostitute, scrubber *Brit & Aust sl*, slag *Brit sl*, streetwalker, strumpet, tart *Inf*, trollop

wicked abandoned, amoral, bad, corrupt, debased, dissolute, evil, heinous, immoral, iniquitous, nefarious, shameful, sinful, unrighteous, villainous

wide *adj* broad, comprehensive, encyclopedic, expansive, general, immense, inclusive, large, sweeping, vast; ample, commodious, full, roomy, spacious

widen broaden, dilate, enlarge, expand, extend, stretch

widespread broad, common, extensive, general, popular, prevalent, rife, universal, wholesale

width breadth, compass, diameter, extent, range, span

wield handle, manage, manipulate, ply, use; apply, exercise, exert, have, hold, maintain, possess, utilize

marriage, married woman

wig n artificial hair for the head

wiggle v (cause to) move jerkily from side to side ~n wiggling

wild adj not tamed or domesticated; not cultivated; savage; stormy; uncontrolled; random; excited; rash **wildcat** n any of various undomesticated feline animals **wild-goose chase** search that has little chance of success **wildlife** n wild animals and plants collectively

wildebeest n gnu

wilderness n desert, waste place

wildfire n raging, uncontrollable fire; anything spreading, moving fast

wile n trick **wily** adj crafty, sly

wilful adj obstinate; self-willed; intentional

will[1] v (past tense **would**) forms future tense and indicates intention or conditional result

will[2] n faculty of deciding what one will do; purpose; volition; determination; wish; directions written for disposal of property after death ~v wish; intend; leave as legacy **willing** adj ready; given cheerfully **willingly** adv **willingness** n **willpower** n ability to control oneself, one's actions, impulses

will-o'-the-wisp n elusive person or thing

willow n tree with long thin flexible branches; its wood **willowy** adj slender, supple

willy-nilly adv/adj (occurring) whether desired or not

wilt v (cause to) become limp, lose strength etc.

wimp n Inf feeble person

wimple n garment framing face, worn by nuns

win v winning, won be successful, victorious; get by labour or effort ~n victory, esp. in games **winner** n **winning** adj charming **winnings** pl n sum won in game, betting etc.

wince v flinch, draw back, as from pain etc. ~n this act

———————— THESAURUS ————————

wife helpmate, mate, partner, significant other US inf, spouse

wild adj ferocious, fierce, savage, untamed; free, native, natural; barbaric, brutish, ferocious, fierce, primitive, savage, uncivilized; boisterous, chaotic, disorderly, lawless, noisy, riotous, rough, turbulent, uncontrolled, undisciplined, unrestrained, unruly, violent; berserk, crazy, delirious, demented, excited, frantic, frenzied, hysterical, mad

wilderness desert, jungle, waste

wilful headstrong, inflexible, obstinate, self-willed, stubborn, unyielding; conscious, deliberate, intentional, voluntary

will n choice, decision, option; aim, determination, intention, purpose, resolution, resolve; desire, fancy, mind, pleasure, wish; testament ~v

choose, desire, elect, opt, prefer, see fit, want, wish; bequeath, confer, give, leave, pass on, transfer

willing agreeable, amenable, consenting, content, eager, enthusiastic, game, happy, prepared, ready

willingly eagerly, freely, gladly, happily, readily

willingness agreement, consent, desire, inclination, volition, will, wish

willpower determination, drive, grit, resolution, resolve, self-control

wilt droop, sag, shrivel, wither

wily artful, astute, crafty, cunning, designing, foxy, scheming, sharp, shrewd, sly, tricky

win v be victorious, come first, conquer, overcome, prevail, succeed, triumph; accomplish, achieve, acquire, attain, earn, gain, get, obtain, procure, receive, secure ~n Inf conquest,

winch *n* machine for hoisting or hauling using cable wound round drum ~*v* move (something) by using a winch

wind¹ *n* air in motion; breath; flatulence ~*v* render short of breath, esp. by blow etc. **windward** *n* side against which wind is blowing **windy** *adj* exposed to wind; flatulent **windfall** *n* unexpected good luck; fallen fruit **wind instrument** musical instrument played by blowing or air pressure **windmill** *n* wind-driven apparatus with fanlike sails for raising water, crushing grain etc. **windpipe** *n* passage from throat to lungs **windscreen** *n* protective sheet of glass etc. in front of driver or pilot **windsurfing** *n* sport of sailing standing up on board with single sail

wind² *v* **winding, wound** twine; meander; twist round, coil; wrap; make ready for working by tightening spring ~*n* act of winding; single turn of something wound

window *n* hole in wall (with glass) to admit light, air etc.; anything similar in appearance or function; area for display of goods behind glass of shop front **window-shopping** *n* looking at goods without intending to buy

wine *n* fermented juice of grape etc.; purplish-red colour

wing *n* feathered limb used by bird in flying; organ of flight of insect or some animals; main lifting surface of aircraft; side area of building, stage etc.; group within political party etc. ~*v* fly; move, go very fast; disable, wound slightly **winger** *n* *Sport* player positioned at side of pitch

wink *v* close and open (one eye) rapidly, esp. to indicate friendliness or as signal; twinkle ~*n* act of winking

winkle *n* edible sea snail **winkle out** extract, prise out

winsome *adj* charming

winter *n* coldest season ~*v* pass, spend the winter **wintry** *adj* of, like winter; cold

wipe *v* rub so as to clean ~*n* wiping **wiper** *n* one that wipes; automatic wiping apparatus (*esp.* **windscreen wiper**) **wipe out** erase; annihilate; *Sl* kill

wire *n* metal drawn into thin, flexible strand; something made of wire, e.g. fence; telegram ~*v* provide, fasten with wire; send by telegraph **wiring** *n* system of wires **wiry** *adj* like wire; lean and tough **wire-haired** *adj* (of various breeds of dog) with short stiff hair

wireless *n* *Obs* radio, radio set

────────────── T H E S A U R U S ──────────────

success, triumph, victory

wince *v* blench, cower, cringe, draw back, flinch, quail, recoil, shrink, start

wind¹ *n* air, breath, breeze, draught, gust, zephyr; breath, puff, respiration

wind² *v* coil, curl, loop, twine, twist, wreathe; meander, ramble, twist, zigzag

windy blustery, breezy, gusty, inclement, squally, stormy, wild

wing *n* annexe, extension; arm, branch, circle, clique, coterie, faction, group, schism, section, side

wink *v* bat, blink, flutter; flash, gleam, sparkle, twinkle ~*n* blink, flutter; flash, gleam, glimmering, sparkle, twinkle

winner champion, conqueror, first, victor

winnings booty, gains, prize(s), proceeds, profits, spoils, takings

wintry chilly, cold, harsh, icy, snowy

wipe *v* brush, clean, mop, rub, sponge, swab ~*n* brush, lick, rub, swab

wipe out annihilate, destroy, eradicate, erase, massacre, obliterate

wise *adj* having intelligence and knowledge; sensible **wisdom** *n* (accumulated) knowledge, learning **wisdom tooth** large tooth cut usu. after age of twenty

wish *v* desire ~*n* expression of desire; thing desired **wishful** *adj* too optimistic

wishy-washy *adj Inf* insipid, bland

wisp *n* light, delicate streak, as of smoke; twisted handful, usu. of straw etc.; stray lock of hair **wispy** *adj*

wistful *adj* longing, yearning; sadly pensive

wit *n* ability to use words, ideas in clever, amusing way; person with this ability; intellect; understanding; humour **witticism** *n* witty remark **wittingly** *adv* on purpose; knowingly **witty** *adj*

witch *n* person, usu. female, who practises magic; ugly, wicked wom-an; fascinating woman **witchcraft** *n* **witch doctor** in certain societies, man appearing to cure or cause injury, disease by magic

with *prep* in company or possession of; against; in relation to; through; by means of **within** *prep/adv* in, inside **without** *prep* lacking; *Obs* outside

withdraw *v* -drawing, -drew, -drawn draw back or out **withdrawal** *n* **withdrawn** *adj* reserved, unsociable

wither *v* (cause to) wilt, dry up, decline **withering** *adj* (of glance etc.) scornful

withhold *v* -holding, -held restrain; refrain from giving

withstand *v* -standing, -stood oppose, resist, esp. successfully

witness *n* one who sees something; testimony; one who gives testimony ~*v* give testimony; see; attest; sign (document) as genuine

———————— THESAURUS ————————

wiry lean, sinewy, strong, tough

wisdom astuteness, discernment, enlightenment, foresight, insight, intelligence, judgment, prudence, reason, sagacity, sense, smarts *Sl, chiefly US*

wise aware, clued-up *Inf*, discerning, enlightened, informed, intelligent, judicious, perceptive, prudent, rational, reasonable, sage, sensible, shrewd, sound

wish *v* crave, desire, hanker, hunger, long, need, thirst, want, yearn ~*n* desire, hankering, hunger, longing, thirst, urge, want, will, yearning

wistful longing, melancholy, mournful, sad, yearning

wit banter, fun, humour, levity, pleasantry, repartee; comedian, humorist, joker, wag; brains, cleverness, discernment, insight, intellect, judgment, perception, reason, sense, smarts *Sl, chiefly US*, wisdom

witch crone, enchantress, sorceress

witchcraft enchantment, magic, sor-cery, wizardry

withdraw extract, remove; absent oneself, back out, cop out *Sl*, depart, drop out, go, leave, pull out, retire, retreat

withdrawal extraction, removal; departure, exit, exodus, retirement, retreat

withdrawn aloof, detached, distant, introverted, quiet, reserved, retiring, shy, silent, taciturn

wither decline, dry, fade, languish, perish, shrink, wane, waste

withering hurtful, scornful, snubbing

withhold conceal, hide, hold back, keep, keep back, refuse, reserve, restrain, retain, suppress

withstand bear, brave, combat, cope with, endure, face, hold off, hold out against, oppose, resist, stand up to, suffer, take, take on, weather

witness *n* observer, onlooker, spectator, viewer, watcher ~*v* mark, note, notice, observe, perceive, see, view,

wizard *n* sorcerer, magician; *Inf* virtuoso **wizardry** *n*

wizened *adj* shrivelled, wrinkled

wobble *v* move unsteadily; sway ~*n* unsteady movement **wobbly** *adj*

woe *n* grief **woebegone** *adj* looking sorrowful **woeful** *adj* sorrowful; pitiful; wretched

wok *n* bowl-shaped Chinese cooking pan

wolf *n* (*pl* **wolves**) wild predatory doglike animal ~*v* eat ravenously

wolverine *n* carnivorous mammal inhabiting Arctic regions

woman *n* (*pl* **women**) adult human female; women collectively **womanish** *adj* effeminate **womanize** *v* (of man) indulge in many casual affairs **womanly** *adj* of, proper to woman

womb *n* female organ in which young develop before birth

wombat *n* Aust. burrowing marsupial with heavy body, short legs and dense fur

won *past tense and participle of* WIN

wonder *n* emotion excited by amazing or unusual thing; marvel, miracle ~*v* be curious about; feel amazement **wonderful** *adj* remarkable; very fine

wondrous *adj* inspiring wonder; strange

wont *n* custom ~*adj* accustomed

woo *v* court, seek to marry

wood *n* substance of trees, timber **firewood** tract of land with growing trees **wooded** *adj* having many trees **wooden** *adj* made of wood; without expression **woody** *adj* **woodland** *n* woods, forest **woodpecker** *n* bird which searches tree trunks for insects **wood pigeon** large pigeon of Europe and Asia **woodwind** *adj/n* (of) wind instruments of orchestra **woodworm** *n* insect larva that bores into wood

woof *n* barking noise

wool *n* soft hair of sheep, goat etc.; yarn spun from this **woollen** *adj* **woolly** *adj* of wool; vague, muddled ~*n* woollen garment

word *n* smallest separate meaningful unit of speech or writing; term; message; brief remark; information; promise; command ~*v* express in words, esp. in particular way **wordy** *adj* using too many words **word processor** keyboard, computer and VDU for electronic organization and storage of text

——————— THESAURUS ———————

watch; attest, bear out, confirm

witticism clever remark, epigram, one-liner *Sl*, play on words, pleasantry, pun, quip, witty remark

witty amusing, brilliant, clever, epigrammatic, funny, humorous, original

wizard enchanter, magician, necromancer, sorcerer; adept, buff *Inf*, expert, genius, maestro, master, prodigy, virtuoso

woe anguish, distress, grief, misery, pain, sadness, sorrow, suffering, wretchedness

woman female, girl, lady, lass, lassie *Inf*, maid, maiden, wench *Facetious*

womanly female, feminine, ladylike

wonder *n* admiration, astonishment, awe, curiosity, fascination; curiosity, marvel, miracle, prodigy, rarity, sight, spectacle ~*v* ask oneself, conjecture, meditate, ponder, puzzle, query, question, speculate

wonderful amazing, astounding, extraordinary, marvellous, miraculous, remarkable, staggering, surprising; admirable, brilliant, cracking *Brit inf*, excellent, magnificent, mean *Sl*, outstanding, sensational, stupendous, superb, terrific, tremendous

wood *also* **woods** coppice, copse, forest, grove, thicket, trees, woodland; timber

word *n* expression, name, term; bul-

wore *past tense of* WEAR

work *n* labour; employment; occupation; something made or accomplished; production of art or science; *pl* factory; total of person's deeds, writings etc.; mechanism of clock etc. ~*v* (cause to) operate; make, shape; apply effort; labour; be employed; turn out successfully; ferment **workable** *adj* **worker** *n* **workaholic** *n* person addicted to work **working class** social class consisting of wage earners, esp. manual **working-class** *adj* **workman** *n* manual worker, **workmanship** *n* skill of workman; way thing is finished **workshop** *n* place where things are made

world *n* the universe; the planet earth; sphere of existence; mankind; any planet; society **worldly** *adj* earthly; absorbed in pursuit of material gain

worm *n* small limbless creeping snakelike creature; anything resembling worm in shape or movement; *pl* (disorder caused by) infestation of worms, esp. in intestines ~*v* crawl; insinuate (oneself); extract (secret) craftily; rid of worms

worn *past participle of* WEAR

worry *v* -rying, -ried be (unduly) concerned; trouble, pester, harass; (of dog) seize, shake with teeth ~*n* (cause of) anxiety, concern **worried** *adj*

worse *adj/adv comparative of* BAD *or* BADLY **worsen** *v* make, grow worse **worst** *adj/adv superlative of* BAD *or* BADLY

worship *v* -shipping, -shipped show religious devotion to; adore; love and admire ~*n* act of worshipping **worshipful** *adj* **worshipper** *n*

letin, dispatch, information, intelligence, latest *Inf,* message, news, notice, report, tidings; assurance, guarantee, oath, pledge, promise, solemn oath, vow ~*v* express, phrase, put, say, state, utter

wordy garrulous, long-winded, loquacious, rambling, verbose

work *n* drudgery, effort, exertion, industry, labour, slog, sweat, toil; business, calling, craft, employment, job, occupation, profession, trade; composition, creation, handiwork, opus, piece, production ~*v* function, go, operate, perform, run; control, direct, drive, handle, manage, manipulate, operate, ply, use, wield; drudge, labour, slave, sweat, toil

workman artisan, craftsman, employee, hand, labourer, mechanic, tradesman

workmanship art, artistry, craft, craftsmanship, expertise, handicraft, handiwork, skill, technique

workshop factory, mill, plant, shop, studio

world earth, globe, planet; area, domain, environment, field, kingdom, province, realm, sphere; everybody, everyone, humanity, man, mankind, men

worldly earthly, mundane, physical, secular, temporal, terrestrial; avaricious, grasping, greedy, materialistic

worn frayed, ragged, shabby, tattered, tatty, threadbare; exhausted, fatigued, spent, tired, weary

worried afraid, anxious, bothered, concerned, nervous, perturbed, tense, troubled, uneasy, upset

worry *v* agonize, annoy, bother, brood, disturb, fret, harass, hassle *Inf,* perturb, pester, trouble, unsettle, upset, vex ~*n* annoyance, care, hassle *Inf,* problem, trial, trouble, vexation

worsen aggravate, decline, degenerate, deteriorate, exacerbate, get worse, go downhill *Inf,* go from bad to worse, sink

worship *v* adore, exalt, glorify, hon-

worsted *n* woollen yarn ~*adj* made of woollen yarn

worth *adj* having or deserving to have value specified; meriting ~*n* excellence; merit, value; usefulness; quantity to be had for given sum **worthless** *adj* **worthwhile** *adj* worth the time, effort etc. involved **worthy** *adj* virtuous; meriting

would *v* expressing wish, intention, probability; *past tense of* WILL **would-be** *adj* wishing, pretending to be

wound[1] *n* injury, hurt from cut, stab etc. ~*v* inflict wound on; injure; pain

wound[2] *past tense and past participle of* WIND[2]

wove *past tense of* WEAVE **woven** *past participle of* WEAVE

wow *interj* exclamation of astonishment

wraith *n* apparition

wrangle *v* quarrel (noisily); dispute ~*n* noisy quarrel; dispute

wrap *v* **wrapping, wrapped** cover, esp. by putting something round; put round ~*n* loose garment **wrapper** *n*

covering **wrapping** *n* material used to wrap

wrath *n* anger

wreak *v* inflict (vengeance); cause

wreath *n* something twisted into ring form, esp. band of flowers etc. as memorial or tribute on grave etc. **wreathe** *v* form into wreath; surround; wind round

wreck *n* destruction of ship; wrecked ship; ruin ~*v* cause wreck of **wreckage** *n*

wren *n* kind of small songbird

wrench *v* twist; distort; seize forcibly; sprain ~*n* violent twist; tool for twisting or screwing; spanner

wrest *v* take by force; twist violently

wrestle *v* fight (esp. as sport) by grappling and trying to throw down; strive (with); struggle ~*n* wrestling **wrestler** *n* **wrestling** *n*

wretch *n* despicable person; miserable creature **wretched** *adj* miserable, unhappy; worthless

wriggle *v* move with twisting action, squirm ~*n* this action

──────── T H E S A U R U S ────────

our, love, revere, venerate ~*n* adoration, devotion, exaltation, glorification, glory, homage, honour, love, reverence

worth *n* credit, estimation, excellence, goodness, importance, merit, quality, value, virtue; cost, price, value

worthless insignificant, meaningless, paltry, pointless, rubbishy, trashy, trifling, trivial, unimportant, useless

worthwhile beneficial, good, helpful, productive, profitable, useful, valuable

worthy commendable, creditable, decent, deserving, estimable, good, honest, laudable, meritorious, reputable, respectable, righteous, upright, virtuous

wound *n* cut, gash, harm, hurt, inju-

ry, slash ~*v* cut, damage, gash, harm, hurt, injure, pierce, slash; distress, grieve, hurt, offend, pain, sting

wrap *v* bind, cover, encase, enclose, enfold, envelop, fold, pack, shroud, surround, wind

wrapper case, cover, envelope, jacket, paper

wreath band, coronet, crown, festoon, garland, ring

wreck *v* break, demolish, destroy, devastate, ravage, ruin, shatter, smash, spoil; founder, shipwreck

wreckage debris, fragments, pieces, remains, rubble, ruin

wrench *v* twist, wrest, wring; rick, sprain, strain

wrestle battle, combat, contend, fight, grapple, struggle

wretched abject, dismal, hopeless,

wring *v* **wringing, wrung** twist; extort; squeeze out

wrinkle *n* slight ridge or furrow on skin etc. ~*v* make, become wrinkled **wrinkly** *adj*

wrist *n* joint between hand and arm

writ *n* written command from law court or other authority

write *v* **writing, wrote, written** mark paper etc. with symbols or words; compose; send a letter; set down in words; communicate in writing **writer** *n* one who writes; author **writing** *n* **write-off** *n Inf* something damaged beyond repair

writhe *v* **writhing, writhed** twist, squirm in or as in pain etc.

wrong *adj* not right or good; not suitable; incorrect; mistaken; not functioning properly ~*n* that which is wrong; harm ~*v* do wrong to; think badly of without justification **wrongful** *adj* **wrongly** *adv*

wrote *past tense of* WRITE

wrought ~*adj* (of metals) shaped by hammering or beating

wrung *past tense and past participle of* WRING

wry *adj* turned to one side, contorted; dryly humorous

———————— THESAURUS ————————

miserable, pitiful, poor, unhappy

wriggle *v/n* squirm, turn, twist, writhe

wrinkle *n* crease, crow's-foot, crumple, fold, furrow, line, pucker, rumple ~*v* crease, crumple, fold, furrow, ruck

write compose, copy, create, draft, inscribe, pen, record, scribble, take down, transcribe

writer author, columnist, essayist, hack, novelist, scribe

writhe squirm, twist, wriggle

writing calligraphy, hand, handwriting, print, scrawl, scribble, script; book, composition, document, letter, opus, publication, title, work

wrong *adj* bad, criminal, crooked, dishonest, evil, illegal, illicit, immoral, sinful, unlawful, wicked, wrongful; improper, inapt, incorrect, not done, unacceptable, unfitting, unseemly, unsuitable; erroneous, fallacious, false, faulty, inaccurate, incorrect, mistaken, untrue; amiss, askew, awry, defective, faulty ~*n* abuse, crime, injury, injustice, misdeed, offence, sin, transgression ~*v* abuse, harm, hurt, ill-use, injure, malign, maltreat, mistreat

wrongful blameworthy, illegal, illegitimate, illicit, immoral, improper, reprehensible, unfair, unjust, unlawful

wry dry, ironic, mocking, sardonic

X x Y y Z z

xenophobia *n* hatred, fear, of strangers or aliens

Xerox *n Trademark* machine for copying printed material ~*v* copy with Xerox

Xmas *n short for* CHRISTMAS

X-ray *n* stream of radiation capable of penetrating solid bodies ~*v* photograph by X-rays

xylophone *n* musical instrument of wooden bars which sound when struck

yacht *n* vessel propelled by sail or power

yak *n* ox of Central Asia

yam *n* sweet potato

yank *v* jerk, tug; pull quickly ~*n* quick tug

yap *v* **yapping, yapped** bark (as small dog); talk idly

yard[1] *n* unit of length, .915 metre **yardstick** *n* standard of measurement or comparison

yard[2] *n* piece of enclosed ground, oft. adjoining building and used for some specific purpose

yarn *n* spun thread; tale

yawn *v* open mouth wide, esp. in sleepiness; gape ~*n* act of yawning

yd. yard

ye *pron Obs* you

year *n* time taken by one revolution of earth round sun, about 365 days; twelve months **yearling** *n* animal one year old **yearly** *adv* every year, once a year ~*adj* happening once a year

yearn *v* feel longing, desire

yeast *n* substance used as fermenting agent, esp. in raising bread

yell *v/n* shout; scream

yellow *adj* of the colour of lemons, gold etc.; *Inf* cowardly ~*n* this colour **yellow fever** acute infectious tropical disease

yelp *v/n* (produce) quick, shrill cry

yen *n Inf* longing, craving

yeoman *n Hist* farmer cultivating his own land

yes *interj* expresses consent, agreement, or approval

yesterday *n/adv* (on) day before today; (in) recent past

yet *adv* now; still; besides; hitherto ~*conj* but, at the same time, nevertheless

yeti *n* apelike creature said to inhabit Himalayas

yew *n* evergreen tree with dark leaves; its wood

yield *v* give or return; produce; give up, surrender ~*n* amount produced

yob *also* **yobbo** *n Inf* bad-mannered aggressive youth

yodel *v* **-delling, -delled** warble in falsetto tone

yoga *n* Hindu system of certain physical and mental exercises

yogurt, yoghurt *n* thick, custard-like preparation of curdled milk

yoke *n* wooden bar put across the necks of two animals to hold them together; various objects like a yoke in shape or use; fitted part of garment, esp. round neck, shoulders; bond or tie; domination ~*v* put yoke on; couple, unite

---

THESAURUS

yearly annual, annually, every year, once a year, per annum

yearn ache, crave, desire, eat one's heart out over, hunger, languish, long, pine

yell *v* bawl, holler *Inf*, howl, scream, shout, shriek ~*n* cry, howl, scream, screech, shriek

yet already, now, right now, so soon; however, still; as well, besides, fur-

yokel *n* (old-fashioned) country dweller

yolk *n* yellow central part of egg

yon *adj Obs or dial* that or those over there **yonder** *adj* yon ~*adv* over there, in that direction

Yorkshire pudding baked batter made from flour, milk and eggs

you *pron* (*second person*) refers to person or persons addressed; refers to unspecified person or persons

young *adj* not far advanced in growth, life or existence; not yet old ~*n* offspring **youngster** *n* child

your *adj* of, belonging to you **yours** *pron* **yourself** (*pl* **yourselves**) *pron emphatic or reflexive form of* YOU

youth *n* state or time of being young; young man; young people **youthful** *adj*

Yule *n* Christmas season

yuppie *n* young highly-paid professional person ~*adj* of, like yuppies

zany *adj* comical, funny in unusual way

zap *v* **zapping, zapped** *Sl* attack, kill or destroy

zeal *n* fervour; keenness, enthusiasm **zealot** *n* fanatic; enthusiast **zealous** *adj*

zebra *n* striped Afr. animal like a horse

zenith *n* point of the heavens directly above an observer; summit; climax

zephyr *n* soft, gentle breeze

zero *n* (*pl* **-ros, -roes**) nothing; figure 0; point on graduated instrument from which positive and negative quantities are reckoned; the lowest point

zest *n* enjoyment; excitement, interest, flavour; peel of orange or lemon

zigzag *n* line or course with sharp turns in alternating directions ~*v* **-zagging, -zagged** move along in zigzag course

zinc *n* bluish-white metallic element

zip *also* **zipper** *n* fastener with two rows of teeth that are closed and opened by a sliding clip; short whizzing sound; *Inf* energy, vigour ~*v* **zipping, zipped** fasten with zip; move with zip

zither *n* flat stringed instrument

zodiac *n* imaginary belt of the heavens along which the sun, moon and chief planets appear to move

zombie *n* person appearing lifeless

zone *n* region with particular characteristics or use

zoo *n* (*pl* **zoos**) place where live animals are kept for show

zoology *n* study of animals **zoological** *adj* **zoologist** *n*

zoom *v* move, rise very rapidly; move with buzzing or humming sound

——————————————— THESAURUS ———————————————

ther, moreover, still, to boot

yokel countryman, peasant, rustic

young *adj* early, new, recent; adolescent, green, growing, immature, infant, junior, little, youthful

youngster boy, girl, juvenile, lad, lass, teenager

youth boyhood, girlhood, immaturity; adolescent, boy, kid *Inf,* lad, stripling, teenager, youngster

youthful boyish, childish, immature, juvenile, puerile, young; active, fresh, spry, vigorous

zero naught, nil, nothing, nought

zest appetite, enjoyment, gusto, keenness, relish, zeal; flavour, kick *Inf,* piquancy, pungency, savour, spice, tang, taste

zone area, belt, district, region, section, sector, sphere

CHEMICAL ELEMENTS

1 hydrogen H
2 helium He
3 lithium Li
4 beryllium Be
5 boron B
6 carbon C
7 nitrogen N
8 oxygen O
9 fluorine F
10 neon Ne
11 sodium Na
12 magnesium Mg
13 aluminium Al
14 silicon Si
15 phosphorus P
16 sulphur S
17 chlorine Cl
18 argon Ar
19 potassium K
20 calcium Ca
21 scandium Sc
22 titanium Ti
23 vanadium V
24 chromium Cr
25 manganese Mn
26 iron Fe
27 cobalt Co
28 nickel Ni
29 copper Cu
30 zinc Zn
31 gallium Ga
32 germanium Ge
33 arsenic As
34 selenium Se
35 bromine Br
36 krypton Kr
37 rubidium Rb

38 strontium Sr
39 yttrium Y
40 zirconium Zr
41 niobium Nb
42 molybdenum Mo
43 technetium Tc
44 ruthenium Ru
45 rhodium Rh
46 palladium Pd
47 silver Ag
48 cadmium Cd
49 indium In
50 tin Sn
51 antimony Sb
52 tellurium Te
53 iodine I
54 xenon Xe
55 caesium Cs
56 barium Ba
57 lanthanum La
58 cerium Ce
59 praseodymium Pr
60 neodymium Nd
61 promethium Pm
62 samarium Sm
63 europium Eu
64 gadolinium Gd
65 terbium Tb
66 dysprosium Dy
67 holmium Ho
68 erbium Er
69 thulium Tm
70 ytterbium Yb
71 lutetium Lu
72 hafnium Hf
73 tantalum Ta
74 tungsten W

75 rhenium Re
76 osmium Os
77 iridium Ir
78 platinum Pt
79 gold Au
80 mercury Hg
81 thallium Tl
82 lead Pb
83 bismuth Bi
84 polonium Po
85 astatine At
86 radon Rn
87 francium Fr
88 radium Ra
89 actinium Ac
90 thorium Th
91 protactinium Pa
92 uranium U
93 neptunium Np
94 plutonium Pu
95 americium Am
96 curium Cm
97 berkelium Bk
98 californium Cf
99 einsteinium Es
100 fermium Fm
101 mendelevium Md
102 nobelium No
103 lawrencium Lr
104 rutherfordium Rf
105 dubnium Db
106 seaborgium Sg
107 bohrium Bh
108 hassium Hs
109 meitnerium Mt

GROUP NAMES AND COLLECTIVE NOUNS

barren of mules
bevy of quails
bevy of roes
brace or lease of bucks
brood or covey of grouse
brood of hens or chickens
building or clamour of rooks
bunch, company, or knob of wigeon (in the water)
bunch, knob, or spring of teal
cast of hawks
cete of badgers
charm of goldfinches
chattering of choughs
clowder of cats
colony of gulls (breeding)
covert of coots
covey of partridges
cowardice of curs
desert of lapwings
dopping of sheldrakes
down or husk of hares
drove or herd of cattle (kine)
exaltation of larks
fall of woodcocks
field or string of racehorses
flight of wigeon (in the air)
flight or dule of doves
flight of swallows
flight of dunlins
flight, rush, bunch, or knob of pochards

flock or flight of pigeons
flock of sheep
flock of swifts
flock or gaggle of geese
flock, congregation, flight, or volery of birds
gaggle of geese (on the ground)
gang of elk
haras (stud) of horses
herd of antelopes
herd of buffaloes
herd, sedge, or siege of cranes
herd of curlews
herd of deer
herd of giraffes
herd or tribe of goats
herd or pod of seals
herd or bevy of swans
herd of ponies
herd of swine
hill of ruffs
host of sparrows
kindle of kittens
labour of moles
leap of leopards
litter of cubs
litter of pups or pigs
litter of whelps
murmuration of starlings
muster of peacocks
nest of rabbits
nye or nide of pheasants
pace or herd of asses

GROUP NAMES AND COLLECTIVE NOUNS

pack of grouse
pack, mute, or cry of hounds
pack, rout, or herd of wolves
paddling of ducks
plump, sword, or sute of
  wild fowl
pod of whiting
pride or troop of lions
rag of colts
richesse of martens
run of poultry
school or run of whales
school or gam of porpoises
sedge or siege of bitterns
sedge or siege of herons
shoal or glean of herrings
shoal, draught, haul, run,
  or catch of fish
shrewdness of apes

skein of geese (in flight)
skulk of foxes
sloth of bears
sord or sute of mallards
sounder of boars
sounder or dryft of swine
stand or wing of plovers
stud of mares
swarm of insects
swarm or grist of bees or flies
swarm or cloud of gnats
tok of capercailzies
team of ducks (in flight)
troop of kangaroos
troop of monkeys
walk or wisp of snipe
watch of nightingales
yoke, drove, team, or herd
  of oxen

PLANETS OF THE SOLAR SYSTEM

Earth   Jupiter   Mars   Mercury   Neptune   Pluto   Saturn
Uranus   Venus

CHARACTERS IN CLASSICAL MYTHOLOGY

Achilles	Dionysus	Menelaus
Actaeon	dryads	Mercury
Adonis	Echidna	Midas
Aeneas	Echo	Minerva
Agamemnon	Electra	Minos
Ajax	Europa	Minotaur
Amazons	Eurydice	Muses
Andromeda	Galatea	Narcissus
Antigone	Ganymede	Nemesis
Aphrodite	Gorgons	Neptune
Apollo	Harpies	Nereids
Arachne	Hector	Niobe
Ares	Hecuba	Oceanids
Argonauts	Helen	Odysseus
Ariadne	Hera	Oedipus
Atalanta	Hercules	Orestes
Athena	Hermaphroditus	Orion
Atlas	Hermes	Orpheus
Aurora	Hippolytus	Pallas
Bacchus	Hyacinthus	Pan
Boreas	Hydra	Pandora
Calypso	Icarus	Paris
Cassandra	Iris	Penelope
Cassiopeia	Ixion	Persephone
Castor	Jason	Perseus
Charon	Jocasta	Pleiades
centaurs	Janus	Pluto
Circe	Jason	Pollux
Cronus	Jocasta	Polydeuces
Cupid	Juno	Polyphemus
Cybele	Jupiter	Poseidon
Cyclopes	Leda	Priam
Daedalus	Mars	Prometheus
Diana	Medea	Proserpina
Dido	Medusa	Psyche

CHARACTERS IN CLASSICAL MYTHOLOGY

Pygmalion
Pyramus
Remus
Romulus
Saturn
satyrs
Selene

Semele
Sibyl
Sirens
Sisyphus
Tantalus
Thisbe
Titans

Triton
Ulysses
Uranus
Venus
Vulcan
Zeus

The Fates

Atropos

Clotho

Lachesis

The Graces

Aglaia

Euphrosyne

Thalia

The Muses

Calliope	epic poetry
Clio	history
Erato	love poetry
Euterpe	lyric poetry and music
Melpomene	tragedy
Polyhymnia	singing, mime and sacred dance
Terpsichore	dance and choral song
Thalia	comedy and pastoral poetry
Urania	astronomy

WEDDING ANNIVERSARIES

YEAR	TRADITIONAL	MODERN
1st	Paper	Clocks
2nd	Cotton	China
3rd	Leather	Crystal, glass
4th	Linen (silk)	Electrical appliances
5th	Wood	Silverware
6th	Iron	Wood
7th	Wool (copper)	Desk sets
8th	Bronze	Linen, lace
9th	Pottery (china)	Leather
10th	Tin (aluminium)	Diamond jewellery
11th	Steel	Fashion jewellery, accessories
12th	Silk	Pearls or coloured gems
13th	Lace	Textile, furs
14th	Ivory	Gold jewellery
15th	Crystal	Watches
20th	China	Platinum
25th	Silver	Sterling silver jubilee
30th	Pearl	Diamond
35th	Coral (jade)	Jade
40th	Ruby	Ruby
45th	Sapphire	Sapphire
50th	Gold	Gold
55th	Emerald	Emerald
60th	Diamond	Diamond

BOOKS OF THE BIBLE
(including the Apocrypha)

Acts of the Apostles
Amos
Baruch
Chronicles
Colossians
Corinthians
Daniel
Daniel and Susanna
Daniel, Bel and
  the Snake
Deuteronomy
Ecclesiastes
Ecclesisticus
Ephesians
Esdras
Esther
Exodus
Ezekiel
Ezra
Galatians
Genesis
Habakkuk
Haggai

Hebrews
Hosea
Isiah
James
Jeremiah
Job
Joel
John
Jonah
Joshua
Jude
Judges
Judith
Kings
Lamentations
Leviticus
Luke
Maccabees
Malachi
Manasseh
Mark
Matthew
Micah

Nahum
Nehemiah
Numbers
Obadiah
Peter
Philemon
Philippians
Proverbs
Psalms
Revelation
Romans
Ruth
Samuel
Song of Solomon
Song of Songs
Song of the
  Three
Thessalonians
Timothy
Titus
Tobit
Zechariah
Zephaniah

COUNTRIES, CURRENCIES AND CAPITALS

COUNTRY	CURRENCY	CAPITAL
Afghanistan	Afghani	Kabul
Albania	Lck	Tirana
Algeria	Dinar	Algiers
American Samoa	U.S. Dollar	Pago Pago
Andorra	French Franc; Spanish Peseta	Andorra la Vella
Angola	Kwanza	Luanda
Antigua and Barbuda	East Caribbean Dollar	St John's
Argentina	Argentine Peso	Buenos Aires
Armenia	Dram	Yerevan
Australia	Dollar	Canberra
Austria	Schilling	Vienna
Azerbaijan	Manat	Baku
Bahamas	Bahamian Dollar	Nassau
Bahrain	Dinar	Manama
Bangladesh	Taka	Dhaka
Barbados	Barbadian Dollar	Bridgetown
Belarus	Dukat	Minsk
Belgium	Franc	Brussels
Belize	Belizean Dollar	Belmopan
Benin	CFA Franc	Porto Novo
Bermuda	Bermuda Dollar	Hamilton
Bhutan	Ngultrum	Thimphu
Bolivia	Boliviano	Sucre/La Paz
Bosnia and Herzegovina	Dinar	Sarajevo
Botswana	Pula	Gaborone
Brazil	Real	Brasília
British Virgin Isles	U.S. Dollar	Road Town
Brunei	Brunei Dollar	Bandar Seri Begawani
Bulgaria	Lev	Sofia
Burkina-Faso	CFA Franc	Ouagadougou
Burundi	Burundi Franc	Bujumbura
Cambodia	Riel	Phnom Penh
Cameroon	CFA Franc	Yaoundé

COUNTRIES, CURRENCIES AND CAPITALS

Canada	Canadian Dollar	Ottawa
Cape Verde	Cape Verdean Escudo	Praia
Cayman Islands	Cayman Islands Dollar	Georgetown
Central African Republic	CFA Franc	Bangui
Chad	CFA Franc	N'djamena
Chile	Peso	Santiago
China	Yuan	Beijing
Colombia	Peso	Bogotá
Comoros	CFA Franc	Moroni
Congo (Democratic Republic of)	Kinshasa	Zaïre
Congo (Republic of)	CFA Franc	Brazzaville
Costa Rica	Cólon	San José
Côte d'Ivoire	CFA Franc	Yamoussoukro
Croatia	Kuna	Zagreb
Cuba	Peso	Havana
Cyprus	Lira; Cypriot Pound	Nicosia
Czech Republic	Koruna	Prague
Denmark	Danish Krone	Copenhagen
Djibouti	Djibouti Franc	Djibouti
Dominica	East Caribbean Dollar	Roseau
Dominican Republic	Peso	Santo Domingo
Ecuador	Sucre	Quito
Egypt	Egyptian Pound	Cairo
El Salvador	Cólon	San Salvador
Equatorial Guinea	CFA Franc	Malabo
Eritrea	Birr	Asmara
Estonia	Kroon	Tallinn
Ethiopia	Birr	Addis Ababa
Faeroe Islands	Danish Krone	Thorshavn
Fiji	Fiji Dollar	Suva
Finland	Markka	Helsinki
France	Franc	Paris
French Guiana	French Franc	Cayenne
Gabon	CFA Franc	Libreville
Gambia	Dalasi	Banjul
Georgia	Lari	Tbilisi

COUNTRIES, CURRENCIES AND CAPITALS

Country	Currency	Capital
Germany	Deutschmark	Berlin
Ghana	Cedi	Accra
Gibraltar	Gibraltar Pound	City of Gibraltar
Greece	Drachma	Athens
Grenada	East Caribbean Dollar	St George's
Guadeloupe	Franc	Bass-Terre
Guam	U.S. Dollar	Agaña
Guatemala	Quetzal	Guatemala City
Guinea	Guinea Franc	Conakry
Guinea-Bissau	Peso	Bissau
Guyana	Guyana Dollar	Georgetown
Haiti	Gourde	Port-au-Prince
Honduras	Lempira	Tegucigalpa
Hungary	Forint	Budapest
Iceland	Krona	Reykjavik
India	Rupee	New Delhi
Indonesia	Rupiah	Jakarta
Iran	Rial	Tehran
Iraq	Dinar	Baghdad
Ireland	Punt	Dublin
Israel	Shekel	Jerusalem
Italy	Lira	Rome
Jamaica	Jamaican Dollar	Kingston
Japan	Yen	Tokyo
Jordan	Dinar	Amman
Kazakhstan	Tenge	Akmola
Kenya	Kenya Shilling	Nairobi
Kirghizia	Som	Pishpek
Kiribati	Australian Dollar	Tarawa
Kuwait	Kuwaiti Dinar	Kuwait City
Laos	New Kip	Vientiane
Latvia	Lats	Riga
Lebanon	Lebanese Pound	Beirut
Lesotho	Loti	Maseru
Liberia	Liberian Dollar	Monrovia
Libya	Libyan Dinar	Tripoli
Liechtenstein	Swiss Franc	Vaduz
Lithuania	Litas	Vilnius

COUNTRIES, CURRENCIES AND CAPITALS

Luxembourg	Luxembourg Franc	Luxembourg-Ville
Macao	Pataca	Macao City
Macedonia	Denar	Skopje
Madagascar	Malagasy Franc	Antananarivo
Malawi	Kwacha	Lilongwe
Malaysia	Ringgit	Kuala Lumpur
Maldives	Rufiyaa	Malé
Mali	CFA franc	Bamako
Malta	Maltese Lira	Valletta
Marshall Islands	U.S. Dollar	Majuro
Martinique	French Franc	Fort-de-France
Mauritania	Ouguija	Nouakchott
Mauritius	Mauritius Rupee	Port Louis
Mexico	Peso	Mexico City
Micronesia	U.S. Dollar	Palikir
Moldova	Leu	Kishinev
Monaco	Franc	Monaco-Ville
Mongolia	Tugrik	Ulan Bator
Montserrat	East Caribbean Dollar	Plymouth
Morocco	Dirham	Rabat
Mozambique	Metical	Maputo
Myanmar (Burma)	Kyat	Yangon
Namibia	Namibian Dollar	Windhoek
Nauru	Australian Dollar	Yaren
Nepal	Nepalese Rupee	Kathmandu
Netherlands	Guilder	Amsterdam/ The Hague
Netherlands Antilles	Guilder	Willemstad
New Zealand	New Zealand Dollar	Wellington
Nicaragua	Córdoba	Managua
Niger	CFA Franc	Niamey
Nigeria	Naira	Abuja
North Korea	North Korean Won	Pyongyang
Norway	Krone	Oslo
Oman	Rial Omani	Muscat
Pakistan	Pakistani Rupee	Islamabad
Palau	U.S Dollar	Koror
Panama	Balboa	Panama City

COUNTRIES, CURRENCIES AND CAPITALS

Papua New Guinea	Kina	Port Moresby
Paraguay	Guaraní	Asunción
Peru	New Sol	Lima
Philippines	Philippine Peso	Manila
Pitcairn Island	Pitcairn Dollar	Adamstown
Poland	Zloty	Warsaw
Polynesia, French	CFA Franc	Papeete
Portugal	Escudo	Lisbon
Puerto Rico	U.S. Dollar	San Juan
Qatar	Riyal	Doha
Réunion	French Franc	St Denis
Romania	Leu	Bucharest
Russia	Rouble	Moscow
Rwanda	Rwanda Franc	Kigali
San Marino	Italian Lira	San Marino
São Tomé and Príncipe	Dobra	São Tomé
Saudi Arabia	Riyal	Riyadh
Senegal	CFA Franc	Dakar
Seychelles	Seychelles Rupee	Victoria
Sierra Leone	Leone	Freetown
Singapore	Singapore Dollar	Singapore
Slovakia	Koruna	Bratislava
Slovenia	Tolar	Ljubljana
Solomon Islands	Solomon Islands Dollar	Honiara
Somalia	Somali Shilling	Mogadishu
South Africa	Rand	Pretoria/Cape Town
South Korea	South Korean Won	Seoul
Spain	Peseta	Madrid
Sri Lanka	Rupee	Colombo
St Christopher and Nevis	East Caribbean Dollar	Basseterre
St Lucia	East Caribbean Dollar	Castries
St Vincent and Grenadines	East Caribbean Dollar	Kingstown
Sudan	Sudanese Pound	Khartoum
Suriname	Suriname Guilder	Paramaribo

COUNTRIES, CURRENCIES AND CAPITALS

Country	Currency	Capital
Swaziland	Lilangeni	Mbabane
Sweden	Krona	Stockholm
Switzerland	Swiss Franc	Berne
Syria	Syrian Pound	Damascus
Taiwan	Taiwan Dollar	Taipei
Tajikstan	Rouble	Dushanbe
Tanzania	Tanzanian Shilling	Dodoma
Thailand	Baht	Bangkok
Togo	CFA Franc	Lomé
Tonga	Pa'anga	Nuku'alofa
Trinidad and Tobago	Trinidad and Tobago Dollar	Port of Spain
Tunisia	Tunisian Dinar	Tunis
Turkey	Turkish Lira	Ankara
Turkmenistan	Manat	Ashkhabad
Turks and Caicos Islands	U.S. Dollar	Grand Turk
Tuvalu	Australian Dollar	Funafuti
Uganda	New Ugandan Shilling	Kampala
Ukraine	Gryvna	Kiev
United Arab Emirates	Dirham	Abu Dhabi
United Kingdom	Pound Sterling	London
Uruguay	New Uruguayan Peso	Montevideo
U.S. Virgin Islands	U.S. Dollar	Charlotte Amalie
United States of America	Dollar	Washington
Uzbekistan	Som	Tashkent
Vanuata	Vatu	Vila
Vatican City	Italian Lira	Vatican City
Venezuela	Bolívar	Caracas
Vietnam	Dong	Hanoi
Western Sahara	Peseta	Laâyoune
Western Samoa	Tala	Apia
Yemen	Riyal; Dinar	Sana`a
Yugoslavia (Serbia & Montenegro)	Dinar	Belgrade
Zambia	Kwacha	Lusaka
Zimbabwe	Zimbabwe Dollar	Harare

TYPES OF CALENDAR

The number of days in a year varies among cultures and from year to year.

GREGORIAN

The Gregorian calendar is a 16th-century adaptation of the Julian calendar devised in the 1st century BC. The year in this calendar is based on the solar year, which lasts about $365\frac{1}{4}$ days. In this system, years whose number is not divisible by 4 have 365 days, as do centennial years unless the figures before the noughts are divisible by 4.
All other years have 366 days; these are leap years.

Below are the names of the months and number of days for a non-leap year.

January 31	July 31
February 28★	August 31
March 31	September 30
April 30	October 31
May 31	November 30
June 30	December 31

★ 29 in leap years

JEWISH

A year in the Jewish calendar has 13 months if its number, when divided by 19, leaves 0, 3, 6, 8, 11, 14 or 17; otherwise, it has 12 months. The year is based on the lunar year, but its number of months varies to keep broadly in line with the solar cycle.
Its precise number of days is fixed with reference to particular festivals that must not fall on certain days of the week.

Below are the names of the months and number of days in each for the year 5471, a 12-month year (1980 AD in Gregorian).

Tishri 30	Nisan 30
Cheshvan 29★	Iyar 29
Kislev 29★	Sivan 30
Tevet 29	Tammuz 29
Shevat 30	Av 30
Adar 29	Elul 29

★ 30 in some years

TYPES OF CALENDAR

In 13-month years, the month Veadar, with 29 days, falls between Adar and Nisan.

MUSLIM

A year in the Muslim calendar has 355 days if its number, when divided by 30, leaves 2, 5, 7, 10, 13, 16, 18, 21, 24, 26 or 29; otherwise it has 354 days. As in the Jewish calendar, years are based on the lunar cycle.

Below are the names of the months and numbers of days in each for the Muslim year 1401 (1980 AD in Gregorian).

Muharram 30	Rajab 30
Safar 29	Sha'ban 29
Rabi'I 30	Ramadan 30
Rabi'II 29	Shawwal 29
Jumada I 30	Dhu 1-Qa'dah 30
Jumada II 29	Dhu 1-Hijja 30*

* 29 in some years